Reader's Digest

How to do Just About Anything

Reader's Digest

The Reader's Digest Association, Inc.
Pleasantville, New York/Montreal

How to do Just About Anything

STAFF

Project Editor
Sally French

Project Art Director
Joel Musler

Senior Editor
James Dwyer

Associate Editors
Joseph Gonzalez
Robert V. Huber
Gayla Visalli
Gerald Williams

Food Editor
Ben Etheridge

Art Production Editor
Lisa Drescher

Art Associate
Morris Karol

Research Editor
Tanya Strage

**READER'S DIGEST
GENERAL BOOKS**

Editorial Director
John A. Pope, Jr.

Managing Editor
Jane Polley

Art Director
Richard J. Berenson

Group Editors
Norman B. Mack
John Speicher
David Trooper (Art)
Susan J. Wernert

CONTRIBUTORS

Contributing Editors
Ellen Coffey
Virginia Colton
Don Earnest
Wade Hoyt, SAE
Carter Smith

Contributing Writers
Paul Ahrens
Ian A. Anderson
Gene Balsley
Robert G. Beason
Deborah Beaulieu
Susan Brackett
Therese Hoehlein Cerbie
Valentin Chu
Sarah Clayton
Eric N. Compton
Michael Dann
Thomas Dickey
Paula Dranov
Barbara Ensrud
Mark Gasper
Caroline Grant
Gordon Hardy
Ray Hill
Penny Hinkle
Victor H. Lane
Peter Limburg
Linda Lombri
Neil D. Mackay
H. J. Maidenberg
Brian McCallen
William T. McKeown
Miranda Morse
Wendy B. Murphy
Lilla Pennant
Betsy Stilwell Petersen
Tom Philbin
Barbara Gilder Quint
Harry Roberts
Peter G. Rose
Mary-Ann Tirone Smith
Tim Snider
Mark Sosin
Ted Spiegel
Joanne Tunney Stack, J.D.
Sara Stein
Larry Tabak
Elizabeth Tener
Denise Van Lear
Jeanne Voltz
John Warde
Daniel E. Weiss
Paul Weissler, SAE

Contributing Artists
Susan Brahinsky
David Lindroth
Ed Lipinski
Ken Meads
Max Menikoff
Mort Perry
Ken Rice
Bill Shortridge
Ray Skibinski
Judy Skorpil

Contributing Researcher
Mary Hart

Copy Editor
Elaine Andrews

Indexer
Sydney Wolfe Cohen

Editorial Assistant
Jean Ryan

Consultants
Paul Ahrens
Antonio Bartolino
Aaron Bisberg
Frances Cohen
John L. Costa, M.D., F.A.A.P.
Johanna T. Dwyer, D.Sc., R.D.
Thomas H. Everett
George B. Feldman, M.D.
Alan F. French
Michael S. Garvey, D.V.M.,
   Dip. A.C.V.I.M.
Francine Gellerstein
Harvey Gold
Leon Grabowski
Julia Grodin
Walter A. Grub, Jr.
Tom Hallinan
Kenneth G. Hubbard, Ph.D.
David Kaufman, M.D.
Carolyn Klass
Lee Kraft
Steven Lamm, M.D.
Joseph Laquatra, Ph.D.
Michelle Lester
Walter LeStrange
Willard Lubka
Cynthia J. Mackay, M.D.
L. Mankowski
Robin Pearlstein
James R. Petersen
Henry H. Printz, C.P.L.
Mary E. Purchase, Ph.D.
Larrie S. Rockmacher, D.P.M.
Victor J. Selmanowitz, M.D.
Damon Sgobbo
Robert L. Smith, Ph.D.
Stanley H. Smith, Ph.D
Tim Snider
Clifford C. Snyder, M.D.
Joanne Tunney Stack, J.D.
Paul Weissler, SAE
Thomas A. Wilson, D.D.S.
Clifford A. Wojan
Bob Young

**The editors thank
the following for
their assistance:**
Robert C. Baker
Reg Barnes
BernzOmatic
Kay Buttenheim
Juliet E. Carroll
Casablanca Fan Co.
Con Edison
Robert Cudney
Kent and Donna Dannen
Erwin J. Ernst, Ph.D.
The Fan Maven
The Fone Booth
Jon S. Fossel
Geysir Hardwood Flooring Inc.
Ronald C. Holcombe
Ronald A. Howard, Jr.
Frank Malara, Jr.
Metuchen Marine
Lt. Frank Martinez
Noris Stone & Sons, Inc.
Joseph J. Ogilvie
Otis Elevator Company
William Roisen
Gertrude Rowland
Donna L. Scott
Joan Harris Spencer
Thomas B. Tenfelde
Tomahawk Live Trap Company
United States Water Polo, Inc.
Derek A. Van Lent

The acknowledgments that appear on page 448 are hereby made a part of this copyright page.

Library of Congress Cataloging in Publication Data: page 448

Printed in the United States of America
February 1997 1/SC

About this book

HOW TO DO JUST ABOUT ANYTHING is a comprehensive guide to solving everyday household problems. More than 1,200 alphabetically arranged articles cover home repair and improvement, auto and appliance maintenance, sewing, cooking, pest control, plant care, gardening, money matters, game and sports rules, housekeeping, medical and legal questions, etiquette, and personal grooming. In short, this is the book you'll reach for first whether you want to unclog a sink, fix a chair, cut your child's hair, write a résumé, paint a house, play gin rummy, grow tomatoes, soothe prickly heat, make a will, bake bread, or handle hundreds of other common challenges and difficulties.

It is also a wonderful book for browsing. On just about every page you'll find something to capture your interest. Look up *Pilot lights* and you'll probably find yourself reading about how amazingly simple it is to make pimientos.

How to use this book
Look up a subject in alphabetical order as you would in a dictionary. You'll usually find it right away. If you don't, turn to the complete index in the back of the book. If your topic is covered under some other name or in an article on a related subject, the index will lead you to it.

The index can also guide you to all articles in a given category. Under *Gardening,* for example, you'll find all the various articles on outdoor plants, growing techniques, and yard care—even one on scarecrows.

To help you obtain additional information, an article may refer to another article. If the reference reads "see *Gluing,*" look up that article; it contains information essential to performing the task at hand. If the

reference reads "See also *Cameras,*" that article covers a related subject that may interest you.

What skills do you need?
Most of the jobs in this book can be done by anyone who is reasonably handy. As you read the simplified instructions, you might be inspired to try tasks that you've previously hesitated to undertake. Before you start, think how a procedure applies to your home or special situation. Jobs in such areas as auto repair, electric wiring, and plumbing occasionally require specialized skills. If you feel uncomfortable about a task, get help from someone with more experience.

Similarly, seek professional advice when necessary. Call a lawyer about an important legal problem. Have an architect or an engineer inspect a potential structural problem in your home. Consult a physician if a medical problem seems serious. In a medical emergency, the first-aid index just inside this book's front and back covers will quickly direct you to the relevant article. If a situation is life threatening, do whatever seems necessary and reasonable to lessen the danger, and send for medical assistance at once.

Checking local regulations
Before making an improvement, such as installing a partition, putting in a concrete driveway, or even planting a hedge, consult your municipality's building department about zoning regulations and permit requirements. You'll find more information on this in the article *Building permits* on page 53.

Cooperative Extension Service
Regional differences in climate and soil greatly affect what you can grow in your garden, orchard, or yard. A reliable, free source of information on this—and many other home problems—is the the Cooperative Extension Service. There's an office

in nearly every county in the United States and its territories. They give expert advice on agriculture and related subjects, including home repairs and improvements, energy conservation, and home economics. Look in your telephone directory under the county government listings; the Cooperative Extension Service is usually listed there—sometimes as County Agent or County Agricultural Agent or as a state university's extension service.

Other sources of help
A horticultural society or botanical garden can also advise on gardening and a utility company on energy conservation. People who sell paint, hardware, lumber, plumbing, and electrical supplies can usually tell you how to use their products. When you go to buy a replacement part, always take the old part so that you can get an exact duplicate.

Manufacturers' trade associations offer information on many products, ranging from foods to building materials. They're listed in the *Encyclopedia of Associations* (Gale Research Company) at your library.

While you're at the library, look at the directory of 800 telephone numbers. Many companies provide free advice on their products. For example, a manufacturer can tell you where to buy a replacement part or can send you an owner's manual for an old appliance. You can also get toll-free 800 numbers by calling (800) 555-1212.

We have tried to pack HOW TO DO JUST ABOUT ANYTHING with as much helpful, easy-to-follow information as possible. We hope you'll find it the most useful book you ever bought.

—The Editors

Selecting tools

Good tools will make your work easier, faster, more accurate, and much safer. Look for sturdy, well-balanced tools that are made of smooth, finished metal—preferably drop forged if they're to be used for heavy-duty work. Moving parts should work smoothly without binding or having excessive play.

The tools described here will handle most of your repair jobs. Buy additional tools only as needed; consider renting expensive tools, especially if you'll use them only once. If a job requires a special tool, it's noted in the article on how to perform that task. You'll also find information on tools in articles such as *Chiseling, Drilling, Power saws, Routers,* and *Wrenches.*

Basic tools for home repair
A screwdriver with a 6-inch shank and a ¼-inch blade will drive most slotted screws. But it's good to have screwdrivers of different widths and lengths, including a longer one with a square shank that you can turn with a wrench and a stubby one for tight places. You can handle most cross-slotted screws with a No. 1 and No. 2 Phillips screwdriver.

Other good choices for a basic kit are a 16-ounce claw hammer and an 8-point (8 teeth per inch) crosscut wood saw. A utility knife and a craft knife are useful, versatile cutting tools; a wood chisel is a handy supplement. To hold things in place while you cut or while glue dries, get pairs of C-clamps with 2½-, 4-, and 6-inch openings.

For gripping and turning things, it's useful to have an adjustable wrench and locking-grip pliers, each about 8 inches long, as well as regular slip-joint pliers. A 10-foot-long flexible steel-tape rule, a combination square, and a framing square will handle most of your measuring and marking chores. The only indispensable power tool is a drill with a set of high-speed twist bits. For maximum convenience and versatility, buy a ⅜-inch reversible, variable-speed model. It should be double insulated for safety.

More specialized tools
Electrical and appliance-repair jobs require electrician's and needle-nose pliers and a wire-stripping tool; all should have insulated handles. For more advanced work, you'll also want a continuity tester to tell if a circuit is wired properly and a neon test light to check if a circuit is live; both functions—and several others besides—can be handled by a device known as a multitester, or volt-ohm meter. Basic plumbing jobs require a 10- and a 12-inch pipe wrench, a plumber's snake (auger), and a plunger with a fold-out bottom to unplug toilets and drains.

To work with metal, you'll need a hacksaw, tin snips, a combination file, a center punch, and special drill bits. Drilling holes in masonry also requires special bits.

Additional tools for auto care
Many auto tools come in versions for specific makes and models of cars. Before buying a tool, read the article describing the job you want to do.

Depending on your car, you'll need a set of combination wrenches ranging from ⅜ inch to 1 inch or from 6 mm to 19 mm. Supplement this with a ⅜-inch-drive socket wrench set covering the same range. It should include a universal joint, a spark-plug socket to fit your plugs, and extensions that total at least 1 foot when joined. Another essential is a set of Allen (hex) wrenches, ranging from .05 inch to .25 inch or from 2 mm to 12 mm.

Other useful auto tools are a ball peen hammer, an offset ratchet screwdriver, an oil-filter wrench, an antifreeze hydrometer, a gooseneck funnel, a tire-pressure gauge, a 12-volt test light, a small wire brush, and battery jumper cables. Some cars require hose-clamp pliers. For working under the car, you'll need two jack stands.

Tool safety
Use a tool designed for the task, especially when the task involves force. Never use dull, loose, or damaged tools.

Wear a respirator mask for jobs that will produce dust or toxic fumes. Wear safety goggles if a job might produce flying particles or if it will produce debris at eye level or above. Protect your hands with thick work gloves when handling rough materials and with vinyl gloves when using strong or toxic liquids. For more safety tips, read the article *Power tool safety* on page 307.

A

Abalone

Preparing and cooking abalone

Abalone is a large mollusk that clings to rocks and is covered with a single iridescent shell. The edible part is the muscular foot that holds the shell to the rock. Fresh abalone is available only in California; canned or frozen is available in the other states.

To prepare fresh abalone, cut out the foot with a sharp knife. Trim away the dark fringe, stomach, and intestines. Rinse the foot and cut it across the grain into ½-inch slices. Pound the slices with a mallet until soft.

Sauté abalone less than 1 minute per side in butter, oil, or bacon drippings; serve with lemon wedges. For variety, cut the slices into strips for stir-fry dishes or chop them for chowder.

Absorbent powders

What they are; how to use them

Absorbent powders soak up moisture, grease, or odors. They can be used effectively as body powders and as spot removers.

Talc (French chalk), a finely powdered mineral, and *cornstarch,* from corn kernels, can be used either mixed with each other or alone as moisture-absorbing body powders.

Fuller's earth, a white or brown claylike powder, removes grease from clothing and carpets. Spread the soiled fabric on a clean cloth. Sprinkle a dense layer of powder onto the spot and rub the powder gently into the fabric. When a light crust has formed, scrape away the powder. For a stubborn spot, leave the powder in place for 10 to 12 hours. To lift grease from carpeting, sprinkle the affected area generously, let the powder stand for several hours, then vacuum.

Baking soda absorbs unpleasant odors. Place opened packages of it in the refrigerator or bathroom. To deodorize carpets, sprinkle on, let stand, and vacuum.

Accident prevention

Avoiding falls, burns, poisoning, and suffocation

It's almost impossible in a normal, active life never to have an accident. But every year thousands of people die from accidents around the home—accidents that could easily be avoided.

Nearly one-third of these fatalities are from falls, the greatest number of which involve the elderly. To prevent these tragedies, fallproof an older person's home. Remove small, loose rugs and low furniture, particularly if they obstruct traffic. Never leave debris on the floor or stairs. Stairs should have solid handrails, and rails may be needed in the bathroom near toilet and tub. Keep all areas well lit.

Poison and fire precautions

Poisoning is the second largest cause of death in household accidents. Keep drugs in their original containers and throw away leftovers when you have taken the prescribed doses. Never leave medicine by the bedside. It is unexpectedly easy to take a medication while drowsy without realizing it.

Store household cleaners and pesticides in their original containers. Never transfer them to drinking cups or soda bottles. Read and follow their warning labels carefully.

Gases, particularly odorless carbon monoxide, also cause many poisoning deaths. Don't leave a car motor running in the garage. Be sure there is ample ventilation for indoor fires. Keep space heaters in good repair.

The third leading cause of accidental death in the home is fire. Instruct the family to leave the house immediately if a fire starts. Call the fire department from a neighbor's house. Practice alternative escape routes. (See *Fire survival.*)

Preventing suffocation

Thousands of deaths occur each year from suffocation. Choking on food is a major cause. Because this happens

without warning, learn to do abdominal thrusts (see *Choking*).

Children, especially those under the age of four, are in danger of choking on small objects. Never give a child anything small enough to fit into his or her mouth. Suffocations are often caused by thin plastics, such as dry-cleaning bags, and by strangulation with cord and string. Keep them out of children's reach. (See also *Bathroom safety; Childproofing; Firearms; Ladders; Power tool safety.*)

Aching feet

What causes and what comforts sore, aching feet

Foot pain has many causes. One of the commonest is the "overuse syndrome" resulting from unaccustomed walking or standing. Resting is one solution, and rolling the feet onto their outer edges at intervals may prevent aches caused by standing. Choosing shoes for comfort rather than fashion helps too. Shoes should cushion the feet, support the arches, and allow toes space.

Recurrent aches can often be traced to fallen arches. Orthotics (arch supports) help; buy them only after examination and prescription by your physician. Alternating hot and cold foot baths and resting the feet may bring temporary relief.

Insensitivity, discoloration, or persistent pain or swelling may warn of diabetes or other disorders. Seek medical care. (See also *Bunions; Calluses; Corns; Flatfeet; Ingrown toenails; Jogging injuries; Warts.*)

Acne

What to do about acne; when to see a doctor

Although acne is not exclusively a young person's problem, almost all teenagers will suffer from this condition to some degree. Acne that occurs in teens is caused by the increased production of hormones that stimulate the secretion of an oily substance called sebum in the skin.

When sebum becomes trapped in hair follicles, it clogs the pores and produces blackheads or whiteheads. If the clogged pore bursts, bacteria spread to surrounding tissue, forming a pimple. White blood cells gather to fight the infection, causing a blisterlike eruption, or pustule.

Treatment of mild acne

Mild cases (mostly blackheads and whiteheads) generally run their course within a year or two and usually don't require medication or professional medical treatment. The best remedy is cleanliness. Wash the face twice a day with an unscented or medicated soap to help prevent the buildup of oils. Rinse thoroughly with lukewarm water. More frequent washing may only irritate the skin.

Over-the-counter creams and ointments containing benzoyl peroxide may help control mild cases, but stop their use if they cause excessive dryness or chapping. Keep hands away from the face. Girls should use medicated cosmetics or none at all.

It was once believed that such foods as chocolate, cheese, and fried foods contributed to acne. These theories have been largely discredited, but any food that seems to worsen acne in an individual should be avoided.

Although acne is rarely a threat to physical health, it can cause severe emotional distress. Many affected teenagers are self-conscious about the condition, and some may withdraw or use their acne as an excuse to avoid school or social activities. If such behavior becomes a problem, seek professional counseling.

Severe acne

For persistent and severe cases, see your doctor. Frequent—and neglected—pimples and pustules can cause disfiguring scars.

Acrylic plastic

Cutting the nonbreakable substitute for glass

Rigid acrylic plastic, sold under a variety of trade names, is used as a building or craft material. In sheet form it can be cut with ordinary woodworking tools. The sheets come with a protective paper covering; to avoid scratching the plastic, leave the paper in place while cutting.

Use the score-and-break method to cut acrylic that is up to 1/8-inch thick. Pencil a cutting line on the paper and align a straight edge along it. Draw a scoring tool (available at acrylic dealers) along the straight edge five to ten times, cutting deeper into the acrylic each time. Place the acrylic along a table edge, the scored line at the edge; apply a sharp, downward pressure, snapping the acrylic in two.

To get a smooth edge on acrylic plastic that is thicker than 1/8 inch, use a power saw. Support the sheet by clamping most of it on a table surface. Leave only enough overhang for sawblade clearance.

Action photography

Anticipation is the key to photographing fast action

Select activities of importance to you. Think about and research the action that is likely to occur. Visualize where and when the action will be at its peak—a pole vaulter at the apex of the jump, for instance. Decide how to frame the action to fill the picture, then choose your viewpoint. That choice can be to move yourself closer to the action or to pull the action close to you with a zoom or telephoto lens (see *Cameras*).

Before the activity starts, practice framing the areas of likely peak action in your camera's viewfinder. Then wait for the expected action, and fine focus just before shooting. This technique frees your mind to concentrate on the subject's action.

Shooting fast action outdoors

If you are using an adjustable camera outdoors, first measure the light. Then set your camera's shutter speed at no less than 1/250 of a second in order to "stop" such action as a person or an animal running. A programmed camera that cannot be adjusted will probably deliver 1/125 of a second under most automated exposure programs. Normal shutter speeds—1/60 or 1/125—will capture normal action, such as a person walking.

Photographing indoor action

Indoors, an electronic flash, which generally gives a burst of light lasting 1/500 of a second or less, will freeze action within 12 feet of the camera. You can sometimes control the action. At a child's birthday party, for example, say, "3-2-1-blow," and click to catch the flicker of candles on the cake. The same trick works to set off a water fight between siblings in the bathtub: say, "3-2-1-splash."

Action can be captured with slower than normal shutter speeds in a technique called panning. Follow the moving subject with your camera, trying to synchronize your movement with the action. The background will look blurred, but the subject should be reasonably sharp.

Photographing people

To catch fleeting facial expressions, the most revealing "action" of all, set your shutter speed at 1/125 of a second when you are using lenses up to 100 mm. A telephoto or zoom lens allows you to observe people's expressions from a distance. But with longer focal-length lenses, use faster film (ISO 400) so you can use faster shutter speeds—for example, with a 200 mm. lens use at least 1/250.

Aerobics

Exercising to strengthen heart and lungs and to build endurance

Aerobic exercise promotes physical fitness by strengthening the heart and increasing lung capacity. Jogging and running are the most popular aerobics, but any activity that is rhythmic and sustained and uses the body's large muscles qualifies. This includes walking, swimming, cross-country skiing, jumping rope, climbing stairs, bicycling, and even vigorous dancing. To get the full benefit of aerobic exercise, you must do it for a minimum of 20 minutes at least three times a week.

The word aerobic means "occurring in the presence of oxygen." All forms of aerobic exercise stimulate more rapid and efficient transport of oxygen through the bloodstream. Oxygen is needed to burn the fuel (calories) that provides the energy for the exercise. In essence, the blood flow to the heart increases, requiring the heart to pump harder. Since the heart is a muscle, the harder it pumps, the stronger it becomes.

Calculating your training level
The object of all aerobics is to increase your heart rate to what is called a training level and to maintain that level for at least 20 minutes. Your training level depends on your age. The maximum human heart rate is 220 beats per minute, but the rate declines by one beat for each year of life. The maximum heart rate for a 20-year-old, therefore, is 200 beats; for a 40-year-old, 180 beats.

Your training level is between 70 and 85 percent of your maximum heart rate. For a 20-year-old, this would be between 140 and 170 beats per minute; for a 40-year-old, between 126 and 153. To determine whether your heart rate has reached training level, take your pulse for 10 seconds immediately after exercising hard for several minutes. Then multiply by 6. Work up gradually to your training level. Anyone over 35 should check with a doctor before embarking on an exercise program. (See also *Exercise; Pulse*.)

African violets

How to care for this popular flowering houseplant

Given the right conditions, African violets bloom nearly year round. They thrive in temperatures between 60°F and 75°F. In temperatures much higher or lower, they may stop growing and blooming.

Light
In summer African violets do best in an east or north window. In winter they may need extra light from incandescent or fluorescent fixtures or from a southern exposure where the sun's rays are filtered. In fall and spring, shade the plants from direct sun. Too little light or light that is too weak may result in extra-long leafstalks and unhealthily soft foliage with few or no flowers. Light that is too strong may cause yellowing foliage and drooping leafstalks.

Watering and feeding
African violets like a humid atmosphere and moist soil, but the soil should not be constantly soggy. To provide humidity, stand the pot on pebbles in a partly water-filled saucer. There should be no contact between pot and water. When the soil surface begins to dry out, water well with lukewarm water but take care not to wet the foliage. Once a month except in winter, feed plants with a water-soluble houseplant fertilizer.

Potting and repotting
African violets bloom more freely when their roots are a bit crowded; repot them only when more than a third of the rosette of leaves extends beyond the pot's edge; use a pot a size larger. Spring or early summer is the best time to repot. Buy African violet soil or make your own from equal parts of peat moss, perlite, and garden soil.

If plants grow extra rosettes of leaves, nip them out with a knife. If leaves rot, turn yellow, or become crowded, break or cut their stalks at the main stem. Don't leave any stem parts on plants; they will rot.

African violets can easily be propagated from leaf cuttings. Select mature, healthy leaves; retain 1 to 1½ inches of stem (see *Propagating houseplants*). In 3 to 6 weeks, when tiny new leaves appear, transplant the rooted cuttings to separate pots. Cover them with plastic bags in which a few small holes have been punched. Keep them in a warm, shaded spot for 2 to 3 weeks.

Air conditioners

Cleaning the filter; removing bad odors; stopping water drips

To get the maximum efficiency from your air conditioner, seal or weatherstrip all air leaks and gaps around the unit and in the room (see *Weather stripping*). Use a unit with a high Energy Efficiency Rating and which is the proper Btu size for the space to be cooled. In an area of high air pollution, a serviceman should clean the unit at least once a year.

Caution: Before performing any operations, turn off and unplug your unit.

If performance falls off, inspect the filter. Clean or replace it if clogged by dust. In most units the filter is on the room side behind a grille. The filter lifts out, or it can be removed after a front panel is taken off. Remove any screws or release any latches holding the panel and pull it from the unit.

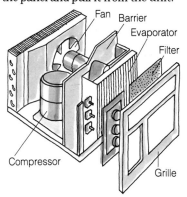

Wash a reusable filter in detergent and water, rinse it, and reinstall it. If there is a break in the filter, dust may have collected on the evaporator fins. Vacuum the fins clean. But be careful not to cut yourself or damage the fins.

If the cabinet is not tilted toward the outdoors, water may drip into the room. Tilt it so that the outdoor side is slightly lower than the indoor side.

The smell of oil or tobacco calls for professional cleaning. A musty odor means clogging of the drain hole under the barrier between the evaporator and compressor or of the channel under the evaporator. Remove the screws and take off the grille to get at the hole or the gap. (On some models

A

you may have to pull the unit partly out of its cabinet.) Clean the hole with a bent wire hanger or clean the gap with a bulb baster filled with water.

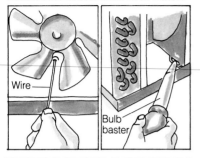

Air filters

Changing your car's air filter

A dirty air filter in your car reduces air flow into the engine, resulting in less power and often lower gas mileage. The typical filter is made of pleated paper. Inspect the filter every 6 months or 12,000 miles. Your owner's manual will advise you how often to replace the filter, but it may clog up beforehand, especially if you drive in dusty areas.

If the car stalls or is hard to start, road-test it briefly (but only briefly) without the filter. If the problem then disappears, the filter is probably clogged.

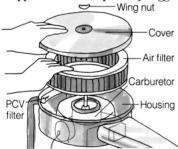

Replace it with a name-brand filter recommended for your car make, model, year, and engine.

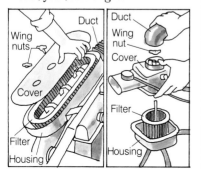

In most cars, the filter is in an air cleaner housing at the top of the engine. Remove the wing nut or open the clips securing the housing cover and lift the cover off.

In other cars, especially those with fuel injection rather than a carburetor, the housing may be connected to the engine's air intake by a duct. The housing may be located alongside the engine, under a fender, or in front of the radiator. Locate the housing and remove its cover. On some cars you may have to disconnect the ductwork to locate all of the retaining nuts or clips.

Remove the paper filter, which may be cylindrical, oval, or rectangular. Tap the filter against a hard surface to dislodge loose dirt, then examine it. A light oily film on the filter is normal as a car ages, but if the filter is very oily, you should have a reliable mechanic check the engine. If the filter is dirty all around, replace it. Most replacement filters today are marked *Top*. If not, either side can go up.

Many air cleaner housings contain a small foam filter for the positive crankcase ventilation (PCV) system. This filter, too, should be changed if it is dirty.

Alpine skiing

Getting started in downhill skiing

Your best bet if you are a newcomer to alpine, or downhill, skiing is to rent skis, boots, and poles. Lessons are not essential, but if you feel a bit shaky and need direction or encouragement, sign up for a lesson or two.

Have your equipment checked and the binding releases set by the ski shop or a ski patrolman. Bindings should be equipped with a ski brake or a runaway strap to prevent the skis from shooting downhill if they release during a fall. Practice stepping in and out of the bindings several times so that you know how to operate them. And learn to hold your ski poles properly. Insert your hands into the loops from underneath so that your hands close around the poles and the straps.

Before skiing down a hill, spend time getting used to your skis. Slide them forward and backward. Take side steps. Push with your poles and walk around in circles. Watch the people around you as they walk with skis. Walk up and then slide down slight rises and dips in a flat area. Next, find a very gradual slope with a wide, level runout. Walk up a small portion of the slope (sidestep up if your skis slide backward) and, using what you have learned about balancing with your arms and your poles, push off and slide down. Point your skis in the direction you want to go—and most of the time you will. Gradually climb higher and slide farther. You may fall a few times, and you may be unsure of your balance, but this is entirely normal for a beginner.

When you fall, relax and fall easily. Hold your poles so that you don't land on them, and try to fall on your side with your skis downhill from your body and parallel to the slope. To get up, pull your legs up under your hips, place your hands or poles uphill from your body, and push.

As your ability improves, try sliding downhill with the tails of your skis pushed slightly apart and the tips close together but not touching. Relax in a slightly flexed stance. Your weight should be evenly distributed and centered over both skis.

Always look in the direction you want to go. Keep your hands relaxed and in front, with your ski poles pointing to the rear. Allow your skis to come back together, push them apart for a longer distance. Practice over and over. Next, while sliding along comfortably with the tails slightly apart, turn your body gently to one side, then the other. Just looking in the direction you want to go will start you in that direction. Try these gentle turns many times, with an occasional straight run for fun.

As you practice, remember to turn with your feet. Keep your upper body relaxed and faced in the direction you intend to go. Take larger, longer turns; make short, quick turns. Try turns with your skis pushed slightly apart, then farther apart. Ski across the slope with your skis parallel, and try pressing the uphill edges of the skis into the slope. Turn uphill to stop. As you become more sure of your

balance, try turns with your skis parallel, turns to the rhythm of a tune, alternating with long, straight runs.

Before you attempt riding a ski tow or lift, watch other skiers do it, and ask them for advice. Let the lift attendant know that it's your first time. Use awareness and common sense as guides to better skiing.

Altering clothing

Improving fit; adjusting for weight loss or gain

Before altering any garment, examine it carefully. If its seam allowances have been clipped or its darts slit, you will be limited in how much you can let the garment out, if at all. For neat results, always iron the creases after you open any seams or darts and again after restitching them.

Adjusting waistlines

A dress or skirt waist or women's pants should fit snug at your natural waistline. If a waist is too large, open the waist seam or the waistband at the sides. Take in both side seams the required amount (equalized between the two). Remove the old stitching and press the new seams open.

On a dress, after side seams are restitched, reattach the waistline seam along the original stitch line. On a skirt or pants, after the waistband sides are taken in, reattach the trimmed, pressed band as before.

A too-tight waist can be let out about 2 inches, depending on the original seam allowance. Open the

side seams and apportion one-half the total ease needed to each seam. A little extra ease can be added to a skirt waistband by simply moving the button or hook and eye.

Adjusting for a large abdomen

Open the front waist seam and the side seams. Let out the side seam fronts up to ⅜ inch. Lower the fabric in the front at the waistline as much as ⅜ inch, tapering the new seam to the original stitching at the sides.

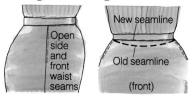

Adjusting for a swayback

Open the back waist seam. Raise the waistline by taking a deeper seam at the center back. Taper the new stitching to the original stitching.

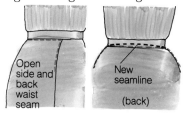

Realigning darts

Darts should point to the fullest part of the body area being fitted and end about ½ inch from the most rounded part. To realign waist darts, open the darts and pin fit them on the right side of the garment. On the wrong side, mark new stitching lines with tailor's chalk. Baste the new darts and try on the garment before final stitching. Press newly stitched darts toward the center of the garment. This same technique can be used on bustline, shoulder, and elbow darts.

Hipline adjustments

If a garment is too loose across the hips, determine how much needs to be taken in. Then open the waist seam at the sides. Allotting each seam half of the desired decrease, stitch new side seams parallel to the original seams and tapering to the waist. Remove the original stitching and trim the new seams. Press them open and restitch the waist seam.

For a too-tight hipline, reduce the seam allowance the required amount

equally along each of the lengthwise seams. If a skirt is long enough and if it isn't too straight and narrow, you can add a couple of inches to its hipline by raising the skirt at the waistline. (This applies also to dresses with waistline seams.) Try on the skirt or dress. Raise the skirt until the hipline feels comfortable and tie a string around the new waistline. Mark the new waistline with tailor's chalk. Remove the waistband or open the waist seam. Trim the top of the skirt ⅝ inch above the chalk marking. Take in the darts (lengthening them as needed) and the side seams at the waistline to fit the waistband or waist seam.

Adjusting for shoulder wrinkles

If you have square shoulders, garments may be taut and wrinkled in that area. To correct this, remove the sleeves. Open and restitch the shoulder seams, gradually narrowing each seam as it tapers from neckline to armhole. To compensate, raise the underarm seams an equal amount.

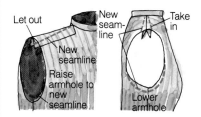

If you have sloping shoulders, your garment may wrinkle diagonally from the neck to the armholes. To correct this problem, remove the sleeves. Open and restitch the shoulder seams, this time gradually widening each seam as it tapers from the neckline to the armhole. Compensate by lowering the underarm seams an equal amount. (See also *Hems; Pants.*)

Aluminum siding

Patching, cleaning, and repainting aluminum siding

Small punctures or cracks in aluminum siding can be filled with good-quality caulking compound.

Cleaning aluminum siding

Siding that is 15 to 20 years old may chalk, or discolor. Apply a piece of

A

masking tape to the siding; then pull the tape off. If a whitish residue remains on the tape, the siding is chalking. To remove chalking or corrosion, scrub the siding with a wire brush and detergent solution. Carefully rinse the surface and let it dry. Rent a pressure washer for large areas.

If the cleaned surface is in good condition, give the siding a coat of clear metal sealer or diluted varnish to prevent the chalking from recurring.

Painting aluminum siding

If the surface of your siding is in poor condition or if you want to change the color, first clean the siding. Then brush on two thin coats of an oil- or latex-base metal primer designed for bare aluminum. Using fine sandpaper, feather, or sand smooth, any ridges or irregularities. Finally, add a thin top coat of an acrylic paint with a flat or semigloss finish.

Because aluminum expands and contracts with changes in the weather, make the paint coats thin to avoid cracking. For some paints you have to apply an intermediate bond coat. Check with your paint dealer.

Anagrams

How to play this word game

Any number from two to eight can play anagrams. A set of 200 anagram tiles is needed, each bearing a letter on one side.

If you do not have a set of tiles, you can substitute two sets of Scrabble tiles or make your own from 3 x 5 index cards. Cut the cards into eighths and print a letter on one side of each piece. The number of tiles for each letter should be roughly in proportion to the frequency that the letter is used in English. Here is one way of doing it:

A	15	J	2	S	12
B	4	K	2	T	14
C	6	L	8	U	8
D	8	M	5	V	4
E	20	N	14	W	4
F	5	O	15	X	2
G	4	P	4	Y	5
H	8	Q	2	Z	2
I	12	R	15		

Place the tiles face down on a table, leaving the center of the table clear.

Going around the table, each player turns over one tile and places it in the center of the table. The object is to spot a word of at least four letters from the turned-over tiles.

Any player to spot a word calls it out (whether it is his turn or not), removes the tiles from the center, and sets up the word in front of him. A word can be captured from another player by adding one letter or more from the center stockpile to the word to form a new one. The first player to assemble 10 words wins. If all the tiles are used before anyone has 10 words, the player with the most words wins.

Animal odors

Eliminating dog and cat odors

To control a pervasive odor of a dog or cat, establish a permanent sleeping place and wash any bedding regularly. Where a pet has slept on carpets, scatter baking soda or carpet deodorizer, then vacuum. Also, keep your pet well groomed. (See *Cats; Dogs.*)

Abnormal body odors

If your dog or cat has an extra strong body odor even when it is brushed and clean, consult a veterinarian. It may have a skin disorder known as seborrhea, an ear infection, or, in dogs, an impaction of the anal glands. Seborrhea can often be controlled by a medicated shampoo or, in mild cases, a human dandruff shampoo. Signs of a glandular problem are biting or licking abnormally at the rear end or scooting on it. This and ear infections require professional treatment.

An older animal may develop halitosis from deposits on its teeth. Prevention is the best course: give a dog a rawhide bone to chew on for short periods; occasionally feed a cat crunchy dry food. In addition, brush your pet's teeth, using baking soda or toothpaste and a soft brush or a gauze square wrapped around your finger. Clean carefully along the gum line.

Cleaning up animal messes

Whenever an animal messes in the house, scoop up the deposit and blot the area with paper towels. Apply vinegar, lemon juice, or ammonia to neutralize the stain. Scrub the area with

soap and water to remove the odor. Commercial preparations are available for applying directly to urine spots to neutralize the odor and the stain. (See also *Skunk odors.*)

Animal tracks

Identifying common footprints

Because wild creatures usually stay in hiding after a snowstorm, look for tracks about 24 hours later. You can also find tracks in mud or wet sand along beaches, streams, and lakeshores almost any time.

Tracks made by members of the dog family are among those most often seen. Domestic dog tracks, however, are difficult to distinguish from those of the dog's wild relatives—the wolf, coyote, and fox. To decide if tracks were made by a wild animal, study the course or route of the tracks. A domestic dog will go directly up to a house or other place used by people, whereas a wild animal will cautiously skirt around it.

The tracks of a domestic cat are recognizable by the small, neat paw marks and a cat's habit of placing its hind paws in the marks of its front paws.

Tracks tell you not only which animal passed by but also the speed and mode of its movement. A rabbit, for example, places its powerful hind feet right up through and ahead of its front feet with each hop, leaving a fan-shaped cluster of footmarks.

Mice and some of the tree climbers, such as raccoons and squirrels, leave long prints resembling human handprints. When running, tree climbers place their front feet together.

Front and hind prints of a :
1. Cottontail (all 4 feet in snow)
2. Gray squirrel (in snow)
3. Raccoon
4. Meadow vole (field mouse)
5. Coyote
6. Red fox

Antennas

Replacing a car antenna

If the shaft of a car antenna is broken or damaged but the antenna base is intact, you can attach a replacement shaft rather than installing a complete antenna. Buy a flexible shaft made of a rubber-covered conductor. Using pliers, break off the remains of the old shaft close to the base. File the remaining end of the old shaft to a slight taper and push on the new shaft. Tighten the retaining screws.

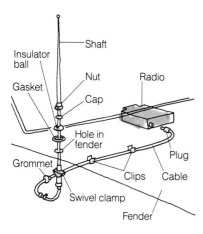

Installing a new antenna

If the antenna is broken off at the base, replace the entire assembly. There are many types of replacement antennas, including one that disappears into the fender and can be lifted only with a special key. This type is almost as resistant to damage as a power antenna but it costs far less.

Reach under the dashboard, locate the antenna cable in the radio, and disconnect it. Loosen the antenna nut and work the antenna assembly out of the mounting hole. Cut the cable from the old antenna and tape the plug of the new antenna to the cut cable. To draw the new cable into place, carefully pull the plug end of the old one. You may have to remove a fender shield to reach in and guide the new cable through a body grommet.

Once the wire is in place, push the new antenna mount through the hole on the fender and secure it. Plug the antenna cable into the radio.

Antifreeze

Flushing a car's cooling system; installing antifreeze

Check your car's cooling system every 6 months. Flush the system and add antifreeze at least once a year. In areas where dumping is forbidden, catch the drained antifreeze and bring it to a garage with coolant recycling equipment, or have them flush and refill the system.

To check the system, remove the radiator cap and look inside. If the contents are very dirty, pour in a can of cooling-system cleaner; operate the car according to the can's instructions.

Flushing with water

Flush the system with water after using the cleaner or if the system is only a little dirty. (If your car has no flushing T, get a flushing-T kit at an auto parts store and install the T following the kit instructions.)

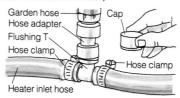

Remove the flushing-T cap and attach a hose adapter. Then connect a garden hose. If the radiator tubes are vertical, remove the radiator cap and install the water-deflector nozzle in the cap neck. If the radiator tubes are horizontal, disconnect the upper radiator hose at the engine and aim the end away from the engine.

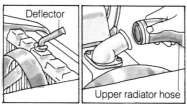

Start the engine, turn on the heater, and set the temperature to *Hot.* Turn on the water to the garden hose; fluid will pour out of the deflector or upper hose. When it runs clear for 2 minutes, shut off the heater, the engine, and then the water. Remove the deflector or reconnect the upper radiator hose.

Depending on your car's setup, open the radiator petcock, or remove the drain plug, or disconnect the lower radiator hose. Let the water drain. Then tighten the petcock, or refit the drain plug or the hose.

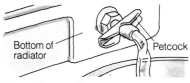

Installing antifreeze

Install an amount of undiluted antifreeze equal to between 50 and 70 percent of the capacity of the cooling system (see your owner's manual). The antifreeze will mix with the water remaining in the system (only the radiator has been drained).

Usually the radiator won't hold all the antifreeze called for. In that case, see if there is an overflow reservoir connected by a hose to the radiator neck. If so, empty the reservoir and add the remaining antifreeze.

If there is no reservoir, run the engine with the cap off the T, the heater on, and the temperature lever on *Hot.* As fluid dribbles out, add antifreeze to the radiator until the required amount is in. Then stop the engine, cap the T, and refit the radiator cap.

Caution: Antifreeze is poisonous. Keep it away from children and pets. Do not work with it when the engine is hot. Keep away from electric fans in the car unless they are disconnected.

Antiquing

Refinishing furniture to give it an heirloom look

In this method of finishing, three coats of finish are applied to a serviceable but uninteresting piece of furniture to give it a patina of age.

Glazing supplies

For the first, or base, coat use a semigloss, oil-base enamel in a color that will mask the old finish. Off-white is often the choice. You may have to mix the second coat—a tinted, nearly transparent glaze. Many paint and wallpaper stores carry clear glaze, as do arts and crafts suppliers. But you can make your own by mixing three parts satin varnish with one part turpentine. Color the glaze by adding oil-base tinting colors (burnt sienna, for example). The final coat is clear polyurethane satin-finish varnish. Experiment with glazing on scrap wood.

Doing the work

Remove knobs and hardware. Wash the piece with detergent and water, and remove old wax with mineral spirits. Lightly sand the piece with medium sandpaper. Put on the base coat with a coarse brush. Let it dry for 24 hours or more.

Brush on the glaze and let it set for a few minutes until it begins to dull. Then begin wiping the glaze off with cheesecloth, leaving some residue. Wipe with the grain, working out from the center of each flat surface. Leave more glaze on depressions, less on high spots and areas that would naturally become worn with use. To produce different textures, try wiping with steel wool, crumpled paper toweling, burlap, a sponge, or a dry paint brush instead of cheesecloth.

Glaze takes about 6 hours to dry, so don't rush. Work glaze like finger paints, then let it dry thoroughly. Sand lightly with fine paper, dust with a tack cloth, and apply a coat of clear satin varnish.

Ants

Getting rid of ants

The cheapest and most permanent way to keep ants out of the kitchen is to eliminate their access to foods that attract them, such as jam, sugar, crumbs, and grease. Get rid of foods you will not use and seal the rest in airtight containers. Scrub down all counters and shelves and leave a few bay leaves on cupboard shelves.

In wet weather ants may come into the house to escape from waterlogged nests. They will disappear again as soon as the ground dries out—if there is no accessible food.

To get rid of persistent ants, your best bet is to place commercially available sweet-baited ant traps on floors or in cupboards where ants have been seen. Be sure to locate them out of reach of children and pets. (See also *Carpenter ants; Termites.*)

Apartment security

Locking up and keeping safe

When moving into a new apartment, have the lock cylinders changed. Equip the door with a heavy-duty dead-bolt lock or a high-quality rim lock, and lock it every time you go out.

Be sure that the door panels and door frame are strong and that the door fits snugly into the frame. A space between the door and the frame makes it easier to pry open the latch.

Lock any windows and doors that open on balconies, fire escapes, or rooftops. If you live on the first or second floor, lock all the windows.

Never allow anyone you don't know into the building. If suspicious persons try to get in, notify the superintendent. Don't leave messages on your door or in the lobby indicating that you are out. Install a peephole in your door, and check who is there before opening your door. (See also *Burglar alarms; Burglarproofing; Door locks; Elevator safety; Peepholes; Window-locking devices.*)

Aphids

Controlling these garden pests

Tiny, slow-moving, soft-bodied insects that come in a variety of colors, aphids feed on plants by sucking out their fluids. Aphids multiply rapidly, especially in hot, humid weather. If your plants are healthy and well nourished, they should survive a brief infestation. But don't overfeed your plants, or the aphids may increase.

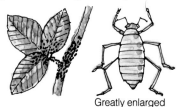
Greatly enlarged

Two or three vigorous hosings will usually combat a mild aphid infestation. A long-term solution is a supply of aphid predators such as ladybugs and parasitic wasps, available from mail-order nurseries.

For severe infestations outdoors, spray with malathion. If you use it on food crops, you must wait before harvesting them. Check the label or with your Cooperative Extension Service for the exact number of days. Indoors, wash plants with insecticidal soap or spray them with resmethrin. Wrapping the bases of plants with aluminum foil discourages aphids.

Appliqués

Stitching cutout shapes to background fabric for decoration

Choose fabrics for shapes and background that are compatible in weight and care requirements—preferably smooth, firmly woven ones of a light to medium weight. Ideas for appliqué color schemes and designs abound in magazines, in collections of stencil shapes, in design publications, and in coloring, art, and needlework books.

To transfer designs most easily, cut a cardboard template (pattern) in the shape of each appliqué piece. Trace the shape onto the appliqué fabric. Before cutting, add a ¼-inch seam allowance for hand appliqué, ½ inch for appliqués to be sewn by machine. Layer the design shapes so that you work from the background to the foreground. Shapes that do not stand by themselves should overlap slightly.

Hand-done appliqué

Cut out the appliqué, including the seam allowance. Staystitch it just outside the traced outline of the design. To reduce bulk and make it easier to turn raw edges, clip inside curves and notch outside curves. Trim outside corners and points, and notch angles.

Place each shape right side down, and position the template inside the staystitching. Press raw edges over the template. Remove the template.

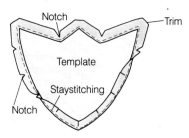

Hand baste the folded edge. Pin or hand baste the appliqué to the fabric. Attach the appliqué with whipstitches.

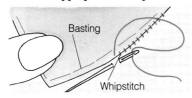

Basting

Whipstitch

Machine zigzag appliqué
Hold the appliqué in place for stitching with iron-on fusible web, a glue stick, or machine basting. If you decide on fusing or gluing, trim away the seam allowance beforehand. If you use machine basting, stitch along the design (traced) line and trim close to the stitching, taking care not to cut stitches or background fabric.

Use a short, narrow zigzag stitch and keep most of the stitches' length on the appliqué rather than on the background. Stitch slowly around curves. Pivot at the corners.

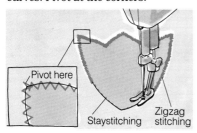

Pivot here

Staystitching

Zigzag stitching

Aquariums

Stocking a freshwater aquarium; choosing, setting up, and maintaining a tank; feeding the fish; treating ill fish

Start with only a few fish. Goldfish are ideal for a beginner's aquarium. Some other popular freshwater species are guppies, medakas, swordtails, and Siamese fighting fish. Select fish that appear lively, well fed, and free of fungus and other growths.

Choosing the tank
A rectangular glass tank is the best container. The traditional fishbowl has a narrow neck that does not allow enough contact between the water and the air. There should be at least 50 square inches of water surface for each fish, and the tank should hold at least 1 gallon of water for each inch of

fish. Thus if you have two fish, each about 2 inches long, you need a 4-gallon tank with an opening of 100 square inches. Buy a stand for the aquarium, or at least make sure that it is on a level surface.

Equip the tank with a glass or clear plastic cover. This keeps dirt out of the water, minimizes evaporation, and helps maintain an even water temperature. Sudden changes in temperature can be fatal to fish. Goldfish thrive in cool water, but most tropical fish must be kept in water between 68°F and 80°F. Get a thermometer and water heater for tropical fish.

Plants play an important part in an aquarium by removing potentially dangerous nitrates from the water. Plants also absorb carbon dioxide and give off oxygen during the day. At night, however, they use up dissolved oxygen; so you should install an air pump with a filter to ensure proper oxygenation of the water at all times.

Setting up the tank
A day or so before you buy the fish, wash the tank with clear water. Cover the bottom with 1½ to 3 inches of well-rinsed aquarium sand or gravel. Slope the sand or gravel to form a slight hollow in the middle—it will catch dirt, making cleaning easier.

Soak the plants for 15 to 20 minutes in a solution of 3 tablespoons of salt per gallon of water to get rid of parasites. Rinse the plants in clear water and embed them in the sand or gravel. If you like, add a few rocks or ceramic pieces to the tank.

Fill the tank with tap water, trying not to uproot plants. Let the tank stand, uncovered, at least 24 hours.

When you add fish to the tank, float them in their plastic carrying bag for 5 to 10 minutes or until the water temperatures correspond. (Do not leave fish in a plastic bag for more than 45 minutes.)

Maintaining the tank
Place the tank where it will receive diffuse light; keep it out of direct sunlight. Direct sunlight may cause overheating and overgrowth of algae. If you cannot get proper natural light for your aquarium, install a fluorescent light on the top of the tank. Pet stores carry special light fixtures to fit any size tank.

To clean the tank, scrape algae from the sides with a long-handled glass scraper. Remove sediment, decaying plants, and uneaten food with a dip tube. Both tools can be purchased from a pet shop. Trim plants occasionally and siphon off some water from the bottom, replacing it with water that has been sitting for 24 hours.

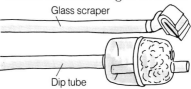

Glass scraper

Dip tube

Feeding
Feed your fish twice a day with commercial fish food. If this is not possible, morning is the best time. Give the fish only as much as they can consume in 10 minutes. (Uneaten food pollutes the water.) Occasionally offer the fish a fresh or frozen food, such as daphnia (a water flea) or tubifex worms, or bits of cooked liver, canned salmon, shrimp, or hard-cooked egg yolk. If you are out of fish food, use ground-up dry cat food or baby cereal flakes. If you are going away for a day or two, the fish can go unfed.

Fish illnesses
Fish gasping at the surface means insufficient oxygen due to overcrowding, heat, or dirt. Improve tank conditions.

Move fish that appear ill to a separate tank for observation. Trailing feces indicates constipation. Give the fish greens or other fresh food.

Fungus, appearing as a white, slimy coating, may infest a fish. Place the fish into a tank containing 3 teaspoons of salt per gallon of water. If the fish does not improve in 3 or 4 days, dispose of it.

Arthritis

Simple measures to relieve pain

Arthritis is not a single disease. More than 100 conditions, each characterized by inflammation of one or more joints, are considered forms of arthritis. Medical treatment can control arthritis and can cure certain forms of the disease. Many forms of arthritis may occur only once; others recur.

A

See a doctor if any of the following symptoms persist for more than two weeks: swelling, recurring pain, or tenderness in the joints; morning stiffness; inability to move a joint normally; redness and warmth in a joint; unexplained weight loss, fever, or weakness combined with joint pain.

Osteoarthritis

When people speak of arthritis, they usually mean osteoarthritis, the most common form. This condition stems from wear and tear on the joints. Any joint can be affected, but those of the hips, knees, shoulders, and spine are most often involved.

Treatment for osteoarthritis usually includes aspirin to relieve the pain and inflammation; exercises to keep the affected joints flexible and build muscle strength; some form of heat (hot baths or showers, compresses, hot tubs, or paraffin treatments); and rest—it often helps to lie down for 15 to 30 minutes several times a day. Other helpful measures include sitting in a straight chair, avoiding stairs, and elevating the leg if the knee is affected. Surgery may be indicated in severe cases of osteoarthritis.

Rheumatoid arthritis

Although less common, rheumatoid arthritis (rheumatism) afflicts many people, and it too is characterized by pain in the joints. Early diagnosis, important with all forms of arthritis, is crucial with rheumatoid arthritis. Mild cases are treated much like osteoarthritis—with aspirin, exercises, heat, and rest. (See also *Bursitis; Gout.*)

Artichokes

Preparing, cooking, and eating globe artichokes

To prepare an artichoke for cooking, cut off the sharp tips of the leaves and trim the base and the outer green layer of the stalk. Place artichokes in a stainless steel or enamel saucepan in 1 inch of boiling salted water with a little lemon juice or vinegar added. Cover and steam until the bottoms of the artichokes can be pierced easily with a fork—about 35 to 40 minutes, depending on size. Remove the artichokes and drain them upside down.

Serve the artichokes with lemon juice and melted butter or vinaigrette or hollandaise sauce (see *Hollandaise sauce*). To eat, pull off a leaf, dip its fleshy stalk end into the sauce, and pull the stalk through your teeth. Cut the inedible hairy part (the choke) from the tender bowl-shaped heart and eat the heart and the stalk.

Remove choke with knife or spoon

Cut along dotted lines

Asphalt driveways

Sealing and patching blacktop

Protect your asphalt driveway with annual applications of petroleum-based asphalt sealant. Ready-mixed sealants are available at building supply dealers in 5-gallon cans—enough to coat 200 to 300 square feet of drive. Sweep the drive clean, then pour sealant over one section of the drive at a time and spread it with a push broom. Apply a second coat within 48 hours.

Fixing small cracks and holes

Repair holes and cracks in your driveway as soon as they appear, preferably in warm or, better still, hot weather. Heat makes asphalt more malleable.

To repair narrow cracks, either squeeze in latex pavement-crack filler, or pack sand into the crack and apply driveway sealant. Pass a piece of lumber over the repair to smooth it.

Repair small holes and cracks wider than your finger with asphalt patching material, available at home centers and lumberyards in 50-pound bags. First, clean debris from the problem areas and probe the subsurface. Fill any voids in the foundation with crushed rock and tamp it down with a sledgehammer, 4 x 4, or other heavy object. Ladle asphalt patching into the crack or hole with a trowel. Tamp it down as you did the crushed rock. If the patching compacts below the surface, add more and tamp again.

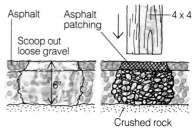

Asphalt · Asphalt patching · 4 x 4 · Scoop out loose gravel · 6" · Crushed rock

Making larger patches

Large holes and broken pavement indicate a problem in the foundation. Dig up loose and broken pavement, using a pickax, if necessary, and scoop out the loose gravel below to a depth of 6 inches. Fill the opening with crushed rock and compact it with a sledgehammer or a (rented) square-head tamper. Leave enough space for the patching material. Pack the patching into the area and tamp it down until the new surface is level. Drive a car over the spot to pack it further. If a depression develops, add more patching. After any repair, apply two coats of sealant to the entire driveway.

Aspic

Preparing and clarifying aspic; using and unmolding it

Aspic is a chilled jelly used to coat foods or mix with them. It can also be served plain as a first course.

To prepare and clarify aspic, skim all the fat from 4 cups of cold, well-seasoned meat, fish, or poultry broth, or use a vegetable broth. Pour ½ cup of the liquid into a 3-quart saucepan, sprinkle it with 2 tablespoons of unflavored gelatin, and let it stand for 5 minutes until the gelatin is soft. Add the remaining liquid and 3 egg whites beaten until frothy.

Bring the mixture to a boil, stirring constantly. When a dense foam appears on top, remove the saucepan from the heat.

Line a sieve with a dish towel (cheesecloth is too porous) that has been rinsed and tightly wrung out. Pour the liquid aspic through the lined sieve into a bowl. Let the aspic stand undisturbed until it is perfectly clear.

Using the aspic

To encase food in aspic, pour ⅛ inch of the aspic into a shallow dish and refrigerate until set (about 30 minutes). Place sliced meats, fish, poultry, or vegetables, and any garnish, on this bottom layer. Pour liquid aspic two-thirds of the way up—the food should not float. Refrigerate until the second layer is set, completely cover the food with aspic, and refrigerate again.

You can also use aspic to make a mold of cold foods, such as paté or salad. Coat a decorative mold or loaf pan with a thin film of unflavored oil. Pour in ⅛ inch of liquid aspic and chill until set (about 30 minutes). Pack the food on the chilled aspic and smooth the top. With a blunt knife gently pull the food away from the container's sides. Fill the crevices with aspic,

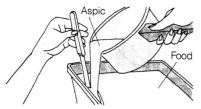

then cover the food with aspic and chill until set. To unmold, run a knife around the edges, dip the mold into hot water for a few seconds, cover with a plate, and invert.

Athlete's foot

How to treat it, avoid it, and protect others from infection

Athlete's foot is caused by fungi that flourish on warm, sweaty feet. It passes readily from foot to foot via the locker-room floor, but you can catch it at home too. The symptoms are cracked or peeling skin, itching or burning, and sometimes blistering, especially between the toes and on the soles. Occasionally there are severer results, such as oozing blisters or deep cracks that should be treated by a dermatologist or podiatrist.

Home treatment
Mild cases may clear up with extra cleanliness and exposure to fresh air. Wash the feet with soap and water, then separate the toes and gently rub away peeling skin with a towel. Repeat and dry well. Sprinkle the feet and between the toes with fungicidal foot powder or baby powder. Repeat

the treatment whenever the feet get sweaty or damp. A fungicidal ointment, obtained at a drugstore and applied two to three times daily, sometimes helps.

The more air circulates around the fungi, the faster they will die. In the summer, wear open sandals. Canvas or perforated shoes are the next best choices. Wear polypropylene or other synthetic socks and change them daily, or oftener if they become damp.

If you have athlete's foot, avoid spreading it by always wearing socks or sandals, even at home. To prevent reinfection, keep your feet dry and don't walk barefoot in public places.

Auctions

Buying and selling at auctions

Most auction houses are in large cities, but their services are available to everyone. Buyers can bid by phoning or writing or by hiring an agent for a modest fee.

Auction houses regularly publish catalogs of upcoming sales, and you can subscribe to those of particular interest, such as antiques, stamps, and art. The descriptions in these catalogs, however, are sometimes suspect as to condition of the items and other vital factors. So are the "expected prices" the items may fetch.

It is best to inspect the items before a sale. Unless you know the market, engage an agent. He'll probably charge between 5 and 10 percent of the price paid for an item. Auction houses can usually recommend an agent in almost any area of expertise.

Before taking your possessions to an auction house to sell, have them appraised by a qualified appraiser. (The Appraisers Association of America, headquartered in New York, qualifies appraisers in various fields.) The appraiser will advise what reserve price to place on an item. This is the minimum price you are willing to accept. The auction house takes a percentage of the final sale price as its fee, usually between 10 and 20 percent.

Buying at a country auction
Here you are usually on your own as to quality, price, and bidding. Some-

times bidding is by hand signal, or you may be given a numbered card to raise. Often you have to pay by certified check or make a deposit at the beginning if you plan to bid. Find out and go prepared.

Arrive early and inspect all items of interest before the auction begins. Set a limit on what you are willing to pay for an item—and stick to it. The bidding itself is like a poker game. Sit near a side aisle and watch other bidders' faces as a clue to how eager they are to buy. If there are several bidders for an item you want, try appearing disinterested and enter your bid only when it looks as though another bidder has nearly won out.

Avocado plants

Starting an avocado plant from a pit; caring for the plant

Easy to propagate and fast growing, the avocado makes an excellent indoor plant, but don't expect it to bear fruit. Remove the pit from the fruit,

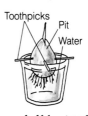

clean it with lukewarm water and insert three or four toothpicks into its sides. Rest the toothpicks on the rim of a glass so that the pit is suspended blunt end down. Add water to barely cover the lower end of the pit. Check the water level daily.

Roots should appear in 2 to 4 weeks, but it may take longer. Keep the pit in a warm, draft-free spot away from strong light for a few more weeks until the roots are well developed.

When the roots begin to spread and look bushy, plant the avocado in potting soil in a 4- or 5-inch pot. Set the pit deep enough for the soil to cover half of it. Water with lukewarm water, keeping the soil moist but not soggy.

Caring for the plant
As the plant develops, the seed splits and a stem with tiny leaves pushes up. You can then move the plant to a place where it will get direct sunlight or bright light at least 4 hours a day. Or put it under two 100-watt bulbs or a frosted white fluorescent tube. Feed

A

the plant liquid houseplant fertilizer once a month.

Without pruning, an avocado becomes spindly and may grow excessively tall. For a bushy, compact plant, cut the main stem back halfway when it is 6 to 7 inches tall, even if it is still growing in water. New branches will sprout below the cut.

To keep an older avocado plant from growing too tall, prune the main stem to the desired height. Encourage branches to sprout from the lower trunk by trimming back the upper branches partway. Also cut away lopsided, asymmetrical growth.

Awnings

Cleaning and repairing fabric awnings and their frames

Awnings can shade a terrace or keep a house cool in summer. Fabric awnings have two main parts, the cover and the frame. Covers can rot, rip, fade, and stain. Frames may suffer from corrosion and loose fastenings.

Traditional covers are of sailcloth, a cotton canvas that lasts 5 to 7 years before the sun fades and weakens it. (For a higher price, awnings can be made of acrylic fabric that will last 8 to 11 years.) Remove covers and store them for the winter in a clean, dry place to extend their lives.

Rainwater running off the roof will stain covers. Periodic hosing with water and, if necessary, a mild detergent can prevent much of the discoloration. Water-repellent spray or liquid applied to a terrace awning will prevent leaking.

Old canvas rips easily. To mend a rip, cut a patch from a similar fabric large enough to extend 1 inch beyond the tear. Glue it on with flexible outdoor glue; sewing will weaken the old fabric. Think about replacing old covers before the following summer.

Maintaining frames

If frames become corroded or rusted, brush them with a wire brush, apply a coat of rust-inhibiting primer, and then repaint them to match the rest of the frame. Check screws and other fastenings and tighten any that are loose. If the frames sway in a strong

wind, anchor them with ropes attached to their outer corners and stretched to cleats on the house.

Axes

Sharpening and lubricating an ax; replacing a handle

Before using an ax, whether old or new, you should sharpen its blade. Clamp the head of the ax, edge up, in a vise. Use a medium-cut mill file, never a power grinder. Hold the file flat against the blade. Draw the file upward toward the cutting edge, lifting off at the end of each stroke.

File on both surfaces, rounding them to a convex profile. Retain this profile to the corners of the blade; don't taper the corners. Check the edge by sighting down its length.

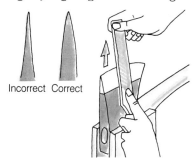

Incorrect Correct

Bright spots indicate dull areas. File these until the edge looks almost invisible. Hone the edge with an oiled, round ax stone, moving it in circles. Use a fine grade of steel wool to apply rust inhibitor or lightweight machine oil. When the ax is not in use, protect its blade in a leather sheath.

Replacing a handle

A loose, split, or broken handle is hazardous; replace it with a new one from a hardware or lumber store. To remove the old handle, clamp the ax head in a vise and saw the handle close to the head. Drill holes in the wood inside the ax head, then force out the wood with an old screwdriver or chisel. Take the ax head along when you buy a new handle to ensure proper fit. Make sure you get a hardwood wedge with the new handle.

If necessary, sand or rasp the handle to fit the ax head; the fit should be tight. Drive the wedge into the slit in

the handle by placing a board against the wedge and hammering it. Saw and sand the handle flush with the head. Finally, smooth the handle with fine sandpaper, and apply linseed oil with a soft cloth.

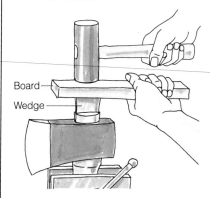

Board
Wedge

Sledge and maul handles are replaced in the same way, except they may require one or two steel wedges hammered into the wooden wedge.

Baby bathing

Safe, comfortable, effective ways to bathe a baby

It is not necessary to bathe a baby every day. Two or three times a week is sufficient, provided the diaper area of the body is kept clean. Don't bathe a baby just after a feeding.

Choose a warm room with no drafts. Have all your needs ready: basin, washcloth, towel, soap, baby shampoo, fresh diaper, safety pins, alcohol, flexible cotton swabs, and clean clothes. Have the water temperature near normal body temperature—between 90°F and 100°F; test it with your wrist or elbow.

Giving a sponge bath

Until the cord falls off and the navel heals, sponge-bathe your baby, holding the infant on a towel in your lap or on a table covered with padding. Wash the baby's face with soap and water, taking care not to get soap in the eyes. Shampoo the scalp once or twice a week, using a nontearing baby shampoo (see also *Cradle cap*).

Gently wash the body, one area at a time, paying careful attention to folds and creases. Wash the genital area last. As you finish each area, rinse it thoroughly and pat dry—don't rub. Clean the navel with a cotton swab dipped in alcohol.

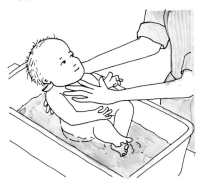

Tub bath
Use a washbowl, large pan, or the kitchen sink lined with a cloth diaper or towel. Have the water just an inch or two deep. Lower the baby gently, talking quietly for reassurance. Hold the baby so that your wrist suppports the head, and the fingers of the same hand are under the shoulder. With your other hand, wash the baby just as you did when sponge-bathing.

After rinsing, wrap the baby in a towel and pat dry. Put on a fresh diaper (see *Diapering*).

Caution: Never leave a baby in a bath unattended, even for a few seconds. Don't use cotton swabs in the baby's nose or ears—clean them with a dampened cotton ball or washcloth.

Baby burping

Getting rid of swallowed air

Whether feeding from the breast or from a bottle, a baby may swallow air that forms a bubble in the stomach and makes the baby feel full. To protect the baby from discomfort, get this bubble up by burping the child in the middle of a feeding and again at the end. Here are three ways to do it:

1. Hold the baby against your shoulder and pat or rub his or her back.

2. Sit the baby upright in your lap, supporting the chest and neck with one hand. Pat or rub the back with the other. It may help to rock the baby back and forth at the same time.

3. Lay the baby face down across your knees, then pat his or her back as you rock the infant gently back and forth.

Whichever way you do it, be sure to put a clean cloth below the baby's mouth to catch any spit-up that may come with the burp.

Baby food

What solid foods to feed infants; how to make your own

It's best to wait to introduce solid foods to your baby until 4 to 6 months of age. Until then, breast milk or formula provides the ideal nourishment (see *Bottle-feeding; Breast-feeding*).

Start with easily digested cereals, such as rice, barley, or oatmeal; applesauce; or pears. Introduce one new food every 5 to 7 days so that you can more easily identify the source of any adverse reaction. Signs of adverse re-

action are vomiting, cramping, excessive gas, diarrhea, or rashes.

Introduce yellow vegetables such as carrots, squash, and sweet potatoes before green vegetables. The best meats to start with are lamb and veal.

Foods that should be delayed till after 1 year of age include all whole-wheat products, fish, smoked meats, all highly seasoned food, egg whites, and honey. Do not add salt or sugar to home-prepared baby food.

Some easily prepared baby foods include mashed ripe bananas, mashed yolk from a hard-cooked egg (start with a teaspoonful), thin oatmeal, cottage cheese, yogurt, fruit sauces, and meat or vegetable puree.

To make a meat puree, grind cubes of well-cooked poultry, beef, or lamb with enough cooking liquid or milk to make it the consistency of applesauce. For a vegetable puree, grind a little freshly cooked vegetables with enough liquid to make a soft puree.

Purees can be frozen in individual portions for later use or refrigerated. Use refrigerated meat purees within 24 hours, vegetable purees within 2 days and fruit purees within 3 days.

Baby-sitters

Finding and using a baby-sitter

When hiring a baby-sitter, try to find one your child will like, and use that sitter whenever possible.

Getting recommendations
Neighboring mothers of small children are often the best source of information on local baby-sitters whom they have found satisfactory. You can also find teenagers who baby-sit by contacting your local high school.

Children 12 or 13 years old often make diligent, enthusiastic sitters when you go out for short periods of time and will be nearby and available by telephone. If you have a small baby or will be away overnight, hire an experienced adult who will be able to deal with any emergency that may arise. Again, ask neighbors.

You can locate professional full-time sitters through advertisements in your local newspaper or through sitter agencies listed in the yellow pages of your phone book. If you find a sitter through an advertisement, ask for at least two references and check each reference carefully. If you use an agency, make sure it is a reputable one. A sitter from an agency is usually costly because of the agency's fee.

Interview prospective sitters and introduce them to your children. Watch how the sitter talks to the children and how the children react to the sitter. Ask about the sitter's experience and what age group he or she is accustomed to handling. Discuss how to deal with such emergencies as choking, fire, falls, and accidental poisoning. Use only a sitter who seems perfectly capable of looking after your children in any emergency.

What to tell a sitter
The first time you use a baby-sitter, have the sitter come early to observe your children's normal activities. In this way both sitter and children will be comfortable with one another and you can leave with an easier mind.

Tell the sitter what time you will be back and where you can be reached in an emergency. Also, specify what foods and beverages the children may have and whether or not they may watch television or play the stereo. Write down your instructions so that the sitter can refer to them. Leave telephone numbers—police, fire department, doctor, neighbors who can help in an emergency—near the phone.

Backache

Relieving and preventing lower-back pain

Painful lower-back muscle strain afflicts almost everyone at some time. Rest, heat, and pain-relieving medication are the basic treatments. A half-hour soak in warm water, lying on a firm mattress, or applying a heating pad to the small of the back may help. Aspirin or acetaminophen may relieve pain. Severe or recurring pain can be caused by a wide range of physical or psychological ailments. See your doctor for diagnosis and treatment.

Preventing backache
Episodes of acute muscle spasm are often brought on by too great an ef-

fort, especially when lifting, or by sudden, awkward motions. To avoid such episodes, let your leg muscles do most of the work of lifting. Bend your knees and hold the object being lifted close to your body. If you are prone to backaches, avoid games like tennis that demand abrupt movements.

Chronic backache, when there has been no spine injury or illness, is a signal that your back can't take the way you are treating it. If you are overweight, your back may be supporting too great a burden—go on a diet. Another cause might be slumping posture. Learn to hold your back straight (see *Posture*), sleep on a firm mattress, and sit on hard, straight chairs.

Weak abdominal and back muscles due to lack of activity can also cause backaches. If your work requires you to sit for long periods, get up and walk about every hour or so. Better yet, undertake an exercise program, worked out with a doctor or physical therapist, to strengthen muscles.

Back-crawl stroke

How to swim facing up

This is an upside-down version of the crawl stroke. Float on your back, palms facing your thighs. Raise one arm out of the water, rotating your palm outward by the time your arm is extended above your shoulder. Lower

your arm backward into the water. As your arm enters the water, it should be slightly outside your shoulder. At a

depth of about 6 inches, pull your hand toward your thigh. When one arm enters the water, begin the same

stroke with your other arm. Kick your legs, which mainly act as stabilizers,

with your toes pointed. Only your toes should break the surface of the water. (See also *Backstroke; Crawl stroke*.)

Backgammon

Rules for playing an ancient gambling game

Backgammon is played on a board by two players, one using 15 black counters and the other, 15 white ones. The board is divided into two identical sides, one for "black" and one for "white." Each side has an inner and outer table with six triangles, or *points*. Those of the inner table are indicated as 1–6; those of the outer, 7–12. No numbers are printed on the board; you must remember them. The tables are separated by a *bar*.

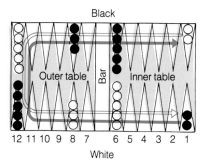

Set up the board as shown above. Then, taking turns with your opponent, try to move all your counters to your inner table and then remove them (*bear off*) from the board. If you succeed in doing so before your opponent, you win. Your counters move along a U-shaped path that passes through your opponent's inner then outer table, then through your own outer table to your inner one.

Making moves
To play, throw a pair of dice and advance one or two of your counters the number of points shown on the dice. A different counter may be advanced for each die or one counter may take all the points; if a doublet is thrown,

you get twice the numbers shown and can move as many as four counters.

Two or more of your opponent's counters on a point create a *block,* which prevents your counter from landing there, but not from jumping over it. A single counter on a point is called a *blot.* If one of your opponent's counters lands on a point with a blot, the blot is *barred*—that is, put on the bar dividing the board.

You must reenter a barred counter before moving another one. To do so, throw the dice. If the number on either die corresponds to an unblocked point on your opponent's inner table, you may move the barred counter there. If not, you lose your turn.

When all your counters are on your inner table, begin to *bear off.* Throw the dice. If the numbers on the dice correspond to the numbers of points you occupy, counters on those points may be removed. If one or both dice are higher than the highest occupied point, you may bear off counters on the highest occupied points. A low throw lets you advance a counter as in a normal move.

Betting, an optional aspect

Traditionally, backgammon is a gambling game, with the stakes set by the players. In fact, this gambling aspect gives the game its name. A losing player who has borne off at least one counter simply forfeits the stake; but a loser who has borne off no counters is *gammoned* (pays double), and a loser who has borne off no counters and has one or more counters on the bar or outside his or her own board is *backgammoned* (pays triple).

Backpacking

Where to go; readying yourself for an overnight hike

Backpacking means carrying life's necessities—food, clothes, bedding, and shelter—on your back. With today's lightweight equipment, a pack load for a weekend trip in summer need not exceed 20 to 30 pounds.

Condition yourself for a trip by walking or jogging daily. Work up to 6 miles of walking; then begin carrying a backpack with a gradually increasing load. It's best to backpack with at least two partners. In case of injury, one can stay with the injured person while the other goes for help.

Where to backpack

National and state parks and forests provide the best backcountry camping. Inquire at park headquarters or at a state parks department about trails and campsites. Other sources are guide books, trail maps (see *Map reading*), and outing clubs.

In selecting a destination, consider the difficulty of the terrain, the physical condition of party members, and the availability and quality of the water, for which you may need pills or filters. It's best to hike 5 to 10 miles per day on easy terrain at the outset. A 10-minute rest per hour lets you remove the burden from your shoulders, drink water, eat a snack, take pictures, and savor the wilds. Allow ample time to reach your campsite before dusk and bring along a flashlight or headlamp.

Food and cooking equipment

Nothing beats a hot meal at the start and end of each day. Rent, borrow, or buy a cookstove and fuel (see *Camp stoves*), nesting pots, a pot gripper, and a pot holder. Take plastic bowls and cups and aluminum spoons.

Dehydrated and freeze-dried foods packaged for campers are convenient but expensive. You can pick up many items from your supermarket, such as instant cereal, dried soups, potato and rice dishes, and pasta sauces. Go heavy on carbohydrates; season with herbs; add canned tuna or frankfurters for flavor. Put the ingredients for each meal in individual plastic bags labeled as to which meal it is. Take dried fruits, nuts, and candies for desserts and trail snacks.

Clothing

Plan your first trip for warm weather. It simplifies your choice of clothing. Cotton is cool next to the skin, but cotton-synthetic blends dry faster if they get wet. On warm days enjoy the freedom of loose-fitting hiking shorts. But for protection against nighttime temperatures, insects, and brambles, bring long pants and a light, long-sleeved shirt.

Cool weather calls for a sweater, long underwear, a down-filled or synthetic-insulated vest or parka, and wool cap and mittens. Prepare for rain with a hooded poncho or a pants-and-parka outfit of waterproof and breathable fabric. The latter, which is very expensive, lets body moisture escape.

Wear lightweight boots of leather or of fabric and leather with ridged soles for traction. To reduce boot friction, wear a pair of synthetic or light wool socks under thick oversocks of light wool or synthetic. Break in a pair of new boots by walking around in them for an hour a day; when they feel comfortable, extend the time and mileage.

Sleeping gear

Although expensive, a good down or synthetic sleeping bag will last many years with care. A closed-cell foam pad or an air mattress under your sleeping bag will make your bed nearly as comfy as at home. A foam pad weighs less and insulates better against cold ground. An air mattress provides better cushioning and is more compact.

Tents

If possible, borrow or rent tents at first, trying different styles before investing in one. A tent should be lightweight and well ventilated and should have mosquito-proof netting at all openings. It should have a seamless, waterproof floor extending up the sides 6 to 12 inches; the top should be of breathable nylon fabric, and there should be a separate rain fly.

The pack and its contents

The pack can be rented. It should have an internal or external frame to help support the load. Proper fit and adjustment of straps are essential; ask an experienced person for help. And include a plastic bag and raincover in the pack.

Carry a flashlight, first aid kit, waterproof matches, candle and backup lighter, a knife with a can and bottle opener, a filled water bottle and water-purification tablets, trail maps, sunscreen, sunglasses, insect repellent, toilet paper, whistle, rope (to hang food from a tree out of animals' reach), and change for emergency phone calls. You may include camera, binoculars, field guides, and fishing gear, but remember that each item adds weight.

Keep the pack's center of gravity high and forward. Put light items at the bottom, heavier ones at top. Items needed on the trail—snacks, water bottle, maps, and rain gear—go in

B

outer pockets or near the top. Pack the sleeping bag and pad in a waterproof bag and lash it to the bottom of the pack with straps or shock cords.

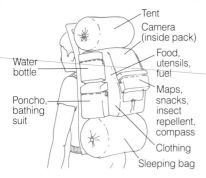

Tent
Camera (inside pack)
Water bottle
Food, utensils, fuel
Poncho, bathing suit
Maps, snacks, insect repellent, compass
Clothing
Sleeping bag

Before setting out, tell at least one friend or relative your plans. Check the weather forecast. At the trailhead or ranger station (if any), sign in and inform the authorities where you're going and when you plan to return.

Backstroke

A restful stroke, easy to do

If you get tired while swimming, switch to the elementary backstroke, as it's properly called. Float on your back with your palms facing downward and your toes pointed. Bring your hands up to armpit level and extend your arms straight out, with your hands slightly above shoulder level. Rotate your palms perpendicular to the water surface. At the same

time, bend your legs so that your heels come directly below your knees.

Pull your hands in to your thighs. Rotate your toes outward and thrust with the legs, making a semicircle. Your hands and feet should return to the starting position simultaneously. When your glide begins to slow, repeat the motions.

Bad breath

Temporary cover-ups; long-term solutions

Covering up bad breath or the scents of tobacco, alcohol, garlic, or onion with mints or other breath fresheners will do only in a pinch. Such products are only camouflages, not cures. The sources of bad breath — the stomach, lungs, and bloodstream — are too distant to be reached.

Better mouth and tooth care may solve the problem. Antiseptic mouthwash kills some of the bacteria that cause mouth odor. But a more effective measure is to clean teeth and gums thoroughly, floss between teeth, and even brush the tongue gently with a soft toothbrush (see *Tooth care*). If cleaning three times a day fails to clear up bad breath, suspect an underlying dental or medical condition and see a dentist or doctor.

Badminton

Playing the racket game

Chalk lines on a rectangular area 20 x 44 feet as shown. Erect a 5-foot-high net across the center of this court.

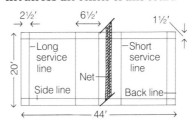

2½'   6½'   1½'
Long service line
Short service line
20'
Net
Side line
Back line
44'

In singles (two players), serve from the back line. Hit the shuttlecock, or birdie (a feathered cork), from beneath with your racket so that it flies over the net beyond your opponent's short service line but remains inside

Birdie
Racket

the side lines and the back line. If you fail to do this, your opponent serves. If his or her service is playable, you must hit the birdie back over the net before it falls to the ground.

Continue volleying back and forth until either you or your opponent fails to return the birdie or hits it out of bounds. If the server misses the birdie, the serve changes sides. If the server's opponent misses the birdie, the server gains a point and serves again. Only the server can gain points. The game is usually over at 21 points.

For surprise effect, try a *drop shot* or a *smash*. When you are close to the net, make a drop shot by tapping the birdie lightly so that it just clears the net and drops on the other side. Return the birdie with a high-speed smash by slamming the birdie downward toward the far corner.

In doubles (four players), you serve from the long service line and use the entire width of the court. At the beginning of the game, the serve passes to the other side as soon as the server makes the first fault, but thereafter the serve rotates to the partner of the server before passing to the other side.

Bail

How to make bail should you or a loved one be arrested

If arrested for even a relatively minor charge, you might have to spend time in jail unless you can make the bail set by the judge. Bail involves your promise to the court to appear for trial if you are freed. The promise is backed by money you or your family agrees to pay if you fail to return for trial.

You do not have an automatic right to bail. The U.S. Constitution requires only that if a court sets bail, it cannot do so in such a large amount that it is the same as not setting bail at all. Federal and state laws provide for bail for most crimes. Check with a lawyer to learn what bail rights you and your family have in your state.

When you make a plea to charges against you, the judge may release you without bail "on your own recognizance" if satisfied that you will not run away. Holding a steady job, living

B

in the community a long time, being active in church or civic affairs, and having good family relationships will usually satisfy a judge that you will return for trial.

Bail bonds

If you have recently moved, lost your job, have no family, or have a criminal record, you might have to post bail. If bail is set at $5,000, for example, you must pay $5,000 in cash to the designated officer. Should you be short of cash, a bail bondsman will provide the money for a fee (typically 10 percent of the bail). The bondsman will require collateral (valuables that can be sold) or promises by you or your family to pay if you fail to appear for trial.

Once you make bail, the court sends your jailer a receipt, or bail ticket. You receive an appearance ticket with the time and place of trial. You are free to go, but bail can be revoked and you can be returned to jail if you are arrested on other charges before your trial.

When you appear for trial, any cash or collateral posted is returned. If you *jump bail* (run away), the judge issues a warrant for your arrest on the new charge of bail jumping, and you lose any money or collateral posted. If, however, you have a good reason for not appearing, such as illness, tell the judge in order to avoid the new charges or the loss of your property.

Bait

Finding, storing, and hooking bait for fishing

Bait should look and smell appetizing to a fish. A worm, minnow, or other live bait should be frisky. Cut or dead bait, such as fish parts or shrimp, works best when it is fresh or well preserved. When fishing, check your bait frequently and change it when it becomes sluggish or when dead bait has a ragged, washed-out look.

Earthworms are surefire fish attracters in fresh water. Look for them beneath rocks or logs, or turn over the soil in a moist garden or dirt pile.

Night crawlers, large earthworms that emerge from their holes in a lawn after dark, can be spotted with a flashlight. Tread softly, and when you see a night crawler, grab it quickly and squeeze it gently until it releases its grip on the hole.

Store worms at cool temperatures (40°F to 60°F) in a container that allows air to penetrate, such as a wooden box or coffee can covered with screening. Fill the container with bits of moist newspaper and fine soil.

Minnows can be caught in shallow water near shore by dragging a 10- to 20-foot seine (a net with weights on the bottom and floats on the top). They can also be trapped in a small-mesh wire trap baited with bread, oatmeal, crackers, or hamburger.

Oxygen is the key to keeping bait fish alive. Use an aerator, or change the water in the bucket frequently. Keep the water in the 60°F range and don't overcrowd a container.

To attach a minnow, run the hook through the lips or in front of the dorsal fin. Don't use too large a hook— the minnow won't swim naturally.

To thread an earthworm, start at the worm's thicker end and let the hook point emerge when the shank of the hook is covered. Or pass the hook through the worm's enlarged band. Worms do not feel pain.

With cut bait, insert the hook through one end and then pass it through a second time so that the hook's shank is somewhat concealed. The point and barb of the hook should protrude slightly.

Bait casting

Setting the cast control on the reel; making a cast

Bait casting is a technique for fishing with either artificial lures or natural bait. The bait-casting reel has a revolving spool, a free-spool mechanism to uncouple the spool from other reel parts, a level-wind mechnanism to distribute the line evenly on the spool, and a drag (magnetic on some new reels) to slow the line when a fish is on it. Some inexpensive reels lack one or more of these features. The rod has a trigger for the index finger.

With the rod rigged and a lure or practice plug on the line (see *Fishing tackle*), tighten the cast-control knob by turning it clockwise. Next, hold the rod with your thumb against the spool. With your free hand, depress the free spool and loosen the cast-control knob by turning it counterclockwise until the lure falls slowly when you take your thumb off the spool. The tighter the setting, the shorter your cast will be.

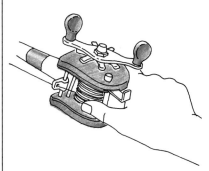

Cast with your right foot slightly ahead and right shoulder facing the target (left foot and left shoulder for left-handed caster). Grip the rod firmly but lightly, focus on the target, and line up the rod with the tip pointing at an imaginary point just above the spot you want to reach. Press the free spool. Then, in a continuous motion, raise the rod to the vertical and, without pause, start it forward, snapping your wrist toward that imaginary point above the target. About halfway between vertical and stop positions, release your thumb but rest it lightly on the spool to prevent backlash. Stop your arm gently if you're using natural bait. Before the lure hits the water, press your thumb against the spool to stop its rotation. A half-turn of the handle releases the free spool.

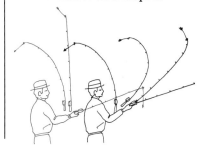

Baking

Techniques for baking a cake from scratch

Baking is cooking with dry heat. Although usually done in an oven, baking can also be done on the stovetop or over an open fire. This article discusses cakes. For other baked foods, see *Breadmaking, Casseroles, Cookies, Gingerbread men; Quiche, Soufflés.*

Preparing the batter

A cake made from scratch takes only a little more time than one made with a mix, and the results, given a good recipe followed with care, will be worth it. Cakes usually combine shortening, sugar, eggs, flour, leavening, a liquid, and flavoring. The last should be of top quality—use real vanilla, fresh spices, the best dark chocolate. Have the ingredients at room temperature. In measuring dry ingredients, level them with the back of a knife.

Often the first step is to cream the butter and sugar together; an electric beater or food processor does this more easily and thoroughly than the traditional wooden-spoon method. Whole eggs can be added in the same way. (If beaten egg whites are to be added, see *Egg whites*). Use cake flour when called for; if you substitute all-purpose flour, reduce the amount by 2 tablespoons per cup. Sift the flour before and after measuring, or as often as the recipe directs. Mix in the flour only until the batter is uniform, using a mixer, a food processor, or a rubber spatula.

Baking the cake

Preheat the oven to the temperature in the recipe while you're mixing the batter. Grease the cake pans, dust them with flour, shake the pans to distribute the flour, then shake out excess flour. Regrease any spot where the flour doesn't adhere. Fill the pans no more than two-thirds full. Place a single pan in the middle of the oven; if the recipe calls for more than one pan, place the pans at least 2 inches from one another and from oven walls. Stagger them so they aren't directly above or below one another. Bake. Insert a toothpick or wire cake tester; if it comes out clean, the cake is done.

Bandaging

Bandaging wounds, scrapes, and minor injuries

Stock your first aid cabinet with adhesive bandages in various sizes and shapes, rolls of gauze in 1- and 2-inch widths, gauze pads, 1/2-inch surgical adhesive tape, and several widths of elastic wrapping bandages. Also consider adding flexible fabric bandages and butterfly bandages. This assortment should equip you to bandage minor wounds and to provide protection in more serious situations until medical help can be found.

There are two reasons for bandaging minor wounds: to close a cut so that bleeding will stop and the edges will heal neatly, and to keep a wound clean and free of infection. Before bandaging any cut, scrape, or puncture, see *Bleeding* and *Wounds.*

Bandages should be changed at least once a day or whenever soiled or wet. By the end of 1 week, most cuts are sufficiently healed so that bandaging is no longer necessary.

Minor cuts and wounds

For a cut that is bleeding very little or has stopped bleeding, use an adhesive bandage. Choose one the right size and shape for the injury. The gauze should cover the entire wound; otherwise, in removing the bandage, you may reopen the cut or pull off the scab. A flexible fabric bandage (an adhesive bandage with stretchy tape) is more comfortable on an elbow, finger, or toe.

After cleaning and drying the area, wrap or pull the bandage fairly tightly to close blood vessels, but don't cut off circulation completely. Within an hour clotting will prevent further bleeding and you can take off the first bandage. Replace it with a clean and looser one.

Open cuts

Butterfly bandages are used to draw two sides of a small (up to 1 inch) cut together so that the wound will heal with a minimum of scar tissue. Apply one side of the butterfly first. Then tug gently as you apply the second side, checking to be sure the edges of the cut meet and align. The pressure should be sufficient to close the cut but not so strong that the edges of the

cut curl inward. You can make an emergency butterfly by cutting a small adhesive bandage.

A doctor should see a cut that is more than 1 inch long, a deep cut across a finger joint, or a cut that is potentially disfiguring—for example, a cut on the lip or nose or through an eyebrow. Use a butterfly bandage on the cut until you can get medical care.

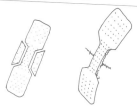

Bandaging scrapes

Scrapes should be covered for only a day or two. By that time a scab has usually formed. A scab is nature's bandage; it seals the wound while allowing air to reach it.

Elbow and knee scrapes are best bandaged with a gauze pad loosely held in place with two strips of adhesive tape so that the joint can bend freely. Gauze may stick to an oozing abrasion. To remove gauze, soak the area in clean water for a few minutes until the gauze can be pulled away easily. Then gently pat the area dry.

Sprains and jammed fingers

Bandaging is also used to relieve the pain of minor joint injuries, such as twists, sprains, and jammed fingers. Once the doctor assures you that the injury isn't serious, provide a wrapping of gauze to support the joint and to remind the person not to move it. Or use an elastic wrapping bandage, following your doctor's directions or those on the package.

Support a jammed finger, sometimes called a baseball finger, with a tongue depressor held in place by a 1½-inch-wide gauze strip wrapped crisscross around the finger and secured by a wrap and tie at the wrist.

Complex bandaging, such as swathing the head, requires experience. It is better left to professionals.

Bankruptcy

Managing debts by legal means

If you are overwhelmed by stacks of bills and cannot honestly cope with them, don't despair. Bankruptcy offers legal help, providing you haven't used it in the past 6 years and haven't hidden or given away assets in the past year to keep them from your creditors. With the advice of a lawyer, you can choose between two types of bankruptcy: liquidation, or straight bankruptcy, and rehabilitation.

To begin proceedings, you must file forms with the clerk of a U.S. bankruptcy court and pay a fee. The clerk can direct you to the proper forms.

Bankruptcy doesn't rid you of all your debts. You are still generally responsible for taxes, government-backed student loans, alimony, child support, and damages (money won in a lawsuit) for deliberate and malicious injuries or fraud caused by you. If you omit a debt from the forms you file, you remain liable for it.

Liquidation

Under liquidation, all your property is sold except for certain things deemed necessary for a reasonable life-style and for your work. (For example, Social Security benefits, an inexpensive car, and tools are exempt.) The court postpones any lawsuits on your unpaid bills, and your creditors must meet you in court to show that they are entitled to the proceeds of the sale.

A trustee handles the sale and sees that your creditors receive their fair shares of the proceeds. You are no longer responsible for those bills, whether your creditors are paid in full or receive only a fraction of what you owe.

Rehabilitation

If you have a regular income, you may use rehabilitation proceedings rather than liquidation. Sale of your property is not required. You need only reach an agreement with your creditors to repay your debts up to a certain amount (either all or part of what you owe) on a monthly timetable.

The court supervises this arrangement, and 10 percent of each payment goes to the court for administrative expenses. Credit bureaus can report either type of bankruptcy for up to 10 years, but lenders generally think better of a creditor who pays off his debts rather than liquidating them.

Barbecuing

Building the fire; controlling the cooking process

Barbecuing can be done over an open wood fire, over charcoal briquettes on a brazier or hibachi, or on a gas-fired or electric grill. Don't burn charcoal in the house because of the danger of carbon monoxide fumes.

To start a wood or charcoal fire, place wadded paper and kindling beneath the fuel and light the paper. Or use an electric igniter for charcoal. Avoid charcoal lighter fluid; it may flavor the food. Never use gasoline or any other highly combustible liquid.

A wood fire is ready for cooking when it has become a mass of glowing embers. Briquettes should burn until they are grayish-white with no black points showing.

The trick to cooking the food to the desired degree of doneness without charring it is controlling the heat. You can do this two ways: by moving the grill higher or lower or by dispersing the coals with a poker or tongs so that the heat is less intense. Start the food 4 to 6 inches from the heat. The thicker the cut of meat, the farther from the fire it should be. Have a squirt bottle of water ready to extinguish flames caused by melted fat.

Bartering

Swapping goods and services

Make a list of what you have to offer: skills; surplus goods (garden produce, unwanted clothing, equipment); or services (housepainting, baby-sitting). Locate other barterers through ads in local newspapers, shoppers' magazines, and company newsletters. Post notices in supermarkets, coffee shops, laundromats, and employee lunchrooms. Inquire whether nearby church and civic groups sponsor barter organizations.

To bring about a swap, know the value of the goods and services being swapped, and be prepared to bargain. Be specific as to what you are offering and when and where you'll deliver. Require the same of the other swapper.

Be aware that barter clubs and indirect exchange organizations may involve costly fees. Members may also be subject to sales and other taxes. In fact, any barter deal can be interpreted, for tax purposes, as an ordinary purchase or sale of goods.

Basement flooding

Getting water out of your basement quickly and safely

If your basement floods, get rid of the water as quickly as possible. If the flooding was caused by a ruptured pipe, shut off the water supply.

Caution: Water conducts electricity. If you have to enter a deeply flooded basement, wear high, heavy rubber boots and thick, dry rubber gloves. Be sure they don't leak. Standing on a wooden stool or chair, turn off the power. Use a dry piece of wood or plastic, such as a broom handle, to flip the main switch or pull out the main fuse block. Don't lean on a wall or touch anything until the power is off.

If the water is only an inch or so deep, use buckets, mops, sponges, or a wet-and-dry shop vacuum cleaner to get it out. Empty the buckets of water into a basement laundry sink or toilet or carry them outdoors.

Using an electric pump

Deeper water must be pumped out. If a plumber is unavailable, your fire department may pump out most of it for you (their equipment cannot get out the last 2 inches of water) or you can get rid of all but the last ¼ inch of water with a rented submersible electric pump. These *puddle suckers* sit flat on the floor, drawing water in through the base and pumping it out through a garden hose.

Connect the hose to the pump and run it out a door or window to a storm sewer or a spot where the runoff will flow away from the house. Lower the pump until it rests on the basement floor. Plug the cord into a neighbor's outlet. Keep debris away from the in-

B

take, or it may clog the machine and burn out its motor.

Pumping without electric power

Flooding may be due to a power failure that stops a sump pump (see *Sump pumps*). You may be able to rent a generator to run your sump pump.

Some electric and marine supply stores sell submersible pumps that are powered by 12-volt automobile batteries. If you use one of these, put the battery in a dry place and put the pump into the water before attaching the battery.

Nonsubmersible gasoline-powered pumps can also be rented for dealing with deep flooding. Run the intake hose down the basement steps or through a window, and the discharge hose far from the house. (See also *Basement waterproofing*.)

Basement waterproofing

Keeping your basement dry

Water gets into a basement by leakage, seepage, or condensation. Problems caused by seepage and condensation are usually easier to fix than leaks. Use a step-by-step approach when waterproofing. Start with the easiest job. If that doesn't solve the problem, proceed to more difficult remedies.

Simple remedies

Wrap sweaty cold-water pipes with fiberglass insulation. If the walls sweat in humid weather, use a dehumidifier.

Check the roof gutters. If they are broken or clogged, repair, replace, or unclog them. Basement drains may be clogged with dirt or tree roots; hire a service to unclog them. If earth has settled around the house, regrade the earth to slope away.

Damp or weeping walls that are without cracks can sometimes be treated. Wait for a dry period or use a dehumidifier to get the walls dry. Scrub concrete or cinder block with trisodium phosphate (TSP) or mild muriatic acid. If the walls get wet only occasionally, a latex masonry sealer paint, applied as directed, may solve the problem. For persistent dampness, try a two-part epoxy masonry sealer. Follow the same procedure for a damp concrete floor.

Advanced remedies

Install a drain or drainage system to combat continual basement flooding. A sump pump may help. (See *Sump pumps*.) If your basement floor is dirt or gravel, consider having a concrete floor poured on top of a plastic liner.

Repair large cracks or gaps in basement walls from the outside if they are above ground level or easily accessible with a little digging. Use mortar. When the patches are dry, coat them with *pargeting* (a thick bituminous solution) or a vinyl spray. If you cannot reach the crack on the outside, you can apply quick-cure concrete patching to the inside for a temporary repair, but it will leak eventually.

If these measures fail, you may have to resort to the tedious and expensive job of waterproofing the exterior foundation walls. Remove the plantings and excavate the earth around the foundation down to the footings. Clean the walls and coat them with pargeting. Finally, replace the earth and plantings. (See also *Drainage*.)

Basketball backboard

Creating a basketball court

You can install a basketball backboard on the outside of your garage or house in just a few hours. Kits are available from hardware stores, home centers, or mail-order houses. Get one with a universal mounting bracket that can be attached to a flat wall, a slanted roof, or even a pole.

Locate the backboard so that it faces a level, paved surface that is safe from obstructions and traffic. Use lag bolts to fasten the bracket into structural framing members such as wall studs (see *Studs*) or roof rafters, or

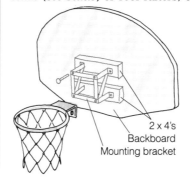

2 x 4's
Backboard
Mounting bracket

bolt 2 x 4s to the wall and bolt the bracket to the boards. Caulk any holes that puncture the wall or roof. (See *Caulking*.)

To install the backboard to the universal bracket, simply insert the supplied bolts between the bracket and backboard and tighten the nuts with a wrench. Check the unit with a level (see *Leveling*) and make any needed adjustments. Play ball!

Basting

How to get a moist roast

Meat, poultry, and fish are often basted while they are cooking in the oven to keep them from drying out and to add flavor. Basting involves covering the food with pan juices, butter, marinade, or sauce.

To keep the oven from losing heat, move the food to the stovetop while basting it. Use a bulb baster, spoon, or brush to pick up juices from the bottom of the pan. Squirt, ladle, or brush the juices over the cooking food. Return the food to the oven. Repeat the basting at regular intervals.

Bathroom cleaning

Keeping bathrooms clean, sanitary, and odor free

Knowing a bathroom's trouble spots helps you plan the cleaning routine. The tub and shower are havens for mildew. Wiping them dry after each use discourages mildew and prevents the buildup of mineral deposits and soap scum. Extend wet shower curtains so that they dry thoroughly Leave the shower doors ajar so that air can circulate.

Scrub the tub, shower, and sink every week. Avoid harsh abrasives; used repeatedly, they mar the finish. Instead, use a mild abrasive, a liquid disinfectant cleaner, or your own homemade mixture; do the scrubbing with a sponge. If stronger measures are necessary, use a brush, plastic scouring pad, or nylon stocking. Clean caulking around the tub with a toothbrush and liquid disinfectant. Clean a suction-backed tub or shower mat occasionally with the same liquid cleaner.

Stains on porcelain

Clean stained porcelain surfaces with a paste of cream of tartar and hydrogen peroxide. Spread the paste over the stain and scrub lightly. Let the paste dry and then wipe or rinse it off.

Use a toilet-bowl cleaner weekly. Bleach poured into the bowl may remove stains. Wash the outside of the toilet with liquid disinfectant cleaner.

Caution: Don't mix any combination of bleach, ammonia, and cleaners in the toilet bowl; a toxic gas results. If you are using two substances, flush away one before pouring in the other. Remove a commercial in-the-tank cleaner if one is in place.

Sweep or vacuum the bathroom floor weekly. Then mop the floor with a damp mop or sponge, using a disinfectant cleaner. An occasional scrubbing with a tile and grout cleaner will help restore grayed grout. Or apply a liquid cleaner, let it stand for about 20 minutes, then scrub the floor with a brush. (See also *Cleaners and polishes; Drain odors; Hard-water deposits; Mildew; Mops and mopping; Shower curtains.*)

Bathroom safety

Avoiding falls, scalding, poisoning, electric shock

Provide good lighting. Put rubber-backed, nonskid rugs or carpeting on the floor. Use suction-backed mats or adhesive decals inside the tub and shower—don't depend on built-in rough patches. Install grab bars in the tub or shower and, if you have an elderly or handicapped resident, next to the toilet. For reliability, fasten these to wall studs (see *Studs*).

Shatterproof enclosures are advisable for tubs or shower stalls. Buy safety glass that is labeled and certified to the American National Standard Institute's Z97.1 standard.

Prescription drugs and other medications can be a hazard when young children are around. Keep medications out of the bathroom cabinet or equip the cabinet with a lock. Store cleaning products in an inaccessible place. (See also *Childproofing.*)

Preventing burns from hot water

If your shower douses you with hot water when another tap is turned on or the toilet is flushed, install a mixing valve with a built-in temperature and pressure regulator.

Electric hazards

Water conducts electricity, so exercise caution with electric appliances. Don't operate light switches or use shavers or hairdryers when your feet or hands are wet. Unplug appliances as soon as you're finished with them.

Most new appliances have built-in cords, but those on some older appliances detach from the appliance. Unplug such a cord from the wall first; a cord dangling from an outlet can cause severe shock if dropped into water.

Portable electric heaters, radios, and tape players are risky in a wet environment. Don't use them in the bathroom. If someone insists on listening to music or news there, get a battery-operated model.

If your bathroom doesn't already have them, seriously consider installing grounded outlets. Even if an outlet has a grounding slot, use a circuit tester to make sure that the outlet is truly grounded (see *Electric receptacles; Ground-fault interrupters*).

Bathroom door locks

Privacy is less important than safety. Remove interior locks from bathroom doors unless a locked door can be opened from the outside.

Bathtub drains

Cleaning and unclogging bathtub drains

Unplugging bathtub drains can be troublesome, so preventive measures are advisable. Keep a bathtub from clogging by cleaning the stopper assembly every few weeks. On most tubs, remove the screws from the overflow plate and pull out the assembly. Then ease the stopper out. Clean both pieces of any hair or soap and reinstall them. With the curved part of the stopper linkage facing down, work the stopper gently back and forth to fit it into place.

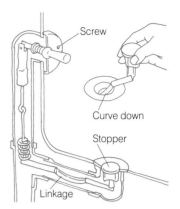

Screw / Curve down / Stopper / Linkage

Chemical drain cleaners, if used frequently, may cause deterioration of the drain system. However, an occasional application may help prevent buildup of hair and soap in out-of-reach parts of the system. Follow the package directions carefully and rinse the drain area thoroughly afterwards.

Caution: Many chemical drain cleaners are dangerous. If you splash any cleaner on your skin, wash it off immediately in cold water. If the drain is clogged and the cleaner doesn't work, it may remain in the tub. Call a plumber. Don't try unclogging the drain yourself by other means; the leftover cleaner may splatter you.

If a bathtub drain clogs, remove the stopper and use a plunger, first stuffing a wet rag into the overflow drain to increase pressure. (See *Drain unclogging.*) If a plunger doesn't work, try using a thin, flexible wire. If the trap is located near the drain hole, insert the wire into the overflow opening. If the trap is situated at a distance from the drain, thread the wire through the drain hole. If you cannot reach the stoppage, call a plumber.

Bathtub recaulking

Fixing the crack between the bathtub and the wall

Over a period of time, the settling of a house results in a crack between the rim of the bathtub and the wall. Cracks may also appear between the sink and the wall or in the shower stall. You can patch these cracks and any cracks between the tiles on the bathroom walls with a tube of waterproof flexible caulking compound.

Clean and dry the area and remove any loose old caulking with a putty knife and then a stiff brush. Cut the spout off the caulking tube sufficiently far back to produce a ribbon of caulking large enough to fill the crack. Squeeze the tube while moving it forward to force the caulking into the crack and to form an even bead the length of the crack. Let the caulking dry overnight before using the bath.

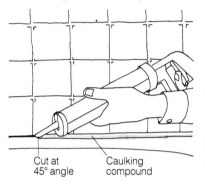

Cut at 45° angle   Caulking compound

Batik

Making fabric prints

Batik is a way of creating a design on fabric by waxing any parts of the fabric you don't want changed and then immersing the piece in a dye solution. When the wax is removed, the design is colored but not the rest of the fabric.

The best fabric for batik is plain, light-colored cotton. Don't use a synthetic fabric—dyes won't penetrate. If the fabric is new, wash it in hot, soapy water and rinse and dry it.

Tack the fabric, stretched tight, to a picture frame or a canvas stretcher. Sketch a design on the fabric with a pencil or a stick of charcoal. Prepare the wax by gently heating 1 pound of paraffin and 5 tablespoons of beeswax in a double boiler until a candy thermometer reads 170°F.

Use only cold-water dyes so that the wax won't melt. If the design requires more than one color, start with the lightest. Prepare the first dye according to package directions. With a small brush, apply melted wax over the parts of the design you don't want dyed with that color. Untack the fabric. Soak it in the dye for 20 minutes, rinse it thoroughly, and let it dry.

Removing the wax

Cover an ironing board with newspaper, and place the dry fabric on it between layers of paper toweling. With a dry iron at one setting below *Cotton*, press the fabric on both sides, changing the toweling as wax accumulates.

Apply the other colors, if any, in the same way. If you are using two or more colors, you needn't press out all the wax after each dye bath; press only the parts you want dyed with the next color, and wax all other parts.

The frog design shown here was drawn on yellow fabric. The frog itself was covered with wax and the background was randomly dribbled with wax. The fabric was then dyed. Wax was pressed out of the frog (except for the eyes), and the background was waxed. Then the frog was dyed green, leaving the eyes yellow.

Bats

Getting bats out of the house

To rid an attic or other part of your house of a bat colony, seal, caulk, weatherstrip, or screen all exterior openings more than ¼-inch wide—except one, through which the bats can escape. Wait 3 days; then, about half an hour after dark (when bats are feeding), seal the last opening.

If an area can't be sealed, install a light that shines directly at the roosting area. In confined areas, suspend mothballs in porous bags as a repellent. Avoid exterminating bats; they are desirable as insect eaters.

If a single bat strays into a room, after dark open the windows and any doors to the outside and turn off all lights. The bat will fly outside.

Caution: Never touch a bat; they can be carriers of rabies. If you are bitten by one, get to a hospital immediately.

Batteries

Maintaining a car battery

Most batteries today are sealed. However, if yours is not, remove the caps and check the water level every 3 or 4 months. If the level is low, add tap water until it comes up to the bottom of the cap hole. If the tap water in your area is hard, use distilled water.

Inspect the brackets that hold down the battery. If they are loose, the battery can vibrate, shortening its life. Tighten as necessary. If the brackets are corroded, clean them with a wire brush and spray them with aerosol penetrating solvent. If corrosion is severe, replace the brackets.

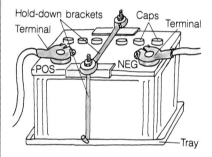

Hold-down brackets   Caps   Terminal
Terminal
POS   NEG
Tray

Disconnect the battery terminals (see *Battery terminals*), lift out the battery, and inspect the tray. Brush off any corrosion and apply a coat of acid-resistant paint. Remove the tray if corrosion has weakened it. Some trays are bolted in, but most are welded and must be chipped out with a cold chisel. Vinyl-coated replacement trays are sold at auto parts stores. To install one, drill holes in the part the old tray was attached to, lining them up with the holes in the replacement tray. Bolt the new tray into place.

Caution: Car batteries contain acid. When working on one, remove jewelry and wear goggles, gloves, and heavy clothes. If acid gets on your skin or in your eyes, rinse for 15 minutes with cold running water. Then get to a doctor. Batteries also emit explosive gas. Never light a match, cause a spark, or smoke near one. Batteries contain lead and should be recycled. Most states require outlets selling them to accept used ones. If your state doesn't, contact environmental authorities for information.

Battery recharging

When and how to recharge a car battery

As a battery ages, its charge weakens, causing slow engine cranking. A battery may need an occasional "jump" to start it, especially when the car is used for short runs or in cold weather. You can simply replace a weak battery, but with an inexpensive recharger, you can nurse it along for weeks, months, or even longer.

If the dashboard warning light comes on (or the ammeter shows discharge during engine operation), there is a charging-system fault. Have it repaired immediately; recharging will not do the job.

If the battery is refillable, remove the caps and lay a damp rag over the openings while recharging. If it is sealed and has a charge-indicator window in the top, use the charger only if the indicator is green or dark. If it is clear or yellowish, replace the battery.

To recharge a battery, use a *trickle charger,* a relatively inexpensive device used to charge a battery at a slow rate. The trickle charger has an electric outlet cord and two wires with alligator clips, one with a red jacket and one with a black or green jacket. Make sure the car's ignition is turned off. Connect the red clip to the battery's positive terminal (marked *POS* or +) and the other to the negative terminal (marked *NEG* or -). Be careful not to let the metal clips touch each other or any other metal or they may spark and

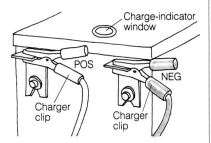

cause an explosion of the hydrogen gas from the battery. After the charger is connected to the battery, plug the charger into an electric outlet and turn it on. Run the charger a few hours or overnight. Disconnect the charger, *not* the battery, until its meter reads less than 1 ampere. Then unplug the charger and disconnect it from the battery.

After recharging, if the battery has removable caps, check it with a hydrometer, an inexpensive device with a float indicating electrical energy in the fluid. If the battery is sealed, test it by trying to start the engine.

If, after recharging, the battery still fails to start the engine, try to jump start the engine. If the engine can be jump started and the charging-system light or ammeter indicates normal operation, the battery is bad; replace it. (See also *Batteries; Jump starting a car; Push starting a car.*)

Battery terminals

Cleaning and replacing terminals on a car battery

Corroded battery terminals and loose or corroded cable terminals are major causes of hard starting, poor charging-system operation, and power failures on the road. Inspect and clean the terminals twice a year.

With the engine off, first disconnect the cable at the terminal marked *Neg* or with a minus sign. Then disconnect the other cable. On batteries with top posts, loosen the retaining nut, then twist the terminal back and forth with an upward motion to remove it. If necessary, tap lightly with a wooden hammer handle to loosen it. If the terminal still doesn't come off, use an inexpensive cable terminal puller. With a wire brush, scrub the battery posts and the cable terminals, inside as well as outside, until all the metal looks clean.

On batteries with side terminals, remove the retaining bolt, and the cable will be free. Even though there is little visible corrosion, carefully wire-brush the surfaces of the disc-shaped electrical contacts. Refit the cables and tighten the terminals securely.

Replacing a cable terminal

On a top-post battery, replace a cable terminal if it is badly eaten by corrosion or if its jaws touch each other. Disconnect both cables as explained. To install the commonest replace-

ment, cut the cable wire close to the old terminal with a hacksaw. Strip 1 inch of insulation from the wire. (If the wire is corroded, cut it back even farther but make sure the cable can

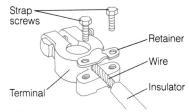

still reach the battery; otherwise, replace the cable.) Loosen the strap screws on the terminal, insert the bared wire end under the retainer, then retighten the screws.

Beadwork

Stringing beads; stitching beads to fabric

Beads can be strung with an ordinary needle. The size of the bead bore (hole) determines the proper needle size. To keep loose beads under control as you work, place them on a scrap of velvet or other napped fabric.

The cording should be thin enough to pass twice through the bead bore. Dental floss makes a durable cording. For a choker-style necklace or a bracelet, use shirring elastic.

Sew beads to clothing with dressmaker's cotton or polyester-covered cotton thread. To add to its strength and reduce tangling, pass the thread across candle wax or beeswax before stitching. On heavy fabrics, attach beads with nylon thread or monofilament fishing line; both are strong and inconspicuous.

Keep the background fabric taut as you work by stretching it on a frame or embroidery hoop. If puckering persists, block the beaded fabric by pinning it to a dampened fabric and letting the fabrics air-dry.

Sewing beads to garments

You can replace beaded motifs on sweaters and dresses by stitching new beads in place singly with a running stitch. Or you can apply the beads one at a time with backstitches. Anchor the thread to the wrong side of the fabric. Draw the needle to the

B

right side and add a bead. Take a backstitch, bringing the needle through the fabric a bead-length behind, then ahead of the first stitch. Continue adding beads, keeping each tightly against the next.

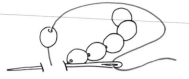

Beads can also be "couched" to fabric by hand or by machine. For handwork, use two threads and two needles. Anchor one thread to the fabric's wrong side, draw it through, and slip on several beads. Anchor the second thread, draw it through, and use it to tack the line of beads to the fabric.

For faster couching, use the sewing machine zipper foot and a zigzag stitch. With the edge of the zipper foot close to the line of beads, tack them in place with zigzag stitches.

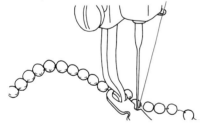

Beards and mustaches

Giving yourself a new image with facial hair.

A beard or a mustache can enhance or conceal a particular feature and make a man look dashing or distinguished. The effect can be just the opposite, however, if the style isn't right.

The first step is to let the beard or mustache grow. Expect your face to look unkempt during this period. Wash it often with soap and water,

and rinse it thoroughly. Be prepared for a bit of discomfort—new hair growth itches. Try an antidandruff shampoo if itching persists.

If your beard is curly, prevent ingrown hairs by turning the curly ends away from your skin with tweezers; if you pull out any ingrown hairs, dab the skin with alcohol or astringent. In about 3 weeks, there should be enough growth to begin clipping.

A full, neatly trimmed beard and mustache disguise a narrow face, irregular nose, pointed or weak chin, or receding hairline. A full mustache without beard directs attention away from a big nose, broad face, protruding chin, or low hairline.

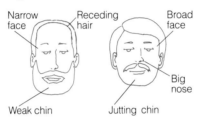

Narrow face Receding hair Broad face
Weak chin Jutting chin Big nose

Many men assume that beard care is less exacting and time consuming than shaving. In fact, whiskers demand daily care for three reasons: first, they trap dirt and bacteria, so a daily shampoo is necessary; apply conditioner to make the hair soft. Second, whiskers quickly get scruffy if you don't keep after them. Trim them at least once a week and with each haircut. And trim them only when they're dry—wet whiskers lie differently than do dry ones. Finally, beards and mustaches can get messy at mealtime; use your napkin often, and after you leave the table, check in a mirror for stray bits of food.

Beauty creams

Making skin softener, moisturizer, cleansing cream

The kind of beauty preparation you need depends on your skin. Dry skin calls for a dense, oily cream, whereas oily skin may need only the protection from weather afforded by a light moisturizing lotion.

Most beauty creams are emulsions—tiny globules of oils or waxy

substances suspended in water. You can concoct them of inexpensive ingredients generally available in drug or health food stores.

These include glycerin, an oily liquid with good emollient (skin softening) properties; beeswax, a mixer and emulsifier; lanolin, a wax that combines with water to hold moisture near the skin; mineral oil, a lubricator and softener; and petroleum jelly, a softener. Scented waters, such as rose water, can be used instead of plain water.

Rich, skin-softening cream
Gently heat 1 cup of white petroleum jelly and 2½ teaspoons of anhydrous lanolin in the top of a double boiler. Small globules of lanolin will form on top of the melted jelly. In a separate pan, warm 2 cups water and 1 teaspoon glycerin. Combine the two mixtures, the water into the oil. Let the combination cool until it starts to solidify, then add a few drops of a non-oil-base perfume or essence. When completely cool, drain off excess water. Put the cream in a jar. Yields about 1⅓ cups.

Light moisturizer
Mix equal parts of vegetable glycerin and rose water or any herbal water. To make an after-shave lotion, add a dash of witch hazel or bay rum.

Cleansing cream
Put 2 cups mineral oil and ½ cup white beeswax (an all-beeswax candle, cut in slivers, may be your best source) into the top of a double boiler and gently heat until the beeswax melts. Let cool to 120°F. In a separate pan, heat 1 cup water to 120°F; add 1½ tablespoons powdered borax; stir gently until it dissolves. Then slowly pour the water and borax mixture into the oil and wax mixture, stirring all the while. Cool the mixture until it starts to solidify, then pour it into jars. Yields about 3 cups.

Bedbugs

Ridding your house of these biting pests

Red-brown creatures up to ¼ inch long, bedbugs may enter a house in clothing, used furniture, or luggage.

They hide in the seams of mattresses and bedding, in the crevices of bed frames, behind baseboards and window and door frames, and in cracks in the wall. Bedbugs emerge at night to feed on the blood of their sleeping victims. In addition to itching, signs of an infestation include a strange odor in the room or tiny streaks of blood on the bedding.

Greatly enlarged

Bedbugs are rare in most homes today, but if you notice any of the signs mentioned above, start to eliminate them by attacking their hiding places. Vacuum your mattress, including the seams and cuff. Thoroughly vacuum the floor and walls, getting behind any picture frames. Wash all bedding. Repeat cleanings often. If you must use a chemical control, try pyrethrum and spray baseboards, window and door frames, and walls.

Caution: Pyrethrum is nontoxic to adults, but never use it on a child's bed.

Bedding plants

Planting for continuous color from spring to fall

Bedding plants are plants put out for temporary display during their peak blooming periods. You can enjoy continuous bloom from spring until frost by interspersing spring bedding plants among bulbs, perennials, and shrubs and by replacing them when their bloom has declined with summer bedding plants. In regions of little frost, spring bedding plants can safely be planted in fall; in colder areas wait until the ground thaws. Buy plants in packs of 6 to 12 or in individual pots, or start your own indoors or in a greenhouse. Set them out before they reach maximum bloom.

Favorite spring bedding plants are pansies, primroses, forget-me-nots, sweet Williams, and English daisies. In regions where winters are very mild, the spring display can include cinerarias, Paris daisies, turban ranunculuses, poppy-flowered anemones, schizanthuses, and clarkias.

Replace spring bedding plants with summer's standbys: ageratum, sweet alyssum, petunias, marigolds, zinnias, dahlias, lantanas, calendulas, geraniums, cannas, and snapdragons for sunny areas. Plants that will bloom in shade or partial shade include balsams, impatiens, begonias (see *Begonias*), and nicotiana. The fall garden can be made colorful with potted chrysanthemums, which will survive light frosts that destroy most summer bedding plants.

Buying and planting

Plan your planting before you go to the garden center so you don't overbuy. Look for plants that are stocky and bushy rather than tall and leggy. Beware of any with yellowing foliage. Set out plants as soon as possible; if you have to wait, keep them well watered and in good light. Plant in dull weather or late in the afternoon so that plants won't droop in the noonday sun. Separate the individual plants in a pack by carefully pulling them apart with your fingers. Set them in at the same soil level as before or slightly deeper; water well. (See also *Flower beds; Mulching, Planting.*)

Bed-wetting

Patience and understanding are the best treatment

It takes some children 4 to 6 years before their bladders grow large enough to retain urine overnight. About 10 percent of children continue to wet the bed into the school years.

The best treatment is no treatment at all. Scolding, shaming, or punishment only turns a transient problem into a chronic one. Equip the child's bed with a rubber pad and keep plenty of no-iron sheets on hand. When the child shows concern, suggest that he or she not drink anything for 2 hours before bedtime and empty the bladder just before retiring. If the child doesn't object, wake him or her at around 11 P.M. to urinate. Or provide an alarm clock to allow the child to control the awakening. Because there may be a medical or emotional cause, discuss the situation with your child's doctor.

Beekeeping

From siting the hive to collecting the honey

Bees can be kept almost anywhere provided there is good forage within a mile of the hive—such pollen- and nectar-producing plants as alfalfa, clover, or goldenrod, or such trees as tulip, locust, or basswood. The honey yield—and whether or not there is a surplus after the bees have eaten their fill—depends on this food supply. Ask your cooperative extension agent about suitable local growth. Put the hive in a sunny, secluded spot with good air circulation and drainage and fresh water nearby (natural or supplied). Provide protection from winter wind.

The most convenient bee source, especially for beginners, is mail order. Your best choice is a 3-pound package of about 14,000 bees and one young queen. As for hives, you are better off buying the standard Langstroth type because it's easier to obtain equipment and supplies. Bees will build their own comb, but they'll do it better—and you'll get more honey—if you install comb foundation (wax sheets similar to natural comb) in the *supers* (honey-storage boxes above the hive chamber).

Collect honey soon after the major local flow (check this timing, too, with your cooperative extension agent). Unless you plan to use honey in the comb, you'll need to buy or rent a centrifugal extractor to remove honey without comb damage.

Any beekeeper must expect some stings (see *Insect bites and stings*). They'll be fewer if you handle bees on warm, sunny days when they're contented. Before removing a comb, drive the bees away with a smoke-blowing device. Wear light-colored, smooth-finish clothing—polished cottons and khakis are ideal. Protect your face and neck with a bee veil. Wear boots and loose-fitting gloves and tie your pant legs at the ankles.

Caution: Although most beekeepers become immune to bee stings, certain people react severely to them. See your doctor if this happens.

Begonias

Starting and caring for begonias, indoors and out

Some begonias are prized for their flowers, others for foliage, still others for both; most are easy to grow. They are categorized by their manner of growth: those that have tubers (tuberous begonias), those with fibrous roots, and those with rhizomes—horizontal surface stems that send up leaves and flowers.

Starting begonias

Nearly all begonias grow readily from stem cuttings; the rhizomatous kind grow from divisions of the rhizomes. Some, such as rex begonias, can be grown from leaf cuttings (see *Propagating plants*). Wax begonias can be started from seeds. Scatter the tiny seeds on top of fine-sifted potting soil and press them down gently. Set tubers, hollow side down, in loose peat moss or peat moss and sand with their bottoms at the surface.

Cuttings and tubers should be started indoors about 2 to 3 months before outdoor planting time. Cover the trays or pots with plastic wrap punched with a few airholes. Keep them warm, slightly moist, and shaded from direct sunlight. When tiny plants (from seeds) or 1-inch shoots (from tubers) appear, move them to individual pots, turning tubers hollow side up. At this time tubers can be divided; cut them with a knife, leaving one or more buds to each section. Dip the cut surfaces in a fungicide such as powdered sulfur.

When all danger of frost is past, move tuberous begonias intended for outdoors to a cold frame. Later, when the soil stays warm (50°F to 55°F) overnight, set the plants in a shady spot with loose, well-drained soil enriched with compost or peat moss. Apply a balanced fertilizer, such as 5-10-5; water with a wand to keep moisture off the leaves.

Some begonia favorites

Tuberous begonias have huge single, double, or semidouble blooms on 1- to 2-foot-tall plants. They are spectacular indoors or out, in beds or in pots. Trailing tuberous begonias do well in hanging pots in shaded locations. Rex begonias, which are rhizomatous, are grown for their beautiful leaves colored in pinks, reds, and greens. They make excellent bedding plants for shade.

Wax begonias—the common bedding plants—bear small white, pink, or red flowers until frost. They like brighter light than other begonias, but not direct sun, and sometimes seed themselves. In fall you can pot the seedlings for indoor bloom.

Indoors, all begonias require room temperature and strong light, but not direct sun except in winter. Provide humidity by placing the pot on gravel in a saucer or tray with water not quite covering the gravel. Check the soil every few days; water when dry.

To save tubers, dig them up before frost, store them in a dry place until the foliage has died, then clean and store them at 50°F to 60°F.

Berries

How to have a garden of berries ripe for the picking

By growing your own, you can enjoy strawberries, raspberries, blackberries, and blueberries at their sweetest and most nutritious. All berries like well-drained soil and full sun. A gentle south- or east-facing slope is ideal. Don't plant berries in a hollow where cold air collects.

Birds are fond of berries, particularly strawberries and blueberries. Cover these crops with a net a few days before they ripen. Pick strawberries in the morning as soon as the dew has dried, raspberries in the late afternoon when their flavor is at its height. Blackberries and blueberries can be picked at any hour; taste them for ripeness before you start.

Planting procedures

Because berry plants are susceptible to disease, start with resistant varieties and disease-free stock. Don't plant them where tomatoes, potatoes, or eggplant have been grown.

Set out new plants as early in the spring as possible so that they become established before hot weather. Keep their roots moist before and during planting. Soak the roots of bare-root plants in a mixture of soil and water before planting. Allow ample space between plants for air circulation. Prune old growth annually and keep plants weed free. Weed by hand; hoes and forks will damage shallow roots.

To start a strawberry bed, dig rotted compost or well-aged manure into the soil. Set plants 8 inches apart in rows 30 inches apart; new leaf buds should be at soil level. Water plants in dry weather, and mulch with straw to preserve moisture and keep the ripening berries off the ground. Remove all but one or two runner plants from each plant. Pick off blossoms the first year. In the fall cover plants loosely with straw or similar material as winter protection. Strawberry plants need replacing every few years, when they bear fewer and smaller fruits.

The bramble fruits

Raspberries, blackberries, dewberries, loganberries, and boysenberries require an acid (pH 5.5), moisture-retaining soil. Choose a sunny spot. Before planting, dig in plenty of peat moss and cow manure or compost. Cut all canes (stems) back to 6 inches.

Set raspberry canes in the soil about 2 inches deeper than the previous soil line, and space them 2 to 4 feet apart in rows 6 to 8 feet apart. Blackberries need even more space. Allow 4 to 6 feet between plants and 6 to 9 feet between rows. Plant blackberry canes at the same depth as the old soil line.

Bramble fruits are subject to many viruses and diseases. To reduce the chance of contagion, use virus-free stock. Plant raspberries and black raspberries 500 feet from one another and from any wild brambles. Prune old canes as soon as they finish fruiting; thin the rest of the canes to about 6 inches apart. Burn all prunings.

Blueberries

Generous rainfall and well-drained, very acid soil (pH 4.8) are essential for blueberries. To prepare the soil, dig a trench or holes at least 2 feet deep and 3 feet wide and fill with a mixture of 2 parts peat moss, 2 parts sand, and 1 part garden soil. Plant at least two varieties (for fertilization), and space them 4 feet apart. Mulch the plants heavily at planting time and every year with leaves, straw, or peat.

Bicycle care

Lubrication; adjusting brakes and gears

To keep your bike riding smoothly, clean and lubricate it regularly. If you ride a lot, every 2 weeks or so lubricate the brake pivots, chain, freewheel, derailleurs, and inner cables with a dry (graphite) spray lubricant; unlike oil, dry lubricant will not attract dirt. Once a year or so, apply a light, water-

difference is mainly in the entrance of the cables into the brake mechanism.

With either type of caliper brake, the pads should contact the rims of the wheels, not the tires. If they don't, loosen the nuts that secure them and adjust their position in the slots of the caliper arms, then retighten the nuts.

Brake pads should clear the wheel rim on each side when the hand levers are fully open. When squeezed, the levers should be at least ¾ inch from the handlebars when the bike stops. If the pads or levers need adjusting,

cable is slack. Loosen the anchor nut and have a helper hold the pads against the wheel (or use a C-clamp to hold them). Using pliers, pull the free lower end of the cable to take up the slack. While holding the cable taught, tighten the anchor nut. Release the pads and recheck the adjustment.

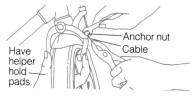

The pads on side-pull brakes sometimes become stuck in the closed position. Loosen the pivot bolt just until the pads come free but do not wobble.

If side-pull brake pads are not equidistant from the wheel, tap the spring on the more distant caliper with hammer and screwdriver until the pads are balanced. If the center-pull brake pads are not equidistant from the wheel, use an adjustable wrench to turn the yoke across the tops of the caliper arms in one direction or the other to bring the pads into position. Be sure that the anchor nut is snug.

Bicycle gears

Derailleur-type gears are used on 10- and 12-speed bikes; hub-and-sprocket type gears are used on most 3-speed and some 4- and 5-speed bikes. The derailleur mechanism shifts the drive chain from one gear to another to vary forward speeds. To prevent derailleurs from slipping out of adjustment, never lay your bike down on its right side, shift only while pedaling, and never backpedal. If the chain slips off the freewheel cogs while you are riding, or refuses to go onto the largest or smallest cogs, the rear derailleur needs adjusting.

Hang your bicycle (or have someone hold it up) so that the rear wheel is off the ground. Look for the adjustment screws on the rear derailleur. They are probably marked *H* and *L* for *High* (the smallest gear on the freewheel) and *Low* (the largest). These screws keep the derailleur from traveling too far to the left or right. Turn the screws a little at a time until the chain centers perfectly on the appropriate cog when you shift and pedal by hand. Adjust the front derailleur in the same way.

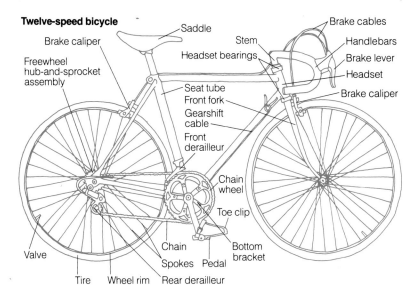

Twelve-speed bicycle

Saddle
Brake caliper
Freewheel hub-and-sprocket assembly
Stem
Headset bearings
Brake cables
Handlebars
Brake lever
Headset
Seat tube
Front fork
Gearshift cable
Front derailleur
Brake caliper
Chain wheel
Toe clip
Valve
Chain
Spokes Pedal
Bottom bracket
Tire   Wheel rim   Rear derailleur

resistant grease (available at bike shops) to the bearings on the headset, bottom bracket, wheel hubs, and pedals. Add light machine oil to the oil holes in 3-speed hubs.

Bicycle brakes

Some bicycles have coaster brakes, which are applied by backpedaling, but most have hand-operated caliper brakes. Caliper brakes may be either center-pull or side-pull brakes. The

squeeze the pads against the wheel rim by hand. Use a wrench to loosen the locknut on the adjuster screw, and turn the screw by hand—turn it counterclockwise to bring the pads closer to the wheel rim and clockwise to move them farther away. Tighten the locknut and test the brakes.

If the levers or pads are still out of adjustment after the adjuster screw has been turned as far as possible, the

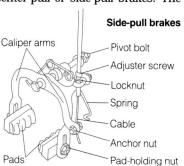

Side-pull brakes

Caliper arms
Pivot bolt
Adjuster screw
Locknut
Spring
Cable
Anchor nut
Pads
Pad-holding nut

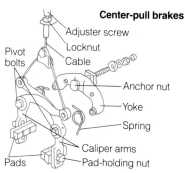

Center-pull brakes

Adjuster screw
Locknut
Pivot bolts
Cable
Anchor nut
Yoke
Spring
Caliper arms
Pads
Pad-holding nut

B

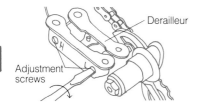

Derailleur

Adjustment
screws

For slipping or binding of hub and sprocket gears, adjust the sleeve nut on the end of the toggle chain. Shift the handlebar lever to first gear, then turn the sleeve nut while looking at the inspection hole in the tunnel nut. When the rivet at the end of the toggle chain is in the center of the hole, shift to second gear, give the sleeve nut another half turn, and shift back to first gear. The cable should be taut, with the lever just managing the shift. Turn the locknut finger tight against the sleeve nut.

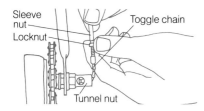

Sleeve
nut
Locknut

Toggle chain

Tunnel nut

Bicycle carrying racks

How to get your bike from here to there

The best thing to do if you're driving to a place where you will ride a bicycle is to rent it when you get there. However, if you have a favorite bike, you'll probably want to take it with you. To reduce the risk of theft, carry it inside your car. If it won't fit, use a rack.

If you have a van, station wagon, or hatchback, put down newspapers to absorb any grease, then place the bike left side down, on top of them. If there's room, you can lay a second bike on top of the first by separating the two with dense foam padding or a sheet of heavy corrugated cardboard.

To carry a bike in a sedan, load it into the trunk, rear end first so that the delicate rear wheel mechanism is protected. The front end will turn down against the car. Tie plenty of foam padding around the protruding end and fasten the trunk lid with a ca-

ble and padlock to prevent bouncing and reduce the chance of theft.

A rooftop rack is the best. It carries several bikes, which are held apart and so will not get scratched. The bikes are out of the way, so that no

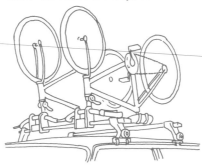

part of the car is inaccessible and the driver's vision is not blocked. The only disadvantages are that it is the most expensive type of rack, it may restrict entry into some parking garages, and it is hard to reach—but thieves will have more trouble reaching it too.

A less expensive type of rack fits over the trunk and is fastened with straps at the top and bottom of the trunk. Its disadvantage is that it has some effect on rear visibility.

Bicycle locks

Protecting your bike from theft

Never lose sight of your bike in a public place unless it is locked; it may get stolen. Use a lock you can pass around an immovable object and then through the bike frame and the front wheel. (If the front wheel has a quick-release mechanism, remove the wheel and pass the lock through both wheels.)

Ideally, use a 9-inch, U-shaped, vinyl-clad shackle of through-hardened metal with a built-in tubular lock. It resists bolt cutters, is hard to pick, and may come with theft insurance.

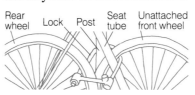

Rear
wheel

Lock

Post

Seat
tube

Unattached
front wheel

Less secure but lighter, cheaper, and easier to fasten around trees or thick posts is a 6-foot coil of plastic-

coated steel cable with loops at both ends or a chain with ⅜-inch hardened steel links. These should be held by a 4-tumbler key lock with a heat-treated ⅜-inch steel shackle.

Bicycle riding

Learning to ride a bike

Teach yourself to ride a bike in an open area that has no traffic. Start with a bike that is small enough for your feet to reach the ground when you are seated on the saddle. Take the bike to the top of a slight incline. If the bike has a gearshift, set it for a middle speed. Sit on the saddle with your feet on the ground. Lift both feet a few inches and let the bike roll down the incline, shifting your body slightly from side to side to keep your balance. Repeat several times, then rest.

Position the right pedal a bit forward of the top of its arc. With your left foot on the ground and your right foot on the right pedal, lean forward. Push off with your left foot, letting it trail behind as the bike goes forward. Push down on the right pedal. If you begin losing your balance, push the handlebars to turn the wheel in the direction you are falling so that the bike comes up under you. Repeat until you can keep your balance. Then do it again, but put your left foot on the left pedal after pushing off with it and start pedaling immediately.

Keep the balls of your feet on the pedals and maintain a steady rhythm. To turn, lean slightly in the direction you want to go and, if necessary, turn the handlebars. Begin with broad turns, then try sharper ones.
Braking and shifting
Your bicycle may have either caliper brakes, which are operated by levers on the handlebars, or coaster brakes,

B

which are operated by foot. To stop with caliper brakes, squeeze both levers, but use less force on the one that controls the front brake (usually the left lever). To stop with coaster brakes, simply reverse the pedaling.

If your bike has gears, shift them to gain momentum going uphill or to help keep your pedaling rhythm on flat ground. If you are approaching a hill, shift into low gear before you start climbing. On a 3-speed bike, stop pedaling before shifting. On a 10-speed, ease up, but do not stop pedaling.

Bicycle safety

Cycling safely in traffic and on the open road

Wear a helmet and equip your bike with a loud bell or horn, rear and front lights, and a 3-inch rear reflector. Ride with the traffic and as far to the right as you can. Comply with traffic signs and signals as though your bicycle were a car. Know and follow your community's traffic laws. Get a copy of the vehicle code from the state motor vehicle department, and request local information from the Automobile Association of America (AAA).

Give turn signals with your left arm, as shown. Focus on the road

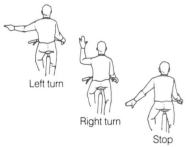

Left turn

Right turn

Stop

ahead, looking out for pedestrians, potholes, bumps, and debris. Watch for cars leaving a parking place without signaling, taxis suddenly stopping to pick up fares, car doors opening without warning, and other cyclists. Try to allow room ahead and on your right. If you must turn suddenly, apply the brakes before turning the wheel. If you must stop suddenly, slide back on the saddle and bring your shoulders down as you squeeze the brakes hard.

Bicycle tires

Fixing a flat on your bike

If your bike gets a flat tire, don't automatically assume it's punctured, especially if the leak is slow. Check the tire's valve first. Simply turn the wheel so that the valve is on top, remove the valve cap, and submerge the entire valve in a glass of water. If bubbles form, replace the valve core. Use valve caps with valve-removing prongs to unscrew the old core. (Certain needlenose pliers will also do the job.)

Valve

If you find a cut or hole in the tire, mark it with chalk to make it easier to find the corresponding place on the tube. Pull out any nails with pliers and pry out glass with a screwdriver. To get to the tube, you will probably have to remove the wheel. Follow the directions in your owner's manual.

Finding the leak

Completely deflate the tire. Use a spoon handle (a screwdriver is too sharp) to pry a small section of the tire from the rim. Leave the spoon in place and run a second spoon handle all around the rim to free the tire on one side. Leaving the valve in place, carefully work the rest of the inner tube out of the tire. Inflate the tube and run

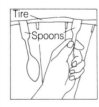

Tire

Spoons

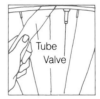

Tube
Valve

your hand around it to find the air flow. Once found, mark the spot with chalk. Check the corresponding place on the tire for nails, glass, thorns, or other sharp objects and remove them.

If you fail to find the leak, remove the valve-holding nut, if any, and push the valve stem out of the wheel rim. Partially pump up the tube and pass it a little at a time through a bucket of water, stretching the tube a bit as you do. Bubbles will form over the puncture. Mark the puncture.

Fixing the leak

Deflate the tube again. Using the materials in a patching kit (available at bike shops), sand the area clean, then apply a light, even coat of adhesive to the cleaned area and let it dry.

Peel the backing from a patch and press the patch, sticky side down, onto the adhesive on the tube. Press down firmly on the edges of the patch with the bowl of a spoon and let the adhesive dry for 5 minutes.

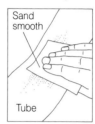

Sand smooth

Tube

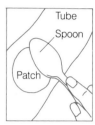

Tube

Spoon

Patch

Push the tube back into the tire, inserting the valve through its hole in the rim. Reseat the tire with your hands, checking that both edges are inside the rim. Replace the valve-holding nut, if any, and inflate the tire to the proper pressure (usually listed on the sidewall of the tire).

Bicycle touring

Planning a long bike trip and pedaling on your way

Pick a destination, then map a route that avoids heavily traveled roads. First tours should cover no more than 35 miles a day—less in hilly country. Be sure your bike is properly lubricated and adjusted. Wear cycling shoes, and use toe clips to hold your feet on the pedals and to lessen leg fatigue.

Travel light and load your bike to maintain good side-to-side balance. Pack about one-quarter of the weight in the rear and three-quarters in the front—on a rack that lies low (around the axle). Remember the essentials: adjustable wrench, screwdriver, air pump, tire repair equipment, pocket knife, flashlight, first aid kit, plastic water bottle, money, and county maps.

Pedal at a steady pace—rapidly, but with as little effort as possible. Lean forward when riding to relieve pressure on your lower back, cut wind resistance, and give balance.

B

Billiards

Playing two basic games

Billiards is played on a table with cushioned rails. The table is like the one used for pocket billiards, but it has no pockets. (See *Pocket billiards*.) Three balls are used: a white *cue* ball for each player and a red *object* ball.

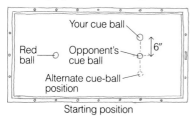

Your cue ball

Red ball
Opponent's cue ball
6"

Alternate cue-ball position

Starting position

Straight-rail billiards is the simplest of the basic games. A player tries to score a point by using a cue stick to drive his cue ball in such a way that it strikes both the object ball and the opponent's cue ball. If he fails to *make a billiard* (score a point), his opponent plays. In three-cushion billiards, a well-known variation, the cue ball must strike three cushions in the course of striking the other two balls. In either game, the first player to get a predetermined number of points wins.

Bingo

A game of chance for groups

Each player buys or is given a card with five columns headed B, I, N, G, and O. Each column has five squares. The center square is marked *Free*; the other 24 are numbered. The numbers under *B* are from the group 1–15; under *I*, from 16–30; under *N*, from 31–45; under *G,* from 46–60; and under *O*, from 61–75. No two cards are alike.

A drawer blindly picks one of 75 counters and announces the number and letter on it. Anyone having these on a card covers that square with a chip. The game continues until a player covers five connecting squares, diagonally, vertically, or horizontally. (The *Free* square may be included.) The lucky player then calls out "Bingo!" and wins either a prize or all or part of the money paid for the bingo cards.

Bird care

Choosing a bird; equipping and maintaining a cage; feeding a bird; training a bird; teaching a budgie to talk; watching a bird's health

Canaries, finches, and budgies all make excellent pets. They are easy to care for, beautiful to look at, and may be pleasing to the ear. When shopping for pets, look for birds that are alert, bright-eyed, and sleek.

There are two types of canary: the song canary, bred for its singing, and the type canary, bred for its color. A song canary can be either a chopper or a roller. The chopper is a loud, jazzy singer, whereas the roller produces a soft melody. The average life span of a canary is 9 years.

Finches are hardy, quiet birds that are kept mostly for their beautiful colors. The most common are the Java sparrow, which is white or gray with a red bill; the society finch, which is white with blotches of color; and the zebra finch. Finches are social and do better when kept with one or more of their own species. The average life span of a finch is 2½ years.

The budgerigar, or budgie, is a small parakeet that is popular for its brilliant color, powers of mimicry, and affectionate nature. Budgies can be taught to talk. It is easiest to train birds 6 to 12 weeks old. (Young birds have stripes on their foreheads.) Budgies may live up to 12 years.

The cage

Choose a cage large enough for the bird to fly around in, and equip it with at least two perches and with dishes for food and water. A cage with a removable tray under a wire mesh floor is easier to clean. Install a bath or place a bowl of water on the cage floor.

A finch's cage should have in the center a branching limb that does not interfere with the bird's flight. For finches or budgies, add a mirror, ladder, or bell to provide amusement. Canaries show no interest in toys.

Place the bird cage out of direct sunlight in a draft-free room that is kept at 70°F. Clean out droppings and wash the bird's dishes every day.

Feeding a bird

Supply your bird with ample food and water. Birds deprived of either food or water die in 24 to 48 hours. When you are going away for several days, get a weekend feeder that dispenses food and water over a period of time. Feed budgies and Java sparrows regular budgie food. Zebra and society finches have smaller beaks and need the smaller finch-seed mixture. Canaries require more fat in their diet and should be fed canary seed. All of these are available at pet shops.

In addition to seed, offer the bird a small portion of leafy greens twice a week. Your bird will also benefit from occasional treats, including fruit, peanut butter, or hard-cooked eggs. Give your bird vitamins daily. They are available in powdered form to be mixed with the seed or in liquid form to be added to the water.

Since birds need grit to digest their food, scatter a little granite gravel, plain or mixed with ground oyster shell, on the floor of the cage. Attach a cuttlebone to the side bars so that the bird can keep its beak trim.

Training a bird

To pick a bird up in its cage, grasp it by its body with its neck between your first and second fingers. Move quickly

and firmly. If you let the bird out of the cage, close all doors and windows in the room and leave the cage door open. Should you have trouble getting a bird back into its cage, darken the room. This will calm the bird and allow you to pick it up more easily. If necessary, drop a lightweight cloth over it.

Never let a canary out of its cage, as it may panic. Budgies should have about 30 minutes of free flight a day. Allow your budgie out of its cage only after it is used to being handled. Begin by putting your hand into the cage and scratching the bird's head. When it gets used to this, press your forefinger gently against its breast and try to get it to hop onto your finger.

Teaching a budgie to talk
Teach your budgie to talk by continuously repeating a word or short phrase. For best results, place the bird in its cage in a darkened room and stay out of sight to lessen distractions.

Give two or three 15-minute training sessions a day. Be patient; it may be weeks before you get results. If you own a tape recorder, record a training session, then you need only play the tape for future sessions.

Watching a bird's health
As soon as you get a bird, find a veterinarian who treats birds. Don't wait. If the bird gets sick, it may be too late.

Major symptoms of illness are ruffled feathers, partially closed eyes, sneezing, loss of appetite, and abnormal droppings. If your bird develops any of these symptoms, keep it warm by covering its cage on all but one side and get it to a vet as soon as possible. Handle the bird as little as possible.

Bird feeders

Feeding the flocks

If you enjoy watching birds, attract them to your window by building a feeder. Birds are interested in food, not design; so the feeder need be no more than a platform with raised edges. Use ½-inch exterior plywood for the platform and common wood lath for the edging.

Cut the wood to the dimensions given in the drawing. Give the top and bottom of the platform (but not the edges) two coats of exterior wood stain. Leave the laths unfinished.

When the stain is dry, fasten the laths to the platform with glue and ¾-inch box nails. Butt the side laths against the rear one, and center the front lath. The gaps at the front corners are for drainage.

Cut a 3- x 7-inch piece of ¼-inch-mesh hardware cloth, and bend under the sharp points. Arch the middle and nail the hardware cloth to the platform near a front corner. Use six ¾-inch box nails, not quite driven in and bent over the hardware cloth.

Nail the feeder to two 8-inch shelf

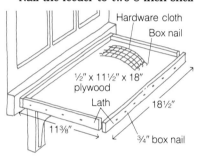

supports. Put a square of lath between each support's rear screw hole and the feeder bottom so that the feeder tips a little to the front for drainage. Nail the feeder to a window sill that is not accessible from an eave or tree—squirrels can leap 6 feet. Put suet and fruit under the hardware cloth, sprinkle birdseed on the rest of the tray, and watch the birdies.

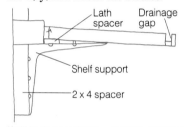

If sill is deep or house siding is masonry, use two lengths of 2 x 4 as spacers. Nail spacers to wood or mount on masonry with screws and masonry fasteners.

Birdhouses

Building for specific species

Birds like a dry house to nest in. No single size house fits all birds, but by adjusting the dimensions, one design can be used for several species.

Cut the six components to the sizes shown in the chart. Use ¾-inch cedar or 1 x 8 redwood tongue-and-groove siding with the tongue and groove sawn off. Cut the bevels and the ventilation and drainage holes as shown. Saw shallow notches the width of the saw blade ½ inch apart on the inside of the front piece. The notches help young birds climb up to the entrance hole. Cut the entrance hole with a keyhole saw, saber saw, or hole saw.

Fasten the two sides and the floor to the back with 6d galvanized finishing nails. Then add the roof. Attach the front by using two plain 6d finishing nails near the top as pivots. Drive a screw through the front into the floor.

Leave the wood raw without paint or stain. Nail the house to a tree or to a post in partial shade. But if the house is for bluebirds, mount it to a post in an open, sunny area and paint its roof white to deflect the sun's rays and keep it cool inside.

Before each nesting season, remove the screw holding the floor in place and tilt the front to clean out the house. The extra inch of length on the front provides a handgrip.

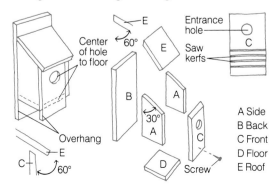

Part	BIRDHOUSE MEASUREMENTS (in inches)				
	Bluebird	House Finch	Flicker	Tree Swallow	House Wren
Sides (two)*	5¾ × 11¾	6¾ × 10¼	7¾ × 22⅜	5¾ × 9⅞	4¾ × 10⅛
Back	6½ × 16½	7½ × 15⅛	8½ × 27¼	6½ × 14⅝	5½ × 14⅞
Front*	5 × 9¾	6 × 7¾	7 × 19¼	5 × 7¾	4 × 8¾
Floor	5 × 5	6 × 6	7 × 7	5 × 5	4 × 4
Roof*	6½ × 8¼	7½ × 9½	8½ × 11½	6½ × 8⅜	5½ × 7⅛
Entrance:					
Diameter	1½	2	2½	1½	1¼
Center of hole to floor	6	4	15	2½	3

*Squared off measurements—before angles or bevels are cut.

Bird-watching

How to observe and identify birds at home and afield

You can learn a great deal about the birds of your area without ever leaving your chair. Position a birdfeeder in view of a window and, aided by an illustrated bird guide, watch. In your yard you can observe even more.

When you decide to go farther afield, it helps to go with a knowledgeable friend or join a bird walk at a nature center. Learn what species are likely to occur in the habitat you'll be visiting and become familiar with them in the guide. The best times of day for bird-watching are early morning and late afternoon, when birds are busy feeding. Spring, when birds migrate and nest, is the season of peak activity—and birds are more visible before tree leaves are full-grown.

Wear dull-colored clothing. Walk quietly, and sit or crouch whenever possible. Try to keep the sun behind you so that you'll see the birds' coloring better.

Most bird-watchers use binoculars with a magnification of seven times. To use binoculars, first find a bird with your naked eye. Then, keeping your eyes fixed on the bird, raise the binoculars to your eyes.

To identify a bird, observe its size, its color and markings, its overall shape and proportions, its posture (is it upside down on a pine cone or creeping up a tree trunk, for example?), the shape of its tail, and any habitual actions. If a bird is in flight, watch its motion (does it swoop, glide, bob up and down?). Estimate its length by comparing it to a familiar bird, such as an English sparrow (6 inches) or a robin (10 inches).

Birth certificates

Acquiring copies

Generally, the physician who attends a birth files a birth certificate with the state department of public health, the state department of vital statistics (usually a branch of the health depart-ment) or, in a few states, with the county clerk. In some large cities, the city itself keeps birth certificates in its own records department.

To get a copy of your birth certificate, write to the appropriate office in the capital of the state or in the city where you were born. The office may be listed in the phone book under the health department or vital statistics department. It may even be listed under "Birth Certificates" in a quick-reference list of state or local government offices. If all else fails, contact the municipal office or county clerk in the place where you were born.

Phone or write to find out the fee required, then mail your request along with a check or money order for the fee. If you live in the city where the records are kept, you can probably apply in person. Death certificates can be obtained in the same manner.

Blackjack

Gambling hard and fast

The object of the game is to get two or more cards totaling 21 or close to but not over 21. Aces count as 1 or 11; face cards, 10; all other cards have face value. After all bets have been placed, the dealer gives each player one card face down, then one card face up.

A player may *stand*—refuse more cards—or say "hit me" and get another card, face up. He may ask for additional cards only as long as the cards in his hand add up to less than 21. A player who has more than 21 points in his hand is *busted* and pays the dealer the amount he bet. If a player gets a *natural* (two cards totaling 21), the dealer pays double.

When all the players are busted or standing, the dealer takes more cards, if he wishes, then turns over his face-down card. If he has more than 21 points, he pays each player still in the game the amount each bet. If the dealer has 21 or less, he collects from those with lower scores and pays those who scored closer to 21 than he did. After five games, the deal moves left to the next player. In gambling casinos, the deal does not move, and the rules of play differ slightly.

Blanching

Ways of blanching foods; reasons for blanching

Foods are blanched in different ways for different purposes. When preparing a fruit or vegetable for cooking or canning, plunging it briefly into boiling water helps retain its flavor, color, and texture. Another type of blanching loosens the skins of such foods as almonds and tomatoes so that you can skin them more easily. Put the food in a sieve or colander and pour boiling water over it.

Prior to freezing, vegetables should be blanched briefly in boiling water to destroy the enzymes that break down foods; after blanching, drop the vegetables into cold water to stop the cooking action. Blanching is also used to remove a strong taste—the saltiness of meats like bacon, for example. Bring the food to a boil in water, boil 3 to 5 minutes, then drain the water.

Bleaching wood

Removing stains and spots; lightening dark wood

Liquid laundry bleach will remove most stains from wood—wood-finishing stains as well as ink, water, and other marks. Strip old finish from the stained area or the entire surface. When bleaching a dark spot, it's best to treat the whole surface so that you don't leave a light area surrounded by dark. Apply the bleach full strength to the raw wood. Leave the surface wet for 20 minutes, then neutralize it with a solution of half vinegar and half water. If after 4 hours a stain remains, re-bleach and re-neutralize the dark area. Before sanding the surface and applying a new finish, let the wood dry 24 hours.

To lighten naturally dark wood, use a two-part commercial wood bleach. Because such preparations contain hydrogen peroxide and lye, they are very caustic. When working with one, follow the directions on the package carefully, wear protective gloves, and work in a well-ventilated place.

Bleeding

Quick responses to severe bleeding wounds

Without delay, press a thick pad of any cloth that's handy directly on a severe wound. Use towels, socks, handkerchiefs. Never mind if you can't get to sterile gauze pads; infection is less

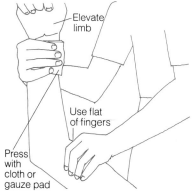

Elevate limb

Use flat of fingers

Press with cloth or gauze pad

worrisome than bleeding. Don't lift the pad to see what's happening; that will renew the bleeding. If the pad gets saturated, top it with another and keep pressing. When bleeding stops or slows, apply a pressure bandage: place the center of a strip of cloth, a necktie, or the like over the pad and wrap it tightly around arm, leg, head, or torso. Tie the bandage over the wound. For a very severe wound, someone should apply pressure manually all the way to the hospital.

Limb wounds

If an arm or a leg is wounded, keep the limb elevated while you press, unless you suspect a fracture. An arm can be held upright by another person, a leg can be propped straight against anything suitable, even a bystander.

Elevating the limb and applying direct pressure may not stop the bleeding. Find the place where the main artery above the wound comes close

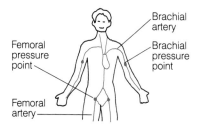

Brachial artery

Femoral pressure point

Brachial pressure point

Femoral artery

enough to a bone to be squeezed against it, and press that place. At the same time, continue direct pressure on the wound itself. For a leg wound, press the heel of your hand into the groin; for an arm wound, press the flat of your fingers into the upper arm.

In the case of very severe injury or an accident where there might be internal bleeding, keep the injured person warm and lying down until medical care arrives. Keep the head lower than the body unless the victim is unconscious or you suspect a head, neck, or back injury (see *Shock*).

Tourniquets

A tourniquet is a last resort, to be used only when bleeding is life threatening or when the injury is a severed limb. Even with a severed finger, foot, or worse, if the bleeding can be stopped by less drastic pressure, a surgeon may be able to reattach the part (see *Severed digits and limbs*).

To make a tourniquet, tear a long, wide strip of cloth (from a shirt or a skirt, if necessary) and find a stick, ballpoint pen, table knife, screwdriver—whatever is handy. Wind the cloth strip twice around the limb above the wound and as close to it as possible; tie a half-knot. Place the

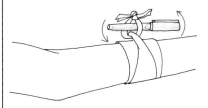

stick over the knot and tie two full knots. Twist the stick until the bleeding stops. Secure the free end of the stick by tying it to the limb with a strip of cloth. Write down when and where the tourniquet was applied and attach the note to the person's clothing in full view. Get medical help quickly.

Once a tourniquet is applied, do not loosen it, or you may throw the person into shock from sudden renewed bleeding. However, if medical help is several hours away and the injury is a deep laceration, release the tourniquet every hour to hour and a half while maintaining direct pressure at the site of the wound. After a few minutes retighten the tourniquet.

Blenders

Problem-solving primer

Before you take a broken blender to a repair shop or buy a new one, check it for some common problems. Unplug the blender before working on it.

Jar leaks may develop in older blenders. In screw-off-bottom types, replace the rubber gasket if a check reveals wear or cracks. To cure leaks at the shaft, buy a new blade assembly.

If the blender operates slowly or erratically, sediment may be caked in the blade assembly. Take the jar off the base and hand-turn the blade. (Be careful not to cut yourself.) If turning is difficult, soak the assembly overnight in water and detergent. If turning is still hard, replace the assembly.

A chipped or broken coupling (the parts in the base and the jar assembly that unite the two) can cause erratic operation. Inspect the couplings and replace them if they are damaged.

Food or water splashing into the switch assembly of a push-button model can prevent operation at some speeds. Unplug the blender, carefully peel off the label surrounding the switch buttons, and remove the screws

beneath. If there is a cap on the *HI-LO* switch, pull it off. On some blenders the switch assembly lifts out; with others you must turn the blender upside down and remove the hex nuts to separate the lower housing and the switch assembly. Use a penknife or a small, stiff toothbrush to scrape off caked food. Reinstall the switch.

Touch-switch models are sealed and so the switches are not likely to give trouble. But if you get the switch wet, you may damage it. Clean the touch panel only with a damp sponge.

If a blender won't run in a working outlet, replace the plug. If it still won't work, open the housing and check the cord with a continuity tester (see *Plugs; Power cords*).

Blinds

Cleaning venetian blinds; replacing cords and tapes

Washing venetian blinds is messy; postpone this operation by dusting regularly. Use a vacuum cleaner or put on cotton gloves and wipe the slats by hand. Don't wash wooden blinds. Spray each slat with furniture cleaner and wipe with a soft cloth.

To wash metal blinds at the window, first dust them. Have two pails of water at hand: one with household cleaner or ammonia in it, the other clear. Extend the blinds fully, with the slats horizontal. Starting at the top, wipe each slat with a sudsy sponge; rinse immediately with clear water and a second sponge.

Metal blinds can also be washed in the bathtub or outdoors and then hung on a clothesline or stretched on a drop cloth. Outdoors, hose the blinds, scrub one slat at a time, and rinse. In the tub, put the blinds in warm suds, scrub, and rinse in clear

water. Let water drip off. But before the tapes dry, rehang the blinds fully extended so that the tapes don't shrink or wrinkle.

Replacing cords and tapes

Kits of cords, tapes, and knobs are sold in most hardware stores. Begin with the blinds fully extended and the slats horizontal. If the tapes are stapled to the bottom bar, remove the staples. If they aren't stapled, remove the end caps and the bottom bar base.

Unknot the cord ends and pull them out of the slats, but leave them on the pulleys. Knot the cord ends. Now slide the slats out. Next, detach the tapes at the top and substitute new ones of the same lengths. Cut new cord the same length as the old and thread it on the pulleys, following the old cord as a guide and unthreading the old cord as you proceed. Replace the slats and run the cord through the slat holes on alternate sides of the tape rungs.

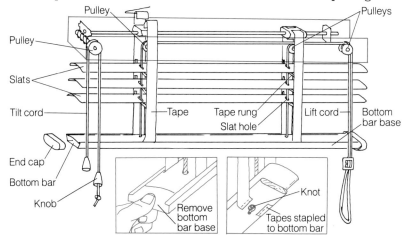

Blisters

Treating water blisters

Blisters often form on heels or soles rubbed by ill-fitting shoes or on hands chafed from gripping a gardening tool, golf club, or similar object. They also develop from burns. The treatment is the same whatever the cause of the blister: protect it from friction, and don't puncture it; the fluid in it will be reabsorbed naturally. Clean the skin and apply a dry sterile gauze pad. If the blister breaks, wash it with antiseptic soap and continue to keep it covered with a dry sterile pad. Don't peel away the dead covering skin. If a broken blister shows any sign of infection—spreading redness or pus—see a doctor.

If you can't avoid the friction that caused the blister, protect it as follows: Make a doughnut of thick adhesive cushioning with a "hole" the size of the blister. Paint the area around the blister with tincture of benzoin to

make the skin sticky. Position the doughnut around the blister and tape it securely with strips of athletic tape. Leave it on until the blister heals.

Blow-dryers

Basic repairs you can make

The typical blow-dryer is a pistol-shaped unit consisting of a handle with switches; a circular housing containing an impeller (or fan); and a barrel 1 ½ to 2 inches in diameter with a heating element inside. The impeller draws air in through a series of holes and passes it over the heating element while expelling it from the barrel.

Replacement is the best answer for a faulty motor, heating element, or switch. However, minor repairs to the plug or cord are worthwhile. Unplug the appliance before working on it.

When a blow-dryer fails to operate at all when plugged into a functioning outlet, replace the plug before attempting any troubleshooting (see *Plugs*).

If the appliance still won't operate, check the power cord. For this, you must open the housing. Remove the screws holding the halves of the housing together (sometimes the screws are hidden beneath a label). Slide the barrel off and part the housing halves with a screwdriver. Use a continuity tester to check the power cord (see *Power cords*). If the cord is defective, install a new one, soldering the bare ends to the switch mounting posts.

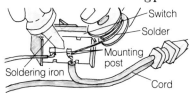

If the power cord is all right, the air-intake grille or the impeller may be stuffed with hair, causing overheating and automatic shutdown. Open the housing and clean out the debris.

A defective cord may also be the problem if a dryer operates only when held in certain positions. Test and proceed as above.

Boat launching

Taking your boat to water

Before you tow your boat, check with your motor vehicle bureau's trailer license office to find out whether state law requires trailer brakes, lights, side mirrors, or special permits for a hull wider than 8 feet.

To launch your boat, you'll probably back it down a ramp. Practice maneuvering in an empty parking lot—your trailer will turn in the opposite direction of your car.

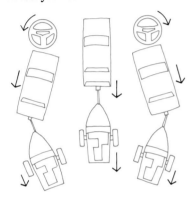

If your boat is small, you can use a second hitch, mounted on the front bumper, for maneuvering at the ramp. It allows you to see what the boat is doing.

Boat refinishing

Repainting and revarnishing

Cracked, peeling, or blistered paint on wood should be removed and the wood repainted. The method of removal depends on the part of the boat you're working on. For contours or details, chemical stripper is the best choice. Brush it on; when the old paint bubbles, remove it with a scraper, putty knife, and bronze wool. You can also use a heat gun, but don't use a propane torch on details.

On large, flat surfaces, a torch or a heat gun works well. Heat the paint until it blisters, then scrape with a putty knife. Don't burn the wood, and be alert to the risk of fire. Antifouling paint on the boat's bottom is best removed with a sander or grinder. The paint may be toxic, so work in a well-ventilated area, wearing protective clothing, mask, and goggles.

Repainting

First sand the wood smooth and dust it with a tack cloth (see *Tack cloth*). Use sealer, undercoat, and finish paint meant for one another. Use epoxy paint for long life, and disposable foam brushes to minimize brush marks. Some paints call for sanding between coats.

Revarnishing

The top coat of varnish may need renewing every 6 weeks or only once a year, depending on conditions in your area. Lightly sand the surface, dust it with a tack cloth, and apply a thin coat of varnish.

When varnish cracks or peels, or the wood beneath gets discolored, it's time to strip it to bare wood. Use a chemical stripper and bronze wool, then fine sandpaper. Revarnish on a dry, windless day in a place that is out of the direct sun. First wipe surfaces with a tack cloth. Use a foam brush and exterior varnish containing an ultraviolet filter. Apply at least three thin coats.

Fiberglass surfaces

Fiberglass has a factory-applied exterior finish called gel coat. Its life can be lengthened with auto polish. Nicks and scratches can be repaired with touch-up kits, but recoating of the entire surface should be done by a fiberglass shop or by a boatyard.

Boat security

Keeping a tight, safe ship

Boats are prime targets for thieves; have your boat insured and take every reasonable precaution to keep it secure. Use a hardened alloy steel chain or vinyl-covered cable to tie a small boat to a dock or mooring. If it's an open boat, run the chain around a seat.

Boats on trailers

A boat stored on a trailer is especially susceptible to theft. If possible, park it out of sight of the road. Remove loose gear from the boat, and remove or lock the motor and prop. Lock the trailer securely. Off-season remove a wheel from the trailer, block the frame, and lock or dismantle the trailer tongue.

Boats with cabins

To make a boat cabin more secure, lay wooden dowels in the tracks of sliding windows. Put strong hinges with long screws on the main hatch and add an exterior lock. On the forward hatch, add special interior hatch fasteners or a padlock. Finally, install an alarm system to discourage intruders.

Marking gear and taking inventory

Mark deck chairs, flotation gear, windbreakers, and other loose items with your name, your boat's name, and your home port. Electronic instruments, communication gear, outboard motors, and the like should be engraved with your driver's license number and state or your Social Security number. (The police can locate you right away if they find an item with your license number; with a Social Security number it takes longer.) You can buy an engraving tool at a hardware store or make one of an electric drill fitted with a burr bit.

Make a complete inventory, including descriptions, serial and model numbers, and manufacturers of your boat and its engine, sails, electronic gear, and other equipment. Boats built after 1972 have a hull number, which you should record. Take photographs from different angles. Keep the inventory and pictures at home.

Other precautions

Ask for bright, all-night lighting at the marina, and encourage the other boat owners to watch your property in exchange for your watching theirs. If you put the boat in dry dock, remove instruments, fittings, canvas, and loose gear. Visit the boat regularly.

Boat trailers

Choosing a trailer; after-launch and off-season care

A boat hull is designed for water. When trailered over rough roads, it can suffer more damage than it does afloat in rough seas unless the trailer's rollers and bolsters are positioned so that they cushion the hull. The trailer axles should be positioned or the boat mounted so that about 5 to 10 percent of the boat's weight rests on the car's hitch. Before attaching

BOCCE

the trailer to the car, place a bathroom scale beneath the hitch to determine the load at that point.

Trailers are rated for the load they can carry. When you're buying or renting one, keep in mind that a 2,000-pound boat can become 3,000 pounds once a big outboard motor, fuel tanks, tackle, and gear are added. (See also *Trailers*.)

Place your gear so that the weight is distributed equally between the stern and bow halves. Too much stern weight can make the rig fish-tail, or sway, dangerously. Too much weight on the hitch lifts the car's front end, throwing the headlight beams too high and making steering difficult.

Trailer maintenance

Because trailer wheels are small and rotate fast, they build up heat on a trip. Then, while submerged during launching, they suck water through the hubs and into the bearings. Inspect unsealed bearings after each entry into the water and, if necessary, repack them with grease. Salt water corrodes; hose down the trailer after every haul-out.

If you store your boat off-season on the trailer, block up the frame to take weight off the tires and springs. Before the next launch, reexamine tires and spare, bearings, frame, winch, hitch, tie-downs, and wiring.

Bocce

Bowling the Italian way

The object of the game of bocce is to bowl four wooden balls closer to the *pallino* (target ball) than your opponent. Bocce is generally played in teams of two or four players, but two can play and take two shots per turn.

The game is commonly played in an alley about 8 feet wide and 60 feet long and bounded on the sides by wooden boards. A *regulator peg* is planted dead center in the playing area, and there is a foul area at each end.

The first player must bowl the pallino from behind his foul line so that it lands about 5 feet beyond the regulator peg and more than 1 foot from the inside of the wooden boards. All players then take turns bowling balls to-

ward the pallino while standing behind their foul lines. You may carom the ball off a side board. You may also hit and move other balls in the playing area, but you must first call the shot—specify which ball you're aiming for. If you miss, the ball you bowled is disqualified and any dislodged balls must be repositioned.

After all four balls have been bowled, add the scores. The two balls closest to the pallino get 1 point each. Bowl more games until one team scores 12 points, the usual winning score.

There is also a popular French variant, called *boules*, which is similar to bocce in most respects. It uses metal balls and can be played in a bocce court or any convenient space.

Body odor

What causes body odor and how to avoid it

At the root of body odor is the perspiration secreted by the apocrine glands under the arms and in the genital region. Acted upon by bacteria, the perspiration emits a strong odor.

The best control for body odor is daily bathing. In addition, keep clothing clean, especially garments that come in contact with apocrine areas. Clothing made of natural fibers allows better air circulation, inhibiting the growth of bacteria.

If these measures are inadequate, resort to a deodorant, which contains agents that destroy bacteria, or an antiperspirant, which checks perspiration. The active ingredient in an antiperspirant is an aluminum compound; of two frequently used, aluminum chloride is more effective than aluminum chlorohydrate but may irritate the skin of some individuals and may also harm clothing. To add to the confusion, some products are designated as antiperspirant deodorants and others that are called deodorants contain aluminum compounds. Try different products, starting with the milder deodorants, until you find one that works and doesn't irritate. Apply it before going to bed or just after waking. If you shave under arms, wait 12 hours before using it.

Stop using any product that irritates. After repeated use, you may find that an application every other day is sufficient. Lotions are most effective; avoid pressurized containers.

Boilers

Draining boilers; routine maintenance; curing a steam boiler of frequent cycling

In a hot-water heating system, a pump circulates water at about 180°F through pipes and radiators. If the pressure gets too high, a relief valve lets water escape. This may indicate a lack of air in the expansion tank (see *Expansion tank bleeding*).

Drain a hot-water boiler only for repairs or in the case of a prolonged power outage when the pipes might freeze. To drain, turn off the power and water supplies and let the water cool (there's a temperature indicator on the boiler). Attach a hose to the drain valve. Lead the hose to a drain or collect the water in buckets. Once water is flowing, open the air vents on top-floor radiators.

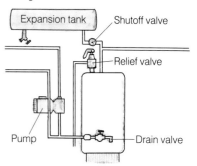

To prevent freeze-ups, an antifreeze compound can be added to the system. This may involve changes in the water supply to the boiler and should be done only by your serviceman.

Refill the boiler by closing the drain valve and turning on the water supply. When you hear water in the top-floor radiators, close the air vents. Later, bleed air from all valves (see *Radiator valves*).

Steam-heat boilers

In a steam system, the boiler turns water to steam, which then circulates through radiators, condenses to water, and runs back to the boiler. If the

42

pressure gets too high, a safety valve lets off steam. Check the valve periodically by lifting the handle. If it won't lift, replace the valve. Drain a steam boiler only for a long absence; do it as you would a hot-water boiler except do not touch the radiator valves.

A glass gauge indicates the boiler water level; the water should be at least halfway up the gauge when the boiler is off. Unless you have an automatic refill valve, check the gauge weekly (more often in very cold weather) and refill the boiler by turning on

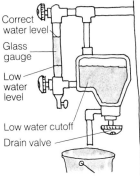

Correct water level
Glass gauge
Low water level
Low water cutoff
Drain valve

the supply valve until the water in the glass reaches the proper level.

To prevent sediment buildup, once a month or whenever the water looks dirty, open the drain valve on the low-water cutoff and drain a pail of water. Be careful; the water will be hot. Refill the boiler to the correct level. If the water remains dirty, add a boiler-cleaning compound. Remove the safety valve and pour in the compound following the package directions.

If a steam-heat system cycles on and off frequently but you're not getting heat, the boiler may need filling. If the water level is correct, an accumulation of sediment may be causing a condition called surging. To relieve it, add an antisurge compound.

Boiling

How water's boiling point is affected by altitude

Heating water to boiling brings it to the same pressure as the atmosphere; it then changes from liquid to vapor, which bubbles up and breaks the surface. Boiling it harder or longer makes it no hotter; only atmospheric pres-

sure alters the boiling point. At sea level, water boils at 212°F. At higher altitudes, where the atmospheric pressure is lower, water boils at a lower point and also evaporates faster.

Elevation	Boiling Point
2,000'	208°F
5,000'	203°F
7,500'	198°F
10,000'	194°F

A lower boiling point may require adjustments in time, temperature, or amounts of ingredients when cooking foods in water and when canning foods at high altitudes. Ask your Cooperative Extension Service (see p. 5) for adjustments in your area.

Bolts

Installing bolts; loosening troublesome bolts

Use a bolt and nut when joining two thin pieces (such as metal), when strength is needed, and when you'll be taking an item apart often. There are three major types of common bolts. *Machine bolts* are made with square or hexagonal heads. *Carriage bolts* have round heads or countersunk flat-topped heads; a square shoulder beneath the head of a carriage bolt keeps the bolt from turning when a nut is tightened on it. *Stove bolts* have slotted flat, round, or oval heads.

Installing bolts

To install a bolt, slide it into place and screw the nut on clockwise. Once the nut is partly on, hold the bolt head stationary with a wrench (or with a screwdriver if the bolt head is slotted). Turn the nut by hand until it is snug, then tighten it with another wrench, but do not overtighten. Use wrenches that fit correctly so as not to damage the bolt head or the nut. Whenever possible, use a socket or a box-head wrench (see *Wrenches*).

Washers can be placed next to the outer surfaces of the parts being joined to protect them from the pressure of the bolt head and the nut. Lock washers or thread-locking solutions, such as Loctite, will prevent nuts from loosening.

Removing troublesome bolts
When removing a bolt, if the bolt head or nut is too worn down to provide a grip, apply locking-grip pliers as tightly as possible. If this fails, file two sides of the nut flat, then try locking pliers or an adjustable wrench.

If a nut or bolt is rusted or frozen, apply penetrating oil, let it sit for a few minutes, then try the wrench again. Repeat the applications if necessary.

A still recalcitrant nut and bolt requires methods that will damage the nut and bolt. Use a hammer and cold chisel to tap a groove into the nut near a corner. Place the chisel in the groove and pound it counterclockwise. If the

Cold chisel
Nut
Bolt

nut still doesn't turn, cut through it with the chisel or with a hacksaw.

If a bolt snaps off while you are trying to remove it, use an extractor. Drill a hole in the broken-off bolt (the diameter of the hole should match the diameter of the extractor's shank), drive in the extractor with a hammer, and apply a wrench to the extractor to unthread the bolt.

Bonds

How to buy Treasury bills, notes, and bonds at auction

Treasury bills, notes, and bonds are forms of U.S. government debt. T-bills mature in a year or less, T-notes in 2 to 10 years, T-bonds in 10 to 30 years. The minimum purchase for T-bills is $10,000; for a T-note of under 4 years, $5,000; and for a T-note 4 years or over and all T-bonds, $1,000.

The Treasury auctions new issues of 13- and 26-week T-bills once a week on Monday, 52-week T-bills every fourth Thursday, notes and bonds monthly or quarterly. T-bills are sold at a discount (less than face value); your return is the difference between the amount paid at discount and the face value reached upon maturity. T-notes and bonds bear interest semi-annually. They too may sell at a discount at auction.

You can buy a new issue directly from a Federal Reserve Bank or one of its branches (ask your bank for the address of the nearest one). Ask the Federal Reserve for dates of upcoming sales, a tender form (or ask what information you must supply if you order by letter), and payment instructions. Check the "noncompetitive" box and provide all the information requested in the tender form. Take the form (or letter) to the Federal Reserve by 12 noon Eastern time of the sale date or mail it postmarked no later than the day prior to auction.

Mail your order to the address given on the tender form. If you order by letter, check with your Federal Reserve branch for the appropriate address. Your order is filled, at no charge, at the average price of all the accepted competitive bids.

For a fee, typically about $50, you can also order a new issue from a bank or broker before the auction. You can sell before maturity securities you bought from a bank or broker; Treasury-bought ones must first be transferred to a bank or broker for premature sale.

You can buy old issues through a bank or broker at a fee, generally $35 to $75. For any trade under $10,000,000 you'll pay a markup above the market price, usually under $10 on every $1,000 invested.

Bonsai

The ancient oriental art of dwarfing trees

Even when fairly young, a bonsai tree looks old. Its leaves, flowers, and fruits are often miniature. A bonsai garden can be either a lone, twisted tree, such as an evergreen, or a group of straight ones, such as maples or birches. Flowering shrubs such as azaleas or cotoneaster can be used.

You can buy an already trained bonsai tree from a garden center. From spring through fall keep it sheltered outdoors except for brief periods of showing indoors. Winter it in a cool

(35°F to 50°F), frost-free place with good light. Water it often enough to keep the soil moderately moist. Mist it daily and whenever it droops during hot, dry spells. Fertilize with a complete houseplant food diluted to ¼ strength once a month except in the one or two hottest months and in winter.

Training a bonsai tree
It takes a year or more to train your own bonsai tree. Buy a young, small-leaved tree with an interesting shape or dig up a seedling from your yard. Study the tree's shape, and try to visualize its final form. Prune it to keep several main branches on each side of the trunk. Work for a composition of pleasing proportion and balance but not symmetry.

Trim the bottom roots to fit a special shallow bonsai tray. If there is a central root, cut it back slightly.

Plant the tree, using insulated electric wire to anchor its roots to the bottom holes of the tray. Then spiral the wire up and around the trunk and branches. Bend them slightly to the

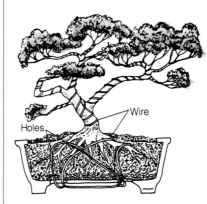

shape you want. Moss on top of the soil gives the appearance of grass.

Rewire the tree annually to allow for its growth. After a year, prune the central root again.

Bookbinding repairs

Restoring damaged books

To fix a *wobbly cover*, pull both covers straight out. Use a knitting needle to apply white (PVA) glue along the joints. Close the book and weight it while it dries for 24 hours.

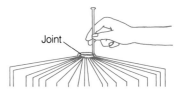

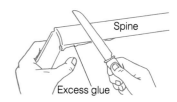

Repair a *loose spine* by brushing white glue along the book's two long edges, but not on the entire back. Align the loose spine with the edges and press it into place. Rub a flat instrument, such as a table knife, on the hinges to force out excess glue;

wipe it off. Cover the spine with waxed paper and wrap an elastic bandage around the book. Dry for 24 hours.

To fix a *cracked endpaper*, apply a thin bead of white glue and press it well into the crack. Cut a waxed paper strip a few inches longer than the book. Fold it lengthwise and position the fold over the glued area. (Excess

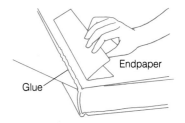

glue will ooze onto the waxed paper, not the endpaper.) Close and weight the book for 24 hours. Glue cloth tape over the hinge for added strength.

Mend *torn pages* by placing waxed paper under the tear. Align the torn edges and brush white glue on the tear. Cover it with rice paper or onionskin, rub gently, and weight it. When the glue is dry, peel off excess paper.

To reattach a *loose page*, cut a narrow strip of paper the length of the book, fold it lengthwise, and apply white glue to the back. Place one half on the loose page, the other half on the next page. Put waxed paper across the paper strip, close the book, and let the glue dry.

Bookcase building

Shelving made with hand tools, power tools, and (almost) no tools

You can construct a bookcase of 1 x 10-inch or 1 x 12-inch pine shelving, using hand tools only. With power tools, you can build the same design of cabinet-grade plywood.

Measure the space where the bookcase is to fit. Draw the bookcase to scale on graph paper. Remember that pine shelving's dimensions are nominal: the thickness is ⅝ inch and the widths are 9½ and 11¼ inches, respectively, for 10- and 12-inch boards.

If the bookcase will sit against a wall with a baseboard, have it rest upon a rectangular base made of 1 x 4 stock so that it will clear the baseboard. Nail it through the bookcase bottom. If the bookcase will hang from the wall, beneath the top shelf add a 1 x 3- or 4-inch hanging cleat the same length as the shelf.

Allow 6 to 8 inches between shelves for paperback books, 8 to 12 inches for hardcover books, and 13 inches for records. If the bookcase will be longer than 3 feet, plan an inside divider. A bookcase longer than 6 feet is unwieldy; build two units.

The shelves can rest on cleats—strips of 1 x 1 wood nailed to the sides and divider (if there is one)—or they can be supported by adjustable shelf rests. Add a back of ¼-inch plywood if the bookcase will hold heavy items.

List all the parts with their dimensions. If possible, have the lumberyard cut the wood to size. If you do the cutting yourself, measure and mark the pieces according to your diagrams and saw them. Then lay like-size boards next to one another to make sure that the finished lengths are identical. Label all pieces.

Check cuts for squareness; if necessary, square them by planing or sanding. Using a try square, mark the sides and the divider for placement of cleats. Nail the cleats with finishing nails, sink the nails with a nail set, and fill the holes with putty. If you are using shelf rests, drill holes for them using pegboard as a guide. Nail the hanging cleat, if there is one, to the underside of the top.

Joining sides, top, and bottom
Hammer the nails through the sides until the points protrude a little. Squeeze a ¼-inch bead of white or yellow wood glue onto the ends of the top and bottom and onto the sides where the top and bottom will abut. Rest the back edges of all four pieces on a level surface and hammer the nails to within ⅛ inch of the wood surface.

Wipe off excess glue with a damp cloth. Measure diagonally from corner to corner. If the diagonals are the same, the bookcase is square; if not, nudge the bookcase with a rubber mallet until it is square. Let it dry overnight. The next day, set the nails and fill the holes with wood putty. Add the back, making it slightly smaller than the edges of the bookcase.

Sand the unit with medium and fine sandpaper. Dust it with a tack cloth (see *Tack cloth*) and apply stain or, if you choose, primer-sealer and paint. If it's a hanging bookcase, see *Wall fasteners*.

Plywood bookcases
Use ¾-inch cabinet-grade plywood in a veneer that blends with your furniture. Cut the wood to size with a table saw or use a circular saw guided by a straightedge. Cut the top and bottom ½ inch longer than the shelves so that you can join them to the sides with tongue-and-groove joints. Make ¼-inch tongues on the ends of the top and bottom and ¼ x ¼-inch grooves in the sides for the tongues to fit into.

Screw cleats to the sides. Glue the top, bottom, and sides, and clamp (see *Cabinet building*). Measure diagonally to check the squareness.

Veneer tape
Plywood edges that will be visible should be covered with veneer tape, which comes in strips to match many woods. Apply it with contact cement, or use veneer tape that comes with adhesive on the back. Trim it with a single-edge razor blade.

Quick bookcases
An attractive, low bookcase can be made with pine shelving and stacked bricks as ends. Use bricks with holes through them so that metal rods can be run through the bricks. Drill holes in the shelving for the rods.

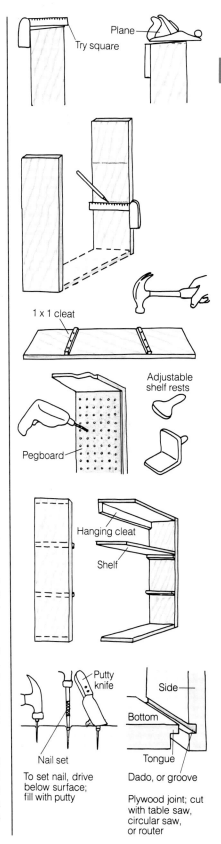

Plane

Try square

1 x 1 cleat

Adjustable shelf rests

Pegboard

Hanging cleat

Shelf

Putty knife

Side

Bottom

Nail set

Tongue

To set nail, drive below surface; fill with putty

Dado, or groove

Plywood joint; cut with table saw, circular saw, or router

B

Book lice

Getting rid of these mold-loving pests

These minute gray or light-brown wingless insects do not eat books. Instead, they thrive on the molds that grow in damp paper, wood, upholstery, and rugs (see *Mildew*). Book lice need heat and humidity to survive.

To get rid of these pests, try correcting the humid conditions by improving ventilation and repairing roofs, leaky windows, and decayed siding—all sources of dampness—or by placing a dehumidifier in the room with books. If book lice are well established in a house, you can spray or dust the affected areas with a spray containing pyrethrins designed for indoor use.

Boomerangs

Throwing an aborigine weapon

Practice boomeranging on a clear day in a large, open area where there's no danger of hitting people, cars, or houses. If there is a breeze, position yourself as shown. Grip one end of the

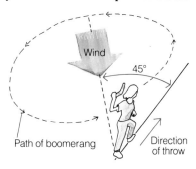

Wind

45°

Path of boomerang

Direction of throw

boomerang with its flat side against your palm and its rounded side toward your body. The free end can point ahead of you or over your shoulder; try both ways.

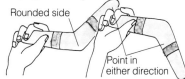

Rounded side

Point in either direction

Step forward with your left foot and swing your arm back. Aim at the horizon and throw the boomerang out in

the direction your feet are pointing. As you release the boomerang it should be tilted slightly away from you. Experiment with this angle; it's different for each boomerang. Snap your wrist as you let the boomerang go and give it a spin with your index finger. Catch the returning boomerang between your palms.

If you're left-handed, you'll need a left-handed boomerang. Follow the above directions in mirror image.

Botticelli

Guessing who It is

A challenging refinement of Twenty Questions, Botticelli requires a group of players to guess a secret identity assumed by another player, who is referred to as *It*. At the start of the game, It gives the first letter of the subject's last name; for instance, "I am R." (R for Teddy Roosevelt.) Using that clue, the players, in turn, ask questions to which It must reply, giving a name beginning with the letter R. (Question: "Are you a great baseball player?" Answer: "No, I am not Babe Ruth.")

It must give an acceptable answer. If not, the same player may ask a question that can be answered yes or no. ("Are you a male?") If the answer is yes, the same player may ask another indirect question. (Question: "Are you a millionaire?" Answer: "No, I am not John D. Rockefeller.") As long as It can think of a satisfactory reply, the game goes on until It's identity can be guessed: "Are you Teddy Roosevelt?"

Bottle-feeding

Safe handling of baby's formula

Breast milk is nature's ideal food for newborn infants, but if you are unable or choose not to breast-feed, a

commercial formula will supply your child with the proper nutrition. Until a baby is at least 6 months old, use liquid or powdered formula, not cows' milk. If a baby has an adverse reaction to the formula (gas, cramps, diarrhea, excessive spitting up), consult your doctor.

For a healthy, full-term baby, rinse the bottles and nipples in cool water, then wash them in the dishwasher or by hand in hot, soapy water. Rinse well and air-dry. Until the baby is 3 months old, boil the water used to make the formula for 6 to 8 minutes.

Bottle the entire contents of each can of liquid formula when you open it. You can mix powdered formula one or several bottles at a time. In both cases, extra bottles can be capped and kept refrigerated up to 48 hours.

At feeding time, have the bottle at room temperature or gently warmed. Check the milk flow through the nipple by holding the bottle upside down. The milk should drip spontaneously, one drop a second.

Cradle the baby in your arm and hold the bottle so that the nipple is filled with milk. When the baby has taken 2 to 5 ounces of formula, burp the baby (see *Baby burping*) and then offer the bottle again.

Bowling

Three strikes and you're in

Basically, bowling consists of rolling a large ball down a 60-foot-long polished wooden lane in an attempt to knock down 10 penguin-shaped pins that have been set up in a triangular pattern at the opposite end. Ideally, you knock them all down at once.

To give the ball momentum when you propel it down the alley, advance to the foul line from a distance of 4½ steps, braking at that line. If any part of your body crosses the line, you commit a *foul*, and any pins you knock down are discounted.

The game is played in 10 *frames*, or turns, and you get two rolls per frame. If you knock down all 10 pins in one roll, you score a *strike*; if you knock down all 10 pins in two rolls in the same frame, you score a *spare*.

Scoring

You score one point for every pin you knock down. In each frame, the score for each roll is noted singly, and the total for the game so far is noted beneath the single scores. If you roll a spare, you get a bonus equal to the number of pins knocked down in your next roll. If you roll a strike, you get a bonus equal to the number of pins knocked down in your next two rolls. If you roll a spare or a strike in the last frame, you get an extra roll or two to determine the amount of your bonus.

On the score sheet, a spare is indicated as a diagonal line and a strike as an X. The bonus points are added into the running total score after the rolls determining the amount of the bonus are made. At the end of the game, the player with the highest score wins.

NAME	8	9	⁻	7	/	8	✕	✕
	8	17	35	55	85	113

✕	8	⁻	7	/	✕	✕	TOTAL
131	139	159	189				189

Equipment

Be sure to use the proper equipment. The weight and span of the ball must be correct for you, and the angle and distance of the thumb and finger holes in the ball must suit you. Balls can be custom drilled for a personal fit.

Bow ties

Hand tying a bow tie

This method also makes a neat bow at the neckline of a blouse. 1. Place the tie around your neck so that one end is slightly longer than the other end. 2. Loop the longer end over, under, and up over the shorter. The two ends should then be of equal length. 3. Flip

the top end out of the way. With the other end make a loop. 4. Bring the loop up to your throat and hold it at the center with your index finger; with the other hand retrieve the top

end and let it hang down. 5. Make a loop of the top end, tuck it up behind the center, and pull it through where your index finger is, making a knot. 6. Pull the loops until they are equal in length with each other and with the two ends; adjust the knot.

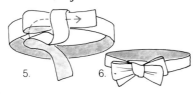

Braiding bread

Three different methods

Any bread dough that isn't too limp or sticky can be braided. Divide the dough into 3, 4, or 5 pieces, depending on the braid style desired. Hand roll each piece into a 12-inch rope. Braid three ropes as you would hair.

To make a 4-rope braid, used for the Jewish holiday bread, challah, place the ropes as shown. Next, reverse the positions of one pair of opposites. Repeat with the other pair. Continue until all dough is braided.

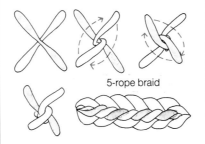

5-rope braid

For a 5-rope braid, roll 3 ropes of similar thickness and 2 thinner ones. Braid the 3 and twist the 2. Lay the twist along the top of the braid and press down to secure it.

In all cases, pinch the rope ends together and tuck them under the loaf. Place the braid on a cookie sheet and let it rise; bake it as the recipe directs. (See also *Breadmaking*.)

Braiding hair

A simple English braid

When learning to braid, encircle the hair at the top of the braid with an elastic band. This keeps the hair neat.

To form a braid, first divide the hair into three equal strands. Wrap your

Elastic

fingers around the outer strands. Second, draw the left strand over the center strand and grasp the left strand (the new center one) between

the right index and third fingers. Grasp the old center strand with the left hand and pull it aside. Third, bring the right strand over the center strand, repeating the motions but

with the opposite hands and fingers (the right strand becomes the new center one). Repeat the second and third steps until the braid is as long as you wish. Wind an elastic around the end of the braid to hold it.

Elastic

Braiding rugs

New rugs from old scraps

Use fabric remnants or scraps of old clothes, preferably wool, in a variety of colors and tones—bright, dark, neutral, patterned. They should be densely woven, medium- to heavy-weight fabrics. You'll need about 1 yard of 54-inch fabric for 1 square foot of rug. You can buy remnants by the pound (¾ to 1 pound for 1 square foot of rug). In addition, you'll need sewing and lacing needles, carpet thread, braiding cones to fold the fabric strips, and a clip clothespin to hold the braid when you stop working.

Tear the fabric along the grain, lengthwise or crosswise, into strips 1¼ to 2½ inches wide (the latter for thinner fabric). To join strips into continuous lengths, put their ends at right angles and stitch on the bias.

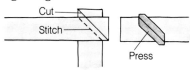

Prepare enough fabric strips for the entire rug. Coil the strips by color in 5-inch rolls until you need them.

Braiding

Insert the ends of three strips into braiding cones and slide the cones a foot or so along the strip. Make a T: join two strips with a bias seam; then attach a vertical strip inside the first two. The single fold of the horizontal strip should face up; it should face left

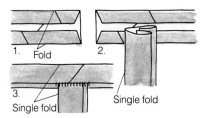

on the vertical. For better tension, sew string to the top of the T and tie the string to a table leg or other stable object. Or clamp the braid to a table or board with a metal braid holder.

Begin the braid by crossing the right-hand strip of the crossbar over the vertical strip, then the left-hand strip over the strip now in the center

(see *Braiding hair*). As you braid, twist the strips so the single-fold edges are always facing left.

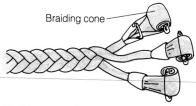

Braiding cone

Making round turns

To shape the center of a round or oval rug, it is necessary to work turns. To start a turn, bring the left strip over the center, then what is now the left strip over what is now the center. Finally, bring the right strip over the center and tighten. This will cause the braid to curve right.

Begin a round rug with a center coil of 6 to 12 round turns; then straight braid as usual. Begin an oval rug by making a straight braid equal to the difference between the rug's planned length and width. Then make 3 round turns, straight braid to the starting end, make 3 more round turns, and straight braid the rest of the rug.

Begin joining braids with a large sewing needle and carpet thread. Work on a table or another flat surface large enough to lay out the rug. Sew through the folds of the inner loops;

Sewing needle

stop just past the second turn. Then, using a blunt-edged lacing needle, begin lacing. Lace under the inside loops (not through the fabric) and out

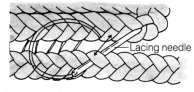

Lacing needle

the top of the braid. As you lace the turns, skip an occasional loop on the

outer braid; this prevents the rug from buckling. Pull the thread tight so that it sinks into the braid.

Skip here

When the rug is the size you want, taper each strip to a point 5 to 7 inches long, each a different length. Fold the raw edges under and stitch them; then stitch the points invisibly into matching loops.

Braising

Cooking meats and vegetables by moist heat

Braising tenderizes tough cuts of meat and helps to accentuate or blend flavors. First, brown the meat or poultry in oil, butter, or fat over medium heat. Remove from the heat and add seasonings and a liquid such as water, stock, or wine to half the depth of the food. For extra flavor, place the food on a bed of chopped vegetables before adding the liquid. Cover the pan tightly to keep moisture from escaping. Simmer the food at low heat on top of the stove or in the oven until it can be easily pierced with a fork.

Whole vegetables such as carrots, celery stalks, and onions can also be braised but do not need browning. Just dot them with butter and add enough liquid to cover the bottom of the pan ¼ to ½ inch deep.

Brake failure

Emergency stopping of a car

If the brakes in your car fail, a warning light on the dashboard should come on. Car brakes are designed so that if a failure occurs at one wheel and the pedal sinks to the floor, you should still be able to stop the car by pumping the pedal. If pumping does not work, downshift and apply the parking brake gradually.

After bringing the car to a stop, turn off the engine, open the hood, and

B

check the brake-fluid level by removing the reservoir cover (unless your reservoir is see-through plastic). You may also have to remove a rubber diaphragm. A slight loss of fluid is normal, but if the level is very low, there's a leak. Add fluid labeled *DOT3* or *4*, which may improve braking enough to let you drive to a garage. Have the brakes serviced immediately. On cars with antilock brake systems (ABS), a computer pumps the brakes if the car begins to skid. This may cause a loud thumping noise and cause the pedal to vibrate. This is normal.

Brass and copper

Cleaning tarnished metals

Most modern commercial polishes contain tarnish retardants, so they help maintain a shine as well as remove tarnish. Choose a polish designed for the metal you are cleaning. Wash the object in warm, soapy water, rinse and dry well, then polish according to the label directions. Buff or wash away all polish; any remaining traces will hasten tarnishing.

You can clean slightly tarnished metals with a homemade paste of equal parts of salt, vinegar, and flour. Rub on with a soft cloth, rinse, and buff. For stubborn stains on brass or copper, rub with salt and vinegar or lemon juice.

To keep outdoor brasses bright, apply a thin coat of paste wax after polishing; indoors, use lemon oil.

Breading

A technique for adding a crispy crust to foods

Meats, fish, vegetables, and other foods are sometimes coated with dry bread crumbs before being fried or baked. To make crumbs for breading, grind stale bread in a blender. If the bread is quite dry, crush it with a rolling pin. Bread that is not dry enough can be crisped in a low (250°F) oven or left out at room temperature. For variety, add seasonings (salt, pepper, herbs, grated cheese) to the crumbs.

If the food is moist (croquettes or chicken, for example), dredge it first in flour; if it's dry (cauliflower, for example), omit the flour. Have ready in a small bowl 1 egg beaten lightly with 1 tablespoon of water. Place the bread crumbs on a plate. Dip the food in the egg mixture, roll it in the breading material, and then refrigerate it for at least 15 minutes to make the breading adhere better.

Breadmaking

What it takes; how it's done

Few things are so tempting as the aroma of fresh-baked bread wafting from a kitchen. Here's what you'll need to produce this small miracle.

Flour: White wheat flour is the mainstay of breadmaking. Rye, buckwheat, or soybean flour or corn meal can be mixed with it for variety. Whole wheat flour can also be mixed with it or used alone. Hard winter wheat is the best flour for yeast breads, but all-purpose flour, a mixture of hard and soft wheat, is satisfactory too; the unbleached kind is preferable.

Liquid: Use water, milk or, in certain recipes, the water in which potatoes have been cooked.

Leavening: Yeast is available fresh in cakes weighing .6 ounces or 2 ounces or dry in ¼-ounce packets or 4-ounce jars. Fresh yeast keeps about 2 weeks in the refrigerator; dry yeast keeps longer and is marked with an expiration date. One packet of dry yeast equals a .6-ounce cake of yeast.

Sugar: As a rule, granulated white sugar is used, but some recipes specify brown sugar, molasses, or honey. Even nonsweet breads may call for some sugar to speed up the action of the yeast.

Salt: Improves texture and flavor.

Shortening: Use butter or vegetable shortening or oil. Shortening makes the bread tender.

Equipment: You'll need a large, deep, straight-sided mixing bowl, measuring cups and spoons, a wooden board for kneading, and 9 by 5-inch metal or glass loaf pans. An appliance with a dough hook makes the mixing easier.

Basic bread recipe
This recipe produces two large loaves of bread. Ingredients are: 6 cups of hard-wheat or all-purpose flour (unsifted); 2 cups of water (or ½ cup water and 1½ cups milk); 1 packet of dry yeast or a .6-ounce cake of fresh yeast; 2 tablespoons of granulated sugar; 2 teaspoons of salt; 2 tablespoons of melted butter or other shortening.

Start by activating the yeast by one of two methods:

Method 1 (dry or fresh yeast): Put ½ cup of warm water (105°F to 115°F) into a bowl, sprinkle dry yeast on top, add 1 tablespoon of sugar, and stir to dissolve. Let stand about 5 minutes. If you are using compressed yeast, the liquid should be no more than 95°F; let the mixture stand until it is bubbly, proving the yeast is active. Meanwhile, add salt, shortening, and the rest of the sugar to the remaining liquid; heat until the shortening dissolves; cool to lukewarm. Combine with the yeast mixture, add 4 cups of flour, and mix thoroughly.

Method 2 (dry yeast only): Stir the yeast into 4 cups of flour. Heat the liquid, together with the shortening, sugar, and salt, to 120°F to 130°F. Add the liquid mixture to the flour and yeast and combine thoroughly.

Kneading the dough
After the yeast has been activated by either method, mix in another cup of flour. Place the dough on a floured board and knead by folding the dough toward you and pushing it away with the heels of your hands. Turn the dough 90 degrees and repeat, incorporating the remaining cup of flour as you knead. Because the absorption rate of flour differs, you may have to add more flour if the dough is still sticky. Knead 8 to 10 minutes, until the dough is smooth and elastic. The kneading procedure can be completed in an appliance equipped with a dough hook.

Wash and grease the mixing bowl. Shape the dough into a ball and place it in the bowl, turning it to grease the top. Cover it. Let the dough rise in a warm, draft-free place (80°F to 85°F) until it doubles in bulk—about 1 to 1½ hours. To check that the dough is ready for the next step, press two fingertips into the dough about ½ inch

B

deep; the indentation should stay. Punch the dough down with your fist.

Divide the dough in half. Roll each half into a rectangle with a rolling pin (to remove gas bubbles); roll up the ends and pinch the edges together. Center each roll, seam side down, in a greased loaf pan. Let it rise until double in bulk. Repeat the finger test with one finger in a corner. Preheat the oven to 400°F. Place the pans in the center of the oven 2 inches apart for air circulation. Bake for 10 minutes. Lower the temperature to 350°F and bake about 20 minutes more. Remove one loaf, turn it out, and tap the bottom of the loaf. If it sounds hollow, it is done. If not, put the loaf back in the pan, return it to the oven, and bake both loaves a few minutes more. Turn the loaves out onto a rack to cool.

Breast examination

A monthly self-exam

All women should examine their breasts once a month, in the week following their period (on a regular date if you are not menstruating). Should you find any irregularity, consult your doctor. Most lumps are *not* malignant, but prompt medical attention is essential.

Standing in front of a mirror with your arms by your sides, study both breasts for any changes in their shape or size; for inversion of the nipples; and for puckering, dimpling, redness, or scaliness of the skin.

Look for the same signs with your hands clasped behind your head and then with your hands pressed down on your hips. Next, gently squeeze each nipple and check for discharge.

Raise your left arm. Using the fingers of your right hand, examine your left breast, feeling for any unusual lump or mass. Working from the outside in, follow a circular pattern. Press firmly in small, overlapping motions, covering the entire breast area from the underarm and the collarbone to the breast and the nipple. Repeat on the other side. (You may prefer to do this in the shower.)

Next, lie on your back, with a pillow under your right shoulder. Plac-

ing your right arm behind your head, examine the right breast area with the left hand, in the same manner as above. Repeat on the other side.

Breast-feeding

The natural way to feed a baby

Surprisingly, both infant and mother have to learn breast-feeding. Some babies learn right away; others need gentle encouragement and guidance during the first few days. If your skin is sensitive, consult your doctor before the baby's birth about preparing your breasts for breast-feeding.

Make sure the infant is fully awake. If the baby seems sleepy, uncover and massage the baby's hands or feet or rub the baby's back. Eliminate distractions so that you can relax and concentrate fully on the baby. Cradle the baby in your arm, and support this arm with a pillow until the baby is big enough to sit in your lap. Make sure that the baby takes the nipple and as much as possible of the areola (the dark skin surrounding the nipple) into his or her mouth.

Build up the length of feedings gradually. On the first day feed the baby for only 2 to 3 minutes on each breast at each feeding. From the second day on, add a minute or so at each feeding. Burp a young infant every 4 to 5 minutes (see *Baby burping*). A typical infant feeds approximately every 3 hours, getting most of the milk in 10 to 15 minutes per breast. An infant should not be on the breast for more than an hour.

Once a day wash your breasts with plain water—not soap. Get plenty of sleep. Eat a well-balanced diet with ample protein, fruits, vegetables, and liquids. Stop eating any food that appears to cause colic. Some babies become colicky when the mother eats

certain foods, such as chocolate, garlic, onions, cabbage, and tomatoes.

Alcohol, smoking, and drugs affect breast milk. Reduce your alcohol consumption and smoking to a minimum, preferrably to zero. Consult your doctor before taking medication.

Breaststroke

A restful stroke for distance and turbulent waters

Start in a facedown position, arms and legs fully extended. Drop your palms down and pull your arms out-

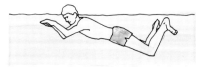

ward and down toward your feet. As your arms move, exhale, bend your elbows outward and drop your wrists

below your elbows. When your hands reach a position slightly forward of your shoulders, bring your hands together in front of your face. At the same time, raise your head slightly and inhale. Your chin should stay in the water.

Lower your head as you kick: rotate your feet outward, bend your knees and, pushing with the bottoms of

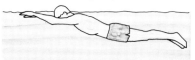

your feet, move your legs in a circular motion. End with your legs fully extended and your feet together, giving your body a forward glide as your arms move forward for the next stroke. Pull, breathe, kick, glide.

Brickwork

Repointing brick surfaces; replacing broken bricks

The mortar holding bricks together can deteriorate over many years or after severe weathering. Repointing is the procedure for restoring cracked or loose brickwork to new strength.

In repointing, you remove cracked and crumbling mortar and fill the joint with fresh mortar. Although the process is not difficult, you should evaluate the job carefully. It's easy to repair small areas, even on a chimney, if they are near the ground. But if your task requires scaffolding and major rebuilding of brick facing, call in a professional mason. Similarly, if your chimney lacks a liner or has holes, large gaps, or smoke coming from anywhere but the top, you should turn to a mason. (See also *Chimneys and flues.*)

Caution: When working with mortar, wear safety goggles and protective clothing, including gloves. Mortar is caustic. If it gets on your skin, wash it off immediately.

Repointing walls and chimneys

Run the edge of an old paint scraper over the joints to remove loose and weakened mortar. Then, with a small cold chisel and a hammer, tap out loose mortar in each joint to a depth of ½ to 1 inch. Brush the joints clean with a wire brush, working the brush firmly. Allow solid mortar to remain, and try not to dislodge any bricks.

Dry-mix mortar is sold in bags at hardware stores and home centers. Pour some dry mix into a bucket, add a little water, and stir thoroughly with a hoe or shovel. Add water until the mix is the consistency of soft ice cream. If it is too thin, add more dry mix. (See also *Mortar mixing.*)

Work the bricks from the bottom row up. Start by brushing water into the joints to prevent the mortar from being weakened by the leaching out of its water. Next, scoop some mortar onto a trowel, hold the trowel up to the joint, and push the mortar into the joint with a tuck pointer (a trowel with a long narrow blade). After filling each joint, smooth the mortar with a sideward motion of the tuck pointer.

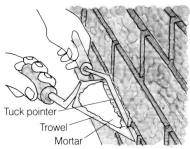

Tuck pointer
Trowel
Mortar

Stir the mortar in the bucket now and then to keep it pliable, and continue working up the rows of bricks. If the mortar on your trowel gets stiff, discard it for new mortar.

When the mortar is firm enough to hold an impression of your thumb, give the joint the same finish as the rest of the brickwork: weathered, concave, V-shaped, or smooth (flush with the surface). Use the edge of the trowel to make a weathered joint. To make a concave joint, press the rounded end

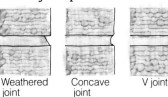

Weathered joint   Concave joint   V joint

of a brick jointer or a bent metal rod into the mortar and draw it along the center. Use the opposite end of the

Brick jointer

brick jointer to make a *V joint.*

If the mortar has left a gray stain on the bricks, wipe it off with a wire brush and water, being careful to avoid the new soft joints. If the stain still shows after the bricks are dry, remove it with a solution of 1 part muriatic acid to 20 parts water. Afterwards hose the surface carefully with a fine spray of water to rinse it.

Replacing a brick

To replace a broken brick, chisel out the mortar and remove the brick with a wide-blade cold chisel, breaking the brick into smaller pieces if necessary. Clean and brush away all remnants of mortar and dust and then brush the cavity walls with water.

Spread mortar over the surfaces of the cavity and butter the top, bottom, sides, and back of the replacement brick with mortar. Force the brick

into the cavity as far as you can, then tap it the rest of the way in with the handle of the trowel. Point the joint and clean off the excess mortar.

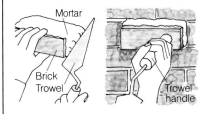

Mortar
Brick
Trowel
Trowel handle

Brick floors

A mortared brick floor can be treated in the same way as brick walls and chimneys. However, if it has large cracks or buckled areas, the foundation beneath may be disrupted, and the whole floor may have to be rebuilt. Call in a mason. For information on brick floors that are laid in sand or stone dust, see *Patio building.*

Broiling

Successful dry-heat cooking

Broiling is a way of cooking steaks, chops, fish, poultry, and certain vegetables by high heat under a gas flame or an electric element (see also *Barbecuing*). Broilers vary greatly with the age and type of oven and fuel, so read and follow the manufacturer's instructions for your broiler. As a general rule, use a gas broiler with the oven door closed, an eleectric model with the door slightly ajar.

Adjust the oven shelves so that the top surface of the food will be 3 inches from the heat source. Meats more than 2 inches thick should be broiled farther from the heat source.

Have the food at room temperature. Preheat the broiler. Oil the rack to prevent sticking. Trim most of the fat from meats to be broiled and slash the remainder at 1-inch intervals. Red meat, if well marbled with fat throughout, needs no further preparation. Tougher meat benefits from marinating 1 to 3 hours. Use tongs rather than a fork to turn the food halfway through the cooking time.

Split a chicken lengthwise and arrange the halves skin side down on the broiler rack. Broil chicken 5 inches from the heat source 15 to 20 minutes per side. Baste during broiling to keep chicken moist and juicy.

Vegetables such as tomato halves, mushroom caps, and thick slices of zucchini can be broiled with meats. Brush them with oil and add them toward the end of the cooking time.

GUIDE TO COOKING TIMES

Broil a porterhouse or sirloin steak the following times:

Steak	Rare	Medium	Well done
1″	6–8	10–12	14–18
1½″	12–14	16–18	20–24
2″	16–18	18–22	30–36

Broil 1-inch-thick lamb chops 8 to 10 minutes for medium rare and 12 to 14 minutes for well done.

To check meat for doneness, remove it just before the end of the minimum broiling time and make an incision. If you inserted a meat thermometer before broiling, it should read 135°F to 140°F for rare; 145°F to 160°F for medium; more than 165°F for well done. Chicken is done if the juice runs clear when you pierce a thigh with a fork.

Broken bones

What to do—and not do—to help a person with broken limbs

More than a few minutes' pain at the site of an injury after a fall or a blow may indicate a broken bone. Unless the normal contour of a limb is visibly distorted or a fragment of bone pokes through the skin, an X ray is the only way to be sure. Until one can be made, use caution; hurrying a person back into action may cause more damage than the fracture itself. Broken bones can pierce arteries, sever nerves, or injure internal organs. To prevent such damage, immobilize the area of a suspected fracture with simple splints, slings, or bindings.

In the case of a leg injury, place towels, a folded blanket, or other padding between the legs. Use neckties, torn strips of cloth, belts, and the like to bind the injured leg snugly to the uninjured one at several points above and below the painful area.

The same technique of immobilization and soft splinting is appropriate

for a suspected "broken hip"—actually a fracture of the upper end of the thigh bone. A hip fracture is indicated if one leg appears shorter than the other and one foot is rotated outward.

If an ankle or a foot seems broken, remove the person's shoes and hose. Tie a pillow around the injured ankle and foot, and keep the leg raised.

Splint an injured arm or wrist with a folded newspaper or magazine and secure it with handkerchiefs or other available bindings above and below the injury. Support the arm with a sling and bind the sling around the chest. If an elbow is hurt, don't attempt to bend or straighten it. Immobilize a straight elbow with a splint of folded newpaper or a magazine; immobilize a bent elbow with a sling bound to the chest. (A sling and bind-

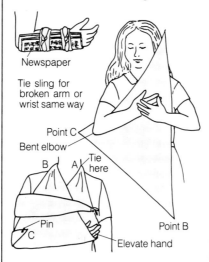

Newspaper

Tie sling for broken arm or wrist same way

Point C
Bent elbow
B   A   Tie here
Pin
C
Point B
Elevate hand

ing will also relieve pain from a broken collarbone or shoulder.) For broken bones of the hand, immobilize the hand and keep it raised until you get medical help.

Bone fractures are usually followed quickly by swelling, so that what began as a snug binding soon becomes tight, cutting off circulation or causing other damage. Every few minutes check the bindings and loosen them if necessary. To relieve swelling, apply ice in a bag or wrapped in thick cloths, but not directly on the injured area.

Be alert to the possibility of shock. Until professional help arrives, keep the person in a resting position, with the head lower than the rest of body (except in cases of suspected head,

neck, or back injuries). Keep the person warm, sheltered, and reassured. (See also *Bleeding; Head and spine injuries; Shock.*)

Budgeting

Taking control of your money

A budget is a guide to help you meet current expenses and put money aside for short- and long-term goals. Whatever your goals—a new car next year, a new house in 5 years, your child's college education 15 years hence—your budget should be structured so that you can achieve your goals within the available time.

Once your goals are set, select a budget period—a time frame for recording and then reviewing actual expenditures against predictions. Most people do this weekly or monthly, but your personal situation may make some other time span convenient.

Estimating your income

First, add up all sources of income, starting with your regular salary (or combined salaries in the case of a couple who both work). Include only what remains of your paycheck after all payroll deductions—taxes, Social Security, union dues, pension or insurance plans, and so on.

Next, add up all other amounts you customarily receive, such as savings account interest, stock dividends, and rents. Include bonuses, commissions, tips, cash gifts from relatives, and income tax refunds only if you are sure of them. In estimating these items, use the minimum you expect to receive. If you are self-employed or work part-time or seasonally, base your estimate on the previous year, even though you expect to earn more. Add up the year's projected annual income, and then divide by the number of budget periods in a year to get a figure for periodic analysis.

Projecting your expenses

There are three broad categories.

1. *Fixed costs.* You must meet these expenses on a monthly, quarterly, semiannual, or annual basis. They are not within your control—that is, you cannot reduce them unless you make a major change in your situa-

tion. They include rent, mortgage, or other housing payments; utility bills (for heat, gas, electricity, telephone,); installment loan payments; tuition; taxes and insurance premiums (other than payroll deductions).

2. *Savings*: Base the amount you set aside during each budget period on the goals you hope to achieve. The first goal of every self-supporting adult or couple should be a nest egg for emergencies. How much you need depends on what other protection such as unemployment compensation or insurance coverage is available in case you lose your job or have health problems. The equivalent of 2 months' income usually suffices.

3. *Variable expenses*. The most flexible of your outlays, these include daily living costs—food and household supplies; transportation (including automobile maintenance and commuting costs); medical care not covered by insurance; household repairs and improvements; clothing; vacations; entertainment; gifts; charitable contributions. Some of the expenses in this category may take the form of a personal allowance, or pocket money, for each family member. You also should set aside an amount for unpredictable expenses, such as repair or replacement of appliances. If last year's records are inadequate for making an estimate, keep track of your spending for a few months to get a more realistic picture.

Adjusting expenditures

After you have made both projections, subtract expenses from income. If you have money left over, you can add it to your savings allocation. If expenses exceed income, review your spending to see what you can cut. Keep in mind that some costs are higher in certain periods than in others and may balance out over the long run. You may decide that some current expense is important enough to delay reaching one of your long-term goals. In trimming your budget, don't make unrealistic cuts that you won't be able to live with; they will ultimately sabotage your plan. Once you have established a workable budget, review it quarterly, annually, or whenever your financial circumstances change. (See also *Net worth*.)

Building permits

When you need one; how to apply; what it is and does

Before building, remodeling, or making an addition to your house, early in the planning stage visit the building inspector in your municipality. He will advise you as to the requirements and standards of the local building code. Because procedures vary widely from one municipality to another, you should telephone first to find out what to bring. You may need a survey of your lot and copies of your plans, especially if it is a large project.

The building inspector can tell you whether your plan varies from zoning regulations—for example, bringing the building too close to the lot line—or creates a nonconforming use—a professional office in a residential neighborhood, for instance. In that case, you'll need a variance approved by a board of adjustment or appeals.

When your plans are more complete, the building inspector will examine them. He may ask for changes to comply with the local building code. These changes might involve the materials or the methods you are using. When he issues a permit, construction can begin. You will have to pay a fee, typically 2 to 8 percent of the project's estimated cost.

Inspections during construction

For your fee you will get something: routine inspections that assure you of a safe and reliable home. At certain stages of construction, the building inspector or a deputy visits the site and makes inspections. The foundation is inspected when all forms and reinforcing steel are in place but before concrete has been poured. Sewage connections are seen before their trenches are filled.

Framing is inspected when the shell, siding, and roofing are in place. Electric and plumbing lines must be seen and sometimes tested before plasterboard or wall surfaces cover them. A final inspection is usually required when all is complete. The building inspector then issues a certificate of occupancy (CO), allowing you to move in.

Bulb forcing

Indoor blooms to brighten winter days

Bulb forcing is the technique of inducing spring-flowering bulbs such as crocuses, narcissi, hyacinths, and tulips, to bloom ahead of time.

Purchase the bulbs in fall, preferably varieties designated for forcing. Plant them in pots or other containers that have a drainage hole in the bottom. Use a porous potting mix; packaged bulb fiber (pulverized charcoal and oyster shell with peat); or equal parts of garden soil, compost or peat moss, and sand or perlite.

Cover the drainage hole with pieces of crock or shell, partially fill the container with gently packed soil, and place the bulbs on the soil so that they are not touching. Pour more soil around them. The tips of large bulbs should protrude and be ½ inch above the pot rim. Small bulbs should be covered. Water well.

Store the planted bulbs in the dark where it is cool (40°to 50°F) but not below freezing; a cellar or unheated garage is convenient. Keep the soil moist. Alternatively, bury the pots outdoors in a trench, with the rims of the pots 6 inches below the ground surface. Cover the trench with salt hay, perlite, or other mulch. This artificial winter should last 12 weeks for hyacinths, crocuses, and daffodils, 16 weeks for tulips.

When shoots of 1 to 2 inches appear, bring the pots into a cool (50°F) room and indirect light for 2 weeks. When the growth is 4 to 6 inches, move the pots to a warm (65°F), sunny spot. Continue to water. Once the buds show color, prolong the flowering by returning the pots to indirect light and by keeping them in a cool room at night.

Once forced, bulbs will bloom again only if planted outdoors. Continue watering until the foliage turns yellow. Then withhold water, and when the soil is dry, remove and clean the bulbs. Store them in a dry place, and plant them in the ground in early fall. It may take two seasons before they bloom again.

Bulbs, corms, and tubers

Planting and caring for these satisfying flower producers

Spring crocuses, narcissi, tulips, and other bulbs make a welcome show of color when the landscape is still drab Equally worth knowing are summer-flowering types such as gladioli, lilies, dahlias, and giant allium, and fall bulbs such as colchicums and *Amaryllis belladonna*. Botanically, this group of plants is divided into true bulbs (tulips, for example), corms (gladioli), and tubers (dahlias), but the common term for all is bulbs.

Most bulbs look their best in small clumps or in drifts or masses, one color to an area. Plant them in borders or in front of evergreens. Some kinds look well planted in lawns or meadows (called naturalizing). Large-flowered bulbs such as trumpet lilies and giant allium are best as accents.

Buy the largest bulbs you can afford; large bulbs mean more and larger flowers. Bulbs should be free of cuts and soft spots. Plant spring-flowering bulbs early in the fall so that the roots can grow before the soil freezes. To prevent rot, plant them where drainage is good. Prepare a new bed by turning the soil spade-deep and adding peat moss or compost, organic fertilizer, and (if the soil is clayey) sand to promote drainage.

In beds where the soil has been made ready, arrange the bulbs on top of the soil in the pattern you prefer. Dig holes to the depth indicated in the chart, using a trowel, bulb planter, or blunt dibble for a small quantity of bulbs. (A bulb planter lifts out a plug of soil.) Add a sprinkling of bonemeal and the bulb; fill the hole. To plant clumps, dig a wide hole to the required depth. Sprinkle in bonemeal, arrange the bulbs four to six per hole, and cover with earth.

To plant individual bulbs in a lawn without disturbing the turf, make a cut with a spade or a mattock. Lean the blade back and forth to create an opening. Put in bonemeal and the bulb, withdraw the tool, and close the cut with your foot. Plant clumps by cutting an H in the sod with a spade.

Fold the sod back, remove soil to the required depth, insert bonemeal and the bulbs, and cover them with soil and sod.

Spade

Hole for bulb

As soon as the leaves emerge, apply bulb fertilizer. Continue feeding the plants monthly until the foliage dies back. Water them in dry spells. Spring bulb foliage must be allowed to die off in place after flowering, but annuals set out later can obscure the browning foliage.

In cold areas the bulbs, corms, and tubers of tender plants (anemones, caladiums, cannas, dahlias, gladioli) must be dug, brushed clean, and stored for the winter in a cool, dry location. Replant them in the spring when the soil has warmed.

PLANTING GUIDE

Plant name	Hole depth	Blooming season
Aconite	1″	summer
Allium	*	summer
Amaryllis	6″	fall
Anemone	2–3″	spring-summer
Begonia, tuberous	1–2″	summer
Caladium	2″	spring-fall
Canna	3–4″	summer-fall
Colchicum	3–4″	fall
Crocus	3″	spring or fall
Cyclamen	1–2″	winter-spring
Dahlia	3″	summer
Gladiolus	4–6″	summer
Glory-of-the-sun	2–3″	spring
Hyacinth	5–6″	spring
Lily (Lilium)	3–4″	summer
Narcissus	6″	spring
Ranunculus	2″	spring-summer
Snowdrop	3–4″	spring
Tulip	6–8″	spring

*3 times bulb depth.

Bunions

Coping with a painful foot problem

Bunions are bony enlargements of the big-toe joint caused usually by an inherited defect. Wearing ill-fitting shoes, especially those with high heels and pointed toes, makes the condition more painful. Bunions can lead to a form of bursitis, an inflammation resulting from a shoe's persistent pressure on the joint.

Bunions can be removed surgically, but this is not always necessary. The pressure can be relieved by wearing a corrective device prescribed by a physician or a podiatrist or by applying a bunion pad—adhesive cushioning with a hole in the center. Acute pain may be alleviated by wearing an old, comfortable shoe with the leather cut away over the pressure point. People with chronic health problems such as poor circulation or diabetes should seek medical help if the pain persists. (See also *Bursitis*).

Burglar alarms

Systems and sensors to warn you and scare off intruders

Although burglar-alarm systems are not infallible (all of them are subject to giving false alarms), they help deter burglars and warn you or your neighbors in the event that someone does break into your home. You can pay thousands of dollars for a professionally installed burglar-alarm system, but you're paying mainly for labor. If you're handy, you can install your own, equally effective, system for anywhere from a few hundred dollars for a small apartment to around a thousand for a rambling residence.

There are two basic choices in do-it-yourself installations: a perimeter system or a motion-detector system. A perimeter system sounds an alarm when someone opens a door or window. A motion detector sounds an alarm when sensors inside the house detect motion. The most effective system often combines two basic types:

magnetic sensors on all the entry doors and motion-detecting sensors in all crucial spaces.

Estimate your needs by drawing a floor plan, showing windows and doors for each room. Buy the components at an electronics store or directly from the manufacturer.

The basic equipment

Both types of alarm systems consist of sensors connected to a control box, a remote-control key switch to turn the system on and off, and a bell, siren, or other warning device. Instead of a key switch, you can install a digital keypad that allows you to periodically change the combination that unlocks the system. Whether you get a switch or keypad, be sure that it has delayed action to allow you to get through the door without sounding an alarm.

Both systems use 12-volt wiring and a transformer to convert 110–120-volt current to 12 volts. Some systems have rechargeable backup batteries to guard against blackouts.

Perimeter sensors detect intrusion instantly, but they require a lot of wiring since every vulnerable entry must have a sensor. This could be an esthetic or safety problem, unless you can hide the wires under moldings or snake them through the walls. Sensors that detect motion require less wiring, but they sound the alarm only when an intruder prowls into a monitored indoor space.

Mount the control box in a closet and rig the key switch or keypad near the entrance so that when you enter, you can quickly disarm the system. Install a panic button in the bedroom so that you can sound the alarm if you detect a prowler at night. Mount the bell or siren on the outside of the house at least 10 feet above the ground.

Perimeter systems

A simple perimeter system can be bought in kit form, with a control box, a bell or siren, magnetic sensors, a remote key switch, and wiring. The kit can be expanded by adding panic buttons and more sensors.

Magnetic sensors are made up of a magnet and a switch. Install the magnet on a closed door or window and the switch on the frame. If possible, recess them in the wood so that they cannot be seen from the outside.

Following the manufacturer's instructions, wire the sensor switch to the control box. When the door or window is closed, the magnet and switch will be close enough to each other to form an electric circuit. When the system is armed, if the window or door is opened, the magnetic field will be broken and the alarm will sound. Each detector needs a shunt switch to disconnect it when you want to open the door or window without shutting off the entire system.

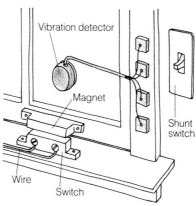

To guard against window breaking, install aluminum-foil-strip or vibration detectors on the glass panes.

Motion-detector systems

The sensors in a motion-detector system might be electric eye (with infrared beam), ultrasonic (with inaudible sound waves), or passive infrared (body-heat sensitive). Install an electric eye and its reflector across a doorway or corridor a few feet from the ground. Mount other sensors in the corners of rooms near the ceiling, aimed at crucial traffic areas.

You can install pressure-sensitive mats under rugs by doors and valuable items. When stepped on, these mats will sound the alarm.

Burglarproofing

Taking precautions to keep your home safe from burglars

A dog is a good guard because its bark alerts you to the approach of intruders. But if you're not home, a burglar may get his work done anyway. Stronger precautions are needed to keep your property safe.

Talk with the police and learn the methods most commonly used by burglars in your area. Pretend you are a burglar and examine your home for weak points. Then fortify them. For example, can a window-mounted air conditioner be stolen easily or pushed in to gain entrance? Install it more securely. Consider what you own that may attract burglars and make those possessions less conspicuous.

How burglars work

Burglars often cruise in pairs. Upon seeing an empty garage or a car pulling out of a driveway, they ring the doorbell. If someone answers, they ask an innocent question and leave. If there is no response, they try to enter the house in the quickest way.

The most common means of access is an unlocked door. If doors are secured with simple locks, burglars can break the locks or use force until the screws burst out of the wood or the frame gives way. Or they can break a cellar window.

Preventing entry

If you have any hollow wooden doors or flimsy door frames leading to the outside or to the garage, replace them with solid wooden or steel doors and firm frames. Install 180° peepholes and stout dead-bolt locks in the outside doors and mount attractive grillwork over all of your lower windows. Trim shrubbery to eliminate hiding places. For added protection, install outdoor floodlights, a fence and gate, and electronic alarm systems. (See *Burglar alarms; Door locks; Peepholes; Window-locking devices.*)

Don't put your name on the mailbox. Burglars will phone to determine if you're home. If they get the answering machine, they know too much.

Getting help

Neighborhood watch programs work well. Encourage neighborly cooperation. Post signs warning strangers that they are being observed.

Before leaving town, arrange to have your home look occupied. Ask a friend or relative to come by daily, but at different times, to park a car in the driveway, put out the garbage on pickup days, take in the mail and newspapers, shovel the snow or mow the grass, and alter the draperies and automatic light-timers.

B

The low-profile approach
Avoid attracting attention. Some of it may prove unwelcome. If a new stereo or home computer arrives, don't put the labeled carton in the trash without flattening it inside out. On the other hand, it is wise to etch your Social Security number on your valuables.

Don't keep cash around; travelers' checks are safer. If you hide valuables, keep a map of their locations in a safe deposit box or with an attorney. Burglars know where people generally keep valuables, and they will look in those places first. In picking places to hide valuables, remember that the kitchen is most often used and that toilet tanks are favorite spots. Leave some money and less-expensive valuables in the open and hope a burglar will overlook the gem collection in the bottom of the goldfish tank. (See also *Apartment security; Bicycle locks; Boat security; Car security.*)

Burns

Treating burns from heat, fire, chemicals, and electricity

The first thing to do for any burn caused by heat or by chemicals is to immerse the burned body parts in cold water or pour cold water over the affected areas. (Don't use ice water; it can cause shock.) Don't waste time removing clothing; a prompt soaking will reduce the effect of a burn and will dilute chemicals.

Next, if the burn is severe, get the person to an emergency room or other medical help. Call for an ambulance to transport the person if more than 10 percent of the body is burned; anticipate shock if more than 15 percent is burned (see *Shock*). Each arm or the head represents 9 percent; the torso, front or back, and each leg represents 18 percent. Facial burns should always be seen by a doctor. Place the victim in a sitting position to alleviate breathing difficulties.

Burns from heat or fire
Soak burns from heat or fire with cold water until the pain subsides. If clothing is charred and the fabric sticks, don't try to pull it off; just cut away loose portions. Remove jewelry, even

from unburned areas, because swelling usually develops. Elevate burned arms and legs above the heart. Don't apply ointments, antiseptics, or bandages. If the person must be wrapped while being transported to an emergency room, use sterile bandages if available; otherwise use a clean sheet.

If hands and feet are burned, put sterile gauze between burned toes and fingers. Keep the victim warm. Unless he or she is unconscious or vomiting, give sips of a solution of 1 teaspoon of salt and ½ teaspoon of baking soda per quart of warm water.

Minor burns, such as those from a hot iron or spattering fat, usually don't require a doctor's care. Flood the burn with cold water until the pain stops. Apply a dry, sterile gauze pad for protection. Don't break blisters. (See also *Sunburn.*)

Chemical burns
Flush chemical burns with water for at least 10 minutes before stopping to call for help. During that time remove any clothing the chemical spilled on, but don't stop rinsing. While help is on the way, continue to flush the burned area for another half hour.

Chemicals in the eye should be flushed for 15 minutes with water poured from a glass or other container before getting the person medical help. For best results, lean the person's head back over a tub or sink or have the victim lie on the floor. Spread the eyelids with your thumb and finger to hold the eye open as you pour.

Electric burns
First, remove the source of electricity: disconnect the power and don't touch a hot wire, appliance, or a person who's been burned until you're sure the power is off. If a hot wire is touching a person and you can't turn off the power, remove the wire with a dry rope or wooden pole; otherwise, you too may become a victim.

Electric burns can be much more serious than the surface of the skin may indicate. They are often accompanied by heart and breathing failures. If the victim is unconscious, begin cardiopulminary resuscitation and continue until heartbeat and breathing are normal (see *CPR*). Watch for signs of shock. Get medical attention as soon as possible.

Bursitis

The causes of bursitis; relieving pain and swelling

Bursitis is traceable to inflammation of the bursas, small sacs of liquid that lie between skin and bones or bones and tendons. The bursas can become inflamed as a result of a blow, constant pressure, or improper movement. The most frequent sites of bursitis are the shoulder, elbow (tennis elbow), hip, knee (housemaid's knee), and big toe (bunions; see *Bunions*).

A bursitis attack usually subsides within 2 weeks. Pain can be reduced by immobilizing the affected area, applying cold compresses, and taking aspirin or another analgesic. Medical treatment in prolonged cases involves drugs for the inflammation or drawing out the excess liquid in the bursas.

Bursitis may become chronic if the affected area cannot be protected from irritation. The bursas can be removed by minor surgery in such a case.

Business letters

Writing clear, correct, effective correspondence

Although the style, content, and form of business letters is important, a letter's effectiveness depends most of all upon the words you use to carry your message. Keep them clear, simple, and direct. Strive for a courteous, friendly tone, proper but not stiffly formal.

Salutation and closing
Use names when you know them. If you don't know a person's name—if you're writing to an unknown committee chairman, say—use *Dear Sir* or *Dear Madam.* If both the name and gender are unknown, use *Dear Sir or Madam* (or the reverse). If the name but not the gender is known, use the full name, *Dear Gerry Dean, Dear P.J. Reed.* Salute an all-male group as *Gentlemen;* an all-female one as *Ladies;* a mixed group as *Ladies and Gentlemen* (or vice versa). If you don't know which courtesy title a woman prefers (Miss, Mrs., Ms.), use *Ms.* or her full name (*Dear Ann Kent*).

The complimentary close can be formal, *Yours very truly, Respectfully yours;* personal, *Sincerely yours, Cordially yours;* or quite informal, *Best wishes, See you Tuesday!*

Format

Surround the letter with balanced, ample margins. Don't cram it all onto a single sheet; use a second sheet even for a final paragraph. Follow the format shown here.

Mr. Luke Reiter
116 W. 43 Rd.
Stephentown, NY 12169

April 28, 1986

Ms. H. Zwack
Sykes Building
Sykes Circle
Madden Corners, NY 12168

Dear Ms. Zwack:

I have reviewed the proposed agreement that you sent me. In general, the terms look good, although I feel a few specifics still need to be ironed out.

Is it possible to arrange a meeting with all the participants in your office sometime late next week? Please get back to me about this soon.

Sincerely,

Luke Reiter

Buttermaking

A kitchen project to try

You can make small amounts of butter by beating cream in a bowl or shaking it in a bottle. But good-quality butter in quantity calls for a churn. Churns come with hand cranks or electric motors and can be ordered from mail-order firms or from country-supply stores. It's worth buying one only if you have a plentiful and inexpensive supply of cream.

Warm the cream to about 60°F to reduce churning time. Butter forms more quickly at an even higher temperature, but it will be soft and will keep poorly. If you are churning by hand, crank fast until the cream gets heavy, then crank more slowly in order not to break up the butter when it forms. With an electric churn, watch carefully and stop the churn as soon as a large lump forms. Strain the butter through a fine sieve. The buttermilk residue is excellent for cooking and is highly nutritious, retaining all the water-soluble vitamins.

Place the butter in a bowl of very cold water. With a wooden spatula or spoon, press and stir the butter until the water turns cloudy. Pour off the water and repeat the process until the water remains clear. Pour off the final water, and work the butter with a spoon or spatula to press out as much more water as possible. Turn the butter onto a wooden board and, using the spatula or "butter hands," press out any remaining water.

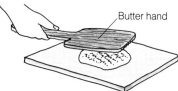

Butter hand

Add salt to taste and work it in. Then shape the butter into decorative pats with two butter hands. Butter will keep several weeks refrigerated, several months frozen.

Buttonholes

Stitching buttonholes by hand or machine

To bind a buttonhole by hand, first stitch around the marked line for the buttonhole by machine or with short

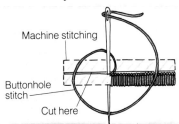

Machine stitching

Buttonhole stitch

Cut here

running stitches. Cut the center and bind the cut edges with buttonhole stitches. One end of a horizontal buttonhole is usually bar tacked (long stitches across the width, then blanket stitches across those). At the end where the button will rest, stitches are fanned. Both ends of vertical buttonholes are finished the same, either bar tacked or fanned.

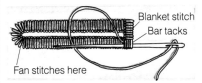

Blanket stitch
Bar tacks
Fan stitches here

You can make buttonholes on your machine using a zigzag stitch, a built-in buttonhole stitch, or a buttonhole attachment, depending on your machine. Stitch along both sides of the marked line, finishing both ends with bar tacks (close zigzag stitches spanning the full buttonhole width). Cut along the marked line, taking care not to cut the stitching.

Buttons

Sewing on a button securely

Thread a needle with a 20-inch strand of thread (heavy-duty thread for coat buttons, finer thread for smaller buttons). Knot the ends of the strand together. Insert the needle in the right side of the garment and pull the thread tight. With the button over the knot, take a stitch from the wrong side up through the fabric and a hole in the button. Then go back down to the wrong side again through an adjacent hole. Place a large needle, as shown, to allow for slack in the stitches for the shank. Make 6 to 10 stitches through each pair of holes. Remove the needle, pull the button away from the fabric and wind the thread around the shank. Secure the thread by passing it through a self-loop.

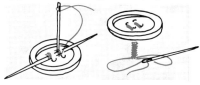

Cabinet building

Construction and installation

A cabinet of pine shelving is sturdy and easily built with nailed and glued butt joints. But its size is limited to the shelving widths. A plywood cabinet has the bottom grooved into the sides, and rabbets must be cut on all four pieces for the back. Exposed plywood edges must be covered with veneer tape. Although a plywood cabinet is more work and requires power tools, it's less limited in size.

In both pine and plywood cabinets, the shelves should fit into ¼-inch grooves in the sides. Corners need reinforcing with triangular blocks cut from 1 x 2-inch pine.

On graph paper draw all details of your cabinet and the location where it

List each part, rechecking the measurements as you do so. Take your list to a lumberyard or home center. If you are using pine, select clean, flat, straight boards. If plywood is your choice, examine the corners and faces of each panel for damage. Purchase finishing nails or screws, wood glue, sandpaper, door hinges and, if needed, drawer glides and veneer tape.

Some lumberyards cut wood to size for a small charge. If you do your own cutting, measure twice and draw your

the top, bottom, sides, and shelves. Then glue the back in place.

In a plywood cabinet, apply glue, and clamp the parts. Wipe off excess glue with a wet rag. Check the cabinet for squareness by measuring diagonally from corner to corner; if the two diagonals are alike, the cabinet is square. If not, adjust the clamps. Let the glue dry overnight.

If the cabinet has a drawer, support it with wooden runners or metal drawer glides. Although more expen-

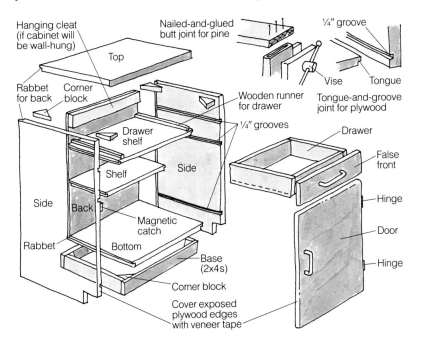

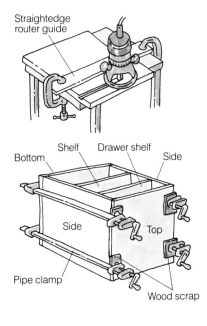

will be installed. Make sure the door and drawer will not obstruct doorways when open. If the cabinet is to stand against a wall with molding, its base of 2 x 4s should be offset at the back to allow for the molding. In the front, set the base in 2 inches to allow for toe space. If the cabinet will hang on a wall, provide built-in cleats.

Materials
Keep in mind that pine shelving, nominally 1 inch thick, is actually ⅝ inch, and the nominal widths of 8, 10, and 12 inches are, respectively, 7½, 9½, and 11¼ inches.

Plywood comes in 4 x 8-foot panels. Use ¾-inch cabinet-grade birch plywood for the top, sides, bottom, shelves, partitions, and doors, and ¼-inch plywood for drawer bottoms and cabinet backs.

cutting lines with a try, combination, or framing square. Saw the wood and check each cut for squareness (see *Bookcase building*). Plane any edges that are not square. Sand each edge lightly. Mark lines for the tongues, grooves, and rabbets; cut them with a table saw or a circular saw or router guided by a clamped straightedge.

When you have all the parts and joints cut, lay them on a level surface. Label each part in pencil and indicate its orientation with an arrow. Try the parts to make sure they fit, holding them with pipe clamps (tape wood scraps to the clamp jaws to protect wood surfaces). This is a rehearsal for the actual gluing.

Gluing the parts
This is the order of gluing: with the parts resting on their front edges, join

sive than runners, metal glides give the drawer a smoother ride. Install the door (see *Hinges*). Make sure you like the finish you've chosen by testing it on a wood scrap.

To mount the cabinet on a wall, find the studs, use a level to mark, and fasten the cabinet into the studs (see *Leveling; Studs; Wall fasteners*).

Gluing and finishing a pine cabinet
If your cabinet is pine, tap nails partway in between the joint lines, then spread wood glue on the edges to be joined. Hammer the nails in, leaving the heads protruding ⅛ inch. Set the nail heads with a nail set. Check for squareness; if necessary, move parts by tapping them with a rubber mallet to make them square. Putty the nail holes. Sand, first with medium, then fine sandpaper. Paint or stain.

Cacti

Bringing the desert indoors

Most cacti are desert plants with sharp spines for leaves and thick stems that store water. They make fine houseplants for people who can't manage a regular watering schedule.

A cactus needs sun, warmth, and dryness. Turn the plant often so that it grows straight. In the spring and summer growing seasons, water only when the soil becomes bone-dry. During winter, when the plant is dormant, keep it cool (40°F to 50°F) and water it even less often. Overwatering causes rot.

Pot a cactus in 1 part coarse sand or perlite and 2 parts peat or potting mix. Repot annually if the roots fill the pot. Wrap newspaper around the cactus so you can handle it. Feed it lightly, if at all, during the growing season with a high-potassium fertilizer.

Jungle species such as Christmas and Easter cacti, unlike the desert varieties, need a humid and shady spot.

Cactus gardens

Desert plants in your garden

Desert cacti grow best in the warm, dry conditions of the Southwest, but some *opuntias* (prickly pears) succeed well into the north and in higher humidity. Certain cacti such as *lobivia*, *rebutia*, and night-flowering cereuses produce magnificent blooms.

Desert cacti need full sun and well-drained soil. An ideal soil is two parts each of fertile topsoil and sand, one part each of perlite and peat moss or leaf mold, plus a generous sprinkling of bonemeal. The best sand is sharp sand; builder's sand is suitable if it feels decidedly gritty to the fingers.

Water a cactus garden only when the soil is dry, but then do it thoroughly. Fertilization is unnecessary.

Never dig cacti from wild areas; in most states it is illegal, and such specimens are less likely to survive than nursery plants. You can grow cacti from cuttings, seeds, offsets, and divisions (see *Propagating plants*).

Cake decorating

Enhancing a cake with homemade decorations

Some cakes need only a dusting of confectioners sugar or a thin glaze of icing. Others call for the grand treatment: a frosting that compliments the cake's flavor and texture (see *Frostings*) and decorations that make the cake an occasion.

Simple, natural embellishments can be charming. Place fresh flowers, stemmed or stemless, on the cake's top or arrange them in a small tumbler in the hole of a cake baked in a tube pan. Fresh or preserved fruits make easy, delicious decorations.

To add flavor and cover flaws in a frosting or glaze, you can use sprinkles, coconut, or ground nuts. Press them against the frosted sides with a long metal spatula or by hand.

For writing messages, fill a clean squeeze bottle with a free-flowing frosting. Pastry bags with decorator tips are available at hardware stores, gourmet shops, and supermarkets. A pastry bag comes with instructions for creating rosettes, scalloped borders, and flowers, but success takes patience and practice. You could also try making hand-shaped flowers. They are easy and fun.

Hand-shaped flowers

Blend 2 ounces of cream cheese and 2 cups of confectioner's sugar. Divide the mixture into several parts and add food coloring—pink or yellow for rosebuds, green for leaves. Leave some white for daisy petals. To shape a rosebud, roll a small ball. Flatten it with your thumb into an oblong, then gently roll it with your fingers. To make a leaf, form a small rope, flatten it, trim its edges with a knife, and place it alongside the bud. Make daisy petals in the same way and add a tiny yellow ball in the center.

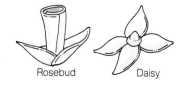

Rosebud   Daisy

Calligraphy

The art of beautiful handwriting

Practice with a calligraphy pen, not a ballpoint, and use calligraphy ink. Working on white bond or typing paper over a printed alphabet, imitate the strokes. Hold the pen at a 45° angle, pulling it toward you, top to bottom and left to right. Keep your hand relaxed. Vary the stroke width by turning your hand to change the angle of the point.

A calligraphy pen consists of a nib (point), an ink reservoir, and a barrel

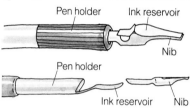

Pen holder   Ink reservoir
Nib
Pen holder
Ink reservoir   Nib

(handle). As you press the pen to the paper, the nib splits, letting the ink flow from the reservoir. Standard calligraphy pens must be dipped in ink repeatedly; calligraphy fountain pens are available, as are left-handed nibs for both types of pen.

Body of small letter is 5 pen widths high, as are ascenders and descenders. Capitals are 7 pen widths high

Hold pen at 45° angle

a b c
defghijklmnop
qrstuvwxyz
A B C D E

Follow arrows for stroke direction

Before buying a pen, put a nib into the holder; the nib should form a straight line with the barrel from tip to end. Check that the nib-gripping device fits the handle tightly; this helps avoid wobbly strokes. Test the weight and thickness for comfort. A lightweight barrel gives you more feel for the nib on the paper; a heavier barrel makes the strokes seem lighter with less friction. A plastic barrel may feel slippery after hours of use, causing hand tension.

During long writing sessions, rinse the nib occasionally in water, shake it, and wipe it, first with tissue, then with a lint-free cloth. When finished, clean the used nibs with a special pen cleaner sold in art supply stores.

Calligraphy ink should flow easily, be consistent in color, and have permanence, or resistance to damage from light. If you find the colored inks you buy thin and opaque, try making your own ink of acrylic paint thinned with water. This "ink" dries quickly, so clean the nib often in warm water.

Calluses

Removing calluses; preventing their recurrence

Calluses are thickened areas of skin that function as natural protection in spots subject to frequent pressure. They often occur on the heels or the balls of the feet because of ill-fitting or high-heeled shoes. They may also appear on the hands of manual workers.

Foot calluses may disappear on their own once you switch to properly fitting shoes. Calluses can be gradually removed by first softening the skin in warm water and then gently rubbing away the dead skin a little at a time with a pumice stone. If this doesn't help, a doctor can remove calluses surgically or chemically. Using cushioned innersoles can sometimes prevent calluses from forming, as can arch supports for people with high insteps. Women should avoid wearing high-heeled shoes constantly.

Calorie counting

Keeping track of what you eat

The number of calories you consume controls your weight. A calorie is the amount of heat required to raise the temperature of 1 kilogram of water 1°C. Our bodies take the calories from the food we eat and convert them into energy. If more calories are taken in than are used up as energy, the body stores the surplus calories as fat. It takes 3,500 surplus calories to make 1 pound of fat.

Estimating your needs

The number of calories burned each day varies widely from person to person, depending on sex, build, age, metabolism, health, and activity. To get an idea of how many calories you need per day to maintain weight, multiply your present weight by 13.6 if you are largely sedentary, by 16 to 18 if you are moderately active, or by 20 if you are very active. The result will give you a general figure that you can further refine by experience.

The only true way of finding out how many calories your body needs is to keep track of the total number of calories you consume and watch the scale. If you gain weight, you are consuming more calories than your body needs and vice versa.

When you establish the number of calories you need to keep your weight stable, use that figure as a guide, increasing your intake for periods when you are more active and reducing it for periods of less activity. Always maintain a balanced diet to insure proper nutrition. (See *Menu planning*.)

Keeping track

The accompanying table (based on charts prepared by the U.S. Department of Agriculture) lists the caloric values of some common foods. More complete lists are available; get a good one and use it. Become a label reader; most canned, frozen, and packaged foods show caloric values on their labels. Include in your count anything that is added to your food, such as sauce, cooking fat, or salad dressing.

CALORIES IN SOME FOODS

Food	Amount	Calories
Almonds	½ cup	345
Apple (2¾"dia.)	1	80
Apple juice	1 cup	120
Asparagus	1 cup	30
Bacon, crisp	2 slices	85
Banana	1	100
Beans, boiled		
green	1 cup	30
kidney	1 cup	220
lima	1 cup	160
Beefsteak,		
broiled, lean	4 oz.	230
Beer	12 oz.	160
Beets	1 cup	60
Bread		
American rye	slice	60
white	slice	70
whole wheat	slice	65

Food	Amount	Calories
Broccoli	1 cup	40
Brownie		
(1¾" x 1¾" x 1")	1	95
Butter	1 tbsp.	100
Cabbage		
chopped raw	1 cup	22
cooked	1 cup	30
Cantaloupe		
(5" dia.)	½	80
Carrots, sliced	1 cup	50
Celery, diced	1 cup	20
Cheddar cheese	2 oz.	230
Chicken, broiled	6.2 oz.	240
Corn	1 ear	70
Crabmeat	1 cup	135
Crackers	4	50
Distilled liquor,		
80 proof	2 oz.	130
Egg	1	80
Frankfurter		
(2 oz.)	1	170
Grapes, green	10	35
Halibut, broiled	4 oz.	195
Ham	3 oz.	245
Honey	1 tbsp.	65
Ice cream	1 cup	270
Jam	1 tbsp.	55
Lamb roast	4 oz.	315
Lettuce, iceberg	1 head	70
Mayonnaise	1 tbsp.	100
Milk		
whole	1 cup	150
skim	1 cup	85
Mushrooms	1 cup	20
Noodles		
cooked	1 cup	200
Oil, vegetable	1 tbsp.	120
Orange juice	1 cup	110
Peach	1	40
Peanut butter	1 tbsp.	105
Pear, Bartlett	1	100
Pie (9" dia.)		
apple	⅙	405
pecan	⅙	580
pumpkin	⅙	325
Pizza, cheese	4¾" slice	145
Potato		
baked		
(5½ oz.)	1	100
French fried	10	135
Potato chips	1 oz.	160
Radishes, raw	4	5
Raisins	½ cup	210
Rice, cooked	1 cup	225
Salami	2 oz.	235
Shrimp	4 oz.	105
Spaghetti		
al dente	1 cup	190
tender	1 cup	155
Spinach	1 cup	35
Squash,		
acorn (baked)	1 cup	110
summer (boiled)	1 cup	30
Strawberries	1 cup	55
Sugar, white		
granulated	1 tbsp.	45
Tomato juice	6 oz.	35
Tomatoes	1	25
Turkey, roasted		
dark meat	3 oz.	175
white meat	3 oz.	150
Veal chop, loin		
broiled	4 oz.	265
Wine	3 oz.	80
Yogurt, low fat	1 cup	145

Cameras

Choosing and using the right camera, lens, and film

The best camera for you is one that suits your pocketbook and your individual purpose. Below are listed two main types of cameras and their capabilities.

Point-and-shoot cameras have become popular and they have replaced *cassette and disc cameras*, which once dominated the market because they were cheap and easy to operate. The point-and-shoot cameras produce excellent slides or prints using 35mm film. Aperture and shutter speed are set automatically by a built-in light meter. A few accept alternate lenses or additional lens elements. They now come in very inexpensive models as well as costly ones.

Single-lens reflex cameras (SLRs), still more expensive, are so named because a single lens brings the identical image to the film and to the user as he looks through the viewfinder. An SLR uses 35mm film and accepts interchangeable lenses (see below). On most SLRs, the exposure settings are controlled by a built-in light meter; the user has only to focus the lens.

The newest point-and-shoot and SLR cameras include automatic film advance, useful for photographing sports and other fast-moving events; automatic focusing; and a range of automatic exposure-control modes.

Camera lenses

Photographic lenses vary from a single piece of polished plastic in the cheapest cameras to a dozen or more carefully ground and coated glass elements. SLRs usually come with a 50mm focal-length lens, which produces pictures with a "normal" 47-degree angle of view (an angle similar to what the human eye takes in).

Interchangeable lenses range from the 8mm "fish-eye," which gives a 180-degree panorama, to a 1000mm telephoto, which takes in only 2.5 degrees but pulls in distant subjects. Zoom lenses adjust to various focal lengths, widening or narrowing the field of view without a change of lenses.

Photography basics

On each lens you'll see an *f* followed by a number. This is the aperture of the lens. The aperture works like the human-eye lens: it opens in the dark and closes in bright light. The lower the *f* number, the wider the lens opening, which means that more light affects the film for any given time, or shutter speed. Shutter speed, indicated in fractions of a second, is the length of time the shutter stays open when you push the shutter-release button.

The aperture and the shutter speed control the amount of light entering the lens. The film registers the light as a two-dimensional image. The sharpness of that image is determined by focusing correctly.

The amount of light affecting the film is the exposure. To keep the exposure constant, any change in size of aperture (f/5.6 to f/8, for example) must be accompanied by a change in shutter speed ($^1/_{125}$ of a second to $^1/_{60}$, for example) and vice versa. To increase or decrease exposure, only one—aperture or speed—need be changed. Each change to a smaller aperture (higher number) or faster speed will halve the exposure. At the smaller aperture settings, more of the scene from foreground to distance comes into focus.

Film and film speed

A film's speed—ability to respond to light—is indicated by the ISO (or ASA) number on the box or roll. Films range from slow, ISO25 to 100, for normal activity and light, to ISO200 to 1000 for fast action or low light.

Extra light for dark situations

Many cameras have a built-in flash system that tells you when more light is needed; others require a flash attachment. When using a flash, you should ordinarily be within 10 to 15 feet of the subject.

There's little you can do to repair a camera; the best course is preventive care. Keep it free from dust, dirt, moisture, jolts, and extremes of temperature. If its exposure system fails, try replacing the battery. If it still doesn't work, take it to a repair shop. (See also *Action photography; Landscape photography; Nature photography; Pet photography; Photographic lighting; Portrait photography.*)

Campfires

Successful fire building even with damp wood

Locate your campfire carefully. It should be on level ground away from tree roots and overhanging branches. A stone at the back helps; it deflects wind and reflects heat. Scrape aside any flammable leaves, pine needles, and forest duff (half-decayed organic material) from a circle at least 8 feet in diameter; get down to damp earth that won't burn. Pile the debris in one place; you'll need it later.

Gather your firewood from dead and downed trees; don't cut live trees or branches—they don't burn well. Use a hatchet or camping saw to lop side branches and a saw to cut the wood into lengths.

The easiest fires to build are the *pyramid* and the *cone.* The pyramid is the best heat source. It starts slowly, lasts a long time, and doesn't scatter sparks. Begin by laying tinder: dry twigs, pine cones, birch bark found on the ground (stripping a tree will kill the tree), or bits of paper. Place several courses of wood, one on top of another, log-cabin style. Top the pyramid with two courses of wood to form a box. Light the tinder.

The cone makes a better cooking fire. It lights quickly, works even with wet wood, and provides a small, concentrated flame. Lay your tinder and erect sticks around it in the shape of a miniature teepee. If the wood is damp, make some sticks into "fuzz sticks" with your pocketknife.

Fuzz stick

Never leave a fire unattended, even in a fireplace. Drown it thoroughly with water before you leave. If your fire was on the ground, bury or disperse the drowned ashes and spread the pile of duff over the ground. Leave the site looking undisturbed.

In many backcountry areas and campgrounds, open fires are not permitted or they are allowed only in an fireplace or firepit. Be prepared: take a stove with you (see *Camp stoves*).

Camping

How to make camping fun for the whole family

Camping offers a welcome break from daily routine and an unparalleled opportunity for family fun in a pleasant setting. It can be an immensely rewarding experience—or a disaster. Forethought makes the difference.

Equipment
Begin with a firm idea of what you want to do while camping. If you plan to spend the time fishing, swimming, hiking, and boating, you'll want simple, serviceable equipment that fits into a car that may already be loaded with gear for your activities and even a boat on the roof.

On the other hand, if your idea of camping is a recreational vehicle, a comfortable chair, a battery-powered TV, and some good books, you'll have room for luxuries.

Simple or luxurious, the gear must function well. A tent should be waterproof, well-ventilated, bugproof, easy to erect, and secure in a wind (see *Tents*). Your sleeping bag should have a nylon shell for ease of maintenance but it need not be the latest and lightest backpacking bag. The pad that goes under the bag should be the best you can buy. You'll be using muscles that don't normally get much of a workout, and a comfortable night's sleep can avoid stiffness.

Keep your cooking gear and your meals simple. If a meal can't be cooked in one pot and eaten from a bowl, it's probably too complicated.

Some simple rules
One of the pleasures of camping is living a simple life uncluttered with gadgets and machinery. But simplicity has its price. You can't just pop wet clothes into the dryer, toss a meal into

the microwave oven, or run a vacuum cleaner through the tent. Hang those wet clothes on a line strung between two trees. Leave muddy shoes outside the tent. Eat meals at regular times, and put the food away immediately afterward so it doesn't spoil or attract animals. Keep your campsite neat and your gear stowed where you can find it when you need it.

Camping with children
Camping can be a memorable family experience, but you have to make some concessions to children. Plan activities with a youngster's attention span in mind. A 4-year-old is a marvelous companion on a short hike—but only if you hike at the pace of a 4-year-old, to whom each leaf, flower, or pebble is a thing of wonder. Better three short walks than one long one. Better a little fishing in the morning and at twilight than a whole day in a boat. Don't forget some books, paper, coloring books, and crayons.

Older children will enjoy having their own tent. It gives them a sense of self-reliance and you some privacy.

Clothing
Good rain gear is a must, as is a warm jacket, a nylon windbreaker, and a long-sleeved shirt and long pants for chilly evenings and mosquito protection. Take one pair each of "wet" shoes and "dry" shoes per person. Because children invariably dirty their clothes, they need extra outerwear. Hats are essential as sunshades.

Where to go
If you're a first-time camper, making a reservation will ease your worry about where you'll spend the night. Always reserve in popular areas. Directories of public and private campgrounds, available in libraries, list facilities such as pools, tenting areas, playgrounds, and trailer sites. The basic fee usually includes campsite, picnic table, grill, and rest-room facilities. At campgrounds for recreational vehicles and trailers, you pay an additional fee to plug in your power cord, run your hose to an outlet, and connect your holding tank to a sewer line.

As a rule, state and national forest campgrounds offer the most scenic sites: they are designed primarily for tent camping with widely spaced wooded sites and a woodsy ambience.

Privately owned campgrounds are more likely to be designed for recreational vehicles and trailers. Site spacing is closer, often on open fields.

Camp stoves

Operating and maintaining gasoline and propane stoves

Choosing a camp stove is simple once you recognize that your basic choice is between the high-heat output of a gasoline stove and the easy operation of a stove fueled by canisters of pressurized propane or butane. Each has advantages and disadvantages.

If you camp in chilly weather, the gasoline stove will heat water quicker than the propane or butane stove; in fact, butane won't work below 32°F. But you get that performance at the cost of fussier operation. Most gasoline stoves require refueling (use only special cookstove fuel), pressurizing, and preheating before they are ready to cook. Repairs and maintenance must be done on a cold stove, and the fuel tank should be depressurized and emptied before removing any of the unit's elements. The generator tube can get plugged with carbon; to prevent this, clean it before each outing by blowing it out with compressed air. (Veteran campers keep a spare generator in their kits.) Each month in the camping season, oil the pump plunger by putting a drop of oil in the hole. After a trip, dismantle and clean the valve assembly.

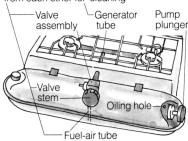

Withdraw these parts and unscrew from each other for cleaning
Valve assembly — Generator tube — Pump plunger — Valve stem — Oiling hole — Fuel-air tube

A propane or butane stove is simple to operate: just open the control valve and light the burner. Ease of operation is offset by the inconvenience of bulky refillable gas bottles and the high cost of disposable bottles. About the only thing that can go wrong is a clogged orifice. If the burner won't light, clean the orifice with a thin wire or needle. Or take it to a gas station and blow it out with compressed air or have it cleaned ultrasonically.

Both kinds of stoves are less efficient in wind. Position your stove so that its cover serves as a windscreen. If it has no cover, try to find some shielding for it, but don't use it inside a tent. And guard against children touching it until it is cool; some parts stay hot long after shutdown.

Canapés

A tempting array of ideas

Canapés are tiny, savory, open-faced sandwiches, party dressed in pretty shapes and colors and daintily decorated and garnished. They can be served hot or cold, as a part of a tea, with drinks at a social event, or as a special snack. Aim for intriguing combinations of bread, butter, and topping that either complement or contrast. Three or four kinds of canapés arranged on a doily-covered plate make a pleasing presentation.

Start with a base of thin-sliced bread (white, whole wheat, rye, pumpernickel) cut into rounds, rectangles, or cookie-cutter shapes. Spread each with butter, margarine, or cream cheese to keep the bread from getting soggy. These spreads can be mixed with other ingredients for extra taste, or they might become the topping itself, perhaps piped on with a pastry bag. For a simple herb butter, combine 4 ounces of lightly salted whipped butter with 2 tablespoons each of minced parsley and chives.

Ideas for toppings

Turn to the dairy case for sliced cheese; add a wedge of apple or pear at the last minute. Use hard-cooked eggs either sliced or as salad. Flaked fish, crab, lobster, shrimp, and other seafoods make delicious toppings by themselves or mixed with mayonnaise and herbs. For a special treat try pink, black, or golden caviar, sliced smoked fish such as salmon or trout, or pickled herring. For an easy spread, combine a 3¾-ounce can of sardines,

drained and chopped, with 1 chopped hard-cooked egg and 1 tablespoon of mayonnaise; garnish with pickle.

Duck, chicken, turkey, or other poultry is delightful sliced thin or mixed with mayonnaise and seasonings. Try slices of duck topped with a dab of orange marmalade.

Use roasted meat—beef, ham, or veal—or patés, cold cuts, or corned beef. For dieters, turn to vegetable toppings: lightly salted, paper-thin cucumber slices with a sprig of dill, or coarsely grated carrot sprinkled with lemon juice and minced parsley.

Canasta

Playing with two full decks

A card game of the rummy family, canasta is generally played by four persons (two sets of partners) with two standard 52-card decks plus four jokers. The object is to make *melds* (combinations of three or more cards of the same rank) to earn points. The first team to score 5,000 wins.

Each player is dealt 11 cards. If a player gets a red three, he puts it faceup on the table and gets a replacement card. The rest of the deck is placed facedown on the table and the top card is turned faceup beside it. If it happens to be a red three, another card is turned up on top of the three. Each player, in turn, draws from the top of the *stock* (remainder of the deck) and then discards one card.

Jokers and deuces are wild and so can be used to help form melds, but there can't be more than three wild cards in any one meld. A player can lay his melds faceup on the table and can later add to them, as can his partner.

A player can pick up the entire discard pile if he can use the top discard in a meld and the pile is not *frozen* (does not contain a wild card or black three). The pile can be unfrozen by a player with a natural pair (no wild cards) of the rank of the top discard.

A hand ends when a player can put down all his cards and has a *canasta*—either a *natural* (a meld of seven cards with no wild cards) or a *mixed* (a meld of seven cards including wild cards). In scoring, each natural

canasta is worth 500 points, each mixed canasta, 300 points. The player who goes out first gets 200 points. Each red three gets 100 points, and a player who has all four red threes gets 800 points. The value of each card in a meld is added, and the value of each card left in a player's hand is subtracted. The values are as follows: joker, 50; deuce or ace, 20; king through 8, 10; all others, 5.

Candied apples

Coating apples with hard candy

Prepare the apples by washing and drying them thoroughly. Remove the stems and in their place insert wooden popsicle sticks.

Boil a syrup of 2 parts sugar and 1 part water to the hard-crack stage (300°F) on a candy thermometer. Tint the syrup with food coloring if desired, and flavor it with a dash of cinnamon. Keep the syrup liquid over hot water in the top of a double boiler.

Swirl each apple in the syrup until it is covered. Allow excess syrup to drip into the pan. Dry the apples upright by pushing the sticks into a block of florist's plastic foam or rest them on a buttered cookie sheet.

Candlemaking

Lighting up your life with your own homemade candles

With only a few materials and tools, you can have the fun of designing and making your own candles. Paraffin is the most practical wax to use. It comes in 10- or 11-pound slabs, one of which melts down to about 4 quarts of liquid wax. To raise the melting point of the wax and make the candles burn longer, add 10 percent stearin (stearic acid) to the paraffin. Supplies are available at crafts shops.

Break up the paraffin with an ice pick. Bring water to a boil in the bottom of a double boiler, then add the paraffin to the top of the double boiler a few chunks at a time. Melt the wax, checking the temperature with a candy thermometer. Don't let the wax get hotter than 210°F or it will begin smoking (paraffin is flammable).

When the wax has melted, stir in the stearin. When the stearin has dissolved, slice in slivers of dye or add dye pellets or liquid dye. (Use only commercial dye made for candles.) Test the color by dropping a bit of wax onto white paper. The finished candle will be somewhat darker.

Molded candles

You can buy a candle mold or use a gelatin mold, a smooth-sided can, a milk carton, or other improvised device. Lubricate the inside with silicone spray or vegetable oil to make it easier to slide the candle out later.

Secure the end of the wick to the bottom of the mold with tape, or weight it with a lead sinker. Position a rod across the mold and tie the wick to the rod so that the wick is taut.

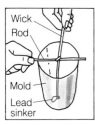 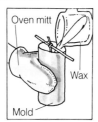

Have the wax at 190 to 200°F for metal molds, 150 to 165°F for other molds. Wearing an oven mitt, pour the wax into a measuring cup and then slowly into the mold. For layered candles, pour one color wax, let it harden, then pour in the next color. Place the filled mold in a bucket with cool water up to the level of the wax. Weight it down. After 30 minutes, remove the weight, puncture the crust around the wick, and pour additional wax into the cavity that has formed around the wick.

Let the wax harden overnight. Then gently pull the candle by the wick to slide it out of the mold, or tear the mold away. If the candle has a seam, pare it away with a knife.

Candymaking

Homemade candy know-how

Fondant, fudge, penuche, pralines, butterscotch, brittles, or taffy are some of the sweets that are fun and easy to make. All involve the steady boiling of a syrup, usually about 3 parts of sugar to 1 of water, to reach a certain stage of crystallization. A candy thermometer tells when the correct temperature for each type of candy has been reached. Here are those temperatures, stages, and types:
230°F-234°F—thread (sugar syrup)
234°F-240°F—soft ball (fondant, penuche, fudge, pralines)
244°F-248°F—firm ball (caramel)
250°F-266°F—hard ball (taffy)
270°F-290°F—soft crack (butterscotch)
300°F-310°F—hard crack (brittle)

At high elevation, decrease the final cooking temperature of any syrup stage by 2°F for each 1,000-foot increase in elevation.

Candies are best made on a cool, dry day. Use a heavy-bottomed pan and stir with a wooden spoon. Check the temperature often while the syrup is boiling.

Even one large crystal can start premature crystallization, causing the candy to be grainy. To prevent this, corn syrup or glucose is often added to the syrup. If crystals form on the side of the pan, remove them with a wet pastry brush or cloth. If necessary, wash utensils to keep them free of crystals. Once the syrup has boiled, don't stir it. Regulate the heat to prevent boiling over.

When the syrup reaches the correct temperature, pour it into a lightly greased container and allow it to cool undisturbed. Don't add the scrapings from the pan. If the recipe calls for beating the candy, wait until the candy cools to 110°F.

Pecan pralines

Lightly butter a large sheet of aluminum foil. Combine 1 cup of firmly packed light brown sugar, 2 cups of granulated sugar, 1 cup of milk or light cream, and ⅝ teaspoon salt in a large saucepan. Bring to a boil, and cook without stirring over moderate heat until a candy thermometer registers 238°F. Remove from the heat and let cool undisturbed to 110°F. Stir in 2 tablespoons of butter and 1 teaspoon of vanilla extract. Beat until the mixture begins to thicken, then stir in 3 cups of roasted pecan halves. Quickly drop by tablespoons onto the aluminum foil. Spread with a spatula to form patties about 2½ inches in diameter. Let harden for 1 hour, then remove from the foil. Store in an airtight container.

Caning a chair

Replacing cane webbing; reweaving a cane seat

Cane chair seats can be replaced with prewoven webbing if the seat has a continuous groove around the opening. Chairs with holes and no groove must be rewoven with strand cane.

Prewoven webbing

The webbing is held in the groove with a tapered strip, or spline. Soak the webbing and spline in warm water until pliable. Squeeze white glue into the groove in the chair and force the webbing into the groove with half a wooden clothespin. Drive the spline into the groove with a mallet. Preserve the webbing with tung-oil sealant.

Reweaving a cane seat

Select the width of strand cane that best fits the holes in your chair frame. You'll need approximately 250 feet of cane for an average seat. The cane will come with the appropriate binder, a broader strand that is used to form a border around the seat. Soak the cane in warm water for at least 15 minutes and weave it while it is wet and pliable. When it dries, it will shrink, keeping the seat taut.

Use an awl to clean out the holes in the chair. Push a strand of cane up through the front center hole, leaving 4 inches hanging below. Wedge the cane into place with a caning peg or golf tee. Pass the strand, shiny side up, across the seat, down through the center back hole, and up through the hole to the left of it.

Continue threading the cane in parallel rows. Keep the tension uniform but loose enough to depress the strands ½ to ¾ inch. If the seat is wider in front than in back, skip some holes at the corners to keep the rows parallel.

Whenever you come to the end of a strand, trim it off, leaving 4 inches hanging below the seat. Tie off the end of a completed or new strand by winding it twice around the cane running between the holes on the underside and pulling it tight.

When the left side of the seat is covered, unplug the end of the first strand and do the right side in the same way. Thread a set of canes from side to side over the tops of the front-to-back strands.

Add a second set of front-to-back strands over the others. Then weave a set of strands from side to side, passing them under the bottom rows of strands and over the top rows.

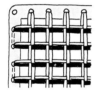

Starting in any corner, weave a set of strands diagonally, passing them under the front-to-back strands and over the side-to-side strands. Add a second set of diagonal strands at right angles to the first, passing them over the front-to-back strands and under the side-to-side strands.

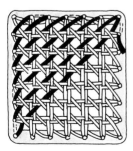

Cut the binder a little longer than the circumference of the seat. Peg down one end of it in the center back

hole, draw it tautly over the holes in the frame, and stitch it down. To stitch it, knot the end of a strand of cane and thread it up through the fourth hole from the peg until the knot catches. Then stretch the strand over the binder and down through the same hole. Use an awl to separate the strands in the hole enough to accept the stitching. Continue stitching all around the seat. When you reach the peg, remove it and stitch past it. Trim the loose ends.

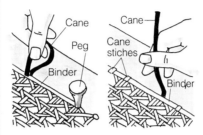

Push a peg through all the octagonal openings in the caned seat to even out the pattern. While the cane is still wet, singe off any frayed cane with a moving match flame. Stain the seat if you wish. Treat both sides of the seat with tung-oil sealant.

Canning

Home methods and equipment

Foods are canned by one of two processes: boiling-water bath or steam pressure. In both, foods can be prepared by the raw-pack or the hot-pack method. Both processes heat foods hot enough and long enough to destroy spoilage organisms.

High-acid foods such as fruits and pickles can be safely processed in a boiling-water-bath canner. For other vegetables, meat and poultry, certain new varieties of low-acid tomatoes, or other products, use a steam-pressure canner. Processing these low-acid foods safely in a reasonable length of time requires a temperature higher than that of boiling water.

Water-bath canners should be deep enough for the water to cover the jar tops by at least 1 inch, with an additional 2 inches above the jars to allow for brisk boiling. The canner must have a tight-fitting cover and a rack.

Steam-pressure canners should be cleaned and checked before each use. Clean the petcock and the safety-valve openings by drawing a string through them. Check that a weighted pressure gauge is clean. Have a dial pressure gauge, old or new, checked for accuracy by a dealer.

Glass jars and closures must be perfect. Discard any with cracks, chips, dents, or rust. Rubber rings for glass-top jars and metal lids for screw-top jars should be used only once. Wash the jars, lids, rings, and bands in hot, soapy water and rinse them well. Metal lids may require boiling; follow the manufacturers' instructions.

Canning procedures

Use only fresh, perfect fruits and vegetables. Wash them in several changes of water; avoid bruising. Pack the raw fruits or vegetables into jars and fill the jars with boiling syrup, juice, or water. Pack foods tightly, except for peas, corn, and lima beans, which need room to expand.

For the hot-pack method, preheat fruits or vegetables in syrup, water, steam, or extracted juice. Pack them in jars, leaving some space between packed food and closure unless otherwise indicated. Cover them with the boiling liquid.

Closures and how to use them

If your jars have metal screwbands and flat metal lids with sealing compound, wipe the jar rims clean after packing and put on the lid with the sealing compound next to the glass. Screw the metal band tight; do not tighten it further after canning. For jars using a separate rubber shoulder ring (porcelain-lined zinc capped and glass-top jars), fit the wet rubber ring on the jar shoulder; fill the jar; wipe ring and jar clean. Screw the cap on firmly and then turn it back ¼ inch.

Processing in a water bath

For raw pack, put the filled jars into the canner with hot water; for hot pack, use boiling water. Add enough hot or boiling water to bring the water at least 1 inch above the jar tops; but don't pour boiling water directly on glass jars. Cover the canner. At a rolling boil, start timing the processing. Boil steadily for the time specified in your cookbook for that food. Add boiling water as needed to keep the jars covered. Remove the jars when the time is up and air-cool them.

Pressure-canner processing
Carefully follow the manufacturer's instructions and these general rules: put 2 to 3 inches of boiling water in the canner; set filled jars on a rack (for steam circulation); fasten the cover securely so that steam escapes only through the petcock. Let steam pour out steadily for 10 minutes before closing the petcock or putting on the weighted gauge. When the pressure has risen to 10 pounds, start counting the processing time. Regulate the heat to keep the pressure constant.

When the time is up, remove the canner from the heat and let it stand until the pressure drops to zero. Wait another few minutes; then carefully unfasten the cover, tilting up its far side to allow steam to escape. Remove the jars to a towel or folded cloth. Screw porcelain-lined caps tight to complete the seal. When the jars are cool, test the cap seals by turning each jar partly over to see if it leaks. With a flat metal lid, press the center; if it is down and won't move, the jar is sealed. Take off the bands. Wipe the jars, label, and store in a dry place.

The above also applies to the canning of meat and poultry, but these require extra care because of the risk of botulism. They must be canned in a pressure canner to destroy bacteria.

Before processing, keep meat or poultry cold, clean, and sanitary. If refrigeration isn't available and the daily temperature rises above 40°F., process meat or poultry as soon as its body heat is gone. Keep everything that touches meat or poultry clean; scrub pans, knives, and kitchen tools in hot, soapy water and rinse with boiling water. If you use wooden utensils and surfaces, scour them with a stiff brush and hot, soapy water. Then rinse and disinfect them with household bleach diluted according to label directions. Leave the solution on for 15 minutes. Wash off well with boiling water. Before tasting or using canned meats, boil them 20 minutes in a covered pan.

Compensating for high elevation
Hot-water bath: Increase the processing time by 1 minute for each 1,000 feet above sea level.

Pressure canner: At sea level it takes 10 pounds of steam pressure to reach the required temperature of 240°F. To reach 240°F at high elevations, the pressure must rise an additional ½ pound for each 1,000 feet of elevation above sea level.

Canoeing
Safety, boarding, basic strokes and turns

Always wear a Coast Guard-approved Type III life jacket, often called a PFD, which stands for "personal flotation device." Tie ropes, each at least 15 feet long, to each end of the canoe; use them to tie to a dock or to grab if the canoe capsizes. Take along a spare paddle and lash it and any other loose gear inside the canoe.

Carry the canoe into the water so that it's afloat. The stern (rear) paddler boards first. To do so, crouch and hold onto the far gunwale with one hand and the near gunwale with the other. Swing one foot in, placing it at the centerline of the canoe, and swing the other foot in. Sit or kneel in the center while your bow partner boards. When you get out, do so in reverse order. Don't run the canoe onto shore; it can damage the hull.

Canoes don't tip over easily—people tip them by making sudden movements or by unbalancing the canoe. Tipping is part of the learning process, similar to falling on skates or skis. If you tip, stay with the canoe. Swim it into shallow water and empty it. Practice tipping so that you know what to do when it happens.

Paddling in a straight line
Sitting on a seat, extend your legs as if driving a car. In this position you use all your body, not just your arms. Hold the paddle with one hand on the grip and the other about 6 inches above the blade; gripping it closer to the blade causes the canoe to roll with each stroke. Begin with the bow person paddling on the left and the stern person on the right. (Eventually you'll learn to paddle on both sides.)

With arms moderately straight, both paddlers swing their paddles forward simultaneously. Rotate your up-

per body a bit and reach the paddle forward, but don't lean at the waist. Thrust the paddle blade into the water with the shaft nearly perpendicular to the water. Push the grip forward with your upper hand, pull back with the lower hand, and return your body to a squared-off position.

Take the paddle out of the water by dropping your upper hand—the one on the grip—toward your lap; the blade will slice neatly out of the water. Swing the paddles forward and repeat the strokes, with the stern paddler following the bow paddler's rhythm. Paddling in unison makes a canoe run smoothly and safely. Think of it as dancing with your paddling partner and the canoe.

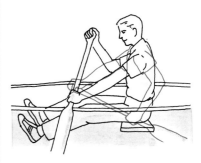

Keeping the canoe straight
The least efficient way to keep the canoe traveling straight ahead is for the stern paddler to trail the paddle behind like a rudder—this slows forward motion. The better way is to take advantage of the fact that the canoe wants to turn left when the stern paddler is on the right side, and vice versa. Take 10 easy strokes together, then switch your paddles so that the bow person is paddling on the right and the stern on the left. Take 10 more strokes and switch again. The stern paddler can more easily sense when the canoe is starting to drift off-course, so it's the stern paddler's job to indicate when to switch sides.

Before long the stern paddler will figure out that a little twist of the wrist keeps the canoe tracking well. Thereafter, you'll switch sides more to equalize the load on your muscles than to keep the canoe straight.

Turning the canoe
The simplest turn is for the stern person to paddle backward, and the bow

C

person to paddle forward. The canoe will turn to the stern paddler's side; however, the canoe nearly stops.

A quicker turn is the *post*. The bow paddler thrusts the paddle blade into the water with the shaft nearly vertical and the power face of the paddle— the face that pushes water—at a 45-degree angle to the canoe's centerline. The stern paddler keeps paddling; the canoe turns without losing speed.

Don't stop learning

Play with your canoe. You'll quickly learn that it responds to every little twitch of the paddle. To make the canoe go sideways (helpful when landing at a wharf), the bow paddler posts as above, and the stern paddler pushes his paddle away from the canoe. You'll soon figure out several other ways to do it.

Car belts

Servicing car drive belts

Drive belts operate the water pump, power steering, air conditioning, compressor, alternator, and other accessories. Loose or broken belts cause problems. The first sign of a belt problem may be a squeal, but inspect even silent belts periodically.

Change a belt if it has a glazed look, deep cracks, or pieces missing. Replace a multigrooved belt if it is missing sections ½ inch or longer across two or more ribs (minor cracks in its grooves are normal).

Check belt tension with a gauge or press your finger on the belt midway between the pulleys. Tighten it if it deflects more than ¾ inch. Some cars have a single belt that zig-zags between several pulleys. It needs no adjustment because a spring-loaded pulley maintains proper tension.

To replace a belt, decrease the tension, slip the old belt off the pulleys, slip the new one on, and readjust the tension. Following are the most common ways of adjusting tension:

If the belt-driven accessory is bolted to a slotted bracket, loosen the bolts and move the accessory toward the engine to decrease tension or away from the engine to increase tension. When the belt has the correct tension,

retighten the bolts.

There are several ways of moving the accessory. If the bracket has a

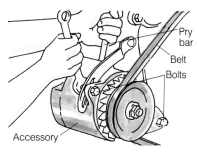
Pry bar / Belt / Bolts / Accessory

square hole, use a ratchet wrench in the hole as a lever for moving the accessory. If there is a hex head on the bracket, use a socket wrench on the hex as a lever. Otherwise insert a pry bar between the accessory and the engine, lean the bar against a sturdy surface, and push the accessory.

The accessory may be held by a jackscrew, which moves the accessory on

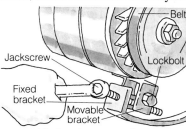
Belt / Lockbolt / Jackscrew / Fixed bracket / Movable bracket

a movable bracket away from or toward a fixed bracket. Loosen the lockbolts or nuts and turn the jackscrew.

Caution: Turn the engine off before touching a belt. Keep clear of an electric fan until the engine is cold, or disconnect it to be sure that it cannot run.

Carbon monoxide poison

Fast action may save a life

A colorless, odorless gas, carbon monoxide is produced by automobile engines, by burning charcoal, coal, or wood, and by incorrect combustion in oil burners or space heaters. Prevent poisoning by regular checkups of heating and car-exhaust systems and by providing adequate ventilation.

A person who is being poisoned by carbon monoxide will have a headache, feel dizzy and nauseous, and seem drowsy. If not removed quickly

from the source of fumes, he or she may turn red, lose consciousness, and die—sometimes within minutes. Get the person outside into fresh air, or open all the doors and windows. Call an ambulance or the police or fire department for oxygen. If breathing has stopped, begin mouth-to-mouth resuscitation (see *CPR*), and have someone else call for help.

Carburetor adjustments

Setting the idle speed on your car

Older cars with carburetors need periodic idle-speed adjustment. For this job you need a tachometer, an instrument that reads the engine's speed. Note the *curb-idle* specification on your car's under-hood tune-up decal.

Finding the controlling solenoid

Many carburetored cars have solenoids that control the idle speed. To determine which is the controlling solenoid on an air-conditioned car, have a helper hold the gas pedal to the floor and then turn the ignition switch to *On* (not *Start*). If a solenoid plunger moves out, it controls the idle. If it doesn't, have the helper turn on the air conditioning (engine still off). If the plunger moves this time, it is not the curb-idle control. A certain type of General Motors solenoid has an additional internal adjuster that controls the curb-idle speed when the air conditioning is off. It also controls a second *low-idle* speed on non-A/C cars.

If no solenoid controls the idle, you'll find a spring-loaded adjusting screw bearing against the throttle linkage. Don't confuse this screw with the one that controls *fast idle* when the engine is cold. The fast-idle screw bears against a stepped, curved part called the fast-idle cam.

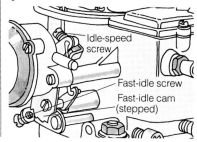
Idle-speed screw / Fast-idle screw / Fast-idle cam (stepped)

If the decal specifies curb idle and low idle, and there is an idle solenoid, that solenoid controls the curb idle alone (except on GM cars with the special solenoid). Also look for a throttle-linkage screw; set low idle on it with the solenoid wire disconnected.

Adjusting the idle

Warm up the engine. Observe any special instructions for idle-speed adjustment given on the decal, such as hoses to disconnect and plug. Connect the tachometer in accordance with its instructions. Typically, attach the negative wire to an electric ground (such as an engine bolt) and the positive lead to the ignition coil's negative terminal.

On GM cars with High Energy Electronic Ignition and the coil built into the distributor cap, connect the positive lead to the *TACH* terminal in the cap flange. On models with a separate coil, connect the positive lead to the *TACH* terminal of the coil (the one without a pink wire).

Next, in very small steps, make the adjustment. Each time you turn a solenoid adjuster, push down slightly on the throttle and allow the solenoid plunger to extend. Then release the throttle and allow 10 to 15 seconds for the idle to stabilize before taking the reading on the tachometer.

The most common adjusters

Adjusting screw against the throttle linkage or the plunger of a nonadjustable solenoid: Turn the screw with a

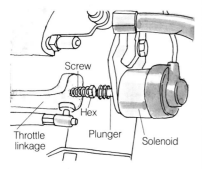

wrench on the screw's hex end. If there is no solenoid, turn clockwise to increase idle speed, counterclockwise to reduce it. With a solenoid, turn in the opposite directions.

Hex or square tip on a solenoid plunger: With a wrench turn the plunger counterclockwise to increase idle speed, clockwise to reduce it.

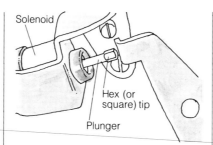

Two-piece solenoid bracket with one part fixed, the other movable along a screw: Turn the long bracket screw clockwise to increase the idle speed, counterclockwise to reduce it.

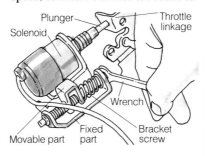

Adjuster on back of solenoid: Turn clockwise to increase idle speed, counterclockwise to reduce it.

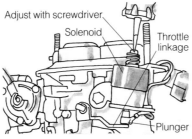

GM solenoid on cars without air conditioning: Use a wrench to turn the solenoid body on the hex at the back, clockwise to increase the idle speed, counterclockwise to reduce it.

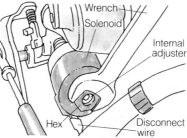

Disconnect the wire from the solenoid. With a ⅛-inch Allen wrench, turn the internal adjuster whichever way is required, until engine speed matches the low-idle specification.

GM solenoid on cars with air conditioning: Use a ⅛-inch Allen wrench to turn the internal adjuster clockwise

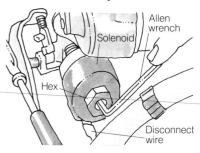

to a stop (do not force). Disconnect the wiring at the A/C compressor, turn on the A/C dash control, and set the idle to the specification listed for the solenoid. Then turn off the A/C, reconnect the compressor wire, and back out the ⅛-inch Allen adjuster until the speed corresponds to the low-idle specification.

Car CD Player

Installing a compact disc player; antitheft designs

Most new cars have a factory-installed sound system. The most popular is a combined cassette tape player and an AM-FM radio. Newly available compact disc (CD) players offer a dramatic improvement in sound quality.

You can upgrade your car's sound system to include CD's in several ways. Some CD players are combined with an AM-FM radio and are designed to replace the unit already in your car. There are five standard sizes for dash-mounted sound systems, so look for a unit that's the same size as the one you're replacing. You can get a self-contained single-play CD unit, or a CD changer that can play 6, 10, 12, or more CD's without stopping. CD changers are mounted in the car's trunk.

If you don't want to give up your cassette collection and the ability to play tapes, you can add a CD player to your present system. If your current car radio has a CD input jack, you can just plug in a portable CD receiver. Or you can buy an FM add-on CD player that works through a frequency on the FM radio already in your dash. This system includes three or more components:

(1) the CD changer; (2) an FM modulator; and (3) a controller for selecting the CD's you want to hear. The FM modulator is mounted in a hidden location inside the car (usually under one of the seats or in a center console). The modulator splits the signal received by the antenna into two parts. One part goes to the CD changer, the other to the radio receiver. Although the sound quality of such a system is not quite as good as a hard-wired CD player/changer, it's less expensive and easier for a do-it-yourselfer to install. Some systems come with a battery-powered wireless remote controller that you can mount on the center console with Velcro.

You can also buy compact CD players specially designed for smaller cars that will fit under a seat or in the glove compartment. No matter which system you choose, follow the manufacturer's installation instructions carefully. Before you buy any aftermarket auto sound equipment, make sure that it's compatible with the sound system components already in your car. If the dealer cannot guarantee compatibility, make sure you can return the unit if it doesn't work properly.

Security features

You may want to shop for systems with special security features. Some in-dash units can be mounted on a slide-out tray so you can take the unit with you when your car is parked. Others come with a detachable control panel. When the control panel is removed, all that remains is a blank panel that won't attract a thief's attention.

Car chasing

Training your dog to ignore cars

Chasing cars not only annoys drivers, it is extremely dangerous for the dog. To prevent the habit from developing, train your dog while it is a puppy and keep it leashed, confined, or under voice control whenever it is outside.

Training a dog to retreat

First teach the dog to follow you on a leash (see *Obedience training*). Then, with the dog on the leash, approach a road or driveway. At the moment that the dog shows interest in a passing car, turn and hurry away, calling to the dog to follow you. When the dog does so, praise and pet it.

Repeat the procedure often, using a long leash. Don't pull the dog unless necessary; try to get the dog to make the decision. When this habit is well established, proceed without a leash. Always praise the dog lavishly.

If your dog is already an habitual car chaser, try training it as described. Don't shout at the dog while it is pursuing a car; that may only increase the dog's urge to chase.

Stronger measures

As a last resort, try frightening the dog with a cold shower from a passing car. Have someone drive while you sit in the passenger seat with a pail of water. As soon as the dog comes close, throw the water over it. Keep out of sight of the dog; if it realizes that you are causing its discomfort, it may become afraid of you instead of cars. Repeat the procedure with as many different cars as possible.

Car horns

Fixing continuously blowing horns and silent horns

If a horn won't stop blowing, tap the horn button—it may be stuck. If that doesn't help, find the horn under the hood, disconnect its wire, and tape over the terminal screw temporarily.

Usually, continuous horn blowing is caused by a faulty horn relay. Buy a new relay (it is inexpensive) and substitute it for the old. The appearance of the replacement will help you find the original. It may be under the dashboard or in the fuse box.

If a horn won't blow at all, check for a blown fuse or a defective relay, horn, or horn button. First check the fuse and replace it if it is blown.

Further testing requires two thin jumper wires (lengths of wire with alligator clips at each end—*not* jumper cables). Disconnect the horn wire and connect a jumper from the battery's positive terminal to the horn terminal. If the horn doesn't sound, attach a second jumper from the horn body to the battery's negative terminal. If the horn blows, its electric ground is bad.

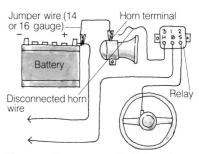

Remove the mounting bolt, brush its threads clean, and refit and tighten it.

If the horn doesn't work either way, replace it. If the horn blew when you connected the first jumper, do this test: remove the relay to identify its terminals, then reinstall it. Connect a jumper to body metal and to the *S* or *2* terminal. You may have to insert a nail into the back of the wiring connector to make contact. Turn on the ignition. If the relay clicks and the horn sounds, the relay is good and the problem is in the horn button switch inside the steering column. Have it serviced. If the horn doesn't sound, the relay is probably defective. Replace the relay.

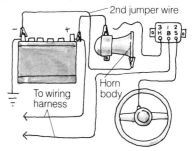

Unlabeled horn relay terminals

If a black wire is connected to one terminal, probe that terminal with a jumper wire connected to body metal; the relay should click. If it clicks and the horn sounds (ignition on), the relay is good and the horn button apparently is bad. If there is no click, the relay apparently is bad.

If there is no black wire, probe each wired terminal with a 12-volt test lamp connected to body metal. At one terminal the lamp will light. Ignore that terminal and, with a jumper wire connected to body metal, probe the other two. The relay should click and the horn sound when you probe one of the remaining two (ignition on). If so, the horn button is bad. If the relay doesn't click, it apparently is at fault.

Car insurance claims

Filing a claim after an auto accident

Send your claim as quickly as possible to the company that insures the other driver (or car owner). If your state doesn't have no-fault insurance, you must be able to prove that the other driver caused the accident in order to collect. If the other driver has no insurance, ask your agent or the state insurance department whether your state has an uninsured motorists' protection fund and, if so, how to file a claim against it. Otherwise, you'll have to sue the other driver to collect.

If your state has no-fault insurance, file your claim with your own company, regardless of who caused the accident. You still might have to sue the other driver if your claim is for an amount larger than that covered.

Filing a claim

Ask your agent what information or special forms you need. Typically, for every car involved you must provide the following information on the official accident report: names, addresses, and telephone numbers of the drivers; the drivers' license numbers and dates of expiration; license plate numbers, make, model, year, and color of both cars; the names of the insurers and policy numbers; a brief description of the accident and the damages. Attach a copy of the accident report to your claim. Be sure to date and keep a copy of your claim and all other materials.

Car damage

The insurer usually requires you to get written estimates on the cost of repairs to your car. It might even send someone to examine the car. If you can't have your car fixed for the amount the insurer offers, tell the insurer in writing how much additional money you need. If you can't agree, ask your lawyer or state insurance department for help.

Have your doctor send detailed reports of the nature and extent of any physical injuries. You might have to be examined by a doctor from the insurer. Submit bills for doctors, hospitals, medicine, rental of crutches, and homemaker's services, if needed; estimates of the costs of future treatments; and statements of income lost during recuperation.

Car keys left in car

Getting into a locked car

Locking your car with the keys inside is embarrassing, but forget pride. Call the police; they have unlocking tools and the know-how to use them properly. Try to unlock the car yourself only if it has bolt-shaped locking buttons. Here's how:

Open a coat hanger and form a ⅜-inch-wide hook on one end. Work it between the door or window and the car body. Catch the lock button under its head and pull the button up.

On other locking systems, the only way to reach the lock is by using specially shaped tools that slide between the glass and the weatherstripping. A better solution is to carry a second car key in your purse or pocket. Thin plastic key blanks that fit in your wallet are available from many car dealers and hardware stores. You can have one cut to match your door key.

Car locks

Opening a frozen car door

If a door lock is frozen, try the one on the other side or the hatch on a hatchback. If you get in, warm up the car and keep the heater on until the heat defrosts the frozen locks.

If all locks are frozen, heat the key with a cigarette lighter or matches. Wear gloves so that you can hold the key until it gets hot enough to melt frozen moisture inside the lock. You can buy an aerosol lock de-icer (an alcohol-lubricant mixture) to squirt into the key slot. However, it isn't as effective as a heated key. If electricity is available, use a hairdryer to thaw the lock.

When washing the car in winter, cover the keyholes with masking tape beforehand to keep out water, which may freeze the locks.

Operating the lever or button a few times should free a frozen latch. If not, use an aerosol de-icer with a narrow, flexible tube several inches long. Work the tube in between the car door and the body to reach the latch.

Car noises and rattles

Diagnosing what they mean

Although car noises are sometimes just irritants, many signal trouble. Tracing a noise to its source can be hard because noise travels along the chassis or body. However, careful observation will help you isolate many noises. If an under-hood noise occurs with the car stopped and the engine running, the source is most likely in the engine, its belt-driven accessories, or the exhaust system. A noise that occurs only when the car is moving is probably in the suspension, the transmission, the rear axle, the tires, or the exhaust system. Following are the most common noises:

Underhood squeals. Loose or glazed belts often are responsible. As a test only, not as an attempted cure, spray them with aerosol belt dressing. If the noise abates, the belts are the cause. Tighten loose belts or replace glazed ones (see *Car belts*).

Worn bearings in an accessory can also cause a squeal. Temporarily remove an accessory's belt as a test. If the noise goes away, refit the belt and adjust it. Then, with the engine running, probe the accessory bearing area with a mechanic's stethoscope.

Clunking on acceleration or deceleration usually indicates worn universal joints in the drive shaft or the front-drive axle shaft (see *Universal joints*). If the joints are OK, excessive wear in the rear axle or front-drive final-drive unit may be responsible.

Underbody roaring, loudest on acceleration, may be from the exhaust system. Patch any holes (even pinholes can cause noise) in the muffler or piping with a patching product. Also look for loose or broken clamps, which may allow separation of pipe joints, creating exhaust noise.

Noise on braking. Squeals usually are caused by worn brake shoes. Clunking on braking may come from loose brake calipers, worn tires, defective shock absorbers, or loose suspension components.

Engine noises

Metallic rattling in the engine, mainly on acceleration, is called ping. Occasional ping is normal. If ping is frequent, using higher-octane gasoline may cure it. If not, have a mechanic check the ignition timing advance controls and the exhaust gas recirculation (EGR) valve.

Clicking noise is normal as the engine starts, since it takes a minute for oil to flow to the hydraulic lifters. But if the noise continues as you drive, either the oil level is low (check the dipstick) or the hydraulic lifters need servicing. Some cars have nonhydraulic lifters that allow a clicking noise as the engine accumulates mileage. In this type, a mechanical adjustment to compensate for wear is necessary.

Hissing indicates an air or vacuum leak, typically from a bad hose connection, a split hose, or a damaged vacuum reservoir. Check under the hood for the noise. You may trace it to a hose you can simply reconnect.

Hissing during mode selection of the heater-air-conditioning unit is normal. However, continuous hissing indicates a vacuum leak. Remove the cover bezel surrounding the A/C controls and, if necessary, the panel itself; look for a vacuum hose connector that has come off.

Vibration in the floor and seats, felt mostly over 35 mph, probably comes from the driveline (transmission mounts, drive shaft or front-drive axle shafts, or a faulty vibration damper). Have these checked. Or the exhaust system may be making contact with the chassis. Check for loose or broken clamps. If the vibration occurs at high speed only, have your tires balanced.

Other noises

Under-body whine, audible from 20 mph to cruising speed, and most prominent on acceleration and coasting, may be in the rear axle or front-drive final-drive unit. Have them checked and serviced.

Dash vibration is normal on some older transverse-engine front-drive cars. If the vibration produces a rattle, move your hand over the dash, applying pressure to panels and brackets. If the noise goes away when you press, you may be able to reduce or eliminate the noise by tightening retaining screws. If that doesn't work, loosen the part, slip in a piece of sheet rubber as an insulator, and tighten the screws.

Wind noise may occur from the failure of window weatherstripping to seal properly. To pinpoint its location, tape the windows shut and if the noise goes away, gradually remove pieces of tape until the noise recurs. Replace bad weatherstripping at the trouble spot or readjust the window.

A broken section of a grille also may cause wind noise. Temporarily tape over the grille opening and test-drive the car. But don't leave the tape in place; overheating may result.

Carpenter ants

Locating their nests; exterminating the ants

These large black ants (about ½ inch long) excavate wood to build their nests. If they colonize a house's supports, they can significantly weaken the structure. If you see carpenter ants or notice bits of sawdust anywhere, there is probably an ant colony nearby. You may have to pull away siding to locate the nest. Carpenter ant galleries have a clean, polished appearance, whereas termite nests are lined with a thin coating of mud. Because there can be more than one colony of ants in a house, the entire house should be treated. It is therefore best to seek professional help.

Carpenter bees

What to do about these large, destructive bees

Signs of carpenter-bee activity are little piles of sawdust on decks or porches and neat, round ¼-inch-diameter holes in the woodwork. Carpenter bees are startlingly large, but rarely sting. However, they can cause con-

Smaller than life-size

siderable damage when they tunnel into exterior woodwork and porches to make their nests. Because carpenter bees nest individually, the damage starts slowly. Exterminate the bees as soon as you notice them. Spray the nest holes with any commercial wasp or hornet aerosol spray. Use the insecticide after dark on a cool evening, when bees are less active. A few days after spraying, fill the openings with a caulking compound.

Carpet beetles

Battling the damaging pests

These ⅛-inch-long black or mottled brown, black, and white beetles may be noticed on windowsills in spring. However, it is the larvae of the carpet beetle that cause damage, feeding on rugs, fabrics (including synthetics), fur, and lint accumulations. They thrive beneath furniture, at baseboards, in floor cracks—any place where it is dark or there is no traffic.

To avoid infestations, vacuum and clean carpets and upholstery often. If possible, change the position of large pieces of furniture. Dry clean slipcovers, blankets, and clothes. Dry cleaning kills carpet beetles.

If you see signs of carpet beetles, vacuum thoroughly and throw away the vacuum bag immediately. Spray with the household formulation containing either chlorpyrifos, tetramethrin, or diazinon; first test an inconspicuous area of fabric for colorfastness. (See also *Pesticides*.)

Carpet cleaning

Getting the dirt out

Because dirt wears at carpet fibers, it is a good idea to clean carpets regularly, even before they look dirty. When selecting a cleaning product, read the label carefully to make certain it is suitable for your carpet. Before you apply the cleaner, test it on a small, inconspicuous area.

Try to work on a clear, dry day. Open the windows wide to prevent a buildup of chemical fumes and to hasten drying. Remove all furniture. If a piece cannot be moved, wrap its legs in aluminum foil. Start by vacuuming thoroughly. If possible, fold the carpet back and vacuum the backing, pad, and floor. Pretreat heavily soiled spots with the cleaning agent.

Types of cleaners

If your carpet is only lightly soiled, you may be able to clean it with a canned spray foam. Apply the foam evenly, allow it to dry, then vacuum.

For a dirtier carpet (except shag), try a shampoo that you scrub into the fiber with a brush or a home-type carpet shampooer. To clean the entire surface evenly, overlap your strokes.

Most effective for cleaning any carpet, but particularly a heavily soiled one, is a machine that sprays hot water and detergent into the fiber. Such equipment can be rented at hardware and grocery stores. Be sure that you get the manufacturer's instructions and buy the recommended cleaning product. With this and other water-base shampoos, be careful not to over-wet the carpet, otherwise water may penetrate the backing.

For carpets that might be damaged by water, use dry-cleaning granules. Sprinkle them on the surface, brush them in, then vacuum. When testing this method, make sure your vacuum will completely remove the granules.

To slow dirt buildup, spray your clean carpet with a soil retardant or an antistatic chemical. (See also *Stain removal; Vacuuming.*)

Carpet laying

Calculating yardage; installing carpet over tackless strips

Using the proper equipment, some of which is rentable, you can install wall-to-wall carpet the professional way.

An accurate scale drawing will help you determine how many yards of carpet to buy and how best to lay it out. Measure the room, including any alcoves or bays; add 3 inches on all sides so that the carpet can be trimmed to fit precisely. If seaming is necessary,

keep in mind that any major seam should lay perpendicular to the principle source of daylight and away from areas of heavy wear. Also, carpet pile should all lean the same way, preferably toward the main door. Allow extra yardage for matching a pattern.

Use your drawing to calculate padding (the square footage of the room plus a few extra feet) and tackless stripping (the perimeter of the room plus a few extra feet).

Tackless stripping comes with pins of varying lengths. Test a carpet sample; you should be able to feel the pins but not be pricked by them. Be sure that preset nails, wood or masonry types, are appropriate for your floor.

Pins angled toward wall

Padding

Tackless stripping

Laying the carpet

Clean the floor, nail loose boards and, if possible, remove any quarter-round moldings. Install tackless stripping around the room (excluding the door-ways) 1/8 inch from the wall with pins leaning toward the wall. Lay the padding between the strips: staple it to wood flooring; adhere it to concrete. Rough cut the carpet, in an adjoining room if possible, allowing a few inches of excess. For a cut pile, use a utility knife along the back; for a loop pile, cut through the face, preferably with a *row-running knife.*

Lay out the carpet, kicking it into place. Slash the excess at corners so that the carpet will lie flat.

To seam, overlap the carpet edges 1 inch; cut the bottom layer with a row-running knife. Lay hot-melt seaming

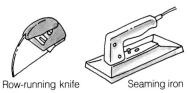

Row-running knife   Seaming iron

tape under the carpet edges, melt the adhesive with a *seaming iron,* then press the edges together over the tape.

Use a *knee-kicker* to anchor the carpet at two adjacent walls, then a

Knee-kicker

power stretcher (if you can find one, otherwise continue with the knee-kicker) to work the carpet into the opposite two walls. Hammer the carpet onto the tackless stripping. Trim the excess with a knife and tuck all edges behind the stripping. Secure the carpet at doorways with metal edging. Replace the quarter-round moldings.

Carpet repairs

Fixing indentations and burn holes; making a patch

To remove indentations left in a carpet by furniture, lay a damp bath towel over the depression and press with an iron. When the towel is dry, the indentation will be gone.

To repair a burn hole, first trim away the burned fibers with scissors. Dab rubber cement into the hole with a toothpick. From an unseen area of the carpet or a leftover scrap, cut enough matching tufts to fill the hole. Dab their ends with rubber cement and insert them in the hole. Work the tufts upright with a pin. When dry, trim them if necessary and use a pin to blend them with surrounding pile.

If you have carpet scraps, you can patch a damaged area up to 8 or 9 inches square. On the carpet back, mark off an area slightly larger than the damaged portion. Lay a board under it and cut it away with a sharp utility knife. Gently dab rubber cement along the edges of the hole at the carpet base to prevent loose strands from pulling free. Across the opening on the back, place strips of household adhesive tape (available in hardware stores) or glue a piece of burlap.

Using the damaged square for a pattern, cut a new piece that matches the old one in pattern and pile direction. Dab rubber cement around the edges of the backing; let it dry. (If your hole is patched with burlap, put double-face carpet adhesive on the back.) Press the piece firmly into the hole.

C

Car radios

Getting yours to work again

When a car radio stops working, don't assume the worst. The cure may be simpler than you think.

Turn on the radio. If you hear static, the problem may be in the antenna (see *Antennas*). Or the radio housing's electric ground may have loosened. Connect a jumper wire (a length of wire with an alligator clip at each end) securely to body metal and to the radio housing. If the radio then plays normally, look for a grounding wire, usually black, leading from the radio housing to body metal or to a dashboard brace. Clean and tighten the connections at both ends or replace the wire if it is broken.

Other possibilities are a poor connection at a speaker or failure of a speaker. Some speakers are readily accessible under detachable panels at the dash or on the rear package shelf. Disconnect and inspect the speaker connections. If they are corroded, wire-brush and reattach them. If a spade-type connector is loose in its terminal, crimp the edges of the terminal with pliers to restore a tight fit.

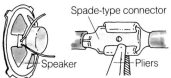

Spade-type connector

Speaker — Pliers

The most accurate way to check a speaker is to plug a new one into the wiring and see if the radio plays normally. Or you can inspect a speaker for obvious physical deterioration. None? Disconnect the speaker wires and connect an analog (needle and dial type) ohmmeter, set at a low-resistance scale, to the speaker terminals; you should hear a staticlike click if the speaker is good.

If you hear no static, check the fuse box for a blown fuse. If the radio fuse is good, look for a second fuse in the wire carrying current to the radio. If your car has such a fuse, you'll find it in a round holder that you can take apart. Replace the fuse if it is bad. Clean and tighten the metal terminals on wires going to the radio.

Car security

Protecting your car from theft

Automobiles are prime targets for burglars, so take every precaution against having your car stolen. Set the emergency brake, put the car in *Park* or in gear, turn the wheels sharply to the curb, and lock the steering column. Roll up the windows, put valuables out of sight, and lock the doors.

A wide variety of antitheft devices is available, including theft-resistant door-lock knobs and locks for the hood, trunk, wheels, and steering column. Use as many of these as make you feel secure. If you cause a thief difficulties, he'll look for easier quarry.

Car alarms are so popular that they are often ignored. But they still attract attention, which is what scares off thieves. A good alarm should set off a siren and flash the headlights to identify the car in a crowded area. It should turn itself off and rearm after 2 to 5 minutes, so as not to drain the car battery. A remote control allows you to set or disarm the alarm from the outside. A *Panic* button on the remote control allows you to trigger the siren if you're attacked near the car.

Carving meat and poultry

Slicing a roast neatly

Meat and poultry consist of thousands of long, thin strands of muscle. If you carve across these strands, that is, against the grain, the meat will usually be tenderer than if you cut parallel to them. Use the proper equipment—a two-pronged carving fork, preferably with a thumb guard, and a well-sharpened carving knife (see *Knives*).

A leg of lamb or a whole ham

Hold the meat steady with a fork. Take several lengthwise slices from the thin side to create a flat base; then rotate the meat so that it sits on that base. Slice the meat perpendicular to the bone. Then cut parallel to the bone to detach the slices. Cut the remaining meat from the other side of the bone in one piece and slice it. An

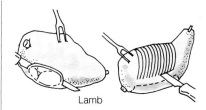

Lamb

alternate way of carving lamb is to remove lengthwise slices down to the bone on one side, then turn it over and repeat on the other side. Lamb is tender enough to slice with the grain.

Beef rib roast

If necessary, remove a slice from one end of a rib roast to form a flat base. Set the roast on the base as shown. Slice the meat across the top. Then cut vertically along the rib to remove the slice. Pick up the slice by inserting

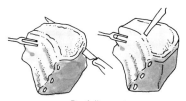

Beef rib roast

the knife under it, the fork steadying it from above. Rib roast can be cut very thin or as thick as half an inch.

Pork loin roast

Ask the butcher to remove the backbone from a pork loin. Slice down the center of the meat between the ribs so that there is a bone in each serving. Or you can slice right along each side of each rib bone, making thinner slices, and alternating one with and one without a bone.

Turkey

Carving a turkey is similar to carving other poultry—all fowl have basically the same anatomy, though their proportions are different. Begin by cutting off the drumsticks and second joints, slicing through the joints. Then hold the bony end of the drumstick and slice downward, parallel to the bone. Next, slice the meat from

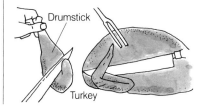

Drumstick

Turkey

the thighbone. Remove the wings by slicing through their joints. Finally, cut the breast meat in thin slices from either side of the breastbone.

Car washing and polishing

Maintaining a car's finish

Ideally, wash your car every few weeks. Hose off loose dirt first. Then use a sponge to wash the surface with a sudsy solution of water and a detergent made for car washing. (Don't use household detergents; they may be too harsh and can streak a car's finish.) Rinse the car, working from the roof down.

Remove bugs and road tar with a tar remover. Tree sap, bird droppings, and other stubborn stains may require a spot application of cleaner-polish, a product sold for weathered car finishes. Rinse the car again after using any special cleaners, then wipe it dry with an old terry-cloth towel or similar soft, absorbent cloth.

When to wax
Renew wax whenever water no longer forms into small, distinct beads on the flat surfaces of a car, usually every few months. Apply the wax according to the manufacturer's instructions.

Spray-on, wipe-off products work well on new cars and those with finishes in good condition. If your car is more than 2 years old, chances are its finish has weathered. In this case, use a cleaner-polish that contains a mild abrasive to remove the weathered top layer of paint. Wipe the polish off and buff the car's surface by hand with a clean, soft cloth. (A power buffer may leave swirl marks.)

Casino

A card game for two

The object is to capture cards from the table. A game ends after playing the sixth deal—the player with the highest number of points wins—or after one player reaches 21 points.

Deal two cards to your opponent, the table (face up), and yourself, then repeat. After each hand, deal eight more the same way, but none to the table. At the beginning of the sixth deal, you must say, "Last."

During play, an ace counts as 1; numbered cards, face value. Face cards can only be played as pairs.

The nondealer plays first. He can take from the table one or more cards of the same rank as a card he holds or two or more cards that add up to the one he is playing. For example, he can take a five and a four from the table by playing a nine. Or he can *build* by laying one card from his hand on top of a table card, announcing the combination he is building. For example, laying an ace on a four he would say, "Building five" (his hand must contain a five). He can also build like-numbered cards, not face cards. On his next turn, he takes the build, duplicates it with an additional five or increases it (once duplicated, a build cannot be increased), unless, meanwhile, his opponent has increased or taken it. If he cannot take any cards, he *trails* by laying a card on the table.

Cards taken (placed facedown) cannot be reexamined except for the last pickup. If you take all table cards in one play (a *sweep*), turn one faceup in the pile. After the last round, remaining cards on the table go to the taker of the last card (this is not a sweep).

Tally as follows: 27 or more cards = 3; 7 or more spades = 1; big casino (10 of diamonds) = 2; little casino (2 of spades) = 1; ace = 1; sweep = 1.

Casseroles

Preparing tasty main dishes

A well-planned casserole can be a culinary triumph. Too often, however, a casserole consists of nondescript leftovers and bland sauce, or fillers such as rice and potatoes are used so heavily that meat appears only as a surprise. Another sort of casserole fiasco is a few pieces of vegetable or meat afloat in a pasty sauce. To avoid this, combine three parts solids with one part sauce (see *White sauce*). If the sauce is thin, use just enough to keep the main ingredients moist.

Casserole ingredients are usually cooked, cut into bite-size pieces, then mixed with a sauce and turned into a well-greased baking dish. Or solid ingredients and sauce can be layered into the baking dish, ending with the sauce. Fish, pasta, and vegetables should be slightly undercooked to prevent overcooking in the heating. Leave ½ inch of bubble-up space at the top of the casserole to prevent sauce from spilling over. For flavor and color sprinkle shredded cheese, buttered crumbs, or paprika on top just before baking. Or cover the casserole with biscuit or corn bread dough.

Preheat the oven to 350°F or 375°F. Place the casserole just below the center of the oven. Bake uncovered, unless the recipe specifies a cover, 30 to 45 minutes. It's done when the sauce bubbles lazily at the edges and a spatula inserted in the center releases a puff of steam. If you're not serving the casserole right away, cover it to keep it warm and prevent drying.

Casseroles can be assembled in advance, refrigerated or frozen, and whisked into the oven (don't thaw a frozen one first). But plan ahead; a casserole that is frozen or very cold requires at least twice the baking time as a freshly made one. Fish, poultry, meat, pasta, rice, and vegetables freeze and reheat well. Avoid freezing potatoes; they tend to get watery.

Cassettes and recorders

Fixing jammed tape; cleaning cassette recorders

If a cassette tape snags, fish out the tangled portion from the cartridge with a bent paper clip. Lay the tape on a flat surface, press the wrinkles out with your fingers, then rewind it, using a pen cap to turn the reel.

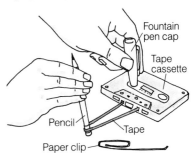

It may be easier to get at a jammed tape by opening the cartridge: unscrew the cartridge or, if there are no screws, pry it open along the weld line (you won't be able to reuse the cartridge). If a tape breaks, splice it, using a splicing kit from an electronics shop. After repairing the tape, screw the cartridge together or fit the reels into a replacement case.

Cleaning the recorder
Weekly cleaning of your recorder (or after 10 playing hours) will make your tapes last longer. Oxide buildup from the tape onto the tape heads and guides eventually decreases sound fidelity. Also, magnetic buildup can, in time, cause distortion. To get rid of oxide, use a cleaning kit from an electronics store or swab the heads, capstan, rollers, and guides with cleaning solution (denatured alcohol on

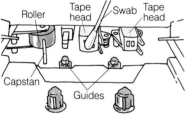

rubber parts, trichloroethylene on metal). Rid the tape head of magnetic buildup by running a demagnetizing cassette in the recorder as instructed. Never lubricate the mechanism.

Complex microcircuitry in cassette recorders makes servicing of electronic parts difficult. Major problems may call for professional repairs or even a new machine.

Cast-iron cookware

How to care for it

Cast-iron cookware heats slowly and evenly, and holds heat well. It is ideal for fried foods, stews, and soups. But it rusts easily, so a new pot or pan should be seasoned before use, even though labeled "preseasoned." Scrub it thoroughly; coat the inside thinly and evenly with melted, unsalted shortening or salad oil (not olive oil, which may leave a taste). Set the pot in a 325° to 350°F oven for 2 hours. When it is cool, wipe off the excess oil,

rinse the pot, and dry it on a burner set at low heat.

After each use, wipe cast iron with a damp cloth or paper towel. Dry it immediately. If charred food adheres to it, scour it with coarse dry salt. To remove caked-on food or rust, scour in soapy water; rinse, dry, and reseason.

Store cast-iron cookware in a dry place, leaving the lids off to allow trapped moisture to escape; place paper towels between stacked pots. Do not store food in cast iron.

Caterpillars

Preventing plant destruction

A well-maintained garden is one of the best defenses against damage from caterpillars—the larvae of butterflies and moths. Feed and water plants adequately. Cultivate and weed weekly. Be alert to drooping stems and partly eaten foliage and remove them. By avoiding pesticides, you'll encourage the presence of caterpillar predators, such as birds, parasitic wasps, lady beetles, and praying mantises.

Promptly after harvesting, burn or trash old leaves and stems; caterpillars can overwinter in them. Dig or rototill your garden in the early spring to expose and destroy pupae.

Leaf-eating caterpillars
Wearing gloves, handpick large caterpillars and drop them into a pail of warm soapy water or water topped with ½ inch of kerosene. For major infestations, spray with *Bacillus thuringiensis,* a natural control toxic only to caterpillars.

Stem-burrowing caterpillars
These borers are invisible and immune to most pesticides. Stunted or yellowing leaves are signs of their presence. Remove squash-vine borers by making a lengthwise knife cut in the stem of a yellowing leaf; discard the pest. Press the split stem together and put some soil over the incision. If damage is widespread, uproot and destroy all affected plants. As a preventive, spray with methoxychlor around the base of squash plants when they begin to produce vines and at 10-day intervals three times thereafter. Wait 1 day before harvest.

Stalk borers, which kill tomato and pepper plants by tunneling in their stems, cannot be controlled by pesticides. Rid your garden of weeds—their breeding places.

Tree- and fruit-eating caterpillars
During winter, look for egg masses on trunks and branches and under loose bark; scrape them off and destroy them. In spring and early summer, trap caterpillars by banding trunks and thick branches with burlap or sticky bands. As the season progresses, replace the sticky bands as necessary and destroy pupae that accumulate in the burlap. Tear out webs of tent caterpillars as soon as they appear. Check with the Cooperative Extension Service (see p.5) on advised spray programs in your area. (See also *Cutworms; Gypsy moths; Pesticides; Tomato hornworm.*)

Cats

Feline feeding, training, grooming, and health care

Before buying or adopting a cat, examine its general health and disposition. Its coat should be sleek, with no bare patches, and completely clean on the hind legs and under the tail. Observe how the cat responds to your holding and petting. Invite it to play by trailing a piece of string. Lack of alertness and playfulness may indicate poor health or former neglect.

Housebreaking
Allow the new cat to explore your home freely, but keep it indoors for 10 days. Provide a litter box, partially filled with an even layer of commercial kitty litter. Remove soiled litter daily with a slotted spatula; the box should be emptied and scrubbed with a disinfectant twice a week. If you have doubts about your new cat's housetraining, restrict it to an area near the litter box for several days. Even if you plan to allow your cat outside eventually, you will need a litter box during the first 10 days while your cat is adjusting to its new home.

Diet
Cat food, whether canned, moist (in packets), or dry, will provide your cat with well-balanced nutrition. To keep

a cat from becoming a finicky eater, remove any declined meal, refrigerate it, then present it, returned to room temperature and freshly stirred, at the next feeding.

An occasional table scrap is a treat, but don't feed your cat pork, very fatty meats, poultry skin, or bones of fish or fowl. Fish should be on its menu only once or twice a week. Most cats enjoy looking for additional treats from food left on the table. It's best to remove the temptation.

Some cats eat too fast, causing vomiting. To slow a fast eater, spread its food thinly over a large container such as a roasting pan.

You may be able to discourage your cat from hunting birds, rodents, or other small creatures by tossing a few pebbles at it (while you are out of sight) whenever it stalks one. If your cat hunts, it may pick up diseases from its prey.

Grooming

Groom your cat with a brush or a comb with rounded tips; this stimulates the skin and removes loose fur. Long-haired cats, especially when shedding, need daily grooming; other cats need brushing every few days.

Even regularly groomed cats swallow fur while cleaning themselves. This can lead to hair balls in the stomach, causing retching and occasionally a blockage in the intestine. If your cat has this problem, add a teaspoon of petroleum jelly to its food twice a week; groom it more often.

When grooming your cat, check for fleas; they may be apparent only from tiny black specks (their droppings). Some cats are allergic to fleas and develop eczema after a few flea bites. To rid your cat of fleas, use only those flea products marked safe for cats.

Health

Have a new cat or kitten examined by a veterinarian. Shots against panleucopenia (distemper) and rhinotracheitis and calici (serious respiratory infections) are musts. Rabies shots are advisable, too. Checkups should be done annually, at which time booster shots can be given.

Have a kitten checked for worms. Worming medicine is a mild poison; don't give it to a sick cat, young or old, without the advice of a veterinarian.

Any cat not intended for breeding should be spayed or neutered as soon as it matures sexually (around 6 months for a female and 8 to 9 months for a male). Contrary to popular belief, this will not cause obesity, and it makes a tom cat less likely to wander.

If your cat is off its feed, sneezes often, or seems lethargic, check its temperature with a rectal thermometer that has been lubricated with petroleum jelly. Raise the tail and hold the cat firmly while slipping the thermometer 1 inch into the anus. Read after 3 minutes. A cat's normal temperature ranges between 100°F and 103°F. Report a temperature above 103°F to your veterinarian.

Never give a cat any drug without checking with a veterinarian. Cats are very sensitive to many drugs, prescription and over-the-counter. (See also *Animal odors; Clawing cats; Fleas; Housebreaking pets; Traveling with pets.*)

Cat's cradle

Having fun with string

Cat's cradles have been made by peoples as diverse as Japanese school girls, African tribesmen, and Alaskan Eskimos. All you need to make one is 2 yards of string or yarn tied at the ends in a square knot (see *Knots*) and your two hands.

The basic cat's cradle is made by passing the string behind the backs of both thumbs and little fingers (but in front of your other fingers) while holding your palms parallel. Draw your hands apart so that the string is taut, then bring your palms closer together so that the string loosens. Insert your right index finger under

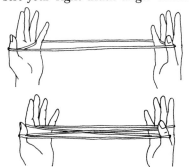

your left palmar string (the string lying in front of your left palm). Do the same with your left index finger and your right palmar string. Finally, draw your palms apart, tightening the string, and there you have it!

Working with the same string, you can make endless variations of this basic design. Use your imagination and experiment. It can be lots of fun.

Caulking

Filling house cracks that cause heat loss

As winter approaches, check inside your house for cracks. Search for drafts by placing a lighted candle near shut doors, window frames, and corner and wall joints. If it flickers, there's a crack. Look for these cracks on the outside of your house. In addition, examine areas where the siding and steps meet the foundation. Seal

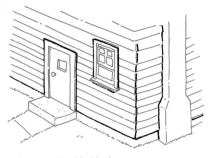

Areas outlined in black may need caulking

any cracks on the exterior with a flexible caulking compound. Work while the temperature is above 50 °F.

Most caulking needs renewing every 5 years or so. Sizable cracks in wood siding, concrete, roofing, and masonry surfaces may require a permanent repair job.

Caulking compounds

The most durable have a base of latex, Butyl rubber, polyvinyl acetate, or silicone. Some are better than others on particular surfaces and some require priming. Read the label. Caulking compounds come in bulk cans, in cartridges for use with a gun, in squeeze tubes, and in ropelike strips, good for temporary seals around storm windows or air conditioners.

Preparation for caulking

Scrape away dirt, grease, and old compound with a putty knife; finish with a wire brush. To ensure adhesion, clean the crack with a solvent such as mineral spirits. Fill cracks wider than ½ inch with oakum before caulking. When dealing with a lacquered aluminum surface, first remove the lacquer with xylol, then wire-brush the surface, and finally apply a quality metal primer with a rust-inhibiting agent.

Applying caulk

For an average-size job, use a cartridge inserted in a caulking gun. Cut the end of the nozzle diagonally at a width that is equal to that of the crack. To apply evenly, pull the trigger while moving the gun down the crack

Rope-type caulking | Caulking gun

at a 45-degree angle. For smaller jobs use compound in squeeze tubes. To caulk around an air conditioner or a window, push in rope-type caulking with your fingers. (See also *Bathtub recaulking; Weather stripping*.)

Ceiling boxes

How to install an electric box for a ceiling fixture

Inspect the ceiling; you may find that an old ceiling box was covered. If so, use existing wiring. But first have the wiring checked by an electrician; it may need replacing.

Caution: Before working on wiring, turn off the power to the circuit you are working on (see *Circuit testing*).

If you must add wiring, the easiest installation is a metal raceway running from a wall outlet to the point where the ceiling fixture will hang. Because a raceway is visible, it isn't suitable for every room. Some local codes regulate its installation; check with your municipality's building department.

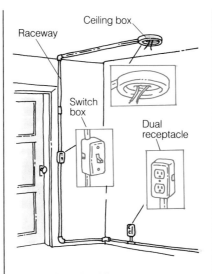

Plasterboard ceilings

Locate joists: look for nails holding the plasterboard to the joists or use a stud finder (see *Studs*). Put on goggles and drill a ⅜-inch hole between joists where you want a fixture to hang. Draw a 6-inch square around the hole; cut out the square with a keyhole saw. Extend a tape measure into the opening and measure between one edge of the opening and the nearest joist. Add 1 inch to this dimension and mark that distance on the ceiling. Repeat, measuring from the opposite edge of the opening.

Using your marks as guides, draw a square around the opening. With a straightedge and a utility knife, cut along the lines drawn, then cut the square into four truncated triangles. Wearing goggles, hammer the triangles from the ceiling. Cut away the inner layer of paper holding the plaster fragments. Using a brick chisel and ball-peen hammer, cut away plasterboard on the joist sides of the hole.

On new plasterboard measure and cut a square ⅛ inch narrower than the opening. Center the ceiling box on

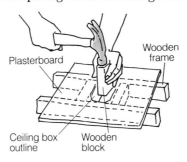

this square and trace its outline. Cut along these lines, then cut the outline in half. Resting the outline on four pieces of wood, knock out the halved form with a hammer and a block of wood, then trim the rim. Run wiring to the box (see *Wiring*) or call in an electrician.

Attach the box to an adjustable bar hanger. Nail the hanger to the joists, making the box flush with the replacement board. Support the plasterboard square, dark side up, with your forearm as you nail its corners to the joists. Nail the joist sides fast with nails spaced several inches apart. To fill and tape cracks, see *Plasterboard*.

Plaster-and-lath ceilings

Tap the ceiling with a cloth-wrapped hammer to locate two neighboring joists, then mark a spot midway for the fixture. Chisel away plaster at that point to expose a lath. Chisel a path along the lath, from one joist to the

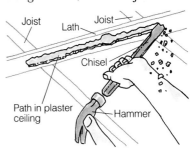

other, then trace the outline of the box where the fixture is to hang. Drill a ⅜-inch hole in the center of the outline; cut out the outline with a keyhole saw while supporting the outer rim with your hand. The inner edges of the joists should be visible.

Saw the exposed lath from the joists and remove lath nails. Screw the box to an offset hanger. Place the hanger into the ceiling groove and adjust the

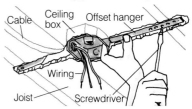

box to fit the hole. Wire the box. Screw the hanger to the joists. Fill the channels with patching plaster; after it has dried, apply spackling compound. Sand smooth, then paint.

Ceiling fans

Their use, installation, and maintenance

A slow-turning ceiling fan cools your skin temperature by increasing the airflow in the room and evaporating your body's perspiration. When used with an air conditioner, a ceiling fan can make less cooling feel like more. In winter, ceiling fans can reclaim heat by returning the rising warm air to floor level. For safety, a ceiling should be at least 10 feet high.

Installation

A ceiling fan can replace a chandelier (some fans incorporate lights) or it can be mounted on newly installed wiring (see *Ceiling boxes*). Mounting systems vary with the manufacturer. Many feature a ball-and-socket system that reduces fan vibration.

To install such a fan, turn off the circuit power (see *Circuit testing*). Screw a mounting crossbar across the ceiling box. Extend the ceiling wires through or over the crossbar. Screw the cradle (or the canopy that doubles as a cradle) to the crossbar, then insert the down-rod ball into the open side of the cradle's socket. Attach the ceiling wires to the fan's wires (like to like, or as instructed) and secure them with wire connectors. Place the canopy over the ceiling box and screw it fast. Attach the blades to the motor housing according to factory instructions.

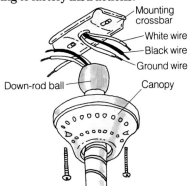

Mounting crossbar
White wire
Black wire
Ground wire
Down-rod ball
Canopy

A ceiling fan's large motor usually doesn't get overworked; it may last a long time without repair. Twice a year wipe the blades and the housing with a damp cloth.

Centipedes

How they differ from millipedes; controlling both

Centipedes—fast-moving, multisegmented arthropods up to several inches long—prey on household and garden insects. House centipedes are harmless to humans, but the bite of some other species is poisonous. They bite humans only if disturbed. You may be allergic to their venom; if you are bitten, consult a physician.

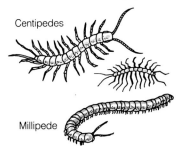

Centipedes

Millipede

Millipedes, often mistaken for centipedes, are harmless, slow-moving arthropods with two pairs of legs per segment (centipedes have one pair). Millipedes feed on decaying organic matter. Both hide in damp places: in decaying vegetation, beneath scrap lumber, and in other debris.

To rid your house of an infestation, clear the foundation and the basement of all such hiding places. Locate your compost pile well away from the house. If the problem persists, spray infested areas with the household formulation of malathion or with diazinon or carbaryl (see *Pesticides*).

Ceramic tile

Tiling a wall or floor; replacing a broken tile

Ceramic tile comes in a variety of sizes, shapes, colors, and patterns. The most common sizes are 1, 4¼, 6, 8, and 12 inches square. Use glazed tiles on walls; unglazed or mat-glazed tiles are better for floors. Coat unglazed tiles with a waterproof sealant. On uniform surfaces, you can use tiles that come on prespaced backing sheets that make installation easier.

Measure the area to be tiled accurately, choose your tile, and ask the dealer how many tiles you need. Consult him also about the proper adhesive to use.

Preparing the surface

You can lay tile on concrete or exterior plywood. The surface must be firm and level. Uneven concrete surfaces can be made smooth and level with a layer of mortar. Springy wallboard and subfloor should be nailed securely. Cover a disfigured but firm surface with ⅜-inch exterior plywood.

Laying tile

The first row of tiles is crucial. On a wall surrounding a bathtub, for instance, draw a tile-height line right above the bathtub rim. Hammer in tacks at either end of the line and stretch a chalked string between them; level the line (see *Leveling*). Snap the string to mark a horizontal line. Next, mark a yardstick with lines the width of your tiles. Shift the stick left and right to find a starting point for laying tiles so that fractional tiles at either end will be equal. After marking the tile widths on this line, snap a vertical chalk line at each full-tile end, making a squared-off area.

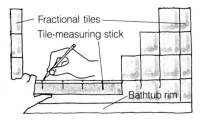

Fractional tiles
Tile-measuring stick
Bathtub rim

Start at either vertical line. Spread the adhesive evenly on the bottom half of the square area with a notch-edge trowel, as specified on the adhesive package. Press the wall tiles gently into place. Then do the top half. Apply fractional tiles after you have tiled the squared-off area.

Notch-edge trowel
Adhesive

Cutting tiles

To cut a fractional tile, draw a line on top with a china-marking pencil; score the line with a glass cutter. Lay a pencil or a nail under the scored line and press down on both halves, snapping the line. For cutting out a curved portion, score a line; then, using tile nippers, remove small bits until the curve has been achieved.

Grouting

Let the adhesive set for at least 2 days. Trim excess at the joints with your fingertip and wipe the adhesive thoroughly from tile surfaces with a damp sponge. The next day, fill the joints with grout. Press this paste (commonly purchased as a water-soluble powder) into the joints with a rubber squeegee. After the grout has cured for 72 hours, coat it with silicone sealant to protect it from water splashes.

Tiling a floor

To tile a floor, first snap a line from the middle of the doorsill to the opposite wall. Mark the line into tile widths, leaving a $1/16$-inch gap between tiles. At the edge mark off the last full tile, nail a room-width wooden batten 90 degrees to this line. Nail a second batten 90 degrees to the first. Using floor-tile adhesive, start tiling at the 3-foot-

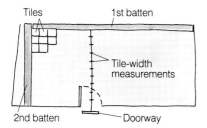

square area within the batten corner. After pressing the tiles into place, insert $1/16$-inch plastic spacers (available from your tile dealer) between them. Install the fractional tiles last. Grout as above.

Replacing a broken tile

Dig out the grout around a damaged tile with a stiff putty knife. With a hammer, tap a cold chisel lightly but sharply on one corner until the tile breaks. Pry out the broken bits with the chisel. Scrape off old mortar or adhesive with a stiff putty knife; brush the area clean. Spread adhesive on the back of the replacement tile, and set it flush with the surface of the surrounding tiles. Grout and seal the joints.

Chafing dish cooking

Many uses of an old-time convenience

A chafing dish, fashionable in Edwardian times, is still useful for slow, even cooking, for flambéing, and for keeping foods warm on a buffet table. It can cook such foods as scrambled eggs, Welsh rarebit, panned oysters, and lobster newburg, or sauces in which to heat precooked foods. The fuel can be alcohol or canned heat.

To cook in a chafing dish, fill the fuel vessel and light the fuel with care. Insert the water pan and pour very hot water into it. Set the cooking pan over the water bath; if there is a wick, adjust it so that the water stays just below boiling. Proceed with your recipe. (See also *Flambéing.*)

Chain saws

Refueling; basic maintenance; lubricating, tensioning, and sharpening the chain

Caution: Wear heavy gloves when handling a saw or its chain. Turn off the ignition switch or unplug an electric model before touching the chain or performing any other maintenance or repairs.

Before refueling a gasoline-powered chain saw, brush away any sawdust from the machine and clean the passages that permit air to pass through the housing. Keep the fuel clean by brushing dirt from the container and straining the gasoline.

Refuel with 2-cycle oil and regular gasoline—don't use automotive oil or

Before heavy use, check the spark plugs. If they are heavily coated with oil deposits, replace them.

After every 5 to 10 hours of cutting with a gasoline saw, clean the cylinder fins with a stiff brush and a vacuum-extension tool. Remove sheet metal covers and the muffler to get at the fins. Take out the air filter, usually housed under the carburetor cover. Wash the filter in detergent and water, rinse, and dry it thoroughly.

At the start of the season, clean the fuel filter in automobile carburetor cleaner. Pull the tube from the tank with a wire hook, detach the filter for cleaning. Reinsert the filter and tube. During the season, replace the filter if the engine sags upon acceleration.

Fill the oil reservoir of any saw with chain oil (sometimes called bar-and-

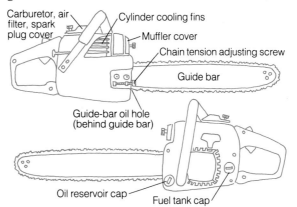

unleaded gasoline in a chain saw. If you can get 1–40 oil for your make of saw, use it in preference to conventional 2-cycle oil. Mix the oil and gasoline in a clean container in the ratio given by saw manufacturer.

chain oil) each time you refuel. On a manual oiler, check the oil level often during cutting. Allowing an automatic oiler to run out of oil will damage the chain. Check the guide-bar oil hole for dirt; clean it out with a wire.

Continued next page

C

Check the chain tension before cutting and often during the work period, especially the first half hour. Chain tangs (projections on back of chain) should be invisible when cold; half their length should show when hot. If it's necessary to increase tension, let the saw cool down, then slightly loosen the guide-bar mounting nut or nuts and turn the tension-adjusting screw, usually clockwise. Retighten the nut or nuts.

Sharpening a chain

Dirt dulls a chain; brush dirt from logs before cutting; keep the chain off the ground. Sharpen the chain every 4 hours of use rather than waiting until you must force the saw to cut.

Use the round file specified by the manufacturer and a file holder that you position at the specified sharpening angle (usually 35 degrees). Hold the chain in place by turning the ten-

sion adjusting screw or by tripping the chain brake on saws with this feature. File the teeth in the center of the guide bar, working from inside toward the outside, then release and advance the chain and file the next group of teeth. Two or three file strokes per tooth is enough. Halfway through, rotate the file in the holder.

After three sharpenings, file the depth gauges (the round projections at the back ends of tooth links), using a depth-gauge tool and a flat file; make the gauges alike in height. Afterward round off the corner of each gauge.

After a chain has been filed to half its original height, use the next smaller diameter file. When chain teeth require constant sharpening, replace the chain, following instructions in the owner's manual. If the saw's guide bar is reversible, reverse it top to bottom after 5 to 10 hours of cutting.

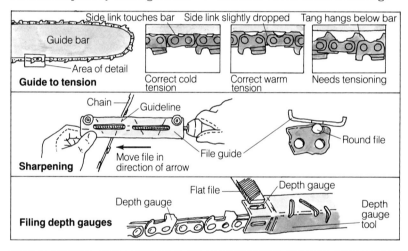

Chair repairs

Regluing and repairing joints; repairing breaks; leveling legs

A chair's strength depends on the firmness of its joints. Chair parts are joined by dowel-and-socket or mortise-and-tenon joints. One loose joint

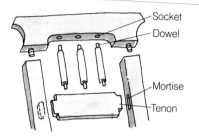

can cause other parts or joints to weaken or break unless repairs are made. Old, brittle glue can crumble, allowing joints to wiggle and gradually enlarge their socket or mortise.

If possible, reglue and clamp a shaky joint without disassembling the chair. Pull the joint apart slightly and use a stiff wire to scratch off all the old glue. Squirt in fresh wood glue and wiggle the joint to work the fresh glue into the wood. You can also insert the glue from a glue injector into a small hole drilled through the wood behind a socket or mortise, or you can push the glue in with a toothpick.

If a socket is enlarged, you may be able to stabilize the joint by jamming bits of matchsticks or toothpicks into the fresh glue around the edges. Some hardware stores carry a liquid synthetic that swells the fibers of wobbly joints so that they fit firmly. Another way to fill an enlarged socket is to mix a bit of sawdust with the glue.

If you have to disassemble a joint, remove any reinforcing nails, screws, or braces; then tap the joint apart with a mallet or padded hammer. Work carefully: screws or brads may be hidden by wood filler or wooden plugs. Sometimes older chairs have joints that cannot be disassembled without splitting the wood.

If these measures fail to cure wobbliness, you must either enlarge a

Chair marks

Protecting wood floors; removing scratches

Chairs that are often moved around can mar wood floors. Prevent this by putting rubber or smooth metal tips on chair legs. Lay a clear plastic mat or an area rug under a rolling chair.

If a waxed floor is lightly scratched, a liquid solvent-base wax or paste wax may disguise the marks. Otherwise go over the area with fine steel wool and a solvent, such as mineral spirits, then rewax. If a polyurethaned floor is

hazed with scratches, you can revive it with a light overall sanding and a fresh coat of polyurethane.

To blend a deep scratch with the surrounding wood, remove old wax with solvent, then fill the scar with a tinted wax, wood stain, a wood-toned crayon (available in hardware stores), or matching wood putty (sand the wood putty when dry). If the floor has been finished with varnish, shellac, or polyurethane, touch it up with the same finish, feathering your brush strokes to blend with the surrounding finish. If the floor has been treated with a penetrating finish or wax, apply a fresh coat.

dowel or tenon or make the socket or mortise smaller. You can fatten a dowel or a tenon by wrapping it with thread before applying glue. Or you can saw a slit in the end of the dowel or tenon and drive a thin wooden wedge into the slit. As the part is pushed into the socket, the wedge will widen it to fit. To make a socket smaller, plug it with glue and a tight-fitting dowel. Let the glue dry, saw the dowel flush with the surrounding wood, and redrill a socket the correct size.

Before regluing a joint, make a practice run so you know just how you're going to clamp it while the glue dries. Use nonmarring wood clamps or protect the chair with blocks of scrap wood placed under the jaws of C-clamps. Web clamps are particularly useful for working on chairs. You can improvise one by tightening a rope with a stick, tourniquet style. Protect the wood with padding.

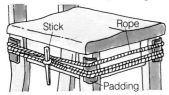

If a rung or leg breaks along the grain of the wood, glue it together then wrap masking tape or wax paper and string around it until the glue dries. Breaks that occur across the grain must be reinforced with dowels or, for small rungs, metal pins.

If your chair wobbles because the legs are of different lengths, set it on a level surface to identify the faulty leg. Put a glide on the shortest leg or cut a sliver off the longest one.

Chairs with padded seats set in a frame usually have reinforcing corner blocks where the legs meet the frame. If these are wobbly, take them off and reattach them with fresh glue and slightly larger screws. To increase the strength of joints, add reinforcing blocks where there are none.

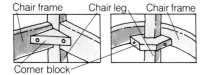

Chandeliers

Installation and rewiring

Caution: Before working on a chandelier, be sure to turn off the power to its circuit (see *Circuit testing*).

Unscrew the nut or the setscrew holding the canopy of the old chandelier. Lower the canopy. Your installation may have a steel bracket instead of a hickey, but the procedure is similar. Disconnect the wires, unscrew the hickey or bracket from the ceiling box stud, and lower the old fixture.

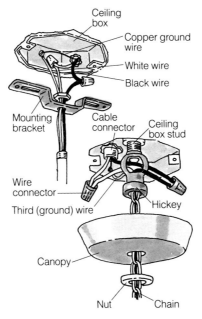

Construct a sturdy wire hook from a twisted coat hanger. Use this to support the new fixture while you rewire: attach one hook end to the ceiling box, the other to the new fixture, and the new hickey to the ceiling box stud. Connect the chandelier to the hickey.

Run the chandelier wires through the hickey and attach them to the ceiling wires (black to black, white to white) with wire connectors. If there is a third wire, attach it to the box or to the line ground wire. Raise the canopy and secure it with the setscrew or nut. To mount a chandelier where none existed, see *Ceiling boxes*.

Rewiring a chandelier

Turn off the power to the circuit. Unfasten the arms from the center stem

unit of a disconnected chandelier. Remove old wiring. Thread new lamp cord through the stem and weave it into the chandelier's chain.

Rewire the socket arms with 16-gauge stranded wire, attaching a wire to each socket terminal. Take one wire from each socket arm and twist them together with a wire from the lamp cord at the chandelier's base; secure with a wire connector. Repeat this step with the remaining socket wires and the other lamp cord wire.

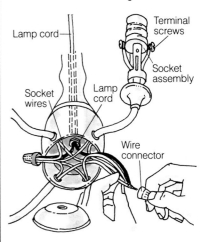

Charades

Making a game of pantomime

In charades, players act out names, titles, or phrases in pantomime while other players try to guess them. The game is usually played in two teams.

Each player in turn is given a subject by the opposing team. The player then attempts to communicate the subject to his or her teammates by acting out key words. The performance is timed, and the team that guesses all of its subjects faster wins.

Special signs can be used. To show that you'll be acting out a book title, for instance, hold your hands together like a book. Show the number of words in the subject by holding up your fingers. Then indicate which word you're acting out; for instance, hold up three fingers for the third word. Divide a word into syllables by placing your fingers on your arm to indicate the number and to show which syllable you are acting out.

C

Checkbook balancing

Reconciling the bank's figures and your own

Balancing your checkbook is the only way to know whether you and your bank agree about the amount in your checking account. The monthly bank statement lists all transactions: deposits, withdrawals, service charges, such as stop-payment orders, and interest (if your account bears interest). The sooner you reconcile the statement with your checkbook, the easier it will be to find and correct an error.

With your statement you probably receive canceled checks for the period covered (some banks are phasing out this service). If checks are included, first compare each one with the figure listed on the statement, then put the checks in numerical order and compare them with your check stubs or register. If your bank doesn't return checks, simply compare each item on the statement with stubs or register. (Keeping careful records, always important, becomes even more so as banks eliminate returning canceled checks.) Next, compare your deposit receipts or records with deposits listed on the statement.

If you find no errors in making any of these comparisons, you're ready to take the next steps: 1. Add up all outstanding checks (those not returned or listed and those written after the statement was issued), including unlisted withdrawals made with bank cards from money machines. Subtract the total from the final balance on your statement. 2. Add all subsequent, unlisted deposits to the statement balance. 3. Subtract from this total any service charges. If the account is interest bearing, add the listed interest.

At this point, you and your bank should agree. If you don't, recheck your figures. Look closely at your handwriting; a confusing or illegible figure may have caused an error. Make sure you haven't overlooked an outstanding check or machine withdrawal. If you find no explanation for the discrepancy, take your records to the bank as soon as possible.

Checkers

Capturing and conquering

The game of checkers is played on a board 8 squares by 8 squares, alternately dark and light, with 12 dark and 12 light disklike *checkers* or *men.* The aim of the game is to capture and remove all your opponent's checkers or otherwise render him or her incapable of moving.

Arrange the 12 dark checkers on the dark squares in the three horizontal rows nearest you while your opponent does the same with the light checkers at the opposite side of the board. Checkers can rest or move only on dark squares. Moves are made forward diagonally one square at a time. Black (dark) moves first.

Captures are made by jumping over your opponent's checkers onto a free square. You may make a series of captures in one move. If you fail to make a possible jump, you lose the checker that failed to jump.

When a checker reaches a square in the opponent's rear (king's) row, it becomes a king and is crowned by placing a captured checker of the same color on top of it. A king can move backward as well as forward.

Cheesemaking

An age-old technique

Cheesemaking is a way of preserving surplus milk, with the aid of certain bacteria, to make a nutritious food that is easier to digest than milk itself. Good-tasting results, however, take time, practice, and patience.

Hard cheeses such as Swiss and Cheddar have been pressed and aged for several months to develop their fine, rich flavor. You must work with at least 4 gallons of milk to make a hard cheese that will age well, so it is better to try soft or fresh cheeses first.

All equipment—of enamel, stainless steel, glass, or wood—should be meticulously clean; unwanted bacteria may introduce unpleasant flavors. Use raw milk that has been pasteurized (heated to 162°F for 20 seconds) or reconstituted dried milk. Homogenized milk is unsuitable.

Basic soft cheese

This recipe, carefully made, produces a slightly granular soft cheese that can be eaten immediately but which will keep for up to 3 weeks under refrigeration. You will need a 5-quart pot, set in a larger pan partly filled with water, or a double boiler of the same size, and a thermometer with gradations of at least 70° to 120°F.

Warm 1 gallon of milk with 1 cup unpasteurized, cultured buttermilk to 92°F. Dissolve ¼ tablet of rennet (available at drugstores) in ½ cup cool water and stir thoroughly into the milk. Then leave the pan of milk undisturbed in a warm place for about half an hour, or until the milk coagulates into a jellylike mass.

When the coagulated milk can be pulled cleanly away from the side of the pan with a knife or spoon, cut the curds (solids) into 1-inch cubes with a long knife. Return the cubes to the

Cuts should be ½" apart

pot and reheat them to around 92°F. Stir gently at this temperature for 30 minutes. Stir in 3 teaspoons salt. Hang the curds to drain in cheesecloth or fine muslin. Drain for 3 to 12 hours depending on how moist or dry a cheese you want. Store the cheese in a clean container in the refrigerator.

Cheese sauces

Flavorful toppings for cooked foods; making an au gratin dish

A Cheddar or process (American) cheese is the most popular for making cheese sauce: Cheddar for a stronger flavor, process cheese for a milder taste and easy melting quality. Colby, longhorn, and Monterey Jack are also suitable. Small amounts of a hard cheese, such as Parmesan or Romano, may be added for extra tang. Mornay, a cheese sauce of European origin, is flavored with Swiss or Gruyère cheese, with Parmesan or Romano usually added.

Classic cheese sauce

Melt 2 tablespoons butter in a heavy saucepan; stir in 2 tablespoons flour, ¼ teaspoon salt, ⅛ teaspoon pepper, and ½ teaspoon dry mustard (optional). Cook and stir over low heat until bubbly; do not allow it to darken. Add 1 cup milk all at once. Cook and stir until the sauce is smooth and thick. Slowly stir in ½ cup shredded cheese; blend until the cheese is melted and the sauce is smooth. Thin, if desired, with cream or chicken broth; heat but do not boil. Makes 1½ cups.

Use the sauce to flavor vegetables, fish, or cooked eggs, or to make an au gratin dish: moisten cooked seafood or bite-size vegetables with a few tablespoons of sauce. Put the mixture in a well-greased, shallow baking dish. Spoon additional sauce thinly over the top; top with buttered bread crumbs. Place the dish under a preheated broiler until the sauce is bubbly and the crumbs are browned.

Chemical toilets

Routine maintenance; replacing pump and seal

Most portable, flushable chemical toilets consist of two sections: a freshwater supply tank—incorporating the bowl, seat, and lid—and a detachable waste-holding tank. Chemicals used to deodorize and help decompose the waste must be handled with care; they may be poisonous. Add them to the holding tank, following the instructions in the owner's manual.

When the holding tank is full, detach it from the upper toilet section and empty it into a permanent toilet. In cold weather, add antifreeze to the water-supply tank.

Keep portable toilets clean with a mild, nonabrasive cleaner suitable for plastics. (Usually the lid and seat can be snapped off for cleaning.) Before storing the toilet, rinse out the holding tank with a solution of 1 cup

household bleach per gallon of water or a cleaner recommended by the manufacturer. If the holding-tank sealing valve begins to stick, lubricate it lightly with silicone spray.

Replacing parts

If a bellows is pumping inadequately, replace it. Pry it out with a screwdriver, placing cardboard padding under the screwdriver blade to avoid disfiguring the toilet top. Spread a Butyl rubber sealant (PTI may be suggested) evenly around the neck and base of the new bellows before you install it. Slip the flush tube well over the neck's barb so that it is against the angle of the tee of the bellows leg. Bending the flush tube downward slightly, press the bellows into place.

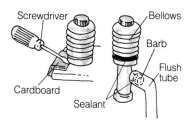

If leaks develop between the bowl and the holding tank, you may replace the gaskets, following the instructions on a kit designed for your unit. Pry out the old gaskets with a screwdriver. Before installing new ones, clean the slot in the base of all traces of old glue with toluol methylbenzine. Take care not to scar the sealing surface; wet the replacement seals before installing them.

Chess rules

How the pieces move in the game of strategy

A game for two, chess is played on a checkered board with pieces that are generally white for one player and black for the other. Each player has one king, one queen, two rooks, two bishops, two knights, and eight pawns. The object of the game is to break through your opponent's defense and capture his king.

Position the chessboard so that black corner squares are at your left. Arrange the pieces on the board.

Arrangement of pieces at start of game

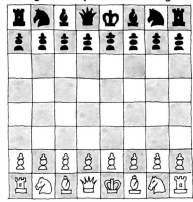

Each kind of playing piece has a unique move. Generally, except for the knight, no piece can jump over or pass through another piece on the board. But any piece can capture any opponent's piece by landing on the same square with it. A captured piece is removed from the game.

The *king* can move in any direction, but normally only one square at a time. A king cannot move to a square that would put it *in check*—that is to where it could be captured with the next move.

The *queen* can also move in any direction. It can also move over as many unoccupied squares as is advantageous, making it the most powerful piece on the chessboard.

A *rook* can move forward, backward, or sideways any number of unoccupied squares, but not diagonally. If you want to bring your two rooks closer together for an attack or move your king to a more protected area, you may *castle*. This can be done only if neither the king nor the rook in question have moved and the squares between the two pieces are unoccupied. In castling, the king moves two squares closer to the chosen rook, and the rook then jumps over the king and onto the square jumped by the king. Castling counts

C

as one move and is the only case in which a king moves more than one square or in which a piece other than a knight jumps over another piece.

A *bishop* can move diagonally forward or backward over any number of unoccupied squares. Each bishop is thus confined to squares of one color throughout the game.

A *knight* can move three squares in two directions: one or two squares forward, backward, or sideways and the remaining one or two squares in a direction at right angles to the first. A knight can jump over any pieces in its path.

A *pawn* can move only forward. From its original position it can advance either one or two squares; otherwise it can advance only one square at a time. A pawn cannot capture a piece in its path (it will be blocked by such a piece), but it can capture a piece that is diagonally in front of it one square to the left or right. If you maneuver a pawn to your opponent's rear row, you can declare the pawn a piece of higher rank—usually a queen because of its power.

Moves alternate; white moves first. Only one piece can be moved per turn, except when castling. You must warn your opponent when you put his king in danger by saying, "Check." He must then move his king out of check or block the attack with another piece. If he cannot, it is *checkmate,* and the game ends. A game also ends if a player cannot move on turn without endangering his king or because of lack of space. This is a *stalemate.*

Chest pains

A cause for concern

Pains in the chest may mean serious, even life-threatening illness. Most alarming is the intense, crushing pain of a heart attack. These pains may radiate from the center of the chest to the jaw, arms, or neck. However, sometimes heart-attack symptoms are less dramatic—discomfort, a feeling of fullness, a squeezing sensation, or excessive sweating. Other possible serious causes of chest pain include a pulmonary embolism or blood clot in a lung or, if symptoms include a cough or fever, pneumonia. A temporary lack of oxygen to the heart may cause a chest pain called angina. Any chest pain lasting longer than 2 minutes requires immediate medical attention.

Less worrisome are pains caused by indigestion, a pulled muscle, or shingles, a viral infection. If you have any doubt as to their cause, see your doctor. (See also *Choking; Coughing.*)

Chewing gum removal

Solving this sticky problem

To facilitate removal, harden the gum by rubbing it with a piece of ice wrapped in plastic. Or, put the gum-stained article in a plastic bag in the freezer until the gum hardens. Use a dull-edged implement to scrape away as much gum as possible.

To remove any remaining stain from a wall, a floor, or furniture, wipe the area with cleaning fluid, mineral spirits, or turpentine (use a detergent solution on asphalt tile).

To clean a gum stain from fabric, place the spot facedown on a clean absorbent cloth or paper towel: rub it lightly with a cloth soaked in cleaning fluid. Keep repositioning the stain as you work so that it is always on a clean area of the blotter beneath.

Chicken raising

Farming your own chickens for fresh meat and eggs

If you're raising chickens for meat, get a breed that gains weight quickly, such as a cross between a White Cornish (male) and a White Plymouth Rock (female). If your interest is in eggs, get light-weight, egg-laying hens, such as White Leghorns. For both eggs and meat, get a dual-purpose breed, such as Rhode Island Reds or Plymouth Rocks.

Housing and health

Day-old chicks are available by mail from commercial hatcheries. If they have not yet been vaccinated, have a veterinarian inoculate them against leukosis and against other diseases that are prevalent in your area (check with your Cooperative Extension Service—see p.5).

Keep the chicks in a brooder or a box warmed with a bulb or heat lamp until they are 6 to 8 weeks old. Set the temperature at 95°F for the first week, and decrease it by 5°F every week.

Once out of the brooder, the chickens will need a waterproof, rodent-proof house large enough to accommodate them without crowding. Allow 4 square feet of floor space per chicken for large breeds and 2 square feet per chicken for small breeds.

Chickens will be less prone to disease and cannibalism (pecking one another) if allowed to range freely, but this is only practical if foxes, coyotes, raccoons, and other predators are no threat. If they are, construct an outside run with 6-foot-high fences that are sunk into the ground. If raccoons are a problem, cover the run too.

If any chicken becomes listless or begins to act in an uncharacteristic manner, isolate it from the others and call a veterinarian. If the chickens become prey to lice, dust the birds and the chicken house with louse powder.

Feeding

Commercially blended feed is available for every type of poultry from baby chicks to laying hens. But if you feed your chickens commercial mixes exclusively, their eggs and meat will taste much the same as store bought.

As a supplement, feed your chickens scratch grains and table scraps such as vegetables, fruit peels, fat, and stale bread. Also give them grit (for digestion) and crushed oyster shells or another source of calcium if they are laying. Keep them provided with fresh, clean water at all times.

Meat and eggs

Meat chickens and surplus roosters will be ready for slaughter when they are 12 to 16 weeks old. Small fryers can be slaughtered younger. Laying chickens will start to lay at around 6 months. A dozen laying chickens should produce about 10 eggs a day.

Chicken soup

Making broth; soup variations

The most flavorful broth, or stock, is obtained from a stewing chicken (an old hen, or fowl). If unavailable, next best are the uncooked necks, backs, and wing tips of frying chickens; rinse and keep them in the freezer until you have several pounds.

To make about 4 quarts of broth, place a trussed chicken or 5 to 6 pounds of parts in a large, heavy pot. Cover with 4½ quarts cold water; bring to a simmer. Skim the foam from the top, then add the following: 2 carrots, 1 medium onion stuck with 4 cloves, 1 bay leaf, 4 sprigs parsley, 2 sprigs thyme, and 3 ribs celery. (If fresh thyme and parsley are unavailable, substitute ½ teaspoon dried thyme and 1 teaspoon dried parsley.)

Cover the pot, leaving the lid slightly ajar. Gently simmer the broth for at least 2 hours; don't allow it to boil. Add salt to taste. If you have used a whole chicken, you can serve it as a main dish. Strain the remaining ingredients through damp cheesecloth. To get a clear broth, refrigerate it until chilled, then scrape away the fat. Use the broth within 4 days or freeze it. To make soup with the broth, try one of the following recipes.

Chicken vegetable soup

Bring 6 cups chicken broth to a boil. Add 1 medium potato, 1 carrot, and 1 rib celery, all diced, ¼ pound sliced green beans and 1 small onion, sliced. Boil 12 minutes. Add ½ cup fresh or frozen peas, 1 cup diced chicken, and ¼ pound sliced mushrooms. Simmer for another 10 minutes. Serve with salt and pepper. Serves 6.

Chicken noodle soup

Cook about ½ pound of your favorite noodles in 6 cups chicken broth until tender; add 1 cup diced chicken. Season to taste. Serves 6.

Cream of chicken soup

Cook ¼ cup rice in 4 cups chicken broth until soft. Strain liquid into an-other pot; puree the rice in a blender with a little broth; return it to the pot. Add 2 cups hot milk or cream and salt and pepper to taste. Simmer a few minutes. Garnish each serving with snipped parsley or dill. Serves 6.

Chilblains

Advice about a painful skin condition

Chilblains is a skin inflammation caused by poor circulation and prolonged exposure to damp and cold. It can occur in above-freezing temperatures. The affected areas—usually the skin of fingers, toes, ears, nose, or legs—develop a burning, itching sensation. The skin may have lesions.

Chilblains should not be warmed in front of a fire or any other heat source. Allow the affected skin to warm gradually. To prevent chilblains, wear warm gloves, hat, socks, and pants, and other protective clothing during winter months. Avoid alcohol and tobacco when you plan to be outdoors for a long period.

Childproofing

Preventing childhood accidents

As soon as your baby learns to crawl, remove breakables from furniture and rearrange the closets so that only safe, sturdy objects are near the floor. To protect a toddler from hazardous materials, have at least one high cabinet that you can lock. Put childproof latches, available at hardware stores, on other closet and cabinet doors. Remove interior door locks; if necessary, install a latch higher up (see *Latches*).

Poisons

Household cleaners, hair dyes, shoe polish, kerosene, and laundry products are just a few of the poisons around a house. Store them in high cabinets and put them back promptly after use. Keep all medicines, including vitamins, in childproof containers and in a locked medicine chest. Don't leave aspirin or other medicines in your purse. Keep a phone number for a poison control center near your phone and have syrup of ipecac on hand in case it is needed to induce vomiting. After spraying your garden with insecticides, don't permit children to play there for a day or two.

Burns and shocks

Keep matches and cigarette lighters out of reach. Put guards in front of radiators, wall heaters, and fireplaces. Use flame-retardant sleepwear. While cooking, turn pot handles toward the back of the stove or use back burners. Avoid hot-water burns by setting the water heater at 130°F. To prevent electric burns and shocks, plug electric outlets with plastic covers available from hardware stores. Use an extension cord only as a temporary connection. Lock up your power tools when not in use.

Avoiding suffocations

Keep all objects small enough to be swallowed away from young children; don't give them toys with parts that might come loose or foods such as carrot or apple pieces or hard candies. Take care, too, with long cords. Plastic bags can suffocate a child; store them out of reach or shred or tie them in knots for disposal; never use one to cover a child's mattress. Be careful of anything in which a child might become trapped, such as a trunk or an unused refrigerator; lock them when not in use, or remove the lock.

Bumps and bruises

Put bars or tight-fitting screens on windows or install latches that keep the windows from being opened more than a few inches. Put gates at the top and bottom of stairs, but avoid accordion types that could trap a child's head. A safer gate is an adjustable wood frame with mesh. (See also *Accident prevention*; *Bathroom safety*.)

Children's party favors

Take-home souvenirs for youngsters to make

Children love the inexpensive party favors—yoyos, bubblemakers, marbles, jacks, crayons, jump ropes, miniature cars—sold in variety stores and oriental import shops. But they'll treasure even more handcrafted favors they make right at the party.

C

C

Story wheel

Cut out five cardboard circles, the smallest 4 inches in diameter, the others 5½, 7, 8½, and 10 inches. Cut a 7- by 2-inch rectangle with a slit down the center through which to read the words written on the disks. Write sentence elements on the perimeters of the disks working from largest to smallest: adjectives, nouns, helping verbs, verbs, prepositional phrases. Fasten disks and rectangle at center with a wing clasp. Twirl disks and read amusing stories.

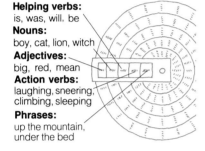

Helping verbs:
is, was, will, be
Nouns:
boy, cat, lion, witch
Adjectives:
big, red, mean
Action verbs:
laughing, sneering, climbing, sleeping
Phrases:
up the mountain, under the bed

Party bags

Give the guests small brown lunch bags, 1- by 12-inch strips of colored construction paper for handles, a stapler, and crayons or magic markers. They can then design their own bags for taking home all their party loot.

Picture puzzles

Cut pictures out of nature magazines and glue them with rubber cement to heavy construction paper. Mark a grid on the back (the construction paper side) and let the children cut out puzzle pieces roughly following the rectangles as guidelines. The size and number of boxes depends on the age of the children (for older children you may even want to vary the shapes). Provide plastic bags to hold (and carry home) the puzzle pieces.

Children's party games

Activities and entertainments for a successful children's party

When planning a children's party, schedule more games than you think necessary because some may fall flat. Arrange the order of the games (long and short) so that the youngsters will not become bored. Your own child's taste may be the best guide as to what will please and for how long. That may range from playground games, such as leapfrog, to guessing games, skill games, and team games.

Hunts

These are good icebreakers. Hide peanuts or wrapped candies around the house or in the yard—finders keepers. Or set up a trail of clues, with each child's clue on a paper of a particular color and each trail leading to a small prize. Or weave a string spider web around a room with each guest's name tagged at one end of a length of string and a prize at the other end. Each guest winds up his or her piece of string but may not move furniture or any other obstacle en route.

Relays

Divide the guests into two teams. Relays might include having each team member in turn put on and take off a complete football uniform or transfer water by the cupful from a pail at one location to an empty pail at another. The team to finish first wins.

Easy skill games

Tossing wrapped candies into a bowl from a line 10 feet away requires a good aim. Each player gets three tries and five candies per try. Dropping clothespins into a bottle or flipping cards into a hat are other simple amusements.

Prizes

Keep a score chart. Give the winner of a game 3 points; the runner-up, 2; everyone else, 1 point. Total the scores at the end of the party and, going from the highest to the lowest points scored, let each child choose a prize. The prizes should be of equal value and nobody loses. (See also *Dodgeball; Fox and geese; Halloween games; Horseshoes; Jackstraws; Kick the can; Musical chairs; Quoits; Scavenger hunts; Soap bubbles; Tug-of-war; Twenty questions.*)

Chimneys and flues

Cleaning and repairing your chimney to keep it safe

Where there's smoke there's a chance of fire, but diligent maintenance of your chimney will keep both smoke and fire in their proper places. Examine a chimney yearly for the safety and security of your family and home. Chimneys get dirty from use, bricks become loose with age and weather, and flues crack and become blocked.

Chimney cleaning

A properly maintained furnace or boiler burns cleanly with little soot accumulation. But if you use your fireplace frequently, clean the chimney at least once a year—more often if you burn softwood. Creosote, a sticky black residue created by burning wood, is carried by the smoke and deposited in the chimney. It reduces the ability of the flue to draw off smoke and, because it is flammable, can cause a chimney fire. Chimney fires often spread to the roof or adjacent houses.

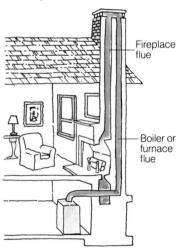

Chimney with two flues

Fireplace flue

Boiler or furnace flue

Cleaning a chimney is a tedious, dirty job and can be dangerous, as you must climb onto the roof. It is safer to call in a professional chimney sweep. He'll block off all flue openings into the house, work the soot down the chimney, and vacuum it away. If you do clean your own chimney, follow the same procedure.

Most stove stores sell special long-handled wire brushes in sizes to fit any flue. You can measure your flue by reaching up the hearth beyond the damper of a fireplace or into the flue opening of a wood stove. If in doubt about the size, buy a brush that is too large and trim its bristles to fit. Sweep out each flue thoroughly with one of these. Take any metal stovepipe down and brush it out with a round wire brush made for that size pipe.

When all interior surfaces of stovepipe and chimney flues have been brushed thoroughly, remove the coverings taped around each flue opening and vacuum them diligently. Work from the highest opening down so that any soot dislodged will fall to lower openings still closed.

Repairing brickwork

If your chimney passes through the house, inspect it wherever it is visible—usually in the attic. Have a helper shine a strong light up the chimney or burn damp rags in the fireplace while you wait in the attic. If any light or smoke comes through, there's a leak. Repair leaks with mortar. Replace missing or badly broken bricks (see *Brickwork*).

For greater safety, new chimneys are built with ceramic flue linings. If your chimney is more than 50 years old, it may not have a flue lining and so may be unsafe. Hire a mason to either add a lining or to lower a prefabricated metal chimney inside your unlined chimney.

China

Dinnerware care and mending

Proper care can do much to preserve china, fine or everyday. To prevent cracks, avoid temperature shock: put only ovenproof dishes in a hot oven; don't put hot food on cold plates; and cool the dishes to room temperature before stacking them. Prevent chipping by placing paper towels or felt between stacked pieces. Hang cups on hooks instead of stacking them. (See also *Dishwashing.*)

Repairing china

Mend breaks with slow-drying epoxy glue, which lets you maneuver the pieces and is waterproof when dry. Clean the broken edges well. Mix the epoxy as the label directs. Apply as thin a coat as you can, join and brace the pieces, then wipe off any excess with the recommended solvent.

The key to successful repair is holding the sections firmly until the glue has cured—at least 12 hours. One

way is to partially sink the larger segment in sand or modeling clay, balancing it so that the piece you attach will stay, at least momentarily, without support. After gluing, hold the smaller piece in place with masking tape or with pinch-type clothespins. Or mold modeling wax or paraffin to the shape of a matching plate and set the pieces in the mold to dry. Devise any system that will work.

If multiple pieces must be glued, determine the order by first putting them together dry, then attaching them one or two at a time.

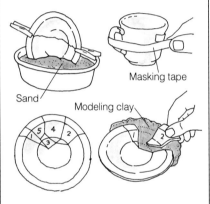

Masking tape

Sand

Modeling clay

Chinch bugs

Preventing infestations; treating brown patches on lawns

These tiny (1/8 inch long) black bugs with white wings suck the juices from the stems of grass and corn. They reproduce rapidly when temperatures exceed 70°F. Infestations of chinch bugs cause spreading irregular brown patches in otherwise green turf. Corn plants remain green but fail to produce good ears of corn.

Enlarged

To protect turf against attack, fertilize it before the weather gets warm; chinch bugs do more damage to underfed lawns. For corn, sow resistant varieties and protect the plant with a collar of building paper dug 1 inch into the soil.

Treat infested lawns with carbaryl, diazinon, or chlorpyrifos according to manufacturer's instructions. If the soil isn't damp, water the lawn first.

Chinese checkers

Traveling across a star

This game for two to six players is played with colored pieces (marbles or pegs) on a star-shaped board with holes for the pieces. The object is to move all your pieces from one of the six star points into the opposite point before any opponent can move his or her pieces across the star.

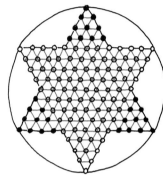

Each player positions 10 pieces of a single color (or 15 pieces if there are only two players) in a point of the star. Then the players take turns moving. When it's your turn, you can move one piece in any direction into an adjacent hole, or you can jump one or more adjacent pieces, either your own or an opponent's. The purpose of jumping is to move your piece to a more advantageous position; you don't remove the jumped piece from the board. When several marbles alternate with open holes in a line, you can jump them all.

Chiseling

Using a woodworking chisel

When you need to pare wood, to make joints, to smooth corners, or to cut recesses (called mortises) for hinges and locks, use a woodworking chisel.

Caution: A chisel is a sharp cutting tool. Always keep both hands behind the blade as you work. Cut away from your body, not toward yourself. For stability, secure the wood in a bench vise, or clamp it to the work surface. Lay the chisel down where there's no danger it will fall on you.

To make a *paring cut*, use a *paring chisel*. It has a thin blade with the sides and end beveled. Use both hands, one on the handle to provide power, the other on top of the blade to control cutting direction. With the bevel up, move the blade along the wood grain, taking thin shavings. To avoid splintering, work from the corner toward the center.

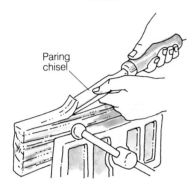

Paring chisel

To make a *chopping cut* across the grain, use a *firmer chisel* (medium-thick blade with or without side bevels; the same chisel can also be used for paring cuts) or a *mortise chisel* (thick blade without side bevels). Hold the chisel vertically and place the blade on the waste side of a penciled cutting line with the bevel facing the waste. Hit the handle with a wooden mallet, making cuts to define the waste area. Then make chopping cuts

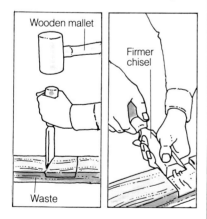

Wooden mallet

Firmer chisel

Waste

across the grain in the waste. Finally, remove the waste by making horizontal cuts with the bevel down. Chisel to the full depth in stages, not all at once. If the waste area is wider than your chisel, overlap the cuts to make the bottom smooth.

When cutting mortises and deep recesses, first remove the bulk of the waste with a saw or drill. Make saw cuts across the grain in the waste or drill a series of holes. Use a chisel to link the holes and clean the corners.

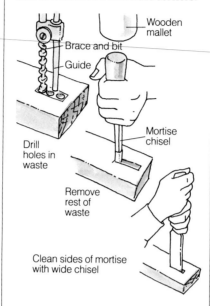

Wooden mallet

Brace and bit

Guide

Drill holes in waste

Mortise chisel

Remove rest of waste

Clean sides of mortise with wide chisel

Choking

Clearing a blocked air passage

Always consider choking an emergency. A person who is breathing while coughing may be able to free a blocked air passage without assistance. Anyone who can't breathe or speak needs immediate help. So also does someone whose coughing is weak, breathing difficult, and lips bluish—*unless he can speak.* Ask the person, "Are you choking?" If he says "Yes" out loud, call an ambulance; he may be having a heart attack.

Abdominal and chest thrusts

If the victim is standing, wrap your arms around him and make a fist with one hand, thumb inward, and place it just above the victim's navel below the breastbone. (Keep your hands below the cartilage that extends down from the center of the rib cage.) Grasp the fist with your other hand and press in with quick inward and upward thrusts. Make as many thrusts as necessary to dislodge the object. If the victim loses

consciousness, give mouth-to-mouth resuscitation (see *CPR*).

If the victim is sitting and cannot stand, move behind his chair, wrap your arms around him and the chair, and apply the thrusts as described.

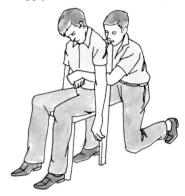

If you start to choke, you can give abdominal thrusts to yourself. Just make a fist as if you were helping someone else. Press your fist into your waist, below the breastbone. Thrust inward and upward, using both your hands. Continue thrusting until the object is expelled.

Another method if you're alone is to position yourself over the back of a chair, the edge of a table, or something similar. Press your abdomen against it so that the edge thrusts in and up toward your diaphragm.

For a pregnant or obese person, use chest thrusts. Hold the victim as shown, clasping your hands as de-

scribed above, and make quick inward thrusts.

Roll a prone person faceup; kneel close to or astride his hips. Place one of your hands over the other and, with the heel of the lower slightly above the navel, give the same hard in-and-up thrust.

For children

If the choking victim is a child 12 months or older, give the abdominal thrusts as described for a standing choking victim, but modify the force of the thrusts according to the child's size.

Hold a child under a year old over your arm or thigh, supporting his head with your hand. With the heel of

your other hand, give up to five quick blows between the shoulder blades. If this technique fails, place two fingers

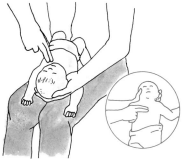

on the center of the chest, just below the nipples, and press straight down (up to five times if necessary). Then look into his mouth and, if you see the object, remove it. Repeat the sequence of back blows and chest thrusts until the object is expelled.

After treating a victim, take him to a doctor as soon as possible.

Cholesterol

Lowering the level to reduce heart-disease risk

Medical research shows that by simple diet changes, you can lower cholesterol levels in your blood and help protect yourself against heart disease. On its own, the body produces some cholesterol, but the foods you eat can add significant amounts of cholesterol to your blood. Cholesterol-rich foods include meat, eggs, and dairy products. Other foods such as animal and chicken fats, and even some vegetable fats, are high in cholesterol-raising saturated fats.

A simple blood test determines your cholesterol level. A level below 200 milligrams per 100 milliliters of blood serum is considered a normal cholesterol level for adults; however, many doctors prefer to look at the ratio of total cholesterol to HDL (high-density lipoprotein).

Formerly, diet changes to lower cholesterol were recommended only for those whose levels were higher than normal. Now doctors know that everyone can benefit from cutting back on such foods as red meats (beef, pork, lamb); organ meats (liver, kidneys, sweetbreads, and brains); egg yolks (limit yourself to four per week); dairy products containing butterfat (butter, cream, whole milk, cream cheese, regular cottage cheese, hard cheeses, ice cream); animal fats (lard, bacon); and vegetable fats (coconut oil, palm oil).

Here are some other cholesterol-cutting practices.

Avoid fried foods.
Use safflower, sunflower, soybean, corn, canola, sesame, or olive oil in cooking.
Get more of your protein from legumes, such as dried beans, split peas, and lentils.
Switch to skim or low-fat milk and other low-fat dairy products.
Use nonstick pans so that you need much less fat when cooking foods.
Trim visible fat from meats and poultry; discard poultry skin.
Eat plenty of foods rich in water-soluble fiber, such as oat bran, wheat germ, vegetables, and beans.
Cut down on sweet baked goods—most are high in fat.

Chopping foods

An easy and efficient method

A cook's or a chef's knife is best for chopping or mincing; it should be very sharp. With one hand, hold the handle of the knife firmly. The thumb should rest against the blade for support, as shown. Hold the other hand

across the back of the blade and near the front of the knife. Keeping the blade tip against the cutting board, and using the tip as a pivot, lift the heel of the knife repeatedly in a rocking up-and-down motion. Gather the ingredients in a heap from time to time as you chop. (See also *Dicing*.)

Chopsticks

The correct way to eat oriental food

Rest one stick (the lower) on your ring finger with its thicker end in the crook of your hand. Hold the other (upper) stick between your thumb and index finger and resting on your middle finger. If possible, use your right hand—the left is considered impolite, even for left-handers.

Tap the narrow ends on the plate to even them. Move the upper stick to widen the gap. Grasp a bit of food by closing the upper stick upon it. The lower stick remains stationary. Eat food in small bites; work rice into a mass for lifting.

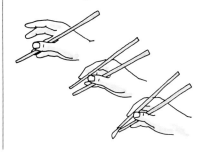

C

Christmas ornaments

Simple ways to make beautiful tree trimmings

Cookie cutters in a variety of seasonal shapes—such as candy canes, stockings, stars, and trees—can be the basis for many projects. Trace them on paper, adding ¼-inch seam allowances. Pin a paper pattern to two layers of fabric and cut out the shape. With right sides facing, stitch them together, leaving an opening at the top for turning. Turn them right side out and stuff lightly with polyester fiberfill. Insert a ribbon loop for hanging and slipstitch the opening closed (see *Slipstitching*).

Another cookie-cutter idea involves nonedible dough. Combine 4 cups flour with 1 cup salt; using your hands, gradually mix in 1½ cups water. Knead for a few minutes, then on a floured surface roll out the dough to ¼ inch thick. Flour the cookie cutter rims and cut out shapes. Use a meat skewer to make make tiny holes at the tops for hanging. Bake the shapes on a cookie sheet at 300°F for 40 minutes. Let them cool, then decorate with acrylic paints.

Cut out cookie-cutter shapes from heavy cardboard. Thinly coat both sides with white glue, then wrap the shapes with closely spaced multicolored or metallic yarns.

Outline cookie-cutter shapes on scrap plywood and cut them out with a jigsaw. Drill hanging holes in the tops. Paint on faces, clothing, or other appropriate motifs. Spray with acrylic sealer or coat with clear shellac.

Ideas with other familiar objects

Trim assorted straw flowers or dried herbs so that the stems are about 1 inch long. Insert the stems in a styro-

foam ball, covering it completely. Attach a ribbon loop with a straight pin.

Buy miniature handled baskets (sold in craft and hobby shops); fill them with dried herbs and tiny dried flowers, such as baby's breath. Tie a ribbon bow on the handle.

Cut rounds, ovals, or diamonds from bright-colored illustration or mat board. Cut motifs from gift wrap or old greeting cards, and use white glue to attach them to the board. Punch a hole at the top for hanging. Spray both sides with acrylic sealer.

Start with two circles of muslin or other plain cotton. Using stencils and acrylic paints, apply color with a small piece of sponge or a stencil brush. Or color the stencil areas with fabric crayons and set the color with an iron. Stitch the circles together, leaving an opening; turn and stuff with polyester fiberfill. Tack on a loop for hanging. A fabric wreath might be decorated with purchased embroidered appliqués for the look of handstitched motifs. Stitch and finish as above.

Make a star of five clip-type clothespins: remove the springs; paint or stain the wood; rejoin the two clothespin parts with white glue. Position the five to form a star; glue them together; let dry thoroughly.

Clothespin halves back to back

To "marbleize" purchased glass ornaments, spray several colors of oilbase paint onto part of the surface of cold water in a bucket. Slowly swirl the colors with a toothpick, leaving some water clear. Dip an ornament into the paint; remove it through the clear spot. Dry ornaments on a rack.

Use patchwork patterns from quilting books or magazines to create paper patchwork ornaments. Cut the patches from gift wraps. Glue them to cardboard; trim away excess backing. Punch small holes in tops; add a ribbon loop for hanging.

Christmas trees

Selecting and caring for one

In shopping for a cut tree, try to identify the type and test it for freshness. The needles of spruce and fir (including balsam) are short and attached to the twigs singly; pine needles are longer and attached in clusters of two, three, or five. Most pines, firs, and the blue spruce have good needle retention and a pleasant fragrance, whereas the white spruce and Norway spruce are poorer in both qualities. Avoid hemlocks, which shed their needles readily.

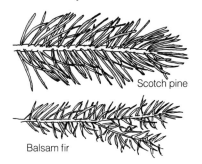

Scotch pine

Balsam fir

The needles of a fresh tree should be pliable. If they are brittle, pop off easily, have a pale or grayish-green look, the tree is not fresh. A tree with at least 80 percent moisture content stays fresh longer if watered. Once moisture content drops below 80 percent, it continues to fall even with watering. When moisture content is 20 percent, the tree is a fire hazard.

If you must carry a cut tree any distance on top of your car, wrap it in burlap to prevent drying and place it with the base facing front. If you're not setting it up immediately, stand it in a bucket of water in a cool, protected place. Before setting up the tree (preferably in a stand that holds water), cut off an inch or more of the trunk to increase it's "drinking" capacity. Water regularly; a fresh tree absorbs up to a quart of water daily.

Place the tree away from fireplaces, TV sets, heaters, and lit candles. Be sure tree lights are UL approved (the box or a tag on the cord should say so) and in top condition. Unplug the lights when not in use. Promptly clean up spilled water or dropped needles (which exude pitch) to prevent staining of your carpet or floor.

Some people buy a live evergreen with burlapped root ball for Christmas and plant it after the holidays. To do so in a cold climate, you must dig a hole before the ground freezes and mulch it. Keep the tree in the house no longer than 10 days; water it daily.

Cigarette burns

How to disguise shallow and deep burns in wood

If a burn is superficial—that is, mars the finish but hasn't reached the wood—first try a commercial furniture cleaner. If the mark persists, rub it with rottenstone in light oil.

Burns that have gone through the finish but not far into the wood also respond to a light touch. Gently rub the charred area with fine steel wool. Remove any remaining blackening by dabbing on straight liquid bleach with a cotton swab. To match the color of surrounding wood, try colored furniture wax or polish, artist's oils, shoe polish, crayon or felt-tip pen, or an oil-base stain, testing first in an inconspicuous area. You can buy stain for touch-ups in felt-tip and small brush-topped containers. In matching color, start light. It's easier to darken an area than to lighten one you've made too dark. Refinish to blend with the rest of the wood.

Burns that go deep into wood

Gently sand or scrape away the blackened wood with a single-edge razor blade or a utility knife. Then fill the area with a stick of tinted wax or shellac; the method is the same with either. Wax is easier and can be removed if you don't like the result.

Select a color that matches the lightest grain in the wood. You'll need a special curved knife, called a burnin knife, or a curved grapefruit knife. Heat the knife over the sootless flame of a spirit lamp or over an electric-stove burner. Hold the wax or shellac stick against the heated blade and guide the melting filler into the depression in the wood. Reheat the knife as needed. Fill the hole slightly higher than the surrounding area.

When the wax has cooled, scrape off the excess with a razor blade. With shellac, scrape off any excess before it hardens, then sand when it's hard. To match the grain, paint darker streaks across the patch with a fine-tipped brush, connecting them to the grain lines of the surrounding wood. Seal a wax patch with clear polyurethane or acrylic varnish spray.

Cigarette odors

Getting rid of tobacco fumes

For an occasional problem—odors left after a party, for instance—there are several remedies: a good airing, aided by a fan; aerosol sprays; or a dish of ammonia or vinegar to cover offensive smells with fresher ones. Burning candles at the party (perhaps scented ones) may help.

Where smoking is constant, consider an air purifier. Small, inexpensive ones that circulate air through carbon filters are best used near the smoke source. True air cleaners are more costly; they circulate air and capture smoke, pollen, and dust particles electrostatically. They can be freestanding or mounted on a wall or ceiling and must be adequately sized and properly placed to be effective. If you have a warm-air heating system, you can have an air purifying unit attached to it to clear smoke from the entire house.

Circuit breakers

Why circuits fail and what to do about it

A circuit breaker is an overload switch that prevents the current in a particular electric circuit from exceeding the capacity of a line. Fuses perform the same function in older systems (see *Fuse boxes*). If too many appliances are plugged into a circuit, calling for more power than the capacity of the circuit, the breaker reacts by switching off (tripping) the circuit. This prevents damage to the wiring, fires, or in the case of a defective appliance, further damage to the appliance.

The maximum current of each breaker or fuse is rated in amperes. Typically a kitchen range requires a breaker of 40 to 50 amperes; a water heater, one of 30 to 40 amperes. These circuits are 240-volt lines controlled by double breakers. The remaining breakers on the power distribution panel are for 15 or 20 amperes, controlling 120-volt general-purpose circuits for lights and small appliances. The large breaker marked *Main* turns off all power in the house.

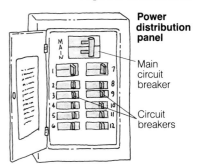

Power distribution panel

Main circuit breaker

Circuit breakers

Most modern breakers have three positions: *On*, when power is flowing in the circuit; *Off*, to shut off power from the line; and *tripped*, a midway position showing that the circuit has been overloaded and is off. A few breakers have only on and off positions. Sometimes a red flag shows in a tripped breaker.

Circuit breaker

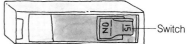

Switch

To restore power to a tripped circuit, remove the overload by unplugging or switching off extra appliances, then move the breaker handle to *Off* and then firmly to *On*. (See also *Circuit map*; *Short circuits*.)

If a major appliance trips the line repeatedly and you're sure the circuit is not overloaded, call a serviceperson.

Circuit map

Its purpose; how to make one

A circuit map tells which circuit breakers or fuses control which outlets; it can help locate wiring problems and prevent overloads. Draw a floor plan of each story, showing out-

C

let and light fixture locations. Stick numbered labels beside all breaker switches or fuses except the *Main* (the largest one), which shuts off all power. (Breakers or fuses may already be numbered on the door panel.)

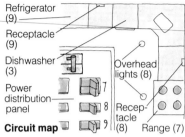

Refrigerator (9)
Receptacle (9)
Dishwasher (3)
Power distribution panel
Overhead lights (8)
Receptacle (8)
Circuit map
Range (7)

Turn on all light fixtures and plug all outlets with lit lamps. As you switch off each breaker or unscrew each fuse, have a helper tell you which lights go out. On your map, number the outlets by their breaker or fuse numbers. Put the plans in an envelope and post near the service panel.

Circuit testing

Checking that power is off; diagnosing circuit failures

When you are going to work on an electric outlet or switch, always turn off the circuit power at the breaker box or fuse panel. To determine which outlets and switches are on a circuit, see *Circuit map*. Then, to test that the power really is off, turn a switch on and off. Test receptacles on an outlet by inserting the probes of a neon test lamp into each receptacle's two openings: if the lamp lights, the power is still on; if it doesn't light, it's safe to begin work.

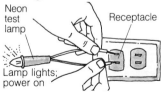

Neon test lamp
Receptacle
Lamp lights; power on

Frequent fuse blowing or circuit tripping may be caused by operating too many appliances and lights on one circuit. Unplug enough of them so that the circuit is not overloaded.

If the problem persists, try to trace the cause by unplugging all appliances and turning off all switches on

the blown circuit. Turn on the power. If the breaker trips or the fuse blows, turn off the breaker or remove the fuse. Unscrew the cover plates on each switch and outlet. Look for broken wires and loose or missing terminal screws; fix or replace them.

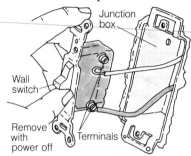

Junction box
Wall switch
Remove with power off
Terminals

If the circuit doesn't blow, re-engage the power and turn on the switches one by one. If during this procedure, the circuit blows again, the problem is probably in the switch or the fixture you just turned on. To determine which, test the switch with a continuity tester; if the bulb lights,

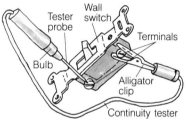

Tester probe
Wall switch
Terminals
Bulb
Alligator clip
Continuity tester

showing the switch is all right, then the problem is probably in the fixture. Remove the fixture; test it and repair or replace it.

If no problem develops, plug in and run appliances one by one. If the cord, plug, or switch of an appliance turns out to be the cause of the blown circuit, replace or repair the faulty part. If none of these suggestions remedies the problem, call an electrician.

Citizen's arrest

What to do when there's no police officer around

If you see a crime being committed and no police officer is in sight, you have the right to make a citizen's arrest. If you do decide to make one, be very careful. Not only do you risk being hurt if the suspect is armed or

dangerous but you may be sued if you make a mistake.

You are entitled to make a citizen's arrest when you see a felony (a serious crime usually involving violence) or someone fleeing from one. Check with your local police department or district attorney to learn if you can arrest someone for a misdemeanor (a minor crime, such as vandalism).

Most citizen's arrests are for shoplifting. If you have only a hunch that someone has committed a crime, don't arrest the suspect. Instead, call the police immediately and give them whatever facts you have. Remember, if the suspect committed no crime, he or she can sue you for false arrest or false imprisonment, even though you thought a crime took place.

You don't need a warrant to make an arrest since there is no time to get one. But be sure to make the arrest during or immediately following the crime; otherwise the arrest is illegal.

Tell the person that you are making a citizen's arrest for the named crime and are taking him or her to the nearest police officer. Ask bystanders for help if you need it and try to get their names and addresses in case they're needed later as witnesses.

The suspect can refuse your request or resist your efforts (but not those of a police officer). If the suspect uses force, respond only with reasonable force to subdue him. Otherwise, you might face charges and a possible civil lawsuit for assault.

After you arrest a suspect, you have no right to question or search him or to seize evidence. Hand the suspect over to the police and remain available to answer their questions.

Although it is your right to make a citizen's arrest in certain situations, the law does not require you to do so. On the other hand, the police can order you to help them apprehend a suspect. If you refuse, you might be subject to criminal prosecution.

Citrus houseplants

Growing citrus from seeds

With their glossy leaves, fragrant flowers, and colorful fruits, citruses make

C

elegant houseplants. They are easy to start too. Just plant fresh seeds of lemon, orange, or grapefruit in a mixture of equal parts of peat moss and perlite or coarse sand. Water well; cover the container with clear plastic and keep it warm (70°F). When the seeds germinate in 3 to 6 weeks, remove the plastic and place the container in bright light (but not direct sun). When the seedlings have several sets of leaves, transplant them to individual pots filled with potting soil.

Feed the plants with a dilute high-potassium fertilizer every 2 to 4 weeks. Water moderately and keep in direct sunlight at least 4 hours a day. In winter, stop feeding, water sparingly, and keep the plants above 50°F.

It may take 7 years or longer for a citrus plant started from seed to flower indoors, so you may want to buy a plant or propagate cuttings from one that is known to flower and fruit. To encourage fruiting, repot every spring in a pot one size larger and place the plant outdoors in summer. Prune leggy branches in early spring. The fruits, although often too tart to eat raw, make excellent marmalade.

Citrus trees

Evergreens with edible fruits for your yard

Citrus trees need the warm climate of Florida, California, and portions of Texas, Arizona, and the Gulf coastal strip to ripen the fruit properly. Even in those areas, it is often necessary in winter to bank soil around the trunks or to wrap the trunks with insulating material such as layers of newspaper. Sour orange (*Citrus aurantium*) and mandarin orange (*Citrus reticulata*), the most hardy, can survive temperatures of 24°F. Citrus trees do best in well-drained loam and in full sun.

Buy budded stock from a local nursery to ensure its hardiness and to avoid varieties locally subject to disease. Plant trees during their winter dormancy, usually February.

Planting citrus trees
A common mistake is planting the trees too close. A grapefruit tree, which may grow 50 feet tall, needs a

clear radius of at least 15 feet (30 feet between trees); an orange tree needs 12 to 15 feet; lemon, lime, and kumquat trees, 8 to 10 feet. Citrus trees can be planted close for a hedge but then they require frequent pruning.

Dig the planting holes large enough so that the roots can be spread fully. Add peat moss and citrus fertilizer to the fill-in soil. Plant trees at their former growing depth or slightly higher, water deeply, and thin and cut back branches (see *Tree pruning*).

Year-round care
Keep the ground beneath a tree's canopy heavily mulched (see *Mulching*). Apply a high-nitrogen fertilizer in spring and summer, a fertilizer without nitrogen in fall. In dry weather give trees a deep soaking weekly. Prune out suckers, dead branches, and crossing limbs. Prune grapefruit trees to keep them low. Ask your Cooperative Extension Service (see p.5) what pesticides to apply in your area.

Clambakes

A seashore feast that you can adapt to the home kitchen

The classic clambake is a beach picnic of clams, lobsters, and sweet corn cooked in a pit dug in the sand. At an elaborate clambake, chicken quarters and white or sweet potatoes wrapped in foil might be added.

Invite easygoing friends who won't mind a little sand in the butter, a few with strong arms to dig the pit and heave rocks into it, some to help cook and serve. Equipment is down-to-earth: clean spade and rake, chicken wire, a piece of canvas big enough to cover the pit; a stiff brush for scrubbing clams; seaweed; and rocks about 2 to 3 inches thick and 6 to 8 inches across. Together, hot rocks, wet seaweed, and canvas create the steam that cooks the food.

Choose a spot above the high-tide line. Dig the pit about 1 foot deep and long and wide enough to hold the foods in a 6-inch layer. Line the bottom and sides with rocks, setting them close together. Build a wood fire on the rocks, using driftwood or any wood that will burn hot for at least 45

minutes. Start the fire. While it burns to coals and ashes, scrub the clams. Dip unhusked corn in seawater.

Rake the ashes and coals from the now red-hot stones, lay a 2- to 3-inch layer of seaweed on them, and place chicken wire over that. Then arrange the food in layers, chicken and potatoes first if they're used, then lobsters, clams, and corn. Top with another seaweed layer, then the canvas. Anchor the canvas with rocks and a 5-inch layer of sand. Let the foods steam for an hour.

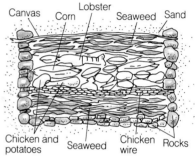

Remove the rocks and brush away the sand; roll back the canvas. Using tongs or barbecue mitts to prevent burns, transfer food to trays. Pass bowls of melted butter for dipping.

You can replicate this feast at home if you have a large, covered enamel pot. Ask the fish store for seaweed. Wash it well and put some of it in the pot; cover with water. (If you can't get seaweed, substitute corn husks or lettuce leaves.) Add each food at about 10-minute intervals with a layer of seaweed on top of each addition. Potatoes go first, then chicken, then lobster, corn, and clams, in that order. Steam until the clams open.

Clamming

Finding, cleaning, and opening clams

Before collecting, check with local authorities; most states and many seashore towns have laws requiring a permit. Inquire whether the waters where you intend to collect are pollution free and the clams safe to eat.

You'll find *soft-shell clams,* known also as steamers or long-necks, on tidal flats in brackish water from Labrador to North Carolina on the East Coast or north of Monterey on the West Coast. At low tide, watch for small holes or squirts of water in exposed flats or sudden small clouds of mud in shallow water. Dig the clams with a garden fork.

Hard-shell clams—called cherry-stones or littlenecks when small and quahogs when full-grown (about 4 inches across)—are found mainly on the East and Gulf coasts. They live in deep water in bays. At low tide probe the bottom with a clam rake that has a basket behind the tines; any clam you strike will be picked up in the basket.

Scrub clam shells with a stiff brush and rinse in several changes of water. For better cleansing, give clams a cornmeal bath: sprinkle a handful of cornmeal into water to cover and leave the clams for 3 to 12 hours. Discard any clam that floats, has a broken shell, or does not close when touched.

To open a raw clam, hold the clam in one hand. Insert the tip of a clam knife between the halves of the shell. Press the blunt edge of the knife with the fingers of the hand holding the clam and move the blade around to sever the muscles.

Press on back edge of knife

Clarifying butter

Removing all but the pure fat from butter

Because clarified butter has a delicate flavor, it's sometimes called for in baking fine cakes. It is less likely than un-clarified butter to burn in sautéing such foods as mushrooms, fish, shell-fish, veal, and chicken breasts, which must cook quickly over high heat. You can also use clarified butter as a sauce for steamed lobster.

To clarify butter, cut 1 stick of un-salted butter into small pieces (for even melting). Melt it in a heavy pan over low heat. Tilt the pan and carefully skim off the foam that rises to the top. Pour off the clear liquid—the clarified butter—leaving the milky residue in the pan. A stick yields about 6 tablespoons of clarified butter. It will keep up to 3 weeks in a covered container in the refrigerator.

Clasps

Putting a new clasp on a necklace or bracelet

To replace a screw-type clasp on a string of beads, work on one end at a time. Snip off the old clasp, leaving as much cord as possible. If there's no knot next to the last bead, make one. Then thread the cord through the link in the new clasp and knot the link against the last knot in the string. Trim the cord, leaving a length equal to the width of the last bead. Apply water-soluble glue to the cord end and let it dry until it is stiff. Then use jeweler's pliers to insert the cord end

through the hole in the last bead. Leave only the knot showing. Dab epoxy cement on the knot and let it dry.

To replace a spring-ring clasp on a necklace or bracelet, simply open the end link of the chain or the jump ring that holds the clasp by grasping it with two pairs of flat-nose jeweler's pliers and twisting it open at a slight angle. Remove the old clasp, put on the new, and close the link or ring by moving its ends together again.

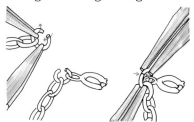

Clawing cats

Protecting your furniture

Cats scratch wood and upholstery to exercise and to sharpen their claws. If your cat doesn't have access to trees, provide a scratching post to prevent furniture damage.

The post should be stable and tall enough for the cat to stretch out. It can be a bark-covered log or a 2 x 2 nailed to a base of ½-inch plywood and covered with burlap or a piece of wool carpet. Attract your cat to the post by rubbing catnip on the post or by attaching a toy on a string to the top of the post.

If the cat still claws, apply a cat repellant to the furniture or squirt the cat with water from a squirt gun when it claws. When training a kitten, restrict it to the scratching post area until it learns to use the post.

Cleaners and polishes

Make-it-yourself formulas for the home

A number of readily available products make effective and inexpensive cleaning solutions. Ammonia is one. Mix 2 tablespoons in 1 quart of warm water to clean painted walls, counter tops, and other kitchen and bathroom surfaces. Or use 2 tablespoons vinegar in 1 quart of warm water.

For a strong cleaning solution suited to tough jobs, mix 1 cup ammonia, ½ cup vinegar, and ¼ cup baking soda in 1 gallon of warm water. Use it on painted walls, vinyl and ceramic tiles, and porcelain tubs and sinks; rinse with water. As with any strong preparation, you should wear rubber gloves and open a window for ventilation while working with it. Store any unused solution in a glass bottle.

To dissolve a thick soap scum around a shower or tub, use a mixture of 1 part deodorized kerosene and 1 part mineral oil. Rinse thoroughly.

Baking soda

An efficient grease cutter and deodorizer, baking soda is less abrasive than commercial cleansers and doesn't scratch polished surfaces. To clean counter tops and the enamel and chrome on appliances, rub with a paste of baking soda. Rinse thoroughly; polish with a soft, dry cloth. To clean and deodorize the inside of a refrigerator or a cutting surface such as butcher block, sponge with a solution of baking soda and water. (See also *Coffee makers; Drain odors.*)

Cleaners for wood

To remove polish buildup on furniture, use a mixture of 1 part vinegar and 1 part water. For cleaning and polishing the wood, mix equal parts of olive oil, denatured alcohol, gum turpentine, and strained lemon juice. Shake well and apply a small amount with a soft, lint-free rag (cheesecloth is ideal). Rub off excess polish with a soft, dry cloth, then buff up a shine with another cloth, preferably of wool. Store this mixture in a tightly sealed glass jar out of children's reach.

Cleaning solvents

Using spot removers safely

Cleaning solvents, or fluids, are used to remove grease spots, stains, and chewing gum from fabrics, most often from nonwashable material. Keep solvents on hand for treating spots and stains promptly.

Any solvent labeled petroleum distillates or petroleum hydrocarbons is flammable. Nonflammable solvents include triethanolamine, perchloroethylene, trichloroethylene, and trichloroethane. Commercial products often contain a mixture of flammable and nonflammable types.

Read labels before each use; see if the product is safe for the fabric you're treating (most cleaning solvents are not safe for rubberized fabrics and certain plastics). Test the solvent on an inconspicuous area to be sure it won't damage color or leave a ring.

Removing a spot

Place the spot face down on a clean, absorbent cloth. Dampen another cloth slightly with solvent and rub the spot lightly, working from the edges toward the center to avoid spreading it; keep moving the spot over a clean part of the blotting material. Use as

little solvent as possible and let it dry well between applications. It's better to repeat the process than to flood the spot, which may spread it or leave a ring. Rinse or air the garment as soon as the spot is gone; launder it or have it dry cleaned without delay. (See also *Stain removal.*)

Cleaning solvent dispensed from a spray can is also effective in lifting grease spots. Simply spray, let dry, then brush off the residue.

Caution: Cleaning solvent is a dangerous chemical. Store it out of reach of children. Never transfer it to a container normally used for food, such as a soda bottle or cup. Work in a well-ventilated area. If the solvent is flammable, don't smoke or work near a stove, active clothes dryer, water heater, or pilot light. Don't put treated clothes in a clothes dryer or near an oven. If anyone swallows cleaning solvent, call a physician, hospital, or poison control center immediately (see *Poisoning*).

Climbing plants

Decorative uses and supports

Climbing plants can attractively fill vertical spaces in your home. Use them to divide a room, curtain a window, cover an expanse of wall, or frame a door. Most flowering climbers, such as passionflowers, bougainvilleas, stephanotis, and black-eyed Susan vine *(Thunbergia alata)*, need full sun or bright light. A few plants grown for their foliage, such as creeping fig, ivy, and philodendron, do well with limited light.

Some, like the passionflower and stephanotis, will wind themselves around almost any support: chickenwire frames, strings stretched between tacks, netting, or  a trellis. Arrange their growing tips to achieve the pattern you want. Other plants need to be tied loosely to stakes or a ladder of lath; use wire-and-paper twisters, garden twine, or transparent tape folded lengthwise at the center so that it doesn't adhere to the stem.

Closets

Organizing them effectively

Whether it's a kitchen cupboard, a clothes closet, or a general storage closet, the principles are the same: store anything you use frequently between waist and eye level. Put items used less often near the floor and the least-used ones overhead. Store small things on a low shelf where you can see and sort through them easily. Because few people can reach more than 10 inches above their heads, higher shelves should hold less frequently used objects, such as luggage.

Clothes closets

A minimum of 3 to 5 feet of rod space holds an average wardrobe. You can increase this by installing two rods, one above the other, to hang shirts, skirts, jackets, and trousers. Leave enough full-length hanging space for long coats, dresses, and bathrobes.

If you can tailor closet shelves to fit your possessions, you'll not only save space but will avoid time-consuming stacking and unstacking. When installing new shelves, use metal tracks and shelf supports that allow you to adjust shelves as your needs change. Or double your present shelf space with some freestanding platforms;

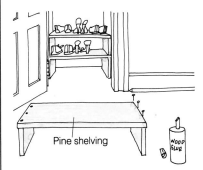

Pine shelving

they can be any length and need not span the entire closet. If your shelves are so deep that you can't reach the back, consider adding slide-out bins.

Try to keep closet floors clear. Place shoes on low shelves or in shoebags. Hang such items as tennis rackets, brooms, and mops from hooks, nails, or spring clips.

Ample light makes it easier to keep a closet neat. You might want to in-

C

stall a light. Battery types are available. Painting the walls with white semigloss paint adds brightness.

To keep closets fresh, allow for good air circulation. Install a vent in the door, or substitute louvered doors. A can of charcoal on a shelf will absorb moisture and counteract mustiness.

Closing a house

Guarding against dampness, rodents, and extreme cold

To minimize dampness, encourage air circulation. Open closet, cabinet, and appliance doors; pull out drawers. Prop up chair and sofa cushions; uncover mattresses. Spread hangers on closet rods so that air can move freely. Clean bedding, towels, and clothes before storing them. In damp areas you might hang bedding rather than fold it. Leave on dehumidifiers and air conditioning only if you can arrange frequent checks of the house.

To discourage rodents and insects, toss out anything that may attract them—food, candles, soap, debris— or store them in airtight metal containers with secure lids. Clean thoroughly; dirt, grease, and soap scum attract pests. Seal exterior cracks (see *Caulking*) and remove tree branches near the house that could give rodents access. Screen chimney tops.

Defrost and clean the refrigerator; leave its doors open. Throw old sheets or plastic tarps over furniture to protect it from dust.

Cold-weather precautions

If you are turning off the heating system in winter and you live where temperatures go below freezing, ask a plumber to drain the pipes. He will blow them out with air pressure, the only way to be certain no water remains in the pipes. Afterwards, to prevent the drains from freezing, fill toilet and sink drains with a solution of half car antifreeze, half water. Pour 1 gallon of the same solution into your clothes washer and another into your dishwasher. Run each unit with its water supply off. This prevents freezing and lubricates the machines. Before using either unit again, run it once with plain water.

If you have a steam-heating system, see *Boilers* for instructions on draining it. A hot-water system can best be protected by adding antifreeze, a job that must be done by a plumber. He will also add a backwater prevention device that stops the solution from entering the drinking-water supply.

Turn off the gas and electric power. However, if the heating system or air conditioning is to remain on, turn off only those circuits not needed to run them (see *Circuit map*).

Clothes storage

Keeping clothes presentable and easy to locate

Unless a garment is going into the laundry, hang it up as soon as you remove it; close the fastenings and adjust the collar and sleeves. Then hang it where it can air. (Put a sweater over a towel bar instead of on a hanger.) Brush suits and coats before you store them. With regular airing and brushing, garments need less frequent cleaning and will last longer.

Invest in thick wooden hangers for suits and coats and padded hangers for other garments (or make your own padded hangers). The shoulders will retain their shape and your garments will be less crushed. To keep pants from slipping off a hanger, glue a strip of felt over the bar (this will also minimize the midknee crease).

Organize your drawer space with dividers or boxes. Minimize creases in folded garments by laying tissue paper on the backs before folding.

Before storing winter or summer clothing, wash or dry clean it; it's best not to starch or iron the washables. Label bags, chests, or boxes with the contents so that you can easily locate items you need. (See also *Mothproofing*.) Don't store wool, cotton, and silk in plastic for more than a few months because these fabrics need to breath; use old sheets or acid-free paper. Where humidity and mildew are problems, avoid all plastic containers.

Accessories

Use shoe trees to keep your shoes in shape and boot trees or cardboard tubes (from paper towel rolls) to hold boots upright. If you store shoes in boxes, air them before storing them.

Suspend handbags from the closet pole with shower curtain hooks or a plastic holder with pockets. Or store them in clear plastic boxes. Hang hats on wall pegs or hooks; organize belts on a belt rack or swinging towel bar.

Cockroaches

Ridding your kitchen of a nasty pest

To prevent an infestation, deprive roaches of their needs: food, moisture, and hiding places. Put all food in the refrigerator or in metal, glass, or plastic containers. Keep counters, shelves, and floors immaculate. Fix leaky plumbing; wring out and dry sponges and dish towels. Caulk openings around pipes, appliance connections, and cabinets. Clean under low furniture and appliances.

If an infestation does occur, take these steps simultaneously: 1. puff boric acid powder into wall openings and under low equipment; 2. after removing all food and utensils, spray suspected hiding places and paths with a commercial roach spray. Place commercial insecticide baits around the kitchen and bathroom.

Caution: Do not treat food preparation areas with any pesticide or poison.

Line shelves with fresh shelf paper after the spray has dried (usually 4 hours). Repeat the procedure 2 to 4 weeks later when a new generation will have hatched.

In an apartment building, you can rid your unit of roaches, but they will return unless all units and hallways are treated simultaneously, preferably by a professional exterminator.

Coconuts

Opening the nut and preparing the meat for cooking

Shake a coconut; if it's fresh, you'll hear liquid inside. Drain the liquid by making holes in the three "eyes" at one end, using an ice pick or screwdriver and hammer. You may have to remove the husk to reveal the holes.

To crack the shell, hold it steady and tap around its circumference with a hammer or the back of a cleaver. Turn and hit the nut until it splits, usually lengthwise.

Another method of cracking is to roast the coconut at 375°F for 15 to 20 minutes (no longer or it loses flavor), then wrap it in a towel and hit it.

Pry the flesh away from the shell with a blunt knife and peel the brown skin with a vegetable peeler. Shred sections of the coconut with a hand grater. Or you can cut the meat into small pieces and grate them in a food processor or blender, about ½ cup at a time. A medium coconut makes 3 to 4 cups grated. Use the meat within 1 or 2 days or freeze it.

Coffee makers

What to do when the coffee won't brew properly

Caution: Unplug any coffee maker before cleaning or repairing it. If a percolator is immersible, return it to the manufacturer for repair.

Start your brew with cold water. Prevent coffee grounds from falling into the perk tube by covering its top with your finger when filling the basket. If the coffee tastes bitter, clean the coffee maker by running a solution of 8 cups of water and 2 teaspoons of baking soda through the cycle.

If a percolator makes weak coffee or only warms the water, examine the perk tube and the valve or the ceramic sleeve. Poke any lodged grounds from them with a pipe cleaner. If the perk tube is bent or the ceramic sleeve is cracked or broken, replace it.

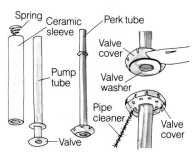

Spring / Ceramic sleeve / Perk tube / Valve cover / Pump tube / Valve washer / Pipe cleaner / Valve cover / Valve

If there's still a problem, the main heating element or the thermostat may be at fault. Each must be replaced by a service center, but you can check them yourself. To get at them, pull the knob from the strength-selector arm and unscrew any screws in the base. Inside there may be an enclosed heating element containing the main heater and the warming element, or the two heaters may be separate and visible. You'll also find a thermostat and/or possibly a fusible link.

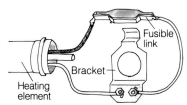

Fusible link / Bracket / Heating element

Always detach the wire from one side of any component before checking it with a continuity tester. Test a separate main heating element or an enclosed one by touching its terminals with a continuity tester; the bulb should light. Test the thermostat similarly, with the strength selector, if there is one, at *Strong.*

If the percolator doesn't heat in a working receptacle, check the cord (see *Power cords*). If the cord is all right, check the terminal pins; if they are pitted or dirty, smooth them with fine emery cloth. If they are loose, tighten their hex nuts; if they are broken, replace them. If the percolator still doesn't work, test the main heating element as above.

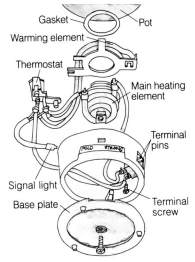

Gasket / Pot / Warming element / Thermostat / Main heating element / Terminal pins / Signal light / Base plate / Terminal screw

If the coffee doesn't stay hot after perking, check the leads of the detached warming element with a continuity tester. If the tester doesn't light, replace the element; replace any gaskets too. If the element is all right, test the thermostat as above.

Reassemble the components. Make sure that the circuitry is not grounded to the pot: make a continuity test from a terminal to the pot; if the bulb doesn't light, everything is OK.

Drip coffee makers

All drip machines have the same essential components: a main heating element, a warming element beneath the pot, a fusible link, a thermostat, and one or two switches. Access is usually gained by removing the back cover plate. On a gravity-feed model, you lift a spring clip and slide out the tank and main heating element. On a pump type, remove the screws.

If the coffee maker doesn't work in a working receptacle, check the cord. If that's not the problem, check the main heating element with a continuity tester. Similarly, take out and check the switch, fuse, and thermostat. A maker that brews weak coffee usually has a defective thermostat.

If brewed coffee doesn't stay warm, the warming element and the switch may be at fault. Unscrew the base plate to release the warming plate, inside of which is an insulated wire heating element (or fine wires on a mica card). Take it out and check it with a continuity tester; check the switch too.

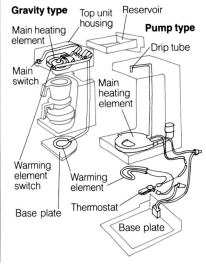

Gravity type / Top unit housing / Reservoir / Main heating element / **Pump type** / Drip tube / Main switch / Main heating element / Warming element switch / Warming element / Thermostat / Base plate / Base plate

C

Mineral deposits build up in the water channels of pump-feed drip coffee makers. Once a month run a quart of half vinegar, half water solution (or one recommended in the owner's manual) through a brewing cycle, followed by 2 quarts of plain water. Use a toothpick to clean residue from the drip tube or dribble notch.

Cold frames and hotbeds

Extending the gardening season with weather protectors

Cold frames and hotbeds are similar; both are glass-covered wooden boxes set over the ground. Both protect plants from frost, wind, and cold weather. A hotbed has an electric heating cable buried in its soil, extending its usage even further.

Seeds can be started and seedlings planted in a frame several weeks before garden planting is possible. Lettuce, radishes, spinach, and scallions can be grown in frames for an additional month to 6 weeks in fall.

A frame should be 1 to 2 feet high in front and 2 to 3 feet in back, producing a sloping top that maximizes the sun's warmth. If possible, locate a frame facing south.

A serviceable frame can be constructed of 2 x 4's and scrap 1-inch boards with discarded window sashes as covers. Much neater is this frame made from a sheet of ¾-inch exterior plywood. Saw the pieces to size, making 15-degree beveled cuts on the top edges of the front and back (to match the slope of the sides).

Cutting diagram

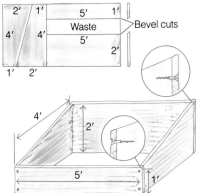

Assemble the parts with waterproof glue and countersunk No. 8 x 1½-inch flathead wood screws electroplated with zinc (see *Countersinking*). Around the top, nail a frame of 1 x 2 furring strips, using 6d galvanized finishing nails.

Furring strip

Make the cover from 2 x 2 pine with lap joints at the corners. Add wire crossbraces with 2-inch turnbuckles to give the frame rigidity. Use two 5-inch T-hinges to secure the cover to the frame. Paint with an exterior paint.

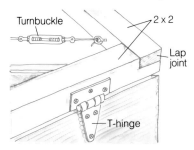
Turnbuckle
2 x 2
Lap joint
T-hinge

For low-cost glazing, staple two-mil clear plastic film to the cover; replace it yearly. For a longer lasting glazing, use ¼-inch acrylic plastic sheet or clear corrugated fiberglass roofing. Fasten it to the frame with No. ½″ x 8 round-head plated screws. If you use the fiberglass, seal its edges with caulking.

Spade the soil where the frame is to be placed to a depth of 1 foot; add peat moss or compost and builder's sand as conditioners. Dig a trench 3 to 4 inches deep to set the frame into.

When the frame has plants in it, keep a thermometer there. If the temperature reaches 75°F, prop up the cover. At night conserve heat by putting an old blanket over the cover.

To convert a cold frame to a hotbed, purchase an electric heating cable at a garden center. Bury the cable about 8 inches deep in a back-and-forth grid pattern with the loops 1 foot apart. If the soil is damp, lay gravel 4 to 6 inches deep beneath the cable. Lay hardware cloth on top of the cable.

Colds

Coping with cold symptoms

Although viruses are known to cause colds, medical science has yet to find a cure. All you can do is relieve the symptoms. With or without treatment, an ordinary cold lasts about a week. If one hangs on longer than 10 days, consult your doctor.

If possible, take to your bed at the first sign of a cold and baby yourself for a few days while your immune system fights the virus. While you may not suffer every possible discomfort, you may have, often in sequence: sore throat, sneezing, a runny and then stuffy nose, perhaps a slight fever with aching and restlessness. Treat only the symptoms you have, each one as it appears.

Natural remedies are often sufficient and lack the unpleasant side effects of some drugs. Drink lots of liquids. Hot soups and drinks soothe a sore throat, as does gargling with warm, salty water. A vaporizer, either the hot-steam or cold-droplet type, will relieve nose or chest congestion.

Aspirin or other analgesics relieve aches and pains, reduce swelling of inflamed tissues, and lower fever. Analgesics also have a mildly relaxing effect that may lift low spirits and help you sleep.

Cold medications

Before buying any over-the-counter cold "remedy," ask your pharmacist what the ingredients are for and whether they're safe for you. Combination cold preparations may contain drugs for relief of symptoms you don't have—or worse, they may duplicate or conflict with other medication you are taking. Don't take any cold preparation for longer than 3 days without a physician's advice. Give drugs to children only on a physician's advice.

Because you are most contagious a day or two before you know you have a cold, it's almost impossible to avoid spreading cold viruses. Once symptoms have appeared, observe these rules: sneeze, cough, and blow your nose into tissues; put used ones in a paper bag and dispose of it daily; wash your hands often; and keep your distance from other people.

Cold sores

Coping with painful blisters on the lips and in the mouth

Cold sores, or fever blisters, in and around the mouth are caused by herpes simplex, a common virus. (A different type of herpes virus causes genital and other herpes infections.) Although uncomfortable and occasionally painful, untreated cold sores usually dry up in 10 days to 3 weeks. To relieve inflammation, try applying a compress soaked in refrigerated Burow's solution (1:40 dilution) for 10 minutes five times daily. A severe outbreak should be seen by your doctor. Beware of touching the blister and then your eyes; this could cause an eye ulcer and infection. Also avoid touching anyone who has eczema; that person can easily get herpes all over his or her body.

After the sores disappear, the virus remains dormant and can be reactivated by illness (usually a cold), exposure to wind or sun, or stress or menstruation. Subsequent eruptions begin with tingling, burning, and itching, followed by the appearance of a cluster of blisters. If you often get cold sores, use a sun-blocking lip balm when outdoors.

Colic

Acute abdominal pain that causes crying in infants

Colic commonly begins when a baby is 2 weeks old and, in most cases, ends when a baby is 3 months old. No one knows what causes colic or why some babies are affected and others not. Breast-fed as well as bottle-fed babies get colic. An immature digestive system or an irritable nervous system may be to blame.

A feeding often prompts an episode of colic. In some babies, colic begins right after they nurse. They draw up their legs in pain and may cry for an hour or more.

You can try one or several ways of soothing the baby: gentle rocking, rubbing the baby's back, warm pads on the baby's abdomen, giving the baby a pacifier. Sometimes nothing works. Inform your pediatrician of the problem so that he can determine whether there's another cause for the pain. Colicky babies usually thrive and gain weight normally.

Collage

How to create a work of art by just gluing things down

The simple art of collage (from the French *coller,* "to glue") consists of arranging and fixing elements on a background to form an original composition. The elements can range from paper, fabric, dried flowers, or shells to machine parts, thumbtacks, or just about anything with an interesting shape, color, or texture.

To begin, cut a mounting board of Masonite, particle board, or plywood to the desired size. Use either ¼-inch or ⅛-inch board, depending on the weight of the materials. Prevent the board from buckling by coating the front and back with white glue or gesso that has been thinned with water to the consistency of light cream. If you wish, glue paper or fabric over the board to form a background.

Assemble assorted papers such as colored tissues, foil, illustrations, and greetings cards or assorted fabrics or other materials or a combination of various materials and move them about to find the most satisfactory arrangement. Cut or tear the paper or fabric for different effects. Glue the pieces into place and let the glue dry.

Collages can also be made of more solid materials. Try a pasta lacework collage, elaborating on the simple design shown here. Use a compass to draw concentric circles on a sheet of colored Masonite; then divide the circles into equal sections. Use the drawing as a guide to create symmetrical

arrangements of diferent types of pasta. Position small pieces of pasta with tweezers. Glue the pasta into place.

Collection agencies

Standing up for your rights with bill collectors

Falling behind in paying your mortgage, medical bills, or other debts doesn't give bill collectors the right to hound you. The federal Fair Debt Collection Practices Act protects you against abusive efforts by collection agencies to get you to pay overdue bills. It doesn't, however, eliminate your debts or stop collectors from using reasonable methods to get paid.

A collection agency can contact you by mail, telephone, telegram, or in person, but not before 8 A.M. or after 9 P.M. unless you allow it. It can't contact you at your job if your employer disapproves, nor can it tell anyone but you and your lawyer about your debts. A collector can, however, ask others where you live or work.

After you hear from an agency, it must send you within 5 days a written notice of how much you owe, the name of your creditor, and instructions on what to do if you don't owe the money. You have 30 days to write back if you dispute the debt. This stops further collection efforts unless the agency has a copy of the bill or some other proof of the debt.

If you write the collection agency telling it to stop contacting you, it must do so, but it can take other action, such as a lawsuit. An agency cannot notify you that it will take some other action, however, unless it or your creditor intends to do so.

It's illegal for a collector to use harassing tactics, such as communicating with you in an obscene manner; threatening your person, property, or reputation; making anonymous or frequent phone calls; or

C

publicizing your debts. Also prohibited are lying about what you owe; implying that you committed a crime; or giving out false credit information about you.

State laws also protect your rights. If you think you've been subject to abusive collection efforts, contact the Federal Trade Commission or your state attorney general.

Compasses

Finding your way with or without a map

A compass needle is a magnet that points toward magnetic north, not the North Pole. The difference between the two, called the angle of declination, varies from area to area and is shown on most topographic maps.

If you are traveling cross-country without a map, the difference doesn't matter. Simply aim the direction-of-travel arrow at the place you want to go and turn the dial, or bezel, until the needle points toward 360 degrees. Keep the needle on this heading as you travel. To find your way back, rotate the bezel halfway around.

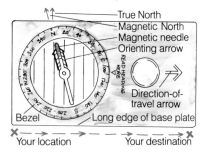

Finding your way with a map
To compensate for the angle of declination, place your compass on a topographic map with the long edge of the base plate connecting where you are to where you want to go. Then turn the bezel so that the orienting arrow aligns with magnetic north, as shown on the map. Now take the compass from the map and hold it level in front of you. Turn your body until the needle aligns with the orienting arrow. The direction-of-travel arrow is pointing at your destination.

Don't try to get there all at once. Pick out a landmark at which the ar-

row is pointing, walk to it, and find another landmark beyond.

If you have to skirt an obstacle, turn 45 degrees from your bearing and count each time your left foot hits the ground. When you've cleared the obstacle, turn back 90 degrees, walk the same number of paces, and turn 45 degrees again, back to your original bearing. (See also *Map reading.*)

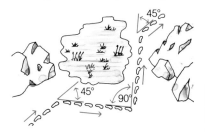

Compost

Recycling yard and kitchen scraps for garden soil

A well-made compost pile turns waste material into rich garden humus in a few months. Build the pile in layers, alternating 8- to 12-inch thicknesses of waste with 2-inch layers of soil. Include green plants, grass clippings, old leaves, egg shells, and shredded newspaper (not more than 10 percent of the latter). Don't compost wood, diseased plants, corncobs, cheese, milk, meat, or grease. Press down each layer. For fast results, sprinkle on a little 10-6-4 fertilizer and, on alternate layers, a generous dusting of lime. Water each layer and subsequently keep the pile damp.

Compost can be piled unsupported, but a bin is neater—and because air must reach the compost, the bin cannot be solid. The easiest kind to make is a wire-mesh pen 3 feet or more in diameter. Form a cylinder from a length of mesh 3 to 4 feet wide and secure it by hooking the cut wire ends around the mesh.

For a more sightly bin, make four slatted wood frames about 3 feet high, using redwood, cedar, or pressure-treated lumber. Nail three of them together, and complete the rectangle with two stretchers. Hinge the fourth side or attach it with hooks and eyes to make it removable.

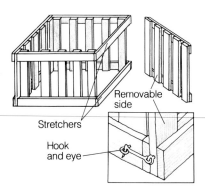

Dig a shallow pit for the bin and put a layer of straw or loose brush in the bottom. Then add waste, layer by layer. Periodically rebuild the heap, moving outside matter toward the center. The compost is ready when it is dark brown, crumbly, and nearly odorless.

Computers

How to buy and care for a home computer

With a home computer, you can entertain and educate, compose music, balance budgets and checkbooks, analyze investments, prepare taxes, run a cottage industry, manage a farm, and manipulate words, numbers, and graphics with amazing speed. With a *modem,* a device that lets a computer use the telephone, you can gain access to large stores of information on many subjects, exchange mail with other computer owners, leave messages at computer "bulletin boards," and participate in classes.

The physical body of a computer is its *hardware.* It includes a processing unit with silicon chips mounted on *boards* or *modules* (plug-in devices that extend the computer's capabilities), a keyboard, a monitor (you may be able to substitute your television set), a disk drive for storage, and an optional printer.

The machine's intelligence is its *software:* the *operating system* that tells the hardware how to perform basic functions and the *programs* that run specific tasks. Most programs are magnetically stored on hard or "floppy" disks. A program that runs in one operating system will not run without alterations in another. An operating system generally works only in the hardware it was designed for.

Buying a computer

First, decide what you want the computer to do for you. Then, through reading books and computer magazines and talking to people who own computers, find the best software programs for those tasks. Then, and only then, buy the hardware to fit.

Look for a helpful dealer. Read the instruction manuals to make sure you can follow them. Test the machine with programs you will use; don't be satisfied with a 5-minute demonstration.

Computers vary in price and capability according to the size of their memory and the speed with which they execute instructions. The size of a computer's *Random Access Memory* (RAM)—the temporary memory that stores program instructions and data—is measured in kilobytes (K), or thousands of bytes (letters, numbers, or other symbols the machine will process). A computer with 24K, or about 24,000 bytes, of memory may be fine for games and simple programs, but some programs that process words or huge batches of numbers require 64K or 128K or 256K.

Check the computer's speed. An "8-bit" machine, which can handle 1 byte of information at a time (8 bits equal 1 byte), is slower than a 16- or 32-bit computer.

Prices range from less than $100 to thousands of dollars. Be aware of additional costs for the monitor, disk drives, printer, connecting cables, or extra boards to allow special functions, such as graphics. Get a fixed price for the package you want, and if prices are too high, look at used computers.

Read the warranty carefully. Exactly what does it promise? Will the dealer service the unit or must you return it to some distant factory? Will the computer's manufacturer still be in business in 2 years? Who pays for shipping? How long for repairs? After the warranty expires is a service contract available? These typically cost 10 percent of the purchase price per year and put a cap on repair bills.

Within the warranty period, use the computer heavily; leave it on several days; let it heat up; test all its func-

tions and report malfunctions. Don't mail the registration card until after initial testing; if the unit's a lemon, the dealer may exchange it quickly.

Computer care

Plug the computer into a house circuit that is free of interference from heavy appliances, especially air conditioners or refrigerators that cycle on and off. A separate circuit is safest. Be sure the computer is well grounded. You may need surge suppressors, noise filters, or line isolation devices to protect against glitches in the power that cause random errors.

Other enemies of a computer are heat, dust, cigarette smoke, static electricity, and magnetic fields. Allow space for air to flow freely around the air intakes and vents. Maintain a room temperature of between 50 and 80°F. Keep the computer clean and cover it when you're not using it.

Every electric or electronic device generates an electromagnetic field. A telephone placed next to a box of computer disks may garble or erase the disks' contents when the phone rings.

Protect against static electricity. You can buy antistatic sprays for the rug and your clothes. Apply often to the surrounding surfaces, but don't spray the computer equipment itself. If static persists, remove carpets from the work area, use a humidifier, or lay antistatic floor mats.

Concrete

Buying, mixing, and pouring this durable material

Concrete is a mixture of portland cement, sand, coarse aggregate (gravel), and water. Use it within 1½ hours after it has been mixed. Arrange to have someone help you with your project.

Caution: Wet concrete is caustic. Wear goggles, waterproof gloves, long pants and sleeves, and high rubber boots. Promptly wash splatters off your skin. Rinse clothing when you finish working. Use lanolin cream to relieve mild irritation. See a doctor if discomfort persists.

Planning a project

Make your measurements on the ground or in a scale drawing, then cal-

culate your needs in cubic yards: multiply the dimensions of your area and divide by 27 (there are 27 cubic feet in

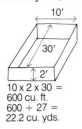

10 x 2 x 30 = 600 cu. ft.
600 ÷ 27 = 22.2 cu. yds.

1 cubic yard); add 10 to 15 percent for a safe margin. If your project is over 3 cubic yards, call a supplier of ready-mixed concrete; he sells by the cubic yard.

Buying and mixing

When you need a small amount—for setting fence posts, for example—buy dry mixed concrete in 90-pound bags (⅔ cubic feet) from a lumberyard or home center. Pour part of the dry mix into a large metal bucket or a contractor's wheelbarrow (rent one from a tool rental store). Add a little water and stir with a shovel or hoe. If still too dry, add a little more water. It's right for pouring when it will hold a mound shape, the smoothed surface of which retains a trowel slash mark.

To mix concrete for a job requiring 1 to 3 cubic yards, rent a portable mixer. Don't exceed its capacity, which is just over half its total volume. The concrete-mix ratio for a driveway or walk is 1 part cement, 2 parts sand, 4 parts aggregate, and ½ part water. Place the mixer at the work site to avoid wheelbarrowing. Hose the drum after each batch; spray other tools often.

Pouring, finishing, and curing

Pour only on a level gravel bed (see *Concrete driveways*) or level and slightly damp ground. Pour on a dry day, with the temperature between 50°F and 70°F.

For a large job have ready-mixed concrete delivered and dumped directly into the formwork if possible (see *Concrete formwork*). In regions that have frost, be sure to order air-entrained concrete.

When pouring from a mixer or barrow, deposit each load against the previous, beginning in a corner. In a slab, spread the concrete with a shovel or hoe. In a wall formwork, ram the mixture up and down with a square-end shovel to remove air bubbles and rock pockets; give particular attention to areas near the forms.

To level the surface, place a strike-off board across the side forms. Move it back and forth to shift the excess concrete into the voids. Use a bull float to level any gaps and embed the aggregate below the concrete surface.

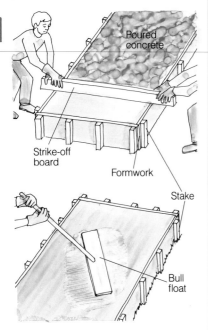

Poured concrete

Strike-off board

Formwork

Stake

Bull float

After the concrete has set enough to hold its shape, run an edger back and forth between the side forms and the concrete. Next, cut control joints in the slab to allow for expansion (one every 4 feet for a walkway; one every 10 feet for a driveway). Next, use a wooden or metal float to level lumps and voids, then smooth the surface several times with a trowel. For a nonskid finish, sweep with a damp, stiff

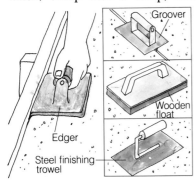

Groover

Wooden float

Edger

Steel finishing trowel

broom. Carefully remove the forms from the "green" concrete one day after the pour.

Curing should take 5 days in 70°F weather, 7 when cooler. During this period, keep concrete moist by sprinkling, or cover it with a plastic sheet.

Concrete driveways

Staking, excavating, building formwork, and pouring

Make your driveway about 9 feet wide and 4 inches thick for passenger cars or 5 inches thick for an occasional truck. To calculate the amount of concrete needed, see *Concrete*. While planning, check with your municipality's building department about local regulations. Arrange for delivery of ready-mixed concrete. On the delivery day have several helpers on hand.

Staking the area
Drive a stake at each driveway corner, 8 inches wider than intended: stake from garage apron to sidewalk or, if there is none, to the street. Mark the length by running string from stake to stake on each side. Using the string as a guide, drive additional stakes on each side every 10 feet.

Drive two stakes 10 feet apart on the street side of the walk. Measure 19 feet down the walk from these stakes. Drive stakes at these points. Hammer a nail partway into the top of each stake. Tie string to each nail and fasten a stake to each string's free end; the strings should be 19 feet long. Use them as radii to mark off curves at staked at 1-foot intervals.

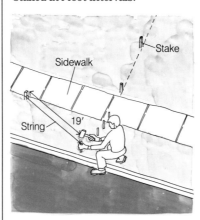

Stake

Sidewalk

String

19'

With a backhoe excavate the apron-to-sidewalk area 5 inches (for cars) or 6 inches (for trucks). Between the sidewalk and street, excavate 10 inches; slope the excavation toward the street. Fill the excavations with 4 inches of gravel. Level and compact the gravel with a tamp.

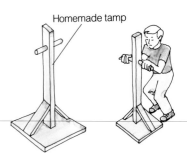

Homemade tamp

To stake the formwork, drive a 2 x 2 stake into the ground at either side of the apron, 9 feet 3 inches apart. Drive four more, two on each side of the walk (observing the same width). As before, use a string guide to position the other stakes, this time at 4-foot intervals. Mark the curved portion from the walk to the street, this time with a 15-foot radius. Again stake at intervals of 1 foot.

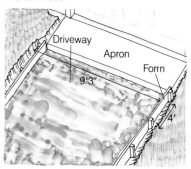

Driveway

Apron

Form

9'3"

4'

Line 2 x 6 form boards in the stake-outlined area (apron to walk) and fasten them to the stakes with duplex-head nails. Where forms meet, secure their ends with a 1 x 6 board, backed by a stake and a rock for added support. Wipe the insides of the forms with motor oil for easy removal after the concrete pour. For the curved portions use ¼-inch plywood the same height as the curb and the walk (see *Concrete formwork*).

After you've ascertained that the driveway will be level (see *Leveling*), adjust for drainage by raising the forms nearer your house 1 inch higher than the other side; use a crowbar.

Dampen the area and line it with tar paper or plastic sheeting. Place 2 x 6 construction boards, supported by stakes, at 10-foot intervals. Place expansion joints (a material you buy from a masonry supplier) on each side of the walk and where the driveway meets the street.

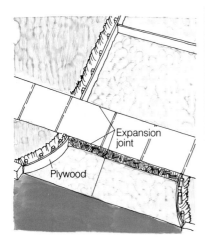

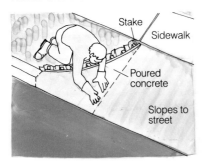

Have the truck pour one section. Strike off, then remove the adjoining construction board and have the truck pour the next, and so on. Later you'll cut control joints where the boards were (see *Concrete*). Wearing gloves, hand shape the slope of the curved area from sidewalk to curb.

Concrete formwork

Building wooden frames for pouring concrete

Concrete exerts tremendous lateral pressure as it is being poured and as it hardens. Build a formwork of sturdy, straight boards to contain it. The desired thickness, size, shape, and purpose of the concrete should determine the formwork's dimensions. Before building formwork, call your municipality's building department to find out the local requirements and whether your formwork must be inspected (see *Building permits*).

To guide excavation and formwork building for a rectangular slab, outline the intended area with four lengths of twine. Extend the twine 4 feet beyond each corner and tie it to the stakes driven there. Check for squareness by measuring diagonally, corner to corner; if the diagonals are equal, the corners are square.

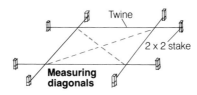

Outline the shape by driving 2 x 2 stakes (1 foot long for hard ground; up to 2 feet for soft) into the prepared ground at 4-foot intervals. Warning: wooden stakes are likely to split while being hammered into rocky terrain; steel stakes are worth the extra cost. Wipe one side of your 2 x 6's (for a 4-inch slab) with motor oil, then place them (oil sides inward) within this perimeter; use wider lumber to make a thicker slab. Check in both directions that they are level (see *Leveling*).

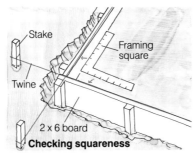

Fasten the end stakes to the forms with duplex-head nails (they are easier to extract later). Check again for

squareness of the shape—this time by placing a square tool in each corner of the formwork. If the tool and the corners don't exactly meet, reposition the stakes until they do and realign the boards. Recheck for level; correct by hammering the corner stakes at the higher end. Nail the remaining stakes to the form boards. Drive in extra stakes where boards join, and nail the three surfaces together.

If the formwork wiggles under hand or foot pressure, give it additional support with kicker stakes. Resting the kicker against the outer edge of

the board, at a generous angle, place your foot at its base to guide it while you hammer it into the ground. Nail the kicker to the top side of the board.

Make curved forms from ¼-inch-thick plywood. Wipe one side with motor oil. Curve the plywood (oiled side inward) and place it in the corner of a rectangular formwork, resting against the forms.

Push the bowed center of the plywood into the desired position, then drive a stake on the inside of the curve to hold it while you nail it to the two forms, using about two dozen ¾-inch roofing nails. Drive additional stakes against the outside of the curve at 1-foot intervals, then nail them to the plywood; brace the outer curve with dirt. Rasp the plywood ends so that they blend into the straight forms. Remove the stake inside the curve.

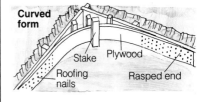

Concrete patching

Filling small and large cracks

Fill a hairline crack with concrete sealer. Clear rubble from a large crack with a steel brush. Widen the crack with a cold chisel; it should be wider at the base than at the top and at least ½ inch deep. Brush out the chips, then scrub the crack clean with a solution of TSP (trisodium phosphate) and water, following the recipe for heavy cleaning on the TSP package.

Using a trowel, pack the still-damp crack with masonry patching compound or with vinyl concrete patching cement. Although more expensive, the latter is easier to work with and has greater bonding strength. Cover the patch with wet burlap and keep it damp for a day or two.

C

Condolence letters

The form to use; what to say; whom to write

A condolence letter is an expression of sympathy and support to a bereaved family or friend. The most personal of personal letters, condolences should be handwritten, never typed, and should follow the form of the personal letter—that is, with address and the date on the upper right-hand side of the paper.

Your choice of stationery is important. Good-quality white, cream, or gray letterpaper is appropriate. Personal letterhead is correct if it is dignified and the color subdued, but avoid bright or whimsical notepaper.

Etiquette experts disagree about whether or not it is correct to use a commercial sympathy card. Some feel it is inappropriate at such a sad and deeply personal time; others find it proper provided the message on the card is warm and personal. If you do use one, don't just sign your name; add a personal note.

It can be difficult to know what to say in a condolence letter, since nothing you can possibly say is really adequate. If the bereaved is a personal friend of yours, write to that friend, recounting a fond memory of the relative who died if you knew the relative. If you didn't know the deceased, concentrate on your friend and how he or she must be feeling. Whatever the situation, make yourself available for help or counsel. Be sure to follow up your letter with a telephone call and, in a month or two, an invitation to do something quiet. Grieving people are most in need of help several months after the funeral.

If a friend of yours has died, write to that friend's closest relative. If you and the relative aren't acquainted, explain who you are (college friend, work colleague, fellow club member) and express how much your friendship with the deceased meant to you. Relate specific examples or anecdotes about your deceased friend; such memories will cheer and touch the bereaved family—as will, again, an offer of help and support.

Condos and co-ops

Buying a home in a multifamily development

The dream of owning a home no longer evokes only a house on its own plot but, to many, calls to mind visions of a condominium (condo) or cooperative (co-op). Both are units of rooms in either an apartment building or a group of attached townhouses. Your home is an individual unit, but you share with your neighbors such common areas as entrances, elevators, the grounds, and parking and recreational facilities.

When you buy a condo, you receive a deed. You own the unit you live in and, if it's a townhouse, the land it's on. You share ownership of the common areas with the other residents and pay a monthly maintenance fee for the upkeep of such areas. The residents elect an association to make rules for the development.

When you buy a co-op, you get shares of stock in the corporation that owns and manages the building. The number of shares depends upon the size of your unit. Your monthly maintenance charges, based on how many shares you have, are a portion of the principal and interest on the building's mortgage, taxes, and maintenance costs. The co-op board of directors—shareholders elected to run the co-op—approves the sale of any unit and sets and enforces bylaws and rules to operate the building.

What to look for

Before buying a condo or a co-op, investigate its location. A convenient area with stores and public transportation protects your investment. Carefully inspect your unit, the entire complex, and its common areas for potential and existing problems that might change your mind about buying or help you negotiate a better price. If you don't know much about structural problems, hire an engineer to inspect the premises.

Talk to other owners about their units and the management of the complex. If the developer has built or owns other complexes, find out whether the owners of units in those complexes are satisfied with the management. Read the prospectus carefully. Check the financial background of the owner or builder, especially if the units are new: consult your local consumer affairs office to find out whether there are any outstanding claims against the owner or builder.

Documents

Once you decide that a condo or co-op is for you, you should read certain documents before signing on the dotted line. Have your lawyer explain what documents your state requires. Those most commonly required follow.

The *declaration of condominium* (or *prospectus* for new condos) states the physical extent of the complex and plans for its management, the value of each unit, any conditions and restrictions on your rights as an owner, and the election process for the association. For a co-op, you receive a copy of the same lease that is given to all the tenants. It declares your rights and duties as a shareholder and the powers of the board.

A *financial disclosure statement* for the last 3 years tells you in dollars and cents how well the condo or co-op management runs the complex and whether there is a separate fund for emergencies or large repairs. This gives you an idea of the accuracy of the estimated monthly charges and the need for special assessments—extra fees for unexpected expenses.

The *bylaws and rules* detail the procedures governing the board and define unacceptable behavior—such as unleashed dogs and noise after midnight—and the remedies.

The *management agreement* explains the responsibilities and costs of operating the complex. Often the service employees contract accompanies this agreement. It lets you know how much the employees make and when they are due for a raise or a new contract—expenses that affect your maintenance charges.

The *purchase and sale contract* for a condo describes the condo's size and location, the buyer and seller, the purchase price and down payment, the monthly fees, the real estate taxes on the unit, and the closing date when you become the owner. For a co-op, the contract states the number of shares bought, the price and down payment, the monthly charges, and any special assessments. It should also provide that if the sale depends on board approval, you'll get back your down payment if rejected. For both condos and co-ops, financing terms, the right of the seller to sell the unit, and repairs to the unit are just a few of the provisions you might want to add to your contract.

Conjunctivitis

Help for an eye problem

An inflammation of the conjunctivas (the membranes that cover the eyeballs and line the eyelids) may be caused by chemicals, dust, bacteria, viruses, or allergens such as ragweed pollen. The eyes may be reddened, weepy, itchy, and sensitive to light. One common bacterial form, popularly called pinkeye, produces redness and a discharge. If only one eye is inflamed, suspect a foreign object (see *Eyewinker*).

Bathe affected eyes several times a day with warm water on a pad of cotton. Use soothing eyedrops. Applying moist, warm compresses may also help. If your eyes don't improve within 3 days, or are in pain or if your vision is in any way affected, see an ophthalmologist (eye doctor).

Because this infection is contagious, the affected person should use a separate washcloth and towel. Do not rub your eyes and warn children not to rub theirs.

Constipation

Eating and exercising to avoid bowel problems

Before you start worrying about constipation, be sure you really have it. A bowel movement every 2 or even 3 days may be normal for you.

You can do a lot to keep your movements regular by drinking enough fluids and eating enough roughage to give the feces bulk, which allows them to pass easily, and by exercising daily. An adult should drink 2 quarts of liquids (water, juice, or milk) daily. For roughage, eat bran cereals, whole-grain breads, leafy vegetables, and fresh and dried fruits. Sprinkle bran flakes on salads or fruits. Use such lubricants as cooking or salad oil in foods. Walking, jogging, swimming and other exercise stimulate the bowel muscle. Avoid laxatives and enemas; they will worsen the problem.

Nervous tension can cause constipation. If you believe this is your problem, or you are constipated for more than 2 weeks, consult your doctor. Chronic constipation can be a symptom of a serious condition.

Consumer complaints

What your rights are; how to complain; where to seek information and help

After centuries of *caveat emptor* ("let the buyer beware"), the law now offers the consumer better protection. Products must be fit to be sold and used in the conventional way as well as in a particular way that you describe to a merchant. A merchant must understand a product well enough to know whether it will suit your purpose. The exception is when a merchant or manufacturer makes a clear disclaimer and you buy the product anyway.

If a product is defective, the seller or the manufacturer must fix it provided you have used it properly. If after several tries it still isn't fixed, you can choose to get a refund or a free replacement. The law further mandates that professional services must be performed in a reasonable way. For example, doctors, dentists, and lawyers must explain possible choices and difficulties and give you time to decide if you want to go ahead.

How to complain effectively

Your first recourse should be to the seller of the defective item or service. To retain your goodwill, a store may exchange an item or give a refund even for a trivial complaint.

If a store refuses to make good on an item, complain in writing to the consumer affairs department of the item's manufacturer. Briefly and unemotionally give all pertinent facts: dates, an exact product description with model and serial numbers, where and when you bought the product, the nature of the problem, and your name, address, and business and home telephone numbers. Include *copies* of sales slips and other relevant documents. State how you would like the problem remedied and by what date. In some cases, especially if a large sum is involved, have a lawyer write your letter.

If you still get no satisfaction, try writing to a company officer (president, vice president).

Where to complain

If you get poor service from a local business or store, complain to the Better Business Bureau (BBB). Write a letter giving all particulars; send a copy to the dealer. The BBB may contact the merchant directly. Although the BBB has no enforcement power, no business wants to be listed by it as a company that renders poor service.

To complain about professional or personal services, look to a licensing agency. Most medical societies, bar associations, and state boards (real estate, for example) have grievance committees and are eager to root out problem professionals.

Consumer's Resource Handbook, a publication of the federal government, lists corporate consumer contacts, industry groups, trade associations, Better Business Bureaus, and government agencies that can help in resolving your complaint. For a free copy, write: *Handbook*, Consumer Information Center, Pueblo, CO 81009.

Other sources of information and help are state and local consumer affairs offices. Congressmen and state legislators can direct you to consumer groups and agencies. Contact your municipal office or the office of the district attorney, the state attorney, or the state attorney general.

Arbitration and mediation

Many communities sponsor mediation centers where citizens can take disputes with local merchants. The usual format is a face-to-face meeting, with a mediator present to help work out a solution. Look in a telephone directory for names like Neighborhood Justice Center or Community Mediation Center.

Continued next page

Many trade associations, consumer action groups, and advisory panels offer mediation and arbitration services. Consult your local consumer affairs office or ask the public library for *HELP: The Useful Almanac* or the Consumer Federation of America's *Directory of State and Local Consumer Groups.*

One possible way to draw attention to your complaint is to send it (with full details, plus your name, address, and telephone number) to an "action line" of a newspaper or of a radio or TV station. Or look in your telephone directory for the nearest office of Call for Action, a national, nonprofit organization with affiliates in about 25 locations, mostly major cities. It dispenses advice and referrals and serves as a consumer advocate, all free and confidential. If you find no local listing write Call for Action, 575 Lexington Avenue, New York, NY 10022.

Contact lenses

Types and their differences; living comfortably with lenses

Contacts can be fitted to the eyes of most people, even those needing bifocals or correction for astigmatism. An eye-care professional should decide which type is best for you.

Rigid gas-permeable lenses are the most durable and least expensive to maintain. They cause less risk of eye infection, for they let more oxygen reach your cornea and resist bacteria better than soft lenses. It takes 1 to 2 weeks to adjust to them.

Soft lenses are the most comfortable (the eyes adjust in a week), but are more costly to maintain and require rigorous cleaning. They last 6 months to a year and may tear and deteriorate from contact with cosmetics.

Disposable and planned-replacement lenses avoid protein buildup that clouds lenses, but they may cost more to maintain. Depending on the type, disposable lenses can be worn for 1 to 2 weeks and then must be discarded. Planned-replacement lenses can be worn for 2 to 12 weeks.

Extended-wear lenses that can be worn for 7 days come in several lens types: rigid gas-permeable, soft, or disposable. Some eyes adjust quickly, but others won't tolerate the constant contact. An eye doctor should check your eyes at least twice a year.

Lens care

Keep lenses immaculate; wash your hands before touching them or your eyes. Keep your contact lens case clean and replace it every 3 to 6 months. Have an eye exam yearly.

Repositioning a slipped lens

Lubricate your eyes with drops. Close your eye and massage the lid gently above the spot where the lens has lodged, nudging it toward the center. It helps to roll your eye toward the lens. You may have to push the lens with your fingertip.

Finding a lost lens

Always insert your lenses over a clean towel or a sink with stopper in it. If you drop a lens, search the floor and yourself inch by inch. Darken the room and beam a flashlight over the area; the lens will glint in the light.

Contractors

Finding a reliable contractor; getting bids; making a contract

The best way to find a good contractor for a job you want done is to consult a friend or neighbor who has recently had a similar project completed. If you can't easily get a referral, ask at building supply yards or your municipality's building inspector's office. They generally know who uses good materials, has his finances in order, and completes jobs promptly. As a last resort, check with your local trade association or look in the classified telephone directory.

In all cases, get financial and professional references from the contractor and check them out. Go to see other jobs he has done if possible.

A builder who takes on big projects and coordinates crews of tradesmen is usually known as a general contractor. He supervises all aspects of a project, arranges for tests and inspections required by law, and makes sure that the work is done on time and to a specified quality. As much as one-third or more of the cost of the job will be his fee.

An individual tradesman, such as a plumber, carpenter, or landscaper, who works for a general contractor or directly for you is called a subcontractor. You can save money by acting as the general contractor yourself and hiring the subcontractors directly. To do this successfully, you must be able to visit the site at least once a day, to understand and coordinate the different trades, and to deal with banks and the local building department (see *Building permits*). And you must have insurance to cover any potential claims or liabilities that could occur.

Getting bids

If your project is large, you may already have an architect who can recommend contractors or who may act as general contractor. If you don't, draw up sketches or plans and list what you want done. Include materials by brand name, where possible, and appliances by make and model.

Submit the same plan and list to at least three different licensed contractors and ask for bids and time schedules. When the bids come back, evaluate the cost, the quality of the contractor's past work, and the time it will take him to complete the work. Don't hire on price alone. Base your decision on the best quality at the most convenient time as well as price.

If a price seems too high or if the job is small, you can pay for time and materials rather than a fixed price, but this is a gamble. The job will be cheaper if the work goes quickly but more expensive if any difficulties arise.

Contracts

A contract can be prepared by the contractor, by your lawyer, or by you if the job is small (see *Contracts*). It should be a written agreement specifying what, when, and how all aspects of the project are to be accomplished. It should include exact dates for start and finish, prices and brand names, and exact descriptions and specifications of the work to be accomplished. Anything not written down could lead to an unpleasant surprise later on.

Include a written procedure for changes you decide to make during construction; changes are where most conflicts arise. They can interrupt a job and add costs, but if both you and the contractor agree and "sign off" changes, it won't be a surprise when the final bill is higher than the contract price.

The contract should also specify when payments are to be made. Always reserve a substantial payment until after the job is 100 percent complete. This will keep the contractor responsive and give you the power to insist that details be completed to your satisfaction. Also make sure that the cleanup is included so that sawdust is swept and debris is hauled away.

Contracts

Making a contract that will hold up in court

You can make a contract with just about anyone for just about anything. Not every agreement you make qualifies as a contract, however. To be a contract, an agreement must provide that something of value be received by both parties involved. Generally, one party offers to pay money in return for which the other party will give up certain goods or perform a service.

The words in a contract should leave no doubt as to what both parties are to do. If you suggest a change in the terms after they have been agreed upon, the change is binding only if the other party agrees to it. If both of you shake hands on a deal, but leave an important term, such as price or quantity, open until later, you have nothing but an "agreement to agree," which is legally worthless.

You don't have to put a contract in writing unless a state law specifically requires it, but doing so protects you against later trouble. Generally, state laws require that contracts for land, for goods over $500, and for long-term employment be in writing.

Caution: Get your lawyer to advise you on the best ways to protect your interests when you make an important contract.

Read a contract—particularly the fine print—carefully before you sign on the dotted line. The courts won't help you if you're careless in making a deal. But if the other party unfairly exploits or tricks you, a court might help if you can prove that you were duped.

Don't make a contract with a minor (usually under age 18) or someone with a mental disability. Their legal representatives can cancel the contract as long as they return anything received under it.

If the other party fails to fulfill the terms of your contract, there's a breach of it. Try to work out a mutually satisfying solution outside of court, perhaps with a lawyer's help. If you can't find a solution, ask a court to cancel the contract, to give you money (called damages) to compensate for your losses, or to order that the contract be performed if there's no reasonable substitute for what was to be done.

Cookie cutters

How to make rolled cookies

Cookies made with cookie cutters are festive, especially if before baking you decorate them with sprinkles, colored sugar, or nuts. Their shapes can be flowers, rounds, diamonds, rectangles, or holiday symbols; their sizes can vary from 1 to 5 inches or more.

On a floured surface, preferably one covered with a pastry cloth, roll dough uniformly to the thickness specified in the recipe. Dough rolled to 1/4 inch or slightly thicker makes chewy or soft cookies; thinner dough, 1/8 inch or less, will be crisp.

Dip the edge of the cutter in flour, and shake off excess. Set it level on the rolled dough, then press down firmly. Lift the cutter, set it close to the first cut, press and cut again. (If the cutter

begins to stick, reflour it lightly.) Continue until all the dough is cut. Carefully lift away uncut dough, then, with a spatula, move cookies one by one to a baking sheet. Set aside all scraps and reroll them at one time; too much reworking adds excessive flour, which will make cookies tough.

Crisp sugar cookies

Preheat oven to 375°F. Cream until fluffy 1 cup butter or margarine, 1½ cups sugar, and 2 teaspoons vanilla. Beat in 2 eggs, adding them one at a time. Sift together 3¾ cups all-purpose sifted flour, 1½ teaspoons baking powder, and 1 teaspoon salt. Add these to the creamed ingredients and stir the mixture just until blended. Wrap the dough in waxed paper and chill about 1 hour. Roll out one quarter of the dough at a time to a thickness of 1/8 inch or less. Cut shapes.

Space cookies 2 inches apart on a lightly greased baking sheet. If you sprinkle them with sugar, brush them first with milk. Bake in the top third of the oven 8 to 9 minutes or until pale golden. Transfer to wire racks. Makes about 7 dozen 2-inch cookies. (See also *Gingerbread men.*)

Cookies

Cookie-making basics; drop cookies with variations

Most cookies are classified as one of five types, depending on the way they are shaped: drop (from a teaspoon); molded (by hand or by cookie press); rolled (see *Cookie cutters* and *Gingerbread men*); bar (cut into rectangles after baking); and refrigerator (sliced from a chilled roll).

For best results, measure ingredients level and preheat your oven for at least 15 minutes. Except for bars, use baking sheets—or turn baking pans upside down (high-sided pans don't allow heat to flow evenly over the cookies). Grease the sheets with unsalted shortening or, for delicate cookies, line the sheets with foil.

Place the dough on a cool sheet and fill the sheet so that the cookies will bake evenly. (If the last batch won't fill a sheet, use the reverse side of a small pan.) Place sheets at the center of the oven or higher and at least 2 inches from oven walls. As soon as cookies are done, transfer them to wire racks. Should they harden on the sheet, pop them back in the oven for a minute.

Drop cookies

This good, plain, basic recipe can be varied with additional ingredients. It makes about 3½ dozen 2½-inch cookies. Preheat the oven to 400°F. Cream ½ cup butter or margarine, ¾ cup firmly packed brown sugar, and 1 egg. Stir in ¼ cup buttermilk or sour milk (if you have none, add 1 teaspoon vinegar to milk). Sift together 1½ cups sifted all-purpose flour, ½ teaspoon baking soda, and ¼ teaspoon salt. Add these gradually to the creamed ingredients and mix until blended. Drop by rounded teaspoonfuls about 2 inches apart on greased baking sheets. Bake 8 to 10 minutes, or until a fingerprint barely remains when a cookie is touched lightly.

Oatmeal-raisin: Reduce flour to 1 cup; add 1 cup raw oats, 1 cup raisins, and 1 teaspoon cinnamon.

Chocolate chip: Add 6 ounces semisweet chocolate bits and ½ cup chopped nuts.

Coconut-orange: Substitute ¼ cup orange juice for the milk. Add 1 cup shredded coconut and 1 tablespoon grated orange rind to the dough.

Cookware

Choosing among and caring for different types

Look for durable materials and sturdy construction. Make sure that pans stand steady and have firmly attached handles and stay-cool knobs.

Aluminum is inexpensive and an excellent heat conductor. However, it discolors and must be scoured. Soaking or long exposure to alkaline foods causes pitting. If you choose aluminum, buy medium to heavy gauge; thin aluminum heats unevenly and gets battered quickly.

Nonstick linings, often used in aluminum ware, allow you to cook with little or no fat. They clean with a wipe of a sponge. Because they scratch easily, use wooden or plastic utensils to stir or turn food.

Stainless steel is relatively maintenance free but expensive. It conducts heat poorly, but a heat-conducting metal core in the bottom compensates for this. Prolonged contact with acid or salty foods can cause pitting in stainless steel. Excessive overheating (for example, burning food or allow-

ing a kettle to boil dry) darkens it; such stains can't be removed. To keep this metal sparkling, dry it with a towel and polish it occasionally with a stainless-steel cleaner or silver polish.

Cast iron heats slowly and evenly, holds heat well, and is inexpensive. Its main disadvantage is its weight.

Enamelware—enamel on metal—is easy to clean and attractive enough to go from stove to table. Iron-based ware makes fine casseroles but lacks the porous surface needed for frying. Thinly coated enamelware chips easily and has hot spots.

Copper—beautiful, expensive, and a fine heat conductor—needs frequent cleaning to keep it shiny. And it must be relined when the tin lining wears thin or gets nicked. If you choose copper, buy heavy gauge; thin copper has hot spots.

Ovenproof glass is inexpensive and usually comes clean with just a sudsy rinse. Because it conducts heat slowly and evenly, it is fine for baking casseroles, pies, and puddings.

Freezer-to-oven ceramic is a durable white material for use on top of the stove and in the oven. It withstands sudden temperature change and can thus go directly from freezer to stove.

Plastic bakeware for microwave or conventional oven use can tolerate up to 400°F and also go into a freezer.

Copyrights

Protecting your work from theft

U.S. copyright law automatically protects any original literary, dramatic, musical, or artistic work that you compose from being used without your permission. A copyright is the exclusive right you receive from the federal government to publish, copy, adapt, and publicly display and perform your work. It is good from the moment you create your work until 50 years after your death. If, however, you create the work as an employee or are especially commissioned to create it, under an appropriate written contract, you create a "work for hire" and the employer owns the copyright, unless you have agreed otherwise.

The work must be original. Merely

reprinting general information, such as the metric table, work in the public domain, or principles or theories, does not entitle you to a copyright. Nor does copying someone else's work.

To be eligible for copyright protection, your work must be set down in some physical form, such as a book, film, sound recording, or videotape. Once you set it down, you have copyright protection. You needn't publicly sell or distribute the work, but if you do, you should include a copyright notice.

For most works, your notice should contain the word "Copyright" or its abbreviation "Copr." or the symbol © (or ℗ for sound recordings); the year the work was first published; and the name of the copyright owner—you. This information should appear where it can be easily seen—for example, on either the title or following page of a writing or on the label of a record—to let everybody know that they must get your permission to copy or sell copies of your work. In exchange for your permission, you can request a fee, called a royalty, when your work is used.

You don't have to register a copyright, but you may do so for a small fee. It's best to protect your rights. For an application form or more information, call the Copyright Forms Hotline, (202) 707-9100, or write Copyright Office, Library of Congress, Washington, D.C. 20559.

Corks and corkscrews

Uncorking the wine

A cork seals a wine bottle, yet permits a tiny amount of air to penetrate. Some feel that this is beneficial to the wine aging process; others say no. As long as corks remain in use, however, there must be mechanisms for removing them with finesse.

Start by cutting off the foil or plastic covering to just below the bottle's bulge; wipe the area clean if necessary. For extracting the cork you need a corkscrew, the most important part of which is the spiral, also called the worm. Look for a thin, widely spaced spiral at least 2¼ inches long with a sharp point but without a sharp edge that could fragment the cork; make

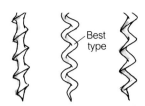

Best type

sure it is well secured. Most corkscrews have levers or braces (or both) designed to make the task foolproof. Four efficient types are illustrated.

To operate (A), set the guide frame on the bottle; check that the crossbar covers the top of the screw post. Screw the spiral clockwise all the way into the cork, then flip the crossbar so that the screw post can move up through the hole. As you continue to screw, the cork will be raised from the bottle. To operate (B), twist the spiral into the cork with the larger crossbar; twist the cork out of the bottle with the smaller one. With (C), as you twist the spiral into the cork the two levers will rise; when the spiral is all the way in, push the levers down to extract the cork. To operate (D), set the guide frame over the neck of the bottle and grasp the frame firmly. Screw the spiral clockwise into the cork; continue screwing until the cork has climbed up the spiral and out of the bottle.

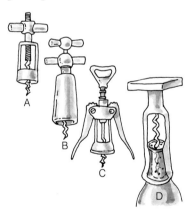

Corncob pipes

For an old-fashioned smoke prized for its mildness

A good pipe requires a dry cob at least 2 inches thick. Field corn is the best source; sweet-corn cobs are too small. If the cob is not dry, keep it in an oven at 120° to 140°F for 8 to 12 hours.

To make the bowl, cut a cross section from the cob 2 inches long. For the stem, use a short piece of bamboo and the plastic stem from an old pipe.

Hollow out the cob, leaving a wall and bottom ½ inch thick. Drill a hole for the bamboo ¼ inch above the interior bottom. Taper the bamboo to fit tightly and glue it in with epoxy. File the outside of the bowl partly smooth and apply a thin coat of plaster of Paris. Finish with fine sandpaper, varnish lightly, and glue on the stem.

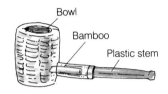

Bowl
Bamboo
Plastic stem

Corn earworms

Protecting your corn crop

This striped, green, brown, and yellow caterpillar, also known as the tomato fruitworm and the cotton bollworm, attacks a variety of crops but is most destructive to sweet corn. After feeding on silk, the corn earworm enters the ear and feeds on the kernels.

To protect your crop, apply a few drops of mineral oil to the silk of each ear as soon as it has wilted and before it dries out. You may find that long, tight-husked varieties, such as Silver Cross Bantam, Country Gentleman, and Dixie 18, are more pest resistant.

Corn earworms can be controlled by spraying with carbaryl or diazinon when the ears appear and every 5 days thereafter until the silking period ends—when the cornsilk tassles turn brown and wither. These same insecticides are also effective against the European corn borer, a pest that eats into corn stems.

Cornhusk dolls

A craft from the early days

Take the soft inner husks from six ears of corn and spread them out to dry on a sheet or between layers of

newspaper. They'll be ready for dollmaking in about a week, when they are pale golden. (You can skip this step by buying packaged dried husks at a Mexican food store.)

Sprinkle the dried husks with water and place them in a plastic bag overnight, or soak them in warm water to soften. Keep them in damp towels as you work.

Begin forming the doll's head by trimming the ends of six husks. Roll them widthwise together, then tie the roll tightly with thread about an inch from one end. Turn the roll upside down and peel the husks back singly over the thread, so that the bound end is covered. Smooth out the husks and tie a thread tightly around them just below the knob, forming the head. For the neck, tie a ¼-inch-wide cornhusk strip over the thread.

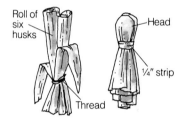

Roll of six husks
Head
¼" strip
Thread

Make arms by rolling two husks around 6 inches of thin wire. Tie the ends of the rolled husks with thread; trim the ends. Insert the arms between the front and back husks, right under the neck; center them. Secure the arms to the torso with a length of husk strip crisscrossing the breast and the back, over and under the shoulders. Tuck loose ends into the torso. Tie narrow strips of husk to make elbows and wrists.

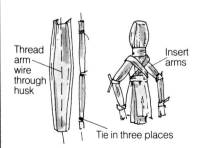

Thread arm wire through husk
Insert arms
Tie in three places

Wrap a ¾-inch-wide strip over each shoulder, cross them at front and back, then secure them at the waist with a ¼-inch husk strip.

Continued next page

C

To make the skirt, position several husks, with wide ends down, around the doll's waist. Tie them in place with thread, then trim the husk ends at top and bottom. Wrap a wide strip of husk over the thread to form a waistband, and tie it in place with two narrow husk strips. Arrange the skirt, then let the doll stand for several days or until it is thoroughly dry. For hair glue dried corn silk onto the head. Draw facial features with ink.

Dried corn silk

Several husks with wide ends down

Corns

Relieving a foot problem

Corns are small, dead-skin buildups caused by pressure or friction from ill-fitting shoes or from bony prominences. Hard corns form on the tops of toes where shoes press directly; soft corns develop between the toes.

Corns are seldom painful enough to require medical treatment. Comfortable shoes will keep them from worsening and even, in time, encourage them to disappear. Protect them, meanwhile, from pressure or friction with adhesive cushioning or sponge rubber rings, both sold in drugstores.

If a corn is sensitive, soak it in warm water for 15 minutes; then rub it with pumice stone to remove surface skin (never trim or pare a corn). Afterward apply a mild softening ointment, such as petroleum jelly or a lanolin preparation. If, after five daily treatments, the corn is still painful, ask your doctor or podiatrist about surgical or chemical removal. (See also *Blisters; Bunions; Calluses.*)

Cosmetics

Using makeup to bring out your best features

Makeup can give your face a smooth finish, conceal flaws or blemishes, and add expression and color. Never borrow cosmetics or share yours with other people. Discard those that are older than a few months; they may harbor bacteria.

If your skin is dry, use an oil- or cream-base foundation. For an oily skin, choose a water-base or oil-free foundation. Before you buy, test a foundation shade by dabbing a bit on your face and neck, in natural daylight if possible. The right shade will almost disappear as you blend it into your skin. If you use a concealer (for hiding blemishes), choose one that's slightly lighter than your foundation.

Cheek color needn't match lipstick exactly but it should be in the same color family. Coral (orangish-pink) cheek color, for instance, shouldn't be used with bluish-pink lipstick. For oily skin, powder blusher is preferable; people with dry skin can use cream rouge.

Preparing your skin

Before applying cosmetics, wash your hands, pin back your hair and, using soap and water, cleansing cream, or lotion, cleanse your face and neck; rinse well. Dab breakouts with a cotton ball or swab dipped in alcohol, witch hazel, or an astringent lotion. Next, apply moisturizer, preferably while your face is slightly damp.

A concealer stick or cream can be used to hide pimples, dark spots, fine lines, or spidery veins. Apply the concealer; then blend it in, taking care to leave no line between concealer and surrounding skin. To minimize dark circles under your eyes, cover them with concealer; pat to blend.

Applying foundation and powder

To give your face an even color, smooth on a bit of foundation with your fingers or a slightly dampened sponge. Stroke upward and outward away from your nose. Blend foundation to your hairline (don't get any in your hair) and just over your jaw to avoid a demarcation line at the neck.

Keep several foundations on hand in shades a bit lighter and a bit darker than your basic color, so that you can match your skin when you get a tan (or lose it). Use these extra shades to experiment with facial contouring. For a receding chin, dot a crescent of slightly lighter foundation over your chin, then blend it with the main foundation shade on your jaw and cheeks. Pull back a protruding chin by doing the same thing with a slightly darker foundation. Check your contouring in daylight to be sure it looks natural; blend a bit more if it doesn't.

Powder-type blusher and eye shadow work best if you powder your face before using them. If you use rouge and shadow with a cream base, apply them first; then dust with powder. Apply loose, translucent powder with a powder brush; use a powder puff or cotton ball for pressed powder.

Contouring with blusher or rouge

Apply a blusher or rouge to the outside of your cheeks, temples, and forehead. To position it, locate the "apples" of your cheeks (the parts that are most prominent when you smile) and the hollows (the areas just below the intersection of cheekbone and jaw). Then shape your face into a more perfect oval. To make a long, narrow face appear wider, stroke the color from the outermost hollows of your cheeks toward your ears. To slim a round face, put color on the apples of your cheeks in tiny crescents below the eye area. Soften a square face by brushing the undersides of both apples back toward your ears and along the jawbone. Keep cheek color two fingers width from your nose and above the nose's bottom.

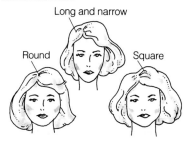

Long and narrow

Round

Square

Next come eye shadow and mascara (see *Eye makeup*). Finish off with lipstick. First, outline your lips with a lip pencil. Apply lipstick with a lipbrush. (See also *Eyebrows; Facial care.*)

Cottage cheese

Two kinds to make at home

You can make cottage cheese with rennet (a substance that causes milk to curdle) for large-curd sweet cheese or without rennet for old-fashioned, small-curd tart cheese. To prevent the curds from getting tough and rubbery, it's essential to control the temperature rise, limiting it to 5 degrees or less during each 5-minute period of cooking. For this purpose you'll need an accurate, easy-to-read thermometer and two large pans in a double-boiler arrangement. The more milk you work with, the easier it is to raise the temperature gradually. For additional information about basic steps and ingredients, see *Cheesemaking*.

Large-curd sweet cottage cheese
Heat 2 gallons pasteurized skim milk or reconstituted nonfat dry milk to 90°F; add to it ½ cup unpasteurized buttermilk. Crush ¼ tablet rennet and dissolve it in ¼ cup cool water. Mix well into milk. Keep the temperature at about 90°F but no higher for 5 hours, or until milk coagulates and breaks cleanly away from a spoon or finger dipped into curds.

Cut curds into ½-inch cubes and heat curds and whey (the liquid residue) very slowly to between 110°F and 115°F; maintain this temperature for about ½ hour, or until a lump of curd holds together when pressed gently between thumb and forefinger.

Strain through cheesecloth and hang to drain until the dripping becomes very slow. Immerse the bag of curds in cold water and stir the cheese gently with a spoon to rinse curds in center. Drain again, then gradually mix in 5 to 6 teaspoons salt. If you like a moist cheese, add a little cream.

Small-curd cottage cheese
Heat 2 gallons pasteurized skim milk or reconstituted nonfat dry milk to 72°F; stir in thoroughly ¼ cup unpasteurized buttermilk. Cover pan with plastic wrap; leave in a warm place from 16 to 24 hours, or until milk sets or coagulates.

Cut the curds into ¼-inch cubes. Cook, drain, and salt as for large-curd cottage cheese.

Coughing

Coping with minor coughs; recognizing serious ones

Coughing is symptomatic of a variety of physical complaints, some mild, some serious. It may be triggered by something incidental such as inhaling a small bit of food (see *Choking*) or noxious chemical fumes. But most often it's a result of the common cold, when secretions of mucus irritate the upper respiratory tract. Coughs due to colds usually disappear without treatment within a few weeks. In the meantime, the ill person may need relief in order to sleep or work.

You can often soothe a cough by drinking warm or cold liquids, or by inhaling steam from a vaporizer or a hot shower or mist from a humidifier. Or put a towel over your head and put your face over a sink full of steaming water. Sucking hard candies or lozenges sometimes gives relief.

Cough medicine may help, provided it does not contain ingredients that work against one another, as some over-the-counter remedies do. There are two types of cough medications: *expectorants* that loosen secretions so that they can be coughed out, and *suppressants*, drugs that suppress the cough reflex. Read ingredient labels. Expectorants include glyceryl guaiacolate and potassium iodide. Suppressants include codeine and benzonatate (prescription drugs) and dextromethorphan hydrobromide.

When coughs are more serious
Coughs requiring medical attention are those accompanied by fever and those that persist longer than 3 weeks. A cough with fever may indicate flu or bronchitis—and if you're short of breath, pneumonia. A severe productive cough (one that entails spitting up thick, yellowish mucus) may be a sign of bronchitis (either acute or chronic), croup (in children), or other serious conditions. Consult a doctor promptly if you or a family member coughs up blood or if any cough persists more than 3 weeks and seems to be getting worse. (See also *Colds; Flu; Laryngitis; Postnasal drip; Smoking.*)

Countersinking

Drilling holes for screwheads

To get a screwhead flush with the wood, you must countersink it in a shallow, tapered hole. Drill a pilot hole with a straight bit (in hardwood, drill a hole for the screw's shank too; see *Drilling*). Then center a countersink bit in the pilot hole and drill. The countersink bit should be the diameter of your screwhead, but a slightly larger bit will do if you stop short of its full diameter. Test for fit by inserting the inverted screwhead.

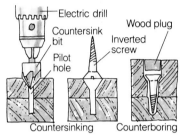

Countersinking   Counterboring

A faster method is to drill the pilot and countersink holes simultaneously with a combination bit specific to one size and length of screw. Unless you use the same screw size many times, this is an expensive method.

To counterbore (sink the screw below the wood's surface), use a bit exactly matched to your screwhead.

CPR

Restoring breathing and heartbeat in emergencies

Cardiopulmonary resuscitation (CPR) is a lifesaving technique for restoring the breathing and heartbeat of an unconscious accident or heart-attack victim. It combines mouth-to-mouth breathing and external heart massage (chest compression). The same method applies in other emergencies—near drowning, drug overdose, strangulation, suffocation, electrocution, or carbon monoxide poisoning.

Speed and persistence are essential. A delay of 5 minutes can be fatal. Although an untrained person can perform mouth-to-mouth breathing, ideally only someone trained in CPR should administer chest compressions. CPR is best performed by two people while a third summons medical help.

There are three basic steps, called the ABC's of CPR: clear the *airways;* *breathe* for the victim; restore *circulation* by chest compression.

Clearing airways
Place the patient on a firm, hard surface, such as a floor or a table, not a bed or a couch. Then tilt the victim's head with one hand pressing on the forehead and the other lifting the chin.

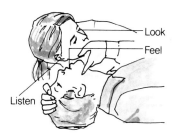

Put your head down and listen and feel for breathing; look to see whether his chest rises and falls.

Breathing for the victim
If the person is not breathing, begin mouth-to-mouth breathing. With one hand, tilt the chin up; place the heel of the other hand on the victim's forehead as shown. The chin should be tilted so that the teeth are nearly together. Use your thumb and index finger to pinch the nostrils shut.

Take a deep breath and place your mouth over the victim's. With an infant or small child, the rescuer's

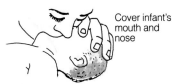

mouth may cover the victim's mouth and nose simultaneously.

Make a tight seal so that no air escapes, and blow two slow, deep breaths in rapid succession. If you can't make a tight seal over a victim's mouth, give breaths mouth-to-nose as shown.

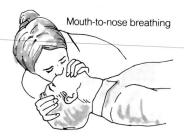

Pause long enough to inhale deeply and resume mouth-to-mouth (or mouth-to-nose) breaths. As you blow, the victim's lungs expand, and you should see his chest rise. If this doesn't happen, retilt the head to make sure the airway is open. Then try mouth-to-mouth (or mouth-to-nose) breathing again. If you still can't establish air exchange (the chest doesn't rise), suspect an obstruction in the air passage and follow the procedure described in *Choking* to dislodge the obstruction.

If you see the victim's chest expand, take your mouth away so that he can exhale and then repeat the mouth-to-mouth procedure (about one breath every 5 seconds for an adult, every 3 seconds for a child). Continue until he is breathing on his own or help arrives. Don't give up.

Restoring circulation
Take the pulse as shown; in an infant under 1 year, take it on the inside of the arm near the armpit. If there is no pulse, mouth-to-mouth breathing must be accompanied by chest compression, preferably done by a second rescuer with CPR training.

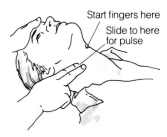

Place one palm on the lower end of the breastbone and the other hand on top and at right angles to it. Then,

keeping both arms rigid, thrust down 1½ to 2 inches. Repeat this pressure rhythmically 80 times per minute (count "one and, two and, three and"). For children ages 1 to 8, use the heel of only one hand; thrust down 1 to 1½ inches at a rate of 100 times per minute.

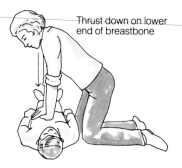

If the victim is an infant, use two fingertips and compress the breastbone ½ to 1 inch, at a rate of 100 times per minute.

One person performing adult CPR
Do mouth-to-mouth breathing for two breaths, then 15 chest compressions at the rate of 80 per minute, then two breaths; move rapidly from one to the other. Continue until breathing and pulse are restored.

Crabgrass

Controlling the tenacious weed in lawn and garden

A fast-growing annual that sprouts from seed each year about the time forsythia blooms, crabgrass crowds out other plants with its flat-lying blades. In the garden, the best preventives are early and repeated cultivation or application of a mulch to keep young plants from maturing.

In the lawn, apply a pre-emergence herbicide such as benefin, bensulide, DCPA, oxadiazon, or siduron before seeds sprout. Except for siduron, these herbicides will retard or possibly prevent germination of some desirable grasses as well, so use them with care. Later on, after shoots have appeared, use a postemergence herbicide, such as a methanearsonate (DSMA, MAMA, or NSMA). Read and follow package directions carefully. (See also *Lawn care; Pesticides.*)

Crabs

Cooking and eating hard- or soft-shell crabs

Hard-shell crabs are best boiled whole. Grasping a live crab from the back or with tongs, rinse it in cold fresh water, then drop it into boiling salted water seasoned with your own combination of spices or with commercial crab-boil seasoning. When the water returns to a boil, continue cooking for 20 minutes (25 to 30 minutes for Dungeness crabs), then drain.

To eat a crab, lift off the apron—a circular shell segment on the female's belly, a pointed section on the male's—and pull off and discard the entire top

Apron

shell. Pull out and discard the long, whitish gills and the spongy stomach.

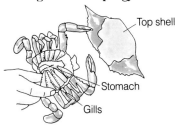

Top shell

Stomach

Gills

Bend and snap off the claws. Snap the body in two and remove the meat with a nutpick or your fingers. Crack the claws with a nutcracker or wooden mallet and pick out the meat.

Soft-shell crabs

Soft-shell crabs (hard shells at the molting stage) can be broiled, sautéed, or deep-fried. In all cases, they must be killed and cleaned first; you can usually have this done at the fish market.

To kill a soft-shell crab, grasp the body between the back legs, and cut across its body just behind the eyes with kitchen shears. Reach into the cavity created by the cut and pull out and discard the stomach. Pull off the apron. One at a time, fold back each side of the top shell and remove and discard the gills, but don't remove the shell. Wash the crab and dry it.

To sauté a soft-shell crab, flour it lightly and brown it in butter for 3 to 4 minutes over moderately high heat. Sprinkle it lightly with salt and pepper. Eat the entire crab, shell and all.

Cradle cap

Getting rid of baby's dandruff

An oily, scaly, yellowish crust called cradle cap sometimes appears on an infant's scalp. A form of the same problem that causes dandruff—excessive secretion by the skin's oil glands—it may cover the scalp, occur in patches, or spread to the forehead.

To remove cradle cap, apply mineral or baby oil or petroleum jelly. Leave it on overnight. Then gently brush or comb the softened crust, using a baby brush or a fine-toothed comb. Finally, wash the scalp with a tearless shampoo. Repeat this treatment daily until the cradle cap disappears or is reduced. If it persists after 3 or 4 weeks, consult your pediatrician.

Cramps

Coping with abdominal pain

Like all cramps, those in the abdomen are intermittent, caused by involuntary muscle tightening. Many women have abdominal cramps before or during menstruation (see *Menstrual cramps*). Cramps can also occur in the leg or arm muscles (see *Muscle aches*) or as a result of overactivity in hot weather (see *Heat exhaustion*).

Without other indications, abdominal cramps are usually a symptom of acute gastroenteritis, an inflammation of the lining of the stomach and intestines that has many possible causes, among them food poisoning, food allergy, flu, constipation, or overindulgence in alcohol. Treatment is bed rest and no solid foods until the cramps have subsided and any other symptoms such as nausea or vomiting have passed. Usually this takes 24 to 48 hours. Meanwhile, nibble on ice chips; take frequent but small amounts of clear liquids: tea, bouillon, ginger ale, or water.

Get prompt medical help if cramps persist more than 3 or 4 hours or are accompanied by such symptoms as high fever, rigid abdomen, continuous vomitting, blood in stools or vomitus, or pain radiating to the right hip or to either shoulder. (See also *Food poisoning, Stomachaches.*)

Crawl stroke

How to master the fastest swimming stroke

Floating prone, with your face submerged and arms extended fully over your shoulders, begin to exhale slowly through your nose and mouth. With your hands flat and your fingers together, pull your right arm downward, bending your elbow slightly so that your hand passes beneath your body. Start turning your head to the side—always the same side, whichever is comfortable.

Complete the pull at your hip or upper thigh and bend your elbow upward. Simultaneously begin the pulling action with your other arm (your arms should be at fairly opposite positions throughout) and complete the head turn so that your mouth breaks the surface.

Inhale deeply, then roll your face back into the water, exhaling slowly. Your arm should exit the water elbow high, wrist low, with your fingers

slightly above the surface. Bring your arm forward and extend it fully; your fingers enter the water first.

Flutter kick

Scissor your legs with your feet staying just below the surface. Flex your knees slightly and point your toes

C

downward. Push downward with the tops of your feet; recover upward. The movement should come from your hip joint (avoid hip rolling). Kick relaxed but fast: six kicks to each stroke cycle of both arms.

Crazy eights

A fast-moving card game where the eights are wild

Deal seven cards to each player if two are playing; deal five cards to each if three or four are playing. Place the remainder of the deck facedown on the table and turn the top card faceup beside it to start a discard pile.

Each player, in turn, discards a card that matches either the suit or the rank of the top card on the discard pile. For example, if the top card is the 7 of spades, you can discard any spade or any 7 on top of it. You can also discard an 8 of any suit and name the suit you wish it to be. If you don't have a proper card to discard (you are not obliged to use an 8), you must draw from the stockpile until you come to a card you can play.

The first player to discard his or her last card gets points for all the cards remaining in the other players' hands. Each 8 counts 50, each face card 10, and each ace 1. Other cards score at face value. A game is 100 points.

Credit

Establishing and managing credit; bad rating; lost cards

Credit isn't just convenient. It lets you take advantage of price breaks and make major purchases without waiting (and, in inflationary times, before the price goes up). Those who extend credit, however, exact interest for the use of their money. Compare lenders' interest rates before making any commitment for a mortgage, installment purchase, or even a credit card.

Credit is granted on a lender's confidence that the borrower will repay. Therefore, the lender usually checks your credit history with one or more of the credit bureaus that collect data about a person's bill-paying practices and debts. These bureaus don't rate you; they simply report what they learn from subscribing stores, banks, and credit-card issuers. They have limited responsibility for accuracy.

Most credit bureaus give a "current" or POS (positive) rating to people who pay bills within 30 days. Those who take 90 days or more will be rated "delinquent" or NEG (negative). Between those extremes there lies a gray area, called NON (nonevaluated) because individual creditors apply their own standards. Unused credit lines are considered debt because you could use them at any time.

Establishing credit
To establish credit you must borrow something and repay it. For those with no credit history, the best way is to set up a savings account, then take out a passbook loan with the savings acting as collateral.

Credit card companies will often let young borrowers start with an account cosigned by their parents. A cosigner may be the answer too for older people who have always paid with cash. The Equal Credit Opportunity Act sets up a special "user" category that could help women with accounts in their husbands' names to build a credit record. Ask for an ECOA/TYPE account or loan.

Managing credit
Credit counselors think most people can afford 10 percent to 15 percent of their take-home pay, excluding mortgages, in installment debt. Over 15 percent means it's time to cut back; over 20 percent means trouble ahead. Similarly, most banks look for a debt-to-income ratio of 10 percent to 20 percent, home mortgages excluded.

Generally, avoid credit transactions under $25. Try to make credit-card purchases just after the monthly closing date, and you'll have about 6 weeks to make the next payment. Pay promptly to avoid interest charges.

Avoiding a bad credit rating
If you have a backlog of debt, pay bills before the grace period ends to avoid triggering a "late" charge on the computer. Next best: pay the minimum amount by the due date. Failing that, send what you can, with a note promising more payments soon.

Federal law now requires a creditor to explain why it rejects you for a loan or a credit card. If a credit bureau was responsible, the creditor must tell you which one. That bureau must let you examine your file without fee within 30 days. For a small fee anyone can see his or her file at any time.

Get the addresses of local bureaus from your bank or department store or check the classified directory under "Credit Reporting Agencies." Call for an appointment or ask if a copy of your file can be mailed to you. The Fair Credit Reporting Act requires all credit bureaus to reinvestigate disputed facts and to delete any that are inaccurate or unsubstantiated—or at least to include your explanation.

Lost cards
Federal law limits a cardholder's liability to the first $50 of purchases on a lost or stolen card; most companies don't charge that. But you must notify the issuer immediately. Some companies won't replace a card lost twice. Special insurance is costly and generally unnecessary. Some homeowners' insurance covers losses.

Credit complaints
If you think your bill is in error, write the creditor within 60 days, giving your name, address, account number, the dollar amount, and an explanation of what you think is wrong. The creditor must acknowledge your letter within 30 days.

Once you have notified a creditor of a supposed error, he cannot act to collect the disputed amount or report it as delinquent. If the dispute is not resolved within 90 days, the creditor can notify the credit bureau and other creditors. He must again notify them when the problem is resolved.

Crepes

Delicate filled pancakes

Crêpe is the French word for a thin pancake that is usually rolled or folded around a filling; it can be served for a main course, snack, or dessert.

Prepare crepe batter at least 1 hour before cooking to allow the flour time to swell—the secret of a soft crepe. (If you haven't time for this, substitute a quick-mixing or an instant-blending flour for regular flour.) The batter should be the consistency of heavy cream and should thinly coat a spoon.

Use a heavy skillet with a 6-inch bottom. Brush it lightly with a few drops of oil or a little butter and heat almost to smoking, or until a bit of test batter sizzles and bubbles. Use a ladle or measuring cup to pour in about ¼ cup of batter. Quickly tilt the pan in all directions so that the batter coats the bottom.

Cook the crepe until the edges are lightly browned—about 1 minute. To turn, loosen the edges with a spatula, slip it under, and flip quickly. Cook the second side for no more than 30 seconds: overcooked crepes are tough or crisp and difficult to roll.

As the crepes are done, stack them. They can be refrigerated for 2 to 3 days or kept frozen for a month; separate them first with sheets of wax paper and wrap them with aluminum foil.

Basic crepe batter
Put ½ cup cold water, ½ cup milk, 2 eggs, ¼ teaspoon salt, 1 cup sifted flour, and 2 tablespoons melted butter into a blender jar in the order given. Blend at top speed for about 1 minute or until mixture is smooth. Or put all the ingredients in a bowl (flour first, then the liquids) and blend with a whisk or an electric beater until smooth. For dessert crepes, add 1 tablespoon sugar to the batter. If batter is too thick, add a few drops of milk. Makes about a dozen 6-inch crepes.

Crepe fillings
For breakfast, sprinkle crepes with cinnamon and sugar, or spread them with jam, maple syrup, apple sauce, or sliced fresh fruit; roll them up. Add a dollop of whipped butter or sour cream, if you like.

For lunch, brunch, or dinner fill each crepe with a blend of 2 tablespoons white sauce, 2 tablespoons sautéed, chopped mushrooms, and a dash of nutmeg (see *White sauce*). Or use Welsh rabbit or creamed chicken, seafood, or vegetables. Or fill crepes with chili con carne with sprinklings of minced onion and grated cheese.

For dessert fill each crepe with 2 to 3 tablespoons crushed or sautéed fresh fruit, lightly sugared. Top with ice cream or whipped cream.

Cribbage

Playing a 17th-century English card game for two

The object of the game is to score points from combinations formed during play and from combinations made in your hand after play. The dealer gives his opponent and himself six cards each, singly. Each player places two cards facedown to form the *crib*, which goes to the dealer. Cut the remaining deck and turn the top card (the *starter*) faceup.

Playing
The dealer's opponent leads by laying down any card and announcing its value. Face cards count as 10, aces as 1, and all other cards at face value. (The announced value is *not* a score.) The dealer then plays a card, announcing the total value of both cards played. (Players keep the cards they play in front of them.)

The play continues until someone is unable to play without making the total count go over 31. That player announces "go," and the other plays all the additional cards possible without pushing the count over 31. The player who couldn't play then starts a new play, from zero, using the remaining cards in his or her hand.

Scoring
You keep score on a board with four rows of 30 holes each (two rows for each player) and 2 or 4 extra holes. Each player has two pegs. If you don't have a board, draw one on paper and use coins as markers.

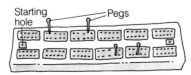
Starting hole / Pegs

At the beginning of the game, starting from an extra hole, a player advances his first peg one hole along the outer row for each point scored. At the second turn, he marks his score with his second peg, counting the hole be-

yond his first peg as 1. This system lets a player keep track of his former score as well as his most recent. He walks the pegs first along the outer row, then the inner, as he plays, for a total score of 61 or twice around, for 121, if agreed upon in advance.

The opportunity for scoring begins just before the first play. If the starter is a jack (*his nibs* or *his heels*), the dealer gets 2 points. During play, a card that brings the announced value to exactly 15 scores 2. A card that brings the announced value to exactly 31 scores 2; if 31 is not reached, the card bringing the value nearest to 31 scores 1. Playing the last card scores 1.

A pair, or a card having the same value as the card previously played, scores 2; a triplet, 6; a four, or fourth of a kind, 12. The last card of a run, or sequence, of three or more cards of the same or mixed suits scores 1 point for each card in the run.

At the end of play, the dealer's opponent takes the scores for the cards in his hand. Then the dealer takes the scores for the cards in his hand plus those in the crib. A player with *his nobs,* the jack of the same suit as the starter card, adds 1 point to his score.

Pairs, runs, and other combinations earn the same scores as when playing, but the starter can be used to form them. A single card can be used in more than one combination.

In addition, a double run of three, a three-card sequence with a pair to any of the three cards (for example, 9-9-8-7), scores 8; a double run of four (9-9-8-7-6) scores 10. A triple run, or a triplet with two other cards in sequence with it (9-9-9-8-7), scores 15. A quadruple, or two pairs and a card in sequence with both (9-9-8-8-7), scores 16. A four-card flush, or four cards of the same suit, scores 4 if in either hand but not if in the crib. A five-card flush, or 4 cards in a hand or the crib of the same suit as the starter, scores 5.

If your opponent overlooks points in his hand, you can cry "Muggins!" and make them your own. The first player to reach 61 (or 121) wins. If the loser fails to score at least 31 or 61, he is left in the *lurch* (the first half of the run on the cribbage board) and the winner is credited with winning two games. The loser of any game deals the next game.

C

Crocheting

Making the basic stitches

All crochet begins with the *chain stitch*, abbreviated *ch* in instructions. Chains form the foundation row and are also incorporated into many pattern stitches. Keep the tension even and slightly loose; if chains are too tight, the work will pull.

Form a loose slipknot about 6 inches from the yarn end (A); insert the

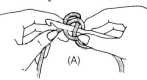

(A)

hook in the loop from right to left. Tighten the loop by pulling both yarn ends. Wrap the ball end of the yarn around the little finger of the left hand, under the fourth and third fingers, and over the top of the index finger (B). Leave about 2 inches of yarn

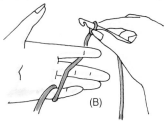

(B)

between the index finger and the hook and keep it taut as you work.

Holding the slipknot between the thumb and middle finger of your left hand, slide the hook forward, catch the yarn (C) and draw it back through

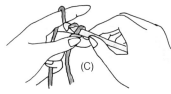

(C)

the chain to form a loop (D). Repeat for the desired number of chains. (The loop on the hook is not counted as

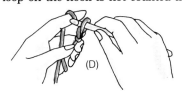

(D)

part of the foundation row.) Try to keep the chains uniform in size.

Single crochet (sc) is the shortest stitch; it forms a firm, compact fabric. Insert the hook in the second chain from the hook (E), catch the yarn and draw up a loop; two loops are on the hook. Catch the yarn again; draw it through both loops; one loop remains on the hook (F). Repeat in each chain

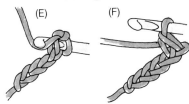

(E)   (F)

across the row. At the end of the row, chain one; turn. Begin a new row by inserting the hook in the first stitch.

Half-double crochet (hdc) is slightly taller than single crochet. Make a yarn over (bring yarn once around the hook from back to front), insert the hook in the third chain, and draw up a loop; three loops are on the hook (G). Yarn over, draw a loop through all three loops; one loop is on the hook (H). Repeat in each chain across the

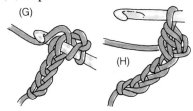

(G)   (H)

row. At the end of the row, chain two; turn. To begin a new row, yarn over and insert the hook in the first stitch.

Double crochet (dc), which is twice the height of single crochet, provides the basis for many pattern stitches. Yarn over, insert the hook in the fourth chain, catch the yarn (I), draw up a loop; three loops are on the hook. Yarn over, draw the yarn through two loops, yarn over and draw the yarn through the last two loops (J). Repeat

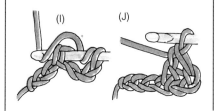

(I)   (J)

in each chain across the row. At the end of the row, chain three and turn. To begin a new row, yarn over and insert the hook in the second stitch.

Triple, or *treble*, *crochet (tr)* makes an airier fabric than any of the previous stitches. Yarn over twice, insert hook in the fifth chain (K), catch the yarn, and draw up a loop; four loops are on the hook. Yarn over, draw through two loops, yarn over, draw through two more loops, yarn over, draw through the last two loops (L).

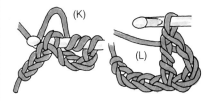

(K)   (L)

Repeat in each chain across the row. At the end of the row, chain four; turn. To begin a new row, yarn over twice; insert hook in the second stitch.

The *slip stitch (sl st)* is used for joining rounds of crocheted motifs, also for seaming and as an edge for finished crochet or knitting. Insert the hook in a stitch, catch the yarn (M) and draw a loop through the stitch as well as the loop on the hook (N).

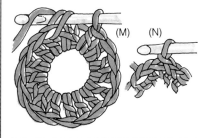

(M)   (N)

Croquet

A game for the entire family

Up to 10 people can play this lawn game, competing singly or in teams. Each player has a colored wooden ball and a mallet striped with the same color. The object is to drive your ball through a course of nine wire wickets and two wooden posts (see diagram). One post marks the start of the course, the other the turning point. Each post must be hit with a separate stroke after the nearest wicket has been cleared.

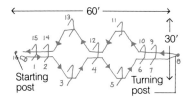

Starting post

Turning post

To decide the order of play, each player drives his ball toward the starting post from about 15 feet away. The player who comes closest goes first, the next second, and so on.

To play, place your ball halfway between the starting post and the first wicket and strike it with the mallet, driving it through as many wickets as possible in the order indicated. For each wicket your ball rolls through, you get an extra shot.

If you hit an opponent's ball, you get two extra shots. If you wish, you may use the first to drive your opponent's ball from the playing area in one of two ways. To make a *croquet shot*, place your ball against the other and put your foot on your ball to keep it in place; then strike it so that the other scoots off. To

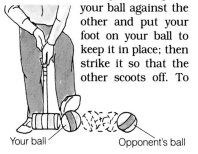

Your ball   Opponent's ball

make a *split shot*, strike your ball without holding it, so that both move. You may not hit the same opponent's ball again until you have passed through another wicket.

The winner is the first player or team to finish the course and hit the starting post. Upon finishing, a player may immediately reenter the game as a *rover* and create mischief for others, thus helping his partner.

Croquettes

A crunchy-coated main dish

Whether they're shaped into balls, cones, cylinders, or flat squares, croquettes are relished for their crunchy coating and creamy fillings. The main ingredient can be cheese, or cooked seafood, meat, poultry, or vegetables

finely chopped and bound with a thick white sauce. You can also incorporate rice or mashed potato. The following recipe yields eight croquettes.

First make a thick white sauce: 4 tablespoons butter, 4 tablespoons flour, and 1 cup liquid (milk or broth; see *White sauce*). Add about 2 cups finely chopped, cooked meat or other ingredients mentioned above. Season with salt, pepper and, if desired, herbs. Simmer 3 minutes. Spread the mixture on a plate; cover it with plastic wrap to prevent a crust from forming.

Chill the mixture, then divide it into 8 equal portions. Roll them into 3-inch cylinders between your palms.

In one bowl have ready 1 egg beaten with 1 tablespoon water; in another, 1/3 cup fine bread or cracker crumbs. Dip each croquette into the egg, then coat it with crumbs. Deep-fry at 375°F until golden (see *Frying*). Remove the croquettes with a slotted spoon and drain on paper towels.

Cross-country skiing

Touring snowy woods and fields

Cross-country skiing dates back thousands of years as a mode of transportation. Now it is a recreational activity that combines a peaceful way to enjoy winter with the benefits of hearty aerobic exercise.

A cross-country skier has many types of skis from which to choose: touring, light touring, backcountry or mountaineering, telemark, racing, and skating. For beginning and intermediate skiing on gentle terrain, the best choice is touring or light touring skis made of fiberglass or composite materials. They are available with waxable or waxless bottoms (see *Ski waxing*).

Select a ski length based on your height, weight, and ability. Touring skis should be slightly longer than your height, but heavier or more experienced skiers should try a longer ski. You'll also need poles, boots, and bindings. Cross-country ski poles have stiff fiberglass or carbon-fiberglass shafts and plastic baskets that keep the poles from going too deep into the snow. Poles should extend from the ground to just under your armpit.

Boots range from lightweight models that resemble a running shoe (for touring groomed trails) to heavier, stiffer, ankle-high styles for backcountry or off-trail skiing. For proper fit, wear two pairs of socks: one thin (silk or polypropylene), the other thick (wool or polypropylene). You should be able to wiggle your toes, but your heel should not slip inside the boot. The bindings hold the boots to the skis by a system of holes or metal loops on the boot's toe piece that clamp into a set of metal pins or a plastic cleat mounted on the ski.

When dressing for a ski outing, wear layers of clothing, starting with underwear that wicks perspiration away from your skin. The next layer can be wool or synthetic, and the outer layer a windproof fabric. Carry a lightweight pack for extra clothing, liquids, and snacks. For skiing in the wilderness, add to your pack: flashlight, matches, food, water, map, compass, whistle, space blanket, jackknife, and rain gear. Watch for signs of hypothermia and frostbite (see *Frostbite* and *Hypothermia*).

Cross-country skiing is as natural as walking. You use a diagonal stride in which the opposite hand and foot move forward simultaneously. Without poles, try walking on your skis. Then try pushing off firmly with one foot. As your heel lifts off the ski, kick that ski backward, shift your weight to the other ski, and glide forward on it. Then push and kick with the gliding ski, and bring the other ski forward and in front of the gliding ski.

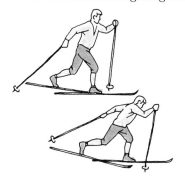

You'll discover a rhythm to kicking and gliding so that you make full use of the ski's forward momentum.

Now pick up the ski poles. They will give you additional power and help you balance. As you kick on the right ski, your left arm plants the pole in front of you and pushes back. With the next stride, as you kick on the left, plant the pole on the right. On level ground, your legs will do most of the work, but on hills you can place more weight on your poles to help pull yourself uphill.

To ski down a hill, keep your knees slightly bent so that your legs act as shock absorbers. To slow down on a gentle slope, you can drag one or both poles behind you as a brake. To slow down on a steep slope or to stop, use the snowplow position: Press the ski tails apart and draw the ski tips together, but not touching. Roll the skis inward slightly so that the inside edges dig into the snow. The steeper the hill, the wider a V you'll need to stop.

You can also turn in the snowplow position. To turn to the right, push your left heel out, digging in with the inside edge of the left ski. Lean to the right, and you'll carve a turn. To turn left, push out with your right heel and lean to the left.

After mastering the basics, try skating, the form that racers and many recreational skiers use. To skate, spread your ski tips apart, and use a stroke similar to that of an ice skater.

Croutons

Bread cubes for garnishes

Slice white bread ¼ to ½ inch thick, trim the crust, butter the slices, and cut them into ¼- to ½-inch cubes. Toast the cubes in a 400°F oven for 3 to 4 minutes; turn and toast the other side. An alternative is to sauté plain bread cubes in butter or oil. Or deep-fry them for 10 to 15 seconds at 350°F. Drain on paper towels.

If you like, flavor the croutons. You can add a sliced garlic clove or a little minced onion to the sautéing pan. Or, while croutons are still hot, sprinkle them lightly with grated Parmesan cheese, paprika, or minced, fresh herbs (an easy method of coating croutons is to shake the ingredients in a paper bag). Store in an airtight container or freeze them. Use croutons as a garnish for casseroles, soups, salads, or cooked vegetables.

Crutches

Learning to walk with an injured leg or foot

To stand up, grasp both crutches with one hand by their handgrips and hold them upright on your injured side. With your free hand against the chair seat or arm, push yourself to a standing position on the uninjured leg. Move one crutch to the unaffected side, and put it snugly under that arm. Then put the other crutch under the arm on your injured side. Don't move until both crutches are secure.

Put your weight on the handgrips; your arm muscles should do the work. The padded underarm is only to keep the crutches in position.

There are two ways to walk on crutches: bearing some weight on the injured side or keeping your injured leg completely off the ground. Your doctor will tell you which way to use.

To walk on one leg, carefully place the two crutch ends about 1 foot in front of you and about 4 inches out from the sides of your feet. Put your weight on the handgrips and swing forward, landing on your uninjured leg at or just ahead of the crutches. That's one step. Move the crutches ahead the same way for each step.

If the injured side can take some weight, position the crutches 1 foot ahead as above and take a short step with the injured leg, supporting most of your weight on the handgrips. Then, with the uninjured leg, take a step beyond the crutches.

To go up stairs, the good foot leads, then the crutches. Going down, the crutches go first, then the good foot.

Curry powder

Making your own blend

Curry powder is a mixture of many spices. It may include black pepper, chili pepper, cardamom, cinnamon, cumin, cloves, coriander, fenugreek seed, ginger, nutmeg, turmeric, and sometimes leaves of the curry tree—combined according to individual taste and their availability.

To make your own blend, toast, but don't brown, whole spices in a 300°F oven for 20 minutes. Let them cool; grind them one at a time in a blender or with a mortar and pestle. Sift, if necessary, before measuring. You can substitute already ground commercial spices, but the result won't be as flavorful. The measurements in the following recipe are for ground spices.

Combine 2 teaspoons each cinnamon and turmeric; 1 teaspoon each cumin and ginger; ½ teaspoon each cloves, black pepper, and chili pepper. Use wherever curry powder is called for or try on eggs or poultry.

Curtains and draperies

Sewing panel curtains and pleated draperies

Usually made of sheer or lightweight fabric, panel curtains have a casing, or pocket, for the rod and, sometimes, a heading above the casing. Draperies are generally of heavier fabric, sometimes lined, and are hung on hooks. For draperies you need pleater tape or stiffener (firm, nonwoven interfacing or buckram) to sew across the top.

Estimating yardage
First, install the hardware according to package directions. Then measure from the top of the rod to the desired length (the windowsill, the bottom of the molding, or the floor—less ½ inch for clearance for floor-length draperies). Add hem allowances (2 to 4 inches for curtains, 3 to 6 inches for draperies), headings (2 inches for curtains, 1½ inches for draperies), and casings (the diameter of the rod plus ¼ to ½ inch for ease).

To determine the finished width, measure the length of the rod and double it for fullness (triple it for sheer fabric). Allow for side hems: 1½ inches for curtains, 2½ inches for draperies; also add 1 inch for seams if you are joining panels.

Divide the finished width by the fabric width to determine the number of panels needed. Multiply the finished length per panel by the number of panels and divide by 36 to find the yardage. Add extra yardage, if necessary, for matching a design.

C

Joining panels

Straighten the fabric ends by cutting the selvage and tearing the fabric or by cutting along a line left by a thread pulled across just below the cut edge. Join panels with an interlocking fell seam: place right sides together with the bottom piece extending ¼ inch. Fold back the extension, then both layers together; press. Pin and stitch.

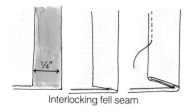

Interlocking fell seam

Finishing the sides

For unlined panels, turn and press the side-hem allowance, turning under the edge ½ inch. Straight stitch or blindstitch along the inside fold.

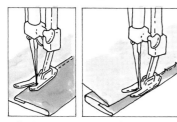

Straight stitch   Blindstitch

For a lining, cut lining fabric 4 inches narrower and 2 to 5 inches shorter than the drapery panel. Stitch a 1-inch hem at the lining bottom. With the right sides together, stitch the lining to the panel at each side, stopping 2 inches from the lining hem; press the seams toward the lining. Center the lining on the panel and press. Unless you're using pleater tape, stitch a ½-inch seam across the top.

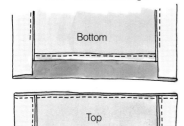

Bottom

Top

Finishing curtain tops

To make a casing for curtains, press the raw edge under ½ inch, then turn

and press the casing the diameter of the rod, plus ease allowance. Stitch ⅛ inch from the edge.

For a casing with heading, press the raw edge under ½ inch, then press the top edge down. Stitch the hem edge, then stitch again at the heading depth, usually 1 inch.

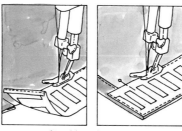

Plain casing   Casing with heading

Finishing drapery tops

To attach pleater tape, first turn its ends under ½ inch and stitch. Lay the tape on the right side of the fabric, lapping edges ½ inch. Stitch the edge. Fold and press it to the wrong side, then stitch on the tape's guideline. Slip a single hook into each end pocket. Insert 4-pronged pleater hooks

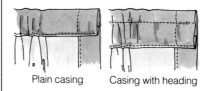

Attaching pleater tape

into adjacent pockets and across the top, leaving 2 to 4 empty pockets between pleats; finger press the folds.

If you are hand pleating lined draperies, attach stiffener as shown; stitch close to the edge. Turn the panel right side out and press all around. Mark

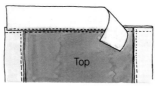

Top

Attaching stiffener to lined drapery

overlaps (center edges) and returns (outer edges) on each panel; space the pleats evenly between them, allowing 5 to 6 inches per pleat plus 4 inches between pleats. Fold each pleat in half and stitch from the top to the edge of the stiffener. Divide each pleat into 3

equal parts and press; machine stitch them or tack by hand.

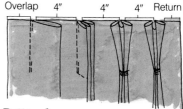

Overlap   4″   4″   4″   Return

Bottom hems

Fold and baste the hems and tack weights in place. Hang panels for a few days, then adjust if necessary.

For a single hem, press the raw edge under ½ inch, then fold and press the remaining hem allowance, mitering the corners. Fuse or sew by machine or hand (see *Slipstitching*).

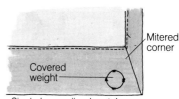

Mitered corner

Covered weight

Single-hem unlined curtain

For a double hem (suitable for sheers), press under 2 inches, then fold and press another 2 inches; sew.

On lined panels, slipstitch the last 2 inches of lining in place. Tack the lining to the hem. Attach weights.

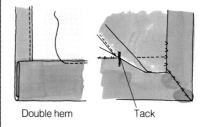

Double hem   Tack

Cushions

Sewing covers; using loose filling material

There are two basic types of cushions: knife edge (thick at the center and tapered at the edges) and box edge (uniform in thickness throughout).

To cover a knife-edge foam cushion, cut two fabric pieces the dimensions of the foam. Stitch piping all around one piece ½ inch from its edges (see *Piping*). With right sides facing and

D

the piped piece on top, stitch a seam ½ inch from the edges, leaving one side open. (The ½-inch seam makes the cover 1 inch smaller than the foam, ensuring a snug fit.)

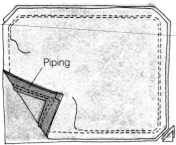

A knife-edge cushion cover

Turn the cover right side out; press. Insert the cushion, slipstitch the opening (see *Slipstitching*). To make it easier to slip the foam in and out of the cover for washing, make an inner cover of plain, lightweight fabric.

To cover a rectangular box-edge cushion, cut two pieces of fabric the dimensions of the cushion's top plus half its depth on all four sides. Following the package directions, stitch an invisible zipper to one side; leave the zipper open. With right sides facing, stitch the two pieces together, beginning and ending at the zipper placket. With the pillow inside, pin the corners to fit smoothly. Take the pillow out. Stitch where you pinned; clip off the excess. Turn the cover right side out; push out the corners.

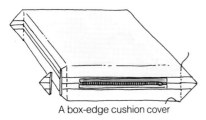

A box-edge cushion cover

Using loose fillings

With loose filling you can make a cushion any size and shape you like. To contain the filling, first cut and stitch an inner cover of firmly woven fabric, leaving one side open. Cut a hole in a corner of the bag of filling (polyester, kapok, feathers, or down), insert it into the cover, and ease out the filling. Slipstitch the opening. Make an outer cover, following the directions for a knife-edge cushion.

Custard

Stirred and baked varieties

A good custard should be velvety and (if baked) firm. But don't overcook it—this can cause the eggs to curdle. Some recipes call for scalded milk; you can substitute cool milk provided it's pasteurized. Hot milk, however, shortens the cooking time.

Stirred (or boiled) custard

This is a soft custard, generally served as a sauce. In the top of a double boiler, combine 4 lightly beaten egg yolks, ¼ cup sugar, ⅛ teaspoon salt, and 2 cups milk. Stir constantly over simmering water until the sauce leaves a thick coating on the spoon; don't let it boil. Remove the pan from the heat; beat the sauce for a minute or two as it cools. Add 1 teaspoon vanilla extract.

Should the custard begin to curdle while cooking, you may be able to save it by immediately pouring it into a cool bowl and beating it vigorously.

Baked custard

Preheat oven to 325°F. Heat 2 cups milk. Meanwhile, beat lightly 2 whole eggs plus 1 yolk, ¼ cup sugar, and ⅛ teaspoon salt. Slowly beat the hot milk into the egg mixture, then add 1 teaspoon vanilla and, if desired, ⅛ teaspoon nutmeg. Pour the custard into five or six 5-ounce custard cups or a 1-quart baking dish. Set the cups or dish in a pan with hot water halfway up their sides. Bake for about 1 hour or until a knife inserted midway between the center and the edge comes out clean; the center will finish cooking while the custard cools.

Crème caramel

In a heavy-bottomed pan on low heat, melt ½ cup sugar in 2 tablespoons water, stirring constantly until the mixture turns thick and golden (8 to 10 minutes); do not boil or it will burn. Quickly pour the caramelized sugar into custard cups, a baking dish, or a metal flan mold; rotate the container to spread the caramel evenly over the bottom. Fill with baked custard mixture; bake, cool, then chill thoroughly. To unmold, run a knife around the edge of the custard, set a dish or serving plate over it, and quickly turn the mold upside down.

Cutworms

Stopping these plant killers

These fat, smooth caterpillars vary from brown to black and may be spotted or striped. They feed at night on stems and leaves of seedlings as well as more mature plants. Signs of cutworms are plants cut off at the soil line and holes in leaves or fruits.

Cultivate the soil in late fall and early spring to expose pupae. Weed regularly to remove their breeding places. Encircle vegetable transplants with bottomless paper cups or milk cartons inserted 1 inch below the soil with 3 inches above.

With susceptible crops, such as corn or beans, lay boards close to the rows; later destroy the cutworms that gather underneath. A light dusting of diazinon or carbaryl worked into the soil before planting can be effective. For an already planted garden, a cutworm bait is available. Follow the package instructions exactly. (See also *Pesticides*.)

Dandelions

A bothersome weed that can be used as food

Unchecked, these broad-leaved weeds choke out grass and other plants. Their roots deplete the soil of nutrients; their leaves shade nearby plants and exude a growth-inhibiting gas.

One method of control is to pull out individual plants as they appear, but you must get *all* of the long taproot to prevent recurrence. Pull them when the soil is wet, using a long weeder to free the roots. For a large crop, apply a broadleaf weed killer such as 2,4-D directly to young plants. You may need to repeat this treatment several times.

Rich in vitamins A and C, dandelions are a food, too. The roots can be peeled and cooked like parsnips or roasted and ground for coffee. The leaves can be dried for tea or used as fresh greens. The leaves taste best (they are always somewhat bitter) when picked in very early spring while the flower bud is still close to the ground.

Rinse the leaves thoroughly in several changes of water. Use them raw in salad or cook them like spinach.

Caution: Don't harvest dandelions from contaminated areas: chemically treated lawns, roadsides with chemical spillover, or dog-walking spots.

Dandruff

How to control it

Simple dandruff—the flaking of dead skin—can afflict any scalp, dry or oily. The condition is controllable but not curable. The best control may be a daily shampoo with your regular soap or detergent shampoo. If you decide to try an antidandruff shampoo, read the labels carefully before buying or using. Here are some common anti-dandruff ingredients, ranging from gentlest to strongest.

Salicylic acid: shampoos with this ingredient can be used every other day. *Pyrithione zinc* shampoo can be used every third day. A shampoo that contains *selenium sulfide* should be used only once a week with your regular shampoo between. Don't use selenium sulfide shampoo if you are pregnant or nursing; note other warnings on the label.

Tar shampoo is equally strong and should be used only once or twice a week, followed by three rinses and a hair conditioner to prevent dryness. Don't use tar shampoo if your scalp is inflamed, and be warned that it can cause discoloration if your hair is light, white, bleached, or tinted. It can also cause inflammation of the scalp (pimples or bumps).

When dandruff is under control, return to your regular shampoo. For severe, uncontrollable dandruff, consult a dermatologist. For dandruff in babies, see *Cradle cap*.

Darkrooms

Space and equipment for developing and printing black-and-white photographs

You've become adept enough at photography to want to develop and print your own pictures. Before you invest in the equipment, try working in a darkroom with someone knowledgeable; a local camera club or an adult education course may be your best source. Work first with black-and-white film; try color later.

Basic darkroom necessities are an absence of external light, a source of electricity, and hot and cold running water. If you don't have a permanent site for your darkroom, use a darkened kitchen or bathroom. Cover countertops with heavy plastic sheeting or use sturdy folding tables with plastic laminate surfaces.

To exclude light, cover the windows with curtains of black felt or sheets of plywood. Block light leaks with black photographic masking tape. Maintain room temperature around 68°F so that chemical solutions will work effectively; 70°F to 75°F is recommended for color work. Ideal humidity for both is roughly 50 percent.

Arranging the equipment

Place the equipment in the order shown; this will make your work flow smoothly. Have a wet side for processing film and prints and a dry side for exposing and print finishing. The print washer should sit in the sink. The enlarger, the heaviest piece of equipment, must be well supported on a stable surface.

Caution: Fumes from some processing chemicals can be dangerous. For this reason, a darkroom needs a fresh-air source and an exhaust fan. If you have allergies, wear rubber gloves to protect your hands from chemical solutions.

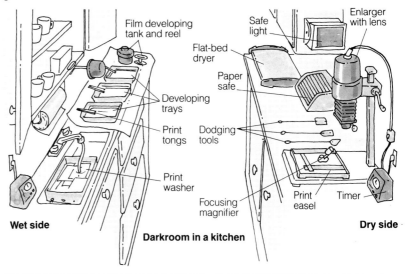

Darkroom in a kitchen

Wet side — Film developing tank and reel, Developing trays, Print tongs, Print washer

Dry side — Safe light, Flat-bed dryer, Paper safe, Enlarger with lens, Dodging tools, Focusing magnifier, Print easel, Timer

Darning

Reweaving fabric by hand

Darning is suitable for mending small holes or frayed areas. If skillfully done, it can be nearly invisible.

Use a wooden darning egg for a sock or other knitted fabric or a sleeve; an embroidery hoop for a flat piece of woven fabric. Don't overstretch or distort the area to be darned. If a hole is large, baste a patch of net or sheer fabric to the wrong side as a base.

Darn under good light and with a fine needle. If possible use a thread from an inside seam or fabric scrap. Otherwise, choose a thread as nearly like the fabric thread as possible.

Working on the right side, take a tiny backstitch near the edge of the hole to anchor the thread (don't knot it). To reinforce frayed edges, make small running stitches around the hole. Fill the hole with side-by-side

D

stitches running parallel to the fabric yarn. Then weave across these stitches at right angles. Keep the stitch tension even and not too tight; pulling the stitches taut can cause puckering. (See also *Mending; Patching.*)

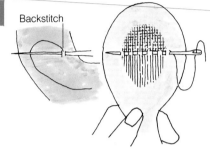

Backstitch

Dart boards

Making your own dart board

You can build a simple dart board by painting a face on a cork-and-plywood base. With a saber saw, cut a disk of ½-inch plywood 19 inches in diameter. With a matt knife, cut a matching disk of thin (about ¼ inch) cork. Join the two with contact cement.

With a pencil, lightly draw two diameters across the face of the cork disk to locate its center. To make a target-type face (see *Darts*), use an extended compass to draw six equally spaced concentric circles from that center. The outside rim is the sixth circle.

You can make your own compass by tying one end of a piece of string to a nail and the other end to a pencil so that the points of the pencil and nail are the desired distance apart when the string is pulled taut. Hold the nail at the center of the board and pull the pencil around the board, keeping the string taut, to draw the circle. Paint the spaces between the circles in alternating bands of contrasting colors of nongloss enamel.

To make a clock-type face, find the center of the board, as above, and position a protractor with its center on the board's center. Make dots every 18½ degrees around the circumference of the protractor and draw lines extending through the center of the board and the dots to the outside edge

of the board. This will create the wedges. Draw the circles as shown in the diagram below and paint the shaded areas with nongloss enamel. Stencil the numbers onto the outside band (see *Stenciling*).

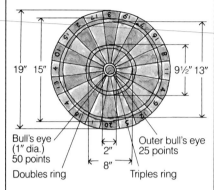

19" 15"   9½" 13"

Bull's eye
(1" dia.)
50 points

Outer bull's eye
25 points

2"

8"

Doubles ring   Triples ring

Darts

Games for two types of board

In darts, players throw small missiles at a target board to demonstrate their marksmanship. There are two types of dart board. The *target-face board* consists of concentric rings. The *clock-face board,* used in the game of tournament darts and its variations, has wedge-shaped sectors as well as rings. Mount either board so that its center, the *bull's eye,* is 5 feet, 8 inches from the floor. Mark a *throwing line* on the floor 7 feet, 9¼ inches away.

The basic game

Any number can play using either type of board. Each player in turn stands behind the throwing line and throws three darts at the board. Point values for the sections hit are as shown here and in the illustration in *Dart boards* above. If a dart lands in the doubles

or triples ring of a clock-face board, the score is doubled or tripled. Darts must stay in the board to be counted. The highest score wins.

The game of tournament darts

One, two, or three individual players or teams of two or more can play tour-

nament darts, using the clock-face board. Each individual player begins with a score of 301 (or each team with a score of 501) and subtracts the points earned from throwing until a score of zero is reached.

Each player throws three darts per turn. Each side must throw a dart into the doubles ring or bull's eye to begin its scoring. Point values are the same as for the basic game.

There are three *legs* (games) in a match. To end a leg, a player must score a double or bull's eye that brings his or her score to exactly zero. If the player fails, all three darts thrown in that turn are discounted and the player tries again at his or her next turn.

Caution: Never play darts where people are likely to walk in front of or behind the target board. Don't let young children play unless they are carefully supervised.

Decoupage

Designs with cut paper

Découpage, French for "a cutting out," is the art of snipping, arranging, and gluing pictures to wood, glass, metal, or porcelain. Basic working needs are shears, cuticle scissors, a sponge, brushes, a sealer (acrylic spray or 3 parts shellac to 1 part alcohol), a burnisher or a small spoon, white glue, a brayer or a child's rolling pin, No. 240 garnet and No. 400 wet-dry sandpapers, varnish, and a tack cloth (see *Tack cloth*).

Any smooth-surfaced object can be decoupaged: tables, boxes, wastebaskets, trays, and lamp bases and shades. Sources of cutouts include books, prints, catalogs, gift wrap, greeting cards, and seed packets. Look for detailed pictures on uniformly thin paper.

Before cutting, stiffen a paper with 2 coats of sealer. Cut out the basic shapes with shears; trim the details with cuticle scissors. Hold the scissors at an angle so that the cut edge will be beveled.

Preparing the object

Wood should be sanded with garnet paper, then dusted with a tack cloth. Next apply stain, followed by a coat of sealer. If the object is to be painted, apply sealer first, then paint. Metal objects should be cleaned of rust, painted with a rust inhibitor, then sealed before painting.

Use plastic-based putty adhesive to arrange the picture elements temporarily until you get a pleasing design. Remove the cutouts and the adhesive. Apply glue thinly to the object's surface. Place on it the large pieces, then add the small and overlapping pieces. Squeeze out excess glue and air bubbles with your fingers; clean off excess glue with a damp sponge.

Next lay a damp cloth on the design and roll it with the brayer or the rolling pin; work from the center toward the edges. Allow 2 to 3 hours for the glue to dry, then press down the edges of the cutouts with the burnisher or the back of the small spoon.

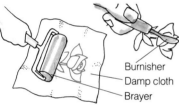

Burnisher
Damp cloth
Brayer

Apply 10 coats of varnish 24 hours apart; dust with the tack cloth before each new coat. Then wrap No. 400 wet-dry sandpaper around a small sponge, dip it in soapy water, and sand to a smooth, dull finish.

Apply 6 to 10 more coats of varnish with a wet sanding after every third coat, including the last, and a dry sanding after the others. Finally, rub with No.0000 steel wool, then a mixture of 1 part pumice and 2 parts lemon oil or linseed oil applied with a soft cloth. Polish with white wax.

Deeds

Transferring ownership of real estate

When you buy real estate, such as a house or a plot of land, the seller gives you a deed as proof that you own the property. The law generally requires that a deed be in writing to prevent disputes. But the language of a deed is so standardized that you can get a preprinted form in a legal stationery store. Each form has blanks to be filled in by the seller with specific information about the land. The seller is the *grantor* and you are the *grantee.*

Protecting your interests

Any land being sold *(conveyed)* must be described in detail. The description is usually in technical language— "parcel lies 124 degrees northerly of Main Street, bound 90 degrees easterly by Fox Lane." Read that description carefully against the description in the most recent survey of the land; once you accept a deed, you own exactly what it says and nothing more.

Most deeds are *bargain-and-sale deeds* giving you complete ownership. Watch out if you are offered a *quitclaim deed.* Such a deed gives you no more than what the seller owned—often less than full ownership. For example, the state may have filed a claim against the property because the seller neglected to pay property taxes; in such a case, you would own the property only after you paid the back taxes from your own pocket.

To make sure that the seller can give you complete ownership of the land, it's important to check into the history of ownership (chain of title). Ask your lawyer to have a title search done to uncover any existing or potential problems.

Signing and filing

The seller signs and dates the deed. Some states require witnesses to ensure that the seller is not being forced to give up the property.

Take your deed to the office of the clerk of the county where the property is located and record it there as soon as possible. If you don't record it and someone buys your property, not knowing that you already own it, you might lose your land.

Deer damage

Protecting your garden

A wire-mesh fence at least 8 feet high is the surest way to keep deer out of your garden. To make a lower fence more effective, stretch a single wire above it, 7 to 8 feet off the ground— deer hate to jump under things. Hang rags on the wire to make it visible.

And because deer fear strong odors, soak the rags in kerosene.

Other odors, especially the smell of human beings, repel deer too. Try hanging small mesh bags of mothballs or of human hair. Or dump your cat's litter box just outside the garden fence. Commercial repellents are also available; they must be renewed often and should not be used on food crops.

If electric fences are legal in your community (check with the local authorities), they can be quite effective. Kits, available from many garden supply centers, include wire, insulators, and a charger that can be powered by a 12-volt battery or by household current. One hot wire is all you should need with a 4- to 5-foot mesh fence. For best results, add outriggers to the fenceposts so that the hot wire is a little higher than the top of the fence and about 3 feet out from it—deer hate broad jumping too. To prevent the wire from shorting out, keep weeds and brush cut back.

Protect fruit trees and ornamentals from winter damage by ringing each with wire mesh. Or fence the entire area and let your dog run there. (Hungry deer will soon learn the limits of a tethered dog's line.) If heavy damage continues, report it to the state wildlife agency. It may indicate a population crisis among deer.

Defrosting a refrigerator

The most efficient way to do it

If a refrigerator doesn't defrost automatically, defrost its freezer when 1/4 inch of ice crystals accumulates. The freezer will function better and the task will take less time.

Turn the refrigerator dial to *Defrost* or *Off;* remove all food from the freezer and from the tray under the freezer (if the freezing compartment is inside the refrigerator). Wrap the food in newspaper or put it in an insulated chest to keep it cold. If your refrigerator has a drip spout to drain water, put a pan under the spout. Leave the freezer door (but not a refrigerator door) open while the frost melts.

Check the manufacturer's instructions to see how long you must leave

D

the refrigerator turned off for proper defrosting. Some must be left at room temperature for 24 hours if more than ½ inch of frost has formed; ¼ inch of frost may melt in an hour.

To hasten thawing, you can place pans of boiling water on the freezer floor. Never use an ice pick to gouge out the ice; you might damage the freezer's lining. Use a soft spatula to scrape away slush and a pair of sponges to mop up water; squeeze out one sponge while the other soaks up water. If the freezer has a tray under it, empty the tray frequently.

Before you return food to the freezer, wipe the food packages dry. The less moisture you introduce into the newly cleaned compartment, the less quickly a new layer of frost will form.

Dehumidifiers

Maintaining and troubleshooting a room dehumidifier

Caution: Before cleaning or repairing, unplug the appliance, let the motor stop, and allow hot components to cool off.

A dehumidifier's fan draws air from the room and pulls it over the chilled coils of its evaporator. The resulting moisture drops into the drip bucket. The dry air then passes over the condenser, regaining some warmth.

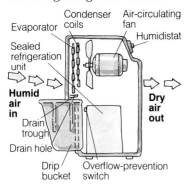

Clean the unit every 6 months of use. Unscrew the front and rear panels; vacuum the inside with a crevice-cleaning attachment, concentrating on the fan and coils. Scrub mineral deposits from the coils with a stiff brush. Tighten screws and nuts.

Water overflow

The drip bucket may overflow because of a faulty overflow-prevention switch. Disconnect the switch and test it with a continuity tester. If the tester lights when you press the switch's push button, get a new switch. If the drain trough under the coils overflows, look for and remove any obstruction in the drain hole.

Short-cycling

Quick on-offs are usually caused by icing, the result of dirt clogging the condenser fins. Clean the coils as described above. Run an old comb between bent fins to straighten them.

Noisy operation

If a fan rattles, it may be loose on its motor shaft. Turn the blades by hand; if the fan wobbles, tighten the setscrews on its hub; if there are none, replace the rubber hub that connects it to the shaft.

If you suspect there's a worn bearing in the fan's motor, dismount the fan from the unit by unscrewing the two mounting nuts. Unscrew the fan from the motor shaft. If you can move the shaft up and down or left to right, a bearing is worn. Get a new motor.

If the unit doesn't operate in a working receptacle, unplug it and check the cord (see *Power cords*). Next, disconnect one lead to the humidistat. Test the humidistat with a continuity tester while you rotate the control knob. If the tester doesn't light, replace the humidistat.

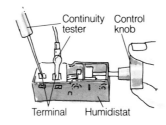

Dehydration

Recognizing and responding to its symptoms

Adults usually take in 2 to 3 quarts of water a day in fluids and foods; dehydration results when the loss of water caused by illness, overexertion, extreme heat, or medication exceeds the intake. The very young and very old are most susceptible. Dehydration can lead to shock and can be fatal.

Symptoms of severe dehydration are a dry mouth, coated tongue, thick saliva, a pinched look in the face, lethargy, irritability, sunken eyeballs, pallor, and low urine output.

Vomiting or diarrhea or both can lead to dehydration in an adult if the condition continues more than 24 hours. An infant under 3 months of age who has three copious, loose bowel movements within a 6-hour period or who vomits up all feedings in a 6-hour span may be dehydrated. Telephone the doctor for advice. With an older baby who has loose stools and vomiting, you can wait up to 24 hours before telephoning the doctor; give the child the diarrhea diet in the meantime (see *Diarrhea*).

Get medical advice, too, if a child or adult cannot replace lost water by drinking because they vomit up anything they swallow. Lost fluids may have to be replaced intravenously.

Excessive water loss from sweating in high heat or during exercise can result in dehydration. Strenuous physical activity in very hot weather can lead also to muscle cramps because salt as well as water is lost in perspiration. Drinking a glass of salted water (1 teaspoon salt to 1 quart water) may relieve the cramps; the dehydrated person should also drink plain water, juice, or other liquids, but not alcoholic beverages.

If you are taking certain medications—for example, a diuretic—discuss with your doctor changing the regimen during hot weather. (See also *Heat exhaustion.*)

Deicing car windows

A vital first step for safe winter driving

Clearing snow or ice from a small circle of windshield glass may be enough for you to see your way out of the driveway, but it isn't adequate for safe driving. You can do a better, safer job with a little extra effort.

First, use a push broom to brush snow from the hood and the roof. Otherwise, snow will blow onto the windshield from the hood as you accelerate and from the roof when you brake.

Next, brush snow from the windshield, then scrape off any ice underneath. If the ice is thick, apply an aerosol deicing spray, which typically contains alcohol. But be careful not to spray it on the car body, for it may damage the paint. (Once diluted with water from the ice, the aerosol will not cause a problem if some dribbles onto the body.)

Use a scraper to remove all traces of ice; the spray itself can cause moisture to evaporate, lowering its temperature and re-freezing it on the windshield. Clear side windows in the same way. Break ice from the windshield wiper blades and squeegees so that they can work properly. If winters in your area are severe, use special winter blades, which are encased in rubber to avoid clogging with ice.

Even if your car has a rear defogger, scrape ice from the rear window. The defogger cannot melt ice rapidly in cold weather. If you are driving at night, scrape ice from the headlamps and wipe them clean.

After 1 to 2 miles of driving, the engine coolant should be warm enough to provide heated air for the defroster. Turn on the defroster and use the windshield washer and the wipers to keep the windshield clean. Winter windshield washer solution, like the deicing aerosol spray, also contains alcohol (although a different type). Do not use the washer before the defroster can supply heated air, or freezing may result. (See also *Car locks.*)

Denim fading

How to bleach denim clothes

Before deciding to give new denim clothing a worn, faded look, be aware that a heavy application of bleach weakens the structure of a fiber. If you want a faded look immediately, you limit the life of your garment.

The more conservative way to fade denim is gradually, by adding 1 cup of chlorine bleach to your washing machine each time you wash your jeans, until they are the color you want.

If you are willing to risk fading a new pair of jeans quickly, follow these instructions: wash jeans twice to remove sizing (starch). Add 1 quart of chlorine bleach to a full machine of water, mixing well before adding the jeans. Agitate a few moments, then allow the denims to soak for up to ½ hour, checking the amount of fading periodically. Wash the garment and add fabric softener to the rinse.

Dentures

Preventing problems with diligent daily care

Dentures are of two types: those that replace all the teeth (full upper and lower dentures) and those that replace some missing teeth and can be anchored to adjacent healthy teeth (removable partial dentures).

Improperly fitting dentures place abnormal forces on the gum tissue and the bony supporting structure. This can lead to painful irritation, to mouth ulcers, and eventually to degeneration of the gum tissue and reabsorption of the jawbone. Even if they fit properly, full dentures can cause shrinkage of gums and jawbones, eventually forcing you to close your jawbones further than normal in order to chew.

The same problems occur with partial dentures. In addition, food can become trapped between the denture and the adjoining natural teeth, leading to tooth decay, inflammation of the gums, swelling, bleeding and, eventually, periodontal disease.

See your dentist twice yearly; regular checkups and, if necessary, a refitting can forestall some problems. If you have pain, sores in the mouth, or bleeding, call your dentist.

Daily care

Dentures may last 5 years or more if you follow these practices. Clean daily with a brush and cleanser recommended by your dentist. Soak removable full dentures (no metal parts) ½ hour in a solution of 1 tablespoon household bleach and 1 teaspoon water softener in 1 cup water. Then brush and rinse thoroughly with plain water. Keep dentures in water when not in use.

Rinse your mouth and removable dentures after meals. Brush your gums daily with a soft tooth brush, then massage them with your finger or a sponge. Brush your tongue too. Once every 2 weeks soak removable dentures overnight in ½ cup white vinegar to remove calcium deposits.

A temporary repair

In an emergency, you can reattach a broken tooth to a removable denture or repair a broken removable denture with fast-acting, extra-strength glue. Don't use a commercial repair or reline kit; these can permanently damage gums and bone. Get quickly to a dentist for a permanent repair.

Depreciation

Calculating tax deductions on the fixed assets of your business

You can depreciate fixed assets, such as machinery, furniture, fixtures, and real estate (except land), used in a business. Because depreciation laws change, seek a tax expert's advice. For example, the 1986 Tax Reform Act generally provides that for the first year you use an asset, you can take only half the deduction normally allowed for a full year's depreciation. When you dispose of the asset, or in its last year of useful life, you can take the other half year of depreciation.

"Straight line" and "accelerated" depreciation are the two main ways of accounting for the decrease in a fixed asset's worth caused by annual wear and tear.

Straight-line depreciation

Take a fixed asset (for instance, a business computer) and divide its total cost ($7,000) by its useful life in years (5); the result is a $1,400 value loss annually, the amount of your yearly tax deduction on your asset. For the first year you would be entitled to a $700 depreciation deduction.

Accelerated depreciation

The advantage here is in the reduction of taxes during the early years of an asset's useful life. This is done by taking greater deductions for depreciation at the beginning of an asset's life and smaller ones at the end. The double, or 200 percent declining balance, method is one accelerated depreciation method. It allows you to apply twice the straight-line rate per year to the declining balance. For example, you could depreciate that $7,000 business computer with its 5-year working life at 40 percent per year, taking percentages of the yearly *remaining* value of the computer, assuming the half-year convention applies; during the second year the computer is worth $5,600, which is what you depreciate then; in the third year it's worth $3,360. You can also write off up to $17,500 of the amount you spend to acquire depreciable personal property. Ask your accountant if this method is for you.

Deviled eggs

Spicy hard-cooked eggs for appetizers or picnics

Shell hard-cooked eggs and halve them lengthwise. (See *Eggs* for how to cook them.) Gently loosen the yolk and remove it, taking care not to break the white. Mash the yolks with a fork or, if there are many, process them in a blender or food processor.

For each yolk, add 1½ teaspoons of one of the following: mayonnaise, sour cream, French dressing, or softened butter mixed with a little vinegar. Blend to a smooth paste. Season with salt, pepper, and dry or prepared mustard. If you prefer spicier eggs, add one or more of the following to taste: curry powder, Worcestershire sauce, cayenne, or hot-pepper sauce. For variety, try minced seafood, ham, onions, herbs, or anchovy paste.

Use a teaspoon or a pastry tube to fill the whites with the mixture. Top with a sprig of parsley or dill, sliced pimiento or olives, caviar, or paprika. Cover loosely with damp paper towels and chill 1 hour before serving.

Diapering

From choosing to changing

It's best to decide before your baby is born which approach to diapering you prefer: cloth diapers that you wash yourself, a diaper rental and laundry service, or disposable diapers. Disposables are the most convenient but also the most expensive. For a somewhat smaller cost, a rental service will collect dirty diapers and deliver clean ones once or twice a week. Least costly is buying 3 or 4 dozen cloth diapers. You'll need to launder them two or three times a week.

Changing the baby

Set up a waist-high changing table; cover it with waterproof padding. Never leave the baby alone on the table even for a moment.

Make diapering a time of play and conversation instead of just a chore. When the baby is tiny, hang a mobile above the changing table. Later on, give the baby a toy to hold. Pick up the baby's feet with one hand. Put the diaper under the baby's bottom, then between the legs and pin it as shown.

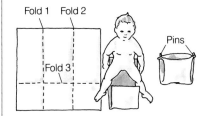

Change a diaper whenever it becomes soiled with urine or stool. Wash the skin in the diaper area, rinse it, and pat it dry. Rinse solids from the diaper into the toilet.

Apply talcum powder or cornstarch sparingly, if at all, and carefully so that the baby doesn't inhale the powder. Don't use cream and powder together; they tend to cake in the skin folds. (See also *Diaper rash.*)

Diaper rash

Relieving an infant's discomfort

Red spots on a baby's skin in the diaper area come from an irritation—the ammonia in urine, bleach or detergent residue in laundered diapers, diarrhea or a fungal infection, or from wet diapers left on too long.

To clear up a mild rash, wash the baby's skin gently but well each time you change a diaper; rinse, dry, and expose the afflicted area to the air for as long as possible. Before putting on a fresh diaper, apply one of the many over-the-counter diaper creams. If you wash your baby's cloth diapers, give them an extra rinse or two, adding ½ cup white vinegar to the final rinse. If possible, dry the diapers in sunlight; it helps destroy bacteria.

If the rash recurs simultaneously with episodes of diarrhea, or if it persists or worsens, consult your doctor.

Diarrhea

Probable causes; suggested remedies

Simple diarrhea, unconnected to disease elsewhere in the body, can have many different causes. It may be a viral or bacterial infection that clears up in a few days. Bouts that are accompanied by nausea and vomiting may be a consequence of contaminated food or water. A brief, mild episode may originate in unwise eating or drinking, or it may be a response to stress. Recurrent attacks may signal a food allergy or a condition known as irritable bowel syndrome.

Notify your doctor if loose, watery bowel movements continue for more than 3 days, if blood or mucus is in the stool, or if fever or vomiting accompany diarrhea.

Because an infant can quickly lose enough fluid to become dehydrated (see *Dehydration*), diarrhea is a cause for concern; be sure to call your doctor at the outset. If you are using a bottle and formula or are breast-feeding your infant, you should go on with the same feedings.

To replace the fluid and mineral loss resulting from diarrhea, give a child special drinks, called oral rehydration solutions. Ask your doctor where to buy them. As bowel movements abate, offer constipating foods: mashed banana, rice or rice cereal, apple pieces, toast, yogurt, baked potatoes.

Older children and adults should be treated similarly for mild diarrhea. A day of clear liquids, then a day or so of bland, nonfatty foods, may suffice. An over-the-counter remedy containing kaolin or pectin, or the two in combination, may help firm up the bowel movement. If these steps fail to arrest the problem, call your doctor.

Traveler's diarrhea

On a foreign trip diarrhea can usually be traced to uncooked foods or untreated water. As a precaution, wash and peel fruits before eating them, eat cooked vegetables, and drink bottled or boiled water or other liquids. When you are planning a foreign trip, ask your doctor what remedies to carry.

Dicing

Cutting vegetables and fruits into cubes

Holding the vegetable or fruit firmly with your fingertips tucked under, cut uniform slices lengthwise with a sharp chef's knife. Stack two or three slices and cut them lengthwise to the same thickness as before; you now have square sticks. Holding the pile firmly, cut crosswise to form cubes.

To dice an onion finely, cut it in half from stem to root; place the cut side against the board. Make thin slices from root to stem, inserting the tip of the knife first, then pushing downward; do not cut all the way through the root. Next, make thin slices horizontally, as far as the root. Finally, cut across the onion to form tiny cubes.

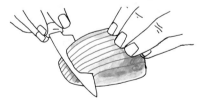

Dieseling

Fixing a car engine that won't stop

When you turn off the ignition and the engine sputters on, it's called dieseling. High-octane gas may help; if not, look for a mechanical fault.

Check the engine idle speed, for which you'll need a tachometer. If the idle speed is too high, a carburetor adjustment may cure dieseling on older cars (see *Carburetor adjustments*). If the carburetor has a solenoid, its plunger may not be retracting when the ignition is cut off (have a helper look). If it is not retracting, replace the solenoid.

The idle may be too high because the throttle linkage is sticking. With the engine running, push the linkage. If the idle drops, the linkage apparently is sticking. Spray it with aerosol solvent to remove dirt.

If it still sticks, install a new throttle return spring. Disconnect the old spring. The universal replacement spring will have straight ends rather than hooks. Make a hook on the straight wire at one end and engage it in the less accessible slot, usually on the throttle linkage. Then extend the spring and, exerting just a slight bit of tension, line up the other end with the slot in the fixed bracket. Use pliers to form a hook and fit it into the slot. Clip off excess wire from the ends with cutting pliers.

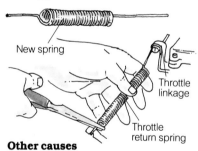
New spring
Throttle linkage
Throttle return spring

Other causes

Check the temperature gauge. If the engine is running hot, suspect a faulty thermostat or try flushing the cooling system (see *Antifreeze*).

The ignition timing may be too far advanced. On older cars that do not have computer-controlled timing, you can check this with a timing light. Follow the instructions with the timing light and the specifications on the underhood tune-up decal.

Certain cars have an antidieseling relay, which triggers the air-conditioning compressor when you turn off the engine. But if the compressor does not click on when you turn off the ignition, have a mechanic check it. Chrysler cars with 1.7- and 2.2-liter engines, General Motors cars with the 2.5-liter 4-cylinder, and some Fords with 3.8-liter V-6s use such relays.

Dieting

Guidelines for safe and lasting weight loss

The secrets of successful dieting, according to leading nutritionists, are to lose weight slowly—no more than 1 to 2 pounds per week—and to change your eating habits. "Miracle" diets may result in quick weight loss, but many are unhealthy, and the pounds lost are often rapidly regained.

One pound of body fat equals 3,500 calories. To reduce weight steadily, eliminate 3,500 to 7,000 calories per week from your diet. You can do this by reducing portion sizes and by eliminating such high-calorie foods as rich desserts and fried foods (see *Calorie counting*). To burn extra calories, increase your exercise; vigorous exercise also reduces appetite.

Any weight-loss diet should daily include foods from the four basic food groups (see *Menu planning*) and should be varied to ensure adequate intake of vitamins and minerals.

Differential oil checking

A part of complete car care

It's natural to check oil levels under the hood, but if you have a rear-drive car, you should periodically check the oil level in the rear-axle differential, adding or changing the oil if necessary. Car manufacturers do not usually recommend routine differential oil changes, and many do not provide drain plugs. But they always provide filler holes (sealed by plugs) to add oil, a small amount of which may be lost from evaporation and seepage.

To check the differential oil level, jack up the car and support it on safety stands at all four wheels. This is necessary so that the car (and the oil in the differential) will be level.

Remove the filler-hole plug. On most cars it is a threaded plug, but on Chrysler products it may be a rubber plug that you pull out and push back in. With the plug out, oil should ooze out at the bottom of the hole or at least be within ¼ inch of the hole.

127

D

If the level is lower, add oil until it is even with the bottom of the hole. If the oil level is very low, check the differential housing for a leak.

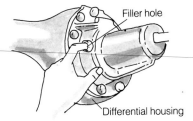

Filler hole

Differential housing

Install a gear oil marked "For service GL-5," with a viscosity in the range of 80–90 or 85W–90. Use a funnel with a hose attached or a clean household squeeze bottle.

If you drive your car into water deep enough to submerge the rear axle, change the differential oil shortly afterwards. If there is no drain plug, use a siphon pump to draw out the oil (and any water) from the filler hole. Then add fresh oil.

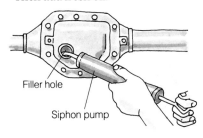

Filler hole

Siphon pump

Dimmer switches

Installing a dimmer switch for an incandescent fixture

A dimmer switch controls the power reaching a light fixture, allowing you to dim or brighten the light at the turn of a knob. The switch's wattage capacity must exceed the total wattage of the lamps in the fixture.

Most dimmer switches are for incandescent fixtures; check the package. An electrician should install a dimmer for a fluorescent fixture.

Caution: Before working on a switch, turn off the power to its circuit. To check that it is off, turn the existing, working switch on and off; the fixture should not light.

Unscrew the cover-plate screws. If paint holds the plate to the wall, slit the paint with a utility knife. Set aside

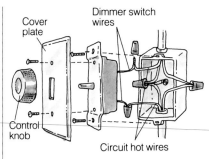

Cover plate

Dimmer switch wires

Control knob

Circuit hot wires

the screws and plate. Unscrew the screws holding the switch in the box and disconnect the circuit wires held by the switch's two terminal screws. Straighten the wire ends.

Connect the wires from the box to the wires on the dimmer switch as shown. Twist the bared ends together and insert them in a wire connector (see *Wiring*). Twist the connector clockwise, making sure that no bare wire is exposed.

Fit the wires and the switch into the box; screw the switch to the box. Mount the cover plate, push the control knob onto the protruding shaft, and turn on the power.

Dirndl skirt

Making a full, gathered skirt

A dirndl is made with at least two fabric panels, depending on the desired fullness and the fabric weight; the heavier a fabric, the less width needed. If the fabric itself is narrow, you might need four panels for a full skirt.

Cut fabric rectangles equal to two to three times your waist measurement and the desired length plus 3 inches for a hem. Cut a waistband the length of your waist plus 1 inch for ease and 2½ inches for seams and an extension; it should be twice the finished width plus 1¼ inches for seams.

Stitch the skirt with ⅝-inch seams, leaving an 8-inch opening in the left seam for a zipper. Finish the seam edges; press. Insert a zipper by the lapped method (see *Zippers*).

Loosen the top tension on your sewing machine slightly and set the machine for a long stitch—at least 8 per inch. Stitch ½ inch from the raw edge on the right side of the fabric, breaking stitches at the seams. Leave long

thread ends. Stitch again ¼ inch away in the seam allowance.

Divide and mark the skirt in four equal sections. Do the same with the waistband (excluding the extension). Pin the skirt to the waistband, matching the four markings. Anchor the bobbin threads at one end by winding them around a pin in a figure eight.

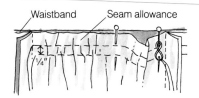

Waistband

Seam allowance

¼"

To gather, pull the bobbin threads at the other end and slide the fabric along them until the skirt fits the waistband; fasten the thread ends.

Even the gathers all around and pin; baste the skirt to one edge of the waistband. With the gathered side up, stitch just to the left of the gathering stitches, holding the fabric firmly on both sides of the needle to prevent pleats from forming. Stitch the waistband ends; slipstitch the inside of the waistband to the skirt (see *Slipstitching*). Add a button and buttonhole (see *Buttonholes*) or a hook and eye.

Dishwashers

Cleaning your dishwasher; repairing nicks; making minor adjustments and repairs

If your dishwasher displays computer messages telling you what's wrong with it or if it comes with its own repair manual or parts kit, use those to solve any problems. Otherwise, try the following remedies.

Caution: Before working on a dishwasher, unplug it. If you have a built-in unit, turn off the power to its circuit.

Cleanliness is important. Every 2 weeks remove the spray arm or arms (some simply lift out, others require the removal of screws). Shake out the arm and use a pipe cleaner to clear its ports. Scrub the filter screen (strainer) or basket with a stiff brush. Clean the tub of debris and wipe down the detergent dispenser and the inside

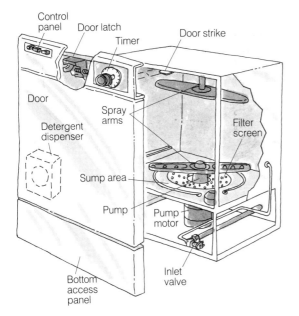

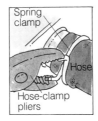

Dishwashing

The best procedures

To protect glazes, rinse dinnerware soon after use. Use cold water to rinse off egg or milk, hot water for other foods. Acid foods can be especially damaging; tea or coffee can stain permanently. To bleach a stain, use a solution of 1 part 30 percent hydrogen peroxide to 3 parts water with a drop of clear ammonia. Or try rubbing with baking soda, but take care not to damage the pattern. If food dries on plates, don't scrape with abrasives or sharp objects; soak them.

To soften burned-on food in pots and pans, fill them with water, add detergent or vinegar and put them on the stove to simmer. To soak a broiler pan, fill it with soapy water, then spread wet paper towels on the broiler rack. The towels will keep the surface damp and help loosen charred food.

Hand washing

Prevent chipping by using a plastic dishpan and a protective rubber collar on your faucet. Fill the pan with hot soapy water, then wash the least greasy items, usually glassware, first. Next wash cutlery, then dishes, and finally pots and pans. To protect against cracking, do not put cold dishes into hot water, and avoid overcrowding the dishpan. Rinse dishes in a pan of hot water, or put them in a rack and pour hot water over them.

To obtain a bright shine, dry silver and crystal pieces by hand. Use lint-free towels (linen is best) to dry and polish each piece while it is still hot from rinsing. Dinnerware, glassware, stainless-steel flatware, and pans are better left to air dry.

Dishwashers

A dishwasher is safe for most modern dishes, even fine china. Exceptions are china that is antique or hand painted or has gold, silver, platinum, or cobalt-blue decoration. Be sure dishes won't collide during the cycle. Use only detergents designated for dishwashers; others create too many suds. To save energy, interrupt the cycle after the dishes are rinsed; open the machine's door and let the pieces air-dry. (See also *Glassware.*)

surfaces. If mineral deposits form, dissolve them by pouring a cup of vinegar into the empty tub and running the machine through the wash cycle.

Cover any fresh nicks in the enameled surfaces or racks with an epoxy coating made especially for the purpose. If the nicks are left unattended, rust may develop beneath the surface and eventually result in leaks. Get rid of rust immediately; don't try to cover it up (see *Rust*).

Remedies for poor washing

The most common cause of poor washing is low water temperature. Run hot water from a kitchen faucet over a glass thermometer for 2 minutes. (Use a thermometer that registers over 212°F.) If the temperature is not between 140°F and 160°F, adjust the setting of your water heater.

Dishes may be insufficiently scraped or rinsed, or the machine may be overloaded or poorly stacked. Avoid nesting dishes one inside the other—water must reach all surfaces. Make sure that no dishes block the spray arm and no utensils protrude through the bottom of the silverware basket.

The detergent dispenser may be stuck. Scrape and wash out the cup, and never fill it quite full. Also avoid wetting the detergent beforehand.

Eliminating noisy operation

Dishes may clatter when struck by water; make sure that they lean against the racks. A grinding noise

may mean low or no water. Open the door during the wash cycle to check. Most machines require at least 1 inch of water above the sump area (the depression around the pump). If the water is too low, the trouble may be with the timer, inlet valve screen, or overflow switch. Call a repairman.

Fixing leaks

In certain locations a bowl may cause water to splash out around the door. Move the bowl. Trickles around the door may indicate that the door isn't tight. Loosen the screws in the lock strike and realign the strike with the door latch to create a firmer seal. Check the door gasket; if it's worn or brittle, replace it. Gaskets are mounted with clips, screws, or pop-in fasteners.

If water comes from under the machine, disconnect the power, turn off the water supply, remove the bottom access panel (usually held by two screws), and check all hose clamps. Tighten leaking worm-drive clamps with a screwdriver. If a leaking clamp is of the spring type, use special hose-clamp pliers to remove it; replace it with a worm-drive clamp. Catch drips in a pan when undoing hoses.

If the washer won't start

Check that the door is properly locked and that the push button or dial setting is correct. Then look for a blown fuse or an open circuit breaker to be sure the dishwasher is getting power. If it still won't start, call a repairman.

D

Dislocated joints

Understanding the causes; avoiding the consequences

A joint becomes dislocated when the bone ends are knocked or pulled out of position. Suspect dislocation if the joint suddenly doesn't work normally, if moving or putting weight on it is painful, or if it starts to swell and discolor. A dislocated limb or digit may look different from its counterpart; it may have a lump or a distorted angle.

Dislocation occurs most often in a shoulder or the jaw, but it can happen to any joint: toes, fingers, ankles, wrists, elbows, hips, even joints between vertebrae. Get medical help right away; the sooner the treatment, the lower the risks. Meanwhile, keep the injured person comfortable, using the same cushioning and immobilizing techniques as for breaks (see *Broken bones*).

It usually takes a considerable blow to dislocate a joint, so other injuries are likely: stretching or tearing of ligaments that hold the joint in position; damage to the joint capsule—the surrounding membrane; crushed muscles, nerves, and blood vessels; perhaps a broken or chipped bone.

What to do—and not to do

Don't try to reposition the joint or to straighten an arm or leg. Remedial steps should only be taken by professionals, guided by X-rays. Depending on the extent of swelling and other injuries, the procedure may require anesthesia. You should apply ice packs to relieve swelling and pain, but in case anesthesia is required, don't give the injured person food or drink.

Relief is often so great when the joint is returned to its normal position (it may even "pop" back by itself) that people are tempted to consider the injury healed. Far from it; damaged ligaments and tissues require weeks to heal. A premature return to normal activities may cause pain and swelling to recur. A person may even risk permanent damage, recurrent dislocations, or the beginning of arthritis in the joint.

Sometimes dislocations occur for no apparent reason. A too-wide yawn can dislocate the jaw; a knee might "pop" unexpectedly; a shoulder may dislocate during some quite ordinary activity. There may be an underlying cause, such as a previous injury, or a predisposition because a joint was always abnormally shaped.

Young children often suffer what is called "pulled elbow"—a term to be taken literally, since the dislocation is caused by pulling a child along by an arm. (A shoulder can be similarly dislocated by yanking a child off the ground by one arm.) Such a dislocation, being only partial, doesn't show up on an X-ray. It can be slipped back into place by a simple maneuver the doctor performs in the office.

Distemper

Safeguarding your dog; symptoms to watch for

Prevention is the only real cure for distemper, a highly contagious canine disease. Once weaned, a puppy quickly loses the protection of its mother's immunity, and should be vaccinated against distemper and other major dog diseases. The initial series of shots should be followed by annual boosters (see *Dog care*).

An unvaccinated dog can contract distemper from the air or by direct or indirect contact with an infected dog. Humans can't catch it, but they can carry the virus on their hands or clothes. Symptoms are loss of appetite, lassitude, runny eyes or nose, a cough, diarrhea, fever, twitching, jaw chomping, and convulsions. Distemper is quickly fatal in many young puppies and may leave older dogs with severe muscle twitches, epilepsy, or temporary or permanent paralysis. Prompt treatment is crucial to survival. At the first signs of the disease, call your veterinarian.

Distress signals

Universal calls for help

If you're in distress in the wilderness during the day, signal with sounds (gun, whistle, tin pans) in series of threes, each followed by a brief silence. Continue until someone responds. In areas where a sound's effect might be limited (a valley or heavily wooded area), use visuals. Build a fire with fuel that will burn slowly and send up a thick, steady column of white smoke; use hardwood, leaves, moss, and ferns. Before igniting the pile, clear the ground around it. Stack the pile high so that the signal will have a long life. When rescue comes, extinguish the fire completely.

If there are aircraft in the area, flash a mirror, a shiny metal object, or glass. Draw attention to yourself by spreading bright-colored clothing on the ground.

If you are on a large expanse of snow, tramp out the words *HELP* or *SOS* 30 feet high with a 10-foot space between each letter.

At night

Use a flashlight to signal SOS (3 short flashes, 3 long ones, 3 short ones) to an airplane. Knowing international Morse code will enable you to relay and receive detailed messages. Carry a copy of it with you (see *Morse code*).

On the water

Maritime distress signals include red flares, an orange smoke signal, a signal mirror, an upside-down national flag, and continuous foghorn blasts. Announce "Mayday" (*m'aider*, French for "help me") on radiotelephone channel 16 (156.8 MHz), the VHF-FM distress, safety, and calling frequency.

On the highway

Tie a white cloth to your car's antenna or door handle and raise the hood. In any situation, stay calm and conserve your energy while you await help.

Diving

Slicing the water headfirst

Caution: Never dive into water of an unknown depth; at least 5 feet is needed for a standing dive from the side of a pool or lake. Check for underwater hazards, such as rocks or logs. People with chronic ear infections or sinus problems should consult their doctors before diving.

The best way to learn a standing forward dive is through a series of confidence-building steps. Start by sitting on the side of the pool with your legs spread. Stretch your arms straight above your head, touching your ears. Lower your head and tuck your chin to your chest. Now, exhale through your nose, then fall downward and forward, continuing to exhale until you resurface. To resurface quickly, turn your hands and head upward.

Next, dive from a kneeling position, as shown. Stretch your arms overhead, tuck your chin to your chest, and fall downward and forward. As your kneeling knee leaves the deck, push your hips upward and propel yourself into the water with your feet. Straighten your legs and bring them together as you enter the water.

Now try a standing position. Curl your toes over the edge of the pool, arms overhead. Bend forward at the waist, tuck chin to chest, roll downward and forward, entering the water hands first—2 to 4 feet from the edge. A standing front dive with a spring can be done next. Take the standing dive position, bend your knees and push upward, arching your body

slightly, as if passing over an imaginary barrel. Next start a standing dive with arms at your sides. As you spring forward, swing your arms forward and arch your body.

Dodgeball

A game for groups of children

The object of dodgeball is for the members of one team of players to hit players on the opposing team with throws of a volleyball or a soccer ball. Chalk out a playing area 30 feet long and wide enough to let all the players stand side by side. Divide the area in half by chalking across its width.

Divide the players into two teams, then withdraw with your players to one side of the court while your opponents go to the opposite side. Throw the ball across the center line and try to hit the players on the other side. The players struck are *out* and must leave the field. Players may try to dodge the ball, but anyone who crosses the center, side, or back line is out.

To win, your team must strike out all opponents. Your team repeats its turn when it hits someone. If you or a team member throws and misses, the opposing team has a go at it.

Dog barking

Correcting the chronic barker

Barking becomes a problem when it is triggered by random noises, telephones, passing cars, or loneliness. Because barking is more easily controlled in a young dog, begin corrective training early.

If your dog barks excessively in your presence, give it a firm "no" and, if necessary, a mild, but sudden jerk of the leash or collar. As soon as the dog is quiet, praise and pet it. Follow this procedure consistently until the dog responds to the initial "no."

The solitary barker
More difficult to treat is the dog that barks when left alone. Make sure your attitude is not encouraging anxiety in the dog. As you prepare to leave, chat with the dog reassuringly. Leave the radio on or a familiar object lying around—something that will make the house feel lived in.

If this doesn't work, try leaving as usual, but wait outside. When the dog barks, reenter, tell it firmly "no," and

jerk its collar if necessary. Praise it when it obeys. Leave again; repeat the procedure several times daily, gradually increasing the time the dog is left alone. (See also *Obedience training*.)

Dog bites

What to do when bitten

The first concern for anyone bitten by an animal is rabies, a usually fatal viral disease carried most often by wild animals but also by cats and dogs. A rabid dog will behave strangely, sometimes biting without reason or foaming at the mouth.

If you are bitten by a stray dog or one whose owner can't be found, wash the wound with soap and water and see a doctor immediately. He will probably prescribe a tetanus shot; antirabies injections aren't usually needed for dog bites. To be safe, if the animal can be captured, have it impounded and observed for signs of rabies.

If the dog's owner is known, find out whether the animal's rabies shots are current. If they are not, the dog will have to be observed by the health authorities for 10 days. Antirabies shots can be delayed that long and won't be needed if the dog stays healthy.

The wound itself, if shallow, can be treated like an ordinary cut (see *Bandaging*). If it is deep, requires stitches, or is potentially disfiguring—or if you haven't had a tetanus shot in 5 years—see a doctor.

Dog care

Choosing a dog; feeding, grooming, and exercise; the sick dog; the older dog

Never buy a dog on a whim, as a surprise gift, or without consulting the rest of the family. Consider first whether you or the intended owner can accept the responsibility of feeding, walking, and training a dog and of providing proper medical care.

If the answer is yes on all counts, then consider the type of dog. Do you want a guard dog or a pet for the children? Small or large? An inexpensive

D

mongrel or a purebred? In considering a purebred, study the American Kennel Club breed descriptions. Try to buy a dog directly from the breeder.

A dog acquired from a pet shop or an animal shelter may have changed hands several times under stress. Ask for a medical guarantee and for an agreement that you can return the dog within a reasonable time if it becomes overly aggressive or shy.

What to look for in a puppy

The best time to choose a puppy is at 7 to 8 weeks of age, when it should be weaned, is lively, and can walk and run. A healthy puppy has clear eyes, a smooth coat, and is alert and playful. Avoid a dog with runny eyes or nose, a potbelly, a cough, or diarrhea.

A friendly puppy will approach you, happy to be petted. If a puppy nips at your ankles and resists petting, it may turn into an aggressive, hard-to-train dog. A puppy that shrinks away from you may be ill or already showing nervous or shy tendencies.

Have a veterinarian examine your dog as soon as possible for worms and general fitness. Give him the dog's immunization record, if any, and schedule further shots. Puppies should be inoculated against distemper, hepatitis, leptospirosis, parvovirus, and parainfluenza at 6 to 8 weeks, at 9 to 11 weeks, and again at 3 to 4 months. Annual boosters are essential. (See also *Distemper.*) Rabies shots are given at 3 to 6 months and thereafter at 1- to 3-year intervals. Unless you plan to breed a dog, ask your veterinarian about the pros and cons of altering it.

Proper feeding

Feed your puppy a commercial puppy food three times a day (twice daily after 6 months). By 1 year it should be eating adult dog food once a day. Most canned, dry, or semidry dog foods provide balanced nutrition. You can add cottage cheese, cooked eggs, or cooked lean meat, but such supplements should constitute no more than 20 percent of the dog's diet. Provide plenty of fresh water; change it twice daily. Follow your veterinarian's advice on vitamin supplements.

Grooming a dog

Accustom a puppy early to regular grooming sessions. Hold it in your arms and gently brush it while talking reassuringly. The average dog needs brushing once or twice a week. While brushing, check for skin problems (see *Fleas; Ticks*).

Bathe a dog if its coat becomes dirty or foul smelling. Wash it in a tub or sink with warm water and a mild dog shampoo. Rinse and towel dry it thoroughly. Keep the dog indoors and away from drafts until it is dry.

Unless a dog's nails are worn down by outdoor activity, trim them periodically with special clippers; cut only the pointed tip of each nail. A mild boric-acid wash will usually clear up eye discharge; if it doesn't, see your veterinarian. Chewing on a rawhide bone once a month helps prevent the buildup of tooth tartar.

Daily exercise

Take your dog for a long walk in the morning, before bedtime, and after its main meal. Keep to a regular schedule; don't overexercise a dog after a large meal or on weekends to make up for a sedentary week.

Training your dog

As soon as you bring your puppy home, start housebreaking it (see *Housebreaking pets*). By 5 months it can begin learning to heel, sit, lie down, come, and stay on command. Be firm but patient and reward success with praise and petting (see *Obedience training*).

When your dog gets sick or old

Some signs of canine illness are loss of appetite, dull eyes, a dry coat, listlessness, vomiting, diarrhea, and excessive thirst or urination. If your dog seems sick, take its temperature and call the veterinarian.

To take a dog's temperature, lubricate a rectal thermometer and insert it in the rectum, leaving it there for 2 minutes while you or an assistant holds the dog still. Normal canine temperature is 100°F to 102.4°F. (See also *Pet injuries; Pet medication.*)

With age, a dog may gain weight, lose its sight or hearing, or become sick. It should be fed smaller amounts—perhaps of a commercial food for aging dogs—at more frequent intervals. Take an older dog to the veterinarian twice a year. (See also *Car chasing; Dog barking; Dogfights; Doghouses; Lost cats and dogs; Traveling with pets.*)

Dogfights

Preventing the fight; breaking up a fight in progress

The best way of dealing with a dogfight is to keep it from happening at all. If your dog is leashed and shows signs of aggression toward another dog (growling, raised hackles, a stiffly wagging tail), pull hard on the leash, say "no" in a firm, low voice, and move on quickly. When your dog is off leash outdoors, monitor its activities and leash it at the first sign of trouble.

Once a fight has started, direct intervention is dangerous. Try instead to distract the dogs long enough so that they can be separated. Dowsing the fighters with water, throwing a blanket over them, or creating a loud, clanging noise may do the trick.

If the dogs are of manageable size, or if one of them seems endangered, two people working together may be able to break up the fight, but they risk being bitten. Each person should seize his dog's hind legs or tail, pull hard and heave the dog behind him. Restraining only one dog can result in injury to both dog and human.

If none of these tactics is possible, you may have to let the fight run its course, despite the risk of serious injury to one or both dogs. When one of them submits by rolling over and exposing its abdomen, the fight is usually over. (See also *Dog bites; Obedience training.*)

Doghouses

An all-season shelter

If your dog spends long hours outdoors, it needs a warm, dry shelter in winter and shade and rain protection in summer. A two-room design provides both, and a removable panel makes the house easy to clean.

Base the dimensions on the size of your dog. Body heat will be the only source of warmth, so the inner room should be just large enough for your pet to lie down. To determine the size, have the dog curl up on a piece of cardboard; then outline its body. Add 4 to

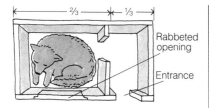

Rabbeted opening

Entrance

6 inches to both dimensions. Make the outer room half as wide as the inner one. To determine height, have your dog sit; then measure the distance from the floor to the top of its head and add 6 inches (12 inches in a warm climate). Make the doorways shoulder high and 2 inches more than shoulder wide.

Use ¾-inch exterior plywood for the floor and roof, and frame the floor with pressure-treated 2 x 4s to make an insulating space below. Make the walls and the partition from ¾-inch particleboard. Rabbet the opening for the removable panel so that the panel

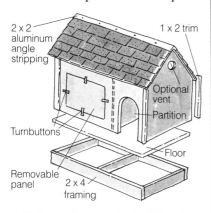

2 x 2 aluminum angle stripping

1 x 2 trim

Optional vent

Partition

Turnbuttons

Floor

Removable panel

2 x 4 framing

will fit snugly; it can be held in place by turnbuttons as shown, or it can be hinged on top to make an awning in summer. Shingle the roof.

In very cold regions, insulate the inner room by gluing 1½-inch solid foam to the walls and roof during construction. Cover with ¼-inch hardboard. Use layers of scrap carpet to insulate the floor. In warm climates, cut vents near the peaks of the end walls and the partition.

Dominoes

Playing the basic draw game

There are many domino games, but most of them are variations of the ba-sic draw game. All domino games use a set of 28 rectangular tiles made of bone, ivory, plastic, or wood. These are the *bones*, or dominoes. The face of each bone is divided by a center line into two *ends*. Each end is marked with dots, or *pips*, in the same way as dice, although a few ends are blank. The number of dots indicates the value of the bone. A blank is zero.

Place all the bones facedown on a table and mix them thoroughly. Draw seven bones from the facedown pile, or *boneyard*, while your opponent does the same. (If there are three or four players, each draws five bones.) Hold the bones in your hand or stand them on edge facing you.

If you find that you have the highest doublet (a bone with both ends of the same value), place it on the table face-up. Your opponent must then lay down a bone with a like half touching it. For example, if you played a double six, your opponent must play a bone with a six at one end. Place a doublet crosswise. Place other bones end to end unless there is no room on the table, in which case place the next bone at a right angle.

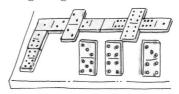

Turns rotate. If you haven't an appropriate bone to play, you must draw from the boneyard until you get one. When the boneyard is used up and you cannot play, you pass. If you get rid of all the bones in your hand first, you win all the points still in your opponent's possession. The game can be 50 or 100.

Doorbells and chimes

Checking the transformer, push button, wiring, and signal unit

Signaling systems such as doorbells and chimes consist of a push-button switch, a signal unit, wiring, and a transformer to reduce the house voltage—usually to 12 to 16 volts. Before testing a system that won't work,

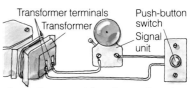

Transformer terminals

Transformer

Push-button switch

Signal unit

check the circuit breaker or fuse (see *Circuit breakers; Fuse boxes*).

Normally, because of the low voltage involved, you needn't turn off the circuit power while working on a signaling system. But on the chance that the transformer is faulty, sending a full 120 volts through the system, check the voltage at the push button. Unscrew the plate surrounding the push button or pry open the button housing. Touch the probes of a neon test lamp to the button's terminals. If the lamp lights, the transformer is faulty; replace it (see next page).

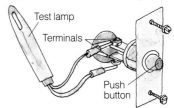

Test lamp

Terminals

Push button

Troubleshooting the push button
If the neon test lamp doesn't light, test the push button by placing the blade of an insulated-handle screwdriver across its two terminals. If the bell or chime rings, the button unit is corroded or defective. Disconnect its wires and use fine sandpaper to remove any corrosion from the contact points and the wires. Reconnect the wires and retest the button. If it works, reinstall it; if not, replace it.

Checking the wiring
If the bell or chime didn't sound when you first tested the button, look for loose connections at the button, signal unit, or transformer. The transformer is usually mounted on the side of a metal junction box in the basement or in a hall closet.

Disconnect the bell wiring from the transformer and the push button. Twist together the ends of the wires at the button and test the ends of the wires at the transformer with a continuity tester. If the tester doesn't light, check for broken wires. If you find any, twist the bared wire ends together and wrap them with electric tape or twist them into a wire connector.

Continued next page

The transformer and signal unit

If the wiring is intact, the transformer may be bad. With the power still on, test the transformer's outside terminals with a 12-volt test lamp (available at auto parts stores). If the lamp doesn't light, replace the transformer.

Caution: The transformer is connected directly to the house power. Turn off the power to the circuit before working on it.

Bolt the new transformer to the outside of the junction box. Using wire connectors, join the wires (black to black, white to white) inside the box.

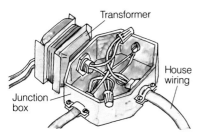

If the bell still won't ring, replace the signal unit with one of the same type and rating. Install it according to the manufacturer's instructions.

Door closers

Adjusting a pneumatic closer

If your screen or storm door shuts too quickly or too slowly, adjust the closer by turning the air-adjusting screw at the end of the closer tube clockwise (slower) or counterclockwise (faster).

If the door doesn't latch after it has closed, remove the split pin from the small bracket to disengage the closer

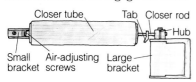

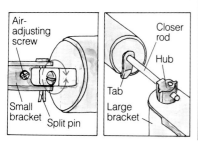

tube. While holding the spring in position, remove the closer pin to release the closer rod. Disengage the spring's hook from the slot of the large bracket and, turning the spring clockwise (with a wrench if needed), insert its hooked end in the neighboring slot (or the one next to it for extra force). Reinsert the closer rod in the hub and fasten with the closer pin; reconnect the small bracket to the closer tube, using the split pin.

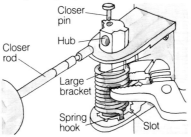

If the snap-action latching force (quick momentum as the door begins to close) is too swift and the slamming too noisy, reduce it: disengage the split pin from the small bracket and advance the closer tube so that its second hole is in line with that of the small bracket; reinsert the pin.

Once a year lubricate the working surfaces of the large bracket and the closer rod with lithium grease.

Doorknobs

Tightening loose knobs; installing new ones

An old-fashioned doorknob has a small setscrew at the base, which secures it to the end of a spindle that runs through the door. When the knob comes off, it is usually because the setscrew is loose or lost; tighten or replace it. If the spindle is so worn that the screw will not seat, rotate the knob ¼ turn and try a new spot. You may have to do this to the knob on the other end, too, to maintain tension.

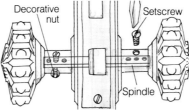

Sometimes the knob itself screws onto the spindle, and these threads become worn. Try putting a wad of putty or modeling clay inside the knob and screwing the knob back on, or wrap the spindle with plastic tape. If these tricks fail, replace the spindle. Or, as a final alternative—say, to save an antique doorknob—position the knob on the spindle and drill all the way through the base. Then insert a bolt and cap it with a decorative nut.

Some spindles screw together in the middle. When the threads become worn, replace the whole spindle.

New doorknobs

Modern doorknobs are part of the latch assembly, which includes a spring catch and perhaps a lock as well. Install these as you would a deadlock (see *Door locks*), following the manufacturer's instructions.

Usually, one knob is attached to the spindle and to an escutcheon, or rose. The rose includes two stems that penetrate the latch mechanism; they are threaded inside to receive mounting screws, which secure the other knob.

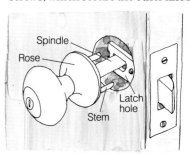

Some assemblies have no stems; instead the mounting screws go into a lock cylinder connected to one knob.

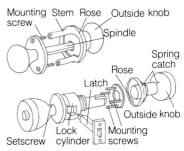

Most problems can be solved by tightening the mounting screws. If no screws are visible, look for a spring catch under the knob. Depress it, remove the knob, and tighten the screws that are revealed.

Door locks

Adding locks for security

It takes three locks, placed at least a foot apart, to keep a burglar from levering your door open. One is probably part of the knob or latch (see *Door-knobs*). You can add deadlocks, rim locks, or police locks in any combination. For best results, install one above and one below the latch. Always use different keys for each lock.

Types of locks

A *deadlock* is a solid bolt embedded in the door. The bolt shoots into a keeper embedded in the jamb.

A *rim lock* is secured to the inside face of the door so that it overhangs the edge and meets with a keeper on the frame. The most secure have interlocking latches (see illustration).

A *police lock* is also secured to the door's inside face. The commonest are the double-throw type, in which two bars slide into keepers on the frame, and the vertical prop type, in which a steel rod reaches to the floor.

Bolts   Keeper

Dead lock   Rim lock

Rod

Double-throw police lock

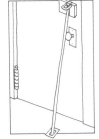

Vertical prop police lock

Installation

The latch on the door must align with its keeper on the frame. Install the door side first; then position the keeper. When you buy a lock, tell the locksmith whether your door opens in or out and which side is hinged. The lock should come with a template showing what size holes to cut and where to position them. The package should also contain hardware, although it is often better to use longer screws than those provided. For more security, drill holes through the door and secure the casing with carriage bolts, putting the nuts inside. Cover the heads with a hardened steel plate, available from most locksmiths.

To install a deadlock, cut two holes in the door: a large one for the lock cylinder and a smaller one for the bolt. After positioning the centers of both holes with the template, use an expansive drill bit or a hole saw to cut the cylinder hole (see *Drilling*).

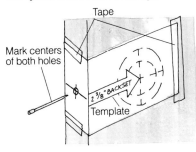

Tape

Mark centers of both holes

2 3/8" BACKSET

Template

Drill the smaller hole in the edge of the door so that it meets the cylinder hole; use a drill guide to keep the bit level and square. (If you don't have a guide, ask a helper to watch at eye level while you watch from above.) You may have to shape the small hole with

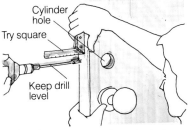

Cylinder hole
Try square
Keep drill level

a chisel to accommodate the bolt assembly and mortise the faceplate into the door's edge (see *Chiseling*).

To mark the position of the keeper on the jamb, dab a little lipstick or crayon on the end of the bolt, close the door, and turn the knob. Then drill a hole in the jamb large enough for the bolt. Center the strike plate over it and trace the plate's outline. Chisel a mortise so that the plate sits flush with the jamb; screw the plate in place.

To install a rim lock or a police lock, only the lock-cylinder hole must be cut. Position the keeper of a rim lock by closing the door and marking where the latch hits. If the door is inset into the frame, cut a mortise for the keeper. Use a chisel to cut a little at a time until the door closes properly.

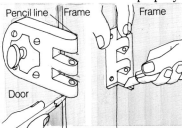

Pencil line   Frame   Frame

Door

To position the keepers of a double-throw police lock, turn the knob until the bars are fully extended; then place the keepers over them and mark their positions. For the prop type, put the top of the steel rod in the casing, with the lock closed, and mark the place where the bottom hits the floor. Then cut a mortise for the plate that holds the rod and screw the plate into place. (See also *Apartment security; Burglarproofing; Doors.*)

Doors

Fixing a door that squeaks, sticks, binds, or fails to close

All that is usually needed to quiet a squeaking door is a drop of oil on each hinge. At the same time that you apply the oil, tighten all the screws. If squeaking persists, an adjustment is needed to align the pins.

Lubrication and screw tightening may also take care of a door latch that sticks or that doesn't close properly. Apply a graphite spray (not oil) to the latch mechanism and tighten the screws in all hardware, including any faceplates in the edge of the door and strike plates on the frame.

If the problem persists, rub a pencil on the end of the latch bolt and close the door. The bolt's path will be marked on the jamb. If it is in line with the hole in the strike plate but fails to reach it, look at the stop molding. It may be out of line or it may contain an obstruction, such as paint buildup or dirt. Chipped paint or loose nails will tip you off. Tighten the molding with small finishing nails, move it slightly, or scrape it clean, as needed.

If the latch bolt is out of line with the strike plate, the frame has probably shifted. If the door works properly in all other respects, simply enlarge the hole in the strike plate with a file. Or, if necessary,

move the strike plate: extend the mortise into which it is set and drill a fresh hole for the bolt.

Binding

The same shifting process can cause a door to bind against the jamb. The tip-off is a spot rubbed bare of paint. To check the alignment of the door within the frame, put a strong light behind the door and close it slowly.

There are several ways to correct binding, depending on its severity. Try sandpapering first—that might do enough to free the door. For a heavy paint buildup see *Paint removal*.

The next recourse is planing. With a pencil, scribe a line on the door face ⅛ inch in from the frame. If the door is binding on top or along the upper edge, use a wedge to hold it open while you plane to the line (see *Planing*). Prime and paint the newly bared wood.

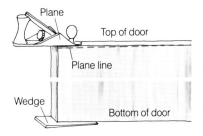

If your door binds on or near the bottom, or if you must plane the entire edge, remove it from its hinges. Most door hinges have loose pins that you can pry up with a screwdriver. First tap gently with a hammer to loosen the pin; if the pin is rusted, apply penetrating oil. If the pins are permanent, prop the door open with a wedge and remove the screws from

the frame side, leaving the hinges attached to the door. Always start with the bottom hinge.

After planing to the line, replace the door and insert the pins halfway (or drive the top screws), starting with the top hinge. If the problem is fixed, tap the pins down (or drive the rest of the screws); if not, plane some more.

If the door is badly out of alignment, it may be easier to insert a cardboard

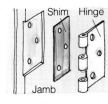

shim under one of the hinges as shown. Remove the screws from the frame side of the hinge, insert the cardboard, and replace the screws. (See also *Folding doors; Garage doors; Shower doors; Sliding doors; Storm doors and windows*.)

Double-entry bookkeeping

What it is; types of accounts; debits and credits

If you are going into business, you'll need an accountant to set up your books and a bookkeeper to gather and record your financial data. Businesses record their transactions by the double-entry bookkeeping process.

Double-entry bookkeeping is based on an equation which states that a business's *assets* (cash, accounts receivable, inventory, real estate, and equipment) minus its *liabilities* (any amounts owed to suppliers and other creditors) equals *proprietorship* (the company's worth to its owners). Income increases proprietorship, expenses decrease it. Every business transaction affects more than one component of the equation but in such a way that the two sides always balance. A sale of goods for cash increases an asset (cash) and proprietorship (income). Payment of a loan in cash decreases an asset (cash) and a liability (loans payable). In both cases, the balance of the equation is unaffected.

Business transactions are recorded in five basic types of accounts: asset, liability, proprietorship, income, and expense. These accounts, which may be subdivided, are contained in a book called the *general ledger*.

Debits and credits

Each ledger page contains information on one account only. A page is divided into a left, or *debit*, side and a right, or *credit*, side. (In bookkeeping, the terms debit and credit refer only to the left and right sides of a ledger page.) Increases and decreases in an account are entered on opposite sides of a page. Increases in assets and expenses are entered on the debit side; increases in liability, proprietorship, and income on the credit side. Thus, payment of a loan in cash is credited to cash (an asset decrease) and debited to loans payable (a liability decrease). The difference between total credits and debits in one account at the end of a bookkeeping period is called the *balance*—a credit balance if credits are greater; a debit balance if debits are greater.

For every debit entry in one account there must be a corresponding and equal credit entry in another; hence the term *double-entry bookkeeping*. Total debits in all accounts in the ledger must always equal total credits. Similarly, the sum of debit balances in the ledger must always equal the sum of credit balances. If they don't, the records contain an error that must be found and corrected.

Dowels

Joining wood with wood

In making or repairing furniture, it's easier to join pieces of wood with short wooden pins, or dowels, rather than with hand-cut joints. In many situations dowels are stronger than nails or screws, and they need not show unless you want them to.

You make dowel joints by drilling corresponding holes in two pieces of wood. Then you insert glue and the dowels and clamp the pieces together until the glue dries. In this manner, boards can be joined edge to edge to form tabletops or countertops, or parts of furniture can be securely fastened together.

The dowels

Ready-to-use dowels are available in various sizes from woodworking suppliers and hardware stores. Choose a dowel with a diameter equal to one-third the thickness of the wood into which it will be installed. The length should be 1/8 inch less than the combined length of its two installation holes, which should be drilled through at least one-third of the thickness of each piece of wood being joined.

If you prefer to make your own dowels, purchase lengths of dowel rod in the required diameter and cut them into suitable segments. Cut a groove along the length of a homemade dowel so that air and excess glue can escape

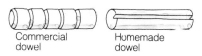

Commercial dowel   Homemade dowel

during installation. To make this groove, clamp a handsaw upside down in a vise and rub the dowel on the teeth. Then use a file to bevel the ends of the dowel so that it will enter the holes easily.

Aligning and drilling the holes

A dowel will seat properly only if the two holes are aligned with each other and drilled perpendicular to the surfaces being joined. If you plan to install a number of dowels, a commercial doweling jig is a worthwhile investment. Jig designs vary; for best results get one with guides for different size drill bits.

If you don't have a jig, align the installation holes by nailing brads at the centers of the hole locations on one piece of wood. Then clip the brad heads, leaving the shanks protruding about 1/16 inch. Align the mating piece, then press down on it so that the brads indent its surface. Remove the brads with pliers. Before drilling the holes, enlarge the brad marks in both pieces of wood with an awl.

Brads

The holes must be precisely centered on the marks. Choose a bit the diameter of the dowel. To ensure that the bit enters the wood perpendicular

Depth guide

to both the length and width of the surface, it's best to use a drill guide (see *Drilling*). If you use a doweling jig you run less risk of error. To make your holes the correct depth, measure the dimension on the bit and mark it with masking tape to show you where to stop drilling.

Another way to align the holes is to use commercial dowel centers of the appropriate diameters. Drill the holes in one piece of wood and insert the dowel centers. Align the mating piece and press down so that the doweling centers mark the surface. Drill holes at the marks and remove the dowel centers from the first piece.

Dowel center

Installing the dowels

Blow wood chips from the holes. Apply glue to one end of the dowel and around the edges of the hole in one of the surfaces to be joined. Insert the dowel into the hole and tap it home with a mallet. Then apply glue to the other end of the dowel, the other hole, and the surfaces of the two pieces. Use clamps to draw the pieces evenly together. Wipe off the excess glue. Keep the pieces clamped overnight.

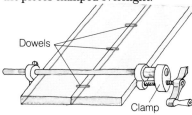

Dowels

Clamp

If a hole is misaligned, fill the hole with a dowel, saw it flush with the wood, sand it, and start over.

Down comforters

Care, repair, and storage

The best shell fabric is tightly woven cotton or a cotton-polyester blend. Each lets the down breathe and trap air properly, yet has fine enough

thread counts that the down can't work its way out.

Buy a washable cover to protect the shell from dirt and stains. Or make a cover by seaming two sheets on three sides and closing the fourth side with a zipper (see *Zippers*).

To dry-clean or wash?

Whether you dry-clean or wash a comforter, check and repair any open seams or loose stitching. For dry-cleaning suggestions, see *Down pillows*. As for laundering, some experts advise handwashing or using only an oversize commercial washer and dryer. Others say the agitator of a top loader may weaken stitches. If in doubt, consult the label.

In a home washer, use the gentle cycle, warm water, and a mild detergent—half the amount for a normal load. Agitate the water and soap until mixed. Stop the machine, immerse the quilt, and continue the cycle. To aid rotation, add a pair of sneakers without laces. Repeat the rinse cycle until the water runs clear.

Set the dryer to *Low*. Tumble the comforter until dry; this may take 3 to 4 hours, during which you should periodically remove the comforter so its cover doesn't get too hot. At the same time, loosen the clumps of down with your fingers. Include the sneakers; they'll help distribute the down evenly.

Repairing rips

You can make a temporary repair with pressure-sensitive cloth tape. To mend a rip, use a fine needle and fine thread. Abut the two edges; close with tiny slipstitches (see *Slipstitching*). Hand-stitch a fabric patch over the mend (see *Patching*).

Down pillows

Keeping them in fluffy shape

With normal use, down pillows need cleaning but once a year. To protect the outer shell from stains, keep it in a zippered, washable pillow protector sold in linen departments.

If you would like your pillows dry cleaned, find a reputable cleaner who is experienced with down products. Air a dry-cleaned pillow well before sleeping on it. If you prefer to wash your pillows in a home washer and dryer, do two at a time and follow the instructions in *Down comforters.*

In time, a down pillow loses the ability to trap air. To revive it, put it in a dryer with a sneaker or tennis ball; set the dryer on *Low.* Tumble for 10 minutes. If that fails, add more down. Shake the filling to one end of the shell; open part of the opposite seam and insert the neck of another pillow or a bag of down in the opening; add down a bit at a time. Sew the opening with a fine needle and small stitches.

Drainage

Diverting water away from your house

Seasonal standing water or swampy areas around your home can cause damp basements and eventual deterioration of house foundations and driveways. Water flowing onto your property or changing runoff caused by construction must be diverted.

You can dig earthen ditches for temporary relief and even pave them for more permanence. But open excavations fill with leaves and debris and require regular cleaning. Drainage pipe installed in covered trenches, while more expensive, works best.

The water must be sent to a pond, stream, drainage ditch, or other outlet that is lower than the lowest problem area. Dig a trench 2 or 3 feet deep to the outlet, making sure that it slopes downward at least 6 inches for every 100 feet. Line the bottom of the trench with about 6 inches of gravel or crushed-rock filler. Use filler of uniformly sized pieces to provide fairly equalized radial pressure throughout the length of the line. Lay sections of drainage pipe 4 to 6 inches in diameter on top of the fill. Cover the pipe with 8 to 10 inches more filler and a layer of fiberglass or 15-pound roofing felt. Then replace the soil.

Drainage pipe is available at building supply outlets. Traditional earthenware or concrete drainage tile is laid with ⅛-inch gaps between the sections to let the water in. Less expensive, lightweight PVC tubing is laid in long connected sections. Water

enters through perforations in the tubing. In sandy soils, wrap PVC tubing in sheets of fiberglass or cover the joints of earthenware or concrete tile with strips of 15-pound roofing felt to keep out fine sand.

If you don't have access to an existing outlet, you may be able to empty into your municipal storm sewer system (consult your public works department). If not, build a dry well (see *Dry wells*). If a steep slope is involved,

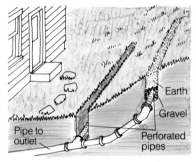

run perforated drainage pipes across the slope and connect them to pipes running down the slope to your outlet. (See also *Retaining walls.*)

Permanent wet areas can be contained in ponds. Specialists from the Soil Conservation Service of the U.S. Department of Agriculture will offer you free advice and help you design a pond. Call your local office. A nuisance swamp could become a family fishing pond or swimming hole. (See also *Basement waterproofing; Gutters and downspouts.*)

Drain odors

How to cope with them

One way to keep a drain free of odors is to run very hot tap water through the drain after each use. Also, try to avoid getting vegetable matter or grease in a kitchen drain or letting hair accumulate in a bathroom drain (hair entraps other odorous matter). Treat any partially clogged drain promptly (see *Drain unclogging*).

To rid a drain of odors, about once a week pour in a handful of baking soda, then run very hot tap water through it. Or, pour in 1 cup of vinegar, let it stand for 30 minutes, then rinse with a stream of hot water.

Drain unclogging

Clearing a stopped-up sink

Keep drains clear by treating them monthly with boiling water and 2 tablespoons of baking soda or, infrequently, with a liquid drain cleaner. These cleaners may also clear partially clogged drains. If you use a chemical cleaner, follow the directions and rinse the drain afterwards.

Caution: Chemical drain cleaners are dangerous. If you splash any on your skin, wash it off immediately in cold water. If a drain is clogged and the cleaner remains in the sink, call a plumber. Don't try unclogging the drain by other means; the leftover cleaner may splatter you.

Using a plunger

If a drain is totally blocked, first try to free it with a plunger. Remove the sink stopper or strainer. Most wash basins have pop-up stoppers that can be removed by simply pulling them up. On some models, you must first reach under the basin and remove a nut that retains the ball joint and the pull control. If the sink has an overflow opening, block it with a wet cloth to prevent air from being drawn in as you work the plunger. Run enough water into the sink to cover the rubber force cup of the plunger.

Place the cup over the drain, tilting the cup to get rid of trapped air. Vigorously pump the plunger up and down 10 times to create a surge in the water trapped in the drain. On the last up-

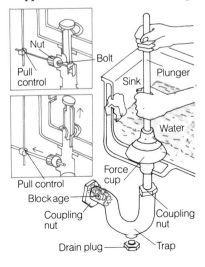

stroke, lift the plunger abruptly from the water. If the water rushes out, you may have dislodged the blockage. Run more water into the sink. If it doesn't go down easily, try the plunger again. Don't give up—keep trying.

Working with the trap

If the above won't work, place a bucket beneath the gooseneck trap under the sink. Unscrew the cleanout plug on the bottom of the trap with a wrench and let the water run out. Clear the stoppage by hand or with a bent wire coat hanger. Replace the plug.

If there is no plug, remove the entire trap, which is held on by two coupling nuts. Remove the higher coupling nut with a pipe wrench. (Wrap the jaws of the wrench with tape to protect the chrome on the slip nuts.) Then support the trap and remove the lower coupling nut. Clean out the stoppage and replace the trap. Do not overtighten the fittings, or they may leak.

Using a snake

If the clog is out of reach, try dislodging it with a "snake"—a thin wire with a coiled spring on the end. Use a flexible-bulb auger with a cable diameter of ¼ inch. Crank the handle of

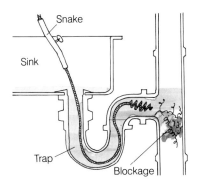

the snake clockwise, both pushing into and pulling out of the drain. Rotate the snake into the drain, working it through the trap under the sink until it contacts and cuts through the stoppage. (You can distinguish between the mushy resistance of a blockage and the hard resistance of a bend in the pipe.)

If the clog is beyond the trap, work the snake into the drain pipe that leads from the trap into the wall. Run the snake through the cleanout or, if you have removed the trap, directly into the pipe. The snake works more

effectively if it does not have to go around a lot of bends.

If the drain is still stopped up, the blockage may be in a main drainpipe; call a plumber. (See also *Bathtub drains; Toilets.*)

Drawer construction

Making and installing drawers

A drawer is nothing more than an open box. It can fit flush with the front of a cabinet or it can be made with a false front, a board that overlaps part of the cabinet front, concealing the gap between the cabinet and the drawer sides. A flush drawer must be more precisely made because this gap remains visible.

Plan drawers on graph paper with the rest of the cabinet (see *Cabinet building*). Design the back and bottom to fit into ¼-inch grooves cut into the sides. In calculating the size of the front and bottom, allow for the thickness of the drawer sides minus the depth of the grooves the front and the bottom will fit into. Also allow room for wooden runners or metal slides. A standard slide takes up ½ inch.

On false-front drawers, butt the front between the sides and add a false front that is ⅜-inch larger on each side than the drawer opening. On flush-front drawers, cut rabbets into the drawer front to fit it over the edges of the drawer sides.

Make the false front (or the actual front in a flush drawer) of the same material as the rest of the cabinet. You can use cheaper plywood for the rest— ½ inch for the sides and invisible front; ¼ inch for the back and bottom.

Cut all the pieces; cut the grooves and rabbets and test their fit. Then assemble and glue the drawer. If needed, reinforce the joints with brads driven through the drawer sides. Clamp the drawer until the glue is dry. Attach a false front by driving screws from the rear.

If you use metal slides (available at hardware stores and home centers), follow the manufacturer's directions to install them. Or make your own wooden runners. Simply glue and nail strips of wood along the sides of

the drawers and on the insides of the cabinet so that the strips on the drawer sides rest on the strips on the cabinet at the proper height. Also nail a strip of wood, or *kicker*, to the cabinet above each drawer side to keep the drawer from tipping as it is pulled out. Be precise in positioning runners or slides; otherwise, the drawer will jam.

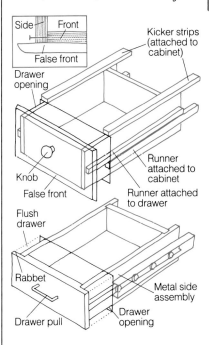

Drawer repairs

Fixing stuck or broken drawers

High humidity may temporarily swell wooden drawers, causing them to stick. If sticking persists in drier weather, lightly sand and then lubricate wooden runners with wax or soap, or clean metal slides and apply a small amount of grease. If you see any loose joints in the drawer, reglue them.

To fix a split drawer bottom, glue a canvas strip along the underside of the split and the bottom edges of the drawer sides. Use white glue.

Flush-front drawers sometimes get pushed too far into the cabinet. To prevent this, glue or tack small blocks of wood to the rear of the drawer runners to serve as stops.

If a drawer tilts when you pull it out, add kickers (see *Drawer construction*) to hold it horizontal.

D

Drawstrings

Replacing lost or broken ones

A simple replacement for the drawstring in a child's garment is a shoelace. It should be the length of the waist or hood of the garment plus sufficient extra to tie. Slip the tip into the opening and push it around to the other side. At each end, make a knot larger than the opening to prevent the shoelace from slipping out.

For an adult garment, you can make a drawstring of cord, fabric tubing, braid, a leather strip, or ribbon, all of which can be purchased by the yard. Attach a safety pin to one end and push it through the casing. Remove the pin; tie a knot at each end.

Drilling

Making clean holes in wood, metal, and other materials

Equipped with the proper bits, a ⅜-inch portable power drill can make holes in wood, metal, masonry, ceramic, plastic—even glass—and do many other jobs as well. For heavy-duty work, such as drilling through steel beams, look for a ½-inch drill with a shoulder brace. (The size refers to the opening of the chuck and also reflects the power and weight of the unit.) Drills with variable speed and reverse drive are costlier than those without, but are well worth the money.

High-speed steel twist bits are good for holes up to ½ inch in diameter in wood, metal, and most plastics. For larger holes in wood, use a spade bit (to 1½ inches), an expansive bit, or a hole saw. For drilling into concrete, brick, or stone, use a masonry bit with a carbide tip. Special carbide-tipped bits are also needed for glass.

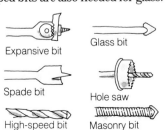

Expansive bit

Glass bit

Spade bit

Hole saw

High-speed bit

Masonry bit

Drilling straight holes

First make sure that the piece you are working on is secure: clamp a board in a vise, wedge a door in place, and so forth. If possible, position the work so that you are drilling straight down or horizontally.

Mark the center of the hole with a center punch. Position yourself so that the bit enters at the proper angle and you can maintain steady pressure. Place the bit against the center point and start drilling slowly, speeding up after the bit has penetrated.

You can usually keep the drill fairly straight with the help of a try square or a combination square. If the precise angle is important, use a drill guide. Commercial guides are available that adjust to any angle, or you can make your own guide from a block of wood.

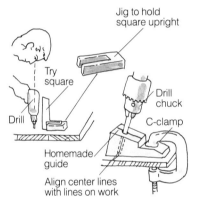

Jig to hold square upright

Try square

Drill chuck

Drill

C-clamp

Homemade guide

Align center lines with lines on work

If you are drilling into metal, stop from time to time and apply a drop of light oil to the work. With masonry and plastic, keep the speed slow to prevent overheating.

To prevent wood from splintering where the bit emerges, clamp a piece of scrap behind the workpiece and drill into it. Or stop drilling when the tip of the bit emerges, then turn the piece and drill from the other side.

To drill a hole of a given depth (in making a mortise, for example), wrap a strip of masking tape around the bit. Drill until the tape touches the surface of the material.

Hand-operated drills

When electricity is not available, use a twist drill (also called an eggbeater) for light jobs; for heavy work, use a brace and bit. High-speed steel bits work in a twist drill. A brace requires its own bits. (See also *Countersinking.*)

Drive belts

Remove, replace, adjust

Household drive belts transfer power from a motor to a pump, fan, or drum. They typically wrap around pulleys but may wrap around a drum at one end. A correctly tensioned belt should deflect ½ to ¾ inch midway between pulleys under thumb pressure.

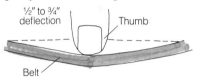

½" to ¾" deflection

Thumb

Belt

Caution: Unplug or turn off an appliance before servicing its drive belt.

A cracked belt or one that can't be properly tensioned must be replaced. Loosen the belt-tensioning device. If the motor bolts go through slotted

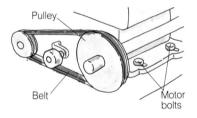

Pulley

Belt

Motor bolts

holes, loosen them and push the motor toward the pulley it drives.

Push on a spring-loaded idler pulley to compress the spring, then slide off

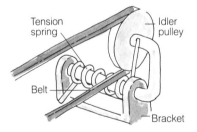

Tension spring

Idler pulley

Belt

Bracket

the old belt. If a pulley is a take-apart type, remove the bolt holding its halves together; the belt will come off.

Take the old belt to the hardware store to get an exact duplicate: same width, close in diameter (perhaps a bit smaller to allow for stretch), and its cross section the same.

If you have replaced a belt or if it is loose, adjust the tension so that the belt deflects less than ¾ inch. Tensioning is basically the reverse of the removal procedure. However, you also may have to pry on the movable part to hold adequate belt tension while you tighten the bolts.

Reassemble a take-apart type with the number of shim washers originally between the pulley halves. Belt too loose? Take apart the pulley again, remove the shims, then reassemble

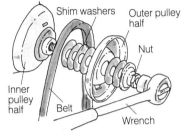

Shim washers — Outer pulley half — Nut — Inner pulley half — Belt — Wrench

(storing the shims against the outside pulley half). The pulley halves will move closer together, forcing the belt to ride higher in its grooves and increasing tension. To reduce tension, insert shims between pulley halves. For drive belts in cars, see *Car belts*.

Driver's licenses

How to apply and renew

Requirements for driver's licenses vary from state to state. Usually, you must be at least 18 years old. However, some states will issue a junior license (around age 16) for limited driving if you complete an approved driver education course and have your parents' consent.

Many states require a learner's permit. To get one—or a license—you must pass a vision test and a written (and sometimes an oral) exam on the rules of the road, traffic signs, and driver courtesy. With a learner's permit, or without it in states that don't require one, you can practice driving only if a licensed driver is with you.

The last step in getting a license is a road test. An examiner joins you for a drive and directs you to perform such moves as parallel parking and U-turns. He or she observes whether you obey traffic signs and the rules of the road. In many states, you must also have a photograph taken for the license.

Renewals

A driver's license is good for 2 to 5 years, depending on the state. Usually you'll receive renewal forms in the mail. If you don't receive them before the expiration date, renew the license in person at the office that issued the original. Car registrations should be renewed annually in the same way.

Driving in bad weather

Fog, rain, snow, ice

The first rule when the weather is bad is to slow down. In fog use low beams; you'll get less glare than with high beams. If necessary, drive at a crawl so that you can stop within the range of visibility. Another car's taillights may shine through fog, but you can't assume that they will.

If you decide to stop, don't do so suddenly; cars behind may not be able to respond quickly. Signal and pull off the road completely so that cars behind won't mistake you for a moving vehicle and plow into you. Put on your hazard flashers.

In heavy rain at speeds above 35 m.p.h., beware of hydroplaning (tires riding on a cushion of water, causing loss of steering control). If it occurs, take your foot off the accelerator to slow the car and hold the steering wheel as straight as possible. Don't hit the brakes.

Crawl through deep puddles; otherwise water may splash the ignition wires, causing the engine to stall. Water may also affect the brakes. Drive slowly and apply the brakes several times to revive their stopping power.

On dirt roads or salted snowy roads dirt may coat the headlights, reducing night visibility. Pull off the road periodically to wipe the lenses.

Winter driving

In heavy snow, you need snow tires. Don't rely on all-season tires; they are designed for light snow. Consider premium snow tires with treads that perform better than ordinary ones at low temperatures.

Carry a shovel and sand or traction mats. Stuck? A gentle acceleration, then a release, may pull you out. Don't spin your wheels, and don't rock more

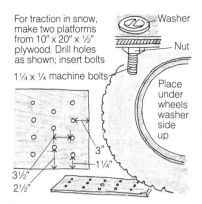

For traction in snow, make two platforms from 10″ x 20″ x ½″ plywood. Drill holes as shown; insert bolts

1¼ x ¼ machine bolts

Washer — Nut

Place under wheels washer side up

3″
1¼″
3½″
2½″

than a few times or you'll damage an automatic transmission.

On ice, make no sudden moves. If you skid, turn the steering wheel in the direction the car's rear is sliding. Be especially cautious at temperatures around 32°F; ice is most slippery then. (See also *Deicing car windows*.)

Drug overdose

Emergency treatment for ingested or injected drugs

If someone has accidentally or deliberately taken too much of a medication or an illicit drug, get expert advice immediately. Phone a poison control center, physician, or hospital emergency room, give what facts you can (kind and amount of drug, approximate time of taking, age and condition of patient), and follow instructions to the letter. Save the container with any remaining contents. Until medical help arrives, apply these emergency measures.

Overdose by swallowing

If the victim is not breathing and has no pulse (see *Pulse*) and has swallowed a drug, perform cardiopulmonary resuscitation (see *CPR*).

If the victim is conscious and has swallowed a drug within the last 30 minutes, induce vomiting with a dose of ipecac syrup preceded and followed by ample fluids. It takes 15 to 20 minutes for ipecac to take effect; if no vomiting occurs, repeat the dose in 20 minutes. *Never induce vomiting in someone who is unconscious or having convulsions.* If your adviser has recommended a different method of

D

inducing vomiting or has advised against it, do as instructed.

When vomiting begins, be sure the victim is bent over, facedown, so that the vomitus cannot enter his lungs. Afterward have the victim drink 2 to 4 teaspoons of powdered activated charcoal mixed in a glassful of water. (If charcoal is available only in capsules, open the capsules and measure out the powder inside.) If the drug was a tranquilizer or sleeping pill, keep the victim awake.

Overdose by injection
If the victim is not breathing, lacks pulse, and the drug was injected, administer CPR. If he is conscious, get the victim to an emergency medical facility immediately.

Sometimes a parent inadvertently administers a drug overdose to an infant by failing to measure medication accurately. To avoid such accidents, use a calibrated medicine dropper or syringe or a measuring spoon. Never increase the dosage unless the doctor so instructs. Don't give a child two doses to make up for one missed earlier without first asking the doctor. (See also *Poisoning*.)

Dry cleaning

Getting good results; the pros and cons of bulk cleaning

Garment labels tell you whether your clothing must be dry cleaned; most woolens, silks, acetates, and many rayons require it. A garment made of washable fabric may need dry cleaning to hold its shape or if it's lined with another fabric. A professional dry cleaning may remove stubborn spots or stains from washable garments.

Take clothing and household items to the cleaner before they become heavily soiled, immediately if they are spotted or stained. Clean all parts of a suit or ensemble together, or colors may fade differently. Point out stains and the location of any sugar-based spills, such as juice, wine, or ginger ale. If you tried to remove a stain at home, tell the cleaner what you used.

Bulk, or coin-operated, cleaning
You can usually save money with a bulk cleaner, who will charge you by the pound. Follow these procedures: turn out pockets, turn down cuffs, and brush off accumulated dirt and lint. Fasten all openings so that garments will retain their shape. Turn knit garments and anything made of napped or piled fabric inside out. Do not clean heavily soiled garments with less dirty ones, or dark or heavy clothing with your light and delicate things. To minimize wrinkling, hang garments, as soon as they come out of the machine, on metal or wooden hangers (the chemicals can soften plastic ones). Air all items thoroughly before wearing or storing them.

A disadvantage of bulk cleaning is that the operator may not know whether his chemicals are safe for your fabrics; many delicate materials, ones with metallic threads, and fluffy or bulky knits can be harmed by certain cleaning chemicals. Nor do most bulk cleaners use special stain-removal techniques or press garments. To be safe, do not bulk clean tailored suits and coats or any clothing that is marked "professional dry clean only."

Dryers

Cleaning your clothes dryer; troubleshooting; replacing the drum belt

Caution: Before servicing a dryer, unplug it or turn off the power to its circuit (see *Circuit testing*). On a gas dryer, also turn off the gas valve. Don't smoke or light a match near the dryer. If you smell gas, turn off the gas-supply valve; call a repairman.

The most common cause of poor drying is a clogged lint filter, exhaust hose, or air vent. Remove lint from the filter after each use. Once a year remove the exhaust hose and shake out lint; insert a straightened section of coat hanger into the outdoor vent to clean the damper and its hinge. Eliminate any sags in the hose that can trap lint or water. Replace a damaged hose with a new type of smooth-wall ducting that is less likely to trap lint.

Gas dryers
If your dryer has a pilot light instead of a flameless igniter, read the service manual for instructions on relighting the pilot. With the power off, periodically remove the front-panel grille over the burner assembly, wipe the burner area clean, and vacuum with a crevice tool. If the dryer heats poorly, inspect the flame with the dryer running. A roaring noise or a yellow flame indicates an incorrect air-gas mixture. This, and all other burner problems, should be left to a repairman. If you move from a natural-gas area to a bottled-gas area, have the gas company change the burner orifices.

If the dryer won't start
Make sure the door is firmly shut and the start switch pushed or turned on. Replace a blown fuse or reset a tripped circuit breaker. Electric dryers are usually connected to two fuses or circuit breakers. If one is out, the dryer may run but won't heat. If the power supply is all right and the dryer still won't start, call a repairman.

Replacing the drum belt
If the dryer starts but the drum doesn't turn, the drum belt may be broken. Unplug the dryer and rotate the drum by hand. If it turns very easily, the belt is broken. To replace it, insert a putty knife under the top panel near a front corner. Push the knife against the spring clip holding the top to the cabinet, and raise the top. Unscrew any screws holding the front panel to the cabinet. Note how the wires from the door switch are connected and disconnect them. Lift off the panel. If the operating thermostat is in the front panel, you won't be able to remove the panel. Set it aside, taking care not to damage the wires. If the drum is supported by the front panel, prop it with a block of wood.

Reach under the drum to locate the idler pulley that controls belt tension. On some dryers, you may first have to remove lower front- or rear-access panels; check your service manual. Push the idler arm away from the pulley and disengage the belt from the drive shaft and pulley. Handle the idler arm carefully; it may be under high tension and could snap back on your hand. Lift the drum slightly and slide off the belt. Slip on a duplicate belt so that its ribbed side is against the drum. Rethread the belt over the idler pulley and drive shaft. Rotate the drum in both directions to make sure that the belt is properly aligned.

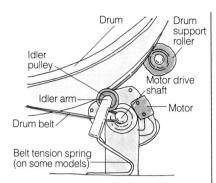

Drum
Drum support roller
Idler pulley
Motor drive shaft
Idler arm
Motor
Drum belt
Belt tension spring (on some models)

Eliminating dryer noises

Remove any objects caught in the drum holes. Tighten the screws on the trim and on the exterior panels. If the noise persists, try to locate its source by opening the dryer door and rotating the drum by hand. If you hear a slow thump that varies with the speed you turn the drum, the drum belt may be worn; replace it. In dryers with sliding drum supports, a scraping sound means the supports are worn. Unscrew the screws holding the supports to the cabinet front; remove and replace the supports.

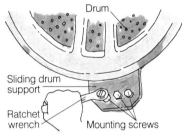

Drum
Sliding drum support
Ratchet wrench
Mounting screws

A worn idler pulley makes a rattle. Many thumps per revolution of the drum indicate a worn drum support roller. To replace these parts you must first remove the top and front panels of the dryer and the drum. Check your service manual or have a repairman to do the job.

Drying foods

Preserving fruits and vegetables by drying

Select only ripe, unbruised fruits and vegetables and wash them thoroughly. Peel vegetables and fruits you would normally peel; slice them $1/8$ to $1/4$ inch thick. Quarter large tomatoes and halve plum or cherry tomatoes;

dry them skin down. Dry peas, asparagus, and small mushrooms whole.

Dip sliced apples, pears, and bananas in lemon juice to preserve their color. Or drop them in a solution of 1 teaspoon ascorbic acid and 1 quart water and leave them for 2 to 3 minutes. Halve and pit apricots, plums, peaches, cherries, and nectarines; treat these also to prevent darkening.

Most fruits and vegetables should be blanched before drying to destroy enzymes that cause deterioration. Put the produce in a metal colander or wire basket set over 1 to 2 inches of boiling water. Cover and steam for the specified time (see chart below); rinse in cold water. Mushrooms, onions, peppers, bananas, figs, grapes, and plums do not need blanching.

Drying food in the sun

In a hot, dry climate (daytime temperatures above 90°F), lay blanched fruits or vegetables on trays of wooden slats or nonmetal screening and set them off the ground in a sunny spot. At least once a day, turn the foods. At night cover the trays with plastic or carry them indoors. Most foods will dry in 3 to 5 days. If rain interrupts the drying, finish it indoors.

Drying food indoors

A homemade or commercial dryer is best for indoor drying. An oven can be used if its temperature can be maintained between 95°F and 145°F; it generally works faster than a dryer. Arrange the food in a single layer on drying racks or cookie sheets; place the sheets in the oven, allowing 3 to 4 inches between racks. Leave the oven door open a crack and direct a fan toward the opening. Periodically rearrange the food to ensure even drying.

Fruit is dry when it is pliable and leathery with no moistness in the center. Most vegetables should be crisp.

To prevent spoiling during storage,

BLANCHING AND DRYING TIMES

Produce	Blanch	Dry at 140°F
Apples	5 min.	6–12 hr.
Apricots	3–4 min.	10–36 hr.
Bananas		6–24 hr.
Grapes		6–20 hr.
Pears	6 min.	10–36 hr.
Plums		24–36 hr.
Eggplant	3 min.	12–14 hr.
Peas	3 min.	8–10 hr.
Tomatoes	3 min.	10–18 hr.
Zucchini		4–12 hr.

pasteurize dried foods for 15 minutes in an oven set at 175°F. Leave dried food in covered bowls or jars for 5 to 10 days. If condensation appears, dry the food for a few more hours.

Store dried foods in airtight containers in a cool, dark place. Most vegetables will keep for 6 months, fruits for a year. (See also *Jerky.*)

Dry mounting photos

Preparing pictures for display

In dry mounting, a photo is bonded to a mat board by melting adhesive tissue sandwiched between them. Photo shops sell special tools—a tacking iron to fix the tissue to the photo and board, and a heating press to seal the layers together—but they're expensive. A regular iron will do, but experiment first with a disposable print to determine the exact temperature setting. You will also need mat board and dry-mounting tissue (both available from photo shops), brown wrapping or heavy tracing paper, a steel ruler, and a utility knife.

Set the iron on *Synthetics* (about 230°F). Place the photo, faceup, on a clean surface and cover it with wrapping paper. Gently iron the photo and then the mat to dry them completely. Wipe photo, mat, and mounting tissue free of dust.

Turn the photo facedown and place the mounting tissue on top. Tack the tissue to the back of the photo by touching the center with the tip of the iron. Using the ruler and utility knife, trim the tissue to the size of the photo.

Position the photo faceup on the mat. Carefully lift two corners of the photo and tack the tissue to the mat

Wrapping paper
Dry-mounting tissue
Mat board
Photo
Tack tissue to board here

with the iron. The tissue should lie smooth. Cover the photo with wrapping paper and gently iron, from the center out, to seal.

Let the photo cool. Trim the mat to the size of the photo or leave a margin (see *Matting*).

Dry rot

Recognizing and repairing it

Dry rot is not really dry; it's a fungus infesting wood that is repeatedly in contact with water. Sometimes the fungus itself is visible; more often, the wood surface is brown and crumbly or whitish and spongy. The rotten wood may yield easily to the probe of an ice pick, or it may sound hollow when tapped with a hammer. Replace or repair rotten wood quickly so that the fungus will not spread.

Look for dry rot in wet basements, near plumbing, and in wood that touches the soil or is exposed to weather. The fungus usually enters at the end grain—the base of a foundation post, the joint of a beam, the place where the window frame butts against the sill, and so forth. Pay particular attention to the windward side of your house; wind can force rainwater deep into a joint or crack. Flaking or discolored paint are symptoms.

Structural members of a house are usually difficult to replace; call in a professional for such jobs. (See *Sagging floors* for help in replacing cellar posts and joists.) You may be able to fix windowsills, door frames, porch rails, siding, and the like by cutting away the affected area (plus 6 inches on either side) and splicing in fresh wood, but it is generally better to replace the whole piece.

Carefully saw or pry the old part away, keeping it intact if you can, for use as a template. Check that the area beneath is not affected. Then make or buy a new part and fit it into place.

If dry rot has infested a small area, you can often repair it with an epoxy resin, available in most boating supply stores. Drill several ¼-inch holes deeply into (but not through) the affected wood. Then mix the two parts of the resin in a plastic squeeze bottle,

and inject it slowly into the holes. Over the course of several days, the resin will seep into the pores of the wood—in effect, replacing the decayed wood with plastic. Add more resin as the first dose soaks in. Finish the job with an epoxy filler.

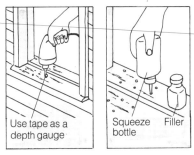

Use tape as a depth gauge

Squeeze bottle

Filler

Dry wells

Getting rid of standing water

Excessive rainwater runoff or standing water near your house may leak into the basement. It must be carried a safe distance away. Call your local public works department about connecting the main downspout from your roof into a municipal storm sewer. If this is impossible, connect it to a dry well—a below-surface collecting basin that allows water to drain slowly into the soil.

You can construct a dry well using a 55-gallon oil drum or concrete blocks. Locate the well at least 20 feet from the house and, if possible, lower than the surface around the house. If you're connecting the dry well to the house gutters, it should be accessible to the main downspout. Excavate a hole big enough to bury the dry well and deep enough for it to be covered by 18 inches of soil.

If you use an oil drum, cut off its ends with a hammer and cold chisel. Make an inlet opening on one side near the top and punch random holes in the sides for drainage. Position the drum in the hole with the inlet opening facing the house.

If you use concrete blocks, lay each block on its side in rows, forming a hollow square at least 3 feet by 3 feet. Create an inlet opening near the top by facing the opening of a concrete block toward the house.

Dig a trench from the downspout or the area you want drained. It should slope down ½ inch for each foot of its length. Install drainage pipe in the trench with one end emptying into the inlet opening (see *Drainage*).

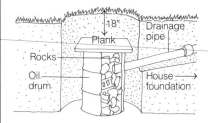

18" | Drainage pipe
Plank
Rocks
Oil drum
House foundation

Fill the dry well with rocks and cover it with treated wooden planks or concrete slabs. Cover the well with soil.

Over many years a dry well fills with sediment. When it no longer holds water, excavate it and add new fill.

Dusting

Suitable methods

Dustcloths can be cut from discarded clothing of soft cotton or wool. These fabrics absorb dust naturally and will not scratch furniture. Or you can buy a chemically treated cloth that attracts and holds the dust.

The cloth should be clean, otherwise dirt particles may scratch your furniture. Keep turning and folding it as you work so that dust is trapped inside and you are wiping with a clean surface. Shake it outdoors. If you use an oil- or wax-base polish, spray it lightly onto your dustcloth, not the furniture. Use an oil-base polish for oiled furniture, a wax-base for waxed.

For light dusting, especially of small objects and hard-to-reach places, use a duster with a handle and a fluffy lamb's-wool head. This is better than a feather duster because wool attracts dust instead of wisking it around. To remove cobwebs from the ceiling, cover a mop with a dustcloth or use the long-wand and small-brush attachments of your vacuum cleaner.

It's best to work from high places— tops of bookcases and frames—to the lower ones—tables, chair rungs, and baseboards—to avoid settling dust on freshly cleaned surfaces.

Dyeing fabric and yarn

What fibers to use; synthetic and natural dyes

Before dyeing fabric or yarn, test a piece to see if the dye will take well and produce the color you want. Animal and vegetable fibers—cotton, wool, linen, silk, and rayon—absorb dye better than chemical synthetics such as polyester and nylon. Dye takes poorly to permanent-press fabrics.

Certain dyes work better on certain fibers; check the manufacturer's advice carefully. If you are unsure what the fiber is, pull out a few threads to test. Holding them over a sink between two coins, bring a lighted candle or match to them. If the threads burn only in contact with the flame and smell of burning hair, the fiber is wool or silk; if they burn then glow afterward like a coal, the fiber is cotton, linen, or rayon; if they do not burn but melt and drip or form a ball, the fiber is a chemical synthetic.

If possible, dye over white or a light neutral. Overdyeing colored fabric takes skill, and the results are frequently not as desired. Dark fabrics, or those that are unevenly colored or faded, should be bleached first, using a packaged color remover or chlorine bleach (for cottons and linens only).

Equipment

Use an enamel, stainless steel, or glass container large enough to hold the fabric without crowding. Manipulate the material with a wooden or stainless steel spoon or a smooth stick such as a dowel. The fabric's dry weight determines the dye quantity; look for yardage equivalents of various fabric weights on the package.

Hot-water synthetic dyes

Hot-water dyeing can be done on the stove or in a washing machine. First mix the dye in hot water in a glass jar, measuring cup, or pitcher. Strain it through paper toweling or cheesecloth into the dyeing container. Wet the fabric, immerse it in the dyebath, and simmer or agitate it for the recommended time, all the while stirring. Rinse it in cool water until no color appears in the rinse water.

To get maximum heat in a washing machine, let the machine stand full of hot water for 15 minutes, then empty and refill it with hot water. Add the dissolved dye, agitate for 1 minute, then put in the material.

To minimize shrinkage and prevent matting of wool in hot-water dyes, use the stove method. Put the wool first in lukewarm water, slowly heat to a simmer, then transfer the wool to the simmering dyebath. Move the wool gently in the liquid, pushing it up and down rather than stirring it. After dyeing is complete, rinse the wool first in very hot water; gradually make subsequent rinses cooler.

Natural dyes

To prepare fabric or yarn for a natural dye, scour it (cook it) to remove oils and fabric finishes. Use 3 gallons of soft water (treated tap water, rain water, or distilled water) per pound of material. Add enough detergent to form suds. Simmer silk for 30 minutes, wool for 45 minutes. Boil linen or cotton for 1 to 2 hours with ½ cup of washing soda added to the solution.

Treating with mordant

Before application of most natural dyes, the fabric or yarn must also be treated with a mineral mordant— alum, chrome, tin, copper sulphate, or iron—so that the dye will be permanently fixed. These are available from drugstores, craft stores, and herbal suppliers. All are poisonous, should be handled with care, and stored out of children's reach. Do not use a mordant in any cooking utensil. Each mordant will bring out a different color or shade in a natural dye. Alum is the most popular as it is inexpensive and less toxic than others.

To mordant 5 pounds of wool or silk, dissolve 4 ounces alum and 1 ounce cream of tartar in 4 gallons water. Add the wet material, bring the liquid to a simmer, and leave at this temperature for 1 hour. Rinse in hot water and cool slowly before drying.

Cotton and linen require more mordant. For 1 pound, use 4 ounces alum and 1 ounce washing soda to 4 gallons water. Add the fabric; bring to a boil. Boil for 1 to 2 hours (the longer time for thicker fabrics). Cool; leave fabric in the mordant for 12 hours. It can then be dyed directly without drying. For color recipes see *Dyes.*

Dyes

Chemical and natural

Modern synthetic dyes are convenient to use, usually colorfast, and available in a wide range of colors. (For good dye sources, check craft magazines.) Natural dyes are more complicated to prepare and apply, but they produce a range of subtle, interesting colors. In fact, rarely is it possible to duplicate a color exactly, even using the same formula; the maturity of the plants and the season in which they were gathered can vary results.

For the best penetration and colorfastness, most dyes must be applied with hot water. However, there are special cold-water dyes for use in batik work and for dyeing wool without shrinking it. Cold-water dyes will take only on animal or vegetable fibers— wool, cotton, linen, silk, and rayon.

Natural dyestuffs

Many flowers, leaves, bark, berries, nuts, and roots yield dyes, especially those that easily stain your fingers. Most flowers produce a brown or yellow dye no matter what the blossom color. Mature plants yield the best dyes. Pick flowers at their prime, berries when fully ripe, and most nuts just after they've dropped. The strongest dyes come from fresh materials, but dried ones can be used. Soak woody materials, such as bark, for at least a week before cooking.

To make a natural dye, put the plants in a large stainless steel or enamel pan with enough soft water (treated tap water, rainwater, or distilled water) to cover. Cook them for a specified time, strain out the plants, then add enough soft water to the dye to cover the article. The following recipes will dye 1 pound of fabric or yarn.

For a bright light-green, simmer 1 bushel (8 gallons) of stalks and flowers of Queen Anne's lace for ½ hour. After preparing the fabric with mordant (see *Dyeing fabric and yarn*), simmer it in the dyebath for ½ hour.

To make a soft yellow dye, use yellow onion skins. Save the skins in a bag in the refrigerator until you have 1 pound. Boil for 1½ hours; strain. Add yarn or fabric, and simmer for 1 hour.

Earaches

Different types; remedial measures

An earache is usually the sign of infection. If anyone has severe ear pain or sudden loss of hearing, get prompt medical care; delay can lead to permanent ear damage.

Pain in the outer ear may result from boils in the ear canal or from "swimmer's ear." The latter infection is frequent in summer; treat it with Burow's solution or an equivalent applied four times daily. Take aspirin or another analgesic for pain. See your doctor if the pain worsens or persists more than 2 days. To prevent swimmer's ear, wear a bathing cap or earplugs in the water and dry both ears after each swim.

Middle-ear infection, common in childhood and often following a respiratory illness, is mainly characterized by partial hearing loss and a feeling of stuffiness in the affected ear. There is no home remedy; immediate medical care is required.

Ears

Care; preventing hearing loss

Clean your outer ear with soap and water on the corner of a washcloth or with a cotton swab. Don't try to remove wax in the ear canal with a swab or other instrument; you may impact it further and injure your eardrum. An over-the-counter wax-dissolving agent may help, but the safest course is to have a doctor flush out impacted wax with a syringe.

Hearing and balance may be temporarily or permanently affected by an ear infection (see *Earaches*), by certain drugs, or by an obstruction such as a correctable bone abnormality or overgrown adenoids. Some loss of hearing may accompany aging.

Increasingly, experts blame permanent hearing loss on the high noise level of modern life: prolonged exposure to loud noise at work or intermittent exposure to loud music, machinery, or traffic. A very high-decibel sound, such as an explosion, can cause immediate damage.

Protect your ears by observing the following practices: wear earmuffs or earplugs in an excessively noisy environment. Don't fly when you have a respiratory infection. Have your hearing tested every 6 to 12 months if you work in noisy surroundings.

Earthquakes

What to do before, during, and after a tremor

If you reside in an earthquake-prone area, you can do a number of things around the house to lessen the possibility of injury during an earthquake.

Put secure latches on cabinets. Anchor any top-heavy furniture with L-shaped brackets attached to wall studs and the top of the piece. Lock the rollers on the refrigerator. Stabilize a water heater by wrapping it with steel plumber's tape and attaching the tape to wall studs. Install flexible connectors where gas lines meet appliances. Learn how to turn off the gas, electricity, and water where they enter the house.

Consider hiring an engineer to determine whether your home is solidly attached to its foundation, if its walls are sufficiently braced, and if the chimney is adequately reinforced.

Besides taking precautions in your house, find out what the emergency plans are in your place of work and, if you have children, the local schools.

To help in the aftermath of an earthquake, keep on hand a battery-powered radio, a flashlight, fresh batteries, candles, fire extinguishers, a first-aid kit, a few days' supply of canned foods, and a 5-gallon container of water for each family member.

During and after the quake

If you are indoors, move away from windows, ceiling fixtures, mirrors, and tall furniture. Stand at an inner wall or in a central doorway or get under a desk, bed, or table. Don't head for the exits or elevators of a high-rise building. It's better not to go outside.

If you're outdoors, try to move away from power poles and other objects that might fall; if possible, get to an open area. If you're in a car, pull over until the tremors stop.

When the quake is over, turn on the radio for instructions; use the telephone only for an emergency. If you smell gas, turn it off at the main valve; open windows and leave. If there is no incoming water and you have none stored, you can get emergency supplies from the water heater, toilet tanks, or canned fruits; boil doubtful water for 20 minutes before drinking or cooking with it. Don't flush toilets until you know that sewage lines are intact. Stand to one side as you open any closets or cabinets. Check the house for structural damage.

Earwigs

Combating a house and garden pest

These dark-brown insects with the forbidding rear pincers are harmless to humans—they don't pinch. Ear-

wigs feed at night on decaying vegetation, dead insects, and sometimes on plants and ripe fruits. If you find small, ragged holes in leaves, petals, or fruits, look for earwigs by flashlight. Try trapping them in rolled-up newspapers left out overnight. Shake the traps over warm, soapy water the next day. Or spray or dust plants and soil with carbaryl, diazinon, malathion, or chlorpyrifos (see *Pesticides*).

Earwigs occasionally migrate into the house or are brought in on fruits and flowers from the garden. They hide under mops, brooms, rugs, and in piles of laundry. To stem an invasion, apply the household formulation of carbaryl, diazinon, or malathion around foundation walls and door sills and, indoors, along baseboards where you see the insects.

Eczema

Causes and treatment of skin rashes

Eczema is a skin condition with a variety of causes. One type is called *atopic dermatitis*; it often runs in families with a history of hay fever or asthma. In the very young it may occur as an allergy to certain foods. Usually in any eczema, the skin is inflamed, itching, and scaly—often in patches. In a child the eczema typically appears in front of the elbows and behind the knees; in an adult, on the hands.

Another type, *irritant contact dermatitis*, is caused by frequent contact with irritating substances. These can be solvents, soaps, detergents, chemicals. Wear rubber gloves when washing dishes or using household cleaners. Wash your hands and bathe with a nonallergenic soap. For either of the above types, a nonprescription hydrocortisone cream, applied four times daily, may relieve symptoms.

Yet a third type, *allergic contact dermatitis*, results from even a small amount of contact. The substance can be wool, poison ivy and related plants (see *Poison ivy, oak, sumac*), nickel (in jewelry), rubber, or certain chemicals. If the problem persists, ask your doctor about patch tests to determine the substance.

Egg decorating

Dyeing Easter eggs

Among the most intricately decorated eggs are *pysanky* from the Ukraine. Uncooked eggs, or whole egg shells from which the egg has been blown, are colored by a wax-resist method similar to batik. Beeswax is applied with a stylus called a *kistka*. The eggs are then dipped in chemical dyes and varnished. If you want to try this intricate art, you might look for a kit of materials and instructions in a museum shop or a crafts-supply store.

An easier method is to use cooled, hard-cooked eggs, a wax crayon or melted candle wax and paintbrush, and vegetable dyes. Dip the eggs in vinegar so that the dye will adhere better; drain and dry them. Prepare the dyes according to package instructions and let them cool.

With a white wax crayon or a small paintbrush dipped in melted candle wax, paint a design on the part of the egg that is to remain white. Lower the egg into yellow dye with a spoon; leave it there 5 minutes or more, turning it for an even coat. When the color is deep enough, lift it out and let it dry.

Next cover the areas you want to remain yellow with more wax and go on to dye with other colors: orange, red, green, blue, purple. It's best to limit each egg to three colors; otherwise the final shade will be dull.

After the final dye bath, place each egg on paper toweling in a warm oven, leaving the door open. When the wax looks shiny, remove the eggs and wipe away the wax with paper toweling.

Another resist method is to apply lines of masking liquid (sold in art stores) to cooled, hard-cooked eggs. Color the eggs as above, using chemical dyes, then peel off the masking material. Do not eat the eggs.

Eggs

Storing and cooking them

Eggs should be stored unwashed and covered (they absorb odors in an open container) in the refrigerator. They will keep this way for 3 to 5 weeks, but to enjoy their best qualities, use them as soon as possible.

Concerns exist today about *Salmonella enteritidis*, a bacterium in some eggs that causes food-borne illness. Symptoms (fever, vomiting, diarrhea, and cramps) begin 12 to 48 hours after eating contaminated raw eggs or lightly cooked eggs. The bacterium is killed by high heat; thoroughly cooking your eggs will ensure their safety.

Eggs cooked in the shell

In an enamel or stainless-steel pan (aluminum darkens), cover the eggs with cold water. Bring just to a boil, then lower the heat to simmer—cooking eggs in boiling water toughens them. For soft-cooked eggs, simmer for 7 minutes; hard-cooked, 12 to 15 minutes. Drain the eggs and immerse them in cold water to stop the cooking.

Poached eggs

Bring 1 to 2 inches of water to a boil. Break an egg into a saucer. Stir the water to create a whirlpool, then gently slip in the egg. Cook for 5 minutes. Remove egg with a slotted spoon.

Fried eggs

For each egg, heat in a skillet a mixture of 1 teaspoon margarine or butter and a few drops of canola or olive oil. When a drop of water sizzles in the pan, break in the eggs; after 3 minutes turn eggs over and cook for 1 to 2 more minutes. Or if you prefer eggs sunny-side up, cook until the white is firm and the yolk begins to thicken but is not hard (about 7 minutes). You can cover the pan to make sure the top gets thoroughly cooked and shorten the cooking time to 4 minutes.

Scrambled eggs

Allow 2 eggs per person. (For a lower-cholesterol dish, use 1 egg yolk for every 2 egg whites.) Lightly beat the eggs; add salt, pepper, and, if desired, herbs. Pour into a heated skillet coated with a mixture of margarine or butter and canola or olive oil. Cook over medium heat, stirring gently, until the eggs are firm throughout. For softer eggs, add 1 tablespoon milk or cream per egg. (See also *Omelets*.)

Egg whites

Separating whites and yolks; beating; folding

To crack the shell of an egg, give it a quick tap at the center with a knife. Hold the egg upright (so that the yolk remains in the lower half) and open the shell. Empty the egg white from the top half of the shell into a bowl, cutting it free with the edge of the lower shell. Slide the yolk into the top half; empty the white from the lower half. Repeat, if necessary. Drop the yolk into a second bowl. If the yolk breaks, drop it immediately into the

second bowl; yolk in the egg whites will decrease the whipped volume.

Beat egg whites at room temperature in a spotlessly clean bowl (grease or other contamination can adversely affect the results). For maximum volume, use an unlined copper bowl or, after beating to the foamy stage, add ¼ teaspoon cream of tartar for every four whites. Do not overbeat; whites should be whipped to a soft-peak or a stiff-peak stage, never to a dry one.

To fold beaten whites into yolks or a batter, pile the whites on top. With a rubber spatula quickly but gently rotate the mixture from the bottom of the bowl over the whites until all the whites have been incorporated.

Electric blankets

Using them properly; troubleshooting

When the power to a blanket is on, don't fold the blanket, lie on it, cover it, place a heavy object on it, tuck its wired parts under the mattress, or place the control unit near a radiator or windowsill.

If a blanket doesn't heat in a working receptacle, unplug it and check that all the connections are tight. Replace a blown fuse or reset a tripped circuit breaker. If the blanket still doesn't heat, or if it overheats, has hot spots, or repeatedly blows a fuse on a circuit that isn't overloaded with other appliances, then the heating element, control unit, or cords may be defective. Take the blanket to an authorized service shop for repair. Ask the shop to test and replace defective parts (control unit, switch, blanket). If the blanket is out of warranty, you may be better off buying a new one.

If a cord causes shock, have it or the entire control unit replaced. If the blanket shocks, unplug it and look for a stuck pin or metallic object.

Electric circuits

Installing a new circuit; connecting to the service panel

Before you install a new circuit in your house, check with your local electrical inspector about the materials and procedures required to meet electrical code requirements. Buy cable, breakers, connectors, ceiling and junction boxes, and receptacles as he advises.

Readying cable for connection
Shred 8 inches of plastic sheath from the ends of an NM (nonmetallic) cable with a ripper; cut off shreds with a

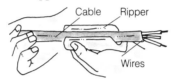

utility knife. If you're using BX cable (wires cased in a flexible spiral of galvanized steel), cut through one spiral at a right angle with a hacksaw. Firmly grasp the cable at either side of the cut and twist it apart. Unwrap a couple of turns of paper directly under the armor; rip it off. Bend the copper grounding strip over the outside of the cable. Push a fiber bushing into the cable end to prevent its sharp edge

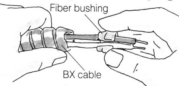

from cutting the wire insulation and causing a short circuit. Strip ¾ inch of insulation from each wire of the NM or BX cable with wire strippers.

Your cable must reach from the service panel to the first new outlet; splicing is not permitted. If you're running the cable along rafters, joists, or studs, staple or strap it fast or run it through ⅝-inch holes.

If you're running the cable behind a wall, you'll need a *fish tape*, a 25- or 50-foot reel of flattened steel spring wire. Drill holes into the wall, floor, or ceiling so that you can fish the cable from one location to another. Loop the stripped ends of cable wires over the fish-tape hook, then secure the bond with electrician's tape.

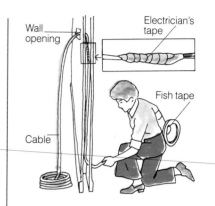

Installing a junction box

Make a template of the box (minus its ears and mounting plate) by placing it facedown on a piece of cardboard. Pencil this outline on the plasterboard wall, then cut it out with a utility knife. Secure the box with bracket tabs. Screw the plate holes to the wall.

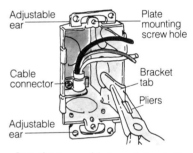

In a plaster-and-lath wall, locate the studs (see *Studs*); plan to install the box on the lath away from studs. Use a hammer and cold chisel to chip away enough plaster to fully expose a wooden lath strip. Make a template (including ears) as described. Pencil the outline so that the box will be centered on the lath. Drill ⅜-inch holes for screw tabs at two diagonal corners of the outline. Insert the tip of a keyhole saw into one of the holes and saw out the pattern. (Use a saber saw with a metal-cutting blade to cut through a metal lath.) Adjust the ears of the box and mark screw holes on the lath for securing the ears; drill the holes.

Slip a cable connector onto the end of the cable sheath; screw it fast. (Skip

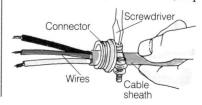

this step if the box is equipped with cable clamps.) Using an old screwdriver, push in a knockout hole in the box, then feed the cable end through this hole. Fit the box into the wall so that it is flush. Screw the box onto the lath, then secure the cable connector to the box. Patch the plaster around the box (see *Plaster patching*). Wire the receptacle (see *Electric receptacles*), then screw it to the box.

Connecting to the service panel

First turn off the main breaker; this shuts off all circuits. With a hammer and nail set, remove the central ring of a multiring knockout from the panel; pry up the next ring by levering a screwdriver with pliers; pull off the

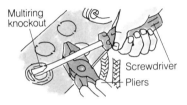

Multiring knockout
Screwdriver
Pliers

pried-up ring sections with pliers. After you have secured a connector to the cable sheath, flush to the stripped edge, connect the cable to the service panel through the knockout hole. If the panel's breaker space is limited, replace a standard breaker with a piggyback to which the leads of the old circuit and the new can be wired, or use two skinny (half-size) breakers.

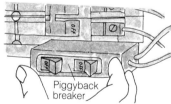

Piggyback breaker

Attach the bare ground and white wire to the ground bus, and the black wire to the piggyback breaker; screw them fast. Don't turn on the new circuit until it has been checked by an electrical inspector.

Electric receptacles

Replacing a faulty receptacle

House outlets for electric power are comprised of a cable that carries the power from a circuit-breaker panel or

a fuse box to a metal or plastic box containing a receptacle.

Caution: Before working on a receptacle, turn off the power to its circuit. To check that it is off, see *Circuit testing*.

If an outlet doesn't work, unscrew the cover plate and receptacle. Fix any loose or broken wires. Reinstall the receptacle; restore power. Plug in a working appliance. If it doesn't run, install a new receptacle.

Turn off the power. Unscrew the old wires. Clip them at the insulation, then strip ¾ inch of insulation from each wire. Hook the wire ends clock-

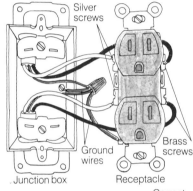

Silver screws
Ground wires
Junction box
Brass screws
Receptacle

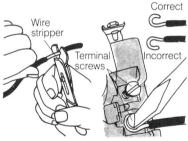

Wire stripper
Terminal screws
Correct
Incorrect

wise around the new receptacle's terminals, black to the brass screw, white to the silver one. Screw them fast. Or use a back-wired receptacle and insert the stripped wires into the two holes in its back. Screw the receptacle to the box. Replace the cover plate and restore power to the circuit.

Electric shavers

Cleaning; checking for wear; basic troubleshooting

To keep a shaver in good condition, clean the head and blades regularly and inspect them for wear. Blow out

hair after each use. Periodically brush the head; clean the blades with commercial spray or liquid cleaner, following package instructions.

Worn blades or screens may cause poor cutting or excessive noise. To inspect these parts in a flat-head shaver, unplug the shaver, set the selector dial on *Clean,* and lift off the shaving head. Push out the blades from the screen. In a curved-head shaver, lift off the screen and remove the cutter or the multiple oscillating blades. Look for gaps in the screen and nicks in the blades. Replace defective parts or the entire head. Return flat-head blades to the slots they came from; put multiple oscillating blades back in their original order.

To inspect a rotary-blade shaver, remove the shaving head assembly and loosen the knob at the back that holds the retaining plate. Remove the plate and inspect the cutters and cutting screens. Defective screens and cutters must be replaced as a unit.

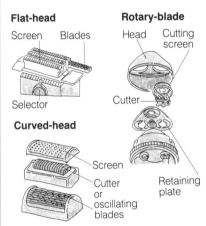

Flat-head
Screen Blades
Selector

Rotary-blade
Head Cutting screen
Cutter
Retaining plate

Curved-head
Screen
Cutter or oscillating blades

If the motor fails to run

Make sure the outlet is working and the shaver's dual voltage switch, if any, is properly set. Test the cord with a continuity tester (see *Power cords*); in cordless shavers, the power pack may have to be replaced.

A jammed head can cause the motor to hum but not run. If the shaver runs normally with the head off, replace the head.

If the power supply and head are all right, the *On-Off* switch, the motor, or the drive assembly may be at fault. Take the shaver to an authorized repair shop for servicing.

Electric slow cookers

The low-heat way to an easy one-pot meal

An electric slow cooker is ideal for stews and pot roasts. Suitable cuts are beef brisket, short ribs, round, or chuck, carefully trimmed of surface fat; also lamb shanks and pork hocks.

In the bottom of the cooker put a layer of quartered potatoes, carrot chunks, and diced medium or whole small onions. Place the meat on top. Add liquid: beef broth, tomato juice, or water; season lightly and cover. If you want to use wine, add it for the final hour of cooking. For 1½-inch-thick cuts, cook on *High* 4½ hours, or on *Low* 12 to 14. Add rice, pasta, or frozen vegetables ½ hour before serving; otherwise they will overcook. Add herbs or spices at the same time.

Electric switches

Testing and replacing a wall switch; mounting a switch box

A single-pole wall switch controls power to overhead lights or to a wall receptacle from one location. If a light fixture fails to work when the switch is turned on, check for a burned-out light bulb, a faulty plug or power cord, or a blown fuse or tripped circuit breaker. If the lamp still does not light, the switch may be worn.

Caution: Before working on a switch, turn off the power to its circuit (see *Circuit testing*). To check that it is off, unscrew the cover plate and mounting screws; carefully pull out the switch. Touch one probe of a neon test lamp to the box's metal shell; touch the other probe to one, then the other, terminal screw. The lamp should not light in either position.

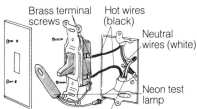

Brass terminal screws — Hot wires (black) — Neutral wires (white) — Neon test lamp — Grounding wires (bare copper or green)

In a middle-of-the-run switch, two black (or a black and a red) hot wires are attached to the switch's brass terminal screws. Loosen the screws and disconnect the wires. Leave the white neutral and bare grounding wires in the box as they are. In an end-of-the-run switch, a black and a white wire will be attached to the terminals; this white wire is hot, not neutral. (It may be marked with black paint or electrical tape.) Disconnect both wires.

Test the switch by attaching the alligator clip of a continuity tester to one terminal and the probe to the oth-

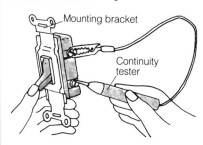

Mounting bracket — Continuity tester

er. Turn the switch on and off. The tester should light only when the switch is on. Next, attach the clip to the mounting bracket and the probe to one, then the other, terminal. Turn the switch on and off at both positions. The tester should not light. Replace a faulty switch with one of the same voltage and amperage.

To install the switch, hook a hot wire clockwise on each brass terminal; tighten the terminal screws. New switches may have a green grounding terminal. If the old switch did not

For steel-armored cable

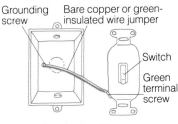

Grounding screw — Bare copper or green-insulated wire jumper — Switch — Green terminal screw

For plastic-sheathed cable

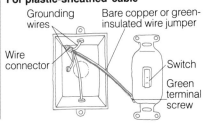

Grounding wires — Bare copper or green-insulated wire jumper — Wire connector — Switch — Green terminal screw

have one, run a bare or green insulated wire jumper from the green terminal screw to the wire connector linking the grounding wires in the box. If the cable serving the box is steel armored, run the jumper from the terminal to the box's grounding screw. Fit the wires and the switch into the box, screw the switch to the box, and remount the cover plate.

Mounting a new switch box

Follow instructions for installing new boxes in *Electric circuits*. Switches should be about 4 feet above the floor. Remove a knockout from the box for each cable that will enter it. Feed 8 inches of stripped cable through each hole; secure the cable at the end of its insulation with the internal clamp

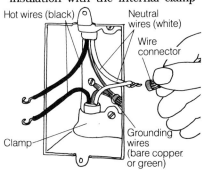

Hot wires (black) — Neutral wires (white) — Wire connector — Clamp — Grounding wires (bare copper or green)

usually supplied with wall boxes. After you have mounted the box, join the stripped ends of the white wires and the bare grounding wires with wire connectors. If the box is metal, run a grounding jumper from the grounding wires to the box. Install the switch as described above. (See also *Dimmer switches; Electric receptacles; Three-way switches; Wiring.*)

Elevator safety

Avoiding crime; if an elevator stalls; safety devices

Don't board an elevator with someone who appears suspicious; wait for the next car. If you're on the ground floor waiting to go up, don't board an elevator headed for the basement; pick it up on its return. Before entering an elevator, check the security mirror, if any. Inside, try to stand near the control panel. If a suspect person enters an elevator you're on, get off immediately. If you are threatened or attacked, press the alarm and as many floor buttons as you can—and yell.

Don't smoke in an elevator. It is annoying to others, a potential fire hazard and, in many cities, illegal. In a fire emergency, use designated stairways or fire escapes—not elevators—to exit the building.

If an elevator stalls

Stay calm. Press the alarm and use the in-elevator telephone, if any. If neither works, bang on the walls or door with a shoe or other heavy object. Then wait for rescue; don't try to climb out without the assistance of a trained emergency crew.

Safety devices

Modern elevators are very safe. If a car's descent exceeds a certain speed, an independently powered speed governor trips a safety switch that activates the brake on the elevator's hoisting machine. If the car continues to accelerate, the governor causes safety clamps to grip the guide rails, bringing the elevator to a smooth, safe stop.

Other devices prevent cars from moving with open doors or doors from opening when a car isn't at a landing. Be careful not to trip or get hit by closing gates when entering or exiting older, manually operated elevators.

Embroidery

Some basic techniques; five basic stitches

To keep fabric taut and easy to stitch, secure it in an embroidery hoop, making sure that the weave is not pulled askew. Cut yarn no longer than 18 inches to avoid fraying and knotting. To secure yarn at the start, hold the yarn end on the wrong side and work stitches over 2 inches of it (A). To finish off yarn, slide the needle under 2 inches of stitching on the wrong side;

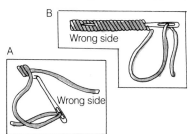

never make a knot (B). For even stitch tension, use a stabbing motion when possible: push the needle straight down through the fabric, draw the yarn through to the other side, then bring the needle straight up. The following are commonly used stitches; work each one as illustrated.

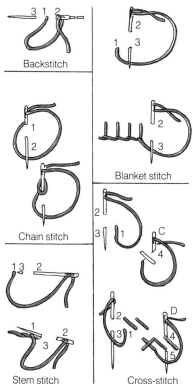

Backstitch: used as a straight outline stitch and as a baseline for other decorative stitches. (Note that the distance between 3-1 and 1-2 are equal.)

Blanket stitch: used as a finishing stitch for edges. Keep the stitch heights even as you work. (Note that point 3 of the first stitch is also point 1 of the subsequent stitch.)

Chain stitch: used for outlining or filling in areas. (Note that point 2 of the first stitch becomes point 1 of the next stitch.) To end a chain row take a small stitch over the last chain loop.

Cross-stitch: used for outlining, filling, or forming geometric shapes. The stitch can be formed in two ways: one stitch at a time, as in (C); or in two rows of slanted stitches, as in (D).

Stem stitch: used for outlining and for stems in floral designs. (Note that point 3 of the first stitch becomes point 1 of the subsequent stitch.)

Eviction notices

Responding to your landlord's efforts to make you move out of your rented home

If you find an official-looking document from your landlord in your mailbox or posted on your door telling you to vacate your home by a certain date, you have received an eviction notice. A landlord has a legal right to demand that you vacate the premises if you fail to live up to responsibilities spelled out in your lease. Generally, if you are late with your rent payments, repeatedly throw loud parties until the wee hours of the morning despite complaints, or refuse to move when your lease is up, your landlord has grounds to evict you.

Each state has its own eviction procedure, but an eviction notice is usually the first step in the battle between you and your landlord. When you receive the notice, don't ignore it and don't put off dealing with it until later. Read the notice carefully to learn why your landlord no longer wants you as a tenant. Then contact a lawyer immediately to see if your landlord has followed the proper legal procedure and whether he or she has grounds to evict you.

If the notice doesn't meet the legal requirements—for instance, stating how much behind you are in rent—it has no effect. You usually have only a short time period, perhaps 3 days, to respond before the landlord can take you to court.

How to respond

Reply in writing. A prompt and well-prepared response to an eviction notice will save you needless time, money, and annoyance. Date the reply and send it by certified mail, return receipt requested. This gives you proof, if you should later need it, that you responded promptly.

In most states you can stop an eviction for nonpayment of rent by paying what is due anytime before the court makes its decision. If your landlord claims that your lease has expired, send him or her a copy of the lease, extension, renewal, or other agreement that proves otherwise.

Examinations

Preparing for and taking tests

There are two main types of examinations: standardized tests, such as the Scholastic Aptitude Tests, and tests made up by a teacher. Each requires a different sort of preparation.

The best way to prepare for a teacher's test is to keep up with the reading and study assignments. That failing, at least keep all quizzes, tests, and graded homework papers. Go over them for clues to your strengths and weaknesses. Note also the teacher's likes and dislikes, pet theories, and ideas that he or she has emphasized. They will probably appear in the test.

Several weeks before the exam, find out all you can about it. What material will it cover? How long will it be? Will it be multiple choice, true-false, fill in the blanks, short or long essay? If a combination of these, how will the time be allotted and how much weight will be given to each section in the scoring? Ask former students what the teacher's tests are like. If you are taking a standardized test, find out whether it is better to guess or to leave an answer blank.

For course exams, ask the teacher the above questions. For a standardized test, get a descriptive bulletin with practice questions from your teacher or guidance counselor or the company that distributes the test. Go over the pamphlet several times. You can also buy books that give extensive practice questions and strategies for almost every standardized exam.

Effective review

Two weeks before the exam, gather all your course material: textbook, lecture notes, reading notes, quizzes, and homework papers. Take a couple of hours to go through this material, writing down the important topics. You might, for example, list the major heads and topic sentences in the textbook. Recall the points emphasized by the teacher. Then check the topics you are least sure of (your homework and quiz papers will come in handy now), and study these. Save your review of more familiar material until closer to the test time.

As you study, interact with your material. Don't just read passively. Take notes on your notes. Underline with color. Make lists of definitions. Rework the math problems that you missed or work out new ones. To review facts, definitions, details, or vocabulary, make up 3 x 5 cards with short questions or definitions on one side and answers on the other. Go over and over these by yourself or with friends; even on essay tests you'll need facts to back up your ideas.

Test taking

Take a clock or watch; pacing yourself is important. Read or listen to the instructions with utmost care. On standardized tests, be sure you understand how to mark your answers. If you're uncertain about any part of the instructions, ask.

On multiple-choice tests, read all answers to each question. If one answer seems right, mark it down. If you're not sure, skip to the next question. Work with care, but don't dawdle. You should consider all questions once; then go through the test again, picking up any you skipped. The second time through, try to get the answer by the process of elimination. If you decide three choices are wrong but don't know which of the remaining two are right, play your hunches—but avoid wild guesses.

On true-false questions, remember that the longer the question, the more likely it is to be true. Words such as "always" and "never" usually signal a false answer; words such as "sometimes," "often," or "usually" may indicate that the answer is true. Your first response is likely to be right; don't change it without good reason.

Essay exams

Read the questions carefully. If you have several essays to choose from and you must write more than one, choose all your topics before starting to write. On the back of your exam book or on a separate piece of paper, write down the ideas that immediately come to mind on each essay. For each essay, underline the key instruction word or words such as "compare," "discuss," "evaluate"; then be sure you do what is asked. Again on separate paper, jot down a quick outline of your first essay. Use about one-

third of your allotted time planning your answers and two-thirds writing. Use the best grammar, spelling, and penmanship you know. Neatness and care will affect your grade.

Exercises

Increasing flexibility and strengthening muscles

Any physical exertion is exercise. At any age everyone benefits from exercise, yet it need not be strenuous (see *Aerobics*). Exercise should be done slowly, at a pace that is comfortable for you. The benefits accrue from repeating the routine at least three to five times a week for a period of 20 to 30 minutes each time.

The stretch-and-flex exercises that follow will improve flexibility. To get their benefit, stretch until you feel mild tension; then hold at that point. Push-ups, sit-ups, and leg raises are for increasing muscle strength.

Head rolls. Turn head to left, back to center, then to right, center. With chin on chest, slowly turn head left, back to center, then right, center.

Shoulder shrugs. Stand with arms at sides, roll shoulders toward ears, drop shoulders. Repeat three times.

Arm circles. Stand with knees relaxed, pelvis tucked under, arms extended. Circle arms in one direction, then the other, first small circles, then larger ones.

Ankle rotation. With knees relaxed, lift one foot slightly, flex and point four times; then circle foot twice in each direction.

Side stretches. Stand with legs apart, knees relaxed. Raise left arm toward ceiling, keeping it close to ear. Bend to right, sliding right arm down leg. On repeat, raise both arms toward ceiling. Bend to right and hold; don't bounce. Repeat to left.

Twists. Standing with arms outstretched, turn upper torso to right; left heel should lift off floor. Repeat to left, with right heel rising. Repeat sequence with elbows bent.

Reach and climb. Stand with legs apart. Reach one arm up as far as possible; then lower it slightly and reach with the other arm. Alternate the reach-and-climb motion from one side to the other.

Arm crossovers. Stand with knees relaxed, hug and cross arms in front of body, then stretch them out to side.

Sitting stretches. Sit tall with legs straddled, toes pointed up, knees relaxed. Reach forward over the leg to a space above the toes. Hold at least 15 seconds; repeat over other leg. Put soles of feet together; hold ankles. Bending from hips and keeping head up, gently pull yourself forward until you feel stretch in the groin area.

Alternate leg raises. Lie on one side, both legs extended (bottom leg may be bent slightly). Move top leg up and down, toes pointed at ceiling. Repeat on other side. Change the muscles worked by turning toes parallel to floor or pointing down.

Cat back. Kneel on hands and knees. Pull stomach in, put chin on chest, and arch back upward like a cat. Reverse arch by bringing head up and dipping spine to form a U.

Side stretch

Sitting stretch

Leg raise

Cat back

Push-ups and sit-ups. These are progressive. Select your own level and pace; move up a level when you can do 16 to 20 with ease. If your feet leave the floor in sit-ups, drop back a level.

Push-up levels. 1. Lift head and shoulders only; hold momentarily. 2. Push up from floor with arms and

roll back onto heels. Reverse sequence, returning to floor. 3. Bend lower leg, weight on upper leg above knee, and push body up, keeping arms straight. Return and repeat. 4. Push entire body up with full arm extension. Do not hyperextend back.

Sit-up levels. 1. Raise arms and shoulders only. When that's easy, raise more of body, pressing hands to floor. Progressively more difficult is raising the body with hands at thighs, with arms across stomach, across the chest and, finally, hands to ears. 2. Do *not* lace hands behind head.

Expansion tanks

Recharging a water-logged tank with air

A layer of air in the expansion tank of a hot-water heating system provides a cushion as the water expands and contracts. If water spurts from the pressure-relief valve on the boiler and the expansion tank feels uniformly hot all over, the tank needs recharging with air.

On some tanks a combination valve lets in air as water drains out through a hose. Turn off power to the boiler; allow the boiler to cool. Attach a hose, turn off the shut-off valve between the tank and the boiler; open the combination valve and empty the tank. Reverse procedures; turn on the power.

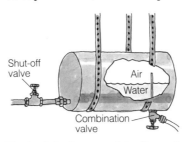

Shut-off valve

Air

Water

Combination valve

If a tank lacks a combination valve, drain the water into buckets. If your system has a diaphragm tank (usually suspended from a pipe) leave the job of recharging it to an expert: the diaphragm is easily ruptured.

Extension cords

Safe usage and repairs

Caution: Always disconnnect a cord at both ends before working on it.

Because extension cords are a safety hazard, some local electrical codes forbid their use. Check your local code before undertaking a repair; you may have to discard your extension cord.

New electrical codes require receptacles every 6 feet along the walls; this rule doesn't apply to older homes. If you must use an extension cord, remember it is only a temporary connection. Unplug it and store it after each use. Most extension cords are marked with an ampere rating. Never exceed the rating; it could start a fire.

If a cord's insulation is frayed or cracked or the wire is exposed, discard the cord and buy a new one. If the cord's plug or its receptacle on the other end is damaged, replace either with a new one (see *Plugs*).

Eyebrows

Shaping and coloring them

A slight tweezing can improve eyebrow shape, as long as you retain their natural look. Keep the eyebrows in proportion to your face by tweezing stray hairs that grow between your brows and below them and that extend too far beyond the outer corner of the eye. Do not tweeze the brow top; this will destroy the natural line.

Just before tweezing, press a warm, wet washcloth over your brow. Heat will make the hair roots a little easier to extract. Pluck hairs one at a time, pulling in the direction that the hairs grow. Refresh the area afterward with a cotton pad soaked in astringent.

Brush your brows daily, using an eyebrow brush or an old, soft toothbrush. A touch of petroleum jelly will add gloss and keep them in shape.

Pale brows can be colored with an eyebrow pencil using light, feathery strokes. Never apply a hair-coloring product to your eyebrows. The strong solution could cause blindness.

E

Eyeglasses

Home repairs you can make on your eyeglasses

If you wear eyeglasses, your eyesight depends on their proper adjustment. Therefore, it's important to know which repairs you can make at home and which are best left to an optician.

The easiest home repair is replacing the tiny screws that hold the earpieces to the front of the frame. You can buy an inexpensive repair kit containing four screws and a very small screwdriver from your optician. (If a screw falls out unexpectedly and you don't have a small enough screwdriver, use the point of a kitchen knife.)

Some repair kits also contain tiny rubber rings meant for tightening loose-fitting glasses. Just slip the ring over the end of the earpiece and slide it down to the hinge. The ring will sit right on the hinge and keep it from bending too far.

Wire frames have tiny screws that hold the top and bottom of the frame together. If a screw becomes loose and a lens falls out, replace the lens, and the screw, and add a small drop of clear nail polish between the two barrels on the frame before tightening. The polish will assure that further vibration will not loosen the screw.

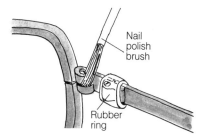

Nail polish brush

Rubber ring

Don't use strong glues to hold a loose lens in a plastic or metal frame. The glue will bond the lens and frame, and if later you wish to have the frame replaced or the lens position adjusted, your optician will be unable to do so.

The tightening of earpieces should be done by a professional; improper adjustment may impair your vision or cause headaches. Temporarily mend a broken earpiece with epoxy, but visit your optician at your earliest convenience to get a replacement.

Eye injury

Emergency treatment for scratches, blows, foreign objects, and chemicals

Cup a hand over an injured eye, try not to blink, and let your tears flow freely. Tears form a protective film, whereas rubbing may cause a foreign object to cut the eye or a liquid irritant to spread further.

If a foreign object can't be removed (see *Eyewinker*), or if the eye still hurts after the object is out, the eyeball may have been cut. Close the eye, and cover it with a pad of cotton wool, gauze, or a folded handkerchief extending from the forehead to the cheek. Tape the pad in place to keep eye movement to a minimum until you get to a doctor.

A blow that causes a black eye can also injure the eye itself, causing internal bleeding leading to infection. Cover the eye with a cold compress, then have a doctor examine it.

Rarely, a splinter or other sharp object impales the eye. Don't pull the object out. Cover the eye and the object with a paper cup, or bend a sturdy piece of paper into a cone. Tape that protection in place while the person is transported to the hospital.

Chemicals splashed into the eye must be washed out instantly before you even take time to call a doctor. Have the person lie flat on his back near a sink or hose. Hold the eyelids open with thumb and finger and pour water gently but generously over the eye for 15 minutes.

Eye makeup

Enhancing your eyes

Choose eye-shadow colors that contrast with or enhance the color of your eyes rather than those that match it exactly. Violet eye shadow, for example, brings out the green in hazel eyes; topaz makes brown eyes look deeper. Mauve, coral, and gray are flattering to blue eyes.

Eye shadow should also complement your skin tone and the color of your clothing. Muted shades look best in the daytime; use iridescent or bright colors at night, if at all.

If your eyes are the classic oval, brush a medium shade from the eye crease to the lashes, a slightly darker shade along the eye crease, and a light shadow along the browbone. Blend the colors up and out.

If your eyes are less than perfect ovals, you can redefine their shape with shadow. Keep in mind that a light color will bring an eye area forward; a dark color will subdue it.

To make small or deep-set eyes seem larger, use a pale shade from the browbone to the eyelashes. Extend them even more by applying a small *V* of a slightly darker shade just beyond the outer eye corners. Prominent eyes will recede if you use a dark shade over the entire lid almost to the browbone.

To make close-set eyes seem farther apart, use a pale shade on the third of the lids near the nose, a darker shade near the temple. Reverse this to make wide-set eyes seem closer together.

 Use a liquid or pencil eyeliner to emphasize shape. Make a thin line as near the eyelashes as possible, also on the outer third of the lower lid; smudge it gently for a natural effect.

For a wide-awake look, use an eyelash curler before applying mascara. Hold the curler near the base of the lashes and squeeze; count to three, then release. Move the curler farther out toward the tips of the lashes and squeeze again.

Apply mascara with your eyes open. Holding the wand vertically, coat the tips of the upper lashes, then sweep the wand horizontally over the lashes from base to tips. If you like, you can also apply mascara to the lower lashes. Should any lashes clump, separate them with the wand tip. Use a cotton swab for cleanups.

Eyes

Eye disorders; what can be done about them

Common eye problems are nearsightedness, farsightedness, astigmatism (distorted vision), and presbyopia. The latter starts at about age 40 when most people have trouble focusing on close objects. All four conditions can be corrected with eyeglasses or contact lenses (see *Eyesight testing*).

Many serious eye disorders can be treated or prevented if you heed certain danger signals. Flashes of light or floating shapes seen before the eyes may indicate a detached retina. See a doctor promptly.

In the course of an eye examination, anyone over 40 should be tested for glaucoma, a disorder that can lead to blindness. Because there are no overt symptoms until sight is affected, it is important to have this test yearly, especially if there is glaucoma in your family. In most cases glaucoma can be stabilized with eyedrops.

Cataracts, another common age-related eye disorder, are opaque areas that cloud the lens, progressively reducing vision. The only treatment is surgery to remove the affected lens. Vision is then corrected with eyeglasses or contact lenses or with plastic lenses implanted during surgery.

Still another threat to sight, macular degeneration, usually develops gradually and painlessly but eventually destroys central vision. Although the condition usually is untreatable, eyeglasses with powerful magnifying lenses can often improve vision. If, as happens rarely, it begins with the sudden onset of distortion and "blank spots," see a doctor promptly; sometimes it can be treated with a laser.

A child with crossed eyes should be seen by an eye doctor as soon as you notice the condition. It is caused by weak eye muscles; youngsters do not outgrow it. Treatment may be as simple as glasses or a patch over the unaffected eye so that the child is forced to use the weak one. A severe case may require surgery. (See also *Conjunctivitis; Contact lenses; Eye injury; Eyewinker; Styes.*)

Eyesight testing

Checking for vision problems

Have a child's eyes tested before he enters school; otherwise, an undetected problem may hamper learning. From childhood on, periodic vision tests are vital: every year until about age 20; less often between ages 20 and 40, when vision changes little; and yearly after that.

Suspect problems if a child rubs his eyes often, shuts or covers one eye, is highly sensitive to light, if one eye turns in or out, or if his eyes burn or are red, teary, or itchy. At any age if there is a sudden change in vision or if you are squinting, holding your work close to your eyes, or making unusual efforts to see, have your eyes tested.

An optometrist is trained and authorized to test visual acuity, using a chart from which you read letters of diminishing size from a set distance. He can prescribe and make glasses or contact lenses and test for glaucoma (see *Eyes*). An ophthalmologist is a medical doctor, who can, in addition, diagnose and treat eye disease, and examine eyes for internal problems.

Eyewinker

Removing a foreign object from your eye

Caution: Never try to remove anything embedded in the eyeball. Cover your eye; don't rub it. Get medical help promptly.

Attempt to remove only an object floating on the white or stuck under an eyelid. Seat yourself before a well-lighted mirror, look up, and gently pull the lower lid down. If you see the speck, pick it off with the corner of a tissue. If not, ease the upper lid down over the lower, then let it slide back. If that doesn't work, look down and lift the upper lid, folding it back over a cotton swab. Pick off the speck if you see it; otherwise, cover the eye and seek medical help. You can do the same for another person; make sure to have good light.

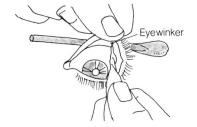
Eyewinker

Facial care

Daily and weekly regimens

A daily routine to cleanse, tone, and maintain moisture level is essential to sustaining healthy facial skin. Clean your skin thoroughly at least twice a day and change your pillowcase often. Particularly important is the nighttime washing, which removes accumulated skin oils, makeup, and dirt.

If you have oily skin, use a liquid or bar soap formulated for your skin type; rinse thoroughly. Dry skins thrive on superfatted soap, creamy washes, or cleansing creams; normal skins can take a mild soap or cleanser. Thorough rinsing is essential. Most skins, except extrasensitive or very dry types, need occasional exfoliation (removal of the top layer of dead skin cells). Do this with a scrub cleanser or by going over your face very gently with a rough washcloth or an abrasive puff moistened with soap.

Toning

Refresh the skin after cleansing and remove any remaining impurities by wiping your face with a cotton ball soaked in skin freshener; avoid the delicate eye area. If your skin is oily, use an alcohol-base astringent. Dry skin benefits from a mild, herbal toner, which often is all the cleansing needed in the morning. A freshener should make your skin tingle and feel taut. If it stings, it's too strong.

Moisturizers and facials

Normal and dry-skinned faces, also dry areas on an oily face, benefit from

155

a thin layer of moisturizer applied after toning and before makeup. If your skin is very dry, or if you live in a cold or dry climate, apply an emollient cream to your skin right after the nighttime wash (see *Beauty creams*).

To remove deep-seated impurities and stimulate circulation, you can give yourself a facial. Boil some water, adding two chamomile tea bags for an herb scent. Remove all makeup and cover your hair with a shower cap. Pour the water into a basin, drape a towel over your head to trap the steam, and hold your face about 1 foot above the water for up to 10 minutes. Blot your face dry, then apply a mask (a clay formula for oily skin, a creamy hydrating mask for dry skin). Don't apply the mask too close to your eyes, mouth, or hairline. Leave on as directed; remove it, then rinse with cool water and apply moisturizer.

Fainting

What to do for a feeling of faintness or an actual faint

Faintness (a weak, light-headed, unsteady feeling) precedes fainting (loss of consciousness). The cause is usually a temporarily diminished supply of blood, and thus oxygen, to the brain. Shock, great pain, or acute stress can bring on a faint, as can ordinary events—standing after stooping, getting winded, skipping meals.

To get over a faint feeling and avoid fainting, lie down with legs raised or sit and put your head between your knees until the feeling passes.

If you notice someone fainting, break his fall, and lay the person down on his back. Raise his legs. Usually he'll revive in a few minutes. If unconsciousness lasts any longer, get medical help. If he's not breathing and has no pulse, in addition begin CPR (see *Pulse* and *CPR*).

Raise him gradually; otherwise he may faint again. Determine whether there are any symptoms that may indicate the need for prompt medical attention. Even if consciousness returns quickly, the person should see a doctor. (See also *Carbon monoxide poison; Shock; Unconsciousness.*)

Family tree

Tracing your ancestry

Start with the newest twigs on the family tree, yourself or your children, and trace your roots back through the generations. A loose-leaf notebook is useful for keeping data in order. An ancestor chart is a convenient way to show relationships; you can draw up

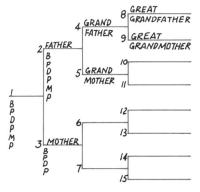

your own or buy printed forms by mail through genealogical magazines or at genealogical libraries.

When you have completed your record of direct ancestry, you might want to attempt a genealogical chart that shows all the branches of your family. Start with a grandparent or a great-grandparent and work forward. This is a far more complicated, but fascinating, task. The illustration below shows a small portion of such a chart.

	JOHN RAIBLE-RUTH			
ERIC-MARY	PHILLIP		LISA-PAUL	
RYAN			BELL	
LOIS-BOB	CHAS	ROGER-JAN	SUE	
KENT		LEE		
JANE	ANDRES	DON	DORIS	GAYLE

With either record try to obtain for each person dates and places of birth and death (see *Birth certificates*), date and place of marriage, and the name of the spouse. To enrich family history, you might also make a biographical sheet for each person and include achievements, occupation, and other news, even photographs, if available.

Gather information first from relatives (take notes or tape record and

note down the source), read through family letters, documents, diaries, baby books, and scrapbooks. Correspondence with distant relatives can lend a special dimension to the quest.

To widen your search, look at the genealogical resources of your library. Other good sources are county and church records, cemeteries, census, pension, and military records (the last three can be obtained from the National Archives in Washington, DC), and the *Catalogue of Genealogies* in the Library of Congress.

Fans

Keeping cool with a well-maintained fan

Caution: Unplug the power cord before cleaning or repairing a fan.

Every 2 weeks of use, vacuum a fan with a crevice-cleaning attachment. At least twice during the summer, sponge dirt from the blades, grille, and other external components with a mild detergent solution. If the owner's manual advises it, put several drops of light machine oil in the oil hole of the motor.

If a fan rattles, tighten the screws or nuts around the blade guard or, if it's a window fan, the screws holding the grilles. A whirring sound may indicate a bent metal blade. Insert a pencil through the grille and hold it so that the leading edge of one blade just touches the pencil's point. Rotate the

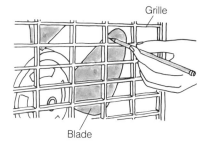

blades by hand to check their alignment. Try to straighten a bent blade with your finger. If you can't, install a set of replacement blades.

Replacing a blade

Open a two-piece blade guard at the clips or remove the screws or nuts holding a one-piece guard and work it off. Loosen the setscrew in the blade hub with an Allen wrench or a screwdriver, depending on the screw style, and slide the blade off. Install replacement blades, and screw the setscrew against the shaft's flat surface. Plastic blades are secured by a spinner that unscrews like a nut. Turn the blades by hand to check for alignment.

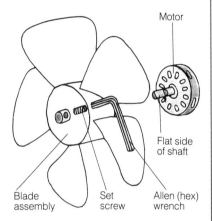

On a fan that won't oscillate, tighten the oscillation nut. If this fails, unplug the fan and oscillate it by hand. If the fan swings freely, the gears are stripped; take the fan to a repair shop. Professional repairs are the answer too if a fan continually blows its circuit or gives a shock when touched.

Faucets

Eliminating leaks

There are several types of faucets, each repaired in its own way. Before working on any faucet, shut off the water under the sink or basin and open the faucet to drain trapped water. Protect finished surfaces of fittings by covering the jaws of your wrench or pliers with electrician's tape. Take any part you are replacing to the plumbing supply store and get an exact duplicate. When reassembling a faucet, coat all parts with heatproof, waterproof grease to provide a good seal, assure smooth movement, and facilitate later disassembly.

Stem faucets

A stem faucet consists of a threaded stem assembly that turns the flow of water on or off, a seat washer that keeps water from leaking out the spout, and a packing nut and sealant that prevents leaks at the top of the stem. To disassemble a stem faucet, remove the handle, unscrew the packing nut or stem nut, and lift out the stem.

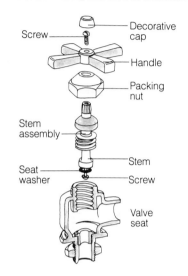

To fix a leak at the spout, remove the screw holding the washer and replace the washer. If your stem assembly has a diaphragm shaped like a top hat instead of a washer, pull off the worn diaphragm and snap on a new one.

If changing the washer doesn't stop the leak, you may need to replace or resurface the valve seat. Examine it with a flashlight to see if it looks pitted and worn. Most newer valve seats can be removed with a seat wrench. Simply insert the wrench, turn it counterclockwise, and lift out the seat. Lubricate the outside of a new seat with pipe-joint compound, push the seat firmly onto the seat wrench, and screw it into place.

If the seat can't be removed, smooth the rough surface with a seat-dress-

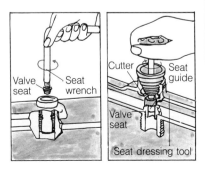

ing tool fitted with a cutter the exact size of the seat. Screw the tool into the faucet so that the cutter is flush against the valve seat and the guide fits snugly inside the valve. Turn the handle of the tool until it moves smoothly. Remove the tool and rinse away the grindings.

Water seeping out around a faucet is usually the fault of the packing. Try gently tightening the packing nut. If the leak persists, replace whatever was used to seal the faucet stem: packing washer, O-ring, or self-forming packing. To replace self-forming packing, remove the old packing and wind enough new packing onto the stem to fill the packing nut, then add half again as much; the nut will compact it.

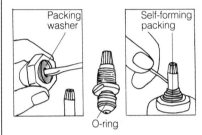

Single-lever faucets

The interior mechanism of single-lever faucets differs from model to model. When repair is needed, a kit of replacement parts or a whole new cartridge must be purchased to fit the specific faucet. Detailed disassembly instructions are included in the kits. Remember to keep the drain closed and lay out the parts in the order you removed them.

Getting at the innards of the faucet may be your biggest repair challenge. As single-lever faucets become more streamlined, their screws are more carefully hidden—tucked under the lever or covered by decorative plates or buttons. When you find the screw, you may need a small Allen wrench to get it out; this usually comes with the kit.

Shower and bathtub faucets

To repair a wall-mounted shower or bathtub stem faucet you may need a plumber's socket wrench to get the stem out of the wall. Chip away plaster, if need be, and insert the socket wrench into the wall. Repair as you would an equivalent sink or basin faucet. Repair a single-lever shower or tub faucet by replacing the cartridge.

Fence pickets

Replacing a damaged picket

When you take a broken picket from a fence, carefully remove an unbroken picket to serve as a pattern for the replacement. Trace its shape onto a knot-free board that is the same width and thickness as the original.

Cut the new picket with a band, saber, or jigsaw. Sand it, rounding the edges slightly so that water will run off. To seal out moisture, paint the pickets and rails where they will join.

While the paint is still wet, nail the two pickets on with galvanized finishing nails. Set the nailheads below the surface, fill the holes with wood putty, and paint or stain the new picket to match the rest of the fence.

Fence posts and rails

Making a rail fence; repair and replacement

Like any wood that comes into contact with the soil, fence posts are prone to decay. If you can't get decay-resistant wood, such as locust, cedar, redwood, Osage orange, red mulberry, or tamarack, use pressure-treated lumber or—as a last resort—apply a nontoxic preservative to the posts yourself (see *Wood preservatives*).

Before starting work, drive a stake at each end of the fence line and stretch a string to serve as a guide in aligning the posts. Level the string to determine how high each post needs to be, and position the posts by dropping a plumb line from the string (see *Leveling; Plumb line*).

At least one-third of a post's total length should be underground (2 feet

Post-hole diggers

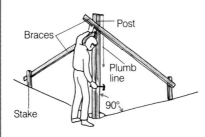

Auger for clay soil   Blade for sandy soil   Clamshell for rocky soil

in any case). With a post-hole digger, excavate a hole twice the diameter of the post, its sides angled outward at the bottom. Make it deep enough to put a large flat stone beneath the post.

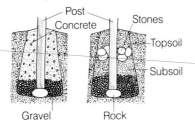

Set the post on the stone and pack 4 to 6 inches of gravel around it. Then align the post with the guide string, plumb it, and brace it as shown.

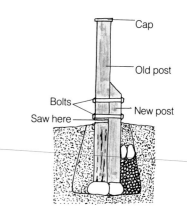

If frost heaving is a problem in your area and flooding is not, fill the hole with heavy subsoil to within 6 inches of the top, using a 2 x 4 to tamp it down firmly as you go. Then force several large stones around the post to keep it in position. Fill the rest of the hole with topsoil, mounding it up around the post. (In warm areas, in sandy soil, or in places where the water level is high, use concrete instead of soil and rocks.)

To protect the tops of posts from moisture, chamfer the edges or attach drip caps of wood or metal.

Attaching rails
The simplest kind of rails are nailed onto the posts. Use the guide string to keep them level; secure them with galvanized nails. The next simplest are split rails that slide into holes drilled through the posts. Rails with tenons that fit into mortises must be assembled as the posts are being set.

Repairs and replacements
A wobbly post can sometimes be firmed by driving wooden wedges around its base. Usually, however, wobbly or skewed posts are rotten beneath the surface. To avoid replacing

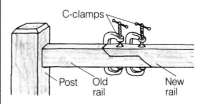

such a post, sink a new, shorter post next to it and bolt the two together; or, if they do not touch, insert a spacer block between them and wrap both with perforated metal strapping. Saw the old post off at the soil line.

To replace a mortised rail, splice a new rail onto the mortised end. Glue and screw the joint in place.

Fern gardens

Hardy ferns for outdoors

North American ferns range from small, lacy maidenhairs to 15-foot-tall tree ferns. Wherever you live, there are some to add a touch of green to a shady nook. Many can survive only in their native environments; others will live almost anywhere. Many are protected by law; do not gather wild ferns unless you know that they are not among the protected ones.

A reputable dealer or your Cooperative Extension Agent (see p. 5) will help you choose ferns suited to your soil, climate, and garden conditions. Soil pH is critical; lime-loving ferns simply will not grow in acid soil, nor will acid-loving ones grow in alkaline soil. Once established, however, most ferns will thrive for years with little care.

Place large plants—such as shield, lady, cinnamon, deer, or royal ferns—

in the center of the bed. Surround them with such medium-size ones as hardy maidenhairs, hart's-tongues, Japanese painted ferns, male ferns, and sensitive ferns. Use polypodys, maidenhair spleenworts, and other small, spreading ferns as a border. Incorporate bulbs and wildflowers to brighten the bed in spring.

Planting and care

Most ferns need loose, well-drained soil rich in humus. Before planting, dig or rototill the bed to a depth of at least 9 inches. Work in a 3-inch layer of leaf mold or compost and a sprinkling of bonemeal. Set each fern so that its crown is level with the soil; then firm the soil around it. Water thoroughly. Apply an organic mulch, such as dry leaves or peat moss, to retain moisture and discourage weeds.

Add mulch in fall; leave dead fronds on nonevergreen species. In spring, remove dead fronds and all other material that cannot be crumbled by hand. Do not use rakes or forks; fern roots are easily damaged. Pull weeds, and add fresh mulch. Fertilize occasionally with a high-nitrogen plant food diluted to half strength. In dry weather, water deeply one to three times a week to keep soil moist.

Ferns

Growing them indoors

Despite their frail looks, many ferns are tough, long-lasting houseplants that survive in sunless corners where most plants cannot grow. They need warmth, humidity, and lots of water.

Keep them out of direct sunlight; they do best in bright filtered light at room temperatures. During the growing season, water generously with tepid water. Mist the fronds daily when temperatures are above 70°F; during hot spells place the pots on saucers full of wet pebbles. Feed once a month with nitrogen-rich plant food, diluted to half the recommended strength. In winter, let the top of the soil dry out between waterings; do not feed.

Repot only when roots fill the pot. Plant in a mixture of 2 parts sterilized potting soil, 2 parts peat moss or leaf mold, 1 part coarse sand or perlite,

and some charcoal granules. When plants get crowded, divide them or cut away some root growth and repot.

Many kinds, such as Boston ferns, mother ferns, Venushairs, and some maidenhairs, are ideal for hanging baskets. Miniatures, such as button ferns and small table ferns, can live in terrariums with virtually no care. The epiphytic staghorn fern can grow on a piece of bark or cork hung on the wall; water and feed it by immersing the mount in a container of tepid water.

Fertilizing houseplants

Keeping your plants healthy

Newly potted plants need no fertilizing, but the nutrients in the soil will soon need replenishing. Fertilize only during the growing season and never when the roots are very dry.

Most plant foods contain three major nutrients—nitrogen, phosphorus, and potassium—in various ratios (see *Fertilizing vegetables*). Most houseplants flourish on the usual 15-30-15 blend, but flowering plants benefit from a high-potassium formula such as 8-6-12 (sold as tomato food). To keep foliage plants lush, use fish emulsion or another high-nitrogen fertilizer instead of a balanced blend for every fifth feeding.

Plant-food concentrates are safe as long as their solutions are not too strong; too much fertilizer can damage a plant's roots. It is generally better to dilute a fertilizer to half the recommended strength and apply more often. For a quick tonic to an undernourished plant, spray the foliage with liquid fertilizer diluted to one-quarter strength. Time-release pills and spikes give long-lasting nutrition. Following the directions on the package, poke them into the soil away from the roots.

Fertilizing trees

For vigor and long life

A midsummer feeding is largely wasted on a tree; the best time is early spring, just as growth begins. A fall

feeding, after the leaves are down but before the ground freezes, is also good. Newly planted trees need phosphorus for root growth. Later on, the main need is nitrogen for leaves (see *Fertilizing vegetables*).

Feed an established tree every other year if it is not making normal growth. If its leaves are severely damaged by insects during the summer, however, feed it that fall to aid recovery. For deciduous trees more than 6 inches in diameter at chest height, use 3 to 5 pounds of granulated fertilizer per inch of diameter; for smaller trees, use 2 to 4 pounds per inch. Evergreens need half those amounts.

Before applying, mix high-nitrogen fertilizer, such as 10-6-4, with peat moss or humus to ensure even distribution. Make concentric circles of small, 12-inch-deep holes around the tree and fill them with the mixture. Start 3 to 4 feet from the trunk and make a new circle every 2 feet, spacing the holes 2 feet apart. Make the last circle 2 feet past the drip line.

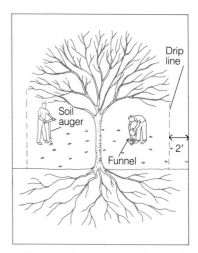

Mix liquid fertilizer according to the directions on the package; space applications as above. Solid spikes of time-release fertilizer are also available for long-lasting nutrition; drive them into the ground according to the manufacturer's directions.

If a tree looks sickly with no apparent cause, test the soil before feeding to be sure that nutrient deficiencies are the problem. Do not feed a tree that has a fungus disease until the disease is cured; the fertilizer helps the fungus more than the tree.

Fertilizing vegetables

What fertilizers are; how to use them for a rich yield

All plants need three major nutrients: nitrogen (N) for leaves and stems; phosphorus (P) for roots, fruit, and seeds; and potassium (K) for all-round health. The numbers on a bag of fertilizer tell you what percentage of each of these nutrients the bag contains. They are called NPK numbers, and they are always in that order. Thus a 100-pound bag of 10-6-4 has 10 pounds of N, 6 pounds of P, and 4 pounds of K. The rest is mostly inert filler. Small amounts of many trace elements, such as iron, magnesium, and zinc, are also present; but unless the soil in your area lacks these, they are of little concern.

Leaf crops, such as lettuce and spinach, need plenty of N. Root crops, such as beets and carrots, should be given little N and some P or they may produce many leaves and small roots. Corn needs N and lots of P. Fruit crops, such as tomatoes and peppers, do best with a balanced fertilizer that leans a little toward the K side.

Plants don't care whether their nutrients come from organic or chemical fertilizers. Organics, such as manure or dried blood (for N) and bone meal (for P), release their nutrients more slowly than chemicals and are less likely to damage roots. (The K of well-burned wood ashes, however, is released quickly.) Most organics also improve the soil's texture. Chemicals usually work faster and their contents are precisely measured.

Applying fertilizer

Dig slow-acting organic fertilizers, such as manure or partly decayed compost, into the soil in the fall for next spring's planting. Well-decayed manure and compost can be applied in early spring. Apply chemical fertilizers according to the manufacturer's directions. When in doubt, remember that too little is safer than too much.

For crops grown from seed, mix chemical fertilizer thoroughly into the top 3 or 4 inches of the soil when you prepare it for planting.

When setting out young established plants, dig holes 2 to 3 inches deeper than needed, work a handful of fertilizer into the bottom, and cover with soil (see *Planting*). Or after setting a plant out, give it a drink of liquid fertilizer, called a starter solution.

Long-term crops, such as squash, corn, tomatoes, and cucumbers, benefit from a midseason side dressing of high-N fertilizer. Sprinkle it along the rows at least 4 or 5 inches from the stems, or encircle each stem with a small trench and fill it with fertilizer. Mix in the fertilizer, then water. (See also *Compost; Soil preparation.*)

FERTILIZERS FOR THE HOME GARDEN

Name	% composition	Quantity per area	Use
5–10–5	5 N, 10 P, 5 K	4–5 lb./100 sq ft.	An all-purpose fertilizer
5–10–10	5 N, 10 P, 10 K	4–5 lb./100 sq. ft.	Good for vegetables
10–50–20	10 N, 50 P, 20 K	Follow directions	Transplant starter solution
Superphosphate	14 to 20 P	1–2 oz./10 sq. ft.	Adds phosphorus
46–0–0	46 N	Follow directions	High-nitrogen side dressing for midseason feeding
Cow manure (dried)	Varies: 2 to 5 N, 1.5 to 3 P, 1.5 to 3 K	1–2 lb./10 sq. ft.	Adds organic matter to soil
Dried blood	12 N	1–2 oz./10 sq. ft.	High nitrogen
Rock phosphate	20 to 30 P	3–4 oz./10 sq. ft.	Very slow acting; use only in alkaline soils
Wood ashes	2 P, 5 or more K	½–1 lb./10 sq. ft.	Quick acting; apply dry
Compost	Varies; small amounts of N, P, K	Unlimited	Supplies valuable organic matter

Fever

Coping with above-normal temperatures

Fever is an abnormal rise in body temperature from the normal 98.6°F (in most people) to 100°F or above. (Normal taken rectally may be up to 1 degree higher.) Although its cause may or may not be serious, no fever should be ignored.

Measure fever with a thermometer. Rinse the thermometer in cool water; shake it with a snap of the wrist until the temperature column drops below 97°F. Put the thermometer beneath the person's tongue; have him close his lips but not his teeth. Leave it there for at least 1 minute.

For rectal measurement use a rectal thermometer and lubricate it with petroleum jelly. If oral or rectal measurement is impractical, take a reading under the armpit for 3 minutes. Bear in mind that some variation is normal from as low as 97°F in the morning to as high as 100°F in late afternoon.

Treatment

A low-grade fever (up to 101°F) rarely requires medical measures except in a very young or very old person, in whom any fever is potentially serious. Report any fever in an infant immediately to your doctor. In an older child, be guided more by looks and actions. A child can have a normal temperature and still be seriously ill.

A fever above 101°F in anyone warrants discussion with your doctor. Aspirin or acetaminophen will lower the fever and help alleviate discomfort. Aspirin in suppository form can be useful if there is vomiting. Never give aspirin to children. A tepid (not cold) sponge bath is comforting but a slow fever reducer: it takes 20 minutes to bring fever down a degree or so.

Chills are a natural accompaniment to fever. The body's "thermostat" senses when its temperature is low compared to the new level. Adding blankets warms the patient to the higher level. The patient may also begin sweating, increasing heat loss. Replace lost moisture with clear liquids—broth, fruit juice, noncarbonated soft drinks, water.

A swift rise in temperature can cause a seizure in a child of 5 years or less. Frightening to parents, it usually results in no brain damage or other adverse side effects, but to be safe, consult your doctor.

Fig trees

Raising figs in a garden or tub

Figs need well-drained soil and full sun. Plant them in the early spring (see *Fruit trees*). Favored varieties for Southern California are Kadota and Mission; for the southeast, Celeste; for colder regions, Brown Turkey. Even if severely frozen, the latter may bear fruit in late summer.

In areas where winters are severe, figs must be protected. As soon as the ground freezes, wrap the fig tree, branches and all, in layers of burlap or other insulating material. Pull it into a tight bundle, then cover it with tar paper or plastic. Make sure water cannot leak in at the top. Remove the wrapping in early spring. Or plant a fig tree in a tub in well-drained, fertile soil. Winter it in a light garage or cellar where the temperature ranges from 30°F to 45°F.

Where summers are long, figs usually bear two crops of fruit: an early one on last year's twigs, a late one on the current season's growth. Prune last year's growth after the first crop.

Figure skating

How to make a figure eight

Figure-skate blades have two edges: inside (the one nearer the inside of your foot) and outside. By skating on one edge or the other it is possible to form graceful curves. Practice skating on these two edges until you feel confident. Then try the figure eight (also called circle eight), one of the formations done in the compulsories of figure-skating competition.

Start in a T-position (see *Ice skating*), mentally envisioning the two circles. Hold your head upright and focus your eyes 2 to 3 feet ahead of the skating foot. Keep your upper body as erect as possible, yet flexible enough for the required rotation.

Place all weight on the left leg, left ankle turned in. Bend both legs and push away strongly onto the outside edge of the right skate. The skating leg should be bent at the start; the free leg should be slightly bent and turned outward from the hip, toe pointed downward, with the blade just above the ice. Keep shoulders parallel with the skating foot to maintain balance.

As you complete three-quarters of the circle, begin to straighten your skating leg and move the free leg forward. At the same time, start to change your shoulder direction (from facing outward to facing inward on the circle). As your free leg moves forward, lean backward slightly to maintain weight on the back edge of the blade and to prevent your hips from rotating at that point.

Nearing completion of the circle, bring the free foot next to the skating foot and bend both knees. As you reach the original push-off mark, turn a full 90 degrees in preparation for the next circle. Push off firmly and strongly onto the outside edge of the left skate, which ideally will touch the ice directly over the original starting line. Make a circle to the left, following the same procedure as for the right.

Filing

Putting your affairs in order

A filing system arranged chronologically, by subject, or alphabetically can help you keep track of your affairs. Use a system or a combination of systems that suits your needs. Before starting, simplify matters: discard clutter such as junk mail, expired coupons, and mail and clippings no longer of interest.

You can, of course, file your papers on shelves or in shoe boxes, but to ensure their safety, a metal box or drawer cabinet is ideal. Mark the sections of your file drawer by inserting guides of reinforced cardboard, or identify a file's subject on the file folder's tab.

Chronological files
Label five folders with the days of the workweek; arrange them in a drawer consecutively, then add an extra folder marked *Next Week*. Hold items in this system until you have acted on them, then move them to another system or discard them. This system is handy for engagement reminders, calls to be made, and errands to be run, as well as for some financial matters.

Drop bills as they arrive into the appropriate date folder; place payment-due reminders in appropriate folders (possibly *Next Week*). Transfer records of all paid bills to a financial file that is organized on a 12-month basis for bank statements and checks.

Subject files
Arrange the subjects alphabetically. Subdivide where appropriate, as in a section marked *Financial*. Subject files lend themselves to considerable flexibility; you can always retitle, subdivide, or consolidate folders in this file as you progress.

Alphabetical files
If you have a lot of correspondence, this system will help you retrieve letters. File alphabetically by last name and put the most recent letters toward the front of each folder.

A box of 3 x 5 index cards is an alphabetical file of many uses. It can help you keep your address list up to date or catalog your books, record collection, or recipes.

Fingernails

Repairing; strengthening them

Weak, soft, or brittle fingernails may be caused by hereditary factors, illness, regular contact with strong household cleaners, or too-frequent use of nail polish remover. To strengthen nails naturally, use rubber gloves for household chores, and keep hands out of very hot water. Rub in cuticle cream daily. Apply hand lotion after washing hands and before bedtime. Try not to use your nails for digging and prying, and keep them filed and snag free (see *Manicures*).

If a nail starts to tear, repair it with a drop of instant-bonding nail glue. Keep the glue away from your eyes. If any glue gets on your skin, remove it at once with polish remover. After the glue dries, file the area smooth.

For nails that tend to peel or snag, try tape wraps that come in kits. Stick the tapes on the ends of your nails, cut the tapes to size, then wrap the edges around the tips and under your nails. Secure them with the finishing liquid in the kit, then polish your nails.

Nail strengtheners

Liquid hardeners, plastic tips, nail wrapping, and artificial nails can cause severe allergic reactions and even injury to nails. Some dermatologists recommend against their use. Should you decide to try such a nail strengthener, be sure to do a patch test following the package instructions. If redness, swelling, or itching develop, do not use the product.

Nail enamel may also cause an allergic reaction, but not always in the vicinity of the nail. Reddish, itchy spots may appear on delicate skin areas, such as the eyelids or sides of the neck and face, touched by the nails.

Finger painting

Creating art with your hands

Finger paints are thick, water-soluble mixtures applied to paper with the hands. Art stores carry them. Or you can make some by adding enough dry wallpaper paste to liquid poster paint to make a smooth, creamy substance.

Purchase finger-painting paper at an art store. Or use a shiny-surface shelf liner, but not the kind that's chemically treated for bugs; it wrinkles when wet. Pencil an "X" on the paper's dull side; you will paint on the shiny side. Dip the paper into water and lay it on a surface that won't be harmed by the paint. Smooth any air pockets by lifting each corner.

Try painting first with one color. Dab some paint on the paper and spread it around. Create designs us-ing your fingers, palm, side of your hand, even objects such as a comb or the rim of a drinking glass. To erase or change a stroke, simply smooth over the paint. Add a little water with your fingers if the paint starts to dry. To work with more than one color, dab each one onto the paper separately. Mix them where you want to create new shades. Clean your hands on a wet cloth between colors.

Finger weaving

Using fingers as a loom

Finger weaving, also known as braiding or multistrand plaiting, is an off-loom technique in which the fingers interlace yarns at 45-degree angles to form a fabric. Any cord is suitable: knitting worsted, rug yarn, twine, jute, or fine yarns doubled or tripled.

A simple pattern is one-direction weave, also called Peruvian flat braid. To make an attractive belt with this technique, you will need 45 yards of knitting-and-crochet cotton or knitting worsted for a band about 1 inch wide (if you use thicker yarn, the belt will be wider). Cut 18 strands, each 2½ yards long; this is 1½ times the finished length of approximately 60 inches. About 6 inches from one end, tie groups of three yarns in overhand knots; secure these six knots side by side under a clipboard hinge.

Holding the yarns firmly in your left hand, use your right hand to plait the far right strand from right to left. Take the strand over the first yarn to the left, under the next, and so forth, then finally over the last yarn on the left, where it becomes one of the strands to be interlaced. Continue weaving, always with the outermost right yarn. (If you're left-handed, you may prefer to work from left to right.)

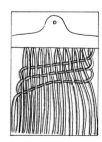

Overhand knots

A weaving strand that passes over a yarn on one row must go under the same yarn on the next row. As you proceed, pull the woven strands firmly together and separate the strands near the bottom to prevent tangling. When you put the work aside, set a paper clip or clamp just below the last row of weaving to prevent loosening. About 6 inches from the end, tie every three strands in an overhand knot.

Fire ants

Their sting; their nests; destroying their colonies

These tiny reddish-brown or black ants, $\frac{1}{16}$ to $\frac{1}{4}$ inch long, will attack anything that disturbs their nest—a mound of debris that can be as large as 2 feet in diameter and 2½ feet high, usually in a sunny spot. They occur in the South and Southwest.

Each ant can sting several times. The sting is fiery and the welt it causes may last a couple of days. Don't scratch an itching welt; it may become infected. A few people may have an acute allergic reaction.

You can destroy much of a fire ant colony by drenching the mound with a solution of carbaryl, diazinon, or chlorpyrifos (see *Pesticides*). Often, however, the queen escapes. When ants that were foraging return, they build a new nest, usually nearby.

Caution: Keep pets and children away from a drenched nest for several days.

Firearms

Safety and care

Before buying a sporting gun, contact your state conservation agency or a local gun club for instruction in its safe handling and use. Check with the police to make sure you are in compliance with ownership laws. Read your gun's instruction manual carefully.

Teach your children that a gun isn't a toy. Explain to them how it works and its potential dangers. Enforce a "hands off" rule until they are old enough to learn safe gun handling.

Guns in the home, car, or camp should be unloaded, but treated as if they were loaded. When handling a gun, open the action and make sure the gun is empty. Always point the muzzle in a safe direction. Don't engage in or tolerate horseplay with guns. Never mix guns and alcohol.

Store firearms out of reach of children, in a locked cabinet, rack, or drawer; or equip your guns with trigger locks. Ammunition should be stored in a locked drawer, separate from firearms and away from heat or electrical sources. Keep keys to storage areas away from children.

Handling a gun

Never aim a gun at anything you don't intend to shoot. Load it only when you're ready to use it, and keep the safety on until just before firing. Don't fire until you have identified your target and know there is nothing endangered behind it. Know your gun's range, make sure its barrel is unobstructed, and use only ammunition intended for it. Wear eye and ear protection when shooting.

Unload your gun when crossing a fence, climbing a tree, or waiting on a shooting line. Carry a gun so that you can control the muzzle's direction even if you trip. Don't leave a loaded gun unattended or rely on the safety as a substitute for safe handling.

Gun care

Inspect your gun after each use and wipe it free of dirt and moisture. Periodically clean the bore with commercial solvent applied with a cleaning rod and patches. Lubricate the working parts and exterior surfaces with a thin coat of light gun oil. Always make sure the gun is unloaded before you start cleaning it.

Fire extinguishers

What to look for; where to install them

An extinguisher's letter ratings tell the types of fire it can put out: Class A (combustible solids such as wood, paper, fabrics, or trash), B (grease and other flammable liquids), or C (electrical). The number preceding the A or B rating (for example, 1-A or 5-B) indi-cates the size of a standard test fire that the extinguisher can put out; the higher the number, the greater the extinguisher's firefighting capacity. The C rating means that the extinguishing materials do not conduct electricity; it has no number.

Match extinguishers to potential fire hazards, or buy multipurpose ABC extinguishers rated at least 2-A 10-B:C. Check the canister for the Underwriters' Laboratories (UL) or Factory Mutual (FM) label and for clear operating instructions. Disposable or gaugeless extinguishers are unreliable; replace them. Do not use water on Class B or C fires.

Install extinguishers in the kitchen and in or near the living room, bedrooms, basement, and garage. They should be in plain view, away from but convenient to fire hazards. Make sure the entire family knows where they are and how to use them. Inspect the pressure gauge periodically. If pressure drops or if the extinguisher is used, even briefly, have it recharged by an extinguisher service company.

Fireplace fires

Starting and maintaining a good, smokeless blaze

A fireplace should be equipped with andirons or a grate to permit air flow from beneath the blaze, and a screen to contain sparks. Before starting a fire, clean out all but 2 inches of ashes and open the chimney damper. Use dry, well-seasoned wood; wet or freshly cut wood is difficult to ignite and is likely to smoke. Hardwood burns longer than softwood and deposits less creosote on the chimney.

Start by laying a large log across the back of the andirons and a slightly smaller log, preferably a slab placed flat side in, about 4 inches in front of it. Fill the trough between the two logs with a few sheets of tightly crumpled, black-and-white newspaper; on top place loosely crisscrossed pieces of dry kindling no more than 1 inch in diameter. Lay a small log on top.

Set a match to the newspaper. After the fire takes hold, see that the top log gradually settles between the lower two. Keep pushing the front log toward the rear; replace it when space allows. Add another top log, if desired. When the back log burns through, lay a replacement on top and gradually work it into position by drawing the fragments of the original forward.

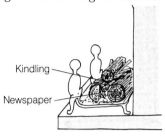

Kindling

Newspaper

If the fire fails to ignite, or if it smokes, one or more of the following may be the problem: (1) The chimney needs cleaning (see *Chimneys and flues*). (2) The room needs more air; open a window. (3) Air is flowing *down* the chimney (the flame of a lighted match held in the flue opening blows downward). Turn off any exhaust fans. Start an upward draft of air by holding a burning newspaper beneath the flue opening (see *Fireplaces*). (4) There are problems with the fireplace structure.

Fireplaces

Keeping them in working order; solving problems

Periodically check the structural integrity of your fireplace and also of the chimney (see *Chimneys and flues*). Inspect the inside with a flashlight for loose bricks, gaps in the mortar, or an obstruction in the chimney. Repair any defects (see *Brickwork*).

Try to operate the damper. This movable plate for adjusting the draft is kept open when a fire is burning; when there is no fire, it is closed to minimize loss of room heat. It should work easily and shut snugly. If it is stiff, spray its hinge or pivot points with silicone lubricant and manipulate the handle until it works freely. If the damper doesn't close completely, remove creosote deposits around it with a putty knife. If there are still gaps when it is shut, fill the spaces with furnace cement.

Continued next page

F

If smoke enters the room

The position and size of the damper are important. It should be 6 to 8 inches above the lintel (see illustration) and the same length as the

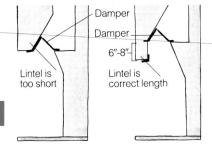

Damper

Damper

6"-8"

Lintel is too short

Lintel is correct length

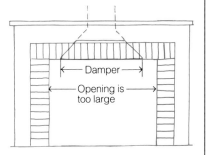

Damper

Opening is too large

width of the fireplace opening; otherwise smoke will flow into the room. If the position is wrong, adding a metal shield or hood at the top of the fireplace opening may solve the problem. If the damper is not long enough, have a mason either install a correct one or make the fireplace opening smaller.

A too-shallow fireplace may cause smoking. Try raising the andirons or the grate on bricks, or use a grate that holds the logs nearer the back wall. If none of the above solves the problem, consult an expert for other solutions.

Fire survival

Preparing your home and family to survive a fire

Install smoke detectors and fire extinguishers bearing the Underwriters' Laboratories (UL) label. Buy portable fire-escape ladders for second- or third-floor windows. Store them near the windows or under beds; practice using them. Check fire safety devices regularly to make sure they are in working order (see *Fire extinguishers; Smoke detectors*).

Planning your escape

Map out an escape plan in advance with your family; hold periodic drills. Establish two escape routes from each room and a safe outdoor meeting place where the family can gather for a head count. Note porch or garage roofs that can aid your escape from a window. Make sure windows open easily. Post the fire emergency number near telephones and find out where the nearest fire alarm box is.

In case of fire

First get everyone out of the house and call the fire department. Then try to fight a small fire if you can. If it gets out of control, leave immediately, closing all doors behind you. When passing through a smoke-filled area, walk in a crouched position, head close to the floor. Try to cover your face with a damp cloth. If your clothes catch fire, don't run. Wrap yourself in a coat or blanket and roll on the floor. Once out of the house, don't go back.

Before leaving a room, feel the door. If it's hot or if you see smoke, don't open it. If the door is cool, put your foot against it, avert your face, and open it slightly. If heat or smoke rush in, shut the door. Leave by another exit or wait at a window for rescue. Stuff bedding or clothes at the bottom of the door, open the window slightly for fresh air, and hang out clothes or a bedsheet to attract rescuers.

First-aid kits

Providing in advance for emergencies

The point of a first-aid kit is to be ready for emergencies—have what you need, know where it is and how to use it—before they happen. You can buy kits in drugstores or assemble your own: ideally, one for home and another for the car or for trips.

A toolbox is ideal. It's sturdy, portable, and keeps everything in sight. Be sure to label medications clearly. Include a first-aid manual, and tape emergency phone numbers to the lid (doctor, ambulance, hospital, police, poison control center). Put the kit away unlocked, out of children's reach but instantly accessible to adults.

Any first-aid kit should contain at least the following:

Triangular bandage and large safety pins (for bandaging and as a sling); elastic bandage (for supporting minor sprains); rolls of 2-inch and 4-inch gauze bandage; box of 4 x 4-inch gauze pads; rolls of 1-inch and 2-inch adhesive tape; adhesive bandages in assorted sizes; bottle of 3 percent hydrogen-peroxide solution (for cleaning wounds); antibiotic ointment; aspirin or another analgesic; ipecac syrup (for accidental poisonings); powdered activated charcoal (for drug overdose); roll of sterile absorbent cotton; cotton swabs; scissors; tweezers and a packet of needles (for removing splinters); tongue depressors (for finger splints); fever thermometer; ice bag (for reducing swelling); flashlight and extra batteries.

Restock short supplies as needed; replace any that have expired (hydrogen peroxide that no longer bubbles) or are doubtful (flashlight batteries). For a travel kit consider adding provisions for special sensitivities: skin or sunburn lotion, antinauseant (for motion sickness), pectin-kaolin compound (for diarrhea). Ask your doctor about antibiotics and kits for allergies, such as bee stings.

Fish cleaning

Preparing fresh-caught fish

Unless you plan to skin a fish, the first step is to remove the scales. Holding the fish by the tail, scrape off the scales from tail to head with a sharp knife or a fish scaler—a saw-toothed instrument. Next cut along each side of the pectoral and pelvic fins and pull them free. Remove the dorsal and anal fins the same way. Leave the fins on if the fish is to be cooked whole.

To remove the viscera of a roundfish, slit the belly from head to tail. Pull out the insides, then scrape loose any blood pockets with a knife. To gut a flatfish, make a small opening behind the gills. After cleaning, rinse the fish thoroughly.

To remove skin from a roundfish, make cuts around the head and tail and the length of the back; working the knife under the skin, pull the skin toward the belly; cut it off. Repeat on the other side. For a flatfish, slit the

Roundfish

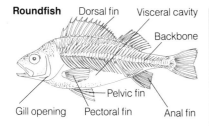

Dorsal fin, Visceral cavity, Backbone, Pelvic fin, Gill opening, Pectoral fin, Anal fin

Flatfish

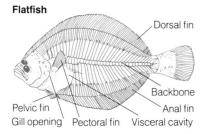

Dorsal fin, Backbone, Anal fin, Pelvic fin, Gill opening, Pectoral fin, Visceral cavity

skin at the tail on the dark side. Holding the skin with a paper towel or a cloth, pull it to and over the head, then down to the tail on the light side.

Cutting steaks and filets

A roundfish, such as salmon or cod, is generally used for steaks. It should weigh no less than 10 pounds. Using a very sharp knife, slice the fish crosswise into pieces at least 1 inch thick.

For filets, use fish that are not too bony—either flatfish or roundfish. To make filets from flatfish, place the skinned fish with the eyes up and cut lengthwise along the center to the bone. Inserting the knife horizontally between the flesh and bone on one side of the slit, cut the flesh from the ribs in short strokes. Repeat on the other side of the slit. Turn the fish over and cut two filets from the other side in the same manner.

To make filets from roundfish, slit along the backbone and across the

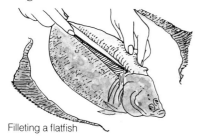

Filleting a flatfish

tail. Then slice through the backbone between the vertebrae directly behind the gills. Using short strokes, run the knife the length of the fish as close to the ribs as possible. Turn the fish over and slice the filet from the other side.

Fish cooking

Baking; sautéing and frying; broiling and grilling; poaching

Cooked fish should be moist. To tell if a whole fish is cooked, insert a skewer near the backbone; it should meet little resistance. A fillet is done when the flesh is opaque at the thickest part; a steak barely flakes when it's pricked with a fork. Allow 10 minutes of cooking time per inch of flesh thickness, no matter what method you use.

Baking is especially suitable for a whole fish. Use a generously buttered dish and brush the fish with butter or oil; or cover it with chopped vegetables or a mixture of bread crumbs, butter, and herbs. Bake in a preheated 450°F oven for the prescribed time.

Another baking method is to wrap fish in oiled foil, add seasonings or a sauce, and bake at 450°F. Wrap the foil loosely to allow steam to circulate, but seal its edges tightly.

Frying and *sautéing* are the best cooking methods for small fish, such as smelts. First dip the fish in beaten egg, then coat with seasoned flour or bread crumbs; or just coat them with flour. To sauté, heat equal amounts of oil and butter in a frying pan over moderate heat. Brown the fish on one side, then the other. To fry, heat oil to 375°F (see *Frying*).

Broiling and *grilling* are suitable for any fish except those shorter than 6 inches. Preheat a broiler or have coals glowing in a grill. (A fish-shaped metal basket facilitates turning a whole fish on a grill.) Cook the fish 4 to 6 inches from the heat source, basting with oil or clarified butter.

Poaching (simmering in liquid) is best suited to firm fish, such as sole, salmon, red snapper, trout, or bass. To poach a large whole fish, leave the fins intact and support it on a rack in the poaching pan. Wrap small whole fish in cheesecloth for easy removal from the pan. Cover the fish with tepid liquid, bring to a simmer, then start timing the cooking.

Court bouillon for fish

In an enamel pan put 2 small whole onions, 1 carrot and 1 celery stalk cut up, 2 sprigs parsley, 2 sprigs thyme (or ½ teaspoon dry), 1 bay leaf, 1 teaspoon salt, 1 quart water, and 2 cups dry red or white wine or ½ cup wine vinegar. If you have some fish heads and bones, add these also. Simmer uncovered for ½ hour. Strain liquid through a double layer of cheesecloth.

Fishhook removal

A simple, time-tested method

Fishermen have a simple trick for removing a hook caught in the skin. It is not a job for anyone with shaky hands or a faint heart; get a doctor to do it if possible. But if medical help is unavailable, here's what to do.

Instead of "backing" the barb out, an action that may tear the flesh and skin, push the barb the rest of the way through the skin, forward and up, in the direction of the curve. Then clip off the barb with wire cutters (which you should have in your tackle box) and gently withdraw the shaft.

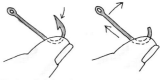

Wash a fishhook wound carefully to forestall infection. Call a doctor if the "hooked" person has not had a tetanus booster in the last 5 years.

Fishing tackle

Keeping gear in good repair

All fishing tackle should be wiped dry after every use. Any equipment used in salt water should be rinsed first in fresh water.

All four kinds of reels—bait casting, open spinning, closed spinning, and fly casting—need regular oiling. Follow the manufacturer's directions. Take a malfunctioning reel to a tackle shop or send it to the manufacturer.

Monofilament line can be weakened by tiny kinks; damaged by suntan oil, insecticide, or gasoline; or fouled by minerals in the water. Before storing line, run it from one reel to another, applying line-cleaning fluid with a dab of cotton and checking for irregularities. Discard weakened line. To keep braided line from rotting, store it in a dry place.

Disassemble rods at least once a week when in use and use nail polish remover to clean the ferrules that join the sections. When a bamboo rod shows signs of wear, apply three thin coats of spar varnish, rubbing briskly with felt before each coat and letting each dry for 24 hours. Fiberglass, graphite, or boron rods need varnish only on the winding thread that holds the line guides. Replace all frayed thread. Replace any nicked guides.

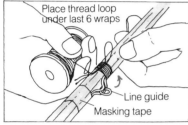

Place thread loop under last 6 wraps
Line guide
Masking tape

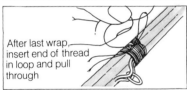

After last wrap, insert end of thread in loop and pull through

Sharpen a hook, even a new one, by pulling the point, barb up, across a fine stone. Replace hooks attached to

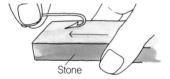

Stone

plugs or lures when damaged or corroded. Touch up scarred plugs with enamel or epoxy paint. Renew bedraggled flies by steaming them briefly. Keep spoons and spinners shiny with fine steel wool. (See also *Bait casting; Fly-fishing; Ice fishing; Spin casting; Surf casting; Trolling.*)

Flagstones

Planning and laying a stone walk or patio

Flagstones are rocks that have been split into slabs and cut into flaglike shapes. They can be of bluestone, limestone, or sandstone. Known as random rectangular flagstones, their sizes start at 12 x 12 inches and increase by 6-inch increments to 36 and sometimes to 42 inches. Thicknesses vary: in an order of 1½-inch stones, you'll find stones from 1¼ to 2 inches thick. Flagstones are heavy; move them by handcart or wheelbarrow. Have someone to help lay them.

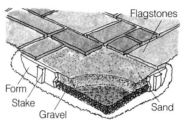

Flagstones
Form
Stake
Gravel
Sand

Flagstones can be cheaply installed (and with reasonable permanence) on a sand bed. After a winter, however, you may have to reset some stones. Laying stones in concrete, although more permanent, is costly and difficult—a job for a contractor.

The length and width of the walk or patio should be divisible by 6 inches. In ordering, tell the masonry supplier the dimensions. Upon delivery, sort the stones by size; then on graph paper, plot the placement of each stone. Break up any long joint lines; frost heaves are likely along such lines.

Lay out the project with string and stakes. Excavate to 7 inches (4 inches for gravel, 3 inches for sand). Set up formwork (see *Concrete formwork*), using pressure-treated boards. Spread and tamp the gravel, then the sand. Check both with a level.

Place the stones, leaving ½ inch between them. Stand on each to make sure it doesn't teeter; you may have to lift it and add or remove sand. Tamp all stones with a rubber mallet. Finally, sweep a mixture of half sand, half topsoil into the gaps. Pack it down with a good hosing, then let it dry. Repeat until the joints are filled.

Flambéing

Creating a flaming spectacle

Sweetened fruits, crepes, and other desserts, as well as meats and poultry, can be laced with liquor and set aflame just before serving. Most of the alcohol burns away, leaving the flavor in the food. To avoid a fizzle, use spirits high in alcohol (vodka, brandy, or whisky, but not wine), and have the food and the alcohol warm.

Caution: Light a dish at the table, rather than carrying it aflame. Do not wear lacy cuffs or flambé near flammable objects.

Crepes Suzette
Make 12 dessert crepes (see *Crepes*), and keep them warm. In a heated chafing dish, melt ¾ cup butter. Add the grated rinds of 1 lemon and 1 orange, ½ cup orange juice, and ¼ cup sugar. Heat, stirring constantly, until reduced to about half. Add crepes, one at a time, coating them thoroughly; fold them into quarters and push them to one side. Warm, but don't boil, ¼ cup each brandy and orange liqueur, and 2 tablespoons rum; pour over the crepes. Ignite by touching a lighted match to the edge of the pan. Serve with sauce spooned on top.

Flashings

Finding and fixing leaks

If you see signs of a leaky roof, check the flashings—those strips of metal that seal the seams around chimneys, vent pipes, dormers, and valleys (low points between roof sections). You may see breaks or pinholes from inside on a sunny day; or you may find discoloration in the flashings, on the roof around them, or on the ceiling or wall beneath.

If the leak is small, fill it with plastic asphalt roof cement, smoothing it carefully with a trowel to eliminate rough spots where water might collect. For a hole of 1 square inch or more, cut a patch from the same ma-

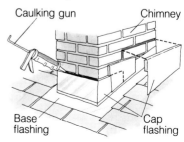

Caulking gun
Chimney
Base flashing
Cap flashing

terial as the existing flashing and 1 inch bigger all around. Coat the area around the hole with cement and set the patch over it. Then coat and smooth the patch and the seam. If you cannot find the leak, apply plastic cement in all logical areas.

The cap flashing around chimneys may separate from the mortar in which it is imbedded. If this happens, chip away the mortar, clean the channel to the depth of about ¾ inch, and reposition the flashing. Fill with fresh mortar or caulking. (See also *Brickwork; Caulking; Roof repairs.*)

Flashlights

Keeping a basic two-cell model operative

Periodically test a flashlight; contact points become dirty and batteries discharge slowly, even when not in use. If practical, store batteries in the refrigerator to prolong their life.

If the beam is dim, rub the battery terminals lightly with sandpaper or emery cloth. Also sand the contact point of the bulb and the contact spring. To reach the spring, remove the cap, reflector, bulb, and batteries; insert a pencil or dowel wrapped with sandpaper. Also stretch the spring slightly with a screwdriver.

If the light blinks, sand and stretch the spring as above. Also check that the switch contact bar touches the reflector collar. If not, bend it slightly and sand it.

If the light doesn't work, check whether the batteries are inserted correctly. If they are and it still doesn't work, replace the batteries, the bulb, or both. To replace a bulb, remove the reflector; unsnap or unscrew the bulb protector, and insert a new bulb. If these measures fail, try cleaning all contact points.

Flatfeet

How to relieve them; helping children avoid them

A person whose arches fall when he stands is said to have flatfeet. The condition may be inherited or develop from overweight, strain, prolonged standing, or poorly supported walking in early childhood. The result can be aching feet, bunions, hammertoes (curving of the toes so they point downward), and pain in the calves.

Wear orthotic (arch) supports and suitable shoes to relieve pain. Avoid long periods of standing. Exercises prescribed by an orthopedist or podiatrist may strengthen the ligaments.

Infants look flatfooted because a pad of fat in the arch covers the bone. The fat pad usually disappears by age two. During the preschool years while the bone is hardening, select shoes with adequate support. Observe a child's posture and walk; check with your doctor if you see irregularities.

Fleas

Their haunts, habits, and elimination

Fleas—small, brown, parasitic insects about ⅛ inch long—jump onto their host to feed on its blood. They spend most of their time resting and breeding where the host rests. Development from egg to adult flea takes about 2 months, less in hot weather. Fleas feed on humans when animals are absent.

The best defense is a thorough house vacuuming, with special attention to your pet's bedding. Wash the bedding and let it dry; spray or dust it with a veterinary insecticide formulation. Give your pet a flea inspection often: look for the tiny black specks that are their droppings. Use flea shampoo, powder, or a flea collar as your veterinarian advises. In case of a severe infestation, calling in an exterminator may be the best answer.

Flies

Decreasing their numbers

House flies, transmitters of serious diseases, feed on and breed in food, garbage, and animal droppings. Discourage their presence by properly storing food, by maintaining a clean kitchen, and by bagging and sealing garbage. Keep your yard free of animal droppings and refuse. Hose down garbage cans, dry them in the sun, and secure their lids (see *Garbage cans*).

Make sure that all door and window screens are in good condition and fit tightly. Flypaper may catch the odd fly that enters despite your precautions. A craftily wielded flyswatter makes a trusty dispatcher.

Pot houseplants with sterilized soil to prevent the fungus gnat, which resembles a small fly, from breeding. Spray diehard flies with pyrethrins.

Floods

Preparations and survival

As a rule, householder's insurance doesn't protect you from losses due to floods. However, if your community participates in the National Flood Insurance Program (NFIP), you should be eligible for special flood insurance. Ask your agent, or dial 800-638-6620.

If you live in a flood-prone area, consider elevating your house or making construction adjustments to keep flood waters out. These measures are costly, however, and they should be planned only by a qualified engineer.

To prepare for the possibility of flood waters entering, move appliances and power tools to a higher floor; for equipment that can't be moved, such as a furnace, find out how to build a floodwall around it. Put a control panel where you can turn off electricity without going into water.

Make a list of personal property, including furnishings, valuables, and clothing. Photographs of your home, inside and out, are helpful for settling insurance claims and proving uninsured, tax-deductible losses. Store insurance policies and property lists in a waterproof or safe-deposit box.

Keep on hand: a portable radio, emergency cooking equipment, nonperishable foods, jugs for water, flashlights, sandbags (if you know how to use them), and plywood and plastic sheeting for plugging holes and sealing doors. If a flood threatens, keep your fuel tank filled for evacuation.

Continued next page

When a flood warning comes

Get your family to a safe area. Stock the car with food, containers of water, a first-aid kit, blankets, flashlights, dry clothing, and needed medication.

Caution: Do not drive across a flooded road. If the car stalls, abandon it.

If you're caught in the house by suddenly rising waters, move to the highest floor, taking along warm clothing, a flashlight, and a portable radio. Fill sinks and jugs with water (rinse them first with household bleach). Wait for help; don't try to swim to safety.

Floor refinishing

Restoring worn wooden floors

If your floor is coated with clear finish, it must be stripped with a sander before refinishing. You can rent a drum-type floor sander and a hand-held disc sander; ask for a demonstration of their loading and use.

Clear the room of furnishings and seal it off from the rest of the house with plastic sheeting. Remove shoe molding from the bottom of the baseboard to permit working close to the walls. Pull out any staples left from carpeting. Repair damaged or loose floorboards; drive protruding nailheads well below the surface and fill the holes with wood putty. Vacuum, then inspect the floor once more.

Sand the floor first with the drum sander and 36-grit sandpaper. Raise the drum off the floor, turn on the power, then lower the drum carefully, keeping a firm grip on the handles. Work across the floor *with* the grain, then return to the beginning and strip the next section parallel to and slightly overlapping the first. Next sand along the walls with the hand sander and 36-grit paper.

Repeat the sanding process twice, using 80-grit sandpaper, then 100-grit paper. Use a scraper to strip the corners. Sand by hand at each end of the room to remove marks where the sander has stripped across the grain. Vacuum thoroughly between stages and wear socks or white-soled sneakers to prevent scuff marks.

Wipe the stripped floor with a tack cloth (see *Tack cloth*) to remove dust. Apply clear sealer or a stain (preferably one combined with a sealer). When dry, buff with fine steel wool. Vacuum thoroughly. Apply polyurethane, shellac, or varnish, using a roller for the center area, a brush around the edges.

Allow to dry at least 2 days, then buff with steel wool again; vacuum. Apply two coats of paste wax, followed by a buffing with lamb's wool. (Note: some polyurethanes do not have to be waxed. Check the label. With a no-wax type, buff with steel wool and wax only if you prefer a softer patina.)

Flour beetles

Preventing an infestation; getting rid of them

Tiny, brown flour beetles, like other pantry pests, will eat almost any type of dry foodstuff—even soup-mix powders, dried fruit, and spices. If you find wormlike larvae or filaments in some newly bought grocery product (one mode of entry into a house), reseal the package and get a refund from the store or put the package in an outdoor garbage can.

If you see the insects in an opened package, get rid of it and check the contents of others. Clear the shelves and brush them; eggs or pupae may be in the corners. Paint the shelves' edges and corners with a household formulation of malathion or diazinon and let them dry. Line the shelves with fresh paper or wash treated areas with soap and water to prevent contaminating stored food. At all times store dry foodstuffs, including pet food, in tightly closed jars, cans, or heavy-gauge plastic bags.

Flower arranging

Keeping flowers fresh; basic design principles

For longer life, cut flowers early in the morning; use a sharp knife or scissors and immerse the stems immediately in tepid water. If the stems are

woody, scrape a little bark from the base to help them absorb water. When buying cut flowers, choose blossoms that are just beginning to open.

Let the stems sit in deep water for several hours. As you arrange the flowers, clip off the bottom of each stem and strip any leaves that would be under water in your vase. Be sure your vase is scrupulously clean.

To hold flowers in place, use florist's foam or a pin holder and florist's clay, available at flower shops. Use the clay to anchor the pin holder to the container. If you are using foam, soak it for several hours until it is thoroughly wet, then pack it tightly into the vase so that it doesn't wobble.

A flower arrangement should have an overall sense of balance. The balance may be symmetrical, as in a round centerpiece, or asymmetrical, as in a scheme of three handsome branches and a single spectacular blossom.

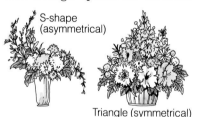

S-shape (asymmetrical)

Triangle (symmetrical)

Scale and proportion of the flowers should be appropriate to one another as well as to the setting and container. Combine a variety of colors, patterns, and textures within a unified whole.

Unity might be achieved by massing similar flowers. Or a few dramatic flowers could provide a focal point to unify several varieties: first place a few stalks to establish the overall shape, then add filling material, usually greenery and light, relatively inconspicuous flowers. Finally, arrange the most dramatic flowers strategically at the heart of the bouquet.

Flower beds

Planning and planting a colorful summer-long display

Whether you want a big, showy patch of color or a narrow border of bloom, choose a place with good drainage that gets at least 6 hours of sun a day.

The first step is planning. Before you buy a seed or lift a spade, make a sketch (graph paper helps) and decide what's to go where. In a large bed, allow for a stepping-stone or two so you can work without doing damage.

Start with the perennials (see *Perennials*). They're the plants that last year after year. Choose plants that are hardy in your area and will give a good blend of color. Some bloom early and some bloom late but the foliage usually lasts all season, so think about the color and texture of the leaves. Allow each plant enough space to flourish. Consider height as well as width, putting taller plants in the back or center.

Next come bulbous plants, such as daffodils, irises, tulips, gladioli, and daylilies (see *Bulbs, corms, and tubers*). Most of these bear showy blossoms that last only a little while. They look best in groups; to heighten the effect repeat the groupings at intervals.

Leave space for annuals from seed or for a succession of bedding plants (see *Bedding plants*). Because these are replaced often, you can let your imagination run free. Try different colors and different groupings. You can even intersperse herbs and such vegetables as lettuce and broccoli.

Planting the bed
Mark out the space and dig or rototill at least 9 inches deep, working in organic matter and fertilizer as needed (see *Soil preparation*). Then divide up the space according to your plan, using stakes in place of individual plants, and string to outline groups.

Plant perennials first, then (according to season) bulbs and annuals. Outline the bed with railroad ties, bricks, or flat stones set flush with the soil so that they won't block lawnmower wheels. (See also *Planting*.)

Flower drying

Preserving blossoms for dried-flower arrangements

Choose only bright, perfect flowers and leaves for drying. Pick them about noon on a clear, dry day, and make sure they are free of moisture, insects, and disease. Begin drying procedures immediately.

Air drying
This method is good for small flowers in clusters, such as yarrow, baby's breath, and hydrangea. Remove all leaves except one near each blossom. Gather the flowers into small bunches and secure them with rubber bands. If you tie them with string or wire, tighten the ties every few days as the stalks dry and shrink. Hang the flowers upside down in a dry, dark place where air can circulate freely around them. Leave them for 2 to 4 weeks, until they are dry but not brittle.

Using a drying agent
To dry flowers with thick heads, such as roses, zinnias, and daffodils, use silica gel, available at craft stores, or perlite from a nursery or florist. The flowers are less likely to mildew and will retain their colors better. If the silica gel has absorbed moisture (the crystals will be pink), set it in a 250°F oven for an hour or until it turns blue.

Spread a 1-inch layer of the drying agent in the bottom of an airtight container. Choose flowers of similar type and size, remove their leaves, and clip off all but ½ to 1 inch of stem.

On top of the agent, place cupped flowers (such as roses) upright, radial shapes facedown, and sprays flat. Completely cover them with additional crystals. Seal and label the container and place it in a cool, dark place.

When the flower petals are almost as crisp as paper (in about a week), gently pour off the agent. Thread florist's wire through the flower heads and secure with florist's tape to provide stems for arrangements.

Flower pressing

Preserving summer memories

For best results, pick flowers and leafy plants around noon. Orange and yellow blossoms retain their colors best; most blues and pinks fade; reds turn brown. Lay each plant between two layers of absorbent paper (best for fleshy flowers) or waxed paper (fine for thin or delicate types). With thick heads, such as roses, press the petals individually. Weight the flowers with a heavy book or bricks; leave them in a warm, dry place for at least 4 weeks.

To make a framed picture, cut a piece of heavy construction paper to fit the frame. Gently arrange the flowers on the paper to form a spray, bouquet, or other pleasing arrangement. With a toothpick, dab a bit of white glue on the back of each plant; press it in place. When the picture is dry, lay it facedown in the frame. Place cardboard backing over it, and push ½-inch brads into the frame to hold the backing. Cut wrapping paper to fit, and glue it to the back of the frame as a seal.

F

Flu

Recognizing and dealing with its symptoms; avoiding its risks

Flu (short for influenza) is an acute, highly contagious, potentially risky viral infection that begins like an ordinary cold but gets worse. Typically it involves fever, chills, sweating, headache, weakness, loss of appetite, runny nose, sore throat, coughing, sore skin, and general achiness.

Usually the only remedy is time and rest, plus a call to your doctor. Drink plenty of liquids; control the discomfort of fever and achiness with aspirin or acetaminophen (for a child use the latter); follow your doctor's advice.

Without precautions secondary infection can develop from the flu virus or from bacteria that thrive on lowered resistance. The very young, the elderly, and those with diabetes, or chronic cardiovascular or pulmonary disease, asthma, or anemia are especially at risk and can be vaccinated against flu; consult your doctor.

With proper care you should feel better within a few days. But that doesn't mean you are fully recovered. A premature rush back to normal activities invites fatigue and a relapse.

Because it is so contagious, flu often comes in epidemics. During an epidemic, caution is the best prevention. Don't get overtired—that lowers resistance. Stay out of crowds. If you get flu, avoid close contact with others. Cover your mouth when coughing or blowing your nose. Discard tissues in a paper bag and trash it daily. Wash your hands often—always before touching others' food or utensils.

Fluorescent lights

Replacing tubes, starter, and ballast

Caution: Before removing a fluorescent tube or working on the fixture, turn off power to its circuit (see *Circuit testing*).

If a fluorescent lamp fails to light, check the service panel; replace a blown fuse or reset a tripped circuit breaker, if any. If the tube still doesn't light or if it flickers or blinks, turn off power to the fixture and twist the tube slightly back and forth to make sure it's firmly seated in the sockets.

If that doesn't work, give the tube a quarter turn toward you and pull it out. Handle the tube carefully. Use long-nose pliers to straighten a bent tube pin. Spray the socket contacts and the pins with electric contact cleaner. Clean a dirty tube with a damp cloth; let it dry before reinstalling it. Tighten the socket screws; replace broken sockets.

To reinstall the tube, line up the pins with the socket slots, push the

If the ends of a tube glow, but the center does not, replace the starter.

If the lamp still doesn't work, hums loudly, or repeatedly blows a fuse on a circuit that isn't overloaded, the ballast, which regulates the flow of power to the tube, may be defective. Turn off the power and remove the tube and the screws holding the lid to the channel (the ballast may be attached to the lid or to the channel). First check the ballast for loose or incorrect wiring; tighten the mounting screws and all electrical connections. Compare the wiring with the diagram on the ballast; reattach the wires if necessary. If the problem persists, remove the ballast. Note how its wires are connected and disconnect them; unscrew the mounting screws. Replace the ballast with a new one of the same type and wattage or with a low-noise type.

Troubleshoot a circular fixture as you would a lamp with straight tubes. To remove a circular tube, turn off power to its circuit, grasp the tube in both hands at the collar, and carefully pull down until the pins come out of the socket; disengage the tube from the tube clips. To install a new tube,

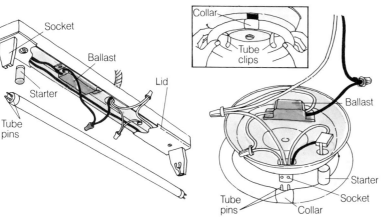

tube in, and give it a quarter turn. Still no light? Install a new tube of the same wattage and type. A new tube may flicker for an hour or two at first. If flickering lasts longer or if the new tube doesn't light, replace the starter with a new one of the same wattage. Rapid- and instant-start fluorescents don't have starters.

Blackening at the ends of a tube means that it's worn out; replace it. If only one end of the tube is discolored, remove it, turn it over, and reinstall it.

gently turn the collar to align the pins with the socket. Hold the tube in both hands and, with thumbs, press the pins into the socket. Push the tube clips in slightly with your middle fingers, and slip the tube into place.

Frequent turning on and off wastes power and shortens tube life. When leaving a room for a short time, leave the lamp on. Most fluorescents won't work below 50° F. Warm the room or install a low-temperature ballast. (See also *Light fixture rewiring*.)

Fly-fishing

Fooling a fish with bits of feather, fur, and fluff

Fly-fishing requires a flexible rod 7 to 9 feet long, a fly-casting reel affixed behind the handgrip, fly line and leader, and the knack of thinking like a fish. It is not enough for the lure to look like a mayfly, mosquito, grub, or minnow; it must act like one too.

Dry flies float, resting on fine filaments (hackles) that dimple the water as an insect's legs do. Wet flies go underwater. Those that look like grubs, nymphs, or drowned things are simply called wet flies; those that look like minnows are streamers or bucktails.

To cast a fly, first strip about 20 feet of line from the reel with your left hand (if you are right-handed). Hold the line lightly as, with a flick of the right wrist, you bring the rod to just

past vertical. The instant the line extends straight behind you (1) flick the rod ahead (2)—again, with wrist action. After several such "false casts" in which you keep the fly in the air while playing out more line, bring the rod forward (3) aiming at the target, and let the fly drop lightly onto the water.

Place a dry fly just upstream of where you think the fish is. Let it drift with the current or breeze for a second or two while you keep the line out of the water; then cast again. Place a wet fly a little farther upstream and let it tumble freely past the fish. Place a streamer or bucktail a little downstream and pull it against the current in slight darts and dashes. Do not jerk a wet fly out of the water.

A fish may leap from the water to take a dry fly, or the fly may just disappear. With a wet fly, you will feel a sudden tug on the line. In any case, the hook must be set quickly, with a firm and gentle pull, before the fish realizes that its mouth is full of feathers. Play the fish by manipulating the line with your left hand; the reel is for storing line, not for fighting fish.

Flying discs

How to hold and throw a plastic saucer

A windless day and a good quality flying disc are all you need to learn this modern version of the ancient sport of disc throwing.

Curl your hand around the disc in the backhand grip—thumb on top, index finger following the curve of the rim, the rest of the fingers fanned out on the underside with the little finger pressed against the inside of the rim. Hold the disc in front of you as shown.

Swing the disc away from your body, smoothly uncurling your hand. Release the disc with a snap of the wrist. Once you've mastered this basic throw, add a short run of up to 10 yards before the release.

To make the disc curve in flight, tilt it at the time of release and use less snap in the wrist. To make the disc hover, then float gently earthward, greatly increase the wrist action and loft the disc into the air like a fly ball in baseball. To skip the disc off the ground, use an underarm delivery and hit a point 10 to 20 feet away.

In flight a disc is unpredictable, so reposition yourself several times, and raise both arms for the catch at the last minute. Grab the edge of the disc with two hands and pull the disc toward your body.

Fly-tying

The basics of the art

Thousands of patterns exist for dry and wet flies, bucktails, and streamers. (For the differences, see *Fly-fishing*.) Some are realistic imitations of living things; others are fanciful creations. The dry trout fly shown, called Grizzly Wulff, imitates a mayfly. It is designed to stay afloat in fast water.

A fly's body is made by wrapping fine thread around a hook, incorporating the tail, wings, and other parts as you go; it is often adorned with fur, floss, or tinsel. The tail and wings are usually the tips of feathers, but animal hair or yarn may also be used. The hackle, usually a feather from a rooster's neck, is stiff and bushy in a dry fly, long and wispy in a wet one. The head is of thread, wrapped and lacquered.

To start, you'll need a miniature vise, hackle pliers that open when squeezed, tweezers, fine-pointed scissors, bobbins for holding thread, and an awl-like dubbing needle for fine work. Supplies include hooks in several sizes, from No. 16 (small) to No. 6 (large); bits of feather, fur, hair, and yarn; mylar tinsel; thread; tier's wax; and head lacquer. Buy a beginner's set and add more as needed.

Making a Grizzly Wulff
(1) Wrap the shank of the hook with waxed thread; add a tail of deer hair by wrapping the base. (2) Use a larger bunch of hair for the wings; cut off the extra and wrap. (3) Push the wing hair upright, divide it into two bunch-es, and crisscross the thread between them. (4) Tie in the bases of one brown and one grizzly hackle feather; then wrap the body with pale-yellow floss. Wind the hackle feathers several times around the body in front of and behind the wings, separating the fibers with a needle. Wrap the head; lacquer it and the body.

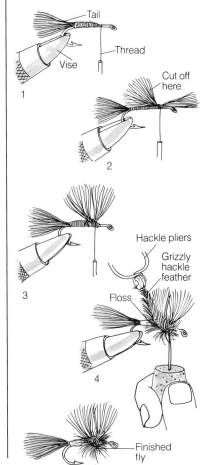

Foam mattresses

Selecting and caring for one

Foam mattresses are available in latex (rubber) and polyurethane. You may prefer the feel of one or the other, but polyurethane usually lasts longer. Also, higher density foams are longer wearing than those of lower density. You can select a soft, medium, or firm mattress (the choice has nothing to do with density). For comfort, choose foam that is at least 4 inches thick.

Maintain a foam mattress as you would any other. Protect it with a quilted mattress pad and air it when you change the bedding. Vacuum the cover occasionally, and if it is removable, launder it about every 6 months. Foam mattresses need not be turned.

To spot clean a foam mattress, use a dry-foam cleaner or a sponge dipped in detergent solution and squeezed dry; allow the bed to dry completely before making it. *Note:* solvent-based cleaners and heat deteriorate rubber.

Folding doors

Installing these space savers

There are two styles of folding doors: bifold and accordion. To work correctly, each must be plumb and hung from level track (see *Leveling; Plumb line*). The track, pivots, pivot brackets, slide guides, rollers, and other hardware are supplied with them.

To hang a pair of bifold doors, first install the track, complete with two top pivot brackets and a plastic or rubber snubber to cushion the impact where the doors meet. Push one pivot bracket to the wall and drop a plumb line from its center to the floor. Install a bottom pivot bracket at that point. Put the door's bottom pivot into its bracket and slide the top pivot bracket toward the center until you can slip the top pivot into it. Then slide the bracket back, inserting the spring-mounted slide guide into the track, and tighten the setscrew. Make

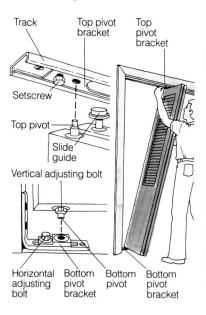

Track — Top pivot bracket — Top pivot bracket

Setscrew

Top pivot

Slide guide

Vertical adjusting bolt

Horizontal adjusting bolt — Bottom pivot bracket — Bottom pivot — Bottom pivot bracket

any fine adjustments with the horizontal and vertical adjusting bolts. Hang the second door in the same way. Then close the doors and mount a pair of aligners near the bottom on the back.

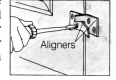

Aligners

To hang an accordion door, first position the track and mark the screw holes. With the doors tied or taped shut, slide the rollers onto the track. Then screw the track in place. Drop a plumb from both ends of the track; use one as a guide for attaching the door's hinged wall panel and the other for placing the strike plate into which the latch fits. (See also *Sliding doors.*)

Fondue

A communal feast

Although there are several kinds of fondue dishes, the most familiar one is cheese. This is especially popular in Swiss cafés where one sees people spearing hunks of bread on long forks and dunking them into hot cheese.

To prepare fondue for four persons, rub the inside of a heavy saucepan with garlic. Pour in 1¾ cups dry white wine and heat slowly until the wine starts to bubble. Meanwhile, dice ½ pound each of well-aged Gruyère and Emmentaler cheeses (if not well aged, they tend to lump). Mix the cheeses with 2 tablespoons cornstarch and toss with your hands.

Add a handful of the cheese mixture to the wine and stir with a wooden spoon until it is almost melted; then add another handful. Continue adding the cheese in batches and stirring until all is blended. The cheese will clump at first, but finally will become creamy. Add ¼ cup kirsch and a dash each of pepper and nutmeg.

Transfer the cheese to a fondue pot set over a table warmer. (If the fondue separates, return it to moderate heat on the stove and stir in a blend of ¼ cup white wine and ½ teaspoon cornstarch.) Give each guest a fondue fork and about ¼ pound of 1½-inch bread cubes, each with some crust on it.

Chocolate fondue can be a fun conclusion for a meal. Melt 1 pound semisweet chocolate pieces in a fondue pot over low heat. Stir in 2 tablespoons rum, brandy, or kirsch. Provide the guests with one or more of the following for dipping: thoroughly chilled cherries, strawberries, or chunks of pears or peaches; also cubed angel food or sponge cake, or plain cookies.

Food mills

Puréeing food without power

A food mill—a metal bowl with a perforated bottom—not only purées food but, unlike a food processor, it strains out seeds, pulp, and skins. A blade fitted closely to the bottom is turned by a handle to force food through the perforations. If the blade jams, you only have to reverse its direction and scrape away the residue with a spoon.

A food mill is ideal for jams, baby food, applesauce, riced potatoes, and tomato sauce. Before adding food to a mill, you should cut it in chunks and, except for soft foods, cook it.

Food mills are available in 1-, 2-, and 3-quart capacities. One type has three interchangeable discs for a fine, medium, or coarse purée.

Food poisoning

Treatment and prevention

Diarrhea or vomiting caused by contaminated food usually lasts no longer than 24 hours. To avoid dehydration, drink water, taking a sip every 15 minutes if you have trouble keeping anything down. Continue with a liquid diet for 24 hours; only then return gradually to bland solids. Medication is rarely necessary.

Consult a doctor if you suspect food poisoning in a child under 3 or if anyone's symptoms last longer than 2 days or are unusually severe. Get emergency medical help if watery diarrhea strikes every 10 or 15 minutes, if it contains blood or mucus, or if abdominal pain or fever is constant.

A rare, life-threatening form of food poisoning is *botulism*. Nausea and vomiting begin 12 to 36 hours after eating a toxin-containing food; they are followed by muscle weakness, dry-

F

ness of mouth and throat, blurred vision, unsteadiness, and difficulty in swallowing, speaking, and breathing. Immediate hospitalization is the only course. Try to identify the food, which may be a canned fruit, fish, or vegetable product; the food may be soft, contain gas bubbles, and smell foul. Take a sample of the food you suspect to the hospital.

Preventing food poisoning
Some bacteria that cause food poisoning are carried on the skin. Harmless in small quantities, they can double in number every 20 minutes in improperly stored food. Illness is caused either by the bacteria or by the toxins they produce; neither necessarily indicates its presence by off-color food or by bad odor. Freezing does not kill bacteria; cooking does but doesn't destroy all toxins or spores.

Wash your hands well before handling food. Cook hamburgers to an internal temperature of 160° F, and chicken to 180° F. Thaw frozen meat completely so that the cooking heat will reach its center. Once food has thawed, don't refreeze it. Serve a cooked food immediately; otherwise, refrigerate it. Avoid picnic foods that nourish bacteria such as custard, cream fillings, mayonnaise, and bologna. Use your nose: don't eat a food with bad odor. When canning, follow instructions to the letter.

Food processors

Doing kitchen chores fast

To make the most of your food processor, find out all the chores that it can do and adapt your recipes and work habits to fit the processor into your kitchen routines.

When preparing dishes that have many chopped or sliced ingredients, start with the hard, solid ingredients, then process the softer ones. If textures are similar, do the chopped ingredients first, then the sliced and shredded ones. To chop, slice, or shred meats and cheeses, have them *very* cold or semifrozen but not hard frozen. Don't attempt to process any hard cheese that can't be pierced easily with a sharp knife.

To make purées for soup, baby food, and thickening sauces, drain any liquid, reserving ½ cup. Fill the processor bowl about half full with the soft or cooked food. Process in 15- to 20-second spurts, adding liquid as needed. Scrape down the sides of the bowl now and then. Purées can be frozen in ice-cube trays for future use.

To mix pastry or biscuit dough, first process the dry ingredients a few seconds, then add the chilled fat in pieces, and process just until mealy. With the motor running, add liquid through the small feed tube; process until the dough forms a ball. Many processors let you mix yeast doughs.

When making cakes or cookies, add the dry ingredients last. If the recipe calls for any chopped dried fruits or nuts, do these first and set them aside. Chill the fruits before chopping, and process them with some of the flour from the recipe.

The processor makes dry cookie or bread crumbs efficiently. Break the ingredients in pieces. Run the motor in 15-second spurts until the crumbs are as fine as you want.

Caution: Always push food down the feed tube with the plastic pusher—not your fingers. Never open the work bowl until blades have completely stopped. When emptying the bowl, hold the metal blade in place with a spatula or spoon, or remove it just before tilting the bowl.

Food storage

Preserving freshness

Most green vegetables need refrigeration and high humidity; shake off excess moisture and store them in plastic bags, preferably in a vegetable crisper. Eat them within 3 to 6 days. Cabbage, cauliflower, carrots, beets, turnips, and celery will keep about 2 weeks in the refrigerator. Rutabagas, thick-skinned squash, dry onions, and potatoes should be stored uncovered in a cool (60°F), dark place. Otherwise, buy small quantities and keep them in the refrigerator for a few days.

Fruits
Ripe cherries, berries, and tomatoes will keep refrigerated and uncovered for a few days. Most other ripe fruits

can be kept in the room for 3 to 5 days, depending on the temperature. Although citrus fruits taste best when stored at 60°F to 70°F, they will keep at cooler temperatures for 3 to 4 weeks.

Breads and staples
Except in humid weather, bread stays fresh for about 5 days in a plastic bag at room temperature. Because bread gets tough in the refrigerator, it's better to freeze it in humid weather.

Flour, sugar, spices, and other dry foods, as well as oil, keep best in airtight containers, away from light and heat. White flour stays palatable for 8 to 12 months; whole wheat for 2 to 4 months. Keep enough oil for daily use in a small container; store a larger quantity in the refrigerator. (Cold oil may cloud; it clears as it warms up.)

Meats and dairy products
Store meats in the coldest part of the refrigerator. They need to breathe, and will keep better if you loosen the store wrappings or rewrap them in wax paper. Roasts, steaks, chops, and poultry will keep from 3 to 4 days; use stew, ground meat, and organ meats within a day of purchase. For longer storage, freeze meat immediately (see *Freezing food*). Refrigerate eggs, milk, and cheeses and use them within a week. (Hard cheeses keep longer.)

Caution: Never taste food that you suspect is spoiled; it may harbor bacteria that could make you very ill. Throw it away.

Wrap or cover all moist foods or liquids that you store in the refrigerator; otherwise the food will dry out and the refrigerator motor may be overworked.

Footings and foundations

Supports for buildings, walls, and other structures

Footings are belowground concrete structures that support and transmit the weight of an aboveground structure or a foundation to the soil. They must be below the frost line.

The building's weight and the soil's load-carrying capacity determine the footing's size. For one-story structures and outbuildings, the rough formula is: a footing's width is twice the thickness of the foundation wall;

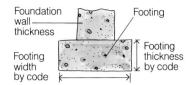

Foundation wall thickness — Footing

Footing width by code

Footing thickness by code

a footing's thickness is the same as that of the foundation wall. How to build footings and foundations is specified by local building code; check with your municipality's building department (see *Building permits*).

Forms and uses

Common types of footings are flat top, for a foundation wall or a slab; keyed, for anchoring concrete or masonry walls; and, for house additions, pier footings, on top of which are piers, posts, or blocks connected by rods. If the structure to rest on the footing will be of concrete blocks or poured concrete, footings must have connectors (steel rods or a keyed channel).

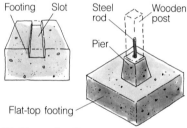

Keyed footing

Footing   Slot

Flat-top footing

Pier footing

Steel rod   Wooden post

Pier

Making a footing

Excavate a trench to the depth required by the local building code and 16 to 20 inches wide—wider if it's so deep you must get into it to work. If you intend to pour directly into the excavation, level the bottom so that the footing's weight will be distributed evenly on undisturbed solid soil.

All footings require rebars (steel reinforcing rods). They are generally available in 20-foot lengths; you may

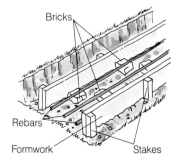

Bricks

Rebars

Formwork   Stakes

have to splice several with wire for the length you need. Before pouring, set the rebars on 2⅔-inch thick bricks.

Build flat-top formwork using the same preparation, tools, and materials as for a basic slab (see *Concrete formwork*). For a keyed footing, start at the center of the long forms and mark every 32 to 48 inches for crosswise 1 x 3 or 2 x 4 lateral braces. Then center and nail an oiled 2 x 4 perpendicular to these braces; nail the braces to the forms.

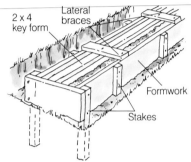

2 x 4 key form   Lateral braces

Formwork

Stakes

Pier forms themselves can be used as footings in areas where there is no frost. Buy premade piers at a lumberyard. For a job that will have footings connected to piers, posts, or columns, pour concrete in two stages: first, the footing, into which you place centered steel rods; then, 24 hours later, the pier or a sono-tube column.

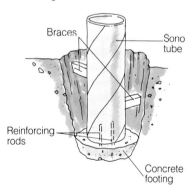

Braces   Sono tube

Reinforcing rods

Concrete footing

Foreclosure

How to avoid losing your home

Put mortgage payments at the top of your priority list of bills. If you can't make a mortgage payment on time (or within the grace period of 10 to 15 days that is usually provided), explain your situation to your bank—or to whomever your lender is. In most cases, you can reach a solution if you have a good track record of paying bills. If you repeatedly miss making your mortgage payments, you might lose your home as a result of a foreclosure. Foreclosure is the process that enables your bank to collect on your debt by selling your home (the collateral for the loan) if you fall behind in paying your mortgage.

Being delinquent in one monthly payment will not result in foreclosure unless your mortgage contains an acceleration clause. Under an acceleration clause, if you miss only a single payment, your bank has a right to demand full payment of the mortgage and to foreclose if you fail to pay it.

A strict foreclosure allows the bank to take your property, even if its value is greater than what you owe. Few states, however, permit it. Usually your property is sold at auction. The money pays the foreclosure expenses and mortgage debt. You receive any money left, but your lender can sue you for a deficiency judgment if you still owe more.

Foreclosure procedures vary from state to state. In many states you can even buy back (redeem) your property within a certain period after a foreclosure auction. Check with a lawyer.

Forms of address

How to address public officials and clergymen

The following models give generally accepted titles to use in the address of a letter, followed by proper salutations. When the person in question is a woman: (a) replace *Sir* with *Madam;* (b) if *Mr.* is followed by a title, as in *Mr. President,* replace *Mr.* with *Madam;* (c) if *Mr.* is followed by a name, replace *Mr.* with *Miss, Mrs.,* or *Ms.*

U.S. President
The President—*Dear Mr. President:*
U.S. Vice President
The Honorable Franklin Jared, Vice President of the United States—*Sir:* or *Dear Mr. Vice President:*
U. S. or State Senator
The Honorable Douglas Jackson, United States Senate *or* The State Senate—*Sir:* or *Dear Senator Jackson:*

U. S. or State Representative
The Honorable Victor Gonzalez, House of Representatives *or* The State Assembly—*Sir:* or *Dear Mr. Gonzalez:*

Judge
The Honorable Robert M. Wright—*Dear Judge Wright:*

Governor
The Honorable Stephen Benson, Governor of (State)—*Sir:* or *Dear Governor Benson:*

Mayor
The Honorable Adam Simons, Mayor of (City)—*Sir:* or *Dear Mr. Mayor:* or *Dear Mayor Simons*

Catholic Archbishop or Bishop
The Most Reverend Francis Xavier O'Shea, Archbishop (or Bishop) of (Archdiocese or Diocese)—*Your Excellency:* or *Dear Archbishop (or Bishop) O'Shea:*

Catholic Priest
The Reverend Laurence Orson—*Reverend Father:* or *Dear Father Orson:*

Episcopal Bishop
The Right Reverend Nigel Damon, Bishop of (Diocese)—*Right Reverend Sir:* or *Dear Bishop Damon:*

Other Protestant Clergymen
The Reverend Peter S. Bates—*Reverend Sir:* or *Dear Mr. Bates:* or, if he has a doctorate, The Reverend Dr. Ray Albertson *or* The Reverend Ray Albertson, D.D.—*Reverend Sir:* or *Dear Dr. Albertson:*

Rabbi
Rabbi Mordecai Levy—*Dear Rabbi Levy:* or, if he has a doctorate, Rabbi Jesse Schwartz, D.D.—*Dear Rabbi Schwartz:* or Dr. Jesse Schwartz—*Dear Dr. Schwartz:*

Fox and geese

A board game for two players

You can make your own board for fox and geese by drilling ½-inch holes into a 12-inch square of ½-inch plywood in the pattern shown. Then get one distinctive marble for the fox and 17 others for the geese. Arrange them on the board as shown. The object of the game is for the fox to kill the geese without getting cornered.

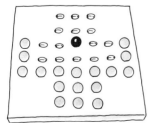

Players alternate. The first player moves the fox; the other moves any goose. The fox can move one hole in any direction or jump over an adjacent goose, landing in an empty hole, or make a series of connected jumps. (A goose that is jumped is considered *killed*; remove it from the board.) A goose can move only one hole forward or sideward and cannot jump. If the fox kills all the geese, it wins. If the geese corner the fox so that it cannot move, the geese win.

Freezing food

Quick and easy preservation

To prevent drying, package all foods to be frozen in moisture-proof wrapping or containers and seal them tightly. Freeze them at 0°F or below.

Heavy-duty aluminum foil is an excellent wrap because it can be pressed to fit the shape of an item; put an extra layer around any sharp protrusions. Heavy plastic wrap, plastic bags, and freezer paper (laminated paper and plastic) plus freezer tape are also suitable. Freezer bags, which require a special sealer, permit you to boil foods right in the bag. With all wraps, eliminate as much air as possible.

Use tempered glass jars, plastic containers, and coffee and nut cans for freezing soft or liquid foods. Leave ½ to 1 inch of expansion space at the top for liquids. Foil baking dishes are ideal for foods to be reheated.

Label packages with masking tape and a freezer pen; show the contents, quantity, and date of freezing. Also include such information as "needs seasonings" or "dilute before using."

What not to freeze
Foods with a high moisture content, such as lettuce, raw tomatoes, cucumbers, radishes, celery, and boiled potatoes do not freeze well. Neither do cottage and cream cheeses and sour cream. Mayonnaise, light cream, and milk usually separate or curdle. Other items that freeze poorly are custard pies, meringue, cream fillings, and cake frostings made with brown sugar or egg whites. Foods made with gelatin may separate. Fried foods tend to turn rancid and become soggy.

Baked goods
Yeast breads can be kept frozen for up to 6 months. Cool freshly baked bread completely before wrapping it. Yeast dough can be frozen and stored for up to 5 weeks wrapped in greased plastic bags, each bag containing enough for one baking.

Cakes are best frozen without frosting; if you do frost one, use confectioner's sugar and butter. To freeze a cake, first chill it in the freezer, then wrap it, protecting the icing with an inner layer of waxed paper. Freezing cake batters is not recommended.

Precooked pastries and unbaked pie crust freeze well. To prepare an unbaked pie for freezing, brush the inside of the bottom and top crusts with shortening, and don't prick the top until you are ready to bake it.

Eggs and cooked dishes
Crack open eggs; either separate whites and yolks or stir whole eggs. Add ¼ teaspoon salt or 1½ teaspoons sugar to each ½ cup of egg yolks to keep them from becoming gummy. It's convenient to freeze the number of eggs you'll need for a specific purpose.

Stews, casseroles, meat pies, and spaghetti sauces freeze well. It's best to add salt and spices upon reheating, as some spices change when frozen.

Fish, meat, and poultry
Freeze fish only if it's absolutely fresh. Scale and clean it thoroughly (see *Fish cleaning*). Fish that weigh 2 pounds or less are best frozen whole and will keep better if frozen in water. Cut larger fish into steaks or fillets. Place wax paper between fillets and steaks before wrapping.

Remove extra fat from meat and bones, if practical. Because meat is subject to freezer burn (dry spots), rewrap packaged meats or add another layer to the store wrapping. Separate chops and patties with wax paper. Freeze meat quickly; slow freezing reduces its quality. Place the portions in a single layer on the bottom and along the sides of the freezer.

Remove poultry innards and freeze them separately. Wash and dry the entire bird; trim any excess fat. Don't stuff raw poultry before freezing it.

Vegetables and fruits
Most vegetables must be blanched before freezing to destroy enzymes that cause loss of color and flavor (see *Blanching*). Leave them in the boiling water for 2 to 4 minutes, depending

on thickness (whole carrots take 5 minutes; corn on the cob 6 to 8 minutes). Rinse and pack the vegetables immediately afterwards.

Fruit usually retains its flavor with freezing, but the texture is softer. A few fruits—cranberries, blueberries, raspberries, grapes, and figs—can be packed dry (unsweetened) if they are to be cooked later. Freeze them in a single layer on cookie sheets, then package them.

If a fruit will be cooked after thawing, add syrup; if it will be served uncooked, add sugar. To fruits that tend to darken, also add ascorbic acid dissolved in water—¼ teaspoon per quart of fruit for sugar pack; ½ teaspoon per quart for syrup.

For a sugar pack, pit and halve or slice the fruit, then sprinkle it with ascorbic acid and ⅔ to ¾ cup sugar per quart of fruit. Stir until juicy. Insert crumpled wax paper under the container lid to hold the fruit under the juice.

For a syrup pack, allow 1 cup syrup per quart of fruit. Dissolve 2 cups sugar in 1 quart hot water. Cool, then pour it over the fruit and pack in containers. (See also *Thawing food*.)

Frostbite

Emergency treatment

The freezing of a body part is most likely to occur in weather below 20°F, especially when there is wind. A frostbitten area looks white and feels rigid to the touch. The part feels numb to the victim and cannot be moved.

Get a victim to a hospital; if that's not possible, warm the frozen area in lukewarm, not hot, water (100°F to 105°F). Handle the frozen parts gently; don't rub them. When the part has thawed, it will be very painful. The victim must refrain from smoking. Don't apply ointment or medication to the thawed areas; instead, dry them and wrap them with sterile gauze. If fingers or toes were frozen, place sterile gauze pads between them. Elevate the thawed limb while transporting the person to a hospital as soon as possible. Don't allow the parts to refreeze. (See also *Hypothermia*.)

Frostings

The icing on the cake

Before frosting a cake, cool it completely, unless the recipe says otherwise. Partially freeze a crumbly cake. Trim any uneven places with a serrated knife. Choose a flat plate 2 inches wider than the cake on all sides. Put a dollop of frosting on the plate and center the cake on top. Set the plate on a lazy Susan, if you have one.

Spread frosting between layers and let it set before coating the top and sides. If you are using a cream filling, spread each cake layer first with a thin coating of melted and strained jelly or preserves (to keep filling from soaking in). Spread filling to within ¼ inch of the edges. Refrigerate the filled cake for 2 hours before frosting it.

To coat a cake with a thick frosting, spread a thin layer all over and let it set. Then refrost the cake, working up the sides first, finishing with the top. Use a metal spatula, dipping it in hot water to get a smooth finish.

To apply thin frosting to a sponge, chiffon, or angel food cake, pour it evenly over the top and let it run down the sides. On a firmer cake, spread the sides and top quickly; dip the spatula in hot water and smooth the surface. (See also *Cake decorating*.)

Basic butter cream frosting
Cream ⅓ cup butter or margarine until fluffy. Beat in 1 pound sifted confectioner's sugar, alternately with 5 tablespoons light cream or milk. Add 2 teaspoons vanilla and ¼ teaspoon salt. To thin, add a little cream; to thicken, add sugar. Fills and frosts two 8- or 9-inch layers or 24 cupcakes. *Chocolate butter cream:* Add ½ cup sifted cocoa with the sugar. *Citrus butter cream:* Substitute orange or lemon juice for the cream; omit vanilla. Add 3 to 4 teaspoons finely grated orange or lemon rind.

Ornamental icing
Beat 2 egg whites and ¼ teaspoon cream of tartar until foamy. Gradually add, then beat until thick, 3 cups sifted confectioner's sugar. If too thick to spread, add a few drops of hot water. Dries hard and glossy; makes enough to frost an 8- or 9-inch cake.

Frozen pipes

Thawing them out; averting catastrophe

Before thawing a frozen pipe, make sure it is not cracked. If it is, turn off the water and repair the break (see *Pipes*). To thaw a plastic pipe, wrap it with rags and pour boiling water over it. Use the same method for metal pipes or, after opening the nearest faucet, use a heat lamp, hairdryer, or propane torch to warm the pipe *gradually*, working backward from the

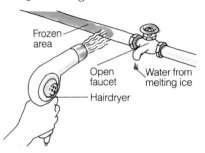

Frozen area

Open faucet

Water from melting ice

Hairdryer

faucet toward the frozen area. Never let a pipe get too hot to touch. Keep metal pipes (not plastic ones) from freezing by wrapping with electric heating cable and insulation.

During a winter cold snap, open all faucets a little. A steady drip may be enough to keep the water from freezing, and even if it does freeze, the open line may save the pipes from bursting. (See also *Boilers; Closing a house; Power failures*.)

Fruit trees

Starting young ones; rejuvenating old ones

Plant fruit trees in a sunny spot with fertile soil and good drainage, at least 8 feet from patios, water pipes, septic tanks, sewer lines, and anything else that could be damaged by their roots. Self-pollinating trees, such as sour cherries, European plums, and most peaches and nectarines, can be planted singly. Japanese plums, sweet cherries, most apples and pears, and some apricots bear fruit only if a different, compatible variety grows nearby to pollinate them.

Most fruit trees are grafted: the trunk grows upon a root of a different kind of tree. Plant dwarf trees with the graft 2 inches above the soil line; standard trees with the graft at soil level. Before planting, mix compost, leaf mold, peat moss, or other organic material into the soil, along with a little slow-acting complete fertilizer.

At planting time, prune off all but three or four of the stoutest branches to form your tree's framework. Cut back the remaining branches and the central leader (main stem) by about one-third. Keep branches that form a wide angle with the trunk—narrow crotches are weak—and keep only one of a pair of branches that grow at the same height on the trunk.

As trees grow, remove any suckers that arise from the roots and any "water sprouts" that come from the trunk. In spring, before growth begins, prune as needed so that light and air can reach all parts of the tree (see *Tree pruning*). Remove any branch that touches another. With apples, cherries, and pears, keep the central leader slightly taller than side branches. For peaches, plums, and apricots, cut the central leader back to form an open, vase-shaped tree with three or four main branches.

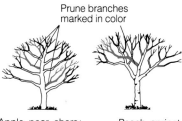

Prune branches marked in color

Apple, pear, cherry, plum

Peach, apricot, nectarine

Your tree is unlikely to bear for the first 3 or 4 years. During that time, mulch around the base and fertilize lightly in spring with manure or compost and with wood ashes or a balanced fertilizer (see *Fertilizing trees*). Thereafter, fertilize only if the tree is in obvious need; overfeeding encourages leaves at the expense of fruit.

Thinning for a good crop

When fruits appear, let them grow to about marble size, then remove any that are wormy, diseased, or undersize. Space the remaining ones 6 to 7 inches apart.

Renewing an old tree

An old, overgrown apple or pear tree can be brought back to fruitful vigor by heavy pruning. In late winter, cut out all dead and spindly branches and any that cross others. Cut out some of the large center branches, opening the heart of the tree to light and air. Thin out or remove knotted-looking spur clusters, where fruit has been borne for many years, and cut back long branches to strong-looking laterals. (See also *Citrus trees; Fig trees*.)

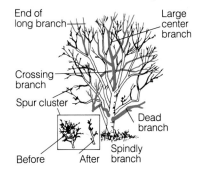

End of long branch
Large center branch
Crossing branch
Spur cluster
Dead branch
Spindly branch
Before
After

Frying

Browning food in deep fat; French fried potatoes

Deep-frying is a way of cooking food quickly in very hot fat. You can use an electric deep fryer with a built-in thermostat, or a deep, heavy pan plus a deep-fry thermometer. You will also need a wire basket, or a slotted spoon or tongs for handling food.

Foods to be fried should be evenly sized and no more than 1½ inches thick, as dry as possible, and at room temperature. Some, such as fish and chicken, brown better with a coating of flour or batter. (See also *Breading*.)

Fill the pan about ¾ full, preferably with an odorless and tasteless vegetable oil (these don't smoke at the usual frying temperatures). Set the thermostat, or immerse the thermometer, before heating the oil. If you have no thermometer, drop in a 1-inch bread cube when you think the oil is hot enough; it should brown in 60 seconds. If the oil temperature is too low, fried foods will be soggy and greasy; if too high, they will brown on the outside, but be underdone inside. At sea level recommended frying tempera-

tures are 350°F to 380°F; subtract about 3 degrees for each increase of 1,000 feet in elevation.

Fry small batches at a time so that the fat temperature does not drop drastically when food is added. Drain food in a single layer on paper toweling. Periodically skim out bits of food.

You can strain deep-fry oil and reuse it several times. Occasionally clarify it by cooking a raw potato in it.

French fried potatoes

Cut mature baking potatoes into square sticks about ⅜ inch thick (see *Dicing*). Soak them in cold water for 10 minutes; pat dry on paper toweling. Heat fat to 375°F. Fry the potatoes in batches, keeping each batch warm in a 250°F oven until all are cooked.

Fuel economy

Getting better car mileage

Where possible, accelerate gently, especially from a stop; an automatic transmission will upshift earlier for better mileage. With a manual, shift to higher gears as soon as possible, but don't strain the engine. Many new cars have upshift lights on the dash to guide you. See a traffic light, toll booth, or slow traffic? Take your foot off the gas pedal and let the car coast to a stop. If you're stopping for more than a minute, turn off the engine.

Hold steady highway speeds. Generally, 40 m.p.h. is most economical, but if your transmission has a lockup clutch or overdrive, speeds of around 50 m.p.h. may be better. Ask your dealer if you're not sure what kind of transmission you have. In climbing an upgrade, increase speed gradually as you approach, then hold as steady a throttle position as possible, even if your speed drops.

Keep windows closed and use the vent in warm weather to reduce aerodynamic drag. If it's very hot, use the air conditioning rather than opening windows at highway speeds. In cold weather, let the engine idle for 30 to 60 seconds, then drive no faster than 40 m.p.h. until the engine warms.

Reduce car weight by leaving unnecessary heavy items out of the trunk. In winter remove ice and snow from the body and underbody. On vacation, pack lightly. Avoid using a roof rack, which causes air drag.

Equipment checks

Inflate tires to the maximum pressure shown on the sidewalls; check pressure often. If tire wear is irregular, have the wheel alignment checked.

Have the engine tuned at least every 2 years or 24,000 miles. Have the choke operation checked on cars with carburetors if you note a sharp drop in mileage. However, it's normal to get lower mileage on short trips, in cold weather, and heavy traffic.

Fuel filters

Replacing them on a car

On most new cars, the fuel filter is inside the gas tank and can only be serviced by a mechanic. It's intended to last for the life of the car. Replace the filter on older cars as recommended in the owner's manual. On older General Motors cars and some others, the filter may be in the carburetor. Otherwise, it's in a fuel line; follow the fuel line away from the engine until you find the filter cannister. On some Japanese cars, the filter is near the gas tank.

Caution: When working with the fuel filter, let the engine cool, disconnect the battery cables, and don't smoke.

Filter in carburetor: Use a wrench to hold the fuel-inlet fitting, a second wrench to open the fuel-line nut. Unscrew the fitting. Catch the filter and a coil spring as they come out. Insert the spring, then a new filter; thread in the fitting and reconnect the fuel line.

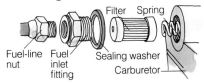

Fuel-line nut   Fuel inlet fitting   Filter   Spring   Sealing washer   Carburetor

In-line filter held by clamps: Using special pliers on spring-wire clamps, loosen or move the clamps away from the filter. Cut apart crimp clamps

Clamp   In-line filter   Clamp

with cutting pliers and replace with a spring-wire or worm-drive clamp of the same size. Work the filter necks free of the hoses. Slide the new clamps out to the hoses. Work the necks of the new filter into the hoses, then center the clamps over the necks; tighten.

Filter at carburetor: Disconnect the fuel hose at the filter. Use a wrench to unscrew the old filter and thread on a new one. Reconnect the hose.

In-line filter held by threaded fittings: Hold the filter's hex flange with one wrench, loosen the fuel-line fittings with a second wrench. Use new sealing washers on the fittings.

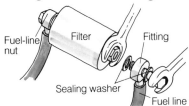

Fuel-line nut   Filter   Fitting   Sealing washer   Fuel line

Filter on fuel pump: Use a fabric-band oil-filter wrench to remove the cover, lift out the old element, and install a new one. Hand tighten the cover; if necessary, use a wrench.

Fuel pump   Fuel line   Filter   Filter cover

Finally, wipe up any spilled fuel, reconnect the battery cable, run the engine, and check for leaks.

Fuel injection

Diagnosing a hesitating engine on a fuel-injection car

If your car has throttle-body fuel injection under the air cleaner, it may suffer from hesitation and stumble if the fuel injector leaks or, on cars with two injectors, if one injector fails.

Remove the air-cleaner cover and unplug the wiring connector or connectors. Have a helper crank the engine. If fuel drips from an injector tip, have the injector replaced.

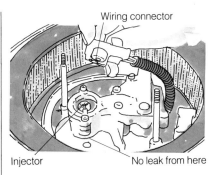

Wiring connector   Injector   No leak from here

If the throttle body has two injectors, crank the engine with the wiring attached as well as detached. Observe whether both injectors spray a cone-shaped spray. If one does not, reverse the wiring connectors and repeat the test. The other injector now fails to spray? The wiring is at fault. The no-spray injector still doesn't work? It is defective and should be replaced.

Furnaces

Cleaning the filter and the blower; adjusting the blower belt and speed; lubrication

In a forced warm-air heating system, cool air from the house enters the furnace through the return-air duct and passes through a filter. A motor-driven blower forces the air over the hot metal pipes of a heat exchanger located on top of the burner or over electric heating elements. Heated air flows

Forced warm-air heating system

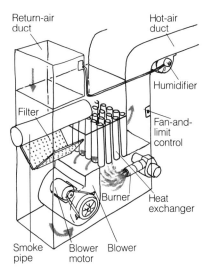

Return-air duct   Hot-air duct   Humidifier   Filter   Fan-and-limit control   Burner   Heat exchanger   Smoke pipe   Blower motor   Blower

into ducts ending in room registers; some systems humidify the air. A fan-and-limit control turns the blower on and off and shuts off the burner if the air passing through the hot-air duct becomes too hot.

Once a year, have the furnace professionally cleaned and checked for leaks. An oil burner and its controls should also be serviced yearly; a gas burner, less often. Basic cleaning and maintenance between servicings will keep the furnace working smoothly.

Caution: Before cleaning or working on a furnace, turn off power to it by switching off the safety switch, usually remotely mounted but sometimes near the furnace.

Cleaning the filter and the blower

A dirty filter reduces air flow and heating efficiency. Once a month during the heating season, remove the filter and hold it up to a bright light. If you can't see light easily through the filter, clean or replace it. Plastic or metal filters can be washed and reused. Hardware stores sell replacements for fiberglass filters. Install a filter so that the arrow marked on it points in the direction of the air flow.

Once a year, remove the blower access panel, and vacuum the area around the motor and the blower. Use a vacuum cleaner and a brush to clean the blower blades.

Adjusting the blower belt

In a belt-driven blower examine the belt for tension and wear twice a season. Check tension by pressing lightly on the belt midway between the motor and the blower pulleys. It should deflect by only ½ to ¾ inch. A tight or worn belt causes blower noise; too much slack reduces air flow. To adjust tension or to replace a worn belt, see *Drive belts.*

Blower and motor pulleys that are out of alignment cause belt wear and power loss. To check alignment, place one edge of a carpenter's square

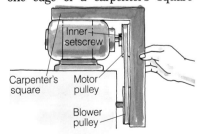

against the outer faces of the motor and blower pulleys. If they are not in a straight line at right angles to the motor, loosen the motor pulley's inner setscrew with a hex wrench and move the pulley forward or back as needed.

Adjusting blower speed

A slow blower delivers insufficient heat. A blower that runs too fast is noisy. To adjust blower speed, loosen the outer setscrew on the motor pulley with a hex wrench. Turn the outer pulley face clockwise to bring it closer to the inner face; this increases blower speed. Turn the outer face counterclockwise to decrease speed. Tighten the setscrew; adjust pulley alignment and belt tension.

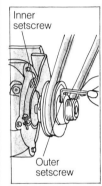

On a furnace with a direct drive blower, turn off all power to the furnace and remove the cover from the blower junction box, mounted on the blower or next to the furnace box. A hot wire, usually red, will be attached

Direct drive blower

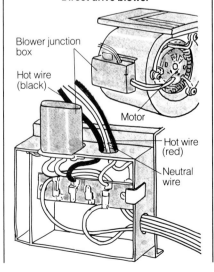

to one of two terminals marked low and medium low; these control the blower when the furnace is working. A second hot wire, usually black, will be attached to the medium high or high terminal used for central air conditioning. To increase blower speed, disconnect the appropriate wire and switch it from low to medium low or from medium high to high; reverse the procedure to decrease speed.

Oiling the motor and the blower

If there are oil cups or grease fittings on the motor and the blower, lubricate them annually. Put a few drops of 20-weight nondetergent oil into the oil cups or two "pumps" of automotive grease from a grease gun into each fitting. Don't overoil. (See also *Gas burners; Oil burners; Thermostat recalibrating; Warm-air heating.*)

Furring strips

Framework for new ceilings and walls

Before installing acoustical tiles or paneling over an irregular surface, you must create a level plane, using ceiling- or wall-width furring strips. These are lengths of wood, usually 1 x 2 or 1 x 3 inches. They may also be needed when installing new siding or shingles or plasterboard over uneven walls. It simplifies the task to make a scale drawing on graph paper. Plot from the center of the area outward: strips on 12-inch centers are usual for tiles, on 16-inch centers for paneling.

Nail furring strips at right angles to the joists or studs (see *Studs*), using two 2½-inch nails at each juncture. Check every two strips with a level. Hammer shims (thin wedges of wood) under any spot where the strips are not level. On a masonry wall, use masonry nails or adhesive, as advised in the paneling instructions or by your paneling dealer.

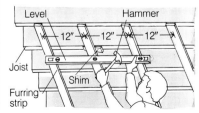

Fuse boxes

Why fuses blow; replacing a blown fuse

In older electric systems, incoming power is divided into branch circuits at a fuse box. Each circuit is protected by one or more fuses containing a metal strip that melts and breaks when the flow of current exceeds the circuit's capacity. In a plug fuse, the metal strip is visible through a plastic window. An overload breaks the strip; a short circuit discolors the window (see *Short circuits*). A blown cartridge fuse shows no sign of damage; test it with a continuity tester (see below). Keep spare fuses handy near the fuse box. Always replace a fuse with one of the same amperage.

Good fuse   Overload   Short circuit

Plug fuses of 15 or 20 amperes protect circuits for basic lighting, kitchen and laundry areas, and individual large appliances. Ferrule-type cartridges, rated up to 60 amperes, control 240-volt circuits for heavy-load appliances such as a clothes dryer. Knife-edge fuses in the large pullout main fuse block protect the main power line. Removing the pullout block or, in some fuse boxes, turning off a main power switch, cuts off all power in the house.

Caution: Before working at the fuse box, pull out the main fuse block or turn off the main switch. Wear shoes with rubber soles; do not stand on a wet spot. Keep one hand free when removing or replacing a fuse.

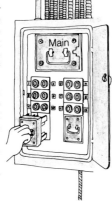

If the power to a circuit goes off, locate and correct the problem (see *Circuit testing*). Then, holding the blown fuse by its glass rim, turn it counterclockwise to remove it. Replace it with a new one; restore the power.

To test a cartridge fuse, pull out its fuse block and remove the fuse with a fuse puller. Touch the probes of a continuity tester to the ends of the fuse. If the tester doesn't light, the fuse is blown. Insert a new fuse into the spring clips by hand.

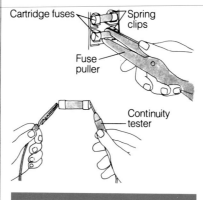

Cartridge fuses   Spring clips

Fuse puller

Continuity tester

Fuses in cars

Testing and replacing blown car fuses

When an electric accessory or a light (except for headlamps) fails to work, the cause may be a blown fuse. Fuses blow when there is too much current flow. However, nonrecurring conditions can also cause a fuse to blow. If a new fuse blows almost immediately, there is a circuit problem.

The fuse box may be under the dash, under the hood, or in the glove box (check your owner's manual). The fuse box is marked so that you can find the fuse for the affected circuit.

There are three types of car fuses: glass envelope, ceramic body, and minispade. When one blows, its metal

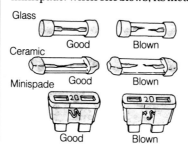

Glass
Good   Blown
Ceramic
Good   Blown
Minispade
Good   Blown

strip breaks (you may not be able to see the break with the fuse in the holder). To check, use a 12-volt test lamp with a pointed probe. Connect the lamp's alligator clip to body metal, turn on the problem circuit, and probe each end of the holder of a glass or ceramic fuse. With a minispade fuse, probe through the holes in the ends of the fuse. The test lamp should light in each case. If it lights in only one, the fuse is blown; if it lights in neither, there is a wiring problem.

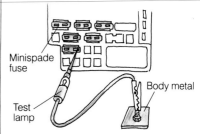

Minispade fuse

Body metal

Test lamp

Turn off the ignition and affected circuit switches. Use a special puller to remove a glass-envelope fuse. Remove a minispade or a ceramic type with a puller or your fingers.

Install a new fuse of the same amperage as that stamped on the old fuse. A higher-rated fuse won't protect the circuit. A lower-rated one will blow even with normal current flow.

Garage doors

Troubleshooting overhead doors; adjusting springs; locks

If an overhead roll-up door binds or sticks, tighten loose screws or bolts in the hinges and in the track brackets. Replace broken or corroded hinges and roller shafts.

Use a level to check that the vertical tracks are plumb. To adjust track that is out of alignment, loosen the track brackets (they have slots for adjustment) and tap the track with a mallet until it is plumb. Bends or crimps in the track impede roller movement. If you can't straighten them out, replace the track.

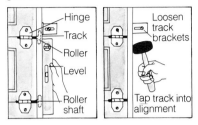

Keep the door's moving parts lubricated. Once a year, apply a few drops of lightweight oil to the hinges and roller bearings. Oil the cable pulleys and wipe the cables with an oiled rag. Occasionally clean the tracks with a rag dampened with paint thinner.

On one-piece swing-out doors, with or without tracks, make sure that the hardware is tight, the moving parts lubricated, and the tracks, if any, are clean and free of bends.

Periodically examine the bottom weather stripping for wear; replace as needed (see *Weather stripping*). Before installing new weather stripping, sand the door bottom and wash it with a mild detergent; let it dry for 2 or 3 days, then paint it with wood preservative (see *Wood preservatives*).

Adjusting the springs
In both types of overhead doors, heavy springs counterbalance the weight of the door to facilitate opening and closing. If a door's springs are properly tensioned, the door should stay in place when raised about 1 foot above the ground. Lifted a foot more, it should continue opening slowly on its own. Lowered a foot, it should gently close and stay closed. If the door closes too quickly or is difficult to raise, the springs may have lost tension.

Check the springs for breaks or rust. If one is defective, replace both with springs of the same size and strength, using the same method of attachment. Garage door springs are under great tension; use caution when adjusting or replacing them.

Some roll-up doors have a pair of springs, each mounted above an overhead track and connected by cables to the bottom corners of the door. The upper cable ends are usually attached to S-hooks that fit into the holes of wall-mounted brackets. To increase tension, open the door as far as it will go, use clamps or a block of wood to hold it in place, and move the hook forward one or two holes. Adjust both cables equally. If the cable is knotted to a hole in a plate above the door, increase tension by retying the holding knot closer to the spring.

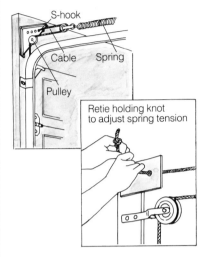

Retie holding knot to adjust spring tension

Replacing or making adjustments to a torsion spring (a single spring mounted across the top of the door opening) is dangerous and should be left to a garage-door specialist.

The springs in swing-out doors are usually mounted vertically at each side of the door. To increase tension, move the spring ends up one or two holes in the doorjamb brackets.

Garage door locks
The bars of a garage door lock should glide easily through the guide brackets into holes in the vertical tracks. If the lock does not work smoothly, try straightening bends in the bars. If that doesn't solve the problem, loosen the guide bracket screws and move the bracket up or down to align the bar with the opening in the track.

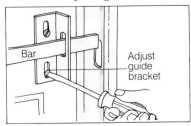

Once a year, unscrew the lock and lubricate the latch mechanism with powdered graphite.

Garage sales

Planning and pricing

Successful garage sales (also known as tag, yard, or barn sales) are usually held on weekends in clement weather. About a month before the sale, check with your municipal government offices: you may need a permit. Ask friends to participate. Assemble, clean, and repair salable items.

Run an ad in a local paper listing the sale date and hours, a rain date, and merchandise range. Post notices at supermarkets, bus stops, and social centers, and on trees and poles if permitted by local authorities.

If you have many valuable items, such as antiques, hire a professional sale manager. He knows the right prices and how to draw the right buyers. He may require a minimum guarantee against his commission.

Pricing
Price goods with removable tags or tape. Use different colors or initials to indicate ownership. As a general rule, price merchandise from 10 to 50 percent of what it would cost new, depending on age and condition. For collectibles and antiques, consult experts. When in doubt, price lower.

Arrange the merchandise on card tables or a picnic table. Group items together: clothes on racks; odds and ends on tables; books on shelves or in boxes. Provide power for testing appliances. Have on hand plenty of wrapping materials (newspapers, bags, and twine) and $30 to $40 in small bills and change in your cash box. Be open to offers; reduce all prices during the final hours of the sale.

Donate sale leftovers to charity or set them aside for another sale next year. Remove the signs you posted.

Garbage cans

Keeping them clean, repaired, and well closed

Get longer wear from your metal or plastic garbage cans by keeping them in a shed and away from moisture; line them with plastic bags.

Continued next page

Periodically hose garbage cans and then scrub them with an industrial detergent containing a disinfectant; when possible let the cans dry in the sun. To deter corrosion, coat their insides and undersides lightly with used motor oil or with asphalt roof cement.

Patch small holes in metal cans with an epoxy-base mending compound from a hardware store. Repair larger holes with a patch of light-gauge (20-24gs.) galvanized sheet steel epoxied in place or fastened with stainless-steel pop rivets (see *Rivets*). Repair splits in plastic cans by sandwiching them between pop-riveted strips of aluminum roof flashing.

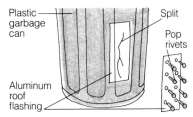

To deter raids by dogs or raccoons, secure the lids of metal garbage cans to the handles with elastic shock cord, available at auto supply stores. Fasten one end of the cord permanently to a can by drilling a hole in one of the handles and hooking one cord end through it; crimp the hook closed with pliers. Hook the free end to the other handle.

For plastic garbage cans with molded lid grips, you can screw a grooved block of wood to the grip, groove down. Run a length of rope or shock cord through the groove and fasten its ends to the can's handles.

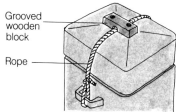

Garden hoses

Care and repair

Don't leave a hose lying on the ground between jobs. Drain and loosely wind it up after each use. Keep it in a cool,

dry place where it won't be damaged by a car, lawn mower, or excessive sunlight. Bring a hose indoors for the winter. Store it on a reel or coiled flat on the floor, not hanging from a nail, which can pinch and weaken it. Straighten out creases and kinks as soon as you notice them.

Repairing a hose

Taping or patching a leaking hose is usually ineffective. Buy an inexpensive repair kit at a hardware store. Simple hose menders employ a connector that is clamped or crimped in place to form a permanent joint. A coupling set allows you to take the hose apart; it is clamped or crimped in place or it may be screwed into the hose with a threaded sleeve.

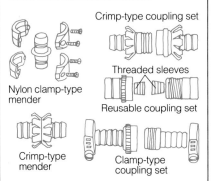

To repair a hose, make straight cuts on both sides of the leak with a utility knife. Take a segment of hose to the hardware store and select a kit whose insert sections match the inner diameter of the hose. The fit should be snug but not so tight that the hose cracks. Soften the ends of a plastic hose with hot water to ease insertion. Follow package instructions for installing the mender or coupling.

If a hose leaks at a coupling, replace the washer. To replace a leaking or damaged coupling, cut about an inch of hose behind the coupling and install a new one. To replace the faucet end, use a female part; replace the nozzle end with a male part.

Gardenias

Growing them indoors or out

Outdoors, gardenias thrive in areas where, during the growing season, days are warm (60°F to 80°F) and

nights are cool (55°F to 60°F). Plant them in sun or light shade in sandy, slightly acid soil mixed with peat moss. Mulch them in summer; feed twice a year with an acid fertilizer.

As houseplants, gardenias like fairly high humidity and bright light, but not strong direct sun; mist them during dry months or keep them on a tray of damp pebbles. Keep the soil uniformly moist and feed them with an acid fertilizer every 2 or 3 weeks from March through September.

For successful flowering, these conditions must be kept constant and temperatures should range from 70°F to 75°F in the day, 60°F to 65°F at night. Gardenias bloom in summer, but you can encourage winter flowers by pinching off summer buds. When the container becomes crowded with roots, or roots grow out of the bottom, repot in an acid potting mixture.

Garden pools

Installing plastic-lined and fiberglass pools

Pick a site for your pool that's sunny enough for aquatic plants to thrive but away from shrubs that might shed into the pool. To support fish and plants, the pool should be at least 1½ to 2 feet deep. In some areas, pools of a specified depth must be fenced; consult local building authorities.

If you want to light the pool or install a submersible electric pump, locate the pool close to a source of electricity. The pump must be within 6 feet of an outdoor receptacle that is equipped with a ground fault interrupter (see *Ground fault interrupters*). Check local electrical codes before running an outdoor circuit to the pool, or have an electrician do the job.

Plastic-lined pools

Garden and landscape supply stores sell flexible plastic pool liners and rigid fiberglass pools; both are easy to install. With a plastic liner you can design a pool in any shape you like. To determine the amount of liner needed, measure a rectangle whose length and width equal those of the pool; add twice the pool's depth plus 1½ feet to the rectangle's length and width.

G

Outline the shape of the pool on the ground with a shovel blade. Dig a hole with sloping sides within the outline to the desired depth. Dig a shallow step along the hole's perimeter in which to place edging material. Remove rocks, roots, and debris that could puncture the liner. Spread a 1-inch layer of damp sand over the soil, and spread the liner. If you have a pump, place it in the pool and drape the cord over the side. Anchor the liner with bricks or stones. Fill the pool

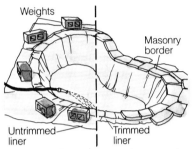

Weights

Masonry border

Untrimmed liner

Trimmed liner

with water from a garden hose. As the liner settles against the sides of the pool, gradually remove the weights. Trim off excess lining, leaving a 6- to 8-inch lip. Conceal the lip with a rock or a masonry border.

Fiberglass pools

Position a fiberglass pool on the site, and scribe its outline with a shovel blade. Dig a straight-sided hole about 6 inches wider than the outline and deep enough so that the rim of the pool will be 1 to 2 inches above the ground when installed. Remove debris from the hole, level the bottom, and spread an inch of sand over it.

If you have a pump and wish to conceal its cord, drill a hole in the pool below the waterline, using a 2-inch hole saw on a portable electric drill. Place the pump in the pool and run the cord through the hole. Plug the hole on both sides with plastic clay.

Lower the pool into the hole. As it fills with water from a garden hose, shovel in dirt around its sides up to

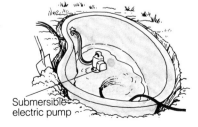

Submersible electric pump

the rim. Line the edge of the pool with rocks or masonry.

Maintaining a garden pool

Top off the pool as water evaporates. Periodically drain it with a siphon or pump and clean it. A submersible pump keeps the water from stagnating without disturbing its surface. To keep pool water fresh even without a pump, stock it with fish, snails, and aquatic plants.

Garden walls

Building mortared-brick or concrete-block walls

Any mortared wall needs a concrete footing (see *Footings and foundations*). Mix only as much mortar as you can use in about 1 hour; when it begins to stiffen, discard it and mix more (see *Mortar mixing*).

Lay bricks in a staggered pattern, with each joint centered on the brick beneath. As you work, be sure that all courses are straight and level and that ends are square (see *Laying bricks*).

A brick wall 4 feet high should be 8 inches thick (one brick length or two widths); cap it by laying a row of bricks crosswise. A 6-foot wall should be 1 foot thick. You can get the extra thickness without using extra bricks by leaving a space in the middle and closing the ends with overlapping bricks. Imbed galvanized steel ties in the mortar atop every fifth course;

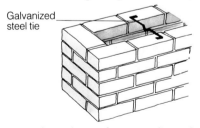

Galvanized steel tie

space them about 2 feet apart. Special caps are needed for the top course.

Concrete-block walls, although less attractive than brick ones, are easier and cheaper to build. The principles are the same, but it takes far fewer blocks for the same size wall. A single 12-inch thickness of concrete block is enough for a wall up to 8 feet high. Use special caps for the top course, or fill the holes in the top blocks with stiff

concrete. Lay small-dimension wire mesh one course down so that the concrete won't fall through. (See also *Retaining walls; Stone walls.*)

Garlic

A pungent, bulbous herb

When buying garlic, choose a head that is plump and firm with no discoloration. Store it in a cool, dry place or in an aerated jar at room temperature; use within 2 to 3 weeks.

To use a clove (individual section), pull it from the head and peel it. The skin will loosen easily if you place the clove on a board, concave side down, and press it with your thumb or hit it sharply with the flat side of a knife.

Garlic can have different degrees of potency; raw garlic imparts more flavor to food than cooked (the longer it cooks, the milder it becomes); cut up or pressed garlic is more potent than whole. For the most delicate flavor, rub the inside of a clove against a bowl in which food will be prepared, or sauté a whole clove in oil, then remove it. (Cook it just until golden; garlic burns easily in hot oil and develops a bitter, acrid flavor.) To obtain garlic juice, crush a clove in a garlic press.

Gas burners

Adjusting the pilot light; replacing the thermocouple

Caution: Don't relight the pilot or attempt to make any repairs if there's a strong gas odor. Close the main shutoff valve, turn off power to the burner at the circuit-breaker panel or the fuse box, and call the gas company immediately.

In a gas burner, natural or bottled gas is mixed with air and ignited by a pilot light or spark ignition. A boiler or a furnace converts the heat to steam, hot water, or warm air. The thermocouple safety device cuts off gas flow if the pilot light goes out.

Twice a year turn off the gas and power to the burner and, with a crevice tool, vacuum the air shutters. Every 3 to 4 years the gas company should service the burner and clean

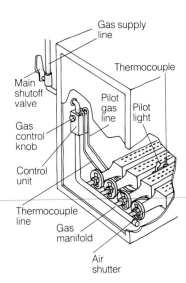

Gas supply line

Thermocouple

Main shutoff valve

Pilot gas line

Pilot light

Gas control knob

Control unit

Thermocouple line

Gas manifold

Air shutter

the fuel passages and the vent. Periodically check the burner flames. If they are yellow, have the gas company adjust the air-gas mixture.

Adjusting the pilot

The thermocouple cuts off the gas supply if the pilot light is too low to heat it. A pilot-adjustment screw on the control unit of some models regulates the pilot flame. Remove the screw cap, if any, and turn the screw counterclockwise to raise the flame, clockwise to lower it.

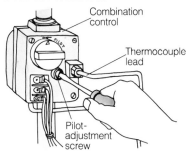

Combination control

Thermocouple lead

Pilot-adjustment screw

To reignite the pilot, set the house thermostat to the lowest temperature setting. Follow the instructions near the control unit. (See also *Pilot lights*.)

Replacing the thermocouple

Do not try to relight the pilot more than twice. If it goes out again, replace the thermocouple or call the gas company. To replace the thermocouple, close the main shutoff valve and turn off power to the burner. When the thermocouple is cool, unscrew the lead from the combination control and wipe the threaded connection at the control with a clean, lint-free rag.

Unscrew the nut holding the thermocouple and the lead to the pilot light bracket. Fasten the new thermocouple and lead to the bracket; connect the other end of the lead to the combination control.

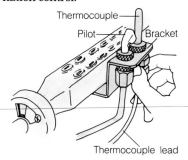

Thermocouple

Pilot

Bracket

Thermocouple lead

Gates

Repairing and building them

For a sagging gate, first tighten the hinge screws; replace them with longer ones if necessary, or drill through the gatepost and use bolts. Then see if the gate is out of kilter; you may be able to square it with a wire and turn-

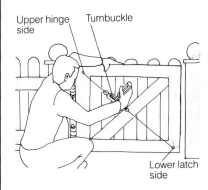

Upper hinge side

Turnbuckle

Lower latch side

buckle. Finally check the gatepost. If it leans, run a wire and turnbuckle from its top to the bottom of the next post. If that doesn't work, reset the post (see *Fence posts and rails*).

Making a new gate

Begin by buying the hardware (see *Hinges; Latches*). The size and design will affect the way you build the gate. Get sturdy, rust-resistant ones; you may need longer screws than are provided. Two hinges are usually enough for a gate 5 feet high and 3 feet wide. Self-closing hinges are a good idea if you have children; loose-pin hinges let you remove the gate easily.

For the width of the gate, measure between the posts, then subtract 1 inch (or more, depending on the design of the hardware). Don't make the gate too wide. A gate wider than 3 feet is likely to sag; make a pair of smaller gates instead. The height depends on the fence; allow at least 2 inches clearance at the bottom.

Make the frame of 2 x 4s, using lap or mortise-and-tenon joints and waterproof glue (see *Gluing*). Make sure that the parts are square. Cut a diagonal brace, also of 2 x 4, to fit tightly between the bottom corner on the hinge side and the top corner on the latch side. Attach it with galvanized 10d nails and steel reinforcing plates. Attach siding to match the fence. Then screw or bolt the hinges to the frame.

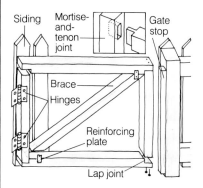

Siding

Mortise-and-tenon joint

Gate stop

Brace

Hinges

Reinforcing plate

Lap joint

Prop the gate in place to be sure it fits. If it does, nail the hinges to the gatepost (one 6d nail in each hinge) and swing the gate open to check the clearance. If it is right, remove the nails, and screw or bolt the hinges to the post. Close the gate and position the latch. For a gate stop, nail a strip of 1 x 2 to the latchpost.

Geraniums

Growing these sun lovers; keeping them over the winter

Geraniums (pelargoniums) thrive in most garden soils. Their showy blossoms range from bright red to pink to white. The variously shaped leaves of some are delightfully scented. In a frost-free climate, they can grow outdoors permanently.

In other areas, after the last frost, set out established plants in full sun in flower beds, in window boxes, or in planters, spacing them 8 to 15 inches apart. (Or simply sink the pots into the soil.) Feed monthly with a fertilizer low in nitrogen; pinch back new growth to keep plants bushy. Keep flowers coming by removing old ones as they fade. Let the soil get slightly dry between waterings.

To keep plants over the winter, bring them indoors well before the first frost. Cut them about halfway back, pot them in the smallest pot that will accommodate their roots, and place them on a sunny windowsill. They do best in low humidity and cool temperatures (65°F to 70°F by day, 5°F to 10°F lower at night). Cut the plants back again when new shoots are 4 to 5 inches long.

Grow new geraniums from 3- to 4-inch tip cuttings taken in August or September. Remove all but three healthy leaves from each and insert the stems in moist sand or perlite. Cover with a clear plastic bag in which you have poked a few holes. After they root, plant them singly in small pots and keep them in a cool, sunny window. Repot in medium-size containers in January or February.

Gift wrapping

Covering a box, bottle, or tube; making a bow

To gift wrap a box, center it top down on a sheet of decorative paper long enough to fit around the box, plus 2 inches of overlap, and wide enough to cover a little more than half the box depth on each side. Bring up one long edge of paper and tape it to the box. Fold under the remaining long side 1 inch and tape it. Stick short lengths of double-stick tape or small circles of regular transparent tape (sticky side out) along the folded edge. Pull this edge over the first one and press it securely in place.

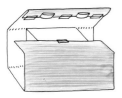

Fold down one side and tape it to the box. Miter the two adjoining sides, then fold them toward the center, creasing the paper along the box edges; tape the two sides together at the bottom. Fold over the lower flap 1 inch; put double-stick tape or a circle of regular tape on the foldover. Bring the bottom flap up, pressing it in place. Repeat for the opposite side.

When a box is larger than a single length of gift wrap, splice two or more sheets together. Lay the sheets wrong side up, fold over two of the edges ½ inch, as shown, and slip them inside each other. Tape the seam.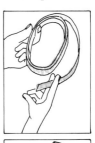

To gift wrap a jar, bottle, or similar item, use pliable paper such as tissue, foil, or colored cellophane; or use fabric and pink the edges to keep it from fraying. Cut two large squares and position them under the container. Bring both sheets together at the top of the container. Tie with ribbon or yarn. Separate the points; fluff them.

To wrap a soft, flat gift without a box, back it first with a slightly larger piece of cardboard. An alternative is to roll the gift into a cylinder and slip it inside a cardboard tube. To wrap the tube, cut paper about 6 inches longer than the tube and 2 inches wider than its diameter. Wrap and tape the paper around the tube, as for a box. Tie ribbon or yarn at the tube ends.

To create a multiple-loop bow, wrap ribbon around your hand seven or eight times, loosely for a large bow,

tightly for a small one. Tape both ends at the center. Cut four small wedges from the loops, then bring the cut portions to the center. Tie a narrow piece of matching ribbon tightly around the center. Remove the tape. One at a time, pull the loops out and toward the center on alternate sides. Fluff and shape the bow. Tape it to the gift.

Gingerbread men

Spicy edibles for children of all ages

Melt ½ cup butter or margarine in a large saucepan. Stir in ½ cup sugar, then ½ cup molasses. Sift together 2½ cups flour, ½ teaspoon salt, and 2 teaspoons powdered ginger. Dissolve ½ teaspoon baking soda in ¼ cup hot water. Alternately add dry ingredients and soda water to the molasses mixture, beginning and ending with dry ingredients. Chill dough 2 to 3 hours.

Make a cardboard pattern, enlarging the design to 5 inches (see *Pattern transfer*); cut it out. Preheat oven to 350°F. Roll out dough to ⅛ inch. Cut around pattern with a sharp knife.

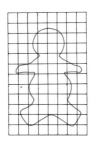 Draw a 6" x 4" rectangle and divide it into ½" squares. Redraw the shape as shown. Cut it out.

Continued next page

Space cookies 2 inches apart on ungreased baking sheets. Press on cinnamon candies for buttons and raisins for eyes. Bake 10 to 12 minutes until lightly browned. If you like, make half a recipe of ornamental icing (see *Frostings*), and outline boots and other details with a decorating tube.

Gin rummy

A rummy by another name

Deal your opponent and yourself 10 cards alternately. Place the remaining cards facedown; turn the top card faceup to start a discard pile. Your opponent plays first, taking this card if he can use it to develop matched sets and discarding one he can't use. If he can't use the faceup card, you can take it. If you can't use it, your opponent draws one from the stockpile and discards. So it goes for the rest of the game, each player holding only 10 cards at a time.

Arrange the sets in your hand: three or more cards of the same rank or in sequence in a suit. Face cards are 10, aces 1, other cards their given value. When your *deadwood* (unmatched cards) is down to 10 points or less, you can *knock* by rapping on the table and discarding a card.

Spread out your hand. Your opponent does likewise and, if possible, lays matching cards on your sets—if you don't go *gin* (have no deadwood). If you go gin, add his deadwood plus 25 points for your score. If he has more deadwood than you, subtract yours from his for your score. If his deadwood equals or is less than yours, he earns the difference plus 25 points. One hundred is the game. Add 25 points to your score for each hand you've won. If your opponent hasn't scored a hand during the game, it's a *shutout*; you get an extra 100 points.

Glass cutting

Making straight and curved cuts

To make a straight cut in a piece of glass, hold a straightedge along the line to be cut. Dip the wheel of a glass cutter into kerosene or light machine oil. Hold the cutter between your index and middle fingers and brace it with your thumb. Stand and lean over the glass for more freedom of movement. Press the cutter wheel down at the far edge of the glass and move the cutter toward you along the straightedge, applying firm, even pressure. (You should hear a sound like radio static.) Score in one continuous motion, ending after the cutter comes off the glass.

Wearing gloves, pick up the glass as shown; break it along the score. Using even pressure, gently push the glass down and outward with your thumbs and up and outward with your fingers. Steadily increase the pressure until the glass snaps in two. To snap off a narrow piece, grasp it with special breaking pliers or with slip-nose pliers.

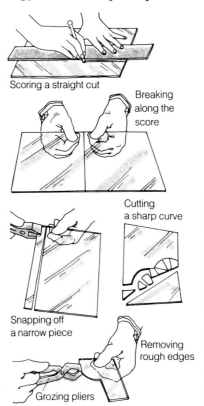

Scoring a straight cut

Breaking along the score

Cutting a sharp curve

Snapping off a narrow piece

Removing rough edges

Grozing pliers

To cut a curve, draw it on the glass with a grease pencil (you can trace it around a cardboard pattern), then score freehand just inside the line. Break the glass as you would for a straight cut, with your hands pointing in the direction of the curve. If the glass won't snap, tap the score gently on the back with the ball end of the cutter, then try again. Cut a sharp curve in stages, removing as much excess glass as possible with straight or gently curved cuts before cutting the final curves. Wearing safety goggles, remove rough edges with special grozing pliers or with needle-nose pliers.

Glassware

Caring for crystal and glass; removing stains

It's best to hand-wash fine glasses. To avoid chipping, wash them one or two at a time in a plastic dishpan or in the sink with a rubber mat. The water should be fresh and hot. For extra luster, add a pinch of laundry bluing or ammonia to the suds. Use a soft brush to clean cut or etched glass. Drain the glasses upside down in a dishrack or on a heavy towel. Dry them with a linen towel.

You can use a dishwasher for everyday glasses, but dishwashing detergent sometimes leaves etchings in glass, which can't be removed. Space glasses in a dishwasher so that they don't touch the dishes or each other.

To remove stains from glassware, including carafes and vases, fill them with water and add 1 teaspoon of ammonia; soak them overnight. Or try rubbing the stain with baking soda, but don't use abrasive cleansers or scouring pads. To remove hard-water calcium deposits, soak glassware for a day or two in distilled water with a little vinegar added. Stained crystal can be soaked in a solution of commercial denture cleaner.

Storing and restoring
Store glassware on shelves lined with flannel-backed plastic, heavy paper, or rubber mats. Don't store it for a long time in newspaper or excelsior; these can bring the sodium oxide to the surface, making the glass hazy.

You can smooth chips in glassware by rubbing with fine, wet emery paper. It's better to have fine glassware and crystal repaired by a professional.

Should stacked glasses get stuck together, put cold water in the inside glass and dunk the outside glass in warm water. Gently pry them apart.

Gluing

Choosing the right glue; making it stick

Almost anything that fits together can be glued. It's a matter of choosing the right glue for the material and of using it properly. But glue is no substitute for a well-made joint; no glue will hold two pieces that don't fit.

Moreover, a joint must be held firmly until the glue sets. Most wood glues require clamping for several hours. Contact cements bond instantly; no adjustment is possible once contact is made. Try to glue on a dry day. Even if humidity doesn't weaken the glue you're using, it might affect the material you're working on.

Before applying any kind of glue, practice putting the pieces together in the allotted time (see chart). If they are to be clamped, decide what clamps to use, how to use them, and in what order. Then try it without glue.

To keep from marring surfaces, tape small wood blocks on the clamps' metal jaws. To keep from gluing a piece to the bench, place wax paper or plastic wrap under the joint; sand-

wich some between the wood blocks and the workpiece too.

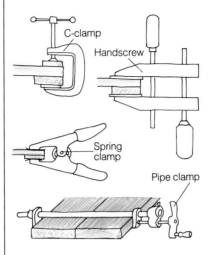

C-clamp
Handscrew
Spring clamp
Pipe clamp

If you lack the clamps needed for a job, you can probably improvise with wedges or a tourniquet. To make a tourniquet, wrap twine twice around the piece and tie it. On both sides of the piece, insert wooden pegs (broken pencils will do) between the two strands of twine. Exert pressure by winding the twine with the pegs, alternating sides to keep the pressure even (see *Chair repairs*).

When joining wood, apply a coat of glue to each piece and tighten the clamps gradually, first one, then the other to keep the pressure even. Continue tightening the clamps until a thin line of glue emerges, but do not overtighten them; a "starved" joint— one with the glue squeezed out—won't hold. Wipe off excess glue with a damp cloth. (On wood that is to be finished clear, however, it is better to let the glue dry, then slice it off with a chisel.)

Instant glues and quick-acting epoxies, meant for joining such non-porous materials as glass and metal, can usually be taped or hand-held; slow-acting epoxies require some kind of clamping (see *China*). The formulas of these products vary, as do the setting times and the lists of materials they will join; read and follow the directions on the container. (See also *Bookcase building; Cabinet building; Dowels; Miter joints.*)

Caution: The fumes from some glues are dangerous. Always use glue in a well-ventilated area, never near open flame. Instant glues bond to the skin; never point a glue tube toward your face.

CHART FOR GLUING

Type of Glue	Uses	Setting/Curing	Remarks
White (polyvinyl acetate—PVA)	Wood, particle-board, paper	1–8 hr./24 hr.	Nonwaterproof; dries clear; clamp within 15 min.
Yellow, or carpenter's (aliphatic resin)	Wood, carpentry	15–60 min./18 hr.	Fairly water resistant; dries clear or yellowish; sandable; clamp within 5 min.
Plastic resin (urea formaldehyde)	Wood, cabinetry, furniture making	4–12 hr./24 hr.	Water resistant; dries tan; mix powder with water; clamp within 30 min.
Resorcinol	Wood, boats, outdoor furniture	10–12 hr./24 hr.	Waterproof; dries brown; mix powder and catalyst; clamp within 1 hr.
Epoxy	Metal, glass, tile ceramics, some hard plastics	4–8 min./12–24 hr.	Water resistant; dries clear, white or gray; mix 2 parts; use quickly
Instant (cyano-acrylates)	Most nonporous surfaces	10–30 sec./12 hr.	Water resistant; dries clear; apply 1 or 2 drops; use within 5 sec.
Cellulose	Wood, china, glass, most fabrics	2 hr./48 hr.	Waterproof; for added strength, apply 2 coats to each surface; clamp
Contact cement	Paper, wood veneer, plastic laminates	On contact/24 hr.	Water resistant; dries amber; apply to both surfaces, let dry; join

Go

Beyond chess

In this ancient Chinese game, you and your opponent alternately place lens-shaped *stones* on unoccupied points (intersections) of the board's grid of horizontal and vertical lines (tournament size, 19 x 19; casual, 13 x 13; beginner, 9 x 9).

One player uses black stones; one white. Black plays first. If your opponent is a rank novice, let him make up to 13 moves before you begin.

The object is to control more of the board than your opponent. You control an area by walling it in with your stones and by capturing any opposing stones inside your walls.

Line-connected, adjacent stones of the same color form a *unit*. Your unit can be captured when all its *liberties* (empty points immediately adjacent) are occupied by your opponent. When your unit's last liberty is occupied, your opponent removes those cap-

G

tured stones. Those empty spaces may then be reoccupied. If you play a stone that captures no opposing stones, hasn't a liberty, and isn't part of a unit with a liberty, remove it and any units connected to it (*suicide*).

To prevent *ko* (a repetitive situation), you cannot make a play that re-creates a position of all stones on the board that existed earlier in the game. Continue play until you can't reduce your opponent's area or expand your own.

Chinese scoring rules: Capture all enemy stones possible. Alternately fill all points that cannot be surrounded by you or your partner. Count 1 point for each intersection you occupy with a stone and 1 point for each empty intersection inside your walls.

Go fish

If two are playing, deal each player seven cards, one at a time. (If there are three to six players, deal five cards to each.) Place the remaining cards facedown on the table to form a *stockpile.* Your opponent then asks you for cards of a certain rank, providing he or she is holding at least one card of that rank. For example, your opponent may say, "Give me your sixes." You must then give up all your sixes. If you have none, say "Go fish," and your opponent takes the top card of the stockpile.

Your opponent keeps playing as long as he or she gets the requested cards either from you or, showing the card as proof, from the stockpile. When he or she doesn't, its your turn. If you get four matching cards (a *book*), place them faceup on the table. When no more cards remain in the stockpile and neither player can make any more books, the game is over. The player with the most books wins.

Golf clubs

Selecting clubs to help your game and give you confidence

When you're ready to buy a set of golf clubs, visit a golf professional before the sporting goods stores. He stocks the top line of reputable manufacturers and knows how to match clubs to an individual's build and swing.

You're allowed to carry 14 clubs; the usual set is four *woods* (numbers 1, 3, 4, and 5), *irons* numbered 3 through 9, plus pitching wedge and sand wedge, and a putter. You can buy a half set (1 and 3 woods; 3, 5, 7, and 9 irons; and a putter), but most half sets are of inferior quality and difficult to fill in later.

The woods may be made of persimmon, laminated maple strips, graphite fibers, or even steel. Persimmon provides a satisfying "click" when it hits a ball; steel drives the straightest.

Iron heads may be cast or forged. Cast heads are more uniform; forged heads give the ball a softer landing on the green.

Try different styles of putter: blade, flange, and mallet head are the most popular. A putter should sit squarely, be easy to align, feel well balanced, and not wobble when you stroke it.

Standard-length clubs fit nearly all players because the fingertips of most men and women, regardless of their height, hang at about the same distance from the ground. However, a short player will need clubs with a flatter *lie* than a taller person. (The lie is the angle of the shaft to the ground when the club rests flat on its sole.)

Shaft flexes range from soft (whippy) to extrastiff. Shaft flex should be matched to the clubhead speed generated by a player's swing. Steel is the best choice for shaft material.

Club weight should be proportionate to a golfer's strength and ability. Average players do best with a light club. Choose rubber grips rather than leather; rubber is easier to clean and retains its tackiness when wet.

After play, wash the irons in warm water and mild detergent; wipe dry. Wipe woods with a clean cloth; apply a thin coat of paste wax and then buff.

Gourds

Making use of nature's store

With little effort you can transform gourds into vases, planters, bowls, ladles, scoops, Christmas tree ornaments, or decorative accessories. Let the gourd's form determine its function. Use store-bought gourds or grow your own by planting the seeds in a well-drained sunny spot and providing a trellis for the vines. Harvest the gourds in late summer when their stems turn dry and brittle.

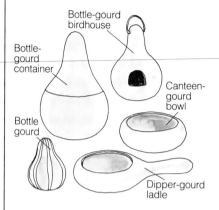

There are two types of gourds: ornamentals and lagenarias. Ornamentals are soft skinned with colorful patterns of yellow, orange, and green. Lagenarias (also called calabashes or hard shells) dry to a tan or yellow. Ornamentals can be picked, allowed to dry for several days, then waxed and polished. Hard shells must be scraped and cleaned before crafting.

To remove a hard-shell gourd's outer skin, wrap the gourd in a cloth soaked in a solution of liquid household cleanser. Keep it wrapped for several hours or until the outer layer is soft. Remove the shell by scraping it with a knife. Store the gourd for several days in a warm place to dry.

Draw a cutting line with a pencil. Use a knife tip to slit this line; then cut the gourd open with a hacksaw. Remove the pulp and seeds and scrape the inside clean with a metal spoon. If some fibers refuse to budge, soak the gourd in water, then scrub with steel wool. If the gourd has a narrow neck, fill it with water, let it soak for a few hours, then scrape it out with a hooked wire. You can waterproof the interior with a coating of paraffin.

Embellish the gourd with stains, water- or oil-base paints, or shallow carvings, or leave it in its natural state. As a final step, seal the exterior with a coating of protective lacquer.

Gout

Its origin, relief, and prevention

Gout is an intensely painful form of arthritis suffered mainly by middle-aged men, less often by women. It stems from accumulation, then crystallization, of uric acid in the joints. Although predisposition, not indulgence, is thought to bring on gout, it is wise to shun "trigger" foods high in uric acid derivatives called purines—mainly red meats and seafood. Alcohol and physical overactivity may precipitate an attack.

Gout begins suddenly, usually as severe, throbbing pain in a big toe, although another joint—ankle, knee, wrist, thumb—may be affected. The area reddens, swells, becomes hot, shiny, and highly sensitive. Aspirin should not be taken to relieve pain; it tends to inhibit excretion of uric acid. Your doctor may prescribe medication to relieve symptoms.

Gravy

Sauce from the juices of roasted or sautéed meat or fowl

Before making gravy, separate the meat juices from the fat. You can pour the pan drippings into a special cup that separates fat and juice. Or pour them into a heat-proof cup and set it in cold water; the fat will rise to the top. Another technique is to siphon the fat from the the pan with a baster, then pour the juices into a cup. Retain ¼ cup of fat in the roasting or sauté pan. To the meat juices add enough hot water or broth and a little wine, if desired, to make 2 cups.

To make a basic brown gravy, heat the fat in the roasting or sauté pan until sizzling. Stir in ¼ cup flour. Stir over moderate heat until bubbly. Add the hot liquid and cook, stirring, until smooth and thick. Season to taste with salt and pepper. If you wish, strain the gravy into a sauceboat.

For thicker gravy, use 5 tablespoons flour. For thinner gravy, reduce the flour to 2 tablespoons.

Giblet gravy: Add finely chopped, cooked poultry gizzards and hearts to gravy after it has thickened.

Mushroom gravy: Sauté ½ cup sliced mushrooms in the drippings before adding the flour.

Au jus gravy: Skim all the fat from the pan drippings. Place the roasting or sauté pan over moderate heat and stir the brown bits up from the bottom. Omit the flour. Add 1 cup meat juices mixed with liquid. Season with salt and pepper. Cook until bubbling.

Red-eye gravy: Prepare just like *au jus,* except use the drippings from sautéed country ham. Hot coffee is sometimes used as the liquid.

Cream gravy: Cook fat with flour as for brown gravy. Stir in 1 cup turkey or chicken broth and cook until smooth and thick. Stir in 1 cup light cream or milk; cook until smooth.

Sour cream gravy: Add 1 cup sour cream to the basic recipe; do not boil.

G

Greenhouse designing

Types of greenhouses; choosing a site; installation

First decide on the type and size of structure you want and how much money you're willing to spend. To provide for expansion, plan for more space than you anticipate using at first. Check with your local building department about permits and other regulations (see *Building permits*).

Ready-to-assemble kits come in a variety of styles from window greenhouses to fully equipped, freestanding structures. Examine as many dealers' catalogs as possible. If you want a nonstandard size or if your property has special problems, you may need a custom-built greenhouse. Or consider building it yourself.

Types and materials

The two basic types of greenhouses are the lean-to, erected on a balcony or against a house wall, and the freestanding. The latter gives you more growing space and is more easily located to take advantage of sunlight. A

Freestanding greenhouse

Lean-to greenhouse

lean-to is usually cheaper, can be hooked into existing house utilities, and is less exposed to wind and weather. It can also provide additional household heat and living space (see *Solar greenhouses*).

Aluminum and wood are the most common framing materials. Aluminum is lightweight, durable, and maintenance free. Wood is cheaper and retains heat better but requires

maintenance. The most popular glazing material is still glass. Sheet plastics are cheaper, but short-lived. If you don't mind a translucent surface, consider rigid fiberglass. It's expensive but very strong and weather resistant and retains heat better than glass. A bed of gravel over an earthen floor provides good drainage; add slate, tile, or wood-slat walkways.

Choosing a site

A greenhouse should get as much light as possible, especially in the winter. Attach a lean-to to a south-facing wall; orient the long axis of a freestanding greenhouse east to west. Pick a site for the greenhouse that's protected from winter winds by trees, a fence, or buildings. A nearby deciduous tree will provide shade in the summer; avoid obstructions that can block light in winter. The site should be level, well drained, and convenient to a source of water and electricity. Run utility lines to the site before putting up the greenhouse.

Installation

Kit manufacturers usually provide foundation plans and installation instructions. In a mild climate, a small, lightweight greenhouse can rest on a sill secured to the ground with tie rods. In colder climates, foundation footings of poured concrete must extend below the frost line (see *Footings and foundations*).

Greenhouse furnishings

A freestanding greenhouse requires its own thermostat-controlled heating system; ask the company that sold you the greenhouse to recommend a unit of the right size and type. If your home has unused heating capacity and if you can set up a separate heating zone, you may be able to warm an attached greenhouse by extending the home system to it.

One or more roof vents, preferably with an automatic opener, is essential for maintaining proper temperature. Other vents may be located on the side walls. In some automatic systems, a thermostat-controlled fan circulates air. In case there is a power or equipment failure, install a battery-

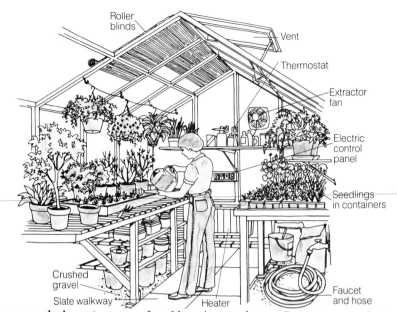

powered alarm to warn of sudden changes in greenhouse temperature.

Roller blinds on the outside of the roof are an efficient way to shade a

greenhouse. Rain-resistant shading paint applied to the outside of the glass is also effective and cheap; wipe it off when it is no longer needed.

Greenhouse gardening

Caring for greenhouse plants; a greenhouse calendar

A "cool" greenhouse, kept at 45°F to 50°F at night, will support a wide variety of vegetables and ornamental plants; with a heated propagator, you can germinate most annual and vegetable seeds. Many more varieties will grow in a "warm" greenhouse, 60°F to 70°F at night, but it's expensive to heat. In an intermediate greenhouse, kept at 50°F to 55°F at night, you can experiment with subtropical and the hardier tropical plants.

Extend the range of your greenhouse by taking advantage of, or creating, microclimates within it. Use a portable heater in conjunction with a humidifier to raise the temperature in one part of the greenhouse. In hot weather, keep the temperature relatively low by ventilating and shading and by damping down walkways and the gravel beneath benches.

Caring for greenhouse plants

Don't use ordinary garden soil. Buy ready-made potting and seeding mix-

tures. Or make your own soil by mixing equal parts of loam, builder's sand, and humus or peat moss; sterilize the dampened mix by heating it in the oven at 180°F for 45 minutes.

Check the soil in the greenhouse every morning; water plants as needed. To increase humidity on hot, dry summer days, damp down two or three times a day or spray all the plants—except those with velvety or hairy leaves—with water. Feed plants in need of a little stimulus every 2 to 3 weeks during the growing season with a complete liquid fertilizer (see *Fertilizing houseplants*).

Controlling pests and diseases

Keep the greenhouse and the area around it clean. Don't use it to store garden tools, which can harbor pests.

Buy plants from reputable nurseries. Inspect new plants for pests and signs of disease. Recheck regularly and remove dead flowers and decaying leaves. Apply pesticides as needed (see *Pesticides*). Isolate unhealthy plants until they improve; throw away badly diseased or infested ones.

A greenhouse calendar

January: On mild, calm, sunny days, ventilate discreetly. Water sparingly

to avoid excessively dry or wet soil. *February:* Sow seeds of Cape primroses, coleuses, snapdragons, petunias, begonias (minimum temperature must be 55°F to 60°F). Toward the end of the month, sow tomatoes for planting out in April in regions where weather permits. *March:* Increase ventilation and start shading plants that may be injured by full sun. Sow the seeds of annuals and of half-hardy and tender perennials for summer flower beds. Start growth of achimenes, amaryllis, and tuberous begonias. Transplant seedlings to pots or flats. Prune climbing plants that bloom on shoots of the current season. *April:* Increase ventilation and shading. Water freely. Sow seeds of asters, campanula, marigolds, cineraria, celosia, false Jerusalem cherries, morning glories. Pot tuberous begonias. *May:* Ventilate freely. Increase shading and damping down. Move seedlings of vegetables and flowers to cold frames, then into the garden. Transplant rooted cuttings to larger pots. Cut back stems of poinsettias; repot them and begin watering regularly (see *Poinsettias*). Pinch out young tips of fuchsia and chrysanthemums. *June:* Ventilate, damp down, and shade as needed. Water and mist freely. Take softwood cuttings of begonias, coleuses, geraniums, and fuchsia; pot them when rooted. Control insects. *July-August:* Sow seeds of cineraria (early July) and calceolaria (late July). In early August sow seeds of lettuce, radishes, spinach, carrots, tomatoes, and herbs for growing in the greenhouse. *September:* Except on cold days, continue ventilating, watering, and damping down. Reduce feeding late in month; stop feeding plants that have finished growing. Sow seeds of annuals to flower in the greenhouse in spring; pot spring-flowering bulbs. *October:* Stop all feeding at month's end. Reduce water for amaryllis bulbs. Remove summer shading except for ferns. Thin overgrown climbers. *November:* Ventilate on sunny mornings. Except on unseasonably warm days, close all vents by midafternoon. Pot fall-sown annuals. *December:* Water as needed; ventilate on mild, sunny days. (See also *Bulb forcing; Houseplants; Potting houseplants; Starting seeds indoors.*)

Grommets

Reinforcing holes; replacing a missing grommet

Grommets are metal eyelets that reinforce hook, rope, or cable holes in fabric or plastic. Kits, available in sewing supply shops, include a setting tap for joining the grommet halves. Hardware stores have kits of heavier grommets for tents and tarpaulins.

Using scissors, cut a hole or an X in the material; make it slightly smaller than the opening of the deep grom-

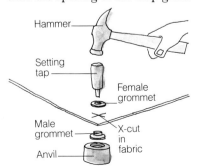

Hammer

Setting tap

Female grommet

Male grommet

X-cut in fabric

Anvil

met half. Push the end of that half through the hole on the right side of the material; put the end of the shallow half over it on the wrong side. Fit the stud end of the setting tap into the opening of the shallow half, and hammer it to crimp the grommet together.

Before replacing a grommet, patch light fabric with seam tape; use nylon webbing with heat-sealed edges for heavy fabric. Burn grommet holes in nylon patches with a soldering iron.

Ground covers

Using vines, creepers, and low shrubs instead of grass

Many low-growing plants carpet the ground with dense greenery, eliminating most of the tedious chores of lawn care. Use them in sun or shade, on slopes or rough ground, under shallow-rooted trees and shrubs, and in hard-to-mow places.

A local nurseryman or Cooperative Extension agent (see p. 5) will help you choose the best ground cover for your needs. Some questions to ask: Does it thrive in your area? Will it do well in the specific conditions where you plan to use it? How tall does it grow? How fast? How wide does each plant spread? What will it look like in 5 years? Before you settle on a plant, look at it on other properties nearby.

Some questions to answer: Do you want flowers? Berries? Something you can walk on? Colored leaves? Fragrant ones? Evergreen foliage? (Snow may cover it anyway.) How much care are you willing to give it?

Spring is generally the best time to plant. Work plenty of compost, peat moss, or well-rotted manure into the area to be covered, along with an all-purpose fertilizer. Then dig a separate hole for each plant. Plant woody ground covers, such as creeping juniper and wintercreeper, on 3-foot centers; such herbaceous plants as periwinkle, pachysandra, and English ivy on 1-foot centers. Plant the slower spreading lily of the valley on 4- to 6-inch centers (see *Planting*).

Apply a 2- to 4-inch mulch between young plants to conserve moisture and smother weeds until the ground

cover can shade them out. Keep the soil moist for most kinds, drier for sedums. Weed as needed.

Once established, a good ground cover requires little care. Some—such as pachysandra, euonymus, and the bright-flowered moss pink—may be mowed yearly to keep them dense and leafy. Use the highest mower setting, and remove clippings.

Some good flowering ground covers are the winter-hardy bearberry and thrift; the sun-loving dwarf germander, chamomile, and various sedums; and the shade-loving periwinkle and lily of the valley. Creeping juniper, with its dense mat of blue to silvery needles, bears light-blue berries in autumn; those of the glossy-leaved bearberry and cotoneaster are bright red. All three need plenty of sun.

Ground fault interrupters

Electric-shock protection

Fuses and circuit breakers protect against short circuits, but even a small current leakage in an electric appliance can cause serious shock if you are barefoot or standing on wet ground. For this reason, the National Electric Code requires that all receptacles in newly installed bathroom and outdoor circuits be equipped with a ground fault interrupter (GFI). This highly sensitive device monitors the current flowing through a circuit's black (hot) and white (neutral) wires. If there's no leakage, the currents will be the same. But a difference of .005 ampere or more causes the GFI to cut off power to the circuit within a fraction of a second, well before the current flow can harm you.

Three types of GFI's are available. A combination GFI—circuit breaker unit installed in the circuit breaker panel by an electrician protects an entire circuit. A portable GFI plugs into a standard three-prong receptacle. A permanent GFI receptacle is installed like a standard receptacle in a wall or outdoor box (see *Electric receptacles*). The GFI leads marked *Line* are connected to the feed cable wires, and those marked *Load* to the outgoing

G

cable wires. Follow package directions or have an electrician install it.

A GFI has a test button, which simulates a current leak when pushed, and a reset button. Test a GFI monthly. If the reset button doesn't pop out when you push the test button, or if a test lamp lights when the reset button is out, turn off power to the circuit and call an electrician.

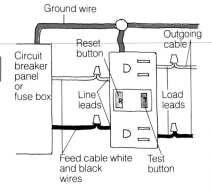

Ground wire

Circuit breaker panel or fuse box

Reset button

Outgoing cable

Line leads

Load leads

Feed cable white and black wires

Test button

Guitar tuning

Keeping the strings on pitch

Many experienced players tune the guitar strings by ear. Others use a piano or a pitch pipe. Still others prefer using a tuning fork (generally in the key of A) to tune the guitar by establishing the correct internal relationship among the strings.

Tuning by piano or pitch pipe

With middle C as your guide, locate the keys E, A, D, G, B, E on a well-tuned piano. Tune each guitar string

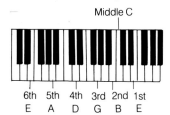

Middle C

| 6th | 5th | 4th | 3rd | 2nd | 1st |
| E | A | D | G | B | E |

to match the piano note's pitch. If a string produces a lower pitch, turn its peg to tighten it. If it sounds higher, loosen it. The principle is the same when tuning by pitch pipe.

Tuning by tuning fork

Strings E, A, D, G, B, E are numbered 6, 5, 4, 3, 2, 1, respectively. Knock the tines of a key-of-A tuning fork sharply

against the edge of a wooden or metal table, then plant its base on the table. Pick the guitar's A string and make it

6 5 4 3 2 1
E A D G B E

match the pitch you hear by tightening or loosening its peg. E, the sixth string, should match that of A when you pick it while holding your finger on its fifth fret. Next press down the fifth fret of the A string; the D string should match its pitch. Press down the fifth fret of the D string; the G string should match its sound. Now press the fourth fret of the G string; the B string should match this in pitch. Finally, press down the fifth fret of the B string; the E (or first) string should match this in pitch.

If you are without a tuning instrument, follow the same procedure, assuming that your E string is reasonably on pitch.

Gutters and downspouts

Eliminating overflow; patching

In spring and fall, clear gutters of leaves, twigs, and other debris. Otherwise, water can overflow and seep into the house. Climb a ladder and clear the gutters by hand, wearing gloves. Wherever possible, lean the ladder against the house, not the gutter, and move it often so that you reach no more than 2 feet each side of the ladder (see *Ladders*).

Use a plumber's snake to clear the upper part of a clogged downspout. Flush the downspouts and cleaned gutters with a garden hose. Insert stainless-steel or copper leaf strainers in the downspouts to prevent future clogs.

Adjusting gutter pitch

Improper pitch may cause overflow. If water stands in a clean gutter, reset its pitch. First, check that the gutter is touching the overlapping shingles at the high end; adjust if necessary.

Drive a nail into the fascia (the board at the very top of the wall) 1 inch below the bottom of the gutter at each end. Draw a string taut between the two nails. Using a line level (see *Leveling*), run a level string a few inches below the first.

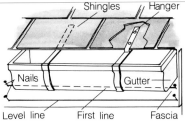

Shingles   Hanger

Nails   Gutter

Level line   First line   Fascia

Measure between the two lines every 4 feet. The distance should increase ¼ inch for each 4 feet. If it does not, reset the gutter. Starting at the downspout end, disconnect and then reconnect three or four hangers at a time.

Patching holes

Holes in any gutter can be fixed with a fiberglass patching kit. If a metal gutter leaks at a joint, the joint overlap may be wrong—water is running against the seam rather than over it. Take the gutter apart and reconnect it with ½-inch No. 6 or No. 7 sheet metal screws. Apply aluminum sealer.

Gypsy moths

Controlling a destructive pest

Dark gray, hairy gypsy moth larvae feed at night in June and July primarily on oaks, but also on other deciduous and evergreen trees and shrubs. Firmly established in the northeastern United States and southeastern Canada, this pest causes extensive and rapid defoliation.

In fall and winter, look for tan, fuzzy, inch-long, oval egg masses on trunks and branches; scrape them off and drop them into a pail of warm, soapy water. In May, after the larvae hatch, spray foliage with acephate, carbaryl, or *Bacillus thuringiensis*. Check with the Cooperative Extension Service (see p.5) for spray programs in your area. For ways to trap the pests, see *Caterpillars*.

When traveling out of an infested area, check your car, camper, and camping equipment for egg masses or cocoons. (See also *Pesticides*.)

Hair care

Brushing, shampooing, conditioning, and drying

The outer layer of each hair shaft, called the cuticle, is composed of overlapping, scalelike cells. If hair is treated gently and the proper balance of moisture and oils plus acidity is maintained, these cells lie flat, and the hair shaft is smooth and shiny. If the cuticle becomes dry, broken, or rubbed away, the hair is dull, lifeless, and unmanageable. The sun, hot appliances, teasing, coloring, straightening, or permanent waving—all tend to break down the hair's cuticle. Correct care helps maintain healthy hair.

Brushing
Brush your hair once or twice daily, especially before shampooing, to distribute scalp oils and to prevent tangling. The coarser and thicker your hair is, the stiffer the brush bristles should be. They can be nylon, plastic, or natural (boar bristle), but should have rounded tips and smooth shafts.

To brush correctly, bend at the waist and gently and slowly pull the brush through your hair from the nape of your neck forward. This protects the more fragile hair at the top of your head and around your face.

Shampooing
If you shampoo daily, lather hair only once (twice, if hair is very oily or scalp is sweaty) and condition it. With less frequent washing, the general rule is to lather twice. Shampoo cleans with a mixture of detergents and water; any extra ingredients—herbs, pro-

tein, beer, or oils—may impart a pleasant scent or feel, improve manageability, or add luster. Whether advertised so or not, most shampoos are pH balanced to protect the cuticle.

The best way to shampoo is in the shower with your back to the spray. Wet your hair thoroughly, lather the shampoo between your palms, and apply it to your hair and scalp. Don't pile your hair on top of your head; instead, start with a scalp massage, using the balls of your fingers, not your nails, then work the shampoo down the hair strands. When soaping is finished, rinse your hair repeatedly until it feels free of shampoo, then rinse once more. Lift sections of long hair to be sure spray penetrates underneath.

Conditioning
Conditioners make hair more manageable by neutralizing the electrical charges caused by shampooing and combing; some also have oils, proteins, and silicone to add sheen. Read conditioner labels and experiment to determine which is right for your hair. Apply a conditioner after each shampoo, following the label directions. Rinse thoroughly. If your hair tends to be oily, condition only the ends. If your hair is fine and also oily, try conditioning *before* shampooing.

Dry your hair by blotting (not rubbing) with a towel. Detangle wet hair with your fingers or a wide-tooth comb; start with the ends and work back toward the scalp. Don't brush fragile wet hair. Air-dry your hair as much as is convenient; use a blow-dryer, rollers, or a curling wand only for finishing touches.

Hair coloring

General procedures for doing it at home

Hair-coloring products can cause allergic reactions, damage your hair, or give you an unflattering color if used improperly. If you decide to change your hair color, select a product from a well-known company. Bear in mind that the greater the color change you make, the harsher the chemical process will be; therefore, it's safer to pick a color only a few shades away from

your natural color. Don't expect the color on the box to be an exact indicator of what you'll get; results depend on your own hair color.

Never color your hair on the spur of the moment. Buy your kit a few days ahead and read the instructions several times. Collect all materials you will need, including a clock for timing and a smock to protect clothes.

At least 24 hours before you color, do a *patch test* for allergic reaction, according to the manufacturer's directions. If redness or itching develops, do not use the product. Return it to the manufacturer for a refund. (Even with a negative allergy test, some people may still develop an allergic reaction during use of the product.) At the same time, do a *strand test* to see how the color will look on your hair. Snip a strand, set it in the solution, and time it as indicated in the instructions. Note the exact number of minutes it takes to get the color you want. Never use a dye or bleach on an inflamed or cut scalp.

During the coloring process, pay exact attention to the timing. It is critical to the health of your hair and to achieving the color you want. Use rubber gloves to handle the solution.

If you wish to permanent wave or straighten your hair in addition to coloring it, check with a reputable beauty salon as to the advisability.

Haircutting

Two basic styles; bangs

Simple haircuts can be done successfully at home. In general, it's easier to trim a good basic cut rather than attempt a new style. On your own head you should trim only the front hair; have someone else help with the rest. As a rule, cut hair when it's wet; keep in mind that it will dry a bit shorter. For best results, invest in good haircutting scissors and keep them sharp (see *Scissors sharpening*).

Layered cut
First divide hair into five sections, two in front, from forehead to crown and back of ears (A), and three in back (B). For a side-part style, divide the front hair at the center of the eyebrow;

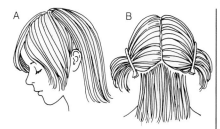

part it at the center for other styles. Clip up all sections except lower back.

Start cutting at the nape of the neck, setting the length at chin level and shaping a slight V at the center (C). If hair grows below the line you've established, clip it carefully with the scissors flat against the neck.

Take down 1 inch of hair from the two upper back sections. Hold about an inch of hair vertically between your index and third fingers, and include some hair that you just cut at the nape. Cut, using the nape hair as a guide to length (D). Continue across the back in the same way.

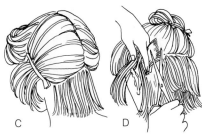

Take down the rest of the back hair (the crown section). Cut it first horizontally (E), using some of the hair below it as a guide for length. Then trim it vertically (F), to make certain that the length is even all around.

Next, take down 1 inch of hair at one side. Establish the length at the earlobe, or from ½ to 1 inch above the lobe. Using this first layer as a guide, layer the hair above it, working first horizontally then vertically. Cut the other side in the same way.

To cut the top hair, pull out a 1-inch strip of hair in front (G) and establish the length at the eyebrow or a little higher. Layer the rest of the top horizontally. Style the finished cut (H).

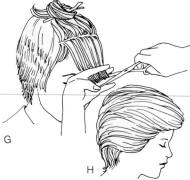

Hair cut to one length

Section the hair as for a layered cut. Separate out about 1 inch of hair all around the hairline; cut it to the length and shape you want. This establishes the outline of the hairstyle.

Bring down the next inch of hair from each section; comb it over the first hair and cut to matching length. Continue to bring down layers of hair and cut them to match the original line until all hair is cut.

Bangs

Before cutting bangs, part off a triangle with the apex about two-thirds of the way back toward the crown and 1½ to 2 inches in from the hairline.

For feathery, uneven bangs, pull the bang hair straight out from the forehead, twist it tightly, and cut straight across the end (I and J).

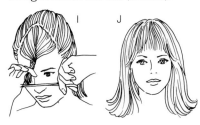

For even, straight-edged bangs, part off ¼ inch of hair near the hairline, wet it and press it against the forehead; cut straight across. Now bring down the next ¼ inch of hair, match it to the first section, and cut it just a tiny bit longer so that the bangs will cup over the forehead. Repeat, cutting each layer just a little bit longer than the previous one, until all hair in the triangle has been cut.

Hair loss

Why it happens; what can be done about it

Daily shedding of some hair is normal. When the loss is so great that thinning or balding becomes evident, you may want to consult a dermatologist. Temporary hair loss has many possible causes: high fever, illness, drug or radiation therapy, nutritional deficiency, hormonal imbalance, an emotional shock, or too-strenuous styling or processing with chemicals.

Most permanent baldness is hereditary and mainly affects men. No treatment has yet been proven to significantly revive hair growth without complicated side effects, but there are corrective options: a toupee or wig (see *Hairpieces*); hair weaving, in which false hair (on a net) is set against the scalp, then woven tightly in with the natural hair; and transplanting healthy hair-growing skin to bald areas. Weaving has to be redone every 4 to 8 weeks and can lead to scalp irritation. Transplanting has satisfied many men, but there can be surgical complications and the final appearance is not entirely natural.

Hairpieces

Wearing them safely

A hairpiece may be worn as a convenience, to conceal hair loss, or to change one's hairstyle temporarily. The best are made of finely textured human hair, but they are expensive and difficult to care for. Wigs of coarser hair are less expensive. A good-looking synthetic wig costs even less and is easier to maintain.

The wearing of a poorly ventilated hairpiece will cause perspiration and oils to build up and can foster bacterial growth and scaling. It's best to wear a hairpiece for as short a time as possible and leave a day between wearings if it is not embarrassing to do so.

If you wear a wig or toupee, wash and condition your hair or scalp daily. Using a proper wig cleaner, keep your hairpiece scrupulously clean.

Chignons, falls, and false braids can cause hair breakage and loss, even baldness with continuous use. Wear a pin-on hairpiece only for special occasions, and attach it carefully.

Hairpin lace

A few basic techniques

Hairpin lace consists of loops held together by single crochet (see *Crocheting*). It is made with a 2-pronged loom, or hairpin (adjustable to different widths); a crochet hook; and any type of yarn. The lace strips are joined to make garments or afghans.

Remove the top bar of the loom. Make a slipknot, slide the loop onto the left prong, and replace the bar.

Wind the yarn around the right prong front to back. Insert the crochet hook under the loop, pick up the yarn (A), and bring it through the loop. Yarn over and draw through again (B). Remove the hook and reinsert it from the back (C), then turn the loom from right to left (D). A new loop is formed around the right prong. Insert the hook under this new loop, yarn over and draw through the loop (2 loops are now on the hook). Yarn over and draw through both loops (E).

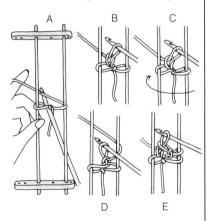

Repeat the directions in the above paragraph until the loom is filled. Remove the bottom bar, slip off all but the top few loops (F), and replace the bar. Continue for the desired length.

To join strips of hairpin lace with a slip stitch (G), use extra yarn held under the work. Insert the hook into one loop from the left and one loop from the right; slip stitch them together.

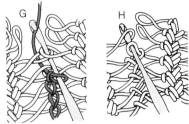

To join strips by weaving (H), insert the hook into one, two, or three loops of one strip, then into the same number of loops from another strip. Draw the second group through the first.

One way to finish outer edges is to work a single crochet in each loop (I).

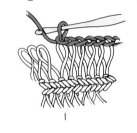

Hair setting

Creating waves with rollers, clips, and tape

If your hair is long or of medium length, set it with jumbo rollers to obtain a sleek look or a loose curl. Use large rollers for more body; medium or small rollers for a tighter curl. Setting short hair with large rollers on the top, sides, and crown creates fullness. Use pin-curl clips or hair-setting tape to wave bangs or very short hair around the ears and nape of the neck.

Wire-mesh and magnetic rollers are kindest to the hair, but must be carefully fastened with hair clips or picks. Brush rollers or plastic rollers with fine teeth cling better, but are more likely to damage hair. Foam-rubber or soft-curl rollers are safe and comfortable for overnight setting, but tend to give an uneven set. Hot rollers are convenient, but damage hair if used daily.

Setting methods

Start with the front, center hair; wind rollers back toward the crown. Then do each side and the back, winding rollers down. Neatly section off hair, using a rattail comb. Each section should be only as wide as the roller's length and as deep as the roller's diameter. Add a little setting lotion, gel, or foam if you wish. Be sure ends are flat and smooth against the roller before winding. The use of endpapers helps guard against split ends and "fish hooks" (ends that bend backwards). Secure the roller right over the section of your scalp where the hair in the roller grows.

To make a pin curl, wind a strand of hair around your finger, slide the curl off your finger against your scalp, and secure it with a pin-curl clip.

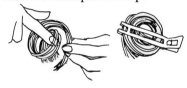

Hair teasing

How to backcomb hair to give it fullness

Teasing can add fullness to a hairstyle and give fine, limp hair greater body. Take a 1- x 3-inch section of hair, comb it out, and hold it away from the scalp at 90 degrees. With a fine-tooth comb, gently comb the section from the ends toward the roots. A slight tangle will form at the base and the hair will stand away from the head. The more times you backcomb, the more fullness your hairstyle will have.

You can tease your hair all over for a very shaped style or do just one area that needs lift. When you have finished teasing, brush or comb the surface of the hair lightly to smooth it.

Avoid too much teasing; it can damage hair badly. Gently comb out the snarls before you wash your hair.

Halloween costumes

Goblins, witches, armored knights, storybook characters

Look through books and magazines for an amusing or frightening character, then combine parts of several commercial costume patterns—or design your own—to fit the character. Keep the garment comfortable and easy to move in. The hem should be short enough to keep the wearer from tripping, and the mask or headdress should provide good visibility.

Salvage fabric from old items you have around the house, such as towels, curtains, tablecloths, sheets, or clothes (you can buy old clothes at a thrift shop). Or purchase unbleached muslin, felt, nylon netting, or fabric lining. Dye the fabric if it's the wrong color (see *Dyeing fabric and yarn*). Use shirt-weight cardboard wrapped with aluminum foil to simulate metal for armor and decorate it with poster or acrylic paints.

Masks

To make a basic mask, cut a pattern from newspaper and make size adjustments. Use the pattern to cut a mask from cardboard or colored mat board. Decorate the mask with poster paints, glitter, sequins, or a crepe-paper ruffle. Punch a hole in each end of the mask and glue on the type of hole reinforcers used for loose-leaf paper. Tie on a length of elastic.

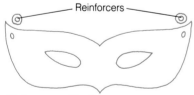
Reinforcers

Makeup and hair

Makeup adds a final touch. Use women's street makeup, burnt cork, or theatrical greasepaint. If you use greasepaint, apply it over a base of cold cream that's been rubbed into the skin, then lightly blotted. Use an eyebrow pencil to create beard stubble, mustaches, or sideburns. To gray your hair, dust it with cornstarch or talcum powder.

Make a "bald" wig by painting a swimming cap flesh color; cut out holes for your ears. Add hair, if you like, by knotting lengths of yarn through holes cut into the cap.

Halloween games

Bobbing for apples and other Halloween party amusements

Bobbing for apples heads the list of favorite Halloween games. Protect the floor with a plastic drop cloth, and float apples in a large pan or tub with about 6 inches of water. Have the bobbers kneel, singly or in groups, and try to bite into one of the bobbing apples and lift it out of the water.

For a drier variant, suspend apples by their stems from strings in a doorway. Have the guests clasp their hands behind their backs and try to bite into the freely spinning fruit.

If your guests are old enough, try this. Once a player secures an apple, have him or her try to peel it in one continuous strip and toss the peel over the left shoulder. Read the initial of the player's true love in the shape the peel forms.

Murder in the Dark

If you're entertaining older children, try Murder in the Dark. Give out slips of paper, one marked "district attorney," one "murderer," and the rest blank. Have the district attorney leave the room, but instruct the other players not to let anyone know what's on their slips. Turn out the lights. In the dark, the murderer prowls and grasps the neck of a victim, who gives a blood-curdling scream and falls to the floor. After the lights are turned on, the district attorney returns to ask questions until the murderer is exposed. The murderer may lie; everyone else must answer truthfully.

Halloween relay races

Give relay races a seasonal flavor. For younger children, try a witches' relay by having members of competing teams race to the end of the room and back, straddling broomsticks. For a spooky nighttime relay, have each team member put on a scary costume, race around the outside of the house, then take off the costume and pass it to the next team member. (See also *Children's party games.*)

Handbag repairs

Cleaning and patching vinyl and leather; fixing straps and clasps

Remove spots from vinyl or patent leather with baking soda on a damp cloth. Then apply petroleum jelly thinly to the entire bag, and buff thoroughly.

Clean heavy leather with saddle soap. For fine leather, use a commercial leather cleaner-conditioner from a shoe or hardware store. Clean dark marks from light leather with a clean pencil eraser. Use an artist's gum eraser to clean spots from suede; renew the nap with fine sandpaper.

If a leather bag is scratched or worn in spots, touch up the damaged areas only with soft, cream-type shoe polish, and buff thoroughly. But never use shoe polish for general cleaning of a bag, or the polish may rub off onto your skin or clothing.

Dealing with tears and holes

To repair tears in a vinyl bag, use a vinyl repair kit from a crafts shop or a piece of matching vinyl and plastic cement. Be sure that the patch and bag are free of grease before applying glue.

If a leather bag is torn, patch it with leather from a crafts store or with pieces cut from an old glove. Turn the patch to the rough side and scrape its edges thin with a single-edge razor blade to keep them from forming a ridge. Then spread contact cement on the wrong side of the patch and over the damaged area of the bag. When the cement has dried slightly, apply the patch and rub it with a soft cloth.

Apply a suede patch from the wrong side, being careful to make the torn edges meet exactly. Then brush up the suede to hide the tear.

Since no patch will be completely invisible, consider using banding or a monogram to hide holes. Or shape the patches to look like decorations. You can also add a pocket of matching material to the outside of a bag to mask a hole or tear.

Straps and clasps

To fix a broken leather strap, trim and overlap the ends and sew them (see *Leatherworking*). Or replace the old strap with a new one from a crafts store or with a costume-jewelry chain.

H

If a clasp on a handbag does not close, check the alignment of the bag's frame and bend it slightly, if neccesary. If the bag has a twisted-prong clasp that won't hold and the frame of the bag is all right, protect the prongs with tape and bend them toward each other with pliers.

Handball

A game for fast reflexes

Two or four can play handball. An official court and ball are required for four-wall handball. Using a tennis ball, you can play a one-wall game against any wall. In both versions, the object is to strike the ball with either hand, bouncing it off the front wall in a way that prevents your opponent from returning it.

One-wall court

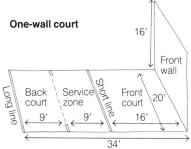

The server stands in the service zone, bounces the ball, and hits it. It comes off the wall and must bounce in the back court—unless the receiver returns the ball before it bounces. The returned ball must hit the front wall without bouncing, although in four-wall handball it may carom off the side walls or ceiling.

Players or pairs hit the ball alternately until one misses. If the server misses, the opponent gains the serve. If the opponent misses, the server gets a point. The game is 21.

Hanging plants

A decorative, space-saving way to display plants

Hang plants at or above eye level around windows and in sunny corners. Keep plants out of the way of foot traffic. Use a plastic, ceramic, or clay hanging pot with a built-in drip tray, a wire basket with an attached drip tray, or a regular pot and saucer in a decorative sleeve. All of these are available at plant shops.

To prepare a hanging basket, detach some of the chains. Line the basket with 2 inches of damp sphagnum moss and a plastic sheet with holes for drainage. Add some potting mixture and trim off excess plastic. Arrange trailing plants around the basket's edge; set upright plants in its center, adding soil to hold them. All plants in the basket should have similar cultivation needs.

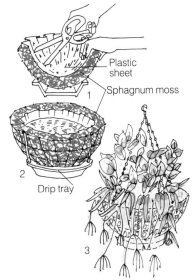

Plastic sheet

Sphagnum moss

Drip tray

Suspend a hanging planter with chain, wire, or rope from a ceiling hook or a wall bracket. Anchor the support with a toggle bolt or a sleeve fastener (see *Wall fasteners*). Install a pulley and chain to lower and raise high-hanging plants for watering.

Hanging plants need the same general care as other houseplants. Check the soil every few days and water as needed. Turn a hanging plant every 2 or 3 weeks so that all sides get equal light. (See also *Houseplants*.)

Plants suitable for hanging
In bright areas, hang oxalis, spider plant, ivy geranium, purple heart, asparagus fern, trailing fig, burro's tail, or Christmas cactus. In shady spots, grow hanging ferns (sword, maidenhair, or rabbit's-foot), Tahitian bridal veil, begonias, trailing fuchsias, creeping Jenny, English ivy, or wandering Jew.

Hangman

A travel and rainy-day game

Paper, pencil, and opponent are all you need to play hangman. Draw an upside down "L" to form the gallows, think of a word of five or more letters, and draw a dash for each letter. Write out the alphabet. The victim (your opponent) calls out letters trying to guess the word.

If the victim calls out a letter in your secret word, write it over the appropriate dash and cross it out in the alphabet. If it appears more than once

in your word, write it in as many places as it appears. Every time the victim calls out a letter not in your word, draw a section of the anatomy on the gallows—head, neck, torso, each arm and leg. If the victim guesses the word before the last leg is drawn, he or she replaces you as hangman. If not, the victim is hanged and you get another turn.

Hangnails

Removal and prevention

A hangnail is a tear in the cuticle or in the skin along the side of a fingernail. It is caused by dryness, picking, or biting. It's best to remove a hangnail as soon as you notice it, before it becomes painful or infected. Use clean, sharp cuticle scissors and clip it close to its base. Wash your hands, apply antibiotic ointment to the area, protect it with a small bandage, then leave it alone. Don't bite or pull on a hangnail. If pain increases or pus forms, see a doctor.

To prevent hangnails, wear rubber gloves when washing dishes, and apply hand cream often. At bedtime, massage in cuticle oil or cream.

Hangovers

How to fight the morning-after blues

The aftereffects of drinking too much liquor are felt throughout the body. Because alcohol is a diuretic (increasing urination), every cell is thirsty. Your mouth is dry, your muscles weak, stomach irritated, head throbbing. Alcohol's toxins, still in your brain, have upset the brain's chemical balance. You can't think clearly; you feel anxious and depressed.

All this is easier to prevent than to treat. If you drink at all, limit yourself to one or two drinks well diluted with water or soda; this helps avoid dehydration and stomach irritation. Before going to bed, drink a pint of water.

A certain amount of morning-after discomfort can be blamed on additives called congeners that give liquor its characteristic flavor or color. Red wine, brandy, and bourbon contain the most punishing amounts; gin and vodka the least. Individual tolerances vary, both for specific congeners and for alcohol in general. To determine what does or does not affect you, keep tabs on the kind and number of drinks you have and your reactions to them.

The morning after
If you have overimbibed, take two aspirin or acetaminophen and two full glasses of water upon awakening. For breakfast eat bland food: poached eggs, a slice of toast, or farina cereal. The caffeine in tea—or coffee, if your stomach can take it—will make you feel more alert. Then take it easy until your body recovers.

Finally, don't succumb to the idea that the "hair of the dog that bit you" will help overcome a hangover. Reliance on an early-morning drink is a sign of alcoholism.

Hard-water deposits

On fixtures; in plumbing

To get rid of chalky calcium deposits left by hard water on your porcelain sink, tub, or toilet bowl, try rubbing the stain gently with a pumice stone. Or cover it with paper towels and soak with vinegar. (Empty the toilet bowl first by turning off the water-supply valve and flushing twice.) After an hour, remove the towels, rinse, and scrub with cream of tartar on a damp cloth. For darker stains, use household bleach instead of vinegar.

Minerals settle more quickly out of hot water than cold, so they collect on the bottom of your water heater, reducing its efficiency; they may also narrow your hot water pipes. To protect the water heater, have a plumber delime it annually. The only remedy for clogged pipes is to replace them. (See also *Water softeners.*)

Hay fever

Relieving seasonal allergies

Hay fever is a catchall term for allergic reactions to pollen from grass, trees, weeds, flowers, spores, or molds. The worst offender is ragweed pollen, which, depending on where you live, is in the air from late summer to early November. Dust and animal dander (particles of shed skin, fur, and feathers) also may bring on hay fever.

Symptoms are sneezing, wheezing, runny nose, and itchy eyes. A recurring or extremely tenacious "cold" may actually be hay fever.

The best treatment for any allergy is avoiding the problem substance. Stay out of woods, fields, or gardens while your hay fever is active; vacation, if you can, in a pollen-free area. Over-the-counter antihistamines and decongestants may help; if not, check with your doctor about prescription drugs. Shots to desensitize you to the responsible allergen may work, but they are costly and bothersome. The newest treatment is by inhaled drugs.

Headaches

Recognizing the serious types; coping with painful ones

Certain headaches indicate serious illness or injury and require a doctor's attention: a sudden, crushingly painful headache; a headache accompanied by blurred vision, convulsions, confusion, numbness, or loss of consciousness; a headache with fever and stiff neck; a headache confined to an ear, eye, or one side of the head; headaches that recur with increasing frequency and severity; and those accompanied by nausea or vomiting.

Other types, although not dangerous medically, can be very painful. *Tension headaches* occur when nerves are irritated by prolonged or chronic tightening of the face, scalp, and neck muscles. You can relax muscles with massage (see *Massage*) or by applying a heating pad or hot compresses to the forehead and the base of the skull; aspirin or another analgesic will relieve the pain. Try, if possible, to avoid the source of strain.

Sinus headaches are induced by swollen sinus tissues caused by infection or an allergy. Over-the-counter painkillers and decongestants will relieve the pain. If the cause is infection, an antibiotic may be needed; if it's an allergy, an antihistamine.

Migraine headaches result from dilation of the blood vessels in the neck and head. Typically a migraine begins with sparkling lights, blurred vision, upset stomach, stuffy nose.

Migraine medication must be prescribed by a physician willing to devote considerable time to working out the type of drug and the timing and dosage that is most effective for each individual. Headache clinics, operated by many major hospitals, offer specialized services to headache sufferers. Such a clinic will probably ask that you keep a record of factors that may trigger attacks: diet (cheese, chocolate, red wine, for instance), menstrual cycle, emotional stress, environmental irritants such as cigarette smoke, perfume, glaring light, or changes in the weather.

Head and spine injuries

What to do and what not to do in a critical emergency

Don't move someone who has suffered a blow or fall of any force until you can ascertain that there is no injury to head, neck, or back. Doing so risks irreparable damage to the brain or spinal cord. If in any doubt, call an ambulance; a serious wound may be invisible or imperceptible.

Head injuries

Any moderate to severe blow can cause *concussion*, a jarring injury to the brain. Telltale signs are pain in the head, dizziness, confusion, possible nausea, memory loss, eye pupils of unequal size. Unconsciousness is likely—short term with mild concussion, prolonged if the concussion is severe. Don't try to rouse the person; get medical help at once.

Sometimes a blow to the head seems too trivial to need attention, its only result a mild, transitory headache. Concussion symptoms don't always show up immediately; over the ensuing 48 hours, watch for worsening headache, drowsiness, nausea, blurred vision, or other symptoms; report them to your doctor. Months later the effect of head trauma may appear as a personality or memory change; inform your doctor.

Skull fracture is similar in symptoms to concussion but carries the added risk of brain damage. Bleeding from a wounded scalp is usually profuse and should be stopped by applying pressure while the person is being taken to an emergency medical facility (see *Bleeding*). If the skull is open, do not probe inside; infection can result. If a clear liquid discharges from the nose, ears, or mouth, blot it but let it drain.

Spinal injuries

Suspect a broken neck or back if there is difficulty moving fingers, toes, or limbs; numbness or tingling in legs or shoulders; pain in the neck or back. Call for an ambulance immediately. Don't move the person or allow him to move. Place pillows or rolled blankets at either side of the victim's head to hold it still. Be calm and reassuring.

Headlights

Replacing a burned-out lamp

When a single headlight fails, the likely cause is a burned-out filament. Testing and replacing conventional headlamps requires only screwdrivers and a jumper wire—a length of wire with an alligator clip at each end.

Remove the cover molding, held by screws; for some cars you may need a Torx-head screwdriver, available in auto parts stores. Next remove the screws that hold the bezel—the metal ring that holds the headlamp to its housing. Don't touch the spring-loaded screws that control headlamp aim, or you'll disturb this adjustment. If the bezel screws are rusted in place, spray them with penetrating solvent, allowing 10 to 15 minutes for the solvent to work.

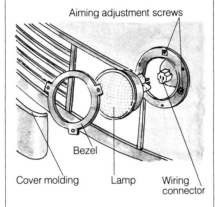

Aiming adjustment screws

Bezel

Cover molding   Lamp   Wiring connector

Pull the headlamp forward to unplug its wire connector. Connect the jumper wire to either battery terminal, and hold one terminal of the headlamp against the other battery terminal. Touch the open end of the jumper wire to the other headlamp terminal(s) one at a time. The headlamp should light if it is good. In that case, check the terminals on the headlamp and wiring connector for corrosion; wire-brush them clean.

A replacement headlamp should be of exactly the same size and type (not necessarily the same brand) as the one you are replacing. If you have halogen lamps, don't install a standard lamp. Be careful to install the headlamp right side up with its locating lugs lined up with the housing.

Some cars have headlamps that contain replaceable halogen bulbs. These come out from the rear of the housing and are accessible with the hood up. Be sure to handle the bulb carefully by its plastic base; don't touch the glass. Follow replacement instructions in the owner's manual.

Headphones

Resoldering loose wires

If you hear intermittent sound or static on headphones plugged into a home stereo unit, it may mean a poorly connected wire in the headphone's plug or in its speakers.

Put on the headphones and gently wiggle the cord where it enters the speaker sections and the plug. Static or intermittent sound at any of these locations may indicate that resoldering is needed. Hold the plug's screw cap and unscrew its prong. (If the plug can't be disassembled, cut it off and replace it with one that can be.) Unscrew or pry off the speaker covers.

Check all connections of the wire leads. Even though only one may be bad, resolder all of them to keep the wire lengths uniform.

Snip off each wire ½ inch from its connection. Using a pencil-type soldering gun, melt the solder that holds the wires to the prong or speaker and discard them. Strip ¼ inch of the insulation from each wire, then reconnect them with fresh solder.

If no sound reaches your ears, clip a jumper wire to the widest band on the plug's prong and to the bottom rim of an AA battery. Place the tip of the battery on the middle band of the plug (1). If you hear static in one speaker, it's working. Test the other speaker by touching the tip of the battery to the prong tip (2). If there's no static, that speaker is dead and must be professionally repaired.

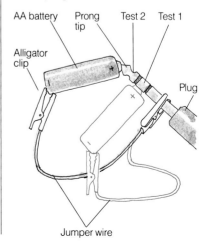

AA battery   Prong tip   Test 2   Test 1

Alligator clip

Plug

Jumper wire

Hearing aids

Determining whether one can help you

There is a hearing aid to help overcome most types of hearing loss, but not all. Before purchasing one, have a doctor or certified audiologist—not a "hearing aid specialist," who is often just a salesperson—test your hearing and recommend corrective measures. It's often possible to correct a hearing loss medically or surgically, but a doctor should make the diagnosis.

The hearing aid does three things: it makes sound louder, it modifies the quality of tone so that words can be understood more clearly, and it prevents excessive loudness from disturbing the user. The working parts of a hearing aid are sometimes in a small plastic case that fits behind the ear. A short plastic tube runs from the aid to a mold that fits inside the ear. More commonly, however, all parts of the aid are combined in a small unit that you insert into one ear. A miniature version of this all-in-the-ear type is the canal hearing aid, the most expensive of these three types.

If your hearing loss results from chronic middle-ear infection or from excessively narrow or nonexistent external ear canals, relatively rare conditions, you may need a bone conduction aid, which transmits sound from a microphone and amplifies it through a vibrating pad worn on the bone behind the ear.

Be sure to secure and understand the guarantee or warranty for your hearing aid.

Heartburn

Relieving pain in the chest

The cause of heartburn is acid juices from the stomach backing into the esophagus. For relief, avoid the substances that aggravate the condition: alcohol, tobacco smoke, certain drugs (aspirin) and foods (garlic, onion, chocolate, coffee). Eat smaller meals. An overstuffed stomach puts extra pressure on the opening into the esophagus. So do tight belts and girdles, even body fat. Obese people often find relief after losing weight.

Let gravity help keep acid down: stay upright for several hours after eating. Prop the head of your bed 4 inches high on bricks or wood blocks.

Over-the-counter antacids help relieve heartburn by neutralizing stomach acid and by coating the lower part of the esophagus; liquids may be more effective than tablets.

If the pain isn't promptly relieved by the antacid or if it's accompanied by sweating or pain in the jaw or arm, report it immediately to your doctor. Such pain can mean a heart attack.

Hearts

A game in which minus is a plus

Ideally four play hearts. The object of the traditional game is to end up with no hearts. Each player gets 50 chips. Deal all cards singly to the left. Cards rank from ace high to 2 low.

The player to the dealer's left leads, placing a card faceup on the table; if others can't follow suit, they must discard one of another suit (preferably a high heart). The player of the highest card of the suit led takes the *trick*; he also leads next.

When all cards have been played, players with hearts get a point for each one; they must put a chip in the pool for each heart. The player with no hearts wins the pool. If others have no hearts, the pool is divided and odd chips are carried to the next pool. If all players have hearts, the pool is untouched and added to the pool for the next hand. The game is 100 points; the player with the *lowest* score wins.

Heat exhaustion

First aid for a person overcome by heat or sun

Heat exhaustion is caused by overexposure to high temperatures or overactivity in hot weather. Although heat exhaustion usually occurs outdoors, a person can be overcome in a hot, poorly ventilated room or workplace. Unchecked, heat exhaustion can lead to heatstroke—often called sunstroke—a life-threatening situation.

A heat-exhaustion victim sweats, losing fluids and electrolytes, but evaporation of the sweat prevents body-temperature rise. Other signs include pale and clammy skin, weakness, nausea, and perhaps headache or muscle cramps. The victim feels extreme fatigue and, if exposure continues, may collapse or faint.

In heatstroke, sweating is absent or very slight, pulse is rapid, the skin flushed, and the victim is lethargic or unconscious or may have a seizure. The temperature shoots above 104°F.

Treatment
Call for medical help if heatstroke symptoms are present or if the person does not respond quickly when treated as follows. Move him to a cool, shady, preferably breezy place or to an air-conditioned room. Lay him down, loosen his clothing, and place cold, wet towels on the forehead and the back of the neck. Cramps will be alleviated if the person drinks cool, lightly salted water (1 teaspoon of salt per quart) or salted fruit drinks, such as those made for athletes. Give him a small amount at frequent intervals—half a glass every 5 minutes.

For heatstroke, in addition undress the victim; wrap him in a wet sheet. Place ice in the groin area and armpits and on the chest. Blow air on his body with your hand or a fan. When temperature drops to 101°F, cover him with a dry sheet; resume treatment if body temperature rises again. Give salted water as described.

Heating pads

Use and care

Before each use, examine a heating pad's permanent inner cover; replace the pad if the cover is worn or cracked. Don't lie on a heating pad or make sharp folds or stick pins in it. Place the pad on top of, not under, the part of the body to be heated. Don't put one on a child or a sleeping person. For a moist pack, use only a wetproof pad.

If a heating pad fails to heat, check the receptacle with a lamp you know is working. Replace a blown fuse or reset a circuit breaker as needed. If the pad still won't heat, heats unevenly, or repeatedly blows a fuse or turns off a circuit breaker on a circuit that isn't overloaded, take the pad to a service shop or buy a new one.

Hedges

Planting and caring for a living fence

A high hedge can shield your yard or garden from the wind or from the eyes of others. Low ones make attractive space dividers. For a dense hedge, space deciduous shrubs 1 to 1½ feet apart, evergreens 1½ to 3 feet apart, depending on their size.

Some deciduous shrubs for tall hedges are the fast-growing buckthorn; the yellow-flowered Siberian pea tree; the thorny, white-flowered English hawthorn; and the silvery-green Russian olive (a fast grower, good for seashores and dry areas).

Evergreens for tall hedges include the hardy, shiny-leaved holly and the slow-growing yew, with its dark green needles and poisonous red berries. The Leyland cypress is fast growing, but survives only in mild climates. Hemlocks are winter-hardy but do not last long in hot climates or in city air. For short to medium hedges, try the deciduous barberry or the evergreen boxwood, cotoneaster, or privet.

Plant the young shrubs in a trench at least 1 foot deep and 1½ feet wide. Before placing them, work 2 or 3 inches of compost or peat moss into the soil on the bottom, then cover with 2 or 3 inches of topsoil. Add some compost or peat moss to the soil you took out of the trench as well, along with superphosphate at the rate of 2 to 3 rounded tablespoons per foot of row. Position the plants and replace the enriched soil (see *Planting*).

To encourage dense growth at the base of deciduous shrubs, cut them back to about 1 foot high after planting. If necessary, to keep young plants upright, tie them with soft twine to a wire strung between posts.

Until a hedge reaches its full height, prune back one-third to two-thirds of the new growth each year, making the plants a little wider at the base than at the top. One such annual shearing, while the plants are dormant, is usually enough. Privets and other fast growers may need a midsummer trim as well. Once the hedge is as high as you want it, prune new growth to 1 inch long (see *Pruning shrubs*).

Hemorrhoids

Help for a painful condition

Hemorrhoids are swollen or enlarged veins at the anus (terminal opening of the rectum); they may be external or internal. They can cause itching, bleeding, and pain; they are likely to recur. Brought on by pressure, they are common among the chronically constipated and those who habitually strain to pass stools.

If they are external, tiny folds of skin may protrude from the anus. They may bleed occasionally and are usually painful only when there is clotting or swelling. Internal hemorrhoids can cause pain, bleeding, and protrusion. Because any rectal bleeding may be a sign of a serious, unrelated illness, see your doctor.

Hemorrhoids may occur during pregnancy or after delivery, but they soon disappear. Other problems that cause pressure, such as a tumor or a cyst, can lead to hemorrhoids.

The usual treatment is a diet high in fiber: whole-grain or bran breads or cereals, fresh fruits and vegetables, and dried fruits (see *Constipation*). And drink plenty of liquids. Although a high-fiber diet may not prevent hemorrhoids, it can relieve the discomfort. Hot baths, rest, and pain medication can all be soothing; cold compresses will reduce the swelling. Good hygiene—washing gently with wet paper and drying carefully after a bowel movement—is important.

Hems

Turned-up hems on garments

To mark a hemline above the hips, lay the garment flat and, from the bottom up, measure an equal amount all around. To mark a hemline below the hips, put on the garment, wearing the undergarments and shoes that go with it. Have someone place pins an equal distance from the floor all around the garment, moving around you with a yardstick or pin marker.

Trim seam allowances within the hem to half width. Press the hem up; baste it ¼ inch from the fold. Mark the hem depth evenly (A): up to 3 inches for a straight garment; 1½ to 2 inches for a flared garment. Trim any excess. To ease in fullness on a flared hem, machine baste ¼ inch from the edge; draw up the stitches until the hem edge fits the garment (B).

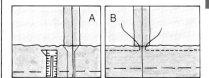

To finish the edge on a lightweight fabric, turn it under ¼ inch and topstitch (C). For a heavier fabric, zigzag stitch ⅛ inch from the edge (D); straight stitch ¼ inch from the edge and pink (G); or cover a straight edge with seam binding (E) or a curved edge with bias tape (F).

To hand-stitch a hem, use a single thread and space the stitches ¼ to ½ inch apart. Use the *blind hemming stitch* for a zigzagged or pinked edge (G); the *slipstitch* for bias tape or a turned-and-stitched edge (H); the *vertical hemming stitch* for a turned-and-stitched edge or seam binding (C). (See also *Slipstitching*.)

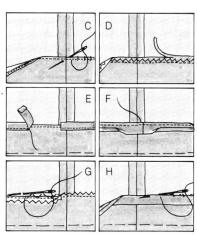

Herb gardening

Growing them for fragrance, beauty, and culinary use

Whether you grow herbs in a high-maintenance formal pattern, such as the knot garden shown, or in an informal kitchen-door patch, pick a spot with full sun and light soil that's a bit on the dry side.

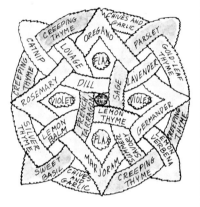

Begin with a scale drawing; allot a specific space to each herb, choosing neighbors according to size, color, texture, and growing needs. Then dig or rototill the soil to a depth of 9 inches, working in compost or well-rotted manure and a balanced fertilizer (see *Fertilizing vegetables*). Use string or small stones to mark out the boundaries of your plan on the soil.

Sow the seeds of annuals such as sweet basil and summer savory in early spring; or start them indoors in late winter and transplant after the danger of frost is past. Buy healthy young perennials from a nursery, herb dealer, or garden center; or take cuttings and divisions from friends' gardens.

The mints, the balms, oregano, and tarragon are easy to propagate by division when spring growth is beginning. (To keep mints and balms from taking over the whole garden, isolate their beds by inserting boards, tiles, or metal dividers at least 6 inches into the soil.) Such bushy perennials as thyme, sage, lavender, rosemary, and bay can be propagated by layering or by taking cuttings about midsummer (see *Propagating plants*). Just let dill, fennel, and parsley go to seed.

Add a little fertilizer after each major harvest. Water sparingly. In future years, weed out any herbs that appear in the wrong beds. Start new perennials from cuttings or divisions when old ones begin to look scraggly.

You can also grow herbs in pots, tubs, or planters on a patio, balcony, or windowsill that gets at least 5 hours of direct sun a day. The easiest are basil, rosemary, chives, and bay. (In all but the mildest climates, bay and rosemary must winter indoors anyway.) The shade-loving chervil and sweet cicely thrive with less light; parsley and mint can also be grown in part shade. To bring chives, mint, and tarragon indoors, pot them well before frost and sink the pots in the soil for 3 to 6 weeks while the roots become reestablished.

Feed potted herbs lightly every 2 weeks (see *Fertilizing houseplants*). Water when the soil feels dry.

Herb preserving

Drying; freezing; under oil

It's best to harvest herb leaves just before blossoming when they contain the maximum amount of oils. Gather seed heads when they are brown and ready to drop. Pick herbs early in the day; wash them; shake or pat them dry. To avoid having to wash herbs, hose them the day before picking.

To dry herbs, tie them in small bunches and hang them upside down in a warm, dark, well-ventilated spot, such as the attic. Or tie up the bunches in paper bags with ventilation holes and hang them outside in the shade for several days (bring them in overnight). Herbs can also be dried in an oven or dehydrator at 70°F to 100°F. Use trays of wood or fabric stretched on a frame—not metal. A microwave oven is also suitable for drying herbs; see the manufacturer's instructions.

When thoroughly dry, the leaves can be easily stripped from the stems and will crumble when crushed. Store the herbs in clean, airtight jars, preferably in a cool, dark place. They will keep about 1 year at the longest.

Herbs can also be frozen, a method particularly suitable for soft-leaved types such as basil and chives. Tie them in small bundles, blanch them for a few seconds in boiling water, dip them in chilled water, then place them in plastic bags and freeze. They will keep for 2 to 6 months. To freeze for a shorter period, omit blanching; snip and freeze the leaves in plastic bags, or chop the leaves and put them in ice cube trays with water. When frozen, drop them in plastic bags.

Herbs for sauces can be kept several months under oil. Put snipped leaves in a jar, cover with olive or vegetable oil, and store them in the refrigerator.

Herbs in cooking

A usage guide; herb blends

Leaves, sometimes seeds, and even flowers of herb plants are used to give special flavor to foods. Chive and nasturtium blossoms, for example, make interesting additions to salads.

Each herb has a particular affinity for certain foods. Here are suggestions for some commonly used herbs.

Basil is especially good with tomatoes, tomato sauces, egg dishes, and salads. Use it fresh if possible.

Chives make an excellent garnish and are delicious in salads and cold soups. Use them fresh or frozen.

Dill leaves enhance cold soups, salads, cooked vegetables, and fish; the seeds are added to pickles.

Marjoram goes with green beans, tomatoes, cabbage, mushrooms, egg dishes, chicken, and salads. It can be a subtle substitute for oregano.

Mint leaves give a fresh taste to fruit cups and fruit drinks. Mint sauce or jelly is often served with lamb.

Oregano is a favorite in spaghetti sauces and pizza; it's also good in soups and salads and with chicken.

Parsley goes with almost any food: salads, soups, stews, potatoes, and cooked vegetables.

Rosemary enhances pork, lamb, chicken, peas, and potatoes. Use the dried herb sparingly; it's quite strong.

Sage is a good addition to meat loaf, sausage, and stuffing.

Savory (both winter and summer) is often added to bean dishes, stuffing for poultry, and salads.

Tarragon is used to flavor vinegar, fish, chicken, and eggs.

Thyme is a fine herb for sausages, stuffing, stews, cooked vegetables, and soups. Like rosemary, the dried version should be used sparingly.

The flavor of herbs is released by heat; to bring out herb flavors in cold dishes, allow them to stand for at least an hour at room temperature. If substituting dried herbs for fresh, use 1 teaspoon of crumbled, or ¼ teaspoon of powdered for each tablespoon of chopped fresh herbs.

Herb blends

For dishes that will cook a long time, such as soups or stews, use a *bouquet garni*, a small, tied bunch of fresh herb sprigs, which is easily removed. The traditional combination is bay leaf, thyme, and parsley.

A standard minced herb mixture, referred to in French cooking as *fines herbes*, is often added to a dish just before the end of cooking, and more may be sprinkled on when serving. It consists of equal amounts of fresh parsley, tarragon, chervil, and chives.

To prepare an *herb vinegar*, place clean sprigs of herbs in a bottle and cover with cool vinegar. Close the bottle and store for several weeks before use. To speed up the release of flavors, you can heat the vinegar (do not boil it), then add it to the herbs.

For a tasty *herb salt*, combine in a blender 7 tablespoons of your favorite dry-herb mixture with 1 cup salt.

To make a *saltless herb seasoning*, whirl in a blender 2 teaspoons brewer's yeast, 2 tablespoons powdered celery leaves, 1 tablespoon powdered parsley leaves, 1 tablespoon powdered onion, ½ teaspoon paprika, ½ teaspoon powdered dill, ½ teaspoon powdered oregano, and ½ teaspoon powdered garlic. Store the mixture in airtight jars. Use as a substitute for salt in salads, soups, and dips.

Hiccups

Overcoming an annoyance

Hiccups are actually interrupted inhalations, caused by the nerves responsible for the smooth rhythm of breathing failing to synchronize. As you inhale, your diaphragm, which ought to be relaxing as your lungs fill with air, has a spasm, and the throat, which should be staying open to let air through, shuts down.

Many kinds of irritation can cause hiccups. Drinking too much alcohol, gulping food down fast, draining an ice-cold drink too quickly, or even laughing heartily on a full stomach are all likely triggers. Nervousness, tiredness, or indigestion can be behind an attack; so can an ordinary intestinal upset or the general physical disruption that follows surgery.

Remedies

To get nerves synchronized again, the trick seems to be to soothe them. One way is to give the diaphragm a forced rest: hold your breath as long as you can, then exhale very gradually. Or try deep, slow breathing. Nonstop, slow sipping of a glass of warm water may have the same effect. A method that children will love involves taking a teaspoonful of granulated sugar.

Some people advocate putting a brown paper bag over one's nose and mouth and breathing in and out repeatedly. The carbon dioxide build-up in the bag will compel the breathing mechanism to work properly.

If none of these tricks works and the hiccups last longer than 3 or 4 hours or if you have recurring attacks, consult your doctor. There are a variety of medications that can stop hiccups.

Hide-and-seek

A game for three or more young children

One child, chosen as *It*, closes his or her eyes and counts aloud to 25 while the other children hide. After reaching 25, It then calls out, "Ready or not, here I come!" and begins looking for the other children. The first child found becomes It in the next game.

In a variation, some place is chosen as *home base*. When It sees one of the other children, he or she calls out, "I spy Rebecca" (or whatever the child's name is) and that child must get to home base before getting tagged by It or (in another variation) before It can reach home base. A child may also sneak out of hiding and get to home base. The first child to be tagged (or beat to home base) becomes It.

Hinges

Installing them on doors, gates, cabinets

A *butt hinge* is mounted on the edge of a door or lid so that, when closed, the two leaves of the hinge lie flat together. The pin protrudes on the side toward which the door or lid opens. If the seam is to be tight, the leaves must be set into mortises in the door or lid and in the frame. Choose hinges that are slightly narrower than the thickness of the door or lid.

Tight-pin butt hinge   Loose-pin hinge

Double-action hinge   Shutter hinge

Continuous hinge

To install a butt hinge, first hold the leaf of the hinge in place on the edge of the door or lid and scribe its outline. Use a try or combination square to make sure the lines are square. Then scribe the depth of the mortise (the thickness of the leaf) on both faces. Use a chisel or router to remove the wood within the scribed boundaries; then drill pilot holes and attach the hinge with flathead wood screws.

Attach any other hinges to the edge of the door or lid in the same way, making sure that all the pins align. Then prop the piece in place and mark the locations of the frame-side leaves. Mortise the areas where they go and screw the hinges to the frame.

Surface-mounted hinges, stronger than butt hinges, are often used on gates, barn doors, and heavy house doors. They are mounted on the face of the gate or door and on the frame; so they are often decorative. Installation is simple: prop the gate or door in position and hold the hinges across it and the frame so that the pins align exactly with the seam; mark and drill holes for fasteners; then attach the hinges with screws or bolts.

Surface-mounted hinges

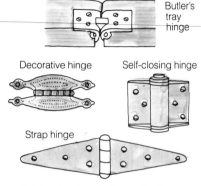

Butler's tray hinge

Decorative hinge   Self-closing hinge

Strap hinge

Cabinetmaking often calls for *concealed* hinges, invisible when the doors are closed, or *semiconcealed* ones in which only part of the hinge shows. Concealed hinges may be intricately formed and sometimes require elaborate mortising. The semiconcealed hinges, on the other hand,

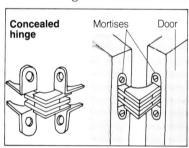

Concealed hinge   Mortises   Door

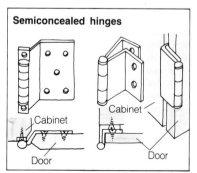

Semiconcealed hinges

Cabinet

Cabinet

Cabinet

Door   Door

may be as simple to install as surface-mounted types. Some have one leaf mounted on the face of a door and another mortised into the frame. Mount

the door leaf first, as with a surface-mounted hinge, then mark and mortise the frame as with a butt hinge. Semiconcealed pivot hinges can often be mounted directly to the top and bottom edges of a door.

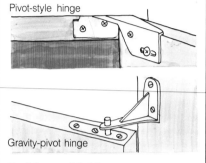

Pivot-style hinge

Gravity-pivot hinge

Problems with hinges
Most problems can be cured by a drop or two of oil. Sometimes, however, a door binds or fails to close properly because one or more of its hinges is out of alignment. Check by dropping a plumb line; the pins of all hinges should align with it. If one does not, remove and reset it. (See also *Chiseling; Doors; Drilling; Routers.*)

Hives

Relieving their itching

Hives are smooth, usually red swellings, ranging from small to saucer-size rounds, that itch and burn. Most are an allergic response to food or medicine, sometimes to dust or pollen. An insect bite or sting can cause hives, as can an individual's sensitivity to sun, cold, light, or pressure (as from a watchband). Hives can even be the first symptom of hepatitis B, for which your doctor can test. Hives may appear and disappear within hours.

Home remedies include cold compresses, calamine lotion, a paste of baking soda and water, or for large areas, a lukewarm bath with 2 cups of old-fashioned laundry starch added. An over-the-counter antihistamine pill may be helpful.

Recurrent hives may require working with an allergist to determine the cause. Giant hives that swell eyes, lips, tongue, or throat are an emergency; get immediate treatment by a physician or an ambulance team.

Hockey equipment

Choosing a stick, skates, and protective equipment

For a beginner the traditional wooden hockey stick (ash or rock elm) is best. A player on an organized team might appreciate the advantages of an aluminum stick: it's lightweight with a foam-filled shaft; the blade of the stick is wooden and detachable if a replacement is needed.

A hockey stick's *lie* (the angle between its blade and shaft) is an important consideration for competition. There are ten lies; No. 6 is the most popular. The angle between the blade and the shaft decreases as the lie numbers advance.

Stick shafts go up to 53 inches; blades up to 14½ inches. To find your correct stick length, hold it with the shaft vertical and the tip of the blade touching the ice; the top of the shaft should touch your chin. A goalie needs a heavier and wider stick than other players.

Wrap some friction tape around the blade; it will give you better control of the puck. Wrap some too around the top of the shaft for a better grip.

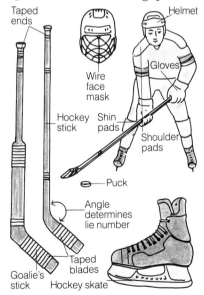

Taped ends   Helmet

Wire face mask

Gloves

Hockey stick   Shin pads

Shoulder pads

Puck

Angle determines lie number

Taped blades

Goalie's stick   Hockey skate

Skates
Hockey skates differ from figure and speed skates: the blades are thinner, shorter, and reinforced with hollow tubing; the boot is higher above the

H

ice. Buy skates in your shoe size or a half size smaller. They should fit snugly over thin woolen socks. For good circulation, leave the top three eyelets of the boots loosely laced; some players don't lace them at all.

Protective equipment

Any form of hockey is a rough game. Broken teeth and bones and facial cuts requiring stitches can result. Buy and wear shin pads, elbow pads, hockey gloves, and a helmet. Strongly recommended, even for pond hockey, is a wire face mask.

Hockey rules

Playing ice hockey on a rink or pond

Official ice hockey is played on a rink by two teams of six skaters wielding hockey sticks. The object is to shoot the *puck* (a vulcanized rubber disc) into the opponents' *goal cage* where a *goalie* tries to block it.

Rink hockey rules

Two blue lines divide the rink into defensive, neutral, and offensive zones. A red line halves the middle (neutral) zone and the rink.

A puck is *iced* (unless it scores a goal) when a player shoots it from his team's side of the red line across the opponents' goal line without any other player touching it. The referee stops the play and signals for a *face-off* in the defensive zone of the shooting player's team. The referee drops the puck between two facing players. When it hits the ice, they grapple for it with their sticks.

When an offensive-team player precedes the puck in the offensive zone or receives a pass that has crossed two lines, *offsides* is called. The referee stops the play; a face-off is held where the pass was made or at a face-off spot near the attacking blue line.

Penalties for tripping, holding an opponent, or hitting him with a stick send the offender to the penalty box for 2 minutes, forcing his team to play shorthanded for that duration or until the opposing team scores a goal. There are also penalties for misconduct, fighting, clipping (falling in the puck's path), and slashing (intimi-

dating an opponent). These may suspend a player for longer periods.

Pond hockey

In pond (shinny) hockey, any number can play, and the playing area may be as large or as small as the pond allows. The only rule observed is that there be no body checking—one player pushing an opponent onto the barrier boards, or in this case, onto the thin ice near the pond's bank. (See also *Hockey equipment*; *Ice skating.*)

Caution: Red Cross recommends 4 inches of clear blue ice; check with local authorities for other safety factors. Don't skate on a pond fed by a swift river or one where a river enters and exits. Bring a ladder and rope in case someone falls through.

Hollandaise sauce

A tangy sauce for vegetables, fish, chicken, and eggs

A traditional hollandaise sauce requires care. The eggs must be cooked slowly over very low heat, and the butter must be added very gradually.

To make 1¼ cups sauce, blend 3 egg yolks, ½ teaspoon salt, 2 tablespoons lemon juice, and a pinch of cayenne pepper in an enamel, stainless steel, or glass pan. Set the mixture over very low heat or hot (not boiling) water. Beat with a wooden spoon, wire whisk, or electric mixer until the eggs are the consistency of heavy cream. Have ready 1 stick of butter (4 ounces), cut into eight pieces. Beat in one piece of butter until it is absorbed by the egg mixture. Then beat in the other pieces one at a time. When the sauce coats the beater thickly, remove from the heat but continue to stir for about another minute. Serve warm.

If the sauce thickens too quickly, remove it from the heat and add 1 tablespoon cold water. If it's too thin, put 1 teaspoon lemon juice and 1 tablespoon sauce into a warm bowl and beat until thick. Then beat in the rest of the sauce ½ tablespoon at a time.

If the sauce curdles, remove it from the heat and beat in 1 tablespoon cold water, a little at a time, until the sauce becomes smooth. If this fails, beat an egg yolk in a clean pan until it thick-

ens, then gradually beat in the curdled sauce until smooth.

Hollandaise should be served immediately but can be kept warm up to 1 hour over a pilot light or set in lukewarm water with plastic wrap on its surface to prevent a skin forming.

Blender hollandaise sauce

Although this has a slightly different flavor and texture from the traditional sauce, it's easier to make. Melt 1 stick of butter in a saucepan until bubbly. Rinse the blender container with hot water. Put in 3 egg yolks, ¼ cup hot water, 2 tablespoons lemon juice, ½ teaspoon salt, and a pinch of cayenne. Cover the blender; whirl at high speed for 3 seconds. Remove the cover but keep the blender on; slowly pour in the hot butter. Makes 1½ cups.

Home video

Taping video movies

To make home video movies, you will need a videocamera (Camcorder) with a built-in or external microphone. Camcorders come in three different models: VHS, VHS-C, and 8mm. You can get one-piece units with everything you need for taping, but some of these require a separate VCR for playback. The model that uses 8mm tapes can only be played back with special equipment that comes with the unit; this model will not play back standard ½-inch tapes. (See *Video cameras*; *Videocassette recorders.*)

Shooting a program

Most of the problems that might crop up in taping a video production have been taken care of in the design of the camera. Focus, color balance, and lighting control are either fully automated or very simple.

When taping a home movie, pay close attention to sound, color, movement, and the selection of images. Tie the piece together with a simple story line; otherwise your tape will be dull—often the case with home movies.

Remember that you are working with moving pictures, not snapshots. Don't pose people or have them line up and wave at the camera. Show a scene, focus on a colorful detail, then bring in the people a few at a time. Let

H

the camera show what they're doing and seeing, get close-ups of the expressions on their faces, and record their comments. Use chance happenings to bring your images to life. If you encounter street musicians or a marching band, tape them. If you prefer, you can dub in music or narration later.

If possible beforehand, map out a tentative scenario with a simple story line. For example, instead of just showing the family eating Thanksgiving turkey, begin with preparing the bird for the oven. Make an image of a clock. Show the cook making other preparations, have someone setting the table. Picture the clock again to indicate the passage of time. Tape the crispy, golden-brown bird coming out of the oven. Then move in on the carver. Finally, tape the smiling family and guests giving thanks and beginning to eat.

Implicit in these suggestions is the notion that you and the camera can select. Pick out details that provide pace, interest, color, and movement. Vary your camera shots. Panning (moving the camera horizontally) and tilting (moving it vertically) are effective pacing techniques and offer visual variety. But don't move the camera too quickly—try to move it at half the speed at which your eye registers the changing subject in the viewfinder. Use zoom shots (coming in close to a subject) sparingly. Instead, use the zoom lens between segments to change the viewpoint, alter the distance from the subject, and select key images.

As a general rule, hold the camera at the same height as your subject (particularly when taping people), just as you would when taking a still photograph. Shooting people from above can be unflattering and disconcerting. While operating the camera, stand still unless the shot calls for vertical or horizontal movement. Walking with the camera requires a great deal of practice to avoid obtrusive shaking and jiggling.

Lighting

Bright sunlight is perhaps the worst illumination for any kind of picture taking, and noon is the least suitable hour. In both cases, the light is overpowering, and the shadows on the subjects faces are unflattering. Over-cast days produce softer, more flattering light, and early morning and late afternoon have great potential for unusual color effects.

If your camera is rated for minimum illumination of less than 15 lux, you can tape indoors with normal household lighting. Otherwise, you may have to supplement the lighting for indoor shots (see *Photographic lighting*).

Caution: Never point a video camera at the sun or at any source of artificial light. Exposure to unfiltered direct light will permanently burn the camera tube and cause streaks and spots on your picture, or may entirely destroy the tube. Also avoid reflections caused by eyeglasses, jewelry, and other metal or glass objects.

Homework

Aiming for better grades

Just before the term begins, fill in an agenda with class time, term-paper and exam dates, team-practice time, work hours, and other commitments. Block out at least 2 hours a day for study—the same time each day if possible. Working within a time frame will keep your mind focused.

Concentration is essential to effective study. Choose a quiet, private place, whether at home or in the library. It should have a desk, a comfortable chair, and good light. If background noise is distracting, wear earplugs or listen to innocuous orchestral music through headphones.

Use the first 10 minutes to outline priorities. What's due tomorrow? The day after? Break any big projects due in the next few weeks into small, manageable units. Save 10 minutes or so for organizing tasks, such as listing items needed for a science project. Jot down what you want to accomplish that day and how long it should take. Adjust your study time accordingly.

Reading to learn

When studying a new textbook chapter, don't just read and underline; take notes. Write down the chapter's title and subheads in your notebook, leaving space to fill in. Now read the chapter and write down the main ideas. You might write them in large letters, supporting ideas in smaller. Write important names and dates in color. Note the review questions at the end, and write down your answers.

Finish by comparing your notes to the chapter. Are they an accurate and complete summary? Discuss concepts you are unsure about with your teacher or friends. (See also *Examinations; Writing a paper*.)

Hood releases

Treating a balky latch; how to get a stuck hood open

Spray a balky latch-release mechanism with an aerosol penetrating solvent; repeat until the latch operates freely by hand. If it remains balky, unbolt and replace the latch.

If the latch of an internal, cable-type release is free but its action is stiff, check the cable along its route; adjust it to eliminate kinks. If there are no kinks, the cable mechanism itself may be at fault. Disconnect it from the latch; if it's still stiff, replace it.

Universal replacement cables are sold but often require improvising of parts to fit. An original-equipment inner cable is the simplest choice.

To install, clip off the wire stop from the old cable at the latch and pull out the cable from the under-dashboard end. Lubricate the new inner cable with silicone or chassis grease, then push it through the cable housing. As it emerges at the latch end, guide it through the latch.

The replacement cable comes with an adjustable stop. Fit it over the cable end, move it up to leave only slight clearance to the latch, then tighten its retaining screw.

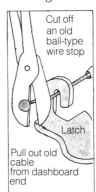

Cut off an old ball-type wire stop

Pull out old cable from dashboard end

Latch

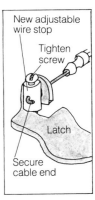

New adjustable wire stop

Tighten screw

Secure cable end

Latch

If the hood won't open on a cable system and you don't hear the latch operate when you pull the cable, the cable is stuck, overstretched, or snapped. To reach it for service, you must open the hood by tripping the latch, perhaps with a screwdriver. On some cars, you can reach the latch by inserting a long screwdriver through the grill or by removing the grill. Or you may be able to reach it from under the bumper, perhaps after removing some plastic panels under the radiator. As a last resort, you may be able to insert a hacksaw blade between the hood and grill and cut apart the latch.

Hook

Correcting a bad golf shot

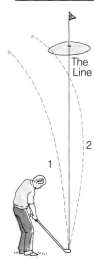

The hook, in which the ball curves from right to left for a right-handed player, has two major flight patterns. One begins left of the target and curves farther left (1); the other heads to the right of the target, then turns left (2). A focus for correcting either is *The Line*, an imaginary line through the golf ball at rest and the target.

The left-to-left hook begins with poor *address* (the position a golfer takes before striking the ball). As a hook becomes worse, the player may aim farther to the right, only aggravating the problem.

Correct it by thinking of a straight line through your shoulder blades and another through your big toes. When you address the ball, set these lines parallel to The Line. Next, reset your grip by turning both hands counterclockwise, placing the right hand on top of the club grip.

During the first 3 feet of the backswing, keep the club head on The Line; during the downswing, follow the same path. The golf ball should fly higher and along the target line.

In the right-to-left hook, the player makes a downswing inside The Line, strikes the ball at an angle, and continues the swing outside The Line. Solve it by raising the right shoulder and rotating it slightly counterclockwise at address. Don't change the grip. Take the club head back outside The Line but keep the club face open.

Turn your hands so that the back of your left wrist faces the sky at the top of the backswing. Start the downswing along The Line. The golf ball should leave the club face along or left of the target and fade to the right slightly. (See also *Slice.*)

Hooks and eyes

Sewing them to lapped and abutted edges

Where garment edges lap, sew the hook on the overlap, ⅛ inch from the edge. First secure the thread with a backstitch (see *Darning*), then whipstitch around each hole in the hook. Pass the needle under the fabric to the end of the hook and whipstitch it also; secure the thread. Close the garment. Mark the eye placement on the underlap; attach a straight eye.

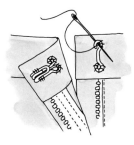

On a garment where edges meet, sew the hook 1/16 inch from one of the edges. Position a round eye on the other edge opposite the hook, extending it ⅛ inch beyond the edge. Whipstitch around both holes in the eye and on each side of the hook.

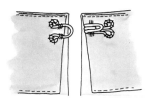

Hopscotch

A playground game: hopping over scotched (scored) lines

Using a stick, scratch a numbered hopscotch pattern of nine compartments on a 10- to 15-foot length of bare ground. Or chalk it on pavement.

Standing in front of space 1, toss a stone into it. Hop on one foot into space 1, pick up the stone, and hop back to the starting point. Now toss the stone into space 2, hop into space 1, then 2; retrieve the stone and hop back to the starting point, one space at a time. Continue this routine until you reach space 9; from there hop back, one space at a time, to space 1. You lose your turn to an opponent if the stone doesn't land in the proper space; if you put both feet down; or if your foot or stone lands on a line. After your opponents have had their turns, pick up where you left off. The first player to make a round-trip wins. Worldwide there are many variations on this basic game.

Horseback riding

Mounting; the English and Western seats; controlling the horse; posting the trot

Learn to ride at a reputable riding school where you'll be mounted on a horse suited to your skills. Wear strong boots or shoes with heels and smooth soles, and a hard hat when it's required. If possible, spend time grooming and leading your horse before mounting. In general, don't approach a horse from the rear.

Mounting a horse
Always mount from the horse's left side. Stand beside its shoulder, facing its rear. Grasp the reins and a lock of mane in your left hand. With your right hand, turn the stirrup iron toward you; insert your left toe. Holding the cantle with your right hand, spring up from your right foot. Balance a moment on the stirrup, then

H

swing your right leg over the horse's back. Settle gently into the saddle; put your right foot in its stirrup. Reverse the procedure to dismount.

The English-style basic seat

The all-purpose basic, or balance, seat can be adapted for dressage, hunting, jumping, and hacking (trail riding). Keep your weight balanced

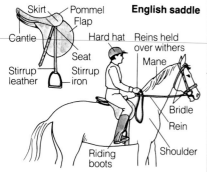

English saddle

over the horse's center of gravity. Sit erect, but relaxed, in the deepest part of the saddle, head up, eyes forward. With your legs hanging straight, the bottom of the stirrup irons should touch your ankles. Place the ball of each foot on the stirrup treads, heels down, toes pointing out slightly. Hold your lower legs back so that your ears, shoulders, and heels are aligned; your knees and toes should be on a line in front of the stirrup leathers. Keep the inside of your upper calves, knees, and thighs against the saddle. Hold the reins in both hands, just above

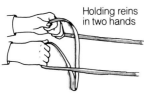

Holding reins in two hands

and on either side of the withers. Keep in contact with the horse's mouth through firmly held, not tight, reins.

The Western seat

In this seat, used for ranch work and trail riding, body placement is the same as in English style. The look is more relaxed, but still erect. Because the Western saddle's stirrup leathers are longer, you sit almost straight legged. Hold both reins in one hand, just above and in front of the horn; rest the other hand on your thigh. Maintain light rein contact with the horse's mouth.

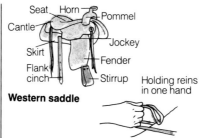

Western saddle

Holding reins in one hand

Controlling the horse

Use your hands, legs, voice, and, in English style, your weight to communicate with the horse. The Western rider remains centered in the saddle, without shifting his weight.

To start a horse or to increase its pace, tighten the reins briefly to get its attention, then slacken them as you lean forward slightly (in English style) and squeeze its sides with your legs. Release pressure when the desired pace is reached.

To turn right, English style, pull steadily back on the right rein while slackening the left; apply pressure to the horse with the inside of your left leg. Reverse the procedure to turn left.

Western horses are neck-reined, not direct-reined as in the English style. To turn right, move your hand horizontally to the right, touching the horse's neck with the reins. Apply pressure with your left leg.

To stop, or slow your pace, pull back slightly on the reins, while (in English style) shifting your weight back and down in the saddle.

Posting the trot

At the walk, keep your body vertical and let your hands be pulled naturally back and forth by the horse's neck action. At the faster trot, the horse lifts one, then the other, diagonal pair of legs. To counteract this gait's bounce, the English rider posts, or rises out of the saddle, when one diagonal pair of legs is lifted, and returns to the saddle when the other pair is lifted. Lean forward and push down on the stirrups, straightening your knees just enough for your seat to clear the saddle. Come down immediately, then go up again.

In Western riding you never lose contact with the saddle seat. To "sit" the jog (a slow trot), relax your lower back and leg muscles and push down into the saddle with the downward movement of the horse.

Horseshoes

A game for ringers

The object: to pitch a horseshoe so that it lands around a metal stake or nearer to it than your opponent's horseshoe. Drive two iron stakes so that they stand 14 inches above ground and 40 feet apart. Center each in a 6-foot-square *pitcher's box.* You and your opponent stand in one box and pitch your horseshoes at the other stake with an underhand throw. As

Underhand throw

Parallel to ground

you release the horseshoe, flick your wrist so that the horseshoe spins and remains parallel with the ground. You each pitch two horseshoes per turn, move to the other stake and evaluate the score, and then pitch them back at the first stake.

A horseshoe encircling the stake (a *ringer*) is worth 3 points. A *leaner* (a shoe leaning against the stake), a shoe touching the stake, or the horseshoe closest to the stake (if it's within 6 inches) each scores 1 point. If both of your horseshoes land closer to the stake than your opponent's, you score 2 points. If you toss a ringer over your opponent's ringer, you void his score. Try to topple your opponent's leaner or knock his horseshoe farther from the stake. The game is 50 points.

Hoses in cars

Checking and servicing them

Coolant circulates through hoses to engine, heater, and emission and performance components. At 6-month intervals, check these hoses; if one feels spongy or hard, looks cracked or oily, or is leaking, here's what to do.

If a coolant hose leaks at a clamp connection, try tightening the clamp. If leaking persists or if it's a spring-wire clamp (which can't be tightened) the problem is apparently in the hose; replace the hose. Loosen the clamp and move it away from the hose neck. Pry open the clamp unless it is on the radiator or heater, where prying may damage the neck. Free a spring-wire clamp by using hose-clamp pliers as shown; spray a corroded screw-tower clamp with penetrating oil; replace either with a worm-drive clamp.

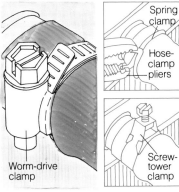

If the hose is stuck to a neck, work a thin-bladed screwdriver between the neck and hose. Or slit the hose parallel to the neck and peel off the pieces. Wire-brush the neck.

Slide clamps on the new hose, dip the hose ends into antifreeze, then slide the hose on. Center the clamp on the neck. If the neck has a flange, put the clamp against its underside.

Heater hose connections aren't always accessible at the heater, but you'll usually find a hose failure close to the engine. Cut the hose a distance away, where it's good. Install a short new hose that will reach the cut end, and connect the pieces with a flushing T (see *Antifreeze*).

There are also vacuum hoses for emission controls. These hoses lack clamps. If such a hose hardens and cracks, a vacuum leak results, possibly affecting engine performance. Check the connections by feel. If a hose is hardened at the neck and is slack, trim it and reconnect it.

Hot tubs
Soaking for relaxation

A wooden hot tub is expensive, both to buy and to operate. A spa of molded fiberglass is somewhat cheaper, but still costly. Both require considerable maintenance. You may be able to deduct the cost from your taxes, but only if a doctor prescribes hydrotherapy for a specific illness. A tub or spa also raises the value of your home, thus increasing property taxes. Have a qualified appraiser estimate the increase in value.

You can have a wooden tub installed and assembled, or you can buy a kit and assemble it yourself. In either case, building permits may be needed, and a licensed electrician and plumber should make the final hookups. A spa needs no assembly, but installation is still a problem. Before installing a tub or spa indoors or on a roof or balcony, consult with an architect or structural engineer.

Fiberglass spa

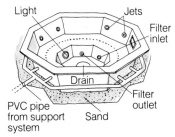

Wooden hot tub

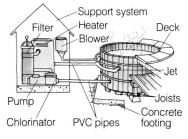

Maintenance
Kits are available for testing pH and disinfectant levels; you must take readings every 2 or 3 days. The pH level should range between 7.2 and 7.8. Any lower (acid) level can irritate eyes and skin and damage the tub, pump, and filter; higher (alkaline) levels leave

deposits and reduce the efficiency of disinfectants. If your water is hard, a softener will protect against additional scale deposits.

Drain and clean the tub or spa every 2 months, using a stiff brush and a garden hose. Then scrub a fiberglass spa with mild detergent and rinse well. Do not let a wooden tub remain empty for more than 2 days.

Caution: The use of a hot tub can be dangerous for the elderly; for those suffering from diabetes, heart disease, or high blood pressure; and for anyone under the influence of alcohol, drugs, or medication. Prolonged use is dangerous for anyone. Do not use the tub immediately after vigorous exercise or within 1 hour after eating. Do not use it alone. Keep it covered when not in use and never allow children to use it unattended.

Housebreaking pets
Toilet training cats and dogs

Confine a new cat to a small area (preferably a bathroom) for several days with a new litter box (see *Cats*). They learn quickly. After this training period, "accidents" are unlikely. If they occur, see *Animal odors*.

Dogs
A puppy should be taken outside after each meal and every 2 hours in between. Praise it highly when it evacuates in a designated area; positive reinforcement is important (see *Obedience training*).

When you won't be home to walk a puppy, confine it to a crate. Puppies take to small, confining areas (boxes, under armchairs); it gives them the comfort and security of a nest. And a puppy won't foul its nest. When confined to a crate large enough for it to stand up and turn around, a young dog learns to hold its bladder and bowels until released in an approved area. Crates are cagelike: some are collapsible, made of stainless-steel wire; others are of durable plastic.

Paper training is another way to housebreak a pup. Confine it to a small area—a back hall, for instance; cover with newspaper that part of the floor where you want it to evacuate.

A puppy can easily forget; place it on the papered section first thing in the morning, after each meal, and at night before you retire. When it uses the newspaper without prompting, reward it with a dog biscuit. If it circles and sniffs, it's ready to evacuate.

Train an older dog to evacuate outside. Follow the same routine as with paper training. When introducing a paper-trained dog to the outdoors, place newspaper where and when you want it to squat. Being familiar with the method, it will most likely oblige. Gradually you may be able to do away with newspaper as a reminder and use it (or a scooper) only for cleaning up after your dog.

House buying

Finding a house; using agents and lawyers; sealing the deal

Because buying a house is probably the most expensive purchase you'll ever make, don't rush into it. Before you even begin to look, think about your present and future needs, then try to find a house that will fill them.

How much space do you need indoors and out to live comfortably? What special needs does your family have? Must you have a downstairs bathroom, north light for the family artist, a garage? Should you buy a new house or an old one? An older house may be built better than a new one, but it may need modernization or major work, such as a new roof.

Shopping for a house

Even before you're ready to buy, periodically check your local newspapers so that you can get an idea of what's available. When the time comes, it may help you to use a broker (see *House selling*). Brokers can quickly tell you what is or might soon become available and can give you an up-to-date picture of local mortgage lending activity. There are brokers who represent sellers and brokers who represent buyers, so make sure that you know whom your broker represents.

Shop for your house in a neighborhood you feel comfortable with in terms of people, prices, and life-style. Try to determine that the neighborhood is stable or improving rather than declining. Establish that it is free of industrial odors, noisy road or air traffic, and other annoyances. Ask about such special problems as frequent flooding and poor TV reception. Be suspicious of a neighborhood with many houses for sale or rent.

Also check to see what highways or major developments may be in the works. In a new development, find out whether sidewalks, sewers, and street lights have been paid for or will be assessed later; ask owners about the builder's willingness to fix problems.

Don't buy a house that is bigger or more expensive than those around it. Resale could be difficult. It may be better to buy a slightly rundown house in a higher-priced area and fix it up.

When you find a house, check its price against the prices of similar houses on the market in the same area. Consider getting an appraisal of its true value to guide you in making an offer. And have an engineer inspect the premises to determine the soundness of the structure and the adequacy of the heating, plumbing, wiring, and insulation. (Local service companies will often oblige by checking out their specialty.) Get a written report on the inspector's findings and an estimate of what it will cost to correct problems. The seller might reduce the asking price or offer to share expenses.

Make your own inspection. Check the water pressure and the fit of the doors and windows. Make sure the roof gutters lead water away from the house. Look in the basement after a rain for signs of water seepage. Find out what is under the carpeting. Unless the owner can present recent certification that the house is free of termites, have a professional check it.

Find out how close the house is to public transportation, shopping, recreation centers, schools, hospitals, and fire and police departments. Also consider the local zoning ordinances and tax rates (get dates of the most recent assessment).

The process of buying

Whether or not you use a broker, hire a lawyer experienced in real estate (or an escrow company if it is more customary in your area). For a fee, which will vary from practitioner to practitioner, a lawyer or escrow company will draw up the contract for sale (purchase agreement), arrange for a title search, execute the closing, and record the deed of sale (see *Deeds*).

Before the contract is drawn up, you may be required to put up *earnest money* as a *binder* to secure your right to purchase the real estate at the agreed-upon terms for a limited time. Unless your agreement specifically says this money must be returned to you if the deal doesn't go through, it may be forfeited. Don't sign a binder without advice from your lawyer.

The contract for sale, which usually entails a 10-percent down payment, is drawn up by the seller's lawyer, but should be reviewed by your lawyer. The contract should be made conditional on your being able to obtain mortgage financing. (See also *Condos and co-ops; Mortgages*.)

Houseplants

Providing the proper environment for healthy plants

Select plants whose needs match the conditions of light, heat, and humidity you can provide. Buy plants from reputable dealers. Before buying a plant, examine it carefully for pests and signs of disease (see chart).

Light

Take advantage of the different light zones in your home. Generally, flowering plants require more light than foliage plants. Observe plants regularly to make sure their light needs are being met. Too much sun may scorch or turn leaves yellow; too little light results in poor growth, thin stems, and yellow leaves. Turn plants periodically to keep them growing straight.

Where light is poor, grow plants under fluorescent lamps. Place the light 8 to 12 inches above the plants (closer for flowering plants; farther away for foliage plants). Keep the light on 14 to 16 hours a day.

Watering

Probe the soil with your finger every 1 or 2 days. If a plant requires moderate watering, let ½ to 1 inch of soil dry out before rewatering. If it needs light watering, allow two-thirds of the soil to dry out. If it needs plentiful watering, the surface should always be moist.

Water plants in the morning, using a long-spout watering can and room-temperature water. Stop when water flows from the drainage hole. Or stand the pot in a deep saucer of water for 30 minutes (water is drawn into the soil through the drainage hole); pour off excess water. (See also *Fertilizing houseplants*.)

Temperature

The usual household temperature range of 65° F to 72° F, with a nighttime drop of 10° F to 15° F, suits most houseplants; a greater drop can be harmful. Don't place plants near fans or radiators or in a draft. On cold winter nights, move plants away from windows. Most plants tolerate summer temperatures up to 90° F as long as the humidity is kept high.

Moisture in the air is essential to a plant's well-being. To increase the humidity level, group plants together on a bed of damp pebbles or place a potted plant in a larger container and fill the space between with moist peat moss. Or install a room humidifier. Misting or washing the leaves of

DISEASES AND PESTS

Symptoms	Cause	What to do
Pale mottling on leaves	Mosaic	No cure; discard plant
Gray-brown powdery spots	Gray mold (botrytis)	Reduce humidity; ventilate
Gray-white powder	Mildew	Ventilate; spray with benomyl
Red-brown spots	Rusts	Spray with Dithane
Mottled, stunted leaves and flowers	Virus	No cure; discard plant
Clusters of tiny yellow or green insects; yellow curled leaves	Aphids	Wash off; spray with malathion
White, powdery insects	Mealybugs	Wash off; wipe with denatured alcohol
Tiny hard-shelled insects; sticky deposits on leaves	Scale insects	Dip in a malathion solution (use 2 tsp. malathion per gallon of water)
Tiny white mothlike flies	Whiteflies	Spray with malathion or rotenone
Black-winged insects on white patches	Thrips	Spray with malathion or rotenone

shiny- or smooth-leaved plants temporarily raises humidity. Don't spray plants with hairy leaves.

Pruning

In spring and summer, pinch off growing tips with your thumb and forefinger to make a plant bushier and to promote flowering. If a plant becomes scraggly, use a sharp knife or scissors to cut off shoots just above a leaf joint. Avoid drastic pruning unless a plant is overgrown or damaged by disease. (See also *Plant care during vacation; Potting houseplants; Propagating plants*.)

House selling

Real estate transactions with or without a broker

The first thing to decide when you're ready to sell your house is whether or not to use a broker. Realtors (members of the National Association of Realtors) and other licensed brokers will bring in many prospects, but their fee is usually 5 to 7 percent of the selling price. Saving that fee gives you the option of lowering the price for a faster sale or keeping the proceeds, but you'll have to finance your own advertising and promotion.

A broker usually arranges an open house, provides a listing fact sheet, takes care of advertising, shows the house, and helps close the sale. Services and fees are negotiable. In some areas, discount brokers offer pared-down services for a lower flat fee.

There are several ways to list your property. With an *open listing* you list your house with several brokers, but only the selling broker gets a commission. With an *exclusive-agency listing,* you pick one broker and pay a commission only if he or she sells the house (not if you do). With an *exclusive right-to-sell* listing, you pick one broker, but you lose the right to sell the house yourself without paying the broker a commission. Any broker you use may handle your house exclusively or may share the listing with other brokers, in a *multiple listing,* which guarantees the broker some commission no matter who sells the house.

Read any agreement carefully be-

fore you sign it and have your lawyer negotiate for any changes you would like. Listing agreements may run anywhere from 30 days to 6 months, and you may still owe a commission if the sale is made up to a certain amount of time after the expiration and if the buyer saw the house while listed. Both time periods are negotiable.

Whether or not you use a broker, you will need a real estate lawyer (or in some areas, an escrow company). Get one involved in the sale as soon as possible.

Pricing your house

Investigate the local market to see what comparable houses are selling for. Check recent sales records with the local tax assessor. Get advice from your broker, if you're using one, or consider using a qualified appraiser—it will cost between $100 and $1,000.

Underpricing sacrifices profit, but overpricing can mean taking longer to sell or maybe not selling at all. You are much likelier to sell the house if the price is close to fair market value.

Advertising and promotion

Prepare a listing sheet giving the age of the house, lot size, room sizes, taxes, and costs for fuel, utilities, and water. A photograph helps. Specify what comes with the house, such as carpets and appliances. Have about 200 copies of the listing sheet printed.

Place ads in several papers. In the ads, stress features that make your house appealing—"Walk to station," "Secluded setting," "Sale by owner." Avoid confusing abbreviations.

Preparing to show

Look at the house for faults as if you were a buyer, then fix it up to look its best. Make sure the lawn and shrubbery are well manicured. Give the place a coat of fresh paint, if necessary. But don't overinvest in new additions or modernizations that someone else won't be willing to pay extra for. Avoid improvements that price the house above its neighbors.

When showing the house, provide such warm touches as flowers, a fire in the fireplace, or cookies in the oven. Don't play music that might offend. Keep noisy children and dogs out of the way. If a broker is showing the house, smile, retreat, and say nothing unless asked. Never lie. You could be sued for concealing known defects.

Continued next page

Legal details

Every real estate transaction is unique. You can start with a standard contract form, but have a lawyer amend it to your advantage. Always try to have a cap put on expenditure liabilities such as termite-damage repair. Make sure that the contract specifically mentions everything that will stay or go (verbal promises don't count). Keep insurance in force until after the official closing of the sale. Don't pay real estate commissions until the closing.

The buyer may ask you to help finance the purchase. Do so only if you're prepared to take back the property or if the tax benefits of installment payments outweigh the benefits of collecting the full purchase price in cash and investing it for a high, trouble-free return.

Humidifiers

Cleaning and fixing portables

Older room humidifiers have a belt or a padded drum to pick up water; a fan vaporizes the water. Ultrasonic humidifiers contain a device called a nebulizer, which vibrates at high speed to turn water into fine mist.

Clean the humidifier reservoir daily to curtail bacteria growth. Use a solution of 1 tablespoon of chlorine per pint of water; rinse with plain water.

Minerals in tap water may build up on the belt or rollers of old-style humidifiers, jamming the machine. Lift out the belt and its rollers, or if your humidifier has a padded drum, lift out the drum and remove the pad from it. Scrub the parts with detergent and hot water. If this doesn't suffice, scrub with a mixture of ¼ cup

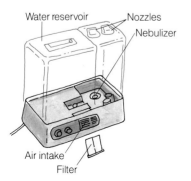

Water reservoir
Nozzles
Nebulizer
Air intake
Filter

vinegar added to 1 quart hot water.

In an ultrasonic, depending on your water's hardness, clean mineral deposits from the nebulizer daily to weekly. Wipe it with white vinegar and a soft brush or cloth, being careful not to scratch it; rinse afterward.

If an old-style humidifier is clean but doesn't run or humidify, a drive belt may be undone or broken. Adjust or replace the belt as required (see *Drive belts*). If an ultrasonic isn't generating air, try cleaning the air filter with cool water. Let it dry completely in a cool place before reinstalling it.

Humidity control

Keeping out the dampness

Left unchecked, excess humidity can create havoc in a house—rotting wood, peeling paint, and fostering rust and mildew. Keep your house well ventilated. Close windows on humid days and open them when the air is dry. If a closet or a room without a window is damp, install a vent, louvered door, or exhaust fan—or all three if the problem is severe. As a last resort, use a dehumidifier.

Install an exhaust fan in the bathroom, or open the window a crack whenever bathing. Install a hood vented to the outdoors over your kitchen range to carry off the water vapor created by cooking.

If you have a clothes dryer in a utility room or basement, check its connections and make sure that it is vented to the outdoors. Amazingly, the average dryer extracts a pound of water out of every pound of clothes. (See also *Basement waterproofing*.)

Attics and crawl spaces

Warm, moist air, such as that generated in cooking, can seep into an attic. In winter it may freeze on the backside of roofing material, then thaw in spring and drip down to rot wood and saturate floor insulation, reducing its effectiveness.

If the insulation has no vapor barrier, install polyethylene sheeting under it or paint the ceiling with vapor-barrier paint (see *Vapor barriers*). Be sure your attic is properly vented (see *Vents*). Cover crawl spaces with 6-mil

polyethylene to keep water vapor from rising from the ground into the house.

House walls

Water vapor can penetrate interior wall materials and reach exterior walls, saturating the insulation or peeling exterior paint. Repaint the interior walls, using a vapor-resistant prime paint under the finish coat, or install tiny vents in the exterior siding to let trapped moisture escape.

Hurricanes

Getting through one safely

Before the start of the hurricane season (June), ask the nearest National Weather Service office if your home area might be imperiled. Most hurricane fatalities are caused by the storm surge—a huge dome of water that is driven ashore. If your area is threatened or if you live in a mobile home or near a river or flood plain, be prepared to evacuate.

Check with your local Civil Defense for a hurricane preparedness plan, which will include such information as shelter locations, what to bring, and the safest evacuation route. Ask how long it would take to get to a shelter in peak evacuation traffic.

Inventory your personal property and stock up on emergency supplies (see *Floods*). Your home owner's insurance probably covers wind damage, but make sure you have adequate coverage (hurricane insurance, flood insurance). Store these important records in a watertight case.

When a hurricane is coming

Keep tuned to your radio or television for a *hurricane watch* announcement. This message informs you that there's a possibility of a hurricane. Listen for further advisories.

After a *hurricane warning* has been announced, double-check your preparations. Anchor outdoor furniture and equipment or bring it indoors. Board up all windows and glass doors; brace garage doors with 2x4's. Moor your boat securely or move it to a designated safe area.

When leaving for a shelter, secure all window and door locks. Leave pets at home (they're not allowed in shel-

212

ters) with plenty of food and water. Take light folding chairs, blankets, and valuable documents.

If your house is inland, well constructed, and on high ground, you may want to stay home. When the storm begins, move to the downwind side of the house, and keep away from windows and glass doors. There's a lull as the eye of the hurricane passes. Don't mistake this for the end; fierce winds will return. Don't go outdoors until local authorities announce that it is safe to do so.

Hypothermia

Handling life-threatening chilling of the body

Hypothermia occurs when body temperature drops to 95°F or below. Be alert to such signs as shivering, pale and cold skin, clumsiness, slurred speech, confusion, irritability, lethargy. Victims, especially the elderly, may not notice symptoms. Ability to sense one's own body temperature decreases with age.

Rewarming must begin immediately; otherwise the victim may perish. Check breathing and pulse (see *Pulse* and *CPR*) and, if necessary, administer CPR. Don't give up; a victim of hypothermia may survive 6 minutes or more without breathing or pulse. Then summon medical help. Move the person to a warm place. If you are far from shelter, get out of the wind; improvise a shelter with anything available. Remove the victim's wet clothing and replace it with dry. Wrap him in blankets or put him in a sleeping bag with another person.

Indoors, if the victim is conscious, use a tub of lukewarm, not hot, water. Provide hot liquids, preferably sweetened, but no alcohol—it lowers temperature. If the victim is unconscious, use heaters and blankets; cover all but his face. Continue rewarming until help arrives or, in outlying areas, until a victim is sufficiently restored to be taken to a hospital.

Prevention

If you will be exposed to the cold for a long period, take precautions. Fuel yourself well with food, especially car-bohydrates; don't smoke or drink alcoholic beverages.

Dress warmly; the best insulation is air trapped between layers of clothing. Wear a hat, gloves, and windproof outer garments to prevent the body's heat escaping. Wet clothing is a double disaster: it loses its ability to trap air and it cools the skin. For prolonged outdoor activity, carry raingear and a change of clothes. Keep active; movement generates heat.

Don't ignore the wind-chill factor. In a wind of 25 m.p.h., 30°F is equivalent to 0°F. Hypothermia doesn't occur only in cold weather. A swim in icy water, even on a warm day, can cause it; so can cold or dampness if exposure is prolonged.

Iceboating

Sailing faster than the wind

An iceboat's hull is mounted on a crosspiece to each end of which skate-like runner blades are attached; a steering runner is located at the hull's bow or stern. The skipper and, in some models, one other person sit in a cockpit in the hull or in a tray on each side of it. The mast supports a mainsail and sometimes a jib.

Iceboating techniques are similar to those for sailing on water (see *Sailing*). Pulling in the sail to catch the breeze starts an iceboat downwind. Sailing at a right angle to the wind results in the fastest speed. In this position, the windward runner may lift off the ice; the boat then skates along on one runner. To stop, point into the wind or release the rope holding the sail so that the wind spills. In either case, allow for a safe gliding distance.

Caution: Check with local authorities on the safety of wind and ice conditions. Wear a helmet, goggles, face shield, padded gloves, and insulated clothing to protect against spills and frostbite.

Ice cream

Churning your own mix

Making ice cream allows you to use seasonal fruits or to create unusual flavors. The task is eased by churning the mix in an electric freezer (some new ones don't even require packing with salt and ice), but hand cranking provides fun for children of all ages.

Make an ice-cream mix (see below). Chill it for 1 to 2 hours. Wash and scald the freezer's can, lid, and dasher; dry and chill them. Follow the freezer maker's directions for the amounts of ice and rock salt. With a mallet, crush the ice in a pillow case or canvas bag.

Fill the can ⅔ full with the mix to allow for expansion (churning incorporates air in the mix). Insert the dasher, cover the can, and place it in the freezer tub. Fill the tub ⅓ full with crushed ice, then alternate layers of salt and ice, using 1 part salt to 6 to 8 parts ice. Attach the motor or hand crank. Let stand about 3 minutes, then turn on an electric freezer or begin cranking a manual one, slowly at first and always in the same direction.

The ice cream is frozen when the hand crank becomes difficult to turn or the motor shuts off or labors heavily. Remove the cranking mechanism, lift out the can, and wipe it clean. Remove the lid and the dasher; pack down the ice cream with a spoon. Replace the lid and plug its hole with a cork. Drain water from the tub and place the can in it. Repack the freezer with salt and ice, cover it with wet newspapers, and let the ice cream ripen for 2 to 3 hours.

A basic ice-cream mix

For about 2½ quarts of ice cream, blend 3¼ cups milk and 1 14-ounce can sweetened condensed milk. Add ½ cup sugar; stir to dissolve. Stir in 3 cups heavy cream; add flavorings.

For vanilla ice cream, add 3½ tablespoons vanilla extract or to taste. For chocolate, combine 1⅓ cups unsweetened cocoa with ½ cup sugar. Bring 1 cup water to the simmer, slowly add the cocoa and stir until it's smooth and syrupy. Add 1⅓ cups chilled syrup to the ice-cream mix.

Ice dams

Preventing leak damage caused by melting roof ice

Snow melting on a roof refreezes on cold overhangs, creating ice dams; these dams trap water that may eventually leak into the house. The permanent way to prevent ice dams is to properly insulate and ventilate your attic (see *Insulation; Vents*). These measures will, in addition, save on heating and electric bills.

A temporary stopgap is to install electric-heat cable bought in a kit. For a roof overhang of 1 foot, you'll need enough cable to run roughly 2½ times the length of your roof, plus the length of the gutters and downspout.

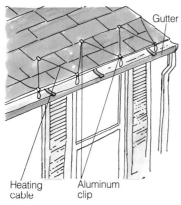

Fix the kit's aluminum clips or clamps to the shingles, following the directions given in the kit, and secure the cable in a zigzag pattern. The correct distance between peaks of the zigzag depends on the amount of local snowfall: space them 1½ feet apart in average snowfall areas and 1 foot apart in snowbelt areas.

Run cable through the gutters and the downspout. To reduce heat loss, keep the cable off the bottoms of the gutters by clamping it to the gutter hangers. Don't let sections of cable touch each other.

Plug the cable into the receptacle of an outdoor waterproof outlet box or bring the cord through a window and plug it inside. Turn it on when snow falls and leave it on while snow stays on the roof. Some cables have a thermostat that turns on the power when the temperature nears freezing.

Ice fishing

Equipment and techniques

Caution: Before going out on a frozen lake or river, check with local authorities for the thickness and condition of the ice and for the number of fishing lines you're allowed to use. Pedestrian traffic requires at least 4 inches of clear blue lake ice; cars, at least 8 inches. Twice these thicknesses are needed if the ice is cloudy or slushy or if it covers a rapid river current.

When you go ice fishing, bring a sled or a large bucket to transport equipment. Rent an ice shanty, buy or build a portable shelter, or set up a windbreak. Wear heavy, insulated boots and many layers of warm clothing.

Bore one or more holes in the ice about 8 inches across with an ax, a spud (a long-handled chisel), or an ice auger. A power auger makes drilling a hole, even in very thick ice, easy and fast, but it's expensive.

Use a skimmer to clear the hole of

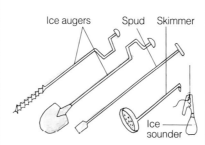

floating ice chips. Because most fish winter on or near the bottom, test the water's depth with an ice sounder or a heavy sinker attached to a hook at the end of a monofilament line.

Drop the hook into the hole; when it hits bottom, clip a bobber to the line and adjust it until the hook is about a foot off the bottom. Then remove the sounder, bait the hook, and drop it back into the hole.

For panfish such as crappies, bluegills, and perch, use a special ice rod, a short jigging rod, or a handline looped around a stick. Panfish hit minnows, mealworms, grubs, mousies (fly larvae), and artificial lures such as tiny spoons, ice flies, and jigs. Make a lure more effective by tipping the hook with natural bait. Jig the bait every few minutes; raise it a few feet if fish are not biting near bottom.

For larger fish such as walleyes and pickerel—or to fish several holes at once—use tip-ups baited with live minnows, shiners, or big chubs. When a fish strikes, the tip-up's spool turns, releasing a signal flag.

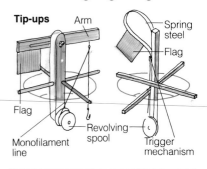

Ice removal

Ridding walks, steps, and driveways of hazardous ice

If you don't want to chop ice away with a handtool, there are several substances that will melt it. Rock salt is the cheapest, but it kills vegetation and damages footgear; moreover it won't work below 10°F.

Calcium chloride pellets are less damaging to vegetation; they will melt ice at temperatures as low as -25°F. Although they are more expensive than rock salt, less is needed.

Granular fertilizer has little melting power but provides traction. It also feeds vegetation along your walk. Cat-box litter, sand, and cinders also provide traction without causing damage.

Ice skating

A few basics for the beginner

Dress comfortably for ice skating. Outdoors wear a hat, sweater, jacket, slacks, long underwear, and gloves. In an indoor rink you won't need long underwear. Remove jewelry for safety.

It's advisable for a beginner to rent skates (most ice rinks have rentals). Figure skates, which have two blade edges, are the best for learning. The boot should fit snugly and hug the heel but have enough room to accommodate a pair of wool socks. With the laces snug, you should still be able to insert two fingers into the boot top on one side. Tie the laces with a double knot and tuck the ends into the boot.

Choose a time when the ice is uncrowded. Walk around a little with guards on the skate blades. When you are ready, remove the guards and carefully step onto the ice. Grasp the barrier and pull yourself away from the entrance. Stand motionless for a moment. Keep your body straight, head up, and knees slightly bent, with feet a few inches apart. Arms should be relaxed, held out to the sides waist high for balance. Feel the inside and outside blade edges grip the ice.

At first, try walking on your skates with short steps. Your ankles will wobble and you will have trouble balancing, but this will soon pass.

Now try the movements that will propel you forward. Place your feet in a T position, the right behind the left at a 90 degree angle. Using the full length of the inside edge of the right blade, push forward. At the same time, shift all your weight onto the left foot and glide, keeping your shoulders pointed in the direction of your movement and your left knee slightly bent. Now bring your right foot forward, parallel with your left, and glide on both blades. Practice pushing off several times, starting first with one foot, then the other.

Pushing off   Gliding

To sustain the forward movement, push off from one foot and then the other, almost as you did in the starting position, but with the thrusting foot angled more to the side. With each stroke, glide as far as you can before pushing off again.

As you approach a corner, turn your body gradually and lean into the curve. Your skates will follow.

As a beginner, you will find the easiest way to stop is by forcing both heels outward and bringing the knees together—called a *snowplow*. Eventually, you should learn the *T stop*, in which you place the free foot at a 90 degree angle to the other and gradually lower the blade onto the ice.

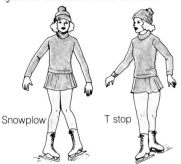

Snowplow   T stop

Don't be afraid of falling. Learn to do it correctly. Keep your hands up as you start to slip, bend your knees, and sit down! To get up, roll over into a kneeling position. Put your hands down flat on the ice, bring one foot forward with the knee about level with your chin, then bring the other foot

Getting up

forward. Stretch your hands out in front of you and stand up. (See also *Figure skating; Hockey equipment.*)

Caution: A pond or lake should have at least 4 inches of clear blue ice; twice that if the ice is cloudy. Check for cracks, weak spots, and broken areas. Don't skate alone.

Immunizations

Protecting your child from contagious diseases

All 50 states require children to be vaccinated against seven of childhood's once most-dreaded diseases: diphtheria, whooping cough (pertussis), tetanus, polio, measles, mumps, and German measles (rubella). These immunizations must be given before a child enters school; some states require a doctor's certificate. Immunization has virtually eliminated these diseases; a worldwide campaign has eradicated smallpox, making that vaccination no longer necessary.

All vaccines are injected, except polio, which is given by mouth. They provide permanent protection by triggering the production of antibodies that attack and destroy disease organisms. Vaccines are made, as a rule, from harmless (dead or weakened) infectious agents unable to cause the disease but strong enough to stimulate the antibody response. Side effects, if any, are usually limited to soreness at the site of the injection, slight fever, or rash. Rarely, there is a severe reaction (fever over 105°F, screaming, convulsions); if this occurs, call your doctor.

Your pediatrician will schedule vaccinations for all seven diseases as appropriate for each child. The DTP vaccine (diphtheria, tetanus, and pertussis) is given in five separate doses: the first three at 2-month intervals starting as early as 2 months of age; the next at 18 months; the fifth just before the child enters school. Thereafter, tetanus alone should be given at least every 10 years. Measles, mumps, and rubella vaccines are given in one injection, usually at 15 months; polio vaccine in four or five doses starting as early as 2 months and ending at start-of-school age.

Adults traveling abroad may need immunization against certain diseases. Well in advance of your trip, ask your travel agent, airline, or the embassies of countries you expect to visit what shots you will require. Or write the Communicable Diseases Division, World Health Organization, 525 23rd Street NW, Washington, DC 20037.

Income tax audits

Avoiding an audit; preparing for an audit; going through one

All federal income tax returns are run through Internal Revenue Service (IRS) computers, which check the arithmetic and flag returns that have errors. The computers may also flag returns with higher-than-average or unusual deductions for someone of a given income level or filing status. Your return may well be flagged if you claim a very large deduction for charity or a casualty loss; if you claim deductions for child rearing and file as a single taxpayer (not a single head of household); if you take deductions for an office in your home; if you deduct exceptionally high alimony payments; if you claim a large number of exemptions for dependents not living in your home; or if you own your own business.

Computers do not decide which returns to audit. They simply bring a questionable return to the attention of an IRS examiner. He or she reviews the return to decide whether it will be audited. Don't be afraid to take large deductions that you are entitled to, as long as you can prove that they are legitimate. Photocopies of bank records showing exceptionally high home mortgage or investment interest payments, proof of business-related expenses, proof of a casualty loss, or copies of receipts for charitable deductions usually suffice.

There is no surefire way to avoid an audit, even if your tax return is uncomplicated. A small number of returns are randomly selected for audit every three years so that the IRS can statistically measure and evaluate the characteristics of taxpayers. The higher your income, the likelier you are to be audited. People who live in certain areas, such as Chicago, Los Angeles, and Manhattan in New York City, may be more apt to be audited than those who live elsewhere.

The IRS can audit a return up to 3 years after its due date or the date it was filed, whichever was later. Keep all tax records handy for at least that long.

Preparing for an audit

If you are called in for an audit (usually by letter), don't panic. An audit notice is not an accusation of wrongdoing; it is merely an invitation to clear up a problem on your return. Up to a quarter of all audits end with no additional payment by the taxpayer or with a refund to the taxpayer.

Although some audits are done by mail, an audit notice usually requests your presence at a local IRS office at a suggested time. You may request a more convenient time, but if you fail

to show up without rescheduling the meeting, the IRS can rule on your return without your being there to explain or challenge. The IRS can also have a court force you to attend.

You can consult an accountant, a tax attorney, or other tax expert to help you prepare for an audit, but often this is unnecessary. There are many books written for the layman about tax law, including some good ones by the IRS, which will give you a clear idea of what you need to know for most audits.

If you feel the issues of the audit are likely to be too complex for you to understand, or if you are afraid you will be charged with tax fraud—such as concealing income or falsifying deductions—consult an expert. If the expert is an attorney, he or she can offer advice on the law and the strategies to adopt for dealing with the IRS.

You can have the expert accompany you or represent you at the audit. If you go alone, but then feel that you cannot adequately explain your position, ask to reschedule the meeting and have an expert return with you.

The audit notice will tell you the items on your return that are in question. Bring in all of your records for those items—canceled checks, cash receipts, credit card receipts, legal documents. Review your records before the audit so that you will be able to discuss them with some familiarity. Do not bring any records that do not pertain to the disputed items. The auditor may review other parts of your return if you draw attention to them.

The audit

At the audit the examiner will discuss the points of the tax law pertinent to your case, examine your records, and listen to your explanations. Treat your auditor in an open, cooperative manner, but don't volunteer information you are not asked for. If you think your examiner is acting improperly, ask to see his or her supervisor.

An audit can end after only one meeting, or it can extend over several. You may be asked to submit additional information by mail. After the audit, the IRS will send you a report, informing you if there is a deficiency (you owe the Government money) and why. If the IRS owes you money, it will

send it to you. If there is a deficiency, you sign an agreement form and pay the tax due. If you disagree, your examiner will explain what you do next to resolve the dispute.

Income tax extensions

Getting extra time to file your income tax return

You can delay filing your federal income tax return for 4 months (for most taxpayers, from April 15 to August 15) simply by filing IRS Form 4868 by the date your return is due, usually April 15. The form is available at local offices of the Internal Revenue Service (IRS). Once you file Form 4868, the extension is automatically granted. This an extension of the filing date *only;* payment is still due.

If you think you owe taxes, pay what you estimate is due when you file Form 4868, or you'll be penalized. When you file your return, you might be subject to interest and penalties if you underpaid your taxes. The IRS will let you know what you owe. If you don't owe taxes or are entitled to a refund, filing for an extension costs you nothing.

If you need still more time beyond the initial 4-month extension, file Form 2688 or ask the IRS for help.

Incorporating yourself

The pros, cons, and hows of incorporating a small business or organization

If you have or plan to start your own business, you may want to incorporate it, even if it involves only yourself or your family. You may also want to incorporate a society or organization you belong to in order to keep its financial involvements separate from those of its members. Incorporating has advantages and disadvantages. Consult an attorney or an accountant to review the ones that apply to you before you take the big step.

Generally, the chief advantage of incorporating is that your liability is limited to the amount you invested in the corporation. If your business fails or is sued, your home and personal property cannot be lost, as it can in a partnership or other unincorporated business. And you can withdraw from a corporation by selling your stock. A corporation can defer tax payments, spread its taxable income over several family members, and provide such fringe benefits as pensions and insurance as a business cost.

On the other hand, corporate profits are taxed, as well as your income from a corporation, and the activities of a corporation are limited to those granted in its charter. A corporation must gain permission to operate in other states, pay additional fees, and observe each state's regulations. A corporation must keep exhaustive records and file numerous reports in each state in which it does business. Finally, attorneys who do corporate work are generally expensive.

To form a corporation, you must file articles of incorporation with the state secretary of state, giving the name of the corporation, its intended duration (how long you want the corporation to continue), its purposes, its address, and the number, names, and addresses of the incorporators. There is a filing fee.

Indigestion

What to do about discomfort after eating

Indigestion covers many complaints, often caused by bad eating habits. Among the discomforts are bloating, belching, passing gas, heartburn, or nausea. Over-the-counter antacids may help temporarily (provided they don't cause adverse side effects; best to ask your doctor), but peppermint tea may suffice.

For more permanent relief, try a change in your eating habits. Eat smaller amounts more often and more slowly. Cut down on tobacco, alcohol, coffee, spices, fats, cucumbers, onions, garlic, beans, cabbage and its kin, and dairy products. If stress triggers indigestion, relax before meals and keep table conversation pleasant.

If your symptoms change markedly, last longer than 2 hours, recur fre-quently, or are accompanied by a gradual loss of appetite, vomiting, bloody stools, or severe heartburn, see your doctor. (See also *Heartburn*.)

Ingrown toenails

Relieving the pain; preventing a recurrence

An ingrown toenail digs into the surrounding skin, causing pain and, often, swelling and inflammation. The usual cause is a toenail cut too short and curved at the corners, shoes that are too tight, or both. Instead of growing out straight, the toenail tends to curve and thus cut into the flesh. Shoe pressure aggravates the condition and the pain.

To lessen the pain and prevent possible infection, soak a bit of absorbent cotton in antibiotic solution or ointment and push it under the nail edge. If the area becomes infected, consult a physician or podiatrist.

Prevent the condition by cutting toenails straight across, not curved. Wear shoes with ample toe space.

Injured wildlife

Getting proper care for disabled animals and birds

Caution: Do not approach a fully grown wild mammal or a bird of prey such as a hawk or owl. It may attack you or harm itself further by trying to flee. Also avoid a mammal that behaves abnormally or one that seems tame and is not wary of your presence. It may have rabies. Never handle prairie dogs or ground squirrels; their fleas can carry plague.

When you spot an injured animal, stop and analyze the source of its distress. Is a leg or wing broken? Does it have an open wound? Or is it lying on the roadside apparently hit by a car?

Then, even if the animal appears safe to handle, report its condition and location to your local wildlife office. In most areas, wildlife protection laws allow only professionals to capture and care for many species. With your report on the animal's condition, a wildlife officer will be able to re-spond with the appropriate help—or advise you what to do. You can get the wildlife office's number readily from the police, the ASPCA, or your neighborhood veterinarian.

You may be asked to bring in a disabled bird. If you do, don't use a cage; a wild bird can hurt itself by crashing against the bars. Carry the bird in a cardboard box or a sturdy paper bag with air holes punched in the sides.

If you find a healthy but apparently abandoned baby animal or bird, leave the area as quickly and quietly as possible. The mother will probably come to its rescue. Even if a well-meaning person has removed it from its natural habitat, the mother is likely to find it if you return it within a day or so.

If you spot a featherless, newly hatched bird on the ground, find its nest and slip it back in. A fully plumed fledgling may become temporarily stranded on the ground during a test flight. If one is in danger from cats or dogs, put it on a nearby branch.

Insect bites and stings

Coping with a painful, sometimes serious problem

The harm done by biting and stinging insects varies. A sting may cause no more than a day's itching or it may inject painful poisons, stimulate severe allergic response, or carry serious disease. Treatment depends on the insect and on individual reactions.

Spider bites

All spiders inject venom when they bite, but few produce it in sufficient strength to injure a human. Black widow and brown recluse spiders are the exception; their bites can be fatal. A tarantula's bite is not in itself serious but may introduce bacteria.

Because most spiders look similar to the untrained eye, it is better to attend to the bite than to try to identify the biter. If the bite is very painful, red, or swollen, assume that it may be dangerous; don't wait for evidence of poisoning. If sweating, nausea, vomiting, muscle cramps, joint pains, chills, fever, or breathing difficulties develop, get medical help promptly. Meanwhile, keep the bite site lower

217

than the heart, and apply ice or a cold compress to it. A paste of baking soda and water will soothe the pain.

Bees, wasps, and ants

Usually one sting from a bee, wasp, or hornet is dangerous only to those highly sensitive to the venom. But multiple stings—from inadvertently disturbing a nest, for example—can make anyone ill. Get to a medical facility promptly and stay there until a physician clears you. If signs of illness appear, you'll be close to help.

Don't waste a minute if someone has a severe allergic reaction to the venom from a single bee sting or from an ant or other insect bite. Signs include swelling beyond the sting site, difficulty in breathing, and faintness. Anyone who already knows he has such an allergy should wear an allergy identification tag and carry a kit with antihistamine pills, a syringe loaded with epinephrine, and instructions. If no such kit is at hand, get medical help immediately.

A person who develops more than a local reaction to any insect bite or sting should see a doctor. Such a reaction might include wheezing, hives, or swelling that begins at the site and eventually puffs up a large area, such as the entire forearm.

Remedies and relief measures

Bee stings and the burning bites of fire ants are painful—and the more venom injected, the greater the pain. Honey bees, the only stinging insect to do so, leave the entire sting apparatus in the wound, and the poison gland continues to release poison after the bee has departed. Don't pull the stinger out with tweezers or fingernails; this squeezes even more poison from the gland. Instead, scrape it out with the blunt edge of a knife. Meat tenderizer, if applied quickly, will break down the toxin and stop the pain. Failing that, ice, baking-soda paste, or calamine lotion will give some relief.

These same three remedies will soothe the itching from other insect bites. When there are many itching bites all over the body, try adding baking soda to bath water; use 4 tablespoons per gallon of water. Avoid scratching a bite; it further opens the wound, allowing bacteria to invade.

Mosquito bites

Mosquitoes, as well as horseflies, deerflies, and blackflies, bite instead of sting. Wash these bites with soap and cold water; use the same relief measures as for bee stings. Occasionally someone has an allergic reaction to such a bite; generally this is treated like an allergic reaction to a sting.

An added risk is that bacterial or viral disease may enter along with an insect's saliva. In some areas, mosquitoes are the carriers of malaria and yellow fever. If you are traveling, ask your travel agent, airline, or the embassies of countries you plan to visit about immunizations for these and other diseases. (See also *Ticks*.)

Insomnia

Overcoming sleep problems

Millions of people experience some form of insomnia. They have trouble falling asleep, they awake very early and are unable to go back to sleep, or having slept a few hours, they awake periodically until morning.

If you function normally during the day, you are probably getting enough sleep. Some people need less than 8 hours, some more.

Temporary insomnia may be related to illness (usually a pain-causing condition) or to a psychological disturbance—anxiety, depression, anticipation, or excitement. More serious is a disorder such as sleep apnea, in which a person temporarily stops breathing, snores, snorts, and then awakes to breathe. This sequence may be repeated many times a night. It is a potentially dangerous condition requiring medical attention.

However, in most insomnia, the cause is far simpler: too much caffeine, too little activity, or nervous tension—the latter often brought on by worry about not sleeping.

Ordinary insomnia is usually relieved by one or more of the following measures. Avoid coffee, tea, and soft drinks containing caffeine after 12 noon. Avoid large, late-evening meals. Exercise daily. At bedtime take a warm bath (not a shower); drink a glass of warm milk—the tryptophan

it contains promotes sleep. In bed read a difficult or boring book, not work-related materials or suspense stories. Engage in sexual intercourse; it has a sedative effect. Learn relaxation exercises to release tension.

If you aren't asleep 10 minutes after retiring, get up and do something; return to bed only when you are really drowsy. Don't habitually rely on alcohol or sleeping pills; in the long run, they make matters worse.

Insulation

Where and how to install it

Tiny air pockets in insulating materials resist the transfer of heat, keeping it inside your home in cold weather, outside in warm. The ability to resist heat flow is measured in R (for resistance) values. The higher the R value, the greater the insulating power. Buy insulation on the basis of R value, not thickness. Look for the R value printed on the insulation or its packaging.

Types of insulation

Batts (precut 4- or 8-foot lengths) or blankets (continuous rolls) of glass fiber or rock wool are sold with or without vapor-barrier facings (see *Vapor barriers*). Loose fill of rock wool, glass fiber, vermiculite, or perlite is poured in place by hand. Loose fill and poly urea foam are blown into enclosed walls with special equipment. Rigid insulation is used for interior or exterior sheathing or around a foundation perimeter.

Insulate surfaces that separate living areas from unheated spaces or the

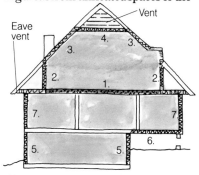

Where to insulate:
1. Unfinished attic floor; 2., 3., 4. Knee walls, Rafters, Collar beams in finished attic; 5. Walls in heated basement; 6. Floor over cold crawl space; 7. Exterior walls

outdoors. How much insulation you need depends on the local climate and fuel costs and the part of the home to be insulated. Ask your utility or a local insulation contractor for the recommended R values for your area.

Insulating an unfinished attic
This is the most cost-effective space to insulate. To determine the square footage of insulation needed, multiply the length by the width of the attic floor. Buy vapor-barrier faced glass fiber or rock wool batts wide enough to fit between joists.

Caution: When working with insulation, wear safety glasses, a breathing mask, and gloves. Consider wearing a hard hat.

Lay temporary plywood flooring and hang one or more work lights. Start laying batts, vapor-barrier side down, at the outer edges of the attic

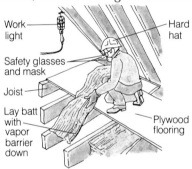

and work toward the center. Make sure the batts butt tightly together. To cut a batt, set it on a board, compress it with a 2 x 4, and cut it with a serrated knife. Compress insulation to fit underneath wiring; leave a 3-inch space around a recessed lighting fixture or a motor-driven device. Adequate airflow above attic insulation is essential to prevent condensation. Don't block the eave vents, if any; install vents or power ventilators in the attic walls or roof (see *Vents*).

If you use loose fill, install a vapor barrier by laying strips of 6-mil-thick polyethylene in the spaces between joists. Cut the strips 3 or 4 inches wider than the spaces, staple them to the side of the joists, then pour in loose fill to the desired thickness. To add more insulation, place new batts or blankets, without vapor barriers, on top of the old, or pour in more loose fill.

If your attic has a finished floor, fit batts, vapor barriers facing you, be-

tween the rafters; staple the outer edges of the vapor barriers to the rafters at 6-inch intervals. Allow at least 1 inch of space between the batts and the roof for ventilation.

Basements and crawl spaces
To insulate an unheated basement or crawl space, fit batts or blankets, vapor-barrier side up, between the overhead joists. Staple wire mesh to the joists to secure the insulation.

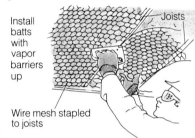

Wrap insulation, vapor barriers facing you, around exposed air conditioning and heating ducts in an unheated basement or attic; seal the edges with duct tape.

To insulate a heated crawl space, lay a 6-mil-thick polyethylene sheet over the entire floor area. Fit strips of insulation against the headers. Using furring strips, nail lengths of unfaced insulation to the sill; the insulation should extend 2 feet along the ground over the polyethylene. Use rocks or bricks to anchor the insulation.

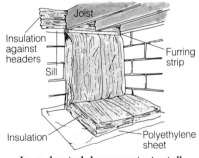

In a heated basement, install a framework of furring strips or studs on the walls (see *Furring strips*). Fit the insulation, vapor barriers facing you, between the studs or furring; staple the insulation in place. Cut pieces of insulation to fit the headers.

Insulating finished walls
Blowing loose fill or foam into walls or installing rigid insulation are usually jobs for a professional. Get estimates from at least three contractors and ask for references.

International road signs

Symbols used around the world to guide drivers

If you plan to drive abroad, learn the system of road signs used in most other countries. Here are some of the less familiar signs you'll see. For a full listing—including individual nations' variations—call your local American Automobile Association club.

Warnings in red triangles

Right curve | Road narrows | Intersection with side road

Bumpy road | Steep descent | Danger

Restrictions in red circles

Do not enter | Road closed | No cars

Oncoming traffic has priority | No left turn | 70 meters (70 yards) between cars

No passing | No parking | No parking or standing

Instructions in blue circles

Right turn mandatory | Minimum speed | Traffic circle

Information in blue rectangles

Hospital | Parking | Tourist information

No through road | Highway | Lane directions

Introductions

Following the rules of etiquette

The standard rule is to introduce men to women, the younger person to the older, and those of lesser rank (or importance to you) to those of higher rank. Just say the higher ranking person's name first. "Mother, this is my friend Julie." "Dr. Brinkerhoff, may I present Mr. Frank Durr." "Debbie, I'd like you to meet Jim Smith. Jim, this is Debbie Donahue."

If you want to introduce two people, but don't remember the name of one of them, make a one-way introduction. In the case of Debbie and What's His Name, simply say, "I'd like you to meet Debbie Donahue." Jim should then introduce himself to Debbie. Since people often forget names, even if they shouldn't, be ready to help your friends when you are being introduced by saying your name quickly if your friend gets stuck.

People often wonder how much detail to give when they are introducing a couple who live together or a group of relatives. The introducer should feel under no obligation to explain the intricate relationships among the people he or she is introducing. Simple names are enough. But it is polite to provide a little background information about the introduced person. "Frank is our office manager." Or "Patty and I went to college together."

When someone is being introduced to a group, everyone (men and women) should stand. Always make an effort to include a new member of a group in the general conversation. When being introduced to an individual, shaking hands is appropriate.

Inventory

Making a room-by-room record of your possessions

If your home is burglarized or damaged by fire, an accurate inventory of its contents will substantiate your insurance claim or tax deduction. An inventory also helps you monitor the number, age, and condition of your belongings, making it particularly useful if you move or sublet your home furnished. Companies selling fire and homeowner's insurance often provide free booklets in which to list household inventory.

Go through your house room by room, writing down the name and quantity of each item, its date of purchase, purchase price, and current value. Check newspaper ads and store catalogs to help you determine current value. Keep separate inventories of clothing, furs, jewelry, silverware, and works of art. Irreplaceable items, and those that have historic or market-determined value, should be professionally appraised (see below).

Photograph each room and take close-ups of works of art and other valuables. Store the photos with the written list in a safe-deposit box; keep a copy of the list in a separate place. Update the inventory annually. Review a new or updated inventory with your insurance company to make sure you have adequate coverage.

You can also take inventory by having someone videotape you as you walk through the house describing and pricing your belongings. Or hire a professional appraiser to draw up an inventory for you. Appraisers charge a daily or hourly rate or a percentage of your property's appraised value.

Invisible ink

Writing secret messages

You can do writing that appears invisible—yet is easily revealed—with lemon or onion juice. Use either bottled or freshly squeezed lemon juice. To get onion juice, grate a peeled onion into a dish, then strain out the juice. Let it set a while before using.

Dip a toothpick in the juice and write on hard-surfaced paper. Let the juice dry thoroughly. To make the message appear, hold the paper next to a hot lightbulb or an electric iron. Don't let the paper catch fire.

You can also do invisible writing with milk. Use a toothpick and allow the milk to dry. To expose the message, rub pencil shavings or fine ashes lightly over the surface.

Invitations

How to answer formal and informal invitations

The formal style of invitation is most often used for weddings, graduations, bar or bat mitzvahs, formal dances and receptions, or large, official dinners. Formal invitations are engraved (or printed to look like engraving) on heavy white or cream-colored vellum. They refer to the host and or hostess in the third person.

Formal invitations require a formal response, handwritten on good quality white or cream paper in blue or black ink, as in the following model:

Mr. and Mrs. Kurt E. Batchelder
Elizabeth and Kurt, Jr.
accept with pleasure
the kind invitation of
Mr. and Mrs. James P. Maclaren
for
Saturday, the twenty-fifth of July

Center each line and spell out numbers. If Elizabeth doesn't wish to attend, her brother's name alone should appear under his parents' names and the following should be added:

Elizabeth regrets
that she is unable to accept

Decline a formal invitation as follows:

Mr. and Mrs. Kurt E. Batchelder
regret sincerely
that they will be unable to accept
the kind invitation of
Mr. and Mrs. James P. Maclaren
for
Saturday, the twenty-fifth of July

Many couples create their own wedding invitations. These may be answered either formally or by a warm, friendly note. A telephone call is not a proper response to any wedding invitation, unless the invitation is issued over the phone or at the last minute.

Informal written invitations to dinner or cocktails may be answered by a telephone call if a reply is requested (see *R.s.v.p.*). Answer the invitation promptly whether or not you choose to accept, giving the host or hostess time to plan food and drinks or to invite other guests if necessary.

Once you have accepted any invitation, do your best to attend. It is not gracious to change your mind for any reason except an emergency. Never take children or other guests who were not specifically invited.

Ironing

The best ways to iron clothing

Iron washed clothes while they are still slightly damp. Otherwise, spray them with water and roll them in a towel for an hour. When ironing a batch of clothes, do the items that require the lower iron setting first.

When possible, iron dark fabrics, acetates, rayons, and silks on the wrong side to prevent surface shine. Steam wrinkles from wool, or use a dampened press cloth and a light up-and-down motion instead of a glide. Iron napped, nubby, embroidered, or appliquéd items on the wrong side with a terry towel between the garment and the ironing board.

Blouses

Start with the collar and cuffs, ironing the wrong side first; hold them taut so that they don't wrinkle. Next are sleeves. If a sleeve has a gathered or pleated cap, it should be pressed on a sleeveboard. Otherwise, avoid the top edge as you iron the sides. Then center the seam underneath and iron the top, taking care not to crease the sides. Iron the sleeve cap over the end of the board, using the tip of the iron for gathers. (See also *Shirt ironing*.)

Skirts and pants

First iron the waistband of a skirt over the end of the board. On a pleated skirt, iron a little below the waist; turn the skirt around and iron the rest of the pleat length. Press a skirt with gathers or unpressed pleats from hem to waist.

Iron the top of pants first. Then lay the pants flat, legs on top of each other, with the side and inseams aligned. Fold back the top leg and iron the inside of the bottom leg. Turn the pants over and repeat on the other side. Then iron the outside of each leg, setting the creases—to the seat in back, to 6 inches below the waistband in front—with a dampened press cloth.

Iron railings

Embellishing stairs, porches, and walkways

With the bolt-together parts available at hardware stores and home centers, you can easily assemble sturdy iron railings that look almost like craftsmen-wrought installations. In addition to the railings—which come preassembled in sections, including slanted versions for stairs—you'll need posts and compatible fittings.

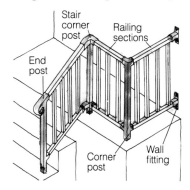

How you install a railing depends on whether you are attaching the support posts to a wooden or masonry surface. On a plank porch or indoor stair, simply screw a base plate to the wood's surface and secure the post to the base plate with the fasteners provided. Then, with a hacksaw, trim the railings to fit, cutting equal amounts from both ends for balance. Slot them into the posts and secure them.

On a concrete carport or on brick steps, you can also use base plates to install the posts; just fasten the plates with masonry bolts and anchors (see *Wall fasteners*). For a more permanent installation, cement the posts

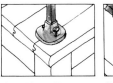

Attaching with a base plate

Cementing in a post

into holes. To make a hole, first draw a square slightly larger around than the post. Wearing goggles, use a carbide-tipped bit to drill a 3-inch-deep

hole at each corner of the square. Then clear out the hole with a cold chisel and a heavy hammer. Wedge the posts in place and assemble the railing fully before filling the holes with fast-setting hydraulic cement.

Throughout, make sure that railings are level, posts plumb, and fittings tight (see *Leveling*). On stair railings, adjust the slant to match your steps' pitch and cut the rail ends at the correct angle to join them to the posts. End with a couple of coats of enamel over the factory finish.

Irons

Repair and maintenance

Caution: Unplug an iron and let it cool before repairing or cleaning it.

If an iron doesn't heat, check first for a blown fuse or a tripped circuit breaker. An iron uses a lot of power and can easily overload a circuit. Unplug all other appliances on the circuit and reset the breaker or replace the fuse (see *Circuit breakers; Fuse boxes*).

A damaged cord can also cause an iron not to heat—or to heat slowly. Check the cord for fraying and loose plug prongs. If bare wire shows, it may be the cause of a short circuit that blew a fuse or tripped a breaker.

Replace the cord only with one that has the same power-carrying capacity, preferably a manufacturer's replacement (see *Power cords*). On many irons you can reach the cord connections by removing the screw or screws on the rear of the iron and lifting off the back section.

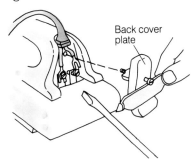

Back cover plate

If an iron's steam vents become clogged, first clean out the residue in the holes with a stiff wire or a straightened paper clip. Then fill the iron with a solution containing equal parts water and white vinegar. Set the iron on a rack over a broiling pan. Operate it on *Steam* until it stops steaming; then run it on the highest temperature for a half hour more. To prevent deposit buildups, use only distilled or filtered water in your iron.

To clean an iron's bottom plate, use a damp sponge with a mild liquid detergent or baking soda. On a metal plate with fine scratches and burrs that catch on delicate fabrics, buff the surface with an automobile polishing compound. If necessary, use very fine steel wool first. Clean well to remove all polish and steel wool residues. Do *not* use these abrasive materials on a nonstick surface.

Itching

Treating it according to the underlying causes

In a superficial sense, all itching is the same: an irritation of the skin that produces an urge to scratch. Its possible causes, however, are many; remedial measures depend on the source. If you buy an over-the-counter remedy, avoid products containing benzocaine or a combination of calamine and antihistamine; they may only compound the problem.

Persistent or generalized itching may be a symptom of internal disease (diabetes, blood or liver disease, parasitic infection, for example). In such a case, it's best to consult a doctor.

In cold weather the cause may simply be dry skin; for this, moisturizing cream, lotion, bath oil, or plain mineral oil may be effective treatment.

Summer rashes

In summer the possible causes multiply. A frequent culprit is prickly heat, best treated by keeping the skin cool and dry (see *Prickly heat*). This is the season, too, for itchy rashes that are caused by allergic contact dermatitis (see *Eczema; Hives; Poison ivy, oak, sumac*). Other summer sources of itchiness are insect bites and stings and sunburn.

At any time of year, household products or chemicals can cause itching. An over-the-counter hydrocorti-

sone cream applied several times a day will relieve discomfort; better yet, shun the offending substance.

In addition, itching may affect the feet (see *Athlete's foot*) or the anus (see *Lice; Pinworms*). If anal itching is a problem, the victim and his or her entire family should be checked by a doctor promptly. Elimination of the problem requires medication and scrupulous personal and household hygiene.

Itching in the groin area (jock itch), the armpits and, in women, in the folds of the breast may be caused by fungi or bacteria. Prevent or treat early signs of irritation in these areas by keeping them dry and dusting with antifungal powder. To relieve itching, apply a compress of Burow's solution (1:40 concentration) three times a day for 10 minutes at a time. Do *not* use petroleum jelly, foot powder, or antifungal ointment intended for the feet.

In women, itchiness in the genital area, especially itchiness accompanied by abnormal discharge, may be a sign of a vaginal or vulvar infection. Such a condition calls for immediate medical attention.

Ivory

Care and cleaning

To retain its warm-white color, ivory must be exposed to light. If you always keep ivory-handled knives in a chest or a piano's ivory keys covered, they will eventually darken and yellow.

Dust ivory with a soft, clean cloth. Wash ivory in mild soap and water, rinse, and dry it. Buff it with a clean woolen cloth. Don't soak pieces such as jewelry or knives; water can soften the glue that holds the ivory in place.

To clean ivory piano keys, pick up a small amount of baking soda with a slightly damp cloth and gently rub one key at a time. Wipe the keys clean with a damp cloth; buff them dry.

To whiten slightly yellowed ivory, try rubbing it with lemon juice diluted with an equal part of water, being careful not to get the mixture on metal parts. Then wipe the ivory with a damp cloth and buff. Let a professional jeweler scrape and repolish badly stained and yellowed ivory.

Ivy houseplants

Attractive and easy to grow in baskets or on supports

Green-leaved ivy prefers bright light without direct sun; a north window is ideal. Variegated kinds are more colorful when they get 2 to 3 hours of sun daily. Summer temperatures of about 65°F are best for the many varieties of English ivy, but they can stand more warmth if the air is fairly humid. The unrelated grape and Swedish ivies prefer somewhat warmer temperatures. Hot, dry air encourages red spider mites in all kinds (see *Mites*).

Grow ivy in equal parts potting soil, peat moss, and sand or perlite. Repot when roots get crowded. During the growing season, let the top ½ inch of soil dry out before watering. Feed every 2 weeks with a balanced plant food (see *Fertilizing houseplants*).

To let the plants go dormant in winter, keep English ivy at 50°F, grape ivy at 55°F, and Swedish ivy at 60°F. Water sparingly and withhold fertilizer.

Ivy in the garden

For a leafy ground cover or wall covering

English ivy and its varieties are evergreens that are hardy as far north as Chicago in sheltered spots. The hardier Boston ivy, a cousin of the Virginia creeper, drops its leaves after a glowing display of autumn color.

Give young plants a good start by working compost, peat moss, or well-rotted manure into the soil, along with a balanced fertilizer (see *Planting; Soil preparation*). During the first year (and during dry spells thereafter), water deeply once a week.

Train your ivy by pruning it in the spring or early summer. Clip away any branches that grow where they're not wanted.

Ivy will not harm a masonry wall, but it can loosen shingles or clapboards. To grow ivy against a wooden wall, install a trellis at least 8 inches in front of it. Propagate from cuttings (see *Propagating plants*).

J

Jacking a car

How to do it safely

The jack that comes with a car is for raising one corner to change a tire (see *Tire changing*); never get under a car supported only by this kind of jack. To lift the car to work under it, get ramps or a hydraulic jack, a pair of safety stands, and chocks. The jack, ramps, and stands should be rated for at least your car's total weight. Jacks or ramps must lift the car at least 8 inches for underbody work.

If all four wheels must hang free, get a hydraulic floor jack. Cheap hydraulic "bottle" jacks with a screwhead are unsuitable for most cars.

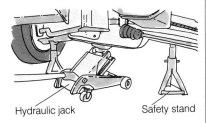

Hydraulic jack   Safety stand

Concrete is the best work floor. On anything softer, first lay down a 2- x 4-foot, ½-inch-thick plywood sheet to spread the load. Whatever the surface, it must be level.

To drive onto ramps, turn the wheels straight, place the two ramps parallel to each other and against the tires, and have a helper guide you as you drive forward in *Low* or *First* (or backward in *Reverse* to raise the rear wheels). Stop when he signals; set the parking brake.

To jack the rear of a front-engine, rear-drive car, place the jack on the bulging center differential on the rear axle. Place a safety stand at each side, under the axle tubes or the spring mounts. To jack the front, place the jack at the center of a rectangular crossmember; position the stands under the suspension arms.

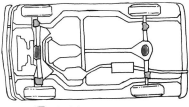

■ Jack here
▨ Place stands here

Center jacking may not be possible on a front-drive car. The owner's manual may recommend jacking under the body side rails. If this is the case, place a jack under the rail on one side, raise the car, and put the safety stand under the control arm in front or under the coil-spring seat in the rear. Repeat at the car's opposite side. Slowly lower the jack until the car rests on the stands. Leave the jack in place for extra protection.

If you lift a car's drive wheels with a jack or ramps, put chocks (bricks, 4 x 4's, or metal chocks) against the wheels remaining on the ground. If the drive wheels are on the ground, put the car's transmission into *Park* or *First.* If the rear wheels are on the ground, also set the parking brake.

The parking brake operates on the front wheels of some Saabs and Subarus. To raise their front wheels, chock the rear; if you lift the rear, put the transmission in *Park* or *First* and set the parking brake. Before jacking a car with air-spring suspension, consult the owner's manual for instructions.

Jack-o'-lanterns

Happy Halloween

Place a flat-bottomed, long-stemmed pumpkin on several layers of newspaper. With a dark crayon or soft pencil, sketch a face on a well-rounded side. Position the mouth high enough so that the candle won't be seen.

With a paring knife, cut out a bevel-edged lid around the pumpkin stem. The opening should be large enough for your hand to pass through. Slice the stringy membrane from the lid.

Dig the seeds and membrane out of the inside of the pumpkin with a long-handled spoon. Carve the face with a sharp knife, using sawing strokes rather than one continuous cut.

Place a candle in a glass holder in the bottom. Keep the pumpkin away from curtains or other flammable objects; don't leave it unattended.

Jacks

A game for nimble fingers

You play this game with a small rubber ball and six multipronged metal or plastic jacks. Start by dropping the jacks onto a flat surface all at once. Using only one hand, toss the ball in the air, pick up a jack, and catch the ball after one bounce. Set the jack aside.

Toss ball up

Keep picking up one jack at a time until you have all six. This is called *ones.* Next, in *twos,* pick up two jacks each time and in *threes,* three. In *fours,* pick up four and two, and in *fives,* five and one, in either order. Last, in *sixes,* pick up all six.

Pick up jacks   Catch ball

You lose your turn if you fail to pick up all the required jacks, don't catch the ball after one bounce, or touch any jack other than the ones you pick up. When your turn comes again, start at the level at which you last played. The first to complete all six levels wins.

Jackstraws

The pick-up sticks game

You play this game with 50 thin wooden sticks. Begin by holding the jackstraws in a bunch just above a flat surface. Release them, letting them fall into a tangled pile.

Pick up one straw at a time. Use only your fingers and be careful not to move another straw. You may twist a straw free, or lever one by pressing down on its end. A jackstraw's color indicates its value. Green is worth 3 points; red, 5; and blue, 10. The one black straw is worth 20 points. Once you have it, you can use it to help lift out other straws.

If another straw moves, your turn is up, and the next player takes over. When there are no straws left, the player with the most points wins.

Jade trees

A houseplant for cool rooms

A succulent that looks like a miniature tree with glossy green, spoon-shaped leaves, the jade tree withstands temperatures as low as 45°F.

In summer, the plant does well at normal warmer temperatures. But from fall to spring, it prefers a temperature around 70°F during the day and 50°F to 60°F at night. It likes several hours of direct sun by a south window during its spring and summer growth period. It also does well in filtered or bright, indirect light.

Water the plant moderately; let two-thirds of the soil dry out between waterings. Fertilize monthly from April to July with liquid plant food diluted to half the recommended strength. During the winter, keep it in a bright area and water sparingly. Repot in early spring every 2 or 3 years; it tolerates a root-bound condition well. Use a mix of 1 part each loam, peat moss or leaf mold, and coarse sand or perlite. Or mix 1 part sand or perlite to 3 parts general purpose potting soil. Propagate a jade tree by leaf or stem cuttings in spring or summer (see *Propagating plants*).

Jams

Preserving fruit pulp

Jam is mashed fruit pulp combined with water and sugar and cooked until thick. It should have a bright color and a soft consistency that spreads easily, but has no runny juice.

The thickening occurs when the correct proportions of pectin and acid (which are present in all fruits in varying degrees) and sugar are combined and cooked to a certain temperature. If sufficient pectin is not present for a good jell, you'll need to add commercial pectin, available as a liquid or a powder. (The powder must be added to fruit before cooking.) Some people prefer to use pectin in all their jam and jelly making; the cooking time is less and a jell is guaranteed. However, pectin does affect flavor and generally necessitates the use of more sugar.

Acid contributes not only to the jelling but to the good flavor of jams and jellies. Mix 1 teaspoon lemon juice with 3 tablespoons water and ½ teaspoon sugar. If your fruit or juice does not taste as tart as this mixture, you will need to add lemon juice—about 1 tablespoon per cup of fruit or juice.

Fruits rich in pectin and acid are cranberries, Concord grapes, tart apples, and damson plums. Strawberries and greengage plums have average pectin and acid; peaches and raspberries have low amounts. By combining a low-pectin fruit, such as pears, with a high-pectin fruit, such as cranberries, you can improve the jelling quality of the low-pectin fruit.

Underripe fruits are higher in pectin and acid than ripe ones. By combining one part underripe fruit with three parts ripe, you can enhance the jelling property of the ripe fruit.

Unless your recipe calls for commercial pectin, you must measure the pectin content of your fruit. Put 1 tablespoon unsweetened, cooked fruit juice and 1 tablespoon 190-proof grain alcohol or rubbing alcohol in a saucer and blend them. If a thick clot forms, the fruit is rich in pectin; if there are stringy clots, pectin content is average; numerous small clumps indicate that pectin must be added.

Caution: Don't taste the mixture containing alcohol; it's poisonous.

Preparing the jam

Unlike fruits for freezing or canning, those for jam can be less than perfect. Hull and crush berries in a bowl. Peel and remove blemishes, stems, and seeds or cores of other fruits; cut them into small pieces and measure them. For best results, cook no more than 6 to 8 cups of prepared fruit at a time.

Some recipes call for mixing the fruit with sugar and letting it stand for a time before boiling. Otherwise, put the fruit into a large, heavy pot of enamel or stainless steel (at least four times the volume of the fruit). To fruits other than berries, add a little water to prevent burning, about ½ cup for every 4 cups of fruit.

Cook the fruit until tender, stirring frequently to prevent sticking. Add the sugar—usually about ¾ cup per cup of fruit—and stir until dissolved. Boil the mixture rapidly until it starts to thicken; then insert a candy thermometer and read it at eye level. Most fruits reach the jam stage—220°F or 8°F above the boiling point of water at high elevations (see *Boiling*)—within 5 to 15 minutes (after 1 minute of cooking with added pectin). Don't overcook jam; it will become too thick.

The thermometer is the most reliable test for doneness. If you don't have one, you can test by removing the pot from the heat, spreading a teaspoon of the mixture on a cold saucer, then chilling it quickly in the freezer. If the skin wrinkles when you push it with a finger, the jam is ready.

Another test for doneness is to dip out a metal spoonful of syrup, let it cool slightly, then tip it over above the pot. If the syrup droplets merge as they slide off the spoon, the jam is done. Remove the pot from the heat. Skim the foam with a slotted spoon.

If you live in a hot climate, it's best to sterilize the jam and the jars in a hot-water bath (see *Canning*). Otherwise, sterilize the jars, then seal them with sterilized canning lids or paraffin. (Sterilize jars and lids in a 225°F oven for 10 minutes; or boil them for 15 minutes, inverted in 2 inches of water. Keep them hot until you are ready to fill them.)

Fill the sterilized jars, leaving ½ inch of space at the top for paraffin, ¼ inch for a sealed lid. Apply the sealing lid with sterilized tongs; or pour ⅛ inch of melted paraffin over the jam, using a circular motion so that the wax adheres to the sides of the jar. Clean the jar rim with a damp cloth.

Caution: Paraffin is highly flammable. Melt it in a double boiler or in a saucepan set in hot water—never over direct heat.

When cool, recheck the seal of each jar, put on outer lids, label, and store the jars in a cool, dry, dark place.

Japanese beetles

Halting their activities

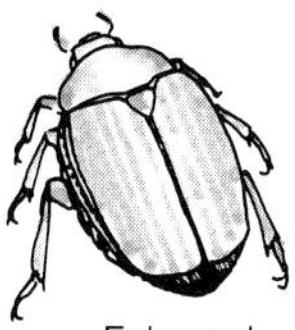

These ⅜-inch-long iridescent beetles, which feed on many kinds of buds, leaves, flowers, and fruit, are especially fond of corn and roses. They overwinter as grubs in soil 8 to 10 inches below the surface. In spring they move nearer the surface to feed on grass roots; in early summer they emerge as adults.

Enlarged

Battle grubs by applying milky spore disease (a preparation sold at garden supply stores) on a mown lawn; follow label instructions. The disease is self-perpetuating and effectively controls grubs for several years.

Shake beetles off plants into a pail of soapy water, or snare them with synthetic bait in Japanese beetle traps bought at a garden center. Effective sprays are carbaryl, malathion, or methoxychlor (see *Pesticides*).

Jars

Opening stuck lids

A partial vacuum in jars and bottles helps the lid form an airtight seal and keep food fresh. But the vacuum also makes lids difficult to unscrew. If you don't plan to reuse a jar, punch a hole in the lid with a can opener or ice pick to break the seal. A slight vacuum also forms when you place a jar with warm food in the refrigerator. To help break the seal, run warm (not hot) water over the jar before opening it.

To get a better grip on a stuck lid, wrap rubber bands, a damp sponge, or a dish towel around it. Or use one of the widely available nonskid rubber pads. You can also get viselike metal jar openers with teeth and long handles. Pliers will open a small lid.

To keep a lid from sticking, wipe all food from it and the jar rim. If dried food does seal a lid, tap gently around its edge with a knife handle. Or run warm water over the lid; heat softens the food and expands the lid, letting you unscrew it.

Jellies

Making them clear and firm

Jelly is made from fruit juice, sugar, and sometimes added pectin (see *Jams*). Jelly should be clear and firm but not rubbery. Although any fruit can be used, the best are crab apples, tart apples, quinces, Concord grapes, cranberries, blackberries, gooseberries, and citrus fruits.

For best results, work with small quantities—no more than 3 to 4 pounds of fruit at a time. Wash the fruit thoroughly. Crush berries to extract the juice. Cut other fruits in pieces but don't peel or core them; the skin and cores are rich in pectin. Put the fruit into a large, heavy enamel or stainless-steel pot (at least four times the volume of the fruit). Barely cover large fruits with water. Add just enough water to berries and grapes to keep them from sticking to the pot. Simmer over low heat until the fruit is soft and mushy. Depending on the fruit, this will take from 10 to 25 minutes. Do not overcook the fruit, or the jelling ability will be reduced.

To extract the juice, pour the pulp into a damp jelly bag or a colander lined with layers of cheesecloth or loosely woven muslin. Set the bag or colander over a bowl and let the juice drip through for an hour or more. If you started with 3 pounds of fruit, you should get about 4 cups of juice. You can get a higher yield if you squeeze the jelly bag or put the fruit through a press, but the juice will be less clear. If you're adding pectin, follow the package instructions.

Heat the juice until it comes to a full boil. Add the sugar (about ¾ cup per cup of juice) and stir until it dissolves. Bring again to a full boil, one that cannot be stirred down. Boil briskly until a thermometer inserted in the center reads 220°F, or 8°F above the boiling point of water at a high elevation (see *Boiling*). For other tests, see *Jams*. If using commercial pectin, boil 1 minute only. Skim off the foam.

Pour the jelly into sterilized jars; seal them with canning lids or paraffin. When cool, add outer lids and labels. Store in a cool, dry, dark place.

Jerky

Making a dried-meat snack

J

With a sharp knife, cut lean, raw beef or venison into strips about 1 inch wide, ¼ to ½ inch thick, and 6 to 10 inches long. Trim away all fat. Freezing the meat for about 20 minutes makes slicing easier. One pound of meat yields ¼ to ⅓ pound of jerky.

For each pound of meat, combine 1 teaspoon salt, ¼ teaspoon each of pepper and marjoram, and ⅛ teaspoon garlic powder. With a meat mallet, pound this mixture into both sides of the strips. Or soak the strips for 1 to 2 days in a solution of 1½ cups pickling salt in 1 gallon of water. Remove the strips and wipe dry.

Hang the strips from the bars of an oven rack, about 1 inch apart (place aluminum foil on the bottom of the oven to catch any drippings). Or arrange the strips on cake racks set in baking pans and place the pans in the oven. Set the oven at 120° F to 150° F; leave the door ajar so that moisture can escape. Dry for 4 to 6 hours, until the strips turn black and are almost brittle (they should bend slightly before breaking). Turn the strips at least once during the drying process.

Place cooled jerky in a lidded container with holes punched in the lid for ventilation; store it in a cool place. Chew jerky as is for a nutritious snack or reconstitute it in stews. Properly made and stored, it lasts for months.

Jet lag

Helping your body adjust to a changed schedule

The abrupt changes in time zones experienced in air travel can seriously disrupt the body's daily cycles. So can a change from day work to night work. The disruption most noticeably affects sleeping and eating patterns. Full adjustment of all bodily rhythms may take a week or longer.

Taking certain steps may minimize jet lag. Prepare your body by gradually changing your sleeping and eating schedules to what they will be at your destination. In flight, avoid alcoholic beverages; they increase fatigue.

Jet-lag diet

You may want to try a four-day regimen that has helped some overcome jet lag. Starting 4 days prior to arrival at your destination, you alternate feast days and fast days. Feast on the first and third days by eating a high-protein breakfast and lunch and a high-carbohydrate dinner; fast on the second and fourth days, eating salads, soups, fruits, juices, and only a slice or two of unbuttered bread or toast. When you arrive, eat a high-protein breakfast.

During the diet's first 3 days, drink caffeinated beverages between 3 P.M. and 5 P.M. only. On the fourth day, drink them in the morning if you are traveling west; between 6 P.M. and 11 P.M. if you are heading east. You can get the full text of the diet by sending a stamped, self-addressed envelope to Antijet-Lag Diet, Argonne National Laboratory, 9700 S. Cass Avenue, Argonne, Ill. 60439.

If you travel frequently, you may want to discuss with your doctor the various drugs that are sometimes prescribed to counter jet lag.

Jewelry

Cleaning jewelry; making minor repairs on costume jewelry

You can maintain the beauty and luster of almost any piece of jewelry by cleaning or polishing it. For the most part, do home repair work on costume jewelry only. Let a professional repair your fine jewelry.

Cleaning jewelry

Most stones and their settings can be cleaned with liquid jewelry cleaner, following package instructions, or with warm water and a little mild detergent. Never use toothpaste or abrasive cleaners. Gently scrub the settings with a soft brush. After washing, dry the jewelry with a soft cloth; then polish it with a piece of chamois.

Diamonds can be cleaned by boiling the stones and their settings in water with a bit of detergent for 5 minutes. But don't boil any settings in which glue has been used, or the heat will loosen the glue. Allow the diamonds to cool at room temperature; don't plunge them into cold water. Diamonds may also be cleaned in a solution of 1 tablespoon ammonia to 2 cups of warm water.

Use silver polish to remove tarnish from silver jewelry. The best way to clean and condition real pearls is to wear them next to your skin; their surface is improved by skin oils.

Loose stones in costume jewelry

If an imitation gem is loose in a prong setting, you can secure it with a pair of smooth-jawed jeweler's pliers. Note that tiny grooves called sets have been cut into the inside surfaces of the prongs. The girdle (widest part) of the stone should fit into the sets.

Open the pliers and place the jaws on facing prongs. Keep the jaws low on the prongs so that they don't slip

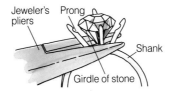

over the top of the stone and damage it. Gently pinch the prongs, moving them closer a little at a time. (Don't apply too much pressure; the metal used for costume jewelry is rather brittle, and a prong may break.) Do the same with the remaining pairs of prongs.

If an imitation stone has fallen from its setting, put a tiny drop of instant glue on its underside before returning it to the setting; then use the pliers as described. Don't put glue on precious or semiprecious stones, and don't try to adjust their settings; precious stones are easily damaged. Emeralds, for example, are so soft that a touch of the pliers can mark them, and even diamonds are vulnerable. (The long points of marquise and pear- and kite-shaped diamonds break easily.)

Loose links and rings

If a necklace or bracelet breaks because a link has pulled open, use jeweler's pliers to squeeze the link shut. Again, use only slight pressure.

Rings can be tightened by installing a ring guard. Just slip the guard into the ring, center it over the bottom of the ring shank, and squeeze the sides

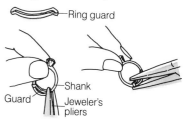

of the guard gently with pliers to tighten. If the ring is then too small, grip the ring shank and the center of the guard, and apply just a little pressure.

Restringing beads or pearls

If a string of pearls or beads breaks, replace the cord; don't try to knot the old one. Do your restringing over a scrap of velvet or other napped fabric to keep the pearls or beads from rolling about. Work on an otherwise clear desk with a drawer open over your lap so that if a bead rolls off, the drawer will catch it. Leave pearls or beads of graduated sizes on their old string, if possible, to keep them in order.

Use nylon cord, thread, or dental floss that is thin enough to pass twice through the bore (hole) in the bead or pearl. Cut the cord 12 inches longer than the total length of the necklace. Thread a needle, and tie a knot in the cord 1½ inches from the end.

Slip the beads over the needle and onto the cord in order. String very small beads right next to each other, and intersperse larger beads with knots as follows. Slip the bead onto the cord, knot the cord, and slip the knot toward the bead with your fingers. As the knot becomes smaller and tighter, insert a needle and push the knot against the bead. Pull the knot tight and remove the needle. Repeat with each bead until the necklace is complete. Add a clasp (see *Clasps*).

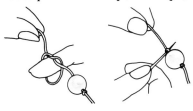

Job application letters

How to write a letter that will get you an interview

Before writing a letter of application or responding to an ad, find out all you can about the company and the job. In the business department of a public library, consult publications such as *Dun & Bradstreet's Middle Market Directory, Standard & Poor's Register*, and *Dun's Employment Opportunities Directory: A Guide*. Or obtain the name of a trade association to which the company may belong; contact the association and ask for particulars about the company. Ask people you may know in the company to share their knowledge.

Reflect on your past and present job and educational experiences. Try to credibly align your talents, skills, and attributes with those that your research shows may be needed or those outlined in the job description.

After you have marshaled the facts, tell them to a friend or to a mirror until you can present your case convincingly. Then write your letter, covering the following points.
1. Get the recipient's attention. Describe one or two characteristics that you think may distinguish you from other applicants. Don't be obviously competitive unless it's a job in sales.
2. Mention the title and duties of your last or current job.
3. Show how your skills and knowledge fit the company's specific needs.
4. Ask to discuss the job in person.

Overcome your modesty by writing the first draft in the third person—as though you were recommending a friend. In your final draft, keep the "I" statements to a minimum. Don't brag or claim traits or skills that you don't possess. Be specific; keep the letter short. Use the appropriate form and stationery (see *Business letters*).

Address your letter to a name, not a department or a title, unless so specified in the ad. Phone the company and ask for the personnel director's name if it wasn't in your research materials. Check your letter for spelling and typographical errors. If you're not a good typist, have the letter professionally typed.

Jogging

Proper equipment; warming up; getting started

An exercise program for a normally healthy person should consist of a warm-up, an aerobic portion, a muscle strength and flexibility section, and a cool-down. Jogging—running at a comfortable pace for 20 to 30 minutes—can be the aerobic portion.

The right equipment is essential to preventing injury: a pair of jogging shoes, *not* tennis or basketball shoes. The shoes should have good support around the heel, a well-cushioned midsole (to reduce impact shock), enough flexibility to bend easily at the ball of the foot (test the shoe with your hands), a wide sole, an arch support, and a thumb's width of space between the big toe and the shoe tip. Most important, the shoes should fit your feet; don't buy a pair just because it matches your outfit.

Clothing should be loose and comfortable, of porous fabric, and light. Once you've warmed up, you'll need less than if you were walking.

It's best to jog on a resilient surface: dirt, grass, or a cinder track. If it must be paving, asphalt is preferable to concrete. Try to find a partner; it's easier and more fun.

First, warm up with about 10 minutes of exercises—walking, arm circles, ankle rotations (see *Exercises*). In addition, stretch the calf muscles and hamstrings (the muscles in the backs of knees and thighs) as shown.

Start out at a slow, comfortable pace. How long you jog is more important than how far or how fast. Jog un-

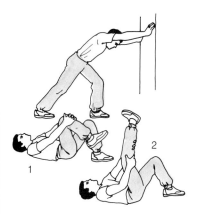

til your heart rate is at your training level for aerobic exercise (see *Aerobics; Pulse*). Keep it there for 20 to 30 minutes. At the start, if you cannot run in your training zone for that long, alternate walking and jogging; gradually increase the jogging.

When you finish, slow to a walk, then cool down with more exercises and stretching so that your heart rate drops gradually to normal. If you have questions about your health and exercise or are over age 35, see your doctor before starting to jog.

Jogging injuries

Treating minor strains

Most jogging injuries are caused by overdoing, improper equipment, or failing to warm up and exercise properly. The result can range from minor muscular soreness to major problems with the ankle, knee, or hip joints or with muscles. Prevent injuries by wearing jogging shoes and setting a training routine (see *Jogging*).

Pain is usually the first signal that something is wrong. Remain aware of your body; don't ignore pain, fatigue, breathlessness, and weakness. Exercising with an injury can result in more complex or permanent damage.

For minor pain in a specific area, remember RICE (Rest, Ice, Compression, and Elevation). Place ice in a bag or towel on the painful area, wrap an elastic bandage tightly over it (not so tight as to reduce circulation), seat yourself, and elevate the part. Leave the ice pack on for 30 minutes, off for 15, then repeat. This treatment can

J

be used for the first 24 to 36 hours. Should the area be very painful or appear to be a worse injury (see *Sprains and strains*), see a doctor. Before resuming jogging, allow plenty of time for the injury to heal; some injuries, such as ankle sprains, require longer than others. Ask your doctor about exercises to prevent recurrences.

If you experience difficulty or shortness of breath, stop jogging immediately and walk; see your doctor. These symptoms may indicate a larger problem. (See also *Shin splints*.)

Juggling

Keeping balls in the air

The first rule of juggling is never to look at your hands. To acquire this basic skill, practice tossing a ball from hand to hand, keeping your hands at about waist level so that the crest of the arc—the spot where the ball seems to hang in midair for a split second before it begins to fall—is directly before your eyes. Concentrate on this spot. Catch the ball in the palm of your cupped hand; toss it by letting it roll off your fingertips.

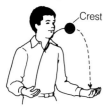

When you can do this about 200 times without looking at your hands, begin working on a simple circle pattern: toss the ball up with your right hand and catch it in your left, then toss it back across your body at waist level. Do this 200 times without missing; then reverse directions and do 200 more.

When you are adept with one ball, try two. Start with one in each hand. Toss one and pass the other quickly to the throwing hand. As the first crests (begins to fall) toss the second. Catch the first, pass it, and—as the second crests—toss the first again. When you can do this 100 times in each direction, try *one-handed circles* with

each hand: toss each ball just as the other begins to fall. Vary the rhythm by varying the height of the toss. Shift to a *piston* pattern: toss each ball straight up in turn, moving your hand back and forth between them.

Circle   Piston

To juggle three balls in a *crisscross* pattern, start with two in your right hand and one in your left. Toss the first from your right hand. As it crests, toss the ball in your left hand so that it rises beneath the first to crest at the same height; then catch the first ball. Toss the last ball as the second crests, and so on.

Julienne

Cutting food into matchstick-like strips

Vegetables cut into julienne strips and quickly cooked make an attractive side dish and soup garnish. Use julienne-cut firm cheeses and cooked meats in salads. To keep food from drying out, cut it just before cooking or dressing it.

To cut julienne, peel the food if necessary and trim off unwanted parts. Cut rounded foods such as carrots or potatoes in half lengthwise or trim a thin slice from one side so that the food rests firmly on a cutting board. Grasp the food as shown and cut it with a sharp knife into ⅛-inch slices. Stack three or four slices and cut

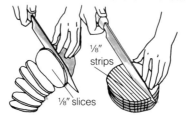

⅛" strips
⅛" slices

them into ⅛-inch strips. Cut the strips into uniform, 2-inch lengths for salads, longer for garnish.

Jump rope

A game for agile skippers

In the simplest group version of this game, two players hold the ends of a 10- to 12-foot rope and turn it as the other players jump, one at a time. The rope turners start by swinging the rope away from the jumper. Then, making a full circle that will pass over the jumper's head, they establish an easy rhythm, with the rope just grazing the ground each turn.

As others in the group look on, each jumper in turn stands just outside of the whirling rope and steps in as it is about to hit the ground. Then the jumper hops over the rope with both feet as many times as possible. The players traditionally chant a counting rhyme, such as "One, two, buckle my shoe," to help keep track of the jumps. When the jumper misses, the turners reestablish the rhythm, and another jumper steps in. Jumpers relieve the turners to give them a chance.

Jump rope variations include hopping on one foot, alternately picking up and setting down a stone every turn, and turning the rope so fast that it goes under the jumper twice each jump. In *salt and pepper*, the rope alternates between going slow and fast. In *running through*, each player in turn steps in, jumps once, and then runs out without breaking the rhythm. Next time, each player jumps twice. The number of jumps progresses until, as jumpers miss, there is only one left. In *follow the leader*, each player must repeat the first player's actions as well as get in and out of the rope swings.

Jump starting a car

Reviving a dead battery

If a car won't start because of a weak battery, it can be started by connecting jumper (booster) cables to a car that will run.

Bring the live car close to the dead one, but not touching it. Set the parking brakes; put both transmissions in *Park* or *Neutral.* Turn off lights, electrical accessories, and the ignitions on both cars. Remove vent caps (if any) from both batteries, then cover the holes with clean damp rags. The rags suppress the emission of the explosive hydrogen gas generated when batteries are charged. Remove jewelry to avoid making sparks. Wear safety goggles and don't smoke.

Connect one jumper cable from the positive post or terminal (marked with a plus sign or *POS*) of the dead car to the positive post or terminal of the live car. Because the bolts on a side-terminal battery have very small heads, the clamps may not make good contact. If they are available, install battery charging adapters; connect the clamps to them.

Connect the second cable to the negative post or terminal of the live car and to an unpainted bolt on the engine, away from the battery, of the dead one. Both cables must be clear of fans, belts, and pulleys.

Start the live car, then the dead car. When both are running, disconnect the cables in the reverse order, starting with the cable clamped at the dead car's engine.

To recharge the dead battery enough to restart the car, drive the car at least ½ hour before stopping. Have the battery fully recharged promptly (see *Battery recharging*).

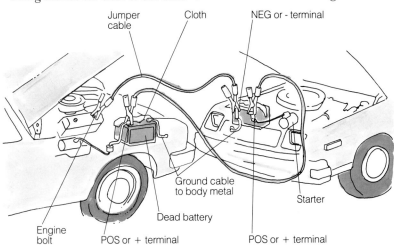

Jumper cable — Cloth — NEG or - terminal — Ground cable to body metal — Starter — Dead battery — Engine bolt — POS or + terminal — POS or + terminal

---

Kayaking

Getting started; boats, paddles, and other equipment

The best place to get the feel of a narrow, tippy kayak is in a pond or a pool with a skilled instructor. Paddling clubs, the Sierra Club, Appalachian Mountain Club, YMCA's, and the American Red Cross often offer courses in kayaking. Always wear a helmet (a lightweight motorcycle helmet is good), sneakers, and a Coast Guard–approved life vest. You should be a strong swimmer.

A wide range of kayaks exists to serve a range of kayaking activities. For example, the *slalom kayak*, with a wide, flat bottom and rounded sides, is easy to maneuver through tight turns and into and out of eddies. A *down-river kayak*—longer, deeper, and with sides sloping to a V—is faster but less maneuverable. For flatwater touring, there are one- and two-person kayaks that are still wider and longer and will carry a heavier load.

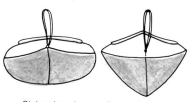

Slalom kayak   Down-river kayak

Slip into a kayak like a pair of pants. First fasten an elastic spray skirt around your waist. Then slide in feet first (have someone steady the kayak if it's your first try). You can use the paddle as a brace. Place your feet against the adjustable braces with knees slightly bent and pressed against the underside of the deck. Wedge your back firmly against the seat back. Finally, snap the hem of the spray skirt over the cockpit coaming tight enough to keep the water out if you roll over, but not so tight that you can't bail out in an emergency.

The double blades of the paddle are

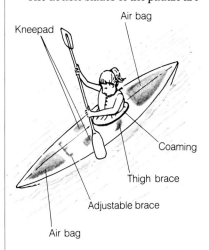

Kneepad — Air bag — Coaming — Thigh brace — Adjustable brace — Air bag

set at 90 degrees to each other so that as one blade leaves the water, it turns, reducing wind drag, while the other blade enters. The basic strokes are similar to canoe strokes.

Keys

Broken, stuck, and lost keys

If a key breaks in the lock, insert a coping-saw blade in the keyhole just above the key's teeth. Hook onto the front of the key shaft and pull it out. If that fails, remove the lock cylinder (see *Door locks*). Many locks let you push out the key by poking a stiff wire through the cylinder. If the break is deep inside, use a coping-saw blade to lift the front tumblers out of the way.

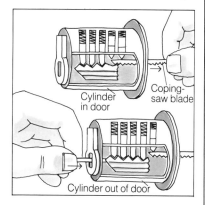

Cylinder in door

Coping-saw blade

Cylinder out of door

If a key is hard to turn, the lock may be clogged. Spray lock lubricant into the cylinder to flush it out. If necessary, disassemble the lock, soak the parts in a solvent, such as kerosene, and lubricate them sparingly.

Keep a list of the code numbers on your keys, especially auto keys. A locksmith can make a new key for any lock, but it costs less with the code.

Kick the can

A field or playground game

If you're chosen to be *It*, place an empty tin can on end in the designated home area, which doubles as a prison large enough to hold all players. Staying in the home area, turn your back and count to 50 while everyone runs and hides. Then search for them. When you find someone, run to the home area, announce the player's name, and say: "Kick the can, 1, 2, 3." That person (if correctly identified) becomes your prisoner and must stay in the home area for the remainder of

the game—unless a free player eludes you and kicks the can as far as he can. This act frees all prisoners. You must then retrieve the can, return it to the home area, and try to catch the players all over again.

You've won the game when you've captured all the players. The first tagged becomes It for the next game.

Kitchen cabinets

Wall-mounting stock cupboards

First, find the wall studs (see *Studs*). A cabinet that is wide enough should be secured to at least two of them.

Mark level lines across the wall for the cabinet's top and bottom (see *Leveling*); mark the center of each stud on both lines. Rule perpendicular lines for the cabinet sides too.

Nail a temporary ledge on the bottom line and prop the cabinet on it to check whether the sides fit snugly against the wall. If the cabinet has a recessed back, you can correct any gaps by trimming the sides: set a compass to the size of the largest gap and

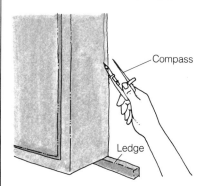

Compass

Ledge

use it to trace the wall contour onto the side. If the back is flush, cover visible gaps with matching wood trim after the cabinet is up. Mark the stud centers on the cabinet's top and bottom; then take the cabinet down and connect the lines on the back.

With a recessed-back cabinet, sand or plane the sides to the wall contour; Then place tapered cedar shingles, one atop the other, centered along each stud line, as shown. Adjust them to the proper thickness and tape them to the back.

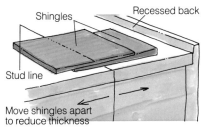

Shingles

Recessed back

Stud line

Move shingles apart to reduce thickness

Reposition the cabinet and drill pilot holes through the back and shingles into the studs 1½ to 2 inches from the top and bottom. Secure the cabinet with screws long enough to extend at least 2 inches into the studs. If the cabinet is wood, countersink the screwheads (see *Countersinking*); on a metal cabinet, use roundhead screws and washers.

To mount a narrow cabinet, nail two 1 x 4 furring strips across the studs and secure the cabinet to them (see *Furring strips*). Notch the sides of a recessed-back cabinet around the strips. The method can also be used to mount a row of cabinets side by side.

Kites

Making a simple diamond-shaped one

Caution: Never use foil or metal on a kite. Don't fly a kite in stormy weather or near power lines; if a kite gets tangled in a power line, don't try to remove it; abandon it. Supervise children who are flying kites.

All you need for a kite are two pieces of ⅛- x ⅜-inch wood, some light string, glue or tape, and covering material. The wood should be light, strong, and straight grained; pine or cypress are good. Notch both ends of each piece, then tie them as shown. The ratio is the same for any size kite: the crossbar is two-thirds the length of the upright; they cross one-quarter of the way down. Stretch string through the notches to form a diamond.

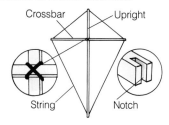

Crossbar

Upright

String

Notch

K

The strongest covering is nylon; the simplest is lightweight paper. Lay the diamond-shaped frame on the material and cut 1 inch outside the string. Snip the corners as shown, then fold the edges over the string, and tape or glue them. To use 1.5- to 2-mil plastic, cut 3 inches outside the string and double the edges over before folding.

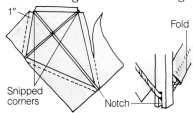

On the back of the kite, stretch a string between the ends of the crossbar and pull it taut until the bar forms a 3-inch bow. On the front, glue a

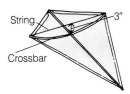

patch of covering material or apply a bit of masking tape where the crossbar and upright intersect. Poke a hole in the patch and insert one end of a 78-inch length of string. Tie it to the

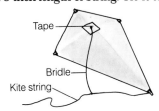

joint and tie the other end to the bottom of the upright. Tie the end of the kite string one-third of the way down this bridle. On a windy day, attach the string higher and tie a tail of 2-inch-wide rags to the bottom of the kite.

Knitting

A review of the basics

Knitting is the craft of making fabric by manipulating loops of yarn with needles. Select the needle size recommended in pattern directions; choose needles that are long enough to hold all stitches without crowding.

When buying yarn, select skeins with the same dye-lot numbers so that the colors match exactly; buy enough to ensure finishing the garment.

Casting on forms the initial row of stitches. Tie a slipknot a measured distance from the end of your yarn (A), allowing 1 inch for each stitch to be cast on. Slide the knot onto a needle and tighten it. Wrap the short yarn end over your left thumb and the yarn from the ball over your left index finger; grasp both ends between your palm and back fingers (B). Insert the needle up through the thumb loop (C), then scoop yarn from the index finger and draw a loop onto the needle. Release the thumb loop; tighten the loop on the needle by drawing the short yarn forward with the thumb (D). Repeat steps C and D for the required number of stitches.

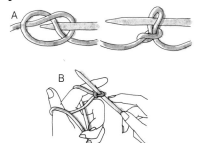

Yarn tension, necessary for a consistent flow of yarn and for even stitches, is maintained by wrapping yarn around one or more fingers and over the right index finger. One method is illustrated (E). Some knitters control yarn with the left hand.

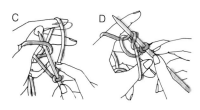

To form the *knit stitch*, hold the yarn behind the knitting and insert the empty needle front to back into

the first stitch on the left needle. With your right index finger, wrap yarn under and over the right needle (F). Pull the loop forward through the stitch

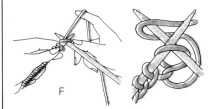

(G); at the same time, use your thumb and forefinger to push the stitch on the left needle toward the tip and off of it. The new stitch is on the right needle (H). Repeat until the row is finished; transfer the knitting to your left hand and begin again.

To form the *purl stitch*, hold the yarn in front of the knitting; insert the empty needle back to front into the first stitch. With your right index finger, wrap yarn over and under the tip of the right needle (I) and pull the new loop back through the stitch (J). At the same time, use your thumb and forefinger to push the stitch on the left needle toward the tip and off of it (K). Repeat until the row is finished; then transfer the knitting to your left hand and begin again.

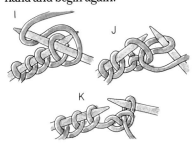

To form the *garter stitch* (L), knit every row. To form the *stockinette stitch* (M), knit and purl alternate rows. To form a *seed stitch* (N), alternate one knit and one purl stitch in the first row. In subsequent rows, knit the knit stitches and purl the purl stitches. (A knit stitch on the reverse side looks like a purl stitch.) To form a *rib*

stitch (O), alternate one or more knit stitches with an equal number of purl stitches in the first row. In subsequent rows, purl the knit stitches; knit the purled ones.

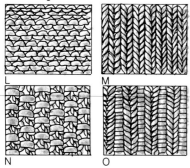

Before you begin a project, consult your pattern for the recommended *gauge* (number of stitches and rows per square inch). Knit a sample square of 4 inches. With the sample flat, count the number of stitches and rows in an inch. If you have too many, try a needle one size larger and test again. If you have too few, use a needle one size smaller and test again.

Always try to begin a new ball of yarn at the beginning of a row. Tie it onto the old yarn (P), tighten the knot,

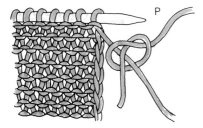

and slide the knot close to the needle. Later weave the yarn ends into the edge with a tapestry needle.

To *cast off*, or remove stitches from the needle, knit the first two stitches of the row, then use the point of the left needle to slip the first stitch over the second one and off the needle (Q).

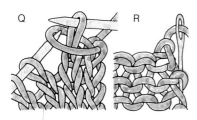

Knit the next stitch; slip the previous one over it. Continue until one stitch

remains. Snip the yarn, leaving about 6 inches; pull it through the final loop. Weave it into the side edge (R).

Knives

Care and sharpening

Always use a knife on a cutting board. Wash and dry a knife by hand right after using it; don't soak it or wash it in a dishwasher (certain high-quality knives are dishwasher safe). Store knives in a wooden knife block or with blades up on a wall-mounted magnetic rack. If you must store them in a drawer, use a divider or knife rack to prevent the blades from bumping against and nicking one another.

Before each use, sharpen a knife with a chef's steel. Grasp the steel in your left hand (if you're right-handed)

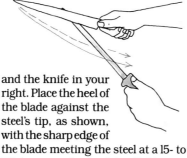

and the knife in your right. Place the heel of the blade against the steel's tip, as shown, with the sharp edge of the blade meeting the steel at a 15- to 20-degree angle. Applying light pressure, quickly draw the knife toward you and to the right so that the entire blade passes over the steel. Repeat the action with the blade beneath and at the same angle to the steel. Alternate strokes until each side has passed over the steel 10 to 20 times.

To restore a badly dulled blade, use a bench stone with coarse and fine sides. Apply light mineral oil to the stone before using it (some stones must soak in oil overnight; check package directions). Place the stone coarse side up and lengthwise in front of you. Place the heel of the blade on the stone so that its sharp edge is at a 15- to 20-degree angle to the stone. Maintain this angle throughout the procedure. Applying pressure with both hands, draw the blade in an arc across the stone so that the entire length of the blade is sharpened. Flip the blade and reverse the stroke. Re-

peat 10 times on each side. Continue with a few light strokes over the fine side of the stone. Wipe the blade and the stone clean. Finish with a few strokes on the chef's steel.

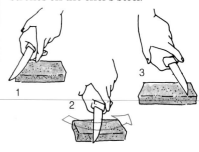

Knots

Tying basic knots

A rope has two parts in relation to a knot: the standing part, which you don't manipulate, and the working end (A). A loop between the two can be overhand (the working end over the standing part) or underhand (the working end under the standing part) (B). The simplest knot, the *overhand*

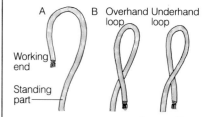

knot, is an overhand loop through which you pass the working end (C). If instead of the working end you pass a second loop through the first one, a *slipknot* is formed (D).

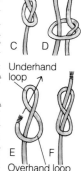

Tie a *figure-eight knot* at the end of a cord to keep it from unraveling. Simply make an underhand loop, then an overhand one (E); pull the working end through the first loop (F).

Use a *square knot* (two overhand knots tied in opposite directions) to join the ends of a cord that has been passed at least once around another object, such as a roast (G). A drawback of the square knot is the tendency of the first half-knot to slip unless it is held down. When a helping finger isn't available, try a *doubled square knot* (H). Because this knot holds tightly after the first half is tied, you can finish it unassisted, without losing the original tension.

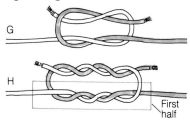

A *clove hitch* is a good knot for attaching a line to a post or a rail. Loop the line around the post and cross it under the standing part (I); loop it around again, then pass the working end under the second loop (J). Be-

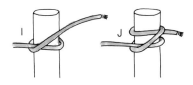

cause a clove hitch needs strain to hold, it's a temporary knot. To keep it from slipping, add a *half hitch*. Pass the working end over and around the standing part and through the resulting loop (K); pull the half hitch up tight against the clove hitch.

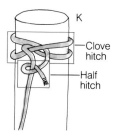

Clove hitch
Half hitch

The *bowline* (rhymes with rollin') forms a loop at the end of a cord. Make an overhand loop; pass the working end through it (L). Pull the working end behind and around the standing part and then back down through the first loop (M). Pull the end to set the knot.

Similar to the bowline, a *sheet bend* is used to join two lengths of cord. Form an overhand loop in one cord (the thicker of the two if they are of unequal diameter) and pass the second cord's working end through it (N). Pull the working end behind and around the first cord's standing part, then back down through the loop.

Lacquering

Spraying and brushing furniture with lacquer

Caution: Lacquer is volatile. Work with good ventilation away from sparks, high heat, or flames (including pilot lights).

Modern lacquer produces a durable, clear or colored finish with good resistance to spills. Clear lacquer is notably free of amber overtones, making it a good choice for light-colored or delicately figured woods. But you may find lacquer tricky to apply since it quickly sets and begins to dry.

Prepare wood for lacquering by filling and sealing (see *Wood finishing*). Sand with fine paper and wipe clean with a tack cloth. Never lacquer over varnish or paint; strip it off first (see *Stripping furniture*).

Because of its fast drying time, lacquer is usually sprayed on. Use an aerosol can for a small piece. For a larger one, use a siphon-feed spray gun with an external-mix nozzle. Suspend or prop the piece so that you can spray all of it without shifting it. Use a movable backdrop to catch overspray. Move the sprayer back and forth in a long, horizontal path. Keep it parallel to the surface and make passes that overlap by a third. Wear a mask and practice first on cartons.

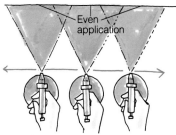

Even application

Move parallel to work surface

Brushing lacquer dries slower than spray lacquer, but you still must work rapidly. Use a large, soft brush and flow the lacquer on generously. Apply each brushful quickly in one long, continuous stroke. Brush out any imperfections promptly with a single, smooth stroke. Apply the next stroke before the previous one starts to set, just barely overlapping the edges.

Most pieces need two or three coats of lacquer—and more on heavily used surfaces like tabletops. Sprayed lacquer dries for recoating in 1 hour; brushed lacquer in 2. After three coats, let a piece dry overnight. Sand between coats only to remove defects.

Ladders

Rules for safe use

Caution: A ladder touching a power line can deliver a lethal shock; avoid using a metal or wet wood one close to a power line. When erecting or moving a ladder, look up to make sure a power line is not nearby. Use double-insulated, grounded power tools while working on a ladder.

If a ladder's rungs or steps aren't skid resistant, buy adhesive-backed anti-slip strips from a hardware store and apply them. Make sure the ladder's feet have rubber or plastic nonslip shoes.

Accessories make ladder use safer. Work trays hold paint and tools; wall grips on ladder tops prevent slipping; and ladder-leg extensions can compensate for uneven ground.

Before using a ladder, check it for cracks, splits, or bent areas. Position a ladder so that the distance between its base and the wall is at least one-quarter of the ladder's length up to its point of support. Don't lean a ladder against a window or a door.

Continued next page

L

Open an extension ladder so that there's at least 3 feet of overlap; be sure to engage the rung locks. When climbing up or down, face the ladder and hold on with at least one hand. If you are working with both hands, hook one of your legs securely over a rung. Overreaching invites a fall; move the ladder instead. Avoid the top three rungs of a ladder or the top step of a stepladder.

Extension ladder

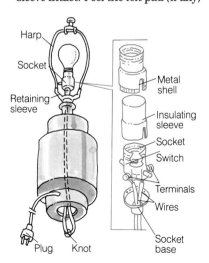

Erecting a ladder

Vertical height

3' overlap

¼ vertical height

Lamp rewiring

Replacing a cracked or frayed lamp cord

Unplug the lamp; remove its shade and bulb. Release the harp from its retaining sleeves by squeezing the arms together. Free the socket shell from its base by pressing your thumb hard against the word PRESS on its side; pull off the shell with its insulating sleeve intact. Peel the felt pad (if any)

Harp

Socket

Retaining sleeve

Metal shell

Insulating sleeve

Socket

Switch

Terminals

Wires

Plug   Knot

Socket base

from the lamp base carefully so that you can replace it later.

Using wire cutters, cut off the existing cord about 1 foot from the bottom of the lamp base. With a knife, strip about 1 inch of the insulation from the old cord still attached to the lamp; do the same to the new cord. Hook the new cord's wire to that of the old cord; wrap the connection with electrical tape. Pull the socket up to feed the new cord through the lamp.

When the new cord appears, snip off the connection and the old cord. Unscrew the terminals that hold the wires and pull out the old wires. Strip ½ inch of insulation from the new cord, then attach its two wires to the socket's terminals. Slip the metal and insulating shells over the socket base. Knot the cord in the base to prevent strain on the wires. Glue the felt bottom in place. Attach a new plug to the cord (see *Plugs*).

Lampshades

Keeping them new looking

Regular dusting is the best treatment for any lampshade. Using a soft cloth, brush, or feather duster, dust inside and out; vacuum a pleated cloth shade. Avoid touching the shade with your hands; oils from your skin can discolor the covering and attract dirt.

To clean a *plastic* or *fiberglass* shade more thoroughly, dust it, then wipe it with a cloth dipped in warm, sudsy water. Rinse and dry it. Avoid wetting glued parts or wires.

Rub spots from *paper* shades with a clean art-gum eraser or the absorbent material made for cleaning wallpaper. To keep parchment paper from drying out, rub it once a year with neat's-foot (leather) oil or castor oil.

Cotton, linen, or *silk* shades should be professionally dry-cleaned because wetting these fabrics may cause them to shrink and warp the frame.

Some *rayon* and *nylon* shades that are sewn, not glued, to their frames, and have colorfast trims, can be washed. Check the label or hang tag. For best results, wash a shade on a clear, dry day when it can dry quickly so that the frame won't rust.

First dust the shade thoroughly. Fill a tub with enough warm water to cover the shade; add a mild detergent. Immerse the shade and swish it up and down. If the water gets very dirty, change it and wash the shade again. Finally, rinse the shade in two or more changes of clear water. Blot it with a towel, then hang it over a bathtub or outdoors in the shade to dry. (Indoors a fan helps to circulate air and speed drying.) Sags in the fabric will disappear as the shade dries.

Don't try to protect a new shade by leaving it in cellophane wrap. The cellophane may shrink from the light-bulb heat, warp the frame, and leave brown marks on the fabric.

Landscape photography

Capturing nature's vistas

When you photograph a scene, decide what is its most visually interesting element—a rushing stream, a barren winter tree. Make this the dominant element in your picture to give it a strong center of interest. Try moving closer to the subject and shifting your camera up, down, and to the sides. Climb on a rock or kneel for a better angle. Leave out details in the scene that distract from the subject.

Centering the subject tends to produce a static image. You can get a more dynamic shot by placing the subject to one side. One widely used guideline, the *rule of thirds*, can help you achieve an interesting visual balance. Mentally draw lines that divide the scene into thirds, both vertically and horizontally. Place the main subject and important subordinate elements along these lines, especially at the points where the lines cross (see illustration). Also try placing the horizon along one of the lines.

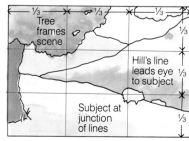

⅓ ⅓ ⅓

Tree frames scene

Hill's line leads eye to subject ⅓

Subject at junction of lines ⅓

L

To create a sense of depth, use fences, paths, and hedgerows as eye-leading lines that draw you into the scene. Use foreground trees and boulders to frame the scene. And shoot in the morning or afternoon when the sun creates shadows that add depth.

Even a simple camera will take good landscape shots, and you can get professional quality with a 35mm model. To get the sharpest images, set the lens for a small aperture and use slow-speed film. Also use a tripod. It lets you compose the scene more carefully and use slow shutter speeds when necessary. If your camera takes other lenses, try a wide-angle lens to take in a broad vista. A polarizing filter will darken the sky, making clouds stand out. (See also *Cameras.*)

Lanterns

Maintaining and repairing a gasoline lantern

Caution: Turn off a lantern and let it cool before starting. Never work near sparks, high heat, or fire (including a pilot light).

Fill a gasoline lantern only with the additive-free fuel sold for that purpose. Wipe off spilled fuel after filling.

When the lantern is on, turn the cleaning-needle lever frequently to remove deposits on the generator's tip. Every couple of months, lubricate the pump through the oiling hole.

If a lantern won't light, the pump may not be creating enough pressure.

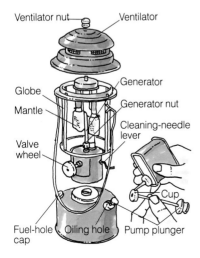

Ventilator nut — Ventilator
Globe
Mantle
Generator
Generator nut
Cleaning-needle lever
Valve wheel
Cup
Fuel-hole cap
Oiling hole
Pump plunger

Unlock the plunger knob, put your thumb over the knob's hole, and pump several times. If you feel little resistance, the leather or neoprene cup on the plunger's inner end needs oiling. Unscrew the plunger and take it out. Apply oil to the cup; then wipe and reinstall it. Replace a brittle cup.

If a lantern flickers, doesn't burn brightly, or burns for a minute or more after it is shut off, it may need a new generator. Before installing one, close the fuel valve and release the pressure in the fuel tank by slowly unscrewing the fuel-hole cap; hold a rag over the cap to prevent spillage. Then unscrew the ventilator nut and lift off the ventilator and globe. Turn the cleaning-needle lever up and unscrew the generator nut. Slip the needle out, and the generator will fall out. Insert the needle in a new generator. Turn the cleaning-needle lever down and tighten the generator nut. Reassemble the lantern; run it to test for leaks.

If one mantle is damaged, replace both. Brush away the old mantles' residue. Tie on the new mantles with drawstrings; arrange the folds evenly and trim the strings. Light the mantles, and let them burn until ashy white. When camping, always carry extra mantles and a spare generator.

Larding

Improving the flavor and juiciness of meat

To *lard* is to thread strips of fat through lean meat before cooking it. Slice chilled fatback or salt pork into uniform, square-cut strips about ⅛ to ½ inch thick and about an inch longer than your cut of meat. Place a fat strip in the groove of a larding needle—a long, narrow, scoop-shaped tool. Insert the needle at one end of the meat, with the grain, and twist it through until about ½ inch of fat protrudes from the other end. Holding the exposed fat against the meat with one hand, gently twist out the needle with the other. Insert fat strips at 1½- to 2-inch intervals. If you don't have a larding needle, use a sharp knife to cut deep slits through the length of the meat; push in the fat with a sturdy

chopstick or the slender handle of a wooden spoon.

Barding is another way to keep lean meat or fowl from drying out during roasting. Cover the meat or bird with thin sheets or slices of fatback, salt pork, or bacon and tie securely at intervals with kitchen string. Or have your butcher do it. Because the bard is discarded after cooking, this method adds less fat than larding.

Laryngitis

Relieving a hoarse voice

Most laryngitis is an inflammation of the larynx (voice box) caused by viral or bacterial infection of the upper respiratory system. The characteristic hoarseness may become so severe that the voice is temporarily lost. Other symptoms are those of any upper respiratory infection: fever, chills, sore throat, headache, and a weakened, run-down feeling.

Treat upper respiratory laryngitis as you would any severe cold or flu—with bed rest, fluids, aspirin or another analgesic, perhaps a cough suppressant (see *Colds; Flu*). Give your voice a complete rest. Don't smoke or drink alcoholic beverages until it has returned to normal.

Hoarseness from irritants

Occasionally the cause is an irritant, such as tobacco smoke or alcohol, or overuse of the voice from prolonged shouting, speaking, or singing. Ceasing the irritant should heal the condition; throat lozenges may help to soothe the irritated larynx.

Laryngitis that persists for more than a week may be chronic. It usually afflicts those who smoke or drink heavily or whose working environment forces them to breathe dust or fumes. Sometimes the underlying cause is chronic bronchitis or sinusitis. If so, treat the root problem.

Don't ignore persistent or excessive hoarseness, especially if no other symptoms are present. It could be a sign of a more serious condition, such as tuberculosis or a tumor of the larynx. See a doctor if any bout of laryngitis lingers more than 10 days. (See also *Sore throats.*)

L

Latches

For cabinets, gates, and doors

To install a *thumb latch* on a door, first position the handle plate on the outside. With a sharp pencil, trace the slot for the lever onto the door. Extend the penciled outline ½ inch or so—just enough to give the lever free play. Then cut the slot: first drill several small holes through the door; finish with a chisel (see *Chiseling; Drilling*). Attach the lever to the handle plate, insert it in the slot you cut, and screw on the plate. Inside, fit the lever plate over the lever and screw it to the door. Attach the latch bar and its keeper as shown. Mount the notched strike on the frame so that the latch bar rests in it when the door is closed.

Thumb latch

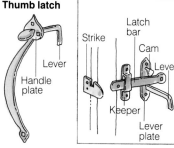

Some thumb latches are fitted with pivoting cams to lock the bar in place. If such a latch is used on a bathroom door, childproof it by removing the cam. To maintain privacy for adults, install a *barrel bolt* or *spring bolt* high on the door, out of a child's reach.

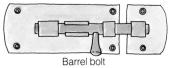
Barrel bolt

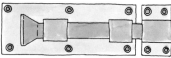
Square spring bolt

Because a *cabinet latch* is opened from the outside only, you need not drill any holes through the door. Simply mount the latch on the door and the keeper on the frame. If the door is inset so that the frame must be mortised for the keeper, dab lipstick or crayon on the latch bolt and use it to mark the position of the keeper.

Childproof cabinet latch

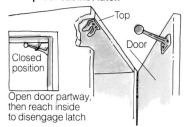

The simplest *gate latch* is a pivoting bar that falls into a bracket on the gatepost; to lift the latch from the other side, attach a string to the bar and run it through a small hole 12 to 18 inches above the latch. A similar string arrangement works for a *self-closing latch*—a good choice for a gate that must be childproof. (See also *Door locks; Doors; Gates.*)

Gate latch

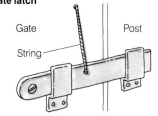

Self-closing latch

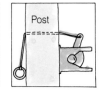

Laundry

Doing it right

Sort your laundry according to color (white, light, or dark), fabric type (cotton, linen, or synthetic), and care instructions; also separate the lightly soiled from the heavily soiled items; make a separate pile for knits and delicate fabrics. White and light colors can be combined as long as you use the water temperature or the cycle for the more delicate fabrics.

Empty pockets, close zippers, turn down cuffs, and tie drawstrings and sashes. Rub stains and heavily soiled areas, such as collars, with an enzyme prewash product, liquid detergent, or a paste of dry detergent and water.

Use *hot water* for white fabrics and very dirty or greasy clothes. (Use cold rinse if permanent press is included.) Use *warm water* for most permanent-press fabrics, light to medium colors, and knits. Use *cold water* for reds or dark colors. Choose a cycle according to machine instructions.

To get maximum cleaning power from a washing machine, mix small and large items in each load, distribute the laundry evenly, and avoid overloading the tub. Use detergent in the amount recommended on the box or bottle. Too little won't get clothes clean; too much can discolor fabrics and leave an unpleasant residue.

Use laundry soap only if your water is naturally soft or has been conditioned with a water softener. Minerals in hard water can combine with soap to leave a dingy scum on clothes. Never wash flame-retardant clothes with soap; it destroys the finish.

To whiten cottons and some synthetics (check the bottle label), add chlorine bleach—no more than 1 cup—about 5 minutes after the wash cycle has begun. Put it through the bleach dispenser or dilute it first with water. Chlorine bleach should not be used on silk, wool, or fabrics with resin finishes; use an oxygen (all-fabric) bleach for these. To soften fabrics and reduce static electricity, add a fabric softener to a rinse cycle or to the dryer.

Lawn bowls

A medieval game played in English-speaking countries

To play lawn bowls, you need a flat lawn 40 yards square surrounded by a ditch 2 inches deep and 2 inches wide. Using string, divide the lawn into six *rinks*, each the length of the lawn and each 19 to 21 feet wide. Place a 14- x 24-inch rubber *mat* on the center string on the lawn, with one of its short ends 4 feet from the ditch. Players must make all shots with one foot on or over the mat.

The *bowls*—brown balls made of wood, composition, or hardened rubber—are flattened slightly at one place; this causes them to travel in a curved path. Their circumference is no more than 14½ inches; they weigh 3½ pounds. When two people play, each rolls four balls per turn; in triples, three; in fours, two.

The game begins with one player rolling the *jack*, a smaller white ball. It must travel at least 25 yards from the front of the mat; if not, an opponent has a try. After the jack has stopped, center it in its rink. The object of the game is to roll your bowls closer to the jack than your opponent's; each bowl that is closer than your opponent's nearest bowl scores 1 point.

Once an *end* is completed, the players take the mat to the far side of the lawn, evaluate the score, and then play the next end from the opposite side of the lawn. The first player to get 21 points wins. (Pairs and fours play 21 ends; triples play 18 ends.)

Any bowl that travels less than 15 yards is *dead* and is placed outside the area of play. Bowls that land outside the strings bounding the rink or that land in the ditch without touching the jack are also dead. Bowls that hit the jack are marked with chalk. These are potential scorers, even if they are knocked into the ditch by an opponent's bowl. To prevent an opponent from getting a good score if he is in an advantageous position, a player can try to knock the jack out of the field of play; this voids the score of that end.

Lawn care

Keeping grass green by keeping it healthy

A lawn needs several hours of sunlight a day and at least 1 inch of water a week. An inexpensive rain gauge can tell you how much water your lawn is getting. Or you can use a spade to open a slit 6 to 8 inches deep; the soil should be damp at the bottom. Grass naturally goes dormant and turns brown in the hot, dry days of summer, reviving with the next good rain. To keep your lawn green in dry spells, give it a thorough weekly soaking, preferably during the morning; frequent light waterings make roots shallow and encourage weeds.

Don't mow a lawn too short; grass needs its leaves to produce food. The ideal height for most grasses is 2½ to 3 inches in hot weather (½ inch shorter in cool weather). Remove only one-third of the blades' length at a time. If the grass is badly overgrown, mow it twice, 3 or 4 days apart. Clippings under 1 inch long may be left on the ground; rake longer clippings for the compost pile.

Fertilizing a lawn

Since grass regularly loses its leaves to mowing, it needs a high-nitrogen fertilizer, such as 10-6-4. An average lawn needs 3 to 4 pounds of nitrogen per 1,000 square feet a year. A 10-pound bag of 10-6-4 contains 10 percent (or 1 pound) nitrogen. Thus, you'll need 3 or 4 such bags for each 1,000 square feet of lawn.

In warmer climates, give the main feeding in early spring, with a small midsummer booster. In wintery areas, give the main feeding in early autumn and a booster just before winter sets in; give another light feeding in midspring, after the first burst of growth has tapered off.

Most grasses do best in neutral to slightly acid soil (pH 7 to 6). With a kit from a garden center, test the soil from several places in your lawn. If the pH is lower than 6, add ground limestone in late fall. Do not apply fertilizer within 2 weeks after applying limestone. Correct alkaline soil (pH 7 or higher) with gypsum, powdered sulfur, peat moss, or well-rotted manure.

Lawn problems

The best defense against weeds, disease, and insects is a well-nourished, properly tended lawn. When weeds *do* appear, pull them before they go to seed, using a long weeder to get all the roots. Herbicides are available, however, both for crabgrass and for such broad-leaved weeds as dandelions, hawkweed, and plantain. Follow the manufacturer's directions carefully. Small doses applied directly to the weeds are better than large-scale applications, which can kill many desirable plants. (See also *Chinch bugs; Crabgrass; Dandelions; Japanese beetles; Weed control.*)

If your lawn gets heavy foot traffic, loosen the soil once a year with a garden fork: thrust the fork into the soil every few inches and wiggle it back and forth. For a large lawn use a mechanical aerator.

Before reseeding bare patches, rake the lawn to remove thatch (accumulated clippings). In the north, the best time to reseed is August or early September. Next best is late winter, before the ground thaws. If you must seed in summer, keep the area moist until the seedlings are well established. In warm climates, seed in late spring or early summer.

Popular lawn grasses

Bluegrass is a favorite in areas with cold winters; it forms a dense turf that takes considerable trampling. Several strains of *perennial ryegrass* are also gaining popularity in such areas. *Fescue*, tough and shade-tolerant, is excellent for playgrounds. In the High Plains, *buffalo grass* is a good choice for its ability to tolerate drought; a slow grower, it needs few mowings.

Where winters are mild and summers hot, *Bermuda grass* is popular. *Augustine grass* and *centipede grass* are also useful. All three are planted by sprigs or plugs instead of seed; they spread rapidly by means of runners. *Zoysia*, another warm-climate favorite, is hardy as far north as Boston. It forms a dense, low-growing turf that turns brown at first frost.

For problem areas such as deep shade, steep slopes, or rough ground, see *Ground covers.*

Lawn chair repairs

Better care, better wear; replacing broken webbing

Hose down lawn chairs periodically to remove grime; scrub stubborn dirt with detergent. At least once a year,

L

clean the exposed aluminum frame with 000 steel wool and kerosene; renew pitted areas with an aluminum cleaner. Wax the frame with car paste wax. Check frequently for loose fasteners and tighten them.

Kits for replacing broken plastic webbing are available at hardware stores and home centers. To measure for a replacement strip, stretch the webbing taut across the chair frame from screw hole to screw hole, then add 3½ inches (for reinforced ends). At one end make a 45-degree fold, then another, forming a triangular tip. Using a leather punch, make a hole ¾ inch from the apex of the triangle. Insert a washerhead sheet-metal screw (these come with most kits) through

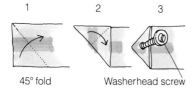

1   2   3

45° fold   Washerhead screw

the hole; then screw it into the fastener hole in the chair frame. Weave the webbing so that it duplicates the position of the broken strip; fold and fasten the other end as before. For chairs that take clip-type fasteners instead of screws, follow the instructions on the kit package.

Lawn mowers

Year-round care of rotary mowers with four-stroke gasoline engines

Before the mowing season, buy a new spark plug. Following the engine maker's specifications, set the gap between the two metal electrodes at the plug's threaded end. Use a spark-plug gauge's bending bracket on the L-shaped side electrode to adjust the gap (see *Spark plugs*). Take out the old spark plug, connect the wire to the new one, and rest the plug's threaded surface on the engine.

Crank the engine; if there is steady sparking between the two electrodes, install the spark plug. If there's no spark or if the spark is erratic, remove the sheet-metal cover over the fly-

wheel, and inspect the magneto coil and the entire length of the plug wire. If either is damaged, replace it; on many mowers it is one component. If you see no damage, have a professional check the electronic ignition.

If you have an older lawn mower with ignition points instead of electronic ignition, you should inspect the points and adjust the gap between the contacts. However, the points are under the flywheel, and to remove the flywheel, you need special tools. You can avoid buying special tools by installing an electronic ignition conversion kit, which is less costly than the tools. Once the kit is in, the points need never again be serviced.

Check that the spark plug wire terminal fits tightly on the plug. If it is loose, push back the rubber nipple and crimp the terminal with pliers.

If the starter is a pull-rope type, inspect the rope for fraying and replace it if necessary.

Remove the air-filter cover and inspect the filter element. Replace the pleated paper type if it's dirty. Clean a plastic-foam filter by immersing it in kerosene, then gently squeezing the kerosene through it; allow it to air-dry. Soak it in clean engine oil, gently squeeze out the oil, and reinstall.

Spray the carburetor linkage with penetrating oil. Also spray penetrating oil on the axles.

If the mower has chain or belt drive, check the chain or belt for looseness. Press on it with a finger. If a belt deflects more than ¾ inch between pulleys, or if a chain deflects more than ½ inch between sprockets, readjust it. In most cases, loosen engine-to-mower bolts, which pass through elongated holes, and move the engine forward or back as necessary. For other, less common belt arrangements, see *Drive belts*. Belts that are automatically tensioned by a spring-loaded pulley cannot be adjusted; replace the loose belt. Tighten the engine-to-mower bolts.

Inspect the blade, and if it is badly nicked, replace it or have a professional sharpen it. Don't try to file away anything other than minor nicks, or you'll unbalance the blade, putting an uneven load on the engine and causing damage.

If gasoline was left in the tank during the winter, gum may have formed, making the mower difficult to start. To clean out the gum, pour a pint can of carburetor solvent into the tank; fill with gasoline. Prime the engine: remove the air filter and pour 2 to 3 tablespoons of clean gasoline into the bottom of the filter housing.

Midseason checkup

Inspect the air filter and if it's dirty, clean or replace it. Do a major cleaning of the mower body. Change the engine oil while the engine is hot. Tighten the engine-to-mower mounting bolts. Check the blade for nicks.

End of season

Drain the gas tank and run the mower out of gas. Immediately change the oil while the engine is still hot. Let the engine cool, remove the spark plug, and pour 5 tablespoons of fresh engine oil into the spark-plug hole. Crank the engine for 3 seconds to circulate the oil; then reinstall the spark plug, but don't reconnect the plug wire. To retard rust, spray penetrating oil on all exposed shafts, linkage, sprockets or gears, chains, and axles.

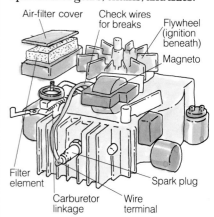

Air-filter cover   Check wires for breaks   Flywheel (ignition beneath)   Magneto   Filter element   Carburetor linkage   Wire terminal   Spark plug

Lawyers

Finding a good one

When shopping for a lawyer, keep in mind that a lawyer's job is to advise a client about how the law applies to a particular situation. A lawyer can't make decisions for you; nor can he or she magically solve your problems when the law is against you.

Ask relatives, friends, and co-workers to whom they turn for advice on legal matters. Listen closely, but critically, to their accounts of experiences with lawyers. Important questions to ask those who recommend a lawyer are: did the lawyer listen to what they said; explain in easy-to-understand language how the law applied and what options were available; treat them in a prompt, courteous manner; and charge a reasonable fee.

If you receive favorable answers to these questions, call to schedule an appointment with the attorney. Ask his or her secretary the charge, if any, for preliminary consultations. You might describe the general nature of your problem over the phone to determine whether the lawyer practices that type of law. (Most lawyers specialize; so a lawyer specializing in tax matters might not want to represent you in an adoption proceeding.)

If you have no luck in getting recommendations from friends and family, ask community groups or civil liberties organizations for referrals. Or contact your local or state bar association—they provide lists of attorneys according to the type of practice, but you'll have to investigate the names on the lists to find the lawyer who can best represent your interests.

Once you arrange an appointment with a lawyer, prepare for it. A lawyer's time is money; don't waste his or her time and your money because you haven't thought out what you want to discuss. Be candid with your lawyer; nothing you say regarding a legal matter can be revealed without your permission. Don't be afraid to ask questions, but if you are, or if you otherwise feel uncomfortable with your relationship, resume your search for a lawyer.

Laying bricks

The basic techniques

Any brick structure needs a footing below the frost line (see *Footings and foundations*). Each brick must rest on, and be joined to its neighbors by, ⅜ inch of mortar (see *Mortar mixing*). All *courses*, or layers, must be level; corners and faces must be plumb (see *Leveling*). Vertical joints must be staggered, each supported by a brick.

Before you start work, make a scale drawing of the structure's elevations and ground plan. Decide on a *bond,* or pattern, then plan each course, calculating how many bricks you need.

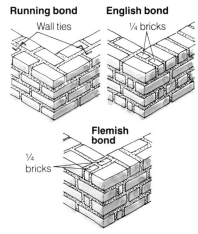

Running bond **English bond**
Wall ties ¼ bricks

Flemish bond
¼ bricks

Order 20 to 30 percent more. Like lumber sizes, the standard brick size, 2⅔ x 4 x 8 inches, is *nominal;* the real measurements are smaller, allowing for mortar joints. Exact measurements vary with suppliers; find out what they are before planning.

Staggered joints means using half or quarter bricks at times. Cut all the bricks before you start. You can use a circular saw with a masonry blade, or you can score the bricks with a chisel and break them off with a hammer.

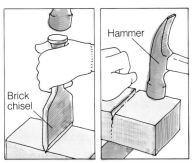

Hammer

Brick chisel

When the footing has cured, outline the structure with chalk and lay out the first course without mortar, leaving ⅜-inch spaces between bricks. Mark the position of each brick with a pencil and remove them. Hose down the footing and about 25 bricks.

If the structure has a corner, begin there. Spread a ¾-inch layer of mortar 3 bricks long and 1 brick wide. Carefully set the first brick ⅜ inch deep in the mortar. *Butter* another

brick as shown, and lay it next to the first; trim off the excess and use it on the third brick. After laying three

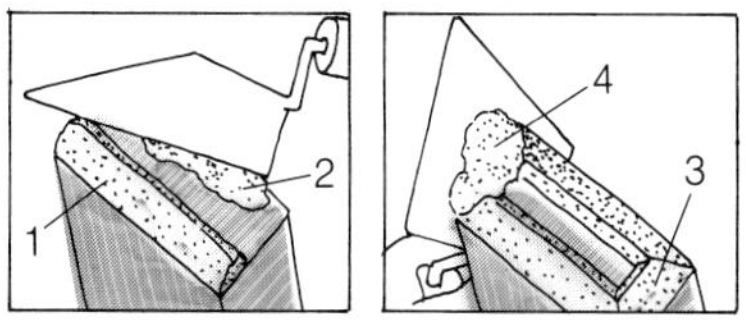

bricks, check the row with a builder's level, tapping bricks down gently with the trowel handle as needed. Use the level as a straightedge, too, to align the front of the row. Then lay three bricks at a right angle to the first three to begin the face of the adjoining wall.

For a wall two bricks wide, lay the first three bricks of the back row next, buttering the end and edge of each; level them with the front row. For a running-bond wall, imbed galvanized *wall ties* at 12-inch intervals atop every third course (see *Garden walls*).

Lay the first brick of the second course along the adjoining wall; if you are building from the end of a wall, use a half brick. Then lay the course in the same way, but make it one-half a brick shorter than the first. Continue, course upon course, until you have built a pyramid with a single brick on top; use a *brick rule* or a homemade *story pole* to position the height of each corner brick. Check the faces of both walls to see that they are plumb. Then build a similar pyramid in the other corner of the front wall.

From corner to corner, stretch a mason's line even with the top of the first course; use it as a guide as you fill in the row. Work toward the middle, laying a few bricks at a time from each end and checking your work with the level. The last brick, or *closer,* must be buttered on both ends. Fill in the back row, then move the line to the top of the second course and repeat. Continue until the wall is filled in.

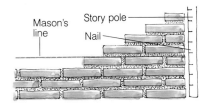

Story pole
Mason's line
Nail

As you work, *point* the joints while the mortar is soft enough to take a thumbprint (see *Brickwork*).

Leaking engine oil

Finding and fixing the source

If an oil leak can't be located, clean the engine with an aerosol degreaser; then spray aerosol foot powder on its sides and bottom. The leak will form a line in the white powder.

You may be able to to fix a leaking oil filter by simply tightening the filter (see *Oil filters*). If the leak is at the oil pan, valve cover, or mechanical fuel pump, tightening the bolts or nuts may solve the problem. On a cover with many bolts, start tightening in the center and work alternately toward the ends. If the leak persists, you may be able to change the gasket, but leave an oil-pan gasket to a pro.

Cover bolt-tightening sequence

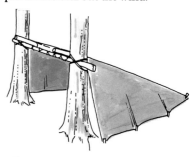

Valve cover. Remove the bolts; if the valve cover is stuck, pry it up. Tape identifying numbers to any hoses or wires you unplug. Using a putty knife, scrape gasket residue from the cover and the cylinder head. If the head is aluminum, take care not to gouge it. If a metal cover rocks on a flat table, it's warped. Sandwich it between flat pieces of wood, then hammer gently on the edges of the upper piece.

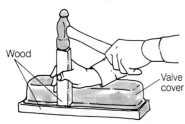

Wood

Valve cover

Apply a film of pliable gasket sealer to the cover's gasket surface, then fit a new gasket. A precut cork-fiber or cork-rubber gasket is best for a sealing problem.

Position the cover and the gasket, then thread in the bolts and washers. Working from the center out, fin-

gertighten, then tighten moderately with a wrench, and then securely.

Fuel-pump gasket. Disconnect the fuel lines. If a pump has a threaded fitting, hold it with one wrench; use another to loosen the fuel-line nut.

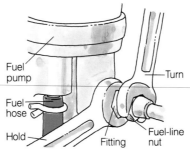

Fuel pump

Fuel hose

Hold

Turn

Fuel-line nut

Fitting

Catch fuel with a rag. Remove retaining nuts or bolts; pull off the pump.

Scrape the pump and engine surfaces. If the gasket is a thin sheet, use two sheets. Apply pliable sealer to the pump surface, then a gasket, another coat of sealer, and the second gasket. Refit the pump and gradually tighten the nuts or bolts. If the engine has a pushrod, suspend it with a paper clip while guiding the fuel pump into place.

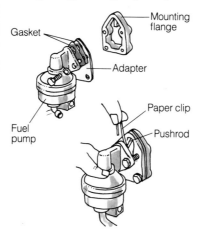

Gasket

Mounting flange

Adapter

Fuel pump

Paper clip

Pushrod

Lean-tos

Simple shelters for campers

A lean-to is an easy overnight shelter to build in a wooded area. All you need to carry are 25 feet of light line and an 8- x 10-foot plastic tarp or drop cloth, equipped with tie lines or grommets.

Look for two trees 3 to 4 feet apart to serve as upright supports. Then find three straight poles for the frame-

work—two 7 or 8 feet long, and the other about 1 foot longer than the distance between the two trees. If you must cut saplings for these poles, choose young birches, poplars, or aspens that grow close to larger trees; they will soon be shaded out anyway.

Lash the short pole to the windward side of the two trees 2 feet from the ground if the shelter is just for sleeping; 3 or 4 feet if you plan to sit up and cook. Rest the ends of the long poles on this crossbar so that the lean-to's open side will face leeward (downwind), and lash them in place. Stretch the tarp over this framework and lash it to the crossbar. Fashion pegs from sticks to hold down the edges; then pile dirt to seal out the wind.

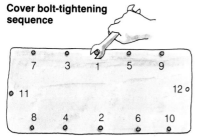

In an emergency, you can make a lean-to that is almost as weatherproof by covering the framework with slender branches and evergreen boughs. Or find an evergreen tree with a low branch, and lean evergreen boughs against it. In winter, pack snow over the boughs for insulation.

Leather garments

Coat, jacket, and glove care

Unless leather clothes are very stained, avoid taking them to a dry cleaner, even one that specializes in leather. The beauty of leather is in the surface patina that develops over time; attempts to restore leather to brand-new perfection destroy the patina.

Clean a smooth-surfaced leather garment yearly. Condition it with oil to prevent drying and cracking. First wipe the garment all over with a damp cloth and a little mild soap (not detergent). Rinse with a fresh damp sponge, pat off excess water, and let the garment dry at room temperature

L

(not near a radiator). Then rub the garment lightly with a little pure neat's-foot oil or mink oil. If the surface feels sticky, wipe off the excess oil with a clean cloth.

Spray a suede or sheepskin garment with a stain-and-water protector when it is new. Brush the surface regularly with a terry towel or a non-wire suede brush to keep it clean and raise the nap. If the inside of a suede garment has a smooth finish, condition it with neat's-foot oil.

If rain causes water spots on suede, let the garment dry thoroughly; then rub it with a towel or brush. Remove minor stains by rubbing them with a gum eraser, an emery board, or very fine sandpaper.

Hang leather coats and jackets on padded or wooden hangers. To store, cover them with a cloth (never a plastic bag) to keep the dust off. Don't fold a leather garment; the creases may become permanent. If a garment gets creased, hang it in the bathroom at shower time. Or press it with an iron at low setting, placing heavy paper between the iron and the leather.

Cleaning gloves

Leather gloves can be washed once a year in cool water with a mild soap. Squeeze water gently through gloves; do not wring. Rinse with cool water, press water out, and dry on a towel at room temperature. When the gloves are almost dry, rub a bit of leather conditioner into their surfaces to restore pliability. (See also *Handbag repairs; Luggage; Shoe care.*)

Leatherworking

Cutting and stitching leather

Leather is sold by the square foot and the ounce: 1-ounce leather weighs 1 ounce per square foot. The weight of leather is related to its thickness: 1-ounce leather is $1/64$-inch thick, 4-ounce leather is $4/64$-inch (or $1/16$-inch) thick. Belts require 7- to 9-ounce-weight calfskin, cowhide, or pigskin. Wallets need 2- to 4-ounce-weight calfskin, cowhide, or pigskin.

Use a cardboard pattern and a utility knife to cut leather. Place the leather, smooth side up, on a cutting sur-

face of linoleum, fiberboard, or hard rubber. Hold a pencil with a sharp point perpendicular to the leather and trace around the pattern. Retrace the penciled line with an awl. Initially cut only partway through thick leather. Then make a second, final cut. Eliminate the initial cut on thin leather, or use scissors if the leather is very thin. When cutting straight lines, use a steel rule or a square as a guide. Cut thick leather with a leather knife.

Before sewing leather, plan the stitches $1/8$ to $1/4$ inch from the outer edge, then use an awl to punch holes partway through the leather to accept them. Use a *glover's needle* (sharp point) for thin leather and a *harness needle* (blunt point) for thick leather with a single strand of nylon or waxed linen thread. The needle and thread should be of the same diameter as that of the prepunched holes. To secure the thread to the needle, pass the needle through the thread near one end; then pass the short end of the thread through the eye of the needle; pull the thread back.

Two of the most common stitches are the *running stitch* and the *saddler's stitch*. Knot a running stitch both at the start and the finish to keep the thread from pulling out, or stitch back to the beginning to create a *double running stitch*, then knot the two ends of the thread together.

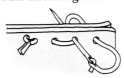
Double running stitch

Use a needle at each end of the thread for a saddler's stitch. To get extra strength, finish with a *locked saddler's stitch* by passing one or both needles back through the last loop or loops, pulling tight, and cutting the ends of the thread flush with the leather.

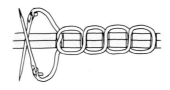
Locked saddler's stitch

Leather edges can also be bound by *lacing,* in which strips of leather are used instead of thread. Use *thongs* (square strips) or *flat lacing.* Screw the thong into the hollow end of a brass lacing needle. Wedge flat lacing between the metal strips of a *two-prong lacing needle.* Punch holes all the way through the leather to accept the lacing instead of only partway as in stitching. A common lacing stitch is the *whipstitch.* Tuck the end of the lacing under several stitches.

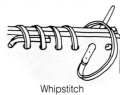
Whipstitch

Left-handedness

Teaching left-handers

Left-handedness occurs in about 15 percent of the population. Although left-handed children tend to have more trouble with manual tasks than right-handers, studies suggest that left-handed people are often unusually creative, inventive, and athletic.

Left-handedness first becomes apparent between 3 and 6 years of age. If your child is left-handed, don't try to change the dominant hand—the child may become frustrated and anxious.

Writing

Learning to write can be difficult for lefties because the left hand, as it moves across the page, covers the words just written. Provide a beginning writer with a pen or pencil that won't smear and encourage him to hold it far enough from the point so that he can see what he has written. Let the child decide for himself be-

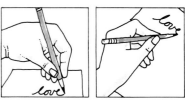

tween the hooked position—with the hand curved above the written line—and the standard position—the hand below the line.

Continued next page

At the table, at study, and at play

At a dining table, some left-handers prefer to sit at a corner of the table and to the left of a right-hander so that their elbows won't collide. Others have no preference. It is more important for lefthanders to sit at lefthanded desks. Otherwise, their writing angle will be extremely awkward, putting them at a disadvantage.

Left-handers seem to have an edge in many sports. In tennis, squash, and other games played with a racket, they have an advantage because their opponents are accustomed to the spin, angles of return, and weaknesses of right-handed players. In baseball, left-handed batters stand on the right side of home plate, several steps closer to first base than a right-hander.

Tools and equipment

In sports and elsewhere, equipment can be a problem for left-handers, though not nearly as much as it once was. Left-handed golf clubs and baseball mitts are widely available. Many tools and appliances come in left-handed models (scissors, for example) or can easily be adapted for left-handers (steam iron cords usually can be shifted to the left side).

Certain right-handed tools, such as chain saws, are dangerous for lefties. Take the time to find left-handed ones.

Leftovers

New meals from old

One basic rule of leftovers is to transform them into a new dish; reheated in their original form, they are seldom as good as they were the first time around. For example, warmed-over roast beef slices are unexciting, but cubed roast beef reheated with spicy curry sauce and served over fluffy rice is both appetizing and an excellent way to stretch a limited amount of beef.

Avoid combining too many different leftovers in one dish—the result will be a mishmash of ingredients. Cook leftovers just long enough to heat them through. Overcooking destroys flavors and toughens meats. To give soft foods texture, add crisp bacon, nuts, water chestnuts, diced sweet green or red peppers, or celery.

Meats, poultry, and fish

Try beef in soups, hash, potpies, curries, noodle or rice casseroles, and in sandwiches; or combine it with onions, celery, leftover vegetables, and dressing (see *Salad dressings*), and serve as a salad. Mix beef with tomato sauce and serve over pasta.

Leftover lamb is ideal for shepherd's pie (chopped meat in gravy topped with mashed potatoes) and curries; turn it into rice pilaf with onions, beef broth, and seasonings. For a change of pace, use lamb instead of beef for stuffing green peppers.

Leftover pork, spread with mustard and relish, makes good sandwiches. Perk up casseroles or turn pasta into a main course with slivers or cubes of roast pork, or heat pork with sweet-and-sour sauce for a Chinese treat.

Chopped ham adds flavor to scrambled eggs, scalloped potatoes, macaroni and cheese, salads, soufflés, biscuits, muffins, and corn breads. Mix ground ham with bread crumbs, a lightly beaten egg, and seasonings for a ham loaf.

Dice chicken for chicken à la king or salad. Add it to soups or combine it with sweet relish and mayonnaise for a sandwich spread. Make broth with the chicken carcass, meat scraps, and fat (see *Chicken soup*).

Combine fish or shellfish with a white sauce (see *White sauce*) and serve over crepes, puff pastry shells, hot buttered toast, or biscuits; or make croquettes (see *Crepes; Croquettes*). Use fish or shellfish mixed with mayonnaise and herbs to stuff eggs, tomatoes, or avocados or to make sandwich spreads.

Vegetables

Use vegetables from yesterday's dinner in salads, soufflés, or omelets. Garnish a casserole with mashed potatoes or shape them into small patties and sauté them in butter. Refrigerate the nutritious liquids from cooked vegetables and add them to soups, sauces, and casseroles.

Egg yolks and whites

Many dishes call for either the white or yolk of eggs, leaving you with the other part. Use egg yolks to make mayonnaise, hollandaise, custards, puddings, and cakes. Freeze leftover egg whites in ice cube trays, one white per

segment. Then transfer the frozen whites to a plastic bag and return them to the freezer. Thaw and use them for meringues, soufflés, macaroons, chiffon pies, angel food cake, and cake frostings. Add an extra white to scrambled eggs.

Bread

Make croutons, French toast, or pudding from day-old sliced bread. Coat meat or fish with bread crumbs before sautéing or deep-frying. Also add crumbs to croquettes and meat loaf and to poultry stuffings. Top casseroles with buttered bread crumbs to add flavor and crunch. (See also *Aspic; Casseroles; Omelets; Potpies; Sandwiches; Soups and stocks.*)

Legal aid

Getting free or low-cost legal assistance

Don't despair of getting competent legal assistance just because you can't afford a high-priced lawyer. You may be able to get the help you need for little or no money.

A dispute over taxes can often be resolved with the help of a local taxpayers' association. An insurance claim can sometimes be settled through your state insurance commissioner. Get assistance on discrimination from the offices of the federal or state attorney general, or contact a special-interest organization concerned with your particular legal problem. The NAACP Legal Defense and Education Fund and the National Organization for Women are among groups that will bring suit for an individual.

A problem involving the courts requires the services of a licensed attorney. If you are a defendant in a criminal case and cannot afford a lawyer, the court must appoint one at no cost to you. Tell the police that you want to speak to the public defender before answering any questions.

Legal Aid Society

In civil and administrative cases, you may be able to obtain a lawyer at little or no charge through a Legal Aid Society office. Found in many cities, these offices give help in three major areas: domestic relations; disputes between a client and a landlord, lender, or installment seller; and small money claims for wages. Eligibility requirements vary, but financial need is always a key determinant.

If you don't qualify for Legal Aid or if you feel you would be better served by a private lawyer, you may want to explore the free or reduced-cost services that some law firms provide *pro bono publico* ("for the public good"). Check the Yellow Pages under "Attorney Referral Services."

Some communities have legal clinics that help with relatively simple matters, such as a routine will or an uncontested divorce. If you are involved in a dispute about a small amount of money, you can bring the matter to small claims court without a lawyer (see *Small claims court*).

Lettering a sign

Centering the words without a ruler

To make a neat sign without complicated measuring, start with pencil sketches on scrap paper, until you find a balanced and pleasing arrangement of the letters. Then print the first line of your message on scrap paper the same width as your poster or

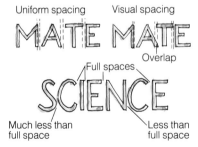

Uniform spacing   Visual spacing

MATE MATE

Overlap

Full spaces

SCIENCE

Much less than full space   Less than full space

signboard. Make the letters with single strokes; you'll widen the lines later.

Blacken the back of the paper with a soft pencil and fold the paper in the center of the line of words. Pencil a light line down the middle of the poster or board. Tape the paper lightly to the board, matching the fold to the line. Trace over the letters to transfer them.

Continue until you've transferred each line of your message. Then go over the letters lightly in pencil, straightening their lines and evening

their height and thickness. If you need to erase, use an art-gum eraser.

Broaden the letters with a broad-tipped marker or a flat-end sable lettering brush and poster paint. As an alternative, you can buy a stencil with the letters of the alphabet and stencil your sign (see *Stenciling*).

Leveling

Finding a true horizontal plane

A number of leveling devices are available in hardware stores. As a rule, the longer the level, the more accurate the reading will be. A combination square with a bubble vial will do for small

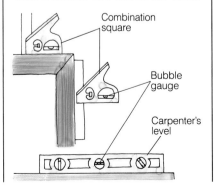

Combination square

Bubble gauge

Carpenter's level

jobs. To level a picture frame, for example, place the square's flat face on top of the frame and shift the frame until the bubble is centered. To check for plumb (vertical), hold the square's ruler against the frame's side and, once again, center the bubble.

Use a carpenter's level for jobs requiring greater accuracy, such as installing shelves. Carpenter's levels are available from 1½ to 4 feet long and have bubble vials for level, plumb, and 45 degrees. For extralong jobs, such as leveling a floor, use a perfectly straight board as an extension. Place the board on edge and set the level at its center. In aligning any work, check the ends as well as the middle. When dealing with a wide surface, such as a countertop, test for horizontal in various directions.

For long horizontal runs, such as a masonry wall or a fence, use a line level—a small bubble tube with hooks

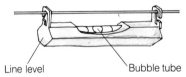

Line level   Bubble tube

that can be hung on a line stretched taut between the ends. For a long vertical line, such as a wallpaper joint, use a plumb bob—a pointed weight hung on a string (see *Plumb line*).

Lice

Detecting and eliminating them

The first sign of body lice may be itching where there is body hair—the scalp, armpits, pubic area, or even the beard or eyebrows. Unless you have sharp eyesight, you may find it difficult to see lice without a magnifying glass. Their tiny bite is also hard to see, but you'll be able to see their nits—small, white egg clusters attached to hair strands.

You may be able to eliminate lice with an over-the-counter shampoo. Do not use one with pyrethrin if the person is allergic to ragweed. Comb out nits with a special fine-tooth comb. Wash linens and clothing in hot water, and iron when dry. If the problem continues, consult a doctor.

Continued next page

Don't be ashamed of lice. They don't signify an unclean home or person, and they don't respect class. Secrecy can lead to epidemics in a family, school, or neighborhood. Anyone with whom an infested person has been in close contact can catch them, and should be told that the problem exists.

Light fixture rewiring

Changing an incandescent fixture to a fluorescent one

Caution: Turn off power to a working fixture's circuit by removing the fuse or turning off the circuit breaker. Check that the power is off by turning on the controlling switch; the fixture should not light.

Remove the old fixture by loosening fasteners and wires. Unscrew the lid from the new fluorescent fixture and use a screwdriver to punch out the center tab on the back of the channel. If the old mounting box has a threaded stud pointing down, add a hickey and a threaded nipple to it (A). If there is no stud, use a locknut to fasten a nipple to a horizontal strap; then screw the strap to the box (B).

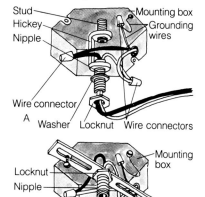

Feed the fixture's wires through the punched-out hole and the nipple; then connect them to the ceiling wires with wire connectors—black wire to black, white to white, grounding wire to grounding wire. Fit the punched-out hole over the nipple, push the channel to the ceiling, and secure it with a washer and locknut.

A heavy fixture with two or more lamps often has a large hole in the center of the channel to accommodate an eight-sided ceiling box. Add a reducing nut and nipple to the stud in the ceiling box (C); feed the fixture

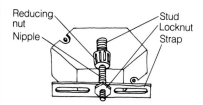

C

wires through the cutout and connect them to the ceiling wires as above. Place the cutout hole over the nipple; then thread a strap to the nipple and secure it with a locknut.

Install a circular fluorescent fixture the same way: add a reducing nut and nipple to the ceiling-box stud, con-

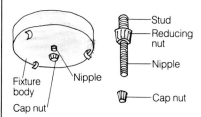

nect the fixture wires to the house wires, and fit the wires into the box. Place the center hole of the fixture over the nipple and secure it with a cap nut. (See also *Fluorescent lights*.)

Lobsters

How to buy, cook, and eat these delicious crustaceans

Live lobsters vary in color from dark greenish blue to reddish brown, but all turn bright red when cooked. Lobsters are best if bought live and cooked just before serving.

When buying live lobsters, select the most active ones. A 1¼- to 1½-pound lobster will satisfy the average adult; a 2½-pound lobster will yield about 2 cups of meat and can feed two or more. Store live lobsters in the refrigerator, not directly on ice; avoid holding them overnight. Use pre-boiled lobsters for salads and cold dishes; additional cooking toughens the meat.

Cooking lobsters

Most lobster lovers prefer the crustaceans steamed or boiled. To steam, fill a large kettle with about 1½ inches of seawater (or add 1 tablespoon of salt to tap water). In the bottom of the kettle, place a rack that stands a bit above the water. Bring to a boil, put in the lobsters, and cover. After boiling resumes, steam 5 to 7 minutes for 1- to 1¼-pound size; 9 to 12 minutes for 1½- to 2½-pound size; for larger lobsters, 5 minutes for the first pound plus 4 minutes for each additional pound. Boiling takes the same amount of time. Lift out with tongs and drain. Serve whole at once, with lemon wedges and melted butter.

Eating a lobster

Most of the meat of a lobster is in the tail and claws. Break off the claws and crack them with a nutcracker to get at the meat. Next, take the lobster in your hands (careful, it may still be hot) and bend it backward so that the tail separates from the body. Break off the flippers and use a cocktail fork to push the tail meat out the front in a single piece or slit open the underside of the tail with a sharp knife and remove the meat with a fork. Finally,

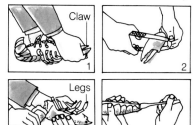

with the body laid on its back, slice or break it open lengthwise. The gray-green "tomalley," or liver, and the coral-colored roe found in female lobsters are considered to be delicacies. Meat can be extracted from the small legs by sucking it out.

Lost cats and dogs

Finding yours; returning other people's

To guard against losing a dog or cat, equip it with a durable collar and attach a tag to it that gives your name, address, and telephone number. A collar should be snug (but not tight) to prevent it from slipping off the pet's head. Even a pet that lives indoors should have a tag; a pet can easily dart through an open door or window.

If you do lose a pet, work outward from the spot where you think the animal was lost, searching in widening circles. A dog may come at your call, but a cat may crouch in hiding (often inside, in closets or under furniture). Use a flashlight when searching dark areas; the light reflecting from its eyes makes the animal easier to spot.

If you cannot find the pet, inform the police or a local animal pound. Tell neighbors; post notices in stores and post offices; advertise in the local newspaper and offer a reward; check the "lost animals" section in that paper. Also check with the mail deliverer and tradespeople who often see stray animals on their rounds, and with neighborhood veterinarians.

Returning a lost pet

If you find a pet that seems lost, first look for an identification tag, then phone the neighbors—it may be a local pet on the loose. If the animal looks thin or sickly, it is probably lost or abandoned; if you cannot determine its owners, contact the local humane society (check the Yellow Pages under "Animal Shelters"), dog warden, or police headquarters for advice.

Be careful about handling a strange animal, particularly one that seems frightened or unfriendly. An animal that is salivating or twitching may have rabies. If you decide to adopt a pet whose owner cannot be found, first try making friends with it. A badly neglected animal may need feeding once or twice before it will trust you. Before taking a stray into your home, have it examined by a veterinarian for mange, ringworm, fleas, and other parasites and diseases.

damp sponge—don't use an abrasive cleaner. For louvers finished with stain, spray furniture cleaner on a clean, dry cloth and wipe the shutters. Dry immediately with another clean cloth.

Painting with a brush

Clean the louvers to remove grease, wax, and dirt. If one side of the piece to be painted is less likely to be seen than the other—the back side of a shutter, for example—paint that side first. Stand the piece so that the louvers slope toward you. Use a brush the width of a single louver. Start with the top louver. Begin your brushstroke at the joint where the louver is mortised into the frame. Stroke halfway across; then stroke from the opposite joint, overlapping the wet edge. Next, paint the edges of the frame, then its top, bottom, and sides. Check your work for runs and missed spots and fill them in. Then turn the piece over and paint the other side in the same way.

Painting with a spray gun

Spray painting should be done outdoors or in a well-ventilated area. Before you begin to paint, practice on newspaper to get the feel of the spray gun (see *Spray painting*).

Position the shutter or door vertically (slats horizontal). Start at the top

and sweep across in one continuous motion. Apply many thin coats—allowing for drying time between—rather than one thick coat.

tors linked to hypertension and high blood pressure. A safe level of sodium is considered to be about ½ to 1½ teaspoons per day ⅛ to ½ for children), but most Americans consume two to three times that amount—10 percent from natural foods, 15 percent from the salt shaker, and 75 percent from processed foods.

You can't rely on salty taste to judge the amount of sodium in a food. Processed foods contain sodium in other forms (sodium benzoate, sodium nitrite, and sodium sorbate, for example). Moreover, the sugar in cookies, cakes, and other desserts masks the taste of salt.

Cutting back at the market

Look for low-sodium, reduced sodium, or unsalted products. Low-sodium foods contain less than 140 milligrams of sodium per serving; reduced sodium means that normal sodium levels have been cut by 75 percent.

Caution: Salt substitutes are available, but persons suffering from diabetes, heart or kidney disease, or receiving other medical treatment should consult with their doctors before using one.

Cutting back in the kitchen

Try halving the salt in your favorite recipes. Then, the next time, halve it again. Taste food first, adding salt a pinch at time. Herbs, spices, fresh garlic, and lemon juice can serve as partial substitutes for salt. By rinsing canned vegetables before using, you can wash away some of the sodium.

Cutting back at the table

Taste your food before reaching for the salt shaker. Use one shake only. Remove the salt shaker from the table or substitute one with smaller holes or put out an herb shaker (see *Herbs in cooking*). The less salt you use, the less salt you will want. Give yourself 2 to 3 months to adjust. You'll find that new flavors emerge.

Louvers

How to clean and paint them

To clean louvers in doors or shutters, first vacuum them with the brush attachment. Wash both sides of painted louvers with warm, soapy water and a

Low-sodium cooking

Cutting back for your health

Sodium, an essential mineral, occurs naturally in many foods. Excessive sodium intake, however—usually in the form of table salt—is one of the fac-

Lubrication

Greasing your car

Some cars still have spring-loaded valve fittings through which grease is injected to lubricate steering and suspension joints. Lubricate all fittings at least once a year—more often if the car maker recommends it—with a name-brand, premium-quality grease.

There are two types of grease guns. The *trigger* type permits one-handed operation so that you can hold the nozzle of a flexible hose against a hard-to-reach fitting with your free hand. With the *lever* type, it is easier

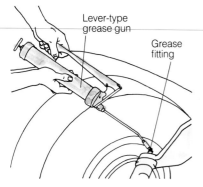

Lever-type grease gun

Grease fitting

to build up pressure, but both hands are required for operation; to reach out-of-the way fittings, you either need a helper to hold a flexible hose, a special nozzle to lock it onto the fitting, or a rigid tube with swivel joints.

Chassis lubrication

First, find all the fittings. They are generally on the suspension ball joints

Typical locations for grease fittings

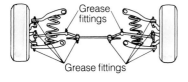

Grease fittings

Grease fittings

Remove factory plug

Install fitting

and the joints of the steering linkage. Dig away any dirt around the joints and inspect the rubber boot on each joint. If it is slightly cut, clean off all dirt, and heal the cut with a coat of silicone paste (available at most auto supply stores). Allow the paste to cure, then lubricate the joint.

If the boot is badly damaged, take the car to a garage. On some cars the entire joint may need replacing, on oth-

ers only the boot may need changing. If in doubt, have the joint replaced.

On an older car, you will find a plug screwed into a joint. Remove the plug with a wrench and replace it with a valve fitting. If the plug is hard to reach, the replacement should be an adjustable right-angle fitting.

Wipe each fitting clean with a rag. Then push the grease-gun nozzle firmly onto it and pump the trigger or lever slowly until you see or feel the fitting's rubber boot swell, or until grease escapes from the fitting just below the boot. If grease escapes from between the nozzle and fitting, rather than below the boot, the fitting is probably rust frozen. Replace it.

Drive-train fittings

The universal joints on the drive shafts of newer rear-drive cars come factory sealed with grease packed in. On some older rear-drive cars, however, and on many four-wheel drive vehicles, you will find grease fittings on the universal joints. You may also find fittings on a joint that has been replaced. They may be recessed and may require a needle-shaped nozzle, sold in auto supply stores. Pump grease into a universal-joint fitting until the grease begins to escape from elsewhere on the joint.

Transmission and manual-clutch linkages do not have grease fittings, but they should be lubricated. Have a helper operate the transmission and manual clutch while you locate the underbody pivot points. Spray all exposed pivot points with an aerosol penetrating oil; then, with your fingers, smear a coating of grease on each joint, working it between the metal-to-metal contact surfaces.

Locate the parking-brake levers at the rear wheels. Spray the joints with penetrating oil, then smear them with grease. Spray penetrating oil on the hood hinges, hood latch, door and trunk hinges, and grease them.

Luggage

Care and repair of suitcases and briefcases

Prevention is the key to a long and healthy life for luggage. Resist cram-

ming too much into a bag and forcing zippers or clasps. Instead, repack the contents. Avoid placing objects with sharp corners—books and the like—along the sides of soft luggage where they could poke through. Spray a balky zipper with silicone compound. Mend small rips with patching tape or sew on a patch (see *Patching*). Take luggage with ailing hinges and large rips to a professional for repair.

Saddlesoap on a damp sponge will remove soil from leather goods. Use a sponge and mild detergent to clean molded plastic, vinyl, and nylon luggage. Soap, water, and a small hand brush are good on canvas; rinse with clear water. Do not immerse any kind of luggage in water.

Lumber

Softwood sizes and grades

The thickness and width of premilled lumber (always given in that order) are *nominal* dimensions; the actual dimensions are always smaller. Thus a 2 x 4 is really about 1½ x 3½ inches.

For softwood that is to receive a natural finish, or for long lengths of narrow 1-inch lumber that are sound and unwarped, buy *clear,* or *A* grade. *B* lumber has more blemishes, but a long 1 x 8 or wider should be sound. For wood that is to be painted, and for any 2-inch construction lumber, the cheaper *C* will usually do. Although *D* lumber has knots and warpage, a long length will often yield several short pieces of high-quality wood.

Macramé

Practicing basic techniques

Macramé is the art of decorative knotting. To practice the techniques, you need some sturdy, even-textured cord, such as twine (yarn is too stretchy); scissors; T- or U-pins; and a rigid work surface that will hold pins. Heavy cardboard will do or you can buy a knotting board, available in different sizes up to 24 x 48 inches.

Cut eight cords, each 4 feet long, and one cord 6 inches long. Knot the short piece (the mounting cord) at each end and pin it firmly to the top of the board. Fold the long cords in half and attach them to the mounting cord with *lark's-head knots.*

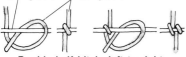
Lark's-head knot   **Reverse lark's-head**

To start a *double half hitch,* one of two basic knots in macramé, anchor the far left cord (the holding cord) with a pin and pull it to the right. With the next cord (a knotting cord), work a *half hitch* over the holding cord. Make a second *half hitch* to complete the stitch; pull it tight. Continue making *double half hitches* over six more strands, then pin the holding cord at the right and work from right to left.

To vary the *double half hitch,* use the holding cord diagonally; or work

Holding cord   Knotting cord

Double half hitch, left to right

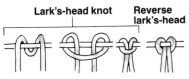
Double half hitch, right to left

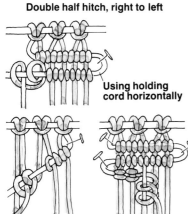
Using holding cord horizontally

Using holding cord diagonally   **Using holding cord vertically**

stitches vertically over the knotting cords with the holding cord.

To make a *square knot,* the second basic macramé knot, use four cords to form a *half knot* (A), then make a second *half knot* in the opposite direction (B). A series of square knots will form a chain (sennit); a series of half knots will form a twisted chain.

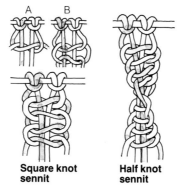
Square knot sennit   **Half knot sennit**

Magic tricks

Principles of magic; basic coin tricks

The hand isn't really quicker than the eye. In fact, you should avoid quick, sharp movements. The art of magic is the art of misdirection. You must focus your audience's attention on a gesturing hand, on your face, on a prop, on another person, on a line of patter—on anything other than the hand that is doing the trick. Sometimes you need only look at what you want your audience to see. Otherwise, look at your audience, not at your hands; above all, don't look at the "working" hand.

Learn one magic trick at a time. Practice it in front of a mirror until your gestures look natural and you can do them automatically.

Disappearing coins
Hold a quarter between the thumb and the index and middle fingers of your right hand. Pretend to take the coin in your other hand. Instead, as your left hand closes around the quarter, push it deep into the palm of your right

hand. Relax your muscles so that the loose flesh folds around the edges of the coin. Later, you can retrieve it with your first two fingers and make it "appear" from almost anywhere.

The basic coin palm is useful in many tricks. Here's another: place a coin in the center of a handkerchief.

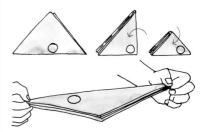

Fold the cloth into three consecutively smaller triangles. Grasp the bottom corners, one in each hand, and hold the cloth out, tilting it back and forth. The coin will slip into your hand; palm it. Wave the cloth with your other hand while you slip the coin into your pocket.

Manicures

Keeping your fingernails shapely; applying nail polish

M

A manicure should be a weekly routine. Start by removing any old nail polish. Hold a cotton pad moistened with polish remover against the nail for a few seconds; then wipe from the base of the nail toward the tip. Use a separate bit of cotton for each nail.

Next, file each nail with an emery board. Holding the emery board on a slant, just under the nail, file from sides to center in one direction only.

To soften cuticles, soak your fingertips for 5 minutes in warm, soapy water. Then, using the blunt end of an orangewood stick dipped in cuticle remover, gently push back the cuticle. Trim hangnails with a small scissors (see *Hangnails*).

Next, scrub the nails with a nailbrush and warm, soapy water. Clean under the nails with an orangewood stick wrapped in wet cotton.

To apply polish, first wipe your nails with remover and be sure they are dry and free of soap. Spread one hand flat on a table. With the other, apply one thin coat of colorless polish. Brush from the base of the nail toward the tip, first down the center, then down each side. Let the polish dry between coats. Then apply two thin coats of color. With a tissue, remove a hairline of polish from the tip of each nail. Finally, apply a colorless sealing coat over the nail and under the tip. (See also *Fingernails*.)

Map reading

Understanding the symbols; finding your way

The legend on a map should include a *scale*, giving the ratio between map distance and real distance; a *key*, giving the meaning of signs and symbols; a *date*, telling when the map was drawn; and a *directional arrow*, showing true north and, perhaps, magnetic north as well. A topographical map, in which fine lines indicate changes in elevation, will also give the *contour interval*, or number of feet or meters of elevation between lines. Before using a map, study the legend and memorize its symbols.

Highway signs

Interstate   US   State or Prov.   Trans-Canada

Map features

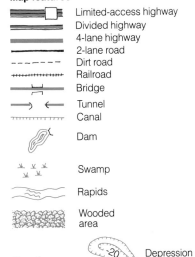

Limited-access highway
Divided highway
4-lane highway
2-lane road
Dirt road
Railroad
Bridge
Tunnel
Canal
Dam
Swamp
Rapids
Wooded area

Elevations   Depression

The scale may be given in numbers (that is, 1:62,500; or 1 inch = 1 mile) or it may be a bar divided into feet, miles, or kilometers. The scale is often shown both ways. To use a bar scale, mark the distance between points of the map on a slip of paper; then hold the paper against the scale.

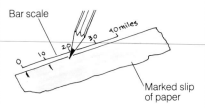

Bar scale

Marked slip of paper

When using a map, align the directional arrow with true or magnetic north (see *Compasses*). Then locate your own position on the map and the place to which you want to go. Figure out how far you must travel and the route you will take; look at signs and symbols to locate landmarks along the route. Road maps have numbers indicating mileage between intersections.

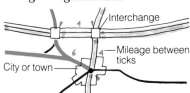

Interchange

Mileage between ticks

City or town

With a topographical map, study the contour lines to get a clear idea of the terrain you must cross. Every fifth line is heavier than the others and is labeled with the correct elevation. The closer together the lines are, the steeper the slope they indicate. Concentric circles indicate a hilltop. A series of V's pointing toward a high spot indicate a ravine or gully; if they point away from one, they indicate a ridge.

On topographical maps published by the U.S. Geological Survey, a blue line is a river; a blue patch, a body of water. A green area is wooded. A black symbol is a man-made structure.

Whenever possible, use a recent map. Older maps may be less accurate, and they don't show new roads, new buildings, and other new construction. For a free list of available topographical maps, write to Branch of Distribution, U.S. Geological Survey, 1200 S. Eads St., Arlington, VA 22202. (See also *Orienteering*.)

Marble

How to maintain, clean, and polish it

Marble is easily stained and scarred. Use coasters under drinking glasses. If there's a spill, wipe it up immediately. Seal doorsills, windowsills, floors, and tabletops with a marble sealer.

Don't drag furniture across a marble floor. Protect heavy traffic areas with throw rugs. Vacuum frequently. Damp mop weekly with clear water or with a mild detergent. If marble gets streaked and dirty, wipe with a damp sponge and buff dry. For stubborn dirt, use dry borax and a damp cloth; then rinse with warm water and buff dry. To clean and polish simultaneously, use a self-polishing marble cleaner. For a major cleaning, strip off any old wax with a wax remover, rinse thoroughly with clean water, and apply sealer followed by paste wax.

Treating stubborn stains

To treat grease stains, make a paste of powdered whiting or chalk dust mixed with acetone. For organic stains—coffee, tea, tobacco, fruit juices, carbonated beverages—mix the powder with hydrogen peroxide, rather than acetone, and add a few drops of ammonia just before applying it. For rust stains, substitute liquid rust remover as the solvent.

Apply mixture to stain, cover with plastic wrap, and seal with masking tape. Let the peroxide and acetone mixtures stand overnight; the rust paste, a few hours. Sponge off the mixture and buff the treated area. Rust stains may benefit from a follow-up treatment with a peroxide paste.

If removing a major stain dulls the surface, wet the area with water and sprinkle it with a marble-polishing powder (tin oxide). Rub with a thick cloth or use an electric buffer.

Marbles

How to play the classic game

Marbles is played with small, translucent, colored balls, most often of glass but sometimes of plastic or agate. The

M

standard marble is ⅝ inch in diameter. However, most players have in their collection one prized ball, designated the *shooter,* which is slightly larger and often exceptional in color.

The most popular game of marbles among American youngsters is called Ringer. To play it, arrange 13 *object* marbles in a 9- x 9-inch cross and mark off a 10-foot-diameter ring with the cross at the center. The goal of the

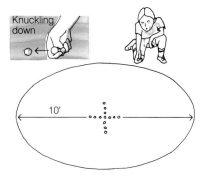

players is to knock object marbles out of the ring with their shooters. The first player to knock out seven marbles wins.

The initial shot for each player of Ringer must be from outside the ring; subsequent shots are taken from wherever the shooter lands. A player continues shooting until he fails to hit a marble; after that the next player takes a turn. All shots must be taken *knuckle down*—a knuckle of at least one finger must touch the ground.

The game can be played *for fair,* meaning each player returns all captured marbles to the original owner after the game; or *for keeps,* in which case the winner takes home his booty.

Another well-loved marble game is Shooting the Ring. A target marble is placed in the center of a ring and more marbles are placed in a wide circle surrounding it. The players must hit the target marble, then call and hit a selected marble in the circle.

Marinating

Making meat more tender and more flavorful

All marinades contain a combination of oil, seasonings, and an active ingredient, such as wine, vinegar, lemon juice, yogurt, or buttermilk. Because of the active nature of the marinade, it's best to marinate in a glass, ceramic, or stainless-steel bowl, using a wooden spoon as stirrer.

Use about ½ cup of marinade for each pound of meat to be marinated. Cubed meat requires 2 to 3 hours of soaking, whereas a large piece should soak overnight. Reduce the amount of wine or other active ingredient if the meat is to soak more than 24 hours. Marinating for 12 hours or more cuts cooking time by one-third.

A simple marinade

For a quick marinade sufficient to cover about 3 pounds of cubed meat, mix 1 cup salad oil or olive oil with ½ cup red wine vinegar or dry red wine in a bowl. Add 1 onion, minced, or 2 garlic cloves, crushed, and salt, pepper, thyme, tarragon, or rosemary to taste. Add meat and toss to coat thoroughly. Cover and let stand about 3 hours at room temperature or 6 hours in the refrigerator. Stir the marinade every hour or two during the marinating period.

When marinating large pieces of meat, turn them from time to time and use a soft food brush to spread the marinade on parts not submerged in the liquid.

Marquetry

Making pictures with wood

Marquetry is a method of creating inlaid designs out of pieces of wood veneer chosen for their contrasting colors and grains.

To do it, you'll need a crafts knife, white glue, assorted veneers, and a cutting board of plywood covered with linoleum. Veneers are available at hobby stores and from companies that sell woodworking supplies.

For your first effort, choose a simple design. Use carbon paper to transfer it onto the veneer you have selected as the background. Place the sheet of veneer on the cutting board and carefully cut out one of the outlined features with the crafts knife. Then slide a sheet of contrasting veneer under the first sheet so that it is visible in the opening. Transfer the shape to the

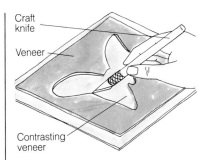

piece that shows through by carefully scoring it along the edge of the opening. Remove the scored piece and cut out the shape. Apply glue to the edges of the opening and press the new piece into place, rubbing it flat with the handle of the knife.

Repeat this procedure until all the outlined features have been replaced with patches of contrasting veneer. For best results, work first with larger background elements, saving the foreground and finer details until last. When the design is finished, trim the edges square; glue long wood strips around the edge to make a border.

Attach the finished marquetry to a mounting board of smooth plywood. Apply a thin film of glue to the board and place the marquetry on top. Cov-

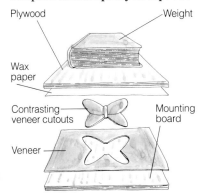

er with wax paper and another piece of plywood; then weight or clamp the pieces to distribute pressure evenly while the glue dries.

Marriage

Applying for a license; tying the knot

Marriage laws vary throughout the country. To learn about local regulations, call or write to the office of your city or town clerk or, in large cities, to the Marriage License Bureau.

Most states require you and your partner to have a blood test within 30 days before you apply for a marriage license. In some states you may need a complete physical examination. Your family doctor can perform the test and the examination. Tell the doctor you intend to be married and ask him or her to fill out all necessary forms. Because you may have to wait several days for lab test results, you should visit the doctor at least a week before you plan to apply for your license.

Some states require a waiting period of a day or more between the issuance of a marriage license and the marriage ceremony. You and your partner will probably have to apply for the license in person. Bring with you all medical documents, identification, and proof of age—a birth or a baptismal certificate, a valid driver's license or passport, a visa or alien registration card, military identification or a draft card—and proof that any former marriages have been terminated by death, divorce, or annulment. All documents should be originals. Many authorities will not accept photocopies, altered papers, incomplete or unsigned forms, or documents that are rubber-stamped rather than signed by hand.

If you are below the age of consent (18 years in most states), your parents may have to accompany you. They should bring identification and proof that they are your parents.

Upon payment of a fee, your license will be issued. Ordinarily it will be valid only for a certain period and only in the state in which it was issued.

Civil and religious ceremonies
A marriage can be performed by a religious leader, such as your priest, rabbi, or minister, or by a civil authority, such as a judge or a justice of the peace. If you choose a religious ceremony, talk with your clergyman well ahead of time about the time, place, and nature of the wedding (see *Weddings*). Make sure you understand any special requirements of the religion in which you will be married.

A civil ceremony can be performed in a judge's chambers or at the license bureau without extensive prepara-

tions. If you plan to have your civil ceremony at home or at a catering hall, discuss arrangements well ahead of time with the judge.

You and your partner may choose to sign a marriage contract. The primary purpose of such a document is to protect financial assets of both partners in the event of divorce or death. The contract should be drawn up by an attorney and must be negotiated with the full consent of both partners. Homemade contracts and contracts signed under duress are unlikely to hold up if contested in court.

Massage
A relaxing routine for the whole body

When giving a massage, keep relaxed. Let your body weight, not your muscles, provide the pressure. Repeat each stroke several times, especially where you sense tension. If you use oil, warm it first in your hands.

The upper body
Have the subject lie faceup on a firm, padded surface, such as the floor or a table. First stroke the person's face gently with your fingertips, moving from the center outward and ending with a circular motion at the temples. Massage along the cheeks and jawbones. Use a firm press-release action along the upper ridge of the eye sockets. With your fingertips, massage the scalp hard enough to move the skin.

Then cradle the subject's head as you work on the neck muscles with your fingers. Give special attention to the big bulges at the base of the skull.

Caution: Avoid rigorously massaging the front of the neck.

Gently lay the head down and, with a hand on each shoulder, push downward toward the feet. Knead the muscles along the tops of the shoulders.

The torso
Place your hands palms down, with heels resting just below the collarbone, thumbs touching. Begin a gliding stroke downward, applying medium pressure to the chest and less to the stomach. Then *pull* firmly up one side at a time: place your hands, fin-

gers down, on the subject's side and pull the flesh upward, alternating hands and squeezing the flesh as you

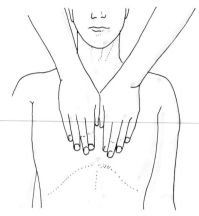

go, along the entire side. Work the top of the chest with your fingertips.

Arms and legs
Grasp the subject's wrist with both hands and apply a firm gliding stroke toward the armpit; continue your top hand over the shoulder. With both hands, pull firmly back down the sides of the arm and over the fingers. Then, *drain* the subject's forearm: with the subject's elbow bent and resting on the surface, encircle the wrist with your hands and slide them downward. Return, applying no pressure. From the same bent-elbow position, massage the inside of the arm with your thumbs. Place the subject's hand on your shoulder and apply the same techniques to the upper arm. Finally, *wring* the arm: grasp it in both hands and rotate your hands vigorously back and forth along the entire length.

Knead the palm of the hand with your knuckles. Work the back, then the front, of the hand with your thumbs. Gently twist each finger, bending it backward and forward as you knead it from the base to the tip.

Use the same gliding stroke for the legs. Pull the inside of the thigh; drain the back of the leg. Then, with your hands supporting the knee, trace the furrow around the kneecap with your thumbs. Drum lightly on the cap with your fingertips; then work circles on either side of the bone. Wring the legs, as you did the arms, and work the feet as you did the hands, applying extra pressure to the heels.

Back

Have the subject turn over onto his stomach, with his head to one side. Knead the buttocks; then twist the knuckles of your index fingers into the hollows on either side. Vibrate the entire area with the heel of your hand.

Use a long, gliding stroke down the back, then work your thumbs up the furrows on either side of the spine. On the return, dig the tips of your index and middle fingers deeply into these furrows. Pull the sides of the torso. Knead the upper back muscles; then rub your palms rapidly over the back.

Finish by raking the body with your fingertips; drum the muscles with the outer edges of your hands. Twist and stretch each limb to its limit, but be careful to test the limit so that you don't go too far. Feather the body with light fingertip strokes.

Caution: Never apply too much pressure to the lower back, and never apply direct pressure to the spine.

Matting

Preparing a mat to frame a picture

Measure, mark, and cut the mat and the backing board to fit your frame (see *Picture framing*). Mat board is available at art supply stores; plywood or heavy cardboard can serve as backing. If the art is valuable, use acid-free matboard and backing.

Place the art on the right side of the mat to determine the size of the opening through which it will be seen or, if the art has a border, measure the area you want to show. Locate the opening so that the side borders of the mat are equal, and the bottom border about ½ inch wider than the top.

Mark the opening a fraction of an inch smaller than the art so that the mat will overlap the edges of the picture. Use a steel ruler or a framing square and either a mat cutter (sold at art supply stores) or a utility knife to cut out the opening. Bevel the edges of the cut inward so that the mat's thickness will show from the front. After cutting all four sides, use a single-edge razor blade to clean the corners

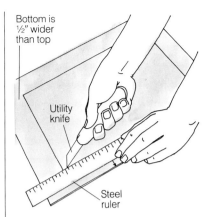

Bottom is ½″ wider than top

Utility knife

Steel ruler

of any fuzz or uncut scrap. Smooth rough spots with an emery board.

Fasten the top of the art to the backing board with tape hinges. Then tape the mat to the backing board.

Mayonnaise

Making it with a wire whisk, a blender, or a food processor

Have all ingredients and utensils at room temperature. To make mayonnaise with a wire whisk, beat 1 egg yolk until thick. Add ¼ teaspoon salt, ¼ teaspoon dry mustard, and a pinch of cayenne pepper. Add ¾ cup vegetable or olive oil, drop by drop, whisking well after each addition. When thick, add 1 tablespoon lemon juice or vinegar. Yield: about ¾ cup.

Blender mayonnaise

Blend at low speed for 15 seconds 1 whole egg, 1 egg yolk, ¾ teaspoon salt, ½ teaspoon dry mustard, and 2 tablespoons lemon juice or white vinegar. Add a dash of tabasco, if desired. Continuing at high speed, add 1½ cups vegetable or olive oil in a thin stream. Yield: about 1¾ cups.

Using a food processor

Whirl 1 whole egg, 2 tablespoons lemon juice or white vinegar, ¾ teaspoon salt, ½ teaspoon dry mustard, and ⅛ teaspoon white pepper for 3 seconds. Continue processing, adding 1¼ cups vegetable or olive oil in a thin stream.

Refrigerated in a tightly sealed container, homemade mayonnaise will keep for a week. To rescue curdled mayonnaise, whisk 1 egg yolk until thick. Beat in a few drops of oil, then gradually beat in the mayonnaise.

Meadow

An easy alternative to a lawn

Start in autumn to turn your demanding lawn into a colorful, work-free meadow of wildflowers. Turn the sod with a spade or rototiller and work the soil deeply. Scatter seeds of wildflowers and wild grasses and rake them in lightly. Sow more seeds in spring, and keep the seedlings watered until well established.

Mail-order seed houses and garden centers sell special meadow mixtures for specific regions. Or you can gather your own ripe seed heads from roadside plants and from vacant lots. Don't try to transplant established wildflower plants; they'll probably die.

To give the plants time to reseed themselves, wait until the following fall to mow your meadow. Keep pulling out weeds and tree seedlings. Once established, your meadow should thrive without fertilizing or watering. Mow it once or twice each season.

Mealybugs

Controlling them on plants

Mealybugs look like cottony blobs on the stems and leaves of houseplants.

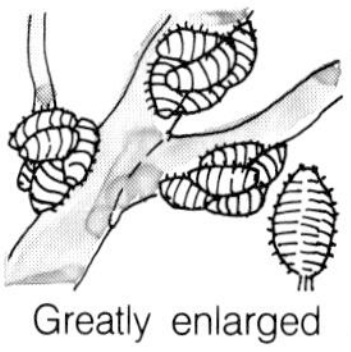

Greatly enlarged

Look for them when leaves begin to yellow and wither. If a plant is small, dip the stem and the leaves into warm, soapy water. Rinse thoroughly 2 hours later. For a larger plant, moisten a cotton swab in rubbing or denatured alcohol and use it to remove the mealybugs one at a time. Try not to get too much alcohol on the plant. Rinse the plant thoroughly with water. Control a severe infestation by spraying with insecticidal soap or resmethrin.

If a plant appears stunted, mealybugs may be on the roots. Wash the soil from the roots in lukewarm water, cut away infested parts, and soak the roots in a malathion solution. Repot in clean soil. Don't use malathion on cacti and ferns. (See also *Pesticides*.)

M

Meat loaf

A simple and popular dish

For a light, fluffy meat loaf, use coarsely ground meat. Spoon the mixture into the pan and do not pack it down. Finely chopped ingredients will make a dense loaf. Use ground beef, pork, ham, or veal, or combine two or more meats.

Basic meat loaf

To 1 pound of ground meat, add 1 cup loosely packed bread crumbs soaked in ½ cup milk or broth with 1 beaten egg. Add 2 tablespoons minced onion, 1 teaspoon salt, 1 teaspoon prepared mustard, and 3 tablespoons ketchup; blend well. Place in a deep roasting pan and shape into a loaf. Or pack the mixture into a loaf pan. Bake at 350°F for 1 hour or until the juice runs clear. Favorite toppings are tomato sauce, barbecue sauce, or ketchup.

Variations

Add minced or grated carrots, scallions, chives, celery, or green pepper, alone or in any combination. Flavor with fresh or dried herbs such as parsley, oregano, or thyme. Vary the size and shape of your loaves, too.

To make a stuffed meat loaf, place three hard-cooked eggs end to end inside the meat; or layer the meat with blanched spinach or carrots (see *Blanching*). Five minutes before you take the loaf out of the oven, arrange sliced green peppers, mushrooms, olives, or capers on top; or spread ¼ cup grated cheddar over it.

To get more servings from a loaf, add 1 cup grated potatoes, cooked rice, or bulgur wheat to the meat mixture. Blend thoroughly.

Meditation

What it is; how to do it

Practitioners of the ancient forms of meditation believe that their disciplines can lead to higher states of consciousness and, eventually, to spiritual enlightenment. In a more practical vein, recent medical studies have indicated that daily meditation can lower blood pressure, reduce stress, and promote a feeling of well-being. The mind is released from the flood of outside stimuli, as well as from the continuous flow of its own thoughts, to achieve a condition unlike either sleep or ordinary wakefulness.

Although some practitioners insist that meditation requires rigorous training, others—including many medical experts—claim that the technique can be learned by anyone.

Basic meditation technique

Choose a quiet place free of distraction. Sit in a comfortable, upright position. Close your eyes and relax your entire body, from your feet to the top of your head. Envision a quiet scene— a blue sky or a green meadow—or concentrate on a word or phrase of your own choosing, repeating it to yourself over and over.

If distracting thoughts, feelings, and sensations intrude, simply concentrate on your chosen word or image. This may be difficult at times of stress, but as you quietly reject distractions, the unwanted thoughts will begin to fade. After 15 or 20 minutes, open your eyes and sit quietly for a minute or so before returning to your daily tasks.

Memory improvement

Curing forgetfulness

With practice, you can improve your memory. When you receive new information, pay close attention to what you are hearing, reading, or seeing.

When you meet someone new, concentrate on getting the name right. To reinforce the art of memory, once or twice a day quickly review what you have learned. If possible, speak the new material aloud, visualize it, and write it down; all three expressions reinforce memory in different ways.

Tricks can help. If you have trouble remembering names and faces in a social situation, connect the name with some aspect of the person's appearance or personality. For example, does Bob bob his head when he talks? Does Rose have rosy cheeks? Is Jean wearing jeans?

Keep a special list of business associates' names and review it often, imagining the people's faces. Put important numbers into an interesting context. Think of 653,645 as two times of day: 6:53 A.M. (your wake-up time) and 6:45 P.M. (dinnertime). Or imagine it as the annual salary of your dreams, $653,645.

Memorizing long passages

Be sure that you thoroughly understand the meaning behind each sentence of a speech or line of a play before you try to remember it. Then work for short, frequent periods rather than long stretches, relaxing your mind when concentration falters. Begin each period by reviewing the material you already know before you go on to something new.

Mending

Repairing broken seams and tears in fabric

A broken seam is best repaired on a sewing machine. Working with the garment inside out, place a row of stitches along the seamline, overlapping the old stitches at the beginning and end of the break. If you mend by hand, make small backstitches along the seamline; at the end of the break, secure the stitches with several small backstitches on top of each other.

If you cannot work from the inside of a garment, repair the break with hand slipstiches (see *Slipstitching*). Secure them with small backstiches.

Tears in fabric

To machine stitch a tear, cut a piece of reinforcing fabric slightly larger than the tear and place this piece under it. Pull the torn edges together and pin and baste them to the fabric beneath; remove pins. With the garment tear

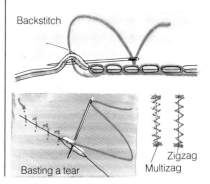

Backstitch

Basting a tear

Zigzag
Multizag

side up and, using short, wide zigzag or multistitch zigzag stitches, sew over the tear. Use a fine needle, and match the thread to the fabric as closely as possible.

On medium-weight fabrics, you can repair a tear with iron-on mending tape. Cut it about 1 inch larger than the tear on all sides. Bond it to the wrong side of the torn area, following the manufacturer's instructions. (See also *Darning; Patching.*)

Menstrual cramps

Understanding how to get relief

Painful menstruation, or dysmenorrhea, is of two kinds: *congestive pain,* which begins before there is any bleeding and is experienced as a continuous, painful tightening; and *spasmodic pain,* which begins with the period and is felt as distinct cramping that comes and goes. (For mood or other changes, see *Premenstrual syndrome.*)

Spasmodic pain is commonest from ages 16 to 25 and is usually ascribed to hormonal changes that make uterine contractions more intense, especially during the first days of a period. Cramps seem to occur only after a girl begins to ovulate. Young girls who are just beginning to have periods and who don't necessarily ovulate before each period are often free of them, as are women who take birth control pills to prevent ovulation. The cramps often disappear after pregnancy.

A mild analgesic, such as aspirin, acetaminophen, or ibuprofen takes the edge off most pain due to menstrual cramps. Ibuprofen is said to be particularly effective, but anyone allergic to aspirin should avoid it. As with all drugs, read and observe the label precautions. If your pain doesn't respond, consult a gynecologist.

Exercising regularly relieves cramps for many women. Others are comforted by curling up with a heating pad.

See your doctor if you first experience pain after 3 or more years of pain-free menstruation or if pain is more severe than usual; either may indicate pelvic disease.

Menu planning

Achieving balance and variety

A nutritious diet is based on a balance from the four basic food groups. Plan your menus to include the recommended servings from each group.

Fruits and vegetables
These prime sources of vitamins, minerals, and fiber should figure prominently in any diet. Aim for four or more servings each day. A serving could be one apple, ¾ cup of juice, one medium potato, ½ cup of vegetables, or a small salad. Because cooking destroys vitamins, several of the servings are best eaten raw. If you snack on a handful of raisins or carrot sticks between meals and quench your thirst with a glass of orange or tomato juice, you have met half the daily requirement from this group.

Breads, cereals, and grains
Grains in the form of complex carbohydrates are important sources of energy and also provide fiber, minerals, and protein. Four or more servings a day are recommended. Because part of a grain's nutritional value is lost in refining, breads made from whole grains, such as whole wheat and rye, are more nutritious than their processed counterparts.

A slice of bread constitutes a serving. So does half an English muffin, one pancake, or a bowl of cereal. One-half cup of cooked pasta equals one serving; thus a good eater can easily pile most of the day's requirement into a spaghetti dinner.

Milk and milk products
Milk, cheese, yogurt, and other milk products are the primary sources of calcium. An 8-ounce glass of milk, ¾ cup of yogurt, 1½ ounces of cheddar cheese, 2 cups of cottage cheese, or 1½ cups of ice cream each provide a serving equivalent in calcium. Children need an average of three to four servings a day, adults two servings, and pregnant or nursing women three to four.

Poultry, fish, meat, and beans
Foods in this group are the primary sources of protein. Two servings a day are recommended. A typical serving is 2 or 3 ounces of cooked poultry, meat, or fish. A ¼-pound hamburger, after subtracting the weight lost in cooking, is a bit more than one serving.

The protein in animal flesh is concentrated. To get its equivalent from eggs, beans, nuts, or seeds one must eat a larger quantity, thus adding extra calories. Keep in mind, though, that most meats also contain fat, and fat contains two and a half times the calories of an equivalent weight of carbohydrates. Combine partial servings: one egg, plus ½ cup of cooked beans, plus 2 tablespoons of peanut butter add up to a full serving. A handful of nuts is a third of a serving.

Vary the ways you meet the requirement. Not only will your meals be more interesting but you will be getting a broader range of nutrients. Each food has specific virtues not exactly duplicated by any other food.

Combine servings in such nutritious mixtures as chili made with beef, beans, and tomatoes, served with rice and topped with sour cream; vegetable stews or creamed chicken rolled into crepes (see *Crepes*); fried rice with meat or chicken; side dishes such as cottage cheese with green onions, cucumbers, and radishes.

Whole-milk products, red meats, and eggs are high in cholesterol. Look for ways to substitute skim milk for whole milk, poultry (without the skin) and fish for red meats, unsaturated vegetable oils for saturated animal fats. Many recipes include more sugar, salt, and saturated fats than the body can easily handle. For better health, keep your meals low in sugar, salt, fats, and saturated oils. (See also *Cholesterol; Low-sodium cooking.*)

Meringue

Making feather-light desserts

Use meringue to top pies and other desserts or bake it into shells and fill it with fruit, ice cream, or custard.

Be sure that the whites are absolutely yolk free (see *Egg whites*). Whip the whites of 2 eggs with a balloon whisk or eggbeater until foamy. Add ⅛ teaspoon cream of tartar and a pinch of salt. One tablespoon at a time, beat in superfine sugar (¼ cup for topping,

½ cup for shells) until stiff peaks form. Add ½ teaspoon vanilla.

For lemon meringue pie, spread the meringue on the filling and bake for 10 minutes at 350°F.

To make shells, preheat the oven to 250°F. Line a baking sheet with heavy brown paper, aluminum foil, or baking parchment. Spoon the meringue onto paper and shape it into a single 8-inch round or into several smaller individual rounds. Bake 1 hour. Turn off the oven, but leave the meringue inside with the door closed for another hour or more. Finish cooling away from drafts, then remove the paper.

Fill or top shells with different combinations of fruit, ice cream, custard, and syrup. Stored in an airtight container, meringue shells will keep for about 2 weeks.

Metalworking

Types of sheet metal; cutting and shaping sheet metal

The thickness of sheet steel, whether stainless, tin plated, or galvanized, is given in gauge number; the lower the gauge, the thicker the sheet. Steel ductwork is usually 28 or 30 gauge; sturdier items call for 26 gauge. Sheet copper is measured by weight per square foot; 16-ounce copper is used for roof flashings, 24-ounce copper for kettles. Sheet aluminum is measured in decimal parts of an inch.

Before cutting a metal sheet, mark the line with an awl or scriber and a straightedge. Wear heavy gloves and cut with tinsnips or aviation sheers. Then smooth sharp edges with a file.

To make a right-angle bend, clamp the sheet between two pieces of hardwood along the line to be bent. Gently

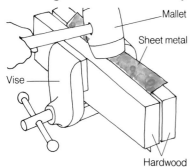

Mallet
Sheet metal
Vise
Hardwood

hammer the metal over with a padded or rubber-headed mallet, working back and forth to keep the bend even. To make a curve, first clamp a length of sturdy pipe in a vise. Then gradual-

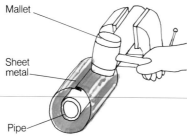

Mallet
Sheet metal
Pipe

ly press and tap the metal while sliding it back and forth across the pipe.

To join two edges, make a hook on each edge and interlock them. Begin with right-angle bends; then hammer each edge over a strip of scrap metal for even spacing. Finally, hook the edges together and hammer the joint flat. For a neater, more secure joint, make a groove punch by chiseling a small channel in a block of wood and hammering it. (See also *Rivets; Soldering.*)

Sheet metal
Groove punch

Meter reading

Calculating electric, gas, and water consumption

Most meters have multiple dials—anywhere from three to seven. The reading on each dial represents a single digit of a larger number. Read the dials from left to right and write them down in that order. If the dials are arranged in a circle, read clockwise, ending with the dial labeled *One,* but ignore dial *One* on gas and water meters.

Whether the hand on a particular dial moves clockwise or counterclockwise, it always advances toward a higher number. If the hand on a dial is between numbers, record the lower number. If the hand is almost directly on a number, check the next dial to the right (or the next dial clockwise). If the hand on that dial has passed 0, record the number the first hand points to; if not, record the lower number.

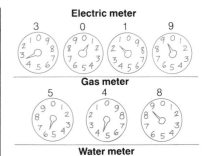

Electric meter
3   0   1   9

Gas meter
5   4   8

Water meter

This meter reads 25028

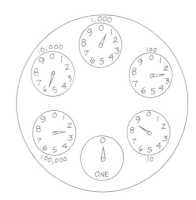

To determine how much electricity, gas, or water you used, subtract the previous month's reading from the new reading. For electricity, multiply the result by the *meter multiplier* given on your bill—usually 10—to get the number of kilowatt hours (kwh) used. Gas and water are shown in hundreds of cubic feet (ccf). To get the number of cubic feet, multiply the reading by 100. To convert cubic feet of water to gallons, multiply by 7.5.

Metric conversion

Easy to do with a calculator

The basic units of the metric system are the *gram* for weight, the *liter* for volume, and the *meter* for length. Other units in the metric system are related to these basic units by multiples of 10. For example, a *kilogram* is 1,000 grams, and a centimeter is 1/100 meter. Additional important units are 1,000 milligrams = 1 gram, 1,000 milliliters = 1 liter, 1,000 meters = 1 kilometer.

Use the following table as a guide in converting from the U.S. system to the metric system or vice versa. For

M

example, to find the number of kilograms when you know the number of pounds, multiply the pounds by .45.

To convert	To	Multiply by
Ounces	Grams	28
Pounds	Kilograms	.45
Grams	Ounces	.035
Kilograms	Pounds	2.2
Teaspoons	Milliliters	5
Tablespoons	Milliliters	15
Fluid ounces	Milliliters	30
Cups	Liters	.24
Pints	Liters	.47
Quarts	Liters	.95
Gallons	Liters	3.8
Milliliters	Fluid ounces	.03
Liters	Pints	2.1
Liters	Quarts	1.06
Liters	Gallons	.26
Inches	Millimeters	25
Inches	Centimeters	2.5
Feet	Centimeters	30
Yards	Meters	.9
Miles	Kilometers	1.6
Millimeters	Inches	.04
Centimeters	Inches	.4
Meters	Feet	3.3
Meters	Yards	1.1
Kilometers	Miles	.6

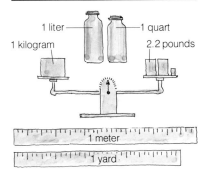

Mice as pests

Keeping them out; getting rid of them

Your first defense against mice is a cat. The cat's scent alone will deter most rodents. The next is neatness; keep all food in metal, heavy plastic, or glass containers. Finally, plug all holes, however small, with steel wool, plaster, or sheet metal, especially around pipes and wiring. Mice climb, so plug high holes too. If you're unable to keep a cat or if the problem persists, try spring traps or poison bait. If you use poison, be sure to place it where pets and children cannot get at it.

Mice usually build their nests within 25 feet of a food source. They forage at night, running along walls and stopping to eat the first morsel they find. Place traps near the wall, baited with food that mice like: bacon fat, peanut butter, raisins, or cheese. Two traps are better than one.

To keep mice from becoming trap shy, bait *unset* traps for 2 or 3 days. Then, to avoid catching your fingers, use a pencil to move the set traps into position. If the mice escape with the bait, secure it with thread or wire.

Traps with a glue surface need no bait. Place them on a pathway; once stuck, the mice will die in 2 or 3 days. Nonlethal traps—safe around children and pets—are expensive and will leave you with live mice to dispose of. Release them in a wild area away from houses (see *Trapping animals*). For poison bait, see *Rats*.

Caution: Place traps or bait out of the reach of children and pets.

Mice as pets

Alert, agile, and delightful

Mice are nearsighted and timid, but once your mouse gets to know you, it may crawl up your arm and fall asleep in the nape of your neck. Spotted, black, brown, or white, these nocturnal creatures delight in exploration; they love to jump and run and climb most of the night.

A cage—either an aquarium with a secure hardware-cloth cover or a rodent cage from a pet store—should be at least 8 x 10 x 6 inches. A larger cage is even better, providing space for romping and special areas for feeding, eliminating, sleeping, and watering.

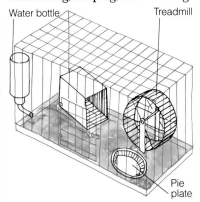

Water bottle · Treadmill · Pie plate

Mice live about 3 years. A buck (male) and a doe (female) can produce up to 17 litters a year, with from 6 to 12 young in each litter. Blind and naked at birth, the young are weaned at 3 weeks of age and are themselves ready to breed at 3 months. If you don't want a proliferation of mice, buy a pair of females; two males will fight. The pet-store owner can identify the sex for you.

A mouse eats a teaspoonful of food each day; seeds, bird grain, nuts, dry dog food, bits of brown bread, green vegetables, and fresh fruit are all good. Commercial pellets are also available. Change the water in the water bottle weekly.

A mouse usually urinates and defecates in the same spot; place a disposable aluminum pie plate filled with sand or kitty litter at that spot. To avoid a "mousy" odor, clean the plate every 2 days.

Microwave cooking

Preparing food quickly and cleanly

Microwave ovens cook with invisible radiation rather than heat. They have become popular because they cook small portions of food in a fraction of the time required by conventional ranges and because they can reduce cooking time even for larger portions. Baking a potato, for example, takes almost an hour in a regular oven but only about 4 minutes in a microwave (increasing the quantity of food, however, increases the time—four potatoes take about three times as long).

Microwaves are good for thawing frozen foods quickly, for cooking fresh or frozen vegetables, and for preparing light meals or snacks. They can also be used to reheat cooked foods without affecting flavor or texture—a boon for family members who may be late for meals or who eat at different times.

A microwave oven melts butter or chocolate without lumping or burning it, and fries bacon or crisps such appetizers as pretzels. Microwave ovens also require less cleanup and release less heat into the kitchen.

Continued next page

A microwave, however, is not perfect. It may cook unevenly, resulting in hot and cold spots. It can cook poultry, roasts, breads, or cakes in less time, but it won't brown them or give them a crust. Special coatings must be added for color. Also, you cannot use it for cooking eggs in their shells, deep-frying foods, making pancakes or French toast, home canning, or baking airy cakes or breads, such as chiffon cakes or popovers.

A number of special techniques and recipes have been devised for cooking with microwaves. Consult one or more of the microwave cookbooks on the market.

How to use a microwave

Center the food in an oven-tempered glass or ceramic dish or in a plastic one designed for microwave use. Do not use a metal container or one with metal trim. Metal can cause an electric arc that may damage the oven. Place the dish in the center of the oven so that the food will cook evenly on all sides. For juicy meat, use a drip pan made of a safe material or a rack made for microwave ovens.

Meats can be cooked uncovered, but most vegetables and combination dishes should be covered with a lid or plastic film so that they won't dry out; leave a corner of the film turned back to let hot gases escape. Periodically turn roasts, stir dishes toward the center to distribute heat, and rotate dishes that cannot be stirred. When cooking or reheating unevenly shaped foods, arrange the thicker or denser parts around the outside of the dish, and the thinner or more tender parts in the center.

A microwave oven begins cooking the moment you start it, so don't wait for a warm-up; time the cooking from that point, using the manufacturer's manual as a guide. Most microwaves have automatic timers that turn the unit off after the period you have set. Some adjust cooking time to food weight, and some have probes that can be inserted in roasts and casseroles to stop the cooking when the desired internal temperature has been reached. Foods continue cooking after they are removed; their internal temperatures can increase as much as 10°F to 15°F.

Taking care of your oven

To keep your oven safe, do not allow food residues to build up, particularly around the door. Check the door gasket regularly to make sure that the seal is tight so that no stray radiation can escape. For instructions in cleaning your microwave, see *Oven cleaning.*

Mildew

How to avoid and remove this common fungus

A dull black mold with a musty odor, mildew thrives in hot, humid places. It often attacks shoes, fabrics, books, luggage, wallpaper, basement walls, and shower curtains.

Avoiding mildew

Eliminating dampness is the key to preventing mildew (see *Humidity control*). Improve ventilation by opening doors, windows, closets, and dresser drawers on muggy days. Trim shrubs and trees that brush against or shade your house.

Absorb excess moisture in closets and drawers with small cloth bags containing silica gel or activated alumina (available at drug and hardware stores) or cornstarch, cornmeal, baking soda, or talcum powder. Leave closet lights on. To protect books, put a container of baking soda nearby.

Install exhaust fans in damp places such as laundry rooms and bathrooms. The basement is often the dampest area in a house. An electric dehumidifier may cure damp air, but if you have leaking or severely sweating walls, you'll need to waterproof (see *Basement waterproofing*).

Removing mildew

To tackle persistent mildew on ceramic tile or concrete, scrub with a mixture of 1 cup chlorine bleach to 1 gallon water; rinse and allow to dry. Scrub painted surfaces with 1 cup ammonia, ½ cup vinegar, and ¼ cup baking soda per gallon of water. Ventilate the area and wear rubber gloves when using either solution.

Spread the pages of mildewed books fanwise to dry. Or sprinkle pages with cornstarch or talcum powder to absorb moisture. Wipe off loose mold with a clean, soft cloth.

Brush or vacuum upholstered furniture and mattresses and air out mattresses and cushions in bright sunlight. For severe mildew, brush the material with a whisk broom; then sponge with a mixture of equal parts of rubbing alcohol and water and follow with a fungicidal spray. A persistent moldy odor indicates deep penetration and may require professional fumigation.

Mirrors

Hanging, cleaning, and restoring them

A simple, secure way to mount an unbacked, unframed mirror on a wall or door is with J-shaped mirror clips on the bottom and Z-shaped clips along the top and sides. The number and size of clips needed depend upon the size and weight of the mirror. Ask the advice of a glass dealer or a hardware dealer that carries the clips.

First draw a level guideline on which to position the base clips (see *Leveling*). Secure 2 or 3 J-clips along the pencil line, using hollow-wall fasteners, toggles, or wall anchors if necessary (see *Wall fasteners*). These clips will support most of the mirror's weight, so be sure they are securely

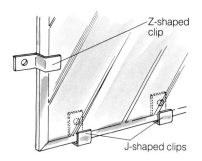

Z-shaped clip

J-shaped clips

anchored. If the clips are unpadded, add thin adhesive-backed felt to prevent the mirror's being scratched. With a helper, gently lower the mirror into position. While your helper holds the mirror, install Z-clips at regular intervals around the sides and top so that the mirror hugs the wall.

As an alternative, have the glass dealer drill holes through the corners of the mirror. Mount the mirror with long screws sunk in preset wall an-

M

chors; cover the screwheads with decorative rosettes.

Cleaning a mirror

Use liquid glass cleaner on a mirror's surface. If it is badly soiled, wipe with a warm solution of tea, water, and detergent, or use 2 tablespoons of vinegar, ammonia, or denatured alcohol in 1 quart of water. Do not allow any cleaner to touch the rear of the mirror; it can discolor the reflective backing. To discourage fogging, trail a soapy finger a few times across the mirror, then shine with a cloth.

To disguise a worn spot in the reflective backing, tape a piece of tinfoil to the back. Don't remove it later; the backing may come with it.

Miter joints

Making attractive corner joints in wood

A miter joint is a corner joint formed by cutting two pieces at 45-degree angles so that when joined, they make a right angle. Miter joints are commonly used for picture frames, door frames, and cabinets where you don't want end grain to show.

Miter joints are best cut in a miter box, either an inexpensive one made of hardwood with 45-degree slots or a metal one that gives greater precision and can be set at other angles. Use a crosscut saw with 8 to 12 teeth per inch for rough work, a backsaw with 13 or more teeth for finer cuts.

Mark the cut line on the wood with a combination square. Brace the miter box with its lip against a bench edge,

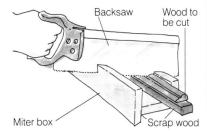

Backsaw / Wood to be cut / Miter box / Scrap wood

place a piece of scrap wood in the box, and put the piece to be cut on top of the scrap, right side up. Hold the piece against the far side; align the mark with the 45-degree slot so as to cut just on the waste side of the line.

Make gentle pulling cuts at the far edge; when the cut is established, saw with smooth, pushing strokes. On a wide piece, make a second pulling cut at the near edge; then alternate between the cuts, making the final strokes in the center.

Cut the adjoining piece with a 45-degree cut slanting the other way. Check the joint for squareness. Glue the cut ends and clamp them in a spe-

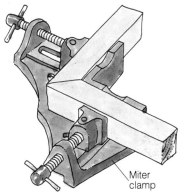

Miter clamp

cial miter clamp. To strengthen the joint, drive finishing nails into the glued pieces from each side; in hardwood, drill pilot holes first.

Mites

Protecting people, pets, and houseplants

Mites infest houseplants, pets, and sometimes human beings. Invisible to the naked eye, they are often detected only after they've caused damage.

When mites attack human beings, they cause itching and redness. In furred animals, mites cause mange and runny, itchy ears. Any infestation should be treated immediately by a physician or a veterinarian.

In houseplants

To detect spider mites on plants, hold a sheet of white paper under a discolored leaf and tap the leaf gently. If mites are present, you will see tiny moving specks on the paper. Signs of infestation in plants vary with different kinds of mites. Cyclamen mites may cause leaves to twist or curl and can produce deformities in buds and flowers; cut off the damaged parts and submerge the entire plant in 110°F water for 15 minutes.

False spider mites cause brownish spots on leaf veins; spray with dicofol three times, 10 days apart. Spider mites spin webs on a plant and cause light, yellowish spots on the leaves; spray vigorously with water to clean leaves or dip plant in insecticidal soap (see *Pesticides*).

Mobiles

Make a moving sculpture

A mobile is a delicately balanced assemblage of lightweight objects suspended by strings. The slightest movement of air will set a mobile in motion.

To make a simple mobile, tie or glue various shapes (circles, squares, animal forms, flowers) to a central string. Cut the shapes from construction paper or mediumweight cardboard. To add texture and interest, incorporate balsa wood, colored glass, or natural objects such as shells and nuts.

More complex and interesting mobiles can be created by incorporating one or more horizontal arms into the

M

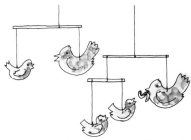

structure. The arms should be rigid, yet lightweight. Slender wooden dowels or 14- to 20-gauge galvanized steel wires make good arms.

Use string or nylon fishing line to hang an object or shape from each end of an arm. Hold the arm between your thumb and forefinger to determine the balance point, knot a string there, and lift the mobile by the string to make sure it hangs level.

Create other arms by the same procedure and add them to the structure. Work from the bottom up, checking the balance of the assemblage whenever a new arm is added. For visual interest, vary the size of the shapes and the lengths of the threads. Display the finished mobile in an open area where it can move freely.

Moldings

Where and how to use them

Molding has been called "the carpenter's friend" because it hides construction seams, minor faults, and any gaps caused by settling and hu-

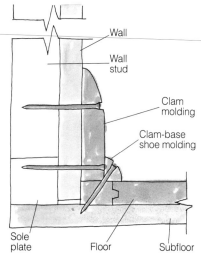

Wall

Wall stud

Clam molding

Clam-base shoe molding

Sole plate

Floor

Subfloor

midity changes. It also serves esthetic purposes, blending adjoining surfaces harmoniously and creating a feeling of spaciousness.

For a simple baseboard, choose a *clam molding,* secured as shown. Hide the seam where the baseboard meets the floor with a strip of quarter-round or *clam-base shoe molding.* Secure it with finishing nails driven at an angle into the subfloor.

On paneled walls, or when you wish to accentuate a ceiling, install *crown molding* where the wall and ceiling meet. To make a narrow room or hallway seem wider, install a strip of *chair-rail molding* (or two closely placed, parallel strips) all around the room about 2 feet above the floor.

Installing molding in a room

Mount the first piece of molding opposite the main entrance so that later pieces will be on the side walls, where any irregularities in the joints will be less obvious.

To fit molding to an outside corner, miter the ends of each piece (see *Miter joints*). An inside corner can be mitered too, but unless the room is perfectly square, there will be a gap. To make a perfectly matched joint, use

the woodworking technique known as *coping.* Saw the end of one length of molding at a right angle, and install it butted against the corner. Miter the end of the mating piece. Then, with a

Coping molding

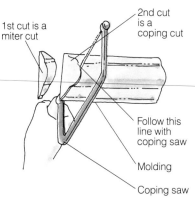

1st cut is a miter cut

2nd cut is a coping cut

Follow this line with coping saw

Molding

Coping saw

coping saw, follow the contours of the molding's front face, slanting the cut slightly inward. It should fit snugly against the first piece.

Molds for foods

Shaping desserts and rice

Use molds to shape gelatin, ice cream, rice, cakes, or puddings. Prepare a mold for gelatin by rinsing the mold with cold water or by oiling it lightly. Oil, however, will leave a film on the surface of the gelatin. A cake, rice, or pudding mold should be buttered or greased before it is used.

To make a layered dessert, fill half of the mold with gelatin or pudding and chill until firm. Then pour in a slightly cooled mixture of a compatible flavor and chill it.

To unmold a gelatin dessert, run a knife around the edge, dip the mold in warm water, put a plate over the mold, and reverse the mold. To loosen hard-frozen ice cream or delicate gelatins, wrap a warm, damp towel around the mold before reversing it.

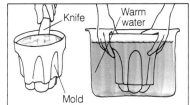

Knife

Warm water

Mold

Monograms

Personalizing clothing and accessories

Before embroidering a monogram, you'll need to draw the letters on the fabric. Stylized letters are available as iron-on transfers, or you can copy letters from a magazine or book. For the iron-on transfers, follow package directions. Enlarge other letters on paper (see *Pattern transfer*), then transfer them to the fabric with dressmaker's carbon and a tracing wheel.

To hand embroider a monogram, stretch the work right side up over the smaller ring of an embroidery hoop; then clamp on the outer ring. Using six-strand floss and a crewel needle, fill in the letters with straight or slightly slanted satin stitches.

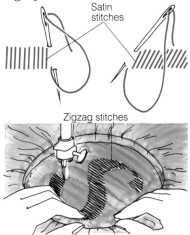

Satin stitches

Zigzag stitches

To machine embroider, use closely spaced zigzag stitches and free-motion sewing. Remove the presser foot and lower the feed dog or cover it. Clamp the work right side down over the smaller ring of a hoop and position the work right side up under the needle. Lower the presser bar and bring the bobbin thread up through the fabric. Holding both upper and lower threads to the left of the needle, take a few stitches to secure them. Clip off threads close to the stitching. Stitch slowly, guiding the hoop and following the outlines.

Before monogramming a stretchy fabric, reinforce it by basting a piece of lightweight cloth to its underside. After embroidering, trim the excess.

M

MORTGAGE PREPAYING

Mops and mopping

Day-to-day floor care

Dry mop often to pick up dust and grit. Wool or synthetic mop heads are best; their static cling attracts dust. Oil-treated mops also trap dirt but can turn floor wax gummy; use them only on wood floors with oil finishes.

Lifting the mop head scatters dust. Plot a course that lets you wipe the mop across the entire area, pulling dust along as you go. Then, shake the mop into a paper bag.

Wash a soiled mop head by hand in mild detergent; or tie it in a net bag and put it in the washing machine. When dry, store the mop head up.

Damp mopping

Most nonwood floors can be kept clean by damp mopping with clear water. First, sweep or vacuum to remove loose debris. Then dip a string or sponge mop into clear water, squeeze out the excess, and wipe a 3-foot-square section of the floor. Do not mop linoleum too often, and dry each section promptly; water eventually makes linoleum brittle.

To clean more thoroughly, mop with water and a cleaning solution recommended for your floor. Be sure to read the label when choosing a product; abrasives and alkaline cleansers can damage vinyl, asphalt tile, and other resilient flooring.

For a fast cleanup, use two mops and two buckets, one with cleaning solution and one with clear water. Wet a section of the floor with the solution, let it stand, then mop to remove dirt. Rinse with the clear water. Flood high-traffic areas with the cleaning solution. Don't flood seamed areas, however; seepage will dissolve floor adhesive.

When the job is finished, wash and rinse the mops well, let them dry, and store them head up.

Morse code

The international signals

You can use sound or a flashing light to send messages in Morse code. The dot is a very short sound or flash; a dash equals three dots. The pauses between sounds or flashes should equal one dot. Leave an interval the length of one dash between letters; two dashes between words.

```
A .-        J .---      S ...
B -...       K -.-       T -
C -.-.       L .-..      U ..-
D -..        M --        V ...-
E .          N -.        W .--
F ..-.       O ---       X -..-
G --.        P .--.      Y -.--
H ....       Q --.-      Z --..
I ..         R .-.
```

```
1 .----      7 --...
2 ..---      8 ---..
3 ...--      9 ----.
4 ....-      0 -----
5 .....      Period .-.-.-
6 -....      Comma --..--
```

Mortar mixing

Premixed or from scratch

Caution: Mortar is a caustic. Wear goggles, waterproof gloves, long pants, and a long-sleeved shirt. Promptly wash splatters off your skin. Rinse clothing when you finish working. If mortar gets in an eye, flush with clear water and call a doctor.

Mortar is composed of portland cement for bonding, hydrated lime for workability, and sand for strength and bulk. Mix only as much mortar as you can use in 1 hour; after that the mortar becomes unworkable.

For a small job, it is easiest to buy ready-mixed mortar, which comes in packages of 10 to 80 pounds. Mix it with water according to the directions on the package.

For larger jobs, such as building a brick barbecue, it is less expensive to buy masonry cement, which contains only the cement and the lime. Mix it with clean builder's sand in a ratio of 1 part masonry cement to 3 parts sand. You can also buy portland cement, hydrated lime, and sand separately; mix them in a ratio of 1:1:6. Masonry cement comes in a variety of colors; if you like, buy pigments for coloring any mortar.

Making the mix

To prepare mortar, measure out the materials by the pail or shovelful in a wheelbarrow or on a mixing board made of scrap plywood with planks nailed to its sides. For small batches, you can use any shallow container, even a garbage-can top.

Blend the dry materials thoroughly with a shovel, trowel, or hoe; then gradually add water, working the mix until it is plastic and smooth. Workable mortar should spread easily, cling to a vertical surface without smearing or dropping, and stay in place (not flow) while stones or bricks are being placed.

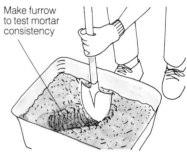
Make furrow to test mortar consistency

To test the mortar, make a furrow across it. If the furrow holds its shape, the mortar is the right consistency. If the sides of the furrow slump, the mortar is too wet; add more dry materials to stiffen it. If the mortar sticks tenaciously to the implement, the mix is too dry; add water.

Mortgage prepaying

Paying off the principal ahead of schedule

Read your mortgage to see if you can prepay without being charged a fee. If it has no prepayment penalty clause, you can prepay in one of two ways: by increasing your monthly payments or by paying one lump sum. If you decide to make larger monthly payments, tell your lender you are going to do so. Then write these words on each check: *Extra principal payment included.* Watch your statements; the bank may simply credit the extra money toward subsequent installments rather than reducing your principal. Before making a lump-sum payment, discuss it with your lender.

Why prepay?

During the first few years of a mortgage, most of your monthly payment goes toward interest. If you have a $65,000 mortgage at 13½ percent,

259

you may pay $200,000 in interest over a period of 30 years. Prepaying during the first 5 years can save much of that money.

Prepaying may not be to your advantage, however. If you have been paying the mortgage for 5 years or more, you may have already paid most of the interest. If you have a mortgage at a low, fixed rate, you might want to continue your monthly payments and put your extra money into a higher-interest savings account or in an investment. The bigger payments may leave you short of cash. Or you may need the tax deduction your mortgage interest payments allow.

Before making a decision, study your mortgage agreement and examine your financial situation carefully. (See also *Mortgages*.)

Mortgages

Types available; how to apply

A mortgage is a loan to finance a real estate purchase, using the property itself as collateral. You generally must pay part of the purchase price down; the rest becomes the *principal* of the mortgage. You may also have to pay the lender a certain number of *points*, each point being 1 percent of the principal. The principal is usually paid off in monthly installments that include *interest*. Your down payment, plus the amount of principal you have paid, is your *equity* in the property.

During a mortgage's early years, most of your payment goes toward interest; you gain little equity unless you can prepay all or part of the principal (see *Mortgage prepaying*).

The federal government, private mortgage insurance companies, and the Veterans Administration all insure mortgages and may make it possible for you to qualify for several different types. Before you make a decision on any mortgage, find out what you are eligible for and what terms various banks, savings and loan associations, and mortgage insurance companies will offer.

Types of mortgages

In a *conventional*, or *fixed-rate* mortgage, you promise to pay a set rate of interest over a number of years (usually 25 or 30). Most older mortgages are of this type, often at a substantially higher interest rate than a new mortgage. If you are buying a house or condominium, it is seldom to your advantage to take over the balance of such a high-interest mortgage. Read the original mortgage contract to see if such a takeover is permitted.

When inflation is high, interest rates rise and conventional mortgages become costly and difficult to obtain. At such times, you may want to take out an *adjustable-rate* mortgage, often called ARM. Under its terms the bank adjusts the interest rate periodically to bring it into line with current market rates. The mortgage contract spells out the time interval between adjustments—generally 6 months to 5 years—and the maximum change in interest rate, either up or down, at each adjustment.

Banks need not increase your rate, but *must* lower it when the standard dips. Federal law requires that an adjustable-rate mortgage contain a *cap* on how high any single increase can be and on the total increase over the term of the mortgage.

In order to make adjustable-rate mortgages attractive, a bank may offer an artificially low rate for the first year of the mortgage period. If you take out an adjustable-rate mortgage, make sure you understand its terms; otherwise you may find your later payments drastically increased.

Another alternative is the *graduated-payment* mortgage. This allows you to begin with smaller monthly payments, with the rate rising annually for several years. After that, payments become fixed. If you know that your income will rise in the future, this type may make sense.

Second mortgages

A homeowner who needs to raise a substantial amount of money—to remodel the kitchen, say, or undertake major repairs—can often obtain it by taking out a *second* mortgage or a home equity loan. Because the second-mortgage lender does not have first claim on the property, second mortgages tend to have higher rates than primary mortgages, and must be approved by the primary lender.

Applying for a mortgage

When you submit a mortgage application, the bank will require a list of your assets and debts, a statement from your employer about your salary, information about the property, and an application fee. A few days after mailing the documents, check that the bank has everything it needs; ask how long it will be before you hear its decision.

If you haven't heard within a reasonable time from the specified date, contact the bank. If your application has been rejected, you may request the reasons and take steps to try to improve your credit record. If you feel you have been treated unfairly, contact your lawyer. (See also *House buying; House selling*.)

Mosaics

Creating pictures from fragments

Mosaics are usually made from bits of colored glass or ceramic tile, but almost any material—plastic or shells, for example—can be used. The pieces are glued to a wood or metal backing, and the spaces between them are filled with grout.

Draw your design full-size on a sheet of paper; the design is called a cartoon. Use tile nippers to cut your material into small fragments to fit the cartoon—the smaller the fragments, the greater the detail you can achieve. Using carbon paper, trace the cartoon onto the backing (the surface you want to cover with the mosaic). Then position the fragments on the original cartoon. Transfer the fragments to the backing one by one,

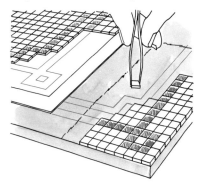

securing each with the appropriate adhesive (see *Ceramic tile; Gluing*). Use tweezers for very small pieces.

After all fragments are transferred and the glue is thoroughly dry, fill the spaces with grout. Use a commercial mosaic grout, or mix 1 part lime with 5 parts portland cement and add water until the mixture is smooth and creamy. If you want colored grout, add mortar dye to the dry ingredients. Apply the grout with a rubber spatula, forcing it into the spaces between fragments. Remove excess grout with a damp sponge. Let the mosaic dry overnight, then re-grout it and let it dry again. Vigorously brush the mosaic with a stiff, bristled scrub brush to smooth out the grout. Sponge the mosaic clean and apply liquid wax.

Mothproofing

Storing clothing safely

Before storing clothing made of wool or other animal fiber, launder or dry-clean it to destroy moth eggs that will hatch into small fur- and fiber-eating worms. Garments that are stored without cleaning often contain food or beverage spills or traces of perspiration, all of which attract moths.

A less effective method is to air garments in the sun, shake them vigorously, and brush them well on both sides, turning out pockets, seams, and linings. However, soft or napped fabrics may still harbor moth eggs.

Extreme temperature changes will destroy moth eggs. If you have a deep freezer, place garments in the freezer at -5° F for 4 to 5 days.

Prepare storage areas by cleaning and thoroughly vacuuming all cracks and crevices. Store cleaned clothes in sturdy cardboard boxes, plastic garment bags with zippered closings, or clean trash cans with tight lids. Put clothes on hangers into heavy plastic bags, and tape the bags closed or heat-seal them. Or wrap the garments in heavy brown kraft paper, and close all openings with strong tape.

Cedar chests and closets will keep out moths only if they have no gaps or open seams and if the cedar is at least ¾ inch thick. Periodically sand the ce-dar so that it continues to release the oils that repel the moths.

If you must use a chemical moth repellent, choose camphor over the more toxic naphthalene flakes. Use repellents as directed on the label.

Caution: Moth balls and flakes are poisonous. Do not scatter them where children or pets can get at them. Don't put mothballs in a bedroom closet or drawer; escaping vapors are harmful. Avoid paradichlorobenzene crystals: they are a suspected carcinogen.

Professional clothes storage

If you are short of storage space, you can store your clothing with a dry cleaner you know and trust. Ask for a signed receipt and a contract stating the full price of cleaning and storage. Keep a detailed list of all stored garments, including the condition they are in when they leave your home.

Motion sickness

Avoiding that queasy feeling

There is no cure for motion sickness once it strikes, but it can often be prevented. Dramamine and other over-the-counter drugs may help, but they also cause drowsiness. If you are prone to motion sickness, ask your doctor about scopolamine, a drug that must be applied in the form of a skin patch one hour before traveling. The patch is attached behind the ear. One application lasts for about 72 hours. Scopolamine should not be given to children, pregnant women, the elderly, or those who suffer from liver disease, kidney disease, gastro-intestinal obstructions, bladder problems, or glaucoma. Possible side effects are dry mouth, drowsiness, and blurred vision.

A surprisingly effective alternative to motion sickness drugs is powdered ginger, and it has no adverse side effects. Capsules are available from pharmacists and health food stores. Take two or three 500-milligram capsules ½ hour before you leave on a trip.

Preventive measures

If you suffer from motion sickness, don't travel on an empty stomach; have a light, bland, easily digestible meal before you leave. Avoid alcohol before and during a journey. Don't read in a car or bus; instead look at the horizon. Position yourself in the most stable areas of a vehicle: near the driver on a bus, forward on a plane or train, in the front seat of a car. Ventilation helps. Open a car window or turn on the air conditioner; stay on deck rather than in the cabin when you're on a boat; use the overhead vent in a plane, train, or bus.

If you feel the early symptoms—dizziness, quickened pulse and respiration, a general feeling of discomfort—lie flat with your eyes closed, breathe deeply, and let your body flow with the motion. (See also *Nausea*.)

Motorcycles

Riding safely; maintenance

Always wear a helmet when riding a motorcycle. If the helmet has no face shield, wear goggles too. Protect your body from abrasion in case of a spill by wearing a leather jacket, long pants, leather gloves, and boots. At night wear clothing with reflective strips.

Drive defensively; motorists often don't see a motorcycle until it is too late. Even if you have the right-of-way at an intersection, slow down and be prepared to stop or swerve. Never weave in and out of traffic, and never pass a vehicle on the right. Look well ahead so that you can avoid sand patches, potholes, obstructions, and animals. Even a small animal can cause an accident.

Check your rear-view mirrors often, especially when you stop at an intersection. If you see a car approaching rapidly, tap the brakes repeatedly to make the brake light flicker.

The front brake supplies most of a motorcyle's stopping power; keep two fingers wrapped around the brake lever and be prepared to use it. Keep your foot resting lightly on the pedal that controls the rear brake. Use the rear brake whenever you're stopping; it will help prevent you from tumbling forward, especially if you have to make a fast stop.

When entering or leaving a toll booth, brake gently or accelerate slowly. Leaking oil from cars accumulates there and can cause a skid. Oil and

M

water is even more slippery, so be extra careful when it's raining.

Preventive maintenance

Keep your motorcycle in good repair. Read the owner's manual and follow all recommendations. Be sure that the tires have sufficient tread and are properly inflated. Maintain proper tension on the drive chain (see your owner's manual) and check the engine-oil level whenever you refuel. If you have hydraulic brakes, keep track of the brake-fluid level in both of the master cylinders. Inspect the machine regularly for loose fasteners, leaks, and other irregularities.

Motorcycle safety courses are offered by the Motorcycle Safety Foundation and other organizations. Ask your motorcycle dealer for details.

Movie cameras

Caring for a super-8 camera

A cartridge-loaded home movie camera is easy to maintain. To keep dust and grit from damaging the film, whisk the camera's interior with a camel's hair brush; then blow any remaining particles away with an ear syringe (not your breath). Pay special attention to the film gate—the rectangular window between the lens and the film. Dirt and film emulsion collect in the guide channels in this area.

Remove hardened deposits with a round toothpick or an orangewood

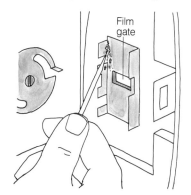

Film gate

stick. For a stubborn spot, wrap a clean, lint-free cloth around the stick and put a drop of lighter fluid or rubber-cement thinner on it. Don't scrape with a metal tool; it can create burrs that will scratch film.

Lens care

Cleaning the lens too often or incorrectly may scratch it or wear away its coating. To keep the lens clean, point it downward and blow out any dust with the ear syringe. Gently whisk off any remaining dust with a camel's hair brush that you use only for cleaning lenses. Keep a lens cap over the lens when you're not using the camera.

If the lens does become smudged, clean it immediately with lens tissue and a few drops of lens cleaning solution; use photographic, not eyeglass, tissue and cleaner. To prepare the tissue, roll it into a tube and tear the tube in half; hold the torn ends side by side and apply a little lens cleaner to those ends. Wipe the lens with a circular motion from the center out, keeping the pressure very light. Don't ap-

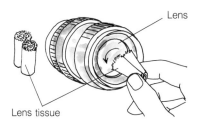

Lens

Lens tissue

ply cleaner directly to the lens; it can seep inside and ruin the optics. Use each lens tissue only once.

Care during use

Always take care when using a camera. At the beach, screw a clear or ultraviolet filter into the lens to protect it from spray and sand. On cold days, keep the camera under your coat except when shooting. Don't leave the camera in a hot or freezing car trunk or in direct summer sun. Before storing a movie camera, remove the batteries; otherwise they may leak.

Movie projectors

Cleaning and maintenance

To keep a projector running smoothly, examine the gate and the pressure plate before each use. One piece of grit on either can scar a film from end to end. Clear away dust with a camel's hair brush and an ear syringe and remove any film emulsion buildup with a round toothpick or an orangewood

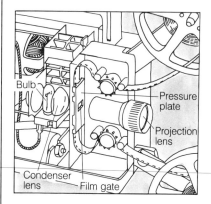

Bulb

Pressure plate

Projection lens

Condenser lens

Film gate

stick. Clean the projection lens only when necessary (see *Movie cameras*). If your owner's manual so directs, oil the projector, being careful not to get oil along the film path.

Clean the light bulb, the reflector, and the condenser lens with a soft cloth at least once a year. Check the bulb a few times a year and replace it if it develops a bulge. To increase the bulb's life, turn it off and let the fan run for 1 or 2 minutes after each use.

Let a bad bulb cool before taking it out. Leave the cover on the new one until you put it in; oil from your skin can damage it. If you do touch the new bulb, wipe it clean with a cloth moistened with rubbing alcohol.

If your projector won't operate, check that the wall receptacle is receiving power by plugging in a working lamp. Then check to see if the power cord has shorted (see *Power cords*); if it has, buy a manufacturer's replacement.

If the projector's motor goes on but the film fails to move or advances in jerky starts and stops, the drive belt may be broken or worn. To replace it,

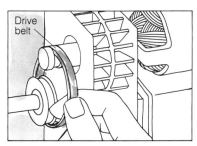

Drive belt

pull the old belt off the pulleys and clean the pulley surfaces with a cloth moistened in rubber-cement thinner or rubbing alcohol. Then slip on a new belt from the manufacturer.

M

Moving

Planning the move; packing

Before moving, measure the rooms in your new home to be sure that your appliances and furniture will fit into allotted spaces; and measure all doors to be sure that everything will go through them. Arrange with your plumber, utility company, or your appliance service company to disconnect major appliances such as washing machines and kitchen ranges. Movers will not do this, nor will they take down a television antenna.

Whether you rent a truck or hire a mover, get comparative prices beforehand. Always get written confirmation for every step of the move.

Moving yourself may save hundreds of dollars, but beware of such hidden costs as mileage rates, drop-off charges, overtime charges, and rental of dollies, pads, and packing cases. A truck rental agency should provide guidelines to help you take an inventory of your possessions and estimate the size vehicle you need. Find out the truck's capacity in cubic feet, not just length. The rental agency's literature should also tell you how to pack—do it carefully; when you move yourself, you pay for any damage.

Hiring a professional

If you are moving within your state, seek out a local mover with a good reputation. Their charges are generally lower than interstate movers. If your move crosses state lines, check the moving company's performance records through the Interstate Commerce Commission (it maintains offices in most major cities). Written estimates are not binding; ask the ICC how often the company's estimates are within 10 percent of their final charges. Send out change-of-address notices as soon as you have contracted with a mover. Arrange to disconnect utilities and to connect them in your new home. To avoid false billing, confirm these in writing. Change your bank and charge accounts.

Packing

Make a floor plan of your new home and label each room with a name and number. As you pack, label each box accordingly. Keep track of the number of boxes for each room. Mark items that you will need as soon as you arrive. Move these and important documents yourself. Take an inventory of each box. Clothing and linens can be packed in dresser drawers, but not too densely. Rent wardrobe boxes for hanging clothes; pack books and records in small boxes so that they are light enough to lift. To protect breakables, line the bottom of the box with wads of crumpled newspaper and wrap each piece in newspaper. Pack the heaviest items in the bottom and add crumpled paper between the layers. Don't stack plates; stand them on edge.

Wrap lampshades in clean paper and pack them in cartons separate from the lamps. Stand mirrors and pictures in cartons; protect them with layers of paper and separate them with corrugated cardboard.

Several days before moving, disconnect the electric power from major appliances and drain off any water. Clean each appliance inside and out and leave it open to air for a day or two. Then tape its doors and lids shut with a strong tape such as filament tape, and tape the power cord to the back of the appliance. Protect the appliance with blankets. Some appliances, such as washing machines, may require special buttressing to withstand the move; check with the mover or consult your owner's manual for each appliance.

When everything has been unloaded, make sure that all your possessions are in good condition before signing the mover's inventory. Do not allow yourself to be rushed. Make any claims for missing or damaged property in writing to the agent or moving company as soon as possible. Your local Interstate Commerce Commission office may be helpful in the event of an unsettled claim.

Mulching

Keeping soil moist and warm while smothering weeds

An organic mulch, such as leaf mold, well-rotted compost, dry grass clippings, shredded bark, or buckwheat hulls adds humus and nutrients to the soil; inorganic mulches, such as plastic and gravel, add nothing, but they last longer.

Apply an organic mulch after the soil has warmed up and your plants are tall enough not to be buried. Most mulches should be 2 to 5 inches thick; a 1- to 1½-inch layer of sawdust is enough, however, and five or six sheets of newspaper make good cover. Weed the garden, fertilize it, and if the soil is dry, give it a good soaking before putting on the mulch. Do not mulch right up to a plant stem or a tree trunk; leave a small space around it.

At the end of the growing season, dig the mulch into the soil or rake it off and add it to the compost pile. Add fresh mulch in late fall for winter protection for perennials or bulbs.

Lay black plastic mulch in early spring after preparing the soil for planting. It will quickly increase the

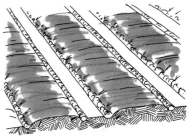

soil temperature by several degrees. If the soil is dry, soak it first. Work on a windless day, and anchor the edges of the plastic with soil or stones. Make slits for planting seeds and cut X's in the plastic for transplants; poke more small holes 6 to 12 inches apart so that rain can seep in. With care, black plastic can last as long as three seasons.

A new kind of mulching material is a fabriclike substance through which water and fertilizer can pass. It is expensive but needs no holes cut in it.

Muscle aches

Easing soreness, stiffness, and cramps

Any unaccustomed exertion can make muscles sore and stiff. Take aspirin or another analgesic to relieve the pain. Relax the muscles with a hot bath or shower, with a heating pad (preferably the moist-heat type), or with hot towels. Heat-producing rubs and lotions may help. Gently exercise stiff muscles to get them back to work. (See also *Massage.*)

A pulled muscle will be swollen as well as painful. Again, take aspirin or another analgesic for the pain; reduce swelling with an ice pack. Bind an arm or leg muscle lightly with an elastic bandage. Don't use a pulled muscle until it stops hurting. If the pain or swelling is intense, or if it lasts longer than 48 hours, see a doctor.

A sudden cramp or spasm may be caused by unusual exertion or the stress of an awkward position. To help the muscle relax, gently massage and stretch it; moist heat helps too. Stretch a cramped hand by pushing the fingers back. For a charley horse in the upper arm, pull the arm straight; if it's in the calf, straighten the leg and pull the foot upward.

Foot and calf muscles often cramp at night, especially if you sleep on your stomach with your feet pointed downward. Get up and walk to increase circulation. Face toward a wall and lean against it at arm's length so that your heels are raised off the floor; then press the heels down to the floor.

To prevent nighttime cramps, sleep in a different position, or raise the foot of your bed slightly. Relaxing with a glass of warm milk before bedtime will also help. For recurrent cramps, or for those that cause acute or long-lasting pain, see a doctor.

Musical chairs

A party game for children or adults

Any number can play. Supply a lightweight chair for each player *except one;* stand the chairs in two rows, back to back. To the accompaniment of a rollicking tune, have the players march around and around the rows of chairs. Stop the music suddenly, whereupon everyone must rush for a seat. The person left standing is *out* and must leave the circle, taking one chair away with him.

Repeat until only two players and one chair remain. The player who captures the last chair is the winner. Adults sometimes play a version of the game called *musical laps:* the men sit in the chairs and the women sit on their laps, or vice versa.

Nailing

Which nails to use; basic techniques

Common nails are best for most carpentry because their broad heads won't pull through the wood. For extra holding power, use *coated nails* or nails with *spiral shanks* or *annular rings.* For cabinetry and other fine work, use *finishing nails;* hammer them almost home; then use a nail set to sink the heads below the surface of the wood. Fill the holes with putty or wood filler. Buy nails specific to such jobs as roofing, flooring, and installing wallboard.

When joining two pieces of different thicknesses, drive nails through the thin one into the thick one. Use nails three times as long as the thickness of

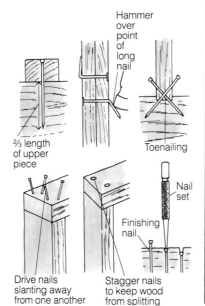

Hammer over point of long nail

⅔ length of upper piece

Toenailing

Nail set

Finishing nail

Drive nails slanting away from one another

Stagger nails to keep wood from splitting

the upper piece so that two-thirds of their lengths will be securely anchored. For more security, drive the nails at angles, slanting toward or away from one another. For maximum strength, drive a long nail through both pieces, and hammer the point over.

To prevent the wood from splitting, stagger nails rather than placing them along the same grain line. In hardwood, drill pilot holes slightly smaller than the nails. Before driving a nail near the end of a piece, blunt the nail's point with a hammer so that the point will shear through the wood instead of wedging it apart.

Use an ordinary 13- or 16-ounce claw hammer for most nailing jobs. Hold a nail between your thumb and forefinger and tap the nail until it stands alone; then strike the head of the nail squarely with increasingly heavy blows. To remove a nail, cushion the hammer's head with scrap wood and use the claw as a lever.

Nasal congestion

Relieving a stuffed-up nose

The common cold is the usual cause of nasal congestion, a condition characterized by swollen and irritated nasal passages and constant production of thick mucus. If the cold is associated with fever, pain along the sinuses, and a yellow-green discharge; see your doctor.

There is no quick cure for a stuffed-up nose—any more than there is for a cold—but there are a number of things you can do to ease the discomfort. Blowing your nose is obvious. Press one nostril closed, and firmly but gently blow through the other one to clear it. Don't blow too hard; you can damage your eardrum.

One of the most effective ways to ease congestion is to breathe moist air. Humidify the air with either a cold-steam vaporizer, which sprays out tiny droplets of water, or an old-style hot-steam vaporizer. Place a hot-steam vaporizer in a stable position where no one will trip over it or touch it; it could cause a burn. Another way to loosen mucus is to fill a sink or basin with hot water, drape a towel over your head, and inhale the vapors.

Using a nasal syringe, you can clear the nasal passages of a child. Hold the child on your lap with his head back, and put a few drops of warm, salty water in one of his nostrils with a dropper. Wait a few minutes for the mucus to soften, suck it out with the syringe, then do the other nostril the same way.

Nasal decongestants work by drying and shrinking mucus-producing tissues. Go easy on their use; they may damage nasal tissue if used too often for too long a period of time. In addition, there may be a rebound effect resulting in the production of more mucus rather than less. As a rule of thumb, limit usage to 3 days. And don't use decongestants at all for young children without first consulting a physician. (See also *Colds*.)

Nature photography

Getting intimate portraits of flowers and wildlife

With a good 35mm single-lens reflex camera (see *Cameras*) and the proper lenses, you can take close-ups of flowers and wildlife. Each requires different techniques and accessories.

Taking close-ups
Use either a close-up lens that screws onto the front of your regular lens or an extension tube that fits between the regular lens and the camera's body. The latter should be automatic so that your camera functions normally. If you have a zoom lens, it may have a "macro" mode that will let you shoot at close range.

Use a tripod for close-ups. It will steady the camera and allow you to compose the picture better. Focus carefully to get the most important parts of your subject sharp; a lens has a very shallow depth of field at close range. To increase the sharpness of the picture, use a small aperture (f/11 to f/22); if there is sufficient light, use slow-speed film (ISO 25 to 125).

Movement is exaggerated in a close-up. To avoid a blurred image, try to work on a calm day. If it's breezy, tie a flower to a stake to steady it or erect a wind shield with stakes and fabric.

Pay special attention to the light. Backlighting will give a translucent effect to leaves and flower petals; sidelighting will sharply define textures. Hold up a white cloth on a frame cut from cardboard to soften harsh sunlight; position a white card to reflect light into shadowed areas.

Photographing animals
Most wild creatures are timid. Move quietly and slowly to avoid frightening them. Wear muted colors, and cover the shiny surfaces of your equipment with dull tape.

Seek out locations where animals feed or water. Or put out food to attract birds and small mammals. Find natural cover with a good view or hide from view in your car or tent. Often, like a hunter, you must stay quietly in one place for hours, or return day after day, until your "prey" gets accustomed to your presence.

To pull in subjects from a distance, you need a 200 to 400mm telephoto lens. A telephoto lens can be tricky to work with; it exaggerates camera movement and has a limited depth of field. Steady the lens on a tripod. Focus carefully. Anticipate your subject's actions, focus on a spot it will move into, and take the picture when it gets there. Use high-speed film (ISO 400 to 1000) and fast shutter speeds ($\frac{1}{250}$ second or more).

Nausea

Relieving the symptoms

Nausea—that sick, queasy feeling that usually precedes vomiting—can be a symptom of many disorders, among them viral infection, reaction to antibiotics or other drugs, motion sickness, morning sickness during pregnancy, a skull injury, and such serious illness as appendicitis, ulcers, food poisoning, and diseases of the heart and gall bladder.

The most common cause of nausea is overindulgence in alcohol or food. The best treatment is to eat little or nothing for 12 hours or so; then, for another day or two, restrict your diet to simple, bland foods that you know agree with you. Ginger ale, tea, and clear broth can ease symptoms of

nausea. If you feel an attack of nausea coming on, take several deep, regular breaths. An over-the-counter antacid can ease the heartburn that often accompanies nausea, but avoid aspirin. (See also *Motion sickness; Vomiting*.)

Necktie tying

Tying a four-in-hand knot

A four-in-hand knot is rather small and tubular shaped. Here's how to tie it. 1. Place the tie around your neck with the wider end on the right and about 2 inches longer than the narrower end. 2. Bring the wider end over and around the narrow end 1½ times so that it is pointing to the left. 3. Take the wide end up behind the knot, bringing it back out at the throat.

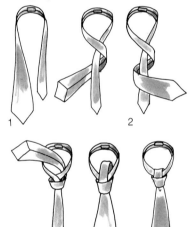

4. Tuck it through the lower crosswise piece in front and pull to tighten. 5. The wide end should cover, and be a bit longer than, the narrow end.

Needlepoint

How to form basic stitches

Needlepoint stitches are formed on a gridlike, open-weave canvas that has precisely spaced holes between the threads. The basic types of canvas are single mesh (mono) and double mesh (penelope); the latter can be worked with stitches of different sizes. Needlepoint stitches are formed either

N

parallel to the lengthwise or crosswise threads or diagonally across their intersections. Some stitches span only one mesh; others span two or more. Stitch size depends on the gauge (meshes per inch) of the canvas.

To secure the yarn end at the beginning of your work, leave 1 inch of yarn at the back of the canvas and work the first stitches over it. When ending a yarn, weave it through the back of the last few stitches and cut it short.

The needlepoint stitch used most often is the *tent stitch*. It passes over just one mesh and can be done in three ways: as the half-cross, the continental, or the basket weave.

Make the *half-cross stitch* on double-mesh canvas, working each row from left to right. At the end of a row, turn the canvas completely around; form the new row next to the first. Work the *continental stitch* from right to

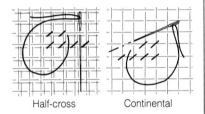

Half-cross   Continental

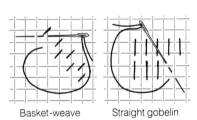

Basket-weave   Straight gobelin

left, turning the canvas with each new row. Begin the *basket weave stitch* near the upper right; work in rows alternately down, then up, the canvas.

A basic straight-stitch is the *Gobelin*. It's worked alternately from right to left and left to right. The yarn can pass over from two to five crosswise threads (two are shown).

Net worth

Finding out how much money you are worth

To determine your net worth, first list all your assets at their current value.

Include checking and savings accounts, credit unions, time deposits, the cash value of your life insurance, the current value of savings bonds, how much you could withdraw from employee profit-sharing plans and retirement programs, and the current cash value of stocks, mutual fund shares, bonds, or other securities. Add in any accrued interest when listing the values of these assets.

Also list the market value of your home and any other real estate you own. Include the value of your car, household goods, jewelry, art works, antiques, and anything else you could convert into cash; evaluate items at the price for which you could sell them, not at their current retail price. Include any money you are owed and can reasonably expect to collect.

Liabilities

Now list your liabilities: the current amounts of outstanding loans, such as mortgage and car loans; how much you owe on credit cards, bank cards, and other installment debts; how much you owe in nonwithheld income and real estate taxes; your college tuition commitments for your children; and all other outstanding debts and financial commitments.

Total the two columns and subtract your liabilities from your assets. The result is your net worth.

Noisy pipes

How to stop banging or rattling

"Water hammer" occurs when water flow is abruptly cut off by a valve, causing the pipes to vibrate and bang. To prevent it, install shock-absorbing air chambers atop the pipes that lead to your fixtures. An air chamber can be a capped length of pipe, a coil of tubing, or a sealed chamber containing a flexible diaphragm. The first two may eventually fill with water, and hammering will resume. In that case, drain the plumbing system (see *Closing a house*) to readmit air to the chamber.

Another type of pipe noise can result from a loose pipe banging on a wall stud or a basement beam when water is turned on or off. Secure the pipe with a U-shaped strap cushioned

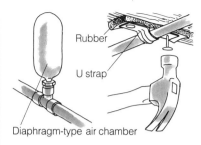

Rubber

U strap

Diaphragm-type air chamber

with a piece of rubber—not too tight on a hot water pipe, which must expand and contract.

Water hammer is common with washers and dishwashers that have automatic valves that turn water on and off quickly. To end it, have an air chamber installed between the valve and the pipes. Sometimes a loose washer causes rattling. Turn off the water supply, remove the faucet housing, and tighten or replace the washer (see *Faucets*).

North Star

How to find it

When you're lost at night, find the North Star, a "fixed" pivotal star around which all others seem to turn. It's over the North Pole. First locate the Big Dipper; four stars make up its bowl and three its handle. Envision a line between the two pointer stars on the outside of the bowl, and extend it five times its own length. You will

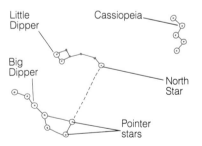

Little Dipper   Cassiopeia

Big Dipper   North Star

Pointer stars

come to the North Star, or Polaris, never more than 1 degree from true north. It is the end of the Little Dipper's handle.

Below a latitude of 40 degrees north (approximately that of Philadelphia or Denver) the Big Dipper slips below the horizon at times. In that case, use the W of the tightly clustered Cassiopeia to locate the North Star.

N

Nosebleeds

Treating minor ones

Although it is shocking to see blood running down someone's face, a nosebleed is seldom serious. The tiny capillaries in the nose are delicate and can be ruptured by blowing the nose too hard. Usually a nosebleed starts when the nasal membranes are irritated by a cold or by chilly or dry air.

Pressure alone will usually stop a nosebleed long enough for a clot to form. Use your thumb to press closed the soft part of the bleeding nostril for 5 to 10 minutes. Breathe through your mouth during this period. For a child, gently pinch both nostrils shut.

If the bleeding continues, hold an ice bag or a cold compress on the bridge of the nose while applying pressure for another 10 minutes. If the bleeding still won't stop, see a doctor.

When the bleeding stops, don't blow your nose for 3 or 4 hours, and don't remove the crusted blood; otherwise the bleeding may resume.

Caution: Do not try to stop a nosebleed that follows a head injury; the bleeding may be relieving pressure on the brain. Get medical help immediately (see *Head and spine injuries*).

Recurrent, spontaneous nosebleeds that are not associated with colds or dry air may be symptomatic of a serious ailment. See a doctor at once.

Obedience training

Teaching your dog commands

In training a dog, praise is your main tool. When your dog obeys say, "*Good* dog," and pet it gently. Praise quietly; exuberant petting will make the dog want to play. Never strike a dog for not obeying a command; that will make it fear you and dread the training sessions. Just say, "No," in a firm, low voice and then show the dog what you want it to do by repeating the exercise. Begin with 10-minute sessions; later extend them to 20 minutes.

Keep the dog to your left. Use a 6-foot nylon or leather lead and a chain

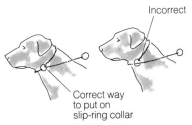

Incorrect

Correct way to put on slip-ring collar

or nylon slip-ring collar. Hold the end of the lead in your right hand and the middle of the lead with your left; let your left hand hang by your side.

To teach a dog to sit, press down on the dog's rump and pull up on the lead while saying, "Sit." Praise the dog immediately when it sits. Always give the command for an action in the same word and tone of voice.

To teach your dog to heel (to walk next to your left leg with its nose slightly in front of your knee), stand with the dog sitting beside your left leg and say, "Spot, heel," in a firm voice. Step forward, left foot first, and walk briskly. If the dog lags behind or forges

Walk with lead loose

ahead, jerk the lead sharply and say, "Heel!" If your dog continues to forge ahead, begin circling; turn sharply and make figure eights. This will keep the dog at heel until it learns from your praise where you want it to walk.

Next teach the dog to stay. Have it sit beside your left leg. Say, "Stay," and bring your left hand, palm facing the dog, from about a foot in front of the dog to within an inch of its nose.

Holding the leash loosely, step away on your right foot; then turn to face the dog. If it follows you, return to the original position and repeat the procedure. When the dog stays for a minute or so, walk back and praise it.

The come command is an extension of the sit exercise: walk away from the sitting dog, turn and face it, then say, "Spot, come!" and tug on the leash. Praise the dog when it runs to you. Gradually increase your distance from the dog; finally, when the dog's response is prompt, practice with the dog off its lead.

Obedience training classes are held in many localities. Consult the Yellow Pages or inquire of your veterinarian.

Obscene telephone calls

How to deal with them

If you answer the phone and the caller says nothing, breathes heavily, or makes obscene, harassing, or threatening remarks, say nothing. Hang up quickly and quietly. Any expression of anger, fear, or disgust—even slamming down the phone—may encourage him to call again.

Instruct your children to do the same. Tell them never to say that their parents aren't at home but instead to say, "My mother can't come to the phone right now. Can she call you back?" No one should give a name, address, or any other information to an unknown caller. Tell no one outside the household about such calls; they may come from someone you know, and word of your annoyance may bring more calls.

If the calls continue, inform your telephone company's service representative; or check the front of your directory for a special number to call. The phone company can work with the police to help solve the problem.

Odors

Keeping your home smelling fresh

Baking soda, vinegar, and lemon juice will help rid your home of most unpleasant odors. The best way to keep a house smelling fresh, however, is to keep it clean. Air rooms, closets, and drawers regularly. Use disinfectants such as chlorine bleach to prevent mildew and garbage smell. If smoke is a problem, see *Cigarette odors*.

In the kitchen, open a window after cooking; wipe up spills promptly. To get rid of strong cooking odors, place a pan of white vinegar on the stove and let it simmer. Remove fish, garlic, and onion odors by washing utensils, pans, cutting boards, and even your hands in lemon juice. Use a solution of baking soda and water to freshen a thermos and to deodorize inside the refrigerator and the garbage compactor. Grind lemon or orange peel in the garbage disposal to clear it of odors.

Bathroom odors

To rid a bathroom of odors, light a match, candle, or bit of string and let it burn for a few seconds. Then put it out and leave it in a dish in the bathroom for 5 minutes or so. (See also *Animal odors; Drain odors; Mildew; Skunk odor*.)

Superdeodorizers

If strong odors persist, use a concentrated deodorizer that destroys smells instead of covering them up. These deodorizers—available in hardware stores, pet stores, and many variety stores—come in tiny bottles and are used a drop at a time. Use them sparingly; if you can smell the deodorant, you have used too much.

Caution: Do not use superdeodorants on pets. Keep them away from your eyes and mouth and out of children's reach. Follow manufacturer's directions carefully.

Office plants

Adding a touch of green

The office environment can be hard on plants. The air tends to be warmer, drier, and draftier than in most houses. Lighting is often uneven, with sun-drenched windows and dim, fluorescent-lit interiors. Heat and air conditioners are turned off on weekends so that in winter, 5 warm days are followed by 2 cold ones; in summer it is the reverse.

If you choose plants carefully, however, they will survive to brighten and soften your workplace. Unless you have a sunny window, forget flowering plants; many foliage plants do well, though, under fluorescent lights. In general, avoid plants that need moist air or dislike warmth. For a cool spot, choose a spider plant. For a moderately warm area, try a snake plant, grape ivy, wandering Jew, dracaena, dieffenbachia, parlor palm, or spathiphyllum. For warmer spots use a ponytail plant, heart-leaf philodendron, or Chinese evergreen.

For watering and feeding requirements, see *Fertilizing houseplants; Houseplants*. If you have a number of plants, you can simplify their watering by sinking their pots in a planter full of moist peat moss. Avoid placing plants directly under air conditioning or heating outlets.

Oil burners

Regular maintenance; emergency measures

An oil burner should be checked, cleaned, and adjusted by a professional serviceman before each heating season. Consider taking out a yearly service contract. Some companies offer lower rates for service at the end of the heating season.

You can do several things to keep your burner operating efficiently. If the motor has oil cups (some have sealed bearings that require no added lubrication), put a few drops of high-grade machine oil in each one every 2 or 3 months during the heating season. Using a crevice attachment, periodically vacuum the openings that admit air to the burner's blower.

When the burner is on, the draft regulator on the pipe leading to the chimney should automatically tip open 1 or 2 inches to admit air; if it

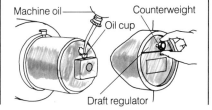

Machine oil / Oil cup / Counterweight / Draft regulator

doesn't, adjust the small counterweight on the circular metal flap.

If your burner has an observation window, look at the flame in the combustion chamber; it should be bright yellow, tipped with orange, and should produce no smoke. If the flame is dark orange or seems sooty, or if you can see black smoke coming from the chimney outside, have your serviceman adjust the burner.

Malfunctions

If your oil burner fails to start, try the following before calling for service: 1. Check the emergency switch. There may be two of these, one on the burner and another on a nearby wall or at the head of the stairs. 2. Check your house electrical panel for a blown fuse or tripped circuit breaker. If a fuse blows or a breaker goes off right after you replace or reset it, call for service. 3. Check your oil supply. Don't trust the gauge; open the filler pipe and measure the level with a long stick. 4. Check the thermostat. If it has a *DAY/NIGHT* switch, make sure it is set correctly; pass a piece of stiff paper or a crisp dollar bill between the contact points to clean them. 5. Push the reset button on the burner or flue. Push it only once, or you may fill the combustion chamber with oil. If the burner starts but immediately stops again, call for service. 6. If the burner motor has a restart button, push it to see if the burner starts.

If the burner sputters or goes on and off, there may be dirt in the oil filters, normally located in the pump housing at one end of the motor. Switch the burner off, unbolt the lid, and clean the filters in kerosene. (See also *Boilers; Furnaces; Warm-air heating*.)

Oil changing

Servicing your own car

Change the oil and the oil filter as directed by your owner's manual—usually every 6 months or every 6,000 to 7,500 miles. If the car is often used to pull a trailer, for trips under 10 miles, or in heavy traffic, change the oil and filter twice as often. Diesels and turbocharged gasoline engines may need a change every 3,000 to 5,000 miles.

Draining the old oil

Hot oil flows better; drain the old oil while the engine is warm. Remove the oil-filler cap and raise the front end of the car (see *Jacking a car*). Place a 1½-gallon plastic catch pan under the drain plug. The plug resembles a large bolt in the oil pan, the metal cover on the bottom of the engine. Loosen the plug with a wrench; then unscrew

it by hand, pulling it away quickly so that oil won't splash you.

An air-cooled VW engine has no oil pan. Instead there is a circular cover plate held by six screws. Remove it to drain the oil and to clean the strainer.

When the oil stops draining, screw the plug back in by hand. You can reuse the washer on some cars, but must replace it at every oil change on others. Check your owner's manual. Don't force the plug; it may "cross-thread," damaging the threads. When it goes in smoothly, tighten it with a wrench. Then change the oil filter (see *Oil filters*) and lower the car.

Adding the new oil

To refill with fresh oil, first check your owner's manual for oil capacity and for the thickness (viscosity) recommendation; the latter may vary according to season. Refill a gasoline engine with an oil marked "For service SG." Also look for the American Petroleum Institute seal marked "certified for gasoline engines." An SG-CD oil is usually recommended for a diesel, but check your owner's manual.

Start the engine and check for leaks. Tighten the plug and filter if necessary. Stop the engine, wait 5 minutes, then check the oil level. Add more oil if needed.

Pour the used oil into a plastic jug and give it to a service station that has a used-oil holding tank for recycling.

Oil filters

Changing one on your car

Carmakers sometimes specify a new oil filter with every second oil change, but it is better to replace it with every oil change. Buy a name-brand filter with the right part number for your engine; check your owner's manual.

At the same time, get a suitable filter wrench. If the filter on your car is easy to reach, a simple strap wrench with a handle will do; if not, use a strap wrench that accepts a ratchet and extension. A wrench with a fabric strap fits all sizes of filters. If the strap is metal, make sure that it closes tightly around the new filter. If you choose a cap-type wrench that fits over the end of the filter, check the fit.

Removing the filter

After jacking the car and draining the oil (see *Oil changing*), move the catch pan underneath the filter. With a filter wrench, loosen the filter, turning

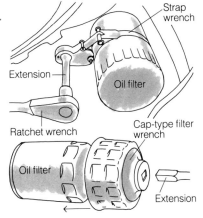

it counterclockwise. Then remove the wrench and unscrew the filter by hand. Dump the oil it contains into the catch pan.

If the filter sticks, drive a large screwdriver through it and use the shank as a lever. If the filter is so firmly stuck that the can portion of the filter

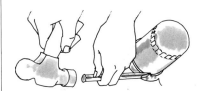

tears away, leaving the base in place, try to drive it off with a cold chisel.

Installing the new filter

Wipe dirt from the mounting stud and the engine's mating surface. Apply a coat of clean engine oil to the new filter's rubber gasket. Screw the filter onto the mounting stud until you feel the gasket contact the engine.

Put the strap wrench around the filter so that it closes with clockwise force. Then tighten the filter 180 degrees (one-half turn) with the wrench. Install fresh oil. If oil leaks from around the filter, tighten it an extra quarter turn.

Oil lamps

Using and caring for an oil or kerosene lamp

Caution: Keep an oil lamp well away from sparks, high heat, and flames.

If you live where power failures are frequent, it's wise to keep one or two oil lamps on hand. Fill a lamp only with kerosene or bottled lamp oil. Be sure to seal the fuel container and put it away before lighting the lamp.

Before lighting a new wick, let it become saturated all the way to the top. To light the lamp, remove the chimney and turn up the wick just far enough to be able to apply a match. Quickly put the chimney back on and turn down the wick until the flame is smokeless. The wick's tip will usually be well below the flame orifice's top

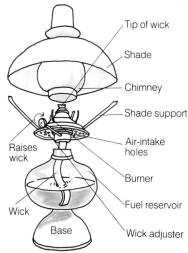

edge. If the flame stays smoky, clean out the burner's air-intake holes with a straightened-out paper clip. If it burns unevenly, trim the wick square with scissors. Always put out the flame and let the chimney cool before fixing the lamp. To extinguish the lamp, just blow into the top of the chimney; don't turn down the wick.

After each use, wash the chimney with soap and warm water. You can buy new wicks, chimneys, and burners at most hardware stores.

Oleanders

For a bright-flowered hedge or specimen planting

Oleanders are fast-growing shrubs with narrow evergreen leaves and large flower clusters of red, pink, yellow, cream, or white. Semitender (they survive brief exposure to temperatures of 18°F), they must have full sun and warmth to bloom profusely. They can stand drought, salt spray, and smog, and will grow up to 20 feet high in most well-drained soil.

Oleanders need little care other than pruning in late winter to eliminate weak branches. They can tolerate more severe pruning, and thus make good hedges; because flowers are borne on the current year's growth, none are lost by pruning. In cold areas, grow oleanders in tubs outdoors and bring them indoors for the winter. Keep them in a cool greenhouse or a cool, light, well-ventilated cellar, and give little or no water. Allow the soil to become nearly dry between waterings.

Caution: All parts of the plant, if eaten, are poisonous. Warn children against them.

Omelets

Basic and variations

For a fluffy omelet, start with the eggs at room temperature. The pan and the butter must be hot enough to cook the bottom layer of egg almost instantly. Because salt tends to toughen eggs, add it after cooking the omelet or let the filling do the seasoning.

For a two- or three-egg omelet, use a 5-inch skillet that flares to 7 inches at the top. For a larger omelet, use a pan that will allow the eggs to spread to no more than ¼ inch deep. Use a skillet with a smooth, unpitted surface so that the eggs will spread freely.

Mix two or three eggs and 1 tablespoon water in a bowl with a fork. Beat just enough to blend. In the pan, heat 1 tablespoon clarified butter (see *Clarifying butter*) until it is hot but not brown; swirl the pan to coat the sides. Pour in the eggs, moving the pan backward and forward to keep them sliding over the bottom. Stir the eggs with a fork in a circular motion from the edges to the center, keeping the fork parallel to, but not scraping, the bottom.

When the omelet has set, loosen the edges with the fork and shake the pan sharply to free the omelet from the bottom. Carefully fold one side of the

omelet over the other, using the fork, and slide it from the pan onto a warmed plate. Season and serve immediately.

For extra flavor, add herbs (see *Herbs in cooking*) or ½ to ¾ cup cooked ham or mushrooms, grated cheese, tomatoes, or sautéed garlic or onions—on top of the eggs before you begin to stir. Most ingredients should be warmed up so as not to cool the eggs.

Orchids

Growing them as houseplants

Most orchids require special care in a greenhouse, but more than a dozen types, including hundreds of varieties, thrive indoors if given adequate warmth, light, and humidity.

Orchids are classified according to their preferred nighttime temperatures: cool (50°F to 55°F), intermediate (55°F to 65°F), and warm (65°F to 70°F), with day temperatures 5°F to 15°F higher. Begin with easy-to-grow intermediates: *paphiopedilums, cattleyas,* and *phalaenopsises* (warm, but adaptable); grow *coelogynes* in cool, sunny rooms. Paphiopedilums are ground-growing orchids; the others are epiphytes—plants that grow perched on trees or other plants. Most epiphytic orchids have thick stems, called pseudobulbs, that rise from a horizontal rhizome.

Place orchids on a windowsill with bright, filtered light; keep them out of direct sunlight except in midwinter. Orchids require at least 10, but not more than 16, hours of light daily to flower. In winter you can supplement available sunlight by placing orchids at least 6 inches under fluorescent lights for 6 hours a day or more.

In general, water orchids moderately during the growth period, allowing the top inch of the potting mix to dry out before rewatering. For cattleyas, let the mix dry out almost completely between waterings; keep coelogynes thoroughly moist during the growth period. With every third or fourth watering, apply liquid plant food diluted to half the strength suggested on the label. Water lightly and stop feeding during the fall or winter rest period.

All orchids require high humidity. Stand pots on trays of wet pebbles; don't place them directly in water. Mist orchids two or more times a day in temperatures over 70°F.

Plant ground growers in standard pots; use a mix of equal parts topsoil, shredded fir bark, peat moss, and coarse perlite. Attach epiphytes to a piece of rough bark or tree-fern stem, or grow them as shown in a mix of 7 parts shredded fir bark, 1 part peat moss, and 1 part coarse perlite.

Repot orchids every 2 years in the spring. Cut off dead roots; carefully remove any clinging potting mix. If the plant has a rhizome, place it on top of the potting mix, with the oldest pseudobulb near the rim of the pot and the growing point toward the middle. Pack potting mixture around the feeding roots.

Orienteering

The thinking sport

Orienteering is like a cross-country treasure hunt: guided by a map and an orienteering compass (see *Compasses*), participants try, in the fastest possible time, to find markers set over an unfamiliar area. Speed and stamina are important, but the real test is figuring out the quickest route—in rugged terrain, rarely a straight or obvious path.

Organizing a meet

To stage a simple orienteering event for family or friends, first select a site. It should have plenty of identifiable natural and man-made features that will serve as checkpoints (called *controls*) and as guides or obstacles to the controls. State and county parks are often ideal, but be sure that any site has clear boundaries, is free of serious hazards, and has been mapped, preferably on a scale of 1:24,000.

On the map, mark out a course, ranging from a 1-mile to 2-mile hike with five controls. A good course has varied terrain—woods, hills, fields, marshes, water—as well as *legs* of varying lengths (300 to 1,500 feet) between controls. Pick controls that offer route choices—short but arduous routes versus easier but longer ones.

Go into the field to check control sites, to make sure your map is accurate, and to place control markers. These are usually red and white flags hung from a tree or a tripod. Each

marker should bear a number and a distinctive symbol or code that a runner can copy onto a card as proof of reaching the control.

At the starting point, provide a master map displaying the course and, for each runner, an unmarked map, control card, and slip of paper describing the controls. Get friends to serve as starter, timer, and judge. Start runners at 1- to 2-minute intervals; each runner copies the course on his or her map, then starts off. (See also *Map reading*.)

Origami

Creating art by folding paper

All you need for origami is a square piece of foldable paper of any size or type. If you prefer, you can get special origami paper at a Japanese novelty shop. The paper is colored on one side and white on the other and usually comes in packets with directions for folding traditional models. Books of origami models are also available.

Basic folds

In directions, folds are indicated by arrows and broken lines. A line of dots and dashes indicates that you should fold down, away from you, to make a *mountain fold*. A line made up solely of dashes indicates that you should fold up to make a *valley fold*. To make

Mountain fold   Valley fold

a *reverse fold*, begin with doubled paper, make a diagonal valley fold, then

unfold it. Open the doubled paper slightly, push the creased area inside, and smooth the folds.

Many origami models begin with the *preliminary fold*. Fold a square of paper diagonally in half twice. Lift the top

triangle until it is perpendicular to the bottom one. Push down on its up-

per tip, squashing it against the bottom triangle. Turn the model over and repeat with the unsquashed triangle.

Lucky crane

The most popular origami model is the crane, which is considered lucky by the Japanese. Begin with a preliminary fold and turn its top flaps in to the center and out again (A); then fold the top down and up again (B). Gently pull the bottom corner of the top layer of paper above the top of the model until its edges come together at the center (C and D). Smooth down the fold (E), then turn the model over and repeat on the back.

Fold in the sides of the model (F), front and back, and pull up the bottom pieces in reverse folds (G). Make a reverse fold to form the head (H); then gently pull the wings apart and blow into the hole in the bottom to inflate the crane (I). (See also *Paper airplanes; Paper hats*.)

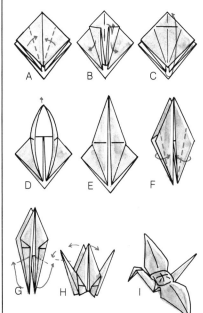

O

Controls:
1. Under two pine trees
2. On the hillside
3. A rock pile
4. Atop the cliff
5. Stone wall corner

Stone wall

Cliff

Leg

Trail

Control point

Shortest distance course

 Runner's probable course

Outboard motor care

Off-season maintenance

When the boating season ends, ideally you should remove your outboard motor from the boat's transom, clean and lubricate it, and mount it on a storage stand. However, many owners just tow the boat home and leave the motor in place, perhaps throwing a tarpaulin over it. After several years of this kind of neglect, a motor will need expensive professional service.

There is a compromise approach, in which you service the motor on the boat to prepare it for the off-season. When the boat is home, clean the cooling system, using a garden hose connected to an adapter on the motor's water intakes. Remove the propeller,

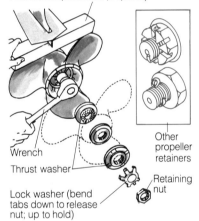

Wood block (to restrain propeller)

Wrench

Thrust washer

Lock washer (bend tabs down to release nut; up to hold)

Other propeller retainers

Retaining nut

then run the engine at idle to circulate water through the passages until only clean, fresh water comes out of the exhaust (dip a finger in the water and,

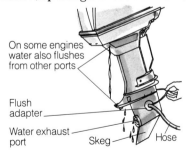

On some engines water also flushes from other ports

Flush adapter

Water exhaust port

Skeg

Hose

without swallowing, taste it to be sure it is not salty). Even if you operate only in fresh water, flush the cooling system to remove silt and dirt. In either case, also hose off the motor housing.

Greasing and draining

Use a grease gun with a cartridge of high-quality, water-resistant chassis grease, such as type NLGI No. 2 EP, sold in auto parts stores. Grease all linkage fittings as specified in your owner's manual (for use of a grease gun, see *Lubrication*). With your fingers, work grease into those linkage joints without fittings. Also smear the propeller shaft with grease.

Drain the oil from the gear case; if a significant amount of water comes out with the oil, this may indicate leaking gear-case seals or gasket or both. Have a marine-engine mechanic pressure test the gear case to confirm the diagnosis; have the seals or gasket replaced as necessary.

Disconnect the fuel line at the carburetor fuel pump. Remove the filter screen and clean it by sloshing it in a pan of automotive solvent. Run the engine to use up fuel in the carburetor.

Drain the fuel tank and lines. Disconnect the fuel-line gauge assembly from the top of the tank and lift it out. Pour the gas in the tank through cheesecloth to filter out dirt. Pour some gas back into the tank, slosh it around to collect more dirt, then empty again. Clean the in-tank filter (if used) in a pan of solvent.

If the fuel line has drain valves, open them. Otherwise blow fuel out of the line with compressed air.

Remove the spark plugs, pour in 2 tablespoons of fresh two-stroke engine oil, and crank the engine for a second to distribute the oil. Then reinstall the plugs.

Supporting the motor

To support the weight of the motor and to take the strain off the boat's transom, build up a row of concrete blocks, topped by a piece of wood, under the finlike *skeg* at the bottom of the shaft. Cover the motor with a waterproof tarpaulin and tie it in place.

In the spring, after you've performed the tune-up services as specified in your owner's manual and repainted the motor housing where needed, inspect the engine paint.

If it's bad, apply fresh paint to keep the engine from rusting. Remove the cowl from the engine, spray degreaser solvent on the engine, then spray with water to neutralize the solvent. After

the engine has air-dried, disconnect its wiring and move it out of the way.

Wrap accessories and other parts that you do not wish to paint with clear household plastic wrap. Wire-brush loose rust and paint from the engine, spray on two coats of primer, then two coats of engine enamel. Reconnect the wiring; spray it with a demoisturant, such as a silicone spray.

Oven cleaning

Using cleaners; self-cleaning and continuous-cleaning ovens

The easiest way to keep an oven clean is to wipe up spills when they occur and to regularly wash the surface. To clean burnt-on grease from an electric oven, pour 1 cup of ammonia into a glass or ceramic bowl and leave it in the cool oven overnight. In the morning, wipe the oven clean with a solution of 1 cup ammonia in a pail of water. Wear rubber gloves and follow other safety precautions recommended on the bottle label. Scrub a gas oven with an abrasive cleanser.

Any commercial cleaner is effective for a heavily soiled gas or electric oven. These are very caustic, however; follow directions precisely and handle with care. Protect the floor with newspapers; cover thermostats, heating elements, and light bulbs with aluminum foil; and wear rubber gloves.

To clean a microwave oven, cover any spill with a damp paper towel and turn the oven on *High* for 10 seconds. When the oven is cool, wipe it clean.

Self-cleaning ovens

Many ovens offer a self-cleaning feature. Refer to the owner's manual for your model and follow instructions to the letter. When the cleaning cycle is finished, a light gray ash remains on the oven floor. Wipe it away with a sponge. Don't attempt to burn the charred food off pots and pans with the self-cleaning setting. The oven system cannot handle this task.

A continuous-cleaning oven has a special lining that converts spattered grease into water and carbon dioxide whenever you use the oven. Even so, heavier spills that drip onto the oven floor must be scrubbed away. When

O

baking, protect the floor with aluminum foil directly under pans that are likely to drip. Clean up any spills quickly. If you must scrub the oven floor, use washing soda, ammonia (in an electric oven), or dry dishwasher soap. Don't use abrasives, steel wool, or commercial oven cleaners.

Overheating engine

What to do when your car overheats

If the *TEMP* warning light comes on or the needle on the temperature gauge moves into the red area and you're stuck in traffic, turn off the air conditioning. On a car with a belt-driven radiator fan, shift into *Neutral* and rev the engine; this pulls more air through the radiator and increases coolant circulation. *Don't* pull over and turn off the engine; it will likely boil over. Do stay well behind the car ahead to avoid the heat of its exhaust. If possible, get off on a side road where you can move faster. If all else fails, turn on the heater; it pulls heat away from the engine.

When you do stop, raise the hood and let the engine cool before looking for the source of the problem. Check for a leaking hose or a faulty drive belt (see *Car belts; Hoses in cars*). Look for leaves and bugs clogging the radiator or air-conditioner condenser. Clean away the debris with a brush and, if necessary, detergent and water.

When the radiator cap has cooled, remove it. Check the antifreeze level (antifreeze raises the coolant boiling point). Fill the radiator and overflow reservoir with a mixture of half antifreeze, half water. Lacking antifreeze, add water; then as soon as possible, flush the system and add new antifreeze (see *Antifreeze*).

Check the antifreeze concentration with a hydrometer, an inexpensive instrument sold in auto supply stores. The concentration should be between 50 and 70 percent. If not, drain the radiator and add antifreeze.

If none of these measures corrects the problem, have a mechanic check the cooling-system thermostat, the radiator cap, the fan, and on cars with electric fans, the fan switch. If overheating occurs when the car is running at highway speed, have the radiator checked for clogging.

Overseas telephone calls

Calling foreign countries by direct dialing

You can save money on your overseas calls if you dial direct. Look up the country and city codes in your telephone directory. Dial the International Access Code (011), the country code, the city code, and the local number. For instance, to call Geneva, Switzerland, dial 011 plus 41 (country code for Switzerland) plus 22 (city code for Geneva), then the local number.

If you need to charge your call to a third number, to call person-to-person, to call collect, or to use a telephone calling card, dial 00 and ask the operator to put through the call. Also dial 00 for operator assistance if you need help in completing a call, if you want to receive credit for a wrong number, or if you need a city code not listed in your directory.

If you have the name as well as the address of your party but do not have the telephone number, the operator will get it for you for a charge. Then dial the number direct.

Oyster shucking

Opening and eating oysters

Oysters are edible all year long, but they tend to be less plump and tasty during their spawning season, from May to August (months with no *R* in their names). To assure freshness, use only oysters that are tightly closed.

Scrub the oysters with a stiff brush to remove any sand. To open an oyster, grasp it firmly in a thick towel with the flatter shell facing up. Push the tip of an oyster knife—or a knife with a short strong blade—about ½

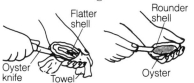

Flatter shell

Rounder shell

Oyster knife

Towel

Oyster

inch into the hinge, or pointed side, of the oyster. Twist the knife to pry the shells apart, then slide the knife around the inside of the upper shell to cut the muscle that holds the shell to the oyster. Pull off and discard the upper shell. Pass the knife under the oyster to cut it from the bottom shell, and flick out any bits of broken shell with the tip of the knife.

Serve the raw oysters on a half shell with a little lemon juice and black pepper or dip them into a mixture of ketchup, horseradish sauce, lemon juice, and liquid red-pepper sauce.

Packing

How to travel wrinkle free

Unless you're on a cruise, travel light. When flying, limit yourself to a carry-on garment bag, a bag that fits under the seat (the sum of its length, width, and height must not exceed 45 inches), and a tote or briefcase. If you check your luggage, include essential medicines, travel papers, valuables, toiletries, and a change of clothing in a bag you keep with you at all times.

Pack shoes and heavy items along the bottom (opposite the handle) of a suitcase or garment bag. Stuff shoes with socks; cover them with plastic bags. Place belts around a bag's perimeter; do not coil them.

Carrying clothes in a garment bag that you can hang up in transit avoids wrinkles. If you pack in a suitcase, place tissue paper or plastic bags in garment folds and in the shoulders and sleeves of dresses and jackets. Lay trousers out flat, creases aligned; fold both legs up about 6 inches below the knee, then fold again above the knee. Fold the sides of a flared skirt inward so that it forms a rectangle; fold a skirt in half and a dress in thirds, with the first fold just above the hem and the second fold at the waist.

Continued next page

Organizing a suitcase

Layer clothes in the following sequence: trousers at the bottom; heavy dresses and skirts; jackets; shirts, ties, light dresses, and sweaters; and lingerie on top. Tuck underwear in corners and crannies.

To pack a jacket, button it and place it facedown with its collar against the bottom edge of the suitcase. Fold the sleeves in toward the center back. Place shirts or sweaters on top; fold the jacket bottom over them.

Carry shampoo and other liquids in leakproof plastic bottles filled three-quarters full. Use a rubber-lined kit or cosmetic bag for toiletries. Don't pack matches, cigarette lighters, or spray cans in luggage you plan to check.

Remove old destination tags. Put an identification tag on each bag; inside tape a business card or a label with your name, address, and phone number. Mark luggage with tape or yarn so that you can recognize it in the baggage-claim area.

Padlocks

Selecting a portable lock

Match a padlock's size and quality to the value of the property you want to protect. For top security, buy a *pin-tumbler cylinder padlock* with a case-hardened steel shackle and a laminated steel or solid brass body; look for the word "hardened" on the shackle. The best, most expensive, locks have a five-pin cylinder and a double-locking mechanism that independently locks each leg of the shackle. If you're using a group of padlocks, buy them keyed alike. Outdoors, use a corrosion-resistant padlock with all brass or stainless steel parts.

A *combination padlock* provides medium security and convenience—there's no key to be lost. Look for reinforced double-wall construction and a case-hardened steel shackle.

Use a *warded padlock* with a laminated steel body to protect property of

Pin-tumbler-padlock key

Warded-padlock key

limited value. These medium-priced, low-security locks closely resemble pin-tumbler padlocks; you can tell them apart by their keys.

A cheap, wrought-steel *shell padlock* is easily forced open. Use it only for nuisance protection—to keep a child out of a toolbox, for example, or to restrict access to a cabinet.

Select a hasp that matches the padlock in size and quality. Look for hardened steel construction, a nonremovable pin, beveled edges, and hidden screws. (See also *Bicycle locks*.)

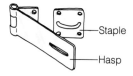

Staple

Hasp

Paintbrushes

Selecting, cleaning, and storing brushes

A good-quality brush makes the paint go on smoothly with less effort. Examine the bristles closely. They should be "flagged," or finely split at the ends to carry more paint. When you brush the bristles against your hand, they should be springy and elastic. When pressed down, they should fan slightly without separating into clumps.

Hit the brush against your hand and fan the bristles to see if any are loose. Tug on them to see if they come out easily. The bristles can be either natural or synthetic for a solvent-thinned paint, such as alkyd. For water-based latex paint, use synthetic; latex swells natural bristles.

A brush should suit the job. For rough masonry surfaces, pick a 4- to 6-inch brush with special durable bristles. For clapboard and interiors, choose a 3- or 4-inch brush. On trim, use a 1- to 2½-inch sash brush, depending on the trim's width. An angled sash brush makes it easier to do hard-to-reach trim, and a round sash brush is useful on narrow, curved surfaces such as railings and pipes. A chisel-cut varnish and enamel brush helps you paint furniture and fine trim smoothly without lap marks.

Clean a brush thoroughly before storing it. To remove latex, lay the

brush on newspapers and squeeze out the paint with a scraper. Then immerse the brush in warm water and detergent. Knead the bristles, working the paint out all the way to the heel of the handle. Rinse the brush in clear water and shake out the excess.

To remove a solvent-thinned paint, squeeze out the excess paint. Then, wearing rubber gloves, immerse the bristles in the recommended solvent and knead them. When the solvent is totally discolored, repeat the procedure with fresh solvent. Wash synthetic bristles in warm water and detergent; then rinse and shake. Clean natural bristles with solvent again.

To store a brush, first dry it; then wrap it in foil or heavy paper to help it retain its shape. For overnight, when you'll paint again the next day, drill a hole at the handle's base. Then slip a wire rod through the hole and rest it on top of a can with the brush suspended in solvent—or water for latex.

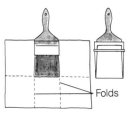

Folds

Painting exteriors

Refinishing your house's siding and trim

Plan to paint your house in spring or fall when the sun's heat won't cause problems. Wait at least 2 days after rain. Latex is the easiest paint to use, but make sure it's compatible with the previous finish. Use flat paint for siding; gloss or semi-gloss for trim.

Your dealer can determine how much paint you need from the dimensions of the walls and the number of windows and doors. Most houses require only one coat; a badly weathered one may need two. You can paint most surfaces with a brush, pad applicator, or a roller, but a roller with ½-inch nap covers rough masonry best. (See also *Aluminum siding*.)

To prepare the house, replace any damaged siding (see *Wood siding*),

P

hammer in any protruding nails, and repair the caulking (see *Caulking*). Remove loose paint and repair paint flaws (see *Paint problems; Paint removal*). Scrub grimy areas with detergent; then hose well and let dry fully. Fill in holes, cracks, and scraped areas with an exterior spackling compound. If a scraped area is large, taper the compound along the edges—no need to cover the entire area. Sand all scraped and patched areas and coat them with the recommended primer.

Painting the siding

Try to work in the shade; the paint will dry better and you'll be more comfortable. As you go, cover shrubs, steps, and walks with drop cloths; remove screens or tape newspaper over them. Stir the paint thoroughly and work out of a half-full can. To load a brush, immerse it about one-third its bristle length; then tap both sides gently on the can's edge to remove excess paint.

Start painting at the top, doing dormers or gables. (For safe use of a ladder, see *Ladders*.) Paint an area about 3 or 4 feet square at a time, working across a wall. Paint from a dry area toward one you just painted. On lapped siding, paint the lower edges first; then paint the surface, going horizontally

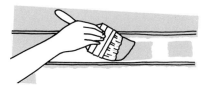

or vertically with the grain. On clapboard, apply three or four short dabs across a board; then spread the paint with smooth, even strokes.

Painting the trim

Wrap rags around the upper ends of the ladder to avoid marring the siding. On the eaves, carefully brush a 2-inch paint band to separate them from the siding; then finish them with a roller. For other trim, use 1- to 2½-inch brushes. Paint a 12- to 18-inch area; then skip ahead the same distance and paint back toward the wet edge. On windows, paint horizontal dividers, vertical dividers; then sides and surrounding wall trim. On doors, do the panels; then horizontal and vertical boards. On flush doors, go across the top first; then down.

Painting interiors

Preparing and finishing a room's ceiling, walls, and trim

You'll find it easier to paint a room with latex paint. Latex is almost odorless, cleans up with water, and dries within a few hours. Check the label to make sure a latex paint is compatible with a previous finish.

Use flat paint on most walls and ceilings, gloss or semi-gloss where dirt and moisture resistance are important: on doors, windows, and trim or in a kitchen or bathroom. Plan on a gallon of paint for every 450 square feet of wall. For the preparation, you'll need a flat-blade paint scraper, a putty knife, spackling compound, masking tape, and drop cloths; for painting, a roller, paint tray, extension pole, stepladder about 3 feet less than ceiling height, brushes for trim and corners (see *Paintbrushes*), and rags.

Getting the room ready

Move out lightweight furnishings. Cluster heavy pieces in the center and cover them with a canvas or plastic drop cloth; make sure you can reach the ceiling above. Also cover permanent installations such as built-ins and radiators. Cover the floor with overlapped newspaper or a drop cloth; make paper paths in other rooms.

Remove or cover door and window hardware; take down picture hooks. Turn off the power to the room's circuits (see *Circuit testing*) and remove cover plates from switches and receptacles. Loosen the canopy on a ceiling or wall fixture and enclose the fixture in a plastic bag. If you need light, run a work light from another room.

Preparing the surface

The more carefully you prepare; the better and longer lasting the paint job. Fix cracks and holes in the plasterboard or plaster (see *Plasterboard patching; Plaster patching*). Scrape off loose paint with a scraper or a putty knife and fill scraped areas with spackling compound. On large areas, spackle along the edges just enough to taper smoothly between painted and scraped areas. Remove old, built-up layers of paint that make the trim look unsightly or that prevent a door

or window from working properly (see *Paint removal*). Sand patched and raw surfaces; then coat them with the recommended primer and let it dry thoroughly. Coat water-stained areas with an alcohol-based stain killer. Finally, dust the walls and ceiling and vacuum debris from the floor; re-lay newspaper or a drop cloth. Put masking tape around windowpanes.

In kitchens and bathrooms, wash off grease and steamed-on deposits with a household detergent or cleaner. If a wall is mildewed, see *Mildew*.

Painting the ceiling

Do the ceiling first. Start by cutting in, that is, brushing a narrow strip of paint around the edge. Then, using a roller, cover an area 3 to 4 feet square at a time. Load the roller in the pan until it is fully and evenly saturated but not dripping. Then roll it across the area in a zigzag. Begin by pushing

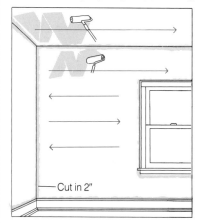

Cut in 2"

the roller away from you and finish by crisscrossing over the area to fill in missed spots and smooth the paint. Paint toward a light source, and cover only what you can easily see and reach. Always start in a dry area and roll toward one that was just painted.

When you have completed several squares, roll back over them to pick up drips and smooth laps. Roll slowly to reduce splattering. Wipe up drops on the floor with a dry rag as you go.

Walls and trim

On the walls, start by cutting in along the edges and around doors and windows. Be sure to make a straight, even line at the ceiling if the walls are a different color. Then roll each wall, working from the top down. Do an area 3 to 4 feet square at a time. Start each with

P

an upward stroke and zigzag as you did on the ceiling.

Use 1- to 2½-inch brushes for the trim. Paint a 12- to 18-inch strip; then skip ahead the same distance and paint back toward the wet edge. Hold thin cardboard next to the baseboard to shield the floor. Paint windows and doors in the same manner as their exteriors (see *Painting exteriors*).

Paint problems

Fixing common flaws

Alligatoring can be caused by applying a second coat of paint before the first has dried. Or two incompatible layers may have expanded at different rates. For a mild case, sand and fill the

Alligatoring

area with exterior spackling compound. For a severe case, strip the paint (see *Stripping furniture*).

Blistering that occurs soon after painting may be the result of hot, direct sunlight, which dries the paint's surface, trapping solvents before they

Blistering

can evaporate. After the paint dries fully, scrape off the blisters, sand, and repaint early or late in the day. Later blisters usually result from moisture in the siding. Locate the cause: excess house humidity; water from damaged roofing, flashing, or caulking; moisture from the ground. Correct it before repainting (see *Caulking; Flashings; Humidity control; Roof repairs*).

Chalking is a powdery surface residue. Many exterior paints are meant to chalk; it allows rain to carry away dirt. If it's down to the paint layer below, brush the chalk off, coat with a primer-sealer, and repaint.

Crusting and *flaking* on a masonry wall result from a moisture-caused granular buildup under the paint.

Clean the area with a wire brush and scraper. Then, wearing gloves and goggles, scrub with a mixture of 1 part muriatic acid and 2 parts water. Rinse well and let dry; correct the source of dampness (see *Basement waterproofing* and the sections listed under blistering above). Before repainting, apply a masonry sealer.

Peeling results from painting over a greasy or dirty surface or from moisture getting trapped beneath the paint. Scrape and sand the surface. Before repainting, correct any source of dampness. On masonry, peeling can have the same cause as crusting.

Running and *sagging* are driplike formations that occur when you apply paint too thickly. Prevent them by making sure to brush out and smooth each paint stroke. Sand off dried runs and sags before repainting.

Wrinkling occurs from applying a paint too thickly. The surface dries first, then wrinkles when the paint under it dries. Sand the surface smooth and apply a thinner coat.

Paint removal

Preparing a surface for refinishing

Caution: Wear goggles and a mask when removing paint with power tools. Handle a propane torch or an electric paint remover with care to avoid burning yourself. To prevent fire, do not use a torch indoors or on walls that are splintered or cracked.

To remove peeling or chipped paint from small areas, use a pull scraper or a putty knife to get under and free the

Pull scraper

loose layers. For larger areas, use an orbital power sander, first with coarse paper, then with medium and fine. Avoid using a disk sander on a drill; it can leave visible circular cuts. To remove flaking paint from a metal surface, use a wire brush or a wire-brush attachment on a drill.

To take thickly layered paint off a broad surface, use a propane torch

with a flame spreader. Hold the torch an inch or so away from the surface just long enough to soften the paint.

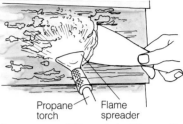
Propane torch   Flame spreader

Then scrape off the paint with a putty knife. Scorching the wood slightly is inevitable, but take care not to char it.

If torch flames seem risky, rent an electric paint remover; the higher its wattage, the faster it works. To use it, hold the heating element over the paint until it starts to sizzle. Then scrape off the paint with the built-in blade or with a putty knife.

After removing paint, sand the surface smooth. Then coat it with the recommended primer before repainting. When you plan to use a natural wood finish, strip the paint with a chemical paint remover (see *Stripping furniture*). Also strip encrusted paint on uneven surfaces, such as moldings with curves and grooves.

Paint touch-ups

Fixing scratches in your car's finish

Repair minor paint damage on your car before rust spreads and makes a difficult job. With a single-edge razor blade, cut away loose paint around the damaged area. Then scrape off loose rust, being careful not to let it slip into good paint. Clean with detergent and water to remove dirt and wax.

Apply a combination metal conditioner and primer to the area. Sold in auto parts stores, this product stops the rust, etches the metal, and primes it for touch-up painting.

If you can't find the combination product, use a drill with a tapered grinding bit to remove rust. If all you have is sandpaper, mask the surrounding area with double layers of masking tape and work carefully to avoid sanding good paint. Wipe away sanding or grinding grit.

P

Apply a single-purpose metal conditioner; allow it to dry thoroughly; then with an artist's brush, apply as even a coat of primer as possible. You must use primer; touch-up paint won't adhere to bare metal. If you use spray-can primer, make a mask from a piece of cardboard, cutting a small hole in the center so that only the damaged area is exposed.

After the primer or combination product dries, apply the touch-up paint. Shake the jar to mix it, then use the brush in the cap to dab on the paint neatly. If you can get a color match for your car only in a spray can, spray some paint into a paper cup; apply it with an artist's brush.

Touch up wide scratches similarly, but don't use sandpaper. If there's rust, grind it off or use the combination product. Learn to live with hairline scratches; they may not rust for years. Touching up only makes them more noticeable.

Paneling

Putting up a woodlike wall covering

To determine how many standard 4- x 8-foot panels you will need, measure each wall's width and divide by 4 feet. Allow the panels to adjust to a room's humidity and temperature for 3 or 4 days. Buy colored nails to match the paneling, and molding to finish the paneling at the ceiling, floor, corners, and around windows and doors. Also get box extenders to move electric outlets even with the paneling's surface; if possible, get a box template to mark outlet locations (otherwise, make cardboard templates).

Remove old moldings. Install furring strips (see *Furring strips*) if the wall is uneven or of masonry or has studs spaced other than on 16- or 24-inch centers (see *Studs*). Turn off the electric power (see *Circuit testing*), then remove the cover plates and take out the receptacles or switches (see *Electric receptacles; Electric switches*).

Starting in one corner, drive a nail every 4 feet, marking the stud positions. Drop a chalked plumb line from each nail and snap it (see *Plumb line*).

Install the first panel at a corner. Cut it to fit between the floor and ceiling with ½-inch clearance. Then set it in place and check that it's plumb by holding a level at the edge away from the corner. If it's not, use a compass to mark the adjoining wall angle as shown. Trim it— from the back with

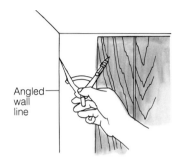

Angled wall line

a power saw, from the front with a handsaw. When installing remaining panels, make sure the outer edge is along the next chalkline.

Nail panels to the studs. Space nails 6 inches apart along the edges, 12 inches apart on the middle studs. To cut an opening for an electric outlet, slip the template into the the box and press the panel against it so that its points outline the box on the panel's back. Drill ½-inch holes at the corners and cut out the rectangle with a saber or keyhole saw.

For a door or window, tack the panel in place and trace the opening on the panel's back. If you can't get behind the opening, measure and mark its position. Before cutting, enlarge the outline by the amount your molding's base will take up when it is nailed around the opening.

Finish by installing molding. Insert a box extender in each electric outlet and reinstall the receptacle or switch. (See also *Plank paneling*.)

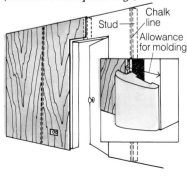

Chalk line
Stud
Allowance for molding

Pants fitting

Adjusting pants on the figure

Within the limits of the seam allowances, pants can be made to fit a little better. Have someone help you pin the adjustments with the pants on right side out. If the pants are being made and have no waistband, tie elastic around the waist. When pinning is complete, remove the pants and re-mark the new seamlines on the inside. Remove the pins, baste the new seamlines, and recheck the fit. Whenever you adjust only part of a seam, taper the new line as smoothly as possible into the original seamline.

If pants fit snugly across the derriere, and side seams are pulled toward the back, let out the back seam allowances on the side seams and raise the seam at the center back. If they are still too tight, lower the crotch curve.

If pants sag in the back because of a flat derriere, take a deeper waist seamline in the back. You may also have to take in the back seam allowances on the side seams.

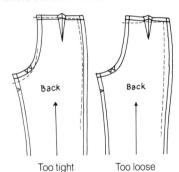

Too tight   Too loose

If pants wrinkle like a smile in the crotch area, the crotch curve must be made deeper. Lower the curve, ¼ inch at a time, until pants no longer smile.

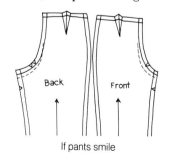

If pants smile

Continued next page

If pants wrinkle like a frown in the crotch area, the crotch curve must be raised. If they still wrinkle after you've raised the curve as much as possible, take a deeper waist seamline.

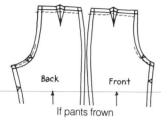

If pants frown

If the pants legs are too tight or too loose, you can add or subtract up to ⅜ inch at the side and inner-leg seams. Adjust an equal amount on both, or the creases will be off-center.

Hemming pants

Put on the pants along with the shoes that you'll wear with them. Pin the hems of pants with straight or slightly flared legs to just touch your shoes in front and cover the line where the shoe joins the heel in back. The back will be slightly longer than the front; adjust the sides to span the two. Baste the hems and recheck the length. Adjust the hem depth, then finish the hem edges and sew them (see *Hems*). Press the pants and set the creases (see *Ironing*).

Paper airplanes

Folding your own aircraft

Michaelangelo made paper airplanes almost 500 years ago. You can be as adventurous by designing your own models. But first try the *dart* shown here, using any type of foldable paper.

Begin by folding a rectangle of paper in half lengthwise, then unfolding it, to form a crease along the center. Fold the corners on one end to meet the center crease (A). Fold the two slanting sections of the sides in to the center (B). Fold the sides in to the center again (C). Turn the model over, fold it in half along the center crease, and snip ½ inch from the nose (D). Finally, open the wings. To make the dart fly straight without crashing to the ground, bend the rear corners of the wings up. To make it climb, create flaps by making ½-inch cuts in the

backs of the wings and tilting the flaps up (E). Hold the plane by the keel and launch it into the air.

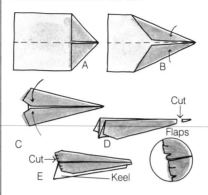

Paper hats

Making party favors

Brighten a children's (or even an adults') party with colorful hats. Make them yourself or give the guests the fun of making their own. Supply heavy construction paper or cardboard cut to the correct shapes and sizes, crayons or felt-tip markers, feathers, and glue-on decorations (such as paper curls, cut-out flowers or polka dots, bits of lace, cotton balls, ribbon, and shiny foil). Let the guests fold the hats as shown, and decorate them to their own tastes.

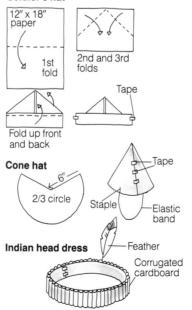

Paper logs

Making fuel of newspaper

Paper logs reduce fuel costs, get rid of old newspapers, and ignite a fire with a minimum of kindling. They are not safe to burn in some wood stoves (see *Wood Stoves*).

Experiment to find the right mix of paper and wood logs for your fireplace. Try laying a fire of three logs, one of them paper.

To make paper logs, use only dry black-and-white newspaper. Roll the papers tightly, leaving space at the center of the roll; or roll them around a dowel. Bind the paper with thin wire or masking tape; remove the dowel.

Another method involves using a metal can with both ends removed. Roll the papers and slip the can over one end of the roll. Put can and all into the fire. When the paper has burned, extract the can with tongs; reuse the can for another fire.

Papier-mâché

Sculpture from paper and paste

Masks, bowls, window blinds, or fanciful sculptures—all can be made with paper and paste or glue of any kind. Newspaper and white glue or wallpaper paste are most popular.

To build up a papier-mâché figure, you will need a base, or *armature.* Use any lightweight material that approximates the shape of the figure you're planning: wadded-up aluminum foil, a cardboard model, wire mesh, tin cans, plastic, or inflated balloons. Shape the desired figure on the armature by applying strips of paste-soaked paper, a mash of paper and paste, or a combination of the two. For example, you can create a mask by

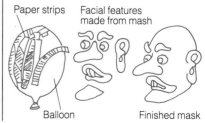

laying strips over an inflated balloon, adding facial features with mash, then puncturing the balloon and removing it when the mask is dry.

When preparing strips, don't cut the paper, tear it against a straight-edge. The rough edges will mesh to make a smoother surface. Mix white glue with an equal amount of water. Prepare wallpaper paste by slowly stirring 1 part powdered paste with 10 parts water. To fireproof your papier mâché, add 1 teaspoon sodium phosphate (available at drug stores) to each cup of adhesive. Before using the strips, either soak them in the adhesive for a few minutes or apply the adhesive with a sponge. Don't oversaturate the strips; they may fall apart.

To make 1 quart of mash, tear 4 large newspaper sheets into small pieces and soak them overnight in 2 quarts of water (you can add 8 teaspoons of sodium phosphate for fireproofing). The next day, boil the mixture for 20 minutes, then whip it with a whisk until the paper is soft and pulpy. Strain the pulp and squeeze it gently until it is a soft, moist lump. Stir in 2 tablespoons of white glue, then 2 tablespoons of wallpaper paste. Stir until no lumps remain. Use the mash like modeling clay.

Let the modeled piece dry overnight (or dry it faster in a slow oven). Sand a piece made with pulp for a smoother finish. Paint papier-mâché with any water-base paint. To waterproof it and make it more durable, spray it with a clear vinyl sealer or give it three or more coats of lacquer.

Parquet flooring

Putting down prefinished wood blocks

You can lay parquet over most flooring, provided it is smooth, level, and dry. Cover an uneven subfloor with ¾-inch plywood or particle board, laying wood strips beneath to level it. On concrete, fill in low areas with a fast-setting patching cement, or rent a grinding machine to level high spots. In all rooms, remove base molding.

Most parquet blocks have tongue-and-groove joints. You install them

over mastic that you spread with a notched trowel. Before starting, let the loosely unpacked blocks adjust to indoor conditions for 3 or 4 days.

Draw a floor plan on graph paper; let each square represent a block. Leave a ½-inch margin for expansion along each wall. If you aren't using a centered symmetrical design or a diagonal one, minimize cutting by running whole blocks along at least one wall, especially a doorway wall.

Snap two chalklines at right angles to each other on the floor as shown. Locate the first line exactly four blocks plus ½ inch from a wall. (For a symmetrical pattern, cross the lines in the center of the room, and for a diagonal pattern, run them at 45-degree angles to the walls.) To check a right angle, mark a point 4 feet from the intersection on one line and 3 feet on the other. The points should be 5 feet apart.

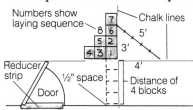

Trowel a ⅛-inch layer of mastic over the floor, just missing the chalklines. Let it dry. Then, starting at the chalkline intersection, lay blocks one quadrant at a time in a staircase-step sequence. Interlock adjacent blocks and gently tap them into the mastic with a mallet and a protective wood block. Trim edge blocks with a fine-toothed backsaw. Trace odd cuts on paper.

Fit ½-inch cork strips in the expansion spaces. Then replace the base molding. In doorways, install reducer strips; they slope to the adjoining rooms' floor level.

Partitions

Dividing a room with a new wood-frame wall

You can build a partition's frame with 2 x 4's and 16d nails. Remove the baseboards and the trim from the walls it will abut; reinstall them afterward.

Locate the wall so that you will be able to nail it to studs in the existing

walls and to a ceiling joist (see *Studs*). To transfer the position of a ceiling joist to the floor, have a helper on a ladder drop a plumb line at several points along the joist while you mark the floor (see *Plumb line*).

Begin by snapping a chalkline on the floor to mark the wall's position. Center a 2 x 4 of the appropriate length over the line and nail it in place. This is the lower soleplate.

Assemble the partition frame on the floor. The 2 x 4 frame consists of studs nailed between a top plate and a second soleplate. Cut the studs 4½ inches less than ceiling height to allow for the three 2 x 4 plates. Space the studs 16 inches apart from center to center if you will cover them with ⅜-inch plasterboard, 24 inches for ½-inch plasterboard. Mark each stud's position; use two nails in each joint.

To frame a doorway, put a horizontal 2 x 4, or header, between studs at the opening's top. Use two uprights on either side and put short studs above, at the usual stud interval.

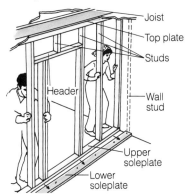

Slip the upright frame on top of the lower soleplate. Use small wooden wedges to shim it, if necessary, and, with a level, check that it is plumb. Nail it at the sides, then at the top and bottom. Saw out the doorway soleplates. After running electric wiring, enclose the wall (see *Plasterboard*).

Passports

Applying for and renewing your travel identification

Everyone, even an infant, needs a passport for travel to almost all foreign countries with the exception of

Canada, Mexico, and some of the Caribbean islands and for re-entry into the U.S. Apply for a passport at a regional branch of the passport office (look in the phone directory under government listings), at a clerk of the county court's office, and at designated post offices. If there is no such facility in your area, contact the Washington Passport Agency, 1425 K Street NW, Washington, DC 20524.

You must apply in person for your first passport. You will need 1. a certified birth certificate, a naturalization certificate, or a consular report of your birth (if born abroad); 2. identification, such as your driver's license, that includes your photo or description and your signature—Social Security or credit cards are unacceptable; 3. two identical 2- x 2-inch photos with a light background, not older than 6 months. Snapshots and vending-machine photos are unacceptable. Go to a photographer who specializes in passport photos. (Most will process your photos while you wait.) You may need extra photos for visas or an international driver's permit.

At the passport office you will fill out an application and pay a fee. Your passport will be mailed to you; in some cases, you can pick it up. Exact cash will be accepted; a check or a money order is preferred.

It's best to renew a passport before it expires. However, if yours has expired and was issued within the last 12 years and you were over 18, you can obtain a new one by mail. Pick up a renewal application at a passport office, courthouse, post office, or travel agency. Fill it out and mail it with your current passport, two identical photos, and the required fee. It takes about 3 weeks. Currently, passports are vaild for 10 years if you are 18 or older, 5 years if you are 17 or younger. (See also *Visas*.)

Pasta

Making fresh noodles by hand; cooking pasta

On a board, mound 1½ cups flour and form a well in the center. Drop 2 large eggs into the well. Beat the eggs with a fork, then gradually blend in the flour with your hands, working the dough into a stiff ball. If it's sticky, add a bit of flour. Clean the board thoroughly.

Beating the eggs in the flour well

Knead the dough until it's smooth and elastic, about 8 to 10 minutes (see *Breadmaking*). Flour the board lightly. Divide the dough in two and cover half. With a long, untapered rolling pin, roll out the other half to ⅛ inch, rotating it one-quarter turn after each roll to keep it round. Press outward on the roller, not down.

Next, stretch the dough by rolling it over the pin, simultaneously sliding the palms of your hands toward the

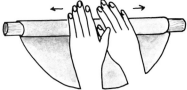

ends of the pin. Roll and stretch this way until the dough is paper thin. Set the dough aside to dry while you roll the second half. After each piece has dried about 30 minutes, roll it into the shape of a jelly roll. With a very sharp knife, cut dough to desired width—⅛ inch for *fettuccine*, ¼ inch for *tagliatelle*. Separate the strands; dry for at least 5 minutes before cooking. Makes 1 pound, or four servings.

Cooking pasta

Allow 4 quarts of water per pound of pasta; bring it to a boil, then add 1 tablespoon oil and 1½ tablespoons salt per 4 quarts of water. Slip pasta all at once into the rapidly boiling water and stir immediately to separate the pieces. For a large quantity, cover the pot briefly to bring the water back to a boil. Fresh noodles are usually done within a minute. Stuffed, frozen, and commercial pastas take from 5 to 10 minutes. Stir and taste the pasta periodically for doneness. When it is *al dente* (firm to the bite), drain immediately. (If cooking 2 pounds or more of commercial pasta, rinse with very hot water.) Toss with some sauce or flavored butter or oil; serve immediately.

Patching

Covering large holes in garments

Apply a fabric patch to holes that are too big for darning. If possible, use fabric from an unnoticeable part of the same item. Shape the hole into a rectangle. Cut the patch to match the fabric grain, making it 1 inch larger than the hole all around.

To handsew, lay the garment right side up; center the patch under the hole and pin it. Clip the corners of the hole diagonally ¼ inch. Fold under the edges of the hole; slipstitch them to the patch (see *Slipstitching*).

To apply a patch with a machine zigzag, set the dials to a wide stitch

Slipstitch patch

Zigzagged patch

width and a short stitch length. Pin or baste the patch to the right side. With the garment faceup, stitch the edge of the patch, then sew a row of medium-length straight stitches just inside the zigzag stitches.

It's convenient to use ready-made iron-on patches on the knees of children's pants. If you use a contrasting color for decoration, fuse it to the outside. Otherwise apply it inside. On heavy cottons, slip a piece of aluminum foil under the garment before ironing the patch to intensify the heat.

You can use suede or suede cloth to patch damaged elbows of jackets and sweaters. Buy them ready-made, or cut two oval patches about 5 x 6 inches. On a sweater, apply patches by hand with a buttonhole stitch (see *Buttonholes*). For a jacket, free the lining at the cuff. Pull it out of the way and pin the patch to the outer fabric. Sew it with buttonhole stitches or straight machine stitches. Resew the lining to the sleeve with slipstitches. (See also *Darning; Mending*.)

Patchwork

Making a pieced-block design

Patchwork is the sewing together of fabric pieces to make a larger fabric. When the pieces form a design, it's called *pieced-block patchwork*.

To try your hand at this traditional craft, make the Simple Star design illustrated, then finish it as a pillow cover. You'll need firmly woven, medium-weight cotton fabric: ⅓ yard of the main color and ¼ yard each of two secondary colors (or use scraps). You will also need thread, a 12-inch knife-edge pillow form, and heavy paper.

On the paper, draw each of the four basic patchwork shapes in the specified dimensions; add a ¼-inch seam allowance all around. Using these as patterns, trace the shapes onto your fabric with a dressmaker's pencil, aligning the arrows with either the lengthwise or crosswise grain, then

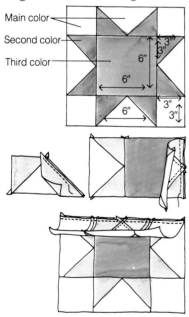

Main color
Second color
Third color
6″
6″
6″
3″
3″
3″
3″

cut them out. Make 4 large triangles and 4 small squares of the main fabric color; 8 small triangles of one secondary color; and 1 large square of the third color. Also cut a 12-inch square of the main color for the pillow back.

Join the pieces in the order illustrated, pressing seam allowances to one side as you proceed. Use a machine or small running hand-stitch-

Running stitches (about 9 per inch)

es. Join the patchwork to the pillow back with a ¼-inch seam (see *Cushions*) and insert the pillow form.

Patents

Protecting your invention

Do you think you've built a better mousetrap that will put you on easy street? Before you quit your job, obtain a patent, the best legal protection for an inventor.

A patent is the right, given by the federal government, that prevents others from making, using, or selling an invention. If your invention is a machine, process, or item used in manufacturing, your patent is good for 17 years. If it's an ornamental design for furniture, jewelry, or the like, you're entitled to exclusive rights for up to 14 years. Once you have a patent, anyone who wants to use your invention must get your permission and pay you a fee. Otherwise, you can sue and win damages (money) for any losses you suffer.

To qualify for a patent, your invention must be original and useful. If you've merely improved on an existing item or a known principle in an obvious way, you've no right to a patent.

Although you can apply for a patent without a lawyer's help, an experienced patent attorney will help it go more smoothly. Before applying for a patent, you or your attorney must review information compiled by the U.S. Patent and Trademark Office, Washington, DC 20231, to learn if any similar or identical invention has already been patented. If none exists, quickly file your application. If your brainstorm is already patented or was discussed in an American or foreign publication within a certain time period, it's ineligible.

Your application must include a detailed account of what your invention does and how it works—the *specifications*. It must also explain how it was built—*claims*. You may have to

submit drawings or models. You must sign an oath that you are the original creator and submit the designated fee, payable by check or money order, to the Commissioner of Patents and Trademarks at the address mentioned.

Patio building

An easy way to make a brick terrace

You can build a patio by laying bricks on a bed of fine sand. Use either regular building bricks spaced ½ inch apart or paving bricks placed tightly together. Select ones rated SW (for severe weathering). Shun thin ones and those with a slippery glaze.

To avoid cutting bricks, pick a design, such as the basket-weave pattern, that doesn't require half bricks at the edges. You will need about five bricks for each square foot. For borders, buy either pressure-treated 6 x 6's or extra bricks to stand on end. To make a tamper, nail a 1-foot square of plywood to the end of a 4 x 4.

Outline the area with a row or two of bricks. Then mark it off with stakes and strings. Dig out about 4 inches (brick depth plus a 2-inch sand bed). If the area has clay soil or receives frequent heavy rains or snowfall, excavate another 4 inches and fill it with washed gravel. For drainage, slope the bottom away from the house slightly. Tamp well. Dig a trench for borders along two adjacent edges, allowing for 2 inches of sand beneath.

Spread the sand. Level it with a board on edge. Then moisten with a fine spray and tamp well. To keep out weeds, cover the sand with 15-pound roofing felt or plastic sheeting.

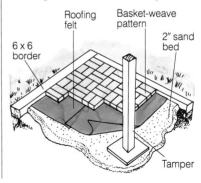

Roofing felt
Basket-weave pattern
2″ sand bed
6 x 6 border
Tamper

P

Continued next page

Set the two borders in place; make sure they are at patio-surface level. Beginning at the corner they form, lay the bricks.

Tap each brick firmly with a rubber mallet. Adjust the level by adding or digging out sand. After laying several bricks, put a piece of plywood over them and tamp them down. Be careful not to shift the bricks. Put in the other borders last.

Pour sand on the bricks; sweep with a broom to fill the joints. Dampen with a fine spray. Wait 15 minutes. Repeat until the joints are filled.

For more permanence, substitute a bed of hard-tamped limestone dust for sand. Put ½ inch of sand on top of the weed barrier for leveling the bricks. Then fill the joints with a dry mixture of 1 part portland cement and 5 parts sand. To avoid staining the bricks, apply the mixture when they are dry and brush off all traces before wetting. (See also *Flagstones.*)

Pattern transfer

Tracing and enlarging flat patterns; copying three-dimensional patterns

To make an exact-size reproduction of a flat pattern, first trace the pattern. Then position the tracing with a sheet of carbon paper over the new surface, and retrace the lines, using a hard pencil, a ballpoint pen, or (on wood and other rough surfaces) a dressmaker's tracing wheel.

If you wish to enlarge a pattern, draw a grid of uniform squares over the original tracing; then draw a proportionally larger grid onto the new surface, dividing it into the same number of squares. Copy the pattern

by hand from the original onto the new surface, using the relationships of the squares to the pattern lines as a guide. For very precise work, add di-

agonal lines to all or part of each grid, further subdividing the squares.

To copy a three-dimensional pattern or some other pattern you cannot trace, such as the contours of a wall on which you want to fit a cabinet, first place the new surface at a right angle to the original. Set the point of a compass on the original and the compass' pencil point on the equivalent part of the new surface. Draw the compass along both surfaces so that the point of the compass follows the edge of the original, and the pencil point draws its contour onto the new surface.

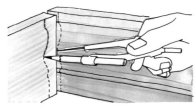

Another way to copy a three-dimensional pattern is to make a template by pressing a profile gauge against the surface you want to copy. A profile gauge is an assembly of tightly packed needles that draw back when pressed against a surface, taking on its shape.

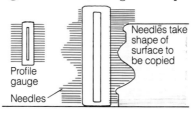

Peanut butter

Homemade from fresh peanuts

For about 1 cup of peanut butter, shell enough peanuts to make 2 cups and blanch them for 1 minute (see *Blanching*); remove the skins.

Creamy style peanut butter: Put half the nuts into the container of a blender, all of them into a food processor; grind for 1 minute. Scrape down the sides with a rubber spatula, then process for another minute. Add 2 teaspoons butter or peanut oil and ⅛ teaspoon salt (optional). Process until smooth. Scrape the peanut butter into a jar. Repeat the process with the rest of the peanuts in a blender.

Crunchy style: In a food processor, grind ⅓ of the peanuts coarsely; set aside. Process the remaining nuts and other ingredients to a paste; mix the paste with the coarse peanuts. If you're using a blender, process as for creamy peanut butter, but for less time. Fresh peanut butter keeps for about 1 week at room temperature, about 2 weeks refrigerated.

Peepholes

Look before unlocking

A peephole contains a lens providing anyone answering the doorbell with a 180-degree field of view, making it impossible for someone outside to be out of sight. There are two kinds, both available at hardware stores. One is small, usually ½ inch in diameter; the other, 1½ inches in diameter, has a one-way mirror so that the person outside can't see you.

At a height that's convenient for the shortest adult, drill a hole in the center of a wood or metal door (see *Drilling*). Use a high-speed steel twist bit as wide as the viewer shank for the small-diameter peephole; drill for the large-diameter kind with a hole saw attached to your electric drill. Screw the adjustable halves of the viewer together through the hole. Tighten with the edge of a coin.

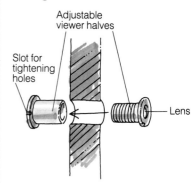

Perennials

They bloom year after year

Because a perennial lives for a long time, it is important to start it in good soil. At planting time, dig the bed deeply and work in organic matter and a balanced fertilizer, such as 5-10-5 (see *Planting; Soil preparation*).

Once a perennial is established, cultivate its soil 1 inch deep as spring growth begins, being careful not to harm its roots. Work in a tablespoon of balanced fertilizer such as 5-10-5; water well. Cultivate and feed again in 4 to 6 weeks, then apply a 2- to 3-inch mulch. Provide stakes for top-heavy plants (see *Staking plants*). Water deeply in dry spells.

To keep blossoms coming, remove faded ones quickly. To make such fall bloomers as chrysanthemums bushier and more productive, pinch back the stems after each 6 inches of growth until midsummer. For giant mums and peonies, pinch off all but the end bud on each stem.

When leaves wither in autumn, cut the stalks to the ground. After the ground freezes, apply a protective mulch—8 inches of straw is good. Propagate most perennials by division (see *Propagating plants*); this should be done every few years, when an established plant ceases to produce good blooms.

Permanents

How to give yourself a permanent wave at home

Before waving your hair, get a haircut or trim split ends (see *Haircutting*). If you want to color your hair as well, do the permanent first, then the coloring (a home-permanent kit tells you how long to wait between the processes). There are kits for colored and frosted hair; if your hair is color treated, consult a hairdresser before using one.

Your permanent-wave kit will contain an alkaline waving solution, which softens the hair shaft so that it conforms to the shape of the curling rods; a neutralizing solution, which sets the hair into its new curls; and a detailed instruction sheet. Some kits also provide curling rods. If you have to purchase them separately, be sure to buy enough to set all of your hair.

Look at your instruction sheet a day or so before you intend to do the permanent and be certain you have all the items you will need: towels, plastic gloves, a nonmetal comb, endpapers, and a smock to protect clothing.

The length of time you leave the waving lotion on your hair is crucial to the success of a permanent. Different kinds of hair absorb the waving solution at different rates.

Caution: If the chemicals are left on too long, they can severely damage your hair.

To determine the right timing for you, do a strand test 24 hours before you do the permanent, following the kit instructions. If a patch test for allergies is recommended, do this at the same time. If your scalp has a sore or is inflamed, delay your permanent until the condition has healed.

Choose a time for your permanent when there will be no distractions. Take the telephone off the hook. Ask a dextrous friend to help you roll your curls. Take precautions to keep the lotion out of your eyes, and throw away any that's left over; it can't be reused.

Your permanent should last from 3 to 6 months, depending on the degree of curl and the length of your hair.

Pesticides

Using these dangerous substances safely

Caution: Pesticides are poisonous. Before using one, read the label carefully. Study all warnings. Make sure you understand the list of active ingredients—their uses and dangers. Follow directions scrupulously. Never apply a pesticide in the presence of children or pets. Never leave a pesticide, its container, or the equipment used to apply it where children or pets can get at them. Never use a household utensil to measure, mix, or contain a pesticide. Before spraying indoors, put all food away and cover utensils; wash tables and countertops afterward. Don't expose a pressurized spray can to heat or to an open flame.

Use a pesticide only if you cannot control a pest in some other way. If possible, choose a specific agent, such as milky spore disease for Japanese beetle grubs or *Bacillus thuringiensis* for caterpillars. Such general pesticides as carbaryl, chlorphyrifos, diazinon, malathion, and methoxychlor may poison bees and other beneficial insects, as well as earthworms, fish, birds, pets, and humans.

Applying pesticides outdoors
Spray pesticides on calm days, and only after you have warned neighbors of your plans. Wear a waterproof hat and coat and a face mask—especially when spraying a large area. Then leave the area until the spray is dry and the odor has passed.

For localized pest problems, use a hose-end sprayer equipped with a valve to prevent back run. For trees or for medium to large gardens, use a slide-pump sprayer or a compressed-air sprayer that is powerful enough to drive through foliage and wet both sides of all leaves. Stop spraying when the liquid begins to drip from the leaves. Never use a high-pressure paint gun for pesticides.

Dusts are easy to use in the garden, but they don't last long. They adhere best if applied while the morning dew is still on the leaves.

Apply dormant oil sprays to pest-prone trees just before buds begin to open in spring; they smother the eggs and developing larvae of insects. Apply only when temperatures are above freezing. They may discolor evergreen foliage, but the damage is temporary.

Check stored pesticides before use. Lumps are signs of deterioration in dusts and powders. Any dilutible preparation should blend quickly and easily with water; emulsifiable concentrates should turn milky. Dormant oil sprays should be uniform and without traces of sludge at the bottom of the container.

Clean spraying equipment by rinsing it with at least three changes of water. Turn containers upside down to dry. Use separate equipment for pesticides and weed killers.

Applying pesticides indoors
A pump-operated spray can is usually better than a pressurized one because it releases less poison into the air. To avoid the lingering odor of commercial sprays, carefully mix the ingredients yourself in water (the usual oil base intensifies the smell) and apply the mixture with a trigger sprayer. When using a fogger to fumigate a large area, make sure the target area is sealed off from adjoining areas.

Continued next page

Dusts and powders, including boric acid, are most useful in wall voids, cracks and crevices, in tight spaces, and behind cabinets and appliances where children and pets can't reach them. Keep them dry; moisture reduces their effectiveness.

Before applying a pesticide to a houseplant, try sponging the plant with warm, soapy water, or treat a localized infestation with rubbing alcohol on a cotton swab. If this fails, and if the weather allows, take the plant outside to spray it; wait until the spray dries before bringing the plant in. (See also *Houseplants.*)

Accidental spills

In case of a spill, quickly remove splattered clothing and flush exposed skin with water. Wearing rubber gloves, scatter sand or sawdust to absorb liquid pesticide from the floor; then scoop it into a metal container. Outdoors, flush the spill area with plenty of water. Inside, increase ventilation to a maximum. Consult your local Cooperative Extension Service (see p.5) about the handling and disposal of contaminated material. In case of poisoning, call a poison control center immediately (see *Poisoning*).

Pet injuries

Preventing and coping with dog and cat emergencies

Keep phone numbers for your veterinarian, a pet emergency clinic, and the nearest poison control center by a home phone and in your wallet. Consult a veterinarian immediately after any serious accident to your pet.

Assemble a pet first-aid kit. It should contain a rectal thermometer and petroleum jelly, tweezers, a small scissors, adhesive tape, cotton batting and swabs, gauze pads and bandages, a germicidal soap, antibiotic cream, 3 percent hydrogen peroxide to induce vomiting, and powdered activated charcoal to absorb poison.

Car accidents and falls

If your pet is injured by a car or in a fall and remains lying down, move it as little as possible. If it gets up, keep it from walking or running. If possible, have someone else call the veterinari-

an or make arrangements to get you there while you comfort the animal.

Restrain a dog with a muzzle of gauze about 2 feet long, or use a tie or stocking. Remove the muzzle if the dog starts to vomit.

Tying a gauze muzzle

Wrap a panicky cat in a towel or blanket. Or have an assistant hold the cat by the scruff of the neck with one hand and by the rear legs with the other; tell him to place the cat on a table, body extended, uninjured side down, while you administer first aid.

To control bleeding, press a gauze or cloth pad on the wound; wrap it tightly with gauze strips. Don't use a tourniquet. If you suspect a bone fracture, restrict the animal's movement. Even if no wounds are visible, an injured animal may bleed internally and go into shock. Look for pale gums and shallow, uneven breathing. Cover the animal lightly with a blanket.

As soon as possible, get an injured pet to the veterinarian. To transport a dog, slide it gently onto a board or other rigid support. Or use a blanket or a coat as a makeshift stretcher. Gently lift a calm cat under the chest and place it in a carrier or box. Place a struggling cat in a pillowcase if you don't have a carrier.

Treating minor wounds and cuts

Restrain the animal. Clip the coat around the wound; rinse it with water. Gently remove surface dirt with a cotton swab, wash the area with a germicidal soap, and apply an antibiotic cream. Bites, other easily infected wounds, and cuts longer than 1 inch should be treated by a veterinarian.

Heat stroke

Leaving a pet in a closed car or tying it outside in hot weather without shade and water invites heat stroke. If on a hot day, your animal pants and drools

heavily, is warm to the touch, or collapses, douse it with cold water from a hose or immerse it up to the neck in a cold bath; put ice packs on its neck and head. Continue treatment until panting stops and its temperature returns to normal (see *Cats* or *Dog care*); then take it to a veterinarian.

Swallowed objects

Prevent your pet from playing with small, swallowable objects, especially needles and thread. Consult a veterinarian if your pet swallows a foreign object. It may pass naturally or it may cause gagging, excessive salivation, and vomiting. Sharp objects require immediate attention.

Poisons

Keep household cleaners, pesticides, car antifreeze, and other toxic substances away from all pets. In case of poisoning, try to determine what the substance was and call your veterinarian or a poison control center immediately. You may be told to induce vomiting with hydrogen peroxide and to administer a specific antidote or activitated charcoal. After the animal vomits, take it to the veterinarian.

If your pet swallows a caustic or acid substance, or if you suspect poisoning but aren't sure what it has eaten, do not induce vomiting. Rush the animal to a veterinarian.

Electric shock

Don't leave electric cords exposed where a cat or puppy can chew on them. If you leave a young pet alone, unplug lamps and appliances in its confinement area and roll cords up out of reach. Don't touch an animal in contact with current. Cut off power at the circuit breaker panel or fuse box; or stand on a dry surface (newspapers or a rubber mat) and prod the animal off the cord with a wooden pole. Take it to a veterinarian without delay.

Pet medication

Dosing a cat or dog

Administer medicines directly, not mixed in food. Follow the prescribed schedule, but if you miss a dose, don't increase the next one. Don't give an animal human medicine unless so directed by a veterinarian.

When giving medicine, be firm, but gentle; speak reassuringly to your pet. If a cat resists, wrap it in a towel or have an assistant restrain it as shown.

Administering pills

Grasp a dog's muzzle or a cat's head with one hand so that your thumb and forefinger are on opposite sides of the mouth. Press the jaws apart by squeezing the animal's lips against its teeth just forward of the jaw hinge. Keep a dog's lips curled over its teeth to protect your fingers from a bite. Tilt the head back and up. Holding the pill between thumb and forefinger of your free hand, place the pill on the tongue as far back as possible; don't toss it in.

Quickly close the mouth and hold it shut while stroking the throat. With a cat, make sure the pill goes behind the hump of the tongue. Then close its mouth and quickly blow in its face.

Liquid medicine

Gently pull out a dog's lower lip just in front of the corner of the mouth to make a small pocket. Using a syringe or an eyedropper, pour the medicine into the pocket a little at a time. After each partial dose, close the pocket, lift the muzzle slightly, and wait for the dog to swallow. Hold a cat's lips open at one side of the mouth and administer liquid slowly with an eyedropper.

Pet photography

Persuading your favorite animal to pose

A pet is often an uncooperative subject. It may refuse to hold still one minute and then settle into an inaccessible or poorly lit spot the next minute. Pick a setting that helps you control the pet and gain its cooperation. A familiar spot, such as a dog's favorite resting place, can relax a pet. An open outdoor space lets you capture a large animal as it roams about. A hamster, gerbil, or cat will often freeze when set on a glass table.

Have the camera loaded and ready. Then kneel down to the pet's level to get a more revealing, straight-on shot. Move in close for an intimate view that excludes distracting background details. If an animal is restless, quiet it with a bite of food. Evoke a response by talking, whistling, or snapping your fingers. When you see a lively expression, take several shots.

Try to photograph a dog running, leaping to catch a ball, or romping with another dog. Use a shutter speed of $\frac{1}{250}$ second or faster to freeze motion (see *Action photography*). Have someone hold the dog and then release it to run to you or to a bowl of food. Pick a spot along the dog's route and set the camera for that distance. Shoot just as the dog reaches the spot.

Photographing a cat

Try to capture a kitten playing with a toy or a ball of yarn. Photograph an older cat settling into a favorite spot, stretching, or cleaning itself. Subdued light is good for close-ups; it makes the cat's eyes appear brighter.

When shooting a pet with a person, show the two playing or gazing at each other or the pet looking on while its owner is absorbed in an activity.

High-speed film (ISO 400 to 1000) lets you shoot in dimmer light, and it freezes action better. If you use a flash, angle it or bounce it off a wall (see *Photographic lighting*) to avoid creating an unnatural glow in the pet's eyes. If your camera takes other lenses, use a telephoto lens to get candid close-ups from a distance. (See also *Cameras*.)

Pewter cleaning

Restoring old and new pewter

An alloy of tin, antimony, and copper, modern pewter (Britannia metal) resists tarnish and needs only an occasional wash in soapy water. Rinse the item well and dry it with a soft cloth.

Polish modern or old pewter by applying a commercial pewter cleaner as directed on the container. Or make your own modern pewter restorer: for matte finishes, mix a paste of pumice and water (a brighter matte), or rottenstone and vegetable oil (a duller matte); for shiny surfaces use automobile polish or mix a paste of powdered whiting and alcohol.

To maintain old pewter, just dust, then burnish with a soft cloth. The tin and lead in old pewter may cause it to develop a brown tarnish. A bath in washing soda may help to remove this. Because of the lead, don't eat or drink from old pewter utensils.

Philodendrons

Growing a durable houseplant

Striking foliage and easy care make philodendrons ideal indoor plants. Leaves may be heart-, arrow-, lance-, or spatula-shaped; smooth edged, indented, or deeply lobed. The leaf shape in some varieties changes as the plant matures.

Supported on a stake, such climbing species as heartleaf, black-gold, redleaf, and fiddle-leaf can grow up to 8 feet high. Use heartleaf and other small-leaved types as trailers in hanging baskets. Grow large-leaved, non-climbers, such as tree, saddle-leaved, and Wendland's philodendrons, in tubs 12 to 15 inches in diameter.

Use wire-and-paper twists or garden twine to tie a climber loosely to a stake inserted in the potting mixture. For a more attractive display, wrap a 2- to 3-

P

inch layer of sphagnum moss around the stake above the potting-mixture level; bind the moss on tightly with nylon thread. Tie the plant to the stake until its aerial roots take hold. Spray the moss with water daily.

Philodendrons do best in bright, filtered light at room temperatures. In poor light, leaves may grow smaller, and stems may become spindly. Avoid direct sunlight and temperatures below 55°F. During the spring to fall growing period, water moderately, allowing the top ½ inch of soil to dry out between waterings; apply a liquid houseplant fertilizer once a month. In winter, water sparingly and stop feeding. Clean the leaves occasionally with a damp sponge; do not use oils or leaf shiners.

Repot only when roots fill the pot. Use a mixture of 2 parts sterilized potting soil, 2 parts peat moss or leaf mold, and 1 part perlite. To propagate climbing species, take 3- to 4-inch-long tip cuttings, or air-layer them (see *Propagating plants*).

Photographic lighting

Using artificial light to produce natural-looking pictures

The most convenient photographic light source is an automatic electronic flash with a head that tilts. With an automatic flash, you coordinate camera and flash settings as directed; then the flash monitors the light and cuts it off when the subject receives the right amount. A flash that is *dedicated*, designed for use with a specific camera, is the most automatic; you don't have to coordinate settings.

An on-camera flash gives very flat, harsh lighting. To soften this effect, cover the flash tube with a slip-on plastic light diffuser or one or two layers of white tissue. To create shadows that give the subject a more rounded, realistic appearance, connect the flash to the camera with an accessory 4- to 5-foot cord (obtainable at your local camera store), then hold it above and to the side of the camera. For a soft, flattering overall light, you should aim the flash at the ceiling or at a nearby wall. In that way the light

will hit it and then bounce on the subject. Bounce the light from an area that is in front of the subject and make sure the area is a white or neutral color.

A simple lighting setup

You can light portraits or still lifes with three photolamps in reflectors on folding stands. Buy photolamp-compatible color film or use the recommended color correction filter. For a backdrop, choose a light-toned wall. Mount your camera on a tripod; it frees you to adjust the lights.

The main, or *key*, light should look like sunlight beamed from the side. Place it a foot or two above and about 45 degrees to one side of the subject. Check that it doesn't create unflattering shadows. The second, or *fill*, light makes shadowed areas less dark. Put it not quite one and a half times as far from the subject at about camera level so that it hits the subject almost straight on. The last light adds depth;

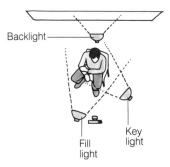

Backlight

Fill light

Key light

put it behind the subject and aim it at the backdrop. Shoot a test roll of film, slightly varying the key and fill lights' distances from the subject.

Pickling

Preserving with salt and vinegar

There are two basic methods of pickling. In *fermentation* (also called brining), vegetables such as cucumbers and cabbage are kept in salt water until a natural fermentation takes place. In *fresh-pack pickling,* fruits or vegetables are often brined briefly, then processed with vinegar and sugar. With either procedure, spices or herbs may be added for flavor.

Virtually any fruit or vegetable can be pickled. For best results, use fresh, firm, unblemished ones (the fruit can be slightly underripe). Wash them thoroughly, but avoid bruising them.

Use pickling salt or pure, granulated salt. Sea, dairy, kosher, or other coarse salts can be substituted, but are not as satisfactory. Don't use the table variety; it contains additives.

If you live in a hard-water area, use distilled or soft water, or boil tap water for 15 minutes and skim off the foam.

Choose vinegar with 4 to 6 percent acidity. Distilled white is best for maintaining the natural color of the pickles; cider, malt, and wine vinegars will add color. Unless a recipe specifies otherwise, use whole spices.

Your pickling equipment should be enamelware or stainless steel for heating, stainless steel or wooden for stirring, and glass or ceramic for storing. For long-term storage you will need canning jars and lids.

Brined dill pickles

Thoroughly wash 4 pounds of pickling cucumbers, 4 to 5 inches long. Line the bottom of a clean, 1-gallon crock with 8 sprigs of dill, 8 garlic cloves, and 15 peppercorns. Add the cucumbers and a brine made with ½ gallon water, ⅓ cup salt, and ½ cup vinegar. Top with more dill, garlic, and peppercorns.

Submerge the pickles with a plate topped by a weight, such as a jar of water. Store at room temperature; skim the scum daily. When fermentation bubbles no longer rise to the surface (after 1 to 3 weeks), the pickles are ready to eat. You can store them in the refrigerator for up to 3 weeks or can them as for fresh-pack dills.

Fresh-pack dills

Soak 4 pounds cleaned cucumbers overnight in a brine made of ⅓ cup pickling salt and ½ gallon water. Drain and pack them into two 1-quart jars. In each jar put 2 garlic cloves, 2 tablespoons dill seeds, and 2 teaspoons mustard seeds. Mix together 1½ cups vinegar, 3 tablespoons salt, 1 tablespoon sugar, and 3 cups water; bring to a boil. Pour the liquid into the jars to within ½ inch of the top. Seal with canning lids and process in boiling water for 20 minutes (see *Canning*). Label and date the jars, then

P

store them in a cool, dry, dark place for at least a month before eating.

Spiced pears

In a 6-quart pot, mix 8 cups sugar, 4 cups vinegar, 2 cups water, 2 tablespoons whole allspice, 2 tablespoons whole cloves, and 8 cinnamon sticks. Simmer for 30 minutes, then add 8 pounds peeled pears; simmer for another 20 minutes. Divide the pears and spices among eight 1-pint jars; cover with liquid to within ½ inch of the top. Seal and process in boiling water for 20 minutes.

Pepper-onion relish

Mince 6 large onions, 5 medium, sweet red peppers, and 5 medium, sweet green peppers; put them into a 4-quart pot. Add 4 cups vinegar, 1 cup sugar, 4 teaspoons salt, and 1 teaspoon mustard seeds. Bring to a simmer and cook, stirring occasionally, until the relish begins to thicken (about 45 minutes). Pack into five ½-pint jars, leaving ½ inch headroom. Process in boiling water for 10 minutes. Store in a cool, dry, dark place for 3 to 4 weeks before using.

Picture framing

Making a decorative case for photographs and prints

You can buy picture-frame molding at art supply and framing stores. Make sure that the picture-holding recess, or rabbet, along the molding's inner edge is deep enough to accommodate the glass, picture, and backing. If you plan to use a mat, also allow for it (see *Matting*). To find out how much molding you will need, add the length and width of the picture or mat and multiply by two. Then add eight times the molding's width to allow for the four joints, plus a few inches for safety. Have a piece of 16-ounce picture glass cut to the picture's dimensions.

Begin by trimming one end of the molding at a 45-degree angle. Scribe a line with a combination square and a penknife. Then cut, using a fine-toothed backsaw in a miter box (see *Miter joints*). To calculate the length of the inside edge of the first piece, subtract twice the rabbet's width from the picture's length and add ⅛ inch

for ease in fitting. Mark the molding's inner edge and scribe a line. Then cut, keeping the saw on the line's waste side. Sand the ends with fine paper.

Use the first piece as a gauge for marking and cutting the piece that goes opposite. Measure and cut the other two pieces in the same manner.

Use carpenter's glue and corner clamps to join the pieces (see *Gluing*). If you only have two clamps, join the pieces in pairs; then join the pairs. Before the glue sets, check for overall squareness by measuring diagonally between corners; they should be the same distance apart. Before removing clamps, drill pilot holes and drive two brads in each corner. Sink the heads and fill the holes. Sand and finish (see *Wood finishing*).

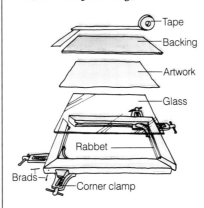

Tape
Backing
Artwork
Glass
Rabbet
Brads
Corner clamp

Set the cleaned glass in the frame. Insert the plain or matted picture and cover with a backing—cardboard, foam-core board, or for more valuable pictures, acid-free museum board. Then press brads or glazier's points into the inner edges of the frame, using padded pliers. Seal the back with wide gummed tape.

Picture hanging

Grouping pictures; fastening them to the wall

Decide whether you want a picture to be viewed from a standing or a sitting position. Experiment by taping a picture-size paper cutout on the wall.

For pictures weighing less than 5 pounds, use a decorative picture hook and a ring that screws into the top of the frame, a sawtooth hanger

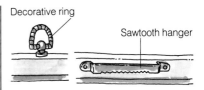

Decorative ring
Sawtooth hanger

hung on a nail, or adhesive- or gum-backed hooks and hangers.

For heavier pictures, make a hanger of braided picture wire of appropriate strength attached to screw eyes. Using an awl, make starter holes for the screw eyes about one-third down

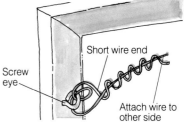

Short wire end
Screw eye
Attach wire to other side

from the top of the frame. Cut a piece of wire about 8 inches longer than the width of the picture. Pull 4 inches of the wire through a screw eye, loop it through again, then twist the end securely around the main wire. Repeat this on the other screw eye. When you pull the wire taut, its apex should be halfway between the screw eyes and the top of the frame. For very heavy pictures, put two extra screw eyes on

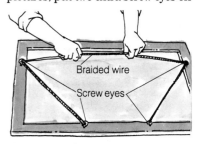

Braided wire
Screw eyes

the bottom of the frame, one-third of the way in from the corners, or on the sides, one-third up from the bottom.

Hook-and-nail hangers can support from 1 to 100 pounds. Space two small hooks a few inches apart (instead of one large hook) to keep a picture hanging evenly. Nail hooks for heavy pictures into studs (see *Studs*).

To hang heavy pictures on thin paneling or plasterboard walls, use hollow-wall anchors or toggle bolts as the package instructs. On concrete or brick walls, use a plastic or lead masonry anchor (see *Wall fasteners*).

Continued next page

P

Have someone hold the picture in place while you make a pencil mark on the wall at the center of the lower edge of the frame. Then slip the picture hook under the picture wire and pull it taut. Measure from the bottom of the frame to the top of the hook. Measure this distance up from the pencil line on the wall, and mark the spot. Reinforce plaster with an "X" of tape, hold the hook firmly on the marked spot, and gently hammer in the nail.

Piecrust

Making a tender, flaky crust

The best piecrust results from accurate measuring, chilled ingredients, light handling of the dough, and minimal stretching when rolling it out.

Basic piecrust

For a two-crust pie, sift into a bowl 2 cups all-purpose flour and ½ teaspoon salt. Using a pastry blender or

two table knives (move the knives parallel to each other but in opposite directions), cut in ⅔ cup chilled vegetable shortening until you have coarse, uneven crumbs. Sprinkle ¼ cup ice water evenly over the mixture. Mix the dough lightly with a fork or knife until it forms large lumps. When the flour appears damp, shape the dough into a ball with your hands and break it open; if it crumbles, add a few drops more water. Reshape into a ball.

Place the dough on a lightly floured marble slab, wooden board, or pastry cloth. Divide it into two balls, one slightly larger than the other. Roll out

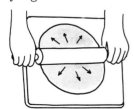

the larger ball with a lightly floured or stockinette-covered rolling pin, working from the center out, not back and forth. Rotate the dough with each roll to get a uniform circle and to prevent sticking. If it tears, pinch it together.

When the dough is ⅛ inch thick and 2 inches larger than the pan, fold it over the rolling pin and lift it into the pan. Press it in place without stretching it. Patch cracks by dampening them and pressing on bits of pastry.

Roll out the top crust 1 inch larger than the pan. Fill the bottom crust. Roll the top crust over the rolling pin and unroll it onto the top of the pie. With scissors or a knife, trim excess dough to ¾ inch. Press the dough around the edge of the pan with a fork; trim the excess. Or roll the edge up and crimp it, as shown. Prick the

top with a fork in several places, or cut vents, so that steam can escape during baking. For a glazed finish, brush the crust with milk or egg white.

Bake a filled pie in the center of the oven. Pies in glass or ceramic pans should be baked at 25°F lower than the recipe calls for. If the edge of a piecrust is browning too quickly, cover it with a strip of foil.

Before baking an unfilled pie shell, prick it with a fork. You can also line the dough with buttered aluminum foil and weight it with a layer of pebbles or uncooked rice or beans. Bake the shell in a preheated oven at 425°F for 8 to 10 minutes. Remove the weights and brush the bottom with egg white or milk; return it to the oven for 7 to 10 minutes. (See also *Tarts.*)

Pilot lights

Relighting and adjusting them

Caution: Don't relight the pilot if there's a strong gas odor. Close the main gas shut-off valve; call the gas company immediately. Before relighting any pilot light, check your owner's manual or look for instructions printed on the appliance (usually on or near the burner control unit) and ventilate the room by opening windows and doors for at least 5 minutes.

To relight the pilot of a gas range surface burner, lift the cook top and hold a match to the pilot. To reach an oven pilot, you may have to remove the oven bottom and the heat baffle beneath it. Turn off the oven and air it out before relighting the pilot.

Gas water heater

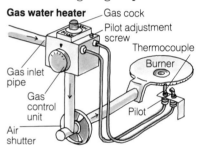

The burner control unit in a furnace, boiler, or water heater usually has a gas cock with *Off, On,* and *Pilot* settings. If the pilot goes out, remove the access panel, turn the gas cock off, and air out the burner chamber. Check the unit's circuit breaker or fuse and its emergency switch to make sure it has electric power. Set the gas cock on *Pilot,* hold a match to the pilot, and depress the cock for 30 seconds. If the control unit has no gas

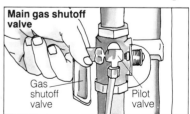

cock, just a reset button, close the main gas shutoff valve, but leave open the smaller pilot valve. Depress the reset button while you relight the pilot.

If the pilot lights, turn the gas cock to *On* or reopen the shutoff valve. If it

P

doesn't, let the gas dissipate, then repeat the procedure, depressing the gas cock or reset button for 1 minute. Don't try to relight the pilot a third time. Replace the thermocouple (see *Gas burners*) or call the gas company.

Adjusting the pilot

A gas burner may not light if the pilot flame is too low. Check your owner's manual for the location of a pilot adjustment screw; turn it counterclock-

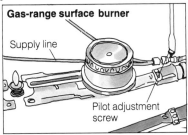

Gas-range surface burner

Supply line

Pilot adjustment screw

wise to raise the flame, clockwise to lower it. If you can't find the screw, or if the pilot flame is yellow rather than blue-green, have a gas company serviceman adjust the flame.

Pimientos

Preserving fresh red peppers

Pimientos are easy to prepare from fresh red peppers and are much tastier than the usual canned pimientos. Wash the peppers. Lay them on their sides in a broiler pan; broil 2 inches from the heat, turning frequently with tongs, for about 15 to 20 minutes; or cook them directly over a gas or wood flame until the skin is charred and blistered. Place the hot peppers in a paper bag; close it tightly and let the peppers steam for 10 minutes or longer. With a small knife, peel off the charred skin, then rub off any remaining shreds of skin.

Remove seeds and pith from the inside; slice the red flesh into strips. Pack the pimientos loosely in jars and cover with vegetable oil. Pimientos will keep in the refrigerator for about a week. Or pack them in freezer containers and freeze for up to 6 months.

Serve pimientos chilled or at room temperature as one of the foods on an antipasto plate. Or use them in salads, pasta sauces, casseroles, stir-fried dishes, or hero sandwiches.

Piñatas

Making and breaking your own

Originating in Mexico, but now popular throughout North America, piñatas are colorful toys shaped like animals, stars, or flowers. At Christmastime, children gather around a piñata

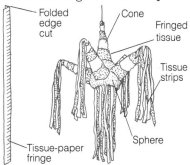

Folded edge cut

Cone

Fringed tissue

Tissue strips

Sphere

Tissue-paper fringe

that is suspended above their heads. They take turns being blindfolded and swinging at the piñata with a stick or baseball bat. Eventually the piñata breaks open, releasing a treasure of sweets and small toys.

Start making a piñata by covering an inflated beach ball with a thin layer of petroleum jelly. Dip newspaper strips into a prepared adhesive (see *Papier-mâché*) and apply them one at a time to the ball. Cover the entire surface of the ball, except for its mouthpiece, with about 10 layers of strips. Then let the paper dry, deflate the ball, and remove it through the mouthpiece opening. Poke two small holes through the surface of the papier-mâché and attach a long, sturdy string. Fill the sphere with candy and prizes. Seal the opening with masking tape.

If you like, add cone constructions to create arms, legs, horns, flower petals, or other features. Simply cut a triangle from cardboard, roll the triangle into a cone, and secure it with tape. Make flaps by cutting 1-inch slits around the cone's base. Fold these flaps out and glue their undersides to the sphere. Cover with paper strips.

Color the piñata with tempera, acrylic, or poster paint. Cut 3- to 4-inch-wide strips of colored tissue paper, fold the strips in half lengthwise, and cut halfway through the folded edge every ¼ inch or so. Separate the tissue into individual strips of fringe.

Glue the fringe to the piñata in parallel layers, using one row to conceal the glued section of the preceeding row.

Hang the piñata by passing its string over a beam or hook and tugging on the string to make the piñata move. Let the children strike out for riches.

Pineapple cutting

Preparing the fruit for serving

To serve pineapple as a dish by itself, cut a slice from the bottom, then cut the entire pineapple, leaves and all, lengthwise into quarters. Cut out the triangular core of each section. With the skin side down, use a small knife to separate the fruit from the peel, then cut crosswise to make wedges. Serve the wedges on the skin. Each quarter pineapple makes a serving.

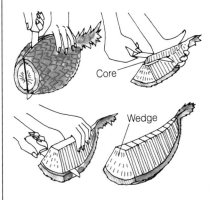

Core

Wedge

To get pineapple slices, cut off the bottom and the top of the pineapple, stand the pineapple on its bottom, and use a large knife to peel the skin. Lay the peeled fruit on its side, slice it, and cut the core from each slice.

Pinochle

Auction pinochle—a popular three-hand gambling variant

Use a 48-card deck: two each of the 9 through ace in the four suits. Points are scored by cards taken in *tricks* and by *melds*, or card combinations.

There are three classes of melds: *sequences*—ace through 10 of trumps (150 points), king and queen of trumps (40), king and queen of all other suits

P

(20); *groups* of different suits—four aces (100), four kings (80), four queens (60), and four jacks (40); *special*—queen of spades and jack of diamonds, *Pinochle* (40); 9 of trumps (10), king and queen of each suit (240). A card used in one kind of meld may be used in others of different classes.

Each card taken in a trick is worth points: ace, 11; 10, 10; king, 4; queen, 3; jack, 2. The last trick won is 10.

The deal and the bid

Give the other two players, the kitty, and yourself the same number of chips. Deal (clockwise) the other players and yourself 15 cards each. Each player *bids* what he believes he can score, or *passes*. The minimum bid is 300 points; bid in multiples of 10.

The play

The highest bidder wins the bid and make melds. Suppose that's you. Show your melds. If they equal or surpass your bid, score your bid; no play is necessary. If not, reinsert them in your hand. Turn over the *widow* (the three cards left from the deal), then add them to your hand. Choose three cards from your hand to *bury* (lay facedown) for the rest of the round. If your opponents concede that you will win your bid, score it; there is no play. If, after reassessing your hand, you concede that you'll fail, there's no play; it's *single bête*. Pay each opponent and the kitty the value of your bid in chips. For a bid of 300 to 340, the value is 1; 350 to 390, 2; 400 to 440, 4; 450 to 490, 6; 500 to 540, 8; 550 to 590, 10.

If none of these shortcuts is possible, announce a trump suit (your strongest) and begin the play by laying down a card. The others must play a card of that suit if possible; the highest card wins the trick. Opponents' tricks are placed in one pile. If you don't have the suit led, play a trump, which beats any suit. If you have no trumps, play another suit; it would have no winning value. If you lead with a trump, the others must play a higher trump if possible. The winner of each trick leads in the next trick. Play goes on until all 15 tricks have been won.

Scoring

If your total score (melds, tricks, and widow) meets or exceeds your bid, you've made contract, and the score is yours. If you fail, it's *double bête*, and you must pay your opponents and the kitty twice the value of your bid. Your opponents get your bid score, which is then subtracted from your total.

Pinworms

Getting rid of an intestinal parasite; avoiding reinfection

Pinworms are tiny white parasites that infest the intestines, mainly of children. They move to the anal area to lay their eggs, causing rectal itching, a sign that worms are present. When a child scratches, eggs lodge under his fingernails and are passed on to others in the family by way of food, utensils, sheets, and towels.

If a child complains of itching or often scratches the anal area or if worms can be seen there or in bowel movements, call your doctor for advice and for a prescription. No over-the-counter remedy is effective.

To avoid reinfestation, make sure that bedsheets, towels, and underwear are changed often and washed in very hot water. Have everyone in the household keep their fingernails clipped and wash their hands well before eating, before handling food, after going to the toilet, and after handling pets. Clean toilet seats daily.

Pipe insulation

Saving heat and reducing condensation

Cut down heat loss by insulating hot-water and heating pipes. Insulate cold-water pipes to reduce condensation (see *Humidity control*). Use premolded sleeves of closed-cell neoprene foam or strips of foam wrapping.

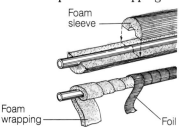

Foam sleeve

Foam wrapping — Foil

The sleeves come in various diameters. To find the size you need, close an adjustable wrench over the pipe and measure the distance between the jaws. Cut little notches in the sleeves to fit around bends.

Install foam wrapping spirally, with a half-width overlap. Cover sleeves or wrapping with aluminum foil. Secure with duct tape every 10 inches and at all joints.

Pipes

Replacing a length of threaded pipe; repairing a leak

Lead pipes, found in some older houses, can contaminate the water; replace them with galvanized steel, plastic, or copper. Brass pipes are safe and durable, but scarce and expensive; replace a damaged one with another material of the same size.

Plumbing pipe is sized by its inside diameter: a ¾-inch pipe has a ¾-inch opening, no matter what it is made of or how large it is outside.

Adapters are available for joining different kinds of pipes so that you can mix materials in the system. Most metal pipes are joined by threaded fittings; the pipe threads must be waterproofed with a *joint sealer* before they are screwed in. Copper pipes are joined by flared or soldered fittings (see *Sweat soldering pipes*), plastic pipes by clamped or cemented fittings (see *Plastic pipes*).

Joint sealers

1. Wrap pipe thread with wicking

2. Cover wicking with joint sealing compound or tape

You cannot unscrew a threaded pipe that has fittings on both ends; as you loosen one joint, you tighten the other. Nor can you screw a new pipe in. To replace a threaded pipe, cut it with a hacksaw and use pipe wrenches to remove each section. Buy two

P

new pipes, threaded on both ends, which—together with a *union coupling*—equal the length of the old

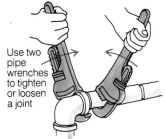

Use two pipe wrenches to tighten or loosen a joint

pipe. Apply a joint sealer and screw a union nut onto one end of each pipe. Then, after slipping the ring nut over the pipe with the unthreaded union nut, screw the other end of both pipes into the fittings. Align the faces of the union nuts and tighten the ring nut.

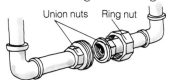

Union nuts   Ring nut

To repair a leaky pipe, look first at the joint; an epoxy compound may do the job. For a pinhole leak in a pipe, use a two-piece *pipe-leak clamp* as shown. For a large leak, use a *dresser coupling*. After shutting off the water supply, cut the pipe with a hacksaw. Pull one section aside and slip a coupling nut, a metal washer, a rubber gasket, and a sleeve of threaded pipe

Nut ————   ——— Bolts

Pipe-leak clamp

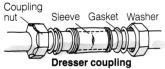

Coupling nut   Sleeve Gasket Washer

Dresser coupling

onto it. Slip the other nut, washer, and gasket onto the other section. Realign the pipe, center the sleeve over the break, and tighten both nuts.

Piping

How to make and insert cording

Piping, also called cording, is inserted in a seam as decoration. It comes ready-made, or you can make your own. To make piping, you need cotton cord, available in several thicknesses where dressmaking or drapery supplies are sold; bias strips of fabric; and a machine zipper foot. The fabric covering the cord can match or contrast with the article it will decorate.

Cut bias strips long enough to cover all the cord and wide enough to wrap around the cord, plus 1¼ inches for seam allowances. Join strips with a ¼-inch seam. Press the seam open and trim protruding edges.

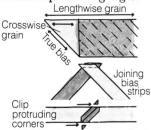

Lengthwise grain

Crosswise grain

True bias

Joining bias strips

Clip protruding corners

Fold fabric over the cord, right side out; pin it. Position the zipper foot to the right of the needle. Stitch close to, but not tightly against, the cord.

To insert piping, pin it to the right side of one fabric layer, aligning the piping stitching with the seamline. Clip the piping seam allowance at corners or curves. Stitch the piping just to the left of the first stitching. With right sides facing and with the piped layer on top, sew the two layers together, stitching just to the left of the stitches that hold the piping.

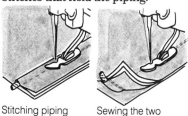

Stitching piping to first layer

Sewing the two layers together

If piping ends must be joined, do so before attaching the second fabric layer. Leave ½ inch free of stitching at the starting end. Cut the cord of the joining end to abut the first one; trim the fabric to ½ inch and fold it under ¼ inch. Wrap it around the starting end. Stitch through all layers.

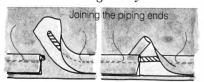

Joining the piping ends

Place mats

Making them from fabric

Place mats must be sturdy enough to form a stable base for dishes and utensils. Reversible quilted material is especially suitable; or use two layers of firmly woven fabric back to back. Avoid slippery or very thin fabrics. Each mat should measure at least 10 x 15 inches to provide sufficient space for a place setting. An oval works well for a round or oval table, a rectangle for a rectangular table. Add ⅝ inch all around for seam allowances.

Stitch two fabric layers right sides together, leaving a 4-inch opening in one edge. Trim the seam allowances to half; trim the corners diagonally or clip *V*'s from the curves. Press the seam allowances flat, then press them

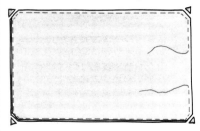

open. Turn the place mat right side out, pushing out corners and bringing the seamlines out to the edges. Slipstitch the opening closed (see *Slipstitching*). Press the mat flat.

To finish quilted fabric or a single layer, use ½-inch double-fold bias tape (see *Pot holders*). Begin binding at the center of one side. At the end, turn under the tape ½ inch; wrap it around the beginning, and stitch.

Place settings

Where to put what

When setting a table, place the flatware on each side of the dinner plate, with the handles about an inch from

P

the edge of the table. Forks go to the left of the plate; knives and spoons to the right. Turn the sharp edges of the knife blades toward the plate. Utensils for the beginning courses of the meal—the appetizer fork or the soup-spoon, for example—should be far-thest away from the plate; silver for the later courses should be near the plate. Unless a salad is being served before the main course, place the sal-ad fork nearest the plate. The dessert-spoon or fork can be placed above the dinner plate or can be brought in on the plates with the dessert.

Salad plates should be placed to the left of the forks, coffee cups and sau-cers to the right of the knives and spoons. Water and wine glasses are placed on the upper right.

If you serve bread and butter, it's best to provide butter plates. Place the butter plate to the upper left of the dinner plate, with the butter knife across the top, blade toward the user. (If you're served bread and there is no butter plate, it's acceptable to put but-ter on the dinner plate and the bread on the tablecloth.)

Napkins may be folded in a variety of ways and may be placed in the cen-ter of the dinner plate, in the water glass, or to the right of the forks.

Planing

Leveling a board; squaring an edge; trimming end grain

To *level* the surface of a rough board with a *jack plane*, set the blade to cut up to $1/16$ inch deep; align the blade by sighting along the base plate. Clamp the board firmly between a vise and a bench dog—or use a wooden jig as shown—so that it is level, solidly sup-ported, and about waist high.

Hold one hand on the plane's knob and the other on the handle. Apply

even pressure as you push the plane diagonally across the wood grain.

When you have removed the high spots from the board, reset the blade of the plane for a shallower cut and be-gin to *smooth* the surface. Plane with the grain in long strokes, holding the plane at a 15-degree angle to the direc-tion of the cut so that the blade slices the wood, rather than chops it. A long, continuous shaving should re-sult. Lift the nose of the plane slightly at the end of each stroke.

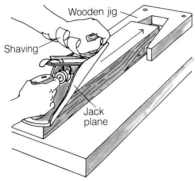

To *square the edge* of a board, al-ways follow the grain. Clamp the work so that it is level. Hold the plane at a 15-degree angle and apply even pres-sure through long, straight strokes.

Use a *block plane* to trim the *end* of a board. To avoid a concave cut, work from both edges toward the middle, then level the resultant hump.

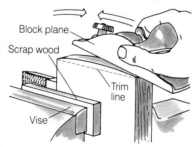

Plank paneling

Finishing walls with solid wood boards

At a lumberyard or a home center, you can buy prejointed planks that are almost as easy to install as 4 x 8 sheet paneling. They come in a variety of woods and finishes and are general-ly between $3/8$ and $3/4$ inch thick and from 3 to 7 inches wide with tongue-

and-groove or shiplap joints. A typical package of mixed widths and lengths will cover 24 square feet.

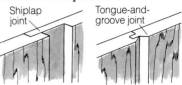

On new framing, use the planks as the basic wall covering. On existing walls, remove base, window, and oth-er trim. Turn off the power to electric outlets (see *Circuit testing*) and re-move the cover plates. If the walls are even and the planks are to be horizon-tal, you can nail them to the studs; otherwise, nail them to horizontal furring strips (see *Furring strips*).

To install planks vertically, start by putting the first plank in a corner, with its tongued edge out. Make sure it's plumb. Using finishing nails, se-cure the plank's inner edge to each furring strip; predrill holes in hard-wood and sink the nailheads with a nail set. Then angle a nail through the tongued edge going into each strip; sink the nailhead slightly. Angle the nails on each subsequent plank and press against the plank for a tight fit.

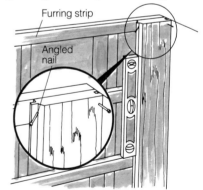

As you work, cut the planks to fit around windows and doors and at wall edges. Use a slip-in template to mark cutouts for electric outlets and a compass to mark uneven cuts along walls (see *Paneling*).

To put up horizontal planks, mark the studs (see *Studs*) and nail into them. Attach the first plank at floor level with its tongued edge up; level it with shims. Then work up the wall.

Finish by installing matching trim along the floor and ceiling and around windows and doors.

Plant care during vacation

Keeping houseplants healthy while you're away from home

If you're going away for a few days, water your plants just before leaving, then put them where they'll be away from direct sunlight. In winter, if you turn the heat down, leave them in the middle of a warm room; place tender plants atop the refrigerator or freezer, where they will benefit from the warm air emerging from the appliance.

A longer absence during the growing season calls for better care. You can have a friend act as sitter, but attach instructions to each plant to keep the sitter from killing the plants with kindness—by overwatering them.

You can safeguard a plant for two summer weeks by watering it thoroughly and putting it, pot and all, into a large, transparent plastic bag. Keep the bag from touching the foliage by inserting sticks into the soil. Seal the top of the bag with a twist. If the plant is very large, enclose only the pot in the bag and tie the bag top around the plant stem—you can safely leave it this way for up to a week.

For longer periods, try any of these self-watering methods. 1. Using individual plant wicks (available at garden centers), connect one or more pots to a container full of water. 2. For plants in clay pots, weight a bath towel with bricks in the bathtub, and run water until it  rises just above the tops of the bricks. Place the plants on the bricks. 3. If the plants are in plastic pots, get a felt capillary mat from a garden center, put the mat into a sink with the drain open, place the plants on it, and let the faucet drip continuously. Or place one end of a capillary mat in a small tub of water and put the other end of the mat on a counter with plants on it. Clay pots are too thick to let the soil come into contact with a mat, but you can use a mat with them if you insert a wick into the pot's drainage hole.

Plant galls

What to do about tumorous growths on plants

Plant galls are abnormal growths on leaves, branches, or roots; they can range from a tiny blister to a sizable irregular swelling. Galls can cause stunted growth; parts beyond the gall may die. Often they have larvae of insects (wasps, mites, aphids) inside. Some galls are caused by fungal, bacterial, or viral diseases.

Although galls look harmful, most do not seriously injure plants. You can try to control them by handpicking them and discarding them. If a shrub is severely infested, cut off and burn all affected parts. This will help prevent future infestations. If the cause is microscopic nematodes on a plant's roots, fumigation of the soil may be necessary. Check with your Cooperative Extension Service (see p.5) or local garden center.

One gall that seriously harms and often kills plants is the *crown gall*. Caused by a bacterium, these rough, spongy tumors, whose color ranges from pink to dark green, appear close to the soil level. Dig up and discard any plant that has them.

Planting

Basic guidelines for putting plants into the ground

Whether you are planting an oak tree or a cabbage, the same rules apply: 1. never lift a plant by its stem; 2. dig a hole at least half again as wide and deep as the plant's root mass; 3. disturb the roots as little as possible; 4. surround them with rich, moist soil.

A *tree* or *shrub* may come with bare roots, with a root ball wrapped in burlap (B and B), or in a container. Keep bare roots in water. Keep container and B and B plants moist.

As you dig a planting hole, put topsoil and subsoil in separate piles. Mix enough peat moss, manure, or compost into the topsoil to increase the volume by half; add a handful of bonemeal for phosphorus. Put enough enriched topsoil back into the hole so that, when packed down, it will support the plant at its original depth. For bare-root stock, make a cone of topsoil and spread the roots over it. Set B and B stock into the hole without removing the burlap. (If the cover is plastic, cut it away carefully, but don't pull it from under the root ball.) Take a container plant carefully from its pot and position it, soil and all.

Add topsoil, carefully working it in around bare roots, until the hole is about two-thirds full. Then cut the burlap from the top of a root ball and peel it back. Pack the soil down firmly and fill the hole with water. Let it drain; then fill with topsoil. Do not tread this soil down. Make a shallow saucer around the stem and give the plant another bucket of water. Make sure the plant gets at least a bucket of water a week during its first summer.

The same process applies to *perennials, ferns,* and *vegetables,* but on a smaller scale. Water the plants well an hour or two before transplanting. If possible, transplant in late afternoon or on a cloudy day so that plants can get established before being subjected to the heat of the sun.

When planting seedlings, there is no point in enriching the soil one hole at a time; prepare the whole bed (see *Soil preparation*). Mark rows with string stretched between stakes. With a hand trowel, dig individual holes at regular intervals. Base your spacing on the mature form of the plants: tall, slender plants can be fairly close; spreading ones need more space.

To take a seedling from its container, tap the container's bottom and sides. Tip it just enough to let the root  ball slide out into your hand. Then put the root ball in its hole as with any container plant. Mark each row with a tag giving the plant's name and the date. (See also *Fertilizing trees; Fertilizing vegetables; Pruning shrubs; Staking plants.*)

P

Plasterboard

Covering a room's ceiling and walls with gypsum wallboard

Use standard ½-inch thick, 4-x 8-foot sheets of plasterboard for most jobs. Choose longer sheets when they will reduce the number of joints; water-resistant sheets for a kitchen or bathroom. Your building code may require fire-resistant ⅝-inch sheets on some walls and may dictate how you attach the sheets; check with your local building department. You also need annular-ring nails, joint compound and tape, and for corners that project outward, metal corner beads. The special tools needed are a crown-head (roundheaded) hammer, 4-inch and 10-inch flat-bladed knives for finishing joints, and an angled tool for finishing corners. If a room's framing is uneven—or if you are covering masonry or plaster—put furring strips over the entire surface (see *Furring strips*). Space them 24 inches apart from center to center for ½-inch plasterboard, 16 inches for ⅜-inch.

Planning the installation

Plasterboard's long edges are usually tapered. When you put two side by side, they form a recess for the joint tape and compound. The short ends are not tapered; it's harder to hide a joint between them. Keep those joints to a minimum. Stagger them to avoid forming a long, noticeable seam. Never join an end to a tapered edge.

Strive for the least number of joints overall. Make sure each sheet edge falls along a joist or a stud or receives support at corners and at regular intervals. Put partial sheets in a ceiling's center rather than its perimeter.

For structural strength, sheets are usually run horizontally on walls. But it's all right to run them vertically when this produces fewer joints. Do not put a joint along a window or door edge; settling and frame shrinkage will cause cracks. Try to cover the door or window area with a sheet; then cut out the opening. A joint midway along a door or window frame is acceptable.

Putting up the sheets

Do the ceiling first with a helper (A). Make a T-brace from 2 x 4's. Cut a piece 2 inches longer than ceiling height; then nail a 3-foot piece across one end. Start in one corner and work across, butting sheets end to end. To lift a sheet into place, climb a ladder, holding one end of the sheet while your helper raises and wedges the T-brace under the other. Keep the sheet level to avoid breaking it. Make sure that the end that will join the next sheet falls along the center of a joist.

Working from the sheet's center out, drive pairs of nails about 2 inches apart into each joist at 12-inch intervals. Along the edges, drive single nails at 7-inch intervals; stay ⅜ inch from the edge. As you nail, press the plasterboard tightly against the joist. Drive each of the nails flush, then in slightly, creating a shallow depression with a crown-head hammer (B), but don't break the paper.

To cut a sheet (C), draw a line on the face side; then score it, using a sharp utility knife guided by a straightedge.

Align a 2 x 4 under the scored line with the sheet's waste part projecting outward. Press the waste part downward to snap the sheet. Then slice through the backing paper. Use a saber saw to cut curves, notches, and openings. Measure and mark cuts to allow ⅛-inch clearance; forcing a sheet in place causes it to crumble.

To install sheets horizontally on a wall, start in a corner. With a helper, position a sheet snugly against the ceiling. To support the sheet while you work, drive two 8d nails into the studs under its lower edge. Nail the sheet as you did on the ceiling, spacing the edge nails at 8-inch intervals. At corners, do not nail an edge that overlaps another. To fit a lower sheet tightly against an upper one, cut it to fit with ½-inch clearance; then raise the sheet with a couple of foot levers made from scrap wood (D).

Make cutouts for windows and doors as you go. For accuracy, measure from the ceiling or from a sheet already in place. Use a box template to mark electric-outlet cutouts and box extenders to bring the outlets even with the new surface (see *Paneling*).

Finishing the joints

Fill any gap wider than ¼ inch with joint compound. To tape a joint (E), spread a layer of joint compound with a 4-inch joint knife. Cut a full length of tape. Press it onto the compound and smooth it with the knife. Hold the knife at a low angle for spreading the compound; raise it nearly perpendicular for smoothing. After 24 hours, apply a second coat 10 to 12 inches wide, using a 10-inch joint knife.

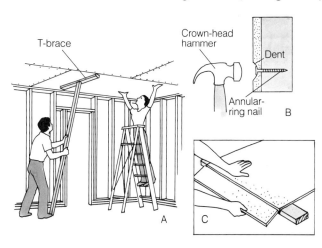

T-brace · Crown-head hammer · Dent · Annular-ring nail · A · B · C

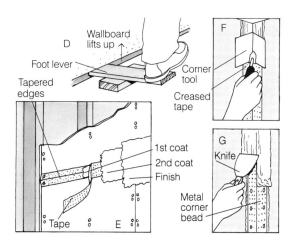

Wallboard lifts up · Foot lever · Tapered edges · D · 1st coat · 2nd coat · Finish · Tape · E · Corner tool · Creased tape · F · Knife · Metal corner bead · G

Feather it at the edges to merge smoothly with the surface. A day later, dilute the compound slightly with water and apply a last coat, feathering it up to 10 inches on either side of the joint. The more smoothly you apply the compound, the less finishing work you will have to do.

In corners, crease the tape lengthwise before pressing it in; use the corner tool for applying and smoothing (F). On corners that project outward, spread compound and press on the protective metal beading. Then nail it in place and finish the joint (G). Also fill and smooth the depressions around nails. To finish, wipe the dried compound smooth with a clean, damp sponge. Or sand thoroughly with fine paper; wear a mask when sanding. Apply a latex primer before painting.

Plasterboard patching

Repairing damaged wallboard

To fix a crack, small hole, or dent, dig out any loose gypsum. Then fill the opening with joint or spackling compound; smooth with a wide putty knife to blend the patch with the wall.

To repair a larger hole, use a keyhole saw to enlarge the area to a rectangular opening. Cut a 1 x 2 about 4 inches wider than the opening. Put construction adhesive on the ends of the 1 x 2. Insert it into the opening and press it against the wall's inside surface. Drill pilot holes and drive a drywall screw into each end through the plasterboard. Cut a piece of plas-

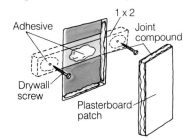

Adhesive
1 x 2
Joint compound
Drywall screw
Plasterboard patch

terboard ⅛ inch smaller all around than the opening, preferably from material slightly thinner than that of the wall. Put construction adhesive on the 1 x 2; put joint compound around the edges of the opening and the patch. Ease the patch into place.

Smooth compound over the area, feathering it to blend with the wall.

For extensive damage, trim the area even with the edges of the nearest studs. Tack 1 x 2 nailing strips along the studs' edges. Then secure a patch

Studs
1 x 2 nailing strips

to the 1 x 2's with annular-ring nails.

To fix peeling joint tape, remove the loose tape, trying not to dislodge chunks of joint compound. Sand the area smooth. Cut new tape to fit. With a joint knife, apply joint compound, press in the tape, and smooth a thin layer of compound over the tape. Apply compound again 24 hours later.

Finish all patches by sanding thoroughly with fine paper. Apply a latex primer before painting. (See also *Popping nails.*)

Plaster patching

Repairing cracks and holes in plaster walls and ceilings

To fix a crack, run an old screwdriver or a beverage-can opener along it to enlarge the opening and knock out loose particles. If a crack is over ¼ inch wide, undercut its edges; that is, taper them inward to widen the crack at the bottom. Brush out loose plaster. Fill the crack with spackling compound; smooth with a putty knife.

To fix a hole, check to see if the supporting wood or metal lath is sound. If it is, clean out loose particles and undercut the edges. Wet the edges thoroughly with water and apply a plaster-bonding agent. Then, starting at the edges and working in, fill the hole to about half its depth with patching plaster. Roughen the plaster's surface with the edge of a putty knife and let it dry for 24 hours. Then dampen the area and apply a second layer of plaster, smoothing it even with the wall.

If the lath is broken, use a keyhole saw or metal sheers to remove damaged portions. Clean and undercut the hole's edges. Cut a piece of wire mesh larger than the hole, and loop a

length of wire through its center. Put the mesh in the hole and pull it tightly against the inside of the wall. Twist

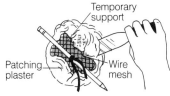

Temporary support
Patching plaster
Wire mesh

the wire around a pencil or dowel to hold the mesh in place. Dampen the hole and apply plaster-bonding agent. Spread patching plaster generously around the edges; make sure it penetrates the mesh. Let it dry. Then remove the wire and finish plastering.

Finish all patches by sanding with fine paper. Prime before painting.

Plastic laminate

Durable coverings

Plastic laminates are available in a wide range of colors, patterns, and textures. Use thin laminates (¹⁄₃₂ inch) for covering vertical surfaces such as walls and doors; thicker, more durable laminates (¹⁄₁₆ inch) for horizontal surfaces such as tabletops and countertops.

Strip paint or varnish from the surface to be covered (see *Paint removal; Stripping furniture*). Fill holes and cracks with plastic wood or a similar agent. Sandpaper the surface smooth and level. When measuring for laminate, add ¼ inch extra on all sides. Mark the laminate for cutting with a pencil and a straightedge.

To cut, clamp the laminate securely, with the cutting line close to the work surface's edge. The decorative surface should be faceup when using a handsaw, facedown for power saws. Hold a handsaw at a low angle; cut slowly. Or use a laminate-cutting scriber; with the decorative side up, score along the cutting line several times. Reverse sides; then place a yardstick along the line and bend the excess piece upward until it snaps off.

Using a paint roller you won't mind discarding, spread a thin, even layer of contact cement over each surface to be joined; allow them to dry as advised in the instructions. To keep the two

P

pieces separated while proper alignment is made, lay thin wood strips or dowels on the surface to be covered.

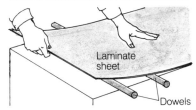

Laminate sheet

Dowels

Gradually remove the strips or dowels, allowing the two surfaces to come into contact. After full contact, expel air pockets by applying pressure over the laminated surface with a rubber-surfaced pressure roller or a rolling pin. Work from the center outward.

Trim off excess with a router and a laminate-cutting carbide bit. Or use a

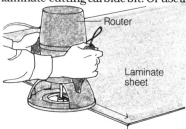

Router

Laminate sheet

flat, fine-tooth metal file in light, downward strokes away from the laminate face and at a 45-degree angle to the edge. To finish table and counter edges, glue on precut edging strips.

Plastic pipes

Kinds of materials; how to use them in home plumbing

Plastic pipes come in many forms. Rigid materials include PVC (polyvinyl chloride), usable for cold-water supply lines; CPVC (chlorinated polyvinyl chloride), for water up to 180°F; and tough, weatherproof, heat- and acid-resistant PVC-DWV for drainage, waste, and vent systems. Each material has its own fittings, its own primer, and its own cement. Make sure that you buy the right kinds for the material you're using. Threaded fittings are also available for joining plastic pipes to metal ones (see *Pipes*).

Regulations vary concerning the use of plastic pipes; before installing them, check local building codes. To find the overall length needed for a

piece of pipe, slip waste pieces of pipe into the fittings and mark how deep they go. Then measure the distance between the faces of the fittings and add the depth figures. Use a hacksaw, backsaw, or power saw to cut the pipe; remove burrs and bevel the ends with a penknife.

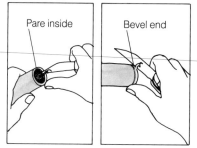

Pare inside

Bevel end

To join a pipe to a fitting, first brush the appropriate primer on the outside of the pipe and the inside of the fitting. Wait about 15 seconds, then apply an even coat of cement to the same surfaces. Push the pipe into the fitting and turn it to spread the cement. Allow the cement to cure according to manufacturer's directions.

PB (polybutylene), a flexible tubing, can carry hot water or cold. It's joined

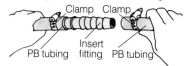

Clamp   Clamp

Insert fitting

PB tubing   PB tubing

with clamps or grip fittings and is especially useful for snaking water supply lines through hard-to-reach places.

Plugs

Replacing a damaged plug on an electric cord

A damaged plug is easy to replace: unscrew it or cut off the power cord. If it's a flat-wire cord, snap a replacement

Flat-wire plugs

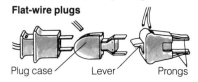

Plug case   Lever   Prongs

flat-wire plug to its end as accompanying instructions direct; no wire stripping is needed.

If it's a round-wire cord, use a multipurpose tool to cut off the damaged

plug; strip the sheathing back about 2 inches; cut off ¾ inch of each wire's insulation. Twist the wire strands clockwise until tight. Before hooking them to the terminals and screwing them fast, tie the wires into an underwriter's knot, as shown; pull the knot between the prongs.

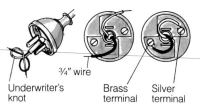

¾" wire

Underwriter's knot

Brass terminal

Silver terminal

Replace the three-prong plug of a heavy-duty cord with one of appropriate amperage (if in doubt, be advised by your hardware salesman). Prepare the wires as for a round-wire plug, knotting all three wires if there is enough space between the prongs; if there isn't, knot only the black and white wires. Connect the ground wire (green) to the green terminal, the black wire to the brass terminal, and the white to the silver. Replace the plug's protective cover.

If a female receptacle (plug) is damaged, buy an exact replacement. Open the old receptacle by undoing the screw or screws that hold the halves together. Note how the wires are connected to the terminals as a guide for installing the new receptacle. If the receptacle is molded, cut it off and install a new receptacle after preparing the wires as described.

Plumb line

Finding the perfect vertical

A plumb line is a piece of string with a weight, or plumb bob, on the end. To use it, suspend the string from a nail, hook, or other object so that the bob hangs freely. The string is perfectly vertical. Mark the spot beneath the point of the bob, or align a structural piece, such as a wall stud or a fence post, with the string.

Sometimes, as when wallpapering, installing tiles, or erecting shelves, it is useful to mark vertical lines on a wall. To do this, rub the string with colored chalk; then, after you have found and marked the plumb, stretch the line taut and snap it. Self-chalking lines are available, in which 50 or 100 feet of string are contained in a reel that doubles as a plumb bob.

Plumb bob

Self-chalking reel

Plywood

The common kinds; how to use them

Plywood consists of panels made from glued layers, or plies, of veneer or wood. Plywood usually comes in 4- x 8-foot sheets, in thicknesses ranging from ¼ to 1¼ inches and greater.

Cheaper and lighter than solid wood, plywood does not shrink or swell with changes in humidity. However, its edges don't hold fasteners or glue as securely as solid wood and are more vulnerable to chipping and moisture; they must be covered for an attractive edge (see *Veneer tape*). Plywood can be used in many applications, including as a facing for walls, roofs, floors, concrete forms, and as a substitute for wide lumber.

Plywood may have a core (center ply) of veneer, particleboard, strips of lumber, or other material. Lumber core's advantage is that you can drive screws into the edge. Particleboard core is cheaper but has less bending strength than veneer-core or lumber-core plywood.

For most uses, choose *construction* plywood. Its face and back are of softwood, usually southern pine or Douglas fir. Each sheet is classified by the quality of veneer used or by its intended end use. In the top veneer grade, *N*, available by special order only, the surface is smooth and evenly matched, suitable for an unpainted, natural finish. Standard veneer grades are *A*, *B*, *C*, and *D*. Look for the stamp on the back of a sheet; it will describe the grade or intended end use. For outdoor use, buy *exterior* plywood, which is made with waterproof adhesive.

Decorative plywood has a hardwood face. It is classified by the species of wood from which the face is made and by the quality of the veneer. *AA* is best, followed by *A* through *E*. *AA* or *A* classifications are usable for cabinetmaking, as is *Specialty* (*SP*), a veneer with a special character, such as wormy chestnut, bird's-eye maple, English brown oak, or prefinished wall panelling.

To cut plywood, use a power saw with a carbide-tipped blade: the adhesive in plywood dulls a steel blade quickly. To avoid splintering the surface, hold the sheet so that the lead teeth of the saw blade cut into the good side. Cover the area to be cut with masking tape, and if possible, place scrap wood underneath. When drilling, place a wood block under the back to prevent chipped edges. Store plywood sheets by laying them flat if possible; otherwise, store them on edge in a vertical position. If plywood is stored at an angle, it is subject to warping.

Poaching

Cooking food in a barely simmering liquid

Poaching preserves texture and prevents protein foods from becoming tough. The liquid can be flavored to complement the food. For poaching eggs or fish, see *Eggs; Fish cooking.*

To poach a whole chicken, wash, truss (see *Poultry trussing*), and immerse it in enough cold water or white wine and water to cover half of it. Add ⅛ teaspoon salt per cup of liquid and herbs, if desired. Bring to a simmer; cook for ½ hour; turn and cook for another ½ hour. To poach chicken breasts with bones, simmer 25 minutes; allow 15 minutes for boneless.

Fruits such as pears, apples, and figs poach well. Combine 1 cup sugar with 2 cups water in a saucepan. Bring to a simmer, stirring until the sugar dissolves. Add a stick of cinnamon, a slice of ginger root, or 2 tablespoons lemon juice. Peel and core the fruit and lower it into the simmering syrup. Simmer for 10 to 20 minutes; test for tenderness with a skewer.

Pocket billiards

The rules for playing pool

Pocket billiards, or pool, as it is usually called, is played with 15 numbered *object* balls and a white *cue* ball on a six-pocket table that is twice as long as it is wide—generally 4½ x 9 feet. Two players compete, and the first to pocket eight balls wins the game.

Arrange the balls as shown and decide who will play first. If you play

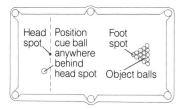

Head spot | Position cue ball anywhere behind head spot | Foot spot | Object balls

first, use a cue stick to drive the cue ball into the group of object balls. On this play, one ball must drop into a pocket or two object balls and the cue ball must strike a cushion (side of the table), or your opponent may demand that you replay the opening.

You get credit for all object balls you pocket on the opening shot. In subsequent plays, you must specify which balls you intend to pocket. If you pocket several balls, they are all credited to you, provided one of them was the called ball. If you pocket an uncalled ball but fail to pocket the called ball, you must *spot* the pocketed ball—that is, put it back on the table, positioning it on the foot spot, or vertically behind the foot spot and as near it as possible. If you pocket the cue ball or if neither the cue ball nor any of the object balls reaches a cushion, you are penalized: you must spot one of the balls you pocketed previously or, if there were none, the next ball you pocket. Whenever you fail to pocket a ball you called, your turn ends and your opponent plays.

There are many other pocket billiard games, among them rotation and eight ball. In rotation, the object balls must be pocketed in numerical order. In eight ball, one player must pocket object balls 1 through 7, and the other player object balls 9 through 15, with the 8 ball reserved for last. (See also *Billiards.*)

Pocket gophers

Controlling and trapping

These chunky, prominently toothed, 5- to 9-inch rodents feed on roots and tubers, which they seek out in their below-ground tunnels. Cats and dogs may help reduce their numbers on your land. Use wire-bottomed planting boxes for small vegetable gardens and flower bulbs. Plant ornamental or fruit trees in large baskets of 1-inch mesh chicken wire.

To trap individuals, dig a hole to the runway about 1 foot from the low side of the fan-shaped mound. Place a pair of wire or box gopher traps in the tunnel, one facing each direction; wire the traps to a stake. Cover your hole with a board and shovel dirt over it. Check daily for sprung traps.

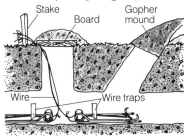

Stake · Board · Gopher mound · Wire · Wire traps

Pocket mending

Fixing holes; loose stitches

On an inside pocket, if the hole or worn area is near the outside (free) edge, make a seam just inside the tear. To mend the pocket by hand, make two rows of backstitches (see *Mending*). If you are stitching the pocket by machine, make one row of straight stitches; then put a row of zigzag stitches next to it in the seam allowance. Trim close to the stitches.

If the hole or worn area is within the body of the pocket, either darn or patch it (see *Darning; Patching*).

If a large portion of the pocket needs mending, replace it with a sew-on or iron-on replacement pocket. They're available at notion or sewing stores.

Patch pockets often come loose at the upper corners. Tack the corners with straight machine stitches, and backstitch ½ inch. Or use narrow, closely spaced zigzag stitches. To sew the corner by hand, whipstitch for about ¼ inch on each side of it.

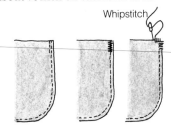

Whipstitch

Poinsettias

Care; getting holiday blooms

A poinsettia's red, pink, or white "flowers" are really bracts, or modified leaves, surrounding its true, nublike, yellow-green flowers.

During the winter flowering season, keep a poinsettia in bright filtered light, at normal room temperatures (above 55°F at night); avoid drafts. Water well, letting the soil dry out slightly between waterings.

To bring a poinsettia into flower the next season, water sparingly after the bracts drop and the leaves shrivel. In May, cut back the stems to about 6 inches. Remove the plant from its pot (see *Potting houseplants*) and pick off most of the old potting mix; repot in as small a pot as will comfortably accommodate the roots (use a mix of 2 parts sterilized fibrous soil, 1 part sphagnum moss, and 1 part perlite). Resume regular watering. Once the weather warms and settles (temperatures above 58°F at night), move the plant to a partially shaded area, outdoors if possible. When it becomes pot-bound, transfer it to a pot 2 to 3 inches wider. When this pot fills with roots, start applying standard liquid fertilizer every 2 weeks until October.

In early September, place the poinsettia in bright filtered light indoors. For 6 to 8 weeks, from late September to mid-November, give it 14 hours daily of complete and uninterrupted darkness by placing it at night in a dark closet or under a cardboard box. The poinsettia should develop colorful bracts 2 to 3 weeks after this short-day treatment.

Poisoning

What to do when someone swallows, absorbs, or inhales a poisonous substance

Most poisonings are caused by accidental swallowing of household products or of drugs that are harmless when properly used for their intended purpose. Children are particularly vulnerable to such accidents. Whatever has been swallowed and whether or not you know it to be dangerous, you must act quickly.

Immediately call your doctor, a poison control center, or a medical emergency service listed under *Emergency Numbers* on the inside front cover or first page of your telephone directory. You can also dial "0" for operator or 911 and report the emergency. Be prepared to give the following information to the person who answers: patient's age; kind of poison; amount swallowed; when the poison was swallowed; treatment being given, if any; whether the person has vomited; and your exact location.

Identify the poison as precisely as you can. Corrosive household chemicals burn the lips. Petroleum products can be identified by smell. Look also for spilled liquids, an open bottle of pills, or the remains of a plant. Keep any such evidence, scraping it up if necessary, to give to medical personnel. Both emergency and hospital treatment will depend upon the kind of poison that has been swallowed. Don't rely on antidotes prescribed on labels—they may be incorrect. Give a specific antidote only if instructed to do so by emergency personnel.

Medicine or plant parts

If the person has swallowed an overdose of medicine or parts of a plant and is conscious, the usual emergency treatment is to dilute the poison and induce vomiting. Have the person drink two glasses of water and then take a dose of syrup of ipecac: 1

P

tablespoon for a child, 2 for an adult. If vomiting hasn't occurred within 20 minutes, repeat the dose—once only. Save a sample of vomitus for analysis by medical personnel.

Cleaners and petroleum products

Do not induce vomiting if the person has swallowed a petroleum product, such as fuel or a solvent, or corrosives, such as an all-purpose household cleaner, a toilet bowl cleaner, or an oven cleaner. If such substances are vomited, they can damage the esophagus and the lungs. You may be told, in this case, to do nothing but get the person to the hospital or call an ambulance immediately. Or you may be advised to dilute the poison with a glass or two of water, unless that causes nausea.

Whatever the situation, don't give any liquid except water unless you are specifically told to do so.

Some poisons will bind to powdered activated charcoal, which carries them, unabsorbed, through the digestive tract. The dosage is at least 2 tablespoons of the powder in a glass of water. The emergency service you contact will tell you whether or not to use this treatment.

A patient who is unconscious or having convulsions cannot be given liquids. For treatment of someone who is unconscious, see *CPR*. Prevent further injury to a person having convulsions by loosening clothing and moving furniture out of the way. Try to prevent tongue biting by inserting a tongue depressor in the person's mouth; turn his head to one side to avoid aspiration (breathing vomitus into the windpipe).

Poisoning by absorption

Some poisons, particularly insecticides, can be absorbed through the skin. Immediately remove contaminated clothing and jewelry, then rinse the body with running water in a shower or under a hose for 20 minutes.

Poisoning by inhalation

Poisonous vapors include such gases as carbon monoxide (see *Carbon monoxide poison*), the fumes from paints and solvents, and vapors from products in spray cans. Get the victim into fresh air immediately. Then, if necessary, apply CPR. When calling for help, mention the need for oxygen.

Preventing poisonings

Be prepared for a poisoning emergency by posting the number of your nearest poison control center (or other medical emergency number if another is more practical for you) next to your telephone. Keep syrup of ipecac and powdered activated charcoal on hand. If activated charcoal is available only in capsules, open the capsules and pour out the powder.

Many poisonings occur because people fail to recognize the toxicity of common household substances. Assume that any medication and all cleaning, maintenance, and gardening products are poisonous. So are alcohol, tobacco, cosmetics, and the leaves, flowers, and berries of many house and landscaping plants. (See also *Bathroom safety; Childproofing; Drug overdose; Food poisoning.*)

Poison ivy, oak, sumac

Getting rid of them; treating the rash

Caution: Wear protective clothing when dealing with these plants. Wash or discard contaminated clothing immediately. Never burn any part of the plants; the smoke carries the irritant.

Poison ivy and poison oak are quite variable. Either may grow as a ground vine, a climbing vine, or a small bush. Their branches may be green and tender looking or brown and woody, depending upon age. The leaves may be pointed, or rounded and lobed like oak leaves; however, they are always in clusters of three separate leaflets, the middle one having a longer stalk. Green in summer, they turn red in fall, when small bunches of white berries appear. Poison sumac, a tall shrub or small tree, thrives in bogs, swamps, or other wet areas. Its 7 to 13 leaflets are paired on a red stem, and its berries are greenish white.

Poison ivy

Poison oak

Poison sumac

To get rid of a small patch of these plants, dig them up by the roots in early spring or late fall. During the growing season, cut them to the ground and cover with black plastic, cardboard, or a 6-inch layer of straw to block the light to the plant. Never burn poison ivy plants.

The herbicide glyphosate, sold at many garden centers, is also effective. Follow directions carefully. It can destroy desirable plants too; so apply selectively.

Prevention

When walking in likely areas, cover your legs, feet, hands, and arms. If you should touch a plant, promptly wash and rinse contact areas twice with strong soap. Wash contaminated clothing. Wash tools too; oil on them can stay potent for years.

After contact, most people get a red, itchy rash with tiny, oozing blisters. Soothe the itching with cold-water compresses; or apply Burow's solution in a 1:40 concentration, followed by plain calamine lotion. It may also help to take an antihistamine pill before going to bed. In the woods, you can get emergency relief by rubbing the affected area with crushed leaves and stems of the orange- or yellow-flowered jewelweed. For a widespread rash or one on your face or genital area, see your doctor.

Poker

Playing five-card draw; the order of the hands

The object of most poker games is to assemble the highest ranking hand of five cards—no matter how many cards are dealt or in what manner—and thus to win the *pot*, the total of all of the bets wagered.

Betting is inherent to the game. Before any cards are dealt, each player puts an *ante* (a chip or a set amount of money) in the pot. Other wagers are made during the course of play (the amounts are often limited by prior agreement), and only a player who matches every bet is eligible to win.

Cards are dealt clockwise, and betting proceeds in the same order. In the basic game of *five-card draw,* each player gets five cards facedown. After the players look at their hands, the one on the dealer's left may *open* the betting; if he does not do so, or *checks,* the next player may open, and so forth. If no one opens, everyone antes again, and the cards are shuffled and redealt. Once betting is open, each player in turn has three options: he may *fold* (quit the hand), *call* (match the bet), or *raise* (make the bet larger). Generally, a player who has checked may not raise, and only three raises are allowed in a betting round.

All players who call the last raise may then *draw* new cards. Each in turn places his discards facedown and gets replacements from the dealer. The previous opener then begins the final round of betting.

Which hand wins

The highest hand, *five of a kind* (five cards of the same rank), is possible only if wild cards are being used—that is, if a joker or some other card can represent any card. Next highest is a *straight flush* (five consecutive cards in the same suit); the highest of these—10, jack, queen, king, and ace—is called a *royal flush.* Then, in descending order, come *four of a kind;* a *full house* (three of one rank and two of another); a *flush* (five of the same suit); a *straight* (five consecutive cards not of the same suit); *three of a kind; two pairs;* and a *pair.*

If two players hold the same kind of hand, the one whose cards rank the highest wins. For example, a pair of kings beats a pair of queens; a jack-high flush of any suit beats one in which the highest card is a 10. In the case of two pairs, the higher pair is decisive; in a full house, it is the three of a kind. (See also *Stud poker.*)

Pool maintenance

Keeping an above-ground vinyl pool clean

When you fill your pool for the first time, have a pool dealer analyze a quart of water taken from an 18-inch depth; he'll recommend an initial stabilizing and a long-range treatment to keep the water chemically stabilized and balanced. Have the water ana-lyzed at the start of each season or whenever water problems occur.

Use stabilized organic chlorine to sanitize the pool water. The most effective form of chlorine is solid pellets fed continuously into the water from a dispenser; powdered chlorine must be added by hand every 1 or 2 days.

Buy a chlorine and pH test kit; test the water daily for the first 2 weeks of the season; twice a week thereafter is probably often enough. Maintain a chlorine residual level of 1 to 2 parts per million (ppm) and a pH (acidity/alkalinity balance) of 7.4 to 7.6. An incorrect pH reduces chlorine's efficiency and can damage the pool liner. Follow label directions when adding pH adjusters or any chemicals to a pool.

To neutralize organic wastes, superchlorinate the pool every 2 weeks, more often if the air temperature is over 85°F and during periods of heavy use. Add a commercial oxidizer or 5 to 10 times the normal daily dose of powdered chlorine (the residual level should be 10 ppm), then run the pump overnight. Stay out of the pool until the "free available chlorine" level falls to below 3.0 ppm. Add an algae inhibitor to the pool every 2 weeks, preferably the morning after the oxidizing treatment.

To filter out sand, dirt, and other solids, run the pump as often and for as long as it takes to clarify the water (experience and your pool dealer will help you determine how long is necessary). Check the pressure gauge daily. If pressure in a sand filter exceeds the level recommended by the filter manufacturer, backflush the filter following the manufacturer's instructions.

Routine cleaning

Make sure everyone showers before entering the pool; ban food and drink from it. Clean the pool surface with a leaf net. Brush down the liner once a week; vacuum as needed. Periodically clean the skimmer's catch basket; with the pump off, remove and clean the hair and lint filter. Repair chipped paint or rust spots on steel walls or frames (see *Paint touch-ups*). Fix liner leaks with a pool-patching kit.

Closing a pool

At the end of the swimming season, treat the water in the pool with a winterizing kit. Clean the pool and backflush the filter. Drain the pool to about 4 inches below the skimmer. Drain water from the pump and filter; store them indoors. Cover the pool with a mesh or solid cover.

Popcorn

Making a popular snack

Popcorn's "popability" depends on the moisture content of the raw kernels. Stored in an airtight jar in the refrigerator, popcorn kernels will stay moist for several months.

Follow manufacturer's directions for popping corn in a popper. Or use a heavy, 4-quart, lidded saucepan or an electric frying pan. Preheat the pan, add ¼ cup of cooking oil, and heat it for a minute. Pour in enough kernels to cover the pan bottom ½ cup of raw kernels yields 3 to 4 quarts of popcorn). Cover, and cook over medium high heat, shaking the pan gently until popping stops. Tilt the lid a few times during popping to vent steam. Pour the popcorn into a bowl; season if you wish with salt and melted butter, or substitute herbs for the salt.

Popcorn balls

A tasty, decorative treat

To mold popcorn into balls or other shapes, coat freshly popped, unsalted corn with a sugar glaze. For 3 quarts of popcorn (a dozen 3-inch balls), mix 2 cups granulated sugar, 1 cup light corn syrup, 1 cup water, and ½ cup butter (1 stick) in a heavy saucepan; cook over medium high heat, stirring until the sugar dissolves. Cook, without stirring, to the hard-ball stage or 260°F (see *Candymaking*). Add food coloring to the cooked glaze if desired.

For a darker glaze, combine ¾ cup molasses, 1½ cups light brown sugar, 1 tablespoon vinegar, ½ cup butter, and ½ teaspoon salt; cook as above to the soft-crack stage (280°F).

Pour the syrup over the popcorn, mixed with nuts or raisins, if desired, and blend thoroughly. When the popcorn is cool enough to handle, press it into shape with lightly buttered fingers. Place on wax paper to cool.

Popovers

Airy muffin puffs

Preheat oven to 450°F. Lightly beat 3 eggs with a whisk, eggbeater, or electric mixer. Beat in 1½ cups milk, 1½ cups flour, and ½ teaspoon salt just until smooth. Heat popover molds, a muffin pan, or custard cups 5 minutes in the oven. Grease well with butter. Quickly fill the cups ⅔ full and bake 15 minutes, then reduce heat to 350°F and bake another 20 to 25 minutes. The popovers should be puffed and golden, but firm to the touch. Serve immediately. Makes 10 to 12.

Popping nails

Fixing protruding wall nails

When a nail pops out of a wall, the cause is usually a framing member that has shrunk or expanded beneath the plasterboard. If the nail comes out easily when you pull on it with pliers, remove it and replace it with a larger nail. Otherwise, drive another nail about 1½ inches directly above or below it; then drive in the popped nail.

Use annular-ring or cement-coated nails. Press the plasterboard tightly against the framing as you hammer. Drive each nail flush with the wall; then in slightly, denting the surface with the hammer's head. If the protruding nail is still not firmly seated, drive it in further, using a nailset. Fill each dent with joint compound and feather it into the surrounding area. Before painting, sand with fine paper, and prime. (See also *Plasterboard*.)

Porcelain repairs

Repairing minor cracks and chips in porcelain or china sinks and toilets

A crack to be repaired must be absolutely dry. Empty a toilet or tank, wipe it dry, then let it dry completely; you can hasten drying with a hairdryer.

Use a two-part epoxy adhesive that takes 30 to 60 minutes to set, not the fast-setting, 5-minute kind; it doesn't stand up well to water. Following the package directions, mix the two components—catalyst and hardener—and use a toothpick, matchstick, or the like to fill the crack. Wipe off the excess; let it cure for 12 to 24 hours.

To hide the crack, use an appliance touch-up paint, available in a variety of colors, sometimes with a tiny brush included. Follow the label directions.

A chip can be covered with porcelain enamel repairer, which can be bought at a plumbing-supply house.

Porcupine quills

What to do if a pet is quilled

A porcupine quill has tiny barbs that work the quill deeper into the flesh. Fast removal is essential so that the quills won't become more deeply imbedded. If there are only a few quills, extract them with needle-nose pliers. First muzzle a dog by closing its mouth and tying the jaws (see *Pet injuries*). With the pliers, grasp the quill near the skin and pull straight; don't bend or twist the quill. Treat the wounded areas with an antibiotic recommended by your veterinarian. Observe the wounds for a week to see that they heal well.

If a quill breaks, move on to the next one quickly: take the animal to a veterinarian as soon as possible to have any broken quills surgically removed. If there are many quills or they are embedded under the surface, a veterinarian should extract them under anesthesia. If you keep pets in porcupine country, keep them in at night.

Portaging a canoe

Carrying between bodies of water or around an obstruction

Before setting out on a canoe trip, review maps and guide books to ascertain how much portaging is involved. In addition to the canoe, you'll have other equipment to carry. A strong person with a light pack may be able to carry everything at once, but usually you'll need two trips each way.

For long portages, reduce shoulder discomfort by wrapping the center thwart with foam padding. Or wear your life jacket as padding. If you'll be doing many portages, equip your canoe with a portage yoke, a shoulder rest that replaces or attaches to the center thwart.

On the trip, when near the end of a lake, check your topographic map for the location of trails to other bodies of water. If you are paddling a river, look for a portage trail well upstream of any obstructions, such as dams or rapids.

Getting the canoe up

Unload your gear and bring the canoe onto dry land. Tie the paddles beneath the thwarts or have your partner carry them. Roll the canoe on its side with the interior facing away from you. Lean over and grasp the center thwart with both hands. Lift the canoe to your thighs, at the same time rolling it toward you. Straighten your knees; this starts the canoe's upward movement. Rotate your hips to

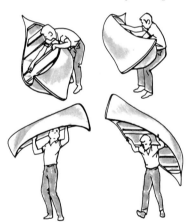

face forward as you raise the canoe above your shoulders. Duck your head into position in front of the thwart or the yoke. Settle the canoe on your shoulders and grasp the gunwales (the sides of the canoe).

Because this is a tricky motion, practice it at home before a trip. If you will have a paddling partner, an alternate is to have him raise one end of the canoe while you back into the carrying position.

To relieve your shoulders without setting the canoe down, rest its end in a tree crotch or on a large rock for a few minutes. Take your time; enjoy the

P

chance to rest your paddling muscles. Hurrying can lead to an accident. At the end of the portage, lower the canoe by reversing the lifting procedure.

Portrait photography

How to get more than a self-conscious snapshot

A good portrait reveals a person's character. Choose clothing, settings, and props that help disclose your subject's personality, occupation, or interests. Keep backgrounds simple.

Pose and expression

For a natural expression, your subject should be comfortable, yet alert. Select a setting in which the subject can sit or lean against something—most people feel awkward standing. Relax your subject with conversation or an absorbing prop. Ask someone with a strained expression to look down and then up; shoot just as the head returns. Or take a shot, then immediately take another while the subject's guard is down. Have a seated subject lean forward a bit to look more alert.

A three-quarter view is best for most faces, but a head-on view makes sharp features less prominent. A profile is rarely flattering. Take full-length portraits at the subject's waist level and closer shots at eye level. Focus on the eyes; if they are sharp, everything else seems sharp.

Photograph on overcast days or on the shady side of a building to get soft indirect light that is flattering and easy to work with. Direct sunlight creates harsh, ugly shadows. Shoot in it only early or late in the day. Pose your subject so that the sun hits from the side. Reflect light into the face's shadowed areas with a white surface: a sheet, poster board, or wall.

Indoor portraits

Inside, work with either all natural light or all artificial (but not fluorescent) light. Pose a subject facing a window that receives indirect sunlight. For a more dramatic effect, try side lighting, which accentuates facial contours and textures; use a reflector to soften the shadows.

When shooting with regular household light bulbs, use compatible tung-

Reflector bounces light into shadow areas

sten color film or the recommended color-correction filter. If your camera takes different lenses, try using a moderate telephoto lens (80 to 135 mm) for distortion-free head shots. (See also *Photographic lighting.*)

Postnasal drip

Reasons and relief for excessive nasal secretions

Because glands in the mucous membranes are always working to keep the nose moist, some postnasal drip—the flow of fluid from nose to throat—is normal. It becomes a problem when mucus is overproduced and drainage is excessive, making your throat sore and producing a constant need to clear it. The underlying cause may be an allergy (see *Hay fever*); an irritant such as smoke, fumes, or a cold; or *sinusitis,* an inflammation of the mucous membranes of the sinuses.

If sinusitis is the problem, besides postnasal drip, you are likely to have a stuffy nose, headache, pain above the eyes and behind the cheekbones, and thick, greenish mucus. Sinusitis often follows a bad cold. If it is painful or chronic or persists for weeks, consult a doctor.

Postnasal drip is most common in cold weather, when air both outdoors and indoors is low in humidity. If you can, stay indoors when it's extremely cold. Add moisture to indoor air by means of vaporizers or humidifiers. It may help to blow your nose *gently* from time to time, even if you feel no need to, and to sleep with your head propped on two pillows.

Posture

What is the best stance; common postural defects

Correct posture is a comfortably erect stance in which head, trunk, and legs are balanced one on top of the other in a relaxed but straight line. Rigidly erect military bearing, requiring exaggerated arching of the spine, is no longer considered advisable.

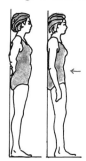

Test   Correction

To test your posture, stand against a wall with your upper back, buttocks, and heels pressed to the surface. Slip your hand behind the small of your back. It should almost touch both your back and the wall. If there is much extra space, your back may be arched more than it should be, a condition called *lordosis,* or swayback.

A simple corrective exercise is to move your feet a few inches out from the wall and roll your pelvis, trying to touch your lower back to the wall. In addition, do head raises and sit-ups to strengthen the abdominal muscles that help support the spine (see *Exercises*). When standing or sitting, concentrate on tilting the lower portion of your pelvis forward.

For a severe curvature of the spine, ask an orthopedic doctor to prescribe special exercises for strengthening back muscles. Or find out whether a nearby YMCA or YWCA has a posture clinic. Avoid high-heeled shoes; they tend to foster or exaggerate the forward curve.

Among adolescents, slumping is common; this usually corrects itself as the youngster grows older. It was once thought that constant reminders to sit or stand straight were needed; medical opinion now is that excessive concern is counterproductive.

However, one problem of youth that can be serious is *scoliosis,* a sideways curvature of the spine that for no known reason mainly affects girls, starting between ages 10 and 15. Evidence of scoliosis is differing heights of the shoulders or the shoulder blades. If you suspect this problem, consult an orthopedic doctor, for the curvature may be worse than it appears. A slight deviation may not require treatment but should be monitored while the child is growing.

A postural defect of older people is *kyphosis,* a convex curvature of the spine as seen from the side. Sometimes called humpback, it is common among those suffering from severe osteoporosis (bone deterioration).

Potato beetles

Spud spoilers

Also known as Colorado potato beetles, these ⅜-inch, yellow-and-black striped insects and their reddish,

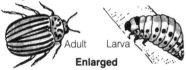
Adult   Larva
Enlarged

black-spotted larvae can rapidly defoliate an entire potato patch.

When the adults first appear in early summer, handpick them. Inspect potato plants several times a week, collecting adults, larvae, and orange-yellow egg masses; drop them into a can of kerosene or soapy water. If you get rid of these first arrivals and their offspring, you will probably be free of potato beetles all summer. Alternatively, you can spray at weekly intervals with carbaryl or methoxychlor (see *Pesticides*).

Potatoes

Growing them successfully in a small garden

Buy certified disease-free seed potatoes from your local garden center. Quarter them with a paring knife; each piece should contain at least one eye. Dust the pieces with a rot-preventing fungicide recommended by your local Cooperative Extension Service (see p.5). Spread them out in the sun; let their cut sides dry hard. Prepare a rectangular bed in light, sandy,

well-drained, and slightly acidic soil. Cultivate 4 inches deep; add compost and well-rotted manure; further enrich the soil with a 5-10-5 fertilizer.

About 20 days before the last frost date in your area, lay the dried pieces in rows, cut side down, eyes up, on the surface of the bed. Allow about 1 foot between pieces in all directions. Press them firmly into the soil, then cover with 6 to 8 inches of hay. Moisten the hay to keep it from blowing away. The potatoes should sprout in 20 days. If frost threatens, cover the sprouts with mulch.

Start harvesting young potatoes 7 to 8 weeks later, when blooming begins. Probe the soil with your fingers, taking care not to disturb the plants or the mulch.

If you see signs of blight—purple blotches on the leaves—spray weekly with maneb. Your crop is full-grown when vine leaves wither. Harvest all potatoes before the first frost.

Pot holders

Quick and easy to make

The basic requirements for a pot holder are that it be large enough and thick enough to protect your hand and wrist from hot pots and pans. To make one, you need quilted fabric, thread, and ½-inch-wide double-fold bias tape. The bias tape is available at notion counters. Or make your own: cut 1½-inch-wide bias strips, fold under both outer edges ¼ inch; then fold the binding in half lengthwise, with one side slightly wider than the other.

Cut an 8-inch square with rounded corners, or an 8-inch circle of quilted fabric. Begin binding at one corner of

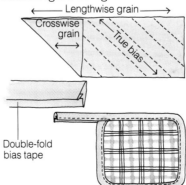
Lengthwise grain
Crosswise grain
True bias
Double-fold bias tape

the square, anywhere on the circle. With the wider side underneath, wrap the bias around the fabric's raw edges; topstitch through all layers. At the end, make a loop for hanging: sew through just the bias for 4 inches, cut the bias and loop the end back onto the bound edge, then stitch the end to the edge with zigzag stitches.

For a casserole pot holder, cut a strip of fabric 5 x 32 inches for the body, and 2 pieces each 5 x 8 inches for mitts. Bind one 5-inch edge of each mitt piece. With raw edges aligned, pin a mitt piece to each end of the body and round out the end cor-

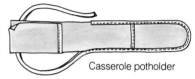
Casserole potholder

ners. Starting at the center of one long edge of the body, bind all around the edge, taking care to catch all layers in the stitching. At the end, make a loop.

Potpies

Meat and vegetables in a crust

The usual filling is meat or poultry, potatoes, vegetables, and a thickened gravy or a sauce. Make potpies with fresh ingredients or leftovers, using the following recipe as a guide.

Peel and cut 2 medium potatoes and 4 medium carrots into ½-inch cubes. Add ¼ cup fresh peas and water to cover; boil until crisp-tender (5 to 6 minutes); if using frozen peas, add them after 3 minutes. Drain liquid into a measuring cup and add enough broth or light cream (for chicken pie) to make 1½ cups.

Sauté ¼ cup chopped onion in ¼ cup butter until transparent. Stir in ¼ cup flour; cook briefly. Add the liquid; stir until thickened. Add the vegetables, ½ pound (1 to 1½ cups) diced meat or chicken, and 2 tablespoons minced parsley. Season to taste.

Make a two-crust pie pastry (see *Piecrust*); fit the bottom into a 9-inch pie plate or into four 4½-inch pans. Top with crust. If you prefer, make a one-crust pastry and put it on top. Bake at 425°F for 30 to 35 minutes.

Potting houseplants

When and how to repot

If a plant's roots protrude from the drainage holes, if it wilts between normal waterings, or if there's little new growth, it may be time to repot. In general, young plants need repotting every year; older ones, every 2 to 3 years. Repot at the start of the growing season, usually in early spring.

Water a plant thoroughly 1 or 2 hours before repotting it. To remove a plant from a small or medium pot, put one hand, palm down, on the soil, with the plant's main stem between two fingers. Invert the pot and tap its rim on a table edge a few times to loos-

en the root ball. Lay a larger pot on its side, and turn it slowly, tapping its rim gently with a wooden block or mallet. If necessary, stand the pot upright and run a knife around the inside of the rim. Hold the main stem while an assistant pulls the pot away.

If the root ball shows mostly potting mixture, leave it in the same pot. If it's covered with roots, move it into a well-scrubbed pot, 1 to 2 inches larger in diameter. Before using a new clay pot, soak it in water for 5 minutes. Cover the drainage hole with a few clay-pot fragments; cover the fragments with sheet moss or a few dry leaves. Add a 1- to 2-inch layer of fresh, moist potting mixture and tap it down.

Center the root ball in the new pot; the top of the ball should be ½ to 1 inch below the pot rim. Pour fresh potting mixture around, but not on top of, the root ball. While filling the pot, tap it repeatedly on a hard surface. Firm the mixture gently with your fingers or pack it with a stick, then water thoroughly.

If a plant is too large to repot, top-dress it every year or two. Scoop out

the top 2 inches of soil without exposing major roots. Refill the pot to its original level with fresh mixture.

Poultry cooking

How to select it; choosing the best cooking method; roasting

Poultry should have smooth skin, no hairs or discolorations, a clean cavity, and no apparent odor. Fresh-killed poultry is best, but some birds, such as ducks, are usually available only in the frozen form. For the correct ways to store and to thaw poultry see *Food storage; Thawing food*.

Almost any cooking method is suitable for a young bird; an older one should be roasted or braised; a very old one (over a year) must be stewed. Whatever the cooking method, remember that breast meat cooks faster than thigh and drumstick meat.

Roasting

Season the cavity of an unstuffed bird with salt and pepper and, if you like, add a fresh herb sprig, peeled garlic cloves or an onion, or half a lemon.

Stuff poultry just before cooking. Do the neck cavity of a turkey first, the tail end only of other poultry. Set the bird on its tail in a bowl. Fill the neck cavity loosely (stuffing expands during cooking) and pull the neck skin over the stuffing. To stuff the tail end, place the bird neck down in the bowl. Sew the openings shut, or close them with poultry pins or small skewers.

Truss the bird (see *Poultry trussing*). Rub it generously with butter or oil (except on a duck or goose; pierce the skin to allow fat to drain out).

Place the bird in a roasting pan, preferably on a rack; put it in a 425°F oven and reduce the temperature to 350°F after 30 minutes. (Cook game hen and squab at 425°F only, allowing 30 minutes per pound.) Roast it for the specified time, basting every 10 to 20 minutes with the pan drippings.

Below are average roasting times; use them only as a guideline. A smaller bird requires more minutes per pound. If the bird is stuffed, add 20 to 30 minutes to the total cooking time. *Chicken:* 12 to 15 minutes per pound. *Turkey:* 10 to 11 minutes per pound.

Duck: 20 to 24 minutes per pound. *Goose:* 11 to 12 minutes per pound.

Chicken or turkey can also be roasted at 325°F for the entire cooking time; allow 16 to 22 minutes per pound.

For even browning, cook the bird for ⅓ the time on one side, ⅓ on the other side, and ⅓ on its back. A large turkey, which is difficult to turn, can instead be placed breast up and covered with foil or a butter-soaked cloth for ½ to ⅔ of the roasting time.

The best way to judge doneness is to insert a thermometer in one thigh before roasting. Otherwise, near the end of the cooking time, insert a skewer in a thigh; the bird is done when juice runs clear. (See also *Braising; Frying; Poaching; Sautéing.*)

Poultry trussing

Tying up a bird

Securing the wings and legs of poultry before cooking it helps to retain a compact shape and prevents the skin from splitting. All you need is white cotton string about 3 feet long.

With the bird on its back and the legs pointing toward you, center the string under the tail, then cross it snugly on top of it. Next bring the string around the drumsticks and cross it on top, pulling the drumsticks as close together as possible. Pass the string under the tip of the breastbone and pull it back toward the wings. Turn the bird over and bring the string over the wings, catching them firmly against the body. Tie a knot; trim the string ends.

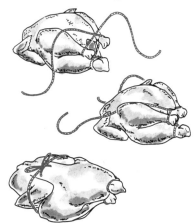

Powder-post beetles

Wood-boring pests

This ¼-inch, brown insect spends most of its life cycle as a whitish larva feeding on the interior of wooden beams that often have a high moisture content (11 percent is normal) and that are often in poorly ventilated basements and attics. A dehumidifier may rectify the problem (see *Dehumidifiers*), unless the moisture problem is due to seepage or leakage (see *Humidity control*).

As the larvae turn into beetles, they bore their way out, leaving small round or oval holes the diameter of a pencil lead and small piles of powdery sawdust on the ground.

If you see sawdust deposits, tap the wood above with an awl handle. Where timbers sound hollow, puncture the area with the point of the awl; if it plunges through, the wood is damaged. If the damage is extensive, you may want to consult a structural engineer about repairs. If the area is small, coat it with deodorized kerosene, then repaint or refinish it.

Power cords

Testing and replacement

Technically, a power cord is any electric cord; but more commonly the term refers to an appliance cord. It contains paired wires of the same length (each covered with heat-resistant plastic insulation) wrapped in a plastic sheath. Or if there's a three-pronged plug, the cord also contains a third, grounding, wire. It may attach at one end inside an appliance and have a plug at the other end; or it may be independently equipped with a male and a female plug.

If an appliance doesn't run in a working receptacle, first check the plug for malfunctioning (see *Plugs*), then the cord. To remove an attached cord, unplug and open the appliance as the owner's manual advises. Using pliers, grasp the strain-relief fitting that holds the power cord to the appliance wall. Rotate the fitting a quarter

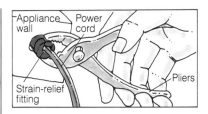

turn; pull it from the housing. Detach the connectors (or wires if they're soldered) from the terminals.

Check the detached power cord for a short circuit by attaching the alligator clip of a continuity tester to one of the prongs of the plug and touching the tester's probe to the other prong. If the tester lights, there's a short. To check for continuity, attach the clip to the connector of one wire (or to the wire); then touch the probe to the cor-

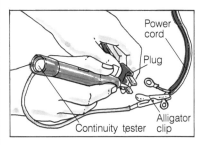

responding prong at the other end. Repeat on the other wire. If the tester doesn't light, there's a break in a wire.

If the cord passes both tests, the problem is elsewhere in the appliance. If the cord fails either test, fit the appliance with a new cord of the same amperage. If you don't know the right amperage, tell the hardware-store salesman the cord's purpose. Buy new connectors and a crimping tool.

Using a utility tool, strip ½ inch of the insulation from the cord's end; fasten the sleeves of the new connectors over the wire ends, using the crimping tool. Reconnect the connectors to the terminals. Replace the strain-relief fitting. Leave the replacing of a power cord on a 240-volt appliance to a serviceman.

Power failures

What to do in a blackout

Turn off or disconnect all appliances and fixtures; leave on a transistor ra-

dio and one lamp to let you know when service is restored. Keep lit candles away from drafts and children. Don't tie up telephone lines with unnecessary calls.

Open the refrigerator as seldom as possible. Food will stay frozen for up to 48 hours in a fully loaded freezer that is kept closed; for 24 hours in a half loaded freezer. Use defrosted food within 1 or 2 days; don't refreeze food that has thawed out completely.

When a blackout occurs during the winter, close off colder rooms and confine your activities to warmer, well-insulated ones. If you have a fireplace, burn wood or rolled newspapers in it (see *Paper logs*). Some gas-fired heating systems can be operated manually. Familiarize yourself with the procedure before the heating season begins (if necessary, have a gas company representative show you how it's done); watch a boiler closely during the manual operation period.

If your house is to be without heat for a prolonged period in below freezing temperatures, the best way to prevent pipes from freezing is to drain the plumbing system (see *Boilers; Closing a house*). If you're not prepared to do this yourself, turn all faucets on to a trickle and flush the toilets periodically. Try wrapping pipes in several layers of newspaper tied with string. These measures may delay freezing. (See also *Frozen pipes*.)

When power is restored, wait 10 minutes before turning on lights and appliances, one at a time.

Preparing for a blackout

Keep on hand emergency supplies of bottled water, canned and dehydrated foods, dry snacks such as cookies and crackers, a nonelectric can opener, and a camping stove with spare fuel. Store candles, matches, fresh batteries, flashlights, and a transistor radio in an accessible place known to all family members.

If you receive advance warning of a storm that could disrupt power and water supplies, fill clean containers and bathtubs with water for drinking, cooking, washing, and toilet flushing (a pail of water poured into the toilet will flush it). Turn the refrigerator and freezer controls to the coldest setting.

P

Power of attorney

How to give it and revoke it

Did you ever wonder who would take care of your financial affairs if you were suddenly hospitalized? Unless you and your spouse share ownership of bank and checking accounts, your family could be left without access to funds held in your name only. To avoid such a situation, tell your lawyer that you want to give your spouse (or a trusted friend or adviser) a power of attorney so that he or she can act in your place if you are unable to do so.

Your lawyer will prepare a document called a power, or letter, of attorney that spells out exactly what powers you are giving to the person. The law requires that you put a power of attorney in writing and that you sign it before a notary public; otherwise, anyone could claim to act on your behalf.

You can revoke your power of attorney at any time, but put it in writing to protect yourself. If you hold a power of attorney and need to sign a check or other document, sign it with the other person's name, then your name, and the phrase "Attorney in fact."

Power saws

Cutting safely; making and using jigs and guides

Control is all-important when using any power saw. Avoid freehand cuts. Whenever possible, use the saw's guides; otherwise make a wooden guide or jig.

Always use a sharp blade; a dull one cuts slowly, puts stress on the saw's motor, and increases the danger of accidents. Tighten all nuts, bolts, and screws regularly, and clean away accumulated sawdust. Never depend on a built-in gauge to set an angle; use it for a rough setting, then cut pieces of scrap wood to find the exact setting.

A *portable circular saw* cuts upward. The teeth of the blade can splinter wood as they emerge; for a neat cut, mark cutting lines on the back of a piece and clamp the piece facedown. Use a square to check that the guide

plate is square with the blade; check that the blade doesn't wobble.

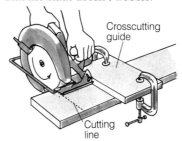

For a crosscutting guide, nail or clamp a straight piece of wood parallel to the cutting line on the part to be saved. To make a long guide for ripping (sawing a board lengthwise), cut strips 8 inches and 15 inches wide from plywood, particleboard, or hardboard. Cut the narrow strip first to include a factory-cut edge; nail or glue it atop the wide strip, with the freshly cut edges flush. Then, using the factory-cut edge as a guide, saw the lower piece to exact width.

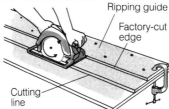

To use the finished guide, align its single-thickness edge with the cutting line and guide the saw along the factory-cut edge of the narrow strip.

A *saber saw* cuts only on the upward stroke. Never force the saw to go faster than it can easily cut. Choose the right blade for the job: the narrower the blade, the tighter the curve it can make; the closer the teeth, the finer and slower the cut.

You can seldom use a guide when cutting curves. Clamp the work good side down and make sure that the

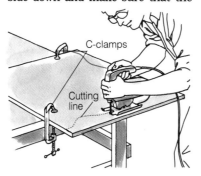

blade has clearance underneath; you may have to reposition the work several times. Stand directly over the work with eyes focused on the line just ahead of the blade.

A *table saw* cuts downward; position the work faceup. Raise the blade so that only two teeth protrude above the surface of the wood. Always feed the wood against the rotation of the blade so that the teeth are coming toward you. Have a helper support the weight of a large piece that overhangs the table. Use the saw's ripping fence when cutting along the wood grain; use the miter gauge when crosscutting. Never use both at the same time.

When cutting narrow or thin stock, use *featherboards;* push the stock through with a *push stick*. To make a featherboard, rip 10-inch slots ¼ inch apart in the end of a 1 x 6; then

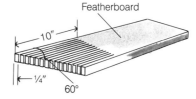

cut the slotted end at a 60-degree angle. Clamp a featherboard to the saw table or to the ripping fence, with the mitered end holding the wood.

If you must hold a piece of wood upright as you pass it over the blade, bolt a wide extension board to the fence or to the guide for support. For greatest precision, as when cutting a tenon on the end of a piece, design a jig into which the piece will fit and pass the entire assembly over the blade.

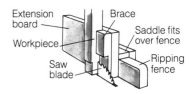

A *radial-arm saw* also cuts downward. It is potentially the most dangerous tool in any shop. Before you turn it on, double-check all of its adjustments; make sure that the tension knob on the side of the arm is tight enough so that vibration won't cause the saw to "walk" toward you.

When crosscutting, hold the work firmly against the fence and pull the saw across it; to cut several pieces the same length, clamp a block of wood to the fence as a jig. Use a featherboard when ripping; have a helper guide the wood after it passes the blade. (See also *Chain saws; Power tool safety.*)

Power steering

Adjusting fluid level

Check the level of fluid in your car's power-steering pump twice a year. If you need fluid each time or if the loss is great, have a mechanic look for leaks.

With the car level, remove the cap from the reservoir, which may be atop the power-steering pump or remotely mounted. Read the level on the cap's dipstick. If the fluid temperature is above 50°F, it should be above the *Add* mark and as high as the *Cold full* mark. If the fluid is hot to the touch, it should be above *Cold full* and as high

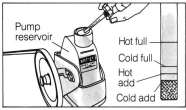

as *Hot full*. If a dipstick is marked only with *Add* and *Full*, the fluid should be between those marks. No dipstick? The fluid level should be up to the bottom of the filler neck. If it's not, install a name-brand power-steering fluid; see your owner's manual for the type.

Power tool safety

Avoiding injury

Nearly all power tool accidents are the result of carelessness. Be alert, use common sense, and know how your tools behave. Do not operate a power tool if you are tired, ill, distracted, or even mildly intoxicated. If your mind wanders, even slightly, stop and do something else until your concentration returns. Keep a first-aid kit handy; never operate a power tool out of earshot of others.

Create a well-lit, well-ventilated, neat working environment. Keep dis-

tractions, including people and pets, to a minimum. Tie back long hair and loose clothing; remove jewelry. Wear eye and ear protection; keep extra goggles and earplugs for visitors. Be sure that tools are grounded and that all wiring is in good condition. Never take off a safety guard except when doing a job that does not permit its use; then use extra caution.

Plan out your work beforehand, looking for potentially dangerous situations. Remove loose hand tools or hardware from a saw table, power tool mounting, or work surface. With a portable tool, clamp the work so that you will have both hands free; unplug the tool and set it safely aside between operations. Disconnect any tool when you make an adjustment or change blades, bits, or attachments. Use a featherboard and a push stick to feed

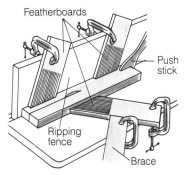

a small piece through a table saw or jointer, and always stand to one side in case the wood kicks back. (See also *Power saws.*)

Premenstrual syndrome

Easy and effective relief measures

Many women experience physical and psychological discomfort during the week before menstruation. Changing hormone levels cause shifts in body fluids. Physical symptoms may include headache, sore breasts, backache, constipation, diarrhea, and bloating. Mental symptoms include tenseness, irritability, and depression.

Mild physical symptoms may be relieved by aspirin or another analgesic. To reduce fluid retention, cut down on salt, which inhibits fluid discharge.

To feel less irritable, reduce or eliminate caffeine and alcohol. Cut down on mood swings by avoiding stressful situations and arguments. Postpone demanding tasks to a calmer time of the month. If your symptoms are severe enough to cause you to stay home from work or to cancel engagements, consulting a gynecologist may be the wisest course.

Pressure cooking

Reducing cooking time

A pressure cooker raises the boiling point of liquid so that cooking time is cut by half or more; it is especially useful at high elevations and for canning. Put ingredients in the cooker with the amount of liquid called for by the manual. Cover, making sure the top is sealed, and heat. If the cooker has a removable weight, put it on the vent when the steam starts to flow steadily. After pressure reaches the desired setting, or a cooker with a weight hisses, adjust the heat to maintain steady pressure, usually on *Low.*

At the end of the specified time, stop the cooking by running cold water over the cooker. Soup can be allowed to cool slowly; let it sit until the pressure drops to 0 (15 to 30 minutes).

Caution: Never remove the lid until the pressure gauge has returned to 0.

When you wash a pressure cooker, do not immerse the cover; soap it with a sponge, then wipe it with a rinsed one. If the vent becomes clogged, clean it with a pipe cleaner. Have the pressure gauge checked periodically by a factory representative. Replace the gasket if it becomes brittle.

Prickly heat

Clearing up hot-weather rash

Prickly heat, or heat rash, is an outbreak of tiny red bumps caused by impeded sweat glands. Perspiration that is unable to reach the skin's surface literally breaks out in minute, itchy blisters. The rash afflicts babies as well as obese people and those with skin disorders that hinder sweat-gland function. It tends to appear where sweat cannot easily evaporate—in body folds or on skin covered or chafed by clothing or bedding.

To avoid it, adults should wear loose, light clothing; babies neither clothing nor covers if feasible. Staying in a room with air conditioning or a fan helps. Take frequent baths or showers without soap.

Baby powder or a powder containing talc will help to keep skin dry and to prevent chafing. Apply it sparingly so that it doesn't cake. Don't treat prickly heat with ointments or petroleum jelly.

Propagating plants

New plants from old ones

Some plants regularly produce smaller ones. *Plantlets* grow on the ends of runners on spider plants, strawberries, strawberry begonias, and a few others; *suckers* or *offsets* appear around the bases of bromeliads, aglaonemas, lilacs, and many others; some lilies produce small *bulbils* at their leaf bases. Separate any of these from the parent plant and grow it (see *Planting; Potting houseplants*).

Use *division* to propagate such clump-forming plants as hardy asters, Boston ferns, chrysanthemums, daylilies, delphiniums, peonies, and primroses. Dig up the root mass or take it from its pot, and pull or cut it apart; replant or repot each part separately. Divide late-flowering plants in spring, early bloomers in fall. Divide the bulb masses of spring-flowering tulips, daffodils, and the like as soon as their foliage dies down.

Divide plants that grow from rhizomes, such as bearded iris, hostas, and lilies of the valley, just as growth

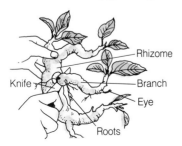

begins in early spring. Dig up the rhizome and clean the soil from it; then use a sharp knife to cut off vigorous young branches, each 2 to 4 inches long, and each with roots and at least one eye, or growth bud.

Taking cuttings

A cutting is simply a piece of a plant. To take a *tip cutting,* cut straight across the stem with a sharp knife just below a leaf. Remove the lower leaves and dip the stem in hormone rooting powder; then plant in a moist mixture of equal parts peat moss and perlite or coarse sand. Enclose the pot in a clear plastic bag and keep it in a warm, shaded place until roots form —perhaps a month or longer.

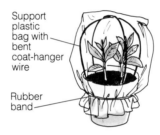

Support plastic bag with bent coat-hanger wire

Rubber band

Tip cuttings of many plants, such as dieffenbachias, gynuras, mints, ivies, and wandering Jews, will root in tap water. A *stem cutting,* from lower on a stem, is treated the same way, but it may take longer to root; pot or plant when the stem begins to sprout.

African violets and gloxinias are among the plants with thick, hairy leaves that can be grown from *leaf cuttings.* Take a healthy young leaf, stem and all, and treat it as a tip cutting. Insert it so that the leaf doesn't touch the soil. Cut the leaves of a snake plant into several 2- to 4-inch sections; each will yield a new plant. To propagate Rex begonias, remove a large leaf and make several cuts on the underside, where the main veins meet. Put the leaf, cut side down, on moist peat moss and weight it with

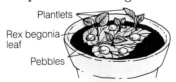

Plantlets

Rex begonia leaf

Pebbles

pebbles. Cover with clear plastic and keep warm. When tiny plants appear, remove the plastic and keep the pot in a warm, shady spot for 3 to 4 weeks.

Layering

The stems of most vines and many shrubs will root where they touch the soil. To *layer* a vine or a shrub with flexible stems, make a small cut in the stem and apply a commercial rooting hormone; then bend the stem to the ground and bury the wounded part 1 or 2 inches deep. Pin or weight it down. When roots form, after 6 weeks or longer, sever it from its parent.

Air layering means bringing the soil to the stem. To rejuvenate a gangly dieffenbachia, dracaena, or ficus, make a slanting cut in the stem and peg the wound open. Apply rooting hormone, then wrap a clear plastic sleeve around the wounded area and

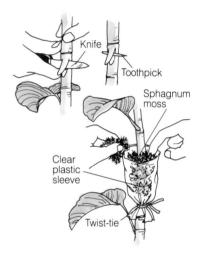

Knife

Toothpick

Sphagnum moss

Clear plastic sleeve

Twist-tie

tie the bottom. Pack the sleeve with damp sphagnum moss and tie the top. When roots appear, cut the stem just below them and plant. (See also *Seed planting.*)

Propane torches

Use, care, and repair

A propane torch burns propane gas at 3,000°F. Use it to sweat solder copper water lines; do heavy soldering (using a soldering tip); soften old paint and tiles; and thaw frozen pipes (using a flame spreader).

The torch's main components—a valve body, an orifice tube, a burner tube, and a burner head—are made of steel or brass; cheaper models are of aluminum. When you screw the valve

Rhizome

Knife

Branch

Eye

Roots

P

body onto the mouth of a fuel cylinder, the valve body punctures the cylinder's self-sealing valve.

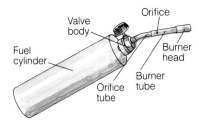

Give the handle on the valve body a quarter turn (from 9 to 12 o'clock) to get the propane gas flowing properly through the torch. Turn the valve handle back (10 o'clock) to reduce the gas flow so that you can safely ignite it at the opening of the burner head; use a flint-and-steel spark maker.

The standard burner head makes a pencil-size flame. Give the valve handle about a half turn (3 o'clock) and start your job. For jobs such as paint and tile softening, replace the standard burner tip with a jumbo model, which produces a flame up to ¾ inch wide. For a still wider flame (up to 2 inches), snap a flame spreader on top of the jumbo burner head.

When the torch has cooled after use, wipe it clean with a cloth. Remove rust with sandpaper. Use a small wire brush to clean the end of the burner head. Some torches have a filtered, clog-proof orifice. If yours doesn't, use a compressed air hose to unclog the orifice hole; otherwise, soak the orifice in alcohol.

A cylinder of propane lasts varying amounts of time, depending on how it's used. Disconnect the torch from the cylinder between uses.

Pruning shrubs

How to guide shrub growth

Examine garden shrubs each spring to determine their pruning needs. Cut out dead or diseased wood, then prune as needed to control size and shape or to encourage flower growth.

You can perform most pruning jobs with a one-hand pruner for shoots and small stems; lopping shears for branches up to 2 inches thick; a pruning saw for larger branches; a pole

pruner for tall trees and shrubs; and hedge shears. Keep tools clean and sharp (see *Sharpening hand tools*).

Pruning techniques

To promote compact, bushy growth,

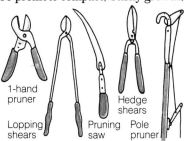

1-hand pruner
Hedge shears
Lopping shears
Pruning saw
Pole pruner

head back, or shorten, a branch to just above an outward-facing bud or shoot. *Trimming out,* or removing stems or branches at the base, produces a taller, less dense shrub. *Shear,* or surface clip, densely foliaged hedge and topiary plants.

Make clean cuts that slope back and away from the bud or shoot. When removing whole branches, cut flush with the trunk or main branch.

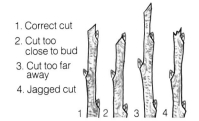

1. Correct cut
2. Cut too close to bud
3. Cut too far away
4. Jagged cut

When to prune

Shrubs that flower in spring on the previous season's shoots (such as acacia, deutzia, forsythia, *Hydrangea hortensis,* kerria, stephanandra) should be pruned by one-third right after blooming; remove older, worn-out branches and weak new shoots. Shrubs that bloom after midsummer on shoots of the current season (*Buddleia davidii,* fuschia, *Hydrangea paniculata,* spirea, tamarisk) should be pruned in early spring; cut back the previous year's shoots to two or three buds from the base.

In general, evergreen shrubs need little pruning, except to remove weak wood in spring, to cut off dead flowers, or to control size. In spring, use a pruning saw to cut back to within a few inches of the ground badly overgrown hollies, yews, and other evergreens capable of renewing themselves from the base.

Rejuvenate an overgrown hibiscus or lilac shrub by cutting it back to within 2 to 6 feet of the ground; remove thin branches and all suckers from around the base. (See also *Fruit trees; Hedges; Tree pruning.*)

Public speaking

How to prepare and deliver a speech effectively

In planning a speech, consider your audience. Who are they? Why is your topic of interest to them? How much might they already know about it? What is the relationship between you and your audience? Jot down these and related considerations and keep them in mind as you proceed.

To organize your speech, write down the three or four main points you want your audience to remember (more than that may diffuse your message). Summarize each idea in a single, clear sentence, then group pertinent information around each idea. Facts and statistics may be important to your topic, but dramatic stories involving real people will also have great impact on your audience. Consider whether visual aids will make certain points more effectively.

Write your speech, using words and sentences that are short and clear. Don't clutter it with unnecessary professional and technical jargon. Write down the main points on 3 x 5 cards.

Rehearse the speech, and time your delivery to match the allotted minutes. Practice in front of your family or a friend; ask for honest feedback. If you can, practice with the audio-visual equipment you intend to use.

If possible, visit the auditorium beforehand. Familiarize yourself with the space, the acoustics, and the technical equipment. If publicity is to be mailed, check it for accuracy concerning the description, content, slant, and duration of your talk.

Speak slowly and loudly. Stand in a relaxed manner: your feet slightly apart, your hands at your side. Your enthusiasm and interest, reflected by your intonation, will help hold the audience's interest. Make eye contact with your audience whenever possi-

P

ble. Try not to read your speech; refer to an outline or to your 3 x 5 cards.

Don't let pre-performance jitters upset you. It's common. Some simple calisthenics or meditation may help prepare you physically and mentally.

Pulse

Counting the number of heartbeats per minute

To take your pulse, place two fingertips on the inside of your relaxed wrist or, alternatively, on the neck below your jawbone. Slide your fingers lightly until you feel the pulsing of the artery. (When taking the pulse on the neck, don't press hard; doing so can slow the heartbeat.) Count the beats for 1 minute while watching the seconds indicator of a timepiece.

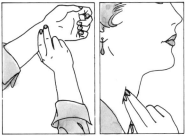

The normal range for resting adults is 60 to 80 beats per minute for males, 70 to 90 for females. Children's pulse rates are higher: as many as 90 beats a minute for a 10-year-old; up to 140 for a baby. At any age, the rate rises above normal just after or during exercise or when a person is anxious or excited. If when taking your pulse, you notice irregularities in the timing of the beats, consult your doctor.

Puppet making

Easy ways to create hand and finger puppets

You can make finger puppets from an old knit glove. Cut off the fingers. Push a cotton ball into each fingertip and tie it with a string to form the head. Then sew on sequins for eyes, red embroidery thread for a mouth, yarn strands for hair, and fabric patches for clothes. Add similar deco-

Knit glove fingers

rations to the other fingers to create a cast of characters.

You can also make finger puppets from construction paper. Cut a piece about 3 inches square for each puppet. Roll the piece into a tube around your finger and tape it. Glue on tissue strands for hair. Draw a face and clothing with markers and crayons, or paste on paper and fabric cutouts.

Paper roll

To make a hand puppet, place your hand on a sheet of paper with the thumb and little finger spread. Trace around it with your pencil about an inch away. Using the paper as a pattern, cut out two thicknesses of a heavy fabric, such as felt or wool. Pin the fabric pieces together wrong sides out; stitch a ½-inch seam around the edges, leaving the wrist end open. Trim the seam with pinking sheers. Hem the wrist opening and turn the puppet right side out. Sew on buttons for eyes and yarns for hair. Use felt cutouts for the other features and outline them with embroidery stitches.

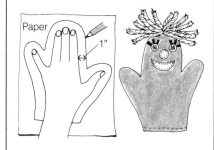

Paper
1"

Puréeing

Making fruit or vegetable pulp

Homemade purées are an interesting way to serve vegetables and an ideal food for infants and people on soft diets. They are also the basis for many sauces and soups. The procedure is to cut naturally soft or cooked vegetables or fruits into small chunks and press them through a food mill or sieve, or process them in a blender or food processor until they are the desired texture. With the addition of some liquid, cooked meats can also be puréed in a blender or food processor.

To purée soup, pour off the liquid; set it aside. Purée the solids; add the cooking liquid, milk, or cream until the soup is the desired consistency.

Season a vegetable purée with salt, pepper, herbs, and butter. If it needs thinning, add a little of the cooking liquid, broth, or cream. If a fruit purée needs thinning, add lemon or orange juice. To thicken it, cook briefly with cornstarch or tapioca starch.

Push starting a car

Using another car to start a manual-transmission engine

Caution: Do not try to start a car with automatic transmission in this way.

Line up a car with a front bumper of the same height and of a shape that won't override the dead car's rear bumper. Tell the driver of the helper car to push the dead car to 15 m.p.h., then apply his brakes (signaling this act by blowing his horn).

Begin with the clutch pedal of the dead car fully depressed, the gearshift in second, and the gas pedal slightly depressed. As the car is pushed up to speed, turn on the ignition. When you hear the horn of the helper car and see the car start to drop back, release the clutch, and the engine should turn fast enough to start. If it doesn't, quickly depress the clutch, shift into neutral, stop, and set up another attempt. Once you start, drive for ½ hour to recharge the battery.

P

Quiche

A custard pie served as a main dish or appetizer

To make the basic pie called quiche Lorraine, preheat the oven to 425°F. Line a quiche pan or a 9-inch pie dish with a single-crust pie shell, building up a crimped edge. Prick and weight it (see *Piecrust*), and bake it for 5 to 7 minutes until firm, but not brown. Sprinkle over the pie shell ½ pound crisp, crumbled bacon and ½ pound grated Swiss or Gruyère cheese.

Lightly beat 4 eggs. Blend in 1¾ cups light cream, 1 teaspoon salt, ⅛ teaspoon white pepper, ⅛ teaspoon nutmeg, a pinch of cayenne pepper, and 1 tablespoon melted butter. Pour the mixture into the pie shell; bake at 425°F for 15 minutes. Reduce heat to 350°F; bake 10 to 15 minutes longer, or until a knife inserted between the rim and center comes out clean. Cool 10 to 15 minutes before serving.

Onion quiche: Substitute 1 thinly sliced, lightly sautéed onion for the bacon. Reduce cream to 1½ cups.

Quilting

Basics of quilting by hand

Quilting is the joining of two layers of fabric with batting (a lofty filler) in between. The top layer can be a printed fabric or a patchwork or appliqué design; it can also be plain, with only the quilting lines for decoration. The bottom layer (backing) can be plain or decorative. Both fabrics should have the same care requirements.

Batting comes in cotton or polyester; the cotton requires more closely spaced stitches to keep it from separating. Both are available in different sizes and thicknesses. A quilting thread or No. 50 cotton is preferred for hand quilting. If you use polyester-

cotton, rub it first over beeswax to minimize tangling. The most suitable needles are "betweens."

When cutting the fabrics, add a few extra inches for shrinkage caused by the quilting process. For an extended, self-binding, cut the backing 1½ to 2½ inches larger than the top.

Below are a few simple quilting designs and the ways of marking them.

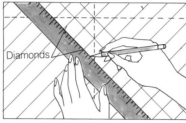
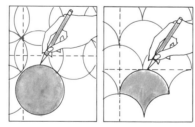
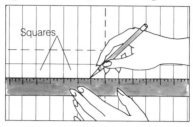

Before marking, press the fabric and designate its center by connecting the side midpoints with basting. A printed fabric can instead be outline quilted along the lines of the design.

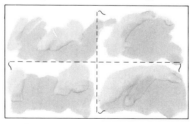

After marking, baste the layers together, working from the center out. Space the basting lines no more than 6 inches apart at the edges (see *Quilting frames*).

To keep the work taut for easier stitching, set it into a hoop or quilting frame; a hoop is suitable for smaller

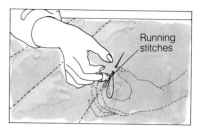
Running stitches

projects, a frame for large ones. Working from the center out and always toward yourself, make short, even *running stitches* (about 12 to the inch) along the design lines and through all layers. Use a single thread, no more than 18 inches long. At the beginning and end of a thread, make a knot and pull it into the batting to hide it.

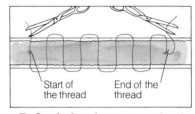
Start of the thread / End of the thread

To finish the edge, turn under the backing edges ½ inch. Fold the backing over the quilted edge; slipstitch it (see *Slipstitching*). Miter the corners.

Mitering the corners

Quilting frames

How to make and use one

Quilting frames are available in different sizes, or you can make your own. You'll need four 1 x 2 boards: two *rails* the width of the quilt plus 12 inches for clamping, and two *stretchers* 3 or 4 feet long; also two sawhorses, eight 6-inch *C-clamps,* two strips of sturdy fabric, such as canvas or ticking, 3 inches wide and as long as the rails, and thumbtacks or staples.

Sand the boards smooth. Attach a strip of fabric to each rail. With the quilt layed on the floor, center it on the canvas and baste it from the center out. Roll the quilt tightly onto each rail leaving the center exposed. Set the stretchers on the sawhorses and

Q
R

311

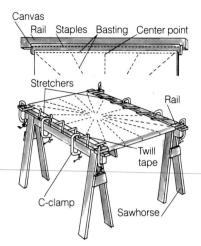

Canvas, Rail, Staples, Basting, Center point, Stretchers, Rail, Twill tape, C-clamp, Sawhorse

clamp them to the rails. Adjust the quilt so that it is taut, and secure it with twill tape looped around the stretchers at 3-inch intervals. Then clamp the stretchers to the sawhorses. When quilting is complete in the exposed section, roll it onto one of the rails; resecure the sides with tape.

Quoits

A pitching game for two

Similar to horseshoes, quoits is a game in which a player tries to toss metal rings, or *quoits,* so that they land around a stake in the ground or at least nearer to the stake than the other player's rings. The stakes, or *hobs,* are driven into the ground 54 feet apart. Each ring weighs about 3 pounds and has a center hole 4 inches in diameter and a rim 2 inches wide.

The players stand behind one of the stakes and take turns pitching their quoits (two each) at the second stake. The players then move to the second stake, evaluate their scores, then pitch back at the first stake.

A quoit that encircles the stake (a *ringer*) scores 3 points; a quoit that leans against the stake (a *leaner,* or *hobber*) scores 2 points; and one that comes closer to the ring than the opponent's scores 1 point. A ringer that tops the opponent's ringer scores 6 points, and a triple ringer gets 9 points for the top ringer. Two leaners against the opponent's ringer count 7 points. A game is 21 points. A match is two out of three games.

Rabbit damage

How to protect your garden, trees, and shrubs

In their quest for food, wild rabbits can cause considerable damage to a vegetable garden. In winter they eat the bark and shoots of leaves and bushes, sometimes girdling the entire base of a tree and thus killing it.

Protect a vegetable garden by enclosing it with a chicken-wire fence 30 inches high with the lowest wire 6 inches underground so that rabbits cannot dig beneath. Surrounding a garden with a double row of onions is another discourager. Protect individual bushes and trees by surrounding their trunks with ½-inch hardware cloth or plastic guards available at

Plastic guard

hardware stores. The guards should start 4 inches below the soil, extend 2 feet above possible snowdrift levels, and allow space for growth.

Cats and dogs can help check the rabbit population. Regularly trapping rabbits alive helps too (see *Trapping animals*). Place droppings near the entrance of a trap to attract other rabbits or use bait, such as apple or carrot pieces. Take a trapped rabbit several miles away, preferably to a suitable wild area, and release it. Spraying trees and shrubs in the fall with rabbit repellent, a distasteful chemical solution available at hardware stores, can also reduce rabbit damage. The repellent may have to be sprayed again after heavy rainfall. (See also *Deer damage.*)

Rabbits

Easy-to-care-for pets

If you plan to keep several young rabbits outdoors, house them in a hutch, as shown, elevated 2 to 3 feet aboveground by posts. Provide bedding of hay, sawdust, or shredded newspaper. Keep mature *does* (females) in a separate hutch; couple them with *bucks* (males) only for mating.

If your hutch will be in a sheltered area, such as a garage or a shed, it can be entirely of wood-framed galvanized rabbit wire: 1- x 2-inch mesh for the sides and top; ½- x 1-inch mesh for the floor. A newspaper-lined drawer beneath catches droppings; empty it daily. Using a stiff wire brush, scour the hutch weekly with a mild disinfectant. Provide fresh bedding.

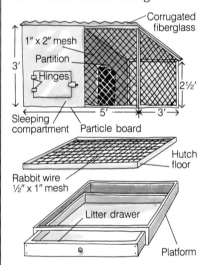

Corrugated fiberglass, 1" x 2" mesh, Partition, 3', Hinges, 2½', Sleeping compartment, Particle board, 5', 3', Rabbit wire ½" x 1" mesh, Hutch floor, Litter drawer, Platform

In addition to rabbit pellets (available at pet stores), occasionally give small amounts of carrots, grass, lettuce, or other green vegetables (except cabbage); too many greens can cause diarrhea. Put all feed in a heavy dish; remove any leftover fresh food within a few hours. Feed young rabbits and females with litters all the pellets they can eat in a day. Feed medium-sized adults 5 ounces of pellets daily. Provide fresh water at all times. Pick up a rabbit by the scruff of its neck (never its ears) while holding its rump and rear legs.

Snuffles, a disease resembling the common cold, manifests itself in runny eyes and nose. If unattended, it may develop into pneumonia. Have your rabbit seen by a veterinarian.

You can keep a rabbit indoors. They're easily housebroken: they usually relieve themselves in the same spot; place a kitty-litter tray there. Clean the tray and provide fresh litter daily. They gnaw, so keep a close watch on a rabbit running free. Remove power cords from its reach; discourage its interest in wicker furniture and straw carpeting.

Raccoons

Keeping them out of garden and house

A watchdog, blaring radio, or floodlighting may deter raccoons temporarily, but the only effective way to keep them from eventually invading your vegetable patch is to electrify the fence surrounding it. Add a single electric wire 2 inches above a strong chicken-wire fence or install a two-strand electric fence with wires 4 and 8 inches off the ground. Keep vegetation trimmed away from the live wires. Raccoons can also be caught in live traps baited with canned fish (see *Trapping animals*).

If raccoons move into your attic or basement, trap them and release them in a suitable area several miles away. If trapping fails, locate their entrance holes; board up the holes in the late evening when the raccoons are out hunting. Cover the holes with hardware cloth, metal flashing, or new boards. Deck a chimney top with a grid of reinforcement rods; secure it with a steel tightening band.

Clear away any raccoon feces you find with a spade; they may contain a parasite that, if ingested by a human, can be fatal. (See also *Garbage cans*.)

Racquetball

A fast game akin to squash

A racquetball court is 40 feet long, 20 feet wide, and 20 feet high; the ceiling and walls are playing surfaces. The basic equipment is two racquets of aluminum or fiberglass and a hollow rubber ball 2¼ to 2½ inches in diameter—slightly smaller than a baseball. Although racquetball is most often played by two, three or four can play.

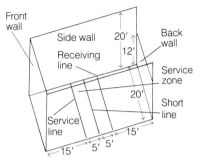

Start the play by serving from the court's 5-foot service-zone area to your opponent, who stands 5 feet behind you. Bounce the ball on the floor once, then hit the ball underhanded at the front wall so that it rebounds past the short line and bounces before hitting the back wall. If the served ball hits the ceiling or side walls before hitting the front wall, it's a *fault;* two faults and you forfeit your serve.

Your opponent can't hit the ball before it passes the short line, but he must hit it before the ball bounces on the floor a second time. The play continues, using any kind of surface combination (side wall, back wall, and ceiling), until one player hits a shot that the other can't return before the ball bounces on the floor twice.

Points can only be scored by the serving player. A game is usually played to 15 points, with two out of three games winning a match. The third game is played only to 11 points.

Radiators

Maintenance; increasing efficiency; eliminating noise

Heat from a hot-water or steam heating system is released through a cast-iron radiator or the metal fins of a convector radiator. At the beginning of each heating season, remove covers or grilles to vacuum the cast-iron tubes or metal fins. Bleed hot-water radiators or convectors (see *Radiator valves*). Straighten bent convector fins with broad-nose pliers. Make

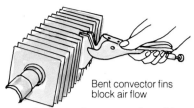

Bent convector fins block air flow

sure the covers have space for cold air to enter at the bottom and for heated air to flow out the top. Add openings if needed; remove obstructions, such as draperies, that block air flow.

You can increase the heat delivered to a room by attaching aluminum foil to the wall behind a radiator. Metallic paint on a radiator absorbs heat. Repaint the radiator with nonmetallic, preferably flat black, paint (you need not remove the old paint); paint the inside of its cover black.

If a steam radiator makes a banging sound, check its slant with a carpenter's level. In a one-pipe system, the radiator should tilt slightly toward the inlet pipe to allow water condensed from cooling steam to flow back to the boiler. In a two-pipe system, it should tilt toward the outlet pipe. To adjust a radiator's slant, lift it

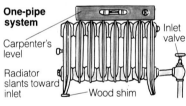

One-pipe system
Carpenter's level
Radiator slants toward inlet
Inlet valve
Wood shim

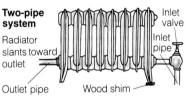

Two-pipe system
Radiator slants toward outlet
Inlet valve
Inlet pipe
Outlet pipe
Wood shim

slightly and use a mallet to drive wood shims under the appropriate legs. A partially opened inlet valve also creates noise. Make sure the valve is completely opened or closed.

Radiator valves

Repairing, "bleeding," and adjusting valves

All cast-iron and convector-type radiators have air valves for venting trapped air. Steam radiators and

Q
R

some hot-water radiators also have individual inlet valves to control the flow of steam or water to the radiator.

To repair a leak around the inlet valve stem, tighten the packing nut. If the leak persists, close the valve, let it cool, then unscrew the packing nut. Replace the packing (see *Faucets*).

Inlet valve

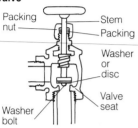

Packing nut — Stem
— Packing
Washer or disc
Valve seat
Washer bolt

Bleeding a hot-water radiator

Air trapped inside a hot-water radiator blocks water flow. At the start of each heating season or whenever the radiator fails to heat properly, bleed, or vent, the trapped air. Some radiators do this automatically; in others, the bleeder valve must be opened and closed with a screwdriver or with a special vent key (sold at hardware stores). With the heat on, hold a cup under the valve and open it slowly. When the air has escaped and water spurts out (it will be very hot), quickly shut the valve.

Bleeding a radiator

Adjusting steam-radiator vents

The automatic air vent on a steam radiator allows trapped air, but not steam, to escape. To balance the heat in your home, install adjustable vents. These will allow you to reduce the speed with which air escapes from and steam enters the radiators in rooms that tend to overheat and to increase that speed in cooler rooms. On

the type of adjustable vent shown, you increase heat by turning the dial to a higher setting with a screwdriver. In another type of vent, you increase heat by pushing a lever from *Closed* to *Open*.

To install an adjustable air vent, turn off the heat at the inlet valve and

unscrew the old vent. Put a turn of plumber's tape or a dab of pipe dope on the radiator's threaded tube, then tightly screw on the new vent.

Radio antennas

Getting better radio reception

In many areas, buildings and land features mar radio reception, producing static or background hiss. A dramatic improvement can usually be made by installing an FM antenna. FM antennas are often combined with television antennas. If you have a television antenna, check it; if it includes an FM antenna, simply wire your radio to it, running the wire through a splitter (see *Television antennas*). Mount an FM-only antenna in the same way you would a television antenna, following the manufacturer's directions. To minimize signal loss, connect the antenna to the radio with 300-ohm wire instead of coaxial cable.

The boom of an antenna should face the origin of the signal. If you want to pull in broadcasts from more than one sending station, install a rotor motor, which lets you turn the antenna toward the signal you want.

If you live in an apartment, where mounting an outside antenna is impractical or prohibited, get an indoor antenna—either an inexpensive dipole antenna, which is mounted on the wall, or freestanding "rabbit ears," which can be fine-tuned. If you want to pull in some hard-to-get stations, try an amplified antenna.

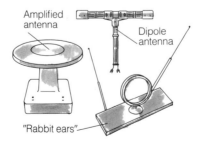

Amplified antenna
Dipole antenna
"Rabbit ears"

To connect any antenna, simply loosen the screws marked *Antenna* or *Ant* at the back of the radio, slip the spade lugs on the antenna wire under the screws, and tighten the screws.

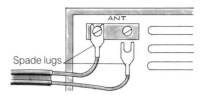

ANT.
Spade lugs

If you want to pull in faraway AM stations, install a 30- to 60-foot-long wire antenna as high as possible (at least 30 feet). Use insulators to couple the antenna to upright poles. Run a wire to the radio. Make sure the radio is well grounded (see *Stereo systems*).

Rag dolls

Charming stuffed toys

To create a rag doll you need only fabric scraps, soft stuffing, thread, yarn, embroidery floss or felt-tip markers, and leftover trimmings.

Make a grid of 1-inch squares and enlarge the doll pattern to 13 inches (see *Pattern transfer*). Trace the pattern twice onto pale pink, beige, or brown fabric. On the right side of one head, pencil in facial features. Embroider the mouth with a backstitch; use a stem stitch for the eyebrows; fill in the eyes and nose with satin stitch (see *Embroidery; Monograms*). Or draw the face with felt-tip markers.

Cut out the bodies. With right sides together, sew a ¼-inch seam all around with a machine or backstitch; leave an opening on one side. Clip curves; turn the doll right side out.

Stuff the body with old panty hose cut into small pieces, polyester fiberfill, or shredded foam. Use a pencil eraser to pack the stuffing tightly into arms and legs. Slipstitch the opening closed (see *Slipstitching*).

For hair, cut lengths of yarn—6 inches long for a boy, 18 inches for a girl—and lay them side by side on a piece of paper until they measure 3 inches across. Stitch through the center of the strands, then again 1½ inches on each side of the center. Tear away the paper backing. Following the lines of machine stitches, sew the hair to the back and top of the head and to each side of it with backstitches. Braid the girl's hair or gather it into pigtails with ribbon.

Q R

Enlarge the clothing patterns on a 1-inch grid. Trace them onto fabric and add ¼-inch seam allowances. Cut them out and sew them, leaving a

2-inch opening at the top center back of each garment. Close the opening with a tiny hook and eye. Hem all edges or cover them with trimmings. Make suspenders out of ribbon, seam tape, or fabric scraps. Add other trimmings if you like.

Raincoats

Choosing and caring for them

When buying a raincoat, you must decide whether you want it to be completely waterproof or merely water repellent. The most popular raincoat, a variation of the World War I trench coat, is usually made of poplin, a tightly woven fabric, treated with a water-repellent finish. Poplin coats supply some water resistance while letting the body breathe, but they get soaked in a prolonged downpour.

To prevent wrinkles and a musty smell, hang a wet coat on a wooden hanger and let it dry before returning it to the closet. Read the care label; some coats should not be dry-cleaned and others should not be washed. If you have a choice, machine wash the coat twice—once with soap and once in clear water. Press the garment yourself or have it pressed professionally.

A water-repellent finish will eventually wear out (when depends on the amount of wear and cleaning it gets). If you notice that water sinks into the fabric instead of rolling off, re-treat the coat with a water-resistant spray, or ask your cleaner to do so.

If you want a truly waterproof coat, get a slicker made from a nonporous material such as rubber or vinyl. A garment made of ripstop nylon coated with polyurethane makes a very lightweight waterproof covering.

Completely waterproof garments usually don't breathe; when you're wearing one, your clothes and body can get overheated and sweaty. A poncho solves this problem; it covers well and yet allows for circulation of air.

Even in nonporous garments, water can leak through the seams. Buy a slicker with flat-felled seams and seal them with liquid sealer, or look for a garment with seams that have been welded (fused) to the garment.

PTFE, a relatively new fabric, is both breathable and waterproof— PTFE is a microporous film that allows perspiration vapor to pass from inside to the outside but keeps moisture from passing from the outside in. The film is either laminated to a single layer of nylon or other fabric or sandwiched between two layers. It is best to add a coat of sealant to the seams. PTFE garments, although expensive, are ideal for anyone who spends a good deal of time outdoors.

Rainwater storage

Inexpensive ways to collect water for nondrinking uses

You can collect and store rainwater in a wooden barrel or in a polyethylene trash can. Shorten a downspout with a hacksaw; take it down if it's hard to cut in place. Then reattach the end elbow and position the container under it. Keep out insects and leaves with a screen cover.

You can make a more elaborate system by mounting two 55-gallon steel drums on a sturdy rack and linking them with pipes. Buy used drums from an industrial supply company or a salvage yard; make sure that they were used for nontoxic substances such as vegetable oil. Clean them well with hot water and detergent.

Build a rack to fit the drums' size; use pressure-treated lumber. Con-

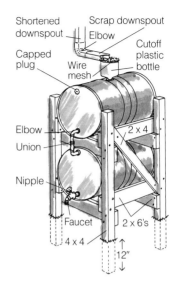

nect each joint with two ⅜-inch bolts. Bury 12 inches of the posts.

A drum end usually has a 2-inch threaded opening and a ¾-inch one. Connect the drums' 2-inch openings with galvanized steel pipe fittings. Screw a 90-degree elbow with one outside-threaded end in each opening. Put a pipe into each elbow and join the pipes with a union coupling (see *Pipes*). In the ¾-inch opening of the bottom drum, screw in a nipple, then a faucet with a spout threaded to accept a hose.

To link the drums with a downspout, remove the plug in the side of the top barrel. If necessary, make a 2-inch hole: drill a hole; then cut the opening, using a metal-cutting blade in a saber saw. Insert a funnel made by cutting the bottom off a large plastic bottle. Put in a ¼-inch wire mesh. Shorten the downspout; then reattach the elbow and extend the unit to the funnel with a scrap piece. Wire the funnel to the downspout.

Raised beds

Constructing an above-ground-level planting bed

A raised bed warms up faster in spring and requires less bending and stooping than an in-ground garden. It provides good drainage and allows you to control soil quality. If the bed is against a wall or a fence, make it no more than 4 feet wide, 6 feet if it's free-standing; 8 feet is a practical length. Consult local building codes if you're planning a bed higher than 3 feet.

For a slightly raised bed, make a rectangular frame with rot-resistant, pressure-treated 2 x 8's fastened at

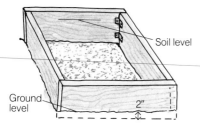

Soil level

Ground level   2"

each corner with two galvanized angle irons. Sink the frame into a 2-inch-deep trench; backfill the trench.

To make a higher bed, use two or more tiers of pressure-treated 6 x 6 landscape timbers. Lay out the timbers for the first course and scribe their outlines in the lawn with a shovel blade. Remove the timbers and dig a 2-inch-deep, level-bottomed trench. Use a ship-auger bit on a heavy-duty

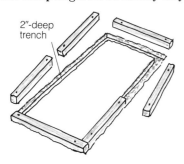

2"-deep trench

drill to drill a ⅜-inch vertical hole 6 inches from the ends of each first-course timber; set the timbers in the trench. Drive a 3-foot length of a ⅜-

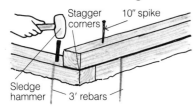

Stagger corners   10" spike

Sledge hammer   3' rebars

inch reinforcing bar (rebar) through each hole with a sledge hammer. Add more courses, staggering the corners as shown. Anchor each timber to the one below with three 10-inch spikes; make sure to stagger the spikes from course to course.

Fill the frame one-third full with crushed rock, then add soil mixture to within 1 inch of the top. Use enriched garden soil or a mix of equal parts peat moss and perlite and 1 tablespoon each of limestone and of high-phosphorus, slow-release fertilizer per gallon of mix. Soak the soil before planting to allow it to settle.

Rats

Getting rid of them with poisoned bait and traps

Chronic anticoagulent rat baits, such as chlorophacinone or diphacinone, are available commercially. These poison baits cause death by internal bleeding and must be eaten in several or more doses. Place the bait along rat runways in the basement, garage, or other suspect locations. The dying rat will leave its nest to look for water, usually outdoors.

Caution: Keep bait locations fenced or locked off from children and pets. Store bait in locked boxes.

Although rats are generally wary, occasionally they can be caught with rat traps. Wash your hands well before baiting a trap; rats are suspicious of human scent. For more details of trapping, see *Mice as pests*.

Preventing entrance is the best way to avoid rat problems. To ratproof a building, cement foundation holes and cracks; pack steel wool into holes in plaster walls and then plaster over; nail sheet metal over holes in wooden walls; stuff gaps around pipe and wiring holes with steel wool and caulking compound. Install heavy screening with ½-inch mesh around windows, vents, and chutes. For a severe rat problem, call in a pest-control service.

Rear window defogger

Test and repair

When a defogger grid works too slowly or cleans only part of the rear window, there may be breaks in the grid lines. If you can see them, repair the breaks from inside the car, using an air-dry kit sold in auto parts stores and discount houses (avoid kits that require the use of high heat).

The typical kit contains a small bottle of electrically conductive material that you apply with a small brush. A template with a slit in it will help you to apply a thin line of the material.

Can't see a break? Find it with the help of a low-cost needle-and-dial voltmeter. Turn on the dashboard defogger switch. Hold one probe (or alligator clip) of each voltmeter wire on each of the wide bars at the sides of the rear window. You should get a reading between 10 and 14 volts. If you get no reading at all, reverse the probes (or clips) and recheck.

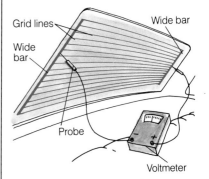

Grid lines   Wide bar

Wide bar

Probe

Voltmeter

When you get a reading of 10 volts or higher, check for a grid-line break: move the probe of the positive voltmeter wire to the center of a grid line, leaving the probe of the negative wire at the wide bar. A reading of 5 to 7 volts means that the line is intact. Test each line the same way.

If, however, the reading is still 10 to 14, the grid line is broken between its midpoint and the wide bar with the negative probe. If the reading is 0, the break is in the other direction.

Now move the voltmeter's positive wire probe slowly in the indicated direction of the break. When the probe passes the break, the voltmeter needle will move sharply.

Q
R

If you get no reading or a very low one when you make the first test across the wide bars, the problem is in the wiring circuit leading to the grid. Have a mechanic fix the wiring.

Record keeping

Keeping financial and personal records in order

Your records are a history of your family's financial and personal growth. Financial records should be organized so that they will be useful at income tax time.

Keep an *active file* (in a file drawer, an accordion file, or a carton) for papers that you accumulate and need during the current year—records needed for taxes (see *Income tax audits*); current car, homeowner's, medical, and personal-property insurance policies; credit- and charge-account statements; employee benefit data; employment and education records; mortgage and other papers related to the home; installment purchase and loan papers; résumés; records of income earned from rental properties; warranties and instruction manuals for appliances.

At the year's end, assemble the papers you will need for tax purposes, throw out dead matter, and divide what remains into what should stay in the active file and what can be put in storage.

Long-term storage
Your *storage file* should contain past tax matters and supporting documents (which must be kept for 4 years), such as bank statements and most of the papers from your active file. Keep old homeowner's and automobile insurance policies until your state's statute of limitations runs out.

Use a *fireproof strong box*, a safe, or a bank safe-deposit box for important, difficult-to-replace documents: birth certificates; marriage licenses; divorce records; passports; social security cards; copies of wills; burial records; life insurance policies; stocks, bonds, and other securities; trust documents; property deeds, titles, and surveys; title to the car; IOU's; IRA or Keogh records. (See also *Filing*.)

Recycling

Extra use from throwaways

Many discarded items made of paper, glass, plastic, metal, textiles, and even old tires and motor oil, can be returned to industry and then recycled into new products or energy. Many communities around the country regularly schedule curbside collections of recyclables, while others offer central collection stations to which residents bring such materials.

If there are no recycling programs where you live, look in the local telephone book under the "Government" section. In both the state and municipal sections, check the listing either for the "Department of Public Works" or the "Department of Waste Management." Most states and municipalities have a recycling coordinator to assist you.

Keep America Beautiful, Inc., 9 West Broad Street, Stamford, CT 06902, will also provide information on recycling options. To start a collection program that will raise funds for your organization, you can contact the Can Manufacturers Institute, 1625 Massachusetts Avenue NW, Washington, DC 20036-2212 regarding aluminum beverage cans.

You can reduce waste in the home by being careful not to buy more food than is necessary, returning clothes hangers to your dry cleaner, trading in car batteries, and donating magazines to hospitals or senior centers. To ensure a large market for recyclables, buy products made from them.

Reference letters

How to write them

Occasionally you may be called upon to write letters of reference for former employees or for friends who are applying for a job or for children who are applying to schools. Begin a letter of reference by stating how long you've known the person in question and in what capacity. Follow with an evaluation of how well the person suits the position for which he or she is applying.

Stress the applicant's positive points and downplay the negative—an unsatisfactory worker or a problem child always deserves a second chance in a new situation, and if you condemn someone in writing, you can be sued.

If you don't think highly of the applicant, show your true feelings by writing a lukewarm recommendation, implying your reservations rather than stating them outright. Personnel departments know well how to interpret unenthusiastic recommendations. On the other hand, if you really like the person you're recommending, be sure to say so openly, with many specific examples of his or her fine character and good work. A reserved recommendation may be interpreted as halfhearted.

You may feel strongly that an applicant who is asking you for a letter of reference is totally unsuited to the position being sought. If the applicant is a friend or a child, you can simply tell him or her that you would not be the best individual to make the recommendation. If you are an employer, and a company requests information on a former employee, you must respond. In this case, have the applicant telephone you. Express your reservations calmly and rationally over the telephone, but don't make any accusations you can't prove.

Letters of reference are important, since your credibility and the future of the person you're recommending often depend on them. They deserve your thought and care.

Q
R

Refrigerators

Maintenance and repair

Caution: Unplug a refrigerator before servicing it.

Once or twice a year, clean the condenser coils beneath or behind the refrigerator. Pry off the bottom grille (or pull the unit away from the wall) and vacuum the coils with a crevice tool. Regularly clean the drain system in a self-defrosting refrigerator. Remove the plug from the drain holes at the bottom of the refrigerator and freezer compartments, insert a piece of stiff wire to unclog the drain, then flush it with water from a basting syringe. Wash the drain pan in soapy water. If water collects under the refrigerator, look for cracks in the drain pan (and in the drain hose in back of certain models); replace them if necessary.

Correcting poor refrigeration

If a refrigerator cools poorly or runs continuously, check that it doesn't need defrosting (see *Defrosting a refrigerator*) and that the temperature controls are set properly. Clean dirty condenser coils. Leaks in the door seal cause rapid frost buildup and poor cooling. For the door to close by itself and form a tight seal, the refrigerator must be level from side to side and tilted back slightly. To level the refrigerator or to adjust its tilt, prop it up in front with a wood block; turn the roller-adjustment screws or the leveling legs counterclockwise to raise the cabinet, clockwise to lower it.

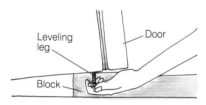

If the door sags, remove the cap, if any, from the hinge at the top of the door. Use a nut driver or screwdriver to loosen the hinge screws (if the unit has a separate freezer door, you may have to open or remove the top door to adjust the lower one). Reposition the door and hold it firmly in place while you tighten the hinge screws.

Check the gasket for wear, tears, and gaps. Before replacing a leaking gasket, make sure a sagging door isn't causing the problem.

Replacing a door gasket

Buy a duplicate gasket and soak it in warm water for a few minutes. Unplug the refrigerator and loosen the gasket-retainer screws around one of

the door's top corners. Pull the old gasket out from under the loosened retainer-strip section.

With the rest of the old gasket still in place, install the new one, pushing its

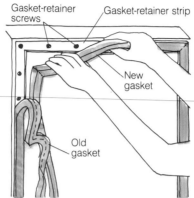

lip fully under the edge of the retainer strip. Partially tighten the screws. Repeat the procedure at the other top corner, then at the bottom. Before tightening the retainer screws completely, check the door for warping; adjust as needed by grasping the door in both hands and pushing or pulling it into alignment.

Testing the door switches

If a faulty door switch causes the inside light to stay on when the door is closed, the bulb's heat causes poor refrigeration. In some frost-free models, a second door switch turns the evaporator fan on when the door is closed. If this switch fails, air can't circulate and frost builds up in the freezer. Test both switches the same way.

Push the switch button by hand. If the light stays on or the fan stays off (with the compressor and fan running, you should be able to feel a draft in the freezer air duct), unplug the refrigerator, gently pry out the switch with a screwdriver, and disconnect the wires. Attach the clip and probe of

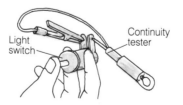

a continuity tester to the switch terminals. On a light switch, the tester should light when the button is out and go off when it's in; a fan switch

should show opposite results. Replace a faulty switch with a duplicate.

Eliminating noise

Make sure the refrigerator is level. Reposition a rattling drain pan so that it clears the compressor.

Refunds

Getting your money back

Unless a product is defective, a seller isn't obliged to take it back. To build goodwill, however, most stores have a returns policy.

You may be able to exchange an item, receive a credit, or get your money back provided you return the item in good condition, with a proper receipt, and within a stated time limit. If an item is defective, the seller or maker must try to fix it and, failing that, offer you a replacement or refund.

To return merchandise, call, write, or go directly to the seller or to a store's returns desk. Calmly state the problem and how you want it solved. If you go, take the item with you if possible; show the receipt, canceled check, or credit-card slip (if you write, send photocopies). Buying with a credit card gives you the added leverage of withholding payment. If necessary, take the case to a company officer or to the owner (see *Consumer complaints*).

Mail-order sales

If an item isn't delivered in the time promised, or within 30 days if no time was specified, you're entitled to a refund. Ask for it in a letter to the company giving the details of the order and method of payment. If the seller notifies you of a delivery delay, he must offer you the choice of a refund or a new delivery date. If you request a refund, he must return your money within 7 business days or credit your account in the next billing cycle.

If you receive wrong or damaged goods, write to the company explaining the problem and asking for a replacement. Don't return the item until you receive instructions from the company, usually within 10 days. If you have a complaint about a mail-order firm, write to M.O.A.L., Direct Marketing Assoc., 1101 17th Street NW, Suite 705, Washington, DC 20036.

Q
R

Relaxation exercises

How to reduce tension

Stress causes muscles to tighten abnormally. Relaxing the muscles reduces the sense of stress. Among the many relaxation techniques, here are some simple ones.

Take a very deep breath. Hold it for a moment, then exhale until the lungs are completely emptied, ending in a sigh with the mouth open. As you exhale, purposely relax your neck and shoulders. Take at least 40 such deep breaths each day. Remind yourself to do so by connecting them to your daily routine, especially to those parts of it that are tense. You might, for instance, take a deep breath each time you are halted in traffic, the telephone rings, or your child calls "Mommy!"

The deep breath takes only a few seconds, yet it slows the sense of time passing. Some people, in fact, remind themselves to relax by putting a piece of bright-colored tape on an office clock or on a wristwatch. Each time they look to see what time it is, they take a deep, relaxing breath.

Slow breathing also eases the feeling of being rushed and under pressure. Breathe in and out slowly while counting backwards from 10 to 1. As you do so, become aware of which muscles are tense, and purposely let them sag.

Telling muscles to relax

Deep and slow breathing can be practiced wherever you are. Other exercises require that you find a special time and place for privacy during the day. Sit comfortably or recline, with your shoes off and your clothes loosened. Close your eyes and breathe deeply several times. Close your mind to activities and cares.

Beginning with your feet, concentrate on one part of your body at a time, and relax it. Then move your concentration to the legs, the knees, and so on, relaxing each part. It may help to first tense the part of the body. For instance, it is easier to relax the face if you first tighten it into a grimace, then let it go.

As your body begins to feel warm and heavy, imagine that you are floating in warm water or drifting on clouds. Ten minutes far from the ordinary world will give you better perspective upon your return.

Rent security deposits

Getting them returned

When you move into rented quarters, your landlord may demand a security deposit in addition to the first month's rent. This deposit, which is equivalent to 1 or 2 months' rent, is set aside to ensure that you'll honor the provisions of your lease. Many states require that the funds be deposited in an interest-bearing account that is earmarked for this purpose. You are entitled to the interest.

When your lease expires, your landlord must return the full deposit, plus any accrued interest, provided the premises are in good shape. The conditions under which you can lose your deposit should be spelled out in your lease; read it carefully. Generally, if you damage the premises and refuse to make or pay for repairs, your landlord can use the security deposit to do so. You may be entitled to get your deposit back even if you break your lease, but it would be a good idea to consult your lawyer.

Reptile pets

Raising turtles, lizards, and snakes

Turtles require little daily care. Keep an aquatic species, such as a mud turtle, in an aquarium filled with water (see *Aquariums*). Always provide a large, easily accessible surface, such as a wood or cork raft, where it can periodically dry out. Keep a land species, such as a box turtle, in a dry aquarium tank. Cover the bottom with washed pebbles and sink in a shallow water dish as a soaking place.

Feed turtles bits of canned or moist dog food mixed with chopped fruits and vegetables, such as melon, tomatoes, spinach, and watercress. Aquatic species also like small whole fish; some will eat only in water.

Snakes and lizards

Keep a lizard or a snake in an aquarium with a soaking dish and a latching cover made of clear sheet plastic with air holes. Put down newspapers for easy cleaning. Provide a hiding place: a piece of curved bark, a box with an

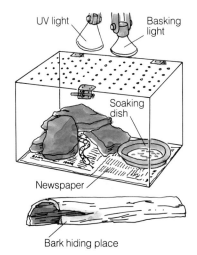

UV light Basking light Soaking dish Newspaper Bark hiding place

opening, or a stone structure. With a lizard, put in a small potted plant and sprinkle it daily; some drink only by lapping droplets from leaves.

Most lizards will eat the same food mix as turtles. But some require live food. Catch bugs in a food-baited jar or buy mealworms and fruit flies from a pet store. Sprinkle them with bone meal or another calcium supplement.

A small snake, such as a garter snake, will eat small frogs and sometimes earthworms. A larger one generally requires a mouse or a chick a couple of times a week. A few species eat only live or freshly killed prey. Stun or kill a combative prey, such as a rat. Before buying a snake, make sure a pet store or another source can supply the proper food year round.

Reptiles are cold-blooded, depending on the environment for their body heat. It's vital to keep the tank between 75°F and 85°F year round. Create a basking area by beaming an overhead light to one side. Also provide an ultraviolet light, such as a black light or a plant light; it helps keep reptiles' bones and shells strong.

Never keep a snapping turtle, a poisonous snake, an alligator, or a crocodile. Choose a safe, easily tamed species that a pet store recommends.

Q
R

Resignation letters

How to write a letter making your resignation official

If you are resigning from a company where you've held a position of some responsibility or where you've worked for a long time, a letter of resignation is appropriate. Set your letter up as you would any business letter (see *Business letters*). Address it to the president of a small organization or, if the company is large, to the director of personnel. In either case, send a copy to your immediate supervisor.

Your letter should state your intention to resign and give the date your resignation will be effective. It should give the reason for your resignation. And it should express appreciation for the experience you have gained on the job, the opportunities you have been offered, or the good friends you have made. In addition, you may want to modestly mention some of your accomplishments in order to jog your employer's memory if he is asked to recommend you for another position sometime in the future.

As you write your letter, bear in mind that it will become a permanent part of your personnel file. As such, it may be made available to a great many people—from future employers to government agencies wishing to check you for security clearance. Therefore, if you are leaving your job under less than favorable circumstances, word your letter carefully. If a company reorganization left you with a job you didn't like, you may refer to the situation in a tactful manner, but avoid angry statements, sarcasm, or name-calling; they will almost surely come back to haunt you. Search for positive things to say about your job experience, and leave the door open for future good relations.

Résumés

Presenting yourself on paper

Your entire future could be changed by your résumé. Take great care in preparing it. Remember that a résumé is basically a sales message designed to interest prospective employers in your background and job qualifications. Write it in the third person and make it clear, to the point, and easy to understand. Keep your résumé to one or, at most, two pages. Have it typed professionally and printed on 8- x 11-inch white bond paper. Make sure it contains no spelling, punctuation, grammatical, or typographical errors.

Put your name, address, and business and home telephone numbers at the top. Write the word "Résumé" either above or below this information.

There is mixed feeling among personnel professionals about including a job objective on a résumé. If you are interested in only one type of job, by all means include it. However, if you are interested in more than one type of job, it may be better to omit it.

Listing past jobs

Describe your most recent job first and work backward in time. Choose active verbs and emphasize your accomplishments. Mention any awards, performance records, or innovations for which you were responsible.

If you have been in the work force for several years, omit summer jobs unless they indicate exceptional merit, such as an internship with a highly regarded organization. If you have reached a professional or executive level, omit any manual or clerical jobs you may have held in the past. Don't explain any long absences from the work force on your résumé; you can do that in an interview. Never give details about why you left a job.

If your work record is spotty, you may use a functional form for your résumé, placing emphasis on your accomplishments rather than on how long you worked. In this case, list your jobs in order of importance rather than chronologically.

Educational and personal data

After your job listing, give your important educational qualifications: high school, if that is as far as you went, or college and graduate school, including any honors. Unless you are a recent graduate with little experience, keep this section brief.

At the end of the résumé, you may add any personal data you wish to make known, such as marital status, number of children, honors, affiliations with professional associations, foreign languages spoken, or skills not reflected in your job record.

Retaining walls

Stabilizing a slope with landscape timbers

A firm retaining wall can keep a slope from eroding and can create level land. You can build one of stone, brick, concrete blocks, or poured concrete, but pressure-treated 6 x 6 landscape timbers are easier to work with and require no concrete footing (see *Footings and foundations*). For a wall higher than 4 feet, call a professional.

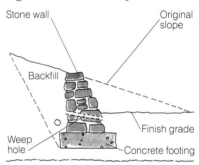

First, excavate the base of the slope, separating topsoil from subsoil; later, when you backfill, use the subsoil first. Then stretch a string between stakes, and along it dig a level-bottomed trench 12 inches below the finished grade. Put 10 inches of gravel in the bottom. Lay the first course of timbers level end to end; pitch them ¼ inch from front to back. Cut the timbers with a chain saw if necessary;

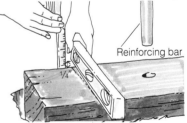

none should be shorter than 6 feet. To anchor them, drill a vertical hole 1 foot from each end and drive 2-foot-long steel reinforcing bars or galvanized steel pipes into the ground.

Set the second course and each subsequent course back ¼ inch. Lay

Q
R

the timbers so that their ends are staggered; secure them by driving 10-inch galvanized spikes into the timbers below. Leave 1-inch gaps, or *weep holes*, between ends of timbers in the second course.

After laying the second course, install drainage pipes: excavate behind the base course and lay the pipes atop a bed of gravel. Cover them with gravel, then fill with soil (see *Drainage*).

Install 4-foot-long anchors atop the ends of the second course, as shown,

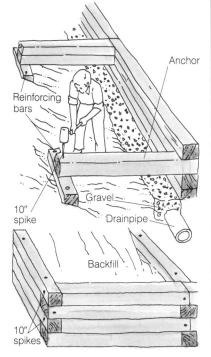

and at 14- to 16-foot intervals between. In subsequent courses, nail timbers atop the anchors, creating a series of three-sided cribs. Backfill with earth and tamp firmly before adding each course. (See also *Garden walls; Laying bricks; Stone walls.*)

Reupholstering

Replacing chair cover and padding

Give new life to upholstered furniture by replacing worn covers and flattened padding. Tools and materials are available at upholstery supply shops; don't substitute other materials. Take badly damaged pieces to a professional.

It's easiest to learn the basics of reupholstering with a simple piece like

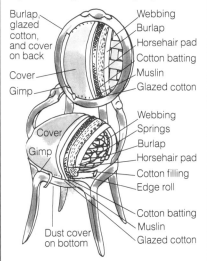

the side chair shown here. First reinforce the springs by tacking new webbing over the old webbing; secure any loose springs (see *Springs*).

Remove the old cover by carefully prying out the tacks along its edges with an old screwdriver. Save it as a pattern for the new cover. If the padding also needs to be replaced, remove the other layers until you reach the burlap covering the springs. Don't take off the edge roll. Refinish the frame if necessary (see *Wood finishing*).

Repadding the seat

Fit rubberized horsehair padding on the seat; trim it flush with the edge roll in the front. Sew it to the roll; then trim the back. Fill the indent between the hair mat and the edge roll with wads of cotton batting to form a smooth surface. Then cover the seat with two layers of batting fitted flush with the frame. Trim batting by pulling it apart, creating a tapered edge.

Cut a piece of muslin 3 inches larger all around than the old cover. Position it over the batting. On each side, tack it at the center. Then, working from the center tacks out, pull and tack it so that it holds the stuffing firmly without compressing it. Use an upholsterer's hammer and 4-ounce upholstery tacks. Always *baste tack* first; that is, put the tack on the hammer's magnetic end and make a single hit driving it halfway in. This lets you remove and replace tacks as you fit the cover. Use the hammer's nonmag-

netic end to drive the tack fully in. Trim the muslin after tacking.

To fit around a post, make a single cut and fold under the edges as shown. Make a Y cut to go around three sides of a post.

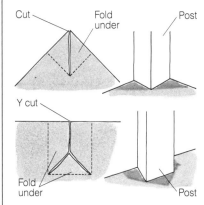

Repadding the back

Replace the back's webbing and its burlap coverings if necessary. The webbing should be just slack enough to conform to the frame's curve. Cut rubberized horsehair to fit with a ¼-inch clearance. Then put in a layer of batting and cover it with muslin. Fit and secure the muslin with fine tacks; then trim the edges.

Covering and finishing

Guided by the old cover and new measurements, cut the fabric for the seat and back covers, leaving a 1-inch allowance. Use sturdy upholstery fabric, and run the design or nap in the same direction on all pieces.

Lay a sheet of glazed cotton on the seat. Trim it ½ inch short all around; pull its edges to taper them. Mark the center of the seat's front and back rails with chalk. Notch the seat cover at center front and back. Match the notches to the marks and tack. Starting at the center tacks, fit and tack the cover around the seat. Tighten the fabric from front to back, not side to side. Trim the edge with a razor.

Cover the back in the same manner. Put one sheet of glazed cotton under the inside cover; two under the outside cover. Glue gimp—a decorative braid—over the cover's edges, and baste tack it in place until it dries.

Cover the seat's underside with a fine-mesh cambric dust cover. Cut it 2 inches larger all around; then turn under the edge as you tack it on.

Rice

How to cook it properly

There are three types of American rice. *Long grain* is slender and the grains remain separate when cooked. It is suited to main dishes, salads, and soups. *Medium grain* is plumper than long grain and more tender when cooked. *Short grain* is almost round; the grains cling together when cooked. Medium- and short-grain rices are best for molds and puddings.

Rice is also classified according to the way it's processed. *Brown* rice retains the bran and germ (and therefore more nutrients), which have been milled from *white*, or *polished*, rice. *Parboiled*, or *converted*, rice has been soaked, steamed, and dried before milling. It retains more nutrients than white rice but takes 5 to 10 minutes longer to cook. *Precooked* white rice has been cooked and dehydrated after milling and needs little cooking.

Rice expands when you cook it; use a large enough pan. For additional flavor, substitute stock or juice for water, or add 1 tablespoon butter or margarine per cup of rice, or sauté the rice before cooking (this may reduce the volume slightly).

To cook white rice in a saucepan, use 2 cups liquid and 1 teaspoon salt per cup of rice. Heat to boiling, stir with a fork, and reduce heat to simmer. Cover tightly. Simmer 15 minutes or until all liquid is absorbed. The rice should be soft but not mushy. To cook white rice in the oven, use boiling liquid and combine all ingredients in an oven-proof dish. Cover; bake at 350°F for 25 to 30 minutes. One cup dry rice yields 3 cups or four servings.

To cook brown rice, use 2¼ cups liquid and 1 teaspoon salt per cup of rice. Simmer, covered, for 40 to 45 minutes on a burner; bake for 1 hour in the oven. One cup yields 3½ cups cooked.

If rice will be held for a while before serving, turn off the heat about 5 minutes before the end of the cooking time. To reheat leftover rice, put it in a sieve, cover, and steam it over simmering water for about 10 minutes. Or heat it in a pan, adding 2 tablespoons liquid for each cup of cooked rice.

Ripening fruit

Speeding up the process; judging when it's ready to eat

In warm weather unripe fruits will ripen quickly if left at room temperature. To hasten ripening in cool weather, enclose them in a paper bag or ripening bowl (a covered, transparent bowl with a perforated lid).

To ripen tomatoes that have been picked entirely green, wrap each one in newspaper and store in a cool, dry place, such as a cellar. Check their condition every few days.

The following will help you judge when certain fruits are ready to eat.

Apricot: evenly golden; slightly soft.

Avocado: resilient but still firm; test at the stem end.

Banana: uniformly golden; green at the tips for a tarter flavor; lightly flecked with brown for a sweeter taste.

Citrus fruits: no green showing.

Kiwi: resilient but still firm.

Mango: ripens from the center out, so test with a toothpick; pick should slide easily through rind and fruit.

Melons: sweet aroma and slight softening at the bud end.

Papaya: fruity to the nose and slightly soft.

Peach and nectarine: aromatic and soft but not mushy.

Pear: resilient but still firm.

Pineapple: fruity aroma; deep golden color; a leaf pulls out easily.

Tomato: uniform, deep red; slightly soft but not mushy.

Fully ripe fruits will keep a few days in the refrigerator (citrus fruits longer). Tropical fruits, such as bananas, will darken but remain edible.

Rivets

Threadless, boltlike fasteners

Solid and blind rivets fasten thin pieces of metal, wood, leather, plastic, or similar materials. Rivets come in steel, copper, aluminum, and brass. Using a riveter (gun) to install blind rivets may be easier and faster, but it doesn't provide the same waterproof seal as solid rivets set by hand. Use blind rivets when you have access to only one side of a work, solid when you have access to both. Rivets should match the material they join.

Before setting rivets by hand, align, then clamp the pieces to be fastened. With a center punch mark rivet positions on the top surface. Using a high-speed steel twist bit, drill holes slightly larger than the rivets' diameter. Back the work against a solid metal surface such as a vise or anvil.

Place the rivet in the hole from beneath the work. The rivet's shank should extend beyond the top surface by a length one and a half times that of the rivet's diameter. Fit the deep hole of the rivet set over the shank, then strike the top of the set with a ball peen hammer. Remove it, then hammer the rivet to make it spread and fit tightly. Place the shallow hole of the rivet set over the rivet head; strike the

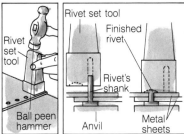

set until the head is rounded off. A split rivet will spread when driven against a metal backing; a two-piece rivet, used in leathercraft, need only be joined and driven together.

Blind rivets are installed from one side and don't need a backing. Prepare the work surface as described. The blind riveter works like a stapler:

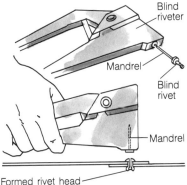

insert the mandrel of the blind rivet into the gun; then slightly squeeze the gun handles to hold the rivet. Insert the rivet into the hole, holding the gun flush to the work. Squeeze the handles to form the rivet head; break off the mandrel.

Roasting meats

Cooking with dry heat

Prime and choice grades of meat that are tender and marbled with fat are good for roasting. These include the standing rib and tenderloin of beef, the ribs, loin, and leg of lamb, and the loin and leg (ham) of pork. Leaner yet tender cuts, such as the eye of round and sirloin tip of beef and the loin or rump of veal can be roasted if they are larded or barded (see *Larding*).

Bring the meat to room temperature before cooking. Season it with garlic or herbs if desired, but do not salt it; salt draws out the juices. Place the roast with the fat side up on a rack set in a lightly oiled roasting pan. Insert a meat thermometer in the thickest part but do not touch the bone. (A newer type of thermometer, which gives an instant reading, can be inserted at the end of the cooking time.)

There are three methods of roasting. For leaner cuts you can preheat the oven to 325°F and roast at this temperature for the entire time.

A second method is to preheat the oven to 450°F, roast the meat at this temperature for 15 minutes, and then reduce the heat to 350°F. This produces a nice brown crust but more shrinkage than the slow approach.

The third way is to preheat the oven to 475°F and roast the meat for the entire period at this temperature. This method is suitable only for roasts that are 5 inches or less thick and are to be cooked rare or medium rare.

Veal and pork should be well done; lamb should be rare or medium. Use the following timing when cooking a roast with a bone by the second method; add 10 minutes per pound for a boneless roast; halve the time when roasting at 475°F. *Beef:* 15 to 20 minutes per pound, rare; 20 to 25 per pound, medium. *Beef, veal, pork:* 20 to 25 minutes per pound, well done. *Lamb:* 10 to 15 minutes per pound, rare; 16 to 18 per pound, medium.

The thermometer should read between 135°F and 140°F for rare meat; 145°F to 150°F for medium rare; and 160°F to 165°F for well done. Above 165°F, most meats will be rather dry. After taking the roast from the oven, let it rest for about 15 minutes to make the carving easier.

If you don't have a thermometer, poke a lean part of the roast. If the meat yields it's rare; more resistant, it's medium rare; firm, it's well done. You can also pierce the meat with a skewer, though you will lose some of the juice. The juice of rare meat is red; medium rare, pink; well done, clear.

Rock gardens

A special world for alpines and other small plants

Ideally, a rock garden should slope at the rate of 1 foot for every 4 to 5 feet of width and should be near a rock outcropping so that it looks natural.

Strip the slope of topsoil and existing plants. If the drainage is poor, dig a series of 18-inch-deep trenches 3 to 6 feet apart down the face of the slope. Half-fill them with stones or brick rubble; then add a 3-inch layer of gravel. Top with a soil mix of equal parts (by volume) loam, peat moss, and rock chips. Use the same mix throughout the garden.

Collect rocks in a variety of shapes and sizes, from grapefruit-size stones to "two-man" boulders that you'll need help moving. Avoid contrasts in color and texture; the rocks should seem to arise from the same bedrock.

Begin placing rocks at the center of the base of the slope, using one of the largest as a cornerstone. Excavate enough subsoil to seat the rock, then position it with an attractive face outward. Excavate for and position two rows of progressively smaller rocks, forming a rough L. Orient them so that the grain runs in the same general direction and tilt them slightly so that water will run toward the slope.

Pack the soil mix between and upon the rocks, all but burying the small ones at the ends. Then build upward a row at a time, setting rocks firmly into the slope and nearly burying them

with the soil mix. Let the soil settle for 7 to 10 days. Then add more as needed and top with ½ inch of rock chips, available from most nurseries and garden supply centers.

Choosing plants

Select a variety of low-growing conifers, ground covers, bulbs, and low perennials that will thrive in your climate. Alpines, such as mountain avens, drabas, and edelweiss, need cold winters. In the desert Southwest, use small, spreading peanut cacti, stonecrops, and other succulents. Ferns, begonias, and many gesnariads can be used in the humid South. Thrift and candytuft are among the plants that tolerate the salt spray of seashores. For the right plants for your area, talk to a local nurseryman, garden supply dealer, or Cooperative Extension Service (see p.5).

Plant dwarf junipers, sand myrtles, or other low shrubs at the bases of large rocks (see *Planting*). In cracks and pockets put rosettes of sempervivum, bright patches of evergreen candytuft or gentians, or clinging stonecrops. Look for bright ground covers, such as thrift, baby's breath, and creeping thyme, to overhang the tops of exposed rocks.

Water and weed well until the plants are established. Thereafter, if you have chosen your plants wisely, little care will be needed beyond watering during dry spells and an occasional weeding.

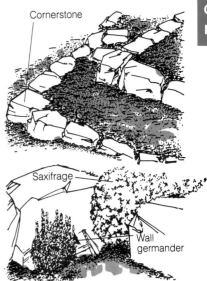

Cornerstone

Saxifrage

Wall germander

Q
R

Roller skates

Buying and caring for skates

Select skates according to where you will use them. Sidewalk skates have soft, wide wheels to give a smooth ride over rough surfaces. Rink skates have harder, narrower wheels for greater speed and maneuverability.

Choose skates with durable, lightweight alloy sole plates and two-cush-

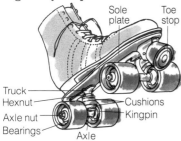

ion ("double action") trucks. Inexpensive loose ball bearings are noisy and must be oiled and cleaned often. Precision bearings are quieter and last longer; sealed ones need little care.

Try on skates wearing your usual skating socks or tights. A boot should fit snugly and hold your heel yet let your toes wiggle. Leather boots let your feet breathe and are more durable. Vinyl boots trap sweat, causing chafing and blisters.

Basic maintenance

Adjust the trucks of new skates with the skates on; then check them regularly. Tight trucks give more stability; loose—but not wobbly—trucks provide more maneuverability. Loosen the hexnut slightly with a wrench; then use a screwdriver or a skate tool to tighten or loosen the kingpin. Try out the skates. Retighten the hexnut.

Each time you wear skates, check that the toe stops and axle nuts are tight. If a wheel doesn't spin freely, back off the axle nut slightly. If a wheel still wobbles after you tighten the nut, it may have worn ball bearings. With loose ball bearings, put a drop of oil on each side of the wheel after 10 wearings and have them cleaned at a skate shop when the wheels' spin begins to slow. Partly sealed precision bearings need oiling and cleaning less often. Rotate the wheels every 6 months. Move each front wheel to the diagonal-

ly opposite rear position; move each back wheel straight to the front. Dry sweat- or rain-soaked boots properly (see *Shoe care and repair*).

Roller skating

Learning to skate on wheels

For safe skating, learn at a rink or on a smooth, litter-free surface. Wear sturdy, nonbinding old clothes and heavy gloves—and elbow and knee pads on pavement. Hold onto a fence or a friend until you gain your balance.

You skate by alternately pushing off with one skate and gliding on the oth-

T position   Pushing off

er. Start with the skates in the *T position:* point one skate forward; put the other at a right angle behind it. Push off by gently pressing against the inside wheels of the back skate. Then shift your weight to the front skate and lift your back leg so that you are balanced over the skate's center. As your momentum slows, lower your back leg. Set the skate down pointing forward, and shift your weight to it. Then push off with the other skate.

For a smooth glide, hold yourself comfortably erect. Don't bend from the waist or look down at your skates. Turn in large arcs by leaning slightly in the direction you want to go.

To stop, bring your raised back skate to the T position; then gradually set it down so that the wheels' edges

T stop

slow you. Avoid dragging a toe stop; this soon wears out the stops and may unbalance you on a rough surface.

Roman numerals

Making numbers with letters

In Latin, numerals were written using letters of the alphabet. These Roman numerals are still used, in addition to our more common numerals based on the Arabic system. The basic principle of Roman numerals is that when a smaller number precedes a larger one, it is subtracted from it. When it follows, it is added.

The first 10 Roman numerals are I, II, III, IV, V, VI, VII, VIII, IX, X. In these you can see the basic principle at work: four is IV, while six is VI. In the first, the one is subtracted from five because it precedes; in the second, it is added because it follows.

A letter repeated repeats its value. For example, XX is 20 (10 plus 10), and XXX is 30 (10 plus 10 plus 10). Other numerals are L for 50, C for 100, D for 500, and M for 1,000; 40 is XL; 60, 70, and 80 are LX, LXX, and LXXX; and 90 is XC. A line over the top of a numeral multiplies its value by 1,000—thus, $\overline{V}$ is 5,000.

Roof repairs

Finding a leak; fixing it

The hardest part of fixing a leaky roof may be finding the leak. The first sign is often a ceiling stain. To minimize ceiling damage, let standing water out by poking a few nail holes through the stained area. Catch the water in a pot.

Since water can travel some distance before it reaches a ceiling, the leak may be anywhere between the stain and the roof's ridge line. Check the flashings first (see *Flashings*).

If the roof rafters in the attic are visible, use a flashlight to look for the leak during a rainstorm or while a helper soaks the roof with a hose. When you find moisture on a rafter, trace it to its source. On a bright day, you may even see sunlight through a hole. When you find the hole, drive a nail or poke a piece of stiff wire through it so that you can locate it outside.

If the rafters on your house are inaccessible from inside, examine the roof

Q
R

itself. Look for cracks, worn areas, rust spots in the flashings, and broken or missing shingles. (Such inspections, carried out periodically, can prevent future leaks; if asphalt shingles show signs of drying and stiffening, cover them with an alcohol-based roof coating.)

Caution: Never work on a roof in wet or windy weather. Wear soft-soled shoes. Make sure the ladder is secure; on a steep roof, use a braced ladder as shown.

Plug holes and cracks in tile and slate roofs with plastic roof cement. If a tile or slate shingle requires replacement, call a professional contractor.

Replace an asphalt shingle on a warm day, when the asphalt is flexible. Gently lift the shingle above and pry out the nails that hold the bad one

in place. Remove it and slip in a replacement; secure it with roofing nails (see *Shingling a roof*).

When replacing an asphalt eave shingle, look at the inverted shingle beneath it; it may also be damaged. Before replacing a ridge or hip shingle, examine adjacent shingles for the nailing pattern; then use the bad shingle as a pattern for cutting and securing the replacement. Cut the shingle on the back, or smooth side, then bend and break it.

If a wood shingle is badly worn or split, use a hammer or small ax to demolish it in place. Pull out the pieces, then slip a hacksaw blade under the shingle above, and sever the nails as close to the surface as you can. Cut a new shingle to fit in the gap; then tap it in place until its edge is aligned with adjacent shingles. Drive a nail in the center of it and dab the nail head with roofing cement.

Flat roofs

If a bubble or blister forms on a flat roof, slit it with a utility knife—take care not to cut through the layer beneath—and use a putty knife to force roofing cement under both sides of the slit. Nail down both sides with roofing nails and cover with more cement. Then apply a shingle or tarpaper patch, nail it down, and cover with cement. For a large damaged area, cut away all tattered or worn material and apply roofing cement to the bare area, overlapping 2 inches all around. Then patch as above.

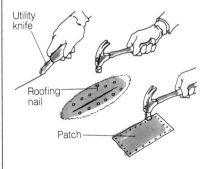

If a flat roof curls at the edges, brush debris out from under the curl and force roofing cement under it. Nail it down with roofing nails and apply more cement over the nail heads and at the edge.

Roses

Growing and caring for them

Plant roses in a well-drained site, protected from strong winds, and receiving a minimum of 5 to 6 hours of sun daily. In cold areas, plant bare-root specimens in early spring; in mild areas, in early fall or late winter. Plant container-grown roses in late spring or early summer.

Buy only quality plants from reputable sellers. Look for the Number 1 rating of the American Association of Nurserymen or for the All-America Rose Selection tag on the package.

Before planting a bare-root specimen, cut back dead or damaged canes to firm, live wood. Trim back damaged or overlong roots. Soak dry roots in muddy water for 24 hours.

Dig planting holes 1 foot deep and across, and spaced 1 foot apart for miniatures, 2 feet for hybrid teas and floribundas, up to 7 feet for climbers and ramblers. For soil preparation and planting directions, see *Planting*.

Plant a rose so that its bud union—the bulge above the roots—is at ground level in mild areas, 1 or 2 inch-

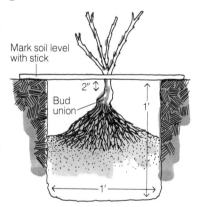

es higher in warm areas, 1 or 2 inches lower in cold. Set a stake for a tree rose before planting it (see *Staking plants*).

Mound 6 inches of soil around the newly planted stems to prevent drying. Gradually remove the mound when buds start to swell in spring.

In dry weather, water roses thoroughly around the roots, preferably in the morning, about once a week. Scratch ½ cup of 5-10-5 fertilizer around each plant in early spring, late spring, midsummer and, in warm areas, again in late summer (don't feed during the first year after planting). Soon after the ground warms in spring, mulch with a fresh 2- to 4-inch layer of coarse peat moss or wood chips. (Rake the mulch aside to feed the plant.) Apply a general-purpose rose pesticide and fungicide weekly from early spring to fall, every 2 weeks during hot spells.

Cut off spent blooms to a point just above a strong shoot or an outward-facing bud. Twist off any suckers—shoots growing from below the bud

union—at the base. To encourage large hybrid tea blooms, pinch off tiny buds below a stem's central terminal bud. Prune most roses as soon as buds begin to swell in spring; prune climbers and ramblers after flowering (see *Pruning shrubs*).

To protect roses in winter in moderately cold areas, twine straw or evergreen branches through the canes, cover the bush with burlap and tie it with string; mound 6 inches of soil around the base. In colder areas, tie up the canes and mound soil 1 foot deep in and around the bush.

Roulette

Gambling on the wheel of fortune; any number can play

Roulette has three components: a 38-compartment wheel, a corresponding betting layout, and chips. Players (any number) bet against the *house* or *bank*. When playing at home, anyone can be the banker, or *croupier*. At the game's start, the croupier gives each player the same number of chips. Bets, placed on the layout, can be played in various ways as shown. When the house numbers, 0 or 00,

come up, the croupier pays bets on those boxes and bets on combinations thereof, and takes in the rest for the house.

The roulette wheel is a solid disc with partitions dividing the rim into 38 compartments or pockets: 1 through 36 are alternately red and black; 0 and 00 are green. The croupier spins the wheel counterclockwise and tosses a small ivory or plastic ball clockwise onto the back track of the bowl above the spinning wheel. When the ball falls into a pocket, the croupier announces the number and color. He pays off the winning bettors and collects the loser's chips.

Betting layout

Line
Five nos.
(1, 2, 3, 0, 00)
Pays 6 to 1

Line
Six nos.
(chip on dividing line at side)
Pays 5 to 1

Square
Four nos.
(chip in center)
Pays 8 to 1

Split
Two adjoining nos. (including 0 and 00)
Pays 17 to 1

High (19 to 36) **or Low** (1 to 18)
Pays even

Straight
Any single no.
(including 0 and 00)
Pays 35 to 1

Column
1 to 34,
2 to 35,
or 3 to 36
Pays 2 to 1

Street
Three nos.
(chip on line at side)
Pays 11 to 1

Dozen
1 to 12,
13 to 24,
or 25 to 36
Pays 2 to 1

**Odd or even
Black or red**
Pays even

Roulette wheel

Routers

How to use this versatile woodworking tool

A router consists of a motor mounted vertically on a horizontal base plate. As you slide the base over wood, a bit rotating at high speed cuts a path. The many bits available allow you to make decorative edges and fluting, to cut designs and lettering, to trim veneer and plastic laminate, and to make interlocking joints. A router can make mortises for hinges and locks and cut dado, rabbet, and tongue-and-groove joints for furniture (see *Bookcase building; Cabinet building*).

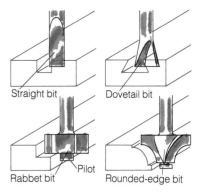

Straight bit   Dovetail bit

Rabbet bit   Pilot   Rounded-edge bit

A light-duty router, rated under ½ horsepower, is fine for many jobs. For a deep cut, you simply make a series of shallow cuts. But cuts that must be made in a single pass, such as a dovetail, require a high-powered model.

Caution: Unplug a router before cleaning it or changing bits. Make sure the bit is locked firmly in place before operating it. Never lift a router until the bit stops. (See also *Power tool safety*.)

To keep a cut straight, many edge-cutting bits have a tip, or pilot, that rolls along the edge. For cuts parallel to an edge, you can attach an edge-guide accessory to the router base. Otherwise, clamp a straight board to your work to guide the router. Measure from the router base's center to its edge. Then align the board the same distance from the cut's center.

For a cut wider than the bit—requiring side-by-side passes by the router—mark the cut's edges with lines. Place the edge of the bit along

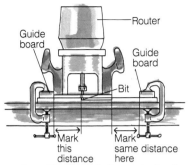

Router
Guide board
Guide board
Bit
Mark this distance
Mark same distance here

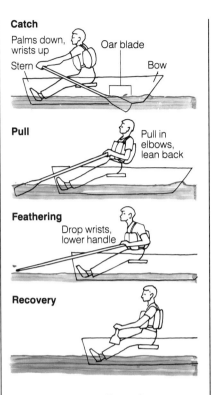

Catch
Palms down, wrists up
Stern
Oar blade
Bow

Pull
Pull in elbows, lean back

Feathering
Drop wrists, lower handle

Recovery

one line. Then mark the router's edge and draw a line parallel to the cut. Align the board along it. Clamp another board the same distance away on the other side of the cut.

Always cut from left to right; this keeps the bit from bucking and damaging the wood. Hold the router firmly with both hands. Practice to learn the best cutting speed. If you cut too slow, the bit may ripple the sides of the cut. If you cut too fast or too deep or use a dull bit, the motor will slow down and cut inefficiently. Listen to the motor; its hum is a good guide to how well a router is cutting.

Rowing

Learning boating basics

Know how to swim before learning to row. Wear a life jacket in rough water or when a storm threatens; nonswimmers should wear one at all times.

Step into the center of the boat and sit erect, facing the stern. Grip the oar handles and push them down slightly and away from you. Raise the handles to lower about two-thirds of the blade lengths edgewise into the water (the *catch* position), then pull straight back. At the end of the pull, lower the handles and drop your wrists so that the blades are out of the water and horizontal (this is called *feathering*). Push the handles forward to return to the catch. Keep your hands parallel and almost at the same height during the rowing cycle.

To row a straight course, work the oars smoothly and in unison. To backwater, or advance stern first, reverse the rowing stroke, pushing instead of pulling the oar in the water.

Turn the boat by exerting greater force on the oar opposite the direction

you want to turn. For a faster pivot, backwater with the other oar.

Approach a dock against the wind or the current, whichever is stronger. Row to shore head on and bow first.

If your boat capsizes, stay with it and try to right it. If it's swamped and isn't overloaded, you can probably row or hand paddle it to shore.

R.s.v.p.

Using the proper form

If you are sending out either formal or informal invitations and want to know who will accept and who decline, include the initials R.s.v.p. at the bottoms of the invitations. An abbreviation for *Répondez s'il vous plaît* ("Please respond"), R.s.v.p. is the correct form to use on an engraved invitation, although you will often see the variations R.S.V.P. or RSVP.

On wedding or other formal invitations, you may also use the phrase "The favour of a reply is requested." (Note that the English spelling of *favour* is used.) When issuing an informal invitation, especially to a large party or one not including a meal, you

may say "Regrets only." This means that the invited persons need inform you only if they will not attend. The polite way to answer an invitation depends upon how formal the invitation is (see *Invitations*).

Rubbings

Copying raised designs

If you want to preserve interesting or beautiful engraved, carved, or textured surfaces, copy them onto paper by rubbing. In rubbing, paper is placed over a surface and then rubbed with a crayon or other marking tool. Sunken areas remain white; raised areas are duplicated on the paper. Rubbings can be made of the designs on coins, decorative brasses, medals, tombstones, or buildings; or on natural items, such as leaves. Surfaces with finely detailed designs work best.

You can make a proof by doing a quick rubbing on plain wrapping paper, but do your final rubbing on high-quality oriental paper (available at art stores), charcoal paper, bristol board, or detail paper (found in architectural and drafting supply stores). Rubbing wax, available at art stores, is the easiest tool to use and gives the best results. The jumbo crayons designed for primary-school children can be used in cool weather, but they tend to melt in warm weather. Choose a dark color, remove the wrapping, and rub with the side of the crayon.

Making the rubbing
Use a soft brush to clean the surface of any foreign matter, such as moss or dirt; gently remove stubborn spots with a gum eraser. Attach the paper to the surface with masking tape and smooth the paper from the center out to avoid puckering. Rub slowly from the center of the paper out, using the fingers of your free hand to feel for flaws beneath the surface. Once the design is worked lightly onto the paper, apply more pressure and work from the edges in. Try to get an even tone throughout.

To remove the rubbing without tearing, peel the tape from the paper—not from the surface of the subject. Fill in missing areas by hand.

Q
R

Rugmaking

Creating pile with a punch needle or a latch hook

With a punch needle you can create a rug that has a definite pattern, such as a mosaic or a floral. To make a rug with rug yarn and a ½-inch pile, you'll need a No. 6 punch needle and burlap or monk's cloth 3 inches wider and longer than the finished rug. Allow 110 yards of rug yarn per square foot and add 15 percent to the total.

Draw or enlarge a design to the size of the rug (see *Pattern transfer*); transfer it to the wrong side of the base fabric with dressmaker's carbon and a tracing wheel. Before you begin, fold under the edges of the burlap and stitch them to prevent raveling. Set the fabric, design side up, into a rug frame or large embroidery hoop. Roll yarn skeins into balls. Thread the punch needle, as shown.

With the open side of the needle facing in the direction you're working,

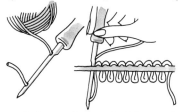

punch the needle into the fabric as far as it will go, and tug the end of the yarn down through the base. For each successive loop, bring the needle up, *slide* it across the fabric, then insert it again, leaving about three threads of fabric between loops. (Lifting the needle too high will pull out loops.)

Work one area of a design at a time, starting with details, and then filling in background. Outline it first, then fill it in by working back and forth or by following the contours of the area.

At the beginning and end of a yarn, pull the end to the pile side of the rug. Later, trim these yarn ends even with the pile. If you want a cut pile, slip the blade of a scissors through a few loops at a time; pull up and cut.

To finish the rug, trim the base fabric to ¾ inch. Working from the right side, lay rug binding along the edge of the pile; sew it to the fabric with heavy

thread and small running stitches. Turn the binding to the wrong side and whipstitch the free edge to the back of the rug, mitering the corners. For a round or oval rug, cut 2-inch bias strips from heavy cotton (see *Piping*). Fold under the edges ¼ inch; press. Attach as for binding, cutting notches around the curves. To keep the pile from pulling out, apply liquid or spray latex to the backing.

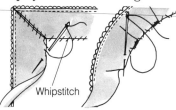
Whipstitch

Working with a latch hook

The latch-hook technique is suited to abstract or generalized designs that rely on texture rather than line. To do a rug with rug yarn, you'll need a No. 6 hook and rug canvas 2 inches wider and longer than the finished rug.

To calculate yarn needs, first determine the number of knots to be made by multiplying the number of meshes in 1 square inch of canvas times the number of square inches in the rug. If using precut rug yarn, divide the total number of knots by the number of strands in a pack to find the number of packs needed. For uncut yarn, multiply the number of knots times twice the height of the pile plus ½ inch. (If the pile is 1 inch, each strand should measure 2½ inches.) Wrap the yarn around a cardboard strip 2½ inches wide; cut the top and bottom edges.

Enlarge your design to the size of the rug. Lay the drawing under the canvas and trace it with waterproof felt markers. Wrap the canvas edges with masking tape to prevent raveling.

Work the rug one row at a time, proceeding from right to left and bottom to top. To form a knot, loop the yarn around the shank of the hook and grasp both ends, pulling them even. Insert the hook under a crosswise

thread; slightly twist it to open the latch. Catch the yarn in the hook and pull the hook down, letting go of the yarn ends as you do so. Pull the knot tight; even the yarn ends if necessary.

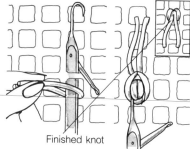
Finished knot

To finish a rectangular rug, sew rug binding close to the first row of knots. Fold under and sew it to the back. On a round or oval rug, trim the canvas to 1 inch and cut notches all around. Fold and sew the canvas to the rug back. Cut bias as for a punch-hook rug and whipstitch it to the canvas.

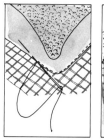

Rust

Removing and preventing rust and rust stains

To remove rust on a metal such as wrought iron, knock off as much as possible with a wire brush or with a brush attachment on an electric drill. Then sand down to bare metal with medium-grit silicon carbide paper, using an orbital sander on flat surfaces. Finish with fine paper or steel wool. Before painting, clean the surface with paint thinner and apply a rust-resistant zinc chromate primer.

Caution: Wear goggles when using power tools and goggles and gloves when using caustic chemicals.

On small tools or other surfaces that are hard to sand, brush off as much rust as you can. Then apply a gel-like rust remover as directed.

On a large job, you can lessen your work by applying a rust converter—a primer that turns solid rust into a protective coating. First, brush off loose material; then apply primer with an old paintbrush. Let it cure as directed before painting. To fix a rust spot on a car, see *Paint touch-ups*.

Rust stains

On siding stained by nailheads, use sandpaper or steel wool to remove as much rust and stain as possible. Sink each nail with a nail set and fill the hole with putty or spackling compound. Then prime the spots with a latex- or shellac-based stain killer. Put two coats over flathead nails which can't be countersunk. Coat a stain on an interior wall with an alcohol-based primer; repeat if it bleeds through. Scrub a rust stain on concrete with a mix of 1 part muriatic acid to 9 parts water.

Preventing rust

Use only rustproof aluminum, stainless steel, or galvanized nails and screws in areas exposed to moisture. Put a rust-resistant primer on any exposed metal piece; prime and paint its hidden sides before installation. Rub a few drops of light oil on hand tools, saw blades, and bits that you store in a damp basement or garage. Use a wax or silicon spray on stationary power tools' work surfaces.

Sachets

Decorative, scented sacks

Sachets are traditionally placed in clothes drawers and closets to scent their contents. Sachets can be filled with dried, fragrant flowers or leaves or with a mixture of dried flowers, herbs, and spices called potpourri.

The simplest sachets are made with frilly handkerchiefs tied with ribbon or lace. You can also sew sachets from fabric scraps and decorate them with ribbon and lace remnants.

For sachets that help repel moths, fill little muslin sacks with southernwood, wormwood, lavender, santolina, or tansy. Put them in pockets or attach them to coat hangers. At Christmas time, make sachets in traditional holiday shapes for package decorations or small gifts.

Homemade scented mixtures

Collect sachet ingredients throughout the gardening season or save the petals from florists' bouquets. (See *Flower drying* for the way to preserve them.) Roses, lavender, and tuberoses retain their scents the best, but other fragrant flowers, such as honeysuckle, carnations, and orange blossoms, can be used.

Before filling sachets, crush petals or herbs and mix them with orrisroot (available at perfumers and some drugstores) to fix their fragrance so that it will last longer. You can also add several drops of an essential oil to intensify the scent.

To make a floral-spice potpourri, use the following: 1 quart dried flower petals; 2 tablespoons dried, grated citrus peel (optional); 1 tablespoon each ground cloves, allspice, and cinnamon; 1 tablespoon each rosemary and crushed bay leaves; 3 tablespoons powdered orrisroot; 10 drops of oil of patchouli, jasmine, tuberose, rose, or lilac, or a combination of these. Place petals in a large jar. Add citrus peel, spices, herbs, and orrisroot; mix together gently. Sprinkle the oils on top; close tightly. Shake the container every few days for 3 weeks, or until the mix is mellowed.

Sagging floors

Reinforcing a floor's understructure

A sagging floor may indicate a structural problem. Call an engineer if the sagging is serious or appears to involve the foundation or a central girder that supports a floor's joists.

A floor that feels bouncy may not have adequate bridging—the diagonal braces between joists. Nail any loose bridging back in place. Then install solid wood blocking, using lumber the same size as the joists. Apply construction adhesive to each joint and stagger the pieces so that you can nail into them through the joists.

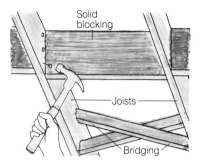

If a floor sags, determine the extent of the sagging with a level and a long straightedge. Measure in from the walls to the sag; then use the measurements to locate the joist involved. To correct a slight sag, drive a hardwood wedge or shingle as a shim between the joist and the subflooring.

If a joist is warped or cracked, jack it up and double it, that is, nail a new joist of the same size to it. Remove the bridging on both sides of the joist. Then install a jack post—or a contractor's jack in a tight crawl space—on a solid, weight-distributing footing, such as a scrap 2 x 10. Lock the jack's telescoping tubes in place with the steel pin; then rotate the jack's screw against a hardwood scrap under the joist. Tighten the jack no more than a quarter turn every 4 days until the joist is straight.

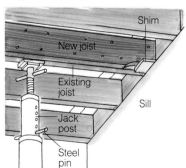

Prepare the new joist by chiseling ¼ inch off its bottom at each end; this will let you slip it easily over the foundation sill and the central girder. Set it in place and shim the ends. Then attach it with 16d nails staggered top and bottom at 12-inch intervals. Install solid blocking to replace the bridging. Lower the jack at the same gradual rate that you put it up.

If the sagging involves two or three joists, put a 4 x 6 on top of the jack and raise them together; use two jacks if it involves more joists. Put spacing blocks under the joists so that you can double them more easily.

Sailboards

Surfing with the wind

Learn boardsailing from a qualified instructor. Know how to swim, wear a U.S. Coast Guard-approved life jacket, and avoid swimming areas and busy harbors.

Position the board at right angles to the wind; the sail should lie in the water downwind, at right angles to the board. Stand on the board's windward

The basic position

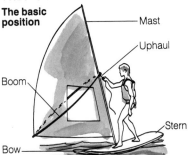

- Mast
- Uphaul
- Boom
- Stern
- Bow

side with the wind at your back; place one foot in front of the mast, the other behind it, straddling the centerline.

Squatting slightly, take hold of the uphaul line with both hands; pull the rig partway up by straightening your body. Continue pulling hand over hand on the uphaul until the far end of the boom clears the water and the sail is at right angles to the board (the basic position). Hold the uphaul with

The crossover

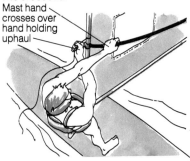

Mast hand crosses over hand holding uphaul

the hand nearer the stern (this will be the "sail hand"); cross the other hand (the "mast hand") over the sail hand to grasp the boom about 8 inches from the mast. Release the uphaul; with the freed sail hand, grasp the boom 20 inches from the mast hand.

To steer a straight course at right angles to the wind, slowly pull in the sail just until it fills and all fluttering stops; keep the boom parallel to the board. Lean back to offset the pull of the sail in a strong wind.

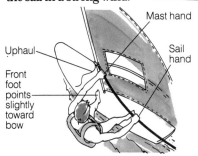

Uphaul

Front foot points slightly toward bow

Mast hand

Sail hand

Tilt the boom forward and pull in the sail to turn the bow away from the wind. Tilt the boom back to turn the bow toward the wind. Sailing directly into the wind stalls the board. (For the points of sailing, see *Sailing*.)

To tack, or change direction by steering the bow across the wind, tilt the boom back until the wind comes from straight ahead and the sail starts fluttering. Take the uphaul in the sail hand and step in front of and around the mast. Reposition yourself; lean the sail against the wind to continue the board's rotation. When the sail and the board are again in the basic position, switch hands on the uphaul, then reposition them on the boom as described.

Sailing

Basic sailboat handling

Know how to swim and learn to sail with an experienced sailor. Start in a small dinghy with a mainsail only. Choose a day with steady, but not strong, winds; check local weather reports before sailing. Know the right-of-way rules and wear a U.S. Coast Guard-approved life jacket. Keep an anchor, bucket, and paddles on board. If your boat capsizes, stay with it.

Step onto the boat's centerline from one side. Start the boat at about a 90-degree angle to the wind (reaching, or going across the wind, is the fastest and simplest point of sailing). Sit on the windward side, one hand on the

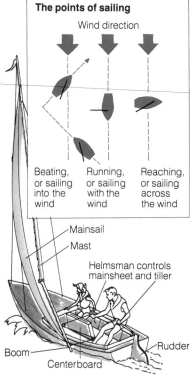

The points of sailing

Wind direction

Beating, or sailing into the wind

Running, or sailing with the wind

Reaching, or sailing across the wind

Mainsail

Mast

Helmsman controls mainsheet and tiller

Rudder

Boom

Centerboard

tiller, the other on the mainsheet (the line that controls the boom's angle).

To control speed, slacken the mainsheet until the sail begins to luff (flap free), then slowly haul in the sheet just until the sail fills and the luffing stops. Direction (course) is controlled with the tiller and by adjusting the angle of the sail in relation to the wind. Counterbalance the boat's tendency to lean (heel) by sitting on the windward rail. If the boat leans too much, slack off on the mainsheet.

To steer to the right (starboard), move the tiller to the left (port), and vice versa. Steering directly into the wind stalls the boat. To change course by tacking, build up speed, then push the tiller away from you to steer the bow through the wind. Duck under the boom as it swings across the boat. Move to the other side, changing hands on tiller and sheet. Jibing, or changing course by taking the stern through the wind, should be avoided

S

by the beginner except in an emergency. When jibing, the boom swings across so rapidly it may injure an unwatchful crew member.

Come into a dock or mooring upwind, luffing the sail to stop. If you must come in downwind, drop the sail 20 to 30 feet away and coast in.

Salad dressings

Vinaigrette and creamy

There are three basic types of salad dressing: vinaigrette, creamy, and mayonnaise (see *Mayonnaise* for a recipe). Variations are created by adding other ingredients.

Standard proportions for a vinaigrette are 3 or 4 parts oil to 1 part vinegar or lemon juice, adjusted to suit individual tastes or the acidity of the vinegar or lemon. Measure the vinegar into a small bowl or bottle; add salt (¼ teaspoon per ¼ cup vinegar) and pepper (⅛ teaspoon per ¼ cup vinegar); stir until dissolved. Add olive, vegetable, or other oil. Stir briskly with a fork or whisk, or shake in a bottle until blended. Taste; adjust the proportions if desired.

You can vary a vinaigrette according to the salad ingredients. Add basil for tomato salad, dill for cucumber. Tarragon, chervil, parsley, and chives are all good with greens. For strong-tasting greens, such as chicory, endive, or arugula, you can add mustard (1 teaspoon prepared or ¼ teaspoon dry per cup of dressing), a crushed garlic clove, or anchovies that have been soaked in water then rubbed through a sieve. For a meat salad, add 1 or 2 tablespoons of the pan juices (fat removed). Curry powder, grated onion, capers, or chopped shallots are other good additions.

Creamy dressings

A creamy dressing can have a base of cream, sour cream, cream cheese, buttermilk, or yogurt. This version makes 1¼ cups. Mix 1 cup sour cream, 3 tablespoons white vinegar, 1 tablespoon sugar, ½ teaspoon salt, and a pinch of cayenne pepper. To thin, blend in a little milk. Cover and chill.

Roquefort or *blue cheese:* Add 2 tablespoons crumbled cheese.

Low-calorie: Substitute yogurt for sour cream. Reduce vinegar to 2 tablespoons and sugar to ½ teaspoon. Add ¼ cup skim milk. Flavor with 2 tablespoons minced chives or 1 tablespoon finely minced onion.

Salads

Making perfect tossed salads

A tossed salad can be a light course to precede, accompany, or follow the entrée, or it can be a meal in itself. An excellent one has first quality, fresh ingredients. Choose greens that are crisp and show few signs of yellowing, wilting, spotting, or bruising. Iceberg should be green and not too hard; very pale iceberg is overmature. Fruits and such vegetables as tomatoes and cucumbers should be used for salads only when they're in season. Meat or seafood should be tender and juicy.

Any edible green can be used in salad. Mild-flavored types, such as bibb, romaine, Boston, or iceberg, are extra pleasing when combined with more pungent greens, such as watercress, dandelion, escarole, endive, arugula, or radicchio. Other flavorful and colorful additions are spinach, red cabbage, carrots, mushrooms, avocado, celery, green pepper, radish, green onion, cucumber, artichoke hearts, snow peas, asparagus, or olives in any combination that pleases you. More exotic additions in the summer are orange daylily or nasturtium flowers, or rose petals.

Allow 1 to 2 cups of greens per serving. Wash them carefully, swirling loose-leaved greens at least twice in a bowl and discarding the water each time. Dry greens thoroughly in a salad spinner or by blotting them gently and rolling them in a clean towel or paper towels. Tear or cut the greens. In general, it's better to tear loose-leaved lettuce and to cut compact types such as iceberg or endive. To crisp them, refrigerate in plastic bags or a covered bowl for 2 to 12 hours. If you're adding fruits or juicy vegetables, prepare but keep them separate from the greens until ready to toss.

Pour the dressing—about 3 tablespoons per quart of greens—over the

salad; toss thoroughly by lifting the ingredients from the bottom of the bowl with a fork and spoon. After half a dozen tosses, taste the salad. If necessary, add a little more dressing and toss again. Serve as soon as possible; salt and vinegar will wilt the greens. (See also *Salad dressings.*)

Sales agreements

When to enter an agreement; canceling one; installment buying; getting the goods

An agreement to buy or sell something is legally binding only if it is a true contract, either written or oral (see *Contracts*). Although the law protects children and persons with mental problems from being victimized in making contracts, the principle of *caveat emptor*—let the buyer beware!—applies to everyone else. You are responsible for reading any written agreement all the way through and for asking questions before you sign.

Try to get in writing any statements the seller makes about the quality of the goods. It will help protect you should the claims later prove untrue (see *Warranties*).

Cooling-off period

When you agree to buy goods in a door-to-door sale or through the mail or by telephone solicitation, most states give you a 3-day "cooling-off" period to decide whether you want to cancel the deal. The salesperson must give you written notice of this right when you make the agreement. (In some states, you might forfeit part of the purchase price if you cancel.) You lose your right to "cool off," however, if you ask for and immediately receive the goods.

Retail installment contracts

When you agree to pay for merchandise in regular monthly installments that equal a portion of the purchase price plus interest, you have a *retail installment contract.* Before you sign it, make sure that its terms are reasonable. Sometimes they are extremely harsh—for example, missing a payment may cause you to lose both the merchandise and the payments you've made. If your agreement seems un-

331

conscionable (so unfair that anyone with average intelligence would consider it shocking and outrageous), you can ask a court to either release you from it or to substitute fair terms.

Getting the goods

If the seller fails to deliver the goods when promised or delivers the wrong goods, you can give him a chance to correct the situation or seek the return of what you paid. If the merchandise is for your business, you can buy comparable goods from someone else and sue the seller for the amount you had to pay above the contract price. You can ask a court to force a seller to deliver an item to you, but only if it is one of a kind, such as an antique.

Salt deposits

Cleaning them off your car

If you live where road salt is used, wash your car's underbody in midwinter with a water hose and spray gun. With a stiff wire, unplug drain holes in door and hatch bottoms.

At the end of winter, repeat and also spray the engine compartment behind the headlamps. Underneath the car body, flush out road dirt by spraying between the bumper and its reinforcing bar and between the fender reinforcement and the fender itself (if there is a gap). Also spray underbody mounting brackets.

Work a stiff wire into holes in the underbody box sections to loosen packed-in road dirt, then flush it out with the spray. Cut away cracked undercoating, which can trap water and promote rusting. Dry and recoat the area with an aerosol undercoating.

Avoid commercial car washes that recycle water. The water may accumulate a lot of road salt.

Sanding

Selecting sandpaper; using it for hand and machine finishing

Sandpaper consists of a paper backing with an abrasive mineral coating. Inexpensive flint paper cuts slowly and dulls rapidly. Use it only for such jobs as removing old paint, where it will clog before the abrasive wears out. Garnet paper is more durable and is best for hand-finishing wood.

Aluminum oxide is a highly durable, all-around paper for hand or power sanding on wood, metal, or plastic. Silicon carbide, harder and sharper, does not last as well. Use it to smooth paint or varnish. If it has a wet-or-dry backing, you can dampen it with water or oil for an extra smooth finish.

Sandpaper is graded by grit numbers. Use coarse (under 80) for shaping wood and removing heavy finishes. Medium (80 to 100) is for smoothing rough edges and cuts and for early sandings of wood and plaster patches. Use fine (120 to 220) for the final sanding before finishing and very fine (280 and up) for smoothing undercoats and polishing finishes. To avoid marring a surface, use no coarser a grade than necessary. Work in steps from coarse to finer grits.

Sanding technique

Fold a large sheet in half and crease it. Align the crease along a table edge and pull down firmly to tear the sheet apart. Fold each half sheet in two so that it's hand size, and use one side at a time. For flat surfaces, wrap paper around a padded sanding block. To make a block, glue felt or low-pile carpeting to a 2 x 4 scrap.

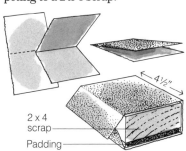

2 x 4 scrap
Padding
4½"

Sand back and forth in straight strokes, using light, even pressure. Do an entire surface, sanding all parts equally. Whenever possible, follow the grain. On a curved surface, sand first with the curve; but finish with the grain. Use a folded edge of paper in tight crevices. Wrap paper around a rounded piece, such as a chair rung. Wear a mask to avoid inhaling dust.

Using electric sanders

Wear goggles and a mask with all power sanders. Use a disc sander on a drill only for rough jobs, such as removing rust or knocking paint off siding. Apply a slight pressure, and tip the disc so that only the half nearest you touches the surface. Keep it moving and take care not to cut swirl marks. Another drill attachment, a drum sander, is good for finishing edges.

An orbital sander, which moves sandpaper in a small oval path, is a good choice for finishing furniture. Tear ordinary sandpaper into halves, thirds, or quarters to fit its pad. Use only minimal pressure as you guide it over the surface. With a dual-action model, use the oval action for initial sanding and the straight, back-and-forth action for finishing.

A belt sander uses a continuously rotating loop of sandpaper. It costs more to buy and use but works fast

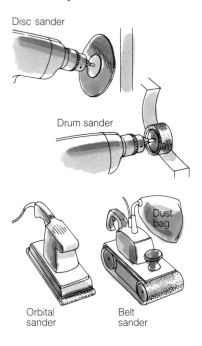

Disc sander

Drum sander

Orbital sander

Belt sander

Dust bag

and handles heavy-duty jobs. To control sawdust, get a model with a built-in, vacuumlike dust bag. Start the sander before touching it to the wood; then keep your strokes even and level. To avoid gouges, never apply excessive pressure and always keep the machine in motion. To sand down a rough surface quickly, use a belt of coarse paper at a 45-degree angle to the grain. Then smooth, using medium and fine paper with the grain. (See also *Power tool safety*.)

S

Sandwiches

How to make better ones; combinations to try

Always use firm-textured, good-quality bread. Take advantage of various bread shapes and flavors to give your sandwiches variety. You can even combine two kinds of bread that are the same size in one sandwich. Don't remove crusts unless you're making delicate tea sandwiches; crusts keep bread from drying out and curling.

Lushly filled sandwiches have more appeal than skimpy ones. Spread butter, mayonnaise, and fillings to the edges of the bread; don't skimp on the fillings. Use several thin slices of meat instead of one thick one. To add flavor and crunchiness, in place of lettuce try watercress, coleslaw, shredded plain cabbage, or sprouts.

Prevent sogginess on made-ahead sandwiches by spreading bread slices with softened butter or margarine rather than with mayonnaise or salad dressing. Wrap tomato and cucumber slices, lettuce, pickles, or relish separately and add them to the sandwiches at the last minute. Make toasted sandwiches just before serving.

Meat or seafood combinations

Layer prosciutto, Swiss cheese, lettuce, and sliced tomatoes between thick slices of Italian bread dribbled with olive oil and red wine vinegar. Combine minced chicken or turkey with finely chopped apple, celery, walnuts, and mayonnaise; spread on white bread. Flake cooked fish or chop some cooked shellfish and combine it with tartar sauce, chopped hard-cooked egg, and snipped fresh dill; serve on an onion roll.

Egg and cheese combinations

Mix chopped hard-cooked egg with chopped green pepper or pimiento or both, chopped celery, diced ham, and mayonnaise. Serve between slices of toasted rye bread. Grate 4 ounces sharp Cheddar cheese, and stir in 1 teaspoon Dijon or spicy brown mustard, 1 tablespoon chopped chutney, and ¼ cup mayonnaise. Spread on lightly toasted English muffins; then sprinkle with curry powder and melt under the broiler.

Here are two new twists to old favorites. Spread buttered whole-wheat toast with cold mashed baked beans; top with crisp bacon and, if you wish, a paper-thin slice of raw Bermuda onion. Mix chopped candied ginger with peanut butter. Serve on raisin bread with orange marmalade. (For open-face sandwiches, see *Canapés*.)

Sauerkraut

Making your own at home

Quarter, core, and finely shred 15 pounds of firm, green cabbage. Wash and scald a 2-gallon stoneware crock. Mix ¼ cup of pickling salt into 5 pounds of the cabbage, place it in the crock, and pack it down with a wooden spoon or potato masher; the brine that forms should cover the cabbage. Continue salting, layering, and packing down the cabbage until the crock is filled to within 3 inches of the rim. Cover with a clean cloth; tuck its edges into the crock. Place a scalded, snugly fitting plate in the crock over the cabbage; weight it down with a water-filled jar so that brine comes up to, not over, the plate. Let the cabbage ferment in a cool place (under 60°F); it will ferment faster at higher temperatures but won't be as good.

Daily during fermentation, remove scum from the top of the brine, wash or replace the cloth, and adjust the weight to keep the kraut under brine. Ferment 5 to 6 weeks, or until no more bubbles rise to the surface. Store the kraut, weighted down in its crock, in a cool cellar (remove scum and wash the cloth weekly), or can it by the hot-pack method. Bring the kraut to a simmer (180°F), pack it in hot jars, and cover it with brine to within ½ inch of the top. Process for ½ hour in a boiling-water bath (see *Canning*).

Saunas

Proper use, benefits, and precautions

A Finnish tradition, the sauna is a dry-heat bath taken in a room lined with untreated, moisture-absorbing softwood. The heat—no higher than 175°F if you've never done it—is generated by superheating rocks. You maintain relative humidity no higher than 10 percent by pouring small amounts of water on the rocks.

Saunas are valued mainly for relaxation and for skin cleansing. The heat raises the temperature of the skin above the normal body temperature, increasing blood flow to the skin's surface. This causes sweat glands to open, cleansing pores in areas that don't normally perspire.

Wear loose clothing (if any) or a draped towel. Remove jewelry, glasses, and contact lenses. Sit on a thick towel. Stay in for 5 to 15 minutes, then leave and shower in tepid water; return for another 5 to 10 minutes, followed by a shower and a 20-minute rest to cool down. Going from a sauna into cold air or rolling in the snow is highly risky—it can lead to a dangerously rapid rise in blood pressure. After a sauna, drink at least two glasses of water to replace lost fluids.

Caution: Saunas should not be used by the elderly, heart patients, pregnant women, or those with diabetes, illness of any kind, or high or low blood pressure. Don't use a sauna by yourself. Wait at least an hour after a meal. Avoid a sauna when taking such medications as antihistamines, vasoconstrictors, vasodilators, hypnotics, stimulants, narcotics, or tranquilizers.

To have a sauna installed or to investigate do-it-yourself installations using prefabricated parts, look under "Sauna Equipment and Supplies" in your local Yellow Pages directory.

Sautéing

Pan frying

Sautéing is the browning or cooking of food quickly in a little fat. To seal in juices and prevent food from sticking to the pan, the food should be dry or coated with flour and at room temperature, the fat very hot before adding the food, and the pan uncrowded. You can any heavy frying pan or a special pan with a long handle and straight sides called a *sautoir*. Enamel, stainless steel, or lined copper is best if wine or vinegar is to be added.

Continued next page

The ideal foods for sautéing are tender meats, poultry, fish, or vegetables that don't require long cooking. They should be thinly sliced or cut in small, uniform pieces.

If you sauté with butter, use clarified (see *Clarifying butter*) or add an equal amount of oil to prevent the butter from burning. When the fat is hot, add the food and move it around quickly or shake the pan to prevent the food from sticking.

Small pieces will be done in a few minutes. Remove them from the pan and keep them warm. Make a gravy or sauce in the sauté pan (see *Gravy*), pour it over the food, and serve.

If the recipe calls for cooking the sautéed food in its own juices or other liquid, cover the pan with a tight-fitting lid after the sautéing period.

Sawbuck

A solid support for cutting firewood

This easily built sawbuck can be disassembled for storage and carrying. Its two sections each consist of two 4-foot legs of 2 x 6 lumber and two shorter 1 x 6 braces. To find the right length for the top braces, subtract the thickness of one leg (about 1½ inches) from the maximum length of firewood that your stove or fireplace can accommodate; subtract the thickness of two legs for the bottom braces.

Lay a pair of legs parallel and on edge; then, using 6d common nails, join them with a bottom brace, its ends flush with their outside edges. Make sure both joints are square. Then nail the top brace in place, its

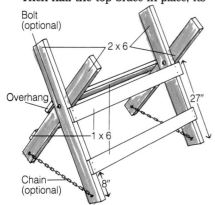

Bolt (optional)

2 x 6

Overhang

27"

1 x 6

Chain (optional)

8"

upper edge 27 inches from the bottom of the legs and one end overhanging a leg by 1½ inches. Build a second frame identical to the first.

To assemble the sawbuck, stand the frames about 30 inches apart and lean them toward each other so that one leg of each is supported by the other's protruding top brace. No metal fasteners should be needed to hold the sawbuck together on soft ground; for added security, however, drill for and insert bolts through the legs and attach a 30-inch chain as shown.

Sawing

Which handsaw to use; how to use it

To work properly, any saw must be sharp and the teeth must be *set*, or angled outward slightly, so that the cut they make is wider than the blade. Have the blades sharpened and set regularly; or buy a sharpening kit, with instructions for its use, and do it yourself. Don't try to sharpen a hacksaw or coping-saw blade; replace it.

The teeth of a *crosscut saw*, meant for cutting across the grain of wood,

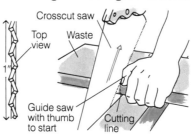

Crosscut saw

Top view

Waste

1"

Guide saw with thumb to start

Cutting line

are like little knives sharpened in alternate directions. As with all saws, the higher the *point count* (teeth per inch), the smoother and slower the cut. For general use, choose an 8- or 10-point crosscut saw.

Hold a crosscut saw as you would a pistol, with your index finger pointing toward the end of the blade. Start a cut by pulling the blade toward you once or twice, using your thumb to guide it on the waste side of the cutting line (not on the line itself). When you have made a small groove, begin pushing the saw through the wood at an angle of about 45 degrees. Relax. Let the saw do the cutting. Use the en-

tire blade and exert a downward push from your shoulder, not your elbow. Apply no force at all when pulling the saw back. As you approach the end of a cut, reach across with your free hand to steady the waste piece.

A *ripsaw* cuts along the grain of wood. It usually has a 5- to 7-point blade, and its teeth are sharpened straight across, like little chisels. The technique for using a ripsaw is similar to that for using a crosscut saw, except that the blade should be held at a steeper angle (60 degrees).

To support a board as you rip it, rest it on two sawhorses, letting one end

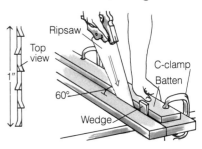

Ripsaw

Top view

1"

60°

Wedge

C-clamp

Batten

project about 1 foot. Rip this length, then readjust the board so that the sawhorse supports the cut end. Continue sawing until you reach the other sawhorse. Then reposition it beneath the cut part of the wood and rip to the end. A third sawhorse may be needed to keep a long board from bowing in the middle. A batten clamped along the cutting line helps to guide the saw. If the blade binds, insert a small wedge in the cut.

A *backsaw* is a short, 12- to 16-point crosscut saw with a stiffener on the back edge. Designed for precision work, it is generally used with a miter box (see *Miter joints*). To ensure a vertical cut when sawing freehand, use a

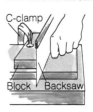

C-clamp

Block   Backsaw

square-edged block of wood as a guide: clamp it atop the piece to be cut, its edge aligned with the cutting line, and hold the saw against it.

A *coping saw*, made for cutting curves in wood, is a metal frame that holds a narrow, fine-tooth blade. Install the blade so that the teeth point toward the handle; saw only on the pull stroke. Use both hands and keep the blade under tension so that it won't bow or break. If the frame gets in the way, rotate the blade carefully, making sure that it doesn't twist.

Use a *keyhole saw* to make an interior cut, such as an opening for an electric outlet. Drill a hole at each corner; then saw from hole to hole along the inside of the cutting line.

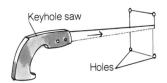

A *hacksaw* cuts metal; it is also used for plastic pipe and similar material. The correct blade for any job allows at least two teeth to rest on the surface to be cut. Install the blade so that the teeth point forward. Use the saw as you would a crosscut saw, but

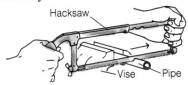

with both hands. It often helps when starting a cut to score the cutting line with a file. To cut very thin stock, sandwich the material between two pieces of scrap wood. When cutting curves, use a carbide-chip blade—actually an abrasive rod.

Scalding

A cooking technique

To scald a liquid, usually milk or cream, is to heat it to about 180°F, or just below the boiling point, when bubbles begin forming at the pan's edge. Scald milk in a heavy saucepan over low heat or in the top of a double boiler over barely boiling water.

Fruits or vegetables may be scalded—plunged briefly into boiling water—to loosen their skins and facilitate peeling. The term is sometimes used synonymously with blanching (see *Blanching*).

Scarecrows

Making a decorative guardian for your garden

Birds soon recognize a scarecrow as an empty threat. But an imaginatively outfitted figure can provide a cheerful centerpiece for your garden.

You can make a scarecrow by putting old clothes on a frame consisting of an 8- to 10-foot upright and a 3- to 5-foot crosspiece. Select clothing that is easy to attach, such as a one-piece union suit, overalls and a shirt, or a long dress. Bright, eye-catching colors make a scarecrow stand out. Durable fabrics weather better.

Fit the frame members through the clothing; then nail them together. Bury the upright 2 feet in firmly tamped soil. Then stuff the clothing with straw. Use twine to tie off openings and to tie clothing together.

To make a head, slip panty hose over the top of the upright, stuff it with fine straw, and tie off the bottom.

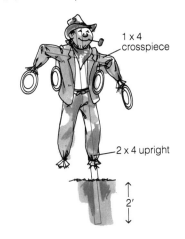

Draw on facial features with markers. Or pin on fabric cutouts. Add a hat, a kerchief, and gloves.

If you want to be certain of scaring away marauders, surround your statuary with a noisy display of pie plates.

Scavenger hunts

Searching for fun

A scavenger hunt is a great way to break the ice when you're entertaining children or adults who don't know one another well. Divide the players into teams of from three to six. Give each team an identical list of objects that they must seek within a defined area and bring back by a certain time.

The objects on the list can be commonplace, humorous, or outlandish. You may call an item by its name or cloak it in intricate clues for the players to decipher. If the hunt is for children, teach them a little nature lore by listing specific types of local rocks, leaves, and flowers. The area of the hunt can be a room, a neighborhood, or a continent, and the time measured in minutes or years.

The winning group is the one that returns first with all of the items. If time runs out before anyone gets through the list, the group that has found the most objects wins.

Scissors sharpening

Keeping a cutting edge

Sharpen scissors only if they're very dull. Frequent touching up whittles away too much metal, causing the blades to cut poorly; professional adjustment may then be necessary. Before you decide to sharpen, tighten the pivot screw holding the blades together. (If the scissors are held by a rivet, slightly spread the rivet head by striking it with the ball end of a ball peen hammer.) If this improves the cutting, there's no need to sharpen.

To sharpen the dull edge of a scissors blade, use an aluminum oxide bench stone (whetstone), available at hardware stores (see *Knives*). Clamp the stone in a vise, coarse side faceup. Spread light machine oil on its surface, then open the scissors wide and, firmly holding one blade and handle, place the other blade on the stone, with the inner face vertical. Tilt it

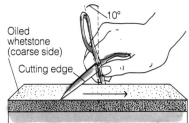

slightly less than 10 degrees so that the cutting bevel is flat against the stone; repeatedly move the blade diagonally across the stone (in the direction of the arrow) until you have the desired edge. Repeat on the other blade. Wipe both blades clean with a soft cloth; open and close the scissors several times to remove the thin wire edges that result from the sharpening. Leave the removal of deep nicks to a professional knife grinder.

Scorched food

Rescuing it; cleaning a scorched pan

Remove a scorched pan from the heat at once. Transfer unburned food to a clean pan, add fresh liquid, and continue cooking until done.

Trim off dark-brown crusts from overdone baked goods. Save burned toast by scraping off blackened crust with a table knife.

To remove burned-on food from a pan, scrape off as much of it as possible with a wooden spoon; fill the pan with hot, soapy water, let it soak, then scour it with baking soda or a nonabrasive cleaner on a plastic scouring pad. Or bring water to a boil in the pan. While the water simmers, scrape off scorched bits with the wooden spoon. After 10 minutes, pour out the water and scour the pan. Repeat the procedure until the pan is clean.

If you can't clean a scorched non-aluminum pan right away, soak it in cold water. Soaking pits an aluminum pan, so clean it immediately.

If a pan is beyond cleaning, discard it or, if it's one you're particularly fond of, have it restored by a professional. To find a professional, check the Yellow Pages under "Metal Finishers."

Scorpions

How to avoid getting stung; dealing with a sting

These nocturnal arachnids are often mistakenly called insects. Their adult size ranges up to 8 inches long. They prey on spiders, insects, and small ro-

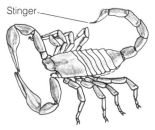

Stinger

dents, and are found mainly in the South and West of the United States. Of the more than 70 North American species, only the bark scorpion, a yellow species found in and near Arizona, possesses a sting that is occasionally fatal to humans.

During the day scorpions rest in dark places such as basements, attics, under stones, in log piles or debris. They may also take refuge under clothing or towels left lying about. If you live in scorpion country, avoid putting your hand into pipes or dark corners where you cannot see. Keep areas around the house free of debris and rotting wood. Seal all possible entryways, especially around a cooling system (see *Caulking*). Wear leather gloves when moving rocks or debris.

Protect a baby's crib by placing each leg in a glass jar (scorpions can't climb glass). When camping, shake out boots, clothing, and sleeping bags before getting into them.

Dealing with a sting

It is difficult to kill scorpions with insecticides; the best way to get rid of one is to crush it with a large board or rock, keeping hands and feet well away from the stinging tail. Look for scorpions at night using a black light—a UV light bulb installed in a battery-operated fluorescent camping light. The scorpions will glow under the light.

If you get stung, call your doctor or the nearest poison control center. Describe the scorpion's color, size, and markings. Trap it if you can. Even if it wasn't a bark scorpion, a sting can be serious if it's on the face, nape, or backbone. Relieve the pain by applying an ice pack to the stung area for 10 minutes; reapply if necessary, *but do not submerge the stung area in ice water*. A stung child under 6 or a person with a history of hypertension should be taken to the nearest hospital for immediate treatment.

Screens

Repairing and replacing screens on windows and doors

To fix a hole in a fiberglass screen, cut a patch from scrap ½ inch larger all around and glue it on with clear all-purpose household cement. A dab of the same glue will fill a small hole.

For a metal screen, cut a patch 1 inch larger than the hole. Unravel a few strands on each side. Turn up the ends. Push them through the screen and fold them flat on the other side.

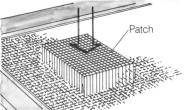

Patch

Replacing a wood-framed screen
Use a putty knife to pry off the molding; work carefully so that you can reuse it. Remove the old screen and all staples or tacks. If the frame's joints are loose, reglue them and reinforce them with mending plates or long wood screws inserted from the sides.

Cut new screen about 4 inches wider and 12 inches longer than the opening. Staple one end of the screen (see *Staple gun*). Work from the center out; on fiberglass screen, turn up a ½-inch hem and staple through both layers. Put the frame on a work surface and bow it as shown. Pull the

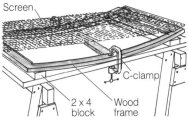

Screen

C-clamp

2 x 4 block

Wood frame

screen taut and staple the other end. Then remove the clamps and blocks and fasten the sides. Do the center rail last. Trim off excess screen with a sharp utility knife. Tack on the molding; sink the brads, fill the holes with putty, and prime. Repaint the frame.

Replacing a metal-framed screen
The screen is held in place by flexible plastic splines forced into grooves. To

S

install a screen, buy a special roller tool that fits over the spline. (Replace old metal splines with plastic ones.)

First remove the old screen: start at a corner and pry out the splines with a screwdriver; you can reuse ones that are still pliable. Cut new screen to the frame's outside dimensions. Trim the corners at a 45-degree angle.

Attach the screen at one end. Force the spline in at the corner; then roll the rest in with short, firm strokes. Pull the screen tight and attach the other end. Then attach the two sides. Trim off excess screen.

Screws

What screws to use; how to get them in and out

Use screws when you need greater holding power than nails can provide, when hammering may cause damage, and when you may later need to take a piece apart.

Wood screws come in plain, plated, and galvanized steel, in stainless steel and aluminum for maximum rust resistance, and in bronze and brass to match hardware. For most joints, the common flathead screw is fine. Sink it flush with the surface or below (see *Countersinking*) and conceal it with

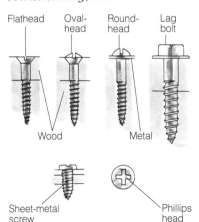

wood putty or a plug. An oval-head screw is more attractive when exposed; a roundhead lets you secure a thin material, such as metal, to wood.

Use a sheet-metal, or self-threading, screw to join metal pieces, such as heat ducts, or as an extra-strong fastener for plywood. A heavy-duty lag bolt (or screw) is for joining large structural pieces; you drive in its square, slotless head with a wrench.

Most screws also come with a cross-slotted Phillips head. You need a special tip to drive it in. But it keeps the screwdriver from slipping, making it ideal when you use a screwdriver bit on a drill to speed a large job.

Installing a screw

Use a screwdriver that fills a screw's slot in both thickness and width. A long screwdriver provides more turning power; a shorter one more control.

Always drill a pilot hole of the proper size (see *Screw sizes*). When joining hardwood pieces, drill again to widen the hole in the upper piece so that the screw's shank can pass through it freely. This lets the screw pull the top piece tightly against the lower one.

To make a screw go in more easily, lubricate the threads with wax or soap. To increase a screw's holding power, apply glue to the threads.

Removing a stubborn screw

Clear the slot with a screwdriver or a hacksaw blade. Insert a small screwdriver in one side of the slot and tap it so that the screw turns counterclockwise. Once the screwhead emerges, twist it out with locking-grip pliers. If that doesn't work, heat the screw with a soldering iron. This expands the screw, enlarging the hole. When the screw cools, it will turn more freely.

If a screw breaks off, drive it in with a nail and cover it with wood putty. If

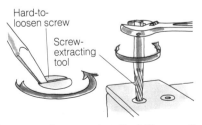

you prefer removing it, drill a small hole in the screw's end and try backing it out with a square-tipped nail or a screw-extracting tool.

Screw sizes

Buying the right size and drilling the proper pilot hole

Screw sizes are designated by length and diameter. Lengths commonly range from ¼ inch to 6 inches. Diameters, indicated by gauge numbers, run from 2 (about $\frac{1}{16}$ inch) to 18 (nearly $\frac{5}{16}$ inch). Screws with the same gauge number come in different lengths. For example, you can buy a No. 8 screw at regular lengths from ½ inch to 2 inches.

To find a screw's length, measure only the portion that enters the material—in the case of a flathead screw, it's the entire length. Select a screw long enough so that two-thirds goes into the lower layer of material.

The chart below lists bit sizes for drilling pilot holes; use a bit $\frac{1}{64}$ inch larger in hardwood. In softwood, an awl or a hammer and nail will make a hole for a No. 5 or smaller screw.

PILOT HOLE GUIDE

Screw size	Bit size
2	$\frac{1}{32}''$
3, 4	$\frac{3}{64}''$
5, 6, 7	$\frac{1}{16}''$
8, 9	$\frac{5}{64}''$
10	$\frac{3}{32}''$
12, 14	$\frac{7}{64}''$
16, 18	$\frac{9}{64}''$

Scrimshaw

Carving teeth and bones—the old-time whaler's art

Whale teeth and jaws—the scrimshander's traditional medium—are no longer available. Nor are elephant and walrus tusks. However, substitutes are easy to find. Seashells and animal bones make good work surfaces for beginners. Hobby shops sell plastic pieces especially prepared for scrimshaw. Boar tusks, cattle horns, and deer antlers are usable; so are the hard white centers of ivory nuts. For real ivory, search in secondhand shops for old billiard balls, knife handles, piano keys, and the like.

Boil bones for several hours to remove all traces of meat and fat. Bake

S

ivory nuts in their shells for 15 minutes at 300°F, then remove the shells.

Cut the material to size, using a fine-tooth hacksaw blade. Polish with very fine sandpaper, followed by superfine. Buff with 0000 steel wool. Seal the surface of bones with butcher's wax or polyurethane varnish.

Caution: Avoid inhaling the dust: work in a well-ventilated area and wear a filtered mask if using a power sander.

Sketch the design on the polished surface with a soft pencil. Or plan it on paper and transfer with carbon paper or by making tiny pricks through the design with a sharp scribing tool.

To hold the material steady, anchor it in beeswax, or make a V-shaped brace from two strips of wood. Carve with a craft knife, engraver's tool, sharp awl, or small-bladed penknife. Using firm, even pressure, cut the heaviest lines first. Then add detail. For shading, scratch parallel lines close together.

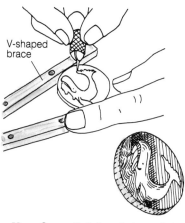

V-shaped brace

Use a fine artist's brush to apply indelible ink, oil paint, watercolor, or dye. The etched lines will absorb the color. Wipe off excess color with a soft cloth. Polish with 0000 steel wool.

Scuba diving

Swimming safely underwater with your own air supply

Scuba diving (the name stands for *Self-Contained Underwater Breathing Apparatus*) should be relaxing and enjoyable. If you find it hard work, you are probably doing something wrong.

Before attempting to dive, complete a certified scuba-diving course; most shops will not rent equipment or fill air tanks without proof that you have done so. Many YMCA's, diving clubs, and equipment shops offer instruction. Make sure the instructor is certified by a reputable agency, such as the Professional Association of Diving Instructors (PADI), the YMCA National Scuba Diving Program, or the National Association of Underwater Instructors (NAUI). Equipment can be rented for the lessons so that you will be able to try this sport before investing in the necessary equipment.

Instructors may require a physical examination by a physician and a swimming test. You must be reasonably fit and free of cardiovascular and respiratory disorders, and your middle ear and sinuses must be able to equalize pressure changes. Swimming tests vary. An NAUI-certified instructor will require you to stay afloat for 10 minutes, swim 220 yards nonstop without fins, and swim underwater for 20 yards without fins and without pushing off. Any course should include 15 to 30 hours of classroom and *confined-water* training (in a pool or enclosed area) and at least five supervised *open-water* dives. Upon completing the course, you'll receive a certificate as a trained diver.

The first rule of diving is *never dive alone.* Use the buddy system; you and at least one other diver should be responsible for each other's safety. The second rule is *maintain your equipment;* never go into the water until you have checked every valve, regulator, and pressure gauge yourself. The third—also contained in the letters SCUBA—is *Stay Calm Underwater, Breathe Always.* Panic means loss of control, something you can't afford underwater. (See also *Skin diving.*)

Seafood cocktail sauce

Adding zest to chilled shellfish

For the classic shellfish sauce, mix 3 tablespoons each of ketchup, prepared horseradish, and lemon juice, 1 teaspoon Worcestershire sauce, hot pepper sauce to taste and, if you wish, 1 tablespoon chopped onion. Serve with chilled, cooked shrimp or crabmeat or with chilled raw clams or oysters.

Green mayonnaise also enhances cold seafood. Mix together 1 tablespoon each of chopped spinach, fresh chives, dill, and parsley. Stir the herbs into 1 cup mayonnaise. Experiment with other green herbs.

Remoulade is another good accompaniment to seafood. To 1 cup mayonnaise add 1 tablespoon chopped parsley, 1 chopped hard-cooked egg, 1 minced garlic clove, and 1 teaspoon Dijon mustard.

Seashells

Collecting and preparing them for display

Search for shells at low tide in coves, along sandy beaches, or in other calm shore areas. Take along a small garden cultivator or similar tool for combing through seaweed and debris and a container for your finds. Wear shoes and gloves.

If you intend to become a serious collector, take a notebook too. Record the day, time, and place that you found each shell and note any special circumstances; also write a short identifying description of the shell.

Number each entry. Later, number the shells accordingly and use the notebook and a shell guide to make labels. As you search, protect the shoreline by replacing seaweed clumps after sifting through them.

Cleaning and oiling

Scrub your shells in soapy water with a stiff brush and rinse them thoroughly. If they are encrusted with hard material, scrape them carefully with a knife or soak them in equal parts household bleach and warm water. Check often during soaking because the bleach can dull the surfaces. Wash and rinse again after soaking. (Some collectors prefer to leave encrustations intact for their scientific interest.)

If you wish to enhance the color and luster of your shells for display, dampen a lint-free cloth with mineral oil or baby oil and rub it over the shells. Buff with a clean, dry cloth.

Seat belts

What to do when one sticks

If a car seat belt fails to retract, pull it out farther and release it. If it won't come forward, it may be twisted or jammed; pull hard and try to remove any twists or impeding debris.

If the belt is still jammed, examine the retractor (you may have to remove a seat cushion or trim panel to get at it). Poke a thin screwdriver into the

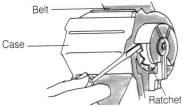

spring side of the case and push the release—a bar, a ratchet, or a hanging weight—while pulling on the belt.

Once the belt comes free, pull and release it a few times. Spray silicone lubricant into the belt's mechanism to help it run freely. Do not remove the retractor case. Any further repair should be done by a dealer or a licensed mechanic.

Seed planting

Sowing seeds in the garden

Mark a row with two stakes and draw a furrow between them with a stick. Follow the instructions on seed packets regarding planting time, spacing, and depth.

For vegetables and flowers with small seeds, dribble the seeds sparingly between your fingers or shake them from a corner of the packet. (Thin the seedlings when they have three or four leaves.) Space larger seeds, such as corn, beans, or peas, farther apart to eliminate the need for thinning. Cover seeds to the recommended depth—most seeds should be covered with a layer of soil that is roughly as thick as the seed itself. Tamp the earth down lightly and water well if the soil is dry. (See also *Cold frames and hotbeds; Greenhouse gardening; Starting seeds indoors.*)

Septic systems

How they work; inspection and maintenance

Most of the waste that enters a septic system is decomposed by bacterial action in a 500- to 1,000-gallon septic tank. Undecomposed solid matter settles as *sludge* to the bottom of the tank; oily waste floats on top as *scum.* The liquid between, known as *effluent,* runs off through an outlet pipe into a drainage field and is absorbed into the ground. To keep sludge or scum from clogging the drainage field, the water level must be maintained and the tank must be pumped out every 2 to 5 years, depending on its size and on the amount of waste it receives. Pumping is a job for a professional septic cleaning service.

Warning signs of an overloaded system include foul odors from your drains or over the drainage field, and lush vegetation over the tank. If water backs up into your drains, it may indicate that the drainage field is blocked by tree roots or clogged by sludge and scum. The roots can be cleared by a drain-cleaning service; a clogged field must be dug up.

To prevent problems, don't put grease or slow-decomposing matter down drains or toilets. If there is no grease trap on the line between your kitchen drain and the septic tank, have a plumber install one. Avoid drain-cleaning chemicals; they kill the bacteria and enzymes that decompose the wastes. To hasten decomposition, mix ½ pound of brewer's yeast in warm water and flush it down a toilet. Don't use a commercial cleaning compound; it breaks up solids, which then flow into the drainage field, clogging lines that can't be cleaned.

Severed limbs and digits

Emergency actions; preventive measures

If someone severs a finger, toe, or limb, get medical help as quickly as you can: call for an ambulance or get the victim to the hospital emergency room. In the meantime, keep the affected limb elevated. The safest way to stem bleeding is by direct pressure: apply a thick wad of cloth directly over the wound and hold it there. If the wad becomes soaked, add to it—don't remove it. At the same time, compress the limb's main artery at the appropriate pressure point (see *Bleeding*).

Don't panic. The emotional shock of an accidental amputation may make the amount of blood lost and the time elapsed seem greater than they are. Avoid applying a tourniquet. If it isn't tight enough, it can actually *increase* blood flow. If it's too tight, it can damage tissue and nerves. A tourniquet should be used only if the person's life is endangered, and then only if an expert is present to assess the situation and apply the tourniquet.

Reattachment of severed digits or, less often, severed limbs may be possible if the tissues are not badly damaged and not too much time has passed. The severed part should go to the hospital with the patient. Put a severed finger or toe in a plastic bag, then put the bag in a container of ice cubes. Wrap a severed limb in a sheet, towel, or other clean material.

Although auto, motorcycle, and train accidents cause many amputations, the most frequent cause of severed fingers and toes is careless operation of appliances: lawn mowers, chain saws, and power tools (see *Chain saws; Power tool safety*).

Another cause of amputations is fireworks. These powerful explosives can blow off the fingers of adults as well as children.

Sewing machines

Threading; inserting a needle; balancing tension

To get good performance from your sewing machine, follow the directions in your instruction booklet carefully. If you have lost your copy, write to the manufacturer and request it; give the model number of your machine.

Although sewing machines vary in the precise way in which they are threaded, there is a general sequence to follow. Bring the thread from the

S

spool through the *tension assembly,* then into the *take-up lever,* and down to the *needle.* Be sure that the thread passes through each of the *thread guides* between these main points. Thread the needle from the direction indicated by the last thread guide; for example, if the guide is to the left, thread the needle from left to right.

Before threading the needle, check

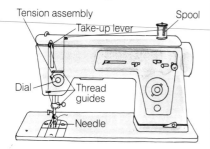

Tension assembly
Take-up lever
Spool
Dial
Thread guides
Needle

that it is straight and free of oil and burrs. Replace it if necessary. Insert a new needle into the machine as far as it will go, with its grooved side facing the last thread guide. Tighten the screw holding the needle in place.

To thread the lower part of the machine, first fill a bobbin with thread. Then, drop the bobbin into its case with the thread feeding *away* from the slot. Pass the thread through the slot, catching it in the tension spring.

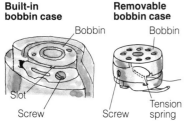

Built-in bobbin case

Bobbin
Slot
Screw

Removable bobbin case

Bobbin
Screw
Tension spring

Before stitching, check for balanced tension by test stitching on a swatch of the fabric you're about to sew. When tension is balanced, the knots between stitches won't be visible, except on very thin fabric. If knots show on the underside, increase the top tension by turning the tension dial to a higher number. If you have tightened top tension to the maximum and knots still show, decrease bobbin-thread tension by turning a screw in the bobbin case counterclockwise. Loose knots on top mean that top tension should be decreased; turn the dial to a lower number.

Sharpening hand tools

Keeping a good working edge

Sharpening means removing metal from a blade to restore the cutting edge. How much metal you must remove depends on how dull or damaged the blade is. For a quick touch-up, rub a blade on a hard Arkansas stone (see *Knives*) or strop it on a leather strap.

The first step in sharpening a dull blade is to restore the bevel. Use a medium-grit stone for such fine-edged tools as chisels, gouges, planes, and spokeshaves; use a coarse-grit stone if the blade is nicked or very dull. You can also use a power grinder, but you risk ruining the blade's temper; dip the blade in water frequently, never letting it become too hot to touch. Use a medium-mill file or a round handstone for axes, mauls, hatchets, and garden tools. Use a rounded scythe-stone for the curved blade of a scythe, sickle, or grass whip.

Study the blade's original bevel and maintain its angle. With a small tool, clamp the stone firmly to a bench and slide the blade back and forth along its length; a honing guide helps to maintain the angle. If you're using a power grinder, use the machine's bevel guide. Clamp a large tool in a vise, and wield a stone or file against it, rubbing toward the cutting edge. Use plenty of light oil or water (with a water stone) to lubricate the work. Stop when the entire bevel shines and your finger can detect a *burr,* or tiny curl of metal, on the edge.

Next comes honing with a fine-grit stone to smooth scratches left by the coarser stone, to remove the burr, and sometimes to add a second slight bevel. Stones are commonly available with a medium-grit surface on one side and a fine-grit surface on the other. Heavy-duty garden tools need no honing; file off the burr.

If you are sharpening fine-edged tools, eight or ten strokes should be enough to smooth the surface; remove the burr by holding the edge of the blade *flat* against the stone and pulling it toward you. With a plane blade or chisel, hone the tip to a sec-

Standard bevel angles

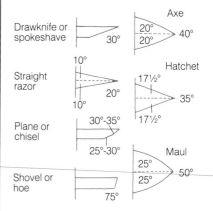

Drawknife or spokeshave — 30°

Axe — 20° / 20° — 40°

Straight razor — 10° / 20° / 10°

Hatchet — 17½° / 35° / 17½°

Plane or chisel — 30°-35° / 25°-30°

Maul — 25° / 25° — 50°

Shovel or hoe — 75°

ond bevel, or *whetting angle,* of 30 degrees (for working with softwood) or 35 degrees (for hardwood).

Finally, for a razor-sharp edge, strop with a leather strap or hard Arkansas stone. Three or four strokes on each side of the blade should do. Test for sharpness by holding the blade below a light and viewing it head-on. If it is sharp along its whole length, it won't sparkle. (See also *Axes; Sawing; Scissors sharpening.*)

Shelf hanging

Making open storage space

For most shelves, use nominal 1-inch boards or ¾-inch plywood with a finished edge (see *Veneer tape*). Mount a single shelf on shelf brackets spaced 32 inches apart, with up to 8 inches of overhang at the ends. For heavier loads, like books, space the brackets 16 inches apart.

To mark the bracket positions, tack a chalkline indicating the shelf's lower edge and pull it taut. True the line with a carpenter's level (see *Leveling*) and snap it. Screw the brackets to studs; on masonry, use wall anchors (see *Wall fasteners*).

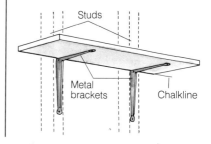

Studs
Metal brackets
Chalkline

S

For a row of shelves, use slotted wall standards with adjustable brackets. Mark the position of the standards' top edges with a chalkline. After putting the top screw partway into each standard, let it plumb itself by swinging free until it stops. Or check it with a level or plumb line (see *Plumb line*).

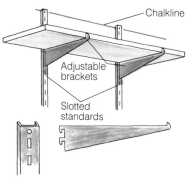

Chalkline

Adjustable brackets

Slotted standards

To hang a shelf between walls in an alcove or a closet, mark the position of the shelf's lower edge with a leveled chalkline along the back wall and then along each side. Cut cleats a shelf's width from ¾-inch molding or from 1 x 2's. Nail them into the studs.

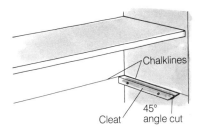

Chalklines

Cleat 45° angle cut

On masonry, use cut or masonry nails; predrill holes in the cleats. Add a back cleat for a wide span or a heavy load. Or nail vertical dividers, cut from shelf lumber, between shelves. (See also *Bookcase building*.)

Shingling a roof

Covering old asphalt shingles with new ones

If the old shingles aren't badly curled, you can nail new shingles directly over them. Use 3-foot-long shingle strips the same width as the old shingles; secure them with galvanized roofing nails long enough to penetrate ¾ inch into the roof deck. If your roof already has two layers of shingles, check with

a building engineer to be sure that it can carry more weight.

Use a utility knife to trim the old overhanging shingles flush with the edge of the roof. It is best to cut shingles from the back, or smooth, side. If

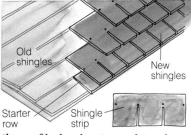

Old shingles

New shingles

Starter row Shingle strip

the roof lacks aluminum drip edges, install them over the trimmed shingles; use aluminum nails and dab the heads with roofing cement.

For the starter row, trim off the notched edges of some new shingles to a width of about 5 inches. This unnotched starter row should overhang the drip edge by about ¼ inch when it is butted against the second row of old shingles. Position the nails 12 inches apart, 3 inches from the shingles' upper edge.

Starting at the left side of the roof, lay the new shingles one row at a time, notched edges downslope, so that each row butts against the lower edge of the old shingles above. The notches should alternate from row to row. Fasten each strip with four nails; one 1 inch above each notch, and one 1 inch from each side.

Before you reach the peak of the roof, carefully remove the row of hip shingles or the metal ridgecap from the peak. Nail a final row of new shingles on each side so that their upper edges meet at the peak. Then reinstall the ridgecap or lay new hip shingles, using the old ones as patterns. Let the sun warm the shingles before you fold them over the peak. (See also *Flashings; Roof repairs*.)

Shin splints

Causes and cures for lower-leg pain

Shin splints, an inflammation of the lower-leg muscles and tendons, causes pain in the front of the leg. Because a

stress fracture (hairline crack) of the shinbone causes similar pain, the two conditions are often confused. Don't try to diagnose or treat yourself—see a doctor.

Shin splints can result from any exercise that overuses leg muscles or subjects the legs to repeated jolts. Given a month or so of rest, the injured muscles and tendons usually repair themselves. If the punishment continues, the condition becomes chronic, or a relapse soon follows recovery.

The wisest course is to avoid the problem by making the activity less punishing. First, ready muscles and tendons for work with a stretching and warm-up routine (see *Exercises*). Second, lessen jolts by wearing well-cushioned shoes and exercising on an even, resilient surface rather than one that is rough or hard.

Shirt ironing

Getting a professional finish

For best results, iron cotton shirts while damp; remove a shirt from the dryer or clothesline before it's completely dry. If the shirt is already dry, spray or flick water on it. Then roll the shirt up with the collar and cuffs on the inside, place it in a plastic bag, and leave it for an hour or so until the dampness penetrates the fabric.

Set your iron for *cotton* and turn off the steam. Place the collar flat on the ironing board, wrong side up, and press from the points toward the center. Turn the collar over and repeat.

Press the sleeves next, beginning with the insides, then the outsides of the cuffs. Place the sleeve flat on the board, taking care to crease it properly; press one side, then the other. Drape the yoke (shoulder panel) over the wide end of the board and iron it.

Lay the back of the shirt flat and press it quickly. Iron the side seams from the inside, then the outside. If the shirt has a pocket, press the inside of the pocket first. Iron both front panels and let the shirt dry on a hanger in an open space before storing it in a closet or a drawer.

Follow the same procedure with shirts of synthetics or cotton blends, but set the iron to a lower temperature. On all shirts, test the iron on a shirttail first to make sure it does not scorch or crinkle the fabric.

Shish kebabs

Cubed or small foods grilled on skewers

Attractive and colorful, shish kebabs are traditionally made of lamb, but chicken, ham, scallops, lobster, beef, and such vegetables as zucchini and mushrooms can also be used.

Adjust the cooking time to the foods you are using: you'll need less time for shellfish and more time for meat. Add tomato wedges to the ends of skewers during the last 4 minutes of cooking. Or put all of the vegetables on separate skewers, brush them with oil, and cook them away from the direct flame.

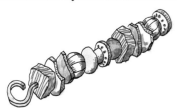

Lamb shish kebab
To serve four, use 2 to 3 pounds of boneless lamb that has been cut into 1½-inch chunks. Mix a marinade of ½ cup vegetable or olive oil, ¼ cup lemon juice, 1 minced garlic clove, ½ teaspoon salt, and ⅛ teaspoon pepper, or to taste. Cover the meat with the marinade and refrigerate for 3 hours or overnight.

Wash and core 2 green peppers, 1 sweet red pepper, and 8 small white onions; parboil 2 minutes. Remove peppers and submerge in cold water. Drain and cut them into 1½-inch squares. Parboil onions 3 minutes longer; cool in several changes of cold water. Stem ½ pound of mushrooms. Drain the meat, reserving the marinade. Thread lamb and vegetables alternately on metal skewers. Coat them lightly with oil. Cook 3 inches from the heat over hot coals or in the broiler for 8 minutes (rare) to 11 minutes (medium rare), brushing occasionally with marinade. Serve with rice and a green salad.

Shock

A life-threatening condition that may follow severe injury

Shock is the term for bodily changes that follow such trauma as dehydration, allergic reaction, or serious injury (burns, fractures, crushing, prolonged bleeding). A person in shock usually has pale, clammy skin; a weak and irregular pulse; and decreased blood pressure. His breathing may be shallow and he may feel faint, nauseated, chilled, or thirsty—symptoms of the body's channeling blood to the vital organs and the brain. In the early stage, he may be agitated; try to reassure him that his injury is being cared for. Later, he may become unresponsive and, finally, unconscious.

Shock symptoms aren't always immediately obvious. Assume they may develop in anyone with a serious injury. In any case, they should be treated only by medical professionals. Summon help immediately; do what you would normally do for the particular injury or other trauma involved.

In addition, aid blood flow by having the victim lie flat; raise his legs about 8 inches unless you suspect a head injury. Cover the victim lightly in mild weather or if he is indoors, more warmly outdoors in winter. Do not use artificial heat (pads, hot-water bottles) except for hypothermia. Offer no liquids, except water for dehydration or burns.

Shock absorbers

How to test them

Standard shock absorbers seldom last longer than 20,000 to 25,000 miles. If your car handles poorly, bottoms out on slight bumps, and rides roughly, check the shocks. For a quick test, park the car on a level area with the engine off, transmission in *Park* (or gears engaged), and parking brake on; then pull up and down on one end of the front bumper so that the car bounces. Release the bumper at the low point of a bounce. The car should settle level after one upward

bounce. If it doesn't, the shock in that corner may be bad. Repeat for the other three corners.

For a more thorough check, jack up the car and support it on safety stands (see *Jacking a car*). Inspect each shock separately. If possible, disconnect the lower end and extend,

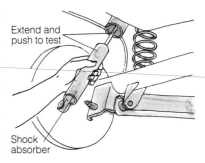

Extend and push to test

Shock absorber

then compress, the shock. If you do not feel smooth, heavy resistance, or if you find dents or significant leakage, replace both shocks on that axle.

Many late-model cars have MacPherson struts, which combine shocks with suspension arms. Have a mechanic check and replace these.

Shoe care

Cleaning, storing, and repairing; salt stains

To avoid damaging the backs, use a shoehorn when you put on shoes. After each wearing, wipe your shoes clean with a cloth or brush. (See also *Shoeshine*). Brush suede shoes with a fine-bristled wire brush made for that purpose. Use a special cleaning compound for shoes made of materials other than leather.

Let the shoes air for a few hours before putting them away. To preserve their shape, use shoe trees. Store them in shoe-storage boxes or shoe bags—not loose on the closet floor.

Check shoes regularly for wear and tear. Have run-down heel lifts replaced before the heels themselves are damaged. To protect the soles, have your repair shop glue *martyr soles* over them. These thin rubber half soles can be stripped off and replaced easily and inexpensively. To lengthen the life of soles and heels, have small hard-rubber taps attached to them.

S

Wet and salt-stained shoes

When shoes get soaked, stuff them loosely with crumpled newpapers and let them dry away from heat. To remove the white stains left by road salt, wipe off loose dirt and mud with a damp cloth; then dab the stained areas with a mixture of equal parts water and cider vinegar. Let the shoes dry, then condition and polish them.

Shoeshine

From a soft glow to a high mirrorlike sheen

Shoe creams clean and condition shoes, heighten their color, and impart a soft shine. They come in a wide range of colors. Paste wax gives a high-gloss shine but it is generally available only in a few dark or neutral colors. Because paste wax builds up on leather surfaces, it's best to apply cream polish or a leather conditioner between polishings.

First wipe the shoes, then apply cream or paste with a clean cloth or applicator, rubbing gently with a circular motion. Then buff to a gloss, using a separate brush for different colors. With paste wax, finish by buffing with a towel or soft cloth. For a high-gloss shine, apply a second light coat of paste wax, using a bit of water-soaked cotton.

Quick-shine liquids are good if you're in a hurry, but the alcohol in them dries out leather; alternate their use with a leather conditioner.

Short circuits

Restoring power

A short circuit is a breakdown in an electric circuit caused by the accidental detour of current through a path of relatively low resistance—as occurs when two wires with frayed insulation touch. In a house circuit, the resulting surge of current will blow a fuse (or trip a circuit breaker) or burn out a wire, causing the circuit to go dead (see *Circuit breakers; Fuse boxes*).

In a lower power circuit, such as the wiring in a car, a short circuit may not blow a fuse but may simply cause the part of the circuit beyond the short to go dead.

There are three main dangers from short circuits: damage to delicate electric components; shock (for example, when a bare wire touches the metal shell of an appliance, a person touching that appliance receives a shock); and fire caused by sparks or overheating wires. Proper fuses or circuit breakers on a line protect against the last two hazards; appliances are usually protected by their own fuses. (See also *Ground fault interrupters*.)

To find a short circuit, follow the procedure given in *Circuit testing*. Test the circuit with all appliances and lamps unplugged and all switches on. If the circuit breaker trips again or a new fuse blows, the trouble is probably in a switch, receptacle, or the wiring. Open and inspect switch boxes and receptacles. If you see charred parts on a switch or receptacle, replace it. If you see a burned wire, a bare wire touching the metal housing, or a wire with a break in its insulation, rewire, using wire connectors. Don't use electrician's tape to reinsulate frayed wires. (See also *Electric receptacles; Electric switches; Wiring*.)

If the circuit works, plug in and turn on appliances one by one until you discover the faulty device. Unplug it and have it repaired.

If the problem is in the house wiring itself, get an electrician to track it down and make the repair.

Shower curtains

How to make them; keeping them clean and mildew free

Choose a waterproof or washable fabric. Estimate yardage by measuring the distance from the shower rod to the floor; add 6 inches for hems. Next, measure the rod. You'll need enough fabric to make a curtain 1 to 1½ times the rod length. To match a pattern in joining panels, buy one extra repeat of the pattern for each yard of fabric. Buy enough shower-curtain hooks and grommets to provide a hook every 6 inches. Check that the grommets are large enough to accommodate the hooks (see *Grommets*). If your fabric isn't waterproof, buy a plastic shower-curtain liner.

If necessary, preshrink the fabric. Join the panels; hem the sides and bottom (see *Curtains and draperies*). Hem the top over a 2½-inch-wide strip of interfacing. Set grommets at each end and at equal distances in between. Hang the curtain and liner on the hooks.

Washing a shower curtain

Unless the care label indicates that a shower curtain is machine washable, wash it in the bathtub with warm water and detergent. (In a machine, put in two or three large towels to balance the load.) To remove soap film, add ½ cup baking soda to the wash water. To keep the curtain supple, add ½ cup vinegar or a few drops of mineral oil to the rinse water. Hang the curtain on its hooks to dry.

To remove mildew from a bleachable shower curtain, sponge with a solution of chlorine bleach (1 part bleach to 8 parts water) and wash; for nonbleachable fabrics, use a paste of baking soda, then wash.

Shower doors

Installing a tub enclosure

Manufacturers offer a variety of shower-tub enclosures with sliding glass doors. Before you buy a do-it-yourself kit, measure your tub carefully. The kit should include instructions and all materials needed for the job: two tempered glass doors, the top and bottom tracks in which they slide, the vertical side rails into which they fit to form a splash-proof seal, and hardware (you may want to use longer screws than those provided). Special caulking should also be provided for sealing the bottom track.

If necessary, use a hacksaw to cut the top and bottom tracks to fit. Center the bottom track on the tub's ledge and mark where its ends meet the walls. Position the side rails on the marks, using a combination square to make sure each is vertical (see *Leveling*). Outline each rail on the wall, and mark the holes for fasteners. Then remove the rails and drill holes

S

for the fasteners, using a masonry bit to cut through ceramic tile.

Apply the caulk to the tub ledge and press the bottom track into it, aligning the track with the marks on the walls. Interlock the side rails with the bottom track and fasten them to the walls. Then attach the top track; in most models, it is simply pushed down onto the side rails. Insert the doors' rollers in the appropriate track (depending on the model) and slip the opposite edge between the guides in the other track.

Shower heads

Cleaning and replacing; attaching a hand-held unit

To unclog a shower head, remove it from the wall pipe, using a pair of padded pipe wrenches to avoid marring the chrome. Disassemble the head and soak the parts overnight in vinegar to soften mineral deposits; then

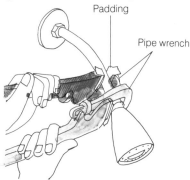

Padding

Pipe wrench

scrub them clean with a stiff brush. Use a toothpick to poke debris and mineral deposits from the shower holes. Before screwing the head back on, apply joint sealer to the wall-pipe threads (see *Pipes*).

To replace a shower head with one that has a nonclogging plastic face plate—or to install a water-conserving head or one that delivers a pulsating flow—remove the old head and screw the new one in its place, following the manufacturer's instructions.

To add a hand-held shower unit, remove the existing head and install a *diverter valve* in its place. Screw the fixed shower head onto the diverter's main outlet, and the hose of the hand-held unit onto the side outlet.

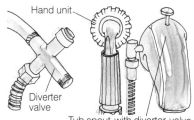

Hand unit

Diverter valve

Tub spout with diverter valve

To install a hand-held unit on a bathtub spout, remove the old spout by inserting a hammer handle and turning it counterclockwise; replace it with a new one that is the same size but includes a diverter valve and an outlet for the hand-held hose.

Shrubs

Using them in the landscape

Shrubs can perform any of several functions in a landscape plan. They can shield your house from winter winds and shade it from the summer sun. Their roots can help hold the soil around the foundation, the driveway, or a steep slope. Shrubs can enclose a private area, define a path or walkway, hide a compost pile or an unsightly shed, or mark boundary lines. Their blossoms and fruits can add color and fragrance to your yard, attract butterflies and songbirds, and even put food on your table. A flowering specimen can be the focal point of an open lawn or the backdrop for a bed of bulbs and annuals.

Shrubs for specific places

For year-round privacy or a winter windscreen, look for large evergreens, such as as myrtle, holly, mountain laurel, yew, or upright junipers. For foundation plantings, select low-growing shrubs that won't block your windows as they mature. To cover a bare slope, try a spreading juniper, euonymus, or heath. For fragrant blossoms near your patio or bedroom window, use a lilac, mock orange, honeysuckle, or jasmine.

For showy blossoms in full sun, choose a forsythia, flowering quince, natal plum, or oleander; in shade, try an andromeda, hydrangea, rhododendron, or witch hazel. If you have problems with browsing deer, look for shrubs that they dislike, including

daphnes, hollies, junipers, and mahonias (see *Deer damage*).

Next, consider the climate. Shrubs are rated for winter hardiness according to a zone map prepared by the U.S. Department of Agriculture; most garden guides and encyclopedias include a copy of this map, or you can write for one to the USDA Office of Public Affairs, Washington, DC 20250. The zone map, however, is only a general guide. For names of shrubs that tolerate local conditions (soil, rainfall, altitude, humidity) consult your Cooperative Extension Service (see p.5). (See also *Hedges; Mulching; Planting; Propagating plants; Pruning shrubs; Staking plants.*)

Shuffleboard

A game of skill, not power

Shuffleboard is played on a smooth, level surface on a court that is 52 feet long and 6 feet wide, with a scoring triangle near each end. The game is played with 6-inch wooden or plastic discs and 5-foot-long *cues* that are used to propel the discs. The cues have curved heads that fit the discs.

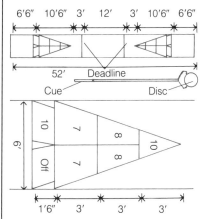

Play begins with eight discs—four of one color for one player and four of another for the other player—in the 10-off section at one end of the court. The players alternate shooting their discs. Each attempts to slide his discs so that they stop within one of the numbered sections in the opposite triangle. Points are scored according to the value of the sections (10, 8, 7) in which the discs lie after all have been

S

shot. If a disc winds up in the 10-off section, that player loses 10 points. Part of the game's strategy is to try to knock the opponent's disc out of a scoring section, preferably into the 10-off area. In order to score points, a disc must be entirely within a scoring area—if it touches a line, no points are credited. If a disc fails to cross the opposite *deadline,* it is immediately removed from the court.

After all eight discs have been shot, total the score and continue play from the opposite end. In a doubles match the original two players' partners shoot. Games are usually played until one side has 50, 75, or 100 points.

Shuffling cards

Ensuring a fair deal

So that the bottom card isn't exposed to the other players, shuffle without lifting the deck from the table. First, square up the deck, long edge facing you. Then: 1. cut the deck in half and hold one half with each hand, your thumb on the near edge, your fingers

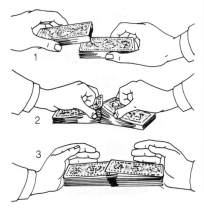

on the back; 2. riffle the near corners with your thumbs as you slide the halves toward each other; use your forefingers to hold the far sides down; 3. push the merged stacks together. Repeat several times.

Shutters

How to fix rickety ones

Exterior shutters develop two problems: the slats or frames can loosen or come apart, and the shutter may fall from the house. If parts of the frame—side, top, or bottom rails—or the slats become loose, you may be able to repair the shutter, using two bar or pipe clamps (see *Gluing*).

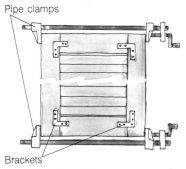

Pipe clamps

Brackets

Lay the frame facedown on a flat surface. Put the parts back in place, holding them together as much as possible with your hands. Clamp the outsides of the side rails and close the clamp gradually and carefully, locking everything into place.

To keep the shutter realigned, screw brackets (available at hardware stores) to the corners with galvanized screws. Release the clamps, and the shutter is ready for service.

Decorative shutters sometimes pull away from the house because the nails holding them are too short. To check, sight along the side of the shutter. Nails should be visible. If they are not, use 10d (or larger) galvanized finishing nails to secure the shutter. Countersink the heads, fill with wood putty, and repaint the shutter. Or, simply leave the heads flush and dab them with a paint that closely matches the shutter paint.

Sidestroke

For swimming long distances

To swim the sidestroke, start in a glide position, with your shoulders and hips perpendicular to the water's surface, your lower arm extended fully forward, and your upper arm placed along your side.

Pull your lower arm downward, palm flat, facing your feet, while sliding your upper arm, palm turned downward, up from your side. When

your hands meet directly in front of your chest, reverse their directions, this time extending your lower arm, fingers forward, so that the arm cuts through the water. Move your upper arm toward your side, palm flat, returning to the original glide position.

Simultaneously, do a scissors kick. Bend both legs at the knees, bringing them back until they are about 12 to 15 inches from your buttocks. Then separate your legs, moving the top one in front and the bottom one behind. When fully extended, snap them forcefully together, so that your feet point straight back just as your arms are returning to their original glide position. When the forward momentum slackens, repeat the stroke.

Sign language

Communicating with the deaf

American Sign Language, the system of communication used by many in the American and Canadian deaf community, is a true language with its own vocabulary, grammar, and syntax. Finger spelling, in which finger movements stand for the letters of the alphabet, is used only to communicate names and unfamiliar words.

Four basic elements make up each word in American Sign Language: the shape of the hand, the way it is moved, the orientation of the palm,

S

and the position of the hand relative to the body. Change any one of these elements and the meaning changes. Facial expressions augment sign language. The raising of an eyebrow signifies a question; the shaking of the head implies disapproval.

Signing can be learned in schools, colleges, and adult education courses and from videocassettes and books. For a list of places it is taught in your area, write the National Association of the Deaf, 814 Thayer Ave., Silver Spring, MD 20910.

Silverfish

Preventing or stopping infestation

Wingless and slender, these silvery insects have long, threadlike antennae and three "tails." They like cool,

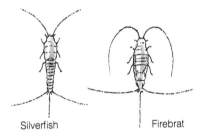

Silverfish   Firebrat

damp environments. Their close relatives, the gray-and-brown mottled firebrats, prefer heat; they live around furnaces and hot-water pipes. Both feed on substances high in starch and sugar, including flour, cereals, food scraps, glue, wallpaper, paste, bookbindings, and some fabrics.

These insects don't thrive if they are often disturbed. Prevent infestation by vacuuming often. Air stored clothing; clean bookshelves and basement and storage areas. Store books and clothes in dry areas or in sealed plastic bags.

To rid a home of an infestation of silverfish, seal cracks and crevices and apply boric acid dust to infested areas that are out of reach of children and pets. Put the dust behind books and into cracks in walls and flooring.

If an insecticide is needed, you may use one containing baygon, bendiocarb, chlorpyrifos, or diazinon. Apply around baseboards, doors, windows, closets, and boxes (see *Pesticides*).

Silver polishing

Keeping silver tarnish free

The best way to clean silver and silver plate is by hand rubbing it with commercial polish or a paste of baking soda and water. Wear rubber gloves to protect your hands. Wash and dry dusty pieces beforehand. Apply the polish with a soft, dry cloth, rubbing lengthwise, not crosswise or in circles. Use a small, soft brush to clean crevices. Coat a string with paste and rub it between tarnished fork tines. Wash the silver, rinse it, and buff with a soft cloth or chamois.

Two other polishing methods, dip polishes and the electrolytic process, are easier, but can dull or whiten the silver. They are not recommended.

To retard tarnishing, store silver in a specially lined chest or drawer, or wrap it in tarnish-inhibiting fabric. Do not use plastic wrap; it can cause hard-to-remove spots. Also, rubber bands can stain silver, even through layers of wrapping.

Skateboarding

Getting rolling

Caution: Skateboarding can be dangerous, and falls are almost inevitable. Make sure your board is in good condition, and wear protective gear—helmet, knee and elbow pads, gloves, long sleeves. Skate only on smooth pavement that is free of vehicles, pedestrians, and debris.

To get acquainted with a skateboard, ride it with one foot on the board and the other propelling it. When you are comfortable with the motion, bring the back foot up, placing it at a 45-degree angle just ahead of the rear wheels. Then turn the front foot parallel with the back one so that you are standing half sideways on the board. Bend your knees slightly and lean forward for balance.

Dismount in the direction you are facing. Hit the ground running or you will fall on your face.

If you feel yourself falling, stay loose; try not to fight the momentum of the fall. Rolling up, or using the forward

motion of a fall to do a somersault, will help reduce injuries.

To *turn,* lean slightly in the direction you wish to go. Lean from the hips, not the waist, and bend your knees as you do so.

Start a *downhill* run on a gentle slope with a safe runout—no walls or traffic. Mount the board; bend your knees slightly; look ahead, not down. Keep your arms forward for balance and your weight centered on the board. If you find yourself going too fast, reduce your speed by turning.

The *kick turn* is a way to avoid collisions or come to a quick stop. Turn sideways on the board with your feet at the ends. Put weight on your rear foot. As the nose of the board rises, push forward with the front foot and you will start turning inward. Stay with the turn, guiding the board back down with your front foot.

Skin care

Maintaining a healthy look

A balanced diet, regular exercise, and proper cleansing are essential to healthy, attractive skin. Avoid eating large amounts of sugar, salt, and fat, and drink at least six glasses of liquid a day. Too much alcohol can cause skin discoloration, and smoking can cause premature wrinkles. Long exposure to sunlight also damages your skin; if you must be in the sun, protect your skin with a sunscreen (see *Suntans*). Daily exercise keeps your circulation healthy and maintains the tone of the muscle layer beneath your skin.

Cleansing your skin

If your skin is very dry or itchy, take short baths or showers; use warm—not hot—water, and bathe or shower no oftener than every other day. Avoid bath salts, which are alkaline; use a bath oil instead. Bubble bath does little for your skin; treat it as an occasional luxury. Whatever your skin type, washing with a sponge, loofah, or thick washcloth will refresh your skin by removing dead cells and stimulating circulation.

After a bath or shower, apply a moisturizing cream or lotion to re-

S

place the natural oils that soap and water strip away. Rub it in while your skin is still damp. Use an extralight moisturizer if your skin is oily. Heavier, thicker moisturizers are suitable for dry or aging skin.

Care of hands and feet

Protect your hands on cold days by wearing gloves. Use rubber gloves while cleaning or gardening, and apply lotion whenever you wash your hands. Keep the skin on your feet smooth by wearing well-fitting shoes with socks or stockings. While bathing, remove rough skin with a brush or pumice stone. (See also *Calluses*.)

Skin diving

A window on the underwater world

All a skin diver needs are a mask for clear vision, fins for easy propulsion, and a snorkel, or breathing tube. Masks and fins that are comfortable on land may not be so in the water; borrow or rent several models before buying. (For diving with an air tank, see *Scuba diving*.)

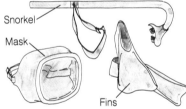

The *mask* should cover your eyes and nose. Look for one that combines the greatest field of vision with the smallest space between your eyes and the water. The tempered-glass faceplate should be firmly encased in a rubber or silicone frame. The sides of the mask should be soft and pliable, with tapered edges that conform to your face. The nosepiece on some masks has a valve that allows you to clear water out of the mask by exhaling through your nose. To check that a mask fits securely, hold it to your face underwater without fastening the strap and inhale gently through your nose. Suction should keep the mask in place.

The *snorkel's* mouthpiece should fit comfortably under your lips and

between your teeth. Breathe normally through it while you swim facedown near the surface. Draw a breath before diving; after you surface, expel water from the tube with a short, forceful breath.

Fins should fit like shoes, whether they have full foot pockets or open-heel straps. Large, stiff fins give the greatest thrust, but they also put the greatest strain on your calf muscles. Use a slow, rhythmical flutter kick from the hips, keeping your knees slightly bent and your toes pointed. Don't let the fins break the surface.

Prolong the life of your gear by rinsing it with fresh water after each use. To keep your mask from fogging, rinse the lens before diving with a commercial defogging solution (follow the manufacturer's directions), or rub it with saliva and wash it out.

Ski repairs

Maintaining a smooth ride

Downhill skis will perform better, last longer, and be safer if you maintain them. Before snow flies, remove dirt and rust from bindings and skis, tighten all screws and bolts, and have the release mechanism checked. Be sure the boots fit the bindings snugly.

To fix scratches, pits, and shallow gouges, use a polyethylene candle, available in ski shops. Secure the ski in a vise, base up. Clean the base with lacquer thinner or ski cleaner, sold in ski shops; both are flammable, so put them and the rag away before using the candle.

Keeping the candle pointed slightly downward, hold a lighter to the polyethylene until a small blue flame appears and the wax runs clear. Hold the stick close to the ski, and let the hot plastic drip into the gouge. (Be careful; hot plastic can give you a bad burn.) Draw the stick backward over the gouge, from one end to the other, until the gouge is filled. Let it cool for 10 to 15 minutes, then scrape off the excess. Rewax your skis (see *Ski waxing*).

Leveling the ski base assures a smooth ride. Set the ski in a vise, base up. Hold the edge of a flat metal

cabinet scraper at a 90° angle to the ski's base. Place your thumbs against the center of the scraper and push it down the base, from front to back. Use firm pressure and long strokes. Wipe the scraper clean after each pass; repeat until the base is flush with the edges of the ski. When you finish, apply a thin coat of wax.

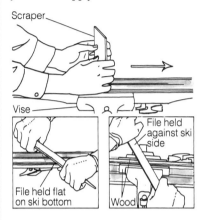

For better control when you ski, file dull or nicked metal edges. With the ski base up in a vise, use a medium-toothed metal file flat against the base. Draw the file toward the tail of the ski. After every pass or two, clean the file with a wire brush. Repeat the process with the file set flat against the side of the metal edge; use a block of wood to hold the file straight up. The ski edges should be sharp enough to score your fingernail.

Ski waxing

For a smooth downhill slide and a fast cross-country glide

Alpine racers wax their downhill skis to increase speed, whereas cross-country racers rely on wax to add both traction and glide. In recent years, most recreational cross-country skis sold in North America have been "waxless," with patterns machined into the ski's base to make the skis grip when climbing hills. Although waxless skis perform well in most snow conditions, they are noisier and slower than waxable skis.

Some cross-country skiers prefer waxable skis, because with the right wax they can ski their best in a variety

S

of conditions, from fresh, dry powder, to icy granules. Hard waxes come in cylindrical blocks and are color-coded to indicate the temperature range for which they are made. There's also a simple two-wax system, with sticky wax for wet snow and harder wax for dry. For snow that has thawed and re-frozen, or at above-freezing tempera-tures, use klister, a sticky wax that comes in a tube.

Check the temperature outside be-fore you apply wax. Peel down the foil covering on the wax, then rub it down the flat part of the ski bottom, work-ing from tip to tail. (Hard wax applies best on cold skis.) Smooth and rub it in with a block of cork. For extra grip, crayon another layer of wax on the middle third of the ski, under the foot.

Apply klister at room temperature. Carefully dab small portions onto the base, keeping the klister out of the center groove and off the ski's edges. Spread the wax evenly and thinly with the plastic applicator that usually comes with the klister. To remove klister or old wax, first scrape with a ski scraper, then wipe off all traces with mineral spirits on a rag.

If your skis slip climbing hills, add grip by applying a wax for slightly warmer conditions. If your skis don't glide on the downhills, scrape off some grip wax. One general rule is that soft (warmer-temperature) wax-es can be applied over hard (colder-temperature), but not vice-versa.

Skunk odor

Ways to get rid of it

To neutralize skunk odor on people or clothing, apply a thick coating of tomato juice or ketchup. An alterna-tive deodorizing treatment for cloth-ing is equal parts of white vinegar and water. Apply, let stand or soak for 15 to 30 minutes, then wash with plenty of soap or detergent.

If a pet is the victim, rub the juice or ketchup into its coat. Wait until the juice or ketchup begins to darken; then wash it off thoroughly. Several treatments may be necessary. A less messy procedure is to bathe the ani-mal with a solution of Massengill douche powder and water mixed ac-cording to the instructions on the package. Rinse out thoroughly.

Commercial neutralizers are also available. Keep one on hand if skunks are common in your area.

Caution: If skunk spray gets into your eyes or your pet's eyes, flush repeatedly with clean water and see a doctor or vet-erinarian at once.

Skylights

Cleaning; fixing leaks; installing a new one

Clean a glass skylight as you would a window (see *Window washing*). Use only a mild soap or detergent solution on a polycarbonate plastic skylight; acrylic plastics can stand a weak am-monia solution. Avoid window-clean-ing preparations and strong solvents such as acetone, alcohol, or gasoline; they can cause the surface to craze.

Remove grease or tar from acrylic with a soft cloth and kerosene, metha-nol, or high-grade naphtha; use ei-ther naphtha or isopropyl alcohol on polycarbonate. Never use abrasive cleaners or pads on any kind of plas-tic, or scrape off stubborn spots with a putty knife or razor blade. Minor scratches can often be obscured with a light buffing of automobile wax—it also protects a skylight's luster.

Leaks

If water stains develop on the ceiling around the frame, or if water drips from the edges of a skylight after a heavy rain, look first at the flashing above the skylight (see *Flashings*). Then check the outside joint where the skylight and the roofing meet. If you see any cracks or gaps, plug them with roofing cement and smooth the surface to get rid of pockets in which water can collect. If you can't see a gap, line the entire joint with cement anyway to seal any invisible pinholes. If this doesn't help, the leak's true ori-gin may be elsewhere on the roof (see *Roof repairs*). If water leaks through the skylight itself, the problem may be that the watertight seal, or gasket, has deteriorated or come loose. Pry out the old seal with a chisel or screw-driver, clean the surfaces, and install a new seal with the adhesive recom-mended by the manufacturer.

A persistent leak in a new skylight may indicate a faulty product or im-proper installation. Check the guar-antee; contact the supplier to have the skylight reinstalled or replaced.

Installing a new skylight

To add a skylight in a cathedral ceil-ing, locate the rafters as you would studs (see *Studs*). Outline the loca-tion on the ceiling, cutting across as few rafters as possible. Allow space at the upper and lower edges for header boards (lumber the same dimensions as the rafters) to be nailed across the cut rafter ends. Turn off power to the area (see *Circuit breakers; Fuses*) and saw a ceiling opening. Drill holes or drive long nails upward to mark the corners on the roof outside.

Remove shingles and roofing felt and saw out the opening from the rooftop. Then saw the rafters, cap their ends with the headers, and nail strips to the tops of the headers to bring them level with the roof. Set the skylight in place and attach it, follow-ing instructions for the particular model to form a weathertight seal when the roofing around it is re-placed. Finish the inside of the open-ing with wallboard or wood.

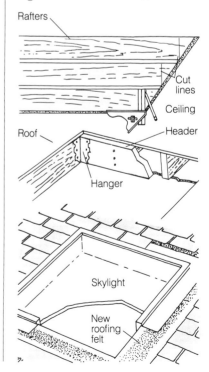

Sleeping bags

Choosing one; basic care

Sleeping bags are graded according to the lowest still-air temperature at which a particular bag will provide comfortable sleeping. This, in turn, depends on the *loft*, or thickness, of the filling when it is fully expanded.

Down fillings have the highest loft per unit weight. They are more expensive than synthetics and hold body heat better, but they flatten out when they get wet. Most synthetic fillings are fairly efficient when damp but deteriorate over time.

The quality of a bag also depends on its design. A good design holds the filling in place so that it doesn't clump, allows the filling to reach maximum loft, and avoids cold spots—areas with little or no filling. If you want the best in a down bag, ask for "slant box with baffles"; for synthetics, ask for "double-quilt sandwich."

Choose a bag suited to your needs; an overstuffed one can be as uncomfortable in warm weather as a thin one in cold. If you camp in various seasons, look for a medium-weight bag with a cold-weather insert and an outer shell of waterproof nylon or breathable resin laminate. If low weight is important, consider down. Mummy bags are the warmest; barrel and rectangular bags are less confining.

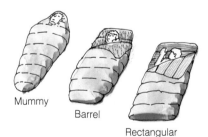

Mummy

Barrel

Rectangular

Proper care

Always sleep on a ground cover (see *Backpacking*). After every trip, air your bag thoroughly. Store it loosely in a large laundry bag (not a stuff sack) or hang it on a wooden or plastic hanger. Clean the bag according to the manufacturer's instructions (see *Down comforters*). Always wash a synthetic bag.

On camping trips, carry a needle and thread, some nylon ripstop tape, and a few safety pins. Tape any rips promptly before filling is lost. Be sure the fabric around the rip is clean and dry; hand stitch around its edges. Make permanent repairs at home (see *Down pillows*). Use the safety pins to replace a broken zipper pull or, in the case of a broken or jammed zipper, to close the bag.

Slice

Correcting a "banana ball"

A slice is a shot that curves widely to the right for a right-handed golfer, to the left for left-handers. It happens when the face of the club is open at impact, imparting a side spin to the ball. It costs distance and accuracy.

Check your *grip* as you address the ball. Your hands are probably turned too far to the left (for a right-hander) so that both your shoulders and your feet are left of *The Line* (see *Hook*).

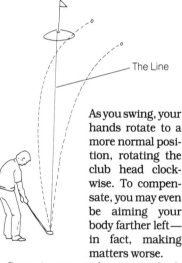

The Line

As you swing, your hands rotate to a more normal position, rotating the club head clockwise. To compensate, you may even be aiming your body farther left—in fact, making matters worse.

Correct your grip by rotating both hands to the right so that, as you address the ball, the V's formed by your thumbs and index fingers point between your chin and your back shoulder. Align your stance with The Line by moving your right foot back a few inches, and thus straightening your backswing. Your head should be slightly behind the ball, cocked a bit to the right.

During your backswing and downswing, keep your head still and look at the ball. Think of your target and follow The Line with your swing. Don't try to power the ball with your hands; let the club's momentum do the work.

Slides and slide shows

Preserving and projecting transparencies

Handle a slide only by the mount. The picture is the actual film image captured in the camera; it can't be replaced if damaged by fingerprints or grit. Heat, light, and moisture are also enemies of slides.

Each projection fades a slide slightly. Don't project any slide for more than 60 seconds. Have a photo store make duplicates of favorite images and use these for showing. To protect valued slides, remount them in plastic-and-glass or all-glass mounts.

Replace a frayed cardboard mount before it jams the projector. If one does jam, turn off the projector light (but keep the fan running) and let the machine cool. Lift off the tray and carefully extricate the slide; remove the projector housing if necessary.

Store slides in a dry, dark place. In a humid climate, store them with packets of moisture-absorbing silica gel. You can keep slides ready to show in projector trays, but return a tray to its box after each use.

It is also safe to keep slides in a metal slide file with baked enamel finish, in the box supplied by the film processor, or in any other acid-free photographic container. Do not use ordinary boxes or desk drawers.

Putting a slide show together

To edit your slides, spread them on an inexpensive slide sorter, which has a translucent rack lighted from below. Examine them through a magnifying glass. Select the best images; weed out bad exposures and repetitive or uninteresting shots.

Put your slides in a logical, storytelling sequence. Start with a picture that establishes the locale or event: a broad vista, a road sign, a door with a Christmas wreath. Move on to more detailed views. Avoid frequent jumps between bright and dark scenes or between horizontal and vertical images.

Number the sequence on the slide mounts. Also, holding the slide to look like the original scene, mark the lower left corner. In the tray, orient the slide so that the mark is at upper right with the dull side forward.

Sliding doors

Cleaning, lubrication, repair

Most sliding doors are suspended from tracks and held in alignment by guides at the bottom. The track should be level and the guides directly beneath and parallel to them; check the track with a level, the position of the guides with a plumb line (see *Leveling; Plumb line*).

If a door hangs askew, adjust one or both of the rollers. Loosen a screw on the mounting, and raise or lower the door until it is level; then tighten the screw. If a door sticks or if the roller jumps the track, check for loose screws, an object lodged in the track, a broken roller, or a bent track.

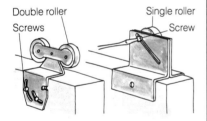
Double roller
Screws
Single roller
Screw

It is easier to replace a broken roller or a bent overhead track than it is to repair one. Remove the door by lifting it until the rollers are free; some can be freed only when they are lined up with key openings, generally when the door is halfway open. Remove the screws that hold the faulty part in place. Install an identical replacement part.

A door that slides on a lower track may or may not have rollers. In either case, problems generally stem from a dirty or bent track. Clean the track with a vacuum attachment or a stiff brush; scrape off any paint or stubborn grit. Lubricate with paraffin, paste wax or with a silicone spray. To straighten a bent track, cut a block of

wood to fit inside it and hammer out the bend from the outside with a rubber mallet.

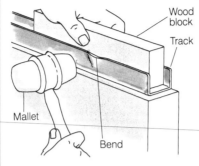
Wood block
Track
Mallet
Bend

With either type of door, apply a little powdered graphite to the axles of sticky rollers; do not use oil on nylon rollers. Also lubricate catches and locks from time to time.

Sliding rugs

How to keep them in place

Small throw rugs are handy but dangerous; someone could take a bad spill if a rug slides from underfoot. For safety's sake, buy rugs that have a nonskid backing. Or apply latex backing yourself. It's available in liquid and aerosol form. The liquid is most effective; apply it with a spatula or a stiff strip of cardboard.

You can also buy nonskid pads or padding by the yard to go under rugs. Thin, rubberized nonskid material provides a firm grip; lay it with the textured side down. Be sure to replace padding after it becomes worn.

Slingshots

Effective but dangerous

A slingshot is a dangerous weapon, not a toy. Even a simple one, made from a Y-shaped branch and a heavy rubber band, can cause serious injury; a metal hunting model, equipped with high-quality elastic, can propel a steel ball at greater velocity than a hunting bow shoots an arrow. Use any slingshot with caution.

Hunting slingshots, available with wrist braces and adjustable scopes, are used for hunting rabbits, squir-

rels, grouse, and other small game. In some states and many towns, their use is forbidden; check with local authorities. They are also used for target-shooting. The National Catapult Association sponsors an annual tournament, in which marksmen shoot steel balls at targets. For information, write to NCA, 129 McDill Ave., Stevens Point, WI 54481.

Slipcovers

Making a chair cover

To determine the amount of fabric you'll need, measure the chair, including the cushions; allow 1 inch for seam allowances and 6 inches for tuck-ins where the arms and back meet the seat. When possible, try to get two narrow sections from one fabric width. Plan extra fabric if you're making a skirt or matching a print. To allow for covering cord (see *Piping*), add an extra 1½ yards of fabric. Approximate yardage for a wing chair is 7 to 9 yards; for an occasional chair, 4½ to 6 yards; for a club chair, 6 to 7½ yards. To calculate how much cord to buy, measure all the seamlines.

If there's an existing slipcover, consider cutting it apart to use as a pattern. Otherwise, drape the fabric on the chair, right side out, with the lengthwise grain running as indicated by the arrows (see next page). Work from the top to the bottom and from the center out, smoothing the fabric and pinning along the upholstery seams with T-pins.

Cut out the pieces, allowing for seams and tuck-ins. Add extra seam allowance at the back of a cushion for inserting a zipper and at the chair bottom. Clip seam allowances at corners and inside curves. Before removing the fabric, spread the seam allowances open; mark the seamlines with dressmaker's chalk. Remove and label all pieces.

Sew the sections together with piping in the seams. Make gathers, tucks, or pleats to control the fullness on a curve.

Insert the zipper in a side back seam; it should extend at least three-quarters of the seam length. Open the

S

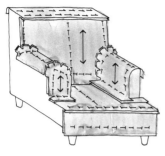

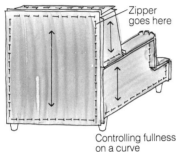

Zipper goes here

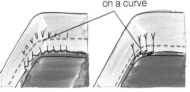

Controlling fullness on a curve

zipper. Place it facedown on the seam allowance that holds the piping with its teeth next to the covered cord and its stop 1 inch from the bottom seamline. Stitch. Close the zipper. Turn under the other seam allowance and stitch the zipper to it. For a cushion, insert the zipper by the centered method (see *Zippers*), extending it across the back and into the sides.

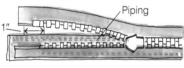

Piping

1"

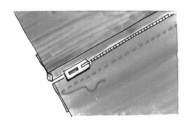

Put the slipcover on the chair; mark the bottom seamline. Attach a skirt or facing. Tack the seam allowances or

facing to the underside of the chair. Or attach two 12-inch lengths of twill tape to each corner of a skirted slipcover; tie the corners to the chair legs.

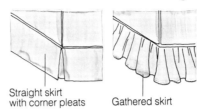

Straight skirt with corner pleats

Gathered skirt

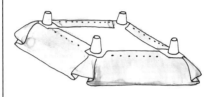

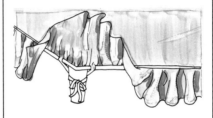

Slipstitching

For invisible mending and hemming

There are two kinds of slipstitches: even and uneven. Use the even stitch to join two folded edges, as in mending a seam or finishing a cushion; use the uneven stitch to sew a folded edge to a flat surface.

For even stitches, bring two folded edges together. Take stitches about ¼ inch long through one folded edge and then the other. Work from the right side of the fabric.

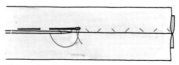

Even slipstitch

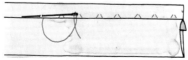

Uneven slipstitch

For uneven slipstitches, fold the edge under ¼ inch; press it. Take a stitch about ¼ inch long through the fold, then a very short stitch through the single layer.

Slugs and snails

Protecting your seedlings and leafy vegetables

Slugs and snails (the former have no shells) hide under stones, leaves, and debris during the day to keep the sun from drying them. At night they emerge to feed, leaving telltale trails of silvery slime. Get rid of their hiding places by keeping your garden cultivated and clean.

To trap slugs or snails, put out grapefruit or potato halves, cabbage leaves, or even wide boards for them to crawl under. In the morning collect the pests and drop them in soapy water. Or set out dishes about 1 inch deep of beer or grape juice level with the soil; the creatures will crawl into them and drown. Don't kill garter snakes; slugs are among their favorite foods.

Protect seedlings and leafy plants by surrounding them with sand or by spreading rings of wood ashes or lime well away from the stems; the pests won't cross them, although these materials will have to be replaced when they get wet. To shield a vulnerable plant, remove both ends of a tin can, tape a sleeve of window screening to it, and sink it into the soil.

Poison baits are often effective; but they are hazardous to children, pets, and wildlife and can be spread by rain or by watering. Only use baits labeled *safe for fruits and vegetables*, and protect the bait from water.

Small claims court

Settling without a lawyer

Most cities and many large towns have a small claims court. Its purpose is to settle minor civil disputes (not criminal charges) at minimal cost. The limit on complaints varies; generally it is about $2,000. Hearings, of-

S

ten held at night, are informal; you need no lawyer to represent you or to prepare paperwork.

To sue in small claims court, go during business hours and file a complaint with the court clerk. Give the name and address of the person you are suing, along with a brief description of your complaint. You will probably have to pay a small fee to cover court costs and the cost of sending a summons. The court will set a hearing date and inform your opponent of the action.

The hearing

Go to the hearing even if you know that your opponent will not be there; he or she is entitled to an adjournment, but if you are absent your claim will be dismissed. Take with you any evidence: contracts, bills, receipts, canceled checks, letters, photos, or witnesses. Don't talk with your opponent; wait quietly until your turn comes. You may be asked to choose between a judge and an arbiter; an arbiter will hear your case sooner but you cannot appeal the decision.

When the judge or arbiter questions you, calmly tell your side of the story. Stick to the facts and don't exaggerate. During your opponent's testimony, listen carefully for statements that you can prove to be untrue. Don't interrupt; you will have a chance to answer later.

If the judge or arbiter decides in your favor, you should receive any payment due within 2 weeks. If you do not, send a copy of the judgment to your opponent by registered mail, return receipt requested, along with a letter asking for payment; keep a copy of the letter. If he or she still fails to pay, notify the court.

Smoke detectors

Equipping your home for safety

Install smoke detectors in halls leading to sleeping areas and at the heads of stairs leading to living areas. Avoid air currents (from vents or radiators, for example), dead-air corners, and ends of halls. A detector on the ceiling should be at least 20 inches from any wall; one on a wall should be from 15 to 30 inches below the ceiling.

There are two types of smoke detectors. *Ionization* detectors contain a tiny amount of shielded radioactive material that breaks air down into charged atoms, through which a small current can flow. Smoke disrupts the flow and sets off the alarm. *Photoelectric* detectors use a small light beam impinging on a light-sensitive photocell; an alarm sounds whenever smoke interrupts the light beam. The light bulb producing the beam lasts about 3 years; then it must be replaced.

An ionization detector responds more quickly to the fumes of a fast-burning fire; a photoelectric type, to smoke from a smoldering fire. The latter is less prone to false alarms from innocuous kitchen fumes.

Either type may be powered by batteries or by house current. A battery-powered detector should have a monitor that signals (usually with intermittent beeps) when the batteries are running down. Change the batteries yearly, or according to manufacturer's instructions.

A smoke detector that runs on house current can be plugged into a receptacle or wired directly into a circuit; with the plug-in type, use a receptacle that cannot be switched off. Choose a detector that has a backup battery in case of power failure.

Test smoke detectors monthly; clean them yearly to remove dust, grease, and other debris.

Smoking

Kicking the habit

First you must make your own decision to stop smoking; if you do it just to please others, you will probably fail. Make a list of the reasons why you smoke. Next to it list the reasons you want to quit. Read both lists often.

When you decide to stop, pick a date in the near future and plan for it. If possible, choose a time when you are faced with a change in routine, such as a holiday or a trip. Tell your family and your friends; they will reinforce your resolve. If you can, team up with another who's quitting—sharing the experience helps. Talk to others who have stopped. Note the moments when you most want to smoke and be ready with a diversion.

Helpful measures

When the date comes, stop carrying cigarettes, matches, or lighters. Hide all ashtrays. Carry nuts or other nutritious snacks to nibble on; stay away from candies. When you feel the urge to smoke, take a few deep breaths (see *Stress*). Drink lots of water and fruit juices.

You will have moments of great anxiety. Endure them; they will pass. Keep active; exercise more. Read an engrossing book; engage in a hobby that keeps your hands busy.

If you backslide, don't give up. Stop again immediately. Nicotine is addictive; a smoker must conquer the habit one day at a time. Don't worry about not smoking ever again; focus on now.

Many have found help from such organizations as the American Lung Association, which has branches in every state, and from commercial smoke-ending programs, as well as from group therapy, hypnosis, yoga, acupuncture, and prescription drugs.

Snails for eating

An appetizer or entrée with a continental flavor

Snails (called *escargots* in French) are usually served in the shell. To eat them gracefully, provide snail pincers and forks. You can buy canned snails (already cooked) at specialty food

Snail pincer

stores. The shells and meat will be packed separately. For four servings you will need 1 pound, or about 4 dozen, snails. Work 1 crushed garlic clove and 1 tablespoon each minced parsley and shallots into ½ cup soft butter. (If using sweet butter, add ¼ teaspoon salt.) Drain the snails and pat them

S

dry. Wash and drain the shells. In each place a dab of seasoned butter and then a snail. Seal the shell entrance with more butter and bake the snails butter-side up in pie plates or snail platters for 10 minutes at 400°F.

Caution: Never eat garden snails; they have ingested chemicals that are poisonous to human beings.

Snakebites

What to do for a victim

All but one of North America's venomous snakes are pit vipers—either a rattlesnake, a cottonmouth, or a copperhead. All pit vipers have triangular heads and slitlike eyes; when disturbed, a rattlesnake usually gives a warning buzz with its segmented tail. A pit viper injects its venom through fangs (usually two, but one may be missing), leaving puncture wounds.

The other venomous snake is the coral snake, found in the southeast and westward into Texas. It has a blunt head, round eyes, and *always* a black snout; its body is banded with red and black rings separated by narrow bands of bright yellow. Its bite leaves a horseshoe-shaped pattern of small tooth marks.

If you think someone has been bitten by a venomous snake, *keep the victim calm, quiet, and lying down if possible;* activity hastens the venom's spread. Immobilize the bitten limb and position it at the level of the heart. Immediately get the victim to a hospital emergency room; carry him if feasible. If he must walk, have him move slowly. Call ahead if possible and describe the snake's appearance. Do not apply ice. Do not give alcohol, sedatives, or other medication.

The initial symptoms of a pit viper's bite are severe pain, swelling, and dark discoloration around the bite. These may be followed soon by nausea, vomiting, shortness of breath, dimness of vision, and shock.

A coral snake's bite produces only slight pain and swelling, but its highly toxic venom (which attacks the nervous system) causes blurred vision, drooling, slurred speech, drooping eyelids, drowsiness, nausea and vomiting, difficulty in breathing, paralysis, and shock (see *Shock*).

If you are in the wilderness

Only if medical help is unavailable within 1 to 2 hours should anyone attempt further treatment—and then only if the bite is a pit viper's. None of the following applies for a coral snake bite; the only treatment is immobilization and relief of the symptoms.

A flat bandage (belt, tie, strips of cloth) should be wrapped close to the bite, between it and the heart, to restrict the spread of venom. The bandage should be loose enough so that a finger can be inserted under it—no tighter than a watchband. Keep the bite area level with the heart.

In a flame sterilize a knife or razor blade or the blade in a snakebite kit. Across each puncture make a linear cut through the full thickness of the skin. Remove the venom with the rubber suction cup from a snakebite kit or by finger massage or by sucking it out by mouth. Continue suction for 20 minutes; then cool (but not freeze) the wound with ice until the victim can see a doctor.

Precautionary measures

In suspect territory—rocky or brushy areas, swamps, around abandoned buildings—wear thick boots, long pants, and leather gloves. Put your hands or feet only on visible surfaces.

Snaps

How to attach and cover them

Small snaps are suitable for necklines and other closures that will bear little strain. Use larger, heavier snaps on jacket closures, waistbands, and garments made of heavy fabric.

Snaps are available in black, silver, and clear plastic, or you can cover large snaps with lightweight fabric to match your outfit. Make a pouch for

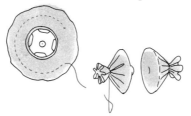

each snap, secure the pouch with a drawstring, trim off excess fabric, and sew the snap in place.

Position the socket half of a snap on the right side of an underlap. Hold it firmly and sew it in place. Place the ball half on the underside of the overlap; align it with the socket half and sew it firmly.

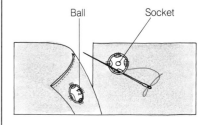

Ball   Socket

Snoring

Reasons and remedies

Experts say that millions of people snore. Snoring occurs when a person breathes through his mouth and the air vibrates across the soft palate and the uvula—the flap of soft tissue suspended at the back of the throat. A nasal obstruction, an allergy, enlarged tonsils and adenoids, or heavy drinking can also contribute to snoring. Sufferers from hypothyroidism (underactive thyroid) and obesity are often heavy snorers.

Prevention

You are more likely to snore when sleeping on your back. Prop pillows on either side to keep from rolling, or sew a pocket on the back of your pajamas and put a tennis ball in it.

If the problem persists, consult a doctor or visit a sleep clinic in a hospital. Professionals can determine if a medical problem exists and can arrange for its treatment.

Some doctors believe that chronic snoring may be a sign of sleep *apnea,* a condition in which breathing ceases briefly, perhaps hundreds of times each night. Apnea can lead to hypertension and heart trouble. It can be treated in a variety of ways, and a doctor should be consulted.

If you are not the snorer but the one whose sleep is being disturbed, earplugs may help. If they don't, you may have to move to another room.

S

Snow blindness

Protecting your eyes in snow

Snow blindness is a painful but temporary condition caused by the glare of the sun's ultraviolet rays on snow. It can occur even on foggy or overcast days, and the symptoms may not appear for as long as 8 hours. The first symptom is difficulty in perceiving variations in the level of the ground. A gritty feeling develops in the eyes; then they begin to hurt when exposed to any light at all.

The best cure is prevention. Wear sunglasses that keep out ultraviolet rays (see *Suntans*). You can also protect your eyes with a mask made by cutting narrow slits in cardboard, plastic, or other material. Blackening your cheeks and nose with soot will reduce reflections.

If snow blindness occurs, the only treatment is darkness. Rest your eyes in a darkened room or cover them with patches or a blindfold until the pain and burning subside, usually within 12 to 24 hours.

Snowbound at home

Preparing for severe winter storms

If you live in the snowbelt, you can easily find yourself housebound for several days. Severe blizzards can hamper snowplows in clearing the roads and may knock out power and telephone lines (see *Power failures*).

The first priority is to stay warm. Keep extra clothing and blankets on hand and have an alternative form of heating such as a UL listed kerosene or propane space heater (along with enough fuel to last several days).

Store an ample supply of candles, gas or kerosene lamps, battery lanterns, or flashlights (and don't forget spare batteries); or consider installing a standby generator to keep basic lights and appliances going.

If your area has a snow-emergency number, keep it near the phone. A battery-operated transistor radio is essential to advise you of storm news and any bulletins from police or the civil defense. Know whom to call in a medical emergency; in many areas, it will be the fire department or a local ambulance corps. In remote areas, a short-wave radio might be your only contact with the outside world.

At the beginning of the winter, check your supply of canned and dried foods. Have on hand at least one week's worth of an assortment of those foods that the family likes. Include crackers, fruit, meats, vegetables, and powdered milk.

If you cook with electricity, provide for an alternative method—for example, a camp stove or a small burner that uses canned solid fuel. A well-stocked first-aid kit and a manual are musts (see *First-aid kits*).

Finally, you may be cut off from television and from other favorite forms of entertainment. Take heart. More than one snowbound household has discovered the old-fashioned joys of reading and of playing family games as a result of a blizzard; consult the list of games in the index at the back of this book for some ideas on how to pass the time.

Snowbound in a car

Surviving until help comes

If you must travel when heavy snow is likely, be ready for emergencies. Take along extra warm clothing, a sleeping bag or blankets, a snow shovel, a flashlight, matches, and flares. Carry a thermos of a hot beverage and a container of fresh water, as well as raisins, bouillon cubes, and cookies or other high-energy food. A metal cup and canned solid fuel will allow you to heat the water for bouillon.

Make sure your car is ready for winter (see *Winterizing a car*). If possible, stick to the main roads and refill whenever the gas level drops to half empty. If the weather is very cold, add gas-line antifreeze to the tank. Listen to radio road-condition reports.

If forced to stop, stay in your car unless you can easily reach shelter. Don't idle the engine; rev it to a moderate speed and run the heater at full blast for about 15 minutes every hour. Then turn it off until the cold becomes unbearable. Before restarting the engine, get out and check that the tail pipe is clear of snow. To further guard against carbon monoxide poisoning, open a window about 1 inch while the engine is running.

Snowmobiling

A checklist for safety

If you're renting a snowmobile, check it out before making a trip even if you are assured that it runs well. Tilt the snowmobile on its side or raise and support the rear end if necessary.

Check that the skis are aimed straight ahead. Make sure that the brake and throttle cables operate freely and that there are no worn or fraying cable ends.

Check the drive belt (see *Drive belts*) and the battery cables and terminals (see *Battery terminals*). Remove the cover and be sure that the chain is tight and that the links are in good condition. If necessary, add oil to the chain case.

Examine the suspension and the track. The parts must be intact and attached. The track must turn freely but without obvious looseness. It should run true, and have no big cuts or punctures. Make sure that the headlights and taillights, including the brakelight, are working.

Check that the engine starts easily and stops when you hit the emergency-stop switch. Road-test the brakes and the steering.

If you have to refuel, mix two-stroke engine oil and gasoline in a can, following the recommended mixing ratio instructions for the oil. Don't try to mix the oil and gasoline in the snowmobile's fuel tank.

Prepare a route and tell it to someone at your starting point. Wear extra-warm clothing, gloves, boots, and a helmet with a face shield or goggles. On a long trip, take survival gear (see *Survival in wild areas*), a tow bar, and such spare parts as a belt, spark plugs, headlamp, installation tools, and extra fuel. If you are a novice, travel with an experienced group willing to trim its pace.

S

Snowshoeing

Choosing the right type of snowshoe; walking; maintenance

There is a snowshoe for each type of terrain. The *Green Mountain* and the *modified bear-paw* turn quickly and handle easily over rough, hilly trails, in forests, and over packed snow and ice. The *Michigan* model is best for long treks across deep powder in open country. Its long, narrow tail keeps it balanced and helps it to track in a straight line.

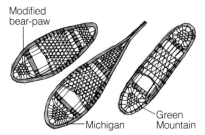

Modified bear-paw

Michigan

Green Mountain

Most high-performance snowshoes have some form of traction device underfoot for steep or icy terrain. Such devices can generally be added to snowshoes that don't have them.

Traditional frames are of wood, usually white ash. Metal is a maintenance-free alternative. Avoid plastic frames for long distances. Neoprene-coated nylon is better than rawhide for bindings and webbing.

Any soft boot or high-topped shoe without a hard heel will do for snowshoeing, but leather-topped, rubber-soled hunting boots are best. Avoid boots with deeply ridged soles; they will wear through the webbing.

How to walk

While learning, use a ski pole or a stick for balance. Keep your knees slightly bent and your feet spread apart as for normal walking. Lift one snowshoe over the edge of the other—not quite as high as in regular walking—and move with a sliding gait.

Sometimes you can glide downhill. On a steep slope, put the tip of one shoe on the tail of the other, crouch on the rear one, and slide.

Hang up wooden snowshoes to dry away from direct heat. If the webbing is rawhide, be sure the snowshoes are out of the reach of rodents. Varnish wood frames whenever the finish becomes worn. Use clear shellac to waterproof rawhide webbing.

Soap bubbles

Fun for children of all ages

You can blow soap bubbles with a bubble pipe, or make your own pipe from a drinking straw by cutting ½-inch-long slits in one end and folding them back. Or fashion a bubble loop from 12 inches of thin wire.

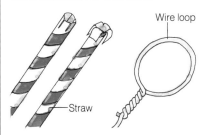

Wire loop

Straw

For a good bubble compound, mix 1 tablespoon each of liquid green soap and glycerin (from a drugstore) with 1 cup warm water. Or mix ½ cup mild liquid dishwashing detergent with 1½ cups warm water. Dip the pipe or straw into the solution, then blow gently until a bubble forms. Cast the bubble free by slightly jiggling the bubble maker. Or dip the loop into the solution so that a thin film spreads across it. Then make multiple bubbles by waving the loop gently back and forth.

Softball rules

A friendly form of baseball

Softball is played on a smaller field than baseball (bases are 60 feet apart rather than 90 feet) and with a larger ball. Fences should be 200 to 275 feet from home plate. A smooth, 6-ounce ball 12 inches in circumference is generally used. Bats are of wood or aluminum, 2¼ inches in diameter, not more than 34 inches long, and weighing 38 ounces. Players may wear cleats or spikes and use baseball mitts. Catchers and plate umpires should wear masks and padding for body protection.

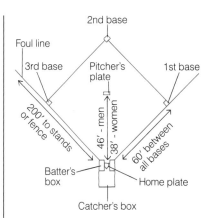

2nd base

Foul line

3rd base

Pitcher's plate

1st base

200' to stands or fence

46' - men

38' - women

60' between all bases

Batter's box

Home plate

Catcher's box

A game lasts seven *innings*. As in baseball, each team is allowed three *outs* per inning. The pitcher must throw the ball underhand and start the pitch with both feet touching the *pitching rubber*.

Most rules resemble those of baseball, with the following exceptions.

In the *slow-pitch* form, teams have 10 players; the tenth player is an outfielder, usually positioned in shallow center field. The pitcher must deliver the ball with a loft, so that it rises 6 to 12 feet above the ground. Base stealing is illegal; runners must stay on their bases until the pitched ball reaches home plate.

In the *fast-pitch* form, the ball need not loft, base stealing is allowed, and a runner may leave the base as soon as the ball leaves the pitcher's hand.

For detailed rules, write to Amateur Softball Association, 2801 NE 50th St., Oklahoma City, OK 73111.

Soil preparation

Groundwork for good gardens

Whether you're breaking new ground or replanting an old bed, nothing is more important to gardening success than proper soil preparation. Begin by testing the soil's pH, or acid level, with a simple kit, available from most garden supply centers, nurseries, and hardware stores.

The pH scale runs from 1 (highly acid) to 14 (highly alkaline), with 7 as a neutral point. Most vegetables do best in a pH of 6 to 7, although cabbages thrive in slightly alkaline soil—

S

about 7.5. Azaleas, on the other hand, need pH 4 to 5.5. An acid soil can be corrected by adding finely ground limestone; a slightly alkaline one by adding peat moss. For a drastic correction of alkaline soil, use a sulfate of iron or aluminum. To get a more complete analysis of your soil's nutrient content, contact your local Cooperative Extension Service (see p.5).

Many gardeners do the basic spadework in the fall. Applied then, slow-acting soil amendments like lime have ample time to take effect.

If you prepare a bed in spring, wait until the ground is dry. Test by squeezing a handful of earth. If it sticks together in a ball, it is too wet. When it crumbles slightly, it is ready.

Go over the soil with a cultivator, spade, or spading fork. Turn it to a depth of at least 10 inches—more if the soil is hard packed. Break up any hard clumps; rake up and remove stones, sticks, and other debris.

Dig in several inches of organic matter—compost, leaf mold, or well-rotted manure—to enrich the soil and lighten its structure so that air, water, and nutrients can get down to roots. Although peat moss lacks nutritive value, it fluffs up the soil as well as affecting pH. Organic matter is especially vital in opening up hard-packed clay soil and in giving sandy soil the body it needs to keep from draining too fast.

Save fertilizing until shortly before planting. Many fertilizers leach away quickly (see *Fertilizing vegetables*).

Solar collectors

Gathering the sun's warmth for house or hot-water heating

In typical solar collectors, water or other fluid is heated by the sun and then circulated to a *heat exchanger,* where it gives up its heat to a domestic hot-water system or to a home heating system. A thermostat controls the flow, shutting it off at night and on gray days. A system may also incorporate a tank or other heat-storage device to hold warmth for sunless days. A common, inexpensive type of collector is the *flat-plate.*

For maximum efficiency, collectors must face south. Their angle from the horizontal should equal the latitude of your area plus 15 degrees. It's best if collectors can be mounted flush with the roof, but if a roof is at the wrong angle, collectors must be tilted—and firmly anchored against winds.

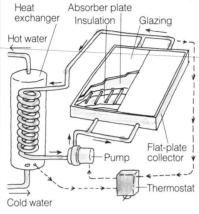

In cold areas, the collector fluid must be protected from freezing at night and on dark days. Some systems contain antifreeze. Others have a *drain-down* or *drain-back* feature that empties the fluid into the heat exchanger or the heat-storage tank.

How cost-effective a system will be depends on your fuel or utility costs, your region's latitude, the number of cloud-free days, and the system's design. Collectors for heating domestic hot water are more likely to be cost-effective than a full home-heating system. A heating consultant or contractor can make these calculations and design a system for your needs. An installation is worthwhile if you can recoup the cost within 10 years.

Solar greenhouse plants

Choosing and growing them

Temperature fluctuations in a solar greenhouse limit its gardening capabilities. In mild climates, a wide variety of annuals, half-hardy shrubs, sun-loving succulents, some orchids, and many bulbs such as lilies, gladioli, and tulips will thrive. On hot days, vent and shade the greenhouse as needed to prevent overheating (see *Solar greenhouses*).

Where winters are severe, a solar greenhouse works best as a season extender, allowing you to start seeds early in spring and to prolong the harvest of such plants as tomatoes and peppers grown in pots. Greens such as lettuce, spinach, and chard may grow slowly all winter. Many houseplants benefit from days spent in the greenhouse but may have to be brought in on cold nights. (See also *Greenhouse gardening.*)

Solar greenhouses

An energy-saving addition to your home

Unlike a conventional greenhouse, which requires a certain amount of artificial heat, a solar greenhouse relies entirely on the sun's rays. Heat captured during the day is retained for several hours after sunset. Attaching such a greenhouse to your home not only gives you additional living and garden space, but may save money on heating costs.

Heat moves from the greenhouse to the main house through vents or an open door or window. For more efficient transfer, install a fan or blower at ceiling height. On winter evenings, close off the greenhouse to prevent heat draining from the main house.

A lean-to solar greenhouse

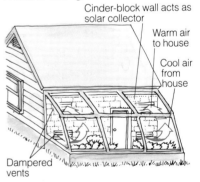

A wide variety of designs are available in kits containing all you'll need except a foundation. Before making a choice, investigate solar greenhouses in your area to determine the amount and angle of year-round available sunlight. Consult a local contractor and check building codes and zoning regulations (see *Building permits*).

S

A solar-pit greenhouse, sunk partially belowground, is relatively simple and cheap to build. If the glazing is well insulated at night, the surrounding earth will keep the greenhouse above freezing in winter.

The light-admitting side of a solar greenhouse should face within 30 degrees of true south, with no trees or buildings shading it; all other sides should be well insulated. In cold areas, use double or triple glazing.

To retain heat at night and on cold days, cover glazed areas with moveable insulation blankets or shutters. Shade and vent the greenhouse to prevent overheating in summer; in hot areas, install an exhaust fan. (See also *Greenhouse designing; Greenhouse gardening.*)

Soldering

Bonding metal to metal

Remember two points when soldering: 1. Clean the metal so that it is free of rust, grease, tarnish, and moisture; 2. except in stained glass work (see *Stained glass*), heat the metal, not the solder. The metal should be hot enough to melt the solder and boil away the *flux*—a substance that cleans the metal, prevents oxidation, and helps the molten solder to flow and adhere.

Solder is available in spools of hollow wire with rosin flux or acid flux in the center of the wire. Use acid-core solder for galvanized iron and zinc; use rosin-core solder for other metals. For some jobs, such as copper plumbing, it is better to use solid solder and apply the flux separately (see *Sweat soldering pipes*).

Heat the metal with a soldering gun, soldering iron, or propane torch (see *Propane torches*). A soldering gun operates with a trigger, heats up and cools very quickly, and is useful for electrical soldering and other fine work. Soldering irons come in a variety of sizes for both small and larger jobs and can work off any wall outlet. Use a torch for large jobs.

Before using a soldering gun or iron, file each face of the tip smooth and clean. Then heat the gun or iron

and hold rosin-core solder to the tip until it is *tinned* with a coat of solder. Wipe off excess with a damp sponge.

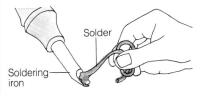

To solder a joint, first clamp the pieces together. Heat the work surface, preferably from below, and apply the solder from above so that it melts upon contact and runs into the joint. Molten solder will automatically move toward the heat. Wash off excess flux.

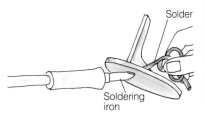

Two flat areas can be joined together by *sweat soldering*. First clean and flux the surfaces to be joined, then tin each separate surface by heating it with a torch and adding a thin, even coat of solder. Let the metal cool, then clean the tinned surfaces and add more flux. Clamp the pieces together and reheat them until a thin line of solder appears along the seam. Let the metal cool again, then wash it.

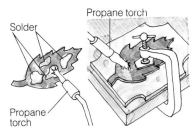

Electrical work

In sound equipment, toys, and handheld appliances such as blow-dryers, wires are often soldered to terminals. To resolder a broken connection, use rosin-core solder and a soldering gun or soldering pencil (a small soldering iron). Clean the wire and the terminal with very fine sandpaper or steel wool; then hold them together, apply solder to the junction, and hold the tip of the gun to the underside of the terminal.

Solitaire

Starting with a standard deck, deal out a row of seven cards, with the first card faceup and the others facedown; then cover the six facedown cards with another row, with the first card faceup. Continue this way, dealing one fewer card per row until you have seven piles, each with a faceup card on top. This is called a *tableau.*

If any faceup card is an ace, move it to a position above the seven rows of the tableau, where it becomes the start of a *foundation.* Turn up the next facedown card in the pile.

The object of the game is to move the cards one at a time and in ascending order, from the tableau into four foundations—one for each suit. Each foundation begins with an ace; then the deuce (two) of the same suit can be played on top of it, and so forth to the king. When all four foundations are filled, you have won the game.

Within the tableau, the faceup card of one pile can be moved to cover a faceup card of the next-higher rank and opposite color in another pile. For example, a black seven (seven of spades or clubs) can be placed upon a red eight (eight of hearts or diamonds) to create a *string.* The string can then be moved as a unit to another faceup card to create a longer string. In the example, the eight could be moved to a black nine to create a nine-eight-seven string. When you move a string or single card, turn over the facedown card thus exposed.

If a pile becomes empty, it can be filled, but only with a king.

Move all eligible cards from the bottom of a string to a foundation. After making all possible moves, turn up the top card on the remainder of the deck. If you can, play it on the tableau or on a foundation and make any other possible moves. If you can't play it, put it faceup in a waste pile and try the next card in the deck. Continue in this way until you have gone through the deck once and no moves remain. You win if all cards have been moved to a foundation.

S

Sore throats

Identifying causes; getting relief

Rawness at the back of the throat may result from nothing more than an evening of drinking, smoking, and loud conversation. It can also be a sign of a serious medical problem.

A sore throat that has been caused by drinking and smoking will respond to rest, soft foods, and gargling with warm water containing salt or crushed aspirin tablets. Throat lozenges may help.

Respiratory illnesses

A sore throat often accompanies such respiratory illnesses as a cold, flu, laryngitis, or tonsillitis. The sore throat usually clears up with the condition. Gargling every few hours can be soothing, as can drinking warm liquids and sucking hard candies or medicated lozenges (don't use the latter too frequently or too long; they can mask more serious symptoms). A humidifier or vaporizer can be comforting. If the sore throat lasts beyond a week, consult a doctor.

Postnasal drip

A persistent postnasal drip can cause a sore throat. Again, clearing up the cause will usually relieve the painful condition (see *Postnasal drip*).

Checking for other symptoms

Inflamed, swollen tonsils indicate tonsillitis. If you see white spots on your tonsils or if you have high fever and tender neck glands, consult a doctor.

A sore throat may be a symptom of a severe illness, such as infectious mononucleosis, a viral infection, or strep throat (the latter a bacterial infection). Initially, mononucleosis seems rather mild but its effects can be long lasting. It temporarily damages the liver. Other symptoms—fever, swollen neck glands, and weakness and fatigue—may persist long after the illness. The victim may also have skin rash and jaundice. Medical care is a necessity; home treatment is limited to bed rest.

Strep throat usually has other symptoms too—fever, headache, and swollen neck glands. See a doctor and have a throat culture. If it is strep throat, he'll prescribe an antibiotic.

Soufflés

An elegant entrée or dessert

Beaten egg whites account for the attractive puffiness of soufflés.

Basic cheese soufflé

Preheat oven to 350°F. Make a white sauce of ¼ cup flour, ¼ cup butter, and 1 cup milk (see *White sauce*); cool slightly. One at a time, beat in 4 egg yolks. Add 1½ cups grated cheddar or Swiss cheese and stir slowly. Season to taste. Set aside the sauce while you beat 4 egg whites until stiff, but not dry (see *Egg whites*). Gently fold them into the sauce.

Pour the mixture into a buttered 1½-quart soufflé dish or a deep baking dish with vertical sides. If there's less then ½ inch between the soufflé mixture and the top of the dish, butter one side of a 4-inch strip of triple-thick aluminum foil, wrap it around the dish so that it extends above the top, and tie it with a string.

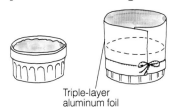

Triple-layer aluminum foil

Bake 35 to 40 minutes, until puffy and golden but still slightly creamy in the center. Serve the soufflé immediately before it has a chance to fall.

For a seafood or meat soufflé, substitute for the cheese 1½ cups minced or flaked well-drained tuna, salmon, clams, ham, or poultry.

Basic hot dessert soufflé

Preheat oven to 350°F. Mix 2 tablespoons cornstarch and ½ cup sugar in a saucepan. Gradually add 1 cup milk; heat, stirring constantly, over moderate heat until boiling. Stir and boil 1 minute until the mixture is thick. Remove from the heat; beat in, one at a time, 4 egg yolks and 2 teaspoons vanilla. Lay a piece of wax paper or plastic wrap flat on the sauce and cool to room temperature.

Beat 4 egg whites with ¼ teaspoon cream of tartar until stiff but not dry. Stir about ¼ cup into the sauce, then fold in the remainder. Spoon into a

1½-quart soufflé dish. Bake, uncovered, 35 to 45 minutes until puffy and browned. Serve at once, with custard sauce or sweetened whipped cream, if you like.

Coffee soufflé: Substitute 1 cup cold, strong black coffee for the milk.

Chocolate soufflé: Increase sugar to ¾ cup. Before adding yolks, blend in 2 ounces grated unsweetened chocolate. Reduce vanilla to 1 teaspoon.

Soundproofing

Reducing noise indoors

Hard, smooth surfaces reflect sound; soft, porous ones absorb it. Heavy draperies, cork paneling, textured wall covering, and thick-pile carpeting can all help to deaden sound. So can an acoustical-tile ceiling.

Soundproofing a ceiling

Install acoustical tiles directly onto a smooth, firm ceiling with an adhesive such as mastic cement. Or nail 1 x 3 furring strips at right angles to the joists and nail or staple the tiles to the strips (see *Furring strips*). For even better soundproofing, install a dropped ceiling—a suspended metal grid in which acoustical panels rest. Staple batts or blanket insulation to the old ceiling.

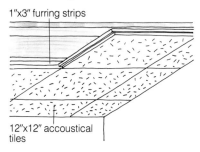

1"x3" furring strips

12"x12" accoustical tiles

Soundproofing walls

To cut down noise between rooms, make the wall thicker by cementing a new layer of plasterboard to the old (see *Plasterboard*). Plan for the edges of the new board to fall along different studs than the old seams. First remove all moldings. Apply beads of construction adhesive along all the stud lines. Press each new board in place and drive nails into the studs along the edges. Finish the joints. Refit the moldings. For added sound-

S

proofing, nail furring strips to the wall, lay insulation between the strips, then attach plasterboard.

Most effective is a *staggered-stud wall.* Strip the old wall to the studs and install a new row of studs just in front of the old ones, spaced midway between them; don't let the top and soleplates touch the old ones or vibrations will be transmitted. Weave insulation batts or blankets between the studs. Finish with new plasterboard.

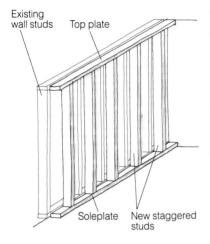

Existing wall studs   Top plate

Soleplate   New staggered studs

Soups and stocks

Starting from scratch

Many soups start with stock, and many gourmet dishes call for stock.

Stocks and consommés

To make a beef stock, brown 1½ pounds beef shinbone and 1½ pounds beef chuck or round in 3 tablespoons oil in a 6-quart pot. Pour off the fat; pour in 3 quarts water. Add 2 medium onions, 2 stalks celery with leaves, 1 carrot, 1 turnip, 3 sprigs parsley, 1 teaspoon thyme, 1 bay leaf, and a few peppercorns. Bring to a boil, then lower the heat; simmer for 3 hours or more, skimming occasionally. Strain the stock through a sieve lined with cheesecloth. Add salt to taste. Chill the stock; the fat will harden on top. Scrape it off with a spoon.

For a veal stock, substitute about 3 pounds veal knuckles or breastbone for the shinbone and chuck. To make chicken stock, see *Chicken soup.*

To make consommé, first clarify strained stock by putting in 2 egg whites and 2 crumbled eggshells; simmer for 10 to 15 minutes. Let the stock stand for at least 30 minutes; strain again. Consommé made with bones will usually jell when chilled and can be served in summer as a refreshing first course. If it doesn't jell sufficiently, add 1 teaspoon softened, unflavored gelatin per quart, heat until the gelatin dissolves, then add a little sherry for flavor, if you like. Chill until firm.

Minestrone

In a 5-quart pot, sauté 1 chopped medium onion, 2 chopped medium carrots, 1 chopped celery stalk, and 2 cups shredded cabbage in ¼ cup olive oil or vegetable oil. Add ½ teaspoon each dried thyme, oregano, and rosemary. Then stir in 1 quart beef or veal stock. Bring the mixture to a simmer and cook it for ½ hour.

Add 4 chopped medium tomatoes or 1 small can Italian plum tomatoes, 1 chopped green pepper or 1 chopped small zucchini, 1 can drained cannellini (white beans), ¾ cup frozen peas, and 1 cup pasta, such as shells or elbow macaroni.

Simmer for another ½ hour, stirring occasionally to prevent the pasta from sticking. Add salt and pepper to taste and more liquid, if needed. Serves six to eight.

Spark plugs

How to replace them

Carmakers recommend replacing spark plugs at intervals ranging from 12,000 to 100,000 miles, depending on the engine and the type of plugs used. Check your owner's manual. If there is at least 2 inches clearance above your spark plugs, you can do the job yourself. Be sure the engine is cool and the ignition is off before starting.

Tape identifying labels to the spark-plug cables before pulling them off; then grasp each at the nipple end, twist to break any heat seal, and pull up. Never pull on the wire itself.

To remove the plugs, you need a ratchet wrench and either a ¹³/₁₆- or ⅝-inch spark-plug socket, depending on your car's plug size. A universal-joint drive-handle attachment and

extension attachments can help you reach awkwardly placed plugs.

Fit the socket firmly over the hex section of a plug and, with the ratchet set to unlock, apply pressure counterclockwise. Hit the handle with the

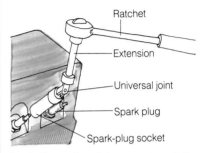

Ratchet

Extension

Universal joint

Spark plug

Spark-plug socket

heel of your hand to unseat a stubborn plug. If it continues to stick, use penetrating oil. If it takes effort from start to finish to unscrew a plug, clean the threads of the hole with a *thread chaser* before installing a new plug.

Replace plugs with the brand and model number recommended by the manufacturer or with a manufacturer's equivalent. If your engine has an aluminum head, apply a film of anti-seize compound (available in tubes from auto parts stores) to each new spark plug's threads.

Use a spark-plug gauge to adjust the gap between electrodes of each new plug. (Refer to your owner's manual or gap specification on the decal under your car's hood.) The gauge wire should fit snugly in the gap. To adjust the gap, use the gauge's bracket to bend the L-shaped side electrode. Recheck with the wire.

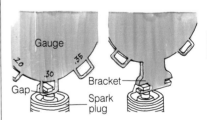

Gauge

Gap

Bracket

Spark plug

Thread each plug into its hole by hand until it seats. If the plug has a gasket, use the ratchet to tighten it a quarter to a half turn more. If there is no gasket, only a sixteenth of a turn should be needed.

Lightly apply silicone dielectric grease to the inside of the cable terminals; then push each terminal onto the nipple of its spark plug.

Spatter prints

Silhouetting designs

Make your own prints by spattering paint around interesting shapes to create silhouettes. Cut paper patterns in simple shapes, such as stars or hearts, or use paper doilies or stencils (see *Stencils*); natural objects, such as leaves or flowers; or any small object, such as keys. (If you want to reuse the objects they must be washable.) Place a piece of construction paper on a newspaper-covered work surface or in a box. Place the shapes on the paper. If possible, pin them down.

Prepare a water-soluble paint, such as tempera or poster paint, by diluting it slightly. Wearing a smock or some other cover-up to protect your clothes, dip an old toothbrush into the paint and, holding the bristles up, lightly scrape a butter-knife blade across the brush *toward* you. This

will send a spray of paint "dots" onto the paper. Or, if you prefer, put the paint into a spray bottle and spray it on. Apply the paint sparingly. Lift the shape from the background. When the paint is dry, position the shape in another area of the paper and spatter with paint of another color, if you wish.

To build a spatter-print frame, nail together four pieces of 1 x 3 pine and thumbtack window screening across the top. Place the shapes on back-

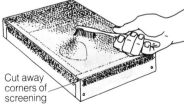

Cut away corners of screening

ground paper and position the frame over the paper. Run the toothbrush across the screen. To clean, rinse the frame with water.

Speakers

Placing them; troubleshooting

Speakers ultimately determine the sound quality of a stereo system (see *Stereo systems*). For best performance, place two speakers roughly 8 feet apart facing the center of the room. In a rectangular room, locate the speakers along one of the shorter walls. Whatever the room's shape, speakers should not face each other.

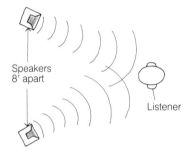

Speakers 8' apart

Listener

If, at certain frequencies (bass or treble), the surface under a speaker vibrates, check that all speaker connections are tight. Place a sound-dampening pad (available at electronics stores) under the speaker.

If a speaker is too near a turntable, a loud howl may result (see *Stylus*). Place the turntable on an isolated surface or on a sound-dampening pad. If nearby glassware vibrates, remove it.

If your stereo system sounds muted, check each speaker: the copper wire should be attached to the positive terminal and the silver wire to the negative on the back of your speakers and at the speaker terminals on the receiver's rear panel.

Spices

Flavorings from plants

Spices are best when freshly grated or ground with a mortar and pestle or a spice or coffee grinder. Ground spices lose flavor quickly. Store them in tightly covered jars in a cool, dark place and try to use them up within a year. In cooking with whole spices, tie them in cheesecloth for easy removal.

These are the spices that most cooks will want on their shelves.

Allspice has a flavor that resembles a blend of cinnamon, cloves, and nutmeg. Long cooking or marinating enhances it. Add it to baked goods, stews, sauces, and marinades.

Anise has a licorice flavor. Use it in cookies and candies.

Bay leaf: Its strong flavor increases with cooking. Use ½ to 1 leaf in sauces, marinades, and for pickling.

Cardamom: Both the small, dark-brown seeds and their creamy white pods can be used. It's good in sweet pastries, hot wine, and curries.

Cinnamon: Use as a baking spice or to flavor cooked fruits, puddings, and hot drinks.

Cloves: Insert them whole in baked ham, marinades, and fruit dishes. Use the ground spice in baked goods.

Coriander: The whole spice is good in punch or pickles, the ground version in gingerbread and curries.

Cumin is one of the main ingredients in chili or curry powder.

Ginger: A light-buff-colored root that is a principal ingredient in oriental cooking. It's best when grated or sliced and used fresh, but is also dried and ground or preserved as chunks in sugar syrup. Ginger is delicious in preserves, chutneys, cakes, cookies, and with meats, vegetables, and fish.

Mace: The skin of the nutmeg shell. Use it in soup and gingerbread and to season seafood, meat, and vegetables.

Nutmeg: Sprinkle it (freshly) grated on vegetables, milk drinks, and puddings, or use it in baked goods.

Peppers: Black pepper, a berry, is picked underripe and allowed to ferment; white pepper, picked when ripe, is preferred for light-colored foods. Either is more flavorful when freshly ground. Prolonged cooking makes them bitter. *Chili* and *cayenne* peppers are fruits with spicy, hot flavor. Use them with caution in sauces and on meat and seafood. *Paprika*, a mild red pepper, can be added in greater quantity to meat and fish.

Saffron: Use it for color and flavor in rice, chicken, or seafood dishes.

Turmeric: It's used to color such foods as butter, cheese, and pickles. Add it to curries and rice. (See also *Curry powder; Herbs in cooking.*)

S

Spider plants

Caring for a popular hanging-basket plant

The arching, ribbonlike leaves of the spider plant can be all green or variegated with creamy stripes. Its long trailing stems bear small white flowers, followed by spidery plantlets—tiny replicas of the mother plant.

Spider plants thrive in bright filtered light and moderate to warm temperatures (above 50°F at night). Keep the soil constantly moist in spring and summer; reduce watering in fall and winter. Apply half-strength liquid fertilizer biweekly. Repot when the roots become overcrowded.

To propagate, place the base of a plantlet in moist commercial potting mix or in a mixture of equal parts sterilized fibrous soil, peat moss, and perlite. When the plantlet is firmly rooted, in about 6 weeks, sever the mother plant's stem.

Spiders

Useful and dangerous sorts

Most spiders feed on live insects and can be of help in keeping garden pests under control. Of the few native American species that bite humans, only the brown recluse and the black widow have bites that can be fatal. There is an antivenom for the latter, but none for a brown recluse's bite. It may, however, be treated by large amounts of antihistamines, cortisone, and antibiotics. In some cases, doctors surgically remove the bitten area and then use plastic surgery to restore the tissue.

The ½-inch-long black widow spider, commonest in the South, has a red "hourglass" on the underside of a shiny black body. It often lives under furniture, in outhouses, and in debris. The ½-inch-long brown recluse, with its dark violin mark on a brown background, inhabits similar places;

Enlarged

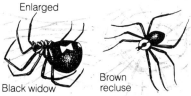

Black widow   Brown recluse

it also hides in folds of clothing. Although mainly a denizen of the West and Southwest, it sometimes turns up in other regions, having been transported unintentionally in luggage and cargo shipments.

If you think you have been bitten by a poisonous spider, contact your poison control center immediately (see *Insect bites and stings*). Such bites are particularly dangerous to children age 5 and under.

To rid your property of all kinds of spider breeding places, clean up debris around the house and in the basement. A few harmless spiders around the house are beneficial: they keep down the insect population. If their webs are unsightly, sweep them away with a brush or a mop head covered with a clean rag; crush spiders and their eggs (silken sacks, up to ½ inch long) with your foot. Don't stand directly under a spider web while sweeping it from a ceiling.

Spin casting

An easy fishing technique

Casting a lure for distance and accuracy is easy with a *spinning reel,* which allows the line to unwind off one end of a nonrevolving spool. The crank handle turns a pickup bail that rewinds the line around the spool. You swing the bail out of the way before casting.

A spinning reel hangs below the rod. You hold the rod in your right hand and reel in with your left. (If you are left-handed or find cranking easier with your right hand, you can get a reel with the crank on the right.) A *spin-casting reel,* or closed-face spin-

ning reel, has a cone over the spool and is mounted on top of the rod. The line emerges through a hole at the tip of the cone.

To cast with either type of reel, position the lure 3 or more inches below the rod tip. Lift the rod to just past vertical, then swing it forward, pointing the tip where the lure should hit. With a closed-face reel, hold down a thumb push button during the backswing; release it for the forward swing.

Before casting with an open-face reel, flip the pickup bail aside. Hold the line over your index finger just ahead of the reel. Release the line as you swing the rod forward.

As soon as the line hits the water, crank either type of reel one turn to engage the line retrieve. Let the lure float, drift with the current, or sink. Then wind in the line slowly or quickly, at a steady speed, or with short, twitching rod movements that make the bait dart like an injured minnow, frog, or insect. Vary your retrieves from one cast to the next. When you see or feel a fish grab the lure, lift the rod to take the slack from the line. Keep the line taut as you reel in.

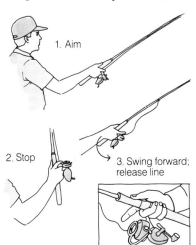

1. Aim

2. Stop

3. Swing forward; release line

Splinters

Removing them safely

With splinters, safety means avoiding infection. Before starting to remove one, wash your hands and the skin surrounding the splinter. Sterilize tweezers and a needle by boiling them in water (for about 10 minutes) or heating them in a flame. Then proceed as follows.

If the splinter is protruding, grasp the end with the tweezers and pull it out at the angle at which it entered. If it's visible but not protruding, use the needle to loosen the surrounding skin and expose the end so that it can be grasped with the tweezers; pull it out at the entering angle.

In either case, once the splinter is out, squeeze a little blood from the wound (this helps to clean it), wash the area, and apply a bandage.

A splinter too deeply embedded to be seen needs a doctor's attention. See a doctor, too, if a splinter breaks off during removal or if pain or swelling occurs after removal.

Split ends

What to do about them; how to avoid them

Abused, overprocessed hairs may virtually come unglued at the tips, resulting in split ends; these can't be repaired. To restore your hair, trim off the split ends, and condition at least once a week with a conditioner specially formulated for damaged hair. Or, warm 2 ounces of olive oil, apply it to your hair, and comb it through; then wrap a towel around your head for 15 minutes. Follow with a shampoo. Between intense conditioning sessions, use a regular conditioner on hair ends after each shampoo.

Prevent split ends by handling hair gently (see *Hair care*). Avoid teasing, use endpapers when setting hair, and confine your use of electric rollers to twice a week at most. Avoid overbleaching; have a permanent wave no more than twice a year. (See also *Hair coloring; Hair teasing; Permanents*.)

Sprains and strains

Relief for two equally painful but different conditions

Many people understandably, but mistakenly, confuse these two condi-

tions. Although they are similarly caused and alike in symptoms and treatment, they happen to different parts of the body. A *sprain* is suffered by a *joint* being pushed or wrenched beyond its normal range; a *strain* is the injury to a *muscle* that is overstretched or twisted past its capacity. Knees, ankles, wrists, fingers, sometimes shoulders, are all subject to spraining; any misused or overused muscle can be strained.

With a sprain, there will be tearing of ligaments; with a strain, tearing of muscle fibers. Both are painful upon being moved; a sprain will, in addition, have swelling and discoloration.

Relief measures are the same for both. Remove shoes or tight clothing from the injured area. The victim should rest, avoid use of the injured joint or muscle for 24 hours, and elevate the limb. Cold compresses on the injury will reduce swelling and help to slow any internal bleeding.

Don't let a person walk or stand on a sprained knee or ankle (see *Crutches*); support a sprained wrist in a sling (see *Broken bones*). Aspirin or another analgesic will dull pain. After about a day, treatment can be modified for long-term results: hot, moist packs or tub soaks to promote healing; gentle flexing exercise to ward off stiffness.

A severe sprain may need a supporting bandage, but not a constrictive one. Avoid tight circular wrapping; instead, apply a bandage so that it

provides support above and below the injury, for example, a figure eight for knee, wrist, thumb, or ankle.

Caution: The symptoms of a sprain are much like those of a fracture. If you suspect a bone is broken, have an X-ray immediately. If swelling and pain don't subside within a few days, consult a doctor.

Spray painting

Coating smooth or uneven surfaces the fast way

A vacuum-cleaner spray attachment or a small, self-contained airless spray gun is fine for painting many household items, such as louvers or wicker furniture. But for house painting, rent a high-pressure, roll-around airless unit; for finishing fine furniture, a compressor-powered, pressure-feed gun. Make sure a unit can handle the paint you plan to use and has the right-size opening. Use an aerosol spray can for small objects; shake it thoroughly before using.

Protect surrounding surfaces with newspaper or drop cloths anchored with masking tape. If possible, suspend or prop a piece so that you can spray it without shifting it; catch the overspray with a movable backdrop.

Caution: Wear a mask and work in a well-ventilated space away from open flames. Never direct a high-pressure spray unit toward a body part; it can inject paint through the skin.

If necessary, thin the paint to the correct spraying consistency. Strain it through nylon-stocking mesh to remove lumps. Point the gun straight at the work surface, 6 to 12 inches away. Move it back and forth, always keeping it the same distance away from the surface. Make strokes up to 3 feet across and overlap them by a third to a half. Move at an even pace. Start spraying just beyond the surface's edge and go past the edge at the end of each stroke.

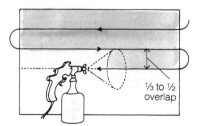

⅓ to ½ overlap

Experiment on cardboard to establish the best working distance, spraying speed, and spray width. Set a narrow width for small pieces and a wide one for broad surfaces.

S

Immediately after use, spray solvent or water (with water-base paint) through a gun. To clean a spray can, turn it upside down and spray until paint stops coming out.

Springs

Fixing sagging and squeaking springs in stuffed furniture

To inspect a chair or sofa's springs, turn it over and use an old screwdriver to pry out the tacks holding the bottom cover cloth. You can see the springs through the webbing.

Reinforcing sagging webbing
If the webbing is sagging but the springs are well attached, you can just put new webbing over the old strips. Tack the end of a roll to the rear center of the frame, leaving an inch overhang. Drive in five 12-ounce barbed webbing tacks; then turn up the end and secure it with five more. Tack first in the center, then at the edges and in between. Stagger tacks to avoid splitting the wood. Use 8-ounce tacks on fragile and hardwood frames.

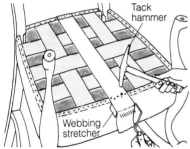

Brace a webbing stretcher at a 45-degree angle against the front of the frame and hook the webbing onto it. Push it down to pull the webbing taut. Then tack the webbing and cut it, leaving 1 inch extra. Turn up and tack the end. Work from the center out, putting in front-to-back strips. Then do the side-to-side strips, weaving them over and under the others.

Retying a loose spring
If a spring has come loose from the webbing, simply sew it back, using a curved needle and stitching twine. Secure the spring at three points and tie off the first and third stitches.

If a spring's innermost coil is untied, remove the webbing. On the inside of the frame, drive a 14-ounce tack halfway in and tie six-ply twine it; then drive it in the rest of the way. Loop the twine around the coil at two points and tie it to an adjacent straight spring. Put in a second tack and run another twine piece, tying it to the coil at two points with a clove hitch. Tie the spring again with two twine pieces at a right angle to the first pair.

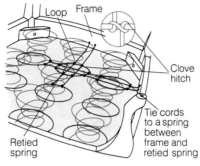

Next secure the springs' bottoms. Put a tack in the rear center of the frame, aligning it with a row of springs. Tie twine to the tack and drive it in. Knot the twine at two points on each spring in the row; then tie it to a front tack. Tie the other front-to-back rows, going from the center out; then tie side-to-side rows. Finally, attach new webbing, and stitch the springs to the strips.

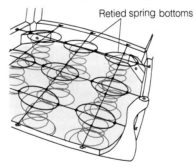

If more than a couple of springs are loose, a piece needs to be professionally rebuilt. (See also *Reupholstering*.)

Sprinkler heads

Replacing and relocating underground lawn sprinklers

If you need to replace a broken sprinkler head, dig out enough around it so that you can grasp it. Then unscrew it and put on a new head. If the riser comes out with the head, clean off its threads and install the new head on it. Then, holding the head, screw the riser into the the underground pipe. If dirt falls into the pipe hole, suck it out with a wet-or-dry shop vacuum.

If a sprinkler head has sunk below ground level, remove the head and the riser and replace the riser with a longer one. If the riser doesn't come out with the head, force an extension for a ½-inch-drive socket wrench into it. Then attach the ratchet handle to the extension and turn it to unscrew the riser. On a riser with a hex around it, slip a deep socket over it instead.

Relocating a sprinkler
You can avoid digging a deep trench in your lawn by running a narrow extension pipe. Buy ½-inch flexible plastic pipe and elbow fittings compatible with your sprinkler system at a garden supply center. Carefully cut and fold back the sod; dig a narrow, 4-inch-deep trench to the new location.

Remove the sprinkler head and riser. Screw an elbow into the opening on the underground pipe. Push the extension pipe onto the end of the elbow and secure it with a worm-drive hose clamp. Dig out more earth if necessary to make the connection. Run the pipe to the new location; cut it to fit, using a hacksaw. Install an elbow on the pipe and screw the sprinkler head onto it. Dig out or add earth under the head to adjust its height.

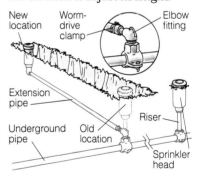

Sprouts

Growing food in a jar

With the exception of potato and tomato sprouts, which are poisonous, the sprouts of almost any seeds are edible and easy to grow. Delicate alfal-

S

fa sprouts are excellent in salads and sandwiches. Bean sprouts, such as navy, kidney, lima, and mung are delicious in stir-fry dishes. Wheat, oats, rye, or rice sprouts are good added to breads, cereals, or main dishes. Mustard or radish sprouts have a tangy, peppery flavor. They taste best mixed with greens or other sprouts.

The only equipment needed for sprouting is a shallow bowl or a jar covered with cheesecloth or a nylon stocking. Or, if you prefer, glass, plastic, or earthenware sprouters are available in health food stores.

How to start sprouts

Seeds need moisture, darkness, and a free flow of air at room temperature in order to sprout. Use only seeds that have not been chemically treated.

Start with no more than ¼ cup of seeds, even less for small ones. Rinse them in a sieve and place them in the container. Cover with warm water and soak them overnight. The next morning drain the seeds well. They should be moist, but not wet. Distribute the seeds evenly in the container.

Keep the seeds in a dark place, such as a cupboard or an oven without a pilot light. Rinse them at least twice a day, four times a day for chick-peas, mung beans, or soybeans. Use cold rinse water in summer, tepid in winter. Drain seeds thoroughly each time. Most sprouts are ready to eat in 2 to 4 days or when 1 to 2 inches long.

Rinse sprouts, discarding any hulls or unsprouted seeds; drain them. If you want green leaves, return them to the jar and leave in the sun for a few hours. Refrigerate sprouts in plastic bags. They will keep for 4 to 6 days.

Squash racquets

A fast-paced indoor game

Although easy to learn, squash racquets—also called simply squash—is demanding to play because it requires speed, intensity, and strategy. The squash court is a four-wall room. A metal strip 17 inches high runs across the front wall. This *telltale,* which the ball must clear when rebounding off the front wall, is the squash equivalent of the tennis net.

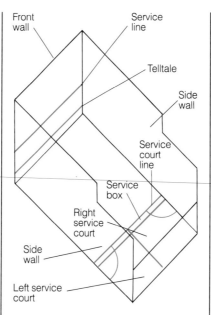

Racquets, a ball, and white-soled sneakers are all the gear that is required for playing squash. A squash racquet is similar to a badminton racquet, but it is much sturdier. The hard rubber balls are small, hollow, and dark green or black. They have relatively little bounce.

Play

The server stands with at least one foot in the service box. He hits the ball at the front wall above the service line so that it rebounds into the opposite service court; he gets two chances to do so. The receiver returns the ball on the fly or after it bounces on the floor. The return must hit the front wall above the telltale. On the way to or from the front wall the ball may carom off the side walls or back wall.

When one player fails to return the ball properly, the other player scores a point. Whoever wins a point serves next. If the server wins the point, he makes the next serve from the opposite side of the court. A game is 15 points; a match three games.

Forehand and backhand strokes are both hit with a whip of the wrist. Good form (as well as your opponent's safety) calls for a minimum of follow through. Considerations of safety and fair play require each player to get out of the way after hitting the ball so that the other can hit. When a player is hindered by his opponent, he may call a *let,* and the point is replayed.

Squeaking floors

Silencing creaking underfoot

You can stop a squeak temporarily by squirting powdered graphite or a white powdered lubricant into the cracks. You can also quiet a loose floor board by driving small triangular metal glazier's points into the cracks. Space them 6 inches apart and use a nail set or putty knife to sink them.

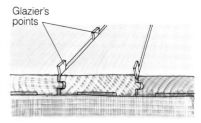

To secure a loose board, drive in pairs of 8d finishing nails angled toward each other. Drill pilot holes and go through the subflooring into the joists. Sink the nails; cover the holes with putty. (See also *Warped floorboards.*)

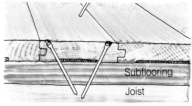

To avoid leaving nail holes or taking up a carpet, work from beneath the floor whenever possible. Have someone walk about to help locate the squeaky area. If a board is loose, weight it down. Then drill a pilot hole through the subflooring and put in a flathead screw. A 1¼-inch screw will normally work; be careful not to go through the surface.

If a joist is sagging, fill the gap above it by tapping in a wood shingle as a wedge; be careful not to raise the floor.

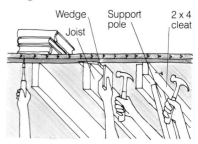

If the gap is over a few inches long, put construction adhesive along the top and side of a short 2 x 4 or 2 x 6 and force it against the subflooring, using a pole from the floor. Then nail it to the joist. Reinforce a sagging or bouncy floor (see *Sagging floors*).

Squeaky shoes

Silencing noisy footwear

When the sole is not sewn tightly enough to the upper part of a shoe, the leather of the upper and the sole may rub together, causing a squeak. The squeak generally stops when the leather softens. If it persists, take off the shoe, twist it in your hands to locate the source of the squeak, and rub some mink oil around the stitches in that area. The oil may soften the leather, stopping the squeaking noise.

If your shoe still squeaks, the leather that is rubbing may be in the interior of the shoe, and you'll have to take it to a shoe repair shop. The shoemaker may put a few tacks in the area of the squeak to hold the sole and the upper together more tightly. If this doesn't work, the shoemaker may have to resole the shoe and use masking tape as interfacing between upper and sole.

Stained glass

Making ornaments or panels

In the Middle Ages, stained-glass windows were made by fitting pieces of colored glass into lead channels, or *cames*. The lead-came method is still used for large windows, but many ornaments and lamp shades are made by the simpler copper-foil technique. In this method, the edges of the glass pieces are wrapped with copper foil and fitted together. Solder is then floated over all exposed surfaces of foil to create the illusion of lead cames and give the piece strength.

Begin by drawing a full-size design and making a carbon copy of it on light cardboard. Cut the carbon copy into glass patterns—templates for the individual pieces of glass in the work. Using the patterns as guides,

cut all the glass (see *Glass cutting*), putting each piece in its place on the original pattern as you cut it.

Wrap the edges of each piece with copper foil and replace it on the pattern. (Rolls of paper-backed copper foil, as well as sheets of colored glass, are available at stained glass specialty shops and some crafts stores.) Peeling off the paper backing as you go, center the edge of the glass on the foil and overlap the ends of the foil. Crimp the foil tightly over the glass.

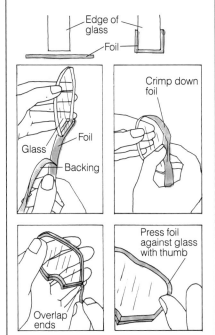

Next, join the foil-covered edges of the glass pieces with solder. Use a tinned heavy-duty soldering iron (see *Soldering*), solid-wire solder (*not* rosin-core solder), and liquid flux (either zinc chloride or oleic acid). To begin, brush the joint to be soldered with liquid flux (1); then hold the end of the wire solder over the joint and touch the hot soldering iron briefly to the solder so that a drop of solder falls onto the joint (2). When all the pieces are joined, float a thin ribbon of solder over all the visible foil, front and back (3). If the solder lumps, spread it along the line with the soldering iron. Gradually add more solder over the first coat until you get a rounded bead (4).

Solder solidifies almost at once, but it cools slowly; don't touch a newly soldered surface. Clean the tip of the iron

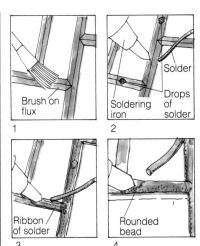

with a damp sponge from time to time as you work. Unless your soldering iron has a thermostat, it will become too hot. Keep unplugging it to maintain the proper temperature. If the solder does not melt freely, the iron is too cool; if the iron smokes or the solder is runny, the iron is too hot.

Wearing rubber gloves, rub down all the solder on the finished piece with copper sulfate or cupric nitrate and a soft cloth. This will discolor the solder and give it the look of antique copper. Wash the finished piece with detergent and water, then rinse and dry it.

Staining wood

Bringing out the wood's grain

Before staining furniture or a floor, strip the wood (see *Stripping furniture*). Scour the stripped surface with gum turpentine and No. 2/0 steel wool, reaching deep into any crevices. Leave the turpentine on for 5 minutes, then remove it with a clean cloth. Let the surface dry overnight, then rub it lightly with very fine (No. 220 to 280) sandpaper, moving with the grain.

If the stripped wood is darker than you want it, bleach it (see *Bleaching wood*). Fill in any gouges with wood filler the color the finished wood will be. Apply the stain as described below, let it dry for 24 hours, then apply the finish (see *Wood finishing*).

Oil stains

Oil stains, although somewhat more expensive than others, are easiest to apply. They work best on softwoods and those hardwoods with open grain (mahogany, for example).

To apply an oil stain, first coat all porous end-grains with thinned shellac (one part shellac and four parts denatured alcohol). This prevents the stain from darkening the end grain too deeply. Let the shellac dry for 3 hours, then cover the entire surface with the stain, either brushing or wiping along the grain. After 15 minutes, wipe the stain off with a clean cloth. Let it sit for 24 hours, then seal it with a coat of thinned shellac.

Water stains and alcohol stains
Water (dye) stains are the least expensive, but you must raise the wood grain and sand it before applying the stain. Water stains come in powdered form, and must be mixed with boiling water. To raise the grain, sponge the surface with warm water. Let the wood dry for 3 hours, then sand it with No. 220 paper. Wipe the surface clean. Apply the stain with a spray gun, if you have one; otherwise, use a cloth or brush. Apply the stain evenly, and work fast—water stains soak in quickly.

Alcohol stains leave a sharp, brilliant color. They're inexpensive and don't raise the wood grain, but they aren't as colorfast as water stains. Coat the end grains with a high-gloss varnish thinned with an equal amount of turpentine. Apply alcohol stain quickly and evenly with a spray gun, brush, or cloth. You can apply several coats, if necessary, but because they dry so fast, you can't correct them.

You can add a sealer over the top of an alcohol stain to prevent its bleeding into the finish, but only if you're not using a penetrating-oil finish, such as tung oil. (The sealer will keep the oil from penetrating.) Use the same sealer you used on the end grain and sand it lightly with No. 220 paper before applying the finish.

Stainless steel

Keeping it gleaming

Stainless steel can be generally maintained by washing and drying it (to avoid water spots) after each use. To keep stainless flatware sparkling, oc-casionally add ammonia to the wash water (2 tablespoons per quart). If it's dull or spotted, clean it with silver polish or (for satin finish) rub it with a soaped steel-wool pad.

Wash sinks, countertops, or stovetops with borax. Glass cleaner or a paste of baking soda is also effective for keeping these polished. Avoid abrasives. See *Cookware* for the way to care for stainless-steel pots.

Stain removal

Treating difficult-to-remove substances on fabrics

Tackle any stain quickly; flood a nongreasy stain with water to keep it from setting; sprinkle a greasy stain with an absorbent, such as cornstarch or talc; after 10 minutes, brush it away. As soon as possible, use the stain removal methods recommended below.

Where several steps are given, not all may be necessary; proceed until the stain is gone. As soon as possible after treating a stain, launder the item or have it dry-cleaned (see *Dry cleaning*).

For best results, work carefully. Follow all fabric-care directions on the label and test any cleaning agent on a hidden part—a seam allowance or facing. Alcohol, ammonia, and vinegar, for instance, may affect dyes.

Enzyme prewash products, not listed in the procedures, are effective for treating protein stains—milk, blood, egg, meat juices, grass—on washable fabrics. Chlorine bleach can be used to remove the last traces of a stain on white and colorfast washable fabrics.

Where alcohol is called for, use the rubbing or denatured type. On fabrics containing acetates, dilute the alcohol with 2 parts water. Before using ammonia on wool or silk, dilute it with an equal amount of water.

Applying cleaning agents
Three basic techniques are softening, sponging, and flushing. To *soften* a hardened stain that can't be soaked, dampen it with a few drops of cleaning agent. Then dampen an absorbent cloth with the same agent; press the cloth against the stain. Keep the cloth on the stain for 30 minutes or longer, repositioning it when it picks up any stain. Add more cleaning agent as necessary to keep the cloth damp.

To *sponge* a stain, place it facedown on a clean, absorbent cloth and gently rub it with another cloth dampened with the cleaning agent. (On a fabric that might be damaged by rubbing, you can instead apply cleaning agent and tap the stain with the bowl of a spoon to loosen it.) Use as little cleaner as possible; reposition either cloth as soon as it picks up any stain. Work from the center of the stain toward the edge to avoid forming a ring.

Flushing is used to get out stain-removing chemicals as well as staining agents. To flush a stain, turn it facedown on a clean, absorbent cloth. With an eyedropper, drip the cleaning agent onto the spot, applying only as much cleaner as the cloth beneath can absorb; reposition the cloth as soon as it picks up any stain.

Wet spotter and dry spotter
These are useful for removing many stains. The formula for wet spotter is 1 part glycerin, 1 part liquid dishwashing detergent, and 8 parts water. For dry spotter mix 1 part coconut or mineral oil to 8 parts commercial cleaning solvent (see *Cleaning solvents*).

Coffee, tea, alcoholic beverages, soft drinks, and fruit juices
Don't use soap on a fruit stain; it may set it. *Washable fabric:* If a beverage contained cream, sponge the fabric first with cleaning solvent. Soak it in a solution of ½ teaspoon liquid dishwashing detergent, 1 tablespoon vinegar, and 1 quart water; rinse. If the stain remains, sponge with alcohol or soak in enzyme prewash. *Nonwashable fabric:* Sponge with water; apply a few drops each of wet spotter and vinegar. Blot with a cloth dampened with the wet spotter plus vinegar; flush with water. If the stain remains, blot with alcohol.

Blood and vomit
Washable fabric: Soak for 30 minutes in a solution of 1 quart warm water, ½ teaspoon liquid dishwashing detergent, and 1 tablespoon ammonia; rinse. *Nonwashable fabric:* Sponge with water; apply a few drops each of wet spotter and ammonia. Blot with a cloth dampened with wet spotter and ammonia; flush with water. Apply a few drops vinegar; flush with water.

Grease, oil-based cosmetics, shoe polish (except white), paint, crayon
Work on a paint stain before it dries. Sponge both washable and nonwashable fabrics with cleaning solvent. If stain remains, apply a few drops of dry spotter; blot with a cloth dampened with the dry spotter; flush with cleaning solvent; dry.

Grass
Treat washable and nonwashable fabrics alike. Sponge with cleaning solvent; dry. Sponge with a nonoily nail polish remover; flush with cleaning solvent; dry. Sponge with water; apply a few drops each of wet spotter and vinegar; sponge with wet spotter; flush with water; dry. If the fabric is colorfast, sponge with alcohol.

Gravy and meat juices
Treat both washable and nonwashable fabrics as for grease. When dry, sponge with water; apply a few drops each of liquid dishwashing detergent and ammonia; blot with a cloth dampened with water; flush with water.

Ink (except red)
Because there are many ink formulas, no one procedure applies to all. Try these in order until one works. *Washable fabric:* Soak the stain in a solution of ½ teaspoon liquid dishwashing detergent, 1 tablespoon vinegar, and 1 quart warm water; rinse and dry. Sponge with alcohol. Soak in a solution of ½ teaspoon liquid dishwashing detergent, 1 tablespoon ammonia, and 1 quart warm water; rinse. *Nonwashable fabric:* Sponge with water; apply a few drops each of wet spotter and vinegar; blot with a cloth soaked in the wet spotter plus vinegar; flush with water; dry. Flush with alcohol; dry. Apply a few drops each of wet spotter and ammonia; blot with a cloth soaked in the wet spotter plus ammonia; flush with water; dry.

Ink (red), perspiration, and urine
Washable fabric: Soak in a solution of ½ teaspoon liquid dishwashing detergent, 1 tablespoon ammonia, and 1 quart warm water; rinse. Sponge with alcohol; rinse. Nonwashable fabric: Sponge with water. Apply a few drops of wet spotter, then a few drops of ammonia; blot with a clean, dry cloth; flush with water. Apply a few drops of wet spotter, then a few drops of vinegar; blot with a clean, dry cloth;

flush with water. Soften with alcohol; flush with water.

Lipstick
Treat washable and nonwashable fabrics alike. Apply cleaning solvent and dry spotter; blot. When dry, sponge with water. Apply a few drops each of wet spotter and ammonia; blot; flush with water. Apply a few drops each of wet spotter and vinegar; blot; flush with water. Sponge with alcohol; dry.

Stair carpeting

Choosing the best type; prolonging carpet life

Many manufacturers rate their carpeting for light, medium, and heavy wear. A heavy-wear rating is best for stairs. If a carpet is not rated, you can judge its durability by the density of the fibers. Roll a corner of the carpet around your fingers. Little or no backing should be visible at the base of the fibers. Look too for a strong backing to which fibers are firmly attached.

Consider how the carpet will look when it gets lots of day-to-day traffic. Good choices are tweeds, patterns, and tightly looped or highly twisted textures in medium colors. Any of these will show fewer footprints and less soil than plush or velvet. If you do buy a plush or velvet, choose one with low pile. Avoid light and dark colors and piles with extreme variations in height. Back your carpet choice with the best quality of padding available.

To prolong carpet life, vacuum stairs frequently and shampoo them every few months (see *Carpet cleaning*). To gain additional life, you can have an extra foot folded under in front of the top or bottom riser when the carpeting is installed. Then, before heavy wear at the front of each stair tread becomes obvious, move the carpet up or down by a few inches.

Staircases

Eliminating a stair's squeaks and wobbles

Repair a stair tread from beneath if the stair's underside is open or if the

covering is easy to remove. Have someone walk up and down the stairs to help you locate a loose tread. Then drive glue-coated wooden wedges into the tread's seams. Or fasten small wooden blocks along the front seam with screws and glue. If the tread's back edge moves, drill pilot holes and

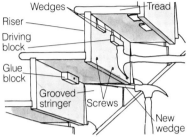

screw it to the riser. If a wedge in a grooved stringer is loose, chisel it out and scrape the dried glue from the groove. Then cut a new wedge; tap it in tightly, using glue.

If you can't work under the stairs, drive wedges into the seams from above. Use thin cedar-shingle scraps coated with glue and trim them flush with a sharp utility knife. Carefully remove and replace any molding.

You can also nail a tread's front edge to the riser. Drill pilot holes and

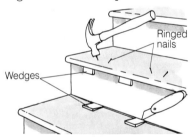

drive in pairs of ringed-shank finishing nails angled toward each other. Sink them with a nail set and fill the holes with wood putty. If the stairs will be carpeted, substitute long, thin flathead screws for more holding power. Because of the intricate joints in most stairs, have a carpenter replace worn or damaged treads.

Stair railings

Fixing loose and broken banisters

To tighten a loose banister, drive a thin, glue-coated wedge into the gap

S

at its top or bottom; then trim the wedge flush. If the handrail wiggles at the newel post, remove the plug under the rail. Tighten the star nut inside, using a hammer and a nail set.

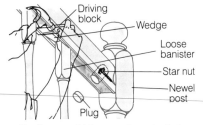

To fix a wobbly newel post, determine how it is attached. One common style goes through the floor and bolts to a joist; you tighten it from below. A larger, hollow old-style newel often has a metal rod running vertically through it; you remove the newel's cap to tighten the rod's top nut.

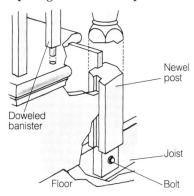

Repairing a broken banister
If a break is not badly splintered, glue it together, using yellow carpenter's glue and clamps. Fill any holes with wood putty; then sand and refinish.

To replace a banister, check to see how it fits into the tread. If it goes into a slot, remove the tread-end trim and pry the bottom out. Then work the tip out of the handrail. Clean out all old glue. Then cut a new banister to fit, put glue on each end, and slip it in. Nail the lower end. If you can't find an identical banister replacement, have a cabinet shop turn one to match.

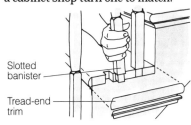

If a banister has a doweled lower end, saw it in half to remove it. Cut the new banister's upper end to fit into the handrail hole with a ⅜-inch space above. If necessary, trim it more and bevel the edge. Trim the lower dowel to a ¼-inch stump. Put glue on each end. Then push the banister up into the rail and drop it into the tread hole.

Staking plants

How to support garden plants

Use bamboo cane or other slender wood or metal stakes, available at garden centers, to support tall-growing (up to 5 feet), top-heavy plants. To prevent damage to roots or bulbs, stake early; for plants such as dahlias and tomatoes, position the stake before setting the plant in place. Make sure that the stake is tall enough to reach just below the flower head or uppermost fruits of the fully grown plant.

To support a single stem, drive a stake into the ground close to the plant. Secure the stem firmly but not tightly to the stake with soft string or paper- or plastic-covered wire twists. Tie at midstem and near the crown; add more ties at 1-foot intervals as the stem grows.

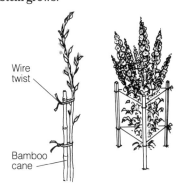

To support a group of plants or a large clump, drive three stakes into the ground in a triangle around the plants; then join the stakes with string or wire. Tie additional string courses at about 1-foot intervals.

Use a cylindrical cage made of 4-inch-square galvanized mesh to enclose and support herbaceous plants that grow more than 5 feet tall. Push three canes into the soil within the cage; secure them with string. Use 6-

inch-square mesh for making a cylindrical cage for tomato plants.

At planting time, support a young tree or a large shrub with a 2-inch-thick, preservative-treated stake that

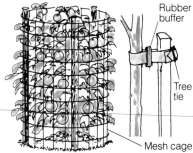

will reach just below the lowest branch. Secure the plant to the stake with rubber or plastic tree ties, available at nurseries or garden centers. Periodically loosen the ties as the plant grows.

Stalling cars

What to do if your car quits

If a late-model car stalls frequently, check with the dealer for a possible factory defect. Have it fixed.

In cold weather, on a car with a carburetor, floor the gas pedal and release it. Then remove the air-cleaner cover and look at the choke plate. It should be fully closed and should open only about ⅛ inch when the engine is started. In hot weather, or after the engine is warmed up, the choke plate should be fully open. Have it adjusted if necessary.

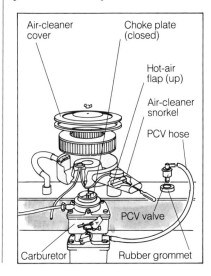

S

When the engine starts on cars with carburetors or throttle-body fuel-injection, probe inside the air-cleaner snorkel with a screwdriver to feel the hot-air flap. It should be up if the weather or the engine is cold; down if the weather or engine is warm. If not, the thermostatic air-cleaner system needs service.

If a carbureted engine idles too slowly or stalls upon starting, turn the fast-idle screw clockwise (see *Carburetor adjustments*). If the air conditioner controls the carburetor solenoid and the engine stalls when you turn on the A/C, the solenoid may be faulty or incorrectly adjusted.

Also check the positive crankcase ventilation (PCV) valve, which is usually contained in a rubber grommet on the engine's top (valve) cover and is connected by a hose to the carburetor or intake manifold. Pull out the PCV valve and shake it. If it doesn't rattle, replace it.

An engine that runs too hot because of poor cooling-system maintenance may stall (see *Antifreeze*). In addition, check the spark plugs (see *Spark plugs; Starting problems*) and the vacuum hoses that run from the carburetor, throttle body, and intake manifold. If any hoses are loose, reconnect them; if cracked, trim or replace them (see *Hoses in cars*).

If these steps don't cure the problem, have a mechanic check the engine.

Staple gun

Choosing and using a fast, efficient tacking tool

Caution: Keep a staple gun's safety handle locked when the gun is not in use; don't point or fire it at anyone or anything other than the work at hand. Keep a staple gun out of the reach of children.

With staples and a staple gun you can perform a wide variety of home repair jobs; where space is too constricted to swing a hammer, this may be the only fastening method possible.

Use a lightweight staple gun to replace screening, install insulation, recover a chair seat, or line a shelf. With a heavy-duty staple gun that accommodates several staple sizes, you can install ceiling tiles and weather stripping, upholster furniture, and lay carpeting. Special attachments are available for stapling electric cable or wire to a surface. Some models have a variable power button that adjusts firing strength to the job requirements.

Lightweight or heavy duty, a staple gun is easy to use. Grasp the hand hole as shown and place the gun firm-

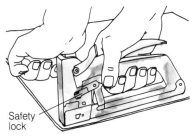

Safety lock

ly against the material to be stapled. Disengage the safety lock, release your grip (the handle will spring up), then squeeze the handle down sharply to fire the staple. To eliminate recoil and increase firing strength, press down on the head of the gun with the heel of your free hand.

For heavy, time-consuming jobs, such as installing insulation or carpeting, consider buying or renting an electric staple gun.

Starting problems

What to do when your car won't start

If the engine won't crank and you hear no click, jiggle the shift lever of an automatic transmission in *Neutral* while holding the key in *Start.* If it cranks and starts, have the neutral-start switch serviced.

If the engine cranks slowly or only clicks, check the battery cable connections (see *Battery terminals*). If the cables are all right, a jump start may work (see *Jump starting a car*). If so, test and recharge the battery (see *Battery recharging*).

If the engine cranks but won't start, on cars with carburetors: remove the air-cleaner cover. In cold weather, a carburetor's choke plate should be closed (see *Stalling cars*). If it's open, hold it closed with a stick while a helper turns the key; the engine may start.

Have the choke serviced. (See also *Fuel injection.*)

If the choke is closed, push it open and, with the ignition off, have a helper pump the gas pedal; a solid fuel stream should squirt into the engine. If there's no stream, check for a clogged fuel filter (see *Fuel filters*). If the weather is very cold, try adding fuel-line antifreeze to the tank.

In hot weather, especially if the car has been driven recently, the choke should be partly open. If not, push it open while a helper cranks the engine; it may start. Again, have the choke serviced.

If you smell a strong odor of gas, the carburetor is flooded. Hold the gas pedal to the floor while cranking the engine; it may start.

If the car still won't start, disconnect a spark-plug cable from one plug and force a key into the rubber boot. Hold the cable between two sticks, with the key ¼-inch from a metal part of the engine. Have a helper crank the

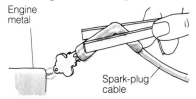

Engine metal

Spark-plug cable

engine; you should see a steady spark jumping to the engine. If not, the ignition system needs service.

If you see a spark, remove the plugs for inspection (see *Spark plugs*). If their electrodes are dirty or if they are past the recommended service interval, install new plugs.

Starting seeds indoors

S

Getting a jump on summer

To determine when to plant, check the seed packet for the time between germination and transplant; subtract this time from the date when you hope to set the seedlings out.

You can use seed flats or individual peat pots filled with sterilized soilless potting mix. Or you can improvise containers from milk cartons, egg cartons, foam coffee cups, aluminum-foil cake pans, and the like. Sterilize used containers with a mild solution of bleach and water. Costlier but handier are self-contained peat pellets; put them in water until they swell, then plant.

Fill a container two-thirds with potting mix. Soak the mix, let it drain overnight, then level it. Sow the seeds as recommended on the packet. With flats and large containers, plant in rows and transplant the strongest seedlings to pots or sectioned containers later. In small containers or peat pellets, plant two or three seeds and snip off the weaklings.

Germinating the seeds

Cover or enclose the container with glass or plastic and put it in a warm, dark spot. Remove the cover as soon as seeds begin to sprout; put the container in a light, but not sunny, place. Keep the soil surface moist with a fine spray. After a few days, when the first true leaves (the second pair) develop, transplant if needed and move the seedlings into the sun or under fluorescent lights. Place fluorescent tubes so that the distance between them and the top of a seedling equals the seedling's height; raise the tubes or lower the containers as seedlings grow. Keep the planting mix moist, not soggy. (See also *Cold frames and hotbeds; Planting.*)

Steaming

Cooking over boiling water

Steamed vegetables, fish, and fruit retain nutrients that might otherwise be lost in the cooking liquid; they also keep their shape and color well.

Place the food on a rack or plate or in a steamer basket. Lower it into a pot with 1 to 2 inches of boiling liquid, resting the food above the liquid. (Artichokes, asparagus, and broccoli can be steamed with the bottoms of the stems resting in the water.) Cover the pot and steam until food is tender. (See also *Pressure cooking.*)

To steam a pudding or bread, spoon the batter into a mold, filling it no more than two-thirds full. Cover tightly with a lid or a double layer of foil tied with string. Place the mold on a rack or directly into boiling water half the depth of the mold; cover the

pot and steam until a pick inserted in the center of the pudding comes out clean—1 to 1½ hours for a 1- or 1½-quart mold. Let the pudding rest for a few minutes, then remove it from the mold. To reheat, return it to the mold, cover, and steam for 30 minutes. Or wrap it in foil and warm it in the oven.

Stenciling

Transferring patterns or lettering

A technique that uses cutouts to transfer patterns onto wood, plaster, tin, paper, or fabric, stenciling is a traditional form of decoration for walls, furniture, or furnishings. You can buy stencils of letters, numbers, and design motifs from art supply stores or make your own (see *Stencils*).

Any type of coloring agent can be used for painting the design. Choose what best suits the material you're stenciling. Latex paints work well for stenciling walls because the colors blend well with the background paint, but apply them with an almost dry brush. You can use acrylic or deck paints for stenciling floors; Japan colors for stenciling glass, polished metal, or varnished furniture; and crayons or poster paints for paper.

If you use paint, blend it to a creamy consistency. If you use a thin coloring agent, apply it in several scant coats to keep it from seeping under the edges of the stencil. Before beginning, test the color on a scrap or an unseen section of the material you're stenciling.

Position the stencil, and brush the color over it, stroking away from the edges toward the middle. For an antiqued effect, apply acrylic paints or watercolors with ½-inch strips of sponge, using straight up-and-down dabbing motions. Clean the back of the stencil before reusing it in order to avoid staining the clean new surface.

For a multicolored design, use a different stencil for each color. Trace the outline of the first stencil on each subsequent stencil and cut a few peep-

holes along each traced outline. Color in the lightest shade first and let it dry; then position the second stencil over the design, using the peepholes to position it correctly. Color in a darker shade. For added protection, coat the finished design with shellac.

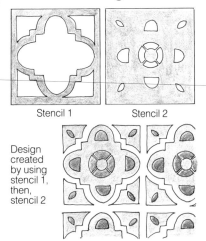

Stencil 1   Stencil 2

Design created by using stencil 1, then, stencil 2

Stencils

Making your own

To make a stencil, draw a design on stiff paper or cardboard and make the cutouts with a craft knife. When designing a stencil, be sure to include *ties*, or strips that separate the shapes and link the cutout areas to the edges of the stencil. Ties should be at least ⅛ inch wide. You can transfer any drawing to a stencil (see *Pattern transfer*), but you must add ties if the original has none.

To make the cutouts, hold the stencil firmly in place and keep the craft knife upright. As you cut, rotate the stencil so that you always stroke the knife in your direction. Mend any broken ties with masking tape, and trim the excess tape to conform with the outlines of the stencil. Trim corners and straighten edges with scissors.

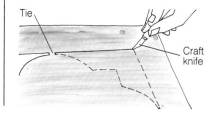

Tie

Craft knife

Stereo systems

What to do when components fail; eliminating noises

If when you operate the phonograph of your stereo system, only one speaker works, jiggle the dead speaker's wire where it connects to the receiver. If no change occurs, switch its jack connections to the receiver. If the problem persists, turn the receiver's program selector from *Phono* to *FM*. If the speaker remains dead, the receiver is probably at fault. However, if both speakers now work, the problem is in the turntable or in the cables or connections between the turntable and receiver (see *Turntables*).

Caution: Unplug the stereo system's power cord from the wall receptacle before cleaning switches, plugs, terminals, jacks, and manual controls and before working on any external component.

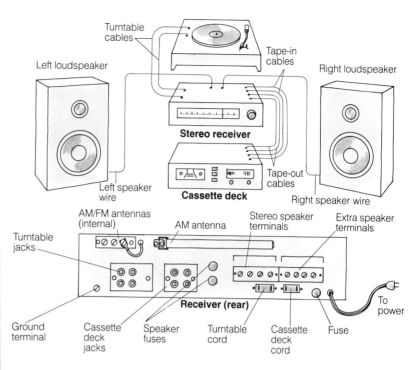

Stereo receiver

Cassette deck

Receiver (rear)

If wire jiggling eliminates the problem, clean all terminals, lugs, connectors, and jacks at both ends of the wire. Use fine sandpaper to remove corrosion from metal surfaces. Spray TV tuner cleaner (available at electronics shops) into all hard-to-reach contact points.

If your stereo suddenly stops working, but the receiver's panel lights do not dim or turn off, check your speaker fuses. Your receiver may have speaker fuses or breakers on its back panel next to the speaker connections. Replace any fuses with duplicates; reset the breaker.

If all stereo components stop working, find the receiver's circuit breaker or fuse, usually on the back panel. (If it's inside the unit, don't open it; call a

serviceman.) Reset the breaker or replace the fuse with one of the same rating. If the blowout recurs, have the receiver professionally repaired.

If your stereo has a low-frequency hum, check all terminal and jack connections. Make sure that the ground wire is connected to the ground terminal on the rear panel of the receiver. Cables from components to the receiver should not touch the power cords. Reduce the distance between the components. If the hum persists, you may need to attach the receiver's ground wire to a house ground, such as a metal pipe, or to the metal screw on the electric receptacle.

If you replace a power cord, use one that meets the specifications in the owner's manual (see *Power cords*).

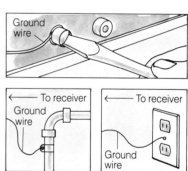

Avoid interference from household appliances by plugging your stereo into a receptacle on a separate circuit. Connecting a low-frequency interference filter, available at electronics shops, between the power cord and the receptacle may also solve the problem. (See also *Radio antennas*.)

S

Sticking windows

Freeing a balky sash; unsticking a painted-in sash

If a double-hung window moves, but doesn't slide easily, lubricate the sash channels with hard soap, paraffin, or a silicone spray lubricant. If paint has sealed the sash to the stop moldings

or parting strip, insert a wide putty knife between the sash and the molding or strip; work the knife up one side of the sash and down the other, tapping the handle with a hammer if necessary. If that doesn't work, place a block of wood in the channel just above or below the stuck sash and tap the block a few times with a hammer. Or try prying open the sash from the outside, using a pry bar under the

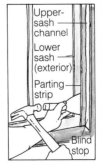

Continued next page

bottom rail of the lower sash or over the top rail of the upper sash. Work at the corners only; protect the sill by placing a wood shim or a piece of heavy cardboard between the bar and the sill.

Once you've opened the sash, use a narrow putty knife to scrape off globs of paint from the edges of the parting strips and both stop moldings. Sand the scraped areas, vacuum the sash channels, then lubricate them.

If the window still sticks, pry out one of the inside stop moldings with a putty knife. Lift the lower sash up and out of the window frame; then remove the cords or chains on both sides of the sash. (To take out the upper sash, pry out the parting strip on the same side as the stop molding you removed.) Sand or lightly plane the sides of the sash, test it in the frame for fit, then reassemble the window.

Stiff necks

Relieving a neck that's stiff and sore

Neck soreness or stiffness has many possible causes. Nervous tension, a muscle spasm, or sitting or sleeping in a draft or in an awkward position are common ones.

Wearing a soft cervical collar usually brings relief; wear it 24 hours a day for 2 days. If you don't have a cervical collar, roll up a turkish towel and fasten it around your neck with a safety pin. Aspirin or another analgesic and applications of heat can reduce pain.

If a stiff neck is severe and accompanied by fever, headache, and nausea, consult a doctor. In children especially, these symptoms may be signs of serious disease. It is also best to see a doctor for a stiff neck caused by an injury, such as whiplash.

Also calling for medical attention is wryneck, or torticollis, a disorder in which the muscles of one side of the neck pull the head down toward one shoulder. It is correctible with massage, careful stretching of affected muscles, perhaps surgery in severe cases. Victims of arthritic diseases may have the condition. Early treatment is advisable.

Stir-frying

Frying food for a short time over high heat

Because it is fast, this oriental cooking method retains the crisp texture of vegetables and preserves nutrients.

Cut all ingredients into uniform bite-size pieces; slice stringy vegetables on the diagonal; thinly slice mushrooms, onions, and meat.

Pour 1 to 2 tablespoons of oil into a *heated* heavy skillet or wok (a bowl-shaped pan designed for stir-frying). When the oil is very hot, put in such

Chopsticks

Wok

Base: large end up for high heat; small end for lower heat

seasonings as garlic and ginger, then add the ingredients one at a time. If meat is included, start with this and cook it until pink; push it up the side of the wok or remove it. Do vegetables next, starting with those that must be cooked longest. Fry, stirring continuously, until the vegetables are almost crisp-tender, then mix the meat with them. Add soy sauce, stock, or other liquid and steam for 1 to 3 minutes.

Stomachaches

What causes and what comforts stomach pain

Most pain in the stomach—the digestive organ high up under the breastbone behind the solar plexus—is a symptom of gastritis (inflammation of the stomach lining). The cause can be food poisoning, infection, a drug, or allergic reaction, even an excess of certain gastric juices. Usually, however, it's overindulgence in food or drink. (For other possible causes, see *Food poisoning; Heartburn; Indigestion; Nausea.* For lower-abdominal cramping, see *Constipation; Menstrual cramps.*)

The irritation should subside within 48 hours. An antacid may give some relief. Avoid aspirin; it irritates many individuals' stomachs. Pain from gastritis comes and goes; if the pain is constant and lasts longer than 3 hours, tell your doctor. Any indication of internal bleeding (blood in vomit, black stools) should be reported immediately. The first day, take small amounts of liquids but no food. The next day, eat bland, easily digested foods, again in small helpings.

If a stomachache persists after 2 days or you have stomachaches often, talk to your doctor. Together you may be able to identify the substances or conditions that cause trouble, such as stress, hurried meals, smoking, or overuse of alcohol or coffee. Hard-to-diagnose stomachaches in children and teenagers may be traceable to mealtime tension or to anxiety about school or social life.

An attack of gastritis can be so acute that it mimics a heart attack, even to the shooting pain in shoulder and arm. Don't take a chance; assume that it *is* a heart attack and get to a doctor. If he recommends an antacid and sends you home, as is likely, it's worth having the reassurance.

Stone tumbling

Polishing rocks for jewelry

A stone-tumbling machine, available at a hobby or lapidary supply shop, consists of an electric motor, a barrel, and a frame with rollers. A belt and pulley connect the rollers to the motor. For raw materials, collect pebbles from beaches or stream beds or wherever you see interestingly colored or patterned stones.

Fill a 3-pound (or less) barrel three-quarters full with stones of ¼ to 1 inch in diameter; add a rough grit of silicon carbide (roughly ½ pound for a 2½-pound load) and water to cover. As the barrel rotates, its contents collide, wearing down the stones.

Every 24 hours, stop the machine, remove six stones, and wash them. Dry them; inspect them under a good light. Return them for further tumbling if they're pitted or cracked;

S

when they are not, remove all the stones. Deposit the sludge in a plastic bag. Wash the stones and the barrel well. Put aside the imperfect stones; place the good ones in the barrel with some other rough-ground (or polished) stones until the barrel is three-quarters full again. Add an appropriate amount of fine grit and water to cover. Again check daily. It may be a week before the stones are perfectly smooth; treat them and clean up as before.

Return the stones to the barrel for final polishing. Add cerium oxide (1 tablespoon for a 2½-pound load) and enough water to cover. Tumble until the stones take on a high luster; it may take a week. Check daily.

Treat the stones and clean up as before. Return them to the barrel with ½ teaspoon of detergent and enough water to cover. Tumble 6 hours to remove the film from the stones. Rinse the stones well. Wrap them in a soft cloth to dry.

Stone walls

With or without mortar

A dry, or unmortared, stone wall is long lasting in wintery regions because it can adjust to frost heaving. It is a good space divider, but cannot be built high enough to give privacy. No footing is needed, but for maximum strength, build the wall on a 5-inch bed of sand in a 6-inch-deep trench.

With careful fitting you can use stones of almost any shape. Collect all the stones before you start. Place the largest at the ends of the wall and at turning points; stones with flat tops and bottoms are best. Then position other large stones flat side down for the base course. The base's width should be ⅔ of the wall's height.

Build up the wall one course at a time, choosing stones that fit snugly and make a fairly even bed for the next

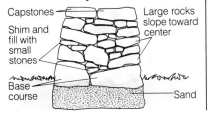
Capstones — Large rocks slope toward center
Shim and fill with small stones
Base course — Sand

course. Use small stones to shim up larger ones and to fill chinks. A curved or bending wall should slope inward

Dig steps to keep stones level on a hill
Original slope

about 1 inch per foot of height so that gravity will pull it together rather than apart. Save some flat, slablike stones to use as capstones atop the wall.

A mortared wall needs a concrete footing (see *Footings and foundations*). Position the stones of the base course as with a dry wall; its width need be only ⅓ of the wall's height. Then, beginning at one end, remove one stone at a time, spread a 2-inch bed of mortar (see *Mortar mixing*), and replace the stone. At the same time, apply mortar to any abutting stones that are already in place. After the course is in place, pack mortar into spaces between stones. Continue building in the same way. placing the stones of each course, then mortaring them one at a time. (See also *Garden walls; Retaining walls.*)

Storm doors and windows

Making and repairing storm windows; installing a storm door

A second layer of glass properly installed on windows and doors reduces drafts, makes heating and cooling systems work more efficiently, and cuts fuel bills. To save even more, make your own storm windows.

Measure the height and width of the window opening just outside the blind stop (see *Sticking windows*). For windows under 5 feet high, you will need four lengths of aluminum storm-window sash fitted with rubber glazing gaskets (available precut at hardware stores), four friction-fit corner locks to hold the sash pieces together, and a single pane of double-strength glass. (Wood-frame storm windows and larger aluminum windows with two or more panes are more difficult to construct.)

Remove the gaskets from the sash pieces and set them aside. Mark the width of the window opening, minus ⅛ inch, on the top and bottom pieces; mark the height of the opening, minus ⅛ inch, on the two side pieces. Using a miter box and a fine-tooth hacksaw, cut each piece to the desired length with 45-degree miters at both ends (see *Miter joints*); file off any burrs. With a rubber mallet, drive a lock into each end of the side sash pieces. Crimp together the sash and lock as shown (hammer the nail just hard enough to dimple the sash, without damaging the lock). Fasten the top and bottom pieces to one side piece to form a three-sided frame; crimp them in place.

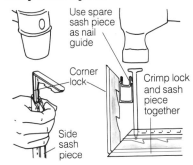
Use spare sash piece as nail guide
Corner lock
Crimp lock and sash piece together
Side sash piece

Have the glass cut 1 1/16 inch smaller than the frame's outside measurements, or cut it yourself (see *Glass cutting*). Wear heavy gloves to handle the glass. Fit the gasket around the rim of the glass, starting at the middle of one side. At each corner, make 45-degree cuts on both sides of the gasket with a utility knife; then fit the gasket to the corner. Trim off the projecting tabs at a 45-degree angle. Slide

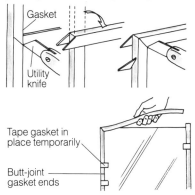
Gasket
Utility knife
Tape gasket in place temporarily
Butt-joint gasket ends

the pane into the frame, then close the frame by adding the fourth side. Mount the storm window to the top of

S

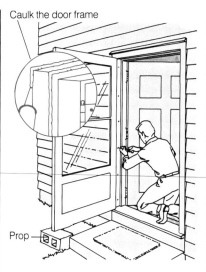

the existing window frame with a pair of two-piece brackets. To make a tighter seal and prevent sweating, weatherstrip both inner and outer windows (see *Weather stripping*).

Replacing a broken pane

If an aluminum storm-window frame has a gasket on only one side of the glass, replacing the pane is simple. Carefully pull the gasket from under the frame's retaining lip; if the gasket has deteriorated, replace it. Buy a new pane of double-strength glass cut $\frac{1}{32}$ inch smaller than the distances between the inner edges of the frame channels. Wear heavy gloves to remove broken glass from the frame; run a screwdriver around the frame to clear out glass bits. Gently lay the new pane in the frame. Starting at a corner and working around the frame,

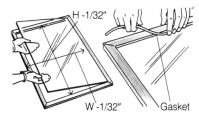

press the gasket under the frame lip. If there are gaskets on both sides of the glass, leave this job to a glazier. To replace the pane in a wood-sash storm window, see *Windowpanes*.

Installing a storm door

Aluminum storm doors are usually sold complete with frames, ready to be installed in standard-size doorways. Measure the width of the doorway from jamb to jamb, its length from head jamb to threshold. If the doorway isn't a standard size, buy a storm door with a frame slightly smaller than required and build out the existing door frame with strips of lumber. If necessary, use a hacksaw to shape the frame to fit the threshold. To install the door, caulk the existing door

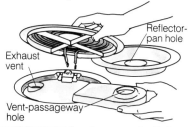

frame as shown (see *Caulking*), then screw the storm-door frame in place.

Maintenance

Once a year, brush aluminum door and window frames with fine steel wool to remove oxidation, then apply paste wax. Paint wood frames as needed. Repair bent or loose hardware and crumbling or missing putty. Reglue a loose joint; reinforce it with a corner plate. (See also *Window insulation; Winterizing a house.*)

Stoves

Troubleshooting an electric or gas range

Caution: Before working on the surface burners or the interior of an electric range, turn off power to its circuit at the fuse box or circuit breaker panel. Power to an electric range is controlled by double fuses or circuit breakers; if you're unsure of their location, call an electrician (see *Circuit breakers; Fuse boxes*).

Before working on a gas range, unplug the power cord (if any). If you smell gas, check the pilot lights. If all are lit, look for the gas shutoff valve under the cook top or at the cabinet bottom; close it by giving the handle a quarter turn so that it is at a right angle to the gas line. Call the gas company immediately.

Simple mechanical adjustments can solve several gas- and electric-range problems. If the oven tends to overheat, check the exhaust vent at the back of the cook top or under one of the surface burners; clear it of any ob-

structions. Make sure the round hole in the vent passageway is in line with the reflector pan's hole.

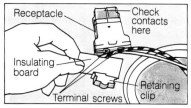

If the oven heats unevenly, fails to maintain a set temperature, sweats, drips water, or is smoky, examine the gasket (the pliant strip that seals the door); replace a worn or cracked one. In some models, pull off the old gasket and clip on a new one. In others the oven liner must be loosened or the door removed; call in a repairman.

If the gasket is good and the oven still doesn't hold a set temperature, have a repairman test the thermostat and recalibrate or replace it.

Electric stoves

If none of the heating elements heats or reaches high temperatures, check the fuse box or circuit breaker panel; replace a blown fuse or reset a tripped circuit breaker as needed.

If a single surface element fails to heat, turn off power to the stove, lift the element, and examine it. If you see bubbles or burn marks on the sheathing or pitting on the terminals, replace the element.

Remove a plug-in element by pulling it gently from its receptacle. Next, inspect the receptacle. Unscrew the mounting screw and pull the receptacle clear of the cook-top opening. If the spring contacts in the receptacle slots are burned or bent, replace the receptacle. Remove its retaining clips and insulating board, unscrew the terminal screws, and disconnect the wires. Install an exact duplicate.

To remove a wired-type element, take off the reflector pan, unscrew the hinge-clip screw, and pull the element

S

up and out of the cook-top opening. Remove the insulating block by prying off its two spring clips. Note how the wires are connected to the element's terminals; then disconnect

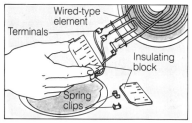

them. Reverse the procedure to install a duplicate element; if the insulating block was burned, replace it too.

When inspecting an element or a receptacle, check the wires as well. If they're brittle or charred, have a repairman replace them.

Bake or broil elements

To remove an oven bake or broil element that's bubbled or burned, turn off the power and unscrew the mounting bracket screws at the rear oven wall. In some ovens, you may have to pull the cabinet away from the wall and unscrew the back panel before you can disconnect an oven element. Pull the element several inches forward. Disconnect the wires from the

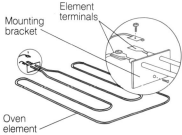

element's terminals, lift out the element, and replace it with a duplicate. Have the wires replaced if they're brittle or charred. If the element is a plug-in type, pull it out gently. Check the plug-in receptacle; replace it if its terminals are burned.

Gas ranges

Except for the mechanical adjustments described above, and relighting or adjusting the pilot (see *Pilot lights*), most gas-range problems are best left to a repairman. If an oven or surface burner's flames are uneven, turn off the burner and let it cool. Use a straightened paper clip to clean the burner ports; if a surface burner has a

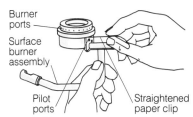

removable cap, wash it in hot water and household ammonia. If the burner flames are yellow, too high, or noisy, have the gas company adjust the air-gas mixture.

If a surface burner doesn't ignite even when the pilot is lit and properly adjusted, raise the cook top, lift out the burner assembly, and unclog the burner and pilot ports with a straightened paper clip. Wash the burner head in hot water and household ammonia. Dry and replace the assembly.

Stranded on vacation

Lost money, passports, and airline tickets

Before leaving on vacation, give a trusted friend or relative your itinerary; the addresses where you'll be staying; and the numbers of your credit cards, traveler's checks, and passport. In an emergency, call your contact and work with him to cancel lost or stolen credit cards and to transfer funds.

Report the loss or theft of traveler's checks to the local police and to an agent of the company that issued them. In most cases, you'll receive a refund the same day; without proper documentation, you may have to wait up to 2 weeks. For prompt action, carry the purchase agreement (the slip of paper listing the numbers of your checks) separately from the traveler's checks and record each check cashed.

If you're out of funds but have a major credit card, try to draw cash with it from a local bank. A U.S. embassy or consular officer will help you cable your bank or your contact at home and arrange a transfer of funds (don't expect him to lend you money or cash a check). Many overseas banks, traveler's checks offices and, in some countries, telegraph offices, offer similar assistance, for a fee.

Report a lost or stolen passport to the local police (you'll need a copy of their report to apply for a new one), then call or go to the nearest U.S. embassy or consulate. If you can provide adequate proof of citizenship, you'll be issued a new passport, often on the same day; it's wise to carry a copy of your birth certificate or other form of personal identification separately from your passport.

If you lose your airline ticket, go to the ticket office of the airline that issued it. In most cases, you'll have to buy a replacement at the prevailing price and wait several months for a refund, provided your ticket hasn't been used. Refund policies vary; some airlines and charter companies offer no refunds for lost tickets.

If you are stranded in a strange city with no money, no place to stay, and no means of transportation, seek assistance from the local police, the Salvation Army, the Travelers Aid Society (its offices are located at many airports and bus and railroad stations throughout the United States), or U.S. consulates in major cities worldwide. Check a local telephone directory for addresses and telephone numbers. (See also *Travel emergencies*.)

Stress

Coping with the strains and upheavals of life

Everyone experiences stress daily at home, on the job, driving to the supermarket. There are ways to counteract it: exercise, meditation, yoga—all appear to temporarily banish tension. Many find relief in deep breathing (see *Relaxation exercises*), a brisk walk, hobbies, listening to music.

More difficult to deal with is the stress caused by any major change. When a new baby is born or a loved person dies, when you get promoted or lose a job, or when you move from one home to another—in all these situations, there is uncommon stress. Unrelieved, it can cause changes in body chemistry. It has been implicated in disorders ranging from headaches and insomnia to depression and heart disease.

Continued next page

Getting some perspective

One way to relieve stress is to talk things out with friends, family, or a wise and trusted counselor. If you decide to seek professional help, ask your doctor, your clergyman, or a friend to recommend a therapist. Often clergymen are skilled counselors.

A therapist need not be an expensive psychoanalyst. There are self-help groups for people under similar stress, such as Parents Without Partners, Al-Anon for the families of alcoholics, newcomers clubs for new residents, bereavement groups for those who have lost their spouses. If someone in your family suffers from a serious disease, such as cancer or Alzheimer's disease, contact the society for that disease to find out if there's a support group in your area.

Live in the present

Talking about the past may help your acceptance of events, but it's best not to dwell on it or to worry excessively about your future course. Instead of trying to deal with *all* the uncertainties you can imagine, deal with one at a time. Take comfort in familiar routines: regular mealtimes, good food, customary standards of dress and grooming, hobbies, companionship.

Finally, take charge of your life with a positive outlook. Those who blame "life" or others for their predicaments handle stress the least well. Taking charge will help you to feel "in control" and competent.

Stretching a canvas

How to prepare a canvas for oil or acrylic painting

Art supply stores sell ready-made stretcher bars in a variety of lengths. For a rectangular stretcher frame, buy two matching pairs of bars and fit their tongue-and-groove ends tightly into each other. With a triangle or carpenter's square, check that all corners are square; adjust as needed by tapping the frame with a hammer.

Canvas, also sold in art supply stores, comes ready to paint (acrylic primed or oil primed) or untreated. After stretching, untreated canvas must be sized, usually with a solution

of rabbit-skin glue, then primed with oil or acrylic primer (sizing isn't needed with acrylic primer).

Buy a piece of canvas 1½ to 2 inches larger all around than the outer dimensions of the assembled stretcher frame. Place the canvas facedown on a work surface; center the frame, beveled side down, on top of it. Fold the canvas back over one long side of the frame. Using a staple gun, staple the canvas to the frame's edge at its center (or use carpet tacks and a hammer). With your fingers or, preferably, with stretching pliers, pull the canvas tightly over the opposite side of the frame; then staple the canvas to the frame edge at the center. Repeat the procedure at the short sides. Then, working outward from the middle of each side, staple at 3-inch intervals, in the sequence shown, stretching the canvas evenly as you go; leave 3 inches of unstapled canvas at the corners.

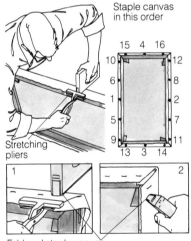

Staple canvas in this order

Stretching pliers

Fold and staple canvas at corners (1) and to back of frame (2)

Fold the canvas at each corner, tucking one part snugly under the other against the frame. Staple the folded canvas in place, with the staple in the widest portion of the wood.

Fold surplus canvas around the frame edge and staple it to the back of the frame at 3-inch intervals. At the corners, fold surplus canvas against the back of the frame and staple securely. Use a flat varnish brush to prime untreated canvas with several coats of acrylic gesso, allowing the canvas to dry between coats. Before using the canvas, sand it smooth.

String art

Circles from straight lines

String art creates abstract or pictorial designs by stretching string across nails in a wood board. Use whatever nails and string, yarn, or wire best fit your design. Pick a wood that will accept the nails easily without splitting (plywood is popular) and cover it with fabric, paint it, or leave it bare.

Begin by drawing your design on paper, connecting dots with colored-pencil lines. Since string cannot be made to curve in midair, all lines in string art must be straight. But straight lines can be used to create the illusion of a curve or even a circle.

To form a curve, draw a set of equidistant dots on each of two perpendicular lines. Number the lines as shown, and connect the dots of the same number with straight lines.

To form a circle, draw a circle with a compass and use a protractor to mark off dots every 20 degrees. (For a denser design, position the dots closer to-

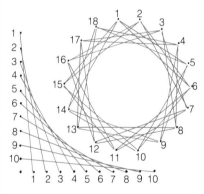

gether.) Draw a straight line from point 1 to point 6, and then from point 6 to point 2, from 2 to 7, 7 to 3, 3 to 8, 8 to 4, 4 to 9, 9 to 5, and 5 to 10. Continue clockwise until you connect your last points (5 to 1).

Prepare the board and pound the nails partway in and to a uniform height. Use one nail for each dot on the design. Tie a piece of string to the first nail. Following the lines of the design, wind the string around the successive nails. Tie it off.

S

Stripping furniture

Removing paint and varnish with a water-soluble stripper

Caution: Work in a well-ventilated, shaded area, not near an open flame; don't smoke. Keep children and pets away from the work area. Wear old clothes, cotton-lined neoprene gloves, and goggles. Store scrapings in a disposable can.

You can remove any finish from wood, using a heavy-bodied or semipaste, water-soluble stripper. Follow the instructions on the container so that you won't damage the wood. A heavy-bodied stripper works well on vertical, grooved surfaces; semipaste, which is active longer, is strong enough to remove polyurethanes and epoxies.

Applying stripper

Remove all hinges and other hardware from the furniture; then, with an appropriate-size paint brush, apply a thick layer of remover in one direction. After a prescribed time (15 minutes, usually), scrape off the softened paint (sludge) with a blunt-edged, round-cornered putty knife or use a wooden scraper. Work carefully; don't gouge the wood. Remove paint from crannies with a stiff toothbrush, a pointed stick, or steel wool. Several remover applications may be necessary. No dark spots should remain. Clean off stripper residue by brushing on paint thinner or mineral spirits. Wipe it off with a clean soft cloth.

Immerse hinges and other hardware in paint remover; scrape off the softened paint with steel wool or a stiff brush. Let the wood dry thoroughly, 24 hours or more, before refinishing.

When paint has been applied over raw, unsealed wood, a bath in a heated, highly caustic solution may be needed to open the grain and dissolve the paint. Have this done by a responsible professional.

Stucco walls

Patching cracks and gaps in a cement-based siding

Stucco comes in premixed, dry form to which you add water according to package directions; or you can make your own by combining 1 part portland cement, 3 parts building sand, and enough water to form a puttylike mixture (for mixing directions and precautions, see *Concrete*). Stucco is applied over masonry or concrete or to wire lath on a wood frame. Don't repair stucco when a freeze threatens.

To fix a crack, use a stiff putty knife to cut open the crack to sound stucco. With a hammer and cold chisel, undercut the crack so that it is wider inside than on the surface. Remove loose material, then wet the crack with a sponge. With the putty knife, pack stucco tightly into the crack. If the crack extends to the base material, overfill it slightly. Let the stucco dry for 15 minutes, then work it into the crack with the putty knife. Scrape off any excess. Moist-cure the patch by wetting it with a fine spray from a garden hose once in the morning and again at night for 3 days.

To repair a large area, scrape away damaged stucco down to the base material. Wearing safety goggles, wire-brush a masonry or concrete surface, and use a hammer and cold chisel to cut slightly into any mortar joints. Clip off and replace damaged lath. Wet the area well. Using a rectangular trowel, scrape stucco from a *hawk*

Applying the scratch coat

Lath — Trowel

Hawk —

onto the wall in a ½-inch-thick layer (the *scratch* coat); press the stucco through the lath to embed it. (If the base is masonry or concrete, omit this coat.) When the stucco is firm but not set, score it with a *scratcher* made of nails driven through a board.

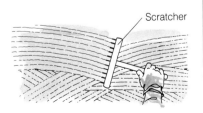

Scratcher

Let the scratch coat dry for 5 to 6 hours; dampen it (or the base wall, if you omitted the scratch coat) just before applying a second, ⅜-inch-thick layer of stucco (the *brown* coat). Rub the brown coat with a *wood float*.

Wood float

Moist-cure it for 2 days; then let it dry for at least 5 days before applying a final ⅛- to ¼-inch-thick coat. Add pigment, if needed, when mixing the finish coat. Trowel it on, then texture the patch with a stiff brush, a wood float, or a trowel to match the existing stucco. Let the finish coat dry for a day, then moist-cure it for a day.

Stud poker

Five-card stud, a poker game for two to 10 players

Deal each player a facedown card *(hole card),* then deal one faceup. Facedown cards are not revealed. The player with the highest faceup card leads the betting, placing X number of chips in the *pot* (see *Poker*). If there's a tie for the highest card, the player who received the card first bets. Other players must bet the same amount or they may drop out by turning over their faceup card. A player can drop out during any betting round.

After the first round, deal the active players another faceup card. Dealing and betting continue until all active players have four faceup cards. At the final betting *(showdown),* the remaining players turn over their hole cards. The high hand wins the pot; for ranking of hands, see *Poker*.

Studs

How to locate the upright supports in a wall

Studs are generally spaced either 16 or 24 inches apart, measured from

S

center of stud to center of stud. To find them, tap a wall lightly with a hammer wrapped in cloth and listen for the solid, rather than hollow, sound that indicates the presence of a stud. Use a 1/8-inch drill to bore test holes just above the baseboard where you suspect there's a stud. Drill several holes side by side until you hit it.

Or locate studs by looking for nail holes in the baseboard and checking the places where sheets of drywall or paneling meet. There will be a stud behind each seam.

An alternative is to use an electronic stud finder, which measures changes in a wall's density. Cheaper magnetic stud finders detect nails used to fasten drywall, paneling, or other framing elements. Both devices are available at hardware stores.

Styes

Treating tiny, painful infections at the eyelid's edge

A sty is a localized bacterial infection of the gland behind the eyelash. It begins as a painful reddening and swelling of the area, followed by a head of pus, which must burst for the pain to be relieved. Left alone, a sty will usually run its course within a few weeks.

You can hurry things along: as soon as the inflammation becomes visible, apply hot compresses to the sty several times a day, keeping them in place for 10 to 15 minutes. The moist heat helps draw the pus to the breaking point. When it breaks, wash the eye area thoroughly to flush away pus.

If a sty doesn't break within a reasonable time or if it recurs, an eye doctor should see it.

After the acute inflammation of a sty dies down, scar tissue forms as the lid heals. Occasionally, an excessive amount of scar tissue builds up, and a painless, firm lump called a *chalazion* develops. Hot compresses may help this disappear, but if the lump is still there after a month, consult an eye doctor.

Stylus

Installing, testing, and replacing a phonograph stylus

The stylus is in the cartridge (a replaceable plastic housing) at the front end of the tone arm. Some cartridges simply plug into the tone arm; others must be connected to it by one or two top-mounted screws and four connector wires. Use a jeweler's screwdriver for this delicate job. Consult your owner's manual or an electronics dealer for advice on the kind of cartridge you need.

If a record in good condition sounds scratchy, adjust, by slight degrees, the cartridge's *tracking force* (the weight of the stylus on the record) so that adequate pressure is exerted on the record. The knob for this is near the base of the tone arm. Older models have a height-adjustment screw on the tone arm's mounting and hinge assembly; raise or lower the screw for correct pressure.

Fuzzy sounds may also be due to grime on the stylus's diamond tip. Clean it with a stylus brush and an appropriate solvent, following package directions. After 1,500 hours of use, your stylus may wear down. Have it checked at a stereo store.

If your cartridge picks up vibrations from noises in the room or from your speakers, those vibrations will be amplified into a howl. Isolate the turntable from the speakers, then place the stylus on a record and tap the turntable chassis lightly. If your tap is amplified and echoed by the speakers, buy and install a new cartridge. If the tap isn't picked up by the speakers, tap the receiver. If this is picked up by the speakers, have your receiver professionally repaired. (See also *Stereo systems*.)

Subletting

Acting as a landlord for your leased property

Before signing a lease to rent an apartment or a house, check whether it allows you to sublet. It may prohibit a sublease. Or it may allow you to sublet only with your landlord's written permission. If so, make sure that there's a clause stating that his permission can't be "unreasonably" withheld (if, for instance, the sublessee has like financial means and like intentions regarding property use). Negotiations may be necessary.

In subletting, you act as a landlord in allowing your tenant, the sublessee, to live on your leased premises for a specified rent and period. You are still legally bound to honor your lease; you can be blamed for a sublessee's acts of irresponsibility. If the sublessee fails to live by the regulations spelled out in your lease, your landlord can demand his or her removal.

Ask your sublessee for financial and character references to protect yourself against possible liability in lawsuits. Require a rent-security deposit (usually equal to one month's rent) to ensure that you will have enough to pay for any damage to the premises. Ask a lawyer or your municipality's local housing authority to explain the finer points of subletting under local landlord and tenant laws.

Succulents

Care and propagation

The best-known succulents are the thick-stemmed cacti (see *Cacti*); others often grown as household plants include deoniums, aloes, kalanchoes, and crassulas (see *Jade plants*).

Give potted succulents as much sunlight as possible, quarter turning them periodically to prevent distorted growth. During the summer, water them moderately and feed them a liquid fertilizer once every month; in winter, water them sparingly. They can tolerate the dry heat of an apartment and occasional neglect.

Repot succulents every two or three years in spring in a mixture of two parts standard potting mixture (see *Potting houseplants*) and one part perlite or coarse sand. Sedums require equal parts of potting mixture and perlite or sand.

Propagate with stem cuttings or, for sedums and crassulas, by a leaf. Let the cutting or leaf dry for a few days (see *Propagating plants*).

Succulents in gardens

Practical, trouble-free, year-round vegetation

Hardy species of sedums, sempervivums, and yuccas thrive in most regions, provided they have the proper sunlight, soil mix, and drainage. The better the soil's nourishment and drainage qualities, the better a succulent's chance of surviving heavy rains and cold winters.

Plant these succulents on a sunny slope in early spring. Excavate to 6 inches, then fill in with a layer of small rocks or broken masonry; follow with a mix of 1 part topsoil, 2 parts sand, and 1 part humus. If you have no sloping areas in your yard, add 1 part gravel to the planting mix to make for faster drainage. If you live in a rainy area, the succulents will need a more nourishing soil: add ½ cup of bonemeal per gallon of planting mix. Pour the soil mixture over the rubble layer in stages; tamp after each deposit. Let the soil settle for roughly a week before planting. Don't crowd the plants, it will reduce ventilation. Pack pebbles around each plant; they'll reflect the sun and help prevent rot.

Every two or three weeks, during dry summer weather, water the soil at the start or end of the day. Weed assiduously. (See also *Cactus gardens; Rock gardens*.)

Sump pumps

Keeping a basement or foundation dry

The sump in which a sump pump sits is a small pit; a 24-inch-diameter sewer tile on a gravel base makes a good one. When water in the sump reaches a given depth, a float-operated switch turns the pump on; when enough water is pumped out, the switch turns off. You can set both levels with the two float clamps. An inlet screen in the base filters out solids.

Use 1¼-inch plastic pipe to carry water from the pump to a drain (see *Plastic pipes*). To prevent backflow, install a brass check valve, its arrow pointing away from the pump. Plug the power cord into a receptacle that is at least 4 feet above the floor and protected by a ground fault interrupter (see *Ground fault interrupters*).

To test the pump, fill the sump with water; do this at least four times a year and any time you plan to be away for an extended period. If the pump works slowly or makes labored noises, clean the inlet screen and check the cord and plug for damage. Be sure the pump is seated firmly on its base.

Clean and inspect the sump, the pump, and the check valve annually. Oil the pump as needed, following the manufacturer's directions. If problems continue, call a plumber or a dealer for service.

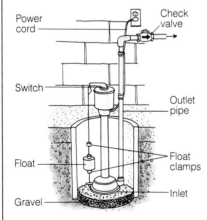

Power cord — Check valve

Switch —

Outlet pipe

Float — Float clamps

Gravel — Inlet

Sunburn

How to treat it

Relieve a superficial sunburn by cooling the skin with cloths dipped in cool Burow's solution (1:40 concentration) or in a mixture of half water, half milk. A hydrocortisone cream or plain calamine lotion may be soothing. Elevate swollen legs or arms. For pain, take aspirin or another analgesic. Later, when the pain is past and dryness and itching develop, use a skin-softening cream or lotion. Stay out of the sun until all signs of the burn, including peeling, are gone.

Blistering signifies a deeper burn. Don't break blisters; it risks infection. If a person is badly burned or if areas become infected, consult a doctor. Started promptly, internal medication may avert a potentially severe burn reaction. For a discussion of the dangers of sun exposure and for ways to prevent sunburn, see *Suntans*.

Sunlamps

Precautions in their use

Caution: Except for the medically prescribed treatment of certain skin diseases, sunlamp use is not recommended by doctors. (For the hazards of tanning, whether under the sun or a lamp, see *Suntans*.) If you have any skin or internal disease, are taking medication, or are especially sensitive to sunlight, consult a doctor before using a sunlamp.

The amount of ultraviolet radiation you receive from a sunlamp depends on your distance from it and the time you spend under it. Overexposure can result in eye injury or a damaging sunburn. Follow the manufacturer's recommended distance and exposure times. Start with short exposures and build up gradually; don't use the lamp more than once a day. If your lamp kit doesn't include a timer/buzzer, use a kitchen timer to avoid falling asleep. Always wear protective plastic goggles, not sunglasses, under the lamp. Anyone else in the room should wear goggles too. Keep pets and children out of the room while the lamp is on.

Suntans

Staying safe in the sun

Tanning is the body's way of guarding against the sun's harmful ultraviolet rays; but this protection is limited. Too much sun, too quickly, causes sunburn (see *Sunburn*). Repeated exposure to ultraviolet rays, whether

S

from the sun, a sunlamp (see *Sunlamps*), or a tanning booth, results over the years in dry, veined, wrinkled skin, and has been linked to precancerous spots and to skin cancer.

Sunlight acting on chemicals in certain perfumes, soaps, cosmetics, and drugs can cause itchy, burning, blistering rashes. If you're taking oral contraceptives or medications, consult a doctor before sunbathing.

If you insist upon tanning, do so cautiously. At first, spend only 15 or 20 minutes a day sunbathing; gradually increase exposure, in increments of 5 to 10 minutes, over the next few weeks. Stay out of the sun between 10 A.M and 3 P.M. Bear in mind that ultraviolet rays can penetrate water, overcast skies, and loosely woven or wet clothes; rays reflected from sand, water, and snow can burn even in the shade. Protect your eyes with optical sunglasses that block at least 75 percent of the light (check the light transmission factor on the label or ask the optician). Plastic lenses should contain an ultraviolet absorber.

Half an hour before exposure to the sun, apply a sunscreen containing a Sun Protection Factor (SPF) of at least 15—the higher the number, the greater the protection. Choose a sunscreen containing avobenzone or oxybenzone, both of which protect against ultraviolet A and B rays. Cover nose, lips, and ears with an opaque sun block containing zinc oxide or titanium dioxide. Reapply sunscreen at least every 2 hours, or after perspiring heavily or swimming.

If you're very fair or tend to burn quickly, don't try to tan at all; you're at greater risk than others. In the sun, wear loose, long-sleeved clothing and a broad-brimmed hat; use a sunscreen on your hands and face.

Superfluous hair

Removing unwanted hair

Shaving is a fast, easy way to deal with thick hair growth, but the hair grows back quickly—within 1 to 3 days—and with stubbly ends. It's best for whiskers, the lower legs, and underarms. On the thighs and bikini line, irritation may occur with regrowth.

To use a safety razor, wet the area, lather with shaving cream or soap, and wait 2 or 3 minutes. Use a sharp blade and shave against the direction of hair growth when possible. Use an electric razor on dry skin; it won't nick the skin as often as a safety razor.

Depilatories

A depilatory is a chemical cream that dissolves hair so that it can be washed away. The treated area stays hair free for 7 to 10 days and regrows without stubbly ends. Depilatories can be used on most parts of the body; on the face, use only creams designated for that area. Before using a depilatory, do a patch test for allergic reaction. If irritation develops after use, apply compresses of Burow's solution (1:40 concentration) for 10 minutes, followed by hydrocortisone cream.

Waxing

Waxing removes large areas of hair by pulling it out from the roots. A warm, melted beeswax formula is spread on the area, and a strip of fabric is pressed over it. After the wax hardens, the fabric is pulled quickly away from the skin. Hair must be at least ¼ inch long. The waxed area will remain hair free for 2 to 3 weeks.

Waxing can be used for hair on the upper lip, legs, or bikini area. The procedure is most often done at beauty or waxing salons, but home-waxing kits are available. Follow the directions exactly. Cosmetic wax is very sticky; protect all surfaces in the area with newspapers. Excess wax can be removed from the skin with mineral oil.

Caution: Wax is flammable; heat it in a double boiler, never over an open flame.

Electrolysis

Electrolysis and other electrical ways of killing the hair root are the only permanent methods of hair removal. Pitted scars are a possible side effect, but some procedures minimize these. Ask a dermatologist to recommend a skilled professional for the job.

Bleaching

To make superfluous hair less noticeable, you can bleach it with a solution of 1 ounce 6 percent hydrogen peroxide and 10 drops ammonia.

Surf casting

Fishing from the beach

In surf casting, you use a spinning reel or a bait-casting reel (often called a squidding reel) and a long, heavy fiberglass rod. The reel should be large enough to hold 150 to 250 yards of 8- to 40-pound-test monofilament line. Ask the tackle dealer the correct size of line and lure to match the rod.

Artificial lures include metal jigs and spoons, plugs, and lengths of surgical tubing shaped like eels. Bait can be crabs, sand shrimp, bloodworms, mussels, or chunks of fish. Ask a local bait shop what works best for the fish you're after. For bait, rig the line with sinkers to resist the surf's pull.

Casting

Hold the rod as shown, with the lure hanging a foot or so below the rod tip. A rig with bait and sinkers may hang almost to the ground. Raise the rod to upright; pivot your body. Near vertical, release the line; stop the rod, catapulting the lure forward; then bring the rod tip almost to horizontal. (For how to operate the reel, see *Bait casting* or *Spin casting*.)

The 2 hours before and after low tide are said to be the best fishing times. At any time, diving birds or surfacing baitfish are signs of large fish feeding on small fish.

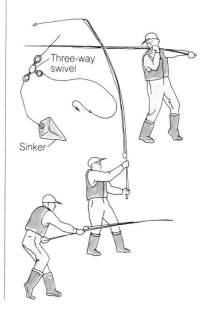

Three-way swivel

Sinker

Survival in wild areas

Stranded; staying alive

When you travel in a wild area, whether on foot or propelled by a motor, be prepared with the three essentials for survival—food, water, and protection from the elements. Carry a kit that includes waterproof matches, emergency rations, a signal mirror, a whistle, a pocket knife, a compass, a candle, first-aid supplies, water-purification tablets, a survival information pamphlet, and 25 feet of light line to secure a lean-to (see *Lean-tos*).

In winter, add a mylar "space blanket" (it can double as a light tarp), a closed-cell foam pad, a collapsible snow shovel, a stove, and fuel (see *Camp stoves*).

If you're stranded

Your chances of being rescued are best if you stay where you are. Keep calm; signal for help (see *Distress signals*). Strike out on your own only after carefully considering the weather, your physical limits, and the probable distance to help.

If you have to spend a night out, find shelter or build a lean-to or snow trench; wait for morning or for better

conditions. Build a fire and sit between it and a rock or wind shelter. To preserve body warmth, stuff dry, fibrous material (leaves, pine needles) between layers of clothing.

Winter survival

In deep snow, scoop out and stomp a trench; roof it over with evergreen branches and packed snow. Protect your clothing from melting snow by lying on the foam pad in the trench. Keep warm with a stove and hot liquids. Wiggle your toes and fingers.

Desert survival

To prevent heatstroke, travel at dawn or at night; rest in the shade during the day. Above all, conserve water. If you run out of it, dig in damp sand (water may seep in) or dig up to 6 feet deep in the lowest point between dunes; if the hole dampens, dig deeper until you strike water. Reedlike desert grass may indicate nearby water. (See also *Backpacking; Campfires; Compasses; Map reading*.)

Sweat soldering pipes

Joining copper pipe

To cut copper pipe with a *tubing cutter,* screw the cutting wheel against the pipe and rotate the cutter, tightening the screw a little for each turn.

To join pipe to a fitting, polish the end of the pipe and the inside of the fitting with steel wool. Apply soldering paste (a noncorrosive flux) to the pipe and fitting; then insert the pipe and turn it to spread the flux. Holding solid-core 50—50 solder to the joint,

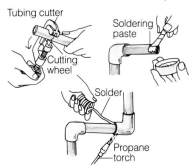

Tubing cutter

Cutting wheel

Soldering paste

Solder

Propane torch

heat the fitting with a propane torch. The solder will be drawn into the joint. Stop when an even bead of solder appears around the joint. (See also *Pipes; Propane torches; Soldering*.)

Swimming

Basic skills; water safety

Learn to swim from a qualified instructor and in shallow water, either in a pool or on a calm, sandy beach.

Stand in chest-deep water; practice submerging your face while holding your breath. Add a bobbing motion: exhale underwater through your nose and mouth, blowing bubbles; then bob up and inhale. Practice seeing underwater by picking up rocks.

Learning basic skills

Rhythmic breathing. Standing in

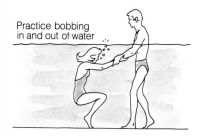

Practice bobbing in and out of water

chest-deep water, lean forward with your face to one side and your ear submerged. Breathe in, turn your head facedown, and exhale through your mouth and nose. Rotate your head sideways again to inhale. Repeat the sequence to the right and to the left to determine the more comfortable side; stay with that side. Practice rhythmic breathing until you do it smoothly.

Prone float. Crouch in chest-deep water so that your shoulders are submerged. Stretch your arms in front of

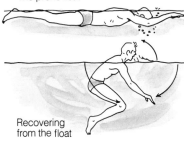

The prone float

Recovering from the float

you. Breathe in deeply, submerge your face, and push off gently from the bottom into the float position. Turn the float into a glide by pushing off from the side of a pool.

Back glide. Crouch in chest-deep water; tilt your head back until your ears are submerged. Push off from the bottom; lift your hips to the surface.

Once you master floating and gliding, combine the prone glide with rhythmic breathing and with the *flutter kick* and arm motions of the crawl stroke (see *Crawl stroke*).

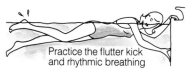

Practice the flutter kick and rhythmic breathing

Water safety

Never swim alone, even in a pool. Swim in supervised areas with a buddy. Watch children at all times. Avoid vigorous swimming for at least 1 hour

S

after eating. Leave the water when you tire; stay out of it during storms.

At a beach, swim parallel and close to shore. If you're caught in a current, swim with it or across it, not against it. If you're exhausted, rest by floating and bobbing, not by treading water. (See also *Back-crawl stroke; Back-stroke; Breaststroke; Diving; Side-stroke; Water rescue.*)

Swollen glands

What they may mean; how to respond

Glands sometimes swell as a side effect of a vaccination or of the use of a drug to treat certain diseases. Usually, though, swollen glands are a symptom of illness or infection. In such instances they are, despite the discomfort, a reassuring sign that the body's defenses are functioning properly.

The glands of the throat often swell during such upper respiratory illnesses as colds or flu; the likelihood is greater if the throat is sore (see *Sore throats*) or the tonsils are involved. More rarely, swollen glands can be a sign of mumps or German measles. If fever and swollen glands persist for a week, the problem may be infectious mononucleosis.

Illness isn't the only possibility. An infected cut or insect bite may cause swollen glands. Whatever the underlying condition, it, not the glands, must be treated. When the condition subsides, the swelling will disappear.

Occasionally a salivary gland in the neck enlarges because its duct is blocked by a chalklike stone. The swelling comes and goes and is not associated with a sore throat. The stone usually comes out by itself.

Swollen glands in the neck, armpit, or groin, usually without pain and possibly with such other symptoms as general weakness, appetite and weight loss, and fever, may be a sign of Hodgkin's disease or another lymphoma. Without fail, bring these symptoms to a doctor's attention. Indeed, anyone with glands that remain swollen for more than a few days or that enlarge or harden, with attendant pain and fever, should see a doctor.

Table repairs

Steadying a wobbly table; leveling a sagging drop leaf

A heavy-duty table may be built with a skirt or apron that reinforces the joints where the legs meet the table-top. An apron may be set into a groove on the underside of the tabletop, screwed directly to the tabletop, or attached with metal clips. If the bond between apron and tabletop becomes wobbly, glue a thin strip of wood or veneer to the apron to make it fit more snugly into its groove; tighten the screws or reposition the clips (they are usually set in a groove on the apron and screwed to the tabletop).

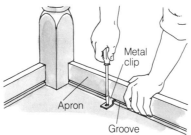

Corners are often reinforced with a wood block or a metal corner plate. If a reinforced joint becomes wobbly, tighten the screws on the wood block or the bolt on the corner plate. If the corners are not reinforced, add your own block or plate. To make a wood block, cut a triangle of hardwood so that the grain runs diagonally across the corner joint, and notch the peak

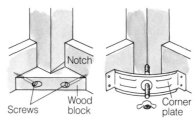

to fit around the table leg. Glue and screw the block to the aprons. Attach a corner plate as shown.

To repair shaky or sagging drop-leaf table extensions, first make sure the hinges are tight. Then, with the drop-leaf support in place, slide a wood shim between the support and the leaf, and plane or sand down the shim until it is just thick enough to keep the leaf level. Glue the wedge in place on the drop-leaf support and let it dry with the leaf up and with a weight on top of the leaf.

Small tables share many of the frailties of chairs and are similarly repaired. (See also *Chair repairs; Cigarette burns; Veneer; Warping.*)

Table tennis

A speedy indoor game

Using a wooden paddle sandwiched by pimpled rubber sheets, serve a hollow plastic ball over a 6-inch-high net that divides a 9- x 5-foot dark-green wooden table, 2½ feet high. Your opponent hits the ball back, you return it to him, and so on.

The table is bordered by a white stripe and dissected lengthwise by another. The room should be large enough to allow for a clearance of 5 feet at each end of the table and 3 feet on each side.

To serve, hold the ball in your palm at table level; toss it up, then strike it with your paddle as it descends. The ball must bounce once on each side of the table before and after it clears the net. (If it brushes the net, serve again.) After 5 points, your opponent serves. A game is 21 points. A 2-point lead breaks a 20-point tie. A match is three out of five games.

You lose the point to your opponent and the *rally* ends if: you fail to strike the ball while serving; your shot is stopped by the net or it goes between a net's end and the post; the ball bounces twice on your side, or strikes

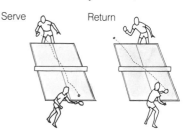

Serve · Return

S

the floor, ceiling, or wall, before you return it; you hit the ball before it bounces; your free hand touches the table or net, or your paddle touches the net; you jar the table while playing; your return misses your opponent's side. You *win* the point if your opponent makes any of these errors.

Tack cloth

A sticky rag for picking up particles when finishing wood

You can buy a tack cloth or make one. Use an 18- to 24-inch square of clean, lint-free cotton, such as finely woven cheesecloth or an old diaper. Hem any raw edges. Saturate the cloth in warm water and wring it out well. Moisten it thoroughly with turpentine. Then sprinkle it with a tablespoon or two of varnish while kneading the fabric to work in the varnish evenly. The cloth should be slightly sticky and yellowish. It should pick up dust but not dampen the surface you are cleaning.

Use a tack cloth just before painting or varnishing to pick up the fine particles you can't get up with a vacuum. As one side fills with dust, refold it to expose a fresh side.

A tack cloth will improve with age and use. Store it in a tightly lidded jar. Two or three times a year, sprinkle it with water and turpentine to restore its stickiness.

Tankless toilets

Repairing a leaking pressure valve; fixing leaking handles

Water flow in a tankless toilet is controlled by a stop valve, a handle, and a pressure valve. The latter can be either a diaphragm or a piston type.

To repair a leaking pressure valve, first shut off the water by closing the stop valve. This valve may be controlled by a small knurled handle or by a screw hidden under a cover nut. To cut off the water supply, turn the knurled handle clockwise or remove the cover nut with a wrench and turn the screw clockwise. Disassemble the pressure valve, lining up the parts so

that you can reassemble them in order. Replace worn parts with new ones from a kit for your model.

Leaking around a handle may be stopped by replacing a worn packing washer. Using a wrench with smooth jaws or with jaws taped, unscrew the retaining nut. Grip the handle assembly with one wrench while unscrewing the packing nut with another. Pry out the packing washer; replace it. If a handle is loose and wobbly or if leaking persists, replace worn inner handle parts with new ones from a kit.

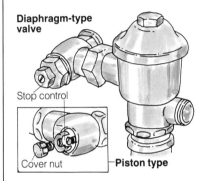
Diaphragm-type valve
Stop control
Cover nut — Piston type

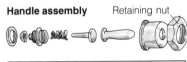
Handle assembly   Retaining nut

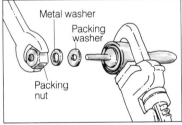
Metal washer
Packing washer
Packing nut

Tapes

Selecting the right adhesive tape for a household job

With a special adhesive tape, you can simplify a task and get better results. Seal food for storage with *freezer tape;* cold strengthens its adhesive power. Wrap packages with *carton-sealing tape,* a thin (usually brown) plastic film, or with *strapping tape,* a clear plastic tape embedded with fiberglass threads. These are stronger than paper tape and don't need wetting.

Tapes for repairs
To mend plastic or a rubberized material, such as a vinyl cushion or a raincoat, select colored *plastic tape* in a matching hue for a less noticeable repair. Similarly, use colored *cloth tape* for such jobs as fixing a ring-binder cover; use heavy-duty clear, plastic tape to seal drafty windows.

When appearance doesn't count, make repairs with *duct tape.* This strong, aluminized cloth tape bonds with nearly any surface and resists heat and moisture. Use it to secure insulation to a pipe, to temporarily fix a cracked window, or to hold boards together for sawing or while glue sets.

For more abrasion resistance, use *aluminum tape.* This noncorroding metal tape conforms easily to curved surfaces; it's perfect for repairing gutters and rainspouts. On a stovepipe, use heat-resistant *flue tape* instead.
Tapes for home-improvement jobs
On a fussy paint job, use *painting tape,* a thin masking tape. It bends more easily along curves than regular masking tape and leaves a neater edge when pulled off. Use a tape roller to attach straight, unwrinkled lengths. On a plumbing job, leak-proof pipe threads by wrapping Teflon *joint-sealing tape* around them (see *Pipes*).

To secure a rug or carpet to the floor, use *carpet tape* that has adhesive on both sides. Stick one side to the floor; then pull off a protective layer and stick the carpeting to the tape. Another double-faced tape, *mounting tape,* lets you attach a picture hook or a towel rack to the wall. This heavy-duty tape forms a strong, long-lasting bond. Its foam backing lets it stick to rough brick and concrete surfaces.

Tarts

Sweet fruit-filled pastries

A tart is a sweetened pastry shell filled with fresh or cooked fruit, usually a pastry cream (custard), and often a glaze. The pastry is easily worked and not as flaky as plain piecrust. To avoid a soaked crust, fill a tart no more than an hour or two before serving.

For a tart shell, work together with your fingertips, an electric mixer, or a food processor ⅓ cup butter, 2 table-spoons sugar, and 2 egg yolks. Grad-ually work in 1¼ cups flour and a pinch of salt. Knead the pastry for about 1 minute; then wrap it in plas-tic and refrigerate it for 1 to 2 hours.

Roll out the dough on a floured cloth or board (see *Piecrust*). Fit it into a 9-inch tart pan, or cut and fit it into six 4-inch tartlet pans. Or, with the dough at room temperature, press it evenly into the pan with your finger-tips. Prick the bottom with a fork. Weight the shell (see *Piecrust*) and bake at 350°F for 20 to 25 minutes (total time), or until golden; cool.

To make pastry cream, beat togeth-er 2 egg yolks and ¼ cup sugar in a saucepan. Stir in 1 tablespoon corn-starch and 1 cup heavy cream. Cook and stir over low heat until smooth and thickened. Lay plastic wrap on the surface to prevent a skin from forming; cool. Stir in 1 teaspoon va-nilla; refrigerate until ready to use.

Fill the pastry shell with the cream and overlap 1 quart strawberries, sliced, on top. To add a glaze, melt ¾ cup red jelly, such as currant or straw-berry. When lukewarm, spoon it even-ly over the fruit; chill.

Other fruits suitable for tarts are sliced fresh peaches, apricots, plums, nectarines, kiwi fruit, banana, pine-apple, or poached pears or apples.

Tea

Different types; the Chinese method of brewing

Teas, like wines, vary in flavor and quality according to where they were grown, when and how the leaves were harvested, and whether or not they've been blended or have additives, such as dried flowers. But the three basic categories are *green*, dried upon har-vesting, which has a delicate flavor; *black*, allowed to ferment before final drying, more robust in flavor; and *oolong*, semifermented, with a char-acter between that of black and green. To preserve flavor, store tea in a tight-ly covered container in a cool place.

For best flavor, brew loose tea leaves in a ceramic or glass teapot. Bring freshly drawn water to a boil. While it's heating, warm the teapot by pour-ing hot water into it. When the water boils, drain the pot, add tea leaves (½ to 1 teaspoon per cup), and fill the pot with water; cover it. Let the tea steep for 3 to 5 minutes, stirring it once. Pour tea into cups. If desired, serve with sugar, honey, lemon, or milk.

Teething

Ages at which teeth appear; symptoms; easing discomfort

Although a few lucky babies produce all their teeth without a single tear, some fret and drool for months before their first tooth even appears.

The drawing indicates the average time of arrival for each of the 20 baby teeth. It's not unusual for teeth to erupt earlier or later than these times.

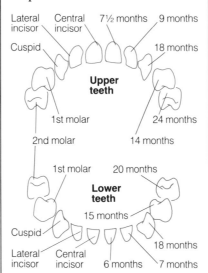

Upper teeth — Lateral incisor, Central incisor, 7½ months, 9 months, Cuspid, 18 months, 1st molar, 24 months, 2nd molar, 14 months

Lower teeth — 1st molar, 20 months, 15 months, Cuspid, Lateral incisor, Central incisor, 6 months, 18 months, 7 months

The symptoms of teething discom-fort include crankiness, a mild fever (up to 101°F), and frequent awaken-ing at night. (However, do not dis-count symptoms of illness, such as high fever or excessive crying, be-cause a baby is teething.) If your baby will not go back to sleep easily at night, a drink of water or milk may help. But try not to let these nighttime feedings become a habit. Talk to your pediatrician about any severe or per-sistent discomfort. To reduce irrita-tion, some doctors recommend rub-bing on the gums a little antiseptic that contains a pain reliever.

Teething makes most babies want to chew; they put whatever they can find in their mouths. Chewing may actually help the teeth come through or relieve teething irritation. Offer your baby a chilled teething ring to suck, a clean washcloth soaked in cold water and wrung out, or soft, washable toys. Keep sharp or small, swallowable objects out of reach.

Telephone answerers

Installing a machine to record incoming calls

A telephone answering machine to re-cord incoming calls during your ab-sence contains two cassette tapes: one for your prerecorded message, the other for the incoming calls. When someone telephones you, your mes-sage plays. This cassette then shuts off and, after a beep, the second cas-sette switches on to record the caller's message. Some models have a re-mote-message-retrieval device, which enables you, with the aid of an elec-tronic beeper, to hear the messages when you dial your phone number from anywhere in the world.

Before installation, give the phone company your answering machine's FCC registration number and ringer equivalency (usually on the bottom of the machine). Insert the three-prong plug of your machine's power cord into an electric receptacle; unplug your telephone cord from the modular outlet (jack) and plug in the ma-chine's cord. If you have a nonmodu-lar jack, buy a converter from your phone company's service center; in-stall it according to instructions. (See also *Telephones*.)

Telephones

Buying phones; adding an extension; troubleshooting

When you buy a telephone from a phone company or from a retail store, make sure that it's compatible with your telephone service and that it has a warranty. At the store, dial some numbers to check the tone quality.

Before installation, report the telephone's FCC registration number and ringer equivalency number to the phone company.

You'll need a *modular jack* to plug in the new phone. For an old, hard-wired junction box, buy a converter to change it to a modular jack. For a non-

Modular jack

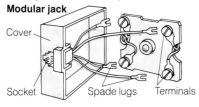

Cover · Socket · Spade lugs · Terminals

modular jack in a room, buy a *four-prong adapter*. To install either device, follow the package directions. For two phones, buy a *duplex jack*.

Wiring for new extensions

Install and wire modular jacks where you want new phones. Connect the four colored station wires (in plastic cable), running from each modular jack, to the color-coded terminals in the *wiring box*. This box connects to a

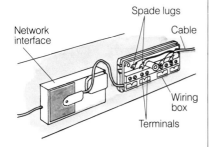

Spade lugs · Cable · Network interface · Wiring box · Terminals

standard network interface (usually in the basement), where the phone company's wiring meets yours.

You can install one additional extension by using a duplex modular jack connected directly to the interface. In one duplex socket, plug the modular-line cord of a phone; in the other, plug an extension cord, the other end of which plugs into a duplex modular jack in a neighboring room.

In either method, you will need to fasten all wiring *before* connecting it to any live phone cable. Staple it around door or window frames and along baseboards if it's permitted by your local fire code. Or, if the electrical code permits, hide it by routing it behind baseboards, between walls, and inside cabinets and closets. You'll need a screwdriver, utility knife, sta-

pler, pliers, hammer, and (if you are going through partitions) an electric drill (see *Drilling*).

Caution: While wiring, take the receiver off the cradle so that the phone won't ring. Use tools with insulated handles. Don't wire during a thunderstorm.

Troubleshooting problems

When you have phone trouble, disconnect the wiring box from the standard network interface. Connect a test phone to the interface. If the telephone works, the problem lies with your phones or station wiring and not with the phone company equipment. If the test phone doesn't function in the interface, have the phone company make the necessary repairs.

If the phone problem is your responsibility, unplug all the phones from their modular jacks, then plug them in one by one. If one doesn't work, its modular cord may be defective. Plug a known working cord into the phone and the jack. If the phone is still inoperative, try a working phone in the same jack. If the test phone works, the other phone is defective; take it to a phone center or retailer.

If the test phone doesn't work, remove the jack cover to see whether any wires have slipped from their slots and are touching; if so, carefully reinsert them in their slots and replace the jack cover. If you don't find the wires dislodged, the problem is probably in the station wires.

Check for defective wiring by investigating the plastic-sheathed cable that runs from the nonfunctioning jack. If you find a section that's bare, broken, or grounded (a bare wire touching a pipe), get rid of the cable; rewire with new cable.

Telephone solicitations

Getting them off your line

People who try to sell you something over the telephone picked your number from a phone directory or from a mailing list; or your number was dialed by machine or by the seller in sequence (555-2223, 555-2224, etc.).

Changing to an unlisted number (a minimum fee in most states) will af-

ford a partial solution. Another approach is to promptly respond "No, thanks" and to request being taken off the list. More effective may be writing a complaint letter to the president of the company.

For information about having your phone number removed from national sales lists, write to Telephone Preference Service, c/o Direct Marketing Association, P.O. Box 9014, Farmingdale, NY 11735.

Television antennas

Installing an outdoor antenna

You need separate antennas to pick up VHF and UHF telecasts, but combination antennas are available. Some also pick up FM radio broadcasts. (See also *Radio antennas*.)

Antennas are categorized by *mileage range* or *gain*. Mileage range indicates how distant a signal an antenna can pull in. Gain is the ability of an antenna to increase the strength of an incoming signal. The mileage range and gain of an antenna are accurate only for one set. If you have more than one, you'll need a stronger antenna.

Direction is another factor. In urban areas, where signals are strong and plentiful, a highly directional, moderate-gain antenna works best. Otherwise, the antenna may be bombarded with unwanted signals. In remote areas, where signals are weak and fewer in number, you'll need a moderately directional, high-gain antenna. If any channels are weak or if the antenna wire will be more than 100 feet long, boost the signal with an *amplifier*. Ask your dealer for help in selecting the best antenna for your area.

Caution: Installing an antenna near power lines is dangerous. If any part of the antenna assembly or a ladder touches a power line, you could be killed. The distance between the antenna and the nearest power line should be equal to at least twice the length of the full antenna and mast. Install an antenna on a calm day.

An antenna can go on the chimney, eaves, or roof, out of the way of trees, power lines, and obstructions. A 10-foot, 16-gauge mast usually suffices;

however, if you live in a hilly area or far from the transmitting signal, you may need a taller mast.

Follow the manufacturer's instructions for mounting the antenna, then turn the antenna until you get the best signal. If signals come from different directions, consider installing a rotor motor to rotate the antenna to different positions as needed.

Any antenna more than 10 feet above its top mounting bracket needs support; add three steel-cable guy wires. Secure them to the antenna and to screw eyes or to bolts and washers screwed into the roof. Then flash the roof (see *Flashings*) and seal it with roof cement. Have a professional install a mast more than 20 feet long.

After mounting the unit, run coaxial cable or 300-ohm wire between the antenna and the television set. Take the shortest route possible, but avoid electric wires—they are hazardous and interfere with reception.

Let the antenna wire hang down the side of the house. Install 4-inch standoffs (large screw eyes) into the siding every 1½ to 2 feet along the wire's path. If the wire runs around a metal gutter, don't let the wire touch it; make a small loop over the gutter, and use a standoff to hold it.

Calculate the location of the television set in relation to the outside wall.

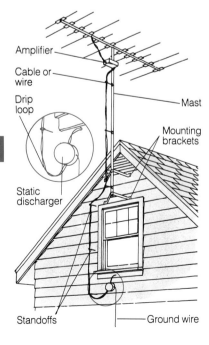

Amplifier

Cable or wire

Drip loop

Mast

Mounting brackets

Static discharger

Standoffs

Ground wire

Drill through the wall with a long ⅜-inch bit for 300-ohm wire or with a long ¼-inch bit for coaxial cable.

Work the wire through the wall with a fish tape or a straightened wire coat hanger. Leave enough wire for a *drip loop*, which prevents water from running into the wall along the wire. Connect the wire to the antenna screws on the television set. If you are using the antenna for more than one frequency (UHF, VHF, and FM radio), connect the antenna wire to a *signal splitter* and connect the terminals of

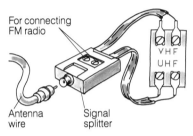

For connecting FM radio

VHF

UHF

Antenna wire

Signal splitter

the splitter to the appropriate UHF, VHF, and FM antenna screws on your equipment. Caulk the hole in the wall.

To protect against lightning, install a static discharger, following the manufacturer's instructions. Then clamp a copper wire to the mast, run it down through the standoffs with the antenna wire, and ground it.

Television sets

Cleaning the tuner and the picture-tube face; getting a better picture

Caution: Don't remove a set's back cover or make internal repairs. Don't block the cabinet's ventilation slots or place the set near a heat source, a computer, or an appliance driven by a series-induction motor (fan, aquarium). Damage to the set's cabinet could result in shock hazard; have it examined by a professional.

The only maintenance that an owner should perform on a set is cleaning the tuner and the face of the picture tube. If the picture is constantly grainy, try this: jiggle the tuner knob. If the picture clears, unplug the set; remove the channel selector knob. Spray tuner cleaner (available at electronics supply stores) through the opening. Replace the knob. The pic-

ture may be distorted for about half an hour afterward.

Let the set cool before cleaning the face of the picture tube. Spray the face with a commercial window-cleaning formula; wipe it with a soft cloth.

Depending on the model, there may be many or a few adjustment knobs and screws on the front and rear panels of a television set. Most are for correcting picture problems and should be used as instructed in the owner's manual. Allow the set to warm up before making adjustments.

Reception problems that defy correction by control knobs may be solved by installing a new antenna or by properly adjusting your old antenna (see *Television antennas*).

Temperature

Using basal temperature to tell when you might conceive

Slight temperature fluctuations may signal ovulation. You'll need a special *basal* body-temperature thermometer to show your temperature precisely. (For temperature taking to detect illness, see *Fever*.)

Temperature changes reflect the cycle: a sudden *drop* at the time of ovulation; a rapid *rise* for 1 to 3 days thereafter; a plateau .5°F to 1°F above the preovulation level until the next menstrual flow starts. Conception is likeliest at ovulation, just prior to the sharp rise in basal body temperature.

To get an accurate picture of your cycle, record your basal body temperature daily for 6 months. Make a graph-paper chart ranging from 97°F to 100°F with five squares between numbers, each square representing .2°F. Take your temperature immediately upon awakening; record it on your graph as a dot.

Tempura

A Japanese dish of fried seafood and vegetables

For batter to coat 1 pound each of shrimp or other seafood and vegetables, lightly beat 2 egg yolks in a bowl;

T

stir in 1 cup each flat beer and flour (rice or all-purpose), and 1 teaspoon salt. The batter should be slightly lumpy. Let it stand for 1 to 2 hours at room temperature or for several hours in the refrigerator. (For extralight batter, fold in 2 stiffly beaten egg whites just before coating the food.)

Shell and devein shrimp but leave the tails intact; cut fish in strips. Leave green beans or okra whole. Cut other vegetables, such as sweet potatoes, peppers, eggplant, zucchini, or carrots, in thin slices or strips. Heat 3 inches of oil in a deep skillet (see *Frying*). One by one, dip the pieces of food in batter, drain the excess, and drop the food into the hot oil. Fry until golden, about $1\frac{1}{2}$ minutes. Drain well.

Serve tempura hot with this sauce: $\frac{3}{4}$ cup chicken or fish stock, $\frac{1}{4}$ cup each soy sauce and sweet sherry, 1 tablespoon grated radish, and 1 teaspoon grated ginger. Add a small amount of horseradish, if desired.

Tennis rackets

Selecting a racket that will be a love match

For the best selection and advice, buy a racket from a tennis facility's pro shop or from a tennis specialty shop. If you play regularly, consider buying a championship-quality racket. The most important factors in choosing a racket are grip size and weight, then head size and composition. Make your choice on the basis of feel. Find a shop with a large supply of test rackets that you can try on a court. Hit with a few you think you'll like; buy the one that feels most comfortable.

The grip circumference of adult rackets ranges from $4\frac{1}{4}$ to $4\frac{3}{4}$ inches. An average size for a woman is $4\frac{3}{8}$ inches; men usually find $4\frac{5}{8}$ inches comfortable. Junior rackets with 4-inch grips are available for young children. Check the side of a racket for the grip size or grip-size number (a 2 racket has a $4\frac{2}{8}$-inch grip; a 3, a $4\frac{3}{8}$-inch grip; a 4, a $4\frac{4}{8}$-inch grip).

The letters L (light), M (medium), or H (heavy) next to the grip size indicate a racket's weight. A light racket is easier on the arm and more maneuverable, especially for a beginner. The larger head size of many of today's rackets makes it easier to hit the ball on the strings and adds power to a well-hit ball. If you tend to hit the ball on the frame or miss it frequently, an oversize racket may be right for you. Buy a midsize racket if you want greater power and hitting area than a standard-size racket offers, but without the bulk of the oversize.

Racket frames made of aluminum, graphite, or a mixture of fiberglass and graphite last much longer than wood frames and will not warp. Aluminum frames, sometimes painted black to give them an expensive graphite look, are the best buy.

The cost of a quality tennis racket seldom includes string. Synthetic gut costs half as much as natural and rivals the latter's playability. Have the shop string your racket within the tension recommendations printed on the side of the frame—tighter for more control, looser for more power.

Tents

Maintenance; site selection; pitching

If you've just purchased or rented a tent (see *Backpacking* for selection information), or haven't used your old one for a while, set up the tent at least once before leaving home; inspect it for defects or damage. This is a good time to use sealant on the seams, which can leak even in a thoroughly waterproofed tent. Apply it to both sides of each seam and allow plenty of drying time to eliminate odor.

You can patch holes with 2-inch ripstop nylon tape. Press a patch firmly over the puncture or tear on the side that has waterproof coating. If grommets are missing or loose, replace them (see *Grommets*). It's a good idea to take ripstop tape and seam sealant on your trip to fix leaks that may develop. Also, for rubbing on small leaks where a hole isn't visible, pack a candle, beeswax, or a chapstick.

Site selection and pitching

Choose a level strip of bare ground. Clear the site of sharp material—rocks and sticks—that could puncture the floor. Avoid ground with many bumps or depressions; these can place undue stress on parts of the tent. Pitch a tent tautly enough so that rainwater can't form puddles in the roof but not so tight as to strain the fabric and stitching.

If you're camping on bare rock and can't sink your tent stakes into the ground, collect small boulders and tie the tent lines around them.

Taking good care of a tent

To prevent punctures, keep the tent floor swept clean and put corrugated cardboard under cot legs. Don't wear shoes inside. Store citrus juices outside; acids are damaging to waterproofing. Cook in a tent only if it has an exhaust vent and a zippered cookhole for placing the stove on bare ground.

Before storing a tent, set it up to dry thoroughly; sweep out debris. Wash a tent only if the manufacturer recommends it; follow instructions. Allow the tent to dry in the sun, or hang it indoors by its suspension points.

Termites

What to do when this pest invades your home

Of the more than 40 species of termites in North America, the $\frac{1}{4}$-inch subterraneans are the most destructive. From their underground colonies, they gain access to structural wood through beams that touch the soil, cracks in concrete slabs, and masonry or concrete-block footings.

Because the workers eat the softer interior parts of wooden beams, they leave no visible trace of damage. Damage is not rapid; however, if left undisturbed for several years, termites will destroy large areas of wood.

Reproductives are dark brown and have four transparent wings of equal

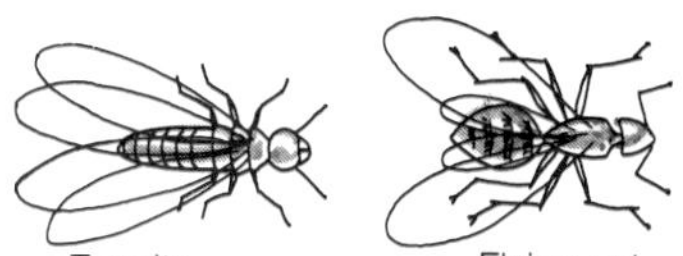

Enlarged

length (flying ants have paired wings of unequal length). Workers and soldiers are yellow or grayish white and wingless. In spring reproductives fly from their settled colonies to establish new ones. They shed their wings and dig a hole in or near a beam that is in contact with the soil. Piles of shed wings indicate multiplying colonies.

A sure sign of infestation is a mudshelter tunnel that leads across a concrete foundation to woodwork. Badly eaten beams may sound hollow when rapped. A pointed tool, such as an awl, sinks easily into the wood.

Controlling an infestation involves special equipment and the use of residual pesticides only permitted to licensed applicators. If you suspect a termite infestation, contact a termite exterminator of good standing to inspect and, if necessary, treat your house foundations.

In a new house, minimize a possible infestation by installing a properly constructed metal termite shield between footings and wooden foundation. Make sure that the woodwork is at least 6 inches above finished grade level. Separate wooden decks, porches, and steps from the house by a 2-inch gap and raise them at least 2 inches above ground.

Terrariums

Making an enclosed garden in a bottle, jar, or fish tank

A properly made terrarium, in which air and water are continuously recycled, can go for months without care.

Use an apothecary jar, untinted jam jar, decanter, brandy snifter, drinking-fountain bottle, fish tank, or the like that can be fitted with a lid. For a small-mouthed container, buy tongs and other long-handled terrarium tools, or make your own by wiring small utensils to dowels.

Sharp blade for pruning

Spoon for digging and planting

Sponge for cleaning glass

Thimble for tamping soil

Clean and sterilize the container. Then, using a funnel if necessary, put a 1- to 2-inch layer of mixed pebbles and charcoal chips on the bottom and cover with 1 to 3 inches of sterilized potting mix—not too much, just enough to anchor plant roots.

Plan the landscape before planting; choose slow-growing plants of similar size and needs. For ground covers, use moss or small creepers, such as button ferns and the small-leaved fig, *Ficus pumilla;* for shrubs, use compact plants like peperomias and marantas; for treelike focal points, use gold-dust dracaenas and other upright species. Add grace to the landscape with maidenhair ferns.

To plant, dig a small hole, then take a plant from its container and shake excess soil from the roots. Position and spread the roots carefully; cover with a thin layer of soil. Moisten slightly with a bulb sprayer.

Put the finished terrarium in a bright but not sunny spot and leave it uncovered for a day; then cover it. A little moisture should collect on the walls or lid from time to time, then drip down as "rain." To adjust the terrarium's atmosphere, open the lid or add a little water.

Thawing food

Normal and quick methods

The best way to thaw any food is in the refrigerator in its original wrapper. Allow 8 to 9 hours per pound for meat and 3 to 4 hours per pound for poultry. A 1-pound package of fruit takes 6 to 8 hours. Use thawed food as soon as possible; except for baked goods, do not refreeze it. Vegetables should be cooked while still frozen.

To thaw meat, fish, or poultry more quickly, submerse it, still wrapped, in cold water. This method takes about one-eighth the refrigerator time.

For even more rapid thawing, place unwrapped poultry in a microwave oven set on *Defrost* or *Low.* Allow 8 to 10 minutes per pound; turn the bird twice during the thawing period. Let it rest for 10 minutes before cooking.

To fast thaw a turkey in a conventional oven, unwrap it, place it in a shallow pan, and heat it at 325°F for about 3 hours. Remove the giblets and neck from the cavities. Season or stuff the turkey; roast it immediately.

Some foods can be thawed safely at room temperature. Fruit thaws in 2 to 4 hours, bread in 3 to 4 hours, cake and sandwiches in 2 to 4 hours.

Thermometers

Installing for the best reading

There are three basic types of weather thermometers: indoor, outdoor, and combined indoor-outdoor. To get accurate readings from an outdoor thermometer, locate it out of direct sunlight, and away from the heat (or coolness) coming from the house. Install an indoor thermometer on an inside wall away from drafts or heat sources.

Indoor-outdoor thermometers generally consist of two thermometers on one base. Connected to the outdoor thermometer is a thin capillary extension tube with a bulb at the end. Install the thermometer on the frame of an airtight window, passing the tube under the window sash and positioning the bulb in a shaded area outdoors where it does not touch any part of the building. Don't expose more than a foot of the tube, and take care not to kink it—kinking can restrict the flow of the liquid inside, resulting in inaccurate readings.

Thermostat recalibrating

When a house heats or cools much above or below setting

Thermostats are designed so that room temperature drops 1°F to 2°F below the setting before the thermostat clicks on. It clicks off before room temperature reaches the setting —but the system continues to deliver heat.

Thermostat models vary widely, and so do recalibration techniques. Refer to the owner's manual for your model. Here's how to recalibrate two common models — one with snap-together magnetic contacts and a calibration screw, the other a round model with a mercury switch. Except for those controlling some electric heaters, thermostats operate on low voltage and there's no danger of shock.

Models with calibration screw

To remove the thermostat cover, unscrew a screw at the top or snap or lift off the cover. Set the thermostat to room temperature. Hold the dial shaft with a wrench and use an insulated screwdriver to turn the calibration screw clockwise or counterclockwise until the contacts stay open when you withdraw the screwdriver. Then turn

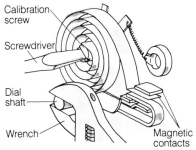

the screw in the opposite direction until the contacts snap shut.

Mercury-switch models

In this type, a drop of mercury in a tube shifts from one side to the other, switching the heating system on or off. Before recalibrating, check that the thermostat is level and not subject to undue heat.

You will need a thin calibration wrench from the manufacturer. Pull off the cover; set the thermostat setting pointer to a few degrees above room temperature. Slip the wrench onto the nut behind the coiled bime-

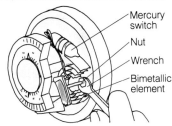

tallic element, hold the dial firmly, and turn the wrench until the mercury shifts. (The direction you turn the nut varies among models.) Next, set the thermostat pointer to a low setting, wait 10 minutes, then slowly turn the dial until the pointer reads the same as the room temperature pointer. Now hold the dial firmly and turn the nut until the mercury slides to the heating contact end of the tube.

Thermostats in cars

Replacing the control of a water-cooled system

If a car's thermostat sticks closed, it can cause overheating in a few miles of driving. If it sticks open, the heater may operate poorly.

Usually the thermostat is housed at the engine end of the upper radiator hose. On some GM four-cylinder cars, it's in a steel housing with a twist-off cap. On water-cooled VW's, it's on the water pump, which is low on the front of the engine.

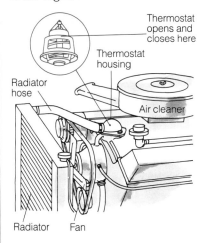

Remove the GM cap and pull out the thermostat by its handle. On other cars, drain the radiator (see *Antifreeze*); unbolt and lift up the housing, noting the thermostat's position for reassembly. On many Ford front-drive cars, you must first make alignment marks on the housing for the thermostat's tabs. Then turn the thermostat counterclockwise and lift it.

At room temperature, the thermostat valve should be completely closed; hold it up to the light to check. Suspend the thermostat and a radiator thermometer in a pot of water so that they do not touch bottom; heat it on a stove. The thermostat should begin to open at the temperature stamped on it (plus or minus 10°F), and should open fully when the water boils.

If it doesn't, replace it with a thermostat with the temperature rating your car requires. Stuff the engine hole with a rag while scraping away

old gasket residue. Apply pliable gasket sealer to the housing, then lay a new gasket on it.

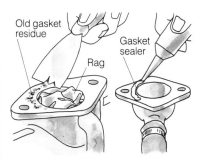

On a Ford front-drive car, turn the thermostat clockwise until its tabs align with the marks you made. If a thermostat has a rubber O-ring, be sure it seats in its groove. On the GM type, push the handle to seat it, then install the cap. On other cars, install the housing and tighten its bolts. Refill the radiator.

Three-way switches

Testing and replacing them

Three-way switches are used in pairs to control one fixture from two locations. If a fixture doesn't light when a switch is on, look for and replace a burned-out light bulb. If that's not the problem, check the fuse box or circuit breaker panel; replace a blown fuse or reset a tripped circuit breaker as needed (see *Circuit breakers; Fuse boxes*). If the fixture still fails to light, test both switches.

Caution: Before working on a switch, turn off the power to the circuit at the fuse box or circuit breaker panel. To make sure the power is off, unscrew the cover plate and mounting screws; pull out the switch without disconnecting the wires. Touch one probe of a neon test lamp to the box's metal shell; touch the other probe to each of the switch's three terminal screws in turn. If the lamp lights, the power has not been turned off. (See also Electric switches.)

A three-way switch has a dark-colored common terminal and two brass *traveler* terminals. Mark the wire connected to the common terminal with masking tape. Disconnect the three wires attached to the switch. Connect the alligator clip of a conti-

389

nuity tester to the common terminal, and the probe to one of the traveler terminals. Flip the toggle up and down a few times. The tester should light only at one position of the toggle. (Three-way-switch toggles don't have *On* and *Off* markings.) Repeat the test with the probe at the other traveler terminal; the tester should light at the opposite position only.

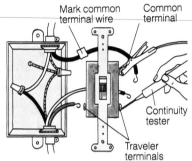

Mark common terminal wire

Common terminal

Continuity tester

Traveler terminals

If the switch passes both tests, reconnect it and test the second switch in the same way. To replace a defective switch, connect the marked wire to the common terminal of the new switch, and the other wires to the brass terminals. Screw the switch to the box; remount the cover plate.

Thrips

A tenacious garden pest

These tiny insects, of which there are 600 species in North America, feed on vegetable leaves (especially onions) and on flowers, such as daylilies, gladioli, roses, and peonies. They cause leaves or flowers to turn silvery and, eventually, brown and dry. You may be able to spot them on plants as tiny, moving, elongated specks.

Thrips often feed between tightly packed leaves and are, therefore, hard to eliminate entirely, even with pesticides. Spraying with malathion at 1- to 2-week intervals may help control their numbers.

If your garden has been seriously hit by thrips, protect future crops by quickly removing and destroying infested blooms and foliage. Weed regularly; weeds act as intermediate hosts for thrips. Don't plant flowers or onions in an area that was infested the year before. (See also *Pesticides*.)

Ticks

Removing one; precautions

Ticks lie in wait on shrubs, grass, and weeds in fields, forests, and lawns. When a human or an animal brushes a tick's perch, it latches on, seeks skin, and sucks the victim's blood. Adult ticks are $1/16$ to $1/4$ inch long; those that carry Lyme disease are smaller than a pinhead. After a full meal, a tick's size may triple.

Remove an imbedded tick with fine-point tweezers. Grasp the tick as close to your skin as possible and pull it straight out. Don't twist the tweezers, but you may have to wiggle them slightly to get the tick to release its hold. Immediately after extraction, wash the bite and your hands and swab the area with antiseptic. Flush the tick down the toilet or immerse it in rubbing alcohol. If you suspect the tick might be a carrier of Lyme disease, save it in a jar of alcohol to show your doctor. If the head remains imbedded, seek medical attention.

When walking in tick country, wear long pants, long sleeves, and tick repellent. Tuck your pants into your socks. Upon returning home, check your clothing, body, and hair carefully. Take a shower and wash your clothing. In season check a cat or dog daily for ticks. Spray your pet's sleeping area and all nearby cracks and crevices with a pesticide labeled for tick control (see *Pesticides*). First make sure that the label says the substance is safe for pets. Wash the pet's bedding and dry it on high heat.

Ticks can carry other diseases, such as Rocky Mountain spotted fever. Both it and Lyme disease often begin with flulike symptoms (high fever, headache, muscle aches, nausea) and a rash. If you have such symptoms, see your doctor immediately.

Tic-tac-toe

The most uncomplicated paper and pencil game of all

Draw a grid with nine boxes, using two horizontal lines and two vertical

lines. The first player marks an X in one of the boxes, and player two marks an O in another. They continue alternating turns until one gets three of his or her marks in a row across the grid either horizontally, vertically, or diagonally. With this accomplished, the winner calls, "Tic-tac-toe!" and draws a line through the winning trio of X's or O's.

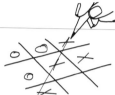

The player going first has the advantage. Hence, players should alternate leading off.

Tiebacks

Tailored or ruffled bands to hold curtains or draperies open

First determine the placement and length of your tiebacks by wrapping a tape measure around one curtain or drapery panel; hold it in place with a thumbtack. Try it tighter and looser and at different levels. When satisfied with the look, insert a cup hook into the window frame or wall on each side of the window, where the tiebacks will

Screw cup hook into wall on both sides

be held. Cut two strips of fabric the length indicated by the tape measure (usually between 20 and 36 inches) and from 3 to 8 inches wide, plus $5/8$ inch all around for seam allowances.

To make tailored tiebacks, fold each strip of fabric in half lengthwise, right sides together, and stitch a $5/8$-inch seam along the length and across one end. Trim away half the seam allowances and trim diagonally across the corners. Turn the band right side out. Turn under the seam allowances at

T

the open end and slipstitch them closed (see *Slipstitching*). Press the band flat. Center a plastic or metal ring at each end; sew it in place.

To sew tiebacks with headed ruffles, first make tailored tiebacks 1½ inches wide. For ruffles, cut fabric strips two to three times the tieback length (the sheerer the fabric the more fullness needed) and 4 to 7 inches wide plus ½ inch all around for hems.

Stitch ¼ inch from each edge. Fold the fabric under along these stitches, then fold again the same amount. Topstitch or slipstitch along the folds.

Place gathering stitches (seven to eight stitches per inch on the machine) 1 to 2 inches from the top edge of the ruffle; place a second row of stitches ¼ inch from the first. Draw up the fabric on these stitches until the ruffle fits the band. Distribute the gathers evenly; topstitch the ruffle to the center of the band. Attach rings.

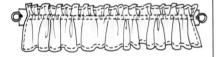

Tie-dyeing

Creating patterns on fabric

The effects of tie-dyeing are created by tightly tying, knotting, or sewing fabric in strategic places, then dyeing it. The tied areas remain untouched while the rest of the fabric absorbs the dye.

Lightweight fabrics of cotton, silk, or linen are best for tie-dyeing; avoid synthetics and blends. For tying, use any kind of string or thread, elastic bands, or pipe cleaners. Natural, cold-water, or hot-water dyes are suitable (see *Dyeing fabric and yarn; Dyes*).

Basic techniques
Wash your fabric first and iron it. Prepare the fabric for dyeing. For a marbled effect, crumple it into a ball; wind string around it in all directions. For a striped effect, iron equal accordion pleats; tie them with thin string at

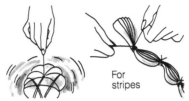

For marbled effect

For stripes

equal intervals. To dye a second color, undo and retie the bindings in different places.

Immerse your fabric in the dye and stir it for the amount of time indicated by the manufacturer. Rinse the fabric until the water runs clear. Remove bindings, knots, or stitches. Unfold the fabric; iron it while still damp.

Making a "sunburst" scarf
Start with a square of light-yellow fabric with hemmed edges. Pick up a point of cloth in the center and tie it. Smooth the fabric into a closed umbrella shape, then tie the rest of the fabric at equal intervals. Dye the fabric orange; rinse it. Tie between the first bindings, then color the fabric in red dye; rinse it; remove the ties. You should have a red, yellow, and orange pattern like a resplendent sun.

Form point in center

1st dye bath

2nd dye bath

Tile regrouting

Freshening a tile surface

In time, the grout between tiles may become mildewed or soiled or may crumble, allowing water to penetrate. Using a sharp-bladed tool, such as an awl or an old, thin chisel or screwdriver, scrape out loose and marred grout. It's not necessary to get out all the old grout; just make sure that what's left is clean and solid. Wipe off the powdery residue with a cloth. Mix fresh grout as specified on the container (it

comes as a powder you mix with water) and apply it over the scraped areas with a rubber squeegee or with your fingers. Wipe grout from the tiles with a damp sponge. Let the grout dry for at least 12 hours; then polish with a piece of clean, dry burlap. (See also *Ceramic tile*.)

Tipping

Guidelines for fair tipping

At restaurants, tip 15 to 20 percent of the before-tax bill, depending on the amount and quality of the service. The rule of thumb is that your waiter gets 15 percent and the headwaiter or captain, 5 percent. If the headwaiter does a special favor, such as reserving a particular table, tip at least $5. Coat checkers get at least 50 cents per coat.

Hotels
For doormen: signaling a parked cab or opening a cab door, no tip; parking your car and carrying your bags into the lobby, $1; braving blizzards or hurricanes to find a scarce cab, 50 cents to $1.

For bellboys: carrying luggage to your room, $1 (more for several bags). You may carry your bags to the lobby when you leave and avoid tipping.

For maids, $1 per room per night. Tip any employee (except the manager) 50 cents for a special errand.

Taxis
Tip cab drivers 15 to 20 percent of the total fare.

Hairdressers and barbers
Tip 15 to 20 percent of the total before-tax bill. If several people have worked on you, ask the owner or main attendant to divide your tip equitably. You don't have to tip the owner.

Planes
Tip skycaps 35 cents to 50 cents per bag for carrying your luggage from the curb to the check-in counter.

Tire changing

How to change a flat

Check the pressure of your spare tire whenever you check your tires. Carry a complete jack assembly, a large ⅜-

T

to ½-inch thick board, and a strong pipe 2 to 3 feet long that fits over the end of the lug wrench.

If a tire goes flat while you're driving, pull off the road at a safe, level spot. (If you can't, call for service.) Turn on the emergency flashers, get the passengers out, put the transmission in *Park* (a manual transmission in reverse), and turn off the ignition. Chock the wheel diagonally opposite to the flat with a large rock.

Take out the jack, pipe, wrench, and spare tire. Pry off the wheel cover with the flat end of the wrench handle. Loosen the wheel nuts with one turn of the wrench.

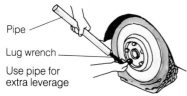

Pipe

Lug wrench

Use pipe for extra leverage

Unless you are on concrete, place the board under the jack, engage the jacking point on the car (see your owner's manual), and check that the jack sits flat under it. Jack until the wheel is 2 to 3 inches off the ground.

Finish removing the nuts (place them in the wheel cover), slide off the wheel, and mount the spare. The wheel must sit flat on its mount. Thread on the nuts finger-tight.

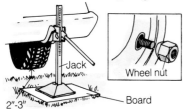

Jack

Wheel nut

2"–3"

Board

Lower the car; remove the jack. Then, using a crisscross pattern, tighten the nuts in stages with the wrench. Tap the wheel cover into place with the heel of your hand. Remove the wheel chock.

Tires

Checking pressure and tread

Check tires every month, not only for correct pressure but for irregular wear. Tire pressure drops when the temperature takes a big drop; check tires often in winter. Check pressure only when the car has not been used for 4 hours or more. If it is low, drive slowly to the nearest service station and add air. Use your tire gauge to re-check pressure; air-tower gauges are generally inaccurate.

Checking for wear

To check the tread depth, stick a penny into the tire groove, head first. If you can see the top of Lincoln's head above the tread rubber, it is less than $1/16$ inch deep, effectively bald. On most tires, also look for wear bars across the tread. If they appear, the tread is down to $1/16$ inch.

Rear tires should wear down evenly. Front tires may wear slightly more at the edges (shoulders) than at the center. If you corner hard, front shoulder wear increases.

If the front tires are worn more toward one side (as opposed to the normal extra wear in the shoulders), have the wheels realigned. Rear tires on front-drive cars may develop wear patterns similar to front tires. If so, rear wheels can often be realigned.

If front-tire wear is spotty, have the tires balanced and the suspension checked for looseness. Large flat spots on the tread may be caused by hard braking in combination with worn shock absorbers. Flat spots can also be caused by grabbing brakes.

Bubbles or waviness in the sidewalls and waviness in the tread indicate internal damage. Such tires must be replaced at once.

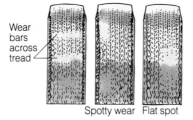

Wear bars across tread

Spotty wear   Flat spot

Toasters

Testing and repairing

After repairing and reassembling a toaster, test it for ground before plugging it in. Press down the lift lever until the carriage locks. Attach the alligator clip of a continuity tester to one

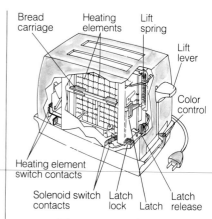

Bread carriage   Heating elements   Lift spring

Lift lever

Color control

Heating element switch contacts

Solenoid switch contacts   Latch lock   Latch   Latch release

prong of the power-cord plug; attach the tester probe to the toaster's shell. The tester should not light. Repeat the test on the other prong. If the tester lights at all, disassemble the toaster again. Check for loose or frayed wiring; bend bread guides away from heating elements. Take the toaster to a repair shop if the problem persists.

Caution: Unplug a toaster before cleaning or working on it. If the internal parts are welded or riveted in place, have a professional service it.

If a toaster fails to heat in a working receptacle, unplug it and gently pry off the knobs from the color-control and the lift levers. Unscrew the screws holding the end plates (if any) and the metal shell. Remove the end plates and lift the shell off the chassis.

Tighten any loose connections between the power-cord leads and the switch terminals. If the connections aren't the problem, free the leads from the terminals; test the cord with a continuity tester (see *Power cords*). Replace a faulty cord with a duplicate.

If the cord is all right, use a small brush or a fine emery board to clean the heating-element switch contacts. Lower the lift lever until the carriage locks; if the contact points don't meet, carefully align the contact arms with needle-nose pliers. If the problem persists, have the toaster repaired professionally, or replace it.

Faulty bread-carriage operation

If the bread carriage doesn't rise or stay down, examine the latch, latch lock, and latch release. Brush off dirt; straighten bent parts with needle-nose pliers. Lubricate the lock and release with powdered graphite. In a

T

toaster with a solenoid, make sure the solenoid switch contacts are clean and aligned. Check the lift spring, if any; slip it back into its seat, or replace it if it's broken or damaged.

Toasts

Paying homage with a short speech and a tinkle of glasses

Informal or formal toasting lends an air of festivity to any celebratory dinner and is a way of honoring people on special occasions. Informal toasting may occur at the beginning of the meal just after the wine has been poured. Everyone raises his or her glass at the same time, and says, "To us," "Cheers," or the like. Guests then touch glasses all around or with the people nearest them, and all take a first sip of wine together.

More formal toasting involves a short speech honoring a particular person and usually occurs toward the end of the meal, when people still have a bit of wine left in their glasses, or at dessert, when champagne is served. The person making the toast stands and makes a short speech about the person or persons being honored. The speech may be sentimental, humorous, or outrageously flattering. At the end of it, the speaker says, "I now propose a toast to . . . ." All guests except the person being toasted rise, repeat the name of the person honored, touch glasses, and sip. Nondrinkers should not toast with water (it's bad luck), but may rise and touch empty glasses. The recipient of the toast does not rise, nor does he or she sip the wine until the toast is completed.

Wedding toasts
At a wedding reception, the best man acts as toastmaster. He begins by toasting the bride. Others, including the groom, then toast the bride. The bride returns her groom's toast and may also toast her parents, her new parents-in-law, or her main attendant.

Other occasions
At a christening, the godfather or godmother begins the toasts; after that, anyone may propose a toast. At an anniversary, the hosts begin the toasting, even if it is the couple themselves.

Toilets

Repairing and replacing tank-toilet valves; unclogging a toilet

When you flush a tank toilet, a trip lever lifts the stopper ball out of the flush-valve seat, releasing water into the bowl. When the tank is almost empty, the stopper ball drops back into the valve seat and seals the outlet. As the float ball descends with the tank's water level, it opens the ball-cock valve, allowing water from the inlet pipe to refill the tank and the bowl. As the tank fills, the float ball rises, closing the ball-cock valve and stopping the flow of water.

A defective ball-cock or flush-valve assembly causes a toilet to run noisily and continuously. To troubleshoot a toilet, remove the tank lid and observe what happens during and after a flush. Make your repairs accordingly.

Repairing a leaky flush valve
The water level in a filled tank should be ¾ inch below the top of the overflow tube. If the water keeps running but the tank doesn't fill, the flush valve is leaking. Close the water supply at the shutoff valve. Flush the toilet. As the tank empties, check whether the stopper ball seats tightly in the valve. If it doesn't, loosen the guide-arm thumbscrews; center the arm over the valve seat. Straighten bent lift wires. Scrub the valve seat with steel wool. Replace a worn-out stopper ball with a more efficient flapper ball.

To install a flapper ball, drain the tank by closing the shutoff valve and flushing the toilet. Unhook the lift wires; lift off the guide arm and the stopper ball. Slide the flapper ball's collar down the overflow tube. Center the ball in the valve seat; tighten the collar thumbscrew. Hook the chain to the trip lever; allow ½ inch of slack.

Fixing the ball cock
If the tank fills but water keeps spilling into the overflow tube, lift the float arm. If the flow stops, the float mechanism is at fault. Remove the float ball by twisting it counterclockwise; replace a cracked or water-filled ball. If the ball is all right, bend the float arm down slightly. Attach the ball to the float arm; flush the toilet. If the water flow persists, the ball-cock washers are probably worn; replace them.

Close the water supply and flush the toilet. Remove the retaining pins holding the float mechanism to the ball cock. Lift out the float arm and the plunger; slide the plunger off the ball-cock lever. Use a screwdriver to pry off the plunger's split washer; unscrew the washer at the plunger's base. Replace the washers. Reassemble the unit. Open the water supply and flush the toilet. If water still spills into the overflow tube, replace the ball-cock assembly with a quieter, less leak-prone inlet or fill valve. Follow manufacturer's directions for installation.

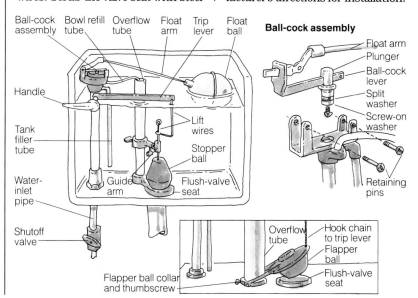

Ball-cock assembly   Bowl refill tube   Overflow tube   Float arm   Trip lever   Float ball

Handle

Tank filler tube

Water-inlet pipe

Shutoff valve

Guide arm

Lift wires

Stopper ball

Flush-valve seat

Flapper ball collar and thumbscrew

Ball-cock assembly

Float arm
Plunger
Ball-cock lever
Split washer
Screw-on washer
Retaining pins

Overflow tube
Hook chain to trip lever
Flapper ball
Flush-valve seat

T

Continued next page

393

Unclogging a toilet

Add or bail out water until the bowl is half full. Use a funnel-cup plunger that fits snugly into the toilet's outflow passage. Pump it up and down rapidly 10 times (see *Drain unclogging*). Pour water into the bowl; if the water level rises, bail out the excess and try again. If the plunger doesn't work after several tries, use a toilet auger. Insert the auger's curved end into the outflow passage and crank the handle until the tip bites into the clog. Slowly pull out the clog or break it up by moving the handle back and forth. If this doesn't work, call a plumber.

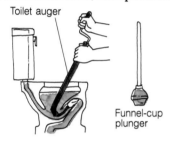

Toilet auger

Funnel-cup plunger

Toilet seats

Replacing a stuck-on seat

The hardest part of replacing a toilet seat is removing the bolts that hold the old seat in place. These bolts are fastened by nuts beneath the toilet bowl. Use an adjustable wrench or a socket wrench to unscrew them.

If the bolts are metal and have corroded, drench them with penetrating oil and let them soak overnight. If the bolts still resist, saw through them: raise the toilet lid and seat, mask the rim of the bowl with cardboard to avoid scratching it, and saw through each bolt with a hacksaw.

Before installing a new seat, clean around the bolt holes. Coat the bolts of the new seat with petroleum jelly to facilitate future removal.

Toilet tanks

Stopping leaks and sweating

A toilet tank sweats when cold water in it causes warm, humid air to condense on its surface. To tell whether moisture dripping from a tank is due to a leak or to sweating, put food coloring in the tank. An hour later, touch white tissue to the bolt tips under the tank. If the tissue colors, there's a leak; if not, the tank is sweating.

Leaks in a wall-mounted tank

Leaks may occur at either end of the pipe leading from tank to bowl. With a spud wrench or large pipe wrench,

Wall-mounted tank

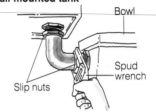

Bowl

Spud wrench

Slip nuts

unscrew the slip nuts at both ends. Wrap the pipe threads with self-forming packing; retighten the nuts.

Leaks in a bowl-mounted tank

To stop a leak around a tank bolt, drain the tank (see *Toilets*). Have a helper secure the bolt with a screwdriver; then tighten the nut under the

Bowl-mounted tank

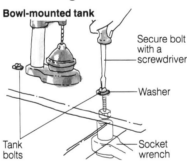

Secure bolt with a screwdriver

Washer

Tank bolts

Socket wrench

bowl rim with a socket wrench. Don't overtighten; the tank may crack. If leaking continues, remove the bolts and replace the washers.

If the tank leaks at the flush valve, drain the tank; use an adjustable wrench to unscrew the nut joining

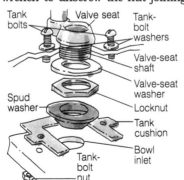

Tank bolts

Valve seat

Tank-bolt washers

Valve-seat shaft

Valve-seat washer

Locknut

Tank cushion

Spud washer

Bowl inlet

Tank-bolt nut

the ball-cock shaft to the water-inlet pipe (see *Toilets*). Remove the tank bolts, lift the tank off the bowl, and lay it on its back. Unscrew the locknut from the valve-seat shaft; pull the valve seat into the tank. Replace the washer at the top of the shaft and the conical spud washer that covers its base. Reassemble the tank.

Preventing tank sweating

Line the inside of the tank with a ready-made liner, or cut ½-inch-thick insulating foam rubber to fit. Drain the tank and sponge it dry. Cut a hole in the front panel of the liner for the flush-handle bracket; make sure the liner doesn't block any moving parts. Glue the insulation in place with rubber cement or silicone glue; wait 24 hours to refill the tank.

Toilet training

When and how to start it

Around 2½ years of age is a good time to start teaching a child how to use the toilet. At this age many youngsters are keen to do things the grown-up way and have enough control of their bodily functions to be able to use a potty consistently.

First decide on certain words to use for bowel movements and urine; use them when changing diapers. As your child learns to recognize bowel movements, he or she may start telling you immediately after one. If he does, or if he shows any interest in the toilet, put a potty or training seat in the bathroom. Explain what it's for; invite him to sit down, clothes and all. Next suggest taking off the diaper and letting the child sit down to see how it feels.

If possible, wait until your child indicates he wants to use the potty. If he shows little interest but gives other signs of readiness for toilet training, such as tugging at his diapers or indicating that he dislikes wearing a soiled diaper, try putting him on the potty at times when bowel movements usually occur.

It may take days or weeks of sitting on the potty for short periods before a child succeeds in eliminating into it. Praise any success warmly. Be patient about a lack of progress or failures fol-

T

lowing an initial success. (Some children learn quickly, then relapse for a few months.) If your child becomes unhappy with this routine, drop the matter for a few days or even weeks until he is willing to try again.

Late development in toilet training is perfectly normal. The best thing a parent can do for a late developer is to be patient and understanding.

Once a child makes a strong effort to succeed, put him in training pants during the day. Staying dry at night usually takes longer to develop.

Tomatoes

How to grow large, luscious fruit

Tomatoes need warm, rich soil. Prepare their bed in fall if possible: dig or rototill 9 inches deep, and work in 2 inches of compost, well-aged manure, or other organic matter. In early spring, rake in 1 pound of 5-10-10 fertilizer for each 25-foot row (see *Fertilizing vegetables*). Or, at planting time, dig a 6-inch hole 2 to 3 feet across for each plant and line the bottom with a 2-inch layer of organic matter mixed with a handful of 5-10-10 fertilizer; cover with topsoil.

Start seeds 8 weeks before you expect to set plants out (see *Starting seeds indoors*), or buy healthy young plants from a nursery or garden supply center. When overnight temperatures average above 55°F, set plants out in rows 3 feet apart. Space plants at 18-inch intervals if you plan to support them, at 3-foot intervals if you are letting them sprawl. An *indeterminate,* or vine, type can be supported by a trellis, stake (see *Staking plants*), or mesh cage. A *determinate,* or bush, type needs no staking but benefits from the support of a mesh cage.

Before planting (see *Planting*), remove all but the top few leaves. Bury the stem to those leaves; roots will develop along it. Place a leggy plant on its side in a sloping trench. Mulch to conserve moisture (see *Mulching*). Water well if tomatoes receive less than 1 inch of rain per week. When the first fruits are about half-dollar size, encircle the stem, at a distance of about 10

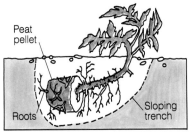

Peat pellet
Roots
Sloping trench

inches, with a tablespoon of 5-10-10 fertilizer; repeat every 3 to 4 weeks.

Pinch off all suckers. When an indeterminate plant has six branches, cut

Mesh cage
Sucker
Pinch off here

off its growing tip to direct energy into the fruit. To prolong harvest beyond frost, cover plants at night with burlap, bedsheets, or plastic tents. (See also *Cutworms; Tomato hornworm.*)

Tomato hornworm

Decimating its ranks

This green, 3- to 4-inch caterpillar, with diagonal white marks on its sides and a curved "horn" projecting from its hind end, feeds on the foliage

of tomatoes, potatoes, eggplants, and peppers. In the adult stage, it is the large (wingspan up to 6 inches), brownish sphinx moth.

Tomato hornworms are easy to control: handpick and destroy worms. Using a twig, knock the caterpillar into a small can of kerosene. To control a more difficult infestation, spray with insecticidal soap or use *Bacillus thuringiensis*.

Don't destroy a caterpillar that has white, rice-grain-size cocoons on its body. These cocoons (parasites actually) will hatch into a kind of wasp that preys on hornworms. (See also *Corn earworms; Pesticides.*)

Tomato sauce

Using fresh tomatoes; variations on the theme

Choose fully ripe, deep red, and richly flavored tomatoes for sauce, preferably a type, such as the plum tomato, that's low in water. Fruit that's too soft for salads can be used, but discard any with signs of decay; these give sauce an unpleasant flavor. If good fresh tomatoes are unavailable, substitute canned ones, whole or puréed.

Basic sauce

For 3 cups of sauce, peel 2 to 2¼ pounds tomatoes. Slice them in half crosswise and squeeze out seeds; then chop the tomatoes. (If you have a food mill, eliminate these two steps and just destem and quarter them.) Chop a large onion and sauté it in 2 tablespoons oil in a large enamel or stainless-steel pot. Add the tomatoes, 1 teaspoon salt, ¼ teaspoon pepper, 2 cloves minced garlic, and 1 tablespoon each minced fresh parsley and basil.

Bring to a boil, cover, and simmer 30 minutes; stir occasionally. If not thick enough, simmer uncovered until it's thicker, or add 1 to 2 tablespoons tomato paste. Force the sauce through a food mill, or purée it in a blender or food processor. (You need not purée if you like a chunky sauce.) If the sauce is too tart, sweeten it slightly with ½ to 1 teaspoon sugar. Serve it with pasta, rice, meat, or vegetables. Serves four.

Bacon sauce: Sauté 3 tablespoons diced lean bacon with the onion.

Creole sauce: Sauté 1 chopped green pepper and 2 stalks chopped celery with the onion. Omit the basil; add two or three dashes hot pepper sauce (or to taste) and a bay leaf. Remove the bay leaf before serving.

Meat sauce: Sauté ½ pound of ground beef with the onion.

Marinara (Italian) sauce: Increase the basil to ¼ cup and add 1 teaspoon dried oregano and ½ cup red wine.

Mushroom sauce: Add ½ pound sliced, sautéed mushrooms to marinara sauce just before serving.

Tomato sauce keeps well in a tightly covered container in the refrigerator for several days. It can be stored in the freezer for up to 1 year.

Toothaches

What to do about the pain until you can see a dentist

Most toothaches are a sign of decay—that is, of tooth deterioration caused by acids formed in the mouth by bacterial breakdown of sugars. (For measures to reduce this risk, especially in children, see *Tooth care*.) Decay begins with erosion of the *enamel,* the tooth's hard outer covering; a small cavity forms. Untreated, decay can progress to the *pulp,* or heart, of the tooth, which contains nerves and blood vessels. See a dentist promptly about any toothache, however mild.

In the interim, you may be able to ease the pain with aspirin or another analgesic. If the cavity's size and location permit, try packing it with a bit of cotton soaked with oil of cloves, a surface anesthetic available at any pharmacy. It may also help to rinse your mouth periodically with a solution of baking soda and lukewarm water.

After dental work, you may get a slightly painful reaction to sweet, sour, or hot foods or liquids. This usually passes quickly, but it can help to rinse your mouth, after eating or drinking, with warm, salted water.

Severely painful toothaches

Extreme pain from heat or chewing may mean that a tooth is dying. If heat causes the pain, try holding ice cubes against the tooth. If chewing causes the pain, the tooth may be fractured, but with prompt attention it may be saved. If you can't get to a dentist immediately and the pain keeps you awake, sleep with your head propped on two pillows.

An abscessed tooth can cause swelling as well as pain. Signs are persistent aching or throbbing that is worse when you chew. It is urgent to get to a dentist as soon as possible, especially if the swelling spreads into your face and neck. Get what relief you can from analgesics; rinse your mouth hourly with warm, salted water. If the abscess bursts (which the warm water will encourage), rinse your mouth thoroughly to wash away the pus. Pain will be relieved—but not the need to see the dentist.

Tooth care

A program to preserve teeth and gums

Tooth care should begin in early infancy. Even while gums are toothless, wipe them twice a day with a gauze pad to reduce decay-causing bacteria. Don't let a baby go to sleep sucking a bottle of milk or fruit juice. Both liquids contain sugar, which feeds bacteria. The longer the bottle stays in the mouth, the greater the risk.

Proper tooth care for children or adults requires regular, thorough removal of plaque, a bacteria-containing film that forms on teeth. You can locate plaque deposits precisely by chewing what is called a *disclosing tablet* (sold in drugstores) or by rinsing your mouth with a few spoonfuls of water containing two or three drops of blue or green food coloring. Color will remain where plaque is collecting; give those areas special care.

Cleaning your teeth

The best toothbrush choice is soft nylon with rounded-end bristles and a flat brushing surface. Hold the brush at a 45-degree angle where teeth and gums meet. Move it back and forth 10 strokes at each location; brush the outside, inside, and chewing surfaces of all teeth.

Then use dental floss to remove plaque and to dislodge trapped food. Wind the ends of an 18-inch length around a finger on each hand. Hold the floss taut and, with a gentle sawing motion, draw it between teeth to the gumline. Gently scrape the gumline, then the sides of the teeth. Brush and floss at least twice a day—if possible, immediately after meals.

Fluoridated water helps to reduce tooth decay. If your community's water supply isn't fluoridated, you can get fluoride tablets or drops for children from a dentist. Choose a fluoridated toothpaste approved by the American Dental Association.

You can further guard against decay by avoiding sweets (particularly those that dissolve slowly in the mouth); heavily sugared fruits; cookies; and pastries. See a dentist twice a year for a checkup and cleaning.

Tornadoes

Recognizing if one may be imminent; how to survive one

Tornadoes are swirling fingers of cloud in which the air motion reaches speeds up to 500 miles per hour. They move over the earth at 5 to 40 miles per hour. Preludes to a tornado are a gathering of huge, dark storm clouds (often tinted green), a sudden silence among animals, insects, and birds, and the appearance of enormous hailstones followed by large raindrops. A tornado begins when part of a cloud bulges downward, forming a funnel.

If you live in a tornado-prone area, you should prepare a specially designated shelter. The best is a storm cellar 15 to 20 feet from the house. It need not be large—8 x 6 x 7 feet high will accommodate eight people. Reinforced concrete is best for the walls, but split logs, cinder blocks, or bricks can also be used. Make a sloping floor with a drainage outlet, and build the shelter deep enough to have at least 3 feet of packed earth above the ceiling. Set the doors preferably to face northeast (most tornadoes approach from the south) and to open inward. The basement is the next safest place. If possible, reinforce a small area of the basement by adding an extra wall.

Equip a shelter with a battery-operated radio, a flashlight, batteries, water, canned food, and a first-aid kit.

Surviving a tornado

If you think you are the first to see a tornado, notify the nearest National Weather Service office or the police or sheriff. At home, open windows a few inches if there's time, but don't go near the windows if the tornado is close; they may explode. Go to a storm shelter or basement. If you can't, proceed to a small room with strong walls on the ground floor. A bathroom offers extra protection because of surrounding pipes. If you're caught upstairs, take shelter in an interior hallway.

In a public building, move to a small room or closet in the northeast corner. If caught in the open, move away at a right angle from the path of the tornado. If escape is impossible, lie facedown in a ditch or depression.

Touch football

No tackle, no chance of broken bones

Divide four or more players into two equally strong teams. Mark goal lines 100 yards apart (or less depending on the plot's size) and sidelines 53 yards apart (often ignored); use chalk or light-colored shirts.

Line up your team along its goal line; your opponents line up along theirs. *Punt* (kick) a football from the goal line down the field. The offense tries to catch the ball as your team (the defense) runs forward to prevent them. When you or a teammate tags an opponent carrying the ball or when the ball hits the ground, the first of that team's four *downs* (attempts to score a six-point *touchdown* at your goal) ends; they have three more.

Place a marker on the field where the ball carrier was tagged. Put the football there. This marks the *scrimmage line* for that team's next down. The offense *huddles* (groups to discuss strategy) then faces your team at this line. Acting on plans made in the huddle, an offense player snatches the ball and throws it to a team member. Some run forward to receive a pass, others to block your team. If one of your players intercepts a pass, your team becomes the offense.

You can run with the ball toward your opponent's goal or pass it laterally or backward; you can make a forward pass *only* after the kickoff play. You can punt the football on the fourth down if you announce it beforehand. If it lands over the goal, your team scores three points.

Each team has four successive downs upon rotation. The game lasts for four 15-minute quarters; the highest score wins.

Touch typing

A home-study method

Sit straight directly in front of the typewriter, your feet flat on the floor. Position your hands over the typewriter's keys, your fingers relaxed and curved, and your forearms at slightly less than right angles to your body. Adjust the chair's height if necessary.

Position your eight fingers over the home keys (a, s, d, f and j, k, l, ;) as shown. Use your left index finger for both the f and g keys; your right one for both h and j. Use a thumb to strike the space bar. Press the shift key with a little finger prior to typing a letter to make it a capital.

Practice finding the home keys by touch. When fully confident, type the home keys under your left fingers in order—asdfg (space) asdfg—while keeping both hands in place. Strike the keys with a light bouncing motion; don't press them. Then, with your right hand, type ;lkjh (space) ;lkjh. Type them over and over, saying the letters as you do so.

To reach the remaining keys, use your fingers above and below the home keys to include all letters and numbers as indicated by the arrows. Get a book of typing exercises and follow them in proper sequence.

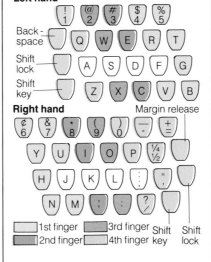

Left hand

Right hand   Margin release

☐ 1st finger ☐ 3rd finger Shift Shift
☐ 2nd finger ☐ 4th finger key lock

Towel racks

Replacing a broken rod; installing the fixtures

To replace a broken towel rod, you must first remove one of the fixtures that holds it in place. Unscrew it. Or, if you find no screws, pry it loose at the bottom, then pull outward and upward to remove it from the clips beneath. Replace the rod with a new one or with a wooden dowel; reset the fixture. Sand a dowel and seal it with three coats of enamel or polyurethane, sanding lightly between coats.

When a broken towel rod is set between ceramic fixtures mounted flush with the wall tile, it's easier to replace it with a metal expansion rod of the same diameter than to remove and reset the fixture. However, if the ceramic fixture has come loose, pry it off the wall; with a stiff putty knife, scrape as much tile adhesive and grout as possible from both the fixture and the wall. Remount the fixture with plaster of paris, which sets quickly; remove excess before it dries.

To install a new towel rack, first mark the positions of the fixtures; then mark all holes in the fixtures or mounting clips. Drill holes for the screws. (To drill through tile, use a masonry bit and the slowest speed of a variable-speed drill; wear goggles. To avoid cracking the tile, apply light drill pressure.) Insert screw anchors in the wall (see *Wall fasteners*); then install the fixtures and rod.

Trailers

Pulling them safely

Before picking a trailer, find out how much weight your car can pull. Check the owner's manual or write for the car maker's towing guide. It will also tell you how to attach the hitch.

If the car's rear sags more than 2 to 3 inches with the loaded trailer attached, the *tongue weight* (weight on the hitch) is excessive. Your car may need rear air shocks to level it.

In some cases—a small car or a car pulling over 2,000 pounds—tongue weight will be too great even with air shocks. If so, buy a hitch that distributes weight to all four wheels. Try redistributing the load in the trailer. Avoid an axle-mounted hitch unless approved by your car maker.

Special equipment
On a trailer over 1,000 pounds, use trailer brakes; don't connect them to the car's hydraulic system. Inflate your tires to the maximum pressure specified for a heavy load. Connect

T

safety chains, trailer lights (including turn signals), and clamp-on side mirrors. Install an automatic transmission oil cooler and, if you're driving in hilly areas, an auxiliary electric radiator fan. Change engine oil every 2,500 miles, automatic transmission fluid every 12,000 miles.

Trailer-towing techniques
Load the trailer more heavily in front and evenly from side to side; secure the load. Keep passengers out of the trailer. Allow extra distance for passing, stopping, and lane changes. Turn off the air conditioning on upgrades to prevent overheating; shift to a lower gear on downgrades to save brake power. If the trailer is more than 1,000 pounds, don't use the overdrive gear, even on level roads.

When you park, apply the parking brake and chock the trailer wheels before shifting an automatic transmission into *Park;* otherwise shifting out of *Park* may be difficult.

Transmission fluid

Checking and adding fluid to your car's transmission

A low fluid level can cause shifting and drive problems or premature failure of an automatic transmission. Check the transmission-fluid level once a month. After you've driven the car a few miles to warm up the fluid, stop on level ground, put the shift lever into *Park* and, with the engine running, pull out the transmission dipstick (on a Honda, shut off the engine and immediately pull the dipstick).

The fluid level should be between the *Add* and *Full* marks. If it's at or below *Add,* shut off the engine and add enough fluid to bring it to *Full.*

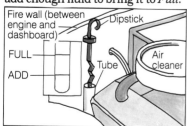

Fire wall (between engine and dashboard)
Dipstick
FULL
ADD
Tube
Air cleaner

Automatic transmission fluid is sold in quart cans, but in most cases the amount needed will be substan-

tially less. Don't simply use the whole can; overfilling can also cause problems. Cap the can with a plastic lid or foil wrap to keep out dirt; save it.

Pour the fluid into the dipstick tube. Use a special long-necked funnel sold in auto parts stores.

Types of fluid
Use only the fluid formulated for your transmission; otherwise shift problems can result. Most cars use Dexron II fluid. Exceptions are Mazda, Volvo, and certain Fords that use Type F. Other Fords use Dexron or Type H. If you own a Ford, check with a dealer to find out which fluid your transmission requires. Dexron and Type F are readily available, but Type H may be available only from a dealer.

If the transmission requires fluid every few months, have it checked for leaks. Smell the dipstick and compare the odor with fresh fluid. If the dipstick sample is discolored or smells burned, the transmission may soon need repair.

Trapping animals

Take 'em back alive

Set a trap, baited with the animal's favorite food, on a well-traveled trail or near recent damage. Take a trapped animal to a suitable environment several miles away (or a distance recommended by your state's wildlife agency) and release it. Not all states permit this transfer without a license; get advice from the wildlife agency and from your local Cooperative Extension Service (see p.5).

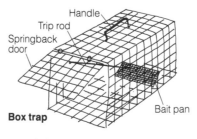

Handle
Trip rod
Springback door
Bait pan
Box trap

Woodchucks
Use a box trap with an entrance at least 9 x 9 inches. Bait the trap with an ear of fresh sweet corn or sweet apple slices. As soon as you have caught the woodchuck, fill in its old holes.

Raccoons
Trap-shy if caught previously, raccoons are canny at stealing bait. Peg down a large box trap (12 x 10 x 32 inches) with a springback door. Bait it with honey mixed with anise oil; place some marshmallows near the bait as a visual attractant. You may have to add hardware screen around the bait end of the trap to prevent a raccoon from stealing bait through the wire. Hose the cage with steam or scrub it with full-strength bleach before reusing or storing it; it may be contaminated by roundworm eggs from droppings (see *Raccoons*).

Caution: Because a raccoon or skunk may be rabid, take extreme care in handling them. Keep pets and children away. If you live in the city or suburbs, contact a humane society for assistance in killing a rabid animal. If you live in a rural area, shooting is the most efficient way to dispose of a diseased pest.

Skunks
Wrap a heavy-duty garbage bag over all but the entrance of a 9- x 9- x 23-inch box trap baited with sardines or cat food. When you've trapped a skunk, slip the rest of the bag around the entrance; stay to the side to avoid being sprayed. Release the skunk as soon as possible. (See also *Mice as pests; Pocket gophers; Rabbit damage; Rats; Skunk odor.*)

Travel emergencies

Finding help away from home

If your car breaks down far from help, turn on the emergency flasher lights and get the car well off the road if you can. Tie a white or red cloth to the handle of the driver's door; raise the hood. Stay in the car until help arrives. If you can't get the car off the road, turn on the emergency flashers, set up flares if you have them, and wait on the roadside. When someone stops to help, ask him to call the police, highway patrol, or your auto club at the next telephone booth or tollbooth. Help can also be summoned on Channel 19 on a CB radio or by dialing 911 or the operator on a cellular phone. Request the same aid from all who stop.

Before your car is towed or repaired, ask for the estimated cost. Many towing companies won't take checks or credit cards. If you're short of cash, try contacting a relative, friend, or your bank to arrange a transfer of funds (see *Stranded on vacation*).

Getting medical help

If you or someone with you gets sick while traveling, go to the nearest hospital. Hotels and motels in major foreign cities and large resorts may have an English-speaking doctor on call. Otherwise, try the nearest U.S. consulate or military post, an American Express office, or the Red Cross. If you anticipate you may need a doctor, the International Association for Medical Assistance to Travelers (IAMAT), 417 Center Street, Lewiston, NY 14092, will send you, for a donation, a list of English-speaking doctors abroad.

Lost luggage and other mishaps

If an airline misplaces your luggage, go to the airline desk immediately. Present your claim checks (but hold on to them) and fill out a claim form. If you need clothing or overnight supplies, ask airline personnel about reimbursement. For ways to reduce the risk of losing your bags, see *Packing*.

When driving in a foreign country, have adequate insurance. If you're involved in an accident or run afoul of the law, contact the nearest U.S. embassy or consulate.

Traveling with a handicapped person

Planning a trouble-free trip

Book your trip early. Travel direct, at off-peak hours. Advise transportation companies and hotels of your needs; ask what their facilities and limitations are. If your companion is in a wheelchair, find out, for example, the width of a hotel room's entrance and bathroom doors, and whether there are grab bars in the bathroom and access ramps where needed.

Air travel

Airline procedures for handling the disabled vary. When making reservations, ask about restrictions on motorized wheelchairs and about boarding and deplaning procedures. Tell the airline agent whether the disabled passenger can stand or walk at all and whether he'll be traveling with his own wheelchair or will need an airline wheelchair. A few days before departure, call the airline to check that the information in its computer is correct.

Almost all airlines preboard disabled passengers, so arrive early. Major U.S. airports have lavatories that are accessible to wheelchairs; most planes don't. If the passenger can't walk at all, he may have to limit liquid intake before and during the trip; consult a doctor about this.

Train or bus travel

Wheelchair accessibility in Amtrak trains and stations varies. Find out what services are offered at your departure and arrival points; book early.

If your disabled companion can't walk at all, you'll have to carry him on and off a bus. Let the bus company know your situation when you book; arrive 30 minutes early.

Ask about special fares for the disabled on Trailways, Greyhound, and Amtrak (a doctor's letter may be needed to qualify). These and most airline companies permit guide dogs to accompany their owners free; check quarantine rules when going abroad.

For further help, contact the Society for the Advancement of Travel for the Handicapped (SATH), 347 Fifth Avenue, Suite 610, New York, NY 10016.

Traveling with children

Keeping young ones safe and happy on the road

When traveling by car, insist that everyone buckle up. An infant or a child under 40 pounds or 4 years old should ride in a federally-approved safety seat strapped securely to the car seat. Don't carry a child on your lap or strap him with your seat belt. Make frequent rest stops in places where a child can run around and expend energy under your supervision.

Bring along a supply of drinking water and nutritious snacks; baby foods, disposable diapers, and a potty chair, if needed; toys and games; blankets and pillows; disposable moist towelettes; and paper or plastic bags and changes of clothing in case of motion sickness or other mishaps.

To avoid motion sickness, keep the car well ventilated, stop often, and provide light, nongreasy snacks. If a child is prone to motion sickness, ask your doctor about medication.

Babies under 6 months old are usually lulled to sleep by noise and motion. Amusing older babies and toddlers can be a challenge. In addition to familiar toys, pack some surprises and pass them out during the trip. Organize sing-alongs and guessing games; older children may like word games (see *Botticelli; Hangman*). An older child can help read maps or look after younger children.

Traveling by air

Look for an airline that preboards passengers with children and which offers children's meals and infant beds. Book early and request seats with extra leg room. Pack a flight bag with snacks, moist towelettes, toys, and a change of clothing. To relieve ear pain during takeoffs and landings, have a child swallow, yawn, or chew gum; nurse an infant or let him suck a bottle or a pacifier. Give children plenty to drink during the flight.

Childproof a hotel or motel room by removing safety hazards. Put tape over the lock of a bathroom door.

Limit sightseeing with children to 2 or 3 hours. Plan excursions to a zoo, amusement park, and similar places.

Traveling with pets

Making your pet's trip safe and pleasant

Before a long trip, have your pet examined by a veterinarian. Make sure that its shots are current. Ask the veterinarian for a certificate of good health and proof of vaccinations; carry the papers with you. If you're going to a foreign country, consult its national airline or nearest consulate about animal health requirements.

Check accommodation guides for places that accept pets; reserve early. Put an identification tag on your pet's collar; for an extended trip, the tag should bear the name, address, and phone number of a friend or relative

T

who can be reached easily while you are away. Prepare a travel kit containing a thermos for water, a water bowl and a feeding dish, food, a leash, flea spray, a brush, a blanket, and a toy.

Transport small dogs and all cats in a comfortable, well-ventilated pet carrier. If you're traveling by car, strap the carrier securely to the back seat; confine a large dog to the rear of the car with a metal grille sold at pet shops.

Taking your pet regularly on short rides several weeks before a long car trip may help it overcome motion sickness. If it doesn't, ask your veterinarian about a tranquilizer.

Don't feed your pet for several hours before departure (3 hours for cats and puppies; 6 hours for dogs; longer if the animal tends to get car sick). During the trip, provide cool water as needed. Exercise a dog frequently on a leash. Don't let a dog put its head out of a car window; flying particles can seriously injure an eye. At your destination, wait at least an hour before feeding your pet. Keep it leashed or in the carrier, away from other animals.

Traveling by air

Because cabin space for pets is limited and airline policies vary, inquire and book early. Otherwise, your pet may have to go as excess baggage on your flight or, as a last resort, as air freight on another flight. Don't ship your pet in very hot or very cold weather. Most trains and buses don't accept pets. (See also *Lost cats and dogs.*)

Treading water

How to stay afloat vertically

Stand in shoulder-deep water; bend forward slightly at the waist. Extend your arms in front of your chest, elbows bent, palms touching, fingers held lightly together. Turning your

thumbs down, push your hands away from each other and down slightly, until they're shoulder-width apart. Turning thumbs up, pull your hands up slightly and back together.

Continue the sculling motion of the hands while adding a modified scissors kick performed upright (see *Sidestroke*). As soon as you finish one kick, start the next one; don't pause between kicks. Or use a slow pedaling motion, bringing each knee slightly above walking level, then down again.

Tree houses

Making an elevated hideout for youngsters

A tree house's design must fit the tree in which it is built; its construction must be flexible enough to give a little when the tree moves in the wind. For a span of 7 feet or less, use 2 x 6's for the frame, 2 x 4's for joists and braces, and 1 x 6's (not plywood) for the floor. Nail floorboards at their ends only.

The easiest treehouse to build is a triangular platform that is secured to the trunk and two limbs of a low-branching tree. Nail the frame with 16d galvanized nails—they shouldn't hurt a healthy tree if they aren't driv-

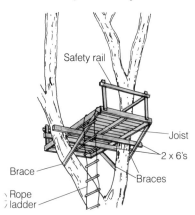

Safety rail

Joist

2 x 6's

Brace

Braces

Rope ladder

en during the spring, when the sap is running. Make sure that the boards are level (see *Leveling*). Install joists every 2 feet or so, at right angles to the longest side of the frame. Using 10d galvanized nails, secure the floorboards to the frame so that they run across the joists. Add walls or a railing at least 2 feet high.

To build between two limbs, nail two 2 x 6's to them, making a crossbeam. Assemble the platform on the ground and lift it onto the crossbeam. Brace the corners. Before building between the trunks of two trees, stabilize the trunks; toenail a 4 x 4 snugly between them, then run a cable and turnbuckle as shown. Pad the cable with garden hose to protect the trees.

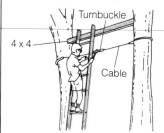

Turnbuckle

4 x 4

Cable

Nail or hinge a ladder to the platform, not to the tree trunk. Don't just nail boards to the tree trunk; such a "ladder" is undependable and dangerous.

Tree pruning

Why, when, and how to do it

There are three reasons to prune a tree: to remove damaged, dead, or diseased branches; to control size and form; and to increase the quality and abundance of fruit and flowers.

At least once a year and after any major storm, inspect all important trees—especially fruit trees, landscaping specimens, and trees growing close to the house, drive, or road. Promptly prune any branches that endanger the tree's health or that pose a safety hazard.

To control shape and form or to improve fruiting and flowering of deciduous trees, prune in late fall or winter when the tree is dormant. Prune evergreens in late winter or early spring. Look for a bud or small branch that grows the way you want the tree to grow. Then cut back to 1 inch beyond that spot. (See also *Fruit trees; Pruning shrubs.*) Use a pole pruner, lopping shears, or a pruning saw.

Don't just cut a branch off flush. Leave the *collar,* or dark ring at the branch's base, attached to the tree; it contains cells that close the wound. To avoid tearing away bark and wood, saw a branch one-third through from the bottom, then finish from above.

Remove a large branch in two stages: first shorten it to a 12- to 18-

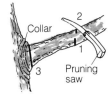

inch stump; then remove the stump. To support a heavy branch while you saw it, tie a stout rope to it and pass the rope over a higher branch; have a helper hold the rope from the ground.

Call a professional for major surgery, such as a split trunk, or to remove high, heavy branches or those that are near power lines.

Trellises

Freestanding support for climbing vines

How solidly you build a trellis depends on the size and longevity of the vine it is to support. For a heavy wisteria, grape, or rambler rose, make a frame of 2 x 4's. Reinforce the joints with galvanized-steel corner braces, and nail

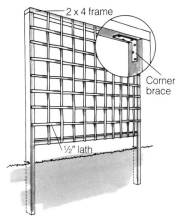

on a latticework of 1 x 2's or interwoven strips of ½-inch lath. For a lighter clematis or honeysuckle, use 2 x 2's and ½-inch lath. Tomatoes, cucumbers, and such annual vines as morning glories can be supported for a season on a frame of 1 x 2's covered by lath or wire mesh; or buy ready-made plastic or wire supports from your hardware or garden supply store.

For a long-lasting trellis, at least 2 feet of the upright posts should be sunk below the soil surface. Use pressure-treated lumber or a resistant wood such as redwood, cedar, or cypress for the posts (see *Fence posts and rails*). If you use a resistant wood for aboveground parts, it can be left unpainted. Apply at least two coats of outdoor paint to other kinds of wood; let it dry before planting.

The face of a trellis built against a wall must be at least 4 inches from the wall to allow adequate air circulation. Hinge it at the base for convenience in maintenance and repair.

Trim on cars

How to reattach a loose piece

If an exterior trim piece has pulled off, it can often be refitted simply by pushing its clip back into a mounting hole or the trim back into its clip. If not, reattach it with *trim adhesive,* a contact cement; follow the instructions on the tube. Remove the clips before applying adhesive. If the mounting holes are rusted, first wire-brush them, then apply rust-resistant paint (see *Paint touch-ups*).

Apply adhesive to both surfaces, then push them together. If the trim must curve around a body part or possibly take impact, as a bumper strip must, use a flexible adhesive designed specifically for bumper strips.

On flat trim pieces, such as medallions and gearshift-pattern indicators, use a quick-setting *cyanoacrylate glue;* the gel type can fill very small gaps. For larger gaps, use a fast-setting (5-minute) *epoxy cement.*

Trolling

Fishing from a moving boat

Troll in deep fresh water for lake trout, landlocked salmon, walleye, or muskellunge. In salt water, troll with heavy bait for such large fish as marlin, sailfish, or tuna. In either case, the idea is to cover a wide territory in a moving boat, towing live bait or a lure at the end of a long line.

Trolling, like any kind of fishing, requires a balanced rod, reel, and line. In fresh water, the tackle can be as simple as a lightweight casting rod, a revolving-spool reel, and 8-pound-test line. For flies, use a fly-casting rod and reel. Rig the line according to the depth at which you are fishing. For early-season landlocked salmon just below the surface, use minnows or streamer flies, singly or in combination, with a sinker attached to the line 1 or 2 feet in front of the bait. For lake trout, walleyes, muskies, and late-season salmon that lurk near the bottom, use a three-way swivel with a heavy sinker on one leg; attach the sinker to a light leader that will break if the sinker gets snagged. Use a longer leader for the bait—use a wire leader for sharp-toothed muskies.

Ocean-going tackle generally includes a heavy rod 6½ feet or shorter and a large trolling reel that can hold up to 1,500 yards of 30-pound-test to 130-pound-test line. The bait can be skipped over the surface or weighted to ride at a depth of about 20 feet.

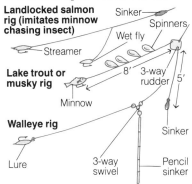

Truffles

A chocolate treat

The melt-in-your-mouth texture of truffles makes them a universally liked treat. Use one kind of dark chocolate (semisweet or unsweetened) or a mixture. Or use white chocolate only.

The following recipe makes about 6 dozen. Cut into small pieces ½ pound unsweetened and 1½ pounds semisweet chocolate. Bring to a boil 1 cup each whole milk and heavy cream. Reduce the heat. Add chocolate to the cream and stir until dissolved. Cool, stirring occasionally to prevent it from separating. Chill until firm.

To shape each ball, scoop out a teaspoonful and roll it between your hands. Roll the balls in chocolate sprinkles, a mixture of equal parts cocoa and confectioner's sugar, or finely ground nuts. Place each in a candy paper or petit-four cup. Store in an airtight container in a cool place.

If desired, flavor the truffles with ¼ cup rum, brandy, or liqueur, 1 tablespoon vanilla (reducing milk by the amount of flavoring), or 1 tablespoon grated orange peel.

Trusts

Gifts on the installment plan

You can provide financially for loved ones or a favorite charity by creating a trust. In a trust, you give another person, the *trustee,* limited control over certain money or property for the purpose of producing income to be paid to someone you name, the *beneficiary.*

The trust continues for a certain prearranged time; then the trustee turns over the remaining property to a designated person, who might be the beneficiary, yourself, or anyone else. For example, you might set up a trust to put a nephew through college, specifying that when he is awarded a bachelor's degree, the balance of the property be divided between your son and your daughter.

Funds can be used only for the purposes specified in the trust agreement. Therefore, if you set up a "spendthrift" trust to support a financially irresponsible person, the funds will be used to pay his normal living expenses but not his gambling debts. If you set up a charitable trust to feed and clothe blind orphan children, the funds cannot be used to add a wing to the orphanage.

Setting up a trust
Before making any binding commitments, consult an attorney experienced in trusts. To protect everyone involved, put the trust agreement in writing (most states require it).

You can establish a trust to operate while you are alive; it is called an *inter vivos,* or *living,* trust. Or you can provide in your will for a *testamentary* trust, to take effect on your death. If you wish to reserve the right to revoke a living trust at a future date, have that right included in the agreement. Otherwise, in order to revoke it, you will have to obtain the permission of all the beneficiaries—not an easy task!

Select as trustee only a person in whom you have great confidence and whose ability to manage money you respect. You may prefer to use a bank or trust company or both an individual and a bank or trust company.

Tub-shower enclosures

Fixing chips in molded bathroom units

Before fixing a chip in a molded fiberglass or acrylic tub or shower enclosure, check to see whether the unit is under warranty. Most are guaranteed for a year; some up to 10. If yours is covered, contact your contractor.

If you decide to undertake the job, write to the unit's manufacturer for a kit containing materials, directions and, sometimes, a special aerosol sprayer. Look for the maker's name on the unit's base or near the drain. Get the address from a fixture or plumbing supply dealer.

The repair involves filling the cavity with a polyester putty mixed with hardener. After sanding the patch, you spray it six or seven times with a liquid resin mixed with a thinner and a catalyst. You finish by sanding with fine paper and rubbing compound. The chemicals are strong smelling, requiring good ventilation.

Tug-of-war

A test of team strength

In an unofficial game, divide eight or more players into two teams that seem equally strong. Players on both sides line up facing their opponents.

Wrap black tape around the middle of a thick rope long enough to accommodate both rows of players. Tape-mark 6 feet either side of this middle mark. Mark the ground under the

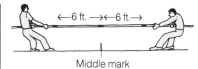

Middle mark

rope similarly with sticks, stones, or chalk. Instruct team members to pick up the rope and hold it firmly with both hands (gloves may be worn); the first player of each team is directly behind the rope's 6-foot mark.

Count to three, upon which each team digs in its heels and pulls. The first team to pull its opponents' 6-foot marker over its own 6-foot marker wins. A team that collectively falls down or lets go of the rope loses.

Turntables

Replacing faulty parts

A turntable platter rotates at 78, 45, or 33⅓ revolutions per minute by *direct drive* (a drive wheel and rubber rollers) or by *belt drive.*

Rubber drive wheels and rollers harden with age and lose their full capacity to grip. When components deteriorate, the turntable's speeds are affected; records sound distorted. To check the speed, chalk a point on the edge of a record and one on the chassis near the platter. Line them up, then turn on the phonograph. Clock how many times the two points meet during 1 minute.

In replacing any part of a turntable, use an exact duplicate or a substitute that is recommended by the manufacturer; consult the owner's manual.

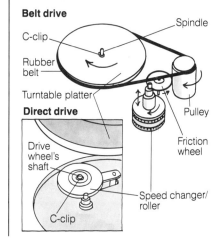

Belt drive

Spindle
C-clip
Rubber belt
Turntable platter
Pulley
Friction wheel
Speed changer/roller

Direct drive

Drive wheel's shaft
C-clip

Unplug the phonograph. Remove the platter by prying the C-clip from the spindle with needle-nose pliers and lifting the spindle out; lift the platter from the chassis.

On a direct drive, the drive wheel is held to the chassis by a C-clip that clutches a drive shaft. While grasping the clip with needle-nose pliers, pry it from the shaft with a small screwdriver. Note the positions of the washers above and below the wheel so that you can replace them correctly.

To replace a broken or stretched belt, remove the turntable platter and wrap a replacement belt around the pulley and the rim under the turntable platter. Reinstall the platter.

Twenty Questions

A guessing game

In Twenty Questions—or Animal, Vegetable, or Mineral, as it is also called—one player secretly selects a person, animal, or object to be guessed and writes it down for later verification. The remaining players then take turns trying to guess the secret subject by asking questions that can be answered "yes" or "no." ("I don't know" and "partly" are also allowable answers.)

The first question is usually "Is it an animal (or vegetable or mineral)?" The remaining questions should gradually narrow down the possibilities until the secret subject is guessed. The player who guesses correctly gets to pick the secret subject for the next game. If no one guesses the subject within the limit of 20 questions, the same player begins the new game.

Twenty Questions can also be played by two players or two teams. Record the number of questions each player or team asked before guessing the secret subject. The lowest score wins.

Typewriters

Cleaning; troubleshooting a manual machine

Keep any typewriter covered when not in use. Periodically clean the machine's innards using a hairblower (on *medium*) or a bicycle pump. Have the typewriter professionally serviced every 2 years.

On a manual, if you have to strike a key extra hard to make it print, there's probably grime in the segment slot at the base of the type bar. Dig it out with the tip of a nail file. Using a stiff typewriter brush, apply and scrub that area with typewriter cleaning fluid (both available at stationery stores). Wipe with a soft cloth.

If the print on the paper is blurred, you may need a new ribbon. Note how you remove it; to install the replacement, reverse the steps.

Blurred or broken print can also mean that the characters are dirty. Brush typewriter cleaner on the characters; blot with a lint-free cloth. Dig out stubborn grit with a common pin.

If a type bar sticks in place, it's probably bent. Press the key. Hold the

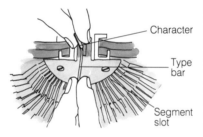

character and its base near the segment slot with your fingers; gently wiggle the character sideways until the type bar straightens and moves easily when you press its key.

If paper slips, swab the platen clean with denatured alcohol. Eventually a platen will become hard; replace it every 3 years. If any characters or type bars are broken or missing, have a service center replace them.

Electrics and electronics
If the machine doesn't function in a working receptacle, check the power cord (see *Power cords*). If the power cord is all right, the problem may be blown fuses in the typewriter. Leave the replacing of blown fuses, as well as other repairs, to a professional.

Ulcers

Simple measures for relief

The usual sign of a peptic ulcer—an acid-caused sore in the lining of the stomach or upper small intenstine—is a steady gnawing or burning pain below the breastbone. Typical cures for ulcers involve decreasing acid production; however doctors now believe that many ulcers are caused by bacteria and can be treated with antibiotics.

An ulcer is worse when the stomach is empty; thus sufferers are usually advised to eat three regular meals a day and to use an antacid in between. Food in the stomach relieves ulcer pain because it neutralizes the acid and acts as a protective coating.

Certain stimulating substances are best avoided. Among them are carbonated drinks, beer, tea, and coffee (decaffeinated as well as regular).

Watching your diet
A milk diet, or even a bland diet, does little either to lessen pain or allow an ulcer to heal. Milk, after neutralizing a certain amount of acid, causes a fresh surge of acid. And there is no evidence that spicy, fatty, or other indigestion-causing foods adversely affect *all* ulcers. Trial and error can tell you which foods, if any, you should avoid. Keeping a food diary helps; jot down what you eat at each meal, then note whether pain follows.

There are prescription drugs for treating ulcers, but many people do well with over-the-counter antacids. Watch for side effects: magnesium-based antacids may cause diarrhea; aluminum-based ones, constipation. Combinations with both minerals upset the bowels less. Avoid calcium-based antacids; they cause the same reaction as milk. Don't take antacids along with other ulcer drugs; they can interrupt absorption. If you are taking any other medication, ask your doctor before taking an antacid.

U

403

Umbrellas

How to buy one that will last; caring for it

Umbrellas come in folding and stick styles. Stick umbrellas are generally larger and stronger than the folding type. There are also windproof models that, when blown inside out, can be quickly restored.

The parts of an umbrella's frame—shaft, runner, ferrule, ribs, springs, caps, stretchers, joints—should be

made of tempered nickel- or chrome-plated steel. A wooden shaft (maple or hickory) is also reliable; periodically treat it with furniture paste wax.

Try out an umbrella before you buy it. It should open and close with ease and stay in position when locked by the top or bottom spring. Some umbrella manufacturers offer a warranty. This generally indicates that the umbrella is well constructed.

Umbrella covers are usually made of water-repellent silk or nylon. The fabric panels (gores) should be joined with a tight stitch of waxed thread. These joints should be stitched to the ribs with waxed thread. The cover edges should also be stitched (not heat sealed) to resist fraying and give a more finished look. Hold an open umbrella up to the light; no pinholes or stray threads should be visible.

Choose an umbrella with a handle of molded polystyrene or sturdy wood. It should be securely attached to the shaft, with no wiggle or give.

Let an umbrella dry open. When a windproof (reversal) umbrella has been blown inside out, place its handle against your midriff, then slowly pull the runner down the shaft; the ribs should snap back into place at once. Have a malfunctioning umbrella repaired professionally or send it to the manufacturer.

Unconsciousness

On-the-spot emergency treatment

Get medical help right away for anyone who is "out cold," drowsy, disoriented, or unresponsive to strenuous efforts to rouse him. These are *all* levels of unconsciousness. Check the person for a medical alert tag, bracelet, or card.

If the person has no pulse and isn't breathing (no rise and fall of the chest, no perceptible exhaled breath, a bluish skin tone) or if breathing is

Recovery position

labored, begin resuscitation immediately (see *CPR*). If breathing is normal, or when it becomes so, move the victim into the recovery position. In this position, he can breathe freely, is less likely to inhale vomit, and will be relatively comfortable.

Caution: Do not move a person into the recovery position if he has a head injury or a possible neck injury.

Stay with the victim. Once a minute check his breathing. When help arrives, treatment of the cause of unconsciousness can begin. (See also *Fainting; Shock.*)

Universal joints

How to check them

If a rear-drive car clunks on acceleration or if a vibration occurs only at certain throttle positions, check the uni-versal joints (U-joints) on the drive shaft. Most shafts have a joint at each end; some have a double U-joint at one end. Many four-wheel-drive vehicles have two propeller shafts.

With the engine off and the transmission in neutral, raise the car at the rear, the front, or both (see *Jacking a car*). Using both hands, grab the shaft each side of a U-joint and try to twist the parts in opposite directions. If you

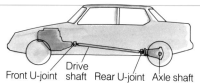

Front U-joint — Drive shaft — Rear U-joint — Axle shaft

feel any free play at all, have the joint replaced. Check all U-joints this way.

When looking for the cause of vibration, check the bolts holding the rear joint together. If you find any loose ones, tighten them.

On a front-drive car, a humming sound indicates a problem with a CV joint on the axle shaft. Have a mechanic check it immediately.

Used cars

How to inspect them

Most used cars come "as is" or with a limited warranty. Evaluate the price against the cost of needed repairs.

A car should start easily and idle reasonably smoothly. Check that all warning lights come on with the ignition. Test-drive the car for at least 10 miles to give warm-running problems a chance to show up.

Reject a car if 1. you hear engine knocking; 2. the oil or coolant warning lights come on or gauge readings are abnormal; 3. an automatic transmission slips on acceleration, grinds or whines, or does not shift smoothly up and down; 4. the clutch shudders or the manual transmission grinds, squeals, or jumps out of gear; 5. there

U

is more than 2 inches of steering wheel free play, roughness when you turn the wheel, or car wandering on smooth roads; 6. the body shakes objectionably at speeds under 55 m.p.h. on a decent road; 7. the exhaust blows blue smoke (oil) or it blows white smoke (water vapor) on a warm, dry day or for more than a few minutes on a cool day. Black smoke is usually a minor fuel problem.

Checking out a car

Brake hard at 25 m.p.h.; the car should come to a straight stop. Some defects are normal with age: a car that rides poorly on rough roads may need new shock absorbers; poor braking may be correctable with work.

With the engine still running, look underneath for an oil leak. Have a trustworthy mechanic evaluate any such leak.

Check all accessories. Except for wipers, their operation may not be critical but will affect price.

Look for lubrication stickers on the door or under the hood for evidence of regular maintenance or look in a private owner's garage for signs of do-it-yourself maintenance.

Take the car to a professional mechanic. He can detect some problems, evaluate your road-test report, and tell you the cost of necessary repairs. If your state mandates inspection, he should tell you if the car will pass.

Vacuum cleaners

Checking for obstructions; changing a drive belt

Caution: Unplug the vacuum cleaner before doing any work on it.

If a vacuum cleaner fails to work properly, first check that the dust bag isn't full. When replacing the bag, check the condition of the filter and clean it, if necessary. Replace the filter at least once a year.

In a canister vacuum cleaner, check for obstructions in the hose and attachments. Plug the hose into the exhaust port, if there is one; run the other end into a paper bag and turn on the motor. Or try pushing a broom handle through the hose. If there are no obstructions and air flow is weak, the hose probably has a hole or split and will have to be replaced.

In a vacuum cleaner with a beater brush, cleaning action may be poor because of a problem with the beater. Lay the machine on its side, remove the metal plate, and see if the rubber belt that connects the beater with the motor is worn or broken. To replace it, release the old belt and lift out the beater bar. Insert a new belt (available at a dealer, or hardware or department store); reset the bar. There should be an arrow indicating which way to twist the belt. If not, turn on the cleaner briefly; the beater should rotate from front to back. If it doesn't, reverse the twist in the belt. Replace the plate.

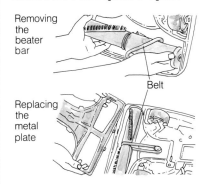

Removing the beater bar

Belt

Replacing the metal plate

If the belt is intact, but the beater doesn't turn, remove the beater and check for tangled hair or threads that could be impeding the action.

Poor cleaning action can also result from worn brushes; they should extend below the bottom plate. Follow the manufacturer's instructions for replacing brushes. If they're not available, replace the entire beater bar.

Vacuuming

Doing an effective job

By vacuuming frequently you can diminish wear on floors, carpets, and upholstery. Before beginning, pick up debris, especially metal objects,

that could damage the hose or the belt (see *Vacuum cleaners*).

For best results on rugs and carpets, use a vacuum cleaner with a beater brush—either an upright or a canister with a power nozzle. The brush agitates carpet fibers and loosens dirt so that it can be sucked away easily. For bare floors, use a floor brush (a beater brush may scratch the finish). For upholstery, draperies, and stairs use the small upholstery attachment. Use a dust brush on walls and a crevice tool at the edge of carpeting, in corners and drawers, and on radiators.

Work slowly, vacuuming with overlapping parallel strokes. If you are picking up any insects or spiders, vacuum a few mothballs into the dust bag and dispose of the bag promptly.

Valances

A finishing touch for windows

Valances are decorative coverings for the tops of curtains or draperies. There are two types. A *soft valance* is a short curtain or drapery in the same style as the window treatment and is usually hung on a separate rod. A *hard valance,* or *cornice,* is a fabric-covered, painted, or stained box, mounted above the window. Whatever the type, valance length should be $\frac{1}{8}$ to $\frac{1}{6}$ the length of the window treatment. Fabric can match or contrast with the curtains or draperies.

For the way to make a short valance see *Curtains and draperies*. Make it wide enough to cover the entire window treatment and with a bottom hem half as deep as the ones on the curtains or draperies.

For an upholstered valance, build a four-sided box, wide enough to clear the rods by at least 2 inches on each side and deep enough to clear the draperies when they're pulled open—usually the depth of rods plus 3 inches. When planning the height, take into account that supporting angle irons will be set above the window frame. Cut four boards, as shown, from pine or fir—1-inch solid or ¾-inch plywood. Glue the top and sides together. When dry, glue the front in place. Reinforce the joints with finishing nails.

Continued next page

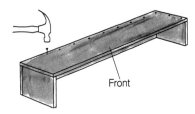

Front

Cut a piece of ¼-inch polyester batting the same dimensions as the front. (Omit this piece if you want a less padded look.) Cut a second piece to cover the entire box, plus 3 inches all around. Spread white glue, thinned with water, on the outside of the front. Glue the smaller piece of batting in place; let it dry. Center the box facedown on the larger piece. Wrap the batting around the box, holding it in place with T-pins. Pull the bottom edges to the underside; trim excess batting in the corners. Anchor the edges with a staple gun or upholstery tacks; where

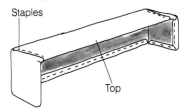

Staples

Top

side and top boards meet, slash diagonally; trim excess batting, then staple or tack the top panel over the side sections. Staple batting inside the back edges of the box; trim any excess.

Cut fabric to cover the box, plus 4 inches all around. Wrap and pin the fabric the same as the batting. Working from the center out, anchor fabric inside the bottom edges; tuck in excess at the corners. Pull the fabric taut over the top and side boards, folding it envelope style on top. Anchor fabric inside the back edges. Mount 1-inch angle irons above the window, 2 to 3 feet apart; set the valance on them.

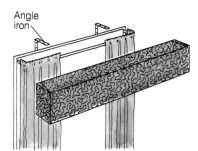

Angle iron

Vapor barriers

Moistureproofing your home

In winter, warm, moist household air moves toward colder, drier air outside. Where insulation has been installed without a proper vapor barrier, water vapor migrating into the walls condenses against the cold inner surface of wall or roof sheathing and inside the insulation. The result is wet, inefficient insulation, and the possibility of mold growth, exterior paint peeling, and structural rot.

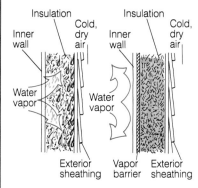

Insulation   Insulation
Inner   Cold,   Inner   Cold,
wall   dry   wall   dry
air   air
Water   Water
vapor   vapor
Exterior   Vapor   Exterior
sheathing   barrier   sheathing

To prevent moisture damage, ventilate your house well (see *Ventilation*), and use insulation with a vapor barrier—usually a layer of nonpermeable aluminum foil, kraft paper, or polyethylene—facing the warm-in-winter side of the wall, floor, or ceiling being insulated. When insulating with loose fill or with unfaced batts or blankets, install a separate vapor barrier of 6-mil-thick polyethylene sheets. More convenient but less efficient as a vapor retarder are insulation batts and blankets with an attached vapor barrier; consider adding polyethylene sheeting to faced insulation.

When installing faced insulation between studs, staple the vapor barrier's flanges to the studs so that the flanges overlap. When covering insulation with polyethylene sheeting, always join sheets at a stud, overlap-

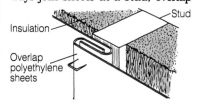

Insulation
Overlap polyethylene sheets
Stud

ping and stapling their edges as shown. Be careful not to puncture or tear a vapor barrier; patch any holes with duct tape for polyethylene.

Use polyethylene as a vapor barrier over an unpaved crawl-space or basement floor. To add a vapor barrier to a finished wall, paint the wall with vapor-barrier paint; vinyl wallpaper or two coats of oil-based paint also provide vapor resistance.

Varnishing

Applying a clear wood finish

Use a tough polyurethane varnish on tables, floors, and other surfaces subject to wear and spills. On other jobs, a less durable alkyd-based varnish can save money. For a clear, nonamber tone, use an acrylic varnish; spray it like lacquer (see *Lacquering*). Reserve a weather-resistant, phenolic-based spar varnish for outdoor trim. Most varnishes come in gloss, semigloss, and satin (dull) finishes.

Sand the surface to be varnished, ending with fine (220) paper. Any previous varnish must be well abraded. To control dust, vacuum the surface and surrounding area. Then use a tack cloth to remove fine particles (see *Tack cloth*). Seal stained wood (see *Staining wood*); avoid shellac sealer if the varnish's label so indicates.

Applying the varnish
Work with good ventilation away from open flames. Use a clean, chisel-cut, natural-bristle brush. Apply varnish full strength; for raw wood, thin the first coat as directed. Avoid making bubbles in the varnish. Don't shake the can. If necessary, stir it gently.

Pour the amount you'll need into a wide-mouth container. Dip the brush bristles a third of the way in. Remove excess by gently tapping the brush on the container; scraping it causes bubbles to fall into the varnish.

Flow the varnish on in long, even strokes with the grain; go a surface's full length if possible. End a stroke by gradually lifting the brush to avoid leaving a ridge. Barely overlap the next stroke. Then wipe the brush dry on paper towels and brush vigorously across the grain to pick up excess var-

V

nish. End by lightly drawing the brush's tip along the grain.

Unless it has worn, older varnish needs only one fresh coat. A new surface needs two; a heavily used surface, three. Between coats, let the varnish dry 24 hours and sand with fine (220) paper; follow the label directions for polyurethane. For a hand-rubbed finish, sand the last coat. Then sprinkle on powdered rottenstone with a little mineral oil. Rub with 0000 steel wool.

Vegetarian diets

Three basic types; a typical meal plan for a pure vegetarian

The three basic vegetarian diets are *vegan,* in which animal products are eschewed entirely; *lacto,* which includes dairy products in addition to plant foods; and *ovolacto,* which includes eggs as well as dairy products.

Every diet must daily include certain amounts of amino acids (protein). Whereas fish, meat, poultry, dairy products, and eggs have all the essential amino acids that we need to build body protein, most plant foods do not. When no animal products are included in a meal, it's necessary to balance the vegetable proteins according to their amino-acid content. For example, legumes (beans, peas, peanuts), which are high in the amino acids lysine and isoleucine, combined with grains (wheat, bulgur, rice), which are high in the amino acids tryptophan and methionine, make a balanced, or complete, protein. Some often used combinations are peanut butter on whole-wheat bread, black beans and rice, and tacos with refried beans.

Legumes combined with seeds, such as a paste of chick-peas and sesame seeds, also make complete protein for the same reason. And the protein value of any grain is enhanced by adding a milk product. Examples are cereal with milk and macaroni and cheese.

If enough calories are not consumed, the body tends to burn amino acids for energy. Because so many foods in a vegetarian diet are low in calories, it's necessary to eat more. Vegetarian diets for children and pregnant and lactating women should be monitored carefully because their protein needs are high and it's especially important for them to get enough calories and complete protein for growth or for producing milk.

Creating a balanced vegan diet
Soybean products, which are high in protein, lend balance and variety to vegetarian meals. Besides the beans themselves, cooked in various ways, there are soymilk, soybean curd (tofu), and meat analogs—foods that resemble meat in flavor and texture.

A typical vegan diet should include a wider than usual variety of legumes, grains, nuts, fruits, and vegetables. Many green, leafy vegetables—broccoli, kale, collards, Brussels sprouts, spinach, and dandelion, turnip, and mustard greens—are important because they provide the calcium normally consumed in milk products. They also supply some of the iron, which would usually be acquired from meat. Legumes and whole grains are other good sources of iron.

One nutrient that can't be obtained from a vegan diet is vitamin B_{12}. Therefore it is recommended that it be taken as a supplement.

Here is a typical daily menu for a vegan adult. *Breakfast:* 1 orange; 1 cup cooked whole-wheat cereal with 1 tablespoon blackstrap molasses, ¼ cup raisins, and ⅓ cup fortified soymilk; 2 slices whole-wheat toast with 2 teaspoons peanut butter. *Lunch:* 2 cups thick vegetable soup; ¾ cup cooked kale; 1 slice whole-wheat bread with 1 teaspoon margerine; 1 banana. *Dinner:* 1 cup black beans on brown rice; ½ cup cooked carrots; ⅔ cup cooked or raw broccoli; 2 slices date-nut bread; 1 cup fortified soymilk.

There are many vegetarian cookbooks on the market. For new recipe ideas look also to some of the cuisines of India, the Middle East, and the oriental countries, where vegetarianism has been practiced for centuries.

Veneer

Fixing a damaged surface layer of fine wood

Soften unpliable old veneer with a few drops of water. Make cuts with a razor knife guided by a metal ruler. Always cut with the grain or at an angle to it.

If a veneer edge is loose, use a thin knife and an emery board to scrape and sand off the old glue underneath. If space is tight, cut the veneer perpendicular or at an angle to the edge, going with the grain as much as possible. Vacuum out the dust. Put yellow carpenter's glue on a knife or a card and work it under the veneer. Wipe off excess with a damp cloth. Put wax paper and a wood block over the area; clamp or weight it overnight.

With a veneer blister, slit through its middle along the grain. Then clean under and reglue the veneer by alternately pressing down one blister half and working under the other half. If the veneer edges overlap at the slit, carefully pare them to fit. On old veneer, try first to remelt the glue under a blister. Using a thick towel, press it with a warm iron for a minute at a time to flatten it. Weight it overnight.

Patching a damaged spot
Buy matching veneer from a woodworking supply house or a craft store. Tape tracing paper over the damaged area, leaving one edge untaped. Trace around the area, forming triangular fingers. (In midsurface, draw a long oval shape.) Slip the veneer under the paper; match the woods' grains and clamp it. Cut through the new and old veneer along the line. Clean out old ve-

neer and glue. Test fit the patch. Dampen it. Glue it in. Clamp, using wax paper and a wood block.

Veneer tape

Finishing raw plywood edges with iron-on wood tape

Select a roll made of the same wood as the plywood's good side. Make sure that the plywood edge is square, smooth, and clean. Wipe it with a tack cloth (see *Tack cloth*).

Unroll enough tape to cover the edge's entire length. Using an iron on a warm, nonsteam setting, tack the tape to the edge by pressing at 6-inch intervals. Smooth and align the tape as you go. Finish bonding it by sliding the iron slowly along its full length.

After 5 minutes, carefully remove any overhanging tape with medium-fine (120) sandpaper. Miter corners where tapes meet, using a sharp craft

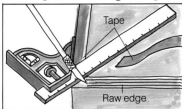

knife. Touch up any unglued spots with the iron. Lightly sand the seams with fine (220) paper.

Ventilation

Using air flow to prevent condensation problems

A well-ventilated attic is especially important in keeping a house comfortable and free of moisture damage all year. (See also *Vapor barriers*.) When installing insulation between attic rafters, leave at least 1 inch of space between the insulation and the underside of the roof sheathing; or install preformed vent channels. Ideally, a rafter cavity should be vented at the soffit and at the roof ridge, allowing air to enter at the roof's base and to exit at its top (see *Vents*).

If venting the soffit isn't possible, install sufficient gable or roof vents to permit good cross-ventilation; consider adding an exhaust fan to supplement air circulation. In an attic equipped with vapor barriers and soffit vents, install at least 1 square foot of open ventilation area for every 300 square feet of floor area; if there are no vapor barriers or soffit vents, double the ventilation area.

Ventilation is also important in a crawl space to eliminate moisture rising from the soil. Install at least two—preferably four—vents high on oppo-

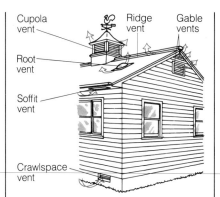

site foundation walls, close to the corners. With a vapor barrier on the ground, provide 1 square foot of open ventilation area for every 1,500 square feet of ground area. Close a crawlspace vent when humidity is high; leave attic vents open all year.

Vent plugs

A way to ventilate an attic or a wall cavity

A vent plug is a metal or plastic cylinder, usually fitted with a screen and louvers; hardware stores sell them in several diameters. To increase attic ventilation, fit vent plugs into evenly spaced holes drilled in the soffits with a spade bit or a hole saw (see *Vents*).

If moisture in a wall cavity causes exterior paint to peel, try lowering indoor humidity (see *Humidity control*). If that doesn't work, you may have to ventilate the cavity by fitting vent plugs into the siding wherever paint is peeling. Plugs in siding reduce insulation effectiveness by up to 50 percent; use them only as a last resort.

Install two plugs between each pair of studs (see *Studs*), one near the bottom of the wall cavity, the other near the top (or, where there's a window, just below the sill). Drill holes in the siding, then push in the plugs, louvers down.

Vents

Installing attic venting

To determine your house's venting needs, see *Ventilation*. Check local

building codes before adding vents. Roofing suppliers sell a variety of soffit vents: individual units and plugs (see *Vent plugs*), continuous strips, or perforated soffit boards.

To install a vent unit, make a template of the side of the vent that will go into the soffit. Trace its outline on the soffit between two lookout beams (look for the heads of the nails attaching the soffit to the lookouts). Drill starting holes in the corners of the outline. Use a saber saw or a keyhole saw to cut a hole; screw the vent in place.

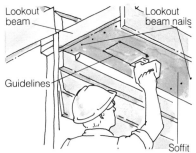

To install a vent strip, snap a chalkline 3 inches in from the outer edge of the soffit. Snap a second chalkline separated from the first by the width of the inside part of the strip. Drill starting holes; saw along the guidelines and between them on both sides of each lookout. Remove the freed soffit sections. With a hammer and chisel, cut along the guidelines into the

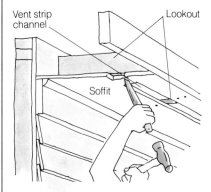

soffit pieces still nailed to the lookouts; pry off the pieces. Press the vent into the channel; nail it to the lookouts. If necessary, chisel into the lookouts so that the vent seats properly.

To install a perforated soffit board, use a pry bar to remove the old soffit (you may first have to remove the fascia board and the rear molding). Nail the new soffit to the lookouts.

Ridge, gable, and roof vents

Whether or not your house lends itself to soffit venting, rooftop vents are essential. Ridge and cupola vents are most efficient, but installing them is a job for a professional.

Rectangular or triangular louvered vents can be fitted into both end walls of a gabled roof, as close to the roof ridge as possible. To install a rectangular vent, draw a rectangle on the inside attic wall ¼ inch longer and wider than the inside part of the vent. Drill corner starting holes; saw out the opening. If you cut through a stud, remove about 1½ inches of it above and below the opening to accommodate two 2 x 4 headers.

Nail the headers to the studs on both sides of, and above and below,

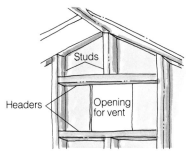

the opening. Apply roofing cement to the vent's outer lip; from outside, fit the vent, louvers down, into the opening. Nail the vent's inner lip to the headers. Caulk the vent's outer edges with roofing cement.

For a triangular vent, trace and cut an opening just below the ridge beam. Saw 1½ inches off the top of any stud below the opening; nail a 2 x 4 header to the cut studs. Cut two more lengths of 2 x 4; nail them to the rafters on either side of the opening. Fit the vent into the opening as described.

Position a roof vent inconspicuously. (See *Roof repairs* for safety precautions when working on a roof.) Measure from the center of the location to the roof ridge and to the nearest side edge of the roof (minus overhang). With these measurements, locate the vent's tentative center point inside the attic. Draw a line from rafter to rafter through this point. At the midpoint of the line, drive a nail through the roof. Find the nail tip on the roof; use it as a center point to draw a circle equal in diameter to the vent hole.

Drill a starting hole on the circle; saw an opening. In the attic, frame the opening with two 2 x 4 headers nailed to the rafters. On the roof, place the vent over the opening. Draw a line around the base; remove the shingles

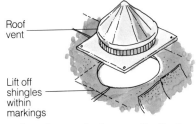

within the marked area. Caulk the the vent's base, place it over the opening, and nail it to the sheathing with roofing nails. Restore the shingles around the vent (see *Roof repairs*). Most attics require two roof vents (one, if the vent has an electric fan).

Video cameras

What to look for in a camera and a portable recorder

Most video cameras attach by cable to a portable, battery-powered videocassette recorder (VCR) that you carry on a shoulder strap. The VCR can be either Beta or VHS format. The VCR and the camera must be fully compatible. Different brands sometimes work together, but you may lose the use of some on-camera VCR controls.

Units that combine the camera and the recorder are called *camcorders*. Besides standard Beta, you can get VHS-C and 8mm units—special compact formats for taping home video.

Lenses and light sensitivity

A camera's zoom range is expressed as a ratio, such as 2:1 or 8:1; the greater the ratio, the greater the lens's wide angle to telephoto capacity. A power zoom and automatic focusing let you do smoother, freer taping. For indoor shooting, look for a low lens f number, such as $f1.2$, which indicates better light-gathering capacity (see *Cameras*). Overall, the lower the camera's *lux* number, the greater its dim-light sensitivity.

Other important considerations

A typical video camera viewfinder shows the image coming through the lens like an SLR camera. Advanced models have a tiny TV screen inside, letting you judge lighting better and replay a take on the spot.

Note the time a single tape can record and a battery can run without recharging. Look for a viewfinder with signals for camera on, too dim light, and low battery. Consider a unit's feel. Will you need a shoulder brace to steady it? Is it compact enough for easy vacation shooting? Try out a unit by renting one. (See also *Home video*.)

Videocassette recorders

Getting the most from a VCR

With a videocassette recorder (VCR), you can record and play back television signals received from the air, a cable system, or a video camera, or you can play prerecorded cassettes. A typical tabletop unit also contains a tuner that selects channels and a timer that turns the unit on and off at the times you set. A portable VCR connects to a separate tuner-timer unit.

Hooking up a VCR

If you have a TV antenna, simply connect the antenna leads to the VCR; then hook the VCR to your set, as directed. With a cable-ready VCR, connect the incoming cable to the VCR; then hook the VCR to your television's cable box or directly to the set if it's cable ready. Either hookup lets you use your TV set with or without the VCR.

If you subscribe to a pay channel or don't have a cable-ready VCR, you may need a special cable connection to use all of a VCR's features. It usually involves splitting the incoming signal and sending it through both the cable box and a device known as a *block converter* and then on to the VCR and television. Another method involves sending the split signal through a cable box and a *channel trap* or a *notch filter*. Cable systems vary. Call your cable office or a knowledgeable dealer.

Repairing a VCR

These complex, delicate machines should be serviced only by a qualified technician. If a problem arises, make sure that the signal or videotape is not faulty or the wiring loose. With a prerecorded cassette, try adjusting the

V

tracking control; it corrects for tapes made on different machines.

The video recording and playback heads are the most frequent trouble source. Have them cleaned if your screen image develops streaks, blips, or snow. Don't use a cassette head-cleaning tape; each use wears the heads slightly. To prolong the heads' life, protect your VCR from heat and humidity. Put a dust cover over it when it's not in use. After years of use, most heads need replacement.

Vines

Choosing and training annual and woody climbers

Such annual vines as morning glories, sweet peas, and canary creepers do best in full sun and moist, rich soil. Once established, they quickly make a colorful display on a trellis, fence, or wall. Start seeds in 3-inch pots 6 to 10 weeks before the last expected frost (see *Starting seeds indoors*). Plant seedlings 3 inches in front of their supports; for best results, give each an anchored string to climb.

Choose a long-lived woody vine according to climate and growing conditions (see *Shrubs*). Consider its habit and size. Left unpruned, a wisteria may reach a height of 60 or 70 feet, its massive stem strangling the tree that supports it or pulling a gutter or downspout from a house; the delicate jasmine seldom grows to 12 feet high.

Training and support

Many vines, such as wisterias and honeysuckles, twine around any available support; train them by pruning them back to desirable buds or branches. Others, such as grape vines and Virginia creepers, cling to walls and trellises with corkscrewlike tendrils or adhesive pads. For sprawling vines, such as jasmine and bougainvillea, which must be tied to supports, erect a wire fence or wood lattice between the plant and the surface it is to cover; train each season's growth with soft twine or gardener's ties.

Prune vines after flowering, usually in late summer or early fall. (See also *Ground covers; Ivy in the garden; Planting; Pruning shrubs*.)

Vinyl sheet flooring

Installing an easy-to-clean, one-piece floor covering

Flexible, do-it-yourself sheet flooring comes 6 feet and 12 feet wide. Try to cover a room with one piece.

Prepare the floor as you would for tiles (see *Vinyl tiles*). Unroll the flooring in a large area and let it flatten for 24 hours. Sketch your room's dimensions. Transfer them to the flooring. Cut it 6 inches wider all around.

Roll up the piece and unroll it in place with edges lapping up the walls. Cut each corner vertically to make the vinyl lie flat; do outward-projecting corners first. Trim the edges, using a utility knife and a metal straightedge. Leave a ⅛-inch space between the wall and the flooring.

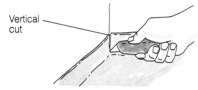

Vertical cut

Following the manufacturer's directions, secure the flooring at the edges, using adhesive or staples (see *Staple gun*). Or fold back half at a time, spread adhesive with a notched trowel, and press it firmly back.

If you must seam two pieces, leave 18 inches of the first piece unattached. Lap the second piece's edge over the first, match the pattern, and weight it securely. Install the piece, leaving the seam edge free. Then cut the seam along a pattern line, going through both layers at once. Fold

Waste   Waste

back the edges, spread adhesive on the floor, and press them back firmly. Apply a sealing adhesive on the seam.

Reattach the perimeter trim to the wall, not the floor; slip a thin cardboard spacer under shoe molding as you nail it on. Don't attach a metal threshold through the flooring.

Vinyl siding

Replacing a damaged panel

To replace a cracked or badly stained panel of vinyl siding, buy from a siding dealer a *zipper tool* along with the replacement panel. Repair weathered siding with a panel from an inconspicuous part of the house and replace that panel with the new one.

Replace a section at least 4 feet long. Use a combination square to mark cutting lines on the damaged panel. Let an edge fall along an existing joint if one is close. Work the zipper tool under the edge of the panel above the damaged one. Pull down on it and draw it along the edge to unlock the

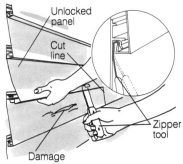

Unlocked panel

Cut line

Zipper tool

Damage

panel. Prop the unlocked panel open with wood blocks. Remove the nails in the damaged panel's top edge. Cut out the damaged area with tin snips.

Cut the replacement panel 1½ inches longer than the opening to allow for a ¾-inch overlap at each end. Slip the panel under one adjacent panel's edge and overlap the other. Follow the existing pattern of overlaps. Make sure the panel's bottom edge locks in place.

Secure the panel's upper edge with aluminum nails at 16-inch intervals. Center each nail in an oval slot. Stop hammering when the head is about ¹⁄₃₂ inch from being flush. Relock the panel above with the zipper tool.

Vinyl tiles

Renewing a floor with easy-to-lay squares

You can install vinyl tiles over most smooth, solid, dry surfaces. Remove

V

all dirt and wax. Secure loose tiles and boards. Remove all perimeter floor trim. Cover a problem surface first with ½-inch plywood or hardboard.

To find out how many standard 12-inch tiles you'll need, multiply a room's length by its width in feet; count a partial foot as a whole foot.

Snap chalklines dividing the room in half in length and width. Check that they are at right angles (see *Parquet flooring*). Lay loose tiles from the lines to the walls. If a wall tile is under 4 inches wide, shift the line 6 inches.

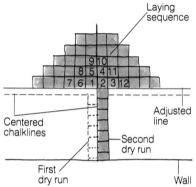

Lay one-half a room at a time. Start with two tiles at the chalkline junction. Work outward to form a pyramid. Peel off each tile's paper backing and press it down firmly. With non-adhesive tiles, use a notched trowel to spread adhesive for a few tiles. Set each tile straight down; sliding a tile pushes up adhesive. Press the tiles down, using a rented, weighted tile roller or a kitchen rolling pin with your weight on it. Alternate the pattern direction of marbleized tiles.

Lay the edge tiles last. Align each over the last adjacent whole tile. Put another tile over it, against the wall. Then score the edge tile with a utility

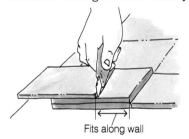

Fits along wall

knife along the top tile's edge. Break the tile along the score. Measure from both walls at a corner. Make a paper pattern for an irregular cut.

Visas

Applying for an important travel document

A visa stamped into a passport by a consular officer of a foreign country permits you to visit that country for a specified purpose and time period.

A U.S. citizen with a valid passport does not need a visa to enter most Western European countries; many Latin American and Caribbean nations require an airline-issued tourist card instead of a visa. Some countries even require visas of airline passengers landing, but not disembarking, within their borders. These are called transit visas. Several months before a foreign trip, phone the consulates of the countries you plan to visit and ask for their visa requirements.

Apply for a visa from a foreign consulate in person, by mail, or through a travel agent. You must present a valid passport (see *Passports*), fill out an application and, in most cases, pay a fee; two or more passport-size photographs may also be required.

A useful U.S. State Department publication entitled *Foreign Entry Requirements* can be obtained by writing to the Consumer Information Center, Pueblo, CO 81009. The charge for the publication is 50 cents.

Vitamins

Getting the quantities you need; vitamin sources

Vitamins help your body to process other nutrients; form red blood cells, connective tissue, and hormones; and generally maintain good health. If you eat well-balanced meals (see *Menu planning*) and have no unusual medical needs, your vitamin intake should be adequate.

If you don't regularly eat all the recommended servings from the U.S.D.A. Food Guide Pyramid or you are on a weight-loss diet of less than 1,200 calories a day, consider a multivitamin pill that supplies the U.S. Recommended Daily Allowances (RDA) of the B vitamins and C.

A deficiency of any vitamin can cause health problems. Megadoses (10 times the RDA) of niacin, folacin, A, C, D, and E can also be harmful.

To get maximum vitamin potential, buy fresh produce and process foods lightly. Retain fruit and vegetable skins. Steam vegetables, cook them in minimal water, or stir-fry them.

GUIDE TO VITAMINS

Vitamin	Good sources
A (Retinol)	Liver; eggs, milk products; fortified margarine; yellow, orange, and dark-green vegetables
Thiamin (B$_1$)	Pork; liver; oysters; whole grains; brewer's yeast; green peas
Riboflavin (B$_2$)	Liver; milk; dark-green vegetables; whole grains; mushrooms
Niacin (B$_3$)	Liver; poultry; meat; tuna; nuts; legumes
Pyridoxine (B$_6$)	Whole grains; liver; avocados; spinach; bananas
Cobalamin (B$_{12}$)	Liver; kidneys; meat; fish; eggs; milk; oysters
Folic acid (Folacin)	Liver; kidneys; dark-green leafy vegetables; wheat germ; brewer's yeast
Pantothenic acid	Liver; kidneys; whole grains; nuts; eggs; dark-green vegetables; yeast
Biotin	Egg yolk; liver; kidneys; dark-green vegetables; green beans
C (Ascorbic acid)	Citrus fruits; tomatoes; strawberries; melons; dark-green vegetables
D (Calciferol)	Fortified milk; egg yolk; liver; tuna; salmon
E (Tocopherol)	Vegetable oils; whole grains; liver; dried beans
K	Green leafy vegetables; vegetables in cabbage family

Volleyball

A game for beach, lawn, or indoor court

On a court roughly 30 x 60 feet, a six-player team tries to hit a 26-inch ball over a net 8 feet high and into the opponent's court. A player may strike the ball with his hand, arm, or any part of his body above his waist. The team to score 15 points first (with at least a 2-point advantage) wins. Only the serving team scores.

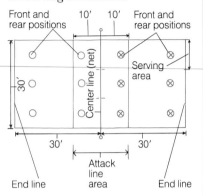

Front and rear positions   10'   10'   Front and rear positions
Serving area
Center line (net)
30'
Attack line area
30'   30'
End line   End line

Each court has a 10-foot attack or frontline area. Three players cover that area while three cover the rear 20 feet. Players rotate positions clockwise with each point gained. The server stands in the service area behind the right-hand third of the end line. Holding the ball in one hand, he gives it an underhand blow with his fist. The ball must clear the net; if it brushes the top *(net ball),* the team loses the serve. (A net ball during a play is good.) The opponents try to prevent the ball from landing by hitting it back. If they can't, the server's team scores a point and serves again. If the server's team can't return the ball, the opponents gain the serve.

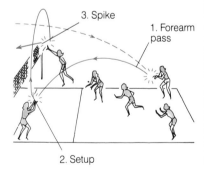

3. Spike
1. Forearm pass
2. Setup

A player may not catch or hold the ball or hit it twice in succession, but he can pass *(volley)* it to a teammate. The ball must go over the net by the third pass. The main purpose of the volley is to set up a *spike,* a hard-to-return downward smash into the op-

posite court. To prevent a spike from landing, opposing front liners may jump up and reach above the net to block the ball.

Vomiting

Comforting and caring for a child or adult who vomits

Vomiting is a symptom with many possible causes. The cause can range from a food that doesn't agree with you to serious illness. However, the most common cause is an intestinal virus. (See also *Hangovers; Headaches; Indigestion; Motion sickness; Nausea; Stomachaches.*) Vomiting may last only a short while or persist for several days.

The best treatment is to eat no solids and to take frequent, small sips of clear fluids: weak tea; decarbonated, room-temperature ginger ale or cola drinks; gelatin; broth; or diluted apple juice. An infant may be kept on the breast or offered one-half-strength formula; it is important to maintain a good fluid intake to prevent dehydration (see *Dehydration*). Once vomiting has ceased (usually within 24 hours) gradually add light, easy-to-digest foods: gelatin desserts, cooked cereals, dry toast, crackers.

Even an adult may want support and reassurance when he is vomiting, but for children these are necessities. Gently sponge off any vomitus. Supply fresh bedclothes and pajamas if necessary. Wipe the toilet and nearby area with disinfectant cleaner. Clean spills from carpeting with a mild solution of ammonia and water.

What to watch for

Be alert for symptoms indicating a serious disorder; report them to a doctor (see *Drug overdose; Food poisoning; Head injuries*). Vomiting combined with abdominal pain and fever may mean appendicitis.

Intolerance to certain medications can cause uncontrollable vomiting. In infants, persistent projectile vomiting (the forceful expulsion of stomach contents) can be easily corrected by surgery. At any age, if vomiting continues longer than a day or if it is unusually severe, consult a doctor.

Waffle irons

Checking and replacing wires, thermostat, and heating coil

If the top and bottom grill plate don't heat, unplug the unit. Unclip the grill plate from the iron's shell, then unscrew and remove the element tray. Inspect the wires in the shell for breaks; check the terminals for corrosion. If replacements are necessary, remove the two heating-unit connecting nuts or screws; if they are frozen, apply penetrating oil. Replace the old wire with a duplicate; clean connectors with fine steel wool.

Further heating problems may be caused by a defective thermostat. Test it for continuity; replace it with a duplicate from the manufacturer or from an appliance repair center.

If the wires and thermostat are not at fault, test the heating coil. Attach a continuity tester's clip to the coil near a terminal; touch the tester's probe to the other coil end. If the tester doesn't light, inspect the wiring under the el-

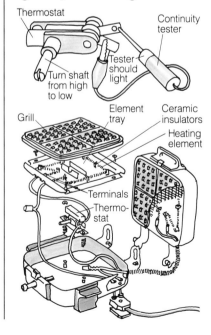

Thermostat
Continuity tester
Tester should light
Turn shaft from high to low
Grill
Element tray
Ceramic insulators
Heating element
Terminals
Thermostat

ement tray; it may be broken or loose. Replace the coil with a duplicate.

Stretch the replacement coil by pulling its ends apart slowly so that the coils are evenly spaced and its total length is just shorter than needed to make the loop. Carefully thread the coil around the ceramic insulators so that it doesn't kink or stretch. Connect the coil ends to the terminals, replace washers, and tighten screws. Plug the power cord into a receptacle to test. Replace grill plates.

Waffles

Crisp batter cakes baked in a waffle iron

Preheat the waffle iron. If properly seasoned, it needs no greasing and no washing. (Follow the manufacturer's instructions or see *Cast-iron cookware* for seasoning.) To test an iron that has no indicator light, put a few drops of water on the grids; the water will skitter if the iron is hot enough.

Sift together 2 cups flour, 2 tablespoons sugar, 1 tablespoon baking powder, and 1 teaspoon salt. Combine 2 egg yolks, 1¾ cup milk, and 6 tablespoons vegetable oil or melted butter or margarine. Pour into the flour mixture; beat just until smooth. Beat 2 egg whites until soft peaks form; fold into the batter. Pour batter in the center of the iron until it covers ⅔ of the surface; close the iron. When the steaming stops, waffles are done. *Buttermilk waffles:* Substitute buttermilk or sour milk for regular milk; reduce the baking powder to 2 teaspoons; add 1 teaspoon baking soda.

Wall fasteners

How to put up an object so that it won't come down

On a hollow wall, attach a fixture to a stud whenever possible (see *Studs*). Use a common nail or wood screw long enough to go through the fixture and wall and well into the stud. Drill a pilot hole for a screw. Secure a heavy item with a *lag bolt* (see *Screws*). Or use a *hanger bolt*. One of its ends is

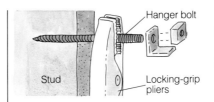

Stud — Hanger bolt — Locking-grip pliers

threaded like a wood screw; the other like a machine bolt. Clamp locking-grip pliers to its center section to drive it into a pilot hole. Support a very heavy load, such as a kitchen cabinet, from a board secured to two or more studs with lag bolts or hanger bolts.

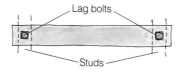

Lag bolts — Studs

Use a sheet-metal screw to fasten to a metal stud. Drill through the wall up to the stud. Dent the metal with a punch. Then drill a small pilot hole.

Attaching to a wall between studs

For a light load, use a *plastic anchor*. Drill a slightly smaller hole or punch one with a large nail. Tap in the anchor. Use a sheet-metal screw.

To hold more weight, use a *hollow-wall anchor* (Molly bolt). Drill a slightly larger hole and slip it in. Steady it with another screwdriver in a flange opening and tighten the screw. You'll feel resistance when the anchor flares out in the wall. Remove the screw and mount the fixture.

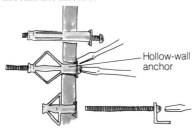

Hollow-wall anchor

You can also use a *toggle bolt;* it has a winged toggle that springs open inside the wall. Drill a hole large enough for the folded wings to pass through.

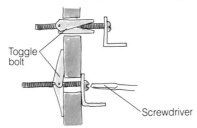

Toggle bolt — Screwdriver

Put the bolt through the fixture, screw the toggle onto the end of the bolt, and slip it all the way into the hole. When the wings of the toggle spring open, tighten the bolt, pulling it toward you to press the open wings against the wall. A *gravity toggle bolt* works similarly; it has a toggle that swivels down.

Attaching to solid masonry walls

Mount a board, such as a shelf cleat, with *masonry nails* or *cut nails* long

Masonry nail — Cut nail

enough to go through any plaster and securely into the masonry. To avoid splitting the wood, drill pilot holes in it. Drill pilot holes in brick, cement block, or concrete. Use a masonry bit and a variable-speed drill on slow speed; keep an even pressure on the bit. Drive the nails in squarely, using a lightweight sledge hammer.

Caution: Wear goggles when driving masonry and cut nails. These hard-steel nails snap easily and can chip a hammer's edge, causing flying particles.

Use a *plastic* or *fiber plug* or a *plastic anchor* for a light load and a *lead anchor* for a heavier one. All expand tightly against a hole in the masonry when you drive in a screw. For the heaviest loads, use an *expansion shield;* a bolt expands it.

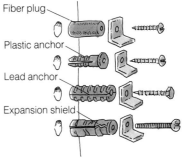

Fiber plug — Plastic anchor — Lead anchor — Expansion shield

For all, drill a hole the diameter and length of the anchor, using a carbide-tipped bit. Clean out the hole before tapping in the anchor.

For moderately heavy loads, you can also use a *wood plug* cut from a ¾-inch or larger dowel. Drill a slightly smaller hole. Grease or soap the plug and drive it in. Then drill a pilot hole in the plug for a wood screw.

W

Wallpapering

Hanging paper or vinyl wall coverings

To determine how many rolls a room will need, add together the widths of its walls in feet and multiply by its height. Divide by 30—the average usable square feet in a roll. Add a roll for good measure. Subtract a half roll for each normal-size window and door.

Buy compatible *paste* and a *paste brush*—or a *water box* for prepasted paper. You also need gluelike *size* for precoating walls, a *plumb bob, chalkline, smoothing brush, seam roller,* and *craft knife* with *extra blades* or a box of *single-edge razor blades.* Devise a worktable: plywood on sawhorses or a table covered with plastic.

Preparing the walls

Walls should be clean, smooth, and sound. Use an alkyd primer-sealer or a latex acrylic primer to cover repairs, new walls, or a regular latex finish. Sand glossy enamel or rub on liquid deglosser. Remove peeling wallpaper, more than two old layers, and vinyl or other paper that strips off easily (see *Wallpaper removal*). Before hanging vinyl, remove old paper. Paint the ceiling and trim. Coat the walls with size, as directed.

Planning the strips' positions

A pattern mismatch will occur at the edge of the last strip you hang. Plan for it to fall along a door's edge, an inconspicuous corner, or a floor-to-ceiling built-in. Normally you start at this point and work around the room. But with a strong, symmetrical design, center the first strip over a fireplace or a sofa or between windows.

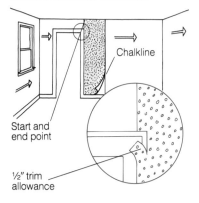

Chalkline

Start and end point

½" trim allowance

Putting up the first strip

Measure out from your ending point a wallpaper width minus ½ inch; mark a plumbed chalkline (see *Plumb line*). For a centered strip, mark a line half a wallpaper width from center.

Cut the first strip with 3 inches trim allowance at top and bottom; make rough cuts with scissors. Coat the upper two-thirds with paste and fold it over itself, paste side in. Be careful not to crease it. Coat the lower third; fold it up. Wait 5 minutes.

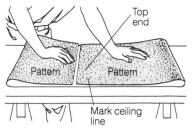

Top end

Pattern   Pattern

Mark ceiling line

Open the top fold, align its edge on the chalkline, and smooth it on with your brush. Then unfold and smooth the lower part. Smooth from the center out to remove all wrinkles and air pockets. Wrap the ½-inch excess onto the adjacent wall; trim it off along a built-in or door frame. Trim the strip at top and bottom. Make all visible cuts with a craft knife or razor guided by a metal ruler; change blades often.

Hang prepasted paper directly from the water box. Roll up the strip from bottom to top, pattern side in. Weight the roll in the box with water to cover. Let it soak as directed. Then pull it straight up and onto the wall.

Water box

Making seams; matching patterns

Cut and hang the remaining strips on the wall. Align each along the previous strip's edge. Push it against the edge slightly so that the two form a slight ridge; it will flatten as the paper dries. After 10 minutes, press the seam with your seam roller. On vinyl paper, *double cut* a seam: overlap the edges and slice through both layers.

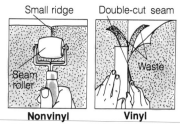

Small ridge   Double-cut seam

Seam roller

Waste

Nonvinyl   **Vinyl**

Match each strip's pattern against the previous strip. With a *drop match* pattern—one that aligns diagonally—it may reduce wastage to cut strips alternately from two rolls.

Turning a corner

Measure from the last whole strip to the corner at three points. Cut and hang a strip ½ inch wider than your widest measurement. On the other wall, measure out the width of the leftover piece; mark a plumbed chalkline.

Measure and cut ½" wider

Chalkline

Lap seam

Leftover piece

Align the piece on the line; lap the seam at the corner; the mismatch won't be noticeable. Glue the lapped vinyl edges with vinyl-to-vinyl adhesive.

On outward-projecting corners, cut the first piece to go around the corner 1 inch. Then plumb and hang the other piece ½ inch from the corner.

At a door or a window, paste the strip over the frame. Make a diagonal relief cut to each corner. Then trim.

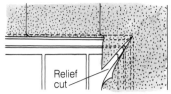

Relief cut

On a window's second side, make the relief cuts as you work down the strip, smoothing and aligning it. At an electric outlet, turn off the power (see *Circuit testing*) and remove the wall plate. Paper over the box, making a small X cut over it. Then trim.

W

Wallpaper removal

Getting ready for a new finish

Peel off vinyl wallpaper. Use a utility knife to free an upper corner; then slowly pull it straight down with the wallpaper almost against itself. Other coverings may strip off easily; always test. Leave the textured paste residue; it forms a good basis for new paste.

Soak off paper that won't strip off. Abrade a nonporous or painted surface with extracoarse sandpaper first. Wear rubber gloves and sponge an entire strip with wallpaper stripping solution. After 10 minutes, rewet a small area and scrape with a wide scraper. Wet the next strip in advance. Scrub off remnants with a strong detergent.

For stubborn paper, rent a steamer from a wallpaper dealer. Hold the flat, perforated steam plate to each area for 2 or 3 minutes. When you've soaked half a strip, scrape it off.

On plasterboard, soak or steam moderately. If it wasn't painted previously, scrape the paper off dry, using a razor-edge wallpaper scraper.

Wandering Jew

Trailing houseplants

Those easy-to-tend tradescantia and zebrina groups commonly called wandering Jew or inch plant have 1- to 3-inch striped leaves, often with purple undersides. In spring and summer, they bear small clusters of flowers. They grow well in pots and in hanging baskets in a warm, sunny window. Cool temperatures slow their growth.

Pot them in a standard potting mix (see *Potting houseplants*). Once or twice monthly during the growing season, give liquid plant food, diluted to half the recommended strength.

In spring and summer, water moderately; in fall and winter, allow the top ½ inch of soil to dry between waterings. When the plant becomes root bound, repot it in a larger container. Propagate by tip or stem cuttings any season. (See also *Houseplants; Propagating plants*.)

War

A fast two-handed card game for youngsters

Evenly divide a facedown standard deck between you and your opponent. Then both simultaneously turn over a top card; the higher (ace high, 2 low) wins. The winner of this *trick* places both cards facedown under his stack.

The game continues in this way until you both play a pair and then there is *war*. Put these cards in the middle of the table. You and your opponent now play three cards facedown; turn over the top one. The higher wins all cards played in the war. If, however, these faceup cards are a pair, a second war is declared; each player adds one card and the play continues in the same way. The taker of all cards or the victor of three wars wins the game.

Warm-air heating

Balancing and maintaining a forced-air heating system

Manually adjusted dampers in the ducts of a forced-air system let you regulate the amount of warm air entering a room. If some rooms are cold and others overheated, balance the system by opening or closing the dampers.

Look for dampers at the beginning of branch ducts leading from a main duct (or, in some systems, from the hot-air plenum) to room registers. Follow a branch duct's path to determine which room it heats; or close a damper to see which room gets cold. Label the damper once you've identified it. A damper is closed when its handle is at right angles to the duct; it's open when the handle is parallel to the duct. Secure a damper in place by tightening its locknut (if any).

Balance the ducts on a cold day. Fully open all dampers and registers.

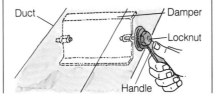

Set the thermostat at normal room temperature and let it operate the heating system for at least 3 hours. Partially close the damper in the duct leading to a room that overheats. Wait an hour, then see how the room feels; check its temperature with a thermometer held 4 feet above the floor. Open or close the damper as needed; check the room again after an hour. Working from warm to cold, repeat the procedure in each room. Because adjusting air flow in one duct affects the others, fine-tuning the system may take several days. If after balancing the ducts, some rooms remain cold, try increasing the speed of the furnace blower (see *Furnaces*).

Maintenance

Periodically vacuum the room registers using a crevice tool. Once a year, inspect ductwork for leaks; seal them with duct tape. For furnace maintenance, see *Furnaces*.

Warped floorboards

Flattening or replacing a cupped board

Warping occurs most frequently in water-damaged or poorly nailed wide boards. Screw down the center of a dome-shaped warp and each side of curled-up edges. Drill a pilot hole for each screw; redrill the part going through the board so that it is large enough to let the screw pass freely and pull the board down. Have people stand on the warp if necessary. Countersink the screws; fill the holes with wood putty mixed with stain to match the floor (see *Countersinking*).

For a stubborn warp, sand or strip off the finish (see *Stripping furniture*). Put wet towels over the area. Cover them with plastic and weight the board with heavy furniture for a day or two before screwing it down.

To replace a severely warped board, drill overlapping ¾-inch holes across the board; be careful not to go deeply into the subfloor. Then use a wood chisel and a mallet to split out the board and square the edge. If there is no subfloor, cut along a joist edge. Drill a hole and use a keyhole saw. Nail on a cleat to support the new board.

Continued next page

W

Cut a new board to fit. Trim off the grooved edge's lower lip. Drill slanting pilot holes for nails. Put carpenter's glue along the tongue and groove. Nail in the board with annular-ring nails; set them and fill the holes.

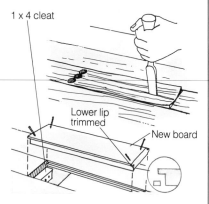

1 x 4 cleat

Lower lip trimmed

New board

Warping

Making a frame loom; calculating warp yarn needed; putting the yarn on the loom

In weaving, the threads stretched onto the loom are called warp. Warping is easy on a small frame loom, which can be used for such projects as cushion covers, bags, and table mats.

You can buy a frame loom at a craft store, or make one with 1 x 2 pine or fir: two pieces 20 inches long and two pieces 15 inches. Lay the two shorter

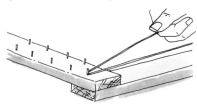

pieces across the longer ones; use an L or T square to form right angles. Glue the joints; reinforce them with 1½-inch screws. Hammer 1-inch brads along the shorter pieces, spacing them ¼ inch apart and staggered, as shown.

A warp yarn should be smooth, springy, and strong. For a frame loom, use knitting worsted, worsted warp yarn, (available at some craft shops), rug warp, or string. To calculate the amount of warp you'll need, multiply the length of the frame loom (20 inches) times the number of strands per

inch (8) times the width of the project; add 2 yards extra. For a pillow cover 14 inches square, you'll need 64 yards.

Tie one end of the warp yarn to a nail at the top of the loom. Run the yarn down the loom to the nail directly opposite, then back up to the next nail, and so on, tying the end at the last nail. Strive for a soft, springy tension—neither taut nor sagging. As weft yarn is inserted (see *Weaving*), the warp will be stretched tighter.

Warranties

Getting your rights under written and implied warranties

Whenever you buy merchandise, you get some form of warranty, or guarantee about the basic quality of the product, that will be upheld by law. The warranty may be written or implied.

Implied warranties
When you purchase an item, you assume that its basic quality and safety meet typical consumer expectations for that type of product. This is the *warranty of merchantability*. If you tell a seller that you need an item to do a particular job, you can reasonably expect it to serve that purpose. This is the *warranty of fitness for a particular purpose*. A seller can exclude these implied warranties only if he makes it clear that he is doing so. For example, an item marked "as is" warns you that you purchase at your own risk.

When a product fails to come up to its warranties, let the seller know at once. He should promptly give you a product that will fill the bill, satisfactorily repair the product, or refund your money. If he refuses, complain in writing. If you still get no results, you can (1) keep the item and sue the seller for the difference in the price of the item promised as compared to the price of the item received or (2) return the goods and sue the seller for the amount of money you paid. If the amount is small enough, you can take it to small claims court without hiring a lawyer (see *Small claims court*).

Limited and full warranties
Manufacturers frequently offer limited or full warranties that promise to repair their product if it malfunctions

within a certain period of time. In a limited warranty you get only what is specified. If a product is covered by a full warranty, the manufacturer is obligated to repair without charge an item that breaks down within the covered period. You need not have mailed in the warranty card, but you may have to produce a dated, itemized receipt or some other proof of purchase, and you will probably have to get the product to an authorized repair service station. If you misused or abused the product or tried to repair it yourself, the warranty is void.

Warts

What to do or not do about these unsightly growths

Warts are caused by viruses. Moderately contagious by contact, they usually appear on hands, feet, or face. *Plantar warts* grow on the soles of the feet, where body weight forces them inward; they can be very painful. *Anal-genital warts* afflict either men or women; they may become secondarily infected with bacteria and are not necessarily contracted venereally.

Most warts, especially in children, disappear in time. If one persists or is painful, if they multiply, or if they are in the genital area or close to a fingernail, see a dermatologist. He may prescribe medication, surgical removal, cauterization, or freezing the wart. Never try to remove one yourself.

Washing machines

Solving clothes-washer problems

Caution: Before servicing a washer, unplug it and turn off the faucets.

If the machine vibrates excessively, adjust the leveling legs so that the cabinet is level from side to side and from front to back (see *Leveling*). Prop up the cabinet with a wood block, loosen the locknut (if any) on a leveling leg with a wrench, then screw the leg in or out; don't extend it too far. Check the adjustment with a carpenter's level.

W

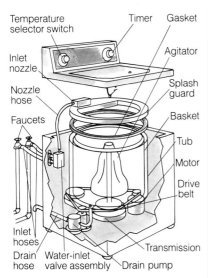

Temperature selector switch — Timer — Gasket — Agitator — Inlet nozzle — Nozzle hose — Splash guard — Basket — Faucets — Tub — Motor — Drive belt — Inlet hoses — Drain hose — Water-inlet valve assembly — Transmission — Drain pump

Cleaning the water-inlet screens

If water doesn't enter the tub or enters too slowly, pull the cabinet away from the wall; use hose pliers to disconnect the inlet hoses from the water-inlet valves (catch the runout in a pan). Straighten out kinks in the hoses. Use needle-nose pliers to remove the domed screens from the valves and (if there are any) from the faucet ends of the hoses. Clean the screens with a small brush under running water; replace a damaged or clogged screen.

Replacing the water-inlet valve

If the tub overflows, unplug the washer. If the water flow stops, the water-level switch may be defective. Leave this and other electrical control problems to a repairman. If the flow continues, turn off the faucets, empty the tub, and replace the inlet valve.

To reach the valve, lift the cabinet top. If the top is secured to the cabinet by spring clips, insert a putty knife under the top and push against the two front clips; if it's held in place by screws, remove them. (In some models, you must unscrew the rear-access panel to reach the inlet valve.) Disconnect the water-inlet hoses. Take out

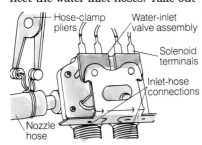

Hose-clamp pliers — Water-inlet valve assembly — Solenoid terminals — Inlet-hose connections — Nozzle hose

the valve-retaining screws; lift out the valve assembly. Loosen the clamp holding the nozzle hose to the valve outlet (use hose-clamp pliers for a pinch clamp; a nutdriver for a screw-type clamp); remove the hose. Disconnect the wires from the valve's solenoid terminals. Reverse the procedure to install a duplicate valve.

Adjusting belt tension

If a washer agitates or spins slowly or not at all, the drive belt may be loose or broken. Pull the unit away from the wall; unscrew the rear-access panel. Inspect the belt for wear or looseness; you should be able to deflect it no more than ½ inch. To tighten the belt, use a socket wrench to loosen the motor-mounting nuts, pull the motor

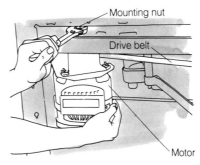

Mounting nut — Drive belt — Motor

back against the belt, then retighten the nuts. If the belt and pulleys are accessible, replacing a worn belt is simple (see *Drive belts*). In many models, the job requires major disassembly; leave it to a repairman.

Fixing leaks

Observe the machine in operation to pinpoint when and where it leaks. If it leaked while filling, look for and replace a cracked inlet hose; use a wrench to tighten the faucets' packing nuts and the hose connections. Lift the top; examine the nozzle hose. Replace it if it's cracked. To tighten a pinch-clamp connection, loosen the clamp and shift it to a slightly different position at the hose's end.

If the machine leaked after filling, look for loose connections and cracks in the pump hoses. To reach them, remove the inlet hoses and rear-access panel. For a closer inspection, bail or siphon water from the tub and lay the machine on its side on a blanket. If the pump leaks (or if it makes a rumbling noise or drains improperly), have it replaced.

Washing walls

The most efficient method

To prepare walls for washing, dust or vacuum them and spot clean heavily soiled areas with a heavy-duty household cleaner. Remove crayon or scuff marks by applying a paste of baking soda and rubbing lightly with fine steel wool. A solution of 1 tablespoon chlorine bleach to 1 cup water is effective for removing ink spots; rinse thoroughly.

For general cleaning, use an all-purpose household cleaner (see *Cleaners and polishes* for a formula) or a paint cleaner from a hardware or paint store. Have ready a pail of clear water and two sponges or rags. (On white paint use white rags or sponges; colored ones may leave stains. Use rags, rather than sponges, on textured walls.) You will also need a step stool or ladder and rubber gloves. Before beginning, test the cleaning solution on an inconspicuous part of the wall.

Work from the bottom up. Start in one corner and work across the base of the wall. Clean an area no more than 3 feet square, then rinse it with clear water and a clean sponge or rag. (On painted wood, also dry each area before continuing.) Change wash and rinse waters when they become dirty.

Many washable wallpapers can be cleaned by essentially the same method, using lukewarm—never hot—water and carefully drying each section of wall after rinsing to avoid water spots. Check the manufacturer's instructions and test your cleaner on an inconspicuous part of the wall.

Wasps and hornets

Getting rid of them

Many wasps, hornets, mud daubers, and yellow jackets build nests near or on houses. Most are black with white, yellow, or orange stripes. Unlike honey bees, they can sting repeatedly. Wasps and hornets, as well as some yellow jackets, build gray, papery nests in such places as trees, attics, or porch ceilings. Other yellow jackets build nests in the ground. Mud daub-

W

417

ers build mud tubes on wood siding, brick, and concrete.

Locate the nest; spray it at night when the insects are sluggish. Wear protective clothing (see *Beekeeping*) and have someone near in case of an extreme reaction to a sting. If you use a flashlight, place it nearby so that escaping insects will fly toward it.

Spray exposed nests with carbaryl or malathion or with a commercially available wasp-and-hornet formula. Some sprays can be aimed from as far as 12 feet away. Destroy ground-nesting insects with a dust that contains malathion or carbaryl. Immediately after directing a few puffs into the entrance, block it with a shovelful of earth. If activity in aerial or ground nests continues after several days, repeat this treatment. (See also *Insect bites and stings; Pesticides*.)

Watches

How to wind and maintain one

Unless your watch is self-winding, wind it in the morning and always at the same time. Wind clockwise to full tension. When changing the time, move the hands clockwise only.

Oil in a watch may congeal or dry out. Have a small watch professionally cleaned once a year; have a large one cleaned every 3 years.

Avoid opening the back of a watch; moisture and dirt may get in. If you accidentally immerse a nonwaterproof watch in water, take it for repairs as soon as possible to prevent rust from forming.

The battery in a digital or quartz watch will last from 1 to 5 years. Ask when you buy your watch. When the battery is about to expire, the seconds in a digital will jump 2 instead of 1.

Watercolor painting

Materials and techniques

Art supply stores sell kits with 12 or more colors in tubes or pans; a palette is often built into the kit's lid. Buy four brushes: one flat; three round (small, medium, and large).

A good, all-purpose watercolor paper is a 140-pound (per ream) stock with a cold-pressed finish. To stretch a sheet of paper, soak it in cold water; let excess water drip off. Lay the paper on a drawing board; smooth out wrinkles. Attach the sheet to the board with gummed tape all around the sheet's perimeter. Let the paper dry.

To mix colors, squeeze dabs from tubes into separate wells of a palette. Wet a brush; touch its tip to a dab (or a pan) of color. Swirl the brush in the palette's mixing area to form a pool of color. Rinse the brush before dipping it in another color. Add the second color to the pool in the mixing area. Swirl the brush to blend the colors.

To paint a landscape like the one shown, draw a light pencil sketch on the sheet. For the sky, wet the paper

with clear water; fill in the area with a *wash*—an even layer of color applied in long, overlapping strokes. While it's still wet, dab off color with a cloth to create clouds. Paint hills, meadows, and the road with washes on dry paper. Overpaint dark shapes (the foreground tree top) on light backgrounds (the sky). Leave voids in dark backgrounds (the hills) for foreground shapes (the tree trunk and house).

Apply paint in ragged strokes with a half-dry brush to create the texture of bark. Dab on paint with a half-dry brush to suggest foliage. Add fine details with a small, round brush.

Water heaters

Saving energy; draining off sediment; testing the relief valve

To save fuel, set heater thermostats at 120°F (140°F for a dishwasher). Cover the heater with an insulating jacket sold in a kit. (See also *Pipe insulation*).

To keep sediment from building up in a heater tank, open the drain valve; drain water into a bucket until it runs clear. Do this monthly if the water is hard; every 2 or 3 months if it's soft.

If the tap water is dirty or the heater noisy, flush out the tank. Turn off power to the heater at the distribution panel (see *Circuit breakers; Fuse boxes*); on a gas heater, turn off the control unit's gas cock. Shut the cold-water valve and open an upstairs hot-water faucet. Attach a hose to the drain valve to direct water outdoors or to a floor drain. Open the drain valve.

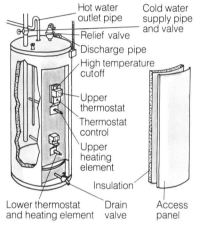

When the tank is empty, open and close the cold-water valve until the water runs clear. To refill the tank, close the drain valve; open the cold-water valve. When the tank is full (water flows out the open hot-water faucet), turn on the heater.

If a faulty thermostat lets tank water overheat, a relief valve will prevent an explosion by venting hot water. You should have the valve tested annually by a plumber. If the valve doesn't release hot water when tested, have the plumber replace it at once.

If an electric water heater doesn't heat—and there's no tripped circuit breaker or blown fuse—turn off power to the heater. Unscrew the access panel; set aside the insulation. Push the reset button on the high temperature cutoff; restore power. If the water still fails to heat, have the thermostats and heating elements tested and, if necessary, replaced.

To relight the pilot and replace the thermocouple of a gas-fired heater, see *Gas burners; Pilot lights*.

Water polo

A rough Olympic sport

A team of 13 players (seven are active; six, substitutes) vies with another in trying to advance an inflated 27-inch ball of waterproof leather past its opponent's goalie and into a netted, 3- x 10-foot metal or wooden frame. A game has 7-minute quarters with 2-minute intervals between them.

The pool, 20 x 30 meters (22 x 33 yards), is just under 6 feet deep; it has horizontal lines at the half mark and at 13 and 6½ feet from each end. No player may touch bottom. Each player wears a numbered bathing cap in his team's color. For an informal game, adjust the dimensions and the rules.

Begin with each team positioned along its goal line, about 3 feet from either goalpost, with teammates 3 feet apart. The referee, at half court, blows a whistle and throws the ball into the pool. The team that gets it moves it by passing it or by *dribbling* (swimming with it). Defense may try to grab the ball from a carrier or knock it away; if they succeed, it's theirs. After a goal, play resumes with teams in their respective halves in any positions and one player from the nonscoring team on the halfway line holding the ball. Upon the referee's whistle, he tosses the ball to a teammate.

Only goalies can put both hands on the ball, slam it with clenched fist, or hold it underwater when tackled. Field players must, while in motion, dribble, pass, or shoot (try for a goal). No team may have the ball longer than 35 seconds without shooting. At least two teammates must handle the ball before a goal can be made. An infraction of these rules is an *ordinary* foul. *Major* fouls include hitting a player, interfering with a free pass, and dunking a noncarrier.

Water pumps and tanks

Curing frequent cycling of a well pump

In a private water system, a pump (usually a piston, jet, or submersible type) lifts water from a well into a pressurized storage tank. A cushion of compressed air at the top of the tank keeps the water within a preset pressure range, usually between 20 and 40 pounds per square inch (p.s.i.). When you open a faucet, the cushion of air forces water into the house plumbing system. As the tank empties, pressure drops. At the low limit of the pressure range, a pressure switch activates the pump. Pressure rises as the tank refills. At the high pressure limit, the pump shuts off.

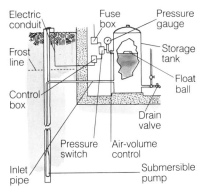

If the pump starts and stops frequently, the tank may be waterlogged—all or part of the air cushion has been absorbed by tank water. Before correcting the tank, look for an open or leaky house faucet. Check and adjust the pressure-switch settings; the difference between *High* and *Low* should be 20 pounds. Test for air leaks by applying soapy water to the tank's upper surface. If bubbles form, tighten a loose fitting, or have the tank repaired or replaced as needed.

To recharge a waterlogged tank, turn off power to the pump. Connect a hose to the drain valve to direct water outdoors or into a floor drain. Open the valve and drain the tank. When the pressure gauge reads zero, remove the air-volume control to let in air (if there isn't a control, remove a plug at the tank's top or open an upstairs faucet). Check the control for stuck parts or a leaky float ball; replace it if necessary. Shut the drain valve, reinstall the air-volume control or the plug; turn on the pump.

To eliminate waterlogging and reduce pump wear, consider installing a tank with a precharged, permanently sealed air cushion.

Water rescue

Safe ways to save a life

If a person in distress is within arm's reach, lie down and, if possible, hold onto a support with one arm or have someone hold your legs. Grab the victim's arm, leg, or hair and pull him to safety. If he is just beyond reach, extend a pole, an oar, a water ski, or a piece of clothing.

Shallow water

Wade in, extending a pole or a towel to the victim. Don't lean toward him; incline your body toward the shore or dock so that you won't be pulled off balance. If there are several of you, form a human chain, as shown.

Stand on the end of the rope while throwing a ring buoy *beyond* the victim. Pull the buoy slowly toward him.

If there's no buoy, throw a floating object: a life jacket, an inner tube, a log.

If you can't throw far enough, row or motor to the victim. Extend an oar or a cushion; pull him slowly alongside. Maneuver him toward the stern; lift him into the boat.

Continued next page

W

Swimming assists

Going into deep water is a last resort; you must be a competent swimmer and able to quickly judge the distance you'll have to swim, the victim's weight, and the water conditions (how cold or rough). If you think that any of these will overwhelm you, *don't attempt a swimming rescue.* Send or go for help; mark your position on the beach with bright clothing.

If you must swim out, bring an object for towing the victim, either a flotation support or a piece of clothing. As you approach, keep the towing device between you and the victim. Tow him to safety using a scissors kick or a back frog kick with a single-arm stroke (see *Sidestroke* and *Backstroke*). If he panics and tries to grab you, release the support and back off. Reassure him; then reapproach him.

Tow an unconscious victim by the chin. Roll him onto his back, cup your hand under his chin, and keep his head above water. Ashore administer artificial respiration (see *CPR*).

Cross-chest carry

If you have no towing device and you're sure you can control the victim, approach him from behind, pause about 6 feet away, and do a *quick reverse:* push your hands forward and,

as your head and shoulders move back, thrust your legs toward the victim. In this postion, scull toward the victim. Reach over and cup his chin with your left hand (if you are right-handed). Pull his head against your arm; press your left arm against his spine to level him off. With your right arm, reach over his right shoulder and across his chest; clasp him under his left arm. His shoulder should be in your armpit. Hold him tightly to your side, with your hip in the small of his back. Tow him, using a scissors kick and a single-arm stroke.

If a panicking victim tries to grab you, put your hand or foot in the center of his chest and push away. There

are a number of release methods enabling the rescuer to escape a victim's grasp. Learn these in a certified life-saving program.

Water-skiing

How to get started

Learn the water-skier's safety code and the water-skiing signals needed to communicate with the towboat (contact the American Water Ski Association, 799 Overlook Drive, Winter Haven, FL 33884. For safety, wear a Coast Guard–approved flotation device designed for water-skiing.

Water skis are made of laminated wood or fiberglass and come in varying lengths for children and adults. Their rubber foot bindings stretch when you fall, releasing your feet.

The motor boat should be able to travel 15 to 35 m.p.h. Use a 75-foot certified towline of ¼-inch diamond-braid polypropylene.

Practicing on shore

Wet your feet and the ski bindings. Slip your foot into the front half of the binding while holding down the heel portion. Pull up the heel piece and adjust the binding's sliding portion.

On shore, crouch on your skis with feet flat and shoulder-width apart, knees to your chest, and arms extended forward outside your knees. As you hold the towline handle, have someone gradually draw the towline taut. Keep your feet flat, knees bent, arms and back straight, head up; let the line pull you to a stand. Practice until you have mastered this motion.

Start in waist-deep water; let your flotation device support you. Grasp the tow handle, crouch as before, and keep your ski tips slightly above water. As the boat idles forward and the line becomes tight, you begin moving.

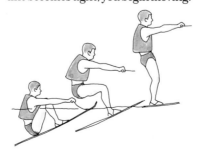

When the rope is tight, yell "Hit it!" The driver will accelerate gradually. Maintain the crouch, and as the skis begin to plane, straighten up slowly. To stop, release the towline and sink into the water.

Water softeners

When and how to soften

Calcium and magnesium, two minerals that make water hard, can form deposits in pipes and water heaters and react with soap to leave a residue on laundry and dishes. To find out how hard your water is, ask your utility or have a plumber or a water-treatment company analyze it. Some Cooperative Extenstion agents (see p.5) also test water. Consider softening water of more than 9 grains per gallon of hardness.

To soften all indoor water or just the hot water, you can install an *ion exchange softening tank* that replaces calcium and magnesium ions with sodium ions. (A person on a low-sodium diet should consult his physician before drinking softened water.) Such systems can be purchased or rented.

To soften water in a washing machine only, add a packaged softener or water conditioner. Where permitted, polyphosphate types are the best. Put in the softener before adding soap or detergent. Add more softener to the rinse if water is very hard.

Water testing

Evaluating household water

If anything about the odor, color, clarity, or taste of your water seems odd, it's a good idea to try to determine the reason why. Even if the water looks and tastes fine, you should consider having it tested if your source is a spring, well, or cistern in a highly populated, industrialized, or farming area. Your county health department or Cooperative Extension Service (see p.5) may test the water for you or send you a list of laboratories that charge fees. A water-treatment company will do certain tests for free.

W

For a test sample, use a sterile bottle; fill it from a cold-water faucet that isn't leaking. If there's an aerator, remove it. Fully open the cold-water tap; let the water run hard for 2 minutes. Reduce the pressure to one-third; let the water run for 2 minutes more. Fill the bottle to within ½ inch of the top, cap it, and get it to a laboratory as soon as possible. A delay of more than 24 hours may affect test validity.

What to test for

A test for coliform bacteria will reveal pollution by human or animal wastes. If an unhealthy count is found, boil drinking and cooking water until treatment equipment is installed.

Nitrates in concentrations of more than 45 milligrams per liter can be harmful, especially to infants. So can a high level of chloroform (a by-product of chlorinating water).

The presence of any lead, cadmium, mercury, or arsenic in the water is dangerous. The occurrence of other metals, such as copper or iron, above certain levels can also be harmful.

A pH test will determine whether your water is acidic (a pH of less than 7) or alkaline (pH above 7). Acidic water corrodes pipes and can leach harmful metals into the water supply. You can test the pH yourself with a kit available where swimming-pool supplies or fish tanks are sold.

Many treatments are available for water problems. Each one's effectiveness depends on several conditions. Before installing equipment, consult an expert.(See also *Water softeners*.)

Weaning

Getting a baby to drink from a cup

Readiness for weaning varies. Some babies do it willingly between 9 and 12 months of age, when the sucking urge naturally decreases. Others need the satisfaction of sucking until age 2.

Introduce your baby to a cup during the latter half of the first year. Start with a few sips of juice or water in a nonbreakable cup. When the baby is willing and able to use the cup regularly, try putting milk in it at mealtimes. If he resists, skip it for a while.

If weaning from the breast, cut out one feeding; a few days later, eliminate a second, then a third, and so on. Substitute a bottle if the baby is under 6 months old; try switching to a cup if he's older. Your milk supply will gradually decrease. When weaning from the bottle, follow the same procedure; eliminate the bedtime bottle last.

Weather forecasting

Reading nature's signs

Although no method of forecasting is infallible, even simple observations may indicate what weather is coming. There's truth in the old saying "Red sky at night, sailors' delight; red sky at morning, sailors take warning." In the Northern Hemisphere most weather comes from the west, and the setting sun shines through tomorrow's weather. If the distant air is dry and clear, the sunset will be red, indicating a fine day to come. Conversely, a red sky around the rising sun shows that dry, clear air has passed to the east, possibly heralding wet weather.

Highs and lows

The weather moves in masses of air, which are propelled into and around pools and eddies of high and low pressure. The air in the masses circulates clockwise away from the center of a high-pressure area, or *high.* It circulates counterclockwise toward the center of a low-pressure area, or *low,* where it escapes upward, cools, and leaves its moisture in the form of rain or snow. A high usually means good weather; a low, poor weather.

Changing winds announce a change in pressure. A wide deviation from the prevailing wind direction indicates a low. If you don't know the prevailing wind directions for your area, consult your weather bureau or a detailed atlas. Often the winds of a low overturn leaves so that you see their back sides.

Reading the clouds

Clouds are among the most helpful weather indicators. They are generally classified as high, medium *(alto),* or low in altitude, and are divided into three basic types: *cirrus* (wispy or feathery), *cumulus* (large and fluffy), and *stratus* (flat and layered). The

Cirrus

Altostratus

Cumulus

Cumulus with thunderhead

types are sometimes combined and any of them may become a rain cloud.

Isolated cirrus clouds indicate the advance of warm, moist air, but not necessarily rain. If they become denser or broader, however, a low is probably on its way. When cirrus clouds develop into long, straight rows (*cirrostratus* clouds), forming a halo around the sun or moon, a prolonged period of rain or snow may be on its way.

Low-lying, gray stratus clouds that cover much of the sky usually bring mists, drizzle, or rain. Higher stratus clouds *(altostratus)* that are flat, gray, and featureless and through which the sun can be seen dimly, mean a few hours of rain or snow, possibly heavy.

Cumulus clouds are favorable signs unless they darken and descend. If a cumulus cloud develops a towering thunderhead, a storm is brewing.

Reading nature's other signs

In the humid atmosphere of a low, smoke stays close to the ground, distant objects look closer, sounds seem louder, and birds and insects turn silent. One or two of these signs indicates a mild low. A combination of most of them indicates a heavy storm developing. (See also *Tornadoes.*)

Weather stripping

Sealing air leaks around doors and windows

Weatherproof thresholds, door shoes, and door sweeps are available to keep air from entering under a door. The simplest to install is a door sweep. Screw it to the inside bottom edge of an inward-swinging door; to the out-

W

side bottom edge of an outward-swinging door. Adjust the sweep so that it's flush with the floor.

Before sealing a door, make sure it fits in its frame (see *Doors*). Mount V- or spring-metal strips on the jambs. Cut the strip on the lock side to accommodate the strike plate. Tubular vinyl strips can be fastened to the face of the stop molding. Heavy-duty stripping is available for garage doors.

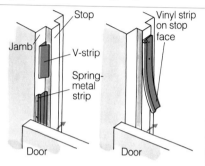

Stop
Vinyl strip on stop face
Jamb
V-strip
Spring-metal strip
Door
Door

Weather stripping windows
Seal double-hung windows by applying self-adhesive plastic V-strips or by nailing spring-metal strips at the places shown in color. Don't cover the pulleys (unless you use a pulley-seal kit that doesn't obstruct the window).

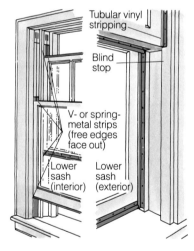

Tubular vinyl stripping
Blind stop
V- or spring-metal strips (free edges face out)
Lower sash (interior)
Lower sash (exterior)

Tubular or foam-filled vinyl stripping is self-adhesive or fastened with nails; it's always visible. With the window closed, fasten strips to the outside bottom edge of the lower sash and to the outside top edge of the upper sash. Mount a strip under the upper sash against its inside edge. Add strips to the blind stops for the upper sash; to the parting strips for the lower sash. (See also *Caulking*.)

Weaving

Making a cushion cover on a frame loom

To make a cushion cover 14 inches square, you'll need a frame loom with warp (see *Warping*); a 16-inch *shed stick;* a *shuttle;* and about ½ pound of *weft yarn.* This can be almost any material, including mohair, chenille, rag strips, ribbon, metallic cord, or a blend of these. Exact quantity will depend on the thickness of the yarns you choose.

Start with the main weft yarn. Loop a weft end around one notch in the shuttle, then wind the weft around

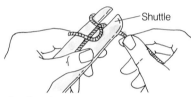

Shuttle

the shuttle. Weave the shed stick over every other warp thread; stand it on edge. Slide the shuttle through the space (shed), leaving a 2-inch tail at the side. Don't pull the weft taut; allow

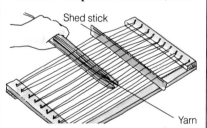

Shed stick
Yarn

it to form slight curves, or bubbles, across the warp. This prevents the warp from being pulled in at the sides.

When you reach the other side, lay the shed stick flat and use it to pack the weft straight and firm; then slide it to the top of the loom. For the return row, weave the shuttle under alternate strands (the ones that lie behind the first weft); this is the second shed. At

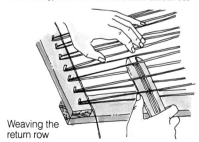

Weaving the return row

the end of this row, weave in the weft tail. Continue weaving, alternating the sheds on each row and packing them with the shed stick, a comb, or a fork.

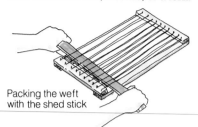

Packing the weft with the shed stick

After completing ½ inch, called a *heading,* introduce other colors and textures. To change yarns at the beginning of a row, leave tails of each yarn; weave them into succeeding rows.

When you have 14 inches of fabric, make another heading. If the shed openings are tight, weave the last row or two with a darning needle. Slip the fabric off the brads. Stitch across the warp ends close to the weave by machine or with a whipstitch.

Weave a second square for the cushion back or buy ½ yard of fabric. See *Cushions* for the way to make a cover.

Weddings

Making the arrangements

If you're planning a large wedding, give yourself at least 6 months of preparation time to assure getting your first choice of sites and to complete all details without a last-minute panic. Even more time may be necessary if you're getting married in or near a large city or during a busy month, such as June. Make sure that the services you choose are reliable by asking friends for recommendations or by getting references.

Here is a schedule for the major preparations for a large, traditional wedding. For a small or simpler affair, some steps can be eliminated.

Six months to a year in advance
Both families should meet and discuss the wedding budget, the time of day, and the wedding style and color scheme. It's traditional for the bride's family to pay most wedding expenses, except for the following: the bride's rings, the marriage license, gifts to the ushers, the clergyman's fee, and

the wedding trip. Often these days the groom's family pays for the rehearsal dinner as well. Other arrangements might be appropriate, depending on how old the wedding couple is and the financial means of each family.

Decide on the number of guests. Allocate them equally to each family, unless the groom's family and friends live at some distance (many on his list would receive announcements instead of invitations). Both families should compile lists and divide them into three parts: people to be invited to the ceremony only, those to be invited to the ceremony and reception, and those to be sent announcements. The lists should include full names and information about which family members are being invited; children over age 18 receive a separate invitation. Index cards are a good way to organize the names.

Speak to a clergyman or judge; begin any premarital religious counseling.

Reserve the wedding and reception places. If the reception is to be catered separately, arrange for a caterer.

Choose and order a bridal dress. Ask one or more wedding attendants to help choose their gowns.

Select china, silver, and household accessories. If you wish, arrange for a bridal registry at a department store.

Four months in advance
Order engraved invitations. These are the only proper type unless the wedding is small and informal. Then the invitations can be issued by handwritten notes, Mailgrams, or the telephone. Consult a book of etiquette for the correct wording for formal wedding and reception invitations.

Engage a photographer.

Plan music for the wedding; make sure your choices are in compliance with those of the wedding place. Arrange for reception music.

Three months in advance
Complete the guest lists. When the invitations arrive, address them by hand in black ink. Write out all names and addresses in full; the only permissible abbreviations are Mr., Mrs., Dr., and Jr. If there are inside envelopes, write titles and surnames on them: Dr. and Mrs. Dwyer, Miss (or Ms.) Ryan, The Messrs. Huber (brothers), The Misses Drescher (sisters). If you

are inviting a family, this is the place to include the children's names (underneath the parents): Mr. and Mrs. French, Alice and Susan. Insert the inside envelope facing the outer flap.

Order attendants' dresses; check on the arrival of the bridal dress.

Select flowers and arrangements for the wedding and reception.

Six weeks to a month in advance
Mail your invitations. Order rings; select gifts for the attendants.

Arrange lodging for out-of-town guests and attendants.

Have final alterations made on the bride's and attendants' dresses.

Plan the rehearsal dinner.

Arrange for announcements in the newspapers.

Write thank-you notes for any gifts that have arrived. It is proper these days for the groom as well as the bride to write these acknowledgments.

Two weeks in advance
Obtain the marriage license.

Begin addressing announcements to be mailed on your wedding day.

Arrange for the bridal party's transportation to the church and reception.

Arrange a time for the wedding rehearsal; inform the wedding party.

One week in advance
Total all positive responses to wedding invitations; give a final estimate of reception guests to the caterer.

Check final details with the photographer, florist, musicians, and any other service people.

Weed control

Eliminating the competition in your garden

The best weed control is prevention: plant dense ground covers under shrubs, use intensive or wide-row methods in the vegetable garden, mulch freely (see *Mulching*).

Annual weeds, such as chickweed and lamb's-quarters, grow fast and produce many seeds, but are shallow rooted. Pull them by hand, cut off their roots with a scuffle hoe, or turn them under with a rototiller before they go to seed. Perennials, such as milkweed and thistle, come back year after year. Dig them up roots and all,

or keep the stems cut back to the ground for at least two seasons.

Use an herbicide only as a last resort, following the manufacturer's directions to the letter. Make spot applications of broadleaf herbicides in spring and fall. Use preemergence herbicides, such as trifluralin and diphenamid, in flower gardens and around established ornamentals to kill weed seeds before they germinate. Never use an herbicide near food plants. (See also *Crabgrass; Dandelions; Poison ivy, oak, sumac.*)

Weevils

Vegetable-garden variety

Relatives of the infamous boll weevil, these plant-feeding beetles have beak- or snoutlike heads. Species vary in shape, size, and color.

Each weevil species attacks certain plants. Larvae of the *carrot weevil* leave zigzag paths in the roots of carrots, celery, parsley, and parsnips. Adult *vegetable weevils* eat all but the central vein of beet, cabbage, cauliflower, and lettuce leaves. *Bean weevils* lay eggs in seed pods; the larvae hatch, grow, and spread in ripening and stored beans. *Pea weevils* nibble notches from the edges of young pea and bean plants.

Most weevils can be controlled by rotating affected crops. In summer, remove all garden debris and weeds where weevils hide; after harvest, remove the crop remains. Early in the spring, cultivate deeply to destroy weevil pupae. To eliminate weevils in stored beans, see *Flour beetles.*

Weight lifting

Exercising with free weights

If you're over 30 or have not been exercising regularly, consult a doctor before beginning weight training. Consider joining a gym where a qualified coach can devise a program for you.

To train at home, buy a barbell and dumbbell set and, if possible, an exercise bench. Begin an exercise with a light weight that you can lift eight

W

times in a row (or for one *set* of eight *repetitions* or *reps*). Over a few weeks, progressively increase the reps in a set to 10 or 12; then add up to 5 percent more weight and start again at eight reps. A beginner's *workout* includes one or more sets for each of 12 exercises. To increase muscle size and strength, do fewer reps with heavier weights; for tone and endurance, do more reps with lighter weights.

Train three times a week on nonconsecutive days. Warm up before a session (see *Exercises*). Rest 2 minutes between sets.

Two basic exercises

Clean and press. Grasp the bar as shown. Lift, or *clean,* the weight by straightening your legs, then your back. Continue the lift with your arms; then snap your elbows in and under the bar, bringing it to shoulder

Palms down
Finish
Midpoint
Feet apart
Knees bent
Start

level. For the *press,* lift the barbell straight overhead. Reverse the procedure to lower the weight.

Squat. Clean and press the barbell; lower it onto your shoulders. Keeping your back straight, squat until your thighs parallel the floor, then recover.

Thighs parallel to floor
Don't bounce at bottom of movement

Wheezing

Easing breathing difficulties

Wheezing—a harsh whistling sound accompanying breathing—is caused by a constriction of the bronchial tubes. Wheezing can occur when breathing in or out or both. If someone wheezes when breathing in, there is an obstruction of the upper airway: a foreign body may be lodged there (see *Choking*); the person may have greatly enlarged tonsils or a tumorous growth; or he may be a victim of croup, usually a childhood disease.

For the latter, humidify the air with a hot or cold vaporizer; keep the patient warm. In case of an acute attack, turn on the shower to *Hot* and sit with the patient in the steam-filled room until his breathing is eased. In any of these cases, see a doctor promptly.

Wheezing upon breathing out is usually a sign of asthma. However, someone with severe asthma may wheeze both upon breathing in and out. Asthma has numerous causes: cold air, a viral infection, food substances, air pollutants (smoke, dust), even exercise can bring on an attack. An asthmatic should be prepared with prescription medication to relieve the wheezing. Never exceed the prescribed dosage; call a doctor if the medication doesn't work.

Whipped cream

A favorite dessert topping

Use heavy cream and whip it as close to serving time as possible. To achieve greatest volume, chill the cream, beaters, and bowl thoroughly. Whip the cream until it begins to stiffen, then slowly beat in 2 to 4 tablespoons confectioner's sugar per cup of cream. If desired, add ½ teaspoon vanilla or ¼ teaspoon other flavoring extract.

For serving on fruit, whip the cream to a soft glossiness. Whip to stiffer peaks for other desserts or for piping through a pastry tube, but be careful not to overbeat. If the cream starts to become buttery, stir in 1 to 2 tablespoons cold milk.

If whipped cream must be held an hour or two, pour it into a strainer lined with a clean cloth napkin and place it over a bowl in the refrigerator.

To stabilize whipped cream for a serve-yourself party, mix 1 teaspoon unflavored gelatin in 2 tablespoons cold water; warm until dissolved. Cool. Whip 1 pint cream until almost stiff, then add the dissolved gelatin. Will keep up to 4 days in the refrigerator.

Whist

The game that fathered bridge

In the American version of this four-player game, partners sit opposite each other. The dealer deals all cards from a standard deck (ace is high), then places the last card faceup on the table; it's the *trump* suit.

The player to the dealer's left leads; others follow suit clockwise. Before playing, the dealer adds the exposed trump card to his hand. If a player can't follow suit, he plays a card of any other suit, including trump. The highest card in the suit led wins the *trick* (round), unless it is trumped. The highest trump takes a trick. The trick winner leads the next round.

Each trick in excess of the first six that a team wins scores 1 point. A game is 7 points. Subtract the losers' score from 7, even if you won more than 7 points, for the score value.

Whiteflies

Dealing with a garden and houseplant pest

Adult whiteflies are about ¹/₁₆ inch long. They feed on cucumbers, beans, tomatoes, and potatoes, as well as on many kinds of houseplants and ornamentals including azaleas, fuchsias, and chrysanthemums. If, when you touch a plant, a cloud of tiny powdery whiteflies appears, it's a sign of a serious infestation.

Immature whiteflies suck juices from the undersides of leaves, causing them to yellow, wither, and finally drop off. Like aphids, whiteflies secrete a clear sticky substance *(honeydew)* which attracts ants and usually causes a black fungus *(sooty mold).*

At certain stages of their development, whiteflies are unaffected by pesticides. When you see flying adults in early summer, spray with insecticidal soap or acephate.

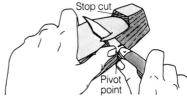

White sauce

The basis for many dishes and for other sauces

To prepare a medium white sauce, melt 2 tablespoons butter over low heat. Stir in 2 tablespoons flour; cook, stirring constantly, until the mixture is frothy but not brown (2 to 3 minutes). Gradually add 1 cup hot milk, stirring briskly until blended. Season to taste. Bring to a boil; reduce heat to very low. Simmer for 4 to 6 minutes, stirring occasionally. If it is lumpy, strain it. Use as the basis for creamed foods and other sauces (see *Casseroles; Cheese sauces; Crêpes*).

Thin white sauce: Halve the butter and flour; use as a basis for cream soup. *Thick white sauce:* Double the butter and flour; use to bind foods (see *Croquettes; Soufflés*).

Velouté sauce: Substitute chicken, veal, or fish stock for the milk in medium white sauce. For *Sauce suprême,* boil down a velouté to half; stir in 1 cup light cream and 2 tablespoons butter.

White-water canoeing

Basic strokes; danger signs

Caution: Do not attempt this challenging sport until you are adept at flat-water canoeing. Always canoe with a partner; practice the basic strokes together before entering white water. If possible, travel with a group. Wear a life jacket; in cold water, wear a wet suit. Tie 50-foot safety lines to bow and stern, and carry a separate throw line as well.

Canoeing in fast water calls for all the skills used in quiet water (see *Canoeing*), but it takes more balance, coordination, and power. In addition, the following paddle strokes are used to change direction, to move from side to side, to slow down, and to stay upright. Work out signals for each with your partner, including the side of the canoe on which to execute them.

A *draw stroke* pulls the canoe sideways; reach out as far as you can, dip the blade parallel to the current, and draw it toward you. A *pry stroke* reverses the motion; dip the blade next to the hull, lever the shaft against the gunwale, and pry outward. A *back stroke* slows the canoe; reach back to dip the blade, and pull it forward. A *brace stroke* gives stability in turns and crosscurrents; reach out to the low side, lay the paddle flat on the water, and push down hard.

Reading the water

A *V* of rippling water pointing upstream has an obstruction at its apex. A *V* pointing downstream has two obstructions, one at each end, with a clear channel between. A *pillow,* or smooth bulge in the water, appears just downstream of a hidden rock; the faster the current and the deeper the rock, the farther the pillow is from it. A *keeper wave* forms over a deep hole; avoid it or speed through at a slight angle. A *haystack,* or standing wave, forms at the foot of a narrow chute or sharp drop-off; to keep the bow from plunging, slow the canoe.

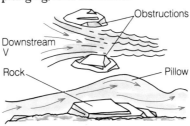

Whittling

A craft that requires only time, patience, and a sharp knife

Whittling is a skill best learned by doing, but here are some tips to get you started. Choose a small-bladed knife that feels comfortable in your hand; keep it razor sharp (see *Knives*). Practice with softwood, such as white pine, before you try to whittle oak, walnut, or any other hardwood.

Block out the work with a soft pencil before you begin removing wood. Sketch outlines on all sides of the wood, including the top and bottom, then carve away the waste. After you have the rough contours of the piece, gradually add the details.

To keep from splitting the wood, always cut with the grain; move the blade from the thickest portion of the piece toward the thinnest. To make a

sharp edge or to limit the length of a cut, use a *stop cut:* press the blade vertically into the wood across the grain, then whittle toward the cut.

Avoid making deep cuts; shave waste wood away gradually, pushing the blade away from you whenever possible. For the utmost control, use your thumb on the back of the blade as a pivot point. If you must draw the blade toward yourself, grip the knife with four fingers and, using your thumb as a brace, cut by closing your hand as if making a fist.

Wicker

Caring for woven furniture; finishing and refinishing it

Rattan and willow wicker can be washed with soapy water, using a soft brush for crevices. If either becomes brittle, drenching with water helps to restore it. Rush, sea grass, or fiber (twisted paper) should only be wiped now and then with a damp cloth.

If rattan or willow has accumulated many coats of unsightly paint, consider having it stripped by a professional. To do the job yourself, work outdoors and use a semipaste stripper; scrub it off with a stiff bristle brush dipped into detergent and water (see *Stripping furniture*).

For a light natural finish, apply polyurethane or clear lacquer. For a darker finish, use stain (see *Staining wood*). You can also paint wicker.

Paint or a clear finish should be sprayed on for best results. Work outdoors on a warm, dry day. Do the underside first. Apply two or three thin coats. Allow each to dry thoroughly.

W

Wills

Protecting your loved ones after your death

Whether you are married or single, you should have a legally binding will. If you die without one, your estate (property) will be passed on according to the state laws of intestacy (for those who die without a will). Your property could end up in the hands of relatives you have never seen or never liked or, if you have no surviving relatives at all, it could go to the state.

Although you don't need an attorney to make a will, it is the best way to avoid the numerous legal tangles that unsuspectingly arise from homemade documents. No two situations are exactly alike; your attorney can explain how the general rules governing wills apply to your situation.

Requirements for a valid will

You must follow the requirements of the laws in your state for making a will if it is to have legal effect. This protects your survivors against dishonest persons who might present forged or otherwise dubious claims against your estate. After your death your heirs will have to submit any document asserted to be your will to the surrogate or probate court, which determines whether the document is genuine. If your will is not drawn properly, the court may decide that it does not reflect how you wanted your property given away.

In most states, you must be at least 18 years old to make a will, and in a few you must be at least 19; check your state law. You must also be competent—you must understand that you are making a will, comprehend its legal consequences, and know who your heirs are. If any doubt exists, the court will treat your will as worthless and direct that your estate be passed on according to the laws of intestacy.

Put your will in writing; verbal wills are rarely acceptable. Use clear, unequivocal language. Words such as "desire" or "wish," rather than "bequeath" or "devise," have cost more than one prospective heir a share of the estate.

Although you have almost unlimited power over your property, you cannot use a will to leave your surviving spouse penniless. If you try to do so, the courts will let your spouse take up to a certain percentage of your property anyway. You can, however, disinherit or leave nothing to anyone else. The best way to do so is to spell out your intentions.

It is a good idea to state that burial expenses, any taxes due, and any other expenses connected with your death must be paid first, before your property is divided.

Naming guardians and executors

If your children are minors, protect their future by naming a guardian to take care of them should they be orphaned by your death. Before you do so, discuss your plans with your candidate to avoid unnecessary legal complications after you are gone.

Name an executor (man) or executrix (woman) to represent you and to handle your will's instructions. Select someone you trust and whom you feel is morally and financially responsible and capable of making decisions. Before you name him or her, make sure that the person is willing to take on the responsibility. After your death, if the person you designated refuses to serve, your estate could be tied up while the court names another executor. It is common to add a provision stating that your executor need not post a bond making him financially liable if he fails to do his job.

Signing and storing the will

Once you have completed your will, sign it at the end. The law requires that two or, in some states, three witnesses be present when you sign and then they must sign it too.

Your witnesses should be persons with no financial interest in your estate, who are likely to outlive you, and who can be easily located. They must include their addresses with their signatures. Should someone challenge your will and the witnesses cannot be found, your survivors face serious legal trouble.

Leave the original signed and witnessed will with your lawyer or with a loved one. Don't leave it in a safe-deposit box unless you check your state law; many states require a special court order to open a deceased person's safe-deposit box to get his will.

Changing your will

Review your will annually to make sure you haven't changed your mind about its provisions. To make a change, add a *codicil.* The codicil must be executed with the same formalities as the will. It should refer to the will by identifying its date of execution and state the changes to be made. The codicil must also be witnessed.

Window boxes

Building your own

A window box should be about 8 inches deep and 8 to 11 inches wide to accommodate two or three rows of plants. Make it no longer than 4 feet, or it may be unwieldy. Use pressure-treated 1 x 10 lumber.

Cut a front, a back, a bottom and two ends as shown, adjusting the

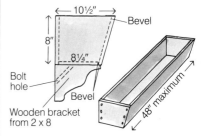

measurements to your needs. Cut a ¼-inch bevel on one edge of the bottom and both edges of the front. In the bottom, drill two rows of ½-inch or ¾-inch drainage holes about 5 inches apart. Fasten all the pieces together with 1½-inch brass screws.

Mount the flower box so that its top is 6 to 8 inches below the window. Use metal brackets from a garden center, or wooden brackets made by cutting right triangles of wood, then sawing a decorative curve on the long side of each triangle.

Attach the brackets to the house siding with lag bolts (see *Screws*); position one bracket near each end of the box and one at the center. (Drill pilot holes in wooden brackets and drill recesses for the bolt heads.) If the house siding is masonry, attach the brackets with screws and masonry fasteners.

For drainage, line the box with crushed rock. Add soil as you would for a raised bed (see *Raised beds*).

W

Window insulation

Reducing heat loss with window coverings

Transparent vinyl sheeting sealed to the inside of a window frame with clear polyethylene tape provides good insulation and light transmission at low cost. But installing and removing the sheets every season can be a chore; they must be replaced periodically, and you can't open a sealed window. Cheaper polyethylene film, sold by the square foot or in storm-window kits, is less effective than vinyl and lasts only one season.

Pop-in shutters made of foam insulation board overlaid with fireproofed fiberboard are inexpensive and easy to make. Cut to fit tightly inside a window frame, shutters insulate better than plastic and, covered with fabric, are more attractive. Daytime storage, however, can be a problem. Hinged shutters solve the problem by folding back against the wall.

Insulated roll-up shades are available ready made or as kits. Running in tracks mounted on the window frame, shades are nearly as effective as foam panels, but can be expensive.

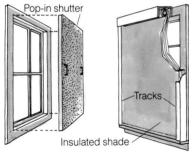
Pop-in shutter
Tracks
Insulated shade

To prevent heat loss, close shades or install shutters before sunset. To avoid cracking window panes on very cold mornings, remove the insulation before turning on the heat. (See also *Storm doors and windows.*)

Window-locking devices

Making a window more secure

A thin blade slipped between the sashes will open a thumb latch. Even a keyed latch pries apart easily.

You can secure a window better with a simple metal pin, sold by locksmiths, that slips into a hole in the sashes' meeting rails. You recess the pin ⅛ inch and retract it with a wire clip that comes with the pin. You can use a clipped-off steel nail in similar fashion and draw it out with a magnet. Another device is a bolt that you insert and remove with a winged key.

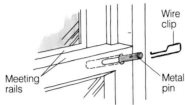
Wire clip
Meeting rails
Metal pin

Install these devices in the meeting rails' corners. Then open the window 3½ inches and put in a second pair so that you can lock it open. Stay ½ inch away from the glass and edges.

You can get a keyed lock that projects a rod through the sashes or one that mounts on top of the lower sash and projects a rod into holes in the top

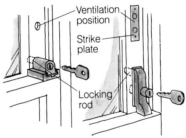
Ventilation position
Strike plate
Locking rod

sash. Another locks to a plate on the top sash and presses against the lower sash. Similar units are available for metal-framed and sliding windows.

On a casement window, replace the latch with a locking latch—either a right- or a left-hand model.

Install locks with nonretractable, one-way screws. Keep a key out of sight and far enough away so that an intruder can't fish it out. Never put a keyed lock on a fire-exit window.

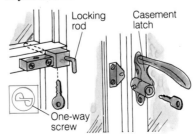
Locking rod
Casement latch
One-way screw

Windowpanes

Replacing broken window glass

Wearing gloves, pick out the broken glass. If the window is sealed with a gasket, first pull the gasket out of the frame. (Wear goggles.) Run a screwdriver around the frame to remove small shards. Scrape off the old glazing compound and pull out the *points* or the *spring clips.* Sand the groove and coat it with linseed oil.

If the points you remove are straight bits of metal, get new ones with horizontal tabs. Straight points are hard to install without breaking the glass.

Buy or cut a new pane (see *Glass cutting*) ⅛ inch smaller in length and width than the opening. Apply a thin bead of glazing compound along all four sides of the frame and press the new pane into place. Replace the spring clips or secure the pane with points spaced 4 to 6 inches apart. Use the putty knife to press the points halfway in. If necessary, tap the putty knife with a hammer.

Two types of points
Spring clip
Putty knife
Point

Roll glazing compound into a rope about ⅜ inch in diameter, press it along the edges of the pane, and draw a putty knife over it to form a triangular bead. Let the compound dry for a week. Paint it, overlapping the glass about ¹⁄₁₆ inch to seal out moisture.

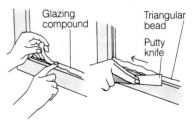
Glazing compound
Triangular bead
Putty knife

If your window had a gasket, don't use glazing compound. Lay the new pane in the bare frame. Press the gasket under the lip of the frame with your thumb, starting at a corner.

W

Window shades

Adjusting slack and runaway shades; dealing with sticking, catching, and wobbling shades

A window shade is held in place by a *pawl*, a small latch that locks onto a ratchet tooth to stop the roller from turning. When you draw the shade down, it pulls the pawl away from the tooth and frees the roller. Spinning keeps the pawl pivoted outward and away from the ratchet. When you stop the shade, the pawl drops onto the ratchet to hold it in place. Tension from the spring raises the shade.

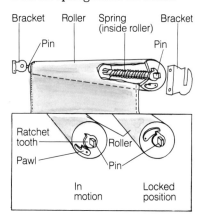

Bracket Roller Spring (inside roller) Bracket
Pin Pin

Ratchet tooth Roller
Pawl Pin
In motion Locked position

A weak spring will cause a shade to roll too slowly. To tighten the tension, roll the shade down partway, remove it from the brackets, and then roll it up by hand and replace it. Test it and repeat if necessary. To reduce tension, roll the shade up completely, remove it from the brackets, unroll it about halfway, and then replace it.

Oil the pawl sparingly if it doesn't hold the shade in place. If a shade catches as it is drawn, bend or move the brackets farther apart. If it draws unevenly, check to see if the brackets are aligned, and make sure that the shade cloth is squared off and mounted evenly at the top of the roller.

To stop a shade from wobbling as it is drawn, straighten the roller pin with pliers. If a shade falls out of its brackets, use pliers to pull the pin out a bit or bend or move in one of the brackets. To move a bracket on an inside mount, sandwich a wood shim between the frame and the bracket.

Window washing

Streak-free methods

Try to choose an overcast day for washing windows. Or do the job when the sun is not shining directly onto the glass. Sun causes streaks.

Some window washers recommend cleaning with clear, tepid water. If windows are very dirty, you may prefer a cleaner. Use a commercial type or make your own, less expensive, version by mixing 2 tablespoons household ammonia or white vinegar with 1 quart of warm water. If temperatures are below freezing, add ¼ cup denatured alcohol or 1 tablespoon glycerine to keep the cleaner from freezing.

Put the solution or water into a spray bottle or apply it with a sponge or a rag wrung out thoroughly to avoid drips. Start at the top of a window. If there are many panes, complete a horizontal row at a time. Use a toothbrush or cotton swab to get dirt out of corners. If using a cleaning solution, rinse.

Dry the window with paper towels, crumpled newspaper, a chamois, or a lint-free rag. Wipe one side of the glass with horizontal strokes, the other vertically; if you leave streaks, you'll know on which side. Remove streaks with a soft, dry cloth.

Windshields

How to clean them

Windshields may be covered by a haze that wipers and washer fluid won't remove. Apply full-strength household vinegar, rinse with water, and wipe with a clean, dry rag.

Air pollution and the silicones applied in many car washes may produce a haze or an invisible coating that causes wipers to streak and chatter. If the wipers are in good condition (see *Windshield wipers*), clean the windshield with a very low-abrasive household cleaner. The glass is clean when water lightly hosed from above sheets across the windshield instead of beading. Clean the wiper squeegees with a cloth dipped in a 50–50 solution of water and gasoline antifreeze.

Windshield washers

Keeping them squirting

A washer that squirts weakly or not at all may be clogged. Disconnect the hose from the nozzle and have a helper operate the dashboard switch. If fluid flows from the hose, clean the nozzle hole with a needle. If the nozzle can't be cleaned, replace it.

If no fluid flows from the hose, look for kinks. Reposition and reshape the hose. If it's still clogged, disconnect the hose at the pump neck. If fluid flows from the pump, blow out the hose with compressed air.

Some hoses have a check valve and filter. Disconnect the hose at this part; if fluid flows through the hose from the reservoir, replace the filter.

If no fluid flows from the pump, check for a blown fuse. If the fuse is good, either the pump or the switch is defective. Connect a 12-volt test lamp to an engine bolt, and probe the two terminals of the washer motor with the pointed tip while a helper operates

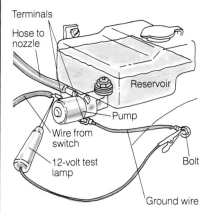

Terminals
Hose to nozzle
Reservoir
Pump
Wire from switch
12-volt test lamp
Bolt
Ground wire

the switch. If the test lamp does not light with the tip on either terminal, the switch is defective. Have a professional replace it.

If the test lamp lights, the pump motor is defective. It's easier to install a universal pump, sold in auto parts stores, than to replace the original pump. Mount the new pump under the hood, splice in new hoses, and leave the old assembly in place.

If the spray is off-target, re-aim the nozzles. Use needle-nose pliers to gently bend a tubular nozzle; don't

W

pinch it. To swivel a ball nozzle, insert a needle in the hole.

Fluidic nozzles are fixed in place and can't be bent, but may be re-aimed by installing a shim, available from the car dealer. Nozzles fitted to wiper arms are not adjustable.

Windshield wipers

Checking and servicing them

If car wipers smear and the squeegees are more than 6 months old, it's time to replace them. On most cars, you release the old ones by squeezing the tangs of a clip at one end or by press-

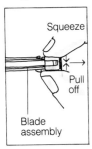

ing a button near the blade's end. Slip a new squeegee into the blade links; it should snap into place.

Replacing a blade

If a blade is bent, damaged, or corroded, replace it. Most have obvious slide locks, levers, or catches; some have a post that you disengage from a hole. On a side-pin type, use a narrow screwdriver to push down on a coil spring while simultaneously prying between the arm and the blade with a second screwdriver.

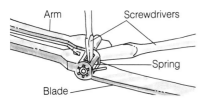

If a blade chatters, the blade or squeegee is frozen, or the arm may be bent. Turn off the wipers with the blade at midstroke; check whether the blade and squeegee are flat on the glass. Straighten a bent arm by gripping it with two pairs of pliers held several inches apart and twisting the arm. If this fails, replace the arm.

Wine storage

Correct methods; providing storage space without a cellar

Store your wines in a cool place well away from light, heat, or vibrations. Ideal temperature is between 55°F and 60°F. But 65°F, even 70°F, won't harm wine as long as the temperature is constant throughout the year; wines will, however, mature faster.

The storage area should be ventilated to prevent accumulation of musty odors, but vents should be kept closed during very hot or cold weather. If possible, maintain the relative humidity constantly around 60 percent.

Except for fortified wines, such as Sherry, keep wine bottles on their sides so that their corks remain moist and fully expanded. If bottles are stored upright, the corks dry out and shrink, admitting air, which spoils wine.

You can convert closet space for wine storage by installing shelves partitioned into bins. Shelves should be at least ¾ inch thick and 14 inches deep. The bins can be of varying sizes, depending on the number and types of wines stored. A bin 13 x 15 inches will hold a case (12) of average-size bottles, stacked on top of one another. To accommodate bottles of different sizes, you may also need some smaller, individual compartments.

Cabinet space can be divided diagonally to create two compartments. Bevel the edges of the dividing board so that it fits neatly. The divider should be strong enough to hold the weight of at least six bottles.

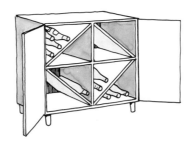

Wine racks, available in attractive units, can be put anywhere that the temperature is right. Their advantage is that each bottle has its own cubbyhole and is easy to retrieve.

Wine with food

Matching wines with foods; the best ways to serve wine

Today people feel free to drink the wines they enjoy without being bound to strict codes. Nevertheless, combinations that have evolved over time continue to provide useful guidelines.

Traditionally, fish and light meats, such as chicken and veal, are accompanied by a dry white wine. But a light-bodied red, such as Beaujolais, is also a good choice. In general, the more delicately flavored the fish or meat, the lighter the wine can be.

Red wines usually accompany red meats, such dark-meat birds as duck, pasta dishes, hearty soups, and the cheese course. The richer the dish, the more full bodied the wine should be.

A sweet white wine, such as Sauterne, Barsac, Muscat, or late-harvest Riesling, is usually served as an accompaniment to dessert (except those of chocolate) or simply on its own.

Some foods don't go with wine at all. Anything very spicy, such as curry or hot Szechuan dishes, overpowers all but the most distinctive wines. So also do foods heavy with salt or vinegar.

When serving different wines for succeeding courses, sequence is important. One moves from lighter to richer, more complex wines as the meal progresses—white before red, young before old, dry before sweet.

The best way to serve wines

All white and pink wines are served chilled. Dry and medium-dry Sherries and light reds, such as Beaujolais and Gamay, can be served slightly chilled. All other red wines are served at room temperature (ideally 65°F. to 68°F). Many red wines, especially less mature ones, improve if opened an hour or so before serving. (See *Corks and corkscrews* for the way to open wine.)

Older red wines often contain sediment. The bottle should be set upright several hours before pouring. It's a good idea also to decant an older wine by pouring it into a clean carafe. Set a strong light or a candle behind the wine so that you can see the sediment. Stop pouring as soon as sediment approaches the bottle's neck.

W

Winterizing a car

Preparing for cold weather

If you live where winters are severely cold, consider installing heaters for the engine coolant and battery. They are sold in do-it-yourself kits in auto parts stores.

Listen underneath the car; if you hear the putt-putt sound of an exhaust-system leak, have it corrected. Change the engine oil, using the cold-weather grade listed in your owner's manual (see *Oil changing*). Do not use oil-thickening additives in winter.

Lubricate the car, including transmission and clutch linkages. Clean and tighten battery-cable terminals; replace them if they are badly corroded. Change the spark plugs and the plug wires if they're heat hardened or oil soaked. Inspect cooling-system hoses and replace any that are deteriorated or leaking. Flush and refill the cooling system with fresh antifreeze. Inspect the engine's drive belts, and adjust or replace them if necessary (see *Antifreeze; Battery terminals; Car belts; Hoses in cars; Lubrication; Spark plugs*).

On cars with carburetors, check the automatic choke (see *Starting problems*) and have it serviced if necessary. Adjust the idle speeds (see *Carburetor adjustments*).

Check that the windshield washers and wipers work properly (see *Windshield washers; Windshield wipers*). Change to rubber-encased winter wiper blades that prevent ice from getting into the blade joints. Install washer antifreeze.

If your car doesn't have all-season tires, mount snow tires on the drive wheels. For safe handling, many makers of front-drive cars recommend using snow tires on all four wheels.

Winterizing a house

A late-autumn checklist

As winter approaches, have your heating system inspected and serviced. If you have a forced-air system, vacuum the duct openings and lay in a supply of air filters. Make sure you have sufficient fuel.

Inspect your roof for loose or damaged shingles and flashings. Check your TV antenna also. After leaves have fallen in late autumn, clean the roof gutters. Trim any tree branches that may damage the house or the outside wiring in a storm.

Remove or cover your air conditioner. Or remove the front panel, place plastic sheeting inside, and replace it.

Shut off the water supply to outside faucets; drain their pipes. Inspect and repair caulking, weather stripping, storm doors, and windows. On the first cold day, search for and seal hidden heat leaks. (See also *Boilers; Caulking; Chimneys and flues; Furnaces; Gutters and downspouts; Insulation; Oil burners; Roof repairs; Storm doors and windows; Warm-air heating; Weather stripping.*)

Wiring

How power is distributed in a house; extending a circuit

Caution: Before working on an electric circuit, shut off power to it at the fuse box or circuit breaker panel. To check that the power is really off, see *Circuit testing.*

Electricity flows along a continuous wire circuit from a power plant to a power-drawing device such as a lamp or appliance and back again. The amount of current flowing past a given point in a wire is measured in *amperes* or *amps*. The pressure that forces current through a wire is measured in *volts*. The use of electricity is measured in *watts,* which are equal to volts multiplied by amperes.

Power enters most houses by means of three wires that pass through a meter to a distribution panel (see *Circuit breakers; Fuse boxes*). Two *hot* wires carry 120 volts each; the third wire is *neutral*. One hot wire and the neutral wire form a 120-volt circuit needed for light fixtures and small appliances. The two hot wires supply the 240 volts used by heavy appliances.

In a typical circuit, a hot wire, wrapped in black (sometimes red or blue) insulation, delivers current at 120 volts to a series of receptacles, light fixtures, and switches. A white- or gray-insulated neutral wire carries current at zero volts back to the distribution panel. Because the neutral wire must provide an uninterrupted path, it is connected to receptacles, but not to switches, fuses, or circuit breakers, which can cut the flow of current. In some circuits, a white wire may be hot; in that case, its ends should be painted or taped black.

Each circuit must have a grounding system to provide a safe path to earth for abnormal current flow (see *Short circuits*). In a well-wired house, a continuous green-insulated or bare copper wire connects every receptacle, switch, and junction box in a circuit to the *neutral bus bar* in the distribution panel. (In some older systems, the circuit wires' metal sheathing acts as ground.) A main ground wire connects the bus bar to an in-ground water pipe or to a copper rod driven into the soil. White wires are also grounded through the bus bar to keep them neutral (at zero volts).

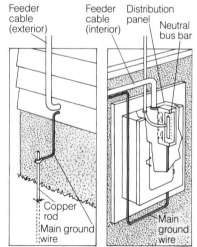

Feeder cable (exterior)   Feeder cable (interior)   Distribution panel   Neutral bus bar   Copper rod   Main ground wire   Main ground wire

Wiring gauges and cable types

Wiring is coded by number; the higher the gauge, the thinner the wire and the smaller the amperage it can carry. A wire too thin for the amperage it must carry is a fire hazard. Don't use a fuse or circuit breaker of a higher amperage than the wire's capacity. Consult local codes and the National Electric Code before starting a project.

Circuit wires are protected by nonmetallic (usually plastic) sheathing or by steel or aluminum armor. Armored

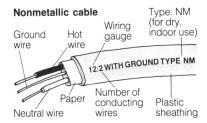

Nonmetallic cable

Ground wire / Hot wire / Wiring gauge / Type: NM (for dry, indoor use)

12/2 WITH GROUND TYPE NM

Neutral wire / Paper / Number of conducting wires / Plastic sheathing

(BX) cable is found in older homes, and in a few areas is required by the local electric code. Nonmetallic (Romex) cable is used in most modern houses.

Wiring connections are made inside wall- or ceiling-mounted boxes. To install an electric box, see *Ceiling boxes* and *Electric circuits.*

Extending a circuit

To extend a circuit to a new box, turn off power to the circuit. Open an existing box near the opening for the new one; see how the box is wired. The easiest point from which to extend a circuit is an end-of-the-run receptacle not under switch control. Run cable from the existing box to the new one (see *Electric circuits*). Secure the cable to both boxes (see *Electric switches*). Install the new box; connect its cable to a fixture, receptacle, or switch

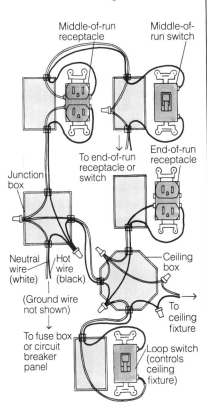

Middle-of-run receptacle / Middle-of-run switch

To end-of-run receptacle or switch / End-of-run receptacle

Junction box

Neutral wire (white) / Hot wire (black)

(Ground wire not shown)

To fuse box or circuit breaker panel

Ceiling box

To ceiling fixture

Loop switch (controls ceiling fixture)

(see *Electric receptacles*). To connect new cable to an existing end-of-the-run receptacle, attach the black wire to the unused brass terminal, the white wire to the unused silver terminal; join ground wires with a wire connector (see *Dimmer switches*).

Wood finishing

Protecting and beautifying a furniture surface

On an old piece, strip off the finish and make any repairs (see *Bleaching wood; Stripping furniture; Veneer*).

If a surface feels smooth, sand it with fine (120) paper; otherwise start with medium (80) and then switch to fine (see *Sanding*). Finish with very fine (220 for softwoods, 280 for hardwoods). Dampen the wood to raise the grain, let it dry, and sand again. The wet wood's color is close to what you'll get with a clear finish. Apply stain for a different color (see *Staining wood*). Vacuum well after sanding and wipe with a tack cloth (see *Tack cloth*). To preserve an antique's look, don't sand it—or sand as little as necessary.

A penetrating oil finish

For a natural-looking finish, use tung oil or a synthetic-resin oil, such as Danish oil or teak oil. Apply the oil liberally with a cloth. With tung oil, rub vigorously to help it penetrate. If an area dulls, add more oil. After 45 minutes, wipe off the excess. Wait 24 hours; then repeat the process. Put a third coat on a heavily used surface. Smooth the dried final coat with 0000 steel wool dipped in oil; wipe dry.

A varnished or lacquered finish

For a hard, surface-sealing finish, use varnish or lacquer (see *Lacquering; Varnishing*). Coat a coarse-grained wood, such as oak, walnut, or mahogany, with a paste wood filler. Mix it with a penetrating-oil wood stain, if necessary, to match the wood's natural or stained color. Thin it as directed. Then rub it vigorously into the pores, using a soft cotton cloth. Work with the grain, then across it. When the filler dulls (10 to 15 minutes), carefully wipe across the grain with burlap to clean off excess. Let it dry overnight. Sand with very fine paper.

You should seal a stained, filled, or antique surface. Mix one part shellac with four parts denatured alcohol. Make thin, even strokes with a clean, natural-bristle varnish brush. Let it dry for 4 or 5 hours. Sand with very fine paper. If you plan to use polyurethane varnish, seal instead with the thinned varnish, as the label directs.

Wood preservatives

Protecting wood outdoors

Except for rot-resistant wood, such as redwood or cedar, raw wood exposed to moisture must be treated with preservative. Avoid highly toxic creosote and penta (pentachlorophenol) preservatives. Select a safer preparation with copper or zinc naphthenate, copper-8-quinolinolate, TBTO (tributyltin oxide), or polyphase. On shingles and siding, apply it liberally, using a natural-bristle brush or a pad applicator. Even these preservatives are hazardous as liquids. Wear a respirator mask, goggles, gloves, and long sleeves.

Whenever possible, dip wood in preservative—for at least 10 minutes. Put a picnic table's legs in a bucket. Soak lumber in a box or trench lined with plastic; use a bulb-operated hand pump to suck leftover liquid back into the can. All low-toxicity preservatives require reapplication every 3 to 5 years. Only copper naphthenate can withstand ground contact.

Pressure-treated lumber

For hard-to-reach spots and for a major project, such as a fence or deck, buy lumber pressure treated at the mill with a long-lasting inorganic arsenical preservative, such as chromated copper arsenate (CCA). Pieces touching soil should be stamped LP-22; others, LP-2. Buy only dry lumber with no surface residue. Don't use it where it will come in contact with food or drinking water. Seal a surface with a polyurethane varnish if young children will use it. Wear a mask to avoid inhaling or swallowing sawdust. Put scraps in the trash pickup; don't burn them. Cutting exposes untreated areas; arsenical preservative is sold solely for coating cut ends.

W

431

Wood siding

Fixing your house's exterior

Fill a small crack in clapboard with caulking compound (see *Caulking*). Wedge apart a larger split with two or three screwdrivers. Use a putty knife to work resorcinol glue along the split's edges. Press the split shut and nail the board's lower edge. Use galvanized or aluminum nails. Set them; fill the holes with putty.

Replacing damaged clapboard

Mark the section to be replaced. If there is no sheathing below, mark along the centers of the studs (see *Studs*). Drive wedges under the lower edge of the section to separate it from

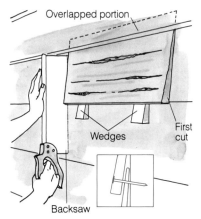

the board below. Cut the board with a backsaw. Then split it out with a wood chisel and hammer. Be careful not to damage other boards or the building paper below.

Drive the wedges under the board above. Then slip a hacksaw blade under it and cut the nails holding the remaining overlapped part of the cut board. Chisel out the part. Replace damaged building paper or fix it with roofing cement. Caulk the cut edges of the opening. Drive in a new board, using a hammer and a protective wood block. Nail it along the bottom and through the board above.

Shingles and shakes

Nail down either side of a cracked shingle; slip building paper under a wide crack first. To replace a warped or badly damaged shingle, cut the nails by slipping a hacksaw blade under it and the shingles above. Split out

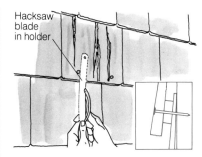

the shingle with a wood chisel; pull out the cut nails. Slip in a matching new shingle. Trim the lower edge, if necessary. Nail it in place. (See also *Painting exteriors; Paint problems*.)

Wood splitting

Making logs into firewood; stacking it

Freshly cut wood is easier to split than seasoned wood. Use a maul to hand split logs 6 to 15 inches across, an ax for smaller ones, steel wedges for larger ones. Split kindling with a hatchet. Protect your eyes with goggles.

To use a maul or an ax, stand the log upright on a 20-inch chopping block, propping it with a forked stick if necessary; a large log section makes a good block. Swing from over one shoulder rather than straight overhead. Aim for the center of the log, in line with the largest knot or branch. Bend your knees as you swing so that the tool strikes the wood squarely.

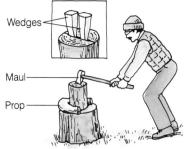

To use wedges, first drive two or three of them partway in with a 2-pound sledgehammer. Place them in a straight line, along a crack if possible. Drive them the rest of the way with a heavier hammer or with the blunt end of the maul. Do not drive wedges with an ax, and do not use an ax or a maul as a wedge.

Check ax, maul, and hammer handles frequently for cracks; make sure the heads are secure and the blades sharp (see *Axes; Sharpening hand tools*). Never leave your splitting tools where they may freeze—a sharp blow can shatter frozen metal.

Stack split wood bark side up in a sunny, open area and on logs to keep it off the ground. Don't stack it against a house wall; it invites carpenter ants and termites. Cover the pile with canvas or plastic sheeting, leaving the sides open for air circulation.

Wood stoves

Using an airtight stove safely

Because wood burns slowly in a modern airtight stove, less heat goes up the chimney than from a blazing fireplace. As a result, chemicals from the wood are deposited inside the flue and stovepipe in the form of *creosote;* the slower the wood burns, the more creosote is deposited. This flammable substance builds up quickly once it has begun, and when a thick accumulation ignites, it burns with intense heat. The resultant chimney fire, the cause of most wood-stove tragedies, can burn through a stovepipe, crack a flue, or ignite a wall.

To lessen creosote buildup, burn only well-seasoned hardwoods. Do not burn trash or artificial logs; burn coal only if the manufacturer's specifications allow it. Never use a flammable liquid to start a fire. Crumple a few sheets of newspaper into tight balls and bunch them in the center of the firebox; then build a "tepee" of dry kindling over them. Light the newspaper and, when the kindling is fully ablaze, add small pieces of firewood. Add larger pieces as the fire grows.

Burn the stove hot (with the door and damper open) for at least 15 or 20 minutes a day, preferably in the morning while the flue and stovepipe are cool. Whenever you add fuel, open the air supply for a few minutes to burn off moisture. Don't overload the stove; put in 1 or 2 hours' fuel supply at a time during the day. Before putting in an overnight load, build up a bed of very hot coals.

W

Clean the chimney at least twice a year, in spring and fall; clean the stovepipe more often, as needed. Have a professional inspect the chimney and stove annually. Repair or replace any component that shows wear.

Before you install a wood stove, check with local authorities. Have the work inspected and certified by your local fire department. Notify your insurance company also; failure to do so may invalidate your policy.

Wounds

First aid for cuts and scrapes

Even a seemingly trivial wound requires care to avoid infection and to promote sound healing. When bleeding has been controlled (see *Bleeding*) and if you are satisfied no stitches or other doctor's care is required, you can treat a wound as follows.

Expose the wound; then wash your hands. Fill a bowl with warm sudsy water (prepared with disinfecting soap, if available). Using a sterile gauze pad, clean washcloth, or newly opened surgical sponge, wash the skin around the wound. Work outward from the wound to avoid contaminating it.

Next wash the wound itself. Copious rinsing with the soapy water is gentler and more effective than scrubbing. Swish a cut hand or foot in the bowl. Flush grit from an abrasion by squeezing the soapy water over it. To protect the wound, see *Bandaging*.

Getting out deep dirt

When dirt is deeply embedded in a laceration (skin tear) or puncture, persist with sudsing and rinsing for at least 20 minutes. Then remove any visible grit or splinters with tweezers. Sterilize the tweezers by boiling them for 10 minutes or by heating their points red hot in the flame of several matches; wipe off the carbon with sterile gauze. Remove what you can easily see and pick out; don't probe. Never squeeze a puncture wound to clean it—this can spread infection.

Check the wound over the next few days. Excessive pain or swelling, redness, or a red streak leading from the wound may indicate infection or the presence of a foreign body in it. See a doctor if a puncture is deep, if foreign matter is embedded in a wound, or if any signs of infection appear.

With a deep wound, there is danger of tetanus infection. Ask your doctor if you need a tetanus booster shot; have one at least every 10 years.

Wreaths

For Christmas or any season

To make a traditional Christmas wreath, collect evergreen branches or use the lower branches of your Christmas tree. Stand them in water for a day or two. For the base, use a 12-inch wire hoop made from a wire hanger or other heavy-gauge wire.

Clip two or three evergreen sprigs 8 to 12 inches long and tie them in a bunch with thin wire. Attach the end of a spool of thin wire to the hoop, then wrap it around the base of the sprigs. Wire another bunch of sprigs behind the first one. Wire a third bunch in place with the tips covering the ends of the first stems. Continue

around the hoop, striving for a full, even massing of greens. Decorate the wreath with a bow and Christmas ornaments, pinecones, or small toys.

For a wreath of small dried flowers, you can use the same wiring technique. If the flowers are very brittle, spray them lightly with water.

For a beautiful wreath to enjoy all year round, gather bare grape vines and soak them until pliant. Choose a long vine for the base. Bend the thick end into a circle and wrap the thinner end around it. Push the thick end of a second vine into the circle, then wrap the thin end around the vines already in place. Continue adding vines until the wreath is several inches thick. If desired, decorate it with dried flowers, seed pods, nuts, or ribbon bows.

Wrenches

The standard types; how to use them

The best wrenches are forged from chrome-vanadium steel or high-carbon alloy steel and are heat treated, oil quenched, and nickel-chrome plated.

Pipe wrenches, monkey wrenches, and *adjustable wrenches* have movable jaws so that their spans change with the turn of a knob. Although versatile, they are imprecise: the movable jaw is a bit loose. In a pipe wrench, this feature is an advantage; when you apply pressure to the handle, the jaws tighten (see *Pipes*). In a monkey wrench, designed to grasp large plumbing nuts like those on drain traps, it matters little. But an adjustable wrench's loose jaw can round off the corners of a tight nut or bolt head; use these wrenches for general work, but if you must apply much pressure, it is better to use a wrench that fits the nut or bolt exactly.

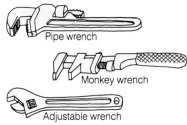

Pipe wrench

Monkey wrench

Adjustable wrench

A *box wrench* fits over a nut to hold it firmly all around. An *open-ended wrench* grasps only three sides. Both are available in metric and fraction sizes; always use the exact size needed. A *combination wrench* has a box head on one end and a matching open end on the other.

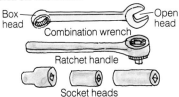

Box head — Combination wrench — Open head

Ratchet handle

Socket heads

A *socket wrench set* includes interchangeable socket heads in metric or fraction sizes and a handle with a built-in ratchet, so that you need not regrasp the nut with every turn of the wrench. The ratchet can be set to tighten or to loosen.

W

Wrinkles

How to prevent premature facial wrinkles and sagging skin

Facial wrinkles occur naturally with advancing age. Elastin and collagen fibers deteriorate, making skin less flexible, and oil and sweat glands become less active, making the skin drier. Also fat beneath the skin often shrinks, causing sagging.

The age when wrinkles begin to appear varies and has much to do with heredity. People with fair skin wrinkle sooner than those with darker complexions. Typically, wrinkles appear first around the eyes, above the upper lip, and on the neck.

Cosmetic creams can soften and lubricate, but their effect on wrinkles is superficial and temporary. Plastic surgeons and dermatologists can remove wrinkles for longer periods with cosmetic surgery, chemical peeling, or the injection of augmenting material beneath them; all involve risks.

Delaying the formation of wrinkles
From an early age on, stay out of the sun as much as possible and always use a sunscreen when out of doors (see *Suntans*). Also avoid smoking; it has been linked to premature wrinkling partly because it lessens circulation to surface capillaries.

Habitual contraction of facial muscles due to stress can also cause premature wrinkling. Several times a day, take a moment to relax your facial muscles. Be aware of frowning and smooth out your forehead.

To prevent crow's feet caused by squinting, be sure that your vision is properly corrected and that you wear sunglasses when you're on the water, at the beach, or in snow.

Keep your hands away from your face. Sitting with your chin on your hand, pushing your face out of its natural position, or rubbing your eyes can stretch delicate skin.

Losing weight too quickly or constantly alternating weight gain with weight loss can cause skin to sag. So, too, can improper dental hygiene and care (the jawbone structure decreases). And poor posture can emphasize wrinkling and sagging that already exist.

Writing a paper

Gathering and assembling research; outlining; writing

Choose a topic that interests you, one you can handle. Make certain that your idea is not too broad or too narrow for the paper's assigned length. Discuss its probable length, thesis (central statement), and proof of the thesis with your teacher. Several weeks before the paper is due, check libraries and bookstores on the availability of references. Consider other sources that might be helpful.

Gathering and organizing research
Assemble as many pertinent and recent sources as you can. List each one on a 3 x 5 card: for books, list the author, title, publisher, and date and place of publication; for periodicals and newspapers, additionally list the volume and page numbers. Alphabetize the cards by author; number each card consecutively.

Take notes on 5 x 8 cards. Give each subdivision a heading; clip together all information relevant to that heading. Number the cards. Organize your notes in a logical sequence.

Outlining
In your introduction, you'll present your main thesis succinctly, stressing its importance and relevance. Briefly outline the background that supports your point of view.

In the main body of the paper, develop your thesis. Present your most important information and strongest arguments with as much backup data as you can muster. Close by summarizing, dramatically stressing the broad significance of your thesis.

Writing
An outline makes the writing easier. Avoid plagiarizing; set material taken directly from a source in quotes. Footnote all quotations and any paraphrase of a fact from a single source.

Complete your first draft; then edit it. As you prepare a second draft, check your transitional sentences: does each point follow from the one before? Be critical; strengthen weak areas. Check spelling, punctuation, and grammar. End with an alphabetically arranged bibliography.

Yoga

5,000-year-old tension-relieving exercises

Hatha yoga exercise is concerned with stretching, posture, and breathing. Practitioners *(yogis)* claim that yoga helps you to relax and that it improves posture, strength of certain muscles, spine elasticity, and flexibility. Some of the exercises may be immediately beneficial. More advanced positions, like the cross-legged *lotus,* may take years to master.

The best way to learn yoga correctly is to attend classes led by a reputable yogi. Improperly performed, the exercises can cause injury. If you are more than 3 months pregnant or have medical problems, don't attempt yoga.

Wear loose clothing and no shoes. Hold a position only as long as it's comfortable. Listen to your body; breathe normally through your nose. Stretch slowly; focus on telling a tight muscle to relax. Attempt an extreme position only after instruction.

Yoga workout
Begin and end your exercises with the *resting posture.* Lie on your back, arms by your sides, palms up, legs outstretched and slightly apart. Close your eyes. Imagine you're floating on water. Unflex your neck muscles: very slowly roll your head from left to right 10 times. Visualize your head; mentally smooth your scalp, eyelids, lines around the mouth and eyes. Relax the other parts of your body: starting with your feet, your ankles, your lower legs, move toward the head. Concentrate on each section of your body until it feels free of tension. (You may become so relaxed that you fall asleep.)

Breathing exercise
Relaxed on your back, slowly inhale to the count of four, pushing out your diaphragm (bulging your stomach) and distending your ribs. As you exhale to the same count, your stomach

flattens and your ribs retract. You can do this while walking or sitting too.

Warm up with the *salutation to the sun* exercise, with one posture flowing into the other. 1. Stand with your hands and feet together. 2. Inhaling deeply, raise your arms over your head and stretch backward. 3. As you exhale, slowly bend forward until you touch the ground. 4. Inhaling, throw your right leg behind you; stretch your neck forward. 5. Throw the other leg behind you, keeping your body in a straight line. 6. Exhaling, lower your knees, your forehead, and your chest to the ground; follow with your hips. 7. Raise your upper torso and, as you inhale, slowly stretch upward with your back arched and your head back. 8. With your feet flat on the floor, raise your hips until your legs are straight. 9. Bring your right foot forward and resume posture 4. 10. Bring the other foot forward and straighten your legs. 11. Slowly stand up; resume posture 2. Return to starting posture. Repeat, using the left leg in posture 4.

Yogurt

Making cultured milk

Milk for making yogurt should be very fresh. Any type is suitable except condensed; the more cream it contains, the sweeter the taste. To obtain a thicker curd, add up to 3 tablespoons of powdered milk per quart of liquid.

In an enamel, stainless steel, or glass pan, bring 1 quart milk slowly to a boil.

Let it cool to 105°F. (If you have no thermometer, sprinkle a few drops on your wrist; it should feel neither hot nor cold.) Add 2 tablespoons starter from a health food store or 4 tablespoons unflavored commercial yogurt. Stir thoroughly, cover, and set the milk to incubate for at least 3 hours.

To keep the incubation temperature around 105°F, use an electric yogurt-maker or set the milk in any slightly warm place such as the top of a radiator, refrigerator, or stove pilot light. Some people wrap the container in a thick towel or a blanket.

Although yogurt can be cultured as low as 70°F, it takes longer to thicken and may acquire a sour taste. Above 115°F the culturing bacteria are killed.

The yogurt is ready to be refrigerated when it retains the impression of a spoon pressed lightly into its surface. It will keep for about a week.

Yo-Yos

Giving it a whirl

Wind the string around the yo-yo's axle. At the string's end make a noose that fits over the first knuckle of your middle finger. Bend your elbow so that your palm faces you. Cock your wrist; as you lower your forearm shoulder height, give your wrist a flick and let the yo-yo roll down the string. Just as the yo-yo reaches the end of the string (it shouldn't touch ground), turn your hand over and give a little tug; the yo-yo will ride up the string and back into your palm.

Zippers

Centered and lapped applications

The centered application is best for a heavy fabric; on a garment it's usually used at a center back seam. Machine baste the placket opening; clip the bobbin thread at 1-inch intervals; press the seam open. With the top of the opening facing you, extend the right seam allowance. Open the zipper and position it facedown on the seam allowance with the top stop ¼ inch below the top seamline (½ inch if your garment has a facing). Using a zipper foot, machine baste the zipper tape along the stitching guideline.

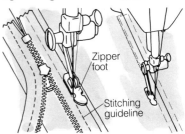

Close the zipper; sew the left tape to the left seam allowance. On the right side of the garment, baste through all layers ¼ inch from the center. Stitch just outside the basting in two steps, starting each time at the bottom center of the placket. Remove all basting.

Lapped application

This is suitable for light to medium-weight fabrics; in a garment, it's most often used at the side seam. Prepare the zipper seam and machine baste the zipper to the right seam allowance, as for a centered application. Turn the zipper faceup; stitch along the fold that lies between the teeth and the seam. On the right side, spread the fabric flat over the unstitched part of the zipper; baste ⅜ to ½ inch from the seam. Stitch close to the basting.

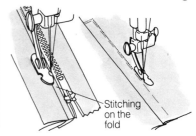

X
Y
Z

Index

436

H

Acknowledgments

Beauty creams on page 30
from THE FORMULA BOOK.
Copyright © 1975 Stark
Research Corporation.
Reprinted with permission of
Andrews, McMeel & Parker, Inc.

After-shave and moisturizing
lotions on page 30 from
NATURAL FORMULA BOOK
FOR HOME AND YARD.
Copyright © 1982 Rodale
Press. Used by permission of
the publisher.

Christmas star on page 90
from LESLIE LINSLEY'S
CHRISTMAS ORNAMENTS
AND STOCKINGS. Copyright
© 1982 Leslie Linsley
and Jon Aron. Used by
permission of St. Martin's
Press, Inc., New York.

Recipes on pages 107, 176,
185–186, 311, 331, 358,
and 413 from THE
DOUBLEDAY COOKBOOK by
Jean Anderson and Elaine
Hanna. Copyright © 1975
Doubleday & Company, Inc.
Used by permission of
the publisher.

Ice cream recipes on page
213 by permission of The
Pennsylvania State University,
Department of Food Science.

Library of Congress
Cataloging in Publication Data
Main entry under title:

How to do just about anything

At head of title: Reader's digest.
Includes index.
1. Handbooks,
vade mecums, etc.
I. Reader's Digest Association.
AG105.H852   1986
031'.02   85-14446
ISBN 0-89577-936-6